Public Administration and Public Policy

FOR CIVIL SERVICES (MAIN) EXAMINATION

Public Administration and Public Policy

For Civil Services (Main) Examination

Volume 1

Lohit Matani, IPS
B.Tech and M.Tech, IIT BHU, Varanasi

Forward for first edition

Late Shri Ram B. Jethmalani
Ex-Senior Advocate, Supreme Court of India
Former Member of Parliament (Rajya Sabha)

Published by
OakBridge Publishing Pvt. Ltd.
M 35, 1st Floor, Old DLF, Gurugram, 122001, Haryana, India
Tel.: +91 124 4305970, E-mail: info@oakbridge.in
www.oakbridge.in

ISBN: 978-93-95764-35-3

Printed and bound at Saurabh Printers Pvt. Ltd.

This book is dedicated to all those men and women who have laid their lives in the service of the nation.

Forward for first edition

The book on ‘Public Administration and Public Policy’ written by Lohit Matani provides a deep insight into the theories and practice of public administration, administrative law, public policy and good governance. Dealing with several topics, and being on line with the syllabus of various recognized universities and the UPSC examination, the book is a must read not only for the students of public administration, law, management and public policy, but also for all the citizens in general.

In the book, Lohit Matani has helped the students to understand the length and breadth of public administration. He has smartly dealt with all the topics in such a manner that all important topics, important scholars, important works and important organizations are discussed in this book while limiting the size of the book. This shows his understanding of the subject.

Moreover, the mind maps he has used in the book are very helpful for the students to remember certain important points from various topics. They are a ready source for the quick revision of the whole subject.

Furthermore, the book is written in a lucid language so that all the students from rural as well as urban background can understand it. There lies the beauty of this book. On one hand, Lohit has tried to discuss the theories of various scholars in their language and style; while on the other hand, he has tried to discuss those topics in such a manner that everyone can understand them with ease.

I wish best of luck to Lohit Matani for the success of this book and his other books ahead.

Ram Jethmalani

Preface

Hello Friends,

Those were the cold days of December 2012 when I was appearing for the Civil Services (Main) Examination, 2012. One of my optional subjects (at that time, there were two optional subjects) was Public Administration. Before appearing for the examination, I thought that my preparation, based on reading some books on public administration and some study material from different coaching institutions, was complete. Owing to lack of time, I had not analysed the previous years' question papers. When I first attempted the examination, I was amused by the difficulty level and depth of the questions. Considering the nature of the questions, I found that my knowledge was shallow. I ended up writing whatever I knew about the questions asked.

Upon returning home, I understood that my answers were general in nature but the questions asked were very specific. Several candidates make the same mistake. They do not understand the subject in depth. They gather superficial knowledge from random notes or books that address only few topics. Superficial knowledge always ends up in failure in the UPSC and State Service examinations. Thus, to fulfil the need for a book that deals extensively with all the topics listed in the UPSC exam syllabus of public administration, I have authored this book. Through it, I have made a humble attempt to share my knowledge with the young students of public administration.

This book is strictly aligned to the syllabus of public administration prescribed by the UPSC. It deals with all the topics extensively. Having said that, I should mention that there are certain 'hidden topics' in the syllabus-topics that are not directly mentioned in the syllabus. A senior student may derive these topics from the existing topics but new students may find it difficult to do that. It is often seen that UPSC asks questions from this 'hidden syllabus'. A knowledgeable person will immediately know that these hidden topics are very much a part of the main syllabus, as they are connected to the main topics. This book helps in connecting the main topics with the hidden topics.

Dealing extensively with the UPSC syllabus and the topics derived from it, this book attempts to cater to the questions asked in the previous 30 years. At the end of each chapter, there is a list of questions asked in the past 30 years from that chapter. After reading a chapter, every reader should try and answer the questions from that chapter. This is the most important strategy to use when preparing for the UPSC examination. When the men/women in the Police and Armed Forces parade, a very important command is followed- 'आगे बढ़ेगा - पीछे मुड़' It means that to move ahead, one has to look back. This command is equally applicable to young students. In order to be successful in the future exams, one needs to diligently analyse and write the answers of the previous 30 years' questions.

Apart from previous years' questions, the book implements the unique idea of mind maps. Mind maps are diagrams that help memorize a difficult topic. As the UPSC syllabus is very large and it is very difficult for a normal mind to remember everything, mind maps help in remembering the key concepts. Each chapter contains certain *mind maps* that deal with the key concepts of that chapter. If a candidate memorizes a mind map, he/she can recall the whole topic in the examination by connecting the concepts shown in it.

Moreover, the book is written in very simple and understandable language. Although, it discusses the actual statements, theories, and ideas given by various scholars, I have made a genuine effort to break down those difficult ideas into easily understandable text. Thus, the book contains both the difficult ideas discussed by learned scholars and their interpretations in lucid language. Wherever possible, I have tried to present the concepts succinctly and point-wise. This has also been done because when concepts are broken down into various points, they are easy to understand and remember. If a student remembers only the headings of the various sections, he/she can write impressive answers in the examination. Remembering the whole text is neither possible nor advisable.

Another unique feature of the book is that it cites various case studies to explain the different theories and concepts. For example, in the chapter on 'Ethics in Public Administration', the various ethics theories are explained using real-life case studies and examples. This helps one to actually understand the essence of the text, while discouraging the habit of gaining superficial knowledge on any topic.

Further, and most important, there are four lists at the end of the book:

(1) Important Terms in Public Administration

(2) Important Books and Papers

(3) Important Scholars and Persons

(4) Important Organizations, Commissions, and Conferences

These lists act as *subject indexes*, mentioning the page numbers of the book where the individual entries are discussed. According to me, these four lists are the most important part of this book, as they provide the key to each and every topic contained in the book. If you analyse the questions asked in the UPSC exam, the questions generally contain difficult terms, names of important persons, names of important books, and names of important organizations. Several students would not have heard those terms before. These lists will familiarize the reader with all the important terms associated with public administration. A revision of the terms mentioned in these lists would be tantamount to a revision of the whole syllabus.

In the end, I would like to say that this book has been written neither to earn money nor to earn name. It has been written with the pure intention of helping students better understand the subject of public administration. Previously, I have helped many students secure good marks in the subject through my blog lohitmatani.wordpress.com. This book goes a step further in that direction. Having completed this book, I feel extremely humble and satisfied and hope that students will benefit a lot from this book.

Lohit Matani

Acknowledgement

I am extremely thankful to all the students who have requested me and gave me the idea to pen down this book on Public Administration. I am also thankful to my parents, who have made me capable enough to write down this book, and my brother, who has always been a guiding light for me.

Moreover, I am extremely obliged by the support and motivation given by wife Manjeet Kaur for helping me in completing this work. She has helped me in remaining physically and mentally fit for writing this book along with the hectic work schedule.

Furthermore, I am thankful to all my teachers and gurus who have shown me the path of knowledge and worship.

Last, but not the least, I am thankful to Sulekh and the entire team of OakBridge for giving me this opportunity to write a book with them.

Lohit Matani

IPS, Maharashtra

Brief Contents

CHAPTERS

Contents

Syllabus Mapping

PAPER - I : Administrative Theory

Introduction

Meaning, scope and significance of Public Administration; Wilson's vision of Public Administration; Evolution of the discipline and its present status; New Public Administration; Public Choice approach; Challenges of liberalization, Privatization, Globalization; Good Governance: concept and application; New Public Management.

Administrative Thought

Scientific Management and Scientific Management movement; Classical Theory; Weber's bureaucratic model - its critique and post-Weberian Developments; Dynamic Administration (Mary Parker Follett); Human Relations School (Elton Mayo and others); Functions of the Executive (C.I. Barnard); Simon's decision-making theory; Participative Management (R. Likert, C. Argyris, D. McGregor).

Administrative Behavior

Process and techniques of decision-making; Communication; Morale; Motivation Theories - content, process and contemporary; Theories of Leadership: Traditional and Modern.

Organizations

Theories - systems, contingency; Structure and forms: Ministries and Departments, Corporations, Companies, Boards and Commissions; Ad hoc and advisory bodies; Headquarters and Field relationships; Regulatory Authorities; Public - Private Partnerships.

Accountability and control

Concepts of accountability and control; Legislative, Executive and Judicial control over administration; Citizen and Administration; Role of media, interest groups, voluntary organizations; Civil society; Citizen's Charters; Right to Information; Social audit.

Administrative Law

Meaning, scope and significance; Dicey on Administrative law; Delegated legislation; Administrative Tribunals.

Comparative Public Administration

Historical and sociological factors affecting administrative systems; Administration and politics in different countries; status of Comparative Public Administration; Ecology and administration; Riggsian models and their critique.

Development Dynamics

Concept of development; Changing profile of development administration; 'Antidevelopment thesis'; Bureaucracy and development; Strong state versus the market debate; Impact of liberalization on administration in developing countries; Women and development - the self-help group movement.

Personnel Administration

Importance of human resource development; Recruitment, training, career advancement, position classification, discipline, performance appraisal, promotion, pay and service conditions; employer-employee relations, grievance redressal mechanism; Code of conduct; Administrative ethics.

Public Policy

Models of policy-making and their critique; Processes of conceptualization, planning, implementation, monitoring, evaluation and review and their limitations; State theories and public policy formulation.

Techniques of Administrative Improvement

Organization and methods, Work study and work management; e-governance and information technology; Management aid tools like network analysis, MIS, PERT, CPM.

Financial Administration

Monetary and fiscal policies; Public borrowings and public debt Budgets - types and forms; Budgetary process; Financial accountability; Accounts and audit.

PAPER – II : Indian Administration

Evolution of Indian Administration

Kautilya's Arthashastra; Mughal administration; Legacy of British rule in politics and administration - Indianization of public services, revenue administration, district administration, local self-government.

Philosophical and Constitutional framework of government

Salient features and value premises; Constitutionalism; Political culture; Bureaucracy and democracy; Bureaucracy and development.

Public Sector Undertakings

Public sector in modern India; Forms of Public Sector Undertakings; Problems of autonomy, accountability, and control; Impact of liberalization and privatization.

Union Government and Administration

Executive, Parliament, Judiciary - structure, functions, work processes; Recent trends; Intragovernmental relations; Cabinet Secretariat; Prime Minister's Office; Central Secretariat; Ministries and Departments; Boards; Commissions; Attached offices; Field organizations.

Plans and Priorities

Machinery of planning; Role, composition and functions of the Planning Commission and the National Development Council; 'Indicative' planning; Process of plan formulation at Union and State levels; Constitutional Amendments (1992) and decentralized planning for economic development and social justice.

State Government and Administration

Union-State administrative, legislative and financial relations; Role of the Finance Commission; Governor; Chief Minister; Council of Ministers; Chief Secretary; State Secretariat; Directorates.

District Administration since Independence

Changing role of the Collector; Union state- local relations; Imperatives of development management and law and order administration; District administration and democratic decentralization.

Civil Services

Constitutional position; Structure, recruitment, training and capacity-building; Good governance initiatives; Code of conduct and discipline; Staff associations; Political rights; Grievance redressal mechanism; Civil service neutrality; Civil service activism.

Financial Management

Budget as a political instrument; Parliamentary control of public expenditure; Role of finance ministry in monetary and fiscal area; Accounting techniques; Audit; Role of Controller General of Accounts and Comptroller and Auditor General of India.

Administrative Reforms since Independence

Major concerns; Important Committees and Commissions; Reforms in financial management and human resource development; Problems of implementation.

Rural Development: Institutions and agencies since independence

Rural development programmes: foci and strategies; Decentralization and Panchayati Raj; 73rd Constitutional amendment.

Urban Local Government

Municipal governance: main features, structures, finance and problem areas; 74th Constitutional Amendment; Global local debate; New localism; Development dynamics, politics and administration with special reference to city management.

Law and Order Administration

British legacy; National Police Commission; Investigative agencies; Role of central and state agencies including paramilitary forces in maintenance of law and order and countering insurgency and terrorism; Criminalization of politics and administration; Police-public relations; Reforms in Police.

Significant issues in Indian Administration

Values in public service; Regulatory Commissions; National Human Rights Commission; Problems of administration in coalition regimes; Citizen-administration interface; Corruption and administration; Disaster management.

Trend Analysis of Previous 10 Years' Questions Papers

If we analyse the trend of questions asked from the different units of public administration, we will see that the UPSC exam can ask questions from any topic. Thus, no topic can be regarded as more important or less important.

As seen in the table below, the UPSC exam may ask many questions from one topic and no question from another. For example, in 2021 only three question was asked from the topic 'Introduction to Public Administration', whereas 5 questions were asked from it in 2020.

Similarly, in 2022, 6 questions were asked from the topic 'Administrative Thought; in 2021, 5 questions were asked from this topic. However, in 2020, only 4 questions were asked from it.

Thus, every year UPSC chooses afresh the topic that would be given more weightage and the topic that would be given less weightage. Therefore, one cannot focus more on one topic at the cost of focusing on another. One should be equally well-versed with all the topics.

Unit	2012	2013	2014	2015	2016	2017	2018	2019	2020	2021	2022
Introduction to Public Administration	1	1	1	2	4	2	5	5	5	3	2
Governance, E-Governance, and Emerging Trends	2	1	3	1	2	1	1	3	2	1	2
Administrative Thought	5	3	2	4	2	3	3	3	4	5	6
Administrative Behaviour	1	2	0	2	2	2	2	0	0	1	0
Organizational Dynamics	2	5	3	2	0	1	2	0	2	2	3
Accountability and Control	2	2	3	2	4	3	1	1	3	1	1
Administrative Law	3	1	1	1	1	2	1	1	1	1	1
Comparative Public Administration	2	1	1	1	2	1	1	1	1	0	0

Unit	2012	2013	2014	2015	2016	2017	2018	2019	2020	2021	2022
Development Dynamics	2	1	2	2	2	3	3	2	1	3	3
Personnel Administration and Civil Services	1	1	0	1	2	6	4	1	0	0	0
Ethics in Public Administration	0	2	3	2	1	2	2	1	1	1	1
Public Policy	2	1	3	3	1	1	1	2	2	1	2
Techniques for Administrative Improvement	3	0	1	1	1	0	1	4	3	5	1
Financial Administration	3	2	6	1	3	5	2	3	3	4	5

Art of Answer Writing

The Civil Services (Main) Examination is a subjective examination in which the candidates are required to write long and descriptive essay type answers. The marks of a candidate, especially in subjects like Public Administration, depend to a great extent on the nature of answers written by him/her. Answers are the only way to portray your knowledge in front of the examiner. Thus, everyone should learn the art of answer writing.

As answer writing is an art, it cannot be learnt in a day. Moreover, the art cannot be described in a few words. I can tell you how to develop that art, but I cannot tell you what that art is. First, I will tell you the broad outline of an answer. Any answer should start with an introduction and end with a conclusion. If a person feels, he can leave some space and write the introduction and conclusion after writing the main answer. However, writing an introduction and a conclusion is very important.

The main part of the answer should depend on the nature of the question asked. The questions in Public Administration are generally in the nature of a statement followed by a word like define, analyze, and so on. There may also be direct questions like 'What are the institutions; where training of civil servants is conducted?' Such questions are rare. They should be answered to the point and efforts should be taken to write a point wise answer as far as possible.

However, the statement based questions are difficult to tackle. For example, one question was asked in 2012—*"Leadership is the 'influential increment over and above mechanical compliance with the routine directive of the organization'" Comment.* [*Katz and Kahn*]. Before writing an answer to a statement based question, a candidate needs to first read the statement carefully and understanding the meaning of the terms used in it. The candidate should also analyze the statement in light of the theories given by the scholar whose statement it is. For example, in the above statement, one needs to understand the four terms- leadership, influential increment, mechanical compliance and routine directive- in light of the teachings of the scholars Katz and Kahn. Thus, for perfectly answering this question, a candidate must know the theories of these two scholars. Therefore, a candidate is required to study deeply. Superficial knowledge is not helpful in this examination.

After analyzing the statement, the candidate has to see the word mentioned after the statement like comment, define, analyze, and so on. In this example, comment is mentioned. Here 'comment' means to give your point of view on the various points in the statement. Thus, in its answer, below the introduction part, you have to first define the various terms used in the statement. Then you have to describe the meaning of the whole statement (in terms of the actual work of the scholars mentioned). Here, you cannot provide a general description of the statement. The description should be the one given by the scholars whose statement it is. A general description will not fetch you good marks.

After explaining the meaning of the statement, you have to give your opinion on it from various angles. For example, in the above statement, you can tell how leadership helps the employees in performing better than what they would have performed while routinely complying with the organizational directions. This angle shows the superiority of an organization with a good leader to the one in which routine procedures are followed. As far as possible, the text should be written point wise and keywords should be underlined.

Apart from the above, there is another angle to the answer. In this angle, the candidate can tell how routine compliance is more important than following a charismatic and a good leader. For example, in some hierarchical organizations like police and army, it is very important to follow routine procedures. Following the commands of a leader with paying lesser regard to routine compliance can make the organization inefficient. In this part also, point wise answer should be written.

Similarly, there could be a third angle to this answer. This angle should describe how to maintain a balance between leadership and compliance in different organizations. It should mention which organizations require more leadership skills and which require more routine compliance. Similarly, there could be various angles to an answer. However, I would like to mention again that all the above points should be written in light of the text written by the scholars mentioned in the question.

Finally, the answer should end with a conclusion. The conclusion should be a one gist of the points mentioned in the answer along with your opinion.

How to tackle with unknown statements and unknown scholars?

Although, if you read my book there would be very less chances that you will face a question regarding an unknown scholar in the UPSC examination, but there can be instances when the statement and the scholar mentioned in the question is completely unknown to you. In that case, your art of answer writing comes in picture. This art of answer writing is gained only by sheer hard work and practice.

If you see an unknown statement and an unknown scholar, you should firstly define the key terms in the statement. Then you should describe the meaning of the statement in terms of any other scholar (whom you have read) who have written on the same topic. Then you should follow the strategy as mentioned above.

How to develop the art of answer writing?

The art of answer writing can be developed by doing two things. Firstly, you should write answers to the questions asked in the last 30 years. These answers should be written by referring the text in this book and from other sources (if required). The answers should be written in the manner described above. If you write answers to the last 30 years questions, you will understand how to write good answers in UPSC.

Secondly, you should join a good online or offline test series for Public Administration. Writing answers within a time limit would help you in developing the skill of writing good answers in the examination hall. However, you have to judge the level of your answer yourself. As the time and resources are very less with a civil services aspirant, you cannot depend on someone else to judge your answers. To judge your answers yourself, you need to see the following things in your answer:

(a) Whether you have explained all the key terms mentioned in the question?

(b) Whether you have explained the statement in the question according to the scholarly work of the thinker mentioned in the question?

(c) Whether you have answered the question from all angles possible and thinkable by a common mind?

(d) Whether you have, if possible, included any current event related to the question in your answer?

(e) Whether you have included all the relevant points in the answer? To verify this you should refer a good book like this one.

(f) Whether you have answered according to the directive of the question? E.g. a question may ask to 'comment', 'describe', 'critically analyze', and so on. These terms are described in the next section.

(g) Whether you have written a good introduction and a good conclusion in the answer?

(h) Whether you have maintained the word limit and still included all the relevant points?

(i) Whether you have underlined the keywords and written the answer as much point wise as possible?

If you can learn the art of judging your answers yourself, you will soon learn the art of writing good answers. Once this art is learnt, the dream of becoming a civil servant won't be far away.

Key Directives in the Civil Services (Main) Question Papers

In a question, UPSC uses different terms behind a statement. It is very important to understand these terms to answer a question accordingly. One of the following terms is mentioned in a question:

1. **Comment/Explain**: When asked to comment, you are supposed to be neutral and write various facts and viewpoints regarding that particular statement.
2. **Critically Comment**: In this case, you need to give both positive and negative sides of a statement. The answer should start with mentioning the positives and then mention the negative aspects of the issue discussed in a statement.
3. **Examine/Discuss**: When asked to examine, you need to first state the meaning of the statement, analyze it from different angles, establish the key facts and issues in the question, show their importance, weaknesses and relate the issue with the happenings in the current scenario. Basically, you have to do complete investigation and write the various aspects of the topic for example, its social, economic, political, cultural impacts, and so on.
4. **Critically Examine**: Critically examine is similar to examine, but in critically examine the student has to focus more on giving the positive and the negative side of the issue. After analyzing both the sides, the student has to give a balanced opinion of his/her own.
5. **Evaluate/Analyze**: Evaluate is similar to examine. The difference is that in evaluate, your answer should give more reference to the current happenings and to the recent government reports released.
6. **Enumerate**: To enumerate means to list out a sequence of points asked in the question. The question would be of asking you to list down all the important points, for example, to list down the Sustainable Development Goals (SDGs).
7. **Justify**: When asked to justify, you have to provide facts, theories and explanations to justify an opinioned statement. After justifying the statement, you should also write 2-3 lines on the non-applicability of the statement in certain situations.

Features – At a Glance

Learning Objectives

At the start of every chapter, Overview of the chapter has bee given to facilitate the better understanding.

After reading this chapter, you will learn the following:

- Meaning of the term administration and its various a
- Meaning of the term public administration, its sc various scholars and its comparison with private adn
- Evolution of the discipline of public administration a
- Comparison between the fields of politics and admin

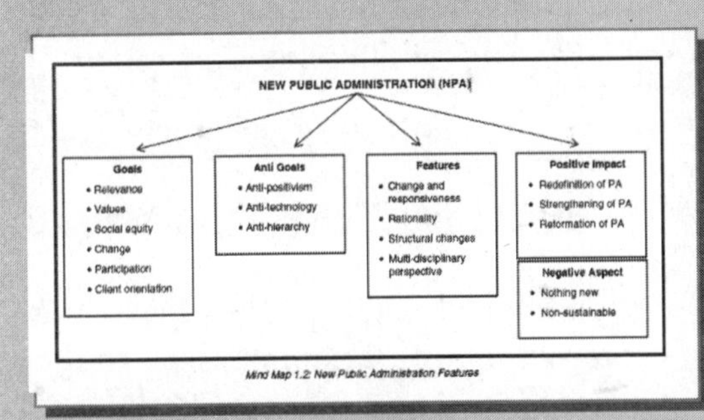

Mind Map 1.2: New Public Administration Features

Mind-maps and Diagrams

In order to facilitate better understanding mind-maps and diagrams have been used to illustrate the key concepts.

Detailed References

In every chapter, detailed references have been provided for further readings.

References

jective of the Theory of Public Administration," in Charlesworth James C., Theo
n: Scope, Objectives and Methods, American Academy of Political and Social Sc

The Study of Administration", Political Science Quarterly, Vol. 2, (June 1887), pp. 1
Hyde Albert C., Classics of Public Administration, Fort Worth, Harcourt Brace Pub
Woodrow Wilson as Administrator", Public Administration Review, Vol. XVI, No.
Prasad V.S., Satyanarayana P., Pardhasaradhi Y., Administrative Thinkers, Sterling

lic Administration and Public Affairs, Englewood Cliffs, Prentice Hall, 1975

Features – At a Glance

Criterion	Types of Goals
Number	Single/multiple goals
Complexity	Simple/easy or difficult/complex goals
Specificity	General or specific goals
Existence	Existence of goals or no goals
Assignment	Self-assigned or imposed goals

Tables and Boxes

Tables and boxes have been provided to compile the important information from the texts.

Practice Question

For the purpose of self-assessment, every chapter ends with the practice questions related to main examination.

Practice Questions (Main Examination)

1. Do you think partisan federalism is acting as impediment to cooperative federalism? Examine how the Supreme Court can end partisan federalism in India.

Ans: Federalism can be defined as the form of government in which the Central or Federal Government is merged with regional or state governments in a single political system. Federalism is a part of the basic structure of the Constitution of India (as provided by the Supreme Court).

Previous Years' Questions

Mayoism, the organizational theory has travelled a long roa
ness." Comment

the Simonian perspective that the 'decisional science envelo
their feedback not in an integrated manner but anything other than t

reasing organizational size gives rise to dialectical forces ha

erits of the classical theory of organization and the systems approac

Previous Years' Questions

Each chapter is followed by the compilation of questions asked in the past 30 years by UPSC, from the chapter.

Important Terms

The book comprises a detailed index at the end, using which, the reader can navigate to the important terms, they are looking for.

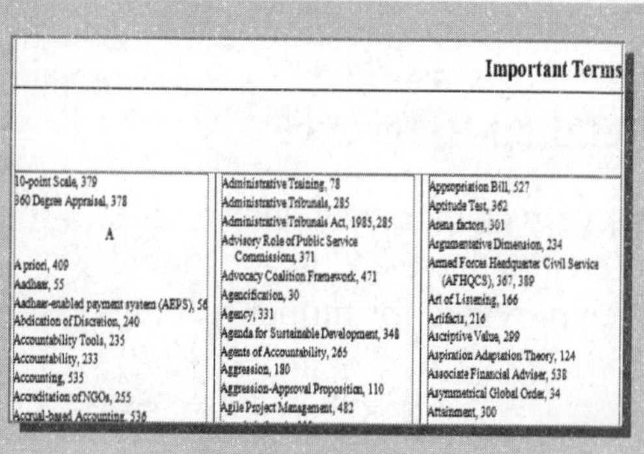

Important Terms

About the Author

Lohit Matani is an Indian Police Service (IPS) officer of the 2014 batch posted in Maharashtra cadre. He holds B.Tech and M.Tech degrees in Material Science and Technology from the Indian Institute of Technology (IIT), Banaras Hindu University (BHU), Varanasi. He has earned accolades during his academic years for publishing 7 US patents in the fields of dielectric materials and wireless power transmission. Before joining the IPS, Lohit has worked for 7 months in General Electric (GE) Technologies Ltd. To fulfil the urge to share his knowledge, and having qualified for the UPSC twice with very good marks in public administration, he always wanted to publish a book on the subject. Lohit loves interacting with young students and candidates preparing for the civil services examination through his articles, blogs, and books. He is the writer of the blog lohitmatani.wordpress.com. Lohit is also the author of *Internal Security* and *Introduction to Civil Services* (OakBridge, 2018).

CHAPTER 1 Introduction to Public Administration

After reading this chapter, you will learn the following:

- Meaning of the term administration and its various applications and forms.
- Meaning of the term public administration, its scope, its nature, its significance, its description by various scholars and its comparison with private administration.
- Evolution of the discipline of public administration and its growth through various stages.
- Comparison between the fields of politics and administration.
- Various features of New Public Administration (NPA), its goals, features and evaluation.
- The three Minnowbrook Conferences and their significance.
- Public Choice Approach to Public Administration.
- The New Public Management (NPM) movement, its theoretical underpinnings, salient features, significance and appraisal.
- Post-NPM reform models including entrepreneurial government, Business/ Government Process Re-engineering, Neo-Weberian State and New Public Service.
- The concept of Liberalisation, Privatisation and Globalisation (LPG), its importance and challenges.

1.1 Meaning, scope and significance of Public Administration

1.1.1 Definition of Administration

The word 'administer' is derived from the Latin word *administrare*, which means to care for or to look after people and to manage affairs. Administration as an activity is as old as society itself.

However, as an area of study, it started with the publication of an essay on the study of administration in 1887 by Woodrow Wilson (ex-President of USA). It is a group activity and involves cooperation and coordination for the purpose of achieving desired goals or objectives. As a process, administration occurs in public, private, and non-governmental organisations.

Broadly speaking, the term *administration* appears to bear at least four different meanings or different senses depending upon the context in which it is used.[1]

As a discipline: It is the name of a branch of learning or intellectual discipline taught and studied in colleges and universities.

As a vocation: It is a type of work, trade, profession, or occupation of an organisation, especially one that involves knowledge and training in a branch of advance learning.

As a process: It is the sum total of the activities undertaken to implement a public/policy or a plan to produce some desired services or goods.

As a synonym, 'executive' or 'government': The word is also used as a synonym for 'government' or for a body of persons in supreme charge of the state affairs, for example, the Narendra Modi Administration and the Manmohan Singh Administration.

1.1.2 Comparison among Administration, Organisation, and Management

The terms *administration*, *organisation*, and *management* are often used interchangeably and synonymously. However, it is important to know the distinction between these three terms (Table 1.1).[2]

Table 1.1: Comparison among Administration, Organisation, and Management

Administration	Organisation	Management
(a) *Administration* is the force (or the policy makers) that lays down the aims and objectives toward which an organisation and its management are to strive. It is the broad policy under which an organisation and its management operate.	(a) An *organisation* is a combination of the necessary human resource, materials, tools, equipment, working space, and other accessories brought together in a systematic and effective co-relation to attain the objective(s) of administration.	(a) *Management* is the force that leads, guides, and directs an organisation for the accomplishment of pre-determined objectives.
(b) The Administration sets the goals.	(b) Organisation is the machine of the management for the attainment of the goals determined by the management.	(b) Management strives to attain the goals set by the administration.

1.1.3 Public Administration

There is an underlying similarity between the administration of public, private, and non-profit organisations. The distinction lies in the different ecological settings in which each operates. The "public" aspect of "public administration" attributes a special character to it. The *Public* can be understood to formally mean *government*. So, public administration is government administration or a socio-economic and politico-administrative confluence in action.

Exhibit 1.1 provides the definitions of public administration given by various scholars. Summing up these definitions, the concept of public administration can be outlined as follows:

1. It is a *non-political public bureaucracy* operating in a political system.
2. It *covers all three branches of government*, i.e., executive, judiciary, and legislature, although it tends to be concentrated in the executive branch.
3. It *provides regulatory and service functions* to the people in order to facilitate an ordered life.
4. It is the *business side of the government* and as such is concerned with public policy-making and execution.
5. It *is interdisciplinary in nature* and draws upon other social sciences such as political science, economics, and sociology.
6. It *deals with the ends of the State,* the sovereign will, the public policy, public interest, and public laws.
7. It *is the study of the authoritative allocation of values by the state*. It is the study of the state in action in the background of the whole political system. It includes the study of public media, legislature, political parties, and other such institutions as a part of the state and the political system.

Exhibit 1.1: Various Definitions of Public Administration

Woodrow Wilson: Public administration is the detailed and systematic application of the law. Every particular application of the law is an act of administration.

L.D. White: Public administration consists of all those operations having for their purpose the fulfillment or enforcement of the public policy.

Luther Gulick: Public administration is that part of the science of administration which has to do with the government. It concerns itself primarily with the executive branch where the work of the government is done; though there are obviously problems also in the connection with the legislative and judicial branches.

J.M. Pfiffner: Administration consists of getting the work of government done by coordinating the efforts of people so that they can work together to accomplish their set tasks.

Herbert Simon: By public administration is meant, in common usage, the activities of the executive branches of national, state, and local governments, government corporations, and certain other agencies of a specialised character. Specifically excluded are judicial and legislative agencies within the government and non-governmental administration.

Dwight Waldo: Public administration is the art and science of management as applied to the affairs of the State.

Nicholas Henry: Public administration is a broad-ranging and amorphous combination of theory and practice. Its purpose is to promote a superior understanding of government and its relationship with the society it governs (theory), as well as to encourage public policies to be more responsive to social needs and to institute managerial practices attuned to effectiveness, efficiency, and the deeper human requisites of the citizenry (practice).

F.A. Nigro and L.G. Nigro: Public administration is a cooperative group effort in a public setting. It covers all the three branches of the government—executive, judiciary, and legislature—and also deals with their interrelationships. It also has an important role in the formulation of public policy and is thus a part of the political process. Moreover, it is closely associated with numerous private groups and individuals in providing services to the community.

1.1.4 Scope

The scope of public administration includes its major concerns as an activity and as a discipline.

Public Administration as an Activity

As an activity, public administration embraces all the activities of the government. So the scope of public administration here is equal to the scope of state activity. In the modern welfare state, people expect a variety of services from the state. In this context, public administration provides a number of welfare and social security services to the people. Besides, it manages government-owned industries and regulates private industries. Moreover, it covers every area and activity under the ambit of public policy.

Public Administration as a Discipline

Public administration as a discipline spans the following views:

POSDCoRB view

According to this view, public administration deals with the planning, organisation, staffing, directing, coordinating, reporting, and budgeting (POSDCoRB) processes of public organisations. This view is given by Luther Gulick and will be discussed in detail in Chapter 3 on Administrative Thought. POSDCoRB activities are common to all organisations. These give unity, certainty, and definiteness to organisations and make their study more systematic. However, this view overlooks the 'subject matter' with which the different agencies are concerned.

The Subject Matter View

Public administration deals not only with the above-mentioned processes but also with the substantive matters of administration, such as defence, law and order, education, public health, and agriculture. Apart from the POSDCoRB techniques, these services require specialised techniques of their own. For example, police administration requires special techniques of crime detection and law and order management. Thus the discipline of public administration deals with both the processes—POSDCoRB techniques and the substantive concerns. To elaborate on this argument, Lewis Meriam has said that

> "Public Administration is an instrument with two blades like a pair of scissors. One blade may be the knowledge of the field covered by POSDCoRB, the other blade is the knowledge of the subject matter in which these techniques are applied. Both blades must be good to make an effective tool."

However, there is no unanimous view on the scope of public administration. Different scholars have given different ideas on the scope of public administration. The views of some important scholars are presented below.

1.1.4.1 Willoughby's View

In his book, *Principles of Administration,* Willoughby said that the study of public administration includes the study of five areas:[3]

General or overhead administration: This administration deals with managerial activities such as planning, organising, staffing, and coordinating.

Organisational structure: This refers to the design of the organisation such as hierarchy and scalar chain.

Personnel administration: This deals with the management of the human resource of an organisation and includes activities such as training, recruitment, and grievance redressal.

Financial administration: This refers to the study of the economic use of financial resources of an organisation.

Material and supply: This refers to the study of the optimum use of material resources of an organisation.

1.1.4.2 Macqueen's View

According to Macqueen, the scope of public administration extends to the three M's.

Man: It refers to human resource management in an organisation.

Method: It refers to the study of the structures and processes of an organisation.

Material: It refers to the study of the optimum utilisation of material resources of an organisation.

1.1.4.3 Pfiffner's View

According to Pfiffner, the study of public administration includes the study of the following two areas:

The principles of administration: It refers to the study of the various concepts, theories, laws, methods, methodologies, tools, techniques, and so on which are used for administering an organisation.

The sphere of administration: It refers to the study of various levels of administration such as local administration, regional administration, internal administration, national administration, international administration, and so on.

1.1.4.4 Walker's View

According to Walker, the study of public administration is extended to the following two major areas:

Administrative theory: It refers to the study of concepts, theories, tools, techniques, methods, and methodologies of administration.

Applied administration: It refers to the study of the various functional areas of administration such as school administration, health administration, law and order administration, and so on.

1.1.4.5 Dwight Waldo's View

Public administration as a discipline includes the study not only of the tools and techniques of administration (POSDCoRB view) but also of the public policy of the government. This expands the scope of public administration to such an extent that everything comes under the umbrella of public administration. This has also made the discipline inter-disciplinary and multi-disciplinary in nature; as a result of this, the contents of many other disciplines, for example, political science, sociology, and psychology, come under the domain of public administration. Due to this, Waldo has said that *public administration has a stable core though a vacillating boundary*. The study of the stable core imparts its identity while the study of the vacillating periphery further enriches it. The study of the tools and techniques of administration is the stable core of public administration. The vacillating periphery is the study of domains such as public policy and state theories in light of the various tools and techniques of administration.

1.1.4.6 Stephen K. Bailey's View

According to Bailey, the study of public administration includes the study of four major areas:

Descriptive theory: Descriptive theory refers to the study of the 'what is' of public administration. It includes the study of organisational structures and organisational processes of public organisations.

Normative theory: Normative theory refers to the study of the 'what ought to be' of public administration. It includes the normative concerns and planned goals of government and public organisations.

Instrumentalist theory: This theory refers to the study of the tools and techniques (POSDCoRB view) of public administration.

Assumptive theory: This theory refers to the objective study of administrative behaviour. It refers to the behaviour of an individual within a public organisation.

Thus, it is clear from the above interpretations of public administration that it carries a wider scope and *is the study of the government in action*. Government inaction is a dependant variable, and being so, it is linked to a number of ecological concerns. The government in action is never static and, thus, its boundary can never be established or delineated.

1.1.5 Nature of Public Administration

The nature of public administration indicates some of its defining characteristics that impart an identity to this discipline. The various views in this regard are as follows.[4]

1.1.5.1 Integral Nature vs Managerial Nature

According to the *integral view*, 'administration' is the sum total of all the activities—manual, clerical, managerial, etc.—that are undertaken to realise the objectives of a public organisation. In this view, all the acts of officials of the government, from the attendant to the secretaries of the government and the head of the State, constitute public administration. Henri Fayol and L.D. White are supporters of this view. According to the *managerial view* of administration, all managerial activities of the people involved in planning, organising, commanding, coordinating, and controlling constitute public administration. This view regards the administration as getting things done and not doing things. Luther Gulick, Herbert Simon, Smithburg, and Thompson are supporters of this view.

1.1.5.2 Narrow Nature vs Broad Nature

If we try to classify the definitions of public administration given by various scholars, we can label them as belonging to either a narrow view or a broad view. *Narrow view* theorists such as Simon and Thomson have emphasised that public administration as a discipline deals with the study of the executive branch of the government. On the other hand, *broad view* theorists such as Willoughby, Gladden, and Dimock say that public administration is the study of all the three organs of the state, i.e., the legislature, executive, and judiciary.

1.1.5.3 POSDCoRB Nature vs Subject Matter Nature

This topic is already discussed under the topic 'Public Administration as a Discipline'.

1.1.5.4 Instrumentalist Nature vs Discretionist Nature

The *instrumentalist nature* of public administration describes public administration as an instrument in the hands of the political class or political community to implement efficiently that which is expressed politically. Under this view, public administration lacks autonomy. On the other hand, the *discretionist nature* of the public administration is an autonomous system. As per this description, it is not an instrument in the hands of the political community, rather it is an instrument of the State. It is responsible for protecting and promoting the public interest, national interest, constitutional philosophy, and social ethos.

1.1.6 Public Administration and Private Administration

As discussed already, the administration is a group activity in which coordination and cooperation are accomplished via the available human resource to attain the desired goals or objectives. Thus, it seems to be universal in all types of organisational settings. However, the nature of administration differs and depends on the nature of the organisational setting and the goals with which it is concerned. On the basis of the institutional setting, the administration is classified into public administration and private administration.

1.1.6.1 Distinction Between Public Administration and Private Administration

Table 1.2 highlights the distinction between private administration and public administration.

Table 1.2: Distinction between public administration and private administration

Public Administration	Private Administration
(a) Public administration is accountable to the public at large as its goals are public in nature. (b) Public administration generally has external financial controls through a legislative body (such as the Indian Parliament). (c) Public administration generally has non-monetary objectives, which cannot easily be measured and accounted for. (d) Public administration operates within a legal framework and is generally rule-oriented. (e) Public administration is subject to political direction and control. It takes place in a political context.	(a) Private administration is accountable to its organisational heads only because its goals are generally not related to public interest. (b) Private administration is financially controlled by their internal mechanisms only. (c) Private administration's main objective is profit, which can easily be measured and accounted for. (d) Different private organisations are regulated by their different sets of rules and regulations, and they are generally goal-oriented.

Public Administration	Private Administration
(f) In public administration, the actions are open for the public to gaze and scrutinises. (g) Often public organisations spend more money than their income or revenue. Thus, they generally have a deficit budget. (h) A public administrator is required to maintain a high degree of consistency in public dealings. (i) Public administration is large-scale administration. Diverse, large, and complex activities fall under the domain of public administration. (j) In the field of public administration, there is generally a monopoly of the government and it does not generally allow private parties to compete with it. For example, the task of national security, foreign relations, and so on. (k) Public administrators generally remain anonymous while working for the public and the government.	(e) Political control does not interfere with public administration. (f) Public scrutiny is not observed in private organisations. (g) A private organisation's income often exceeds its expenditure. (h) A private administration is not bound to maintain consistency of treatment while dealing with its customers. (i) Private administration is, by all means, smaller than public administration, in terms of its size, complexity, and diversity of activities. (j) Private organisations generally deal with matters that involve other competitive players also. (k) Private administrators do not follow the rule of anonymity.

The aforementioned differences between public and private organisations are conventional differences. However, certain other differences provided by some renowned authors are as follows.

Dahl and Lindbloom's Description of Public Administration and Private Administration[5]

Private administration operates in a market economy based on the principle of demand and supply, which primarily promotes individual choice and volition. This mechanism operates through volunteerism and does not use coercion or force. On the other hand, public administration operates under political economies and cannot always be guided by market forces. Thus, public administration has three important limitations as compared to private administration, described in the following.

Problem of free riders: In private administration, all goods and services provided are chargeable as per the market conditions. However, in case of public goods and services, the imposition of market-driven user fees is not possible. In this type of situation, the sense of personal benefit goes down and the tendency to escape responsibility goes up. This gives rise to the problem of free riders in public administration. Free riders are those who are ready to consume the goods and services but try to escape the responsibility of paying for them.

Individual competence: In private administration, individuals are considered rational. Each individual tries to attain the best among the present alternatives and tries to maximise his own utility. However, individuals in public administration are not completely rational as they have to choose between unclear alternatives. This impacts the individuals' competence.

Externalities and spillover: Public administration is prone to externalities and spillover effects. It is impacted by any activity in other agencies, private as well as public. For example, huge investments in the IT industry (unrelated private agencies) can create employment opportunities at all levels. This has the potential to reduce the crime rate and thus influence the role of the police organisation (public administration). This is an example of a positive externality.

Moore's Description of Public Administration and Private Administration

Moore has discussed the difference between public administration and private administration based on the concept of 'public value'. Public value refers to various public goods and services. It is provided by both the public sector and the private sector. Moore says that the public sector provides public value at a cost that is equal to or even less than the cost of production. On the other hand, the private sector provides goods and services at a cost that is more than the cost of production. Thereby, for the public sector, the public value is an end in itself; for the private sector, public value is merely a means to achieve an end.

Benn and Gaus's description of public administration and private administration

Benn and Gaus have brought out the difference between public administration and private administration on the basis of 'the publicness' of public organisations and the 'privateness' of private organisations. The publicness of public organisations is based on the following three characteristics.

Interest: In public organisations, the public at large has an interest. The loss of a public organisation impacts the public at large. However, the loss of a private organisations impacts only a single individual or a group of individuals.

Access: The access and facilities of a public organisation are open to the public at large. However, the facilities of a private organisations are open only to a group of individuals.

Agency: If an agency is owned by a single individual or a group of individuals, it explains the privateness of that organisation. On the other hand, if it is owned by the public at large, it explains the publicness of that organisation.

1.1.6.2 Similarities Between Public Administration and Private Administration

Public administration and private administration have the following similarities:

1. Both public and business administration rely on common skills, techniques, and procedures.
2. Nowadays, the principle of the profit motive is not peculiar only to private administration, as it is now accepted as a laudable objective for public sector enterprises also.
3. In personnel management, private organisations have been influenced greatly by the practices of public organisations, such as job security and regular promotions. Thus both employ similar personnel management techniques.
4. Both public and private organisations are subject to certain legal constraints such as taxation, monetary, and licensing policies.
5. There is a similar type of hierarchy and management system in both the public and private sectors. Both have the same kind of organisational structure, superior-subordinate relationships, etc.
6. Both carry on continuous efforts to improve their internal working and also for the efficient delivery of services to people or customers.
7. Both types of administration serve people, as clients or customers. Both have to maintain close contact with people to inform them about their services and also to get feedback about their services and products. In both cases, public relations help them to inform and improve their services to the people.

1.1.7 Significance

The importance of public administration has grown, both as a discipline and as a profession, over time.

1.1.7.1 As a Discipline

Public administration is an important area of study for the following reasons:

Public interest: The government today has to work towards the public interest. Thus, the study of public administration is necessary for the effective delivery of public services.

Policy impact: The study of public administration is necessary to understand the impact of government policies and programmes on society.

Developing force: A detailed study of public administration, and particularly development administration, is required in developing countries in order to attain speedy socio-economic development.

Touches citizens: Public administration plays a significant role in the lives of the people. For most of their needs, citizens depend on public administration. Thus, it has become an important part of the educational curriculum.

1.1.7.2 As a Profession

In the contemporary age, public administration as a profession has become an essential part of society and a dominant factor. It is important as a profession because of the following reasons:

Basis of the government: Administration, or the executive branch of the government, is the basis of the government. Government can exist without legislature and judiciary, but no government can exist without administration.

An instrument for providing services: According to Felix A. Nigro, "the real core of public administration is the basic service that is performed for the public." These services can be provided only by public administrators; thus this profession is very important.

An instrument for implementing policies: The policies framed by the government are translated into reality only by public administrators.

A stabilising force in society: Public administration is a major force for bringing and ensuring stability in society. Although the government changes periodically (after 5 years in India), an element of continuity between the old and new orders is provided by public administration.

An instrument of social change and economic development: In developing nations, public administration plays a crucial role in rapid socio-economic development.

Technical character: Public administration is important as a profession as it represents a galaxy of all of a nation's occupations. This is so because an increase in the number of functions undertaken by the government has required highly specialised, professional, and technical services.

1.1.7.3 Reason for Growing Importance of Public Administration

The importance of public administration has grown because of the following reasons.

Emergence of welfare and democratic state: The emergence of the welfare and democratic state has led to an increase in the activities of public administration compared to that of the *laissez-faire* state. The state now has to serve all sections of people in society. This leads to enhanced responsibilities of public administration. Public administration is also required to regulate and control private economic enterprises to meet the objectives of the state.

Industrial revolution: The industrial revolution gave rise to socio-economic problems, hence necessitating governments to assume new roles and responsibilities such as the protection and promotion of the rights of workers in industrial establishments. Public administrators have to implement various legislations in order to protect the rights and entitlement of its citizens. Thus, its arena has grown.

Scientific and technological developments: Various scientific and technological developments such as computers and communication systems have given rise to the era of 'big government' and large-scale administration. This has increased the importance of public administration.

Economic planning: The methodology of economic planning has required a large number of experts and an elaborate administrative machinery for plan formulation, implementation, monitoring, and evaluation.

Rapid growth of population: The ever-increasing population has increased the importance of public administration.

Increase in man-made and natural disasters: Frequent disasters have increased the role of public administration in tackling disasters.

Other reasons: Other reasons for increased importance of public administration are decline in social harmony, increase in violence due to conflicts, communal riots, ethnic wars, terrorism, and so on.

1.2 Evolution of the Discipline and its Present Status

1.2.1 Evolution Before Woodrow Wilson[6]

Public administration has developed as an academic and professional field through a succession of six paradigms, as described by Nicholas Henry. The subject has developed in the USA. Many authors start the discussion on public administration from Woodrow Wilson. However, according to this author, prior to Wilson, there were a number of events and structures that undertook a serious study of government in action. The literature relating to the state and the statecraft existed prior to Wilson as well. Some of the examples are the *Ramayana* and *Mahabharata*, literature of Austrian and German scholars (called Cameralists), and literature of Confucius. Also, there were some French scholars (Bonin, Viven, etc.) as well in this regard.

1.2.2 'The Beginning' of Public Administration

Role of Woodrow Wilson: Woodrow Wilson is commonly thought to be the founder of public administration in the United States. In 1887, Wilson introduced Americans to this field with an essay titled 'The Study of Administration'. This essay published in 1887 is considered to be an important landmark for the beginning of public administration as a discipline. Wilson's vision about the need for administration as a separate discipline to study the government in action gave an impetus to this subject.

Role of public service movement: Apart from Wilson's formative essay, public administration's intellectual roots were planted in the reformist 'public service movement' that was sweeping the American political landscape in the earlier twentieth century. This movement led John D. Rockefeller to found and fund the New York Bureau of Municipal Research in 1906. The Bureau was a think tank and was extraordinarily creative in laying the intellectual groundwork of what public administration should be, and it produced some of the early guides for a wide variety of public administrative tasks.

However, by the early twentieth century, public administration stood as a prominent pillar of the discipline of political science.

1.2.3 1900–1926: Paradigm 1—The Politics-Administration Dichotomy[7]

1. **Role of Frank J. Goodnow:** Frank J. Goodnow, in his groundbreaking book, *Politics and Administration* (published in 1900), contended that there are two distinct functions of government—politics and administration. Politics has to deal with the policies or expressions of state will, while administration has to do with the execution of these policies. Goodnow's point—that elected politicians and appointed public administrators do different things—eventually was labelled by academicians as the politics-administration dichotomy.
2. **Impact of this paradigm:** The politics-administration dichotomy offered protection to the fledgling profession of public administration.
3. **Role of L.D. White:** Leonard D. White, in 1926, wrote the first book, titled *Introduction to the Study of Public Administration*, devoted to the field of public administration. The book expressed the progressive values of public administration at that time. According to him, partisan politics should not intrude on administration. The mission of administration is efficiency, and administration in general is capable of becoming a 'value-free' science in its own right.

These perspectives provided an intellectual base for public administration's next paradigm, which rested on the idea that just as there were principles of science, there were principles of administration.

1.2.4 1927–1937: Paradigm 2—Principles of Public Administration

1. **Role of W.F. Willoughby:** In 1927, W.F. Willoughby wrote a book titled *Principles of Public Administration"*. The book appeared as the second full-fledged book on the subject of public administration. In the book, he suggested that public administrators would be effective if they learned and applied scientific principles of administration. This gave birth to the principles of the administration paradigm.
2. **Impact of this paradigm:** The status of public administration soared high during this paradigm. Thus, it was known as a *reputational zenith* for public administration.
3. **High noon of orthodoxy:** The principles of administration were understood to be indeed principles, i.e., they worked in any administrative setting without exception. Such understanding reached its peak in the work *Papers on the Science of Administration* by Luther H. Gulick and Lyndall Urwick. These papers were a report to the President's Committee on Administrative Science and were regarded as the field's high-noon of orthodoxy.

1.2.5 1938–1950: The Era of Challenge

In this era, the discipline of public administration faced dissent from two mutually reinforcing directions. One objection was that politics and administration could never be separated in any remotely sensible fashion. The other was that the principles of public administration were something less than the final expression of managerial rationality.

Doubt over politics-administration dichotomy: The politics-administration dichotomy was questioned due to two subtle intellectual shifts—internal and external. Internally, public administration scholars started noting, in the 1930s, that making public policy remained, certainly, a question for statesmen, but public officials surely affect the process of public policy in some manner.

Externally, in the 1930s, the word 'politics' expanded its scholarly meaning to include public policy-naking, and public administrators, in accordance with the dichotomy, were not allowed to enter this forbidden political zone. It was at this point that the politics-administration dichotomy became ntellectually untenable.

Criticism by Herbert A. Simon: In 1947, Herbert A. Simon published his devastating critique *Administrative Behaviour.* In this work, he dismissed the principles of administration as 'proverbs of administration'. He wrote that a fatal defect in the current principles of administration is that for almost every principle one can find an equally plausible and acceptable contradictory principle, thus rendering he whole idea of principles moot. We will discuss the ideas of Herbert Simon in Chapter 3 on Administrative Thought.

Criticism by Dahl: Dahl found three important problems in the evolution of the science of public administration:

(a) Exclusion of normative concerns: The principles of public administration exclude normative concerns from the discipline. However, it is impossible to exclude such normative concerns from the subject, as the scientific means to achieve efficiency cannot be useful without any clarification of the ends to be attained.

(b) Machine concept of organisation: Dahl says that the principles of administration regard an organisation as a machine and do not embrace the presence of a psychological human being in it. According to him, the science of public administration must include some aspects of human behaviour also.

(c) Parochial nature of intellectual pursuits: According to Dahl, the principles of administration were formed on narrow and parochial research. He suggested that there was a tendency to enunciate universal principles based on a few examples drawn from limited national and historical settings. According to him, the study of public administration must become a much more broad-based discipline, resting not on a narrowly defined knowledge of techniques and processes, but rather extending to the varying historical, sociological, economic, and other conditioning factors.

1.2.6 1950–1970: Paradigm 3—Public Administration as Political Science

n this paradigm, public administrationists wormed their way back into the warm and welcoming vomb of the mother discipline, i.e., political science. This happened because it was understood that political matters cannot be separated from public administration in a democracy like America. Political science clearly had a profound impact on the character of the discipline of public administration. The fundamental principles of American political science, such as democracy, political participation, and due process under law, became important concepts for public administration. Political science helped in laying some of the normative foundations (ends to be attained) for the discipline of public administration.

.2.7 Paradigm 4—Public Administration as Management (1950–1970)

During the 1950s and 1960s, a spate of scholars shifted towards management, which was sometimes also known as administrative science or generic management. Cornell University's Graduate School of Management, founded in 1948, was the first academic unit that embraced the idea of generic management. Generic management was considered as the logical successor to more parochial paradigms such as public administration and business administration. It was said that public, private, and other institutional distinctions of management were false. Thus, management was considered as a 'groundswell development' that tended to pervade all other disciplines.

This era could be thought of as a resurgence of Woodrow Wilson's desire to make the business o government 'less unbusinesslike', and it renewed belief in developing the 'principles o administration'. The years 1950–1970 also featured the 'public management movement'; both halve were emphasised—public (by the political-science-oriented scholars) and management (by th management-oriented scholars). The management paradigm pushed the public administratio scholars into rethinking what the 'public' in public administration really means. It was said tha publicness was composed of *three dimensions: agency* (or *institutional*), *interest* (or *philosophical*) and *access* (or *organisational*). These dimensions have already been discussed earlier in this chapter.

1.2.8 Forces of Separatism (1965–1970)

During the period 1965–1970, public administration sowed the seeds of its own renaissance and too a path of separation from the disciplines of political science and management. As a result, th National Academy of Public Administration (NAPA) was set up in 1967. It was an association o America's most distinguished public administrators and academics, which could serve as a resourc in the solution of public problems.

1.2.9 1970 onward: Paradigm 5—Public Administration as Public Administration

'Public Administration as public administration' refers to the public administration's successful brea with both political science and management and its emergence as an autonomous field of study an practice. This paradigm brought about a reunion of public administration's professors an practitioners, which was lacking after the 1930s. The epistemological independence of publi administration took place only after the birth, in 1970, of the National Association of Schools c Public Affairs and Administration (NASPAA). NASPAA is composed of about 260 of America' Master of Public Administration (MPA) and related degree programmes.

From Politics-Administration Dichotomy to Politics-Administration Continuum

In paradigm 5, politics and administration coexist on the same social continuum, but as separate an distinct constellations of logic, whose activities sometimes overlap. At the far ends of this continuum political acts (such as appointing unqualified relatives to government jobs) can be distinguished fro administrative acts (such as appointing the most qualified applicants drawn from a competitive poo to government jobs). However, it is difficult to separate the political from the administrative in th middle of that continuum. But it is clear that political values relate more to power, communit pluralism, personality, loyalty, emotion, and ideology, whereas public administration's values rela to fairness, hierarchy, elitism, impersonality, professionalism, analysis, and neutrality.

1.2.10 1990–Present: Paradigm 6—Public Administration as Governance[8]

1. Since 1990, changes such as globalisation, the Internet, and related developments hav pressurised governments to reduce their sovereignty. As a result, governments hav relinquished their traditional responsibilities to individual citizens, groups of citizen public-private partnerships, the non-profit sector, the private sector, public authoritie associations of governments, and local governments. This process is known i administrative literature as *withering of state*.

2. Further, we started moving away from *government* (i.e., delivery of public services by institutions of state and control over citizens by these institutions) and towards *governance* (i.e., configurations of laws, policies, organisations, institutions, cooperative arrangements, and agreements that control citizens and deliver public services). *Government is institutional and governance is institutional and networked.* Such a networked nature of public administration is also known as 'making a mesh of things'.

Impact of this paradigm

It is seen that there is a positive correlation between the intense collaboration among public organisations and a high level of satisfaction held by citizens. An example of this collaboration is the *focused deterrence* approach to fight crime in the USA. Focused deterrence was a network-based method designed to reduce gang-related violence by coordinating among police, prosecutors, social workers, clergy, outreach workers, victims, former gang members, social-network analysts, and public and private employers, among others. The approach became spectacularly successful, with the crime rate decreasing by more than half in many cities of the USA.

1.3 Politics and Administration

1.3.1 Distinction Between Politics and Administration

As already discussed in paradigm 1 of public administration, the earlier writings on public administration made a clear distinction between politics and administration as two distinct and separate kinds of activities.

1.3.1.1 Woodrow Wilson's Explanation[9]

According to Woodrow Wilson, the field of administration is a field of business. It is removed from the hurry and strife of politics. In most points, it stands apart even from the debatable ground of constitutional study. It is a part of political life only as machinery is a part of the manufactured product. Administration lies outside the proper sphere of politics. Administrative questions are not political questions. Although politics sets the tasks for administration, it should not be allowed to manipulate administration offices.

1.3.1.2 Locus and Focus of Politics and Administration[10]

According to scholars, politics and administration are institutionally (locus of a field) and professionally (focus of a field) different fields. The institutional locus of politics could be found in legislatures, political parties, and pressure groups, whereas administration is the formalised executive branch of government. In terms of professional focus, politics is what the politicians do and the focus of administration is to turn political objectives into practical reality.

1.3.1.3 Max Weber's Explanation

Purity of administration as a differentiated function (apart from politics) received great intellectual support from Weber's concept of rational bureaucracy. The structural features and the behavioural norms implicit in a bureaucratic form of organisation contributed to the growth of public administration as a fairly autonomous institution bound by rigorous rules and uncontaminated by irrational forces. There may be changes in political leadership, but the civil servant must unfailingly offer technical advice to his political master keeping himself aloof from the politics of the day.

1.3.2 Areas of Interaction Between Politics and Administration[9,11]

Politicians interact with administrators on different forums in various ways. Peter Self-identified four important areas of interaction between politicians and the administrators. These are as follows.

Policymaking

Politicians influence policies by sensing public demands and converting them into election promises. The members of the legislature (politicians) influence policymaking in a limited way through legislative debates and participation in legislative committees. On the other hand, administrators have their own quota of influence at the time of the actual framing of the formal policy document. They have the professional skills to put ideas into practice. The policy document is their handiwork.

Arbitration of interests

Arbitration of interests is palpably a political act and falls within the province of politicians. Individual politicians, the political party, and the legislature engage in arbitration functions of various kinds. In their constituencies, politicians often intervene in group disputes. More powerful interest groups such as labour, industry, big landlords, and even some bureaucratic groups try to tilt public policy in their favour through influential politicians. On the other hand, the administrators get involved in interest group politics both overtly and covertly. When they receive memoranda and visiting groups representing different interests, they deal with group interests in the course of their normal official business. There are usually many consultative committees attached to the ministries which act as conduits for flow of group interests within the administration.

Treatment of individual and localised claims

In this area, administrators defend their distinctive methods of uniformity against politicians' frequent interests in influencing administrative decisions. Take, for example, the case of planning. As the Indian experience shows, the brokerage role of the politician does not end at the planning stage; it extends up to implementation. Block development planning may allocate resources among different sectors such as irrigation, animal husbandry, and so on. However, when it comes to actually spending the money on the ground, political interference takes the form of clientele manipulation and site (village) manipulation. Adherence to the administrative role and political intervention in the interest of the client often clash with each other. The relationship between the politician and the administrator tends to move towards a collision course in a situation where the politician is keen to help his supporters and constituency members by disregarding bureaucratic rules and regulations.

Balance between political accountability and administrative discretion

Administrators need autonomy and discretion in much the same way as politicians need control and intervention. There is thus an inherent clash in public administration between political control and administrative autonomy. The administrator's preference for autonomy might stem from his respect for rules, regulations, and uniformity, and also from his genuine concern for speed and promptitude. The politician from this perspective is a stumbling block in the way of disciplined and expeditious action. On the part of the politician, the administrator appears as an interloper and a competitor. The politician perceives himself as the ultimate controller of administrative affairs and the real guardian of public interest. If the administrator seeks autonomy, the politician looks at him as a usurper of political power and an unwanted intruder in the politician's domain.

1.3.3 Acid Test for Politician and Administrator

The acid test of a minister's statesmanship lies in how much he can delegate to the civil servant without losing control over policy in key areas of concern. The civil servant, in turn, can serve the minister well if he tries genuinely to enter into the mind of the minister and presents policy alternatives for his final choice.

1.3.4 Top Level Management—Vanishing Point of Politics-Administration Dichotomy[12]

The top level management is virtually the vanishing point of the politics-administration dichotomy. Governmental power is used and directed from the topmost level, where the minister and his secretary and other top advisers have close relationships, in the course of identification of problems and framing of public policies. As Peter Self observes, there are significant structural patterns at the top managerial level that have an obvious effect on the actual relations between political executives and administrators. The structural patterns are woven around the following:

1. How members of the two groups come to occupy their respective positions.
2. How sharply the political and administrative roles are differentiated.
3. How much the two groups differ in the degree of cohesiveness in terms of stored beliefs, attitudes, and common ties.

1.3.5 Public Administration and the Prevailing Political Regime (American Perspective)[13]

As discussed already, professional public administrators are educated to have neutral competence in maximising efficiency, effectiveness, and economy in governmental organisations. However, public administration occurs within a larger system directed and controlled by political operatives whose highest priorities do not usually include maximising efficiency, effectiveness, and economy. As a consequence, public administrators should maximise efficiency, effectiveness, and economy in support of, but subordinate to, the higher political priorities. In America, there are four political groupings:

1. Cultural conservatives
2. Economic conservatives
3. Conservative democrats
4. Liberal democrats

Each of these political groupings reflects a distinct political philosophy and seeks to actualise their distinct vision of society.

1.3.5.1 Public Administration Operates Within the Constraints Set by the Prevailing Political Regime[14]

There is a difference between the political administration in control of the executive branch and the prevailing political regime. A regime is defined as the set of institutions through which a political unit makes its fundamental decisions over a sustained period and the principles that guide those decisions. A regime constrains its political actors including those who control the administrative branch.

Individual public administrators work with their superiors to ensure compatibility among the definitions of their job, the public administration model or system in use, and the political grouping in control. By ensuring this compatibility, individual public administrators pursue efficiency, effectiveness, and economy in support of higher political priorities.

A new political administration's principles will either be consistent with the prevailing regime's principles or they will not. If they are not, the new administration will probably be severely constrained in its ability to implement its management plan, if one is defined. In most such cases, the new administration will simply accept the existing administrative system with perhaps some tinkering at the margins (because administration is subordinate to political priorities). Therefore, in pursuing compatibility, the individual administrator needs first to identify the prevailing regime in terms of the political groupings, identify the controlling political administration in terms of the groupings, note incompatibilities and constraints, and identify the intent of the administration with regard to the prevailing administrative system.

1.4 New Public Administration (NPA) and Minnowbrook Conferences

1.4.1 Need for Restoration of Public Values in Public Administration: The Birth of NPA[15]

By the end of the 1960s, American society was faced with a number of problems. These included dissatisfaction with the Vietnam War, population increase, environmental problems, increasing social conflicts, and economic crisis. These problems made the younger generation of intellectuals question the efficacy and speed of the response of the political and administrative systems. It was felt that the dissatisfaction arising from the persisting turbulent environment calls for restoration of values and public purpose in the government. Human and value-oriented administration was suggested. It was felt necessary to inject, in public administration, the goals of being responsive to the needs of clients and ensuring social equity in service delivery. This thinking led to the emergence of a new public administration (NPA). It intended to provide a philosophical outlook for public administration.

1.4.2 Precursors to New Public Administration

During 1967-68, various efforts were initiated in the USA with the aim of providing a multidisciplinary public policy and social-equity-oriented focus to public administration. The three prominent efforts among them were the following:

- The Honey Report on Higher Education for Public Service
- The Philadelphia Conference on the Theory and Practice of Public Administration
- The Minnowbrook Conference –I

1.4.2.1 The Honey Report on Higher Education for Public Service

In 1966, John Honey of Syracuse University prepared a report on the evaluation of public administration as a field of study in US universities. It highlighted the following problems confronting the discipline:

1. Uncertainty and confusion over the status of the discipline
2. Inadequate funds at the disposal of the university departments for promoting the discipline
3. Institutional shortcomings while researching and teaching public administration
4. Lack of communication between the scholars and practitioners of public administration

Thus, it recommended the following for improvement of public administration as disciple:

1. There should be generation of resources for public administration research and practice, both from the government and business sector.
2. There should be encouragement for higher studies in public administration.

3. There should be interlinking of university departments and the government through the appointment of professors to positions in the government, and vice versa.
4. Setting up of a National Commission for Public Service Education for providing leadership in the field of public administration.

This report laid the basis for examining the role of public administration in generating social awareness.

1.4.2.2 Philadelphia Conference on the Theory and Practice of Public Administration

A conference on the theory and practice of public administration was organised, in 1967, by the American Society of Political and Social Sciences under the chairmanship of James C. Charlesworth. The following major viewpoints emerged out of the conference:

Flexibility in the scope of the discipline: There should be flexibility in the scope of public administration to facilitate its development as a discipline. This flexibility will account for the massive increase in the functions and responsibilities of the government.

Dichotomy between politics and administration: The dichotomy between politics and administration is meaningless due to interlinkages between the policymaking and implementation functions of public administration.

Focus on social problems: Public administration as a discipline should focus more on social problems such as poverty, unemployment, and environment.

Promote social equity: Public administration as a discipline should promote values such as social equity, efficiency, accountability, administrative responsiveness, and people's participation in decision-making.

Management flexibility: There should be flexibility in the management of public organisations to avoid organisational hierarchy and administrative rigidity.

Training of public administrators: Training programmes should be conducted in public administration to sharpen the trainees' managerial abilities as well as to deepen their social sensitivities. These programmes should be conducted in professional schools.

Administrative ethics: There should be emphasis on administrative ethics in these training programmes.

This conference was considered very important, as it provided a broad philosophical basis to the discipline of public administration.

1.4.2.3 The First Minnowbrook Conference

The atmosphere in the USA in the 1960s was characterised by the cynicism of youngsters towards institutions such as family, church, media, profession, and government. However, there was an optimistic view that public administration can be useful for solving the USA's technological as well as social problems. It was at this juncture, in 1968, that a conference was organised at Minnowbrook by the young scholars of public administration under the guidance of Dwight Waldo of Syracuse University.

The basic objective of this conference was to examine ways of making public administration responsive to social concerns and assuming the role of a change agent in reforming the society. It also had the objective of analysing the changing perspectives in the field of public administration amongst those who experienced the Great Depression, New Deal, World War II, and those who entered the field in the 1960s. The focus of the conference was on the following important aspects of public administration:

Public policy approach: It gave importance to the public policy approach of public administration, as it had a significant effect on the quality of government.

Significance of social equity: It considered social equity as a key objective while implementing public policies, apart from efficiency and economy.

Values in public administration: It said that public administrators are not mere implementers of fixed decisions, but are agents for implementation of values such as ethics, honesty, and responsiveness in the provision of public service.

Cut back of government agencies: It said that despite the fact that the public needs change, government agencies often outlive their purposes. Hence wherever needed, cut back of government agencies needs to be resorted to.

Change management: It said that the role of a responsive government is to manage change and not just focus on growth.

Participative citizenry: It also said that active and participative citizenry should be a part of public administration.

Anti-hierarchy: It challenged the usefulness of the concept of hierarchy.

Importance of implementation: It also said that implementation plays a major role in the decision-making process.

Importance of pluralism: It said that although pluralism is accepted as a useful device for explaining the exercise of public power, it had ceased to be a standard for the practice of public administration.

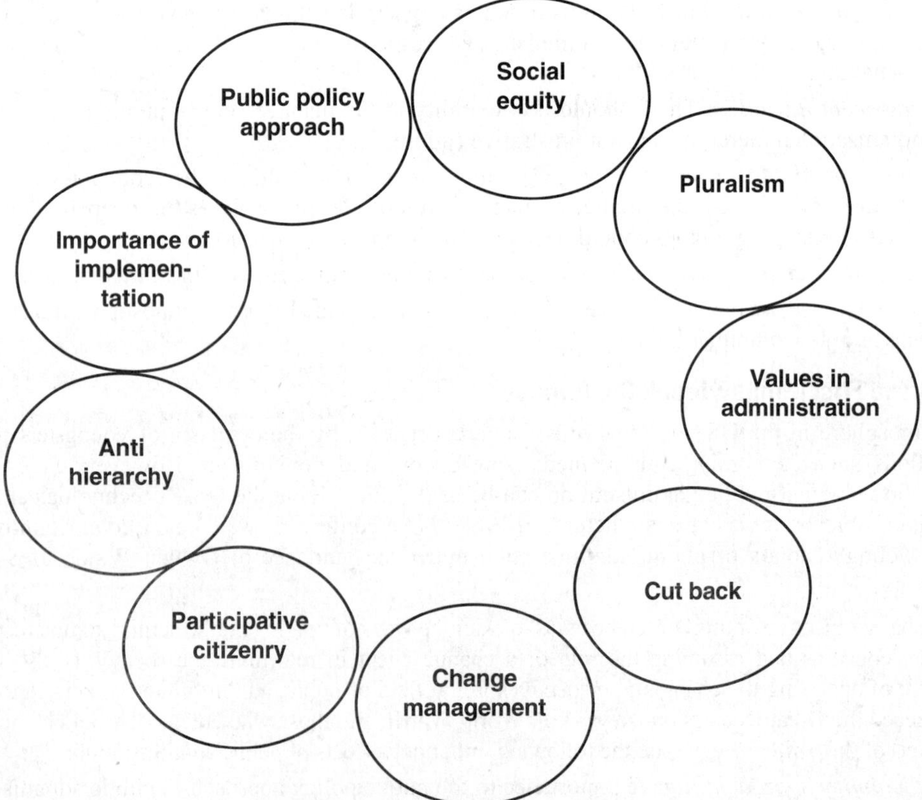

Mind Map 1.1: Features of First Minnowbrook Conference

The conference was sensitive to the problems in the functioning of American democracy; thus it attempted to provide a new focus to public administration. Moreover, it led to the emergence of new a public administration (NPA).

1.4.3 Goals of New Public Administration

The scholars of new public administration (NPA) focused on the following goals for NPA.

Relevance: It was felt that the discipline of public administration should be relevant to the contemporary issues and problems of the society. The excessive management orientation in the discipline needs to be done away with, and public administration should deal with the political and administrative implications of administrative action. The scholars desired radical changes in the curriculum of the discipline to make it more relevant to the realities of public life.

Values: The value-neutral orientation of public administration was vehemently criticised and rejected by these scholars. They made a case for inclusion of concepts such as values, justice, freedom, equality, and human ethics in the discipline of public administration. It was held that commitment to values would enable the discipline to promote the cause of the disadvantaged sections of the society.

Social equity: The NPA movement felt that social equity should be the primary aspect of public administration. It made a plea for distributive justice and equity to be the basic concerns of public administration.

Change: The movement attempted to make the discipline of public administration more relevant and social equity oriented through change and innovation. They considered public administrators as change agents. They wanted the discipline to be receptive to any change in society.

Participation: The movement called for greater participation by all employees in an organisation in matters of public policy formulation, implementation, and revision. In addition, participation from individuals and groups from outside the organisation was sought to make public administration more responsive and client-oriented.

Client orientation: The First Minnowbrook Conference and NPA identified client orientation as the key goal of public administration. Thus, it called for a change in the attitudes of bureaucrats to be people-oriented.

This *normative approach advocated by NPA proponents* called on the government to adopt the objective of reducing the economic and social disparities and enhancing the life opportunities for everyone in the society.

1.4.4 Anti-Goals of New Public Administration

Robert Golembiewski identified three major anti-goals of public administration. They were as follows.

Anti-positivism: Positivism is a philosophical system that recognises only that which can be scientifically verified or which is capable of logical or mathematical proof. It focuses only on administrative concepts such as profit and efficiency. This makes administration more rigid. The NPA movement intended to reduce the rigidities in administration to make it more adaptable, receptive, and problem-solving.

Anti-technology: NPA wanted that human beings should not be treated as mere cogs in an organisational machine to foster the traditional goals of economy and efficiency.

Anti-hierarchy: Hierarchy as an organisational principle promotes bureaucracy, brings in rigidities, kills creativity and innovation, and isolates the administrator from the surrounding environment. Hence, the NPA scholars condemned hierarchical structures as traditionally propagated by public administration.

1.4.5 Features of New Public Administration

George Frederickson has referred to certain key features of the new public administration. These are as follows.

Change and responsiveness: The NPA movement called for appropriate internal and external changes in administration to adapt to the changes in the social, political, economic, and technological environments.

Rationality: The movement said that the efficacy of public administrators' actions should be judged not only from the point of view of the government but also from the perspective of the citizens.

Structural changes: New public administration called for experimenting with different organisational structures in tune with the relevant situation and needs of the environment. It said that there was a need for small, decentralised, and flexible hierarchies to facilitate citizen interaction.

Emphasis on multi-disciplinary perspective: According to the NPA perspective, public administration is influenced not just by one single thought but by several knowledge streams. Hence, an understanding of various approaches, including political, management, and human relations, is essential for the growth of the discipline.

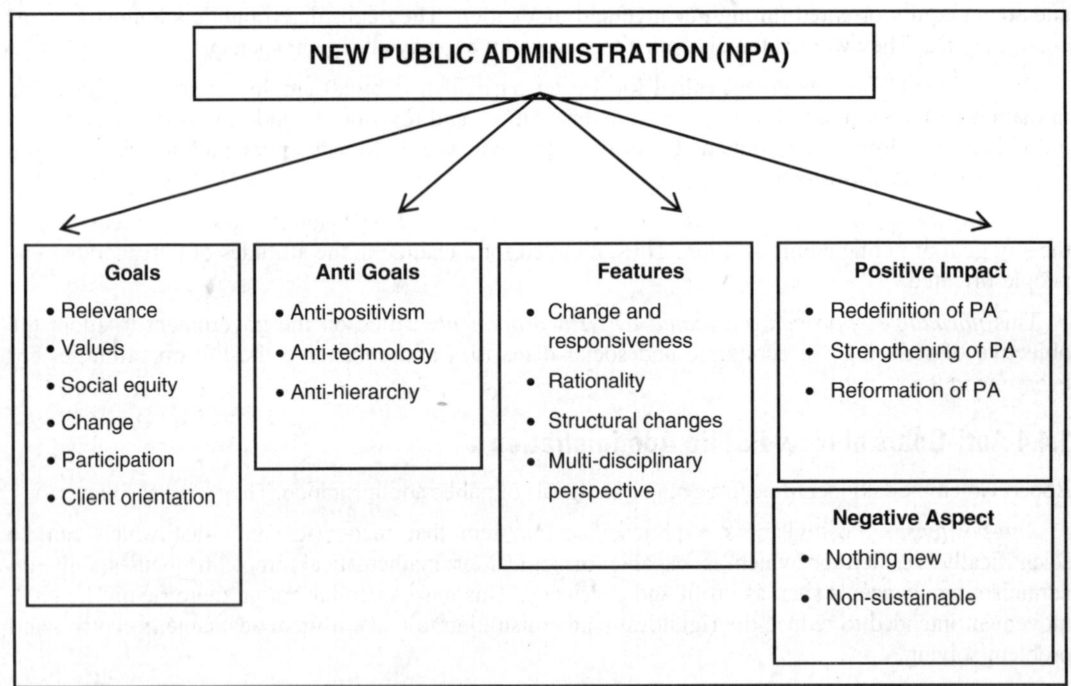

Mind Map 1.2: New Public Administration Features

1.4.6 Evaluation of New Public Administration

NPA was criticised on the following aspects.

Lack of novelty: Some scholars said that there was nothing 'new' in NPA, except that it made a plea for the administration to become responsive to the societal problems prevalent during that period. Regarding NPA, critics said that "newness does not lie in the thread of the fabric rather in the manner the fabric is woven."

Durability: At that time, critics doubted whether the new thinking will sustain for long or not.

However, NPA had the following positive aspects.

Redefinition of public administration: NPA redefined public administration because of its emphasis on key concepts such as participation, responsiveness, client orientation, and so on.

Strengthening of public administration: In NPA, an attempt was made to bring administration closer to the people and strengthen its capacities to solve societal problems.

Reformation of public administration: NPA stirred intellectual thinking towards democratising public administration, building a theory of public administration in tune with its interdisciplinary nature, thereby attempting to reform public administration in its outlook and functioning.

1.4.7 The Second Minnowbrook Conference

The Second Minnowbrook Conference was held on 4 September 1988 under the leadership of George Fredrickson. It was attended by 68 scholars and practitioners of public administration and other disciplines such as history, economics, political science, and psychology.

1.4.7.1 Background of Minnowbrook II Conference

The conference was held in the backdrop of the changing role of the state and the government, more privatisation, contracting out, and increasing role for non-state actors in the governance process. The scenario in the 1980s was dominated by the philosophy of privatisation and a concern for private interest. Due to this, a general preference amongst the American public was towards lesser governance. Apart from this, during the period of this conference, the field of public administration expanded, with many universities in the USA offering programmes in public administration. Also, it became more inter-disciplinary in nature compared to the situation in the 1960s, when it was a part of political science.[16]

1.4.7.2 Objective of Minnowbrook II Conference

Minnowbrook II aimed at comparing and correcting the changing epochs of public administration. This was attempted through a comparison of the theoretical and research perspectives of the 1960s with those of the 1980s and their respective influences on the conduct of governmental and other public affairs.

1.4.7.3 Major Thrust Areas of Minnowbrook II Conference

Minnowbrook II had the following thrust areas.

Social equity: Social equity was a predominant theme at Minnowbrook I. However, it was discussed that this concept was nearer to reality in the time of Minnowbrook II.

Democratic values: In Minnowbrook II, strong concerns were expressed about democratic values and the centrality of public administration in promoting them. The concern was manifested in the focus on ethics, accountability, and leadership in public administration.

Normative-behaviourist debate: The debate between the normative and behaviourist perspectives continued in this conference. The normative perspective refers to the study of the 'what ought to be' of public administration. It includes the normative concerns and planned goals of the government and public organisations. On the other hand, the behavioural perspective of public administration is the analysis of public administration from the micro-level perspective of individual behaviour and attitudes by drawing on insights from psychology on the behaviour of individuals and groups in public organisations.

Acceptance of diversity: Minnowbrook II accepted diversity in a workforce as a basic value. It was identified in three main contexts: (a) the issue of generalists versus specialists; (b) racial, ethnic, and sexual diversity; and (c) gender diversity. However, not much attention was given to the problems being engendered due to heterogeneity and to conflict resolution strategies and arbitration skills.

Emphasis on short-term goals: Minnowbrook II emphasised on short-term goals for public administration, as it was felt that the environment in which public administration performs is so complex that a meaningful long-term vision is neither reasonable nor possible.

Professional ethnocentricity: The discussion in Minnowbrook II gave an indication of 'professional ethnocentricity' or parochialism indicating that public administration, as a field, is not much concerned with examining interdisciplinary issues.

Disdain towards capitalism: In Minnowbrook II, there was a strong negative attitude towards business as an enterprise. The deliberations exhibited a disdainful acceptance of capitalism and business. One of the challenges to public administration, it was felt, is to manage the 'seams' of society rather than building on the best that the business as well as public sector offer.

Innovative personnel practices: In the conference, emphasis was laid on innovative personnel practices to bring out the best in the employees and reinforce high productivity.

Non-addressal of technological issues: In the conference, an unwillingness to address technological issues in public administration was evident.

Not normative: In the conference, there was an unwillingness to look at the specifics of what the government should do.

1.4.7.4 Major Concerns of the Second Minnowbrook Conference

Minnowbrook II focused on the following major concerns of public administration.[17]

Complexity of environment: The environment in which public administration works has became more complex due to the changing nature of public administration as well as due to diversity in the problems faced by the government such as AIDS, nuclear wastes, budget, trade deficit, and so on. This made it essential for public administrators to rely more on facilitation, dialogue, and negotiation. According to Minnowbrook II, the curricula of public administration need to be revised with a view towards highlighting the societal as well as political context, emphasising more on interpersonal skills and techniques.

Requirements of democracy: The participants of Minnowbrook II emphasised the need for administrators to keep in view the requirements of democracy and employ democratic process-based methodologies in the performance of their duties. This was felt necessary due to (a) the need for positive action by public officials for the fulfilment of the potential of democracy by the representative government and (b) the underlying obligation to advance democracy, which is an ethical requirement of public service.

Imbalance between public needs and resources: A major concern of Minnowbrook II was on correcting the imbalance between the public needs of that time and the resources devoted to their amelioration. It was felt that to maximise the efficiency of administration in that situation, a bureaucracy more concerned with dialogue and consensus was required. It was emphasised that practising public administrators need to be more proactive in the performance of their duties. Openness and public participation in administration was also felt to be required to be encouraged.

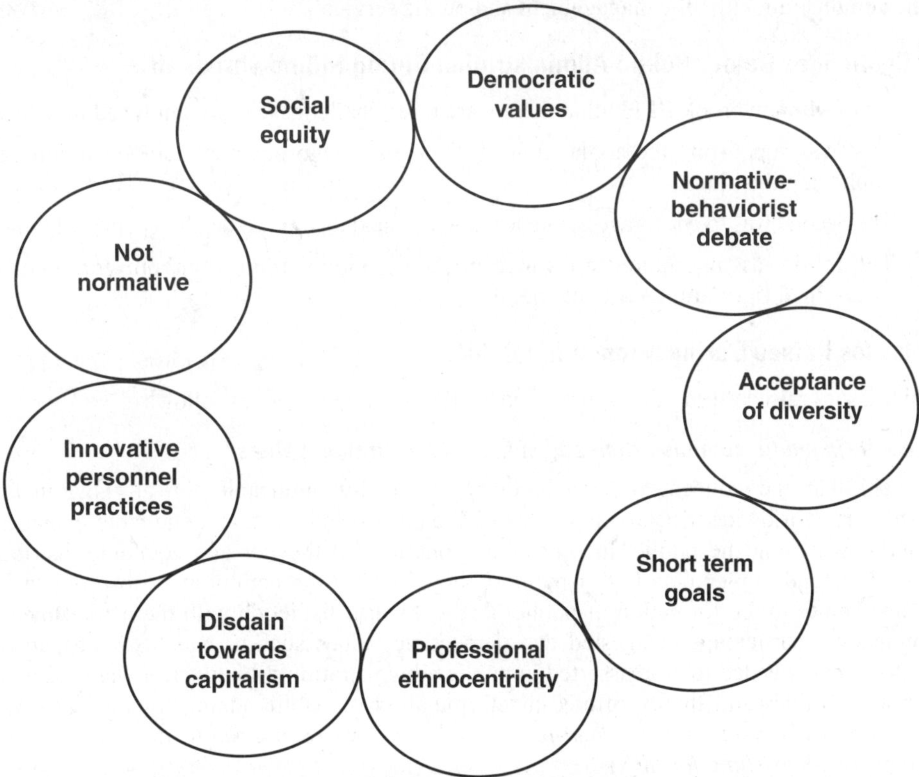

Mind Map 1.3: Features of Second Minnowbrook Conference

1.4.7.5 Significance of Minnowbrook II Conference

The Second Minnowbrook Conference made an attempt to examine the theory and practice of public administration in the changing scenario. It tried to project a future vision for public administration by balancing the business and public sectors. The effort has been on rebuilding the discipline.

1.4.8 Minnowbrook Conference III

The Third Minnowbrook Conference took place in September 2008 and was headed by Rosemary O'Leary. It was conducted in two phases. The first phase was a preconference phase. In this phase, both young and emerging scholars of public administration were asked to contribute a five-page critique of public administration. Almost 56 proposals were accepted and considered. The second phase was conducted in a round table format. It was a get-together of 220 senior scholars from 13 countries. The scholars were divided into various groups based on their areas of concern.

1.4.8.1 Theme and Background of Minnowbrook III

The conference was conducted against the background of the ascendancy of neo-liberal ideology, advocating downsising of government and opening up more space for the market and non-government agencies. Against this background, the theme of the conference was chosen as 'the future of public administration, public management and public service'.

1.4.8.2 Challenges Before Public Administration During Minnowbrook III

Participants of Minnowbrook III felt that there were three challenges before public administration.

1. First was supporting the application of diverse and rigorous methodological approaches in public administration.
2. The Second was to encourage theoretical diversity and theoretical depth in public administration.
3. The third was to promote relevance in public administration without compromising on methodical rigor and theoretical depth.

1.4.8.3 Issues Raised During Minnowbrook III

The major issues raised during the Minnowbrook III Conference were as follows.[18]

Social equity in public administration and public administration values

It was said that the concept of social equity is equally applicable for all governments and administrations worldwide. Social equity was defined as (a) fair, just, and equitable management of all institutions serving the public directly or by contract, (b) the fair and equitable distribution of public services and implementation of public policy, and (c) the commitment to promote fairness, justice, and equity in the formation of public policy. As dissatisfaction with the market mechanisms was dominating, participants suggested that democratic values such as equality, transparency, and representativeness needed to be reasserted in public administration. Moreover, it was said that public administration values and theory offered a reformulation of public administration, *defining public administration as 'a socially embedded process of collective relationships, dialogue and action to promote human flourishing for all'.*

Rethinking of the identity of public administration

According to the participants, various new social problems await the consideration and attention of the state and its administrative systems. They call for taking advantage of multi-disciplinary orientations in the social sciences and finding better ways to integrate them in the current ethos of public administration. They said that such inter-disciplinary ideas, tools, and methods can help in overcoming social problems and creating effective remedies for the new type of social maladies. Interdisciplinarity also meant cooperation, collaboration, and a share of information and knowledge. Participants said that the multi-level, multi-method, and multi-system analyses with a look towards the future are the main frontiers of modern public administration.

Public administration as a field of study

The participants of Minnowbrook III wanted public administration research that is relevant and applicable, practitioner-friendly, action-oriented, context sensitive, done collaboratively, and in an inter-disciplinary fashion, with methodological diversity and the acceptance of different ways of analysing and thinking. They wanted the discipline to produce students that have the needed skills and competencies to meet society's most pressing public policy problems. They also desired a culture within the field of public administration where the scholars were relevant, practical, and making a difference through interdisciplinary and global work.

Intellectual diversity in public administration

Public administration as a field was categorised by great diversity in theoretical approaches and methodological tactics. This wide scope led to potential epistemological and methodological fragmentation, which prevented scholars from appreciating and building on each other's work. In this situation, it was felt that the key to continued progress was the appropriate application and understanding of empirical approaches of public administration so that methodological diversity generates more robust cumulative analyses of a complex phenomenon rather than fragmentation.

Public administration with a global perspective

The conference said that globalisation has been challenging the theory and practice of public administration at an unprecedented level in contemporary times. To advance the progress of the public administration theory, we need to examine issues across national and ethno-demographic divisions in order to better understand and explain context-specific phenomena. Public administration should reach out to the global public administration community in academic exchanges, global innovation and diffusion of best practices, and collaborative education. The conference called for building theories that offer great explanatory power, have higher acceptability, and are more responsive to the demands in diverse and specific contexts. A vast array of emerging issues, such as anti-terrorism wars, natural and man-made disasters, epidemic diseases, economic crises, energy and environmental problems, and ethnic conflicts are all globally interconnected. Even problems within the traditional domestic policy realms, such as public transportation, information management, and defence and security, have been pushed across national boundaries by extended privatisation and contracting efforts, demanding global perspectives in building knowledge and seeking solutions. Thus, there is a need for a new theoretical perspective of public administration that embraces the opportunity to learn at the global level.

Questions for the future of the field

The participants of the conference criticized that research undertaken by academics is focused on publication in academic journals, not on the potential relevance to the problems being faced by the public and private sector managers. From 1988 to 2008, the field of public administration gradually became less dominated by American scholars. A new breed of public administration 'global scholars' sees comparative studies across countries as a crucial methodology for the construction of new knowledge in the field of public administration.

Public administration in dark times is characterised by numerous and growing catastrophic events in the social, political, environmental, and economic areas; significant, persistent, and systemic policy failures across policy domains; and the loss of vibrant public spaces in which citizens can wrestle with important social questions and engage government officials in discussions. These dark times exist around the world and are made worse by the fact that at precisely the moment in which we confront serious political, economic, and environmental challenges on a truly grand scale, the prospects for an organised, collective will capable of addressing and seeking to resolve these problems is very dim. The participants of Minnowbrook III felt that the *government is not capable of governing in the face of the seemingly insurmountable problems that characterise the dark times,* because of two issues.

- Public administration does not adequately acknowledge itself as a *de facto* arbiter of political conflict and therefore as a discipline capable of and responsible for shaping societal affairs.
- Public administration suffers from a bureaucratic pathology that consigns the field to the pursuit of narrow administrative goals and limits its abilities to address complex policy problems.

1.4.8.4 Minnowbrook III: A Missed Opportunity

Minnowbrook III was considered as a missed opportunity to address the problems of public administration in dark times. This happened because the participants were for the most part unrelated to each other and did not have the time to build the bonds of trust needed for such potentially divisive discussions. The conference also failed to find new approaches and ways to collectively search out future growth trajectories of the discipline. Thus, the conference seemed like a good gathering without being able to reap a rich and intellectual harvest at a time when the discipline of public administration badly needed a new direction and a way out of the nagging identity crisis.

1.4.9 The Three Minnowbrook Conferences: An Analysis

The Minnowbrook Conferences represent an extraordinary assembly of intellectual talent, past and present, and new and seasoned. These conferences are intended to take stock of where the field is, where it is going, and where the field needs to go. Minnowbrook is an idea or rather a set of ideas. A comparison of the three Minnowbrook Conferences is provided in Mind Map 1.4.

Minnowbrook I	Minnowbrook II	Minnowbrook III
It occurred in a time of turmoil in the US, which was in the middle of the Vietnam War.	It occurred in a time of privatisation and globalisation.	It occurred in a context of social and political turbulence as well as dissatisfaction with market mechanisms.
The scholars were young and less than 35 years of age.	The scholars were mostly in their 50s.	The scholars were both young and seniors. Phase 1 consisted of young scholars and Phase 2 of senior scholars.
The conference was revolutionary and radical.	The conference was sober in character.	This conference was intellectually rigorous and practical in character.
It was optimistic in character.	The mood was of constrained optimism. They emphasised on the centrality of the state but also provided a note of caution.	It had a negative attitude while talking about public administration in dark times.

Minnowbrook I	Minnowbrook II	Minnowbrook III
There was no presentation of any papers.	It also did not have a presentation of any papers.	It was occupied by the presentation of papers by junior scholars and discussion by senior scholars.
It consisted of participants from the field of American public administration only.	It consisted of American participants from diverse fields including economics, sociology, and psychology, apart from public administration.	It consisted of diverse scholars from 13 countries across the globe. Thus, it was global in nature unlike the earlier two conferences.
It emphasised on the value of social equity for public administration	The idea of social equity became more real during this conference.	Social equity was specially emphasised and defined in this conference.
The objective of this conference was to evaluate the state of the field of public administration.	Its objective was to compare and contrast the changing epochs of public administration.	Its mission was to critique the current state of public administration, public management and public service, and examine the future of the field of public administration.
It was an action-oriented perspective that embraced normative inquiry. It set an agenda for public administration in the form of NPA.	It retreated from an action perspective to the cerebral examination of the classics, and produced discussions that were more practical and less radical.	It tried to set a future and agenda of public administration but ended by only redefining public administration.
It occurred in an era of search for identity and legitimacy as a separate field of study.	It also occurred in an era of search for identity for the discipline.	At this conference, there was no identity crisis for the discipline, as it had its own journal and trained scholars.
It focused on the Waldonian perspective of a more political, theoretical, and philosophical approach to thinking about the tensions between democracy and bureaucracy.	Apart from the normative Waldonian perspective, it also recognised the Simon perspective emphasising a more empirical investigation of organisational parameters.	It focused on methodological diversity for understanding the complex phenomena of today.

Mind Map 1.4: Comparative analysis of the three Minnowbrook Conferences

1.5 Public Choice Approach to Public Administration

1.5.1 Introduction to Public Choice Approach

Public choice applies the methods of economics to the theory and practice of politics and administration. It is an application of economic principles to the study of how collective decisions are made—application to such things as the design and working of the Constitution, election mechanisms, political parties, lobbying of interest groups, bureaucracy, Parliament, and other parts of the government. The title of the approach is formed of two words—'public' and 'choice'. The first word 'public' indicates that the approach focuses on the activities of, and processes in, public organisations. The word 'choice' suggests that the behaviour or actions of people in public organisations or their activities are to be understood in terms of a single dimension, that of the choices the individuals make from the available alternatives and within constraints.

1.5.2 Methodological Individualism and Rationality

The methodology of public choice consists of two related elements. The first one, the idea of *methodological individualism*,[19] propounded by public choice theory, rejects viewing society as an organism. It says that even when studying collective entities and groups, the individuals should be the unit of analysis, both as the basic unit of decision-making and as the unit for whom the decision is made. It says that an organic view of society is misleading. The second element is *rational choice.* This idea suggests that people try to do the best they can, given the constraints they face. People try to rank alternatives in order of preferences and choose the most preferred alternative while being consistent in their choices. Applied to politics, the basic inference of this idea is that politics should not be analysed from a 'public interest' perspective but from an 'individual gain maximising one' perspective. All participants in the political arena—politicians, bureaucrats, voters, and stakeholders—act to maximise their own gains. They do not have 'public interest' but their 'self-interest' in mind while taking actions.

1.5.3 Public Choice as Exchange

Public choice theorists deal with the question of the state in a contractarian paradigm. According to them, the government is an economic institution in two senses. First, it is an end through which people can realise certain ends. Second, it arises as the result of bargaining and exchange among individuals. Governments are not only a party to, but also the result of, this exchange process. Public choice theorists say that political decision-making institutions can be analysed in the same way as economic institutions. They assert that human beings' propensity to barter and exchange is not limited to economic exchanges or commercial transactions but is present in almost all areas of human interaction.

A normative principle that follows from the exchange paradigm is that if voluntary exchange involving consent is preferred to coercion, then those policies that promote voluntary exchange among consenting individuals are to be preferred. This is why public choice theorists are such vocal proponents of market relations. Not only is the market in its idealised form an efficient economic institution that promotes growth and prosperity, but also the voluntary exchange process that underlies the market, and in any sphere, is the best guarantor of human liberty and the best protector against coercion.

1.5.4 Market Failure and Government Failure

Pareto Optimality

Public choice theorists suggest that, provided certain assumptions are met, when people enter into voluntary exchange with one another, each pursuing their self-interests independently, they ensure that competitive markets are the most efficient institutions for allocating resources. On this, sociologist Vilfredo Pareto gave the concept of *Pareto optimality*. It refers to a situation where no one can be made better off without at the same time someone else being made worse off. The price system takes care of resource allocation. Competition, in perfect markets, is so severe that no one has it in his or her power to set a price that would guarantee extra gains for that individual or organisation. Everyone sells homogeneous goods or services, and sellers can enter or leave the markets with ease. Perfect competition means a situation where paradoxically there is no rivalry. Everyone has equal power (or the lack of it).

Before the situation of Pareto optimality (or Pareto efficiency) is attained, a situation of Pareto improvement is witnessed. A change in the market that makes one individual better off without making another worse off is called a *Pareto improvement.* When all the Pareto improvements are made in a market situation, the allocation of resources is deemed as *Pareto optimal.*

Situations of Market Failure

A market failure is a situation where free markets fail to allocate resources efficiently. The following are the situations of market failure.

Positive and negative externalities: An externality is an effect on a third party that is caused by the consumption or production of a good or service. A positive externality is a positive spillover that results from the consumption or production of a good or service. For example, although public education may directly affect only students and schools, an educated population may provide positive effects on the society as a whole. A negative externality is a negative spillover on third parties. For example, second-hand smoke may negatively impact the health of people, even if they do not engage in smoking.

Environmental concerns: Production of a good or service may impact the environment, which may become an important consideration for market failure.

Public goods: Public goods are goods where the total cost of production does not increase with the number of consumers. For example, a lighthouse has a fixed cost of production that remains the same whether one ship or hundred ships use it. Public goods distort markets as people can share the benefits without paying for them or contributing to their growth.

Underproduction of merit goods: A merit good is a private good that the society believes is underconsumed, often with positive externalities. For example, education, healthcare, and sports are considered merit goods.

Overprovision of demerit goods: A demerit good is a private good that the society believes is overconsumed, often with negative externalities. For example, alcohol, cigarettes, and prostitution are considered demerit goods.

Monopoly: Monopoly is a condition when there is only one player in a field. For example, before the 1990s, the Indian Government had monopoly in telecommunication services.

It can be said that theoretical conditions for market success are extremely stringent and rarely to be found in the real world. Hence, cases of market failure are ubiquitous. However, according to public choice theorists, the existence of market failure does not imply that the government will do a good job by participating in economic production and provision.

Government Failure

The situation in which the government shows inefficiency in the provision of goods and services is called *government failure*. According to public choice theorists, there is no guarantee that a real-world government will be more efficient or will automatically enhance social welfare. They explain government failure in terms of the pursuit of vested interests by politicians who try to win elections and by rent-seeking bureaucrats.

1.5.5 Modern Public Choice Thinkers

1.5.5.1 Duncan Black and Median Voter Theorem[20]

Duncan Black is considered the founder of modern public choice. His most important contribution is his *median voter theorem*. This suggests that on straightforward issues—such as how much should be spent on roads—the political parties will gravitate to the centre of opinion, where most votes are to be had. Any party that drifts away from the centre will lose votes to the other side. Further, since political parties aim to win votes, the result is that parties bunch together at the centre, giving voters little real choice.

1.5.5.2 Kenneth Arrow, Impossibility Theorem, and Voting Paradox[20]

According to Kenneth Arrow, the key question for any electoral system is how accurately the group decisions that emerge from it reflect the nature, prevalence, and strength of preferences among the members of the voting public. He found that there is no practical democratic system that can guarantee this happy outcome. He called this the 'impossibility theorem'. Moreover, any election system can be manipulated by people voting strategically or by *agenda setters* who decide the order in which decisions are taken. The purpose of voting is to try somehow to translate the opinions of many individuals into one collective decision. However, the outcome of an election depends on how an election is managed. If there is someone who can set the order in which the votes are taken—say, the chair of a committee that has to choose between several options—that agenda-setter can rig the order in which the votes are taken in order to ensure that his or her own preferences prevail regardless of what other people want. The more options that are on offer, and the more electors there are voting, the more severe this *voting/ cycling paradox* becomes.

1.5.5.3 Anthony Downs, Rational Choice, and Rational Ignorance[20]

Anthony Downs applied the idea of rational choice theory across the workings of the political marketplace. For political parties, rational choices are dependent on the income, prestige, and power they gain from being in office, rather than on any particular policies. Indeed, they would change their policies in search of the votes that would put them in government. Voters, for their part, would choose whichever party delivers the most benefits. In his *idea of rational ignorance* of voters, Downs pointed out that it takes time and effort for voters to find out what policies each candidate supports. But the chance of any person's vote actually deciding an election outcome is microscopic. Thus, it is simply not worth voters' time and efforts to become well-informed. As a result, many people vote on the basis of party labels or do not vote at all. Sadly, this means that since most voters are apathetic, well-informed interest groups can exert a disproportionate influence on the parties.

1.5.5.4 Buchanan and Tullock—The Virginia School[20]

Buchanan and Tullock published a book titled *The Calculus of Consent* in 1962. In this book, they examined the issues raised by simple majority voting systems, the first of them being logrolling. *Logrolling* is a process of vote trading in which an interest group bargains with another group for gaining votes. For example, a group wants better roads in its own locality. Then it makes a simple bargain with other such groups: you vote to improve our roads today, and we will vote to improve yours some time soon. The expression probably derives from the old practice of neighbours assisting each other to move felled timber, which is difficult to do alone. An agreement to exchange votes on separate legislative measures, as in the roads example, is called *explicit logrolling*. On the other hand, *implicit logrolling* happens when the different groups bundle their various proposals into a package before they are voted for. So voters or legislators who feel very strongly about one measure also end up voting for other people's measures too. Buchanan and Tullock founded what is known as the 'Virginia School' of Public Choice, which focuses on constitutional theory and real-world political institutions.

1.5.5.5 Mancur Olson[20]

In his 1965 book, '*The Logic of Collective Action*', Mancur Olson explored the impact of special interest groups on the political process. There are many large interest groups that find it hard to mount effective lobbying campaigns. These include important groups such as consumers and taxpayers. One reason for it is the *free rider problem*. Accordingly, if a consumer lobby were successful in winning concessions from politicians, all consumers would benefit, whether or not they actively joined the campaign. So, why should anyone make any contribution, when they can free-ride on the efforts of others? The disturbing result is that those groups, such as professional bodies and trade unions, which can somehow restrict any benefits they achieve for their own members, are over-represented in the public debate. However, those, such as consumers and taxpayers, that are more numerous but harder to organise are under-represented.

1.5.5.6 William H. Riker, Rochester School—Minimum Winning Coalition and Game Theory[20]

William H. Riker was the leading figure of the Rochester School of Public Choice. He explored how interest groups might form coalitions, offering to support each other for mutual advantage in the political process. Alliances take effort to set up and keep together, however, and Riker found that 'grand coalitions' are short-lived. He concluded that the best strategy for interest groups was to assemble a *minimum winning coalition*, an alliance just large enough to win but not too big to keep together. Riker also bought *game theory* into public choice. Game theory is a branch of applied mathematics that provides tools for analysing situations in which parties make decisions that are interdependent. This interdependence forces the players to take into account what other players might do in order to make their own best decisions, based on their goals. Applications of this theory to political science include the analysis of strategic voting in committees and elections, formation and disintegration of parliamentary coalitions, and the distribution of power in weighted voting bodies.

1.5.5.7 William A. Niskanen and Bureau Shaping Model[20]

The American economist William A. Niskanen tried to identify the interests and objectives of bureaucrats in a 1971 book *Bureaucracy and Representative Government*. Bureaucracy is engaged in the activity of providing public goods and public services. Since these goods and services provided by the bureaucracy are not sold, a political process replaces the market process. Niskanen formulated his theory in a framework of what economists call *bilateral monopoly* or a situation where there is a single seller of a product confronting a single buyer of the product. Consequently, both come to have considerable power, control, and bargaining strength. In his model, the government and not the public is the buyer of bureaucratic services. The bureau is the only seller of its services and the government the only buyer of the 'output' of the bureau. This exchange of the output is for a budget and not a per-unit price. He suggested that people in bureaucracy seek to maximise their budgets—which brings with it power, status, comfort, security, and other benefits. Later an extension of the Niskanen model was provided by Dunleavy, which is called the *bureau-shaping model*. The basic extension was that higher-ranking bureaucrats supposedly place greater emphasis on non-pecuniary gains rather than on maximisation of budgets, as Niskanen had proposed. Thus senior bureaucrats are supposed to shape bureaus that increase their non-pecuniary power and status, since in public bureaucracies, compared to the private sector, there are greater constraints to pecuniary and monetary gains.

1.5.5.8 George Stigler, Chicago School and Regulatory Capture[20]

George Stigler was the founder of the Chicago School of Public Choice. According to him, regulators (in the government) have some basic incentive while regulating some economic activities (say, monopolies) of the private sector. These incentives suggest that influential individuals and units in the private sector and special interest groups 'capture' the regulatory process by influencing the bureaucrats who are in charge of this regulation by appealing and playing on the bureaucrats' incentives. Big businesses or large farmers often benefit from regulation by getting subsidies, by being protected from competition and price control, which ensures large demand. Of course, trying to get regulation would involve lobbying, and being regulated means being subject to rules and regulations, but so long as the costs are lower than the benefits, monopolies would try to get regulated.

1.5.5.9 Vernon Smith[20]

Vernon Smith conducted experiments on how people actually make their choices. From his experiments, he concluded that it is possible to design election systems that reveal the choice of different elector's views and discourage strategic voting. While people do free ride, they do so very much less than is commonly thought. Indeed, many people devote far more energy to politics than their 'rational' self-interest would justify.

1.5.5.10 Jagdish Bhagwati and Rent Seeking[19]

Bhagwati spoke of directly unproductive profit-seeking activities (DUPs). They are means of earning a profit through activities that do not add to social value. They produce goods and services that do not provide utility. Typical examples of DUPs are tariff-seeking lobbying, creating artificial monopolies that generate rents, and even smuggling. The important thing about DUPs is that these use up resources to create profits but produce no output. DUPs can arise both as a consequence of particular policies and be undertaken to influence the making of favourable policies. As examples of the former situation, we can consider lobbying by special interest groups to gain from some policy. Another type of activity within this category is the smuggling that may take place as a consequence of a protectionist policy characterised by high custom duties. As an example of the second category, we can think of strong industrial groups, which lobby for high tariffs and quotas or policies that discourage foreign competition.

1.5.5.11 Ostrom and Democratic Administration[21]

Ostrom gave a new paradigm of public administration, known as democratic administration. His theory had the following basic elements.

Divided authority: According to Ostrom, in view of the corrupt nature of political decision makers, authority should be divided to limit and control the exercise of political power. He focused on shifting the locus of administrative responsibility from a single centre to fragmented and multi-headed authority structures and even to citizens directly.

Against politics-administration dichotomy: There is no dichotomy between politics and administration. There is always political interference while framing administrative rules and regulations, as they concern public goods and services. The politics-administration dichotomy, in view of Ostrom, has been instrumental in the installation of the concept of a *monocratic organisation*.

Democratic competition: Ostrom advocated healthy and democratic competition among government agencies. For this, he said, multi-organisational arrangements are better than monocentric administrative apparatus structured hierarchically. Ostrom said, "If public agencies are organised in a way that does not allow for the expression of a diversity of preferences among different communities of people, then producers of public goods and services will be taking action without information as to the changing preferences of the persons they serve."

Maximise efficiency: The purpose of democratic administration is to maximise efficiency as measured by last-cost expended in time, effort, and resources. According to Ostrom, democracy and efficiency are not merely closely related concepts, but they are virtually synonymous.

1.5.6 Public Goods and Services

Public goods and services may be provided by the public as well as the private sector. They have two characteristics: non-rival competition and non-exclusion.

Non-rival competition: This concept means that for a given quantity of a good available, consumption by one person does not diminish the quantity left for someone else to consume. A classic example is national defence. National defence consumed by one citizen of a country does not reduce the amount left for others.

Non-exclusion: A private good, such as an apple, has the property of exclusion in it. If a person eats an apple, he can exclude another from eating it. For a good with non-exclusionary properties, on the other hand, it is impossible or extremely expensive to confine the benefits of the good to a few persons. A person will derive benefit from the production of the good, regardless of whether or not he or she pays for the good.

Non-rival but exclusionary goods (club goods): A good may be non-rival and yet it may be possible to exclude some people from using that good. A classic example is cable television broadcast. If a programme is being broadcast, then its viewing by one person does not diminish the amount left for others. However, it is possible to exclude some people from viewing the programmes.

Non-exclusionary but rival goods (congested goods): These goods have rival consumption; but in their case, it is very difficult or extremely costly to carry out exclusion in consumption. A congested road is a prominent example. One person driving a vehicle does not mean others can be excluded from driving their vehicles; but, clearly, the space taken up by one person on the road reduces the space available for others.

Pure public goods: Goods that show the characteristic of being both non-rival and non-exclusionary are pure public goods. A classic example of a pure public good is a lighthouse. When the light of the lighthouse is on, it is difficult to prevent any nearby ship from seeing it and being guided by it (non-excludability). Moreover, one ship's use does not reduce the light left for other ships, or, in other words, one ship's use does not affect the ability of other ships to use the light (non-rivalry).

1.6 New Public Management (NPM)

New Public Management has become an area of focus in the developed as well as developing world from the late 1980s onwards. According to Pollitt, NPM has variously been defined as a vision, an ideology, or a bundle of particular management approaches and techniques for the reformation of the public sector. During the 1980s, debates and discussions centred around making a deliberate, conscious choice between the 'old' public administration, which relied on bureaucratic efficiency, and the present-day new perspective of public administration with a significant management orientation labelled NPM. This perspective led to a series of managerial concepts and techniques in the governmental systems with a view to making public organisations efficient, economical, and effective.

1.6.1 Original Sources of NPM

Christopher Hood and Michael Jackson's book[22] *Public Administration* (1991) is considered as the original source of the concept of NPM. The inspiration of NPM came from very different sets of literatures. One was the new institutional economics led by authors such as Williamson or Moe. The other literature was broadly interested in 'mangerialism', drawing inspiration from a range of management theories applied to mainly private sector organisations.

1.6.2 Theoretical Underpinnings and Genesis of NPM

The three main theoretical underpinnings of NPM are *public choice*, *principal-agent theories*, and *new Taylorism*.

Public Choice Theory

The theory criticised the Weberian bureaucratic model as lacking cost-consciousness because of the weak links between costs and outputs. It said that there are no incentives for politicians and bureaucrats to control costs, as the reward system in the public sector is not oriented towards performance improvement. Moreover, it explained that public managers focus more on delivery than on productivity and efficiency, so waste and over expenditure are common in the public sector. This approach led to a new paradigm of government, sensitive to market forces and remodelled according to the concepts of competition and efficiency.[23]

Principal-Agent Theory

According to this theory, the public acts as *principals*, on whose behalf politicians and bureaucrats (as *agents*) are supposed to govern. However, the principal (public) is unable to hold the agent accountable because of insufficient information (information asymmetry), incompleteness of the contracts of employment, and the problem of monitoring the behaviour of public employees. As the officials usually pursue their own narrow, self-interests rather than public interest, the common tendency on the part of public officials is to underperform. Thus, a way out was thought to expose public services to greater competition in the form of NPM reforms.[21]

New Taylorism

Another theoretical root of NPM is hidden in neo-Taylorism. It is concerned with the internal organisation of the bureaucracy. The cause of bad management, according to neo-Taylorism, lies within the administration itself. Things go wrong in public administration because the cost of producing the public services is not known. There is lack of personal responsibility among administrators, and individual administrators play safe rather than show initiative. Public organisations are geared to self-maintenance and routine; service to the community through initiative, imagination, and adaptation is never the motto. To counter this, the following suggestions have been made by neo-Taylorists:[21]

1. Application of performance evaluation techniques to measure actual achievements against preset targets.
2. Assigning personal responsibility for each step in the performance of the production process.
3. Introduction of individual rather than collective incentives for rewarding achievements and punishing underperformance.
4. Following the private sector model of production, imposing increased control by means of economic and financial information with the intention of providing a costing of almost everything produced in the public sector.

The genetic factors responsible for the birth of NPM were as follows.

Increase in government expenditure: During the 1970s and 1980s, the excessive increase in government expenditure in many countries brought to light the wastage, mismanagement, and increasing debts coupled with corruption and inefficiencies in governmental operations. This rise in government expenditure along with poor economic performance led to the questioning of the need for large bureaucracies. Hence, attempts were initiated to slow down and reverse the growth of government in terms of increasing public spending as well as staffing.

Influence of neo-liberalism: Neo-liberalism favoured the dominant presence of market forces over the state. Concepts such as efficiency, markets, competition, consumer choice, and so on gained predominance due to the neo-liberal philosophy. It favoured cutting back the welfare state, maximising individual liberty and freedom, and encouraging market mechanisms leading to equitable outcomes. Free markets unrestrained by the government, removal of barriers to facilitate the free flow of goods and money, and privatisation were considered significant measures for economic growth by this philosophy. It favoured roll-back by the state and the space created by it to be filled by the private sector.

Impact of new right philosophy: The new right philosophy, propagated in the 1970s in the UK and the USA, favoured markets as a more efficient mechanism for allocation of resources. Excessive reliance on the state was not considered appropriate. The new right denounced the role of the bureaucracy and proposed a minimal role for the state in provision of social assistance. This perspective had a global impact in generating a consensus about the efficiency of market forces.

Washington Consensus: During the 1980s and 1990s, it was felt that poverty and economic stagnation in developing countries was the result of the state undermining the operation of market forces. It was considered necessary to bring about adjustments in the economy on various fronts such as in the financial and banking sectors. This led to the emergence of the Washington Consensus. It comprises the reform measures promoted by the Bretton Woods Institutions (International Monetary Fund and World Bank) and other think tanks aimed at addressing the economic crisis in developing countries. This is also termed as the structural adjustment cum stabilisation programme, which emphasised on the need for sound microeconomic and financial policies, trade and financial liberalisation, and privatisation and deregulation of domestic markets. This strategy, gradually adopted in many developing countries, promoted the minimal state that refrains from economic intervention and focuses on sound monetary policy and provision of education, health, and infrastructure.

1.6.3 New Public Management: Salient Features[23]

The core characteristics of NPM are the following:

Productivity: NPM reforms sought to increase the quality and quantity of government services after incurring lower revenues.

Marketisation: This strategy sought to replace traditional bureaucratic structures, mechanisms, and processes with market strategies.

Service orientation: NPM also directed public organisations to keep the needs of the customers as their priority.

Decentralisation: It also sought to delegate service delivery responsibilities to lower levels.

Policy-administration dichotomy: It also directed public agencies to implement policies using the private sector qualities of efficiency and high productivity. It urged that policy decisions should be made by a different central organisation and they should be executed by their implementation agencies.

Apart from these core characteristics, the NPM perspective had the following distinct characteristics:

Managerial skills: Managerial skills such as delegation, motivation, and team building were emphasised to complement policy making skills at the policy level.

Disaggregation: NPM also sought disaggregation of large public organisations into separate self-contained units having their own goals, plans, and requisite autonomy.

Performance standards: Explicit measurable performance standards were sought to be set for public organisations.

Privatisation: Emphasis was laid on the private ownership of public organisations, contracting out, and competition in public service organisations.

Competition: NPM sought to promote competition both among public sector organisations and between public and private sector organisations engaged in the delivery of goods and services.

Strategic capabilities: NPM sought strengthening of the strategic capabilities of public organisations. Strategic capability refers to an organisation's ability to successfully employ competitive strategies that allow it to survive and increase its value over time. It focuses on the organisation's assets, resources, and market position.

Responsiveness: NPM outlined public services to be more responsive to the needs of the customers, providing value for money to the customers.

Steering not rowing: NPM sought for the government to steer the economy rather than grow it by directly providing goods and services. It should become a facilitator for a competitive market.

Information technology: NPM also sought the use of IT for better provision of public goods and services.

As summarised by *Dunleavy* et al., NPM can be synoptically represented as

NPM = Disaggregation + Competition + Incentivisation

Entrepreneurial Government

Osborne and Gaebler came out with the concept of 'entrepreneurial government' in their book *Reinventing Government* (Osborne & Gaebler, 1992). In their vision, the government should be adaptable, responsive, efficient, and effective. For this, they suggested a 10-point programme as follows:

1. Promote competition: Entrepreneurial governments (EGs) promote competition between diverse providers of goods and services.
2. Empower citizens: EGs empower citizens by pushing control out of bureaucracy.
3. Performance measurement: They measure the performance of their agencies, focusing particularly on outcomes, not inputs.

4. Mission driven: They are driven by their missions, not by their rules and regulations.
5. Customer-oriented: They redefine their clients as customers and offer them choices.
6. Prevention rather than cure: They prevent problems rather than solve them afterwards.
7. Profit-oriented: They put their energy into earning money rather than simply spending it.
8. Decentralisation: They decentralise authority, embracing participatory management.
9. Market mechanisms: They prefer market mechanisms to bureaucratic mechanisms.
10. Catalysing role: Rather than only providing services, they focus on catalysing all sectors—public, private, and voluntary—into action to solve community problems.[24]

The authors say that these 10 principles offer a powerful conceptual tool if used as a checklist. One can run any public organisation or system or any of society's problems through the list. The checklist's ultimate value is that it provides the power to unleash new ways of thinking and acting.

1.6.4 Business Process Re-engineering

Business process re-engineering (BPR) is the fundamental rethinking and radical redesign of business processes to achieve dramatic improvements in critical measures of performance, such as cost, quality, service, and speed. According to Fowler, its many features include the following:

Combining of tasks: Separate and simple tasks are combined into skilled and multi-functional jobs.

Natural order: The stages in a work process are performed in their natural order.

Outsourcing: Work is performed where it is best done; some parts of the process may thus be outsourced.

Reduced control: The volume of checking and control of separate tasks are reduced.

Work compatibility: There is total compatibility between processes, the nature of jobs, and structure, management methods, and the organisation's values and beliefs.

Recognition of IT: IT is recognised and exploited as offering many opportunities for the redesign of the work systems and the provision of information to enhance evolved decision-making.

Multiple versions of work processes: Work processes may have multiple versions to cope with varying circumstances.

Such type of BPR leads to the following outcomes:

Flatter organisations: Due to BPR, managerial hierarchies and organisational structures are flattened.

Result orientation: Rewards in re-engineered organisations are given for the achievement of results and not simply for any activity.

Process teams: Due to BPR, work units (i.e., sections or departments) change from functional units to become process teams.

Single point of contact: Due to BPR, customers have a single point of contact with the organisation.[25]

1.6.5 Impact of NPM Perspective

Due to the NPM perspective, a host of initiatives were ushered in the western as well as third-world countries.

1.6.5.1 Impact of NPM on United Kingdom

In the UK, the public administrative system underwent major transformations since 1979 under the Thatcher regime and afterwards. The measures taken were as follows:

Reorganisation of government: An *Office of Public Service* was created in the UK for overseeing the reorganisation of the government. A series of reviews were carried into the work of the various departments and their policies, activities, and functions in order to bring economy in their functioning. These activities were examined by adopting a procedure known as *prior options review*. This procedure analysed whether the work done by a department was necessary or could be done away with, privatised, or decentralised.

Financial devolution: Under the Financial Management Initiative of 1982, measures were directed towards improved financial delegation, financial control focusing on clear-cut objectives, measuring performance against them, and assessing the costs involved in achieving them.

Next Steps: For decentralisation, 'Next Steps' or executive agencies were created for discharge of a specific set of activities. They comprised civil servants and chief executives responsible to the concerned ministry. Their key financial, service, and quality targets were indicated in their business plans.

Citizen's charters: In 1991, John Major intended to bring markets closer to the state through citizens' charters. The citizens' charter programme insisted on public organisations to draw, publish, and work towards a clear set of service standards.

Contracting out: Contracting out of a variety of services such as street cleaning, garbage collection, and so on was done in 1992 in the UK. Gradually it was extended to other areas such as health and social care services. To monitor the activities of private entities, set service standards, prices of privatised utilities, and regulatory organisations were also set up. Public-private partnerships for financing of new public facilities, including transport projects, roads, hospitals, and museums were initiated.

1.6.5.2 Impact of NPM on the USA

The following reforms were initiated in the USA owing to the NPM perspective.

National Performance Review: In 1992, under the influence of Osborne and Gaebler's 'entrepreneurial government', Vice President Al Gore initiated National Performance Review (NPR). The basic objective was to transform the culture of federal organisations by making them performance-based and customer-oriented and to prescribe a new type of government that functions cheaply and efficiently. It identified adherence to the following steps:

(a) Eliminating red-tapism by streamlining the budget process, decentralising personnel policy, and abolishing insignificant rules.

(b) Putting citizens first by providing them the scope to voice their problems, dismantling governmental monopolies, and utilising market mechanisms to solve certain problems.

(c) Empowering employees to get results by decentralising functioning, emphasising responsibility of results, and improving the work environment.

(d) Cutting back to basics (returning to the core activities) by investing in the effectiveness of government institutions, reformulating the programmes to save costs, and eliminating unnecessary tasks and activities.

President's Management Agenda: George Bush's President Management Agenda focused on strategic management of human capital, competitive outsourcing, improved financial performance, expanded electronic government, and budget and performance integration.

1.6.5.3 Impact of NPM on Australia

In line with the NPM perspective, certain activities in Australia were outsourced. *Partial user-pay charges* for health and education services were introduced. Privatisation of government business enterprises was also undertaken. *Service charters* were introduced in all government departments and business enterprises. *Public service reforms* were also ushered in to make the system more efficient, flexible, responsive, performance-oriented, and accountable through a performance-based pay system and decentralisation.

1.6.5.4 Impact of NPM on New Zealand

Apart from reforms similar to those in other countries, the following reforms were implemented in New Zealand:

Senior Executive Service: A Senior Executive Service (SES) was created comprising the chief executives of government departments and a new group of senior officials. They were appointed on five-year renewable contracts.

Social Impact Unit: A special Social Impact Unit (SIU) was created to examine the social consequences of corporatisation of government departments. The SIU was entrusted with the responsibilities of identification of mechanisms by which the central government could work constructively with regions, communities, and employer organisations; policy areas where the government might need to consider alternative means of meeting social objectives; and issues that might be treated as non-commercial and funded on a contractual basis.

1.6.5.5 Impact of NPM on Developing Countries[26,27]

The following NPM reforms were implemented in developing countries. The reforms implemented in India will be dealt with in detail in the later chapters of the book.

Cost-cutting and downsizing: Downsizing strategy was implemented in various developing countries during the 1980s and 1990s primarily to overcome the economic crisis prevailing in these countries. Public sector downsizing and retrenchment operations were implemented in Africa, Latin America, and the transition economies. However, it became counterproductive in many countries because the productive staff left the organisations while the remaining staff got demoralized and corruption increased. India also adopted downsizing. The *Expenditure Reforms Commission (ERC)* of the Government of India examined the structure of various ministries and departments. It concluded that drastic downsizing was the solution for professional and efficient governance.

Agencies in government: The donor agencies played a great role in bringing the concept of agencification in developing countries. Agencification took place in Africa on lines similar to that in western countries. The model in Tanzania was copied from the 'Next Steps' agency model of the UK. Ghana, Kenya, Uganda, Tanzania, and Zambia amalgamated the income tax and customs departments into revenue authorities, which is a good example of agencification in developing countries. However, the concept is only in an experimental stage in developing countries.

Decentralisation of management authority: In many developing countries, this phenomenon was seen in the form of devolution of political power to lower levels of government authorities. It has had a positive impact in many countries, such as Papua New Guinea, Philippines, India, Côte d'Ivoire, and Columbia, and resulted in lesser corruption and improved customer orientation in public services. A major reform of Indian decentralisation was in the form of the 73rd and 74th Constitutional Amendment Acts, under which power was transferred to panchayati raj institutions and urban local bodies, respectively.

Market mechanisms in the public sector: Under it, corporatisation of the health sector was seen in many African countries such as Ghana, Kenya, Zambia, South Africa, Malawi, and Zimbabwe.

Reinventing personnel management and performance management: Approaches towards performance management are being seen in many developing countries. Concepts such as the balanced scorecard (BSC) became popular in Asian countries. The performance appraisals/management systems introduced in Ghana, Namibia, South Africa, Mauritius, Uganda, Kenya, and Mozambique were some initiatives in this direction. In India, tools such as the budgetary exercise, annual reports published by various ministries, performance budgets, and outcome budgets were employed towards better performance management. The *result-based management (RBM)* system in Malaysia, *monitoring and evaluation (M&E) system* in Indonesia, and *program budgeting* in Afghanistan are some of such mechanisms for performance management in the public sector. *Performance-linked pay for civil servants* replacing the traditional seniority-based pay and promotion is a successful example of performance management initiative from the Singapore government.

Service quality and customer responsiveness: In India, *Sevaottam* was adopted as an initiative for improving customer responsiveness. The citizen charter and public grievance redress mechanisms were the major components of this initiative. Countries such as Nepal, Bangladesh, and Ghana introduced citizen charters as part of their service delivery system. The *performance pledges* of Hong Kong, *client charters* of Malaysia, and *People first* movement of Africa were some of the initiatives taken in this direction.

1.6.6 Critique of NPM Reforms' Implementation in Developing Countries

Some of the major criticisms against NPM in the specific contexts of the developing countries are as follows.[21]

Lack of resources and managerial capacity: Doubts have been raised by scholars such as Caiden Polidano and Sundaram that the developing countries lack the kind of resources and managerial capacity necessary to implement the NPM type of sophisticated reforms agenda.

Corruption and nepotism: Public management in many of the developing countries is afflicted by corruption and nepotism, and such deviant behaviour hinders the process of implementation of NPM-type reforms.

Absence of preconditions: Some of the preconditions of NPM, such as the existence of a firm rule of law to ensure compliance with contracts, entrepreneurship, and effective operation of markets, are generally absent in developing countries.

Lack of legal framework: Governments in many of the developing countries are not capable enough to move to sophisticated contractual arrangements for the delivery of public services. In most cases, necessary supportive laws and the enforcement of complex contractual arrangements is not well established.

One-size-fits-all reforms: The one-size-fits-all type of uniform approach to reforms in the developing countries with their varying history, organisational structure, culture, and environment may be counterproductive in the short as well as in the long run.

Non-alert citizenry: A basic requirement for the success of the NPM-type of public sector reforms is an alert and active citizenry, which is generally missing in most developing countries.

NPM needs its enemy: Traditional bureaucracy

Scholar Pollitt has observed that it appears from the operational experiences of developing countries that NPM works best when it is built on the secure foundations of a stable Weberian bureaucracy. When injected into situations where the civil service is highly politicised and unprofessional, the public service ethic is missing, budgets are unstable, and accountability is weak, negative impacts of NPM are seen. The paradox then is that the NPM needs its enemy—traditional bureaucracy—in order to succeed.

1.6.7 Appraisal of NPM

In general, the NPM perspective is criticised on the following grounds.[23]

Clash of values between traditional public administration and NPM: The NPM perspective does not propagate just implementation of new techniques but also makes a case for propagation of a new set of values derived from the private sector. Public service as distinct from the private sector is characterised by certain basic norms such as impartiality, equality, justice, and accountability. These seem to be overridden by market values such as competitiveness, profitability, efficiency, and productivity. Some apprehend that this could lead to weakening of public interest and challenge the legitimacy of public service.

Managerial predominance over policy capacity: New public management gives significance to managerial principles and practices and does not assign importance to policymaking. Moreover, some of the NPM reforms are likely to affect the policy-rendering function of bureaucrats. For example, the practice of contractual employment for civil servants might undermine their capacity to render effective policy advice to political representatives.

Lack of clarity of relationship between citizens and political representatives: NPM fails to establish a clear-cut relationship between citizens and politicians. For the NPM model, market mechanisms play a dominant role and fail to indicate the ways through which people in a market system can contribute towards creating a suitable democratic system.

Absence of a clear-cut concept of accountability: Although NPM envisages enhanced accountability as one of its goals, its focus is more on results or outputs. With the market forces playing a key role, there is a fear of dilution of the concept of hierarchical accountability. NPM is more managerial in nature than political. It lacks clarity in defining the roles of politicians and bureaucrats.

Promotion of individualist ideas in place of collective interests: New public management is considered to be an individualistic philosophy that fails to take cognisance of the collective demands of the society. The market-oriented restructuring, especially, in a developing country is bound to affect certain categories of society, particularly the poor, peasants, and labourers, due to its repercussions such as withdrawal of subsidies, reduction in the workforce, and cutbacks in welfare programmes.

Citizens vs customer orientation: NPM provides customer orientation to the government. It calls for empowerment of the customers, increasing their choices and strengthening the government to meet the needs of the customers. This is in contrast with the conventional public administration, which emphasises effective and equitable public service. NPM initiatives intend to empower consumers by diluting the citizens' rights. It gives prominence to those who can pay for the services, thereby claiming efficient services. The anti-state ideology it pursues leads to a decline in basic social services provision, creating a bunch of inequities.

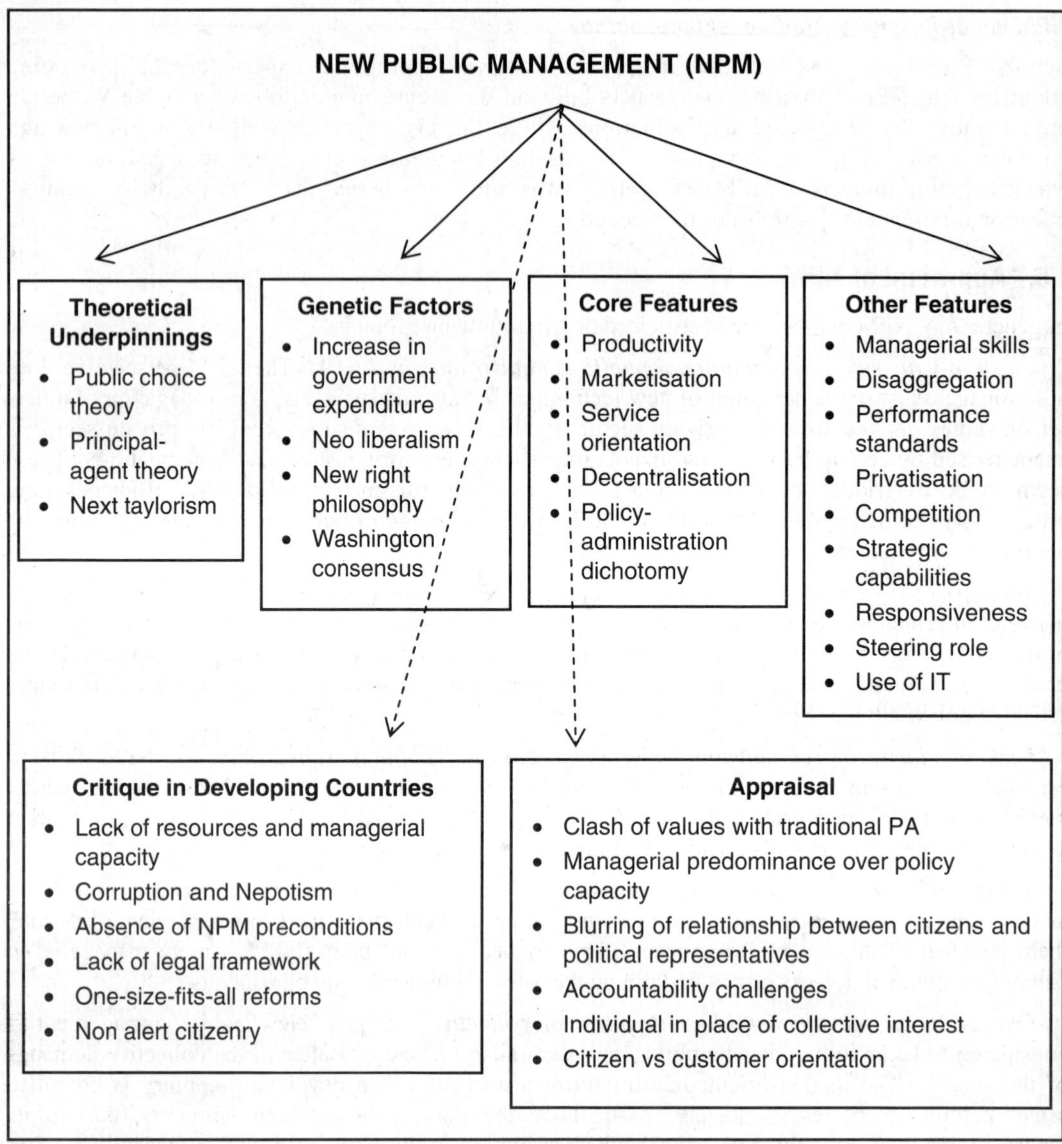

Mind Map 1.5: New Public Management Features

1.7 Post-NPM Models

The four important models of reforms post NPM were (a) the neo-Weberian state, (b) new public governance, (c) digital era governance (DEG), (d) new public service, and (e) public value management (PVM). The second, third, and fifth models will be discussed in Chapter 2.

1.7.1 Neo-Weberian State Model by Pollitt and Bouckaert[21]

Owing to the negative aspects of NPM, an attempt has been made in many countries to retain some of the good features of NPM alongside the old features of traditional bureaucratic organisation. Thus, a hybrid concept has been coined, known as the Neo-Weberian State (NWS), to imbibe the positive elements of NPM and at the same time to retain the basic Weberian foundation of public administration. Worldwide, there have been two major public sector reforms: (a) the Anglo-American NPM 'marketisers' and (b) the continental European 'modernisers'. The reform model of the second group, i.e., the continental group, is what Pollitt and Bouckaert call the NWS. The following principles characterise the NWS perspective.

A. Important Features from Traditional Public Administration

Centrality of the state: According to the NWS perspective, the state should have political, organisational, and managerial capacity to grapple with domestic and international problems such as globalisation, environmental threats, technological innovations, and demographic changes.

Reformation and enforcement of administrative law: This principle helps in guaranteeing equality of all and protection against arbitrary state actions.

Preservation of public service: This is the celebrated Weberian principle of a public service with a distinct status, culture, and terms and conditions of employment.

Representative democracy: This principle emphasises parliamentary control of bureaucracy and is basic to the legitimacy, control, competence, and stability of public bureaucracy.

B. Important Features from NPM

External orientation toward citizens: Similar to the customer orientation of NPM, this principle represents an outward shift away from internal bureaucratic rules toward the needs and values of citizens.

Supplemental public consultation and direct citizen involvement: Similar to the NPM-style citizen and community control, this principle provides for a range of procedures for public consultation as well as direct representation of citizen views.

Results orientation: Emulating the NPM model, this principle encourages a greater orientation towards achievements of results rather than just following formal rules and procedures.

Management professionalism: This principle tends to mix the Weberian idea of professional (basically legal and procedural) expertise with acquisition of 'managerial' knowledge and skills by civil servants.

1.7.2 New Public Service by Denhardt and Denhardt

Denhart and Denhardt[21,28] in their path-breaking publication *The New Public Service: Serving, Not Steering* have succinctly put the central role of government as 'service'. Their arguments were as follows.

Government as democracy: The government should not be run like a business, but like a democracy. Public interest and democratic citizenship are the hallmarks of government.

Increase sense of service: The sense of service should be improved in public employees so that they have better self-esteem, sense of dignity, and self-respect in doing public service.

Co-governance: Public servants should reconnect with the citizens. As they invite citizens to participate in the governance process, there will emerge a new culture of co-governance, with the administrators and citizens working together for the common good of the society.

However, this model is just a normative stand and a mere expectation from public servants. It is a timely warning and an appropriate cautionary note against the trendy 'downsizing' movement in public administration.

1.8 Challenges of Liberalisation, Privatisation, and Globalisation (LPG)

1.8.1 Role of Public Administration under LPG

In the era of LPG, the role of public administration is more towards governance and less direct involvement. In different sectors, public administration has to play different roles as mentioned below:

(i) **Direct Role in Core Areas:** Government has to play a direct role in the following six core areas:
- Defence, International Relations, National Security, Justice and Rule of Law.
- Human Development through access to good quality education and healthcare to every citizen.
- Infrastructure and sustainable natural resource development.
- Social security and social justice.
- Macro-economic management and national economic planning.
- National policies in respect of other sectors.

(ii) **Competitive Role:** Government has to compete with the private sector in certain areas like telecommunications, airlines, insurance, etc. Here regulatory commissions have been established to ensure a level playing field for both the sectors.

(iii) **Partnership with Citizens:** There are certain areas in which the government can partner with citizens for efficient delivery of services like maintenance of schools, hospitals, irrigation water and civic amenities.

(iv) **Partnership with Private Sector:** In areas like electricity, water and transport, the government can partner with private sector.

(v) **Partnership with Third Sector:** Government can have partnership with Non Governmental Organisations (NGOs) and Voluntary Organisations in sectors like protection of forests, empowerment of women, micro credit, health schemes and awareness programmes.

1.8.2 What is Globalisation?

Globalisation[29] refers to the multiplicity of linkages and interconnections between states and societies that make up the present world system. It describes the process by which events, decisions, and activities in one part of the world come to have significant consequences for individuals and communities in quite distant parts of the world.

It can be understood in terms of two distinct phenomena: 'scope' (or stretching) and 'intensity' (or deepening).

- *Scope* of globalisation means the set of processes that embrace most of the globe or which operate worldwide, hinting at a spatial connection.
- *Intensity* of globalisation implies intensification of the levels of interaction, interconnectedness, or interdependence between states and societies, which constitute the whole world.

It has received a boost due to technological developments and market-driven economic development. It creates a free atmosphere for administrative, political, socio-economic, cultural, and technological changes. It implies, from an economic perspective, removal of trade barriers and large-scale entry of multinational enterprises engaged in foreign direct investment.

Inevitable Globalisation

Globalisation has become difficult to resist and repel because it has on its side powerful forces that have already preselected what counts as 'real' and, therefore, shape the world accordingly. The 'neoliberal' portrayal of globalisation as some sort of natural force, like the weather or gravity, tries to convince people that they must adapt to the discipline of the market if they are to survive and prosper. This claim of inevitability, the 'TINA' factor (there is no alternative), implies that nothing can be done about the natural environment of the economic and technological forces; therefore, political groups ought to acquiesce and make the best of an unalterable situation.

1.8.3 Negative Impact of Globalisation on Public Administration

The challenges of globalisation in public administration are multi-dimensional.[30] These are as follows.

Changing role of the state

Globalisation has given way to new reforms such as NPM and governance, from the traditional nature of public administration. This has led to a pro-market and 'anti-state' philosophy. In this era, the biggest challenge for public administration is to recast the role of the state. There is a need for evolving a new regulatory state with an expanded agenda.

Responsiveness of state institutions

The globalising state is said to threaten the lives of common people through promotion of elitist policies. The key challenge to counteract the negative consequences of globalisation is to strengthen and revitalise public institutions in a manner that ensures their legitimacy and effectiveness in the protection of public interests.

Asymmetrical global order

The emerging rules of the game of globalisation have proved to be asymmetrical in terms of construct and inequitable in terms of outcome. The influence of developing countries in multi-lateral institutions that govern the world economy is at best limited. Moreover, the poorest people and the smallest countries are at particular risk in terms of *de facto* exclusion from the arrangements of global governance. In sharp contrast, industrialised countries exercise a disproportionately large influence in the world, not only in the sphere of economics but also in the realm of politics. The undemocratic global governance system is more than reflected in institutions such as the International Monetary Fund (IMF), World Bank (WB), P-5, G7, and even the OECD (Organisation for Economic Co-operation and Development), which make decisions that are of profound importance for global governance. The World Bank, being the largest supplier of development capital to the third-world countries, wields high control over such countries. Consequently, the noose around the developing countries is tightened by the practices and policies of global capitalism. The growth of transnational corporations (TNCs) such as General Motors and Facebook accounts for over half of the world's industrial output. Such TNCs have their headquarters in North America, Europe, Japan, and South Korea. This geographical concentration reflects existing asymmetrical power relations between the North and the South.

Negatives of structural adjustment programmes

Structural adjustment programmes (SAPs) are known as the liberalisation dice of the globalisation game. Emerging from the Bretton Woods system, the IMF and World Bank provided loans to developing countries during the Cold War with the West's political objective of containing communism. Supplying the much-needed loans to the developing countries, IMF and World Bank in return demanded, from their debtor countries, the implementation of the so-called SAPs. They provided guiding principles to improve the capability of the recipient countries to handle development assistance better and utilise it more efficiently. They focused mainly on lean and efficient states, facilitating the growth of market forces. However, large portions of these developmental loans have either been pocketed by authoritarian political leaders or enriched local businesses and the northern corporations they usually serve. Exorbitant sums have sometimes been spent on ill-considered construction projects. Most importantly, SAPs rarely produce the desired results in developing debtor societies because the mandated cuts in public spending translate into fewer social programmes, reduced educational opportunities, more environmental pollution, and greater poverty for the vast majority of the people. Moreover, the recipe of SAPs prescribed by the international economic institutions significantly reduces the autonomy of developing countries in the formulation of economic policies conducive for their path of development.

Changing priorities of policies

Ideally, in a democracy, policy should be expected to meet the needs of efficiency; and rational allocation of resources is required to endorse accountability and thereby dismiss social and political pressures. However, globalisation has led to state power being conditioned by forces lacking any sense of accountability to people. Everything that promotes growth is presented as 'pro-development'. All the political parties across the spectrum have vociferously supported the ideas of neo-liberalism. This has led to distortion of policy priorities in India and has assumed disturbing proportions with rapid deregulation and opening up of the sectors of economy to foreign investors on one hand, with attractive incentives being offered to exploit the unexploited natural resources of the non-industrial regions on the other hand. Sustainability has become the first casualty of this growing scramble for short-term growth and profits.

Employment generation: A failed promise of globalisation

Economic reforms in consonance with SAP may have given a boost to industrial productivity and brought in foreign investment in capital-intensive areas, but the boom has not created jobs as expected. This is most visible in terms of the non-linearity of employment with respect to the revenues in the IT industry. Today two things are happening, one is that the creation of jobs may or may not be greater than the jobs that were lost due to liberalisation; second, the kind of skills required are changing rapidly—job creation is taking place in areas that require higher skills. As on date, there are few well-paid jobs in India because investment has been heavily concentrated in the capital and skilled-labour intensive industries, such as auto-parts and automobiles, two-wheelers, engineering goods, chemicals and chemical products, petroleum refining, telecommunication, pharmaceuticals, and software. Moreover, many of those who lost jobs happen to be women, who, because of other pressures on them, find it difficult to acquire training for the new types of skills required for jobs that emerge because of modernisation.

Negative impact on welfare activities

The experience of adoption of SAPs, with the resolve to bring down fiscal deficit in the third-world countries, has resulted in worsening living conditions in the face of heavy reductions in government spending on social sectors such as food, health, and education, in particular, and overall cuts in public sector investment, in general. Despite the professed concerns for providing a human face to SAP, the experience in the Indian context has also not been very different.

Widening rural-urban divide

SAP-induced development policies focus on enhanced and targeted public investments in programmes to facilitate improvements in the quality of life of the masses; but the disparity between the elite and masses remains more pronounced in the rural sector. For example, in the agricultural sector, the increasing thrust of SAP-related policies towards commercialisation and corporatisation of agriculture is resulting in landlessness and migration. Changes in this sector, such as the patenting of seeds, greater mechanisation, and increased costs of agricultural inputs, have led to loss of work and indebtedness, thereby leading to desperation.

Alienation of tribal communities

In the name of globalisation and rapid growth, even the most culturally and ecologically sensitive areas have been opened to mining, industries, expressways, and so on. This has hugely increased the benefits of corporations, with cheap raw material and labour, and relaxation of land and environment laws. However, corporate leaders of Indian and foreign companies have hardly proved to be the legitimate flag-bearers of sustainable and equitable development. In all tribal areas of the country and, indeed, in most areas with traditional pastoral, peasant, and fisher communities, globalisation-led development has been environmentally and culturally devastating and has hardly benefitted these communities.

Accountability challenge of globalisation

In the era of globalisation, public organisations operate in an environment different from before. Their environments are more open, more turbulent, and continuously subject to changes. In addition, under the influence of new public management, public administrators are now viewed as entrepreneurs in an increasingly privatised government.[28] This has led to two significant challenges to accountability: 'value drift' and 'goal drift' (Galia Cohen, 2017).

Value drift: Public organisations are undergoing a hybridisation process, under which they are adopting businesslike practices and values related to production. The spur of values, such as the attainment of fast and frugal results, production pressure, and 'can-do' attitudes, is fundamental to the decrease in governmental accountability. The global financial crisis of 2007-2008 was preceded by a period where such exclusionary value sets were dominant. In fact, in a report issued in 2011, the US government concluded that the crisis was not a natural disaster, but the result of high-risk complex financial products; undisclosed conflicts of interest; and the failure of regulators, credit rating agencies, and the market itself to rein in the excesses of Wall Street.

Goal drift: Another major challenge to accountability flows directly from public organisations' heavy reliance on third-party contractors. Multiple traditional government functions are nowadays being performed by third parties, which have been characterised as a *shadow government.* Several accountability challenges are associated with this blurring of boundaries between the public and the private sectors and the shift towards hybrid configurations. The first problem is diffusion of political authority. Contractors usually have their own bases of power and hierarchical structure, which may lead to noncompliance and conflicting goals and interests. Moreover, by collaborating with external providers, the government *contributes to the establishment of monopolies*. Competition on a specific product or service becomes limited and providers enjoy the public image of being recognised as a monopolistic authority by the government. A good example is defence contractors whose expertise in producing weapons for the government affords them a superior market position. Evidently, creative service arrangements, such as contracting out, public-private partnerships, and privatisation, pose a risk of 'goal drift' in the government. If contractors do not share the same interests as the government, they can undermine the achievement of national goals. Goal incongruence is a critical barrier to maintaining accountability in the government. Khademian (2010) referred to it as the lack of *purposeful organisations.*

Increase in transnational organised crime

Transnational organised crimes are crimes that are either committed in more than one country, committed in one country but planned or controlled in another, committed in one country by groups operating in more than one country, or committed in one country but impacting many countries. The process of globalisation has outpaced the growth of mechanisms for global governance, and their deficiencies have just produced the sort of regulation vacuum in which transnational organised crime can thrive.[31] Human and commercial flows are too intense to easily distinguish the licit from the illicit. Weak law enforcement and lack of international cooperation have provided sanctuary to those who, however harmful their activities, are of use to the authorities in one country or another.

SUMMARY

This chapter has extensively discussed the various aspects of the discipline of Public Administration. Aiming to introduce the readers to the subject of public administration, the chapter has clearly laid down its meaning and its differences with other forms of administration. Giving a detailed overview of the evolution and various models of the discipline, the chapter has aimed at providing a firm understanding of the subject at the outset. As Public Administration is a new discipline, clarity about its importance and evolution is imperative to understand the other aspects of the discipline. This chapter has honestly attempted to deliver a clear idea of the discipline to the readers.

Practice Questions

1. What is administration and how is it used in different senses?
2. Compare the three terms: administration, organisation, and management.
3. What is public administration? Explain its salient features.
4. Explain the scope of public administration as an activity and a discipline.
5. "The study of public administration involves five areas" (Willoughby). Explain.
6. "The scope of public administration extends to three M's: Man, Method and Material. (Macqueen)" Explain.
7. Explain the view of Pfiffner and Walker on the scope of public administration.
8. "Public administration as a discipline includes not only the study of tools and techniques of administration but also the study of the public policy of the government." In this context explain the views of Dwight Waldo on the scope of public administration.
9. Explain the 'integral vs managerial', 'narrow vs broad', 'POSDCoRB vs subject matter', and 'instrumentalist vs discretionist' natures of public administration.
10. Compare and distinguish public and private administration.
11. Explain the different paradigms of the evolution of public administration from 1900.
12. What was the importance of the New York Bureau of Municipal Research in the evolution of public administration?
13. Explain the shift from politics-administration dichotomy to politics-administration continuum in terms of the evolution of the discipline of public administration.
14. The principles of public administration were the high noon of orthodoxy of public administration. Explain.
15. How did Dahl criticise the principles of public administration?
16. Management was considered as a groundswell development that tends to pervade all other disciplines. Explain.
17. Explain the different dimensions of the term 'public' in public administration.
18. What are the areas of distinction and interaction between politics and administration? Explain in terms of the politics-administration dichotomy theory.
19. How is public administration modified by the prevailing political regime? And at what terms does it remain the same irrespective of the political regime?
20. Public administration occurs within a larger system that is directed and controlled by political operatives. It operates within the constraints set by the political regime. Explain.
21. What is NPA and what were its precursors?
22. What was the impact of the Philadelphia Conference on 'the theory and practice of public administration (1967)' on the discipline of public administration?
23. What were the features of the First Minnowbrook Conference?
24. What were the goals, anti-goals, and features of NPA?
25. Evaluate the importance of NPA in the discipline of public administration.
26. Minnowbrook II had a connection with both the past and new thinking. Explain this in terms of the important thrust areas of the Second Minnowbrook Conference.

27. What were the challenges before the Third Minnowbrook Conference and what were the issues raised during it?
28. Public administration is "a socially-embedded process of collective relationships, dialogue and action to promote human flourishing for all." Explain in terms of the discussion in the Third Minnowbrook Conference.
29. Public administration is undergoing dark times, and the government is not capable of governing in the face of the seemingly insurmountable problems that characterise the dark times. Evaluate in terms of the discussions in the Third Minnowbrook Conference.
30. Minnowbrook III was a missed opportunity for the discipline of public administration to grow. Evaluate.
31. Compare the background, discussion, and impact of the three Minnowbrook Conferences on the discipline of public administration.
32. What do you mean by 'methodical individualism' and 'rational choice'? What impact have these two terms had on the discipline of public administration?
33. Public choice theorists view politics as an exchange process. Explain this phenomenon and its consequences.
34. What are the situations of market failure and government failure?
35. What is the impact of Duncan's median voter theorem on the public choice approach to public administration?
36. What is the impact of Kenneth Arrow's impossibility theorem on the public choice approach to public administration? What is a voting paradox?
37. What is Anthony Downs' contribution to the public choice approach of public administration?
38. Explain logrolling and the impact of Buchanan and Tullock on the public choice approach to public administration.
39. Explain the free-rider problem and Mancur Olson's contribution to the discipline of public administration.
40. Explain the bureau shaping model given by Niskanen.
41. What is the meaning of 'minimum winning coalition' and 'game theory'? Discuss their impact on the public choice approach to public administration? What is regulatory capture?
42. Explain rent seeking and Jagdish Bhagwati's contribution towards the public choice approach of public administration.
43. Describe Ostrom's model of democratic administration.
44. What are the different types of public goods and services?
45. What were the theoretical underpinnings and genetic factors of NPM?
46. What are the salient features of NPM? What has been the impact of NPM on developed as well as developing countries?
47. Give a critical account of the impact of the NPM perspective on developed and developing countries.
48. Explain the model of 'entrepreneurial government' and 'business process re-engineering'.
49. Describe the model of neo-Weberian state given by Pollitt and Bouckaert.
50. Describe the model of new public service given by Denhardt and Denhardt.
51. What is globalisation? What are its negative impacts on public administration?

CHAPTER 2 Good Governance, E-Governance, and Emerging Trends

After reading this chapter, you will learn the following:

- A clear understanding of the terms governance and good governance.
- Various approaches and characteristics of good governance.
- Good governance initiatives taken in India.
- The concept of Digital Era Governance and its worldwide impact on Public Administration.
- The concept of e-governance, its core principles, scope, issues, strategies and successful examples.
- Digital India Mission.
- Social media and its importance in good governance.
- The Public Value Management paradigm of Public Administration.

In the present time, the term *governance* is associated with different concepts, such as citizenship, sustainable development, biodiversity, and so on. In different contexts, the term connotes different meanings. Thus, it is not defined definitely. It has varied definitions and interpretations. However, if we discuss all of them, we will get more confused about the meaning of governance. Thus, we will keep our discussion on the meaning of the term very limited.[1] Governance is defined by two major approaches, as described here.

First Approach: In the first approach, governance is defined as the manner in which power is exercised in the management of the country's economic and social development.[2] According to UNDP, *governance is defined as the exercise of political, economic, and administrative authority to manage a nation's affairs. It is the complex mechanism, processes, relationships, and institutions through which citizens and groups articulate their interests, exercise their rights and obligations, and mediate their differences.*[3]

Second Approach: The second approach in defining governance focuses on the sharing of authority for public management between state and non-state actors. Here governance is viewed as a form of multi-organisational action wherein public, private, and third-sector (non-governmental sector) actors engage together in problem solving for the development of the people.

2.1 Good Governance: Concept and Application

Similar to the term governance, there are two approaches to defining the term *good governance*, both of them are important for holistically defining its significances.[4]

The Liberals Approach to Good Governance: Liberals view state power primarily as a potential threat to the well-being of citizens. Thus, they define good governance as a governance system that has proper legal, constitutional, and other arrangements to protect against the threat of state power. Thus, according to them, good governance is a governance system that is responsive, accountable, transparent, democratic, and participative.

Statists Approach to Good Governance: Statists primarily see the state as a means to aggregate power and resources for the collective good. They view good governance as a governance system that does not have weaknesses such as public disorder, vulnerability to external threat, or failure to provide adequate public services. According to them, a good government should have adequate arrangements to ensure the rule of law, efficient and effective administration, quality public service, human rights, well-regulated market, adequate social security for citizens, and so on. For governance, they prefer terms such as authority, order, capability, and autonomy.

In the context of developing countries, a good government has the qualities of both the liberals as well as the statists.

2.1.1 Rhodes' Different Uses of the Term Governance

Rhodes has mentioned six separate uses of the term 'governance'.[5] They are as follows:

1. **Minimal State:** It focuses on limiting the extent of governmental intervention and extending the role of markets and quasi-markets to deliver public services.
2. **Corporate Governance:** It refers to that system of governance by which organisations are directed and controlled. Rhodes identified three principles which are fundamental to corporate governance as well as the public sector. They are (1) openness or disclosure of information, (2) integrity or straightforward dealing and completeness, and (3) accountability in terms of holding individuals responsible for their actions through a clear allocation of responsibilities and clearly defined roles.
3. **New Public Management (NPM):** This concept is dealt with in great detail in Chapter 1.
4. **Good Governance:** Rhodes also defines governance as a term synonymous to good governance. For him, good governance involves an efficient public service, independent judicial system, and legal framework to enforce contracts, accountable administration of public funds, independent public auditor responsible to a representative legislature, respect for law and human rights at all levels of government, a pluralistic institutional structure, and a free press. It also regards good governance as systemic, political, and administrative—*systemic* in the sense of 'governance' as broader than 'government', *political* in the sense of a democratic state enjoying both legitimacy and authority, and *administrative* in the sense of an efficient, open, accountable, and audited public service endowed with bureaucratic competence to help design and implement appropriate policies and manage the public sector. Thus Rhodes observes, "good governance is a marriage between new public management and liberal democracy."

5. **Socio-Cybernetic System:** Kooiman said that governance stands for a pattern or structure that emerges in a socio-political system as a common result or outcome of the interacting intervention efforts of all involved actors. In a poly-centric state, the task of the government is to enable socio-political interactions to encourage many and varied arrangements for coping up with problems and to distribute services among the several actors. Examples of such interactive patterns are self-regulation, co-regulation, public-private partnerships, co-operative management, and joint entrepreneurial ventures.
6. **Self-organising Networks**: 'Governance as self-organising networks' views governance as broader than government, with services provided by any permutation of the government and private and voluntary sectors. The term 'network' used in this connection denotes several independent actors involved in the delivery of services.

2.1.2 UNDP's Characteristics of Good Governance

The definition given by the United Nations Development Programme (UNDP) is similar to the definition given above. However, it is more elaborate, clear, and provided in a point-wise manner. Thus, it is being mentioned here to clarify the basic concepts of the readers. According to UNDP, the characteristics of good governance are as follows:[6]

1. **Participation:** In good governance, all men and women have a voice in decision-making, either directly or through legitimate intermediate institutions that represent their interests.
2. **Rule of law:** In good governance, legal frameworks are fair and enforced impartially.
3. **Transparency:** It denotes that processes, institutions, and information are directly accessible to those concerned with them, and enough information is provided to understand and monitor them.
4. **Responsiveness:** Good governance institutions and processes try to serve all stakeholders.
5. **Consensus orientation:** Good governance considers different interests to reach a broad consensus on what is in the best interests of the group.
6. **Equity:** In good governance, all men and women have opportunities to improve or maintain their well-being.
7. **Effectiveness and efficiency:** In good governance, processes and institutions bring out results that meet needs while making the best use of resources.
8. **Accountability:** In good governance, decision makers in the government, private sector, and civil society organisations are accountable to the public as well as to the institutional stakeholders.
9. **Strategic vision:** Leaders and the public have a broad and long-term perspective on good governance and human development, along with a sense of what is needed for such development.

2.1.3 Good Governance and India

The idea of good governance is as old as Indian civilisation. The rulers of India were bound by *dharma,* popularly called *raj dharma*, which precisely meant ensuring good governance for the people. The description of good governance is found in many Indian texts such as the *Shanti Parva-Anushasanparva* of *The Mahabharat*, Shankracharya's *Nitisar*, Panini's *Ashtadhyayi*, and especially in Kautilya's *Arthashastra*. While highlighting the principle of good governance, the *Arthashastra* declares, "In the happiness of his people lies the king's happiness; in their welfare his welfare;

whatever pleases himself he shall not consider as good, but whatever pleases his people he shall consider as good."

2.1.4 Steps Taken for Good Governance in India

Many important steps have been taken for good governance in India. These have been a part of the administrative reforms in India and will be discussed in other chapters of this book. However, the following is a list of all the good governance reforms:[7]

1. **73rd and 74th Constitutional Amendment Act, 1992:** These two acts gave constitutional status to panchayati raj institutions and urban local bodies, respectively. They will be discussed in the chapters *Rural Development* and *Urban Development*, respectively.
2. **Right to Information Act, 2005:** It will be discussed in the chapter *Accountability and Control.*
3. **National Rural Employment Guarantee Act, 2005:** It will be discussed in the chapter *Rural Development.*
4. **Right to Education Act, 2009:** It will be discussed in the chapter *Rural Development.*
5. **National Health Mission:** It will be discussed in the chapters *Rural Development* and *Urban Development.*
6. **National Food Security Act:** It will be discussed in the chapters *Rural Development* and *Urban Development.*
7. **Government Knowledge Centre:** The Department of Administrative Reforms and Public Grievances (DAR&PG) launched a web portal named *Governance Knowledge Centre* in 2005. The portal is intended to be a knowledge repository and a platform for sharing ideas and views on governance and is primarily targeted at civil servants and those interested in the practice of, and research on, governance and public management. The knowledge shared by practitioners and researchers facilitates a better comprehension of the nuances of administrative and management practices, and paves the way for taking up appropriate interventions aimed at improving government standards.
8. **Direct Benefits Transfer Scheme:** All government schemes will be discussed in their relevant chapters.
9. **E-Governance**

2.1.5 Critique of Good Governance

There are many views of good governance seeking to prove it as a panacea for 'bad governance' in a changing world demanding more dynamic, result-oriented, transparent, and accountable government on the one hand, and a networking of formal institutions belonging to the government, the market, the private sector, and the civil society on the other. However, the concept of good governance has its pitfalls as described below:[8]

1. **Depoliticising the government:** The tendency of good governance is to depoliticise the government and bring in more technicality and expertise at the cost of the citizens' age-old and hard-earned democratic right to govern politically. Throughout the 'governance' discourse, references are made to reduce the act of governing to an apolitical and technical exercise.
2. **Old wine in a new bottle:** According to Strange (1983), much of the governance literature is a rehash of old academic debates and it is not clear whether something new is brought to the discipline of public administration.

3. **Ambiguous meaning:** The concept of good governance does not have an agreed upon meaning and is an imprecise concept. It is so broad in its application that attaching any precise meaning to it is not possible.
4. **Different values:** The concept of governance is laden with different values. Some models reflect anti-bureaucratic and anti-governmental sentiments, while other models are deeply contextual, based on constitutional, legal, organisational, and political influences. This varied perspective makes the subject of public administration both bigger and grander, a kind of 'un-public administration'.
5. **Devaluation of traditional administration:** Due to the governance debate, investment in the prevailing institutions, cities, states, nations, and their established governments, as well as the accomplishment of the institutions, are devalued. Order, stability, and predictability of traditional institutions are likewise undervalued.
6. **Governance with government:** Governance is often centred around non-state institutions, both non-profit and for-profit contracts, non-governmental organisations, parastatal organisations, third parties, and so on. Thus, it is a general feeling among the advocates for governance that there can be governance without government. However, it should be known that it is still the state and its sub-jurisdictions that deal with the vexing problems of race, poverty, and justice.
7. **Ethnocentricity:** It is said that the good governance thesis is basically ethnocentric, and more specifically, Eurocentric. In the Third World context, ethnocentricity is considered a prerequisite for the sound development of management. This represents, according to Leftwich, a new orthodoxy that dominates official Western aid policy and development thinking.[9]

However, scholars like Niraja Jayal have viewed the universal application of governance in a negative manner, particularly in the Indian context. She argues that democracy and development in India must be seen as intimately related, both functioning under similar constraints, for deeply entrenched social inequality in India both retards balanced development and distorts the logic of democracy. This distorting logic of democracy in an unequal society impels the state's direct and more active role in welfare provisions for the masses, such as education, health, nutrition, and housing. In the interest of distributive justice, the protection of the vulnerable cannot be left to 'governance' alone. So in her view, governance should not be about looking towards the state alone but at different ways of approaching and defining democracy and development.[10]

2.2 Digital Era Governance

2.2.1 Emergence of Digital Era Governance

Digital era governance (DEG) started in the United Kingdom, as described in the famous paper of Dunleavy et al., namely, *New Public Management is Dead—Long Live Digital-Era Governance.* Before the emergence of DEG, in the era of new public management (NPM), the distinguishing features of the development of public sector organisational and managerial change mainly revolved around information technology changes and alterations in information systems. The waves of IT changes that occurred before the 1990s had very limited transformative impacts. Office automation processes were extensively adapted to and fitted in with the preexisting organisational culture of public sector agencies. Agencies became highly dependent on their IT infrastructures, but did not shape their modes of operating as much as might have been expected.

However, in the period of DEG, we saw the growth of the Internet, e-mail, the Web, and the generalisation of IT systems from only affecting back-office processes to conditioning the entire terms of relations between government agencies and civil society in important ways. Internet growth has had especially important implications in political and administrative change in areas far beyond leading-edge advanced industrial countries.

By digital era governance, we signify a whole complex of changes that have IT and information-handling changes at their centre, but which spread much more widely and take place in many more dimensions simultaneously than was the case with previous IT influences. Contemporary IT technology changes also operate via shifts in societal information-handling norms and patterns, as the modes of informing consumers and involving them with corporations change across leading-edge sectors.[11]

DEG 2.0: According to Margetts and Dunleavy,[12] a second wave of digital era governance started in 2010. Owing to the development of social media, this second wave swept the government sector. It also gained extra impetus from the new austerity pressures for the extensive implementation of digitalised cost-saving processes, and from the extraction of real productivity gains from the maturing of earlier waves of digital change from the late 1990s to the mid 2000s.

2.2.2 Impact of DEG on Public Sector (as Compared to NPM)

The three macro themes of NPM that were immensely influential for more than two decades were:

1. **Disaggregation:** It involved splitting up large bureaucracies developed on Weberian lines. The key aspects of this change from the 1980s to 2000 were the agencification of central government functions, more use of quasi-government agencies, creation of micro-local agencies (locally managed schools and hospitals), and introduction of purchaser-provider separation (discussed in Chapter 1).
2. **Competition:** NPM introduced alternative suppliers, as discussed in Chapter 1.
3. **Incentivisation:** Incentivisation, in NPM, emphasised the need to design economic or pecuniary motivations for actors or organisations, forcing them to make the best use of time, assets, and resources. The key tools here include privatisation, private finance initiative (PFI) schemes, public-private partnerships, performance-related pay, charging users, public sector dividends, and 'light touch' regulation.

However, on the other hand, the three macro themes of DEG are as follows:

1. **Reintegration:** It reverses the fragmentation of NPM by joining up and trying to de-silo public sector processes. It stresses bringing back genuine partnership working, 're-governmentalising' issues that must inherently be handled by the state (such as security), creating new central government processes to do things once instead of many times, squeesing process costs and using shared services to drive out NPM's duplicate organisational hierarchies, and aiming at radical simplification of services organisation and policies.
2. **Needs-based holism:** It is a thoroughgoing attempt to create client-focused structures for departments and agencies. It seeks to implement end-to-end redesign of services from a client perspective, put in place one-stop processes, and create agile and resilient government structures that can respond to problems in real time instead of catching up with them only

after long lags. The contrast here is with the brittle, inflexible, and complex structures that NPM typically produced.

3. **Digitalisation:** It covers the adaptation of the public sector to completely embrace and embed electronic delivery at the heart of the government business model, wherever possible.

The components of the above three macro themes on the public sector, in the first as well as second wave of DEG, are beautifully tabulated by Margetts and Dunleavy.[12] It is described in Mind Maps 2.1–2.3.

2.2.2.1 Components of Reintegration

	Centralising, network-based, communications gain developments	Decentralising, database-led, information processing gain developments
First wave of reintegration	• Rollback of agencification • Joined-up governance • Re-governmentalisation • Reinstating central processes • Procurement concentration and specialisation	• Re-engineering service delivery chains—de-duplicationc • Shared services
Second wave of reintegration (DEG 2.0)	• Intelligent centre + decentralised delivery designd • Single tax and benefit systems • Reintegrative outsourcing	• Intelligent centre + decentre-lised delivery design • 'Big data' analysis • Central government disengage-ment and load shedding • Delivery level, joined-up governance

Mind Map 2.1: The components of reintegration in the first and second waves of DEG[12]

The explanations to some of the typical terms used in Mind Map 2.1 are as follows:

(a) **Joined-up governance:** Joined-up governance was the central element of reintegration in the UK under the Tony Blair government. It focused on major departmental amalgamations at the central level. A similar activity took place in India after the formation of the Modi government in India.

(b) **Re-governmentalisation:** The concept involves the absorption into the public sector of activities that had previously been outsourced to the private sector. The biggest example of it has been the transfer of some 28,000 airport security staff from private contractors in the US to the federal civil service, as the only sure corrective to the problems highlighted by the 9/11 terrorist attacks.

(c) **Re-engineering service delivery chains:** It is already discussed in Chapter 1 under the topic of business process reengineering.

(d) **Intelligent centre + decentralised delivery:** This is a design for allocation of functions across tiers of the government. It has been imported from successful private companies such as Walmart and Tesco. In the retail sector, this approach means that comprehensive sales and customer information data are collected electronically at store level (from tills and loyalty cards) to create a 'big data' warehouse, which is analysed centrally by specialist analyst units and central management. The centre then settles strategic decisions, and procures products in a unitary way across thousands of suppliers and distributes them into stores. Famously, Walmart's response to Hurricane Katrina was much more effective than the federal government's, because in intelligent design, it is not left to local decision makers (individual store managers) to set policy or undertake procurement. A similar form of such strategic design has begun to emerge in intelligence and surveillance policy in the USA since the 9/11 attacks.

2.2.2.2 Components of Needs-based Holism

	Centralising, networks-based, communications gain developments	Decentralising, database-led, information processing gain developments
First wave of reintegration	• Interactive and 'ask once' information seekinga • Agile government processes	• Client-based or needs-based reorganisation • One-stop provisions, ask-once processes • End-to-end service re-engineering
Second wave of reintegration (DEG 2.0)	• Social security systems moving online • Single welfare benefits integration • Linked-benefits approvals and payment integration • Single citizen account • Integrated service shops at central level	• Joined-up local delivery of public services • Co-production of services • Client-managed social/healthcare budgets • online citizen testimonialsc/ evaluations substituting central regulation • Open-book government (trans-parent government providing right to information) and citizen surveillance substituting central audit • Development of 'social web' processes within online govern-ment services • 'Big society' changes linked to central disengagement

Mind Map 2.2: The components of 'needs-based holism' in the first and second waves of DEG[12]

The explanations to some of the typical terms used in Mind Map 2.2 are as follows:

(a) **Interactive and 'ask once' information seeking:** It is an equivalent strategy to one-stop provision. Interactive mechanisms, such as using call centres and phone forms or online e-services, automatically facilitate agency staff and systems, taking a more holistic view of people's needs and preferences. 'Ask once' methods involve a commitment by the government to reusing already collected information, rather than recursively gathering the same information many times, as happened under the NPM's fragmented systems.

(b) **Co-production of services:** It means production of services, such as health and education, together by the government, private sector, and civil society.

(c) **Citizen online testimonials:** Customer/citizen testimonials help in accurately identifying problems in government institutions, e.g., identifying hospitals with patient care problems. As evidence, Google-searches for flu symptoms provide accurate advance indicators of the regional and local spread of flu cases, beating federal centres for disease control and prevention monitoring. The UK government replaced central controls by an army of citizen auditors.

(d) **Social web processes within online government services:** The development of the social web process within the government sector is leading to new organisational forms that exploit the capacity of the Internet, mobile access to organise without organisations, and new forms of co-production of government services. For instance, in some Swedish cities, the care of mentally handicapped people has begun to move into mixed care circles, bringing together state professionals and family/friends. Such care networks can be coordinated in real time via online 'social web' mechanisms that make everyone's information available to all partners.

(e) **Big society' changes:** Recent times have seen the sorting of staff and clients across public sector agencies and creation of pooling effects favourable to better performance at lower cost. This has also led to externalisation of roles to NGOs and community organisations, known as the 'big society'.

2.2.2.3 Components of Digitalisation

	Centralising, networks-based, communications gain developments	Decentralising, database-led, information processing gain developments
First wave of reintergration	• Radical disintermediation (cut out the middlemen) • Active channel streaming, customer segmentationa	• E-government • New forms of automated processes using 'zero touch' technologies (ZTTs) or radio-frequency identi-fication
	• 'digital by default' strategies	• Isocratic administration, e.g., quasi-voluntary compliance, do-it-yourself forms • Moving towards open-book government
Second wave of reintergration (DEG 2.0)	• '100% online' channel strategies • 'government cloud' • Free storage, comprehensive data • Government super-sites and enhanced search sites	• Social web shifts to rich technology within online estate • Freeing public information for reuse, mash-ups, etc. (open data initiatives) • Pervasive computing, fuel transition to ZTTs, and capital substitution for labour.

Mind Map 2.3: The components of 'digitalisation' in the first and second waves of DEG[12]

The explanations to some of the typical terms used in Mind Map 2.3 are as follows:

(a) **Active channel streaming:** Active channel streaming occurs when governments face up to the extra costs and difficulties of multichannel access (of providing citizen services), abandoning the common initial position of simply adding electronic service channels to the existing capacity. They use a strategy of segmenting customers and displacing them to active electronic channels.

(b) **'Digital by default' strategies:** The government tries to bring all the users to channels of online service delivery using two strategies. First, they incentivize users to switch to electronic channels by providing e-services with lower costs or greatly improved functionality. Second, they legally compel people or businesses to change how they transact with government agencies.

(c) **Zero touch technologies (ZTTs):** The ZTT approach was pioneered by private sector companies such as Cisco. In ZTT, the ideal is that no human intervention is needed in a sale or administrative operation. For instance, the surveillance and control system for the London congestion charge is an almost ZTT process. Once the entry of a particular car has been paid for, its number plate is automatically counted as valid in the monitoring machinery, or turned up as an apparent exception if not paid for, with the vast majority of cases not requiring staff attention.

(d) **Isocratic administration:** Isocratic administration is one that has citizen-centred (or business-centred or stakeholder-centred) processes, rather than the earlier agency-centred processes, where citizens and businesses substantially run their own interactions with the government. Isocracy is self-government, going beyond simple disintermediation. The self-administration concept reflects greater acceptance of the importance of quasi-voluntary and self-directed compliance with the government in liberal democracies. The key role for the government's administrative apparatus is not necessarily directly collecting taxes or enforcing compliance in a detailed way, so much as holding the ring and solving the assurance problem for people who are initially predisposed to cooperate but are anxious not to be 'suckered' into isolated cooperation when others can defect without penalty.

2.3 E-Governance

The above-discussed DEG movement has taken place in advanced countries such as the UK, USA, European, and Scandinavian countries. However, through globalisation, the wave of DEG has spread over all the countries, including the Third World developing countries. In countries like India, the wave of DEG is often referred to as 'e-governance', having similar components and impact on the public sector as DEG.

2.3.1 E-Administration, E-Government, and E-Governance[13]

E-administration, e-government, and e-governance are three identical but different terms.

E-administration refers to the intra-organisational or intra-governmental applications of information and communication technology (ICT). In simple terms, it refers to the computerisation and networking of an organisation as the necessary background for adopting any citizen-oriented e-governance application. Basically, e-administration involves the back-end operations of ICT in an organisation.

E-government can be defined as the application of ICT—particularly Internet-based information technology—by government agencies to improve the efficiency, effectiveness, transparency, and accountability of the government. It is the next stage of using ICT, which creates an inter-organisational presence and seeks to create an online presence of the government.

E-governance, on the contrary, is about the use of ICT to support the guiding and steering of an organisation—be it a private agency or a civil society organisation—to achieve its goals. In the political context, e-governance is about the use of ICT to steer society and promote public interest. It is the ultimate stage of ICT application in the government, whereby a two-way interface is created between the government and the users, who could be citizens, business entities, and other tiers of the government (state government and local governments).

For example, *e-procurement*, which is concerned with the use of ICT to support the purchasing departments of public or government agencies, falls in the category of e-government. By contrast, an ICT application designed to help lobbyists (e.g., farmers and industrialists) to participate efficiently in political processes, such as influencing a public subsidy policy or new electricity tariff, falls in the category of e-governance.

2.3.2 Moral Framework of E-Government

The United Nations' World Public Sector Report (WPSR)—*E-Government at the Crossroads*—describes the moral purpose of e-government as public administration, which is in the process of transforming its internal and external relationships with the use of modern ICT. Modern ICT relates communication among people, which is the quintessence of human society. In the context of public administration, e-government is bound to have an impact on the creation of public value—a notion rooted in people's preferences.

2.3.3 Core Principles of E-Governance

The core principles of e-governance projects are as follows:[14]

1. **Clarity of purpose:** While adopting e-governance, there needs to be a clear understanding and appreciation of the purpose and objectives to be achieved through it. It should not be taken up merely to demonstrate the capability of an existing technology, but the technology should be adopted to solve an existing problem. *Citizen-centricity* should be at the heart of all e-governance projects.
2. **Environment building:** While implementing an e-governance project, there is a need to change the mindset of all the stakeholders involved, i.e., politicians, government officials, and civil society at large. Government personnel have to be incentivised to change old habits and acquire new skills. Awareness needs to be created in the public, so that there is a constant demand for reforms in governance through the implementation of e-governance.
3. **E-governance as an integral part of reform in governance:** Every government organisation or entity, every government programme or policy, and every law and regulation have to integrate e-governance modules within itself rather than e-governance brought in as an afterthought or introduced as an adjunct.
4. **E-preparedness:** A certain level of preparedness is essential for any e-governance project, in the form of the existence of the basic infrastructure and human resource capabilities of an organisation. Then organisations have to identify the areas/activities falling under their functional domain which could benefit from e-governance. Next, the e-governance projects

need to be prioritised based on the simplicity of the projects, ease of implementation, and benefits to the citizens. Then an organisation has to undergo business process reengineering to make the implementation of the e-governance project simpler. The project then has to invent technological solutions or adopt existing ones for its implementation. After all these steps, an e-governance project has to be tested at the pilot stage to check the technological solution along with procedural and functional inputs. Then, finally, the project has to be scaled.

5. **Disciplined way of working:** E-governance requires a disciplined and systematic way of working in organisations.
6. **Monitoring and evaluation:** Monitoring helps in early detection of problems and hence facilitates prompt corrective action. Moreover, the impact of e-governance initiatives should be evaluated through independent agencies against parameters that would determine whether the objectives have been achieved or not.
7. **Developing secure, fail-safe systems and disaster recovery systems:** The technological architecture of e-governance projects need to be made fail-safe. Further, there have to be integrated sound disaster recovery modules with adequate security features to prevent loss of data and collapse of the system.
8. **Sustainability:** Once it has been established that any particular initiative is the better way of providing services or information to the people or conducting the business of the government, it should not be allowed to relapse on the grounds of expediency.
9. **Allowing for horizontal applicability:** Different states across India face similar types of challenges. To make e-governance more cost-effective and successful, success stories need to be shared and adopted across states and organisations, thereby minimising costly repetitions of mistakes.
10. **Development of local language interfaces**
11. **E-governance—A continuing process:** Bringing in e-governance has to be a continuing process, which would require many adjustments. It has been well-said that e-governance is a journey and not a destination.

2.3.4 Scope of E-Governance

The scope of e-governance extends to the following four relationships:[15]

1. **Government to citizen (G2C):** The G2C relation includes the services provided by the government to the citizens. These include public utility services such as telecommunication, transportation, post, medical facilities, and education. E-governance in a G2C relationship involves facilitation of the abovementioned services using ICT. It includes the following components:
   (a) **E-citizenship:** E-citizenship includes online transactions relating to issue and renewal of documents such as ration cards, passports, election cards, and Aadhaar cards.

   (b) **E-registration:** E-registration covers the online registration of various contracts an individual enters into during her/his lifetime.

   (c) **E-transportation:** E-transportation involves the ICT enablement of government services relating to transportation by road, rail, water, and air. This may involve booking and cancellation of tickets; status of vehicles, railways, and so on; issue and renewal of driving licenses; and registration and renewal of vehicles.

(d) **E-health:** E-health is the ITC enablement of health services, including interconnection of all hospitals and creation of patient and pharmacy databases.

(e) **E-education:** E-education involves facilitation of distance as well as classroom education using ICT.

(f) **E-help:** E-help refers to facilitation of disaster and crisis management using ICT. It includes the use of technologies such as the Internet and sms for the purpose of reducing the response time of government agencies in times of disasters.

(g) **E-taxation:** Online tax-due alerts and online payment of taxes fall under the purview of e-taxation.

2. **Citizen to government (C2G):** The C2G relationship includes the communication of citizens with the government arising in democratic processes such as voting, campaigning, and feedback. It includes the following components:

(a) **E-democracy:** E-democracy is aimed at using ICT for the enablement of the true democratic process including voting, public opinion, feedback, and governmental accountability.

(b) **E-feedback:** ICT can be used for providing e-feedback from the citizens, e-debates, as well as collecting citizens' surveys online.

3. **Government to government (G2G):** The G2G relationship includes the relationship between central and state governments and also that between two or more government departments. It has the following components:

(a) **E-administration:** E-administration includes the implementation of ICT in the functioning of the government, internally and externally. It can reduce the communication time between government departments. It can also substantially reduce paperwork. It also brings morality and transparency into the administration of government departments.

(b) **E-police:** E-police refers to the use of ICT for the purpose of facilitating the work of the police department in investigation and administration. It includes databases of police officers, their performances, criminals, crime trends, and so on. It can help in reducing the response time of the police department.

(c) **E-courts:** E-courts help in the ICT enablement of the judicial process, including distant hearings, online summons and warrants, and online publication of judgments and decrees.

4. **Government to Business (G2B):** G2B is a relationship between the government and businesses and has the following components:

(a) **E-taxation:** E-taxation helps in online payment of corporate taxes and dues. It also helps in cross checking any frauds and deficiencies in payment, bringing in accuracy in government dealings and making up lost revenue by avoiding miscalculations.

(b) **E-licensing:** The ICT enablement of the licensing and registration process for various companies is known as e-licensing.

(c) **E-Tendering: E-tendering** is a facility of online tendering and procurement.

2.3.5 Issues of E-Governance

The following issues are faced while implementing e-governance:[15]

1. **Technical issues:** The following technical issues are faced in e-governance:
   (a) **Interoperability:** In e-governance, the interoperation of various state governments, and various ministries within a government, is a critical issue. Integration, processing, and sharing of information and data is a big problem.
   (b) **Confidentiality:** In the process of e-governance, the confidentiality of any transaction or information provided by citizens to government agencies has to be ensured. Otherwise, the information can be misused by the private sector or other competitors.
   (c) **Security:** The security of transactions such as tax payment, fine, and bill payment needs to be ensured and the system needs to be fail-safe.
   (d) **Authentication:** The credentials of citizens requesting services need to be verified before they access or use the services. The digital signature plays an important role in providing this authenticity.
2. **Economic issues:** There are following economic issues in e-governance:
   (a) **Cost:** In e-governance, implementation, operations, and maintenance cost of services provided should be low enough for maintaining high benefit-cost ratio.
   (b) **Maintainability:** The e-government system must be compatible and maintainable for easy fulfilment of emerging needs.
   (c) **Reusability:** E-governance should be considered as a nationwide plan and the implemented modules must be reusable by other administrations.
   (d) **Portability:** The primary requisite for portable applications is independence of components from the hardware or software platforms, to help in possible reuse by other administrations.
3. **Social issues:** The following social issues are faced in e-governance:
   (a) **Accessibility and digital divide:** The e-governance service should be accessible for anybody from anywhere at any time. Even if the Internet population is growing exponentially, there is a very big portion of the population that may not be able to access e-governance for various reasons. If there is separation of accessibility among individuals, communities, and businesses, then this phenomenon is known as a *digital divide*.
   (b) **Usability:** All the users may not be experts in ICT transactions or the technology used for e-governance. Therefore the service provided must be usable or user-friendly. To make the system usable, guidance on operation may be provided to the users.
   (c) **Acceptance:** E-governance requires reconfiguration of the internal and external structure of public sectors. The main aim is to improve the system efficiently and to provide high-quality services to the citizens. However, there are integration issues in the public sector due to power conflicts over departmental and functional boundaries.

(d) **Use of local languages:** The access of information must be permitted in the local languages for user comfort.

(e) **Awareness in rural areas:** In India, there is a very high percentage of villages where awareness of e-governance is required, since a large portion of the rural population is not aware of new technologies and computer education.

2.3.6 Strategies of E-Governance

The strategies for building e-governance projects across India, and other developing countries, are as follows:[15]

1. **To build a technical infrastructure or framework across India:** The complete implementation of e-governance in India would require building technical hardware and software infrastructure. It will also include faster connectivity options such as broadband and 4G technology and the implementation of advanced zero touch technologies (ZTTs). The technology implemented must also include the concerns of the disabled persons.
2. **To build institutional capacity:** This will require training of government employees and appointment of experts.
3. **To build legal infrastructure:** For better implementation of e-governance, the government will need to frame laws that will fully incorporate the established as well as emerging technology.
4. **To build judicial infrastructure:** The judiciary as a whole needs to be trained in the new technology and its benefits and drawbacks. The government may also set up special tribunals to deal with matters relating to ICT.
5. **To make all information available online:** Online publishing of all government information can be facilitated through centralised storage of information, localisation of content, and content management.
6. **To popularize e-governance:** The people of India need to be educated and made e-literate for e-governance to flourish. People should be educated about the advantages of e-governance over physical governance.
7. **Centre-state partnership:** Centre-state and interstate cooperation is needed for smooth implementation of e-governance. For this, the government can set up a central hub, such as the current Government of India portal, for accessing information on all the organs of the central and state governments.
8. **To set standards:** It is also very important to set various standards to bring e-governance up to the quality and performance level of the private corporate sector. These standards include interoperability standards, security standards, technical standards, and quality standards.

2.4 Digital India Mission

2.4.1 Introduction to Digital India

The *Digital India programme* is a flagship programme of the Government of India with a vision to transform India into a digitally empowered society and knowledge economy.

Many e-governance projects have already been implemented since the 1990s—railway computerisation, land records computerisation, and individual e-governance projects of different states. Though these e-governance projects were citizen-centric, they could make less than the desired impact due to their limited features. The isolated and less interactive systems revealed major gaps that were thwarting the successful adoption of e-governance along the entire spectrum of governance. The ambitious Digital India programme will attempt to address these gaps.[16]

2.4.2 e-Kranti or NeGP 2.0

The national level e-governance programme called *National e-Governance Plan* (NeGP) was initiated in 2006. However, there were some shortcomings in it like the lack of integration amongst government applications and databases, low degree of government process reengineering (mentioned in Chapter 1), scope for leveraging emerging technologies such as mobile and cloud. These shortcomings are aspired to be addressed in the e-Kranti programme with the vision of *transforming e-governance for transforming e-governance*. e-Kranti has the following principles:

(a) Transformation and not translation

(b) Integrated services and not individual services

(c) Government process reengineering to be mandatory in all mission mode projects (MMPs)

(d) ICT infrastructure on demand

(e) Cloud by default

(f) Mobile first

(g) Fast-tracking approvals

(h) Mandating standards and protocols

(i) Language localisation

(j) National GIS (geographic information system)

(k) Security and electronic data preservation

e-Kranti has 44 MMPs under it, including those of financial inclusion, women and child development, social benefits, and urban governance. The focus of e-Kranti is to bring transformation to realise:

IT (Indian Talent) + IT (Information Technology) = IT (India Tomorrow)

2.4.3 Vision Areas of Digital India Programme

The Digital India programme is centred on three key vision areas:

1. **Digital infrastructure as a utility to every citizen:** It includes the following components:
   (a) Availability of high-speed internet as a core utility for delivery of services to citizens
   (b) Unique, lifelong, online, and authenticable cradle-to-grave digital identity for every citizen
   (c) Mobile phone and bank account enabling citizens' participation in the digital and financial space

   (d) Easy access to a *common service centre*
   (e) Shareable private space on a public cloud
   (f) Safe and secure cyberspace
2. **Governance and services on demand:** It has the following components:
   (a) Seamlessly integrated services across departments and jurisdictions
   (b) Availability of services in real time from online and mobile platforms
   (c) All citizen entitlements to be portable and available on the cloud
   (d) Digitally transformed services for improving ease of doing business
   (e) Making financial transactions electronic and cashless
   (f) Leveraging GIS for decision support systems and development
3. **Digital empowerment of citizens:** It has the following components:
   (a) Universal digital literacy
   (b) Universally accessible digital resources
   (c) Availability of digital resources/services in Indian languages
   (d) Collaborative digital platforms for participative governance
   (e) Citizens not required to physically submit government documents or certificates

2.4.4 Programme Management Structure for Digital India Programme

The programme management structure for Digital India consists of a *Monitoring Committee on Digital India* headed by the Prime Minister, a Digital India Advisory Group chaired by the Minister of Communications and IT, and an Apex Committee chaired by the Cabinet Secretary.

2.4.5 Pillars of Digital India Programme

Digital India is an umbrella programme that covers multiple government ministries and websites. It weaves together a large number of ideas and thoughts into a single, comprehensive vision so that each of them can be implemented as part of a larger goal. It is to be implemented by the entire government, with overall coordination being done by the Ministry of Electronics and Information Technology (MeitY). The programme aims to provide a thrust to the following nine pillars of growth areas:

1. Broadband highways
2. Universal access to mobile connectivity
3. Public Internet access programme
4. E-governance: Reforming government through technology
5. E-Kranti: Electronic delivery of services
6. Information for all
7. Electronics manufacturing
8. IT for jobs
9. Early harvest programmes

2.4.6 Digital India Infrastructure

The Digital India programme relies on the following infrastructure for its growth:

1. **State wide area network (SWAN):** Under this scheme, technical and financial assistance are provided to the states/union territories (UTs) for establishing SWANs to connect all states/UT headquarters up to the block level via district/sub-divisional headquarters in a vertical hierarchical structure.
2. **Single-window interface for trade (SWIFT):** The Central Board of Excise & Customs has taken up the implementation of the single-window project to facilitate trading across borders in India. The 'India Customs Single Window' would allow importers and exporters the facility to lodge their clearance documents online at a single point. Required permissions, if any, from other regulatory agencies would be obtained online without the trader having to approach these agencies.
3. **Rapid assessment system:** The National e-Governance Division, a division of the MeitY, has developed a rapid assessment system (RAS) for continuous feedback on the e-services delivered by the Government of India and state governments.
4. **Open data:** The Open Government Data (OGD) Platform India—data.gov.in—is a platform for supporting the Government of India's Open Data initiative. The portal is intended to be used by ministries/departments and their organisations to publish datasets, documents, services, tools, and applications collected by them for public use.
5. **National Supercomputing Mission:** The National Supercomputing Mission has been envisaged to empower the national academic and R&D institutions, spread across the country, by installing a vast supercomputing grid comprising more than 70 high-performance computing facilities. These supercomputers will also be networked on the National Supercomputing grid over the National Knowledge Network (NKN).
6. **Mobile seva appstore:** A mobile applications store (m-AppStore) has been created to facilitate the process of development and deployment of suitable mobile applications for delivery of public services through mobile devices.
7. ***MeghRaj*:** To utilise and harness the benefits of cloud computing, the Government of India has embarked upon an ambitious initiative—a *GI cloud*, which has been named *MeghRaj*.
8. ***Jeevan Pramaan*:** *Jeevan Pramaan* is a biometric-enabled digital service for pensioners of central government, state government, or any other government organisation. It aims to streamline the process of issuing life certificates, making it a hassle-free experience for pensioners.
9. **IRCTC Rail Connect**
10. **Integrated health information system:** An integrated health information platform (IHIP) is being set up by the Ministry of Health and Family Welfare (MoHFW). The primary objective of IHIP is to enable the creation of standards-compliant electronic health records (EHRs) of the citizens on a pan-India basis, along with the integration and interoperability of the EHRs through a comprehensive health information exchange (HIE) as a part of this centralised accessible platform.
11. **Government e-Marketplace:** The Government e-Marketplace (GeM) is a single-window solution for online procurement of common-use goods and services required by various government departments/organisations/ PSUs.

12. **eTrade:** The Department of Commerce is pursuing the project eTrade, the purpose of which is to facilitate foreign trade in India by way of promoting effective and efficient delivery of services by various regulatory/facilitating agencies involved in foreign trade so as to enable the trade to avail services from these agencies in an online environment.
13. **eSign:** eSign is an online electronic signature service, which can be integrated with service delivery applications via an open API to facilitate an Aadhaar card holder to digitally sign a document.
14. **eBasta:** This project has created a framework to make school books accessible in digital form as e-books to be read and used on tablets and laptops.
15. **Bharat Broadband Network:** Bharat Broadband Network Limited is a special purpose vehicle set up under the Companies Act by Government of India with an authorised capital of INR 1000 crore. It has been mandated to create the National Optical Fiber Network (NOFN) in India. A total of around 2,50,000 gram panchayats spread over 6,600 blocks and 641 districts are to be covered by laying incremental fibre.
16. **Aadhaar:** Through the Aadhaar scheme, every resident of the country is being provided with a unique identity or Aadhaar number.

2.4.7 Digital India Services

Many services are provided under the Digital India programme. Some of the important services among them are as mentioned below:

1. **Swayam:** It seeks to bridge the digital divide for students who have hitherto remained untouched by the digital revolution and have not been able to join the mainstream of the knowledge economy. This is done through an indigenously developed IT platform that facilitates hosting of all the courses taught in classrooms from 9th class till post-graduation to be accessed by anyone, anywhere at any time.
2. **mKisan:** The mKisan SMS portal has been conceptualised to provide a quantum leap in the dissemination of timely, specific, holistic, and need-based knowledge among farmers over large geographical areas by leveraging the power of mobile telephony. This has been done so that all relevant sectors can use this platform not only to reach out to the farmers but also to address their concerns and queries.
3. **MCA21:** The Ministry of Corporate Affairs (MCA), Government of India, has initiated the MCA21 project, which enables easy and secure access to MCA services in an assisted manner for corporate entities, professionals, and the general public. The MCA21 project is designed to fully automate all the processes related to the enforcement and compliance of legal requirements under the Companies Act, 1956.

2.4.8 Citizen Empowerment due to Digital India

The various services provided by Digital India have led to the empowerment of citizens. Some of the examples of citizen empowerment are as follows:

1. **PayGov India:** A national payment service platform has been envisaged for a common e-Governance infrastructure that will offer end-to-end transactional experience for a citizen, which includes accessing various services through the Internet with a payment gateway interface for online payments.

2. **MyGov:** The MyGov platform is a unique path-breaking initiative which was launched by the Hon'ble Prime Minister of India, Shri Narendra Modi. It is a unique first-of-its-kind participatory governance initiative involving the common citizen at large. The idea of MyGov is to bring the government closer to the common man through the use of the online platform, creating an interface for healthy exchange of ideas and views involving the common citizen and experts, with the ultimate goal to contribute towards the social and economic transformation of India.
3. **Aadhaar-enabled payment system (AEPS):** AEPS is a bank-led model that allows online interoperable financial inclusion transactions at micro ATMs through the business correspondent of any bank using the Aadhaar authentication. It is a payment service empowering a bank customer to use their Aadhaar card as their identity to access their respective Aadhaar-enabled bank account and perform basic banking transactions such as balance enquiry, cash deposit, cash withdrawal, and remittances through a business correspondent.

2.5 Social Media and Public Administration

2.5.1 What is Social Media?

According to Eric Qualman, "social media are the biggest shift since the Industrial Revolution."

Social media are a group of new type of online media, which share most or all of the following characteristics:

1. **Participation:** Anyone is free to contribute to the content of social media. This has blurred the distinction between media and audience.
2. **Openness:** Social media services are open to feedback and participation. They allow voting, comments, and sharing of information. There are rarely any barriers to accessing and making use of content.
3. **Conversation:** Whereas traditional media is about broadcast, social media is better seen as a two-way conversation.
4. **Community:** Social media allows online communities to form quickly and communicate effectively, sharing common interests.
5. **Connectedness:** Social media are connected to other sites, resources, and people. This has led to the thriving of social media.[17]

2.5.2 Different Types of Social Media

1. **Social networks:** These sites allow people to build personal web pages and then connect with friends to share content and communication. The biggest social networks are MySpace, Facebook, Google Plus, and LinkedIn.
2. **Blogs:** A blog is a form of an online journal where entries are written in an informal and conversational style. Service is provided by companies such as Google and WordPress.
3. **Wikis:** These websites host community documents into which any individual can add or edit information. The best known wiki is Wikipedia.

4. **Podcasts:** It includes audio and video files that are available by subscription, e.g., iTunes of Apple.
5. **Forums:** Forums are online areas for discussion on specific topics and interests. They are a good place to engage in a detailed discussion.
6. **Content communities:** Content communities are the sites that organise and share particular kinds of content. The most popular types are those based on photos (Flickr) and videos (YouTube).
7. **Micro-blogging:** These are social media sites where small amounts of content are updated by members. This content is distributed online, e.g., Twitter.

2.5.3 Web 2.0 and Government 2.0

Web 2.0 is the current state of online technology as it compares to the early days of the Web, characterised by greater user interactivity and collaboration, more pervasive network connectivity, and enhanced communication channels. Due to the advent of social media, there is greater collaboration among Internet users, content providers, and enterprises. Increasingly, due to social media, users are able to provide more input with respect to the nature and scope of Web content and, in some cases, they exercise real-time control over it.

Government 2.0 is used to describe how social media are changing the relationship between government institutions and citizens. Citizens and service users are increasingly expecting a more open government and a greater say in how things happen around where they live and are probably already discussing your local issues online. Government 2.0 refers to open data to make the government more transparent and accountable and the uses of social media tools to engage in those conversations, shape policy, support local democracy, and improve services.[18]

2.5.4 Transformation of Governance through Social Media

Significant trends showing the transformation of governance through social media are as follows:[19]

2.5.4.1 Cry for transparency

Social media are supporting a new wave of sharing information online, leading to increased transparency in governance. The government of Iceland looks at social media as a method of 'sustainable transparency' through a constant flow of information. Similarly, Israel's Defence Forces have a YouTube channel chronicling its activities. Moreover, social media are playing a major role in ensuring that elections in new Arab and African democracies are held in a transparent manner. Likewise, a US site, publicmarkup.org, allows citizens to view and propose suggestions to specific US federal legislation as it is in process.

2.5.4.2 Citizen Engagement

According to Aneesh Chopra, ex-CTO of the US Government, "the opportunity of social media is not economical or technological; it's emotional." For citizen engagement, the US government has started crowdsourcing for public solutions, to make the procurement process more efficient and reduce waste. A US site 'challenge.org' rewards citizens with cash prizes for solving government problems. Similarly, the South African government has employed social media to stimulate a constructive national debate on values and ethics. On similar grounds, the National Aeronautics and Space

Administration (NASA) provides opportunities to social media followers to interact with its leading astronauts.

Studies have shown that *citizens who engage with the government online have a more positive view of government.* Promoting close online engagement:

- Creates better decisions by capturing local knowledge
- Increases the capacity of the society to understand the complexity of problems
- Increases public support by legitimising solutions

2.5.4.3 Humanising the government

Owing to the presence of social media, governments are beginning to appreciate and connect with the emotional side of the people they govern. They are taking lessons from how brands engage and build an emotional connection with their stakeholders. For example, the US embassies in different countries spark discussions among people and give them a reason to belong to the US community. They develop unique and engaging content and post updates on social media regularly.

2.5.4.4 Crisis management

There are plenty of examples to show how social media has been a lifeline to connect with people during disasters. As an example, the US and UK embassies in Tripoli used Facebook to instruct evacuations amidst their democratic revolution, connecting their citizens with ferries out of the way of danger.

2.5.4.5 Real-time response

In the private sector, there are many case studies about companies using social media as effective tools to solve problems in real time. In fact, the biggest brands have established social media 'war rooms' to monitor customer sentiments and use them effectively. These practices are being adopted by the state and city governments as well. The world across, with a tweet or text, potholes, broken street lights, and other issues are being reported and fixed.

2.5.5 Indian Government and Social Media

India has the world's second-largest mobile phone user base with over 1.12 billion users as of 2017, with an average 91.47 connections per 100 citizens. In order to engage with this large online citizen base, share information, and deliver services more quickly and effectively, Indian government agencies are increasingly using social media. With a purpose to create awareness and promote various e-governance schemes and programmes in the country, the Digital India social media team was set up in 2014.

Some excellent examples of government agencies engaging social media tools to great benefit have emerged. MyGov, an Indian Government initiative, is one of the biggest crowdsourcing and citizen-engagement platforms in the world.

2.5.6 Challenges faced by Governments in Using Social Media

Government agencies face the following challenges while using social media:[20]

1. **Why use social media:** Government departments sometimes find it difficult to define the need or objective to use social media. Is it for providing information, seeking feedback

generic interaction, or so on? Due to this lack of clarity, departments often either choose not to use social media or attempt to be present on all platforms at once.

2. **Which platforms to use:** Given the plethora of platforms and even types of social media available, it is very difficult to choose the type and number of platforms on which to engage and to figure out how to create interlinkages between these platforms.
3. **Who will engage:** Government departments have limited resources to engage over social media, which demand a deeper and constant interaction. Closely associated questions are that of authority, i.e., who is authorised to respond on behalf of the department, whether such a response will be made in personal or official capacity and from a personal or official account, etc.
4. **How to engage:** The use of social media is an ongoing process and requires long-term commitment. Many officials have questions around rules of engagement—how to create and manage an account, what should be the response time, what are the legal implications, etc.

2.5.7 Government of India Guidelines for Using Social Media[20]

To help government organisations engage more fruitfully with stakeholders using the various social media platforms, the MeitY has drafted a document titled *Framework and Guidelines for Use of Social Media by Government Organisations*. The guidelines provided in this document are as follows.

2.5.7.1 Defining the objectives

The objective of social media is not just to disseminate information but also to undertake public engagement for meaningful public participation in the formulation of public policy. The objectives of using social media should be

1. Seeking feedback from citizens
2. Re-pronouncement of public policy
3. Issue-based as well as generic interaction
4. Brand-building or public relations
5. Generating education and awareness on national action plans and implementation strategies

2.5.7.2 Choosing the platform

The choice of social media platform should be made based on the following factors:

1. Duration of engagement—Is the engagement sought an ongoing activity or is it being created for a specific time-bound purpose?
2. Type of consultation—Is the consultation open to the public or is it confined to a particular group of stakeholders, such as experts?
3. Scope of engagement—Does the consultation require daily, weekly, bi-weekly, or even hourly interaction?
4. Existing laws—Do the existing laws permit the use of such platforms and what are the requirements under such laws regarding data protection, security, privacy, archiving, etc.?

2.5.7.3 Governance structure

The two most important aspects of social media are its viral nature (news spreads spontaneously) and the demand for instant gratification (queries, responses and counter-responses are posted instantaneously). However, since the official pages of government departments must reflect their official position, some measure of control must be included in the flexible design of communication.

1. **Account governance:** Wherever possible, the same name for the different social networking accounts may be adopted to ensure ease of search on the Internet.
2. **Response and responsiveness:** The major attraction of social media is the spontaneity and immediacy of response and feedback, and those visiting the site would expect some kind of response within a pre-defined time limit. As far as possible, it is important to state upfront the scope of response (given/not given), type of response (official/unofficial), response time (1 day/1 week), and so on, so that the expectations are set correctly.
3. **Content governance:** Content creation and social media profiles overlap, therefore sharing consistent content on all social media platforms should form the bedrock of content policy. While social media tools make it easy for everyone to become a creator, for the official account, the content must be specified and tailored to the site on which it is to be published. A moderation policy should also be published if the platform permits others to add their own content; this informs people what they can post whilst protecting the sensitivities of others who may visit the platform.
4. **Data and information security governance:** The government's communication to citizens via social media should follow the same data retention policy as its communication through other electronic and non-electronic channels.
5. **Legal provisions:** The content should be posted in accordance with provisions of laws such as the RTI Act, IT Act, and IT (Amendment) Act, 2008, and rules and regulations thereunder.

2.5.7.4 Communication strategy

Social media should only be used by the government to communicate existing government information and propagate official policy to the public. Moreover, great care must be taken to avoid propagation of unverified facts and frivolous misleading rumours, which often tend to circulate through miscreants on social media platforms.

2.5.7.5 Creating a pilot

Since social media are relatively new forms of communication, it is always better to test efficiency and efficacy of such initiatives with a pilot project.

2.5.7.6 Engagement analysis

Social media monitoring must be an integral part of any social media strategy. Today a multitude of tools offer solutions for measuring conversation, sentiment, influences, and other social media attributes. The social network analysis (SNA) software facilitates both quantitative as well as qualitative analysis by mining raw data and combining it with the individual and social matrix.

2.5.7.7 Institutionalising social media

The final step in ensuring that a pilot social media project is scaled up and integrated is to link it to the existing administrative and communication structure. For this:

- Rules may be established that all policy announcements will be undertaken simultaneously on traditional as well as social media.
- All important occasions as far as possible may be broadcasted using social media.
- All documents seeking public opinion must be posted on social media sites.
- All updates from the official website should automatically be updated on social media sites.
- All traditional communication should publicise the presence of the organisation on social media.

2.6 Public Value Management

In accordance with the transformation from government to governance, a second paradigm shift has taken place from new public management (NPM) to a new focus on creation of public value, under the paradigm of public value management (PVM).

According to O'Flynn, public value has been described as a multi-dimensional construct—a reflection of collectively expressed, politically mediated preferences consumed by the citizenry—created not just through 'outcomes' but also through processes that may generate trust or fairness.[21]

2.6.1 Mark Moore on Creating Public Value

Mark Moore presented the concept of PVM in his seminal book *Creating Public Value*.[22] He gave the idea that while private managers strive to create private value, those in the public domain try to produce public value. According to Moore and succeeding authors, public value as a concept focuses on[23]

1. A wider range of values than public goods
2. More than mere output
3. What has meaning for people, rather than what a public-sector decision maker might presume is best for them

In order to pursue public value, organisations have to pursue a strategy that has to meet three broad tests, which Moore has conceptualised in the so-called *strategic triangle of Moore* (see Mind Map 2.4). They have to

1. Declare their overall mission or purpose (cast in terms of important public values)
2. Offer an account of the sources of support and legitimacy that will be tapped to sustain the society's commitment to the enterprise
3. Explain how the enterprise will have to be organised and operated to achieve the declared objectives

These three key issues (the public value an organisation strives to create, the societal legitimacy and support it can tap into, and its organisational capabilities to make public value creation a success) are intrinsically linked, as Moore indicates by connecting them in his strategic triangle.

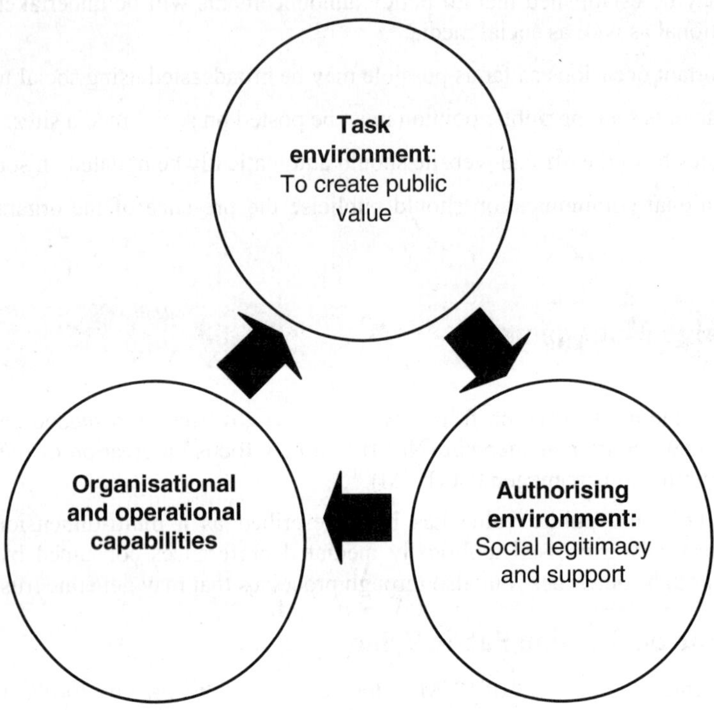

Mind Map 2.4: Moore's strategic triangle for public value management

2.6.2 PVM: A New Paradigm for Public Administration

PVM constitutes a new paradigm in public service provision that is "both post-bureaucratic and post competitive".[21] The key propositions, on which the idea of PVM as an emerging paradigm is based are as follows (see Mind Map 2.5):

1. In this paradigm, public interventions are defined by the search for public value.
2. In PVM, there is a need to give more recognition to the legitimacy of a wide range of stakeholders.
3. An open-minded and relationship approach to the procurement of services is framed by a commitment to a public service ethos.
4. In PVM, an adaptable and learning-based approach to the challenge of public service delivery is required.

	Traditional public administration	New public management (NPM)	Public value management (PVM)
Key objectives	Politically provided inputs: Services monitored through bureaucratic oversight	Managing inputs and outputs in a way that ensures economy and responsiveness to consumers	The overarching goals is achieving public value that in turn involves greater effectiveness in tackling the problems that the public most cares about; stretches from service delivery to system maintenance
Role of managers	To ensure that rules and appropriate procedures are followed	To help define and meet agreed performance targets	To play an active role in steering networks of deli-beration and delivery, and maintain the overall capacity of the system
Definition of public interest	By politicians or experts	Aggregation of individual preferences, in practice captured by senior politicians or managers supported by evidence about customer choice	Individual and public preferences produced through a complex process of inter-action that involves deliberate reflection over inputs and opportunity costs
Preferred system of service delivery	Hierarchical department or self-regulating profession	Private sector or tightly defined arms-length public agency	Menu of alternatives selected pragmatically and a reflexive approach to intervention mechanisms to achieve outputs

Mind Map 2.5: Comparative paradigms of management[24]

SUMMARY

This chapter has dealt with very important topics-good governance and e-governance among others. It deals with important initiatives towards a citizen friendly government. The various models discussed in this chapter like Digital Era Governance, Public Value Management and e-governance are the most recent developments in the field of Public Administration.

Practice Questions

1. Explain the different approaches to describe the term 'governance'.
2. Explain the different approaches to describe the term 'good governance'. What are the characteristics of 'good governance'?
3. Governance is used to mean different things in different contexts. Give the different meanings of the term 'governance'.
4. Describe the steps taken for good governance in India.
5. Give a critical review of the concept of good governance and its practice.
6. How did digital era governance (DEG) lead to the reintegration of public agencies that were disintegrated by the NPM reforms?
7. DEG or e-governance is a concept of intelligent centre + decentralised delivery. Explain.
8. What do you mean by zero touch technologies (ZTTs) and isocratic administration?
9. Differentiate between the terms e-administration, e-government, and e-governance.
10. What are the core principles of e-governance reforms?
11. What are the issues faced while implementing e-governance? What are the strategies to overcome them and successfully implement an e-governance project?
12. What is the Digital Indian mission? How is it similar to the digital era governance of the western countries?
13. What are the vision areas and pillars of the Digital India programme?
14. What are social media? What impact do they have on public service delivery and public administration? What are the challenges that a government agency faces while using social media? How can these challenges be overcome? Explain in the light of the social media guidelines given by the Department of Electronics and Information Technology.
15. What is public value management (PVM)? Why is it called a paradigmatic shift in public administration? Explain it with traditional public administration and new public management.

CHAPTER 3 Administrative Thought

Learning Objectives: After reading this chapter, you will learn the following:

- Importance of various administrative theories propounded by key thinkers of public administration and management
- Various theories including scientific management theory, classical/structural theory, bureaucratic theory, situational theory, human relations theory, systems theory, decision-making theory, and participative management theory of organisation
- About the thoughts of various thinkers such as Woodrow Wilson, Frederick Taylor, Henry Gantt, Frank Gilbreth, Lillian Gilbreth, Harrington Emmerson, Henri Fayol, Mooney, Reiley, Luther Gulick, Lyndall Urwick, Max Weber, Robert Merton, Alvin Gouldner, Peter Blau, Philip Selznick, Robert Jackall, Merle Fainsod, Hegel, Karl Marx, Mary Parker Follett, Elton Mayo, Kurt Lewin, George Homans, William Foote Whyte, Eric Trist, David Easton, Chester Barnard, Norbert Weiner, Stafford Beer, Talcott Parsons, Gabriel Almond, Herbert Simon, Douglas McGregor, Chris Argyris, Rensis Likert, and Peter Drucker among others
- Contributions of these thinkers towards the theory and practice of public administration
- Different approaches to studying the subject of public administration

3.1 Administrative Theory

The subject of public administration has developed from the theories and models given by various renowned scholars of the subject. In this chapter, we will discuss the theories propounded by various scholars that have led to the emergence of the present discipline of public administration.

3.1.1 What is a Theory?

The term 'theory' is derived from the Greek word *theoria*, which means 'looking at', 'viewing 'contemplating', and 'speculating'. A theory is a set of ideas organised in a logical order to reinforc or demolish an existing conviction or to form the basis for a new conviction. It represents systematic explanation of causal factors and their fusion within a conceptual framework.

A theory has three important characteristics, namely, a set of propositions. These propositions ar interrelated, and some of these propositions can be empirically tested. A proposition is a statemer about the relationship between two or more concepts.

3.1.2 Public Administration Theory and Its Objectives

In the present time, the dynamic nature of society and the complex nature of governmental activitie make it difficult for generalist administrators to continue functioning in an old-fashioned way and ye realise the administrative goals. Thus, there is a definite need for the development of administrativ theories that can aid the functioning of public administrators. However, there is a general antipath against theory in the minds of public administrators. This is known as 'ivory tower thinking', wher the administrators feel that the theory is far removed from the reality they confront. They believe th power is knowledge and that their experience is greater than theory.

According to Stephen Bailey,[1] the objectives of public administration theory are to draw togethe the insights gained from the subject of humanities and the validated propositions of the social an behavioural sciences, and to apply these insights and propositions to the task of improving th processes of the government to achieve politically regimented goals by constitutionally mandate means.

3.2 Thoughts of Woodrow Wilson

3.2.1 Scientific Study of Administration

Woodrow Wilson is considered the father of public administration. In his famous essay, 'The Stud of Administration',[2] he emphasised the need to develop a science of administration. His essay laid th base for the development of public administration as an academic discipline and a field o professional specialty.[3] He wanted the study of administration to be methodical, disciplined, an systematic.

The objectives of this academic field, according to Wilson, were as follows:

1. To discover what the government can properly and successfully do and how it can do thes things with the utmost possible *efficiency* and the least possible cost either of money or o energy.[4]
2. To set the discipline on the foundations of *stable principles*, thus removing the confusion o functioning in administrative functions.[1]
3. To find the best way to give *public criticism/public opinion control over administrativ actions*, while ensuring that it does not interfere with the daily functioning of th administration.

3.2.2 Democracy and Administrative Science

According to Wilson, the growth of administrative science is easier in a monarchical state than in a democracy. Thus, administrative science was first developed in Europe by French and German academics. The reasons for the active growth of administrative science in European states were as follows:

1. Governments in European states were not subjected to public scrutiny, thus, the governments in these countries were active in many fields of public life.
2. As there was less interference and competition, governments focused attention on discovering various means of governing well.

However, democracies such as America witnessed a slow pace of growth of administrative science because of the following reasons:

1. In democracies, the administration was continuously responsive to the 'multitudinous monarch called public opinion'. Wherever public opinion was a governing principle of government, administrative reforms were always slow because of compromises.
2. In democracies, governments largely focused on amending and tinkering with their constitutions due to pressure from different political groups. Thus, they were left with very less time to concentrate on the details of administrative science.

3.2.3 Public Administration and Public Law

According to Wilson, *public administration is a detailed and systematic execution of public law.* Every particular application of general law is an act of administration. Government plans do not fall under administrative activities, but the detailed execution of these plans does. The study of administration, viewed philosophically, writes Wilson, is closely connected with the study of the proper distribution of constitutional authority.

3.2.4 Vacillation Between Separability and Inseparability of Politics-Administration Connection

Wilson, at different moments, talked differently about the relationship between politics and administration. While talking about the politics-administration dichotomy, he said that administration lies outside the sphere of politics and administrative questions are not political questions.[1] He said that politics is the special province of a statesman and administration that of a technical official.[5] Moreover, he said, "bureaucracy (or administration) can exist only where the whole service of the state is removed from the common political life of the people, its chiefs as well as its rank and file. Its motives, its objectives, its policy, its standards must be bureaucratic."[1]

While talking about politics-administration inseparation, Wilson said that no lines of demarcation, can set apart administrative from non-administrative functions, can be run between this and that department of the government without being run uphill and down dale over dizzy heights of distinction and through dense jungles of statutory enactment, hither and thither around 'ifs' and 'buts', 'whens' and 'howevers' until they become altogether lost to the common eye. Moreover, he said that no topic in the study of government can stand by itself—least of all perhaps administration whose part it is to mirror the principles of the government in operation. Administration cannot be divorced from the other branches of public law without being distorted and robbed of its true significance. Its foundations are the deep and permanent principles of politics.[1]

F.W Riggs Argument

On this vacillation concept of Wilson, Riggs said that "for Wilson not only politics and administration are closely intertwined but administrative actions are hardly conceivable in any sense except that they are the implementation of political policies. Thus Wilson was under no illusion that administration can take place in a political vacuum."

- For more details on relation between politics and administration, you can read the topic "*Politics and Administration*" in Chapter 1 of this book.

3.2.5 Public Administration and Business

According to Wilson, the field of administration is a field of business and is removed from the hurry and strife of politics. Like business, administration does not involve itself in political questions. It is not subject to the vagaries and vicissitudes of politics, and it functions uninterrupted to fulfil the goals of the political system. Wilson felt that the affairs of public administration were synonymous with those of private administration. Thus, the study of public administration should be akin to the central concerns of business administration, namely, the values of economy, efficiency, and effectiveness. He said that government should not be unbusinesslike and should not have *unbusinesslike traits* such as being politicised, partisan, slow, and corrupt.

3.2.6 Wilson's view on Civil Service

Wilson's views on civil service were as follows:

1. A technically schooled civil service, selected on the basis of merit, is indispensable for a successfully working administration.
2. Civil service should be cultured and self-sufficient enough to act with sense and vigour.
3. It should be intimately connected with the popular thought, by means of elections and constant public counsel, as to find arbitrariness or class spirit out of the question.

   There should be an ethical sense of public duty in the entire intellectual terrain of public administration.[6]

3.2.7 Initiator of Comparative Public Administration (CPA)

Wilson emphasised on the historical and comparative methods for the study of administration. He said that administration is the most suited field for comparative learning.[1] We have a misconception that administration stands on a different basis in democratic and other states. On comparing administrations, we can rid ourselves of this misconception. Due to comparative analysis, we can learn the weakness, strengths, virtues, peculiarities, and modes of operation of other administrative systems.

Engaging in comparative studies, democracies can learn from European autocracies (of that time) their more efficient administrative methods without importing their autocratic spirits and ends. This import of methodology from autocratic countries, according to Wilson, is important in meeting democratic challenges such as chaos from within and of forces from outside.[7]

3.2.8 New Meaning of Government

In his article, "New Meaning of Government", Wilson said the following:

Participation of Citizens: All classes and interests of people should participate in government.

Free from Private Control: The government should be disentangled from all vested interests and free from every kind of private and narrow control.

Responsive to Public: The government should be responsive to genuine public opinion.

National Visions: The government should develop the vision of the nation.[8]

Thorough Implementation of Laws: Laws should be implemented thoroughly, intelligently, fearlessly, and without reference to persons or interests—financial or political.

Government as a Trustee: The government shall administer resources as a good trustee and as an instrument of humanity for social betterment.

Priority Functions of Government: Wilson identified the priority functions of the government such as food security, conservation of natural resources including rivers and forests, maintenance of health and sanitation, and development of agriculture, industries, education, women, and cities.

He termed these seven steps the 'new meaning of government'.

3.2.9 Criticism of the Woodrow Wilson's Theory

The ideas of Woodrow Wilson regarding public administration are criticised on the following grounds.

Naive or Inconclusive Ideas

Richard Stillman has criticised the ideas of Wilson as naive and inconclusive. As per Stillman, Wilson's essays raised more questions than providing answers. For instance, Wilson argued that administration should become businesslike but did not elaborate on how to make it businesslike. Similarly, he recommended giving a balanced role to public opinion in administration, but did not provide a method to do that.

Inconsistency of ideas or lack of focus

Wilson failed to establish a proper relationship between administrative and political realms; he introduced but failed in establishing a science of administration. There is serious inconsistency in his ideas on politics and administration, science of administration, and the role of public opinion.

Contribution is not significant enough to deserve the tag of Father of Public Administration

Paul van Riper has said, "Wilson's essays had no influence on evolution of study of public administration in US. Its main focus was only politics-administration dichotomy". Riper further argued that at the most Wilson was only one of the founders of administration in America but the difficulty with equal and greater recognition for other scholars lies in the fact that none of them went on to become the President of the USA.[9]

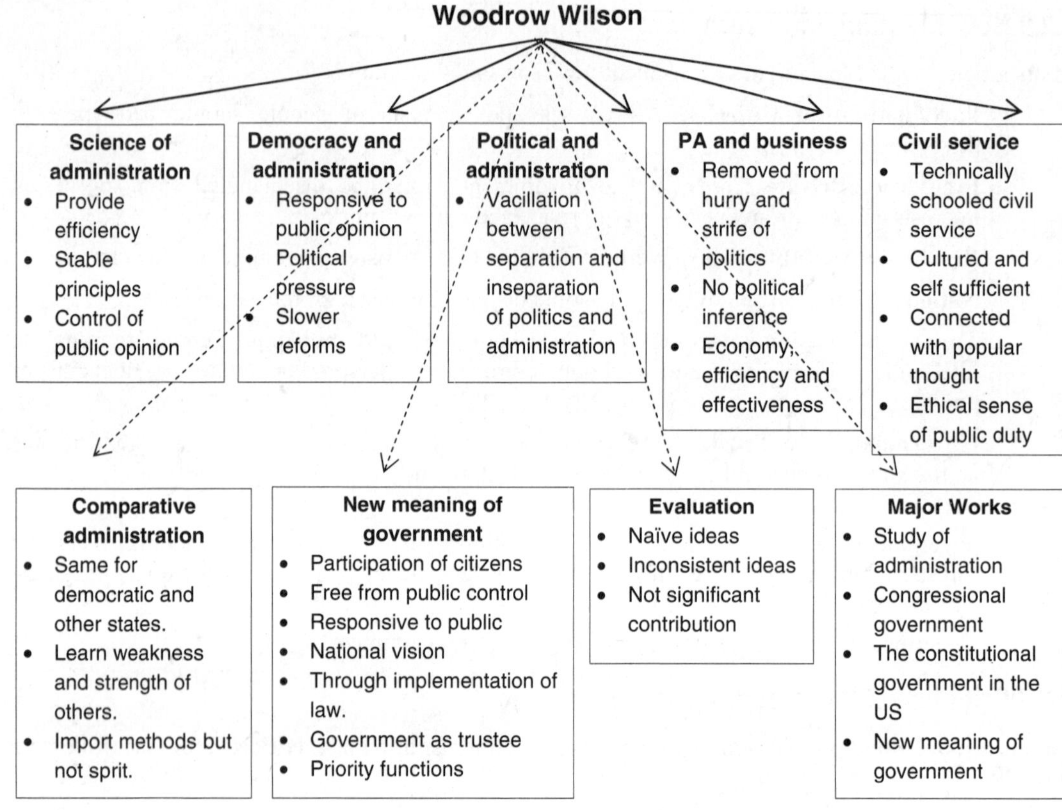

Mind Map 3.1: Ideas of Woodrow Wilson

3.3 Scientific Management and Ideas of Frederick Taylor

The scientific management approach is one of the most important approaches in the field of administrative theory. It came in the wake of the new industrial revolution that has taken place during the later part of the twentieth century. It is an attempt to solve the problems of complex organisations that have emerged as a result of industrial development. Frederick Winslow Taylor is regarded as the pioneer of the scientific management approach.

3.3.1 Backdrop of Tayor's Ideas and Theory

In his research on industrial functioning, Taylor noticed that a phenomenon of workers purposely operating below their capacity existed, and he called this 'soldiering' or 'skiving'. The reasons for such a phenomenon were as follows:

Elimination from Work: Workers did little work as they felt that if they will become productive, some of them would become surplus and would be eliminated.

Non-Incentive Wage System: The non-incentive wage system of that time encouraged low productivity. Employees took care never to work at a higher pace, as higher pace would become the standard, as a result of which the wages of employees may come down.

Unscientific Methods: Workers wasted their time and effort by relying on the rule-of-thumb and unscientific methods and practices other than those scientifically determined.

Taylor undertook various experiments (as will be discussed later) to remove the problem of soldiering in industrial organisations.

3.3.2 Taylor's Prominent Works and Ideas

Taylor's contribution to the development of scientific management is recorded in his papers 'A Piece-Rate System (1895)', 'Shop Management (1903)', 'The Art of Cutting Metals (1906)', and 'The Principles of Scientific Management (1911)'.

3.3.2.1 Piece Rate System

Taylor's work 'Piece Rate System' is considered an outstanding contribution to the principles of wage administration. In it, he proposed a new system of wage administration consisting of three parts:

1. Time study: Observation and analysis of work through time study to set the 'rate' or standard.
2. Differential rate: Giving different rates of working to different pieces of work.
3. Payment system: Giving payment to workers and not to positions, thus giving higher payments to workers working at a higher rate, irrespective of their positions in the organisation.

3.3.2.2 Philosophy of Management (in Shop Management)

In his paper 'Shop Management', Taylor described his philosophy of management.[10] Here he said that the objective of management is to pay high wages and have low unit production cost to achieve increased industrial efficiency. The other objectives of this philosophy are as follows.

Scientific Methods of Research and Development of a True Science of Work

Scientific methods of research and experiment should be applied to management problems. Every act of a worker can be reduced to a science. He said that it is necessary to know what constitutes a fair day's work. This needs the scientific investigation of a 'large daily task' to be done by qualified workers under optimum conditions. The results of these investigations should be classified, tabulated, and reduced into rules and laws to find out the ideal working methods or what is called 'one best way of doing a job'.

Standardisation of Work and Scientific Selection of Workers

In industrial organisations, workers who possess physical and intellectual qualities need to be selected scientifically to ensure the effective performance of the scientifically developed work (as discussed in previous point). This needs a deliberate study of the aptitude, nature, and performance of the workers and a determination of how they can be potentially used.

Scientific Education and Development of Workers

Every worker must be scientifically trained according to the scientific requirements of the work. It is the responsibility of the management to develop workers and offer them opportunities for advancement to do their jobs to the fullest realisation of their natural capacities.

Intimate and Friendly Cooperation between the Management and the Workers

Taylor considered that the management must inspire the workers to do their job scientifically and properly, and not allow them to slip back to the earlier unscientific methods of doing work. Management and workers should come together to bring a mental revolution in them. There should be division of work between the management and workers. In the traditional management theory, the worker was entirely responsible for the work and the management had less responsibilities. However, scientific management divided the responsibility equally between the management and the worker. This division of work creates between them an understanding and mutual dependence.

3.3.2.3 New and Total Concept of Management

According to Taylor, managers, instead of being authoritarian, should develop a new approach, and change to a more comprehensive and broader view of their jobs, incorporating the elements of planning, organising, controlling, determining standards, and devising incentive schemes. The principle object of management is to secure the maximum prosperity for the employer coupled with maximum prosperity for each employee. There is no inherent conflict in the interests of the employers, workers, and consumers. The results of higher productivity should equally benefit all the people, i.e., workers, employers, and consumers in the shape of higher wages to the workers, greater profits to the management, and payment of lower prices for the products by the consumers.

3.3.2.4 The Art of Cutting Metals

In his paper 'The Art of Cutting Metals', presented to the American Society of Mechanical Engineers, Taylor displayed the results of 30,000 to 50,000 recorded experiments conducted over a period of 26 years on efficiently and effectively cutting metals. It answered questions such as the tools to be used, cutting speed, and feed to be used while cutting metals. This presented a major breakthrough in the development of the American industry. Through this paper, Taylor tried to emphasise that in all industrial tasks, scientific fact-finding methods should be used to empirically determine the right ways of performing tasks.

3.3.3 Functional Foremanship

Taylor introduced a new concept of functional foremanship in the management of industries. This system was against the 'linear' system in which each worker is subordinate to only one boss. In functional foremanship, one worker is subordinate to eight specialised supervisors and receives orders from all of them. Of the eight functional supervisors, four are responsible for planning and the remaining four for execution.

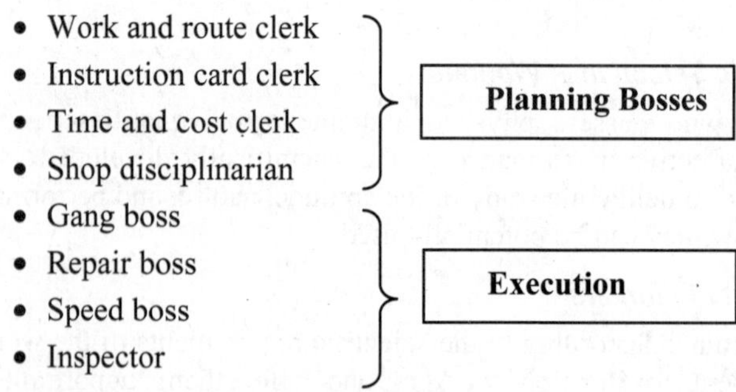

In this functional type of organisation, the foreman can be trained quickly and specialisation becomes very easy. Taylor identified *nine qualities of a good foreman*, namely, education, technical knowledge, manual dexterity and strength, tact, energy, grit, honesty, judgment, and good health.[11]

3.3.4 Mental Revolution

As already discussed, scientific management causes a complete mental revolution on the part of the workers and the management as to their duties, towards their work, towards their fellow workers, and towards all of their daily problems. It involves the following:

1. Mutual cooperation: Workers and management feel that their mutual interests are not antagonistic and mutual prosperity is possible only through mutual cooperation.
2. Increase the surplus: Both parties stop thinking about the division of surplus as the most important factor and together turn their attention towards increasing the size of the surplus until the surplus becomes so large that it becomes unnecessary to quarrel over how it should be divided.[12]
3. Change in mental attitude: Mental revolution brings a complete change in the mental attitudes of both the parties, substitutes peace for war, substitutes hearty brotherly cooperation for contention and strife, pulling hard in the same direction instead of pulling apart, replacing suspicious watchfulness with mutual confidence, and becoming friends instead of enemies.

3.3.5 Basic Principles of Scientific Management

Based on the work of Taylor, the following basic principles of management can be deduced:

- Science, not rule of thumb
- Harmony, not discord
- Cooperation, not individualism
- Maximum output, in place of restricted output
- Development of each man to his/her greatest efficiency and prosperity

3.3.6 Scientific Management Movement

Louis Brandeis first used the word scientific management in the year 1910, which was later adopted by Taylor in his writings. Taylor's close associates such as Henry Gantt, Frank Gilbreth, and Lillian Gilbreth carried out further research in the domain of scientific management. Now we will briefly discuss their contributions.

3.3.6.1 Henry Gantt

Henry Gantt took forward the work of Taylor and propounded two individual contributions, as mentioned below:

The Task and Bonus Wage System: Gantt's task and bonus wage system was introduced in 1901 as a variation on Taylor's differential piece-rate system. With this, the employee received a bonus in addition to his/her regular day rate if he/she accomplished the task for the day; he/she would still receive the day rate even if the task was not completed, whereas Taylor's piece-rate system penalised employees for sub-standard performance. As a result, it enabled workers to earn a living while learning to increase their efficiency.

Gantt's Bar Chart: Gantt's bar chart was created to record the progress of workers towards the task standard. A daily record was kept—in black if the worker met the standard; in red if the worker did not. On developing, the chart showed how work was scheduled over time through to its completion. This enabled management to see, in graphic form, how well work was progressing, and indicated when and where action would be necessary to keep on time. As an example, Fig. 3.1 shows a Gantt Chart for redecorating an office.

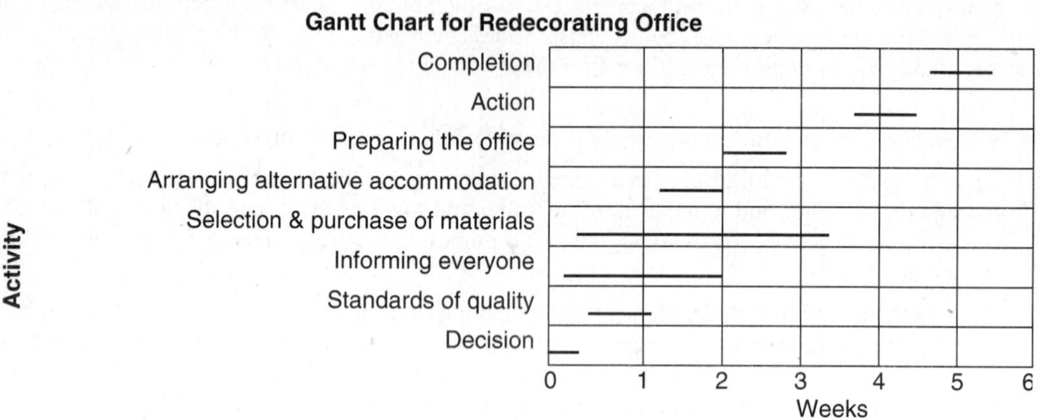

Fig. 3.1: An Example of Gantt Bar Chart

The Gantt chart provided a graphic means of planning and controlling work and led to its modern variation, the PERT (programme evaluation and review technique).[21]

3.3.6.2 Frank and Lillian Gilbreth

Frank and Lillian Gilbreth were a husband-wife team who worked as engineers in the early part of the twentieth century. Their main focus was on the fields of motion study and time study, combined with an interest in the psychology of efficiency and work.

Motion Study: In their motion study, Gilbreth said that it is the duty of an organisation to study motions and reduce them as rapidly as possible to standard sets of least in number, least in fatigue, and most effective motions. Frank developed a list of 17 basic movements to aid him in analysing motion; he called each movement a 'therblig'. These fundamental movements, which could not be broken down into other motions, gave Frank a way to accurately analyse the elements of any movement a worker may make. For example, some fundamental movements (therbligs) are grasp (to gain control of an object), position (to line up, orient, or change position of a part), and use (to apply tool).[22] Frank used a motion picture camera to capture each movement of a job on film so he could easily analyse each motion. These motion studies were conducted with typists, surgeons, nurses, and sports persons.

Fatigue Studies: In their experiments, Gilbreth found that adequate breaks should be given to reduce fatigue in workers. They suggested that working hours should be reduced so that employees had sufficient time to recover and be prepared for the next working day. To make rest breaks more attractive to employees, they suggested that organisations should provide proper reclining chairs, lunch rooms, rest rooms, or other entertainment.[23]

Home Reading Box Movement: The Gilbreth also worked to establish libraries at each job site to check out material to read at home or during breaks.

Ergonomics: Frank Gilbreth is often called the 'father of ergonomics'. The Gilbreth pioneered the use of devices, such as adjustable chairs and improved workstations, to ease strain on the body and to reduce injuries.

3.3.6.3 Harrington Emmerson and Efficiency Through Organisations

Harrington Emmerson propounded the ideas of Taylor in his studies of scientific management. According to him, lack of organisation was a major problem in industries. He proposed the *line-staff organisation* as a way of bringing staff knowledge to assist the line managers. This line-staff idea was similar to Taylor's desire to use the knowledge of functional foremen, but it was an improvement since it did not split the chain of command. He took Taylor's idea of setting performance standards and applied this to cost accounting. He said that standards should be established for what the costs should be, rather than estimating costs from previous records. Moreover, he proposed *twelve principles of efficiency* as mentioned below:[24]

1. **Clearly defined ideals:** The organisation must know what its goals are, what it stands for, and its relationship with the society.
2. **Common sense:** The organisation must be practical in its methods and outlook.
3. **Competent counsel:** The organisation should seek wise advice, turning to external experts if it lacks the necessary staff expertise.
4. **Discipline:** Not so much top-down discipline as internal discipline and self-discipline, with workers conforming willingly and readily to the systems in place.
5. **The fair deal:** Workers should be treated fairly at all times to encourage their participation in the efficiency movement.
6. **Reliable, immediate, and adequate records:** Measurement over time is important in determining if efficiency has been achieved.
7. **Dispatching:** Workflow must be scheduled in such a way that the processes move smoothly.
8. **Standards and schedules:** The establishment of standards and schedules is, as discussed before, fundamental to the achievement of efficiency.
9. **Standardised conditions:** Workplace conditions should be standardised according to natural scientific precepts and should evolve as new knowledge becomes available.
10. **Standardised operations:** Likewise, operations should follow scientific principles, particularly in terms of planning and work methods.
11. **Written instructions:** All standards should be recorded in the form of written instructions to workers and foremen, which detail not only the standards themselves but the methods of compliance.
12. **Efficiency reward:** If workers achieve efficiency, then they should be duly rewarded.

3.3.7 Contribution of Scientific Management to Public Administration

In this section, we will discuss the various contributions made by scientific management to the field of public administration.

Administrative Improvement Techniques

Modern scientific management techniques such as operations research, method study, time study, system analysis, and management by exceptions are all part of Taylor's heritage. These concepts are a part of administrative improvement techniques in public sector organisations.

Spread to Many Countries

Scientific management movement conquered the citadels of old-fashioned industrial management in the United States and had a tremendous effect on industrial practice.[13] It spread to Germany, England, France, and other European countries. It was also supported in Communist Russia and Taylor's principles were included in the curriculum of the education and training of engineers. Lenin referred to Taylor's system as 'a combination of subtle brutality of bourgeois exploitation and a number of its greatest scientific achievements'.

Departmentalisation

Public administration developed as a discipline with the codification and collection of labour information and census data, necessitating the establishment of government departments. This collection and codification of empirical information was derived from the experimental methods of Taylor used for industrial management.

Training for Public Service

The New York Bureau of Municipal Research, regarded to be a pioneer in government administration, established the first National Training School for public service, after being inspired by Taylor's concept of scientific training of workers. This training school was established in the Taylorist tradition of collecting and managing information with the aim of improving municipal government affairs.[14]

Standardisation of Salaries

The New York Bureau of Municipal Research also collected a vast amount of information pertaining to business conducted in New York City. Within that framework, a businesslike approach was taken to analyse teacher's salaries, with the objective of standardising pay grades and managing the provision of educational supplies.[15]

Use of Information for Policy-Making

Frit Marx's seminal work, 'Elements of Public Administration', served as a turning point in time on the matter of scientific management theory and its application in public administration. Here he said that "administrators are interested in the techniques of systematising the process of securing and sifting through relevant information so that the factors involved in arriving at a policy decision can be stated and the consequences of alternatives can be analysed and balanced.[16] This is akin to the Taylorist quest to manage the dissemination of information to all stakeholders involved in the production process.[17] Similarly, Appleby has emphasised the importance of information management (as derived from Taylorism) in public administration and public policy. According to him, information managed properly can benefit the policy; and information purposefully and nefariously withheld by administrators can serve to the detriment of public policy.[18]

Contribution to Industrial Psychology

Industrial (organisational) psychology is the scientific study of the workplace, where rigor and methods of psychology are applied to issues involving personnel management, coaching, assessment, selection, training, organisational development, and performance.[19] To analyse Taylor's contribution to public administration, Pitts[20] studied diversity, race, and performance in public organisations. The research studied and evaluated whether an organisation in the public sector, specifically a department of education, indeed had a *representative bureaucracy* that matched the general population to which it provided public services. In this study, the units of analysis were the relationships or significance between diversity, representation, and performance among teachers, administrators, and students, while segmenting variables heterogeneously by Black, Latino, White, Asian, and Indian races. Thus, Taylorism was used here, and in other similar studies, to measure the effect of diversity on motivation and performance. It was found that management representation (the shop foreman) contributed positively to performance.

Contribution to Psychology of Public Administration

Taylorism laid the base of understanding the mind, behaviours, and psychology of public administrators as they perform their duties in government departments. Frederick Taylor was a psychologist while motivating and experimenting to achieve the highest production output and motivating workers to do so. Taylor was interested in the conscious state of minds of the supervisor (shop foreman) and the worker (machinist), with a goal of improving thought processes. In Taylorism, there was a desire to provide workers with information to inform them of the benefits of being productive. Thus, Taylor's scientific management theories were later used by public practitioners to address social and organisational problems.

3.3.8 Criticism of Taylor and Scientific Management

The scientific management movement is criticised on the following grounds:

Pro-capitalist

The scientific management movement emerged at a time when capitalist development had reached the stage of requiring organisational changes in the functioning of organisational enterprises. Hence it is considered more as a pro-capitalist theory. The critics considered that the scientific management helped more the owners of industries than the workers.

Against Trade Unions

Critics thought that scientific management tends to destroy trade unions and their principle of collective bargaining. They felt that scientific management was a menace to the community at large as it causes continuous increase in unemployment. Trade unions felt that Taylor was more interested in the mechanical aspects of work and not much concerned about the total work situation.[26]

Dehumanisation

Robert Hoxie, in his investigations, found that Taylorism deals only with the mechanical and not the human aspects of production. Scholars such as Oliver Sheldon, M.P. Follette, Elton Mayo, and Peter Drucker also charged that Taylor's principles were impersonal and underemphasised the human factor. Taylor's philosophy that workers were generally lazy and try to avoid work has also been criticised.

Harry Braverman's Criticism

In his book *Labour and Monopoly Capital*, Harry Braverman[25] criticised Taylorism on the following three grounds:

1. *The principle of dissociation of labour process from the skills of the worker:* Taylorism resulted in separation of worker from the knowledge that the worker might possess, particularly the knowledge derived from a craft or traditional process. The labour process was dependent upon managerial practices rather than workers' abilities.
2. *The principle of separation of conception from execution:* There was a division, under scientific management, between manual and mental labour. The implementation of Taylorism leads to a situation where the organisation of work is the prerogative of the management where as the worker has to simply execute the work. In other words, this is separation of 'mind' from 'hand'. This results in alienation of labour from the labour process.
3. *The principle of use of monopoly over knowledge to control each step of labour process and its mode of execution:* Taylorism resulted in the managerial section monopolising the knowledge of work and controlling the worker in each and every aspect of execution of the work.

Criticism by Managers

Managers who wanted quick promotions without any merit based on higher education opposed Taylor's ideas as they advocated training of managers by experts.[27]

Criticism of Minute Division of Work

Taylor is criticised that he did not understand the anatomy of work. His minute division of work was criticised on the following grounds:

1. The work gets de-personalised and the worker becomes a mere cog in the machine.
2. It leads to automation of workers, which has psychological consequences on workers.
3. According to Peter Drucker, due to scientific management, the organisation became a piece of poor engineering judged by the standards of human relations, as well as those of productive efficiency and output.

Criticism of Functional Foremanship

Taylor's functional foremanship was criticised by many, saying that it will lead to confusion when each worker is kept under the control of eight supervisors. A worker may not be able to satisfy eight supervisors in all the aspects.

3.3.9 Antonio Gramsci's Critique of Taylorism

In his text, '*Americanism and Fordism*', Antonio Gramsci has provided an account of the implementation of American models of production, such as Taylorism and Fordism, on European economies after the First World War. Here, among other things, Gramsci said that Taylorism produces a gap between manual labour and the 'human content' of work, leading to mechanisation of the workers. He criticised Taylorism on the following grounds.

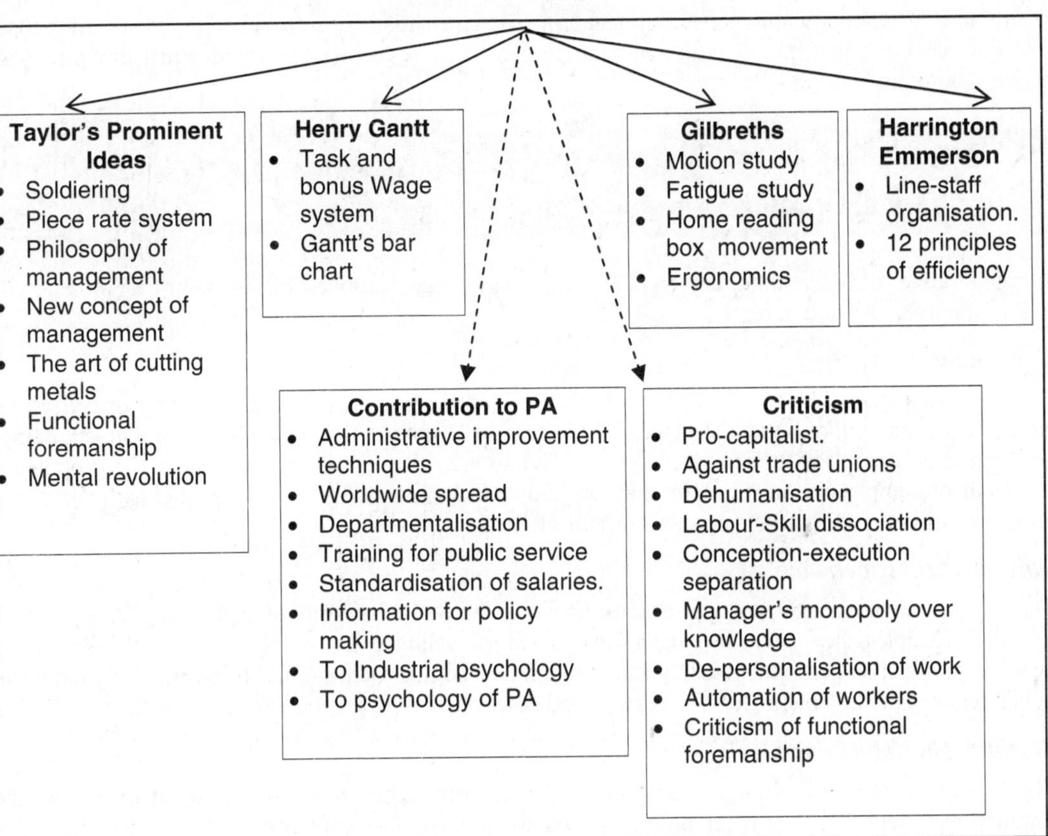

Mind Map 3.2: Scientific Management Ideas

Not Applicable to All Trades

This separation and adaptation to mechanisation is difficult in some intellectual trades such as publication of texts; here the workers are the scribes, compositors, and typists. Here it is hard to reach that level of professional qualification that the worker should forget or not think about the intellectual content of the text he/she is producing. For example, it is not possible for a scribe to put his/her attention only on the calligraphic form of the single letters. Here, he argued in a sarcastic manner, that the worker's interest in the intellectual content of the text can be measured from his/her mistakes. Conversely, his/her qualification is commensurate with his/her lack of intellectual interest, i.e., the extent to which he/she has become *mechanised.*

Complete Freedom of Worker

Once a worker adapts to mechanisation, his/her brain reaches a stage of complete freedom. The only thing that gets mechanised completely is the physical gesture; the memory of the trade, reduced to simple gestures repeated at an intense rhythm, nestles in the muscular and nervous centres and leaves the brain free and unencumbered for other occupations.

Non-Conformist Attitude

Due to mechanisation, when the worker gets no immediate satisfaction from his/her work and realises that the management tries to reduce him/her into a 'trained gorilla', non-conformist thoughts start creeping into his/her mind.[28]

3.4 Administrative Management Approach/Structural Approach/Classical Theory of Organisation

Administrative management approach is an approach of organisational management based on certain major premises as listed here.

Structuralism

This approach gives importance to the structure of the organisation. It considers that organisations cannot function without their structures. Structure is a device through which the human beings working in an organisation are assigned the tasks and are related to each other. Since the proponents of this theory emphasise on structure, they are known as *structuralists*. Structure moulds the nature of human beings according to the needs of organisation.

Universality of Experience

The administrative management approach assumes that there is universality of experience. Thinkers think that the principles they have developed have universal validity. According to Fayol, the distinction between management and public administration is false and misleading. Their theory not only embraces public service but also enterprises of every size and description, of every form and purpose.[29]

Scientifically Valid Principles

Thinkers feel that their principles are scientifically valid. Since they are based on industrial and military experience, they cannot be considered imaginary. They are based on rigorous empirical observations. Scholars believe that it is possible to develop a science of administration based on the experience of organisations.[30]

3.4.1 Henri Fayol's Approach to Administration

Henri Fayol is considered the *founder of managerial approach* to administration and is also considered as the founder of the *management process school.* His prominent works include 'General and Industrial Management (1916)' and 'The Theory of Administration in the State (1923)'.

3.4.1.1 Fayolism: Industrial Activities

According to Fayol, the totality of activities of an industrial undertaking is divided into six groups. These activities are present in all the organisations irrespective of their nature.[31]

1. Technical activities: These activities consist of production, manufacturing, and adaptation.
2. Commercial activities: These include activities such as buying, selling, and exchange. These require, together with acumen and decisions, a thorough knowledge of the market and of the strengths of the competitors, long-term foresight, the use of contracts, and price regulation.

3. Financial activities: These are basically a search for and optimum use of capital. Proper financial management is necessary to obtain capital and to make optimum use of the available funds for the success of an enterprise.
4. Security activities such as protection of property and person.
5. Accounting activities such as stock-taking, balance sheets, costs, and statistics.
6. Managerial activities: Managerial activities are done by persons at all levels of hierarchies and consist of five elements, namely, planning, organisation, command, coordination, and control (POCCC).

3.4.1.2 Fayolism: Elements of Management

Fayol identified the following five elements of management.

1. **Planning:** Administration's chief manifestation and most effective instrument is the plan of action. It enables the separation of short-run events from long-range considerations. Unity, continuity, flexibility, and precision are the broad features of a good plan of action.
2. **Organisation:** Organisation means to provide an agency with all required functional inputs such as raw materials, tools, capital, personnel, and so on. They are classified into material organisation and human organisation (personnel, leadership, and organisation structure).
3. **Command:** The art of command rests on certain personal qualities and knowledge of the general principles of management. A good commander
   (a) has thorough knowledge of their personnel;
   (b) has the ability to eliminate the incompetent;
   (c) is well-versed with the arrangement binding the business and its employees;
   (d) sets a good example;
   (e) conducts periodic audit of the organisation and uses summary charts;
   (f) brings together their chief assistants by means of conferences, at which unit of direction and focusing of effort are provided;
   (g) is not engrossed in details; and
   (h) aims at making unity, energy, initiative, and loyalty prevail among the personnel.
4. **Coordination:** It consists of working together and harmonising all activities and efforts so as to facilitate the functioning of an organisation. Its objectives are to ensure that one department's efforts coincide with the efforts of other departments, and to keep all activities in perspective with regard to the overall aims of the organisation.
5. **Control:** Control is used to establish conformity with the plan, instructions, and principles of the organisation. It comprises sub-activities such as keeping watch, monitoring, checking, auditing, and obtaining feedback.

3.4.1.3 Fayolism: Attributes of a Manager

According to Fayol, a good manager has the following attributes:

1. Physical fitness, including good health, vigour, and appearance.
2. Mental fitness, including the ability to understand, learn, and judge, and having mental vigour and adaptability.
3. Morality for being firm and willing to accept responsibility.
4. General education, including acquaintance with matters not belonging exclusively to the functions performed.
5. Special knowledge of the functions performed.
6. Experience of the work performed and knowledge about other events.

3.4.1.4 Fayolism: Principles of Administration

Henri Fayol formulated 14 principles of administration which, according to him, were not rigid but adaptable to various enterprises and settings.

Division of Work: In order to bring efficiency and effectiveness into an organisation, the work has to be divided and entrusted to the people who are specialised in it. Organisations were invented because humans failed to perform work single-handedly, and division of work was the cause of the genesis of organisations. However, division of work has its own limitations. The important ones are the volume of work, the technology, customs, and physical and organic limitations. Work cannot be divided if it is too less or when the people available do not have skills for it. Moreover, integration of the different parts is equally important as the division of work.

Authority and Responsibility: Authority and responsibility must be coterminous, coequal, and defined. It is not enough to hold people accountable for certain activities; it is also essential to delegate them the necessary authority to discharge that responsibility.

Discipline: Obedience should be observed in accordance with the standing agreements between a firm and its employees.

Unity of Command: For effective functioning of an organisation, the subordinates in the organisation should receive command from one superior only. Confusion, inefficiency, and irresponsibility arise upon violation of this principle. However there are some exceptions to this principle in the case of field office specialists. For example, it may be inevitable for an engineer in a field office working under administrative supervision of the field office manager and under technical supervision of the chief engineer in the central office. In such a situation, Luther Gulick suggested the system of 'integrated dual supervision'.[32]

Unity of Direction or Single Top Executive: One director or executive should head an organisation. Well-managed administrative units in the government are always headed by a single administrator. To support it more, Urwick warned against the use of committees for the purposes of administration. According to him, boards and commissions are slow, cumbersome, wasteful, and ineffective. They do not cooperate with other agencies.

Subordination of Individual Interest to General Interest: The interest of the organisation should prevail over the interest of one or a group of employees.

Remuneration of Personnel: The remuneration paid for services rendered should be fair and afford satisfaction to both personnel and the firm.

Centralisation: The degree of initiative left to managers should vary depending upon top managers, subordinates, and business conditions.

Scalar Chain (Hierarchy): Hierarchy indicates the control of the higher over the lower. In administrative structures, it means a graded organisation of several successive levels or steps. It facilitates the allocation of responsibilities to the different levels of organisation. It also facilitates easy flow of work and easy coordination and control in an organisation. It also fixes responsibility of individuals and makes accountability clear.

Order (Placement): Once the basic job structure has been devised and the personnel to fill the various slots have been selected, each employee occupies that job wherein he/she can render the most effective service.

Equity: For personnel to be encouraged to fulfil their duties with devotion and loyalty, there must be equity based on kindness and justice in employer-employee relations.

Stability of tenure of personnel: Suitable organisational conditions should exist to provide stable work tenure to employees.

Initiative: A powerful motivator of human behaviour is his/her ability to innovate and think creatively. Fayol suggested that suitable conditions should be created in order to encourage employees to take initiatives.

Esprit de Corps: It suggests that harmony and union among the personnel of an organisation are the sources of great strength in an organisation.

3.4.1.5 Fayolism: Administrative Training

According to Fayol, there should be systematic training in administration. Everyone needs to use some concepts of administration. At home and in affairs of state, the need for administrative ability is in proportion to the importance of the undertaking, and for individual people, the need everywhere is greater in accordance with the position occupied. Hence, there should be some generalised teaching of administration: elementary in primary schools, somewhat wider in post-primary schools, and quite advanced in higher social educational establishments.

3.4.1.6 Fayolism: Gangplank

A hierarchical organisation is divided into various levels. Gangplank is a technique for level jumping in organisations where level jumping is in the interest of the business. This Fayol technique is illustrated with the help of Fig. 3.2. If 'F' follows the principle of proper channel of communication, he/she has to send his/her message or file to 'P' through 'E', 'D', and so on, covering nine levels. It is however, possible for 'F' to use a gangplank and avoid going through 'A' and all the other intervening layers as intermediaries. However, recourse to gangplank is possible only when the immediate superiors (in this case 'E' and 'O') authorise such a relationship.

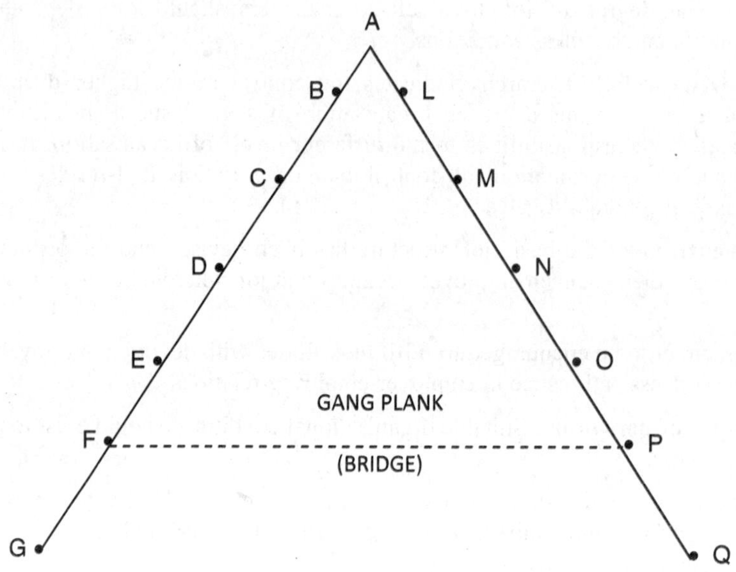

Fig. 3.2 : Gangplank by Henri Fayol

3.4.1.7 Comparison Between Fayol's and Taylor's Approaches to Administration

Taylor and Fayol both have contributed to the development of the science of administration. The similarities in their work were as follows:

1. They both realised that the problem of personnel and its management at all levels is the key to individual success.
2. Both applied scientific methods to the organisation's problems.
3. They both emphasised mutual cooperation between the management and employees.

On the other hand, the theories of Taylor and Fayol can be distinguished on the following points:

Basis	Taylor	Fayol
Human aspect	Taylor somewhat disregards human elements and there is more stress on improving materials and methods	Fayol pays due regard to the human element, e.g., the principle of initiative, *esprit de corps*, and equity recognise a need for human relations.
Status	Father of scientific management	Father of management principles
Efficiency and administration	Stresses on efficiency	Stresses on general administration

Basis	Taylor	Fayol
Approach	It has micro-approach because it is restricted to factories only	It has a macro-approach and discusses the general principles of management that are applicable in every field of management
Scope of principles	These principles are restricted to production activities	These are applicable in all kinds of organisations regarding their management affairs
Achievement	Scientific management	Administrative management
Focus of work	Operative level	Management level

Mind Map 3.3: Comparison of Fayolism and Taylorism[33]

3.4.2 Mooney and Reiley's Theory of Organisation

Mooney and Reiley's primary piece of literature is entitled *Onward Industry! The Principles of Organisation and Their Significance to Modern Industry*, which was published in 1931. They emphasised the importance of organisational structure being governed by universal principles. In their work, they created three universal organisational principles: coordinative, scalar, and functional.

Principle of Coordination

The coordinative principle, known as the *master principle*, involves an organisation coordinating the tasks of multiple workers in order to accomplish their organisational objectives. The principle emphasises that when work is divided and entrusted to different individuals, the work has to be coordinated to achieve the organisational tasks. It is basically bringing together the work done by different individuals.

Scalar Principle (Hierarchy)

This principle has already been discussed in the section of Henri Fayol. According to Mooney and Reiley, the delegation of work should complement the hierarchical structure. They also emphasised a principle governing the superior-subordinate relationship identified as the *exception principle*. It states, "Subordinates should refer only the few unusual and difficult problems to their superiors while handling all easy and routine problems themselves."[34]

Functional Principle

The functional principle focuses on horizontal differences based on the types of tasks. It identifies the method of each individual's work duties and how they contribute to the organisation's goals. One area of functional differentiation is the line and staff principle, which refers to the creation of staff units to advise or support line authorities in the performance of their duties.[35]

3.4.3 Gulick and Urwick

Luther Gulick and Lyndall Urwick have contributed to the administrative management approach in their famous writings 'Administrative Reflections from World War-II', 'Papers on the Science of Administration (1937)', 'The Elements of Administration (1943)', and others. They had a rich experience in the working of the civil service, military, and industrial organisations. Thus, with these two, we saw a coming together of public administration and business administration. They felt that if the experiences of administrators are processed it could be possible to develop a science of administration.

3.4.3.1 Structure of Administration

One notable feature in the writings of Gulick and Urwick is the importance they attached to the structure of administration while almost neglecting the role of people in the organisation. On this, Urwick remarked that it is impossible for humanity to advance its knowledge of organisations unless the factor of structure is isolated from other considerations, however artificial such isolation may appear.[36] He defined organisation as determining activities that are necessary for a purpose (or plan) and arranging them in groups, which may be assigned to individuals.[37]

Moreover, while emphasising the importance of design and structure, Urwick has conceived an organisation chiefly as a designing process. He felt that *lack of design is illogical, cruel, wasteful, and inefficient.*

1. Illogical, because it is inconceivable to appoint a person and pay them wages without an idea of the position they are likely to occupy.
2. Cruel, when an organisational member does not know the qualifications required for the job and the duties assigned to them in the job situation.
3. Wasteful, because if jobs are not arranged properly, functional specialisation is not possible, and training people to occupy jobs falling vacant due to death or retirement becomes difficult.
4. Inefficient, because supervisors have nothing to fall back on except personalities in the event of conflict and confusion.

3.4.3.2 Principles of Administration

Gulick and Urwick devoted their attention to the discovery of principles based on which the structures of organisations may be designed. Gulick enumerated 10 principles of organisation as follows:

1. Division of work or specialisation
2. Bases of departmental organisation
3. Coordination through hierarchy
4. Deliberate coordination
5. Coordination through committees
6. Decentralisation
7. Unity of command
8. Staff and line
9. Delegation
10. Span of control

Similarly, Urwick identified eight principles of organisation as follows:

1. Principle of objectives: Organisation should be an expression of a purpose.
2. Principle of correspondence: Authority and responsibility must be coequal.

3. Principle of responsibility: Responsibility of superiors for the work of subordinates is absolute.
4. Scalar principle (hierarchy)
5. Principle of span of control
6. Principle of specialisation
7. Principle of coordination
8. Principle of definition: A clear prescription of every duty.

After formulating these principles, Urwick felt that the administrative organisation is still an unexplored field and there are many unknown factors for a fuller understanding. He, therefore, suggested that his principles are a framework of thought and an arrangement of ideas that would help others to synthesise them further based on their own experience.

3.4.3.3 Executive Functions

Gulick identified the various functions of the executive and used the acronym POSDCoRB for them. The expansions of the letters of this term are as follows.

Planning (P): Already discussed in the section Elements of Management under Henri Fayol's Approach to Administration.

Organisation (O): Already discussed in the above-mentioned section.

Staffing (S): Staffing is concerned with all aspects of personnel administration such as recruitment, appointment, promotion, discipline, and retirement.

Directing (D): Directing relates to the orders issued by managers to the subordinates concerning the activities of administration.

Coordination (Co): Already discussed in the section Elements of Management under Henri Fayol's Approach to Administration.

Reporting (R): Reporting symbolises the upward flow of information to the executive. A good communication system is imperative through which such progress is reported to the executive. It is through reporting that the executive becomes aware of the problems in the organisation for which he/she may initiate corrective measures.

Budgeting (B): It covers the entire field of financial administration.

3.4.3.4 Explanation of Certain Principles

Many of the principles given by Gulick and Urwick have already been discussed in the section Principles of Administration under Henri Fayol's Approach to Administration. The explanation of the other important principles is given here.

The Theory of Departmentalisation

This principle provides a basis on which work is divided in an organisation and departments are created under it. Luther Gulick identified four bases, popularly known as 4Ps, on which different departments are based.

Purpose: Here departments are created based on the major purposes or functions of the departments, e.g., the welfare department is created based on the purpose of looking after the welfare of the people. Such departmentalisation is advantageous, as these departments are self-contained organisations and low coordination costs are involved in running the department. They are more certain of attaining their goals. These departments, however, also have certain disadvantages such as lack of possibility of work division, failure to update technology, and not enough work for specialists working in the department.

Process (or Skills): Process-based departments are created based on the processes or skills involved in their functioning, e.g., the department of engineering may be considered as a process-based department. The advantage is that it brings together in a single office a large amount of each kind of work, and it is possible to make use of the most effective division of work and specialisation. Moreover, it makes possible the maximum use of labour and machinery for mass production. However, a major disadvantage of this basis is that it leads to purposeless division and growth of department.

Persons (or Clientele): Here departments are created on the basis of the type of clientele, e.g., the 'old-age welfare department' serves a particular kind of persons who need special attention. Its advantage is that people working in these departments acquire specialised skills to serve a particular clientele. However, a disadvantage is that coordination between such departments becomes difficult due to overlapping and duplication.

Place (or Territory): Here place is the basis for departmentalisation, such as a district administration or tribal area department. Here all functions performed in a given area are clubbed together. It is useful for the intensive development of an area. The members become area specialists. However, such departments suffer from lack of functional specialisation and growth.

The theory of departmentalisation is criticised on the basis that the criteria of departmentalisation are incompatible with each other. They are vague and often overlap with each other. For example, the department of medicine can be considered a process-based department (involving medicine skills) as well as a purpose-based department (with the purpose of improving health).

Principle of Staff

In the performance of organisational activities, executives require the help of officials known as *staff*. Staff is of two kinds: special staff and general staff. While the general staff helps the executive (line) in knowing, thinking, and planning functions, the special staff helps the executive (line) in carrying out the basic operations of the organisation. However, the line-staff relationship suffers from the following problems:

1. General staff helps in coordinating the work of organisational specialists without themselves taking any specialised functions. For example, Gulick mentioned that in military organisations general staff assist their supervisors in their central task of command, control, and coordination. This may de-motivate the specialists.
2. Staff assistants who act on behalf of top executive, Urwick mentioned, are often regarded as 'encroaching' upon the authority of senior officials. To overcome this, the staff should act in an anonymous manner.

Principle of Delegation

The principle of delegation requires that the executives should keep the requisite authority to act with and delegate the rest of authority to their subordinates. Such delegation of authority helps the subordinates in discharging their responsibilities. According to Urwick, "lack of courage to delegate properly, and knowledge of how to do it, is one of the most general causes of failure in an organisation." Moreover, the senior executives should be accountable for the actions of their subordinates.

Principle of Span of Control

This principle signifies that a superior cannot control more than a certain number of subordinates. Urwick said that no superior can supervise directly the work of more than five, or at the most six, subordinates whose work interlocks. This principle is based on the psychological concept of 'span of attention'. When the number of subordinates increases arithmetically, there is a geometrical increase in all possible combinations of relationships, which may demand the attention of the supervisor. Gulick identified various factors that may influence the optimum span, particularly the capacity of an individual executive, the nature of work performed, the stability of an organisation, and geographical proximity to those who are supervised.

3.4.4 Human Factor in Public Administration

While commenting on his *The Papers on the Science of Administration*, 70 years from its first edition, Gulick noted that "after all, governments are constituted of human beings and have their main job helping, controlling, and serving human beings."[42] He considered human beings as the major and essential variables for understanding the nature of public administration at that time and guiding the field into the future.

Administrative Structure Designed for War

According to Gulick, the structure of the modern state is specifically designed for war and is distinctly military. It is authoritative, with all authority concentrated at the top, and all the work, but not the authority, assigned to subordinate echelons and field commanders. The vocabulary of public administration is also military in origin. Terms such as 'line and staff', 'field commanders', and 'material and manpower' are military terms.

Time Factor in Public Administration

Gulick emphasised the importance of time as a crucial factor in public administration. Without time, there is no change, no growth, no cause and effect, and no responsibility for management. All public policy innovations are rooted in timing and in *democracy timing is the hallmark of the statecraft.*[43] He identified five aspects of time:

1. Time as an input
2. Time as an output
3. Time as the flow of events
4. Time as the gap between two or more significant events
5. Timing as a management policy

The principles of administration should be eternally tied to the culture in which they work, and the culture must evolve appropriately well before major changes can be successfully undertaken in human organisations. *Timing is essential for any organisation as it is not a machine but an organism.* Time must become a central strategic and moral concern in public management. Thus, governments must plan and work with this flow in time and for time.

3.4.5 Positive Contribution of Administrative Management to Public Administration

Apart from the concepts discussed in the preceding sections, the positive contributions of the administrative management approach to public administration are as follows.

Working Principles: We find the working of principles such as division of work, coordination and delegation in present-day organisations. Organisations cannot function without adhering to these principles.

No Alternatives to these Principles: The principles of administrative management approach have been criticised by many scholars, but no one has been able to search for better alternatives for these principles.

Basis for development of administration: The principles of administration have provided the basis for the development of later theories in administration.

Basis for Functionalism: Fayol was a pioneer of the concept of viewing management as being made up of functions. His functional organisation is still the best way to structure a small business especially a small manufacturing business.[38]

Moral Dimension to Public Administration: Gulick captured the development of the field of public administration and pointed towards the importance of public administration as a managerial, political, moral, and ethical concern. As Denhardt has noted, we now recognise that administrative action is permeated by moral choices, and whether we like it or not, administrators are a model of not only technical and professional but also moral behaviour.[39]

3.4.6 Criticism of Administrative Management Approach

The theories of Fayol, Gulick, Urwick, and other administrative management theorists are criticised on the following grounds.

Neglected Structural Aspects

While devoting considerable attention to functional classification, Henri Fayol neglected the structural aspect, and his treatment of organisation was considered defective.

Single-Dimensional Functionalism

The functionalism of Fayol was found to be deficient in design and logic. It took a single dimension of management to determine all facets of the organisation around it.

Narrow Empirical Base/Low Evidence for Theory

The empirical base used by Fayol for generating a full-fledged theory of management is too narrow. He theorised functionalism on the basis of functions undertaken in a manufacturing company. The principles of the classical theory tend to dissolve when put to test.

Ignored Socio-Psychological Factors

Proponents of the human relations school felt that administrative management scholars ignored the socio-psychological or emotional needs of the employees. They believed that there is a tendency to treat the human being as an instrument incapable of individual contribution based on personal qualification. It is this failure that gave rise to human relations movement and behavioural studies.

Not Universally Valid

The administrative management theory is not universally valid as far as the principles of administration are concerned. They appear more in the nature of postulates of experienced people who have closely observed organisations at work.

Principles as Proverbs

Herbert Simon has regarded the principles as "homely proverbs, myths, slogans and inanities." He said, "it is fatal defect of the current principles of administration that, like proverbs, they occur in pairs. For almost every principle one can find an equally plausible and acceptable contradictory principle. Although the two principles of the pair will lead to exactly opposite organisational recommendations, there is nothing in theory to indicate which the proper one to apply is. For instance, one of the proverbs says that administrative efficiency increases by specialisation. But it is not made clear whether area specialisation is good or functional specialisation. Likewise, there is contradiction between the principle of specialisation and the principle of unity of command. The specialists working in organisations are required to be subjected to the dual control of superiors in administrative and technical matters."

Neglected Informal Organisation

Classical theorists showed concern only for the formal organisation while neglecting the informal organisational process.

Neglected Organisational Dynamics

The dynamic nature of administration and the ever-changing setting in which it functions are not given adequate attention by classical theorists. The organisation, and its goals, undergoes a constant change as a result of the economic, social, or political stimuli and, hence, any study of administration must take into consideration this element of change.[40]

Neglected Organisational Conflicts

Classical theorists had little appreciation of the role of intra-organisational conflict of interests in defining limits or organisational behaviour.

Pro-Management

All the classical theories have a pro-management bias. The theorist only dealt with the problems of management in the organisation and not other operational problems that involve the other levels of organisation.[41]

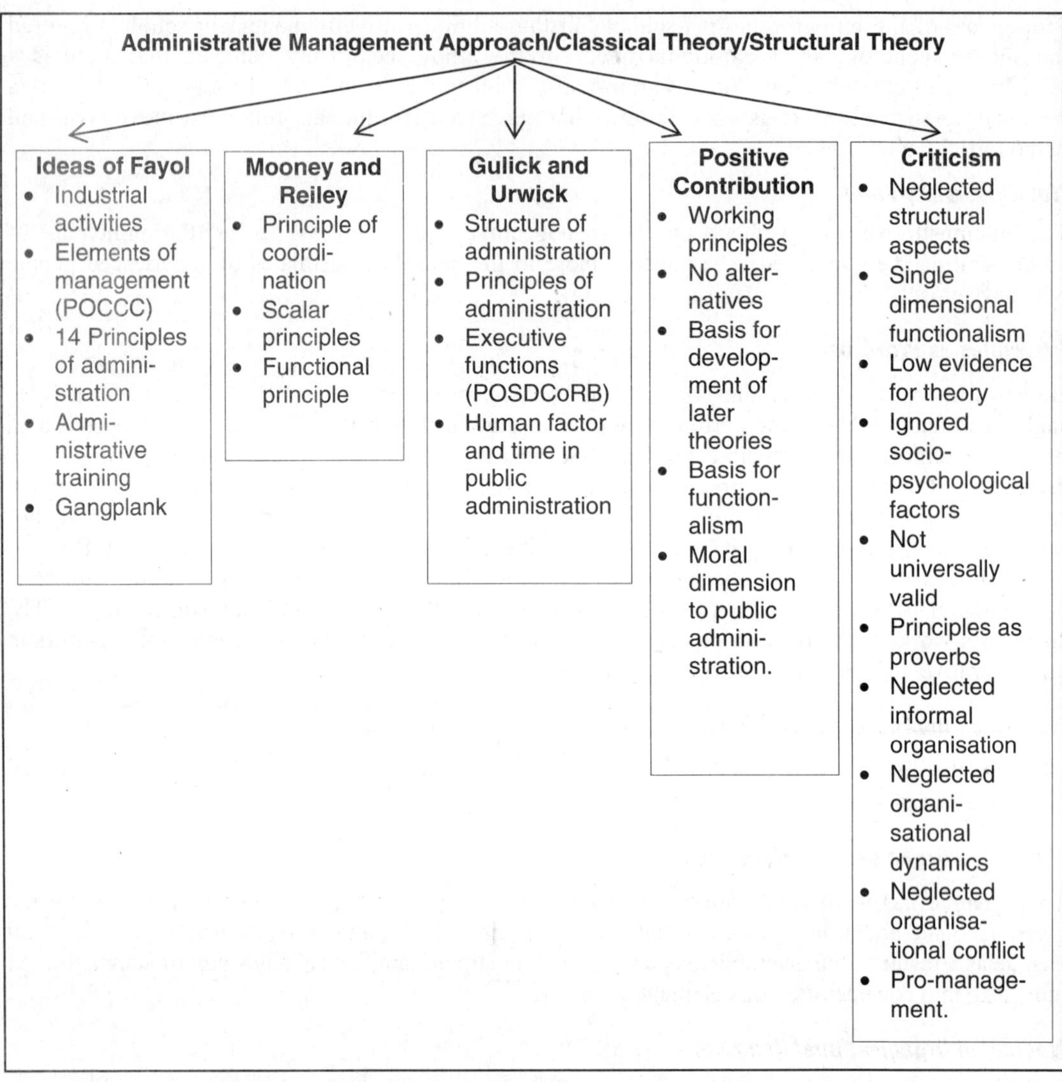

Mind Map 3.4: Ideas of Administrative Management Approach

3.5 Weber's Bureaucratic Model–its Critique and Post Weberian Developments

Weber's bureaucratic model finds a central place in the classical theories of public administration and organisations. Max Weber is considered as the first thinker to systematically study bureaucracy. His major writings were 'The Theory of Economic and Social Organisations', 'General Economic History', and 'Protestant Ethic and Spirit of Capitalism'.

3.5.1 Weber'sTheory of Bureaucracy

According to Weber, the theory of bureaucracy was needed to bring in efficiency in the functioning of organisations. As stated by him, "no special proof is necessary to show that military discipline is ideal model for the modern capitalist factory."[44] It is said that Weber's bureaucratic model is inspired from the Prussian military organisation. According to him, the capitalist market economy required a bureaucratic organisation as it demands the official business of the administration to be discharged precisely, unambiguously, continuously, and with as much speed as possible.[44]

While Taylor attempted to rationalise the functions of the modern factory, Weber made an attempt to rationalise the bureaucratic structures. Before Weber, a French economist invented the term 'bureaucracy' in 1745. The word consists of two terms 'bureau' (meaning writing table and office) and 'cracy' (meaning rule). Thus, it denotes rule by officials.

3.5.2 Max Weber on Authority

Max Weber's concept of bureaucracy is closely related to his ideas on legitimacy of authority. He distinguished between power and authority. Power is said to be possessed if the will of a person can be enforced despite resistance. On the other hand, authority is said to be possessed when a will or command elicits voluntary obedience on the part of specific individuals. It is a state of reality where a person willingly complies with legitimate commands or orders because he/she considers that a person by virtue of his/her position could issue orders to him/her.

3.5.2.1 Components of Authority

The five essential components of authority identified by Weber were as follows:

1. An individual or a body of individuals who rule.
2. An individual or a body of individuals who are ruled.
3. The will of the rulers to influence the conduct of the ruled.
4. Evidence of the influence of the rulers in terms of the objective degree of command.
5. Direct or indirect evidence of that influence in terms of subjective acceptance with which the ruled obey the command.

3.5.2.2 Categories of People in an Organisation

Weber categorised persons in an organisation into the following four types:

1. Those who are accustomed to obey commands.
2. Those who are personally interested in seeing the existing domination continue.
3. Those who participate in that domination.
4. Those who hold themselves in readiness for the exercise of functions.

While explaining these points, Weber concluded that "all administration means dominance."

3.5.2.3 Ideal-type Constructs of Weber

Weber came out with 'ideal-type' models for describing different types of authorities. He defined ideal-type constructs as conceptual patterns that bring together certain relationships and events of historical life into a complex, which is conceived as an internally consistent system. However, these constructs were like utopias, which were arrived at by the analytical accentuation of certain elements of reality. They were formed by one-sided accentuation of one or more points of view and by the synthesis of a great many diffuse, discrete, more or less present, and occasionally absent concrete individual phenomena, which were arranged according to those one-sidedly emphasised viewpoints into a unified analytical construct. In their conceptual purity, these mental constructs cannot be found empirically anywhere in reality.[45] The real historical experience would usually fall in-between the extremes of his ideal-type constructs. Weber approximated the complexity of specific historical situations by bringing various ideal-type concepts to bear upon the specific case under his focus.[45] These ideal types helped Weber in constructing 'ideographic' as well as 'nomothetic' analyses. *Ideographic* in the sense that they tried to specifically understand the meaning of individual, historical, cultural, and subjective phenomena. *Nomothetic* in the sense that they tried to generalise historical situations and derive universal systems that explain the types or categories of objective phenomena.

3.5.2.4 Types of Authority Systems

In his ideal-type constructs, Weber divided authority into three types, based on the sources of legitimacy for each authority. These are (a) traditional authority, (b) charismatic authority, and (c) legal-rational authority.

Traditional Authority

Traditional authority rests on an established belief in the sanctity of immemorial traditions and the legitimacy of the status of those exercising authority under them. Here a command is obeyed because of the belief in age-old customs, traditions, conventions, and beliefs. This is a pure type of feudal, patrimonial regime under which the organisation consists of household officials, relatives, and loyalists. The only documents in the administration of law are the documents of tradition, namely, precedents. This system retains legitimacy as long as the customs and traditions are respected in the organisation.

Charismatic Authority

Charismatic authority rests on devotion to the specific and exceptional sanctity, heroism, or exemplary character of an individual person and of the normative patterns or order revealed or ordained by them.[46] Charisma means supernatural, superhuman, or extraordinary qualities of a leader. Those subject to charismatic authority are 'followers' of the leader, not 'subjects'. The only basis of legitimacy is personal charisma.

Legal-Rational Authority

Legal-rational authority rests on a belief in the legality of the patterns of normative rules and the rights of those elevated to authority under such rules to issue commands. Manifestations of it are found in organisations where rules are applied judicially and in accordance with ascertainable principles valid for all members in an organisation. Weber considers it as the most rational form of authority.

Traditional authority	
Nature of legitimate authority	**Nature of administrative staff**
1. Legitimacy is claimed and accepted on the basis of 'sanctity of orders' 2. Obedience is given not to enacted rules but to persons whose orders are legitimised by: (a) Tradition that govern certain areas (b) The chief's free personal decisions (prerogative) 3. No rules are enacted; new situations are covered by precedents, i.e., the wisdom of the promulgator	1. Staff is recruited from two sources: (a) Patrimonial source: Persons tied to the chief by traditional loyalties (b) Non-patrimonial: Purely personal loyalties (favourites), vassals (relations of fealty), or those who freely contract for such a relationship 2. Many posts are filled on the basis of kinship 3. Staff lacks: (a) Clearly defined sphere of competence (b) Rational ordering of offices in hierarchy (c) Regular appointments or promotions (d) Technical training as a regular requirement 4. Types of staff under traditional authority are: (a) 'Gerontocracy' (governance by old people) or 'patriarchal' (governance by men): there is no personal administrative staff at all (b) Patrimonialism: A personal staff develops, which is under the pure personal control of the chief (c) Decentralised patrimonialism: Here a group of individuals appropriate certain advantages, offices, etc., and thus limit the power and control of the chief (e.g., leasing, tax farming, and sales of offices)

Charismatic authority	
Nature of legitimate authority	**Nature of administrative staff**
1. The individual in power is considered superhuman and supernatural; s/he is treated as a leader 2. Followers do not elect a leader but recognise his/her charisma 3. Consistent failure of charisma may lead to depositioning of the leader 4. Charisma is routinised by finding a successor: (a) Finding a person with specific characteristics	1. In its pure form, there is no administrative staff; only followers and disciples. There are no legal rules: (a) Disciples are chosen on the basis of charismatic qualities (b) No appointments or promotions are made (c) There is no hierarchy or specified sphere of competence (d) There are no salaries or benefits

Charismatic authority	
Nature of legitimate authority	**Nature of administrative staff**
(b) Designation of a successor by the original charisma holder (c) Designation by charismatically qualified staff (d) Charisma transmitted hereditarily (e) Charisma transmitted by ritual means 5. Authority structure of routinised charisma is affected by the manner in which administrative staff secures economic positions 6. Charisma can also be routinised in anti-authoritarian direction by use of plebiscite to legitimise leadership: (a) It is a form of charismatic authority in which authoritarian elements are concealed by plebiscite (b) Anti-authoritarian routinised charisma may lead to emphasis on economic rationality, but at the same time may do away with all rational procedures if this prevents obtaining benefits for followers	(e) Unlike traditional authority, staff is not bound by precedent 2. Routinisation affects the character of administrative staff: (a) Norms are created for recruitment (b) Method for selecting a charismatic successor affects the method for selecting administrative staff (c) Routinised staff secures its economic position through benefits and offices 3. Routinisation of charisma in anti-authoritarian direction also affects the nature of administrative staff: (a) Principle of election may be applied to staff (b) Election of staff may tend to curtail the power of leader (c) As long as election is limited to plebiscitary leader, staff is usually chosen on the basis of personal loyalty.

Legal-rational authority	
Nature of legitimate authority	**Nature of administrative staff**
1. Here obedience is owed to the legally established impersonal order 2. Legal norms may be established on any of a variety of bases (expediency, values, etc.) 3. Intentionally established abstract rules are applied to specific cases 4. Person in authority occupies an 'office' 5. Person who obeys command obeys 'only the law', not the individual 6. Offices are arranged in a hierarchical manner with appeal and grievance machinery 7. Individuals in authority need specialised training for rational application of norms	1. Legal authority in its purest form utilises bureaucratic administrative staff 2. Characteristics of bureaucrats are as follows: (a) They are subject to authority only in official capacities (b) They are organised in hierarchy of office (c) The office is filled by free selection (d) Officials are appointed on the basis of technical competence (e) Officials are paid in money; fixed, graded salary scale; pensions are also provided (f) Each office has defined competence (g) Office is a primary occupation

Legal-rational authority	
Nature of legitimate authority	**Nature of administrative staff**
8. Officials are separated from ownership of means of production; their private property is strictly separated from public property 9. Office is separated from living quarters 10. Official does not appropriate his/her office 11. Written documents are at the heart of all processes; all decisions are taken in writing 12. Ultimate source of authority in a legal-rational system may well be in another order (charisma)	(h) There is career advancement by seniority and/or achievement (i) Official is separated from the means of administration (j) Official is subjected to discipline in conduct of office 3. Appointment is a crucial feature as election impedes hierarchical discipline 4. Specialised knowledge is indispensable 5. Administrative staff in its purest form is of 'monocratic type': (a) It is the most rational means of carrying out imperative control over human beings (b) Primary source of superiority is technical knowledge (c) One can escape existing bureaucratic authority only by creating another bureaucratic authority (d) Capitalism has been a major spur towards bureaucratisation (e) Development of bureaucracy leads to social levelling, and social levelling favours bureaucracy (appointment by merit)

Mind Map 3.5: Comparison of three different types of authority[46]

3.5.3 Max Weber's Elements of Bureaucracy

Weber described bureaucracy as an administrative body of appointed officials. He categorised bureaucracy into (a) patrimonial bureaucracy found in traditional and charismatic authorities and (b) legal-rational authority found only in legal type of authority. He identified certain elements of bureaucracy as follows.

Impersonal Order: Weber said that officials in bureaucracy do their duty in an impersonal manner. Subordinates follow the impersonal order given by their superiors. According to Merton, authority, the power of control which derives from an acknowledged status, inheres in the office, not in the particular person who performs the official role. This leads to the de-personalisation of relationships in an organisation.

Rules: Rules are the basis of functioning of the legal-rational authority. They regulate the conduct of officials in an office.

Sphere of Competence: It involves a sphere of obligation to perform functions that have been marked off as a part of systematic division of labour. It also implies provision of the incumbent with the necessary authority to carry out their functions.

Hierarchy: Every office and every official is a part of hierarchy.

Separation of Public and Personal Ends: Officials are separated from ownership of the means of production. Official position cannot be used for personal ends. Office property is separated from personal property, and officials are accountable for the use of office property.

Written Documents: All administrative acts, decisions, and rules are recorded in writing. These documents make the administration accountable to the people and provide a ready reference for future action.

Monocratic Type: Certain functions performed by the bureaucracy cannot be performed by any other form of organisation. They monopolise certain functions, and only the authorised officials can perform those functions.

3.5.4 Weber's Iron Cage

Max Weber is well-known for his concept of iron cage, originally written in German as 'stahlhartes Gehäuse'. By this he meant that the whole society is captured in the iron cage of rationality and other means followed by the frugal puritanical Protestants. The capitalist economic system was developed as a result of the frugal living style of the Protestants. However, even when Protestantism decreased, the system of capitalism remained, as did the social structure and principles of bureaucracy that had evolved along with it. The bureaucratic social structure, and its values and beliefs, shaped the social life in modern times. This phenomenon was conceived by Weber as an iron cage.

Technological and economic relationships that organised and grew out of capitalist production became fundamental forces in the society. If a person is born in a society where bureaucratic division of labour and hierarchy is a prominent value, he/she is bound to live and adopt those values. His/her life and views will be shaped to such an extent that he/she would not be able to imagine any system other than the bureaucratic and the capitalist system. So, those born into the cage live out its dictates and reproduce the cage in its perpetuity.

3.5.5 Mixed Types of Authority and Administrative Systems

Max Weber was more aware of the social interactional patterns in bureaucracy than his ideal-type construct suggested. Such a consciousness is reflected in his views on the working of the 'mixed' authority systems. Weber said that in the real world, 'pure' legal-rational authority systems, such as the other two ideal-types, had never existed. In the empirical world, elements of various authority patterns are mixed with each other. For example, some bureaucracies may emerge from charismatic movements. Likewise, the supreme head of a bureaucratic group may have a claim to authority on a basis other than the legal-rational, e.g., a hereditary charismatic ruler may have a bureaucratic staff. Moreover, a legal-rational order will generally retain traditional and charismatic qualities. Thus, Weber suggested the need to work with 'mixed' types or with clusters of interrelated characteristics from several of the ideal types. He spoke of mixed types such as 'patrimonial bureaucracy' when referring to specific cases of historical administrative systems.

3.5.6 Structural and Functional Meaning of Bureaucracy

In public administrative literature, there are two meanings of the word bureaucracy: structural and functional. The structural meaning describes bureaucracy as an organisation having structural features such as hierarchy, specialisation, and competent incumbents.

From the functional perspective, a study of bureaucracy involves the study of the impact of bureaucratic behaviour on other subsystems of the general social system, of which bureaucracy is a part. Carl Friedrich has specified four behavioural features of bureaucracy in this sense: objectivity, discretion, precision, and consistency. These features contribute positively to the bureaucracy's capacity to achieve its objectives in a rational manner. Such characteristics (termed by Riggs as 'bureau-rationality') are also useful in the achievement of the goals of the broader social system in which bureaucracy operates.[50]

3.5.7 Politics and Bureaucracy

According to Weber, public bureaucracy is considered as a subsystem of the political system. The political class is responsible for electoral and legislative functions, and bureaucrats are responsible for the implementation of the public policy decided by the politicians.

Neutrality of Bureaucracy

While implementing public policies, bureaucrats are expected to remain politically neutral. They are expected to obey the orders of the political leaders, even during a disagreement with them. Here, a bureaucrat should be neutrally competent, i.e., they should do government work expertly, objectively, and without regard to personal partisanship or other obligations and loyalties.[51] In general terms, neutrality of three kinds is important for the bureaucracy. They are as follows.

Neutrality between Classes: Bureaucracy is expected to allocate resources justly and show a neutral attitude towards different classes of society such as landlords, capitalists, traders, and workers. If bureaucracy is seen as neutral, then conflict between classes can be minimised. Thus, neutrality of bureaucracy is considered as a main instrument of social order.

Neutrality between Cultural Groups: Society consists of various cultural groups, such as those based on religion, caste, language, or religion, whose interests collide with each other. The bureaucracy is required to hold a balance between them and is thus required to be neutral to them. It is important that bureaucrats consciously safeguard the interest of lower socio-economic groups.

Neutrality between Political Parties: In a democracy, various political parties fight for implementing the wishes of the people. Bureaucracy is the instrument used to implement the public policies decided by the various parties. Thus, it needs to be neutral towards them so as to serve the wishes of the general public. This neutrality of bureaucracy suffers due to spoils system as well as due to the frequent and unjustified system of transfer and postings.

Commitment of Bureaucracy

According to Karl Marx, members of bureaucracy suffer from loss of freedom, creativity, humanity, and morality. This leads to alienation of the bureaucracy. This problem can be solved by improving the commitment among the members of the bureaucracy. In other words, the bad effects of bureaucracy can be reduced when employees are imbued with dedication. This commitment is again of three types.

Value Commitment: The bureaucracy has to be committed to the human values of truth, compassion, honesty, and courage. It also needs a commitment towards national and constitutional values such as justice, liberty, equality, fraternity, secularism, socialism, democracy, and nationalism.

Service Commitment: Commitment towards service of the people is an important consideration for a bureaucratic organisation. It is expected that the service interest is put before their own personal interest.

Professional Commitment: Since in the Weberian bureaucracy the contribution of bureaucrats is due to their specialised knowledge, they are expected to keep themselves abreast with the latest developments in their field of specialisation. They must also match the expected standards of the profession. They must adhere to the ethics and etiquettes of their profession.[54]

Competition for Power between Politicians and Bureaucrats: Weber conceived a competition for power among the politicians and the bureaucrats. He recognised that every problem, despite its seemingly technical nature, can assume political significance, and its solutions may be influenced by political considerations. This may lead to a competition for power. He visualised *bureaucracy as a power instrument of the first order for one who controls the bureaucratic apparatus.*[52] The technical superiority and expertise of bureaucrats against the lack of knowledge of politicians leads to greater power for bureaucrats.

Bureaucratic Absolutism: In the above-mentioned condition, if bureaucrats are successful in concealing the important premises of decisions and in avoiding inspection of and control over their functioning, bureaucratic absolutism might result.[53] The accountability of the administration can decrease to its specialised knowledge and secretive functioning in day-to-day administration.

3.5.8 Limiting the Scope of Bureaucratic Power

Max Weber suggested the following mechanisms for limiting the scope for bureaucrats appropriating excessive power as described in the preceding topic.

Decision by Collegium: In a hierarchical bureaucracy, decisions are taken by only one individual at a level of hierarchy. This may lead to appropriation of power. To avoid this, Weber suggested that important decisions should be taken after consultation among the members of a collegium.

Division of Responsibility: Weber suggested that a division of responsibility and functions among different bodies will lead to sharing of power and avoid arbitrary use of absolute power.

Average Competence of Administration: If administrators have average and good enough competence to gain the confidence of the people, they may not indulge themselves in wrongful appropriation of power. However, amateur administrators may not match the demand for expertise in a modern society.

Direct Democracy: Weber suggested direct democracy for bureaucrats, where they have a short tenure, right to be recalled, and are controlled by an assembly. However, such a system is possible only for small organisations and local governments.

Parliamentary Responsibility: The responsibility of the bureaucrats towards the elected representatives limits the power of the bureaucracy. However, this may lead to bureaucratisation of the representatives.

3.5.9 Criticism of Weber's Bureaucracy

Max Weber's theory of bureaucracy is criticised on the following grounds.

Bureaucratic Model is Irrational

Scholars such as Merton feel that the bureaucratic structure conceived by Weber is irrational in its formation, particularly the features such as hierarchy and rules-bound nature. They can lead to unexpected consequences and detrimental results.

Conflict of Purpose

A division of functions in an organisation may lead to subunits setting up their own goals, which may be in conflict with the overall purpose of the organisation.

Ideal-type Constructs are Inconsistent

Talcott Parsons has pointed towards the inconsistency in the ideal-type constructs of Weber. Weber expects the superior staff to be technically more competent and in a position to give orders to the subordinates. However, it is not always possible to appoint superior staff that is more competent than the subordinates. In that case, there exits an inconsistency on whom to obey: the one with more professional competence or the one appointed on a higher position.[47]

Non-compliance with Rules

Scholars such as Alvin Gouldner feel that Weber's bureaucracy does not create conditions that orient the behaviour of the members with the rules of the organisation. The problems of non-compliance arise due to certain conditions that are present in the outside environment of the organisation. Weber has not paid any heed to these outside conditions in his bureaucratic model.[48]

Not Universally Applicable Model

Critics believe that the Weberian model of bureaucracy is not applicable to all places at all times. In all organisations and places, efficiency cannot be guaranteed by the rigid application of rules, hierarchy, and so on. Efficiency can only be guaranteed when an individual identifies himself with the purpose of the organisation and changes his/her behaviour with the changing circumstances of the internal and external environments of the organisation.

Not Applicable in Underdeveloped Societies

The assumptions made about human motivation, in Weberian bureaucracy, are not valid in the context of non-Western societies. As an example, patrimonial bureaucracy may be more conducive to economic growth in underdeveloped societies than the legal-rational bureaucracy of the Weberian type.

Not a Modern Phenomenon

Max Weber observed that legal-rational bureaucracy is a modern phenomenon. H.C. Creel and A.B. Spitzer raised their objection on this idea of Weber. According to them, all the characteristics of Weberian bureaucracy existed in the Chinese administration of 200 BC. Similarly, the functions of Prefect in nineteenth century France were similar to the functions of Weberian bureaucracy.[49]

Neglected Human Behaviour

Weber paid more attention to the structure of an organisation than the human beings that personify it.

Sphere of Competence not Applicable to Development Administration

The idea of the sphere of competence is not always valid for development administration. In development administration, an official has to be proactive and react to a new situation even when he/she does not receive an order for it from his/her superior. An administrator has to be ready to discover new problem situations rather than just wait for a complaint to come to them. However, in the concept of the sphere of competence, a subordinate does only those tasks for which he/she receives orders from his/her seniors.

Hierarchy Impeded Mutual Trust

The concept of hierarchy leads to mutual suspicion in inter-organisational and inter-personal settings. It leads to the growth of authoritarianism among superiors and impedes the creation of a team spirit in the organisation.

Records lead to Formalism

Excessive dependency on written records makes the official a 'glorified clerk'. Recording of each and every oral discussion leads to too much formalism in the organisation. It is deleterious for the efficiency and effectiveness of an organisation.

Ideal Types not Relevant to Developing Countries

Riggs has said that Weber's ideal-type construct of bureaucracy has assumed that administrative systems are autonomous. However, in developing societies, administrative systems do not have the same degree of autonomy from other social structures as their counterparts in developed societies.

No Study on Impact of Economic, Socio-Cultural and Other Factors

Weber has studied the interaction between the political system and its administrative sub-systems. However, he has not analysed the impact of economic and socio-cultural systems on bureaucracy. Alvin Gouldner has said that Weber's ideal-type models are innocent of spatio-temporal cautions and give the impression that bureaucracy has existed in an essentially similar form, regardless of the great differences in which it was enmeshed.

Notwithstanding all the critical points mentioned above, it must be mentioned that Weber's bureaucratic analysis is criticised on the basis of advancements in organisation theory, system theory, and development theory after the 1970s, not in the context of Weber's time and ecology. In his time, the definition of bureaucracy did not include the institutions of the current developing countries. At that time, there were not many developing nations of the kind found today. Weber's bureaucratic analysis should be understood in the context of his ideal-type model, which is methodologically a 'static' system construct.

3.5.10 Post-Weberian Developments in Bureaucracy

The following ideas on bureaucracy, either to support Weber or to criticise him, have been propounded after Weber.

3.5.10.1 Robert Merton and the Bureaucratic Personality

Merton analysed the dysfunctions of bureaucracy, which referred to the negative consequences of structural and normative bureaucratic practices. He talked about 'bureaucratic personality' while analysing bureaucratic dysfunctions. Normative attachment to rules and regulations gives rise to a bureaucratic personality obsessed with procedural compliance. Advancement of rules over the ends of the organisation leads to a *ritualistic rather than a rationalistic character* of an organisation. Moreover, it encourages the 'displacement of goals'. Thus, the bureaucratic structures influence (a) the individual's personality and (b) the ability of the organisation to achieve its ultimate objectives.[55]

3.5.10.2 Alvin Gouldner and the Patterns of Industrial Bureaucracy

In his experiments in industrial enterprises, Gouldner found that not all organisational members had the same interests or goals. Therefore, bureaucratic rules and regulations should be examined to understand whether they are in conformity with the interests of the different parties in an organisation. This analysis led to Gouldner's patterns of industrial bureaucracy: mock bureaucracy, representative bureaucracy, and punishment-centred bureaucracy.

Mock Bureaucracy: Such bureaucracy has rules in which no party in an organisation is interested. Such rules are rarely enforced and routinely violated. For example, the no-smoking rule in an organisation in which neither the managers nor the workers have any interest.

Representative Bureaucracy: This type of bureaucracy has rules in which all parties are interested. Therefore they are followed closely and strongly enforced. For example, all the parties in a mining industry are interested in the rules and regulations pertaining to safety during mining.

Punishment-centred Bureaucracy: This type of bureaucracy has rules in which one group is interested and the other is not. These are often rules imposed by managers on their workers. It generates tensions in an organisation and is the root cause of organisational conflict. These rules are generated due to lack of trust between the management and workers.

On the basis of this analysis, it is deduced that the stability of a bureaucratic rule depends upon the degree to which those subject to the rule willingly accept, rather than resist, the bureaucratic requirement. Gouldner viewed *bureaucracy as an emergent process:* "the degree of bureaucratisation is a function of human striving; it is the outcome of a contest between those who want it and those who do not."[48]

Gouldner: Primary and Secondary Organisational Tensions

Gouldner said that bureaucratic rules serve to create contradictions and tensions in organisational life. Organisations are structurally designed to control those human beings who have interests other than organisational interests. Organisations need to earn their cooperation and efforts for the fulfilment of organisational goals. This is a source of 'primary tension' in an organisation. This tension is served by various forms of supervision and coordination so that organisational members serve in the interest of organisational owners. This supervision generates 'secondary tension' in an organisation. This secondary tension is managed using written bureaucratic rules and requirements. However, while managing these secondary tensions, the primary tension is never addressed.

Primary tension is a specific case of the *agency problem* in the principal (e.g., employer) and agent (e.g., worker) relationship. The agency problem assumes that agents will have different goals from those of the principal and, thus, it cannot be guaranteed that the agent will do what the principal wants. Thus, the principal will tend to supervise the agents, leading to generation of secondary tension and, in turn, bureaucratic rules.

Gouldner: Bureaucracy Indulgency Patterns

Gouldner came out with some non-bureaucratic means to address bureaucratic tensions. He put forward ideas of 'structural adaptation' and 'indulgency pattern' in which there is selective exercise of supervisory authority as well as non-enforcement of certain rules in the benefit of the organisation. Gouldner believed that supervisors should anticipate the consequences of stringent enforcement and settle instead on a posture of tolerance and indulgence because ceaseless exercise of supervisory authority may produce resentment among the workers and create an unpleasant work environment. Supervisors have to exercise flexibility with the workers if they expect workers to exercise flexibility while doing their job. Otherwise, workers may employ a 'work-to-rule' strategy against the managers. Under it, workers do only those tasks that are defined under their formal job description. This strict adherence to a formal job requirement is used as a weapon against management, and it exposes the inadequacy of the formalised procedures.

3.5.10.3 Peter Blau and Dynamics of Bureaucracy

In consistency with Gouldner, Blau introduced the 'functional approach' while analysing the consequences of bureaucratic actions and routines. Bureaucratic efficiency is measured in terms of certain statistical performance standards. However, in the path of achieving these statistical standards, bureaucrats develop certain innovative measures that lead to the *displacement of goals* and members vying for those goals may be against the overall purpose of an organisation.

Adaptive Innovations: Blau observed that dedicated members of bureaucratic organisations find innovative alternatives in place of official procedures to achieve the overall purpose of an organisation. To explain this, he gave the example of a federal agency responsible for enforcing laws regulating corporate financial transactions and accounting. The agents in this agency were responsible for auditing the books and records of firms to determine the accuracy of information and compliance with legal regulations. According to the formal procedure, they had to refer to their senior officer in case of any doubt. However, in practice they rarely consulted their superior; rather they consulted their colleagues who had already faced a similar situation. This action was more efficient as other agents were in close physical proximity than the supervisors. Moreover, this interaction and sharing of information and advice among the agents created a work environment characterised by collaboration and horisontal communication. Thus, workers employ alternative means to achieve goals and thereby force the superiors to revise their strategies for compliance. This generates further bureaucratic tension resulting in the reformulation of bureaucratic procedures.

Redefinition of Bureaucracy: Blau has redefined bureaucracy as an "organisation that maximises efficiency in administration or an institutionalised method of organised social conduct in the interest of administrative efficiency." Thus, he suggested that one should look at the purpose of an ideal-type bureaucracy and then see what structural characteristics suggested by Weber (and in what combination) will help achieve the desired levels of efficiency.

3.5.10.4 Philip Selznick's Idea of Bureaucracy as Institution

In his study on bureaucracy, Philip Selznick identified the uniquely human elements that convert an organisation from a lean, no-nonsense system of consciously coordinated activities into a natural product of social needs and pressures.[56] In his theory of organisation, he viewed, "delegation as a primordial organisational act, a precarious venture which requires the continuous elaboration of formal mechanisms of coordination and control."[57] Delegation on one hand leads to enhanced autonomy and freedom but, on the other hand, leads to increased machinelike control.

Recalcitrant Tools of Action: Selznick has referred to the members of a bureaucracy as "recalcitrant tools of action." These recalcitrant tools are influenced by larger commitments that prevent and constrain organisational rationality. Humans are regarded as recalcitrant tools as they transport and develop commitments that conflict with rational organisational purposes as defined by organisational owners. They operate as 'wholes' rather than mere occupants of a formal position. This is an impediment to formal rationality because non-work-related roles and personality traits tend to deviate from those prescribed by the formal bureaucratic structure. As an institution, a bureaucracy must attend to the needs and commitments of these recalcitrant tools of action and, in the process, adapt and evolve themselves.

3.5.10.5 Robert Jackall's Idea of Bureaucracy as a Moral Maze

Robert Jackall studied how bureaucratic organisations shape moral consciousness and produce a bureaucratic ethic. "Bureaucratic work causes people to bracket, while at work, the moralities that they might hold outside the workplace or that they might adhere to privately and to follow instead the prevailing morality of their particular organisational situation... what matters on a day-to-day basis are the moral rules-in-use fashioned within the personal and structural constraints of one's organisation."[59]

Jackall said that authority is experienced in the day-to-day superior-subordinate relationship. This relationship and the actual rule-in-use that prescribe appropriate behaviour take on the character of a patrimonial bureaucracy. Personal loyalty is the primary rule of behaviour for managers. While this can be placed in an instrumental or rational context, it departs radically from Weberian notions of rational or instrumental action. In the Weber bureaucracy, rewards are given to those who advance organisational goals. However, Jackall said that in reality deferential forms of behaviour (also known as *symbolic substitute*) are used as a substitute for bureaucratic criteria such as effectiveness, efficiency, and competence.

Circles of Affiliation

The personal, patron-client, and senior-subordinate relationships are defined in terms of *circles of affiliation*. These alliances or networks do not conform to the formal or rational-legal channels of communication that might be reflected in the organisational chart. Their crucial feature is the use of informal criteria of admission that are poorly defined and constantly changing.[59] Thus, the task for ambitious members is to shape others' perceptions of oneself in the positive direction. Thus, rationality is creatively adopted by organisational members. It signifies what the sociologist Karl Mannheim described as *self-rationalisation*. This involves "self-streamlining, that is, the systematic application of functional rationality to the self to attain certain individual ends."[59] If organisational rationalisation is the construction of structures to achieve certain goals, then self-rationalisation is the criterion of a persona, or image, as a means to achieve the goal of personal advancement.

3.5.10.6 Merle Fainsod and Patterns of Bureaucracies

Merle Fainsod sketched five patterns of bureaucracies based on their relationship with the political system.

Representative Bureaucracy: This bureaucracy exists in a competitive political process where bureaucratic initiatives are based on the decisions arrived at after consensus among different political groups.

Party-State Bureaucracy: Party-state bureaucracy is found in totalitarian regimes where the bureaucratic actions are guided by the leadership of a single political party. It may also be associated with strong charismatic leadership, as is the case in quite a few African states.

Military-Dominated Bureaucracy: A military-dominated bureaucracy is one where the military virtues of hierarchy and discipline are stressed upon more, and processes such as persuasion and discussion are neglected. It is found in regimes where the military occupies a strategic position.

Ruler-Dominated Bureaucracy: This is the personal instrument of an autocratic ruler used in dominating his/her people. Bureaucracy here has a subservient role, though some individual bureaucrats may be influential due to their personal qualities.

Ruling Bureaucracies: It is the system where bureaucracy is the de facto ruling element. An example of such a system is the colonial rule where administrators used to rule without any discussion or direction from the local elected representatives.[59]

3.6 Hegel's Idea of Bureaucracy as a Universal Class

Hegel viewed the state as the final development in a series of social orders, the other being the family and the civil society. The state provides the ground where unconscious and particularly oriented activities become gradually self-conscious and public spirited.[60] He described three types of classes in a society: the agricultural class, the business class, and the universal class. Each of these classes reflects a mode of consciousness, namely, conservatism, individualism, and universalism, respectively. Here bureaucracy is the universal class that acts as a link between the civil society and the state. The task of this universal class (bureaucracy) is the universal interest of the community.

Regulatory Mechanisms for Bureaucracy

Bureaucrats are recruited from the middle class, which has a self-seeking orientation and instability. However, the class values are not transmitted to the bureaucrats as they become a part of the bureaucratic system. Bureaucrats undergo a series of internal and external pressures, which educate them to the will and knowledge of the universal interest. The internal control refers to the bureaucratic ethos, which is the result of the bureaucratic habits and the motivation that accompany the fulfilment of bureaucratic duties.[60] The external pressures include those from the rulers as well as those from below in the form of grievances and petitions by corporations, free press, and public opinion.

3.7 Marxist Thoughts on Bureaucracy

Karl Marx formed his theory of bureaucracy on the basis of his personal experience of the malfunctioning of the state administration. He deduced the notion of bureaucracy from the bureaucratic relationship existing between the power-holding institutions and the social groups subordinated to them. In France, and in other European states, he observed that the whole administration was run by bureaucrats functioning under the command of a king or a dictator.

3.7.1 Background

In the Marxist theory of historical materialism, the historical origin of bureaucracy is found in four sources, namely, religion, formation of the state, commerce, and technology. Religious bureaucracy consisted of the castes of clergy, officials, and scribes operating various rituals. The formation of a state and its maintenance was propounded by the formation of a large bureaucracy. Similarly, the growth of trade and commerce added a new, distinctive dimension to bureaucracy. Finally, bureaucracy increased due to increase in technology, as it led to increase in mass production requiring standardised routines and procedures to be followed.

3.7.2 Bureaucracy—An Exploitative Instrument of State

Karl Marx considered capitalism as an exploitative system. He considered bureaucracy as an instrument in the hands of the capitalist state to exploit the working class. To explain this, he gave the example of the French ruler, Louis Bonaparte, of that time. Louis Bonaparte accumulated extreme dictatorial powers. To do this he was assisted by the bureaucracy and military. Bureaucracy helped him in making and executing laws to strengthen the base of his despotism. Marx also termed bureaucracy as 'parasitic' as it was designed to maintain status quo and the privileges of the dominant section of the society.

For Marx, unlike Hegel, bureaucracy was a particular closed society within the state. There were three basic elements in Marx's perception of state:

1. State is an organ of class domination.
2. The aim of the state is to create an order that legalises and perpetuates the oppression of one class by moderating conflicts.
3. The state is a temporary phenomenon; it will wither away with the abolition of classes.

3.7.3 Private Ends of Bureaucracy

While the property-owning class possesses private property, the bureaucracy possesses the state power. The state power serves the same purpose for the bureaucracy as the private property serves for the property-owning class. To quote Marx, "bureaucracy holds in its essence of the state, the spiritual essence of the society, it is its private property."[61] For individual bureaucrats, the state objectives turn into their private objectives of getting higher posts and progressing in their career.

3.7.4 Secrecy and Mystery of Bureaucracy

Marx shared the idea of Weber that bureaucracy gains superiority and authority due to its specialised knowledge. He said, "authority is the principle of bureaucracy's knowledge, and the deification of authoritarianism its credo." People look at bureaucracy with awe and veneration and as a mysterious and distant entity. Moreover, bureaucracy keeps secrecy in its matters in order to maintain this mystery. This spirit of mystery is safeguarded within itself by hierarchy and outside by its nature as a closed corporation.

3.7.5 Characteristics of Bureaucracy by Marx

Marx commented on the following characteristics of bureaucracy.

Division of Labour: Due to bureaucracy, the basic division of labour happens between the intellectual and material activities. While the workers perform the productive/material activity, the capitalists and bureaucrats perform only the intellectual activity. While workers do all the hard work in the name of division of labour, the capitalists and the bureaucrats share the maximum proportion of the gains of production.

Hierarchy: According to Marx, the hierarchy of bureaucracy is a hierarchy of knowledge. For him, "bureaucracy is a circle from which no one can escape. Its hierarchy is a hierarchy of knowledge—the top entrusts the understanding of the lower levels, whilst the lower levels credit the top with understanding of the general, and so, all are mutually deceived."[61] The hierarchical structure does not provide a safeguard against greedy behaviour because the hand and feet of the superiors themselves are tied.

Recruitment: Marx was critical of the recruitment of members of the bureaucracy through competitive examinations. According to him, the quality of statesmanship required by a member of bureaucracy cannot be tested by a competitive examination. The main function of the examination is to allow only those members of the higher class who can afford costly higher education. Apart from being costly, higher education inculcates the values and attitudes supportive of capitalism.

3.7.6 Bureaucracy Causes Alienation

In modern industrial settings, workers lose control over their lives after losing control over their work. They cease to be autonomous beings in any significant sense. In industries, workers lose control over the process of production, over the products they produce, and over the relationships they have with each other. Marx said, "as absolute monarchy limits people's autonomy by controlling them in the sphere of politics, capitalism does so by controlling their workplaces and their economic life."

Unlike a capitalist worker, an artist typically works under his or her own direction. They are in total control of their work. The same is not the case with industrial workers. This leads to the following types of alienation among them.

Loss of Freedom: Once a worker accepts a job, he/she comes under the authoritarian command of the management. The workers' freedom is curtailed due to coercion, control, and threat of punishment. Managers also suffer from the same kind of alienation, as they are a part of the same system. Capitalists also suffer the same loss of freedom because they are not free to eat, drink, buy books, go to the theatre, think, love, theorise, sing, paint, etc. as they wish. They are constrained by the nature of their business.

Loss of Creativity: The bureaucracy decreases the creativity of its members. As no worker produces the whole product due to division of labour, the workers cannot apply their creativity. The administration also loses creativity and remains anonymous.

Loss of Humanity: According to Marx, human values play no role in the functioning of a bureaucracy.

Loss of Morality: Loss of freedom and humanity lead to loss of morality in bureaucracy.

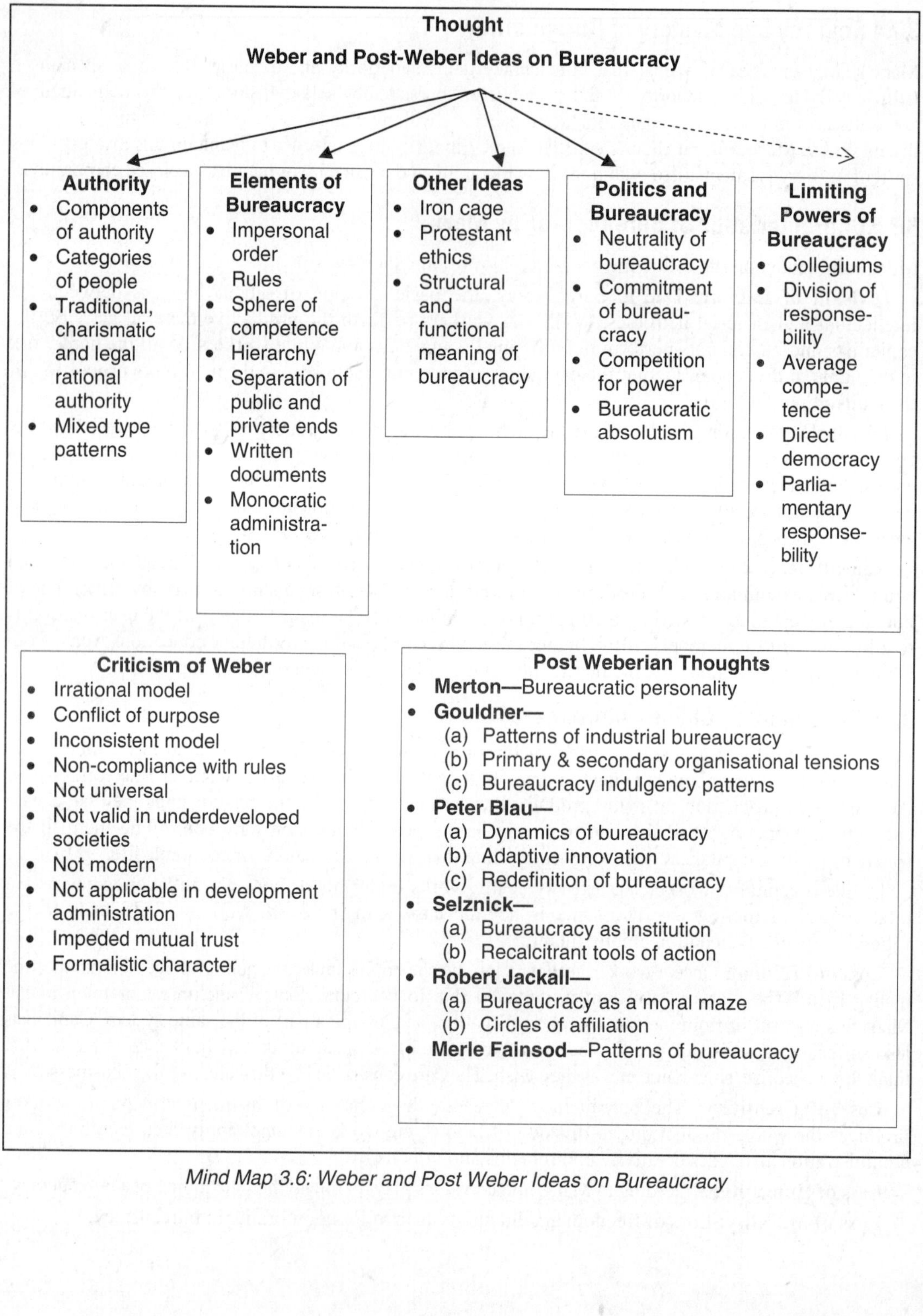

Thought

Weber and Post-Weber Ideas on Bureaucracy

Authority
- Components of authority
- Categories of people
- Traditional, charismatic and legal rational authority
- Mixed type patterns

Elements of Bureaucracy
- Impersonal order
- Rules
- Sphere of competence
- Hierarchy
- Separation of public and private ends
- Written documents
- Monocratic administration

Other Ideas
- Iron cage
- Protestant ethics
- Structural and functional meaning of bureaucracy

Politics and Bureaucracy
- Neutrality of bureaucracy
- Commitment of bureaucracy
- Competition for power
- Bureaucratic absolutism

Limiting Powers of Bureaucracy
- Collegiums
- Division of responsebility
- Average competence
- Direct democracy
- Parliamentary responsebility

Criticism of Weber
- Irrational model
- Conflict of purpose
- Inconsistent model
- Non-compliance with rules
- Not universal
- Not valid in underdeveloped societies
- Not modern
- Not applicable in development administration
- Impeded mutual trust
- Formalistic character

Post Weberian Thoughts
- **Merton**—Bureaucratic personality
- **Gouldner**—
  - (a) Patterns of industrial bureaucracy
  - (b) Primary & secondary organisational tensions
  - (c) Bureaucracy indulgency patterns
- **Peter Blau**—
  - (a) Dynamics of bureaucracy
  - (b) Adaptive innovation
  - (c) Redefinition of bureaucracy
- **Selznick**—
  - (a) Bureaucracy as institution
  - (b) Recalcitrant tools of action
- **Robert Jackall**—
  - (a) Bureaucracy as a moral maze
  - (b) Circles of affiliation
- **Merle Fainsod**—Patterns of bureaucracy

Mind Map 3.6: Weber and Post Weber Ideas on Bureaucracy

3.8 Mary Parker Follett: Dynamic Administration

In the management literature, Mary Parker Follett falls under the category of those ardent thinkers who identify themselves with the study of 'organisational university' and human relationships rather than with closed organisations and narrow business policies. For her, business represented an institution of great value and the sociological system of individual cooperation; and in it, lies a structure of managerial importance. Based on this framework, she developed the theory of human action, which expounded the basic human emotions and forces that underlie the process of organisation.[62]

3.8.1 Social Experiments by Follett

Follett took her illustrations from everyday common occurrences and adapted the same of business situations. She breathed a new vigour into the incidents of common life and made them important for business life.[63] It was this mental character of her work that was known as her 'social experiments'.[64]

3.8.2 Dynamic Aspect of Follett's Thinking

Follett believed strongly in the ever-changing and revolving aspect of life. She considered the dynamic process of change as the sole reality, and everything else was subject to this phenomenon of change. This is evident when she said, "decision is only a moment in process." Likewise, this dynamic character of her writing was clear in her theories on leadership, decision-making, power, control, coordination, conflict, giving orders, and integration.

3.8.3 Paradoxical Nature of Conflict and Integration

Follett understands that conflict in an organisation can be functionalised by positive measures, and thus its negative implications can be minimised by setting it to work for us.[65] Here she advanced the idea of 'constructive conflict', recognising that conflict should be regarded as a normal process in an organisation by which socially valuable differences get registered for the enrichment of all concerned.[64] She said conflicts are neither good nor bad, and should not be seen with passion or ethical prejudgments. Conflict is a medium to showcase differences—difference of opinion and difference of interests—between employer and employees, between managers, between directors, and between all those wherever conflicts appear. As conflicts are unavoidable, these should be capitalised on and something good should be made out of them. Comparing with the universe she said, "all polishing is done by friction. We get the music from the violin by friction and we left the savage state when we discovered fire through friction."[64]

According to Follett, there are three ways to resolve a conflict: by domination, by compromise, or by integration. *Domination* is a victory of one side over the other. It is problematic since it creates discomfort and tendencies such as repression and rebellion against the dominator. It is not a permanent solution and conflict keeps on surfacing again and again. *Compromise* is a way in which each side gives up a little and settles the conflict so that the work goes on smoothly. It is also problematic as it creates a feeling of resentment due to giving up something. *Integration,* the final method of resolving conflict, involves the integration of the desires of the parties, without both the parties losing their desires. It has the following advantages with respect to the other conflict resolution techniques:

1. Integration creates new things and new values.

2. It leads to use of better techniques and saves time and resources.
3. It goes to the root of the problem and solves the conflict permanently.

One interpretation of integration is that it is a harmonious marriage of differences to produce a new entity, and the real leader is the person who can understand the law of the situation and get the most out of it.[66]

3.8.4 Steps for Achieving Integration

Follett has suggested the following steps for achieving integration.

Uncover Differences: First, the differences between two people need to be uncovered, identified, and the real issues in them need to be understood. Significant, rather than dramatic, features of the conflict need to be understood. Managers often have a tendency to focus on the dramatic moments while forgetting the significant moments.

Break down Differences: Second, the demands of both the sides need to be broken into smaller parts. It includes an examination of the symbols used in organisational work, which in turn includes a careful scrutiny of the language used to see what it really means. In integration, it is important to articulate the whole and real demand, which is obscured by miscellaneous claims or by ineffective presentation.

Anticipation of Conflict: Third, conflicts need to be anticipated and responded to in a constructive manner. It is like a game of chess. Anticipation of the response by itself is not enough; there is need for preparation for the response as well. This involves building up of certain attitudes in the people. Responses are of two types: circular and linear. Of these, the circular response is the true basis of integration.

Circular Response

The concept of circular response rests on the principle that the organisation is a pattern of relations between actors, conceived as a single situation produced by a union of interests. A circular response is one that is not wholly predictable, as a person continually modifies his/her behaviour to adjust to the expected responses of others who constitute his/her environment. Thus, circular response consists of a modulation of both the activity and sentiments of the actors in an environment. Follett explains the circular response as, "the most fundamental thought about it is that reaction is always reacting to a relating.... I never react to you, but to you-plus-me; or to be more accurate, it is I-plus-you reacting to you-plus-me."[65]

3.8.5 Hurdles to Integration

The following are the hurdles before a successful integration process.

Requires Intelligence: Integration requires high intelligence and inventive power, which are not possessed by all. It also requires keen perception and discrimination, without which the process of integration can be difficult.

Dominating Tendencies: People enjoy domination over others. This thrill of victory over others hinders a person from resorting to integration.

Theorising the Problem: Theorising the problem, instead of looking for a practical solution, is another obstacle to integration. Constant theorisation of the problem leads to more disagreement and conflict.

Language: Sometimes, language used creates new disputes that were not there earlier. Thus, the language used should be favourable for reconciliation and should not perpetuate the conflict.

Leadership: Sometimes leaders provide undue influence to perpetuate a conflict or favour a party in a conflict. This increases the conflict rather than solving it.

Lack of Training: Organisational members are not properly trained in the art of dealing with conflicts. Mostly, there is a tendency to 'push through' or 'force through' the resolutions previously arrived at, rather than looking into the real-time issues in a conflict.

To overcome these hurdles, Follett thought that there should be courses to teach the art of cooperative thinking and to master the technique of integration.

3.8.6 Law of the Situation and Giving of Orders

According to Follett, there are four important steps in giving an order.

1. Conscious attitude: The order-giver shall realise the principles through which it is possible to act on any matter.
2. Responsible attitude: The order-giver shall decide on which principles one should act on and give orders in accordance with those principles.
3. Experimental attitude: The order-giver shall experiment with different orders, watch their results, and analyse why some are successful and some fail.
4. Pooling of results: The manager shall pool the experiences of all orders and activities, and see to what extent and in what manner the methods of giving orders can be changed if the existing methods are not working.

Implementation of Orders

There are certain obstacles towards following an order, such as past life, training, experience, emotions, beliefs, and prejudices, which form the 'habit pattern' of an individual. For effective implementation of an order, an employer has to manipulate the habit patterns of its employees. Follett suggests the following means to implement an order:

Introduce New Attitude: To bring a change in the habit patterns, one has to build up certain different attitudes in a person; then he/she has to provide for the release of those attitudes; and finally they should augment the released response.[64] For example, a salesperson creates in us an attitude that we want to buy their product; then at just the psychological moment, they produces their contract form which they may sign and release the attitude; then if we are preparing to sign, someone calls in to tell us how pleased he/she is with his/her purchase of this article and that augments the response being released.[64]

Form Habits: To ensure compliance of an order, the employer shall form a habit among employees to ensure acceptance of that order. For this, he/she must make the officials ready for a new method; then he/she must change the rules of the organisation so that it is possible to adopt the new method; then finally a few people should be convinced to change to using the new methods so that it intensifies the attitude of the remaining people.

Change in Environment: The environment of giving orders need to be modified in order to favour the acceptance of an order. The response to an order depends to a large extent on the place and circumstances in which orders are given. The distance an order travels needs to be decreased in order to achieve a favourable response.

Integration with Individual: The order shall seek to unite and integrate the two dissociated paths within an individual through circular behaviour. Giving and receiving orders is a matter of integration. Before integration between the order-giver and the order-receiver, there is need for integration within an individual.[64]

Manner of Giving Orders: The manner of giving orders should be considerate and genuine. Order receivers should be treated with regard to their feelings and self-respect while giving orders. Harassing, tyrannical, and overbearing conduct of officials leads to opposition to an order.

De-personalisation of Orders: Before giving, an order should be de-personalised. This involves a study of the problems to discover the 'law of the situation' and obeying it by all concerned. One should not give orders to another, but both should agree to take orders from the situation. De-personalising refers to exercising the authority of the situation. Orders shall keep on changing with the changing nature of the situation. External orders can never keep pace with the prevalent situations, and only those drawn fresh from the situation can do so.

'With' Proposition: While giving orders it should be known that people resent the feeling of working under someone. However, they like the feeling of working 'with' someone. The study of the situation involves this 'with' proposition. It heightens self-respect and increases efficiency.

3.8.7 Power, Authority, and Control

Follett has defined power, authority, and control in order to explain her law of the situation. She defines *power* as the ability to make things happen, to be a causal agent, and to initiate change. Power is the capacity to produce the intended effects.[64] It is of two types: *power over* (coercive power) and *power with* (coactive power). 'Power with' is better than 'power over', as it is a self-developing entity that promotes better understanding, reduces friction, encourages cooperative action, and promotes participative decision-making. 'Power with' can be attained by obeying the law of the situation and taking orders from it. This power cannot be delegated, as it is the result of knowledge and ability.[64]

Authority, according to Follett, is power vested in a position. It creates status differences, affects human dignity, and creates friction in an organisation. She suggests that *authority should be derived from the function.* The central authority (derivation of authority from the chief executive) should be replaced with the authority of function in which each individual has the final authority within the allotted functions. This authority can be conferred, but not delegated, on others. *Responsibility*, i.e., the answerability of doing a task, also flows from the function and the situation. In the law of the situation, a person is not 'responsible to someone', but is 'responsible for a particular function'. Follett believed in the pluralistic concept of responsibility or cumulative responsibility and rejected ultimate responsibility as an illusion.

Control is the monitoring of the functions of organisational members in order to achieve organisational goals. Follett believes in 'fact-control' rather than 'man-control' and in 'coordinated control' rather than 'superimposed control'. As facts change from situation to situation, control should depend on the fact of a situation (known as fact control) rather than senior-subordination control (known as man control). In coordinated control, control mechanisms are correlated at many places in the organisational structure. This control mechanism should be designed and developed as part of the unifying process of an organisation. This will make the organisation, and its various parts, self-regulating and self-directing.[5]

3.8.8 Coordination Through Control

According to Follett, planning in an organisation is done by self-adjustment and self-coordination of the various and varying interests. Thus, the coordination and control mechanisms are the most important activities of an organisation. On this, Follett has given the following four principles:[67]

1. **Coordination of all factors in a situation:** All factors in a situation have to be related to one another and these inter-relationships are important for an organisation.
2. **Coordination by direct contact:** Influential and responsible people in an organisation must remain in direct contact with each other to enhance coordination in an organisation.
3. **Coordination at policy stage:** Involvement of responsible and influential people should be sought at the policy stage itself rather than at the implementation stage. This increases the motivation and morale in an organisation.
4. **Coordination as a continuing process:** Coordination should remain a continuous process from planning to implement-tation to further planning. Such coordination should be achieved from the free flow of accurate information and adequate research on it.

3.8.9 Situational Leadership

Follett proposed the theory of 'situational leadership'. To Follett, "a leader is a person who can see all around a situation, can see it as related to certain purposes and policies, can see it as evolving into the next situation, and can understand how to pass from one situation to another."[65] According to Follett, a leader has the following qualities.

1. **Energise Group:** A leader is the one who can energise a group, encourage initiative from members, and can use the available resources effectively.[65]
2. **Connect to the Situation:** A leader should be able to show that their orders are integral to a situation.
3. **Relate Factors in a Situation:** A leader should be able to grasp the essentials of a situation and interrelate all the factors involved it. Here, the leader is the expression of a harmonious and effective unity, which he/she has helped to form, and which he/she was able to make a going concern.[68]
4. **Organise Experience:** A leader should be able to organise the experience of the members of a group and use it for achieving organisational goals.

Types of Leadership

Follett has talked about three types of leaders.

Leadership of Position: It is leadership due to holding a respectful and superior position.

Leadership of Personality: It is leadership due to having a forceful personality.

Leadership of Function: It is leadership due to having expert knowledge about a function. People follow this leader because of their influential knowledge. They have complete knowledge of a situation, understands its total significance, and can see through it.

The success of an organisation depends on its flexibility to allow leadership of function to operate fully and to allow people with knowledge and experience to control a situation.[65]

3.8.10 Consent, Democracy, and Participation

In public sector literature, there are three areas of attaining democracy. The first area focuses on citizen participation—advocating participation by citizens, clients, politicians, and representatives of other agencies in public organisation decision-making. The second area is participatory policy analysis, giving citizens a voice in the early steps of policy-making. The third area focuses on the enhancement of democratic administration of public organisations.[69] Follett has given her valuable guidance on all these three areas.

1. **Citizens Participation:** Follett emphasised on citizen forums where a broad range of citizens could deliberate over policy issues and give recommendations.[70]
2. **Focus on Local Communities:** Follett focuses on the importance of local communities and engaging people in debate to develop social and political understanding and participation.[71]
3. **Democratic Citizenship:** Follett's thoughts helped in re-conceptualising democratic citizenship. She emphasised on the involvement of citizens in governing and focused on the use of public spaces for deliberation and utilising education to build knowledge and confidence in civil involvement.[72]
4. **Responsiveness of Public Administrators:** Follett suggested key qualities of a leader that would make him/her a responsive public administrator. According to her, the ability to listen skillfully can reduce the tension between administrative effectiveness and democratic accountability. Follett suggested skilful listening in her concepts of respect for differences, an attitude of openness, and reflexivity. Responsiveness of public administrators is very important for enhancing democratic participation.[73]
5. **Democracy within Public Organisations:** Follett preferred participation over hierarchy, authority from situation, and leadership of function (in place of leadership of position). Such, and other, ideas of Follett were forerunners for enhancing democracy in the functioning of public organisations.

3.8.11 Management: Art or Science

Follett has promoted an image of management as both an art and a science. It is a science in Follett's assertion of analysing each situation methodically and consistently. She has stated that "leadership is not the intangible, incalculable thing we have often seen it described as. It is capable of being analysed into different elements, and many of these elements can be acquired and become part of one's equipment."[64] However, she refers to management as an art when she advises to work with metaphysical understanding along with scientific methods.

Seminal and Prophetic Contributions

The work of Follett is important because of the following reasons.

1. **Prophetic Work:** Follett's ideas on conflict, integration, coordination, control, authority, leadership, and so on had a universal approach and were ahead of time.
2. **Essentials of Leadership:** Follett's prescience in prioritising knowledge as a criterion of leadership and other aspects consisted all the essentials of leadership theories of today.
3. **Emphasis on Democracy:** Follett emphasised democracy as a continuous process of interaction between individuals in an ever-changing society.
4. **Organic Unity:** Follett's sense of organic unity, with all organisations being inherently social constructs, provides a basis for understanding social relations in an organisation.

5. **Interdisciplinary Approach:** The research approach of Follett was interdisciplinary and holistic towards relationships within organisations.
6. **Humane Approach:** Follett had great respect for all human beings working in an organisation, and she placed great emphasis on human relationships.
7. **Sense of Culture:** Follett focused on matching the culture and values of a country with the organisational strategies.
8. **Reciprocal Service:** Follett's concept of reciprocal service, in which there is ethical responsibility to the greater society by all individuals and organisations, is an important concept for management.

3.8.12 Feminist Angle in Follett's Writings

Morton and Lindquist[74] have categorised the work of Follett as being feminist because of the following reasons:

1. Follett's organisation and democracy theory is based on human relationships, which is a primary emphasis of the feminist theory.
2. The law of the situation requires knowledge to be developed through observation and experience. Such a stance is taken in feminist literature.
3. Follett's mechanism of conflict resolution is through integration and by embracing diversity and open communication; this is a feminist approach to conflict resolution.[71]

3.8.13 Ethical Angle in Follett's Writings

Follett's writings focused on the various issues of ethics in public administration.[75] Some of them are mentioned here.

Ethical Manager

Follett says that a leader must learn to 'deal fairly'. This was her approach to the concept of ethical manager. She also considered management as a profession. She asserted that the word 'profession' connotes a foundation of science and a motive of service, because a profession rests on the basis of a proven body of knowledge, and such knowledge is supposed to be used in the service of others rather than merely for one's purposes.[63]

Transcendence and Spirituality in Management

Follett's vision of organisation work was one in which there was something transcendent. She also attributed a religious sense to management. She wrote, "the high adventure of business is its opportunity for bringing into manifestation every hour of the day the deeper thing within every man, transcending every man, which you may call ideal, or God, or what you will, but which is absent from no man."[65] Follett was concerned about the inhumanity of the mechanical age and was in a search of spiritual life in her concept of transcending management. She said, "in commerce we may find culture, in industry idealism, in our business system beauty, in mechanics morals; the ethics of lathe are of a pretty fundamental kind."[63]

In *Creative Experience*, she wrote that "the divorce of our so-called spiritual life from our daily activities is a fatal dualism."'[65] According to her, interaction between people could create spiritual values, and it is more important in a business that manufactures articles. She also suggested that business offers a great opportunity for the creation of spiritual values through intimate human interweaving, through which all development of man has come.[63]

Organisational Ethics

One of the key issues of organisational ethics is the proper use of power, which Follett has discussed extensively. Disregarding the concepts of division of power, she pointed out that "the moral right to an authority which has not been psychologically developed, which is not an expression of capacity, is an empty ethics."[63] She considered that power and authority need to be developed. She also observed that the real authority that implies ethical responsibility comes from a function rather than from a static position. Follett also talks about ethics when she talks about the 'rights of labour'. She did not present rights of labours as confronting capital rights, as her concept was of integration and not of confrontation. She pointed out cooperation as a basic idea for dealing with industrial democracy.

Individual Development

While talking of individual development in an organisation, Follett referred to the preservation of the integrity of each individual. She said that the chief function of business is to give an opportunity for individual development through the better organisation of human relationships.[63] She preferred a management style of educating rather than blaming for fostering individual development. For individual development, she referred to interweaving activities in an organisation. It is related with Follett's doctrine of circular response.

Corporate Responsibility and Collective Responsibility

(i) Follett said, "a business man should think of his work as one of the necessary functions of society, aware that other people are also performing necessary functions, and that altogether these make a sound, healthy and useful community."[63] She talked about how managers could contribute to the welfare of society. She also emphasised the contribution of managers to culture. She said, "through your business itself, if you manage it with style, you are making a contribution to the culture of the world."[63]

She also insisted that managers must be aware of their social responsibility not only as citizens but also as members of the business profession. Moreover, while describing about corporate responsibility, she gives it three purposes: maintenance of standards, education of the public, and development of professional standards.[63] By collective responsibility, she meant the responsibility of everyone to the whole. This collective responsibility is a result of her vision of business as an integrative unity,[63] in which each individual is integrated in the whole. A business should be organised so that all members feel a responsibility towards the whole organisation.

Stakeholders Approach

Follett is considered a pioneer in the stakeholder's approach of management, although she never used this nomenclature. She mentioned a number of groups, apart from employees, related to the firm to whom the managers have to pay heed and maintain human relations, including bankers, stockholders, co-managers, directors, wage earners, competitors, suppliers, and customers.[63] She also proposed to deal with different interest groups from her perspective of 'integrative unity'.

3.8.14 Criticism of Follett's Work

Follett's writings are criticised on the following points:

1. **Illusory Ideas:** Follett's ideas are criticised for being illusory.

2. **Not Scientific:** Follett analysed the social content of an organisation, but she did not do that on the basis of strong scientific footing. She threw out interesting ideas more or less randomly and, therefore, the thread of consistency was hard to find and harder to follow.[66]

3.9 Human Relations School

The human relations movement started in the 1930s as a branch of the scientific management movement. It came as a critic to the classical theories of organisation and was supported by a number of psychologists, sociologists, and anthropologists. It brought a change in organisational thinking after the Hawthorne Experiments in the 1920s. Many scholars did their research work in the field of human relations. Prominent among them are the following:

1. Elton Mayo
2. Chester Barnard
3. Kurt Lewin
4. Fritz Jules Roethlisberger
5. Georges Friedmann
6. Rensis Likert
7. Douglas McGregor
8. George Caspar Homans
9. William Foote Whyte
10. Eric Trist
11. Chris Argyris

3.9.1 Elton Mayo and His Research in Human Relations

Elton Mayo is recognised as the father of human relations theory. His main research hypothesis is that the relation between the employer and employees should be humanistic and not mechanistic. Employees and workers should be treated with dignity and honour rather than as mere factors in a production system. He developed a method of experimentation known as the clinical method.

Clinical Method

Mayo advocated the use of clinical method in the development of a useful approach to securing social skills. This method was designed to help a researcher in doing real-life experiments on human beings and social relations, and developing knowledge on the basis of these experiments. Before this approach, studies on human nature and organisations were based on observations rather than experimentation. The job of a practitioner of the clinical method was to start at the grass-roots level and critically examine all data that may be relevant to the formulation of a theory of social skills. According to Donald Schon, "the clinical method helps the research student to obtain knowledge about group behaviour, to develop simple generalisations, to explain what happens, and to incubate the kind of behaviour which facilitates effective action."

3.9.1.1 Research at Textile Mill in Philadelphia

A textile mill in Philadelphia was a well-equipped organisation with all the modern facilities for workers. The employees were well-trained and intelligent. However, the labour personnel faced problems in the mule-spinning department of the mill.

Issues for Research

1. **Absenteeism:** Due to high absenteeism among workers in the department, the management had to hire 25% more workers.
2. **Low Productivity:** The management consulted various efficiency engineers and introduced several financial incentives and schemes. However, these did not produce any result.

Observations by Mayo

After studying the situation, from physical, social, and psychological angles, of the mule-spinning department of the mill, Mayo made the following observations:

1. **Physical trouble (foot problem):** Every piecer working in the department was suffering from foot trouble for which the company had no immediate remedy. This trouble developed since every piecer had to walk up and down a long alley, a distance of 30 yards or more, on either side of which the machine head was operating for spinning frames with cotton thread.
2. **Overburden:** A single worker had to attend to 10–14 machines due to which he/she felt fatigue.
3. **Disconnect with management:** Workers did not communicate with the company president, as they were afraid of him because he was a colonel in the US Army in France both before and after the First World War. Workers were afraid of protesting in front of him.

Experiments by Mayo

Mayo performed the following experiments on the workers of the textile mill.

1. **Introduction of rest periods:** Mayo introduced rest periods of 10 minutes each, in the morning and afternoon, for every team of piercers. As a result, physical fatigue among workers was eliminated. The morale of workers increased, in turn increasing the production. The labour absenteeism decreased to a very low value.
2. **Introduction of earn bonus scheme:** Mayo introduced bonus for those workers who would produce more than a certain percentage of work. As a result, the workers were initially happy. However, the supervisors opposed these two schemes as they were not brought under these schemes. Therefore, they suggested that workers should earn their rest periods and should not get them for free. However, due to this new system production fell as workers became unhappy.
3. **Rest periods for supervisors as well as workers:** Mayo suggested shutting down of the spinning department for 10 minutes for four times a day, so that every employee (supervisor as well as worker) enjoys his/her rest period. The control over these rest periods was given in the hands of workers. Due to this, the old problem disappeared, production increased and workers started earning high bonus.

Conclusions of Textile Mill Experiment

Mayo made the following conclusions from his experiments at the textile mill:

1. High absenteeism and passivity among workers was a result of postural fatigue produced by spinning.
2. Rest periods brought an end to postural fatigue.
3. Rest periods are more effective when they are regular.
4. Due to rest periods and bonuses, the family life and the behaviour of workers improved.

5. The problems of the mill were not because of the working conditions in the mill but because of the emotional response of the workers towards the work performed.
6. The problems were not due to the monotonous nature of the work but due to the monotonous work being done in an isolated manner.

3.9.1.2 Research in Western Electric Company (Hawthorne Studies)

Mayo conducted research under a research programme of the National Research Council of the National Academy of Science at the Hawthorne plant of the Western Electric Company.

There were some preconceived notions about work in the early 20th century. They were as follows:

1. There was a clear-cut cause-and-effect relationship between the physical work, environment, productivity, and well-being of the workers.
2. There was a relation between the production and given conditions of ventilation, temperature, lighting and other physical conditions, and wage incentives.
3. It was believed that improper work design, fatigue, and other conditions of work were the main hurdles towards high efficiency.

The Hawthorne studies were conducted to establish a clear-cut relationship between man and the structure of formal organisations. The studies were conducted in the following phases:

Illumination Experiment (1924–27)

Objective: The objective of the illumination experiment was to determine the effect of different levels of illumination on worker's productivity. In this, two groups of female workers were closely located in separate rooms, each group performing the same task. Both the rooms were equally illuminated with stabilised room temperature, humidity, and so on. The conditions of work were changed slowly in both the rooms, to observe any change in production due to change in illumination.

Observation: After observations over one-and-a-half year, it was found that there was no change in production with respect to change in illumination for the two groups.

Relay Assembly Test Room Experiment (1927)

Objective: The objective of this experiment was to study the impact of various job conditions, apart from illumination, on group productivity. For this, two groups of girls were formed and asked to do work related to assembly of telephone relays. The productivity depended on the speed and continuity with which the girls worked. The girls were consulted before introduction of any change in the working conditions. They were given the opportunity to express their viewpoints and concerns to the supervisor. They were also allowed to take decisions on matters concerning them. The incentive system was changed so that the incentive of a girl was based on the other five, rather than the output of a larger group. Rests period were introduced. Refreshment snacks were served along with rest periods. The number of working hours and working days were decreased.

Observation: As each change was introduced, morale increased, absenteeism decreased, productivity increased, and less supervision was required. However, when the researchers reverted back to the original position (no rest and other benefits), surprisingly, productivity increased further instead of going down.

Conclusion: Productivity increased not because of change in physical conditions but because of a change in girl's attitude towards work and their work group. Due to group pressure and autonomy, they developed a sense of belongingness and responsibility.

Mass Interviewing Programme (1928–31)

Objective: Around 20,000 interviews were conducted to determine the attitude of employees towards company, supervision, insurance plans, promotion, and wages.

Observation: It was observed that a complaint was not an objective recital of facts; rather it was a symptom of personal disturbance, the cause of which may be deep seated. Employees felt satisfied or dissatisfied after they viewed physical conditions, supervision, and other factors with respect to their personal situation. There was a change in the attitude of the workers, without introducing any reforms, as the workers thought that the working conditions were changed because of their complaints. They also felt that their wages were better although their wage scale remained unaltered.

Conclusion: The following conclusions were made from these interviews:

1. Workers felt elated when allowed to freely express themselves. They felt that the conditions in the environment were changed to their advantage.
2. Subordinates felt good when allowed to freely comment about their subordinates.
3. The personal situation of the worker was a configuration composed of a personal preference involving sentiments, desires, and interests of the person and the social reference constituting the person's social past and his/her present interpersonal relations.
4. The position or status of the worker in the company was a reference from which he/she assigned meaning and value to events, objects, and features to his/her environment such as working hours, wages, etc.
5. The social organisation of the company represented a system of values from which a worker derived satisfaction/dissatisfaction according to the perception of his/her social status and expected social rewards.
6. The social demands of the workers were influenced by their social experience in groups (both inside and outside the company).

Bank Wiring Experiment (1931–32)

Objective: The objective of this experiment was to determine the impact of small groups on individuals. A group of 14 male workers was formed who were engaged in the assembly of terminal banks for use in telephone exchanges. The hourly wage of each worker was based on the basis of the average output of each worker. A bonus was also paid on the basis of group output.

Observation: It was expected that highly efficient workers would pressurise the less efficient workers to increase output and take advantage of the group incentive plan. However, it was observed that the workers established their own standard of output, which was enforced by various methods of social pressure. The following social code of conduct was maintained for establishing group solidarity.

1. One should not work more than the group standard. One going against this was known as *rate buster*.
2. One should not work less than the group standard. One going against this was known as *chesler*.
3. One should not tell the supervisor anything detrimental about a fellow group member. One going against this was known as *squealer*.
4. Within a group, members should not maintain distance and act officious.

Conclusion: The following conclusions were made from the bank wiring experiment:

1. The behaviour of the team was not related to the general economic conditions of the company.
2. The workers viewed the interference of extra-departmental personnel in the group as a disturbance.
3. The workers considered superior officers as representative authorities of the management, whose sole task was to discipline the workers.
4. The logic of efficiency did not work well with the logic of sentiments in a group.
5. The human aspects of the organisation were equally important as the technical and economic aspects.
6. The concept of authority was based on social skills in securing cooperation rather than expertise.

3.9.1.3 Conclusions from Hawthorne Experiments

Hawthorne effect: When workers know that they are under observation, their productivity increased irrespective of any positive or negative change in the working conditions.

Social unit: More than being a techno-economic unit, a factory is a social unit. The social and psychological factors play an important role in motivating the workers.

Group Influence: The workers in an organisation develop a common psychological bond, which unites them into an informal organisation. The behaviour of the individual is influenced by this group.

Group Behaviour: Typical group behaviour dominates or supersedes individual behaviour.

Morale: Social, psychological, and human factors at the workplace play a greater role than the physical conditions in increasing the morale of workers.

Supervision: The style of supervision greatly affects workers' morale and productivity. A worker who takes interest in the social problems of the workers gets easy cooperation from them.

Communication: Output increases when workers are explained the logic behind various decisions and their participation is sought in those decisions.

Balanced Approach: The management has to take into account various physical, social, and psychological factors for increasing the productivity of the workers. A balanced approach to the whole situation is required.

Informal Organisations: A social organisation is divided into formal and informal organisations. The informal organisation is a necessary prerequisite for developing collaboration in an organisation. If the management is skilful enough to get the goals of informal organisation to run parallel with the goals of formal organisation, many management-worker problems can be resolved.

Logics in an Organisation: Three kinds of logics are found within a factory social system: the logic of cost, the logic of efficiency, and the logic of sentiment.

3.9.1.4 Absenteeism in Industries

While the Second World War was on, most of the US industries were suffering from chronic absenteeism. Elton Mayo took the task of studying the reasons for this high absenteeism in industries.

Observation: Mayo observed the following in his research:

1. The industries that had introduced the *group wage scheme* had a lower rate of absenteeism and turnover. The group wage was to be awarded if all workers would attend all their respective shifts in a day. In the event of any shortfall in a day, the cut in the wage was uniformly applied.
2. The workers naturally formed groups under the leadership of an able leader who devoted time and energy in consolidating group solidarity. As supervisory officers did not interfere in the daily affairs, all the work was under the charge of a man who had no official standing and was a *natural leader*.
3. The industries where turnover and absenteeism were high had no *informal groups* and natural leaders to knit the workers into a team.

Conclusion: Informal groups and natural leaders were instrumental in raising the level of productivity by cooperating with the management.

3.9.2 Underlying Philosophy of Human Relations Approach

The human relations experiments conducted by Mayo have been compared with those in physical science by Galileo. Mayo has emphasised on two basic principles throughout his writings on human relations. He states that the "difference between two important principles of social organisation—the one, that of an *adaptive society*; the other, that of an *established society* is extremely important."[76]

Established Society: Established societies were primitive societies in which group codes dictated a certain social order and directed each individual to a patterned and stable kind of life. The individual considered themselves subordinate to the group, which developed their life pattern and gave them stability. In return, the group assures the individual of a definite function and satisfactory participation in the established society.

Adaptive Society: An adaptive society had grown due to the advent of industrial revolution. It is composed of individuals of varied origins, many of whom shift from one group to another in search of better job opportunities. However, this frequent changing of groups makes the individual aimless and unhappy. They find the world around them hostile, and any fleeting moments of happiness coming to them are extremely short-lived.

Every human being has a craving to return to the established form of society. Due to this they show interest in qualities such as collaboration and coordination.

3.9.3 Influence of Le Play and Durkheim on Human Relations School

The work of Elton Mayo and others was specially influenced by two individuals: Frederick Le Play and Emile Durkheim. Le Play did an intensive study on European workers as they were getting industrialised between 1829 and 1855. When Le Play observed simpler communities such as agriculture and fishing, he found in them qualities which Mayo has attributed to an established society.

The studies of Emile Durkheim were attempted to characterise the impact of industrialisation upon an individual. He found out that industrial development had lessened both the capacity of working together and the sum of human happiness. Industrialisation has moved the individual away from qualities such as cooperation, which were characteristic of pre-industrialised societies. Due to industrialisation, there was no longer any direction in living; all orderly resemblances of an established society were destroyed, leaving behind chaotic and lonely rubble. This change was the cause of *anomie* (planelessness in life) leading to community disorganisation.

The ideas of Elton Mayo and other human relationists were heavily influenced by these two concepts of Le Play and Durkheim.

3.9.4 Equilibrium in Industrial Organisations

The conclusive point deduced from Hawthorne experiments was that an industrial organisation is a social system whose functions are economic solvency and the maintenance of employee relations. These two functions lead to two corresponding problems: (a) external balance (economic solvency) and (b) internal equilibrium (maintenance of employee relations). "A factory system, like any stable social system, must be conceived as tending towards an equilibrium in which its different parts are functionally adjusted to each other."[77] The economic aspect of the social system of industry, with its advances in productive techniques, has by far eclipsed the function of maintaining good employee relations, thereby bringing a vast dis-equilibrium in the social system.

3.9.5 Leadership Training

A leader is responsible for maintaining equilibrium in a factory social system. As Alfred G. Larke has stated, "the supervisor who succeeds in developing an enthusiastic, productive and cohesive team is likely to be sensitive to interpersonal problems among his people; to talk of his job in terms of the group rather than of individuals."[78] Mayo has indicated the leader's most important task as integration of groups by means of social skills so that these groups form a stable team that can integrate the goals of formal and informal organisations as much as possible.

According to Mayo, a leader should be trained to give more weightage to the logic of sentiments than to the logic of cost and efficiency. Roethlisberger, Dickson, and Wright[79] have stated the following five rules whereby a supervisor can understand employee sentiments better.

1. "Supervisor should listen patiently to what his subordinate has to say before making any comment himself.
2. Supervisor should refrain from hasty disapprobation of his subordinate's conduct.
3. Supervisor should not argue with his subordinates.
4. Supervisor should not pay exclusive attention to the manifest content of the conversation.
5. Supervisor should listen not only to what a person wants to say but also to what they do not want to say or cannot say without assistance."[79]

3.9.6 Kurt Lewin's Work on Human Relations

Kurt Lewin continued the work of Elton Mayo in human relations. His research focused on the following prominent areas.

3.9.6.1 Leadership Styles and Their Effects

Lewin carried out studies on the impact of different leadership styles on outcomes of boys' group activities in Iowa. He classified three different leadership styles—autocratic, democratic, and laissez-faire.

Autocratic Leadership: He found that in a group with an autocratic leader, there was more dissatisfaction among members; the group became aggressive or apathetic.

Democratic Leadership: In a group with a democratic leader, there was more cooperation and collaboration among members; the group enjoyed their work.

Laissez Faire Leadership: In a group with a laissez faire leader, there was no particular dissatisfaction witnessed, though the workers were not highly productive.

A significant observation of Lewin's study was that when the respective leaders were asked to change their leadership styles, the effects of each leadership style remained similar. This proved that democratic leadership style produced better results than the other two styles. It also showed that it is possible for the leaders and managers to change their styles, and to be trained to improve their leadership and adopt appropriate management styles for a specific situation and context.

3.9.6.2 Force Field Theory

The force field theory says that the activities of people are affected by various forces in their surrounding environment or field. *Field* is defined as a totality of coexisting facts in an environment that are conceived as mutually interdependent. The three main principles of this theory are as follows:

1. The behaviour of individuals is a function of the existing field.
2. Analysis starts from the complete situation and distinguishes among its component parts.
3. A concrete person in a concrete situation can be mathematically represented.

The theory is helpful to distinguish whether factors within a situation or organisation are 'driving forces' for change or 'restraining forces' that will work against desired changes. Examples of driving forces are ambitions, goals, needs, or fears that drive a person towards or away from something. Restraining forces are those which oppose driving forces from acting.

Quasi-Stationary Processes: The interplay of these forces creates a stable routine of normal, regular activities, which are described as 'quasi-stationary processes'. In daily activities, the driving and restraining forces balance out and equalise to fluctuate around a state of equilibrium for an activity. Any increase in the productivity from the current quasi-stationary level requires either of the following changes:

1. Strengthening of driving forces, e.g., paying more money for one's activities; or
2. Restraining of inhibiting forces, e.g., simplifying the production processes.

3.9.6.3 Group Decision-Making

Lewin carried out his research in the United States on exploring ways to influence people to change their dietary habits towards less popular cuts of meat. In his experiments, he observed that if group members discuss an issue themselves and are able to decide themselves as a group, they are far more likely to change their habits than if they had just attended lectures giving appropriate information and advice.

Lewin said that two key ideas emerged from his field force theory, which are crucial in the appreciation of group processes. These are as follows.

1. Interdependence of fate: A normal group comprises individuals of different characters. However, the members are able to see that their fate is dependent on the fate of the group. The members who recognise this interdependence are eager to share the responsibility for the welfare of the group.
2. Task interdependence: Task interdependence means interdependence in the goals of group members. If the group's task is such that the members of the group are dependent on each other for achievement, then a powerful group dynamic is created.

This interdependence (of fate and task) results in making the group a 'dynamic whole'. This means that a change in one member or subgroup impacts others.

3.9.6.4 Three-Step Change Management Model: Unfreeze-Change-Refreeze

Lewin considered that for achieving a change effectively, it is necessary to analyse all the options for moving from the existing present to the desired future state, and then to evaluate the possibilities of each option and decide on the best one, rather than just aiming for the desired goal and taking the easiest and straightest route for it.

There are two kinds of resistance to change: first from social habits and second an inner resistance to change. Both of them are rooted in the interplay between a group as a whole and the individuals within it. The driving forces that are strong enough to change social habits, or challenge the interests or customs of the group, are able to overcome these resistances. In Lewin's view, resistance can be lowered by reducing the value a group attaches to something, or by fundamentally changing what the group values. For this, he suggested a complex step process of unfreesing, changing, and refreesing the beliefs, attitudes, and values that are required to be changed. The phase of unfreesing involves group discussions in which individuals experience other's views and begin to adapt their own.

3.9.6.5 T-Groups (or Training Groups)

Training groups (T-groups) were introduced by Lewin in Connecticut, where he designed a two-week training programme that looked to encourage group discussion and decision-making. Here, the participants treated each other as peers irrespective of their rank, race, gender, and colour. Bringing such groups of people together was a powerful way to expose areas of conflict, so that the established behavioural patterns can 'unfreeze' and then be changed and refrozen. These learning groups were termed T-groups.

3.9.6.6 Action Research

Lewin introduced action research in 1940 as an important innovation in research methods that were especially used in industry and education. Action research includes experimenting by making changes and simultaneously studying the results in a cyclic process of planning, action, and fact gathering. It emphasised a power relationship between the researchers and those researched; it sought the participation of subjects in studying the effects of their own action, identifying their own biases, and working to transform relationships in their community or organisation.

3.9.7 George Caspar Homans: Examination of Small Groups

For Homans, the explanation of how individuals create and maintain social structures requires taking into account the conditions that influence their behaviour. The important conditions considered by Homans were stimuli, rewards, and punishments. Once these social structures are created by individuals, they exert their effect back on the behaviour of their makers.[80] At the bottom, "both the structures and their back effects consist of the behavior of individuals."

George Homans has used the systemic approach in explaining small groups, which he described as 'internal systems' facing 'external systems'. He developed interest in small groups when he was working as a student in Harvard University with Elton Mayo, who at that time was interpreting the results of Hawthorne studies. The idea that influenced him was that "if we wanted to establish the reality of a social system as a complex of mutually dependent elements, why not begin by studying a system small enough so that we could, so to speak, see all the way around it, small enough so that all the relevant observations could be made in detail and in first hand."[81]

3.9.7.1 Activity, Sentiment, and Interaction

Homans identified three variables that can be measured for studying small group behaviour; these were interaction, sentiment, and activity.

Interaction is defined as an event in which an action of one man serves as a stimulus for the action of another.[81] It is a whole class of variables that could be measured in regard to how often and for how long a given person speaks in a conversation; how often and how soon that person initiates talk or other action; how many persons within a given place or time does that person interact with.[82]*Sentiment* is a behaviour that expresses a person's attitude towards other persons and includes the "liking and disliking for individuals, approval and disapproval of the things they do."[83] It can be measured in terms of facial expressions, bodily attitudes, and by what people say.

Activity refers to any action performed by people that may not require interactions with others or express interpersonal sentiments. Activities can be operationalised and measured, e.g., in case of output, the activity of production of the number of goods per hour by a worker can be measured.

These three classes of variables—interaction, sentiment, and activity—are interdependent and are the basic elements of social behaviour.

3.9.7.2 Internal and External Systems

The three variables mentioned already are the components of a group's internal and external system. Every group, as a social system, is constituted of a boundary that separates it from the environment. Within this boundary (in an internal system), all interactions, sentiments, and activities are mutually dependent in determining the behaviour of group members.

Homes gave the example of an industry where a number of workers perform an activity in the same room (internal system). Due to this performance of work activities they engage in interaction. This interaction increases the positive sentiment among workers, which increases their interaction even more. This set of relations forms the group's *internal system*.

A group's *external system* is the physical and social environment that exists outside its boundary. This may consist of required or planned activities and/or interactions, as well as the external physical setting. As the elements of social behaviour (interaction, activity, and sentiment) are mutually dependent on the internal system (or primary system), they are also mutually dependent on the external system (or secondary system). Thus, the pattern according to which the management of a factory lays out the physical equipment of a department may affect the workers' interpersonal relations within it.

3.9.7.3 Social Behaviour as Exchange

In his major work *Social Behaviour: Its Elementary Forms*, Homans articulated basic propositions to explain the 'sub-institutional' or elementary forms of social behaviour in small groups. He put forward a systematic set of general propositions about elementary social behaviour grounded in the notion of reward and punishment, deprivation and satiation, cost and profit, aggression and approval.[84] The general propositions are as follows.

The Success Proposition: For all actions taken by a person, the more often a particular action of a person is rewarded, the more likely the person is to perform that action.[85]

The Stimulus Proposition: If, in the past, the occurrence of a particular stimulus or set of stimuli has been the occasion on which a person's action has been rewarded, then the more similar the present stimuli are to the past ones, the more likely the person is to perform the same action, or some similar action, now.[85]

The Value Proposition: The more valuable to a person is the result of his/her action, the more likely he/she is to perform the action.[85]

The Deprivation-Satiation Proposition: The more often in the recent past a person has received a particular reward, the less valuable any further unit of that reward becomes for him/her.[85]

The Aggression-Approval Proposition: When a person's action does not receive the reward they expect, or receives unexpected punishment, they will be angry; they become more likely to exhibit aggressive behaviour, and the results of such behaviour become more valuable to them. On the other hand, when a person's action receives the reward they expect, especially a greater reward than they expect, or does not receive the punishment they expect, they will be pleased; they become more likely to perform approving behaviour, and the results of such behaviour become more valuable to them.[85]

The Rationality Proposition: In choosing between alternative actions, a person will choose that one for which, as perceived by them at the time, the value V of the result multiplied by the probability P of getting the result is greater.[85]

In essence, social behaviour is an exchange of material and non-material (e.g., symbols of approval and prestige) goods. The more a person gets of something, the less valuable any further unit of that value becomes for them, and the less often they will emit behaviour reinforced by it. Moreover, a person involved in an exchange relationship also expects to receive as much reward from the other as they give to the other. In other words, people expect a fair and equitable exchange of rewards and costs between persons. Homans called this the *rule of distributive justice*.

3.9.8 William F. Whyte

Inspired by the studies of Elton Mayo and Fritz Roethlisberger at the Western Electric Hawthorne Plant, William F. Whyte pursued his line of research in the restaurant and hotel industry in Chicago, wherein in the 'Tremont Hotel' he demonstrated the power of case studies in solving managerial problems.

He chose the methodology of 'objective observation' to study human relations. It was based on the idea that interactions among individuals over a period of time produce a structure of informal leadership,[86] and this informal leadership and the group structure influence the behaviour and confidence of its group members to a very large extent. Whyte discovered this phenomenon when he was a participant of a bowling gang in North End Life in 1938. He stated, "As I later thought about the bowling contest, I became convinced that I had discovered something important: the relationship between individual performance and group structure. I believed then (and still believe now) that this relationship can be observed in all manners of group activities."[87]

3.9.8.1 New Roles of Human Resource Manager

William F. Whyte conducted his research on human relations in the restaurant and the house-keeping department of the Tremont Hotel, where he deduced that frequent interviews with employees and management improve their interpersonal relations and help in solving stubborn and long-lasting problems. This was part of his action research approach. The detailed case studies conducted by him are beyond the scope of this book. He concluded new roles for the managers of human resources (HR) from his case studies. He suggested the following seven features of their roles:

1. Keeping confidences
2. Interpreting rather than blaming
3. Working with the man most immediately responsible

4. Consulting with the top man
5. Utilising research data
6. Assuming responsibility for rewards and punishments
7. Counselling and controlling

These roles of the HR manager were again presented, in a different manner, by David Ulrich in his work *Human Resource Champions*. These are presented in Fig. 3.3.

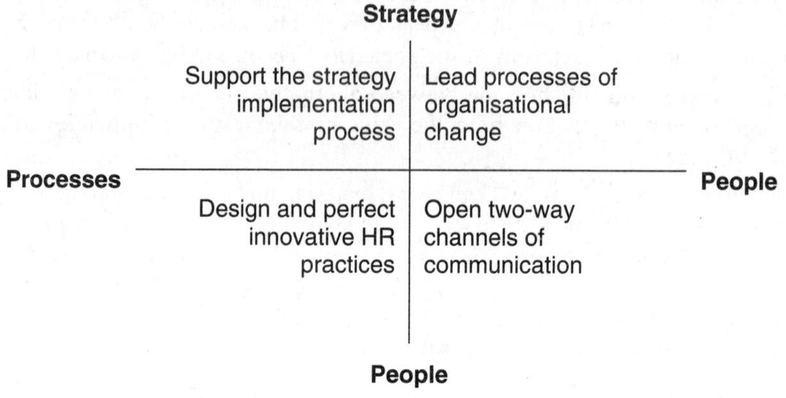

Fig. 3.3: Four roles of HR Manager (David Ulrich)

3.9.9 Eric Lansdown Trist

Eric Trist was influenced by the rising alienation of workers from productive employment, the ideas and research of Kurt Lewin, and studies in the British Army and found that there was high complexity in resolving human and social problems inside a well-established bureaucracy. Pointing out the importance of action research, he said that scientifically oriented observation and carefully controlled changes in operating procedures can help in integrating the gratification of individual needs with the aims of an organisation.

Socio-Technical Theory (Beyond Mayo)

Trist said that for humanising organisations, one has to look beyond Mayo's ideas that with spontaneous cooperation comes friendliness towards workers, which then leads to individual adjustment to task, better cooperation and high production, less absenteeism, less waste, and greater ease of supervision. He said that his socio-technical theory and practice tended to explore the possibility of limited, basic, and structural supervision, which can help in reducing the alienation of workers from the production activity. No matter how advanced social changes and technological upgradation are, organisational change could not be induced when they are induced as a result of a study which they have not controlled. He conducted studies in the US coal industry, where implementation of new mechanisation and new work relations led to the disruption of traditional work relations and autonomy, and thus led to decreased production and increased absenteeism. On the other hand, when new technology was integrated with the traditional single-place mining system, with the participation of members, teams became self-responsible, cohesive, and interested in achieving the goals.

Public Organisation as Open Systems

Trist considered public and private organisations as 'open systems', rather than logico-economic arrangements. He advanced the view that organisations exist in different types of environments, and organisational change can be successful only when there is realistic understanding of the nature of environment.[88]

Participative Democracy

Trist held the view that industrial civilisation would benefit most when the quasi-religious passion for bureaucracy, as the preferred form of domination (authority) at work gave way to participative democracy, when the tightly supervised competitive 'team' was induced to become an autonomous and self-regulating group, and that the goal of industrial organisations was best achieved with efficient, creative, and gratifying use of human effort.[89]

Social Conference

Trist introduced 'social conference', a participative method, for changing organisations to achieve desirable and possible futures. It draws together people who normally work in the field to establish plans for their shared system. This is in contrast to the conventional planning that uses the guidance of elite groups, which are supported by expert staff and external consultants.

3.9.10 Criticism of Human Relations School

The human relations approach to administration, propagated by Elton Mayo and others, is criticised on the following grounds.

Manipulative Tendencies

There is some manipulative tendency in the ideological structure of the human relations approach. The human relations approach taught that instead of becoming dictatorial in achieving its goals, the management should become a "benevolent despot who manipulates his subjects in the interests of his own security and welfare."[90] The logical outcome of this theory is a society where manipulation is the chief form of control.

A form of Totalitarianism

In Kerr's opinion, Mayo's theory of undivided loyalty to the plant (or organisation) can be seen as a subtle form of totalitarianism. According to him, a division of loyalty to the various institutions of the modern industrial society is the guarantee of freedom. Kerr has said that attempting to reinstate the values of the Middle Ages and working for a spontaneous collaboration in an ever-changing capitalist society is a naïve approach of the human relationists.

Bias in Experimentation

Mayo's tests had an underlying bias among the testers. There are certain values enshrined in the tests that the testers tried to achieve. In the words of William Whyte, "what the personality testers are trying to do is to convert abstract rules into a concrete measure that can be placed on a linear scale, and it is on the assumption that this is a correct application of the scientific method that all else follows."[91]

Unions related Criticism

The research of human relations has generally ignored the role of the trade union in a modern industrial setting. Human relationists feel that trade unions were formed because of the influence of the Industrial Revolution. The Industrial Revolution broke the personal relation between the employees and the employer, which was regulated by a system of mutual privileges and obligations.[92] However, Whitehead disagreed with this argument and said that unions were formed not to improve the material conditions of the worker, but to direct a "new ordering of society,"[92] which would restore the task of leadership and organisation to the workers; these were functions that the new working class had lost.

Environmentalist Criticism

It is criticised that the Mayoites have ignored the external environmental factors while microscopically measuring behavioural patterns in a self-contained situation. They have failed to provide full and adequate answers to questions about the underlying uniformities and differences in motivational, attitudinal, and behavioural patterns and relations of people at work in industrial society.[93]

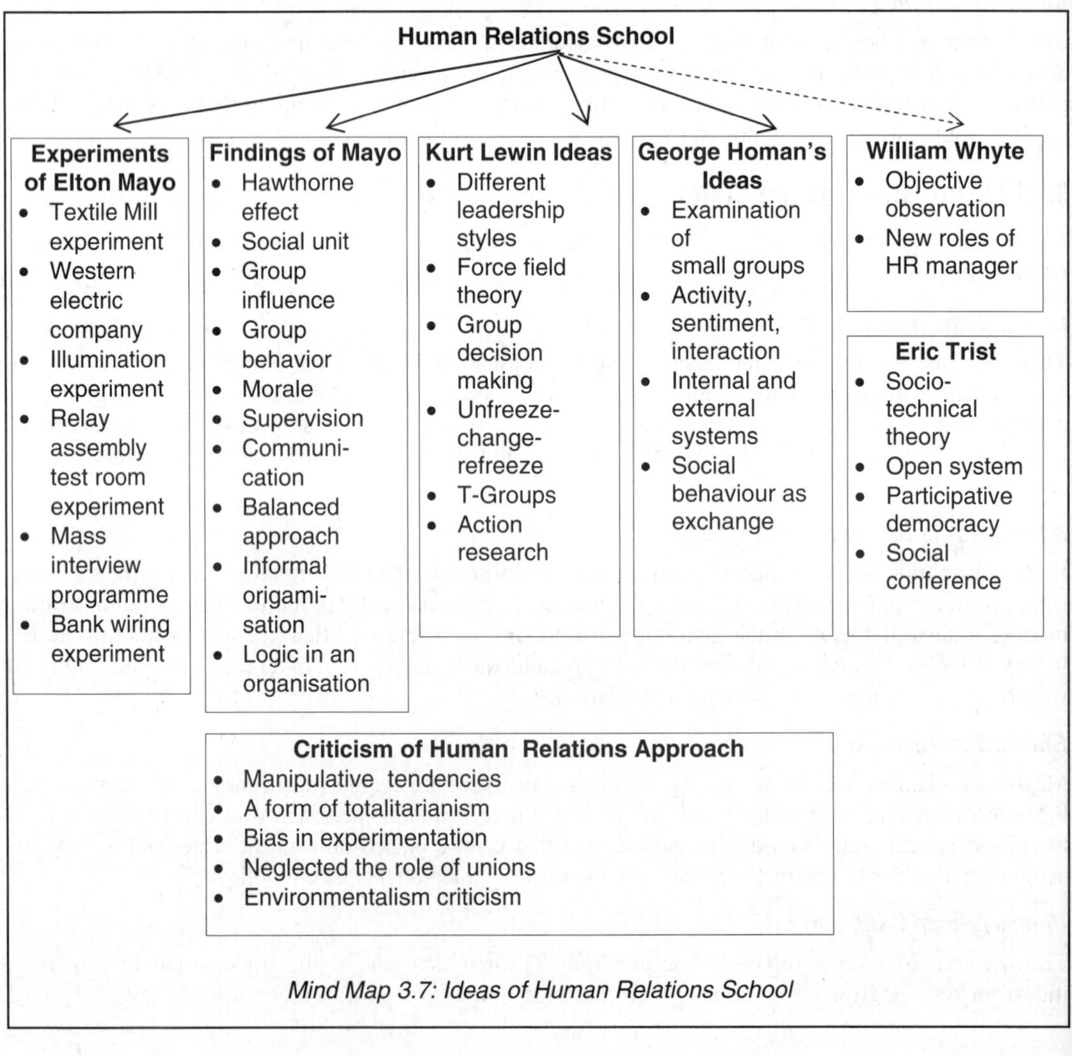

Mind Map 3.7: Ideas of Human Relations School

3.10 System Approach and Functions of Executive

The system approach is an approach of management that describes an organisation as an interconnected set of elements that function as a whole. These elements comprise sub-systems, structure, actions, and interactions that enable the system to perform certain functions. This approach is characterised by three properties:

1. It is a set of interactions taking place within itself.
2. The interrelated activities or elements have a boundary set around them.
3. The system has an external environment that affects the activities of the internal interactions.

The work of a system is to maintain administrative order and equilibrium among its sub-systems and environment. It consists of three distinct processes—inputs, throughputs, and outputs. The systems are of two types: open and closed. First we will discuss open system organisations.

3.10.1 Open-System Organisations

An open-system organisation consists of an internal system and an external environment. The internal system consists of subparts and subsystems. The external environment consists of economic, social, political, and technological factors. The internal system continuously interacts with the environmental factors. The system takes in inputs from the environment and processes them into outputs, which are returned to the environment.

Inputs → Transformation Process → Outputs

Types on Inputs: The types of inputs that are supplied to a system are as follows:

1. Material
2. Energy
3. Information

Transformation Process: The inputs are converted into outputs using human resources and machines in the system.

Environment Influence: The system is affected by forces from the outside environment such as

1. Cultural forces
2. Technological change
3. Educational environment
4. Political situation
5. Natural resources
6. Human resources
7. Economic framework

The task of the administrator is to integrate these variables in meeting the organisational objectives. Thus, a modern administrator has to be a systems' analyst.

3.10.2 David Easton's Political Systems Theory

David Easton's systems theory portrays public policy as an output of the political system. It helps in conceptualising the interaction between the environment, political system, and public policy. While explaining his model, Easton said that the political system is the part of the society engaged in the 'authoritative allocation of values'. The policy alternatives brought out are based on the values held by the policymakers.

A feedback mechanism is developed, through which the effects and consequences of the outputs are put back into the system as inputs. The understanding of this process helps in policy analysis, which in turn helps in explaining the causes and consequences of public policy. Easton has described the policymaking process as a 'black box' that converts the demands of societies into effective policies (see Fig. 3.4).

Environment: Social and Economic Variables in the Polity

Inputs	Black Box (Conversion Processes)	Outputs
• Demands • Resources • Support • Opposition	• Structures • Procedures • Policymakers • Psycho-Social Framework	• Goals • Policies • Services • Symbols to public and other policy makers

Fig. 3.4: David Easton's Political System

3.10.3 Chester Barnard's Social System Theory

Chester Barnard is considered as the spiritual father of the 'social system' school.[96] His work *The Functions of Executive* is based on a series of lectures he gave on administration at the Lowell Institute of Boston. He introduced social concepts in the analysis of managerial functions and processes. Where, on the one hand, the classical thinkers started with managerial functions and focused on improving the task efficiency of an individual, Barnard, on the other hand, started with an individual, moved to cooperative effort, and ended with executive functions.

3.10.3.1 Organisation as a Cooperative System

Barnard said that organisation is a system that is subordinate to a larger system known as society. This was clear when he said, "At roots, the cause of the instability and limited duration of formal organisations lie in the forces outside. These forces both furnish the materials which are used by organisations and limit their action."[97] He viewed organisation as a social system of cooperation of human activity. He said, "Cooperation originates in the need of an individual to accomplish purposes that he individually cannot achieve."[97] Regarding an individual, he said that the most important limiting factors in the situation of an individual are his/her biological, physical, and social limitations. The most effective method of overcoming these limitations is cooperative social action.

He defined organisation as a "system of consciously coordinated activities or forces of two or more persons."[97] An organisation becomes alive when

1. there are persons to communicate with each other
2. the persons are willing to contribute action
3. the persons are willing to accomplish a common purpose.[95]

These clauses (communication, willingness to serve, and common purpose) are also known as *elements of an organisation.*

Barnard rejected the concept of economic man while explaining why a person contributes their efforts towards the purpose of an organisation. At this point, he recommended the concept of contribution-satisfaction equilibrium. Barnard also identified *four characteristics of formal organisation*, namely, systems, depersonalisation, specialisation, and informal organisations.[98]

3.10.3.2 Contribution-Satisfaction Equilibrium

Barnard described that a person contributes towards organisational activities because of the incentives they get from it. A person's contribution depends on the net satisfaction they get from an organisation, which in turn depends on the material and non-material incentives received from the organisation. Material incentives include conditions of salary, chances of promotion, etc. Non-material incentives include hierarchy of the organisation, honour, pride, and so on.

Barnard also analysed a multiplicity of incentives and classified them into specific and general incentives.

Specific Incentives

The four specific incentives described by Barnard were as follows:

1. Material inducements such as money, things, or physical conditions
2. Personal non-material inducements such as distinction, prestige, and personal power
3. Physical conditions at work
4. Ideal benefactions such as pride of workmanship, sense of adequacy, altruistic service for family, loyalty towards organisation and patriotism.[97]

General Incentives

The four general incentives described by Barnard were as follows:

1. Compatibility with associates
2. Adaptability to working conditions
3. Enlarged participation: Opportunity to participate in the course of events
4. Conditions of communication: Communication conditions include personal comfort in social relations and the opportunity for comradeship and for mutual support in personal attitudes[97]

3.10.3.3 Concept of Authority

In his work, Barnard described the term 'authority' as "the character of a communication (order) in a formal organisation by virtue of which it is accepted by a contributor or member of the organisation as governing the action he contributes."[97] For him, authority consisted of two aspects:

1. The subjective aspect which describes that a person accepts a communication as authoritative; and
2. The objective aspect which describes the character of the communication by virtue of which it is accepted.[95]

A person accepts communication as authoritative only when the following conditions are fulfilled simultaneously:[97]

1. The person understands the communication: A communication should be intelligible and well-understood to have any authority. If communications are unintelligible, most of the time is spent in the interpretation of orders to concrete situations.
2. The communication is consistent with the organisational purpose: The communication should be compatible with the organisational purpose in order to be accepted. Any apparent conflict in purpose needs to be explained in order to gain acceptance.
3. The communication is compatible with personal interests: The communication should be compatible with the personal interests of an individual in order to be accepted. They should also provide positive incentives to an individual.
4. An individual has physical and mental ability to comply with the communication (order): Accepting a communication or order should be within the mental and physical capacity of an individual.

Before Barnard, it was thought that authority originated from the top of the organisation. Barnard was the first one to assert that authority rested on the acceptance or consent of subordinates. Enduring acceptance by subordinates can be ensured only when the following three conditions are fulfilled:

1. The orders issued are in accordance with the above-mentioned four conditions of communication.
2. The orders fall within the 'zone of indifference'.
3. A group influences the behaviour of an individual, resulting in the stability of the zone of indifference.

3.10.3.4 Zone of Indifference

The orders issued in an organisation are of three types: (a) those that are clearly unacceptable, (b) those that are neutral and just acceptable/unacceptable, and (c) those that are clearly acceptable. The third category of orders is those that fall in the 'zone of indifference.'[97] This 'zone of indifference' is the zone in which a superior is free to act. In this zone, employees have a disposition to accept authority. The size and nature of this zone depends on the type of inducements provided to a person in comparison to the sacrifices he/she makes for the organisation. Thus, the executive should issue only those orders that fall within this zone.

3.10.3.5 Informal Organisations

Chester Barnard has defined informal organisations as "the aggregate of the personal contacts and interactions and the associate grouping of people."[97] Informal organisations are structureless, transitory, and involve relations and interactions that take place without any joint purpose. They serve an important purpose by establishing general understanding, customs, habits, institutions, and conditions favourable for the rise of a formal organisation.[95]

Moreover, Barnard argues that an informal organisation must establish formal organisations within it to be effective. On the other hand, a formal organisation must create informal organisations as a means of communication and means of protection for individuals from the domination of formal organisation.[5] In Barnard's words, formal and informal organisations "are interdependent aspects of the same phenomenon—a society is structured by formal organisations, formal organisations are vitalised and conditioned by informal organisations."[97]

3.10.3.6 Functions of the Executive

Chester Barnard said that the work of the executive is a specialist function to maintain the organisation in operation. Its function is like that of the nervous system of an organism, including the brain in relation to the rest of the body. The essential functions of the executive are as follows.

Maintenance of Organisational Communication: The function of the maintenance of organisational communication includes the definition of organisational positions and maintenance of organisational personnel system. It requires preparation of organisational charts, specification of duties, division of work, and so on. The personnel system requires recruiting people with appropriate qualifications, offering them incentives, and so on.

Formulation of Organisational Objectives and Purposes: The executive needs to frame organisational objectives that are widely accepted by all members of the organisation.

Securing of Essential Services from the Individuals: This function requires bringing personnel into a cooperative relationship with the organisation and eliciting essential services and contribution from them. This can be achieved by maintaining morale, education, training, and incentives for the individuals, and supervision and control over the individuals.

3.10.3.7 Fiction of Authority

Chester Barnard said that there is an implicit presumption within the authority principle that individuals accept orders from the superior because they want to avoid making issues of such orders and avoid incurring personal subservience or loss of personal status with their colleagues.[5] On the other hand, the superior issues only those orders that fall in the zone of indifference so that their communication is accepted without resistance.

This fiction of superior authority is necessary in an organisation because of the following two reasons:

1. **Delegation of responsibility upwards:** The fiction of authority described earlier allows an individual to delegate responsibility, for an organisational decision, upwards to the superiors. People obey superior authority because they do not like accepting personal responsibility when they are not in a position of accepting it.[97]
2. **To serve the good of the organisation:** If a superior authority is disobeyed, the good of the organisation comes at stake. Non-compliance with the authority because of arbitrary personal reasons is considered as an attack on the organisation.

3.10.3.8 Authority of Position versus Leadership

Authority of position is that authority which is imputed to communications from the superiors when they are consistent with their positions. It is independent of the personal abilities of the incumbent. *Authority of leadership* is that authority which is imputed to the superior personal abilities of a person irrespective of his/her position. It is imputed to what they say and guide. This sort of authority lasts only till a leader is adequately informed.

3.10.3.9 Character of Communication System

The character of a communication system necessary for seeking effective contribution from the organisational members can be described as follows:

1. The channels of communication should be definite.
2. There should be a definite formal channel of communication to every member of the organisation.
3. The line of communication should be as direct and as short as possible.
4. The complete line of communication should be usually used.
5. The competence of the persons serving as communication centres, that is, officers and supervisory heads should be adequate.
6. The line of communication should not be interrupted when the organisation is functioning.
7. Every communication should be authenticated.[5,97]

3.10.3.10 Ideas on Responsibility

Chester Barnard viewed responsibility in terms of morality and defined it as the power of a particular private code of morals to control the conduct of the individual in the presence of strong contrary desires or impulses.[97] It is determined by a complex set of moral, legal, technical, professional, and institutional codes. These codes govern individual conduct and may sometimes also result in conflict among them.

For Barnard, management decisions are concerned with moral issues, and the survival of the organisation depends on moral commitment.[99] Barnard wrote, "organisations endure, though, in proportion to the breadth of morality through which they are governed. This is only to say that foresight, long purposes, high ideals are the basis for the persistence of organisational cooperation."[97]

3.10.3.11 Ideas on Decision-making

Chester Barnard defined decisions as acts of individuals that are results of deliberation, calculation, and thought involving the ordering of means to ends.[97] He classified decisions as being personal and organisational.

Personal decisions are those that may or may not relate to participation in organisational processes. They are taken outside the organisation based on incentives the organisation offers and may not necessarily be logical. *Organisational decisions* are those that are connected to organisational purposes, are based on information, are logical, and cannot be delegated. They are the result of discrimination, analysis, and choice. Barnard regarded decision-making in an organisation as a specialist function; the decisions may be positive or negative. This is clear when he said, "fine art of executive consists in not deciding questions that are not pertinent, in not deciding prematurely, in not making decisions that cannot be made effective and in not making decisions that others should make."[97]

3.10.3.12 Ideas on Leadership

According to Barnard, leadership is the factor of chief significance in human cooperation. He said that while cooperation is a creative procedure, leadership is the indispensable fulminator of its forces.[99] "The inculcation of belief in the real subsistence of a common purpose is an essential executive function."[97] To Barnard, leadership is "linked with knowing whom to consider, with accepting the right suggestions, with selecting appropriate occasions and times—an understanding that leads to distinguishing effectively flanked by the significant and the unimportant in the scrupulous concrete situation, flanked by what can and what cannot be done, flanked by what will almost certainly succeed and what will almost certainly not, flanked by what will weaken cooperation and what will augment it."[97] Thus, leadership is not just deciding what is right, but getting the right thing done.

For Barnard, a leader is a teacher. He/she cannot do his/her work without teaching people. He/she has to provide them with a philosophy to work against adversities; he/she has to set goals and indicate the methods of achieving them. Leaders have to be more effective than others, both in conveying meaning and intentions with a sympathetic understanding.[99] Barnard listed out the five essential qualities of a leader, namely, vitality and endurance, decisiveness, persuasiveness, responsibility, and intellectual capacity.[97]

3.10.3.13 Science of Organisation

Chester Barnard wanted the integration of the two cultures of management, its science and art; and he believed that it is possible to develop a science of organisation. As per him, it requires an understanding of social anthropology, sociology, social psychology, institutional economics, management, and so on. Along with higher-order intellect, it also requires one to inculcate a sense of unity and create common ideals.[97]

3.10.4 Cybernetics and Viable System Theory

3.10.4.1 Cybernetic Approach to Organisation

The approach of cybernetics is an important contribution to organisational thinking. It exemplifies the modern vision of closed-system thinking and is attributed to the work of Norbert Wiener. The development of this field allowed diverse disciplines to communicate their problems in the common language of systems theory. It also allowed a common set of principles to be applied to the problems of control and regulation. For example, the principles of system design that allowed ancient mariners to steer ships with governors were the same principles that allowed mechanical engineers to design thermostats for air-conditioning units. These systems can be seen as returning to equilibrium after being disturbed by regulating themselves through feedback information.[100]

3.10.4.2 The Viable System Model of Stafford Beer

The viable system model of Stafford Beer (Fig. 3.5) is used as a conceptual tool for understanding organisations, redesigning them, and supporting the management of change.[101] This model deviated from the traditional hierarchical models of an organisation where plans were made at the top and implemented by a cascade of instructions through tiered ranks. The old model was considered slow and inflexible to cope with the increasing rate of change and complexity surrounding organisations.

Various technological developments have given way to flatter and networked organisations with a wider distribution of data to reach all those who actually perform the work in real time.[101] The viable system model helps in attaining functional decentralisation (as against hierarchy) along with cohesion among the whole organisation. It is underpinned by fundamental cybernetic principles of communication and control in complex organisations. It provides a framework for designing flexible and adaptable organisations that balance external and internal perspectives and long- and short-term thinking.

Organisations as Recursive Systems

The viable system model recognises that organisations have far less inner complexity than their environments. This is a natural imbalance that needs to be recognised and addressed through various strategies that the organisation employs to bring this complexity within the range of its response.[101] Similarly, a management team has far less complexity than the organisation itself. Thus, the whole organisation needs to be understood without having knowledge about all the details known by others.

An important concept of organisations is their *recursivity*. Recursivity describes the architecture of complex organisations and is based on the presumption that all living systems are composed of a series of subsystems, each having self-organising and self-regulatory characteristics. Each subsystem contains further subsystems, and so on, right down to the level of the single cell. All these subsystems are autonomous. They contain, within them, the capacity to adapt to change in their environment and to deal with complexity.[102]

These recursive structures provide long-term viability to the organisation. They are both efficient generators and absorbers of complexity and highly adaptive to change. They function like this because they consist of a devolving series of primary activities (responsible for producing goods and services in an organisation) supported by sufficient regulatory and communication functions to enable them to operate effectively at every level. Thus, for example, the elementary cell at the shop-floor level in a manufacturing environment is effectively subsumed within larger primary (autonomous) activities. Each primary activity, from the level of the elementary cell to the total organisation, has its own value chain. This architecture of complexity and recursive structures enhances the operational complexity of the organisation and makes it more cohesive.[103]

Five Essential Functions for Viability

An autonomous unit (or viable system) needs to have five functions in place if it has to operate effectively in its environment. These are as follows.

Implementation: Primary activities (responsible for producing goods and services) are at the core of the recursive model. Goods and services are produced at different levels of aggregation by embedded primary activities, and the value chain of the organisation as a whole implements its overall purpose.

Coordination: A viable system has systems in place to coordinate the interfaces of its value-adding functions and the operations of its primary subunits. This coordination is a sense of mutual adjustment between the support functions and autonomous units. It is an area where information technology (IT) systems can be extremely helpful in avoiding direct and intrusive human intervention.

Control: A two-way communication between the subunit and the meta-level management is a prerequisite for viability. It is a channel through which resources are negotiated, management instructions are issued (on an exception only basis), and accountability reports flew upwards.

Intelligence: The intelligence function is a two-way link between the primary activity and its external environment. It provides the primary activity with continuous feedback on marketplace conditions, technology changes, and all external factors. It also projects the identity and message of the organisation into its environment.

Policy: The main role of policy is to provide clarity about the overall direction, values, and purpose of the organisational unit as well as to design the conditions for organisational effectiveness.

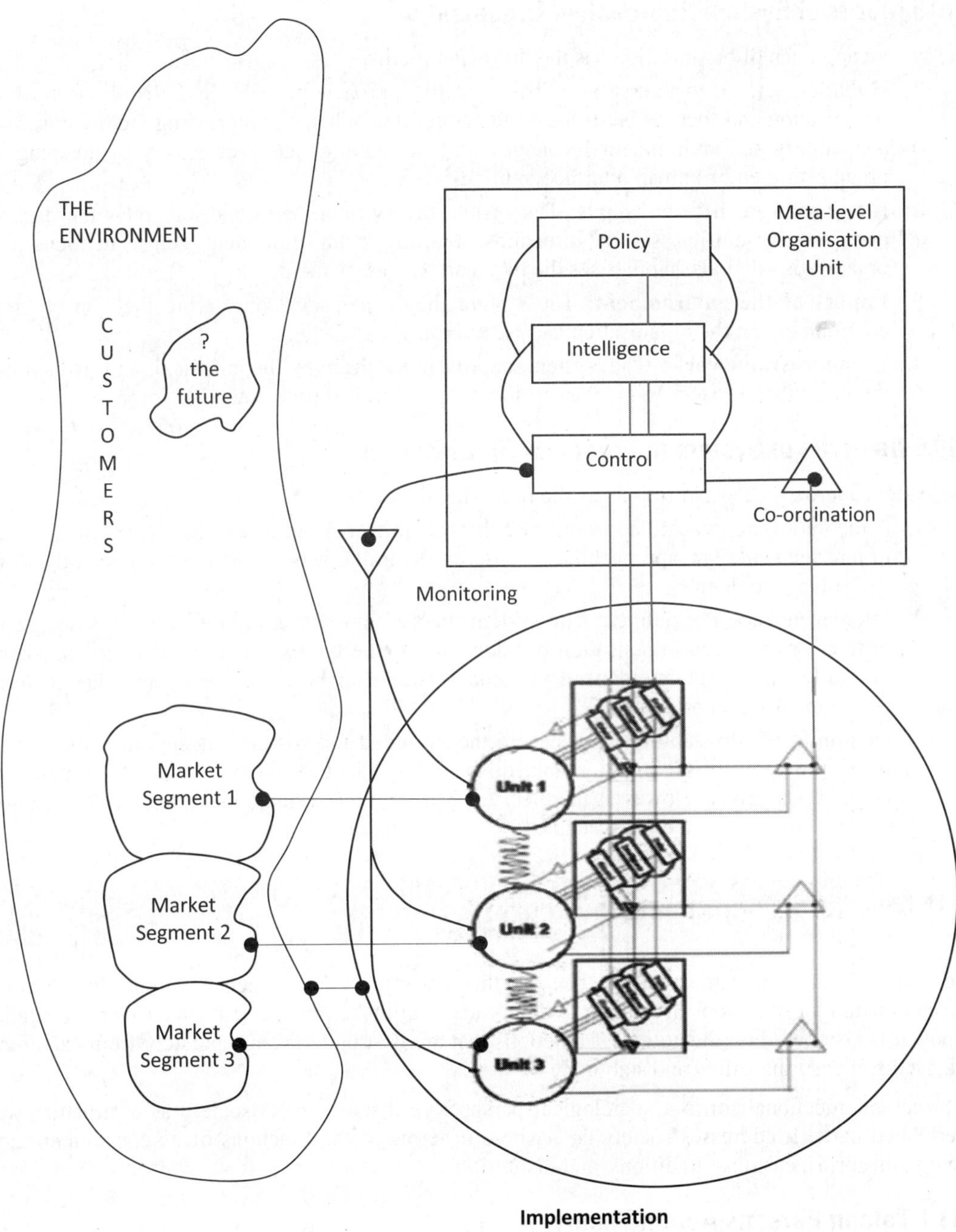

Fig 3.5: The Viable System Model[101]

3.10.5 Merits of System Approach of Organisation

The system approach of organisation has the following merits.

1. **Holistic view of organisation:** The system approach provides a holistic view of the organisation and focuses on its adaptive nature. It also helps in increasing the organisation's adaptability to environmental changes and in making better decisions by keeping the organisation-environment interface in mind.
2. **Integration of different parts:** The system theory interrelates and integrates the different parts into a unified set of directions. Starting from individual goals, it focuses on organisational goals, synthesises the two, and converges them.
3. **Impact of the environment:** The system theory helps in considering the impact of the environment on the organisation and vice versa.
4. **Broader framework:** The system approach synthesises the classical and behavioural theories into a broader framework to solve organisational problems.[104]

3.10.6 Demerits of System Approach of Organisation

The system approach of organisation has the following demerits:

1. A theoretical approach: People criticise the system theory because of its theoretical approach to management. The approach has no usefulness in the way an organisation actually works and solves problems.
2. Interdependence not defined: The system theory emphasises the relationship amongst the different parts of an organisation but does not define the exact nature of interdependence. Similarly, the exact interdependence and relationship between the internal and external environments are not defined.
3. Non-uniform applicability: The system theory failed to provide concepts that apply to all types of organisations. Small organisations are less adaptive to environmental variables than large organisations. However, the theory is based on the assumption that most organisations are big, complex, and open systems.[104]

3.11 Structural Functionalism Theory

The structural functional theory dates back to the time of Aristotle when he studied the ultimate causes in nature or of actions in relation to their ends or utility. Montesquieu's doctrine of separation of power is also based on the notion of functions that are best undertaken separately from each other as a means of ensuring safety and stability.[105]

Structural functionalism is a sociological perspective that interprets society as a structure with interrelated parts. It addresses society as a whole in terms of the functions of its constituent parts, namely, its norms, customs, traditions, and institutions.

3.11.1 Talcott Parsons Action Theory

Talcott Parsons came out with an *action theory* based on the system-theoretical concept and the methodological principle of voluntary action. He said that a social system is made up of the actions of individuals.[106] He said that each individual has expectations of others' actions and reactions to his/her own behaviour, and these expectations are derived from the accepted norms and values of the society they inhabit.[107]

These expectations are entrenched or institutionalised when the behaviours are repeated in further interactions; this leads to the creation of roles in society. Parsons defined *roles* as the normatively regulated participation of a person in a concrete process of social interaction with specific and concrete role partners.[107] An individual is expected to conform to the norms governing the nature of the role he or she fulfills.[108] Some of these roles are bound to institutions and social structures (economic, educational, and legal). They are functional in the sense that they assist society in operating and fulfilling its functional needs.[109]

State of Equilibrium

A state of equilibrium is said to be attained in a society when there is no conflict when everyone knows what is expected of them (what are their roles), and when these expectations are consistently met. The important processes for attaining this equilibrium are *socialisation and social control.* Here socialisation is the mechanism for transferring the accepted norms and values of society to the individuals within the system. When the norms and values are perfectly internalised and become a part of the individual's personality, socialisation is said to be perfect.[110] Parsons said that "this point is independent of the sense in which the individual is concretely autonomous or creative rather than 'passive' or 'conforming', for individuality and creativity, are to a considerable extent, phenomena of the institutionalisation of expectations."[107]

Role Bargaining

Role bargaining is a phenomenon in which individuals interact with, and adapt to, changing situations.[109] Once the roles are created, individuals create norms that guide further action and are thus institutionalised, creating stability across social interactions. If this adaptation process cannot adjust, either new structures are formed or the society dies. This model of social change is described as a moving equilibrium.[109]

3.11.2 Robert Merton on Structural Functionalism

Robert Merton was a follower of Parsons but regarded Parson's theory as being too generalised. He dealt with some of the limitations in Parsons' theory. The limitations he identified were (a) functional unity, (b) universal functionalism, and (c) indispensability. While criticising Parsons' functional unity, Merton said that all parts of a modern and complex society do not work for the functional unity of the society. Some institutions and structures may have other functions and some may be dysfunctional. Some practices are only functional for a dominant individual or a group. Merton also said that there may be functional alternatives to the institutions and structures currently fulfilling the functions of society.

Theory of Deviance

Merton formulated the theory of deviance to explain how internal changes can occur in a system. For him, deviance meant a discontinuity between cultural goals and the accepted methods available for reaching them. According to Merton, an individual faces the following five situations in a system:

1. Conformity: Conformity occurs when an individual has the means and desire to achieve the cultural goals socialised into them.
2. Innovation: Innovation occurs when an individual strives to attain the accepted cultural goals but chooses to do so using a novel or unaccepted method.

3. Ritualism: Ritualism occurs when an individual continues to do things as prescribed by society but forfeits the achievement of goals.
4. Retreatism: Retreatism is the rejection of both the means and goals of society.
5. Rebellion: Rebellion is a combination of the rejection of societal goals and means and a substitution of other goals and means.

The deviance theory says that change can occur in a society either through innovation or rebellion.

Manifest and Latent Functions

Merton distinguished between manifest and latent functions in a system. Manifest functions are those done with the conscious intention of individuals. On the other hand, latent functions are the unintended objective consequences of individual actions.[111]

3.11.3 Gabriel Almond on Structural Functionalism

Gabriel Almond introduced the structural functional approach for comparing political systems. He argued that in order to understand a political system, it is necessary to understand its institutions (structures) along with their respective functions. For better understanding, these institutions need to be analysed in their historical context.

Almond's work was based on the input-output system model of David Easton. According to him, the required inputs in a political system are political socialisation and recruitment, interest articulation, interest aggregation, and political communication. The outputs from a political system are rule making, rule application, and rule adjudication.[112] Political communication links input to outputs in a way that provides the function of a feedback loop.

In this theory, Almond compared the political systems of developing countries on the basis of a common set of categories. He used sociological and anthropological approaches to find this set of categories. He viewed the political system as "the legitimate, order maintaining or transforming system in society."[112] He regarded system analysis for political systems as comprehensive, as it included all interactions, both inputs and outputs. All political systems have similar sets of properties. First, all political systems have a political structure. Second, the same functions are performed in all political systems. Third, all political structure is multifunctional, whether in primitive or in modern societies.[112]

Almond has classified the functions of a political system into three categories:

1. Conversion functions: These consist of interest articulation, interest aggregation, political communication, rule making, rule application, and rule adjudication.
2. The operation of the political system in its environment.
3. Maintenance and adaptation of political systems to pressures for change over the long term.[113]

3.12 Decision-Making Theory by Herbert Simon

Herbert Simon is considered a proponent of behaviour studies in public administration. Behaviour study is an interdisciplinary study of human behaviour using knowledge from various social science subjects. Its objective is to understand human behaviour in an organisation. Where on the one hand, Max Weber discussed the anatomy of organisations, on the other, Simon discussed the physiology of organisations.

Some of the important works of Simon are *Administrative Behavior* (1947), *Fundamental Research in Administration* (1953), *Organisation* (1958), and *Human Problem Solving* (1972). He was awarded the Nobel Prize in 1978 for his contribution to analysing the decision-making process.[114]

3.12.1 Science of Administration

All studies on administration done by Simon had decision-making as their central theme. For him, decision-making was a process of drawing conclusions from premises and, therefore, the premises rather than the whole decision served as the unit of analysis for him.[115] For Simon, the administration was equivalent to decision-making; his studies were based on how to make effective decisions. For understanding decision-making, Simon recommended an empirical approach to the study of administration.

Simon's decision-making approach subsumed several administrative functions such as Fayol's POCCC and Gulick's POSDCoRB. To understand the science of administration (and decision-making), Simon rejected the politics-administration dichotomy and propounded the concept of fact-value dichotomy. He considered that the science of administration should be based on factual premises of administrative decisions. This science of administration, Simon considered, is applicable equally to public and private sector organisations.

3.12.2 Decision-Making Theory

Simon considered an organisation as a structure of decision-makers. He said that some sorts of decisions are made at all levels of organisation. Describing this structure of decision-makers, Simon said that each organisation has three types of employees. The top-level employees have the important function of decision-making. The middle-level consists of supervising staff that affects the organisational work by influencing the work of the operating staff (lowest-level staff). The lowest-level staff implements the actual physical work of an organisation.

The decisions made at different levels are based on a number of premises, and Simon's focus was on how these premises are determined. These premises are based on individual preferences, social conditioning, and communications received from competent units in an organisation. The top-level management influences the premises on which the middle-level and lowest-level employees base their decisions.

3.12.3 Decision-Making Process

Simon divided the decision-making process into three concrete steps: intelligence activity, design activity, and choice activity.[117] These steps are explained below.

Intelligence Activity: This step involves finding occasions to take decisions. It necessitates the executive to understand and analyse the organisational environment. At this stage, the executive identifies the problem that needs to be solved.

Design Activity: The executive searches for all possible alternatives to solve the identified problem. They analyse the merits and demerits of all available solutions. Then the executive critically evaluates the different consequences and costs of all the alternative courses available.

Choice Activity: Finally the executive selects the most appropriate available solutions, which enables the attainment of the objectives at the lowest cost.

These three steps require certain skills such as judgment, creativity, quantitative analysis, and experience on the part of the executive.

3.12.4 Fact and Value Content of a Decision

Simon said that there are two constituents of a decision: fact and value. The 'value' content deals with the preference of an individual and the 'fact' content deals with the information required for a decision. According to Simon, "an administrative science, like any science, is concerned purely with factual statements. There is no place for ethical (value) statements in the study of science."[117] The rules of scientific analysis focus more on factual content than value content; however, the fact and value content is inextricably joint.

The decision-making process is made complicated due to the close connection between the fact and the value content. Speaking of decision-making, Simon said that "each decision involves the selection of a goal and a behaviour relevant to it; this goal may in turn be mediate to a somewhat more distant goal, and so on, until a relatively final aim is reached."[118] Moreover, Simon said that the 'value judgments' are concerned with the selection of final goals in a decision, and the 'factual judgments' are concerned with the implementation of the decided final goals.[118]

3.12.5 Purposiveness of Organisation and Hierarchy of Decisions

Every organisation has a purpose that is described by its purposiveness. The behaviour of an individual in an organisation is purposive as it is oriented towards the attainment of the goals of the organisation. This purposiveness of the organisation for the attainment of the goals brings about integration in the pattern of behaviour, in the absence of which the administration would be meaningless.[114]

In order to achieve this purpose, the organisation divides its work into various functions or units and further into subunits until one reaches the base. This purposiveness creates a hierarchy of decisions, with a step downward in the hierarchy consisting of the implementation of the goals set forth in the step immediately above. Simon concluded that the behaviour of an individual is said to be purposive in so far as it is guided by general goals or objectives; it is rational in so far as it selects various alternatives that are important for the achievement of the previously selected goals.[114]

3.12.6 Types of Rationality

Herbert Simon defined rationality as one concerned with the selection of preferred behaviour alternatives in terms of some system of values, whereby the consequences of behaviour can be evaluated.[118] He said that a decision bridges the distance between rationality and behaviour.[119] Rationality is a criterion used in the decision that is theoretically grounded on the presupposition that the agents are intentionally rational.

Simon defined rationality as a relation of conformance (efficacy) between pre-established ends and the means to reach them. This relation between the means and ends is a question of fact. However, it is difficult to separate the means from the ends because an apparent end may only be a means for some future end.

Simon has given an account of the following different types of rationality:

1. **Objective rationality:** A decision is said to be objectively rational if it is correct for maximising the given values in a given situation.
2. **Subjective rationality:** A decision is said to be subjectively rational if it maximises attainment relative to knowledge of the subject.
3. **Conscious rationality:** A decision is said to be consciously rational if it involves a conscious process for adjusting the means to the ends.

4. **Deliberate rationality:** A decision is said to be deliberately rational if it involves a deliberate process for adjusting the means to the ends.
5. **Personal rationality:** A decision is said to be personally rational if it is directed towards personal goals.
6. **Organisational rationality:** A decision is said to be organisationally rational if it is oriented towards organisational goals.118

3.12.7 Bounded Rationality

Simon said that total rationality is not possible in administrative behaviour. According to him, the following are the limitations towards achieving total rationality:

1. There is a lack of knowledge among decision-makers about the full range of possible solutions to a defined problem.
2. There is a lack of knowledge of the consequences of all possible alternatives.
3. An administrator lacks time to fully examine each possible alternative and its consequences.
4. There is a lack of knowledge about the future events in which the decision will be operating.
5. The decision-makers habits, personal beliefs, and intellectual capacity are also impediments to total rationality.
6. Informal groups, along with their influences, conventions, and behavioural norms, also constrain total rationality.
7. Total rationality is constrained by organisational factors such as rules and procedures of formal organisation, its channels of communication, and so on.
8. The external pressures on an organisation also impact the total rationality of its decision-makers.

While proposing the concept of bounded rationality, Simon rejected the idea of 'maximising' decisions and put forward the idea of *satisficing*. This word is a combination of *satisfaction* and *sufficing*. It involves a course of action that is satisfactory and good enough. This is also known as 'somehow muddling through'. As an administrative official recognises that the world he/she perceives is the simplified version of the real world, he/she makes his/her choices using a simple picture of the situation, which takes into account just a few factors that he/she regards as most relevant and crucial.[118]

While making a decision, an administrative official identifies the various alternatives and evaluates them one at a time. When an acceptable (good enough) solution is found, the search is discontinued. While selecting alternatives, heuristics are used to reduce large problems to manageable proportions so that decisions can be made rapidly. (*Heuristic* is a rule that guides the search for alternatives that have a high probability of yielding satisfactory solutions. For instance, some companies continually hire engineering graduates from the same college because in the past such graduates have performed well for the company.) Finally, the official chooses a satisfactory alternative that meets or exceeds the basic minimum decisional criterion.

3.12.8 Aspiration Adaptation Theory

Aspiration adaptation theory is a part of the concept of bounded rationality. It suggests that the individuals in an organisation have an aspiration level. If a choice promises to satisfy this aspiration level, it is exercised without an extensive search for an optimal strategy. This leads to a *satisfactory* alternative. However, if the individual is unable to find any satisficing alternative, he/she drops his/her aspiration level downwards. Then a decisional choice is made among the alternatives that satisfy the new aspiration level.[121]

An administrative official takes a decision based on bounded rationality and the aspiration adaptation scheme (Fig. 3.6). First, they set the goal. Second, they set an appropriate aspiration level or criterion (that is, when the solution is acceptable if not perfect). Third, they employ heuristics to narrow the problem space to certainly feasible alternatives. Fourth, if no alternative is identified, they lower the aspiration level and begin to search for new alternatives. Fifth, they identify an alternative and determine its acceptability. If it is unacceptable then the fourth step is repeated. If an alternative is acceptable, then it is implemented. Finally, after implementation, an administrative official evaluates the sense with which the goal was (or was not) attained, and lowers or raises the aspiration level for future decisions.

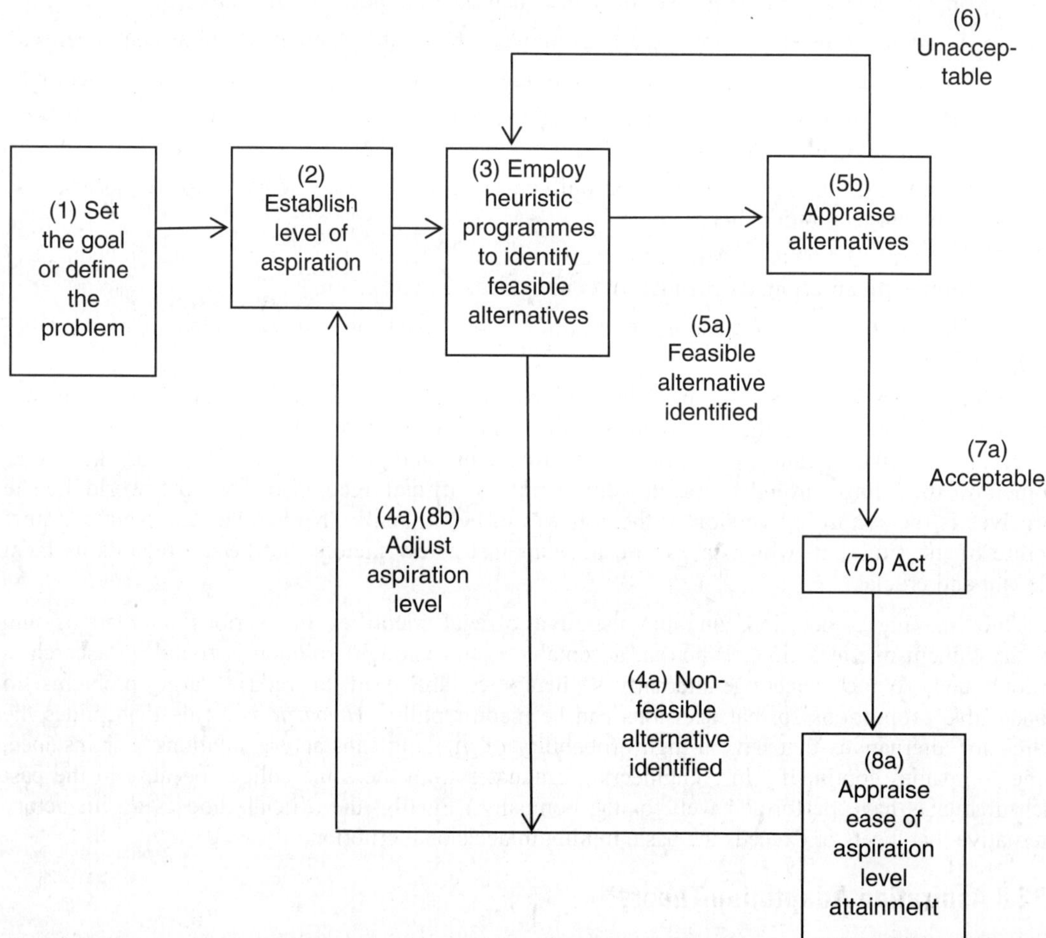

Fig 3.6: Bounded Rationality and Aspiration Adaptation

3.12.9 Programmed and Non-programmed Decisions

Herbert Simon made a distinction between two types of decisions: programmed and non-programmed decisions. The differences between them are tabulated in Table 3.1.

Table 3.1: Differences between programmed and non-programmed decisions

Programmed decision	Non-programmed decision
1. Programmed decisions are repetitive and routine in nature. Thus a definite procedure can be worked out and each decision is not required to be dealt with separately.	1. Non-programmed decisions are novel, unstructured, and have to be tackled independently as no established methods are available for dealing with them.
2. In such decisions, the organisation provides alternatives through routines or strategy.	2. In such decisions, the organisation provides the parameters for searching for various alternatives.98
3. These decisions require techniques such as habit, clerical routines, knowledge, skills, and informal channels.	3. These decisions require techniques such as the rule of thumb, selection, training of executives, higher skills, judgment, innovative ability, and so on.

However, Simon also identified certain similarities between the two types of decisions. They both include definitions of the situation, analyses of the means and ends to link actions to the organisational objectives, division of problems into independent parts, choosing the alternatives based on the 'satisficing' criterion, uncertainty, absorption, and routinisation of the process.[98]

Gresham's Law of Decision-making

Gresham's law of economics (bad money drives out good money) can also be applied to the decision-making process. In the decision-making process, this law states that programmed decisions (or activities) overshadow non-programmed decisions (or activities). Thus, if a decision-maker needs to make a series of decisions, he/she will work on those decisions first that are routine and repetitive. The novel and unique decisions (non-programmed decisions) will be saved for a later time. This happens because a manager likes to clear his/her desk first before getting down to more serious decisions. However, routine decisions do not end easily and non-programmed, and important, decisions suffer.

3.12.10 Procedural Rationality and Substantive Rationality

Simon introduced the concepts of procedural rationality and substantive rationality. Individual behaviour is said to be *substantively rational* when it is directed towards the realisation of organisational ends, subject to given conditions and constraints. It is concerned only with the choice made in an organisation. On the other hand, individual behaviour is said to be *procedurally rational* if it is an outcome of appropriate deliberation. It is concerned with *how* a choice in an organisation was made. Simon's research in the area of cognitive science demonstrated that, in complex situations, the choice is taken and its result strongly depends not only on the process that generated it but also on the objectives that oriented it.[119] Thus, it is indispensable to understand the process by which the choice is made.

3.12.11 Administrative Process of Decision-Making

Administration is a group activity. Therefore, it is necessary to build a process for channeling organised effort towards the group task and goals. This process is known as the *administrative process*. Simon said that this administrative process consists of certain steps. The organisation segregates certain elements in the decisions of its members and establishes regular organisational procedures to select and determine these elements. For example, if the task of a group is to build a ship, the design for the ship is drawn and adopted by the organisation. This design limits and guides the activities of the persons who actually construct the ship. Thus, an organisation takes away from an individual a part of his/her decisional autonomy and substitutes it with the organisational decision-making process. This decisional process consists of the following three steps:

1. It specifies an individual's functions, focusing on the general scope and nature of his/her duties.
2. It allocates authority to a person to make further decisions for the individual.
3. It sets other limits to the choices of an individual that are necessary to coordinate the activities of several individuals in an organisation.[114]

This structuring of behavioural choice in a decision-making process gives rise to the features of specialisation, coordination, expertise, and responsibility.

Specialisation

According to Simon, tasks are delegated to different levels of an organisation, leading to a vertical division of labour. Simon gave three reasons for vertical specialisation in an organisation. First, in the case of horizontal specialisation, vertical specialisation is necessary to achieve coordination among individuals. Second, vertical specialisation provides expertise in decision-making. Third, it provides a system of fixing accountability to the level where the decisions are taken. For example, the accountability for taking wrong decisions is fixed on the board of directors in an industry, rather than on the operating staff implementing them.

Coordination

A decision-making process requires not only the adoption of the correct decision but also the adoption of the same decision by all the operating staff members of an organisation. This requires adequate exercise of authority, influence, and communication in an organisation so that a decided the plan of operations governs the activities of all members of the group. In an organisation, there are two types of coordination: procedural and substantive coordination. *Procedural coordination* establishes the line of authority and outlines the sphere of activity of each organisational member. It gives a general description of the behaviours and relationships of the members of the organisation. *Substantive coordination* specifies the content of the work of individuals. For example, in the automobile industry, an organisation chart is an aspect of procedural coordination and a blueprint of the automobile engine is an aspect of substantive coordination.

Expertise

According to Simon, expertise in decision-making is attained when the responsibility for it is allocated in a manner that all decisions requiring a particular skill can be made by persons possessing that skill.

Responsibility

As the autonomy in decision-making is restricted at various levels and some amount of discretion in decision-making is provided to every level; individuals are held responsible for the amount of discretion they exercise while making a decision.

3.12.12 Organisational Influence on Individuals

The middle-level/supervisory/non-operative staff of an organisation have the task of influencing the decision of the operatives/working staff. In a small organisation, this influence is direct; however, in large organisations, the supervisory staff is interposed between the top executives and the operatives. These several levels of middle-level staff are themselves subject to influence from the above; they further transmit, elaborate, and modify this influence before it reaches the operating staff.[114]

Moreover, Simon said that influence is of two types: internal and external. *Internal influence* tends to create attitudes and habits in employees that help them in reaching a desired decision. The modes of this kind of influence are organisational loyalty and efficiency training. *External influence* tends to impose on employees decisions made elsewhere in the organisation. The modes of this kind of influence are authority, advice, and providing information.

Simon has used the word 'influence' in place of 'direction' because directing is only one of the many techniques used by the supervisory staff in order to influence the decision of the operating staff. The description of the various modes of influence is mentioned below.

1. Authority (external influence): Simon regarded authority as a means to make the organisational man conform to the organisational demands. However, authority does not flow from above. Authority is exercised only when the staff willingly accepts it. This authority may flow in various directions and at various levels, and not necessarily from top to bottom. Authority is said to be accepted if an individual allows his/her behaviour to be guided by the decision of the superiors. An individual obeys an authority only when it falls in his/her 'zone of acceptance'.
2. Advice and information (external influence): Useful information and advice help in greater effectiveness in decision-making.
3. Organisational loyalty (internal influence): Organisational loyalty means loyalty towards organisational goals. It confines the individual interests towards their organisational tasks instead of probing into the basics of the problems. It renders group effort possible.
4. Training (internal influence): Training is a vital mechanism to facilitate greater direction to the individual in decision-making. It is more applicable when the same elements are involved in a number of decisions. It helps in supplying facts, providing frames of reference, and indoctrinating desirable values in the individual.

3.12.13 The Criterion of Efficiency

Simon said that an administrator is guided by the criterion of efficiency. This criterion dictates the choice of an alternative that produces the best results for the given application of resources.[118] It demands that, of the two alternatives having the same costs, the one that leads to greater attainment of the organisation objective be chosen; and of the two alternatives leading to the same degree of attainment the one that entails a lower cost should be chosen.[118] However, Simon cautioned that higher-level decisions are not possibly be measured and compared easily. This criterion of efficiency helps the individual in handling the fact content of a decision.

3.12.14 Computerisation for Decision-Making

Computers and techniques such as mathematical tools, operations research, electronic data processing, systems analyses, and computer simulation are instrumental in decision-making in an organisation. They help in efficient information storage, processing, and dissemination for decision-making. The use of these tools has reduced the dependency on middle-level (supervisory) personnel and has led to *re-centralisation* in decision-making.

Apart from it, the use of computerised techniques has also led to more rational and coordinated communication of decisions. The use of computerisation has also increased rationality in the decision-making process and behaviour of individuals. This has happened due to an increase in the efficiency of programmed decision-making due to computerisation.

3.12.15 Drawbacks of Simon's Decision-Making Approach

The work of Herbert Simon, on decision-making and administration, is criticised on the following points.

Neglected Environmental and Other Factors: Simon has neglected the role of social, political, economic, and cultural factors while analysing the decision-making process. Simon has also neglected the role of factors such as intuition, tradition, and faith in decision-making.

Neglected Value Content: Simon has tried to focus on the fact content while making decisions. However, values are an integral part of decision-making and removing them would make the study of public administration mechanical and routine. His idea of only fact-based decision theory is not relevant to public administration. It may be of some utility to private administration.

Neglected Individual: While concentrating on organisational decision-making, Simon has neglected the role of an individual and their values and emotions. On this, James McCamy felt that the individual disappeared into the organisation and that emotion had vanished in a puff of reason.[13]

Discounted Uncertainty: Chester Barnard observed that Simon did not take into account the amount of uncertainty involved in most decisions. On this, he said that Simon tried to produce physics and at the same time tried to solve the riddle of the universe.

Neglected Communication: Chester Barnard also observed that Simon's theory neglected the process of communication in an organisation.

Not Politically Neutral: Simon was also criticised by Chester Barnard for not taking a politically neutral stance.[13] Simon assumed that administration plays a similar role in all countries. However, administrative systems in developing countries do not have similar roles to those of developed countries, and thus require a different model of decision-making.

Revived Politics-Administration Dichotomy: Critics argue that Simon's use of logical positivists' distinction between fact and value was a sort of revival, in a new guise, of the discredited politics-administration dichotomy.[120] On this, Norton E. Long has noted that bureaucracy is not, and cannot be, a neutral instrument solely devoted to the unmotivated presentation of facts too, and the docile execution of orders from, political superiors.[120]

Criticism of Efficiency: Simon's concept of efficiency was criticised on the ground that it was equivalent to the economy and may lead to a mechanical conception of administration and to an inconsistent relationship between the means and ends.[5]

General Theory: Critics regard Simon's decision-making theory as being extremely general. Although it provides a framework for decision-making, it does not provide a detailed guidelines for organisational planners.

3.13 James March: Behavioural Theory of the Firm

James March, in his book *Behavioral Theory of the Firm*, pointed out the conflict between rational theories and real people's abilities in a firm. His ideas were as follows.

The Goal of a Firm

March said that the goals of a business firm are a series of more or less independent constraints imposed on the organisation through a process of bargaining among potential coalition members and elaborated over time in response to short-run pressures. Thus, it is important to notice that there are no consensus goals for a firm. They are only constraints for the participants, and the participants bargain with each other for these constraints.

Organisational Expectations and Choices

Organisational expectations are those variables that are a result of inferences drawn from available information. Thus, it is determined either by the process of drawing inferences or by the information that is made available to the organisation. The key point for a firm is to decide what type of information is necessary and how to successfully get it. Based on this information and alternatives, a firm makes it choice decisions. The variables that affect this choice are those that influence the definition of a problem within the organisation, those that influence the standard decision rules, and those that affect the order of consideration of alternatives. Moreover, the standard decision rules are affected primarily by the past experience of the organisation and/or the past record of organisational tasks.

Major Relational Concepts

In his work, James March suggested four major relational concepts in an organisation: quasi-resolution of conflict, uncertainty avoidance, problematic search, and organisational learning.

Quasi-resolution of Conflicts: James said that it is inevitable that there will be conflicting goals in an organisation. Thus, he suggested a process to 'queasily' solve these conflicts. In this concept, first all goals are to be listed as independent constraints. Second, local rationality has to be assumed to get some compromised goals among the participants. Third, attention is to be given to the acceptable level of decisional rules and sequential attention to the goal. Through this process, March believed that the conflicts can be smoothed.

Uncertainty Avoidance: According to March, firms can be risk averse and their uncertainty can be avoided. He suggested that short-run, rather than long-run, uncertainty shall get more attention in an organisation. He suggested a feedback-return decision procedure, in which the feedback from the environment helps the organisation in solving emerging problems and waits for the next one. Like this, firms tend to find a way to control the environment rather than treat the environment as exogenous.[122]

Problematic Search: Problematic search is defined as the pursuit (or search) of a solution stimulated by a particular organisational problem. March said that this search is motivated, simple-minded, and biased. Here the biased information is the one that might cost longer computing time for the true solution to come out.

Organisational Learning: The concept of organisational learning denotes that organisations exhibit adaptive behaviour over time. Especially, they adapt their goals, attention rules, and search rules according to the variables in the environment.

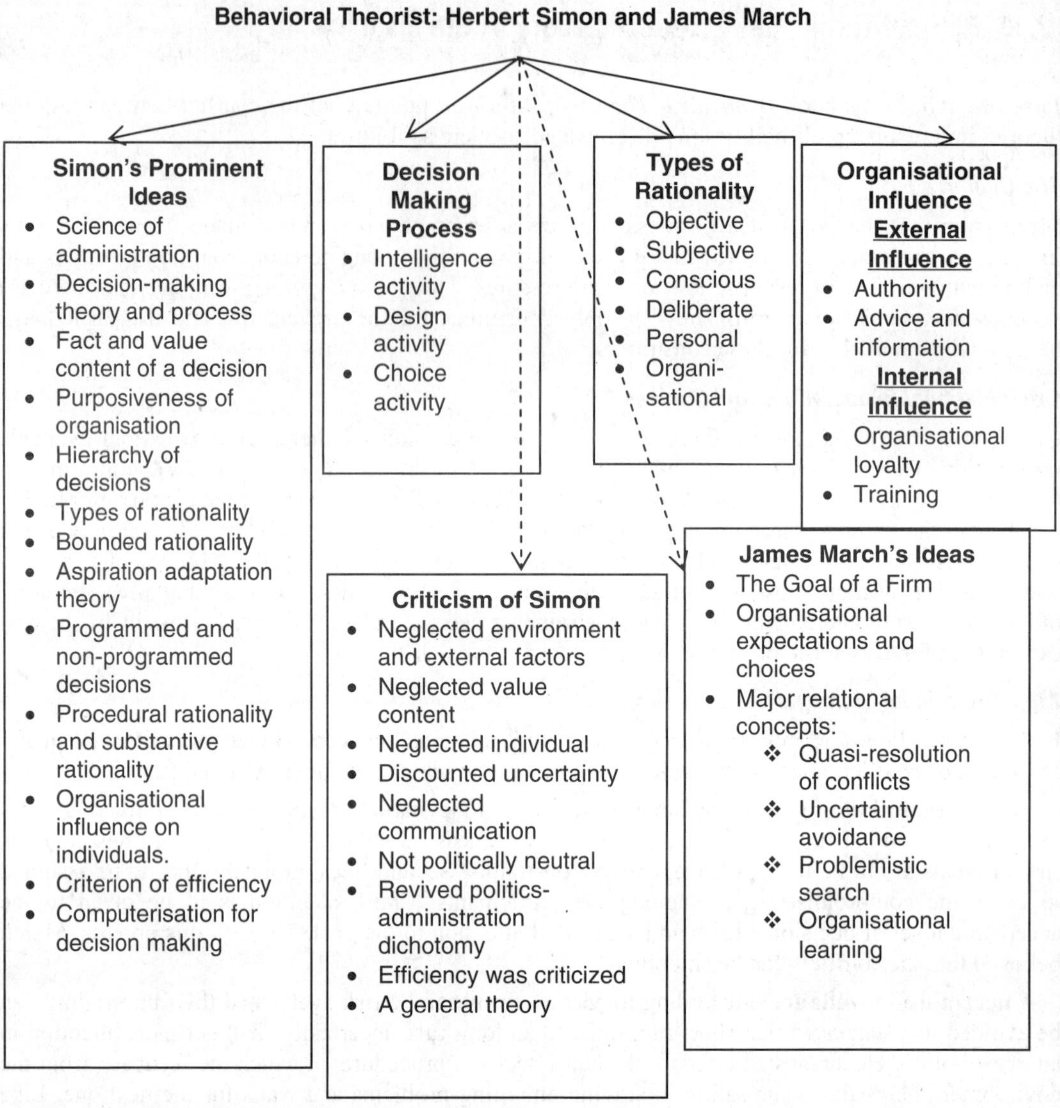

Behavioral Theorist: Herbert Simon and James March

Simon's Prominent Ideas
- Science of administration
- Decision-making theory and process
- Fact and value content of a decision
- Purposiveness of organisation
- Hierarchy of decisions
- Types of rationality
- Bounded rationality
- Aspiration adaptation theory
- Programmed and non-programmed decisions
- Procedural rationality and substantive rationality
- Organisational influence on individuals.
- Criterion of efficiency
- Computerisation for decision making

Decision Making Process
- Intelligence activity
- Design activity
- Choice activity

Types of Rationality
- Objective
- Subjective
- Conscious
- Deliberate
- Personal
- Organi-sational

Organisational Influence

External Influence
- Authority
- Advice and information

Internal Influence
- Organisational loyalty
- Training

Criticism of Simon
- Neglected environment and external factors
- Neglected value content
- Neglected individual
- Discounted uncertainty
- Neglected communication
- Not politically neutral
- Revived politics-administration dichotomy
- Efficiency was criticized
- A general theory

James March's Ideas
- The Goal of a Firm
- Organisational expectations and choices
- Major relational concepts:
  - ❖ Quasi-resolution of conflicts
  - ❖ Uncertainty avoidance
  - ❖ Problemistic search
  - ❖ Organisational learning

Mind Map 3.8: Ideas of Herbert Simon and James March

3.14 Participative Management Approach

Participative management is an approach of administrative theory in which employees are given an opportunity to participate in the decision-making process of an organisation. Douglas McGregor, Chris Argyris, and Rensis Likert are the prominent thinkers of this school.

3.14.1 Douglas McGregor (Socio-psychological Approach)

Douglas McGregor was a pioneer in the study of the effect of different managerial practices on productivity and motivation in an organisational setting. His classic *The Human Side of the Enterprise* is regarded as the most seminal book on industrial psychology. In his next important work, *The Professional Manager*, he showed how the human side of the enterprise can be developed through appropriate managerial intervention and understanding.

In his work, McGregor focused on the most important question in management about whether *successful managers are born or made*. Moreover, he focused on the *assumptions (implicit as well as explicit) about the most effective way to manage people*. He suggested that the making of managers is the result of the management's conception of the nature of its task and of all the policies and practices that are constructed to implement this conception. McGregor said, "the theoretical assumptions which the management holds about controlling its human resources determine the whole character of the enterprise."[123]

3.14.1.1 Theory X and Theory Y

McGregor worked in the area of the theoretical assumptions that the management of an organisation holds. He said that "every managerial act rests on theory."[123] He said that, like in natural sciences, in organisational science, the managerial action has to *selectively adapt* to the nature of the employees in the organisation. To explain the basic theoretical assumptions of low-performing and high-performing managers, McGregor propounded Theory X and Theory Y of managerial control. In these two theories, he described that control of human affairs can be viewed as an integration of human behaviour either through coercive compulsion (theory X) or through motivational self-control (theory Y).

Theory X is also known as the 'carrot and stick theory'. It creates a command and control environment in an organisation, which relies on the low need for motivation. On the other hand, the higher-order motivational needs, McGregor asserts, are satisfied by *Theory Y*. This theory emphasises the need for selective adaptation in managerial strategy. It points to the fact that humans fail to cooperate in an organisation not because of their human nature but because of management's failure in realising the true potential of their human resources. Theory Y attempts to create organisational conditions that facilitate members to achieve their own goals best by directing their efforts towards the success of their enterprise.[124]

The basic features of the two theories are schematically described in Mind Map 3.9.

Variables	Theory X	Theory Y
Basic assumption of management	1. The average employee has an inherent dislike for work and will avoid it.	1. Average employee treats work as natural as play or rest.
	2. Employees must be corrected, controlled, directed, and threatened with punishment to get them to do organisation work.	2. Employee exercises self-direction and self-control while fulfilling organisational objectives.
	3. Employee prefers to be directed, wishes to avoid responsibility, has	3. Employee commitment towards objectives is created due to positive

Variables	Theory X	Theory Y
	relatively less ambition and wants security above all.	rewards.
		4. Average employee seeks responsibility.
		5. Average employee has a high degree of creativity, imagination, and ingenuity in finding solutions to organisational problems.
		6. The intellectual potentialities of the average employee are not fully utilised.
Planning	The superior sets objectives for subordinates.	Superiors and subordinates set objectives jointly.
	There is little participation by subordinates in setting objectives and developing plans. Only a few alternatives are explored.	There is participation by subordinates in setting objectives and developing plans. Many alternatives are explored.
	There is a low commitment to objectives and plans.	There is a high commitment to objecttives and plans.
Leadership	Leadership is autocratic.	Leadership is participative and team-based.
	People follow orders, but there is hidden resistance and mistrust.	People seek responsibility, feel accountable, and are committed to plans.
	Communication is one way, top-down, with little feedback. The flow of information is limited.	Communication is two way with a great deal of feedback. Necessary information flows freely.
Controlling and appraisal	Control is external and rigid.	There is self and internal control.
	Superior acts as a judge.	Superior acts as a coach.
	There is low trust in appraisals.	There is high trust in appraisals.
Focus	Focus is on the past with emphasis on fault finding.	People learn from the past but focus on the future.

Mind Map 3.9: Basic features of Theory X and Theory Y[125]

While describing the two theories, McGregor says that theory X maintains the status quo in an organisation whereas theory Y creates conditions for organisational innovation.[123]

3.14.1.2 McGregor and Scanlon Plan

Theory Y of McGregor is considered consistent with the Scanlon plan. This is because of their association of McGregor with Frederick Lesiaur, who was carrying out research at the union-management cooperation at MIT Sloan. The origin of the Scanlon plan was labour management cooperation, in which both management and employees sit down and try to solve their problems together. The plan had been trusted as a key element and had the workers' suggestions at its heart. In his research on workers' collective bargaining in steel firms, Scanlon formed joint union management committees; these committees were flooded with workers' suggestions. Employees were made to fill out suggestion forms. These suggestions were discussed at a work team level. If a suggestion was up-voted by the work team, it was taken up for implementation. If a suggestion was rejected for any reason, it was taken up by the screening committee for consideration.

In this scheme, Scanlon found that workers have other greater motivations than money. It originated the *gainsharing system,* in which the employee who contributes to improving the functioning of the company finds a share in its gain. The Scanlon plan required the whole-hearted support of the union along with its members. It also required management willing to open its books and innermost production secrets to union members. The principles of the Scanlon plan (explained by Carol Frost), described in short as *EPIC,* are explained in the following.

1. Identity: The Scanlon companies shared their financial, production, and other relevant information with their workers. The workers were introduced to the reality of the company so that they can improve it. The proponents considered reality as the biggest motivator for human beings. When workers understand reality, they will be motivated either to save their jobs or to make their companies better.
2. Participation: Participation is an opportunity the management provides to the employees to influence decisions in their area of competence. In the Scanlon plan, people were not involved only for the sake of involvement. There was an understanding that knowledgeable people would be able to influence decisions, and the person closest to the work knew the most about that area.
3. Equity: The principle of equity emphasised balancing the needs of the key stakeholders: employees, customers, and investors. If the management does not focus on key stakeholders, they try to maximise their area to the detriment of the organisation.
4. Competency: In the Scanlon plan, competency meant continuous improvement personally, professionally, and organisationally.

As described above, the Scanlon plan was a philosophy of management based on theoretical assumptions entirely consistent with Theory Y.[5]

3.14.1.3 Application of Theory Y in Line-Staff Relationship

The assumptions of Theory Y are relevant to the line-staff relationship, which often results in conflict, friction, and lower commitment. As Theory Y emphasises teamwork at all levels of the organisation, it helps in improving line-staff collaboration and in reaching the best decisions in an organisation.

3.14.1.4 Rational Emotive Manager

McGregor said that while a human is a rational being, he/she could realise his/her grandeur only by coming to terms with his/her emotional and human side. The emotional reactions of a manager interfere with his/her perception of organisational reality. In the book *The Professional Manager*, McGregor talks about how managers can manage their emotions while rationally understanding the reality of their organisation. He said that the assumptions of Theory Y are useful in doing this.

3.14.1.5 Working Through Differences

In an organisation, there are often conflicts and differences among employees. The task of the manager is to manage these differences in a manner that the objectives of the organisation do not suffer. However, differences do create some tensions in the organisation. McGregor has suggested a threefold strategy to tackle these tensions:

1. Divide and rule
2. Suppress the differences
3. Work through differences

The first two strategies are based on Theory X and have failed for a long. The third strategy is based on Theory Y. It suggests that a manager should steer through the differences so that the interplay between managers may yield innovation, commitment to decisions, and strengthening of relationships within the group.

3.14.1.6 Criticism of McGregor's Work

The research work of McGregor is criticised on the following grounds.

1. Rejected traditional management concepts: McGregor rejected traditional management concepts such as control and direction. These concepts cannot be ignored and are very useful for understanding employee motivation in all types of organisations.
2. Tough ideas: The ideas of McGregor have been criticised as being very tough for the weaker and self-starter employees because they need superior guidance in their daily activities and are dependent on superiors for moving ahead.[5]

3.14.2 Chris Argyris

Chris Argyris was one of the first theorists who advanced the concept of organisational development and the development of individuals in it. He considered that organisational development was necessary, as there was a basic incongruence between the requirements of a formal organisation and the needs of a mature personality. He felt that there were various forms of control in formal organisations that made the employees dependent on their superiors; these forms of control were perceived as instruments of punishment.

3.14.2.1 Adaptive Mechanisms in a Formal Organisation

Argyris said that individuals in a formal organisation witness a structure where there is task specialisation, unity of direction, a chain of command, and a span of control. Due to these formal organisational principles, individuals feel dependent, subordinate, and passive toward their managers. A feeling of failure, frustration, short-term perspective and conflict is created in them. Due to such conflict, individuals resort to one of the adaptive mechanisms as follows:

1. They try to leave the organisation.
2. They make efforts to climb up the organisational ladder.
3. They try to use certain defence mechanisms.
4. They become apathetic and disinterested in their organisation.

Apart from these listed mechanisms, individuals also seek membership in groups in order to dissipate their organisational frustration.

3.14.2.2 Managerial Assumptions in Formal Organisations

Like McGregor, Argyris also said that the assumptions, about the employees, held by the managers determine the character of an organisation. In formal organisations, the management assumes that the employees are lazy, uninterested, apathetic, money-crazy, commit errors, and cause wastage. Managers feel that employees are disloyal to the organisation. Thus, any change in organisational improvement is directed toward improving employees' attitudes and making them interested in their work.[126] This kind of leadership is autocratic and directive in nature.

3.14.2.3 Organisational Development

As the formal organisation makes the employees passive and disinterested, Argyris has suggested a fourfold strategy to bring in positive organisational change. It includes, first providing an environment for the development of the individual towards personal or psychological maturity. Second, it includes improving the interpersonal competence of the employees. Third, it focuses on changing the organisational structure. And, fourth, it involves techniques for programmed learning aimed at individual change. These strategies are described in the following sections.

3.14.2.3.1 Maturity-Immaturity Theory

In his maturity-immaturity theory, Argyris observed incongruence between the needs of mature employees and the structure of formal organisations. The maturity-immaturity continuum describes seven basic metrics on which people develop as they grow as employees. This continuum is described in Mind Map 3.10.

Immature Employees	Mature Employees
1. **Infant passivity:** Employees are disinterested and passive when organisations restrict them to passively perform a narrow scope of work.	1. **Adult activity:** Employees are adults, interested in their work, and seek active work on their own.
2. **Dependent:** Organisations do not allow employees to exercise their independence through participation in decision-making. This makes them dependent on superiors and affects their self-esteem and productivity.	2. **Independent:** Intrinsically, employees seek to work independently and participate in the decision-making process. They also seek to accept responsibility for their work.
3. **Limited behaviour:** As organisations do not allow employees to play a variety of roles, their motivation decreases.	3. **Different behaviours:** Employees seek to play their roles in different types of work and thus intrinsically show varied behaviours.
4. **Erratic, shallow interests:** When employees do not participate in larger organisational decisions, they develop shallow interests, feel isolated, and are disenfranchised.	4. **Stable, Deeper Interests:** Mature employees have long and stable interests in their work.
5. **Short-term perspective:** As organisations do not allow employee participation in long-term strategies, they develop short-term perspectives. Their morale and productivity decline due to this.	5. **Long-term perspective:** Matured employees seek to pursue long-term perspectives. This keeps their motivation and efficiency high.
6. **Subordinate social position:** Organisations treat employees as children (or as subordinates) and do not trust them.	6. **Equal/super-ordinate social position:** Employees seek an equal position with the management and want to be treated as mature adults.

Immature Employees	Mature Employees
7. **Lack of self-awareness:** Formal organisations think that their employees are not aware of their potential.	7. **Self-awareness:** Mature employees are very well aware of their potential and have the quality of self-control.

Mind Map 3.10: Immaturity-maturity continuum

In this theory, Argyris describes that employees are mature people capable of accepting responsibility, pursuing long-term interests, and are concerned about the fulfilment of higher-order needs.[5] Thus, they should be treated as mature adults for better functioning of an organisation. He suggested that each individual has a set of needs. Related to their needs are their abilities, interests, and skills. *Abilities* are the tools with which an individual expresses and fulfils their needs. These are the communication system for the needs to express themselves.[127] The *interests* of individuals are basically a product of the fusion of their several needs. Thus, interests are indicators of the kinds of needs people have. For example, a person who has a need to be independent and to know more has an interest in being a good scientist. [127] *Skills* are those qualities that are inherent or learned by an individual. For example, finger dexterity and other manipulative skills are inherited, while skills such as leadership can be developed.[127]

3.14.2.3.2 Developing Interpersonal Competence

Interpersonal competence is defined by Argyris as the ability to deal effectively with other human beings. He listed three necessities for the development of interpersonal competence:

1. *Self-acceptance:* A person shall accept their skills and qualities and value themselves in a positive fashion.
2. *Confirmation:* A person shall verify that the image they have of themselves is the same as others perceive of them.
3. *Essentiality:* A person shall be capable of utilising his/her central abilities and expressing his/her central needs in an organisation.

On the basis of these necessities, Argyris postulated certain kinds of behaviour that are evidence of interpersonally competent behaviour. Four of them are described here.

1. Owning up to or accepting responsibility for one's ideas and feelings.
2. Being open to the ideas and feelings of others and those from within one's self.
3. Experimenting with new ideas and feelings.
4. Helping others to own up, be open to, and to experimenting with their ideas and feelings.[5,128]

3.14.2.3.3 Modifying Organisational Structure

Argyris suggested that the traditional form of organisations was more effective for routine and non-innovative activities. However, newer forms of matrix organisations are required for innovative activities requiring employees' commitment. He postulated four forms of organisational structure based on the requirement of their tasks and the nature of decision-making. These are described by Argyris as System 1 (pyramidal structure), System 2 (modified formal organisational structure), System 3 (power according to functional contribution), and System 4 (matrix organisation). A brief description of these is given in Mind Map 3.11.

	Task requirement	Nature of decision-making
Pyramidal structure	Routine, periodical work, or in emergency operations with time constraints.	Decisions are made once and are supposed to be widely agreeable. Individuals do not seek to participate in larger decisions.
Modified formal organisational structure	Here, tasks are routine and require little innovation for growth.	Decision-making allows subordinates' participation, with the option for the superior to pitch in. This happens as the subordinate is a member of the superior's decisional unit.
Power according to functional contribution	Here, tasks are those involving teamwork, group incentives, new product development, inter-departmental activities, and long-range planning.	Depending on an employee's potential contribution to the problem, the decision process allows each employee an opportunity to provide information and control decisions.
Matrix organisation	Here the task to be performed is novel and innovative. For example, technical and research work in universities and industries.	The decision process provides equal power and opportunity to each employee. Employees have ample opportunities to influence the decision in core activities. It brings in individual self-discipline. Members work as a cohesive decisional team.

Mind Map 3.11: Argyris: Different organisational structures

Role of a Leader in Matrix Organisations

While explaining the different organisational structures, Argyris has emphasised on the role of leaders in matrix organisations. The style of leadership needs to be consistent with the real administrative situation. Leaders need to focus on the following tasks:

1. They need to control 'productive tension', which emerges from new challenges, taking risks, and expanding one's competencies.[5]
2. They need to help their employees to understand the internal environment, enlarge their aspirations, and face interpersonal reality.
3. They need to manage intergroup conflicts on constructive issues.

In totality, the leaders have to work towards improving system effectiveness.

Job Enlargement in Matrix Organisations

By job enlargement, Argyris meant stretching the individual's intellectual and interpersonal capabilities by providing him/her more control within his/her sphere of activities and providing him/her more opportunities to participate in decisions relating to his/her area of work. This also means delegating more higher-level work to the lower level. The matrix form of organisation allows such kind of job enlargement.

3.14.2.3.4 Programmed Learning Techniques

Argyris suggested various techniques of programmed learning aimed at an individual as well as organisational change. Some of them are discussed here.

Sensitivity Training (or T Group Training)

Sensitivity training is aimed at improving individual competence. It consists of a laboratory programme in which individuals are allowed to expose their behaviour, give and receive feedback, experiment with new behaviour, and develop awareness and acceptance of the self and sensitivity to the personalities of others.[5] It leads to the following benefits:

1. Group functioning: Individuals are able to learn the nature of effective group functioning.
2. Diminished hierarchy: It helps in forgetting hierarchical identities and developing distributive leadership and consensual decision-making.
3. Delegation of responsibility: Sensitivity training also helps in more delegation of responsibility to the lower level.
4. Information flow: It helps in the free flow of information from lower ranks, which further helps in making efficient decisions.
5. Interpersonal competence: As individuals realise their real behaviour as well as the behaviour of their colleagues, it helps in improving their interpersonal competence.
6. Improvement in organisational culture: It helps in improving the organisational culture or environment by making it free, friendly, cordial, and constructive.

Organisational Learning

The traditional training techniques focused on the learning of individuals while maintaining the structure and processes of the organisation. However, Argyris pointed out that organisations also learn from the experiences and actions of individuals.[129] This happens when individuals act as change agents by detecting and correcting errors in organisational theory-in-use and embedding the results in organisational structure and processes. It takes the form of single-loop and double-loop learning.

Single-loop Learning

In this approach, learning involves the detection and correction of errors. Whenever something goes wrong, an initial part of the call for many people is to look for another strategy that will address and work within the governing variables of the organisation. In other words, the given or chosen goals, values, plans, and rules are operationalised rather than questioned. This is single-loop learning.

Double-loop Learning

In this method of learning, the governing variables of the organisation are themselves questioned and subject to critical scrutiny. It leads to modification in governing variables and a shift in the way strategies and consequences are framed in organisations. It also leads to change in the organisation's underlying norms, policies, and objectivities in order to correct any errors in the organisation.

3.14.2.4 Criticism of Chris Argyris

The research work of Chris Argyris is criticised on the following points.

1. Benign view of man: Critics say that Argyris has a very benign view of man in relation to the organisation. His consideration that employees are mature individuals and organisations must treat them as individuals are not always valid.

2. Utopian concept: His idea of employee motivation and self-actualisation are considered utopian by some critics.
3. Antipathy towards authority: His ideas are considered as strictly against traditional authority. His concept that organisational structure is the biggest devil is unpalatable.
4. Non-methodological study: Critics say that Argyris conducted his studies without any sound methodological grounds. For instance, there is little empirical support in favour of the statement that people in organisations are singularly opposed to authority.

3.14.3 Rensis Likert

Rensis Likert conducted research on the management practices of American government organisations (e.g., railways, hospitals, and schools), business firms (e.g., industrial and commercial firms), and voluntary organisations. His research was based on the working of all sorts of employees from unskilled labour to top scientists. His major works include *New Patterns of Management*, *The Human Organisation*, and *New Ways of Managing Conflict*.

3.14.3.1 Styles of Supervision

Rensis Likert has classified the styles of supervision into job-centred supervision and employee-centred supervision. The characteristics of both styles are described in Mind Map 3.12.

Supervisory Style	Job-centred	Employee-centred
Primary Concern	The primary concern of leaders is to get the task done and maintenance of prescribed standards.	The primary concern of leaders is dealing with the human aspect of their subordinates and building effective teams for high task performance.
Pressure	Superiors exert pressure to get the work done.	Superiors exert little pressure and provide a free environment.
Confidence	They have little confidence in their subordinates	They earn and get the confidence and trust of their subordinates.
Supervision	They exercise close and detailed supervision.	They exercise general rather than detailed supervision and allow subordinates to schedule their own pace of work.
Freedom	They allow little freedom to subordinates.	They increase the achievement motivation of the subordinates and encourage them to accept high performance goals through the group decisional process.
Correction Strategy	They are punitive and critical when mistakes occur.	They help subordinates when mistakes occur.

Mind Map 3.12: Characteristics of job-centred and employee-centred supervisory styles[5,131]

Time Factor in Supervisory Styles

Likert has considered the time factor while analysing the two management styles. He said that the heavy pressure exerted in the job-centred management style may produce good results for a short time period, but the good performance will go down due to the rising resentment of subordinates. On the other hand, giving freedom to employees for positively achieving organisational goals through effective team building may take a little while before producing desirable results. Referring to the two styles of supervision, Likert said that the leadership style needs to be specific to a particular situation. Moreover, who will assume leadership depends on the nature of the situation. Likert sounds similar to Mary Parker Follett while suggesting such an idea of situational leadership.[132]

3.14.3.2 Interaction-Influence System

Likert proposed the *principle of supportive relationships*, which states that a supervisor should be perceived by a subordinate as a person who is primarily interested in building and maintaining the subordinate's sense of personal worth.[133] If a superior is perceived as supportive by the subordinate, the superior's behaviour will have a better effect on the subordinate's performance. To achieve such a supportive relationship between the superior and the subordinate, Likert postulated the concept of an interaction-influence system, which helps in maximising the skills, resources, and motivation of individuals at different levels of the organisation. Organisations possessing this system have the following characteristics.[132]

1. Each member finds his/her personal values, needs, and goals reflected in those of the workgroups and organisation as a whole.
2. Every member is identified with the objectives of the organisation and the goals of his/her workgroup. The member sees the accomplishment of these goals as the best way to meet his/her own needs and personal goals.
3. Pressures for high-performance goals, efficient methods, and skill development come from the members themselves.
4. There is accurate information flow, which helps in providing rational bases for individual and group decisions.
5. Every member of the organisation is able to exert his/her influence on the decisions and actions of the organisation. This influence is proportionate to the significance of his/her ideas and contributions.
6. There is a cooperative motivation, communication, and decision process, which enables the members to influence the decisions in the organisation.

These characteristics are not shown in the traditional form of hierarchical organisations. These organisations preclude the development of well-knit work groups and the cross-fertilisation of ideas, skills, and resources for effective problem-solving and decision-making in an organisation.

3.14.3.3 Linking-pin Model

Likert suggested a linking-pin organisational structure, which can help in removing the deficiencies of traditional organisations. In this model, each individual plays two roles: first, he/she plays the role of a member of a higher-level group; second, he/she plays the role of a leader of a lower-level group. This model enables group functions to become far more important than individual roles. This model has a bottom-up model of organisational structure rather than the top-down model of traditional organisations (see Fig. 3.7).

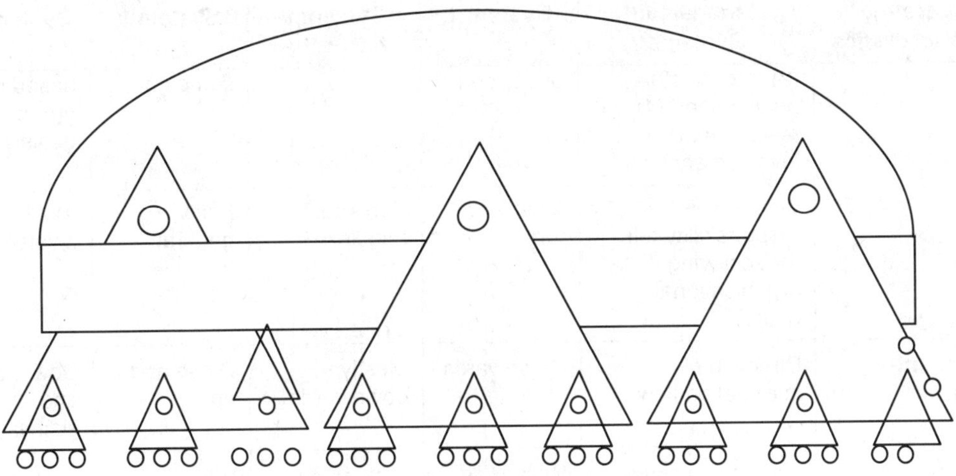

Fig 3.7: Likert's Linking Pin Model

3.14.3.4 Management Systems

Like Argyris, Likert also proposed different systems of management that lie along a continuum. These systems have distinct characteristics. However, they are blended into one another with many intermediate patterns along the continuum. The four managerial systems proposed by him are based on two important characteristics: the first is the type of authority or control an organisation exercises over its members and the second are the operating characteristics (leadership, motivation, communication, interaction, influence, decision-making, goal-setting, and so on) of the organisation used to control and coordinate the activities of the people in the system and the kind of attitudinal responses evoked from them.

Mind Map 3.13 plots the different management systems on the basis of the two characteristics mentioned above. The four management systems are termed *exploitative authoritative system, benevolent authoritative system, consultative system*, and *participative system*. Among these, the fourth system is considered the most productive and ideal.

Operating Characteristics	Management Systems	System 1	System 2	System 3	System 4
Leadership	Confidence shown on subordinates	None	Condes-cending	Substantial	Complete
	Freedom to talk to subordinates	Not at all	Not much	High freedom	Fully free
	Seeking of ideas from subordinates	Seldom	Sometimes	Usually	Always
Motivation	Is predominant use made of (1) fear,	1, 2, 3 most often, and 4	4 mostly and 3 sometimes.	4 mostly and 3, 5	4, 5 mostly

Operating Characteristics	Management Systems	System 1	System 2	System 3	System 4
	(2) threats, (3) punishment, (4) rewards and involvement?	occasionally .		sometimes.	based on group set goals.
	Where is responsibility felt for achieving organisational goals?	Mostly at top	Top and middle	Fairly general	At all levels
Communi-cation	Direction of information flow	Downwards	Mostly downwards	Down and up	Down, up, and sideways
	How is downward commu-nication accepted?	With suspicion	With some suspicion	With caution	With open mind
	How accurate is upward communication?	Often wrong	Censored for boss	Limited accuracy	Accurate
	How well do superiors know the problems faced by the subordinates?	Know little	Some knowledge	Quite well	Very well
Interaction	Character of interaction	Little, always with fear and trust	Little, always with some condescend-ing	Moderate, with a fair amount of confidence and trust	Extensive, high degree of confidence and trust
	How much cooperative teamwork is present?	None	Relatively little	Moderate amount	Very substantial amount throughout organi-sation
Decision-making	At what levels are decisions formally made?	Mostly at top	Policy at the top with some delegation	Broad policy at the top with more delegation	Througho ut but well-integrated

Operating Characteristics	Management Systems	System 1	System 2	System 3	System 4
	What is the origin of technical and professional knowledge used in decision-making?	Top Manage-ment	Upper and middle	To a certain extent, throughout	To a great extent, throughout
	Are subordinates involved in decisions related to their work?	Not at all	Occasionally consulted	Generally consulted	Fully involved
	How does the decision-making process contribute to motivation?	Nothing, often weakens it	Relatively little	Some contribution	Substantial
Setting Goals	How are organisational goals established?	Orders issued	Orders issued with some common involvement	Orders issued after discussion	Group action, except during crisis
	How much covert resistance to goals is present?	Strong resistance	Moderate resistance	Some resistance at times	Little or none
Feedback Control	How concentrated are review and control functions?	Highly at top	Relatively high at top	Moderate delegation to lower levels	Quite widely shared
	Is there an informal organisation resisting the formal one?	Yes	Usually	Sometimes	No; same goals as formal
	What is the control data used for?	Policing and punishment	Reward and punishment	Reward, some self-guidance	Self-guidance, problem solving

Mind Map 3.13: Operating characteristics of different management systems[135]

3.14.3.5 Science-based Management

Rensis Likert has suggested a scheme of causal, intervening, and end-result variables that affect organisational climate and performance. The *causal variables* are management practices such as work standards, budget imposition, performance goals, group decision-making, supportive relationships, etc. The *intervening variables* are the prevailing attitudes and motives in the organisation. These variables are affected by the causal variables including favourable attitude towards superiors, high confidence and trust, good communication, and peer group loyalty. The *end-result variables* are the final results of an organisation; they include variables such as low absence, high productivity, and high earning.

Likert has established a relationship between these three kinds of variables—causal, intervening, and end-result—and has tried to show how System 4 can produce better end-result variables than the other three systems.

3.14.3.6 Organisational Improvement Technique

As discussed, Likert was convinced that System 4 is the best management system for realising high-performance organisational goals. Thus, he provided an improved technique for moving an organisation from System 1 to System 4. He suggested an overall strategy for changing the management system, constituting coordinated efforts such as team building, job enrichment, sensitivity training, participative decision-making, and management by objectives. The organisational improvement cycle proposed by Likert consisted of the following steps:[136]

1. First, an ideal model (System 4) needs to be established.
2. Second, the organisation's score on the key dimensions of the ideal model needs to be measured.
3. Third, the organisational strengths and weaknesses need to be diagnosed after analysing its score on the key dimensions of the ideal model.
4. Fourth, an action plan needs to be developed to build on the above strengths and correct the weaknesses concerning the structure, leader and subordinate behaviour, organisational climate, and so on.
5. Fifth, the above-mentioned action plan needs to be implemented.

While implementing this organisational improvement cycle, Likert has suggested the following guidelines and cautions:

1. Action efforts need to be focused on causal variables and not directly on intervening variables. The intervening variables will improve automatically if efforts are made toward improving the causal variables.
2. A shift from System 1 to System 4 must be gradual and not direct.
3. There should be involvement, in the planning and implementation process, of all the persons who will be affected by the change in the system.
4. There should be the use of objective and impersonal evidence in the action planning process.
5. The improvement programme must have active involvement of the powerful and the influential people of the organisation.
6. The action planning must be conducted in a supportive and helpful atmosphere.[136]

3.14.3.7 Criticism of Rensis Likert's Work

The research work of Likert is criticised on the following grounds:

Farfetched Theory: The hope of Likert that organisations will move from System 1 to System 4 is too farfetched to be considered realistic.

Slows Down Decision-making: The linking-pin model is accused of slowing down the decision-making process. Critics regard it as nothing more than drawing triangles around traditional hierarchical structures.[137]

Improvement Procedure not Clear: Likert's theory has emphasised that management System 4 is better than System 1, but it has not cleared the procedure of transformation from management System 1 to System 4. It has also not answered the question of why managers revert back to System 1 or 2 in time of crisis.

Relationship with society and culture not established: Likert has considered System 4 as superior to Systems 1 and 2 without considering the cultural and sociological constraints in which they operate. During crisis management, System 1 is considered better than System 4. During a crisis, System 4 characteristics such as supportive relationships and group decision processes are not completely effective. Moreover, Likert has not considered the fact that hierarchical and authoritarian societies will give rise to System 1 organisations, and System 1 organisations will work better for such societies. Furthermore, Likert also has not guided on how System 4 can be realised in such authoritarian and conflict-prone societies.

3.15 Peter Drucker

Peter Drucker is a management thinker who took a humanistic approach to management and focused on the people of the organisation, as they are the ones who create the organisation. He is well-acknowledged for anticipating privatisation, decentralisation, the emergence of an information society with the necessity for life-long learning, and the role of knowledge workers. His work focuses on how organisations can bring out the best in people and how employees can find a sense of community and dignity in modern organisations. His work is valued by politicians and managers worldwide. He is considered a bridge between academics and business to the benefit of both. His theory of management focuses on various novel ideas. Some of his ideas are described in the following sections.

3.15.1 General Nature of Management

Peter Drucker considered that management is a generic term and not limited to a profession such as business or government. It pertains to every human effort that brings together in one organisation people of diverse knowledge and skills. It is the specific and distinguishing feature of any or all, organisations concerned with management, and its study began with the emergence of large organisations—business, governmental, civil services, army, etc.[138]

According to Drucker, the basic objective of management is to make an organisation innovative. He has described management both as a discipline and as a profession. Drucker described three basic functions of management as mentioned below:

1. To fulfil the specific purpose and mission of the organisation.
2. To make the work productive and achievement-oriented.
3. To manage the social impact and social responsibilities of the organisation.[139]

Accordingly, Drucker emphasised that a manager has to act like an administrator where he/she has to improve upon what already exists. He/she has to act as an entrepreneur to bring drastic results to an organisation. Drucker said that different organisations have different missions, strategies, and structures but the same underlying management principles. These principles include hierarchy, unity of command, transparency, authority commensurate with responsibility, and so on. Drucker pointed out that these management principles do not tell us what to do, but these principles only tell us what not to do.[5] They do not tell us what will work, but only tell us what will not work. Giving the example of an architect, Drucker said that the principles of architecture do not tell what kind of a building is to be built, but they tell what kinds of restraints are to be made while constructing and designing a building.[5]

This point of Drucker is made clear when one looks at the generic role of management in different organisational settings. The principle of unity of command cautions that there should not be more than one boss. Similarly, the principle of transparency cautions that no manager should be allowed to take arbitrary decisions without the knowledge of the other members. However, these principles do not guide the goals and procedures of the organisation. Thus, they do not tell what to do, but what not to do. This idea of Drucker, of principles playing only the role of restraining, provides much autonomy to managers in achieving organisational goals.

3.15.2 Restructuring and Reinvention of Governmental Organisational Structure

Drucker has emphasised the three basic characteristics of an effective organisation structure as follows:

1. The structure should be based on achieving high performance.
2. The structure should contain the least number of managerial levels.
3. The structure must make possible the training and testing of tomorrow's managers.

However, he said that the governmental organisational structure is characterised by the non-performance of goals. He identified six reasons for this non-performance in government agencies.[140]

1. Governmental agencies have lofty, vague, and non-operational objectives such as 'best medical care for the sick'. They are neither measurable nor achievable.
2. Public agencies do not prioritise their goals and attempt to do several things at the same time.
3. These agencies suffer from the critical problem of overstaffing.
4. The structure of public agencies favours the status quo and disfavours experimentation and innovation.
5. Public agencies do not have a system of learning from experience.
6. Public agencies remain unable to give up programmes, policies, and institutions after they become unnecessary.

While keeping these points in mind, Drucker suggested a radical change in the structure of government agencies and the way they are maintained. He suggested the following methods for it.

Continuous Improvement: Drucker suggested that the concept of continuous improvement should be built into the functioning of government agencies. As per him, improvement should be a continuous and dedicated activity and not a 'patch-and-spot-weld' activity.

Benchmarking: Drucker suggested that the good performance of public agencies should be benchmarked and made a standard. Rest all agencies should be compared to it for their improvement.[141]

Measurable Objectives: Drucker also emphasised that public agencies should clearly define the objectives of performance, quality, and costs.

Negative Incentives: Public agencies should work on providing negative incentives such as budgetary cuts for non-performance. The officials performing below the benchmarked standard need to be punished in terms of low salaries, demotion, and early retirement.

Rethinking of Agencies: Public agencies need to identify activities that are productive and must strengthen and promote them. They should review their policies, programmes, and activities, and 'rethink' their mission. This rethinks and review should be a periodic activity.

3.15.3 Federalism in Organisation

Drucker advocated the concept of federalism in government organisations. It refers to centralised control in a decentralised structure. This system provides a close linkage between decisions adopted by the top management on the one hand and autonomous units on the other. It is like a relationship between the federal government and the state government, in which local organisations participate in the decisions that set a limit to their own authority. It has the following advantages:[139]

1. It keeps the top management free to devote their time to important functions.
2. It defines the functions and responsibilities of the operating people.
3. It creates a yardstick to measure their success and effectiveness in operating jobs.
4. It helps to resolve the problem of continuity by giving managers of various units education in top management problems and functions while they are in an operating position.

3.15.4 Management by Objectives

Management by objectives (MBO) is regarded as one of the most important contributions of Drucker to the field of management. It refers to the collective set of organisational goals, targets, and measurements. It helps in directing the vision and efforts of all managers towards a common goal. It ensures that individual managers understand the results demanded of them. It also ensures that the superior understands what to expect from his/her subordinates. It motivates each manager to give their maximum effort in the right direction. It makes the managers a means to achieve the ends of the business performance, rather than being ends in themselves.[142]

MBO requires each employee, from senior executives to production foremen, to be clear about their objectives, the performance expected from their units, and the contributions expected from their units towards the functioning of other related units. MBO emphasises teamwork and team-based results. Each manager is required to list down the goals of their unit and measure its performance against those goals. As a result, MBO helps in substituting management by domination with management by self-control.[142]

MBO has various advantages. It helps the manager to control their own performance. The self-control in MBO helps in building greater motivation, the desire to do the best, higher performance goals, and a broader vision. On the one hand, it provides strength, direction, and responsibility to the individual; on the other hand, it provides a common vision and direction and helps in establishing teamwork and harmonising the goals of the individual with the organisational goals.[142]

3.15.5 Organisational Changes

Drucker said that rapid changes are occurring in society, and human beings should face these changes as a challenge and use them in building a better society. For this, we need to develop dynamic organisations that are able to absorb societal changes much faster than static ones.

3.15.6 Knowledge Workers

Drucker used the word 'knowledge workers' for the modern age professional managers and specialists whose skills are based on their ability to acquire and use their knowledge. Drucker predicted the information age and the importance of knowledge workers in it. This new worker is based on knowledge and not on physical labour or management. Organisations succeed because of their ability to acquire and use this knowledge.

While describing knowledge-based organisations, Drucker said that knowledge when applied to already known tasks leads to 'productivity' and when applied to new tasks leads to 'innovation'.[143] He defined various characteristics of knowledge workers such as their level of education and training. He described six factors that affect the knowledge workers' productivity, namely, the tasks to be performed, the responsibility and autonomy given to them, continuous innovation in organisations, continuous learning, and the quality of organisational output. Continuous learning is required to keep knowledge workers creative and their knowledge up to date.

Information

Drucker defined information as data endowed with relevance and purpose. The conversion of data into information requires knowledge.

SUMMARY

This chapter dealt with the administrative thoughts of various renowned scholars of public administration and management. Moving forward, the Chapter 4, will deal with the important concept of human behaviour in organisations.

Practice Questions

1. Woodrow Wilson is considered as the father of public administration. Critically analyse this statement.
2. Growth of administrative science is easier in monarchical states than in a democracy. Critically analyse this statement.
3. Woodrow Wilson is considered as the initiator of comparative public administration. Critically analyse this statement.
4. What is the philosophy of management according to Taylor?
5. Explain the work of Gantt and Gilbreth on scientific management.
6. What is the contribution of the scientific management movement to public administration?
7. Compare and contrast the administrative thoughts of Fayol and Taylor.
8. "Lack of design is illogical, cruel, wasteful and inefficient." (Urwick) Explain.
9. Timing is essential for any organisation as it is not a machine but an organism. Explain.
10. The ideal-type constructs helped Weber in constructing 'ideographic' as well as 'nomothetic' analysis. Explain.
11. What do you mean by mixed types of authority systems?
12. Differentiate between bureaucratic rationality and commitment.
13. Bureaucracy is a power instrument of the first order for one who controls the bureaucratic apparatus. Explain.
14. "Advancement of rules led to ritualistic rather than rationalistic character of organisation." (Merton) Explain.
15. "Bureaucracy is an emergent process." (Gouldner) Explain.
16. What are the primary tensions and secondary tensions in bureaucratic organisations? (Gouldner)
17. What do you mean by adaptive innovation in bureaucracies? (Peter Blau)
18. "Bureaucracy is a moral maze." (Robert Jackall) Explain.
19. "All polishing is done by friction." Elucidate in terms of Follet's theory on constructive conflict.
20. " 'Power with' is better than 'power over' as it is a self-developing entity." (Follett) Explain.
21. Leadership is a situational concept. Explain
22. What were the ethical issues in Follett's writings?
23. What is the influence of LePlay and Durkheim on the human relations school?
24. "A factory system, like any social system, must be conceived as tending towards an equilibrium in which its different parts are functionally adjusted to each other." Explain with reference to the human relations school of management.
25. What is Kurt Lewin's force field theory?

26. What is Lewin's three-step change model?
27. "Small groups are like internal systems facing external systems." In light of this statement, explain the theory of George Homans on small groups.
28. What is the rule of distributive justice in the human relations theory of George Homans?
29. "Political system is that part of the society engaged in the authoritative allocation of values." (Easton) Explain.
30. "Contribution originates in the need of an individual." (Barnard) Explain in terms of the contribution-satisfaction equilibrium.
31. Organisations are recursive systems. Explain in the light of the viable systems model.
32. Explain the ideas of Talcott Parsons, Robert Merton, and Gabriel Almond on structural-functional theory of organisation.
33. "The rules of scientific analysis focus more on factual content than the value content, however, fact and value are inextricably joint." Explain in terms of Simon's decision-making theory.
34. What is the difference between procedural and substantive rationality? Explain Simon's administrative process of decision-making.
35. "The theoretical assumptions which the management holds about controlling its human resources determine the whole character of the enterprise." (McGregor) Explain.
36. Explain the techniques suggested by Argyris for organisational development.
37. Supportive relationships, linking-pin model, and management systems are the major contributions of Likert. Explain.
38. What are the major management ideas of Peter Drucker?

CHAPTER 4 Administrative Behaviour

Learning Objectives: After reading this chapter, you will learn the following:

- Meaning of administrative behaviour
- Process, techniques, and various models of decision-making
- Basic elements, channels, and various models of communication
- Various factors influencing the communication process and measures to improve it
- How to give effective feedback and its various models
- Meaning of motivation and its various types
- Need, process, and modern theories of motivation
- Meaning and characteristics of morale, factors affecting it, and its impact on productivity
- Meaning of leadership and its various explanations
- Various theories of leadership—with personality focus, behavioural focus, contingency theory, substitute theory, transactional theory, transformational theory, charismatic leadership, and entrepreneurial theory of leadership
- Difference between leaders and managers
- Role of gender in leadership
- Organisations and the role of leadership in them, the negative impacts of micromanagement, and the concept of servant leadership

4.1 Defining Administrative Behaviour

Administrative behaviour is one of the several approaches to understanding management. It focuses on the human processes within the organisation. According to the *Handbook of Organisation Behaviour*, it is defined as "an applied field of inquiry that encompasses the study of all aspects in and by formal organisations… It treats as units of analysis everything from individuals acting, feeling, and thinking in an organisation to groups, large subunits such as departments or divisions, the organisation as a whole and even populations of organisations and their relationships to larger social structures such as the State and the society."[1] It consists of various important organisational dimensions such as decision-making, communication, morale, motivation, leadership, and so on.

4.2 Process and Techniques of Decision-Making

In an organisation, a decision is defined as "the selection of a proposed course of action."[2] It is the process concerned with what decision-makers do in order to deal with uncertainty.[2] It is a critical aspect of group behaviour in an organisation, as the decision made by one person affects the decisions of others around him/her, as well as the functionality of several other group behaviour dynamics, such as creative processes, conflict, cohesion, group performance, and member satisfaction.

A good decision is seen as a challenge for managers as "decision-making is not an event; it is a process, one that unfolds over weeks, months, or even years; one that's fraught with power plays and politics and is replete with personal nuances and institutional history; one that's rife with discussion and debate; and one that requires support at all levels of the organisation when the time of execution comes."[3]

4.2.1 The Decision-Making Process

As already discussed in Chapter 3, a decision-making process consists of three steps, namely, intelligence activity, design activity, and choice activity. (Please refer to Chapter 3—Decision-making Theory by Herbert Simon.)

According to Herbert Mintzberg, the decision-making process takes place in three phases. He proposed the *three-phase model* as described in Fig. 4.1.

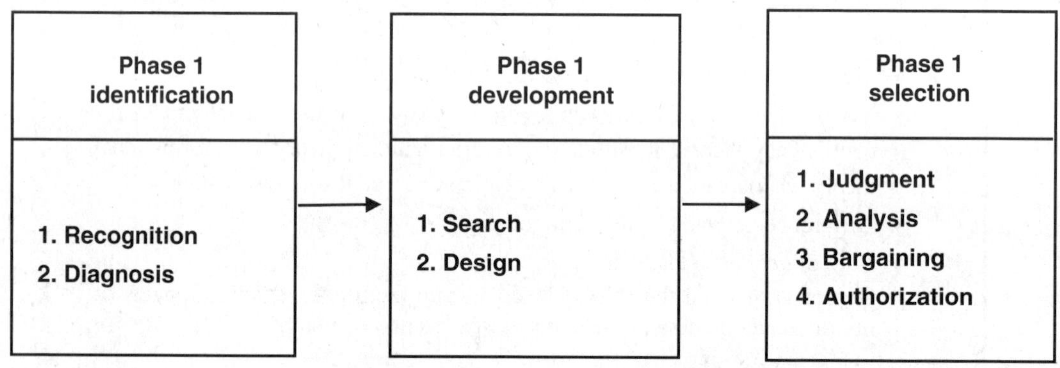

Fig. 4.1 : Mintzberg's Three Phase Decision Making Model

The three phases of the decision-making process described by Mintzberg are as follows:

1. **Identification phase:** In this phase, there is the recognition of a problem, or the opportunity to make a decision arises. A diagnosis of the problem is also made in this phase.
2. **Development phase:** In this phase, there is a search for existing standards procedures, ready-made solutions, or the design of a new tailor-made solution.

3. **Selection phase:** In this phase, a choice of an alternative is made. This selection is made in three ways. It is either made by the judgment of the decision-maker, on the basis of the experience/intuition of the decision-maker, after analysis of the alternatives on a logical and systematic basis or by discussion among various group members. The decision is authorised once it is formally accepted.

4.2.2 Different States of Nature for Decision-Making

While choosing among various alternatives, a decision-maker may not have complete knowledge about the various alternatives and their consequences. His/her status of knowledge is also known as the *state of nature*.

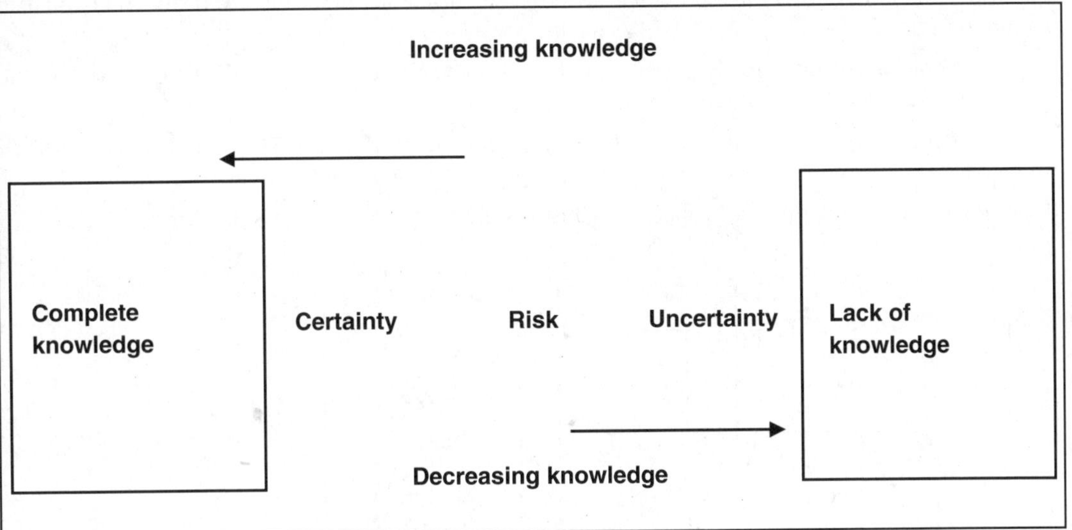

Fig. 4.2 : Decision Making Conditions Continuum[5]

The three states of nature are described in the following (see Fig. 4.2):

1. **Decision under certainty:** A condition of certainty is said to exist when the manager knows the precise outcome associated with each alternative or course of action. The knowledge of the alternatives and their consequences is perfect. A manager only needs to identify the consequences of the available alternatives and select the outcome with the highest benefit or payoff. For example, the purchase of government bonds or certificates of deposits may be called a decision under certainty.
2. **Decision under risk:** A condition of risk is said to exist when the manager knows about the different alternatives but their consequences are probabilistic and doubtful. The consequences of various alternatives are assessed on the basis of past experience, research, and other information. It is the most common state of nature.
3. **Decision under uncertainty:** A condition of uncertainty is said to exist when a single alternative may result in more than one outcome, but the relative probability of each outcome is unknown. Here the manager has no knowledge for estimating the likely consequences of the

various alternatives. There is no historical data to infer probabilities or to make comparative judgments among the alternatives. For example, the selection of a job among various alternatives incorporates a great deal of uncertainty (though not complete). In this case, a number of factors are to be weighed and evaluated, most often without comparable standards.

4.2.3 Models of Decision-Making

There are various models of decision-making that describe how decisions are made and should be made, in organisations. We will discuss several models in this section.

4.2.3.1 Rational Model of Decision-Making/Economic Man Model/Econologic Model

The rational model of decision-making has already been discussed in Chapter 3. It rests on two basic assumptions:

1. People are economically rational. It means they choose a course of action that has the greatest advantage among the various alternatives.
2. People attempt to 'maximise' outcomes in an orderly and sequential process. They search for the most advantageous alternative in a planned, orderly, and logical fashion.

The decision-making process proposed by this model is described in Fig. 4.3.

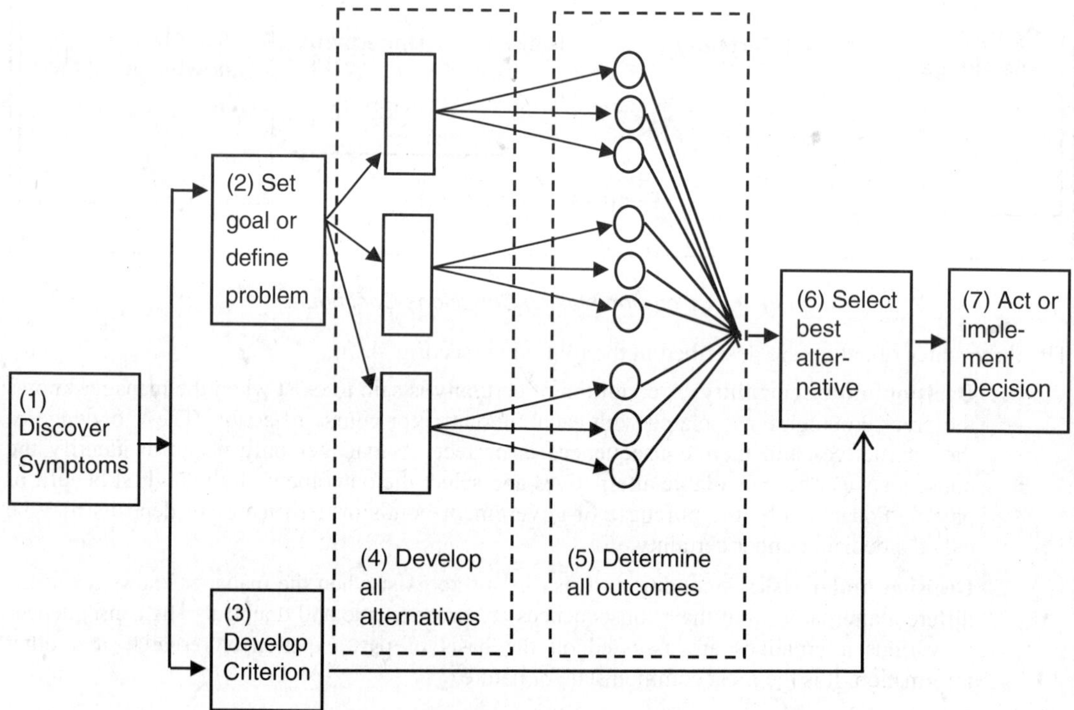

Fig. 4.3 : Economic Man Model of Decision Making[6]

The process of the economic man model consists of the following steps:

1. Discovering the difficulty and symptoms of the problem.
2. Defining the goals and problems.
3. Develop a criterion against which alternative solutions are evaluated.
4. Identifying all the alternative courses of action.
5. Determining the consequences of each alternative.
6. Choosing the best alternative after comparing the consequences of each alternative on the basis of the chosen decision criterion.
7. Finally, acting on or implementing the decision.

Drawback: However, this model does not describe how decisions are actually made as it has many impractical assumptions. It assumes that people have complete information, they can recall all the information, they can manipulate this information to derive expected values, and they can easily rank the alternatives consistently for identifying the preferred alternative.

4.2.3.2 Behavioural Decision-making/Bounded Rational Model of Decision-Making/ Administrative Man Model

There are a series of decision-making models falling under the category of *behavioural decision-making*. Behavioural decision-making describes how people actually take decisions and what they do in the process of decision-making. Many experts consider that people decide on important matters not rationally but by using rules of thumb, or simplified routines and shortcuts for solving problems.[7] There are various behavioural decision-making models such as the bounded rationality model, the political model of decision-making, the utilitarian model, and the garbage can model. Among these, the bounded rationality model has already been discussed in Chapter 3.

4.2.3.3 Gamesman Model/Implicit Favourite Model

This model of decision-making is used for making non-programmed or novel decisions. Developed by Soelberg, it describes that a decision-maker chooses an alternative that seems to be his/her favourite. First, a decision-maker identifies an *implicit favourite alternative*. Second, they continue their search for identifying the best alternative, known as the *confirmation alternative*. Third, they develop a decisional rule on the basis of the positive characteristics of the implicit favourite alternative (showing that the implicit favourite alternative is superior to the other confirmation alternatives). Finally, a decision is arrived at after considering this decisional rule. See Fig. 4.4.

Drawback: However, this model has the drawback that the implicit favourite alternative may be superior to the confirmation alternative only in one or two dimensions. Thus, it may not result in the best alternative.

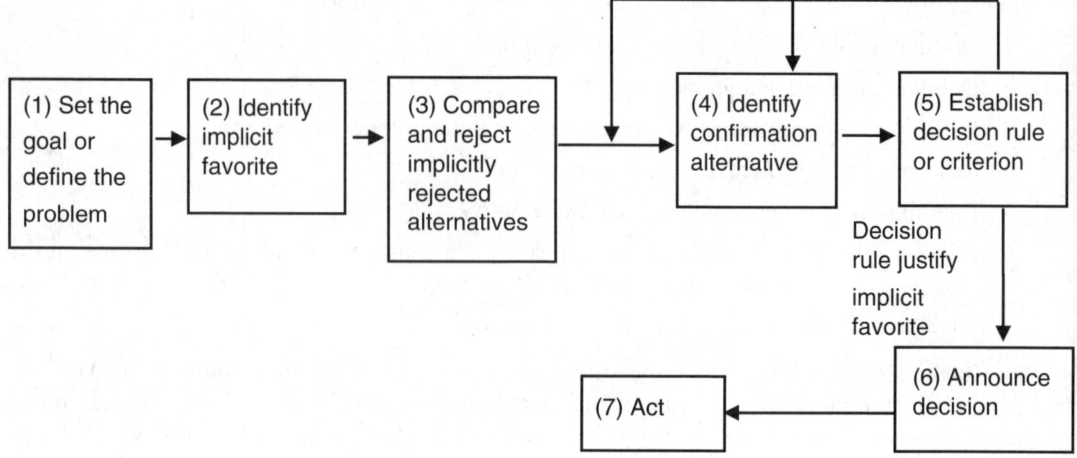

Fig. 4.4 : Implicit Favorite Model of Decision Making[6]

4.2.3.4 Political Decision-Making Model/Bargaining Model

The political decision-making model is adopted when the decision-maker has to seek the cooperation, coalition, and inclusion of the views and perspectives of divergent personalities. The model seeks to highlight that in a decision-making group, members come with their preconceived notions, bringing their own needs and perceptions into the decision-making process. Thus, the process involves bargaining and influencing powerful people in the group.[8] Full information is not available to the decision-maker as the members may try to manipulate information. Here, decision-makers are perceived as political players who may be concerned just with their limited sense of success and benefit; thus, they are described as displaying *rational ritualism.*[9] In this model, Charles Lindblom has suggested incremental change over radical change, as it is easier to build support for a series of incremental changes from the current situation.

Positive aspect: The positive aspect of this model is that it represents how the real world operates and reduces conflict by seeking the support of the powerful members of the group.

Negative aspect: The negative aspect of this model is that the data used in it is unreliable and the analysis is unreal.[9]

4.2.3.5 Utilitarian Model of Decision-Making/Precautionary Model

The utilitarian model of decision-making is a mix of the approaches of the bargaining model and the bounded rationality model. The model says that when a decision-maker is faced with possible harm, danger, or a serious problem, s/he acts in a way that can address the problem in a cost-effective manner. Even if s/he cannot perfectly analyse the cost-effectiveness of every alternative and even in the face of multiple stakeholder preferences, a decision-maker will choose a solution that seems most cost-effective to him/her. Here the decision-maker quantifiably analyses all the variables that appear to her/him as relevant to the decision and then determines the utility of the different options from an economic perspective. On the basis of this analysis, s/he chooses the final decision.

Positive aspect: This approach has the advantage that it canvasses action over inaction and problem-solving over idealism, with the awareness that what seems to be the right decision today might prove to be an ill-informed choice in the future.

Drawback: The solution is not perfect and may prove to be wrong in the long run.

4.2.3.6 Garbage Can Model of Decision-Making

In this model, decision-making opportunities are described as a garbage can in which many problems and their solutions are dumped independently of each other by decision-makers, as and when they are generated.

It assumes that the organisational preferences and processes are unclear to the members of the organisation. The participants involved are also not permanent and the amount of time and effort they put in keeps on fluctuating.[10] In this model, no organisational process exists for finding a solution to a problem, and the decision-makers are disconnected from the problems and solutions. In this chaos, many unnecessary solutions are produced, which is also known as *organisational garbage*. Many solutions may be proposed for which there are no problems. Problems are solved with solutions that are already available.

Some opportunities to deal with a problem arise; these opportunities are called *choice opportunities*. They are treated like garbage cans. Various problems and solutions are flown into these opportunities, just like garbage.

As some people are organised in classifying their waste into wet garbage, dry garbage, and plastic garbage, some organisations are more structured in classifying their problems and solutions into different garbage bins, while others work in a haphazard manner and put all their problems and solutions into one garbage bin.

In the absence of an independent decision-making process, a solution comes as an interplay among four independent organisational streams, namely,

1. **Problems:** They can originate both within and outside the organisation, and require attention. For example, there may be an insufficiency of personnel to handle incoming work.
2. **Solutions:** Solutions are generally the result of someone's hard work. They are usually created before a problem exists. The organisational members then search for ways to apply the existing solutions.
3. **Participants:** Participants, or members of the organisation, leave the organisation frequently and cannot devote their time solely to a given problem. Employees, contractors, and volunteers can all be considered participants in an organisation.
4. **Choice opportunities:** These are decision-making moments in the organisation such as meetings or the signing of a new contract.

For example, in a furniture company in India, managers discuss that the kind of furniture they produce can be in good demand in East Asian countries. This is a solution that is thrown in the organisational garbage can. Now after sometime (choice opportunity) in the life of the organisation (when the participants have changed but the solution has remained), the problem of how to expand the business of this company arises. At this time, the earlier solution of exporting their product to East Asian countries comes into the picture and helps in making the decision.

Positive aspect: A notable advantage of this model is that it provides a real-world representation of the non-rational manner in which decisions are often made.

Negative aspect: This model does not prescribe the most efficient means of taking a decision.

4.2.3.7 Process Model for Decision-Making

In this model, standard operating procedures (SOPs), or pre-established guidelines within the organisation, are used to make decisions. The actions or behaviours of the parties are decided on the basis of these SOPs or guidelines.[11] These SOPs are decided by mutual agreement. For example, the police department has developed an SOP to deal with murder cases. Whenever an investigating officer confronts a murder case, s/he follows this SOP to successfully investigate it.

4.2.3.8 Focused Trial and Error Model of Decision-Making

This model requires an adaptive, and not purely rational, strategy for problem-solving. In the absence of essential data and facts, this model does not require a correct understanding of all the issues and also does not require a logical procedure for decision-making. However, this model requires the following features in a decision-maker:

1. **Tentativeness:** The decision-maker should be able to revise their course of action as necessary.
2. **Willingness to delay action:** The decision-maker should be able to delay their action in order to collect fresh evidence, process additional information, and present new alternatives.
3. **Choosing incremental action:** The decision-maker should be able to choose incremental action over radical ones, where one big decision is broken into several sub-decisions, rather than introducing one large, radical decision and bearing its impact over a long period.
4. **Spreading risk:** If sufficient information is not available, the decision-maker should be able to spread their risk and maintain strategic reserves for meeting unforeseen calamities as well as opportunities, whenever possible.
5. **Avoid over-commitment:** If partial information is available, the decision-maker should avoid over-commitment to a decision and be ready to reverse their decision.

4.2.3.9 Participative Decision-Making

The participative decision-making approach is effectively used in projects on rural and urban development. In this model, decisions are made by the participation of those people who will be affected by the decision. It takes place right from the conception of a project to its implementation, monitoring, and evaluation.

Participative action research (PAR) for community development is a good example of participative decision-making. In this model, research on community development is conducted with the participation of the local people. It provides an opportunity for the involvement of the whole community in the development of projects by allowing for clarifications and reflections that might improve the researcher's understanding of the situations and problems to shape their strategies rather than prematurely intruding on external ideas. This active participation helps in the capacity building of the community members; it builds the knowledge and skills of the participants to act in their community as leaders or agents for creating change.

This model respects the knowledge of the members and their ability to understand and address the issues affecting them.

4.2.3.10 Public Choice Model for Decision-Making

Public choice models suggests that public officials while making decisions, do not act in a rational manner for maximising public gains. They are self-interested individuals who want to avoid risks and promote their own interests and careers. Their motive, while taking decisions, is to enlarge their programmes and increase their budgets. Thus the decisional choices made by public officials are based on the criteria of self-growth and self-interest.

4.2.3.11 Mixed Scanning Model of Decision-Making

The mixed scanning model, suggested by Etzioni, is a mixture of the incremental and rational models of decision-making. To explain this model, Etzioni gave the example of a worldwide weather observatory system utilising satellite data. A rational model would have required a complete survey of the weather conditions, employing cameras capable of detailed observation and frequent reviews of the sky. However, this huge mass of data may subvert the decision-making capabilities. On the other hand, the incremental model suggests focusing on only those parts of the world where similar patterns have been observed, along with a few nearby regions. As a combination of both, the mixed scanning model suggests two cameras to be used, a broad-angle one covering all parts of the sky (but not in great detail) and the other focusing on those areas revealed as irregular by the first camera to ensure an in-depth examination. This model may miss certain areas, but is less likely to miss obvious trouble spots in unfamiliar areas.

The essence of mixed scanning decision-making is to employ two levels of scanning for searching for alternatives, depending on the problem. The first level of scanning is for higher coverage and the second level is for truncated coverage.

4.2.3.12 Organisational Decision-Making

Nicholas Henry has suggested ways in which decisions are made in different organisations. He said that just as the rationality of organisational members is bounded, so is the rationality of the organisations themselves.[12] The different decision-making methods are suggested depending on whether the members agree or disagree on the goals and the causal factors for attaining those goals. The methods are *analytical*, *judgmental*, *compromising*, and *inspirational/authoritarian* decision-making. They are clearly represented in Mind Map 4.1.

Type of organisational decision-making	Organisational goals	Causal factors	Method of decision-making
Analytical	Complete agreement	Complete agreement	Decisions are made analytically with little or no internal debate about values. Decisions are made on shared technical perceptions. The outcomes of various alternatives are computed using techniques such as linear programming, network analysis, and statistical analysis.
Judgmental	Agreement	Disagreement	Decisions are made judgmentally. Here the outcome of various decisional alternatives is unknown. For example, a marketing manager may have several alternative ways of promoting a product, but may not be sure of their outcomes. Here good judgment is required to choose among the alternatives and increase the probability of desired outcomes.
Compromising	Disagreement	Agreement	Decisions are made by bargaining or compromising. This happens mostly in legislative debates.

Type of organisational decision-making	Organisational goals	Causal factors	Method of decision-making
Inspirational/ authoritarian	Disagreement	Disagreement	Here inspiration or authoritarian decision-making is used. Decisions are either inspired from previous decisions or are forced upon the members by the leader of the organisation. Decisions, while being implemented, also need to be adaptive to accommodate new developments.

Mind Map 4.1: Different methods of organisational decision-making[12]

4.2.4 Decision Shaping Factors

Decision-making in an organisation is shaped by various factors. These factors suggest why decisions are not completely rational. Some of these factors are described in the following sections.

4.2.4.1 Bounded rationality

This has been discussed in Chapter 3.

4.2.4.2 Heuristics and biases

Heuristics are the factors that reduce the mental efforts required of decision-makers while making decisions.[13] They are considered as the "unconscious routines to cope with the complexity inherent in most decisions."[14] They help in narrowing down the plane of possible solutions and reducing the complexity of the decision-making process. Heuristics are of the following types:

1. **Representativeness heuristic:** In the representativeness heuristic, the decision-maker makes an inference from a small number of cases and a small sample size. The decision-maker does not consider the probability of all the outcomes.
2. **Availability heuristic:** In the availability heuristic, those events or alternatives are considered more probable that can be recalled more easily by the mind.[13] The ease of recall may be because the information is vivid, well-publicised, salient, fresh in memory, or recent.[15]
3. **Anchoring and adjustment heuristic:** In this heuristic, the decision-maker makes an estimation on the basis of some implicitly suggested reference point, and some adjustments to it.[13] For example, if a newly appointed SP finds a riot situation in their district on the first day of their joining, they tend to make their future law and order decisions considering that the district is prone to riots. Such heuristic blocks the possibility of a realistic appraisal of the situation.
4. **Interpretation on the basis of decision framing:** Under this bias, people try to avoid extremely positive or extremely negative options. This happens when the decision problem is framed in such a way that it highlights the gain or loss alone in the situation. People perform the weighing function while selecting an alternative. For example, when a group of people was asked to choose between the following two alternatives:
   (i) Adopt a programme for saving 200 people
   (ii) Adopt another programme where there are one-third chances that 600 people will be saved and two-thirds chances that no one will be saved.

   more people tended to choose alternative A, even when both will result in the same solution.[13]

5. **Status-quo bias:** Under this bias, the decision-maker chooses the alternative that helps them in maintaining status-quo, because status-quo provides psychological safety to the decision-maker.[14] Organisations that emphasise more on punishment tend to have managers who favour status quo alternatives.
6. **Escalation of commitment:** Under this heuristic, managers tend to defend their past choices and give themselves the false hope that by continuing with that choice, they would succeed as planned (even if reality suggests otherwise). Also known as the *trap of sunk cost fallacy*, it makes people think that since they have already invested some time and money in a particular project, they can rescue it by putting in some more.[16]
7. **Perpetual selectivity/confirmation bias:** In this heuristic, out of many data points available from the environment, a manager filters out those choices that fit into his/her scheme of things and rejects those that shake his/her existing scheme of things. Such a heuristic is found in the implicit favourite model.

4.2.4.3 Personal Limitations

Individuals in an organisation succumb to heuristics and biases because of their limited ability, slow learning, and fear.[9] As an individual has limited ability, s/he can focus only on a limited number of items and calculate a limited number of probabilities. Individuals also suffer from fear while taking important decisions; this fear restricts rational thinking. Fear often leads to undue delay in decisions, impulsive decisions, and even indecision.

4.2.4.4 Interpersonal Barriers in Decision-Making

There are frequent interpersonal barriers such as trust among members in an organisation. These barriers restrict the free discussion of ideas and quality decision-making.

4.2.5 Thinking Disposition and Good Decision-Making[12]

Even after discussing the various factors that negatively impact decision-making, there is ample scope for making good decisions. These good decisions are made by the use of a wide variety of thinking dispositions. *Thinking dispositions* are rational and psychological decision-making techniques such as the following:

1. Thoughtful reflection on the decision and its consequences.
2. Extracting more and more information before making a decision.
3. Trying to match one's degree of certainty with the strength of the evidence.
4. Correcting one's biases and being aware of them.
5. Being willing to wait for a good solution to emerge.[17]

4.2.6 Decision-Making in Public and Private Sectors

Nicholas Henry has very beautifully described the differences between decision-making in public and private sector organisations. This distinction is shown in a tabulated form in Mind Map 4.2.

Public sector	Private sector
1. **Bargaining:** Decisions in the public sector emphasise more on bargaining; they believe that negotiation legitimises decisions.[18]	1. **Analysis:** Decisions in the private sector are based more on analysis than on bargaining.

Public sector	Private sector
2. **Complex decisions:** Public decision-making requires one to tackle vast and complex decisional criteria.[19]	2. **Simple process:** Private decision-making requires one to tackle a single criterion, i.e., financial performance.
3. **Slow and cautious:** Public organisations have a conservative culture, which leads to slow decisions. They are less likely to take risks.[20]	3. **More risky decisions:** Private organisations take more risks and are faster in taking decisions.
4. **Participative:** The decision-making process in the public sector is more participative; they use large group interaction methods, which can involve a large number of people for making decisions.[21]	4. **Less participative**
5. **Lesser communication with oversight bodies:** Public administrators communicate their decisions completely to legislators and other oversight bodies. This happens because legislators are less informed and less consistent in their oversight.	5. **More consultation with oversight bodies:** In the private sector, the board of directors has a greater and consistent say in the decision-making process.
6. **Life and death decisions:** Public administrators get an opportunity to take life and death decisions.	6. The private sector does not get opportunities to make such life and death decisions.

Mind Map 4.2: Distinction between decision-making in public and private sector organisations

4.2.7 Measures for Improving Decision-Making

As seen in the preceding sections, the decision-making process suffers from various lacunae such as individual inability, lack of time, and other heuristics. Some of these problems can be addressed using the following measures.

4.2.7.1 Group Decision-Making

Research has suggested that when the members of a group participate in the discussions leading to a decision, the quality of the decision improves. Participation becomes more necessary when the decisions are complex and their consequences are serious. Group decision-making is better, as a group represents diverse stakeholders in a decision. It helps in collecting more information and examining the issues from a diversity of views. As a result, more approaches and alternatives are generated. If the members of the group are those people who will be affected by the decision, the acceptance of the decision improves.

The group decision-making process is negatively impacted by the following two phenomena:

1. **Risky shift phenomenon:** This phenomenon suggests that groups may indulge in taking riskier decisions. This happens due to the following four reasons:
    (a) Risk-takers in the group persuade the cautious companions to take more risk.
    (b) As the members familiarise themselves with the issues and arguments, they feel more confident in taking riskier decisions.
    (c) The responsibility for decision-making is diffused across the group.
    (d) People avoid appearing cautious.

2. **Groupthink:** This phenomenon suggests that in a group, group norms and concurrence to them become more important than critical thinking. Once concurrence for an alternative is achieved, a realistic appraisal of other alternatives is avoided. Groups also avoid re-examination of their course of action after new information is suggested. They avoid seeking the advice of experts within and outside the organisation. They also ignore possible roadblocks to their chosen decision and, as a result, fail to develop contingency plans for potential setbacks.

4.2.7.2 Creativity in Decision-Making

Creativity in organisations improves their decision-making process. Creativity is defined as the production of novel and useful ideas.[22] It helps in connecting two previously conceived processes in order to gain new and better insight into solving problems. Creativity in organisations is a trainable skill. A related term to creativity is innovation, which is conceived as applied creativity or putting ideas to work. Organisational creativity can be improved by using the following four techniques:

(a) **Brainstorming:** Brainstorming is a technique that was developed by Alex Osborn in the 1950s to stimulate creative thoughts within a group. In it, all participants respond to a problem by contributing their ideas. Other participants comment on these ideas. This leads to the generation of more ideas. The participants are not allowed to criticise or evaluate others' or their own ideas. The focus is only on generating new ideas.[23]

(b) **Creativity in Organisational Processes:** To support creativity, organisational culture must not emphasise control, cohesion, loyalty, strong norms of appropriate behaviour and conformity.[24] The culture must be one of open communication, flexibility, risk-taking, trust, and non-confirmation.[25] Moreover, creativity can also be encouraged by setting clear goals, creating creative and diverse groups, removing constant supervision and supporting functional conflict among the specialists in the organisation.[26]

(c) **Synectics:** Synectics is a technique developed by William J.J. Gordon in which novel alternatives are stimulated by joining together distinct and apparently irrelevant ideas. A synectic group is formed of members from diverse backgrounds and training. A problem is stated for the group to consider. After understanding the problem, the members of the group offer potential solutions. The leader structures the problem and discussion in such a manner that forces members to deviate from their traditional way of thinking. Methods such as role-playing, the use of analogies, paradoxes, metaphors, and other thought-provoking techniques are used. This leads to the generation of creative alternatives; the feasibility of these alternatives is tested with the help of a technical expert. Thus, in contrast to brainstorming, ideas are judged continuously when they are produced.

(d) **Nominal Grouping:** Nominal Grouping is a technique developed by Andre Delbecq and Andrew Van De Ven, in which a nominal (in name only) group of 7–10 individuals is created. These individuals from different backgrounds are brought together and familiarised with a problem. Each group member is asked to silently prepare a list of ideas to tackle that problem. Then each member shares their ideas in a round-robin manner, in which their ideas are recorded on a board. After this, members discuss and evaluate each recorded idea. Ideas are reworked, combined, deleted or added. Finally each member votes by privately ranking the recorded ideas. Group preference is the arithmetical outcome of the individual votes. This technique is used to reduce verbal interaction, as is present in brainstorming and synectics. Thus, it minimises the inhibiting effects of group interactions while initially generating different alternatives.

4.2.7.3 Use of Technology for Group Decision-making

Technology can be used for making group decision-making systematic. It can help in making the contribution of the members fact-based rather than socio-emotionally based. In this technique, the participants meet electronically rather than physically. It helps in avoiding emotional issues. It also helps in avoiding rejection or acceptance of a solution because of the nature of the person from which it has emerged.

Groupware: Groupware is a term used for computer support for conducting such coordination meetings. It allows sharing documents, amending documents and commenting on ideas, similar to a face-to-face meeting. Various examples of groupware are e-mail, electronic bulletin boards, teleconferencing, group writing, and so on.

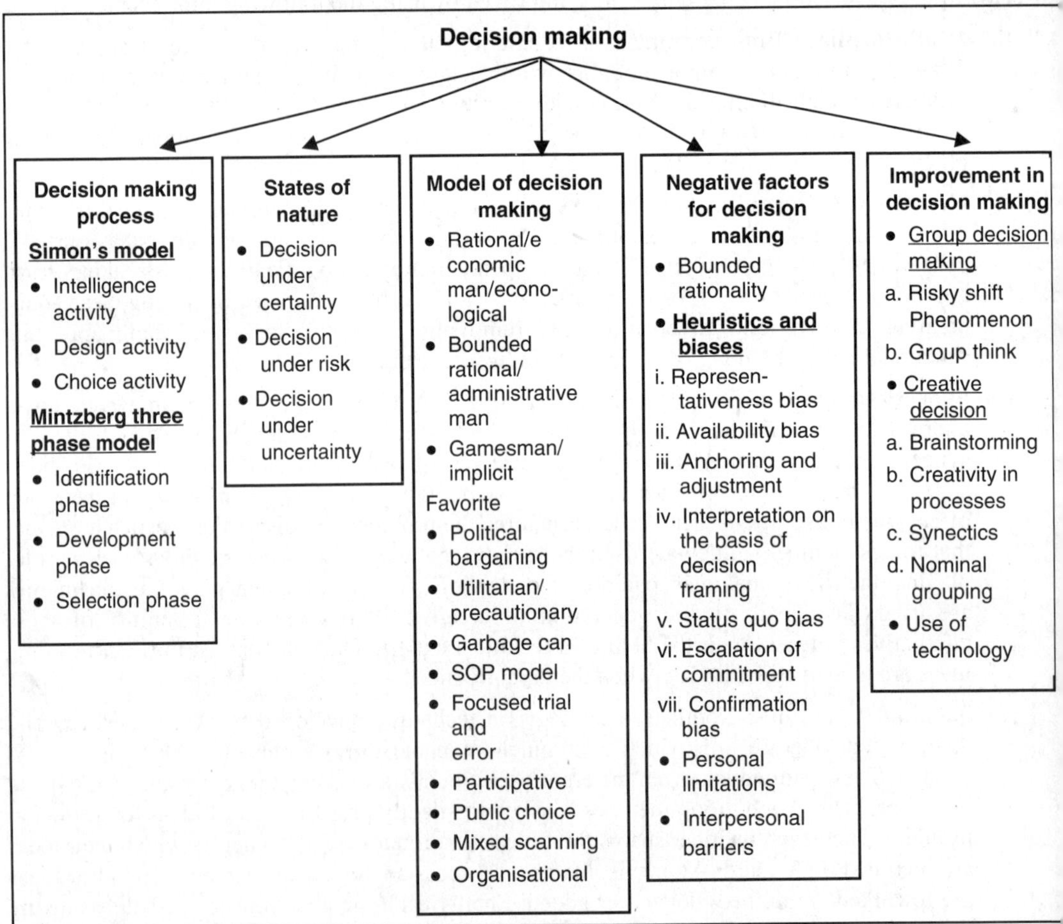

Mind Map 4.3 : Basic Concepts of Decision Making

4.3 Communication

Communication is the basic ingredient of most organisational processes such as the performance of various tasks, decision-making, leadership, motivation, and so on.[27] It is defined as "the transmission and reception of ideas, feelings and attitudes—verbally and non-verbally—which produce a response."[28] It is also "a process by which we assign and convey meaning in an attempt to create shared understanding."[29] The process of communication is instrumental in the following two senses:

(a) **Achievement of Results:** Communication is important for organisational goals. It involves informing, directing, and persuading others to action.

(b) **Expression of Social and Emotional Aspects:** Communication allows people to express themselves, their feelings, and their social, emotional, and aesthetical needs.

The present approach to communication is based on cybernetics. In cybernetics, Norbert Weiner focused on the natural tendency toward disorder and disintegration in society. The entropy of the system (a measure of the tendency to disintegrate) increases naturally. The increase in entropy needs to be controlled by methodical information processing, also known as communication. Information, in the form of communication, is the antidote to entropy.[30]

4.3.1 Elements of Communication

The process of communication consists of the following elements:

(a) **More than one Party ('Who' of Communication):** A communication process consists of at least a sender and a receiver. They are known as the 'Who' of communication.

(b) **Context of Communication ('When', 'Where' and 'How' of Communication):** The context of communication signifies its time ('when' of communication), physical setting ('where'), and its social, situational, environmental, and cultural factors ('how' of communication). These elements affect one another and are also get impacted by external forces. Thus, the communication context keeps on changing.

(c) **Messages and Barriers of Communication ('What' of Communication):** The 'what' part of communication consists of its words, sounds, message structure, gestures, eye contact, posture, voice characteristics, dress, hairstyle, and accessories. They all help in creating the message of communication. Apart from it, there are certain *barriers* that create distortion in communication. They are both, physical and psychological barriers. The barriers are of the following types:

   (i) **Physical Barriers:** Physical barrier occurs when the source is not clearly visible/audible/legible to the receiver and he/she is not comfortable in the environment. Geographical distance is an example of a physical barrier.

   (ii) **Psychological Barriers:** The sender and receiver may have differences in attitude, interest, and motivation level, leading to their different perceptions of things and situations. Apart from it, the varied level of anxiety, inherent prejudices, and previous experiences create psychological barriers to communication. The greatest barrier occurs when there is a tendency to evaluate the other person's message from one's own perspective. When feelings and emotions get involved in the evaluative process, the difference in perspective is so heightened that the two parties miss the main point completely.

(iii) **Socio-cultural Barriers:** The culture of society also impacts the nature of communication. For example, due to Indian culture, women may feel uncomfortable discussing health issues with male health workers.

(iv) **Linguistic Barriers:** Faulty expression, poor translation, verbosity, ambiguous words, and inappropriate vocabulary are certain examples of linguistic barriers. Apart from them, words and symbols may communicate different meanings to different people.

(v) **Technical Barriers:** Technical barriers arise with the use of technology; for example, poor audio quality, weak video signals, and so on.

(vi) **Information Overload:** The supply of too much information may lead to difficulty and assimilation of information.

(d) **Feedback of Communication:** Feedback is a process in which the receiver responds to the message from the sender. The sender can also generate feedback for themselves if they become aware, observe themselves, and listen to themselves in communication. The form of feedback may be positive or negative. Positive feedback is a form of affirmation or appreciation. Negative feedback suggests a gap, deficiency, and inadequacy.

Figure 4.5 shows a schematic diagram representing the communication process.

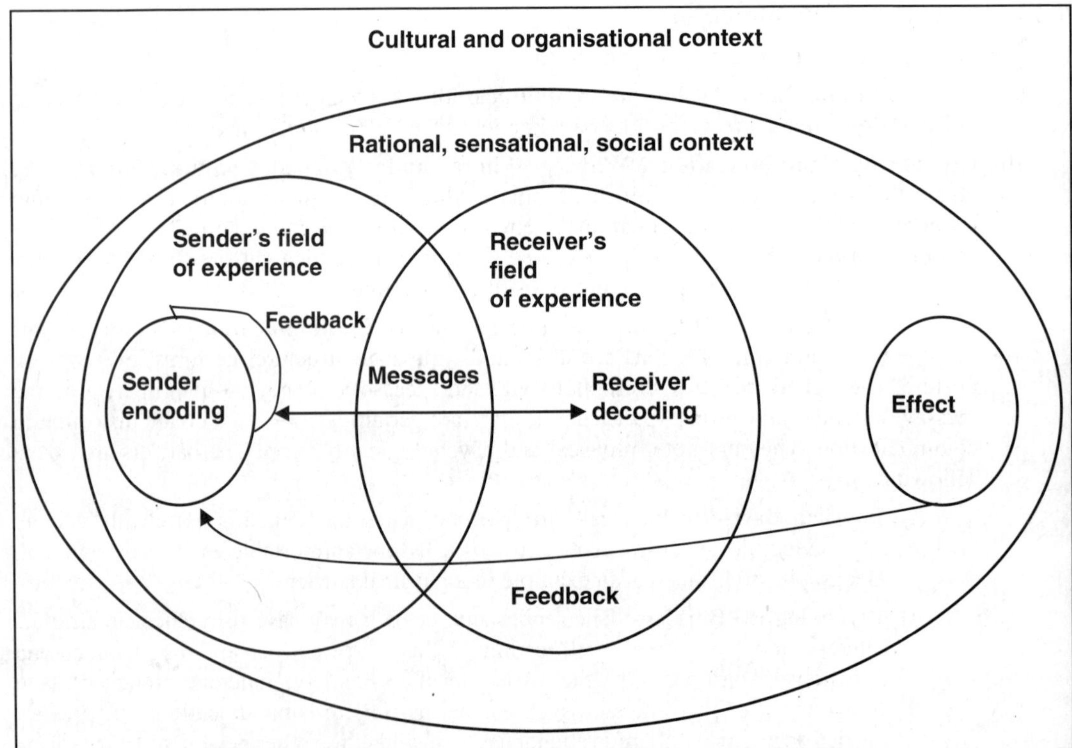

Fig. 4.5 : Schematic of Communication Process[31]

The communication process shown in Fig. 4.5 is as described below:[32]

(i) An event-as-experienced by the sender is communicated first. This happens because the event-as-it-occurred is processed within the sender's field of experience.

(ii) The event-as-experienced by the sender is structured within a message and presented by the sender. This structuring of the message by the sender plays a crucial role in communication.

(iii) At the receiver's end, the message is processed within the receiver's field of experience, leading to the event-as-understood by the receiver. This may be divergent from the event-as-it-occurred and event-as-experienced-by-sender. This divergence may be due to the sender's field of experience, sender's encoding, message structure, receiver's field of experience and receiver's decoding.

(iv) The above-mentioned divergence can be explored by giving and seeking feedback.

4.3.2 Channels of Communication

Channel of communication is the direction, or the path, through which communication takes place. It can be classified on the basis of (1) relationship, (2) direction of flow, and (3) method used.[33]

4.3.2.1 Channel of Communication on the Basis of Relationship

Based on the relationship between the two parties, communication is formal or informal.

(a) **Formal Communication:** A formal channel of communication is deliberately established by an organisation for the formal transmission of messages. In them, a superior gives orders to their subordinates and the subordinate supplies information to the superior. The formal channel helps in maintaining order and seriousness in communication. However, due to the higher number of message levels, formal communication suffers from delay and chances of distortion.

(b) **Information Communication:** Informal communication takes place on the basis of informal and social relations within an organisation. It does not follow the formal channel. It may take place between persons cutting across organisational positions. As the origin of informal communication is difficult to trace, it is also known as *grapevine*. The advantage of informal communication is that it spreads very fast. However, it may not be completely right or maybe an outright rumour. No one can be held accountable for it. It is also liable to distortion when it passes from one person to another.

4.3.2.2 Channel of Communication on the Basis of Direction of Flow

On the basis of direction, communication can be classified as follows:

(a) **Vertical Communication:** Vertical communication takes place between a superior and subordinates in an organisation. It is classified as downward communication and upward communication.

(b) **Horizontal Communication:** Horizontal communication takes place between two persons having equal rank in the hierarchy. It facilitates better coordination of interdependent activities.

(c) **Diagonal Communication:** Diagonal communication takes place between two persons at different levels of hierarchy and in different departments.

4.3.2.3 Channel of Communication on the Basis of Method Used

Communication is divided into the following types on the basis of the method used:

(a) **Verbal Communication:** Messages transmitted orally are known as verbal communication. It gives a personal touch to communication. It is economical and fast. It also helps in seeking the reaction of the receiver immediately. However, it is not very useful when the numbers of persons to be communicated with are high in number. It also does not help in recording the content of the message.

(b) **Written Communication:** Written communication is the most important means of communication in a formal organisation. It consists of orders, instructions, reports, and bulletins. This form of communication is advantageous, as it is permanent, tangible, and verifiable. It is also beneficial when the subject matter is lengthy and needs to be conveyed to a large number of people. However, the drawback of written communication is that it is time consuming, formal, and lacks a personal touch. It is also difficult to maintain complete secrecy in written communication.

(c) **Communication via Symbols:** Communication via gestures or symbols is used to make verbal and written communication more effective.

4.3.3 Models of Communication

A model of communication is a graphical representation of its various elements. Some of the important models of communication are described in the following.[34]

(a) **Lasswell Model of Communication:** The Lasswell model of communication (1948) focused on the basic elements of communication, such as its 'who', 'what', 'which', 'whom', and 'what'. These elements are described under the previous topic 'Elements of Communication'.

(b) **Shannon and Weaver Model of Communication:** Also referred to as the transmission model of communication, this model describes the process of signal transmission. In it the information source produces a message to be communicated out of a set of possible messages. The transmitter converts the message into a signal suitable for the channel to be used. The channel is the medium that transmits the signal from the transmitter to the receiver. The receiver performs the inverse operation of the transmitter by reconstructing the message from the signal. The destination is the person or thing for whom/which the message is intended (Fig. 4.6).[34] The model also describes the concept of noise, i.e. disturbance or errors in transmission. As the noise increases, the entropy of the system increases. This increase in entropy needs to be tackled by the repetition of the message.

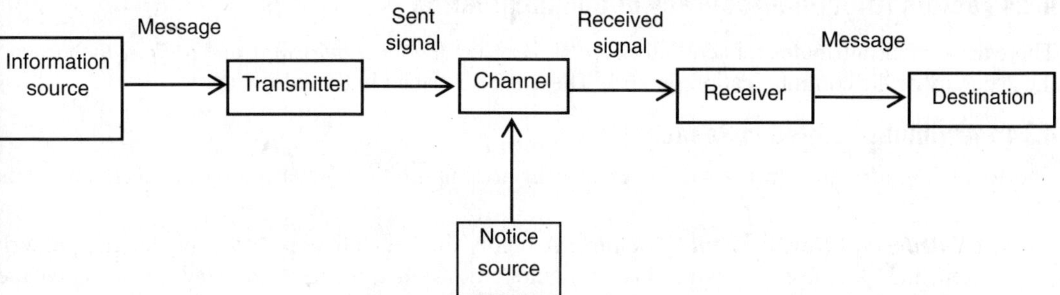

Fig. 4.6 : Shannon and Weavers Model of Communication[34]

(c) **Osgood Model of Communication:** Charles Osgood (in 1954) showed that communication is a dynamic process in which there is an interactive relationship between the source and the receiver of the message. An individual sends as well as receives messages via encoding, decoding, interpreting messages, and sending and receiving feedback (Fig. 4.7). This model is relevant in those communications where the sender and receiver are physically present together. A teacher and student interaction in a classroom is a good example of this communication.

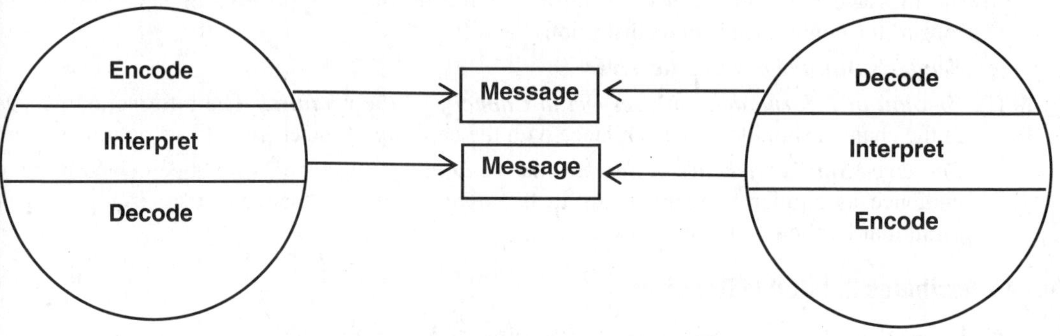

Fig. 4.7 : Osgood's of Communication[34]

(d) **Schramm Model of Communication:** The Schramm model visualised communication as a process of sharing of experience and commonality of experience of those communicating. This model of communication is similar to that described in Fig. 4.5. If the sender and the receiver have a common field of experience, communication becomes easy. On the contrary, if the field of experience is not common, then communication becomes difficult. The model is good for bilateral communication but does not apply suitably to complex and multiple levels of communication. This model describes a form of transactional communication, in which there are both linear communication (flow of message from sender to receiver) and interactive communication (formation of a shared relationship between sender and receiver).

4.3.4 Factors Affecting Accuracy of Communication

There are various attributes related to the *sender*, *receiver*, *channel*, *message*, and *topic*, which impact the accuracy of the communication process. These are described in the following.

4.3.4.1 Attributes Related to Sender:

The following attributes on the side of the sender are important in determining the accuracy of the communication:

(a) ***Intellectual Development of Sender:*** A highly intellectually developed sender can properly encode a message with his/her autonomous judgment, command over language, accommodating nature, and tolerance for ambiguity.

(b) ***Rules for Coding:*** The sender prepares a message by using an implicit or explicit code or set of rules. These rules govern communication within a group. The use of more implicit code of communication makes the message more dependent on the context of a communication and is, thus, restricted to those privileged to access those implicit norms. For example, if some people are invited to a 'Garba' dance, it is implicit that only those wearing traditional attire will be allowed to dance.

(c) ***Divergence of Sender:*** The degree to which a sender differs from the commonly agreed coding rules impacts the accuracy of communication.

(d) ***Sender's Attitude towards Content of Message:*** A neutral attitude towards the content of the message helps in the least distortion of the message. A positive or negative attitude toward the content leads to its distortion.

(e) ***Sender's Attitude towards Receiver***

(f) ***Amount of Information with respect to Capacity of the Channel:*** The information packed in the channel should be in accordance with the capacity of the channel to accommodate.

(g) ***Perceived Similarity between Sender and Audience:*** The sender, who is perceived by their audience as similar to them, tends to be more persuasive than one who is regarded as dissimilar by their audience.

4.3.4.2 Attributes Related to Receiver:

The attributes related to the receiver are similar to those related to the sender.

4.3.4.3 Attributes Related to Channel

The following channel attributes impact the accuracy of communication:

(a) Number of channels available

(b) Opportunity for modification, revision, and correction of message in the channel

(c) Opportunities for feedback in the channel

4.3.4.4 Attributes of Message:

The following attributes of message impact the accuracy of communication:

(a) ***Confirmation between several components of the message*:** A communication is more accurate if the several components of the message convey the same meaning. For example, if the spoken message is also confirmed by the expression, tone of voice, and body language, then the meaning will be accurately communicated.

(b) ***Message Structure:*** The components of the message must be arranged in a specific manner in order to make the message predictable to the receiver.

(c) ***Degree of Objectivity:*** A well-defined message becomes independent of the context and situation of communication.

4.3.4.5 Attributes of Topic:

The following attributes of the topic impact the accuracy of communication:

(a) ***Ambiguity or unambiguity of the topic itself***

(b) ***Complexity of the topic:*** The complexity of the topic impacts the accuracy of communication. This complexity is reflected in the number of parts within the message and their interrelationship.

4.3.5 Measures to Improve Communication

As discussed above, there are many barriers to communication. Apart from them, there are instances where the sender deliberately tries to misrepresent the message or deceive the receiver into drawing a wrong conclusion from the message. These, and other forms of distortion in communication, can be arrested by the following measures:

4.3.5.1 Confirm the Verbal with the Non-Verbal Message

Misrepresentation or deceit in a message can be verified if the receiver checks the sender's message against some facts, evidence, or statements of others. The strongly felt emotions of a person can be witnessed in their non-verbal behaviour. For example, lying, deceit, or similar behaviour may cause stress, increase body movement, speech hesitation, and speech errors such as stutters, repetition of words or omission of words. Such non-verbal behavioural signs should be checked to understand the veracity of verbal communication.

Apart from that, non-verbal messages help in providing further information and keeping the speaker and listener engaged with each other. Thus, non-verbal communication behaviour is related to verbal communication in the following ways:[35]

(i) The sender shall repeat the verbal message in the non-verbal form. For example, s/he shall point towards a place on the map while discussing it with the audience.

(ii) The sender may sometimes substitute a verbal answer with a non-verbal answer. For example, he may nod to convey the message 'Yes'.

(iii) The receiver shall compliment the speaker while listening, using techniques such as leaning forward and smiling in between. The presence of this non-verbal behaviour shows enthusiasm, encouragement, and interest.

(iv) The speaker shall use hand gestures while assenting to verbal communication. For example, s/he may bang a table while communicating "I am sure things will improve in the future."

4.3.5.2 Separate Communication Problems from Other Problems

There are certain problems that are not communication problems but are branded so. For example, verbal assault on others, withdrawal, and refusal to collaborate is not communication problems but problems related to other aspects of the organisation. These problems need to be separated, and effectively dealt with, in order to improve the communication process.

While such problems persist, the receiver shall carefully listen to the total message, compare the message received from one channel with that received from another, and ask questions to unearth the actual message shared. This can help them separate the above-discussed problems from the communication process, and still effectively communicate.

4.3.5.3 Learn the Art of Listening

Listening is a very important part of effective communication. Effective communication needs to balance talking and listening in order to exchange meaning.[36] Listening is much more than just hearing. It involves interpreting, searching for the full and accurate meaning, and understanding the meaning of the message. Listening is of the following four types.

(a) **Comprehensive Listening:** This form of listening is for understanding facts, ideas, and themes in the message.

(b) **Evaluative Listening:** This form of listening involves evaluating the merit/demerit of the persuasive argument of the sender/speaker.

(c) **Empathic Listening:** This form of listening involves understanding the other person's thoughts, beliefs, and feelings, and conveying the same to the other. The parties accept individual differences, and yet openly express their ideas and feelings and receive the ideas and feelings of the other.

(d) **Appreciative Listening:** This form of listening is for pleasure, especially artistic pleasure.

A receiver in a communication shall be an active listener. An active listener reflects on the message, restates, and summarises what they hear. They also allow the speaker to offload those unexpressed emotions that are difficult to deal with. They help the speaker, and give her/him time, to be in better control of their emotions. They make reflective statements such as "you seem to be saying that…;' these statements help the speaker in clarifying the message. The following measures should be taken for effective listening:

(a) **Physical Setting:** The physical setting should be such that it is conducive for listening; all distorting elements and disturbances should be removed.

(b) **Better Command over Language:** The listener should have better command over the language. S/he should ask the speaker to clarify the message where s/he does not understand the content of the message. S/he should reflect and confirm whether s/he has understood the meaning of the message correctly.

(c) **Motivation:** The listener should be motivated to understand the message of the speaker/sender.

(d) **No Premature Response:** The listener shall avoid premature response before the speaker has completed his/her message.

(e) **Non-Verbal Communication:** The listener shall notice the expressions of the speaker and try to relate them with the verbal part of communication.[37]

4.3.5.4 Probing the Message

For understanding information completely and accurately, a person must be skilled at probing and asking questions. It helps the speaker in, bringing out such information to the surface that s/he is unaware of, has difficulty articulating, or has hesitation in expressing. It motivates the speaker to talk in more concrete and specific terms.

4.3.5.5 Art of Giving and Receiving Feedback.

A very important characteristic of a good communicator is giving appropriate and constructive feedback in negative situations. Feedback for poor performance is often regarded as unpleasant by the sender as well as the recipient. Constructive feedback is one that can help the recipient as well as the organisation without damaging the relationship between the feedback giver and the feedback receiver. The following are the qualities of good feedback:

(a) **Descriptive rather than Evaluative:** Feedback should not consist of an evaluative judgment or label on the feedback receiver. A judgment makes the receiver defensive as well as offensive toward the feedback giver. Feedback should be descriptive, i.e., it should make the receiver aware of the latent intention behind the feedback. It should be able to reveal the important and unanticipated consequences of the recipient's behaviour over others.

(b) **Intention of Helping:** The intention of feedback should be to help a person, and not harm, demean, or insult them.

(c) **Specific in Nature:** The feedback should be specific rather than general. Saying "there are many errors in your functioning" is general feedback, and saying "you did not write the introduction of report number 24 correctly" is specific feedback.

(d) **Immediate:** The feedback should be given immediately.

(e) **Sensitive to the readiness of the receiver:** Feedback should be given only when the receiver is ready to accept it.

(f) **Objective:** The feedback should be based on facts rather than impressions, personal preferences, or prejudices.

(g) **Valid:** The feedback should be correct, authentic, and taken from a reliable source.

Models of Giving Feedback: There are certain models of giving feedback. These models may be applicable in different situations and for different people. They are described below:

(a) **Feedback Sandwich Model:** 'Feedback Sandwich' is a popular three-step procedure for giving corrective feedback. In it, praise is followed by corrective feedback, which is again followed by more praise. Thus, corrective feedback is sandwiched between praise and more praise. It helps in softening the impact of criticism and makes the feedback giver comfortable in giving feedback.

(b) **Situational-Behaviour-Impact (SBI) Model:** The SBI tool is an important tool that helps the receiver in reflecting on his/her actions while understanding the feedback correctly. First, it involves the definition of the situation the feedback refers to. This puts the feedback into context. For example, 'in the meeting on Monday…' is a situation. Second, it involves mentioning the specific behaviour that needs to be addressed. It should be specific and non-judgmental. For example, "During yesterday morning's team meeting, when you gave your presentation, you were uncertain about two of the slides, and your sales calculations were incorrect" is specific feedback. Third, this technique involves how the behaviour of the receiver impacts others. For example, "During yesterday morning's team meeting, when you gave your presentation, you were uncertain about two of the slides, and your sales calculations were incorrect. I felt embarrassed because the entire board was there. I'm worried that this has affected the reputation of our team."

(c) **Pendleton's Model of Feedback:** Pendleton's model is a technique in which the sender highlights the positive aspects of the receiver's behaviour with the help of the receiver himself. It is followed by a discussion on how to reinforce the positive aspects of the behaviour. It is finally followed by a discussion on what improvements in behaviour can be attained and how. Thus, this model not only highlights the negative behaviour but also provides strategies to tackle it.

4.3.6 Persuasive Communication

Persuasive communication is a form of communication in which the sender seeks to persuade the receiver(s) to accept their particular points of view. Denhardt, Denhardt, and Aristigueta pointed out three measures for effective persuasive communication in public organisations. These are as follows:

(a) **Credibility of the Source:** Senders of communication regarded as credible are more persuading than those who are less credible. Thus, for effective communication, one must improve his/her own credibility in the eyes of the receiver(s). This credibility can be improved by the experience and trustworthiness of the speaker.

(b) **Character of the Message:** The way in which a message is delivered makes it persuasive/non-persuasive. As Denhardt et al. said, "Although we think of persuasive messages as involving rationality and objectivity, there also are emotional elements that enter into the process of persuasion."[38]

(c) **Range of Acceptance:** According to the authors, the range of acceptance is "a range within which receivers are willing to entertain beliefs or attitudes different from their own."[38] If an argument falls within this range, the receivers will accept it more willingly. Thus, the sender should make a careful assessment of the receiver's range of acceptance before communicating.

4.3.7 Johari Window—A Framework for Effective Communication and Feedback

A communication process reveals a lot about our inner thoughts and feelings. However, sometimes the sender hides his/her inner thoughts and feelings, even from him/herself. Moreover, people have limited or incorrect perceptions about the self and their relations with others; this limits their ability to manage their problems. Feedback from others offers people new information about themselves, which is necessary for developing alternative perspectives on problems.

The 'Johari' (named after the combined names of authors Joseph Luft and Harrington Ingram[40]) window model is a simple and useful technique for illustrating and improving self-awareness and mutual understanding between individuals within a group. It is also used in assessing and improving a group's relationship with other groups.

		Things about self that:	
		Self knows	**Self doesn't knows**
Things about self that:	**Others knows**	**Open self**	**Blind self**
	Others don't know	**Hidden self**	**Unknown self**

Fig. 4.8 : Johari Window[15]

The Johari framework consists of four quadrants, as shown in Fig. 4.8. They are described as follows:

(a) **Open Self:** This quadrant represents knowledge about self which the person is a willing to share, or cannot avoid sharing, with others.

(b) **Hidden Self:** This quadrant represents the area where one knows themselves more than others know them. This happens because s/he may inhibit or mask uncomfortable or unpleasant areas of the 'self' by actively misrepresenting things about himself. This hidden area is masked, consisting of knowledge about the self that a person does not want others to have. If trust between people grows, there is willingness to share and shift towards the 'open self' quadrant.

(c) **Blind Self:** This quadrant represents a situation when we misrepresent facts or truths about ourselves to ourselves.

(d) **Unknown Self:** This quadrant refers to a situation when we realise that neither we know about ourselves nor others know about us. The size of this quadrant often increases with growing knowledge. The more we learn, the more we realise that our knowledge is limited.

4.4 Motivation in Organisations

Motivation is one of the most important concerns of modern organisations, as it influences many other issues within an organisation such as employee performance, employee retention, creativity, problem solving, and other important actions.

Many scholars have provided different definitions of motivation. However, the most precise definition is "a set of energetic forces, both within and beyond an individual's being, to initiate work-related behaviour, and to determine its form, direction, intensity, and duration."[41] Work motivation has the following characteristics:

(a) Motivation results in both from the context (e.g., organisational reward systems, the nature of work) and from forces inherent in the person (e.g., individual needs).

(b) Motivation is inside a person and cannot be observed directly. Only the manifestations of motivation, such as goal attainment, can be measured.

(c) Motivation should be understood with the social side of an individual and the organisational climate of goals and outcomes.

4.4.1 Intrinsic and Extrinsic Motivation

Intrinsic motivation is that motivation which drives a person to perform because of the satisfaction derived from the work itself and from the goal attained by it; it is a need in its own right.[42] In it, a person regards work as an opportunity for new learning, new contributions, enjoying responsibility, autonomy, and being creative.

Extrinsic motivation is that motivation that drives a person to perform not because of the work itself but because of the extrinsic outcome (or rewards) to which the work leads. In it, a person regards work as a means to obtain the rewards associated with the job.[43]

However, extrinsic and intrinsic motivations are not discreet factors. They may work together, as will be discussed in the later part of this chapter. The same reward may be intrinsic as well as extrinsic; while pay is an extrinsic reward, a pay increase can also indicate achievement and increasing responsibility and, thus, overlap with intrinsic rewards.[42]

4.4.2 Persistence

Persistence as a quality suggests that the motivated behaviour of a person continues until a goal is reached through sustained efforts in the face of obstacles and failure. The concept helps in distinguishing motivation from similar concepts like job satisfaction. It is possible to find satisfied employees who are not motivated towards their work. On the other hand, it is also possible to find motivated people who are not satisfied with the various aspects of their work. A similar idea will be discussed in Frederick Herzberg's theory of motivation.[45]

4.4.3 MARS Model: Relationship between Motivation and Performance

Motivation is one of the factors that influence an employee's performance. The four factors that impact performance, as described by the MARS model (Fig. 4.9), are motivation, ability, role perception, and situational factors. They all have a combined effect on individual performance. For example, in a sales job, a person should be enthusiastic (motivation), understand their duties (role perception), have sufficient resources to perform their work (situational factors) and have sufficient knowledge and sales skill (ability). If any of the above factors is missing, job performance will suffer. This suggests that "successful performance involves the co-operation of motivation and ability in a clear and supportive work environment."[46]

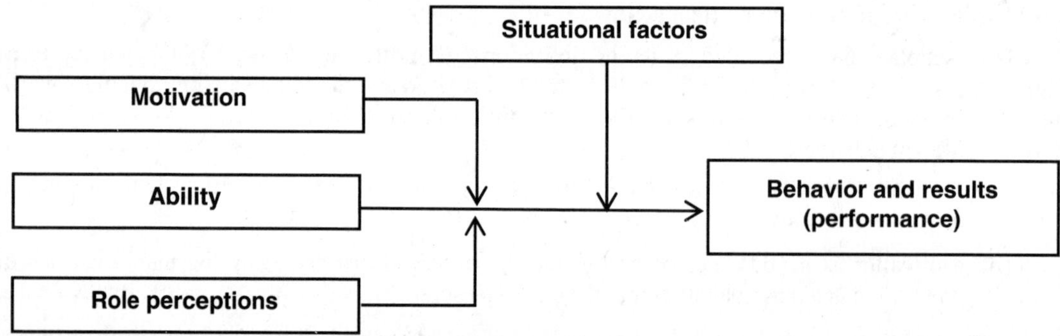

Fig. 4.9 : MARS Model of Motivation and Performance[46]

4.4.4 Theories of Motivation

The major theories on motivation are divided into two categories—content theories and process theories. *Content theories* on motivation describe the 'what' of motivation and *process theories* on motivation describes the 'how' of motivation.

The major content theories are drive theory, *McClelland's secondary motives theory, needs theories, and theory Z.* The needs theories are a sub-part of content theories, and consist of *Maslow's Needs Hierarchy Theory, Herzberg's Two Factor Theory, and Alderfer's ERG Theory.*

The process theories consist of theories such as *Vroom's VIE theory/expectancy theory, positive reinforcement theory, equity theory, and goal setting theory.*

The latest addition to motivation theory is the *Attribution Theory of Motivation.*

4.4.4.1 Drive Theory (Clark Hull)

Hull has described motivation as a drive that is created by unfulfilled needs, deficits, or deprivation (Fig. 4.10).[47] These unfulfilled needs create a disequilibrium or imbalance, which 'drives' the behaviour of a person towards action for satisfying those unfulfilled needs and restoring the balance. For example, if a person has not eaten for many hours, s/he will feel an unfulfilled need known as 'hunger'; s/he will, thus, have the drive to search for food in her/his house (action), and will finally eat food and satisfy the imbalance created in her/him due to hunger.

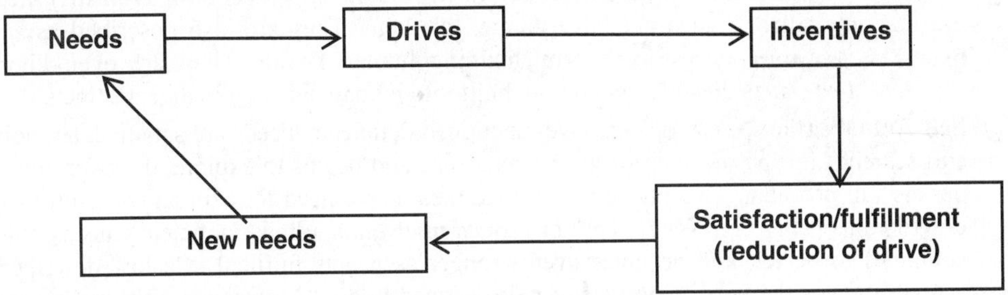

Fig. 4.10 : Hull's Drive Theory

The drive theory has divided the needs into two categories as follows:

(a) **Primary Needs:** These are unlearned needs that are biological in nature, such as hunger.[47] A person is not taught to experience them.

(b) **Secondary Needs:** These are those needs that are learned during our interaction with others. For example, the need for power and status. They are more important in the case of organisational studies.[48]

However, the drive theory is criticised on the ground that it assumes a mechanistic view of humans. People are viewed as machines 'driven' to restore the balance in order to survive. It ignores the value of reward at the end of and the learning during the performance.

4.4.4.2 Maslow's Needs Hierarchy Theory

Maslow's theory is a needs theory. Needs theories share a fundamental focus: a deficit created by an unsatisfied need and motivated behaviour aimed at the restoration of balance or satisfaction (similar to drive theory).

Maslow's theory is based on the idea of the prepotency of needs. According to Maslow, different people have different needs and motivations. Needs are described as the 'third force' in understanding the human psyche after Freud's unconscious desires (first force) and their consequences (second force).

Maslow described a hierarchy of needs in which the lower position is occupied by basic needs. These needs are based on the ongoing cycle of deficiency and fulfilment. The upper position is occupied by those needs that do not arise due to deficiency and are not cyclical. Once the lower needs are satisfied, then the desire for fulfilment of other needs arises in a step-by-step manner; each satisfied lower order need gives way to an unfulfilled higher-order need. Unless the lower needs are satisfied, the middle or higher-order needs do not surface. The needs described in this model are as follows:

(a) **Physiological Needs:** These are biological needs for food, thirst, sex, shelter, and also salary.

(b) **Safety Needs:** This is the need for job security and safety provided by fixed tenure, saving bank accounts, insurance, and so on.

(c) **Social Needs:** These are needs for friendship, contact, relations, recognition from others, and membership of groups and unions.

(d) **Esteem Needs:** These are needs for the recognition of one's achievements. They are divided into two parts. The lower esteem needs represent the need to be respected by others, achieve status, get recognition from others, and gain reputation and dominance. The higher esteem need is self-esteem, which represents the need to build self-respect, confidence, competence, and excellence.

The four above-mentioned needs are described as *deficiency needs* (or *D needs*), i.e., they are felt only till one does not have enough of them. They are also described as *survival needs*, as they are necessary for maintaining human health. They are even known as *instinctoid needs*, as they are genetically built into human beings like their instincts.

(e) **Self-Actualisation Need:** If the above-mentioned deficiency needs are satisfied, an individual still searches for the meaning of her/his existence and begins to explore, discover, and utilise her/his full potential. This phenomenon is termed as the need for self-actualisation. It is also described as *being need* (or *B need*) or *growth motivation.* Unlike deficiency needs, this need continues to be felt and becomes even stronger as it gets fulfilled. Maslow described self-actualisation as the need to do what one is destined to do. "A musician must make music, an artist must paint and a poet must write, if he is to be ultimately at peace with himself. What a man can be, he must be." He gave the following qualities of self-actualised people:[49]

(i) **Reality-centred:** They have the tendency to differentiate between genuine and fake things.

(ii) **Problem-centred:** They treat problems as an opportunity to look for solutions and learn.

(iii) **Need Privacy:** They require privacy and are comfortable being alone.

(iv) **Culturally Independent:** They are independent of culture and environment; they rely on their own experience and judgment.

(v) **Resist Enculturalism:** They are non-conformists and are not susceptible to social pressures.

(vi) **Democratic Values:** They are open to ethnic and individual variety.

(vii) **Sense of Humour:** They have the unhostile sense of humour and prefer jokes about themselves also.

(viii) **Sense of Appreciation:** They have an ability to appreciate even ordinary things and see them with wonder.

(ix) **Simplicity:** They tend to remain themselves and simple.

(x) ***Gemeinshaftsgefuhl***: They have a quality of social interest, compassion, and humanity (known as *Gemeinshaftsgefuhl*). They also have the ability to be creative.

Apart from the above-mentioned qualities, they also suffer from anxiety, guilt, absentmindedness, and unexpected events of ruthlessness. For self-actualised people, motivation is nothing but character growth and character expression.[50] They have special needs such as truth, goodness, uniqueness, perfection, justice, self-sufficiency, and meaningfulness.

Clarifications on the Model

Maslow has provided the following few clarifications to his needs hierarchy model:

(i) **Non-Rigid Hierarchy:** The hierarchy in the hierarchy of needs is not rigid and there is scope for deviations. For example, for some people, having a low level of aspiration, higher-level goals may disappear forever and they get satisfied with very low levels of need fulfilment. Similarly, there may be people who may sacrifice a lower-order need for some time to satisfy their higher-order needs.

(ii) **Non-Watertight Hierarchy:** The hierarchy of needs is not divided into watertight compartments. Satisfaction is not an absolute but a relative term. The emergence of a higher-order need, from a lower-order need, is a gradual and not a sudden process.

(iii) **Unconscious Process:** The emergence of new needs, and disappearance of old needs, is an unconscious process.

(iv) **Culturally Neutral:** The basic needs and desires of all the people are the same, irrespective of all the societies and cultures they live in.

(v) **Multiple Motivations:** Human behaviour is determined by multiple motivations. The need is just one of the variables that motivate human behaviour.

(vi) **Satisfied Need:** The satisfied need ceases to be a motivator again.

Peak Experience

Maslow gave the idea of peak experiences and described the phenomenon as exciting movements involving feelings of happiness and well-being, and an awareness of transcendental knowledge of the higher truth.[51] It is attained by a self-actualised person. These experiences tend to be uplifting, release creative energies, give a sense of purpose and a feeling of integration, and leave a permanent mark on the individual.[49] These experiences open up the vision of a person towards limitless horizons; they create in a person both feelings of powerfulness and helplessness simultaneously.

Eupsychian Management

Maslow described 'Eupsychian Management' as one that is designed to allow the employees to satisfy their safety, love, as well as self-actualisation needs. Happiness at work is the most important criterion of self-fulfilment. Maslow suggested that there should be a study of employees' complaints in order to understand and satisfy their needs.

Criticism of Needs Hierarchy Model

1. Maslow's theory, although appealing, is based on no formal research in management.
2. The theory is also criticised to be of no formal use to managers as it merely classifies the needs that everyone has.
3. The theory fails to identify the cultural and individual differences, and assumes that people experience the same hierarchy of needs.
4. The description of self-actualisation and self-actualised people is based on the writings of, and talking to, selectively chosen people rather than rigorous sampling.

4.4.4.3 ERG Theory (Alderfer)

Alderfer gave the theory of existence, relatedness, and growth (ERG). In it, he classified needs into three categories corresponding to Maslow's needs hierarchy. The existence needs correspond to the physiological and safety needs of Maslow. Relatedness needs correspond to the social needs and recognition needs of Maslow. Finally, the growing needs of the ERG model correspond to the self-esteem and self-actualisation needs of Maslow. However, the ERG model is different from Maslow's model in the sense that it did not specify a hierarchy of needs. In this model, needs can arise in any order and it is not necessary that the lower need will arise first.

4.4.4.4 McClelland Secondary Motivation Theory

The McClelland model focused on the secondary needs, as it considered secondary needs more important from the social and organisational perspective. He described the following three categories of motivation (see Fig. 4.11):

(a) **nAch:** McClelland described nAch as the need for achievement which corresponds to the self-esteem and self-actualisation needs of Maslow. It is described as a need for a sense of mastery over one's environment, accomplishment through one's own abilities, and skills and preference for challenges but moderate risks. Achievement needs also provide a want for feedback from others and personal responsibility for success/ failure.

(b) **nPow:** Described as the need for power, it is the need for autonomy for self and control over others. It corresponds to the social, esteem, and recognition needs of Maslow.

(c) **nAff:** Described as the need for affiliation, it is the need for friendship, love, and group membership, corresponding to the relatedness need of the ERG model.

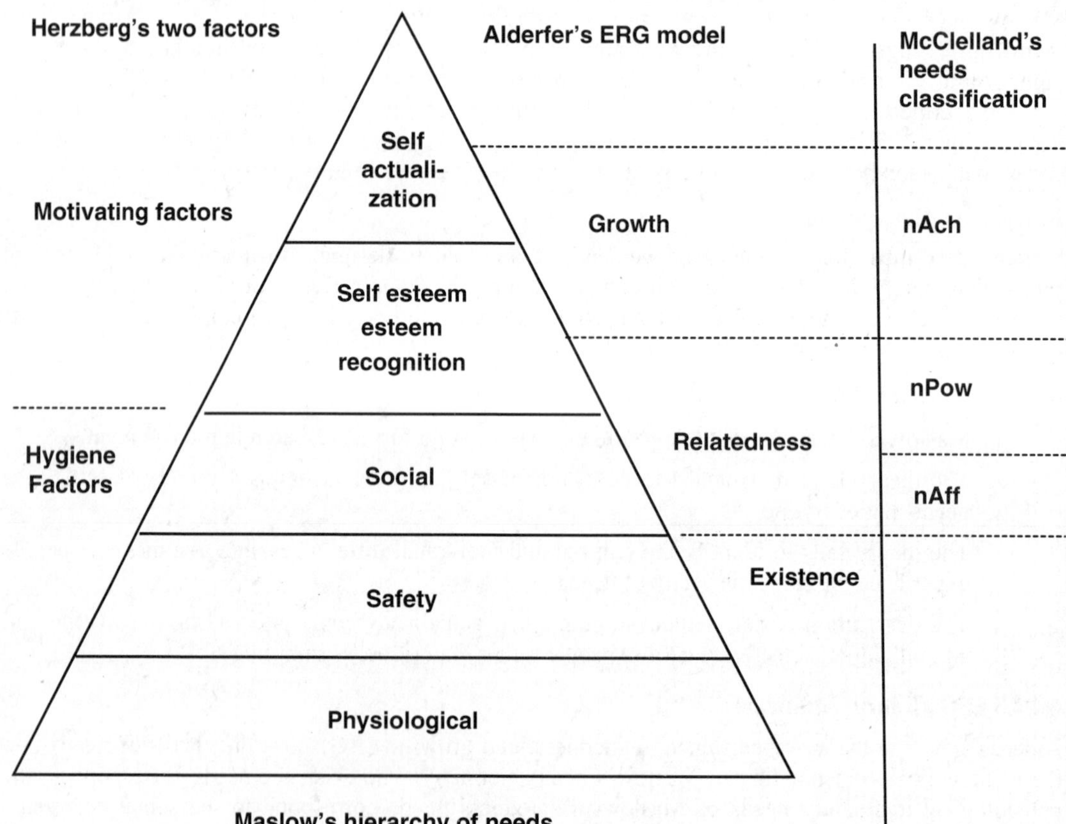

Fig. 4.11 : Different Needs Models of Motivation on Same Scale

4.4.4.5 Herzberg's Two-Factor Theory/Motivation Hygiene Theory

Frederick Herzberg said that an individual has two sets of needs—to avoid pain and to grow psychologically. He called these two sets of needs as those for avoiding job dissatisfaction and earning job satisfaction. The factors for avoiding job dissatisfaction are known as *hygiene factors* and those for earning job satisfaction are known as *motivational factors/motivators* (Fig. 4.12).

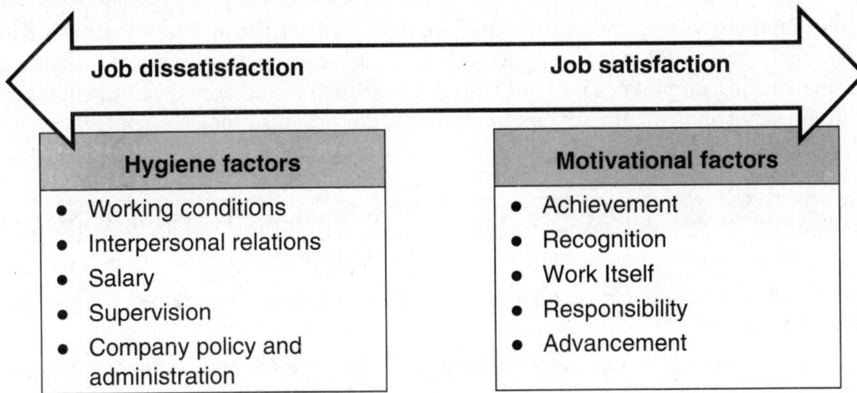

Fig. 4.12 : Herzberg's Motivation Hygiene Theory

The motivational factors/motivators/ satisfiers are described as follows:

(a) **Achievement:** It is the need to independently achieve one's aims and organisational goals. It is similar to the nAch need of McClelland.

(b) **Recognition:** It is the need for being recognised/acknowledged by others for the accomplishment of an organisation or personal goal.

(c) **Work Itself:** It is a need to get motivation from the content, variety, and challenges of the task itself.

(d) **Responsibility:** It is the need to be entrusted with complete responsibility for certain tasks and has authority over deciding how the task is to be performed.

(e) **Advancement:** It is the need for periodical advancement towards higher order tasks.

On the other hand, hygiene factors/dissatisfiers are those factors that are necessary so that the employees do not feel dissatisfied with their organisation. They are environmental factors such as working conditions, interpersonal relations in the company, salary, supervision style in the organisation, and company policy and administration. These factors have no relation to the motivation of specific job-related behaviour. While on one hand, the motivational factors produce long-term changes in human attitudes, the hygiene factors produce only short-term changes in human attitudes. Herzberg described the following characteristics of the two-factor theory:

(a) The factors that create job satisfaction are separate from those that lead to job dissatisfaction. Growth and task performance are attained by satisfaction, and dissatisfaction are unrelated to the task.

(b) The opposite of satisfaction on the job is not dissatisfaction; rather it is no satisfaction from the job. Similarly, the opposite of dissatisfaction from the organisation is not satisfaction; rather it is no dissatisfaction from the organisation. Thus, satisfaction and dissatisfaction are not the opposite of the same continuum. They are 'unipolar traits'.

(c) The motivating factors are self-sustaining and not dependent on supervisory conditions. On the other hand, hygiene factors are those that are never satisfied completely and require continuous attention from the organisation to be satisfied. They need to be replenished periodically.

Motivation Seeking and Hygiene Seeking Employees

According to the motivation-hygiene model, the employees of an organisation can be divided into two categories—motivation-seeking employees and hygiene-seeking employees, described in Mind Map 4.4. Hygiene-seeking employees will not help in the growth of the organisation. On the contrary, they will create an environment of extrinsic rewards in the organisation. Herzberg has also called them 'barrack soldiers' of the organisation.

Hygiene-seeking employees	Motivation-seeking employees
Motivated by the nature of the organisation	Motivated by the nature of task
Get highly dissatisfied with aspects of the job such as salary, job security, and interpersonal relations	Are tolerant towards poor hygiene factors in the organisation
They react with satisfaction after improvement in hygiene factors	They react less after improvement in hygiene factors
They do not get much satisfaction from achievement	They realise ultimate satisfaction from achievement
They show little interest in the kind and quality of work	They are utmost concerned with the quality of work and enjoy their work
They have a negative attitude towards virtues such as life and work	They have a positive attitude towards virtues such as work and life
They do not learn professionally from organisational experiences	They learn and develop professionally from organisational experiences
Their values change through change in surrounding cultures	Their belief systems remain unchanged by change in culture

Mind Map 4.4: Motivation-seeking and hygiene-seeking employees

Measures to Improve Motivating Factors at the Workplace

Herzberg suggested the following measures for improving the motivating factors at the workplace:

(a) **Job Enrichment:** Herzberg said that enrichment of the job is the true source of providing intrinsic motivation to employees. Moreover, it helps in making the work experience more meaningful. It involves making the job sufficiently challenging so as to utilise the full abilities of an employee. It also involves providing an increasing level of responsibility to those employees who demonstrate increasing levels of ability. A job that is not able to utilise the full abilities of a person must be either automated, or the person must be replaced by a person of lesser skills and abilities.

However, Herzberg cautioned that job enrichment is a 'vertical loading of the job' and should not be confused with 'horizontal loading of the job'. *Horizontal loading* means increasing the amount of work by giving a similar nature to the work to an employee. For example, if a person tightens 1,000 bolts a day very nicely, asking them to tighten 2,000 bolts daily amounts to horizontal loading. It does not help in increasing motivation.

(b) **Vertical Loading and Natural Module of Work:** Herzberg suggested developing natural modules of work for which individuals can be given complete responsibility. Here, a module is a set of related tasks that contribute in sequence to the completion of some function. This module of work is related to some natural unit of work, to become meaningful and motivating. Generally, organisations have several employees performing the work of several fragments of a natural work module; this hinders in fixing the responsibility of a single individual for the whole module. However, when an individual is given the responsibility of the full process, s/he develops a sense of proprietorship for the work. This concept of loading the whole process into a job is known as *vertical loading* of the job. Unlike horizontal loading, this addition of additional tasks and responsibilities helps in improving job satisfaction for employees.

Criticism of Motivation Hygiene Theory

1. The motivation approach of Herzberg is criticised as being an industrial engineering approach to motivation.
2. The theory seems to be more applicable to the management than the employees at the shop floor level.
3. Some elements are considered as both satisfiers and dissatisfiers. For example, income, which is dissatisfier when it is low, acts as satisfier when it is high because it provides recognition and enhances self-esteem.
4. Herzberg's methodology is criticised for being egg-bound. It has the basic flaw that people refer to motivating factors when things are going well in their work and organisation. However, they blame the hygiene/ environmental factors when things are not right in their work and organisation. That is a basic human tendency that remained unaddressed in this theory. Moreover, critics have also said that the separation of satisfaction and dissatisfaction is an artifact of the *critical incident technique* used by Herzberg and is not a reality.
5. The theory is also criticised for universalising the satisfiers and dissatisfiers. However, the same factor can cause job satisfaction for one and job dissatisfaction for another.
6. The theory made a flawed assumption that a satisfied and happy person will become a more productive employee.

Comparison between Maslow's and Herzberg's Theory

The motivation theories of Maslow and Herzberg are, both, needs-based theories. They emphasise a similar set of relationships between needs and motivation. Herzberg's hygiene factors are equivalent to Maslow's lower-order needs and Herzberg's motivational factors are equivalent to Maslow's higher-order needs (as shown in Fig. 4.11). However, the two models have certain differences as shown in Mind Map 4.5.

Maslow's model	Herzberg's model
The basic presumption is that any unsatisfied need (whether lower or higher) motivates a person	The basic presumption is that only higher-order needs (satisfiers) are motivating, and lower-order needs (dissatisfiers) only avoid dissatisfaction

Maslow's model	Herzberg's model
This model can be applied to any kind of employees	This model has only limited applicability for higher management and professional employees
It is a descriptive theory and does not makes any suggestion for improving motivation	Along with being descriptive, it prescribes measures such as job enrichment and vertical loading for improving motivation
It deals with all kind of motivation in society	It deals only with work-related motivation in professional organisations

Mind Map 4.5: Differences between Maslow's and Herzberg's theories of motivation

4.4.4.6 Theory Z of Motivation

Theory Z of motivation originated from Japanese management philosophy and was propounded by William Ouchi and Alfred Jaeger. It advocates the establishment of motivational-oriented organisational cultures with special emphasis on employee development and a participative culture. In the theory, there is an integration of the characteristics of American Organisations (Type A) and Japanese Organisations (Type J). The characteristics of Theory Z organisations are described in Fig. 4.13.

Characteristics of theory Z organisations	Type A organisations	Type J organisations
Decision-making by group participation	Individual managers make decisions	Emphasis on group decision-making
Responsibility assigned on an individual basis	Assigned on an individual basis	Responsibility shared collectively by a group
Control is maintained using trust and goodwill	Explicit and formal control mechanism	Implicit and informal control mechanisms
Performance evaluation and promotions are very slow	Slower promotions. Emphasis is on evaluation and training than on promotions.	Very fast promotions leading to job hopping
Career Path—Employees are allowed to learn all areas of operations	Very specified career path—people stick to one area of specialisation	Very general career path—there is job rotation, and broad-based training is given to make the employees feel comfortable in any part of the organisation
Concerned for workers' whole life	Concerned only for worklife	Concerned with workers' whole life—business and social

Fig. 4.13: Characteristics of Theory Z organisations[52]

Some of the characteristics of Theory Z organisations are as described below:

(a) **Recruitment and Promotion:** Employees are recruited for a long time. People of all ages are employed. Promotions are slow and based on productivity performance.

(b) **Organisational Structure:** The organisational structure is hierarchical based on moderate job specialisation, moderate decentralisation, job enlargement, and, where required, a matrix form of organisation. Organisations are built around groups.

(c) **Decision-making:** Decisions are less centralised, with an emphasis on participation and consensus. Verbal communication is encouraged and written communication is used only to verify the execution of decisions.

(d) **Management System:** Management tries to attain high goal congruence by integrating the organisational goals with those of the individuals. Employees are considered valuable assets and they show an inherent liking of work and require very less supervision.

(e) **Employee Relationship:** Organisations show high concern for employees and their welfare.

(f) **Human Resource Development:** In these organisations, the potential skills of employees are recognised and developed. Job enlargement and career planning are given due emphasis. Organisational socialisation, technical training, and research and development are the priorities for these organisations.

Process Theories of Motivation

Process theories of motivation are those theories that focus on how a person is motivated. They consider motivation as a complex psychological process determined by factors on the side of the individual as well as those lying in the organisational context. As they focus on the 'how' of motivation, they are found more useful for application in the work context. Various process theories are described in the following sections.

4.4.4.7 Skinner's Positive Reinforcement Theory

Skinner gave the positive reinforcement theory of motivation, which was fundamentally based on his experiments on rats. He believed that the best way to understand behaviour is to look at the causes of an action and its consequences; he termed this approach *operant conditioning*. Herė *operants* are intentional actions that have an effect on the surrounding environment. According to Skinner's theory, behaviour that is reinforced tends to be repeated and behaviour that is not reinforced tends to die out or weaken.

Apart from reinforcement, there are two more types of operants that can shape behaviour—neutral operants and punishers. These three operants are described below:

(a) **Neutral Operants:** These are the responses from the environment that neither increase nor decrease the probability of a behaviour being repeated.

(b) **Reinforcers:** These are the responses from the environment that increase the probability of a behaviour being repeated.

(c) **Punishers:** These are the responses from the environment that decrease the likelihood of a behaviour being repeated.

Among these three operants, reinforcers are of the following two types:

(a) **Positive Reinforcement:** Positive reinforcement is a response that strengthens behaviour by providing a consequence that an individual finds rewarding. For example, if a police constable is given INR 1000 for every time s/he detects a case (i.e., reward), s/he will be more likely to repeat this behaviour in the future (detect more cases).

(b) **Negative Reinforcement:** Negative reinforcement is a response that strengthens a behaviour by the removal of an unpleasant reinforcer. For example, if police constables do not complete their investigation on time, they are made to do an extra parade. Thus, they will complete their investigation on time so as to avoid doing an extra drills, thus strengthening their behaviour of completing their investigations on time.

Schedules of Reinforcement

Skinner further analysed the impact of reinforcement schedules on the behaviour of human beings/animals. He considered that different patterns of reinforcement had different effects on the speed of behaviour change (*response rate*) and on the extinction of the desired behaviour (*extinction rate*). The different types of schedules and their reinforcement are described in Mind Map 4.6. Accordingly, a slower rate of extinction is provided by variable ratio reinforcement and the quickest rate of extinction is provided by continuous reinforcement.

Type of reinforcement	Response rate	Extinction rate	Description
Continuous reinforcement	Slow	Fast	Reward is given every time a specific behaviour occurs. For example, a constable is rewarded every time s/he detects a crime.
Fixed ratio reinforcement	Fast	Medium	Constable is rewarded only after s/he detects a fixed number (say, 5) of crimes. (Reward given only after a behaviour occurs a specified number of times.)
Fixed interval reinforcement	Medium	Medium	Reinforcement is given after a fixed time interval, provided at least one correct response is made. For example, a constable is given a bonus every 3 months if s/he detects at least one crime in this period.
Variable ratio reinforcement	Fast	Slow	Behaviour is reinforced after a desired behaviour occurs an unpredictable number of times. For example, a constable may be rewarded for detecting 3, 4, 5 or any number of cases, so that s/he remains indulged in her/his task.
Variable interval reinforcement	Fast	Slow	Reinforcement is given after an unpredictable amount of time provided one correct response is made. For example, a constable is rewarded in a period of 1, 2, 3 or any number of months.

Mind Map 4.6: Different types of reinforcement

4.4.4.8 Victor Vroom's VIE Theory/Expectancy Theory

The expectancy theory propounded by Victor Vroom considered that different individuals have different levels of motivation according to the differences in their personal choices and situational factors. It suggests that when an individual is presented with different behavioural options in a situation, s/he selects the option with the greatest *motivational force* (MF). The motivational force for a behaviour or task is a function of three distinct perceptions, as shown in Fig. 4.14.

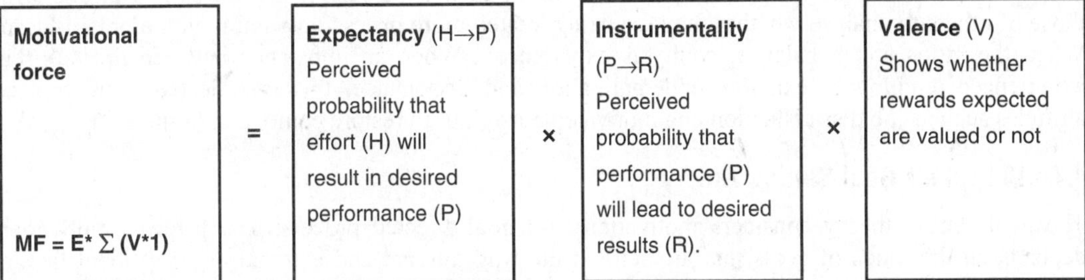

Fig. 4.14 : Victor Vroom's Expectancy/VIE Theory[65]

(a) **Expectancy:** Expectancy perception is the probability that an individual assigns to the belief that if tried (H), there would be a success (P) for meeting the final goals. This perception is based on the following sub-factors:

 (i) **Self-Efficacy:** It is a belief of a person in himself for performing a task successfully. If it is high, the person is confident of achieving the goals and expectancy is high.

 (ii) **Perceived Control of Performance:** Expectancy is high when individuals believe that they have control over expected performance. It depends on the past experience of an individual.

 (iii) **Goal Difficulty:** Expectancy is high if an individual perceives the goals to be within his/her capabilities. On the contrary, expectancy is low when the goals are considered as difficult and unrealistic.

(b) **Instrumentality:** Instrumentality perception is the subjective probability that meeting performance expectations (P) will be instrumental in getting desirable rewards (R) such as an increase in pay, promotion, recognition, or sense of achievement. Instrumentality increases when valued rewards are directly proportional to performance. This perception is based on the following sub-factors:

 (i) **Trust:** If there is higher trust in leaders, subordinates will believe that their performance will be met by valued rewards.

 (ii) **Control:** Instrumentality increases when individuals believe that they have some kind of control over how, when, and why rewards are distributed.

 (iii) **Policies:** Instrumentality increases when pay and reward systems are clearly mentioned in formalised policies.

(c) **Valence:** Valence perception is the value an individual places on particular rewards. It depends on individuals' needs, goals, values, and other sources of motivation.

The process described by Vroom helps managers in understanding the individual motivational process and in identifying where to intervene in order to influence crucial employee perception, to increase employee motivation.[64]

4.4.4.9 Adams' Equity Theory of Motivation

Equity theory describes that people are motivated by a sense of equity in work place. They are not only concerned about the rewards they receive for their efforts but also about the rewards others receive for their efforts. People compare the ratio of their own outcomes/rewards and efforts with those of others to analyse whether they are being treated more or less favourably in the organisation. When the ratios are in balance, equity is experienced. When an imbalance between the ratios is experienced, employees experience demotivation and dissonance; this is reflected in workplace attitudes such as job dissatisfaction and motivated behaviour to restore equity and fairness.[66]

4.4.4.10 Locke's Goal Setting Theory

The goal setting theory considers motivation as a goal-directed process. The level of motivation depends on the kinds of goals that are set and the way internal and external organisational factors affecting the process between goal identification and goal achievement are managed. In the theory, the goals are classified as shown in Table 4.1.

Table 4.1: Goals in Locke's goal setting theory

Criterion	Types of Goals
Number	Single/multiple goals
Complexity	Simple/easy or difficult/complex goals
Specificity	General or specific goals
Existence	Existence of goals or no goals
Assignment	Self-assigned or imposed goals

Goal setting theory has the following principles that describe the level of motivation:

(a) If individuals are committed to difficult goals, and their efforts are supported by specific outcomes and process feedback, then the highest levels of individual performance are achieved.[67, 68]

(b) Specific and difficult goals lead to consistently higher performance. General and easy goals like 'do your best' lead to disinterest in work.[69]

(c) Effective goal setting requires effective feedback (the art of feedback has been discussed in the section on Communication in this chapter) and employee commitment to goals.

(d) Higher number of goals demotivate a person. When a difficult task involves both quantity and quality goals, people may tends to neglect the quality goals and maximise the quantity goals.[70]

(e) A difficult goal is intrinsically rewarding. In the case of these goals, the provision of external evaluation reduces intrinsic motivation.

(f) When the goal is difficult, individuals experience far greater total motivation- both extrinsic and intrinsic, compared to individuals who are assigned easy goals.

4.4.4.11 Porter and Lawler's Performance Satisfaction Model

Porter and Lawler's model is an attempt towards explaining the relationship between motivation and performance. As shown in Fig. 4.15, it is based on the assumption that rewards cause satisfaction and performance produces rewards. Thus, the relationship between performance and satisfaction is linked with another variable—reward. This concept is against the neoclassical view that held a direct relationship between performance and satisfaction.

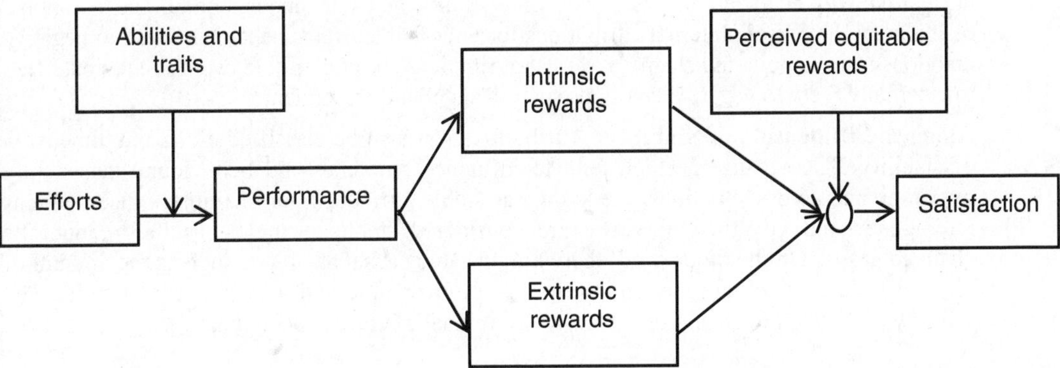

Fig. 4.15 : Porter and Lawler's Performance–Satisfaction Model[72]

In the model, the reward is the one that is positively valued by the individual. These rewards are indirectly related to satisfaction through *perceived equitable rewards*. A perceived equitable reward is a variable that refers to the amount of reward an individual thinks they should get as the result of their performance. In the model, satisfaction is viewed as a deficiency measure, as it is determined by the difference between the actual rewards and perceived equitable rewards. If the actual rewards are higher than the perceived equitable rewards, the situation is one of satisfaction. If the actual rewards are lower than the perceived actual rewards, the situation is one of dissatisfaction.

The satisfaction/motivation of an individual is influenced by various factors such as the value placed on rewards, efforts of an individual, abilities and traits of the individual, role perceptions of the individual, and perceived equitable rewards of the individual. While providing rewards, the following principles must be respected:

(a) Valued and important rewards shall be tied to performance.

(b) Better rewards should be given for higher performance. These rewards should be visible for all to see.

4.4.4.12 Weiner's Attribution Theory of Motivation

Attribution theory is a useful theory that provides managers with a better understanding of the cognitive and psychological mechanisms that influence motivational levels.[53] An attribution is a causal explanation for an event or behaviour. For example, if a police inspector talks very roughly with the complainants, a person may attribute (give reason for) this behaviour to poor police training. The process of attribution helps in understanding the cause of desirable events and in repeating those experiences again. Attribution for desirable behaviours and outcomes ultimately helps in shaping emotional and behavioural responses.[54]

Classification of Attributions

There are various classifications of attributions. They are as follows:

(a) **Along Locus of Causality:** Attributions are classified along the locus of causality. This describes the internality or externality of an attribution. If a murder case remains unsolved and an inspector attributes this to his/her own lack of intelligence, he/she makes an internal attribution. If the same result is attributed to a lack of sufficient investigation tools, the attribution will be external. The locus of causality helps in understanding the emotional reactions of the person. Internal attributions for undesirable events/behaviours lead to negative emotions such as guilt and shame. External attributions for undesirable events/behaviours lead to externally focused negative emotions such as anger and resentment.[55]

(b) **Along the Dimension of Stability:** Attributions can also be classified along the dimension of stability. These causes, which tend to influence outcomes and behaviours consistently over time and across situations, are known as stable attributes. For example, causes such as intelligence and governmental laws are considered stable attributes, as they cannot be changed easily. On the other hand, there are unstable causal attributes such as the amount of physical effort, which are susceptible to change over time and in different situations. The stability dimension of attributes affects an individual's future expectations.[56]

Locus of causality →

Dimension of stability ↓	Internal	External
Stable	Internal and stable attributes e.g. intelligence	External and stable attributes e.g. laws
Unstable	Internal and unstable attributes e.g. efforts	External and unstable attributes e.g. temporary policies

Fig. 4.16 : Different types of Attributes

Thus, attributions can be of four types, as described in Fig. 4.16.

Different Attribution Styles

An attribution style is defined as a tendency to consistently attribute positive and negative outcomes to a specific type of cause, either internal/external or stable/unstable.[53] The attribution styles are of the following types:

(a) **Optimistic Attribution Style:** It is the tendency to attribute negative outcomes to external factors and positive outcomes to internal factors.[57]

(b) **Pessimistic Attribution Style:** It is the tendency to attribute negative outcomes to internal and stable factors, such as intelligence, and desirable outcomes to external factors and unstable factors, such as luck.

(c) **Hostile Attribution Style:** Similar to the optimistic attribution style, the hostile attribution style is a tendency to attribute negative outcomes to external factors and positive outcomes to internal factors. However, in this case, the stability of the negative outcome promotes hostility or anger towards the external entity (e.g., one's manager).[58]

Different Motivational States

The various types of attributions and attribution styles lead to four types of motivational states among individuals. Among them, two motivational states, learned helplessness and aggression, are undesirable and two motivational states, empowerment and resilience, are desirable among individuals. They are described below:

(a) **Learned Helplessness:** Learned helplessness is a motivational state, in which people become passive and unmotivated and remain the same even after modifications in the environment.[59] It describes a situation in which individuals believe that efforts are futile and failure is inevitable. Such a state is attained due to organisational policies/norms and leaders' behaviours that make employees feel that success or recognition is unobtainable.

This tendency of learned helplessness can be explained in terms of the attribution process. If there are external barriers to success in the workplace, failure is attributed to internal and frequently stable factors while success is attributed to external factors. It leads to the pessimistic attribution style, in which individuals blame themselves for failure and appreciate their managers for success.

(b) **Aggression:** Aggression is a state of high motivation directed towards undesirable goals. It is of two types—instrumental and hostile aggression. Instrumental aggression is a behaviour targeted towards obtaining a goal that the organisation is not helping in attaining. For example, a police officer who is not satisfied with their salary and indulges in corrupt activities to earn more money is doing an act of instrumental aggression. On the other hand, hostile aggression is a behaviour aimed at harming others. Both types of aggression are a result of hostile attribution style, i.e., employees who attribute negative work events to external and stable causes are motivated to engage in aggressive behaviour.

(c) **Empowerment:** Empowerment is a state of high motivation caused by the optimistic expectation of rewards associated with personal effort.[60] It results from the attribution of negative work events to factors that are internally controllable or those factors that are external, unstable, and uncontrollable; it also involves the attribution of positive events to internal factors such as intelligence, skills, and efforts.[59] This tendency is found more in individuals possessing the optimistic attribution style.

(d) **Resilience:** The definition of resilience is "a staunch acceptance of reality, strongly held values and an uncanny ability to improvise and adapt to significant changes."[61] It is found in individuals have a tendency to develop accurate attributions.[62] Their attributions are in line with reality. Resilience, thus, can be termed as a factor that helps individuals avoid attributional errors that can hurt motivational levels. By making people grounded in reality, resilience helps in preventing pessimistic and hostile attributional tendencies.

Motivational state	Associated attributional tendency
Learned helplessness	Favour internal and stable attributions for failures; external attributions for success
Aggression	Favour external and stable attributions for failure

Motivational state	Associated attributional tendency
Empowerment	Favour internal and stable attributions for success; external and unstable attributions for failure
Resilience	Favour accurate attributions, not biased towards overly internal or external attributions for success or failure

***Mind Map 4.7:** Different motivational states according to attribution theory*[53]

Techniques for Promoting Employee Motivation

According to attribution theory, the following five techniques have been suggested to improve employees' motivation:

(a) **Resilience Screening:** Organisations should employ the kind of resilient employees they need. For example, organisations such as hospitals require a high level of resilience and, thus, should hire individuals possessing higher resilience. The resilience level of a candidate can be analysed by asking him/her to describe past hardships and his/her response to them.[63]

(b) **Attributional Training:** Employees can be trained to have accurate and optimistic attributional tendencies. This can be done by measuring employees' attribution styles with an assessment device and discussing their attributional biases with them. The realisation of optimistic, pessimistic, or hostile attribution styles helps in correcting them. Another method of attributional training is discussing the causes of employees' successes and failures on a case-by-case basis. This can help the employees in understanding the multiple personal and situational factors responsible for negative and positive outcomes.

(c) **Immunisation:** Employees can be immunised against demotivated attributions by providing success early in the organisational life of an individual. Early failure may lead to a feeling of inability (internal and stable attribution). On the other hand, early success in surmountable tasks may lead to a feeling of strength, intelligence, and ability. This will promote more optimistic attributions throughout the employee's organisational life.

(d) **Improving Psychological Closeness:** Psychological closeness describes the extent to which two or more people form the same perceptions regarding the situation. It helps managers form accurate attributions regarding their employees' performance. Such closeness is found more in managers who have personal experience with the work their employees are doing. Thus, managers should be given an experience of their employees' work so as to increase psychological closeness between managers and employees. This can also be done by internal promotions.

(e) **Multiple Raters of Promotion:** Multiple judges should be used to judge employees' performance, so as to improve the accuracy and motivational capacity of employees' attribution. It ensures that potential biases among one or more judges are offset by the accuracy, or counteracting biases, of other judges. A 360-degree appraisal is a good example of a review by multiple judges.

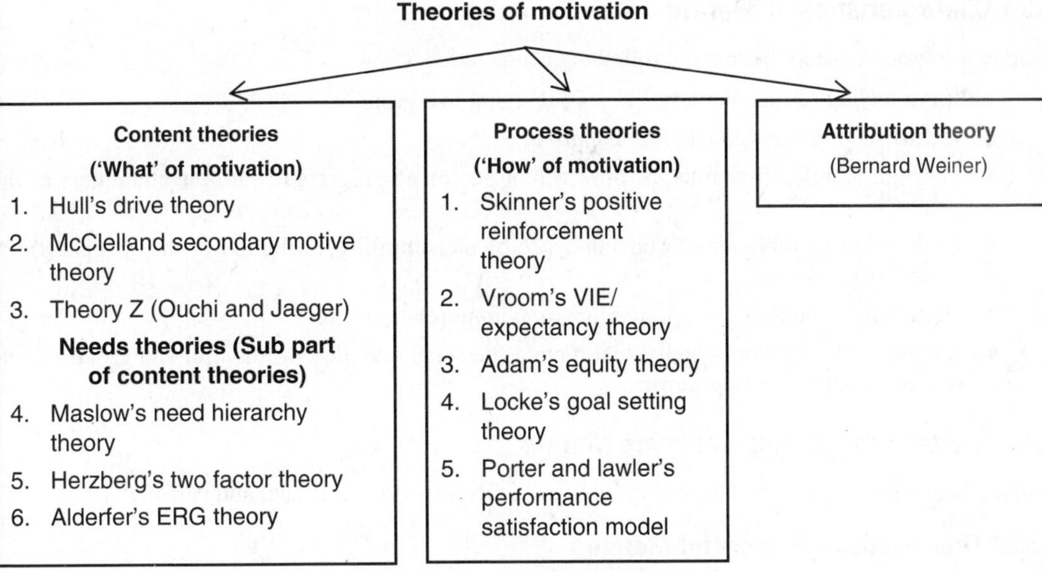

Mind Map 4.8 : Theories of Motivation

4.5 Employee Morale

Employee morale is generally referred to as the willingness to work in an organisation. Being a widely quoted term, there are different definitions of morale. After classifying these definitions, we find three basic approaches to define morale. They are as follows:

(a) **Classical Approach:** Robert M. Guion has defined morale in terms of job satisfaction. He defines morale as the extent to which individual needs are satisfied and the extent to which individuals perceive satisfaction to be stemming from total job satisfaction.[71]

(b) **Psychological Approach:** According to Jucious and Slender, "morale is a state of mind and emotions affecting willingness to work which in turn affects individual and organisational objectives." Here morale is a psychological concept determining the employee's willingness to work. It is also the willingness of group members to cooperate as a work unit.

(c) **Social Approach:** The social approach describes morale as the ability of individuals to live in a society or group for achieving common goals. In the words of Blackmanship, "morale is a feeling of togetherness." It shows the interest of the employee in their work, working conditions, fellow employees, supervisor, employer, and the organisation. Morale is a key factor in the creation of an atmosphere in the organisation conducive to the achievement of the organisation.

Summarising, morale is an indicator of the attitude of employees towards their jobs, superiors, and the organisation's environment. It is a by-product of the group relationships in an organisation.

4.5.1 Characteristics of Morale

Morale is a group concept having the following characteristics:

1. It is a feeling of togetherness, i.e., of belonging to a group.
2. It consists of a clear goal before the group.
3. For high morale, there must be observed or perceived progress toward the attainment of the goal.
4. Each group member should have a sense of meaningful contribution to the group and the overall performance.
5. High morale requires a supportive or stimulating relationship.
6. Morale is of two types—individual morale (personal attitude towards life) and group morale (collective attitude of a group).

4.5.2 Factors Influencing Employee Morale

Employee morale is influenced by two categories of factors—organisational and personal.

4.5.2.1 Organisational Factors for Morale

The following organisational factors influence employees' morale:

(a) **Reputation of the Organisation:** People working in reputed organisations experience feelings of pride and loyalty.

(b) **Goals and Objectives of Organisation:** Employees develop a positive attitude towards work if the goals are worthwhile, useful, and acceptable. Morale is high when organisational goals are in tune with individual goals.

(c) **Organisational Design:** Organisations having bigger hierarchies and longer channels of communication tend to have lower morale. On the contrary, flatter structures have higher morale.

(d) **Nature of Work:** Challenging, meaningful, and satisfying work tends to increase morale.

(e) **Organisational Environment:** Workplace conditions such as cleanliness, safety, comfort, cooperation, job security, and security determine employees' morale.

(f) **Rewards:** A good system of rewards, salaries, promotion, and other incentives keep the morale of the employees high.

(g) **Leadership:** A competent, dependable, and fair leadership is instrumental in achieving high morale. A sympathetic, friendly, and employee-centred leadership is also useful.

(h) **Fellow Employees:** Acceptance, recognition, and companionship of fellow employees are key factors of high morale. Moreover, trust and confidence among employees lead to high morale.

(i) **Self-concept:** How employees perceive themselves in the organisation (self-concept) influences their morale. How employees' needs and values are satisfied by the organisation is a crucial factor for morale.

4.5.2.2 Personal Factors for Morale

The following personal factors influence morale:

(a) **Employee's Age:** Other factors remaining equal, older employees have higher morale because younger employees are more dissatisfied. Older employees have stability, a serious attitude, reliability, a sense of responsibility, and a lesser tendency towards outer distractions.

(b) **Educational Level:** According to research, a reverse relationship is found between employees' education and morale. The higher the education level of an employee, the more s/he compares her/his attainment with others, leading to lower morale.

(c) **Occupational Level:** The occupational level within an organisation impacts the level of morale. For example, executives as a whole may have higher morale than managers; managers in turn may have higher morale than workers.

(d) **Experience:** Other things being equal, morale increases with increasing years of experience. However, it decreases if an experienced employee has not met her/his job expectations from the organisation.

4.5.2.3 Effect of Morale on Productivity

The impact of morale on employee productivity is unpredictable. As expected, there is no direct relationship between morale and productivity. This is because morale is only one of the factors that influence productivity. Productivity can be high with high morale, or can also be low with high morale. There can be four combinations of morale and productivity as follows:

(a) **High Morale–High Productivity:** High morale is an attitude to be more productive only if proper leadership is provided. High morale leads to high productivity when employees are motivated through financial and non-financial rewards.

(b) **High Morale–Low Productivity:** High morale may also lead to low productivity in situations where employees spend their time and energy satisfying their personal objectives unrelated to the company's goals. This happens due to lack of training, faulty work equipment, ineffective supervision, and restrictive norms of informal groups.

(c) **Low Morale–High Productivity:** Low morale may result in high productivity for a temporary period when there is a fear of loss of job, good supervision, and when the work is routine based or machine based, requiring only limited capabilities of employees.

(d) **Low Morale–Low Productivity:** Low morale is ideally expected to result in low productivity.

4.6 Concept and Theories of Leadership

Leadership is the most talked about topic of management. There are thousands of definitions of leadership. For our purpose, we will define leadership as "a process, and a mutual influence relationship among leaders and followers who intend real changes and reflect their mutual purposes."[73] Based on this definition, the following attributes of leadership emerge:

(a) Leadership is a process and not an act.

(b) The influence process in leadership is mutual between leaders and followers.

(c) The influence process is for making some real changes and bringing in significant improvement in the state of affairs of the organisation.

(d) It is beyond goals. Its purpose is to create a vision that connects followers who might have different individual goals.

Mutual Influence Relationship

As described, leadership is a mutual influence relationship between a leader and followers. John French and Bertram Raven have described five sources of this influence:

(a) **Coercive Influence:** Coercive influence is the capacity of a leader to punish his/her followers for not performing the assigned tasks. The influence is based on fear.

(b) **Reward Influence:** Reward influence is the leader's ability to positively recognise his/her followers and provide them with appropriate rewards.

(c) **Legitimate Influence:** Legitimate influence is that which flows from the organisational position of the leader. In it, followers feel the obligation to accept the leader's authority.

(d) **Expert Influence:** Expert influence is the one that is derived from the knowledge, skills, expertise, and information possessed by the leader.

(e) **Referent Influence:** Referent influence is that which is based on the personal attraction that a leader holds for her/his followers. The followers identify themselves with the leader and recognise him/her as their role model.

The first three influences can be categorised as positional influences, and the last two influences can be categorised as personal influences.

4.6.1 Various Explanations of Leadership

Leadership have been explained by various thinkers in different manners. Some of the prominent thinkers are described below:

(a) **Katz and Kahn:** Katz and Kahn have described that the essence of leadership has to do with *influential increment*, which goes beyond the routine and taps bases of power beyond those that are organisationally decreed.[74] They identified three levels of leadership in an organisation. The top-level leadership is concerned with the design of the whole organisational structure and formulation of policy. The intermediate-level leadership functions within the limits of general policy. Finally, at the operative level (lowest level), the task of leadership is to make the best use of the institutional means and procedures for task operation.

(b) **Philip Selznick:** Philip Selznick considered leaders as creative men whose profession is politics, which involves "continuous redefinition of public interest and the embodiment of those definitions in key institutions." Selznick has identified the following key tasks of leadership:

   (i) Definition of institutional mission and role: The primary task of organisational leadership is setting goals in terms of internal and external demands.

   (ii) Institutional embodiment of purpose: The goals and policy devised needs to be percolated down to the social structure of the organisation.

   (iii) Defence of institutional integrity: The leadership has to maintain the core values of the organisation and its distinctive identity.

   (iv) Ordering of internal conflict: The leadership has to understand the various competing interests within the organisation and maintain a balance of power appropriate to the fulfilment of the organisational commitments.[75]

(c) **A.K. Rice:** A.K. Rice conceived of leadership in terms of a boundary controlling function. According to him, "leadership is most conspicuous at points of discontinuities in the organisational structure, where there are breaks between parts of the system."[76]

4.6.2 Leadership Theories

Over the years, various theories of leadership have been developed. They can be classified as personality focus leadership theories, behavioural focus leadership theories, contingency and situational leadership theories, substitute theory, transactional leadership theory, transformational leadership theory, and other leadership theories.

4.6.2.1 Personality Focus Leadership Theories

The two famous personality focus leadership theories are the *great man leadership theory* and the *leader's traits theory*.

4.6.2.1.1 Great Man Leadership Theory

The earliest leadership theory described a leader as a 'great man' who moved history forward because of his/her exceptional characteristics as a leader. The theory believed that a few people are capable of forcing the course of events in an hour of crisis or some great social need so as to write history very differently from what it might have been. The theory is heavily criticised, as there can hardly be a leader personality across diverse contexts. Moreover, hero worship is likely to make a leader out of a person through perception and attribution rather than someone possessing the required leadership qualities.

4.6.2.1.2 Leader's Traits Theory

The leader's traits theory emphasises the traits that make a successful leader. Here 'trait' is defined as a relatively stable disposition of an individual to behave in a particular way.[78] Its examples are high self-confidence, extroversion, and so on. The theory considers that a leader's characteristics and attributes contribute to the effectiveness of leadership. A leader brings personal traits to everything s/he does, enhancing leadership performance and potential.

Some of these traits and skills were identified by Stogdill in 1974. Accordingly, some of the effective leadership traits are:[79]

(a) Adaptability to situations
(b) Alertness to the social environment
(c) Ambitiousness and achievement orientation
(d) Assertiveness
(e) Cooperativeness
(f) Decisiveness
(g) Dependability
(h) Desire to influence others
(i) Energetic
(j) Persistence
(k) Self-confidence

(l) Tolerance to stress
(m) Willingness to assume responsibility

Moreover, according to Stogdill, some of the skills for effective leadership are as follows:[79]

(a) Cleverness or intelligence
(b) Conceptually skilled
(c) Creativity
(d) Diplomacy and tactfulness
(e) Fluency in speaking
(f) High knowledge about group tasks
(g) Administrative ability
(h) Persuasiveness
(i) Socially skilled

Negative Aspects of Traits Theory: Leader's traits theory was not much helpful because of the following problems:

(i) The list of leadership traits grew to more than 1700 words in English language alone. Thus, the numbers of leadership traits are very high and cannot be found in any single person.

(ii) Possession of these leadership traits and characteristics could not predict successful leadership across situations.[79]

(iii) The list of traits contains characteristics that are opposite to each other. For example, decisiveness and flexibility.

(iv) Different effective leaders had different styles and different traits. Thus, effective leadership is not based on common traits.[80]

(v) It is suggested that dispossession of some traits explains ineffective leadership, but possession of certain traits does not surely explain effective leadership.

4.6.2.2 Behavioural Focus Leadership Theories

The leadership theories that focused on the behavioural aspects of leadership are (1) leadership studies at Ohio and Michigan State Universities and (2) McGregor's Theory X and Theory Y.

4.6.2.2.1 Leadership Studies at Ohio and Michigan State Universities

The leadership studies at Ohio State University study the behaviour of leaders. In the studies, two different underlying factors for leadership emerged. They are described as follows:[81]

(a) **Consideration:** It describes leadership behaviours related to inclusion, good feeling for subordinates, and a concern for the development of subordinates.

(b) **Initiation of Structure:** This variable describes leadership behaviours related to defining roles, control mechanisms, task focus, and work coordination.

Similarly, Michigan State University also studied effective leadership behaviours and proposed the following two dimensions of leadership:[82]

(a) **Employee Orientation:** This behaviour of leaders suggests that they consider human relations as an important aspect of their work; they consider employees as human beings of intrinsic importance. They take an interest in employees and understand their individuality and personal needs.

(b) **Task Orientation:** This behaviour of leaders suggests that they stress more on the technical aspect of the work. They consider employees only as means to get the work done.

The Michigan study concluded that leaders' behaviours contained elements of both the above-mentioned factors. However, some leaders are more employee-oriented and some are more task-oriented. This perspective on leadership still forms the basis of most modern leadership theories.

4.6.2.2.2 McGregor's Theory X and Theory Y

Douglas McGregor's theory X and theory Y are already discussed in Chapter 3. It suggests that leaders seem to have certain assumptions about human nature. These assumptions influence their style of leadership and influence subordinates.

4.6.2.3 Contingency and Situational Leadership Theories

The contingency theories of leadership suggest that effective leadership styles differ in different situations. The famous contingency theories are Fiedler's contingency theory, Hersey and Blanchard's situational leadership theory, Blake and Mouton's managerial grid model, House's path-goal theory, and Reddin's three-dimensional model of leadership.

4.6.2.3.1 Fiedler's Contingency Theory

Fiedler suggests that no one leadership style suits all situations. Effective leaders are those who match their leadership style with the demands of the situation. All situations consist of three major variables, as described below:[83]

(a) **Task Structure:** Task structure suggests the degree of structuring of work. It is considered as high when the task entrusted to subordinates is definite, routine, specific, and predictable. It is considered low when the task entrusted is indefinite, non-routine, general, and unpredictable.

(b) **Leader-Position Power:** This variable describes the amount of formal authority a leader possesses due to his/her position in the organisation.[84]

(c) **Leader-member relationship:** This member describes the nature of the relationship between the leaders and followers. It is said to be favourable when employees accept the leader openly. It is said to be unfavourable when employees do not accept the leader openly.

On the basis of these situational factors, Fiedler made the following suggestions:

(a) Leadership style should be high-task-oriented when the situation is highly favourable or highly unfavourable. However, the style should be relationship/employee-oriented in moderate situations. An example of a highly unfavourable situation is that of a natural disaster.

(b) Most leaders are unable to change their leadership style according to situations because the styles stem from their individual personalities, are learned early in life, and are reinforced by continued life experiences.

(c) Thus, organisations should select leaders who possess the matching leadership style for a definite situation.

Least Preferred Co-Worker Scale: Fiedler offered a measure, known as the 'least preferred co-worker scale (LPC)', to distinguish between task-oriented and relationship-oriented leadership styles. The LPC scale requires a leader to describe one person with whom s/he worked the least. On a series of 1 to 8, a leader has to rate his/her least preferred co-worker as follows:

Unfriendly 1 2 3 4 5 6 7 8 Friendly

Uncooperative 1 2 3 4 5 6 7 8 Cooperative

Hostile 1 2 3 4 5 6 7 8 Supportive

Guarded 1 2 3 4 5 6 7 8 Open

A high LPC score of a leader suggests that s/he has a relationship-oriented leadership style and a low LPC score suggests that s/he has a task-oriented leadership style. A leader who rates his/her followers high on the LPC scale derives satisfaction out of interpersonal relationships; on the other hand, a leader who rates his/her followers low on the LPC scale derives satisfaction out of high task performance.[85]

4.6.2.3.2 Hersey and Blanchard's Situational Leadership Theory

Hersey and Blanchard suggested that a leader should adopt a particular leadership style—task-oriented or relationship-oriented—on the basis of his/her subordinate's readiness or maturity for task performance. Here a leader is task-oriented to the extent that s/he engages in specifying the subordinates' duties and responsibilities and relationship-oriented to the extent that s/he acts in a facilitative and supportive manner to his/her employees.

Employee readiness/maturity is defined as the ability and willingness of employees to accomplish a given function. On the basis of employee readiness, there are four leadership styles. They vary from highly directive to high *laissez-faire*. If followers are unable and unwilling to work, the leader has to be task-oriented to compensate for the followers' lack of ability, and also be relationship-oriented to get the employees to follow his/her line of thought. If the followers are able but unwilling to work, the leader needs to use a participative and supportive style. If the followers are able as well as willing, the leader needs to delegate more work to the followers. The four leadership styles are described in Fig. 4.17.

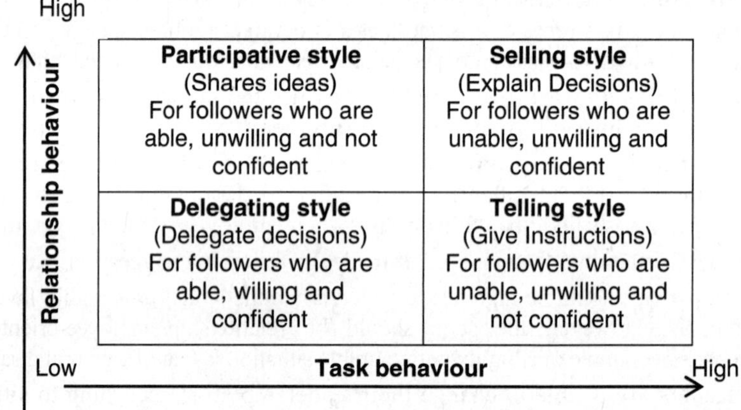

Fig. 4.17 : Four styles of leadership by Hersey and Blanchard[86]

This theory of leadership is very important, as it is intuitively appealing and easy to understand. Its emphasis on the role of the situation and the subordinate's maturity highlights the need for learning leadership skills.[87] Moreover, the theory emphasises that individual subordinates should be treated differently in different situations. It also emphasises on the ability of the leaders to compensate for the ability and motivational limitations of their followers.

However, the theory is also criticised as having questionable validity and utility. Critics suggest that employee readiness/maturity may be an attribution made by the supervisors based on interpersonal attraction rather than identifiable employee qualities.[88]

4.6.2.3.3 Blake and Mouton's Managerial Grid Model

Based on the Ohio and Michigan studies, Blake and Mouton (1962) proposed two dimensions of leadership—*concern for people* and *concern for task*. These two dimensions were used as axes to construct a managerial grid for plotting any manager's style of leadership.

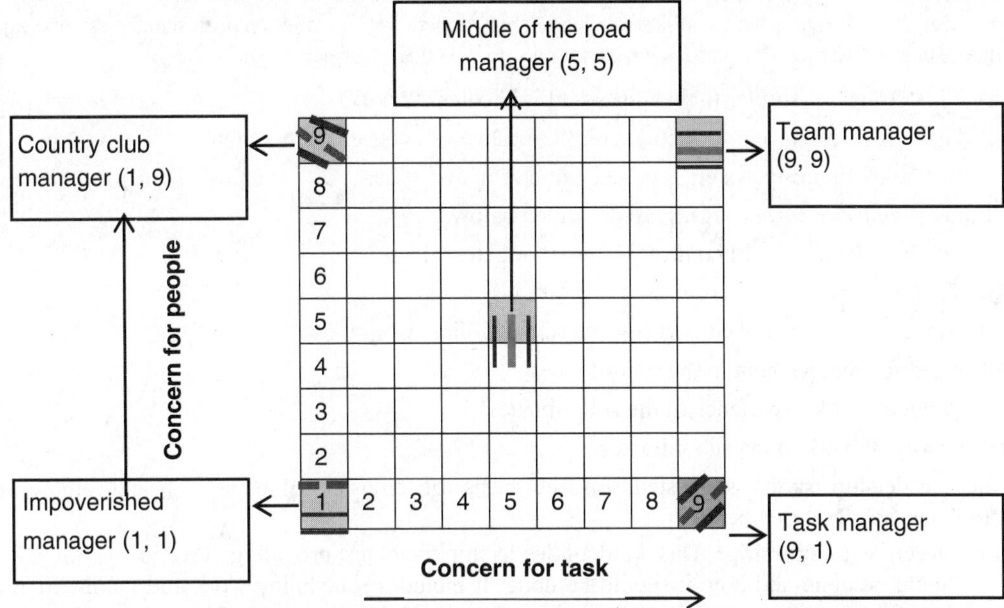

Fig. 4.18 : Different styles of Leadership according to the Managerial Grid Model[89]

Accordingly, Blake and Mouton identified five leadership styles (as described in Fig. 4.18):

(a) **The Impoverished Manager (1,1):** S/he is that kind of manager who is least concerned about people as well as for work. S/he desires to avoid risk, postpones dealing with difficult issues within the organisation, avoids conflict, and attempts to meet the minimum job requirements only. S/he pays attention to the people only to achieve the minimum required production.

(b) **The Task Manager (9,1):** S/he is that kind of manager who is highly concerned about work and least concerned about people. S/he strictly exercises authority and seeks obedience from the staff. S/he allows little consideration for the needs and problems of the employees.

(c) **The Country Club Manager (1,9):** S/he is that kind of manager who has a high concern for people and least concern for work. S/he gives the highest priority to happiness and harmony among the staff and the lowest priority to organisational goals and purposes.

(d) **Middle of the Road Manager (5,5):** S/he is that kind of manager who balances organisational tasks and the needs of the employees. S/he is neither fully people-oriented nor task-oriented.

(e) **Team Manager (9,9):** S/he is that kind of manager who shows high concern for both people and work. S/he maintains employee relationships around task issues. S/he treats conflicts as a natural phenomenon and deals strategically with it.

The managerial grid model is appreciated for its intuitive appeal and simplicity.

4.6.2.3.4 House's Path-Goal Leadership Theory

The path goal theory is formed by combining the Ohio studies on leadership and Vroom's expectancy model of motivation. It states that the basic role of a leader is to help employees stay on the right path towards challenging organisational goals and valued rewards. A leader provides coaching, guidance, support, and necessary rewards to subordinates in order to satisfy their needs contingent on their performance. It suggests several styles of leadership depending on the environmental factors and subordinate characteristics. The various *environmental factors* are described below:

(a) Task structure (similar to that discussed in Fiedler's theory)
(b) Nature of work group—whether conflict-oriented or consensus-oriented
(c) Nature of authority system—bureaucratic or matrix type.

The various *employee characteristics* are described below:

(a) Subordinate's locus of control—internal or external
(b) Task ability of the subordinate
(c) Authoritarianism in the manager-subordinate relationship
(d) Need for achievement in the subordinates
(e) Previous work experience of the subordinates
(f) Clarity of work in the subordinates

The four leadership styles suggested, on the basis of environmental factors and employee characteristics, are described below:

(a) **Directive Leadership:** This kind of leadership involves providing direction about what should be done and how it should be done. It includes scheduling work and maintaining a standard of performance. It can be used when the subordinates have an external locus of control, lack experience, and have a low need for achievement. It can also be used when there is a conflict between work groups.
(b) **Supportive Leadership:** This kind of leadership involves showing concern for the needs of employees and being friendly and approachable. It can be used when the task is highly structured and under bureaucratic and formal authority systems.
(c) **Participative Leadership:** This kind of leadership involves consulting employees while making organisational decisions. It can be used when the task is non-routine and unstructured. It can also be used when the relationship is non-authoritarian and the subordinate's locus of control is internal.
(d) **Achievement-Oriented Leadership:** This kind of leadership encourages employees to perform at their highest level by setting challenging goals, emphasising excellence, and demonstrating confidence in employees' abilities. It is suitable when the task is unstructured and the subordinate's need for achievement is high.

A leader has to choose from the above styles in order to help the employees attain work satisfaction.

4.6.2.3.5 Reddin's Three-Dimensional Model of Leadership Effectiveness

William Reddin, in his model of leadership effectiveness, suggested that leadership becomes effective or ineffective depending on situational factors. He highlighted eight styles of leadership, four among which are classified as effective styles and the other four as ineffective leadership styles.[90] The *effective leadership styles* are as described below:

(a) **Developer:** In this style, leaders have implicit trust in people and are primarily concerned with developing them as individuals. It is preferred in situations where high relationship orientation and low task orientation are required.

(b) **Executive:** In this style, leaders use high task orientation or high relationship orientation, depending upon the situation. They behave as motivators who set high standards, treat everyone somewhat differently, and prefer team management in the organisation.

(c) **Bureaucrat:** In this style, a leader adopts low task orientation as well as low relationship orientation. His/her concern is just to follow rules and regulations and maintain a particular situation with those rules and procedures.

(d) **Benevolent Autocrat:** In this style, a leader adopts high task orientation and low relationship orientation. However, his/her style of leadership depends on the situation. A leader projects themselves by knowing what they want, and also knowing how to get it done without the resentment of their subordinates.

The ineffective leadership styles are as described below:

(a) **Missionary:** In this style, a leader adopts high relationship orientation and low task orientation in inappropriate situations. The leadership is interested in only maintaining harmony and is considered highly ineffective.

(b) **Compromiser:** In this style, the leader uses both high task orientation and high relationship orientation in situations that require focus on only one orientation. Leaders are seen as poor decision-makers as they allow themselves to be influenced by the pressures in a situation.

(c) **Deserter:** In this style, the leader uses low task orientation and low relationship orientation in inappropriate situations. They are seen as being uninvolved and passive towards the work and organisation.

(d) **Autocrat:** In this style, the leader used high task orientation and low relationship orientation in inappropriate situations. The leader is perceived as having no confidence in employees and being interested only in the immediate tasks.

This theory very clearly suggests that similar leadership styles can be effective or ineffective in different situations.

4.6.2.4 Substitute Theory of Leadership

Kerr and Jermier proposed the substitute theory of leadership in 1978. The theory questions the need for leadership in all situations. It suggests that certain aspects of situations reduce the importance of formal leadership. These aspects are related to the individual, task, or organisation. These aspects either 'neutralise' or 'substitute' the influence of formal leadership on subordinates.[91] Here *neutralisers* are those factors that make it impossible for leaders to influence the outcome criteria. They serve to reduce or cancel the leadership-outcome relationship. Some of the neutralisers are mentioned below:

(a) **Individual-Level Neutralisers:** Individual level factors such as indifference towards rewards reduce the impact of leadership on outcomes.

(b) **Organisational-Level Neutralisers:** There are organisational level neutralising factors such as low positional power of the leader, dispersed subordinate work sites, inflexible rules, and policies. They also decrease the influence of formal leadership.

On the other hand, *substitutes* are those factors that delimit or negate the influence of the formal leader and replace this loss of influence with their own influences. Some of the substitutes are mentioned below:

(a) **Individual-Level Substitutes:** Individual-level substitutes are factors such as high individual ability, experience, training, and professional orientation.

(b) **Task-Related Substitutes:** The various task-related substitutes are the routine nature o tasks, high analysability of tasks, and intrinsically satisfying nature of task.

(c) **Organisational-Level Substitutes:** The various organisational-level substitutes are factors such as high formalisation of procedures, detailed job descriptions, minimal hierarchy, high performance standards, and autonomy.

Apart from the abovementioned two factors, there exist *enhancers*, which are variables that augment o strengthen one or more leadership behaviours.[92] However, Kerr and Jermier clearly mentioned that substitutes exist for some leadership activities but not for all.

The importance of this theory is that it helps in crucial and problematic situations by removing leadership neutralisers or creating leadership substitutes and enhancers. This makes leadership more effective and the situation more favourable.

4.6.2.5 Transactional Leadership Theory

Transactional theory of leadership explains a kind of leadership in which the leaders guide or motivate their followers in the direction of established goals by clarifying role and task requirements. The theory was initiated by Max Weber and then developed by Bernard M. Bass in 1981. The theory has several assumptions such as:[93]

(a) High performance is achieved when the chain of command is definite and clear.

(b) Employees are motivated by rewards and punishments.

(c) The followers' primary task is to obey the instructions of the leader.

(d) Subordinates are required to be closely monitored for ensuring expected performance.

This theory describes the following features of the transactional leadership style:

(a) **Contingent Reward:** The leadership clearly defines rewards for meeting expected organisational performance.

(b) **Active Management by Exception:** The leadership closely monitors the performance of the subordinates and takes corrective actions for any deviations.

(c) **Passive Management by Exception:** Here, leadership allows independence in work and intervenes only when standards are not met; s/he even uses punishment for poor performance.

(d) **Laissez Faire:** In it, leaders allow independence to subordinates for making their own decisions. Leaders avoid making decisions and transfer their responsibility to their subordinates.

Transactional leadership is like an exchange relationship between the leaders and subordinates. It is transitory in nature and does not connect the leader and followers at an emotional level. At best, this kind of leadership might get the subordinates to achieve their existing goals while, at the same time contributing to the organisational goals.[94]

An important transactional leadership theory is the leader-member exchange theory.

4.6.2.6 Leader-Member Exchange Theory/Vertical Dyad Linkage Model

The leader-member exchange theory is a theory that explains the one-to-one relationship that a leader shares with his/her subordinates. It assumes that leaders have very less time and energy to devote to multiple matters. Thus, they sort their subordinates into in-group and out-group subordinates with whom they develop different levels of exchange. Similarly, the subordinates also develop different levels of relationships with their leader.

In-Group Members: In-group members are those subordinates to whom leaders assign important tasks. They are thought to be capable and trustworthy by the leader. These subordinates are closer to the leader. They are perceived to be more compatible and have similar attitudes, values, and demographic factors as that of the leader.[95] The leader helps and supports an in-group member beyond the formal role expectations, by sharing information and resources.[96] It is a result of high mutual trust, face-to-face interaction, reciprocal influence, and a sense of common fate.

Out-Group Members: The other subordinates are described as out-group members. Routine and less important tasks are assigned to them, as they do not enjoy the confidence of the leader. It involves low personal trust, low face-to-face interaction, low sense of common fate, and low favour between leaders and followers.[97]

This theory is criticised because in team-based organisations, leaders cannot afford to sub-optimise the potential contribution of the out-group members.

4.6.2.7 Transformational Leadership Theory

The transformational nature of leadership was first proposed by James McGregor Burns. This nature describes a leader as a facilitator of change occurring "when one or more persons engage with others in such a way that leaders and followers raise one another to higher levels of motivation and morality."[98] This kind of leadership aims at influencing changes in the attitudes and assumptions of subordinates and thus building commitment to organisational goals and objectives.[99] It helps in changing the organisational culture. Transformational leadership consists of four interrelated factors:[100]

(a) **Idealised Influence:** Transformation leaders are admired, respected, and trusted by their followers. Followers identify with and want to become like their leaders. The leaders also give preference to the followers' needs before their own needs. They are also consistent in their principles, values, and ethics in all situations.

(b) **Inspirational Motivation:** Leaders motivate their subordinates through meaningful and challenging work. They arouse individual and team spirit in the organisation. They help the subordinates to imagine desirable future states and work towards them.

(c) **Intellectual Stimulation:** Leaders stimulate the subordinates to be innovative by questioning their basic assumptions, reframing problems, and approaching old situations in new ways.

(d) **Individualised Consideration:** Leaders act as coaches to each individual and pay adequate attention to their individual needs. This helps in developing followers to successively higher levels of potential.

The difference between transformational and transactional leadership is made clear in Mind Map 4.9.

Transactional Leadership	Transformational Leadership
Leaders put contingent rewards for desired conduct	Leaders share non-negotiable values such as integrity to improve the subordinates' conduct
Leaders desire stability and control	Leaders desire to change

Transactional Leadership	Transformational Leadership
Leaders meet expected levels of performance	Leaders help subordinates perform beyond expectations
There is conditional trust between leaders and followers through contracts and exchange	There is continuous trust between leaders and followers through admiration and identification

Mind Map 4.9: Difference between transactional and transformational leadership[101]

4.6.2.8 Charismatic Leadership

Charismatic leadership is that kind of leadership which inspires a higher level of action in followers.[102] Like transformational leadership, charisma helps in taking the values, goals, and aspirations of the subordinates to higher levels.[94]

Followers of charismatic leaders view their leader as possessing superhuman qualities. They identify themselves with the leader and accept the leader's missions and directives unconditionally.[103] The charisma is believed to be developed by the first two components of transformational leadership—idealised influence and inspirational motivation—combined with the personal abilities of the leader. The charismatic leader engages with their followers in the following six ways:[60]

(a) **Vision Articulation:** They consistently articulate new and exciting goals for the future.

(b) **Environmental Sensitivity:** They understand the opportunities as well as constraints, barriers, and limitations present in the environment.

(c) **Unconventional behaviour:** The unconventional behaviour of a charismatic leader surprises the followers.

(d) **Personal Risk:** They have a tendency to self-sacrifice for organisational goals.

(e) **Sensitivity towards Members:** They are sensitive to the needs and concerns of their members. It leads to the development of mutual liking and respect between leaders and followers.

(f) **Change Oriented:** They are change-oriented and often question the status quo.

Charismatic leaders engage their followers at an emotional level. They raise their morality to more principled levels of judgment. They also motivate their followers to sacrifice their self-interests for the higher purpose of the team and the organisation.

4.6.2.9 Entrepreneurial Leadership

Entrepreneurial leadership is the kind of leadership that encourages procedural and cultural changes in an organisation in order to dramatically improve its productivity and quality. It is similar to charismatic and transformational leadership in its emphasis on change.[104] However, it advocates radical change through higher zeal, depth of knowledge, and expertise.[60]

An entrepreneurial leader plays a significant role in the change process by engaging in personal transformation and by being a coach and facilitator for subordinates. S/he leads by learning and fully engages in the transformational process through continued initiatives.[105]

An entrepreneurial leader sees learning as a way of organisational development and not as a threat. By developing his/her own skills and reflective ability, an entrepreneurial leader becomes more open minded to change and innovative ideas.[106] S/he accommodates multiple perspectives and copes with complexity. Thus, s/he is at an advantage in the times of complex, changing, and competitive environment.

Leadership theories

Personality focus

Great man theory

Leader's traits Theory
- Stable disposition of a person
- Traits by stogdill

Behavioral focus

Ohio studies
- Consideration
- Initiation of structure

Michigan studies
- Employee orientation
- Task orientation

McGregor's Theory X and Theory Y

Contingency theory

Fiedler's theory
- Task structure
- Leader position power
- Leader member relationship
- Leader preferred co-worker

Hersey & Blanchard's theory
4 Styles of leadership based on employee readiness/maturity

Managerial grid model
- Impoverished manager
- Task manager
- Country club manager
- Middle of the road manager
- Team manager

Path goal theory
4 Styles of leadership based on Environmental factors and employee characteristics

Reddin's 3 Dimensional Model
Effective and Ineffective leadership style depending on situation

Substitute theory
Neutralizers, substitutes and enhancers of formal leadership

Transactional leadership
- Contingent Reward
- Active management by exception
- Passive management by exception
- Laissez Faire

Leader member exchange theory
- In group members
- Out group members

Transformational leadership
- Idealised influence
- Inspirational motivation
- Intellectual stimulation
- Individualised consideration

Charismatic leadership
- Vision Articulation
- Environmental sensitivity
- Unconventional behavior
- Personal risk
- Sensitivity towards members
- Change oriented

Entrepreneurial leadership
Radical change through knowledge and expertise

Mind Map 4.11 : Various Theories on Leadership

4.6.3 Women in Leadership

There has been an underrepresentation of women in leadership in all sectors, either private or public. Women with similar background and experience are evaluated less favourably than their male counterparts for leadership positions. Two terms are used to describe this discrimination against women in leadership—*glass ceiling* and *glass escalator*. Glass ceiling denotes certain invisible barriers, within the organisation, which restrict the upward movement of women to leadership positions. On the other hand, glass escalators denote certain invisible facilitators that accelerate the growth of male members with respect to female members in leadership positions. However, the situation is changing drastically after globalisation. The role of women in leadership is widely recognised now.[107]

4.6.4 Leaders vs Managers

Leaders and managers are two different entities. In organisations, leaders need not be managers and managers need not be leaders. There are several differences between leaders and managers, some of which are pointed out in Mind Map 4.11. However, the two terms are interdependent, as managerial success requires leading effectively.

	Managers	**Leaders**
Basic values	The basic values of managers are to maintain stability, order, and efficiency. They try to change only forced to do that.	The basic values of managers are to bring in flexibility, innovation, adaptation, and risk-seeking attitude in the organisation.
Basic concern	Their basic concern is getting things done and making employees perform better. Their concern is to solve emerging problems rationally and conservatively.	Their basic concern is to help employees find meaning in organisational goals and get them agreed upon as the most important and meaningful things to be done.
Nature	Their nature is to do the things right.	Their nature is to do the right things.
Core process	Their role brings predictability and order through traditional management functions.	Their role is to bring organisational change through vision, its communication, and inspiring subordinates.
Relationship with others	They enjoy hierarchical and authoritative relationships with the subordinates	They enjoy multidirectional influence relationships involving superiors, peers, associates, and subordinates.
Basic culture	They aim at control in order to achieve organisational goals	To achieve organisational goals they bring in disorder, arouse expectations, new thinking, and bring in new choices using imaginative power.

	Managers	Leaders
Basic goals	The basic goals of the managers are those set by the top management and those deeply embedded in the organisational history and culture.	The basic goals of the leaders are those that emerge from the dreams and desires of the employees and management. They are forward-looking and create a suitable culture and history.

Mind Map 4.11: Difference between managers and leaders[101, 108]

Managing and leading requires different skill sets and mindsets. However, both are required in a successful organisational personality. "The best leader has well-developed management skills; the best manager has well-developed leadership skills."[109] John Ketter has explained the idea of leaders and managers clearly in the following paragraph:

"The point here is not that leadership is good and management is bad. They are simply different and serve different purposes. The fundamental purpose of management is to keep the current system functioning. The fundamental purpose of leadership is to produce useful change, especially non-incremental change. It is possible to have too much or too little of either. Strong leadership with no management risks chaos—the organisation might walk right off a cliff. Strong management with no leadership tends to entrench an organisation in deadly bureaucracy."

4.6.7 Leadership and Learning Organisations

Learning organisations are those that keep on learning and improving their strategy and processes in a constantly changing and competitive environment. Some of the aspects of organisational learning were discussed by Chris Argyris and are described in Chapter 3 in the section Chris Argyris. Organisational learning is much more than individual learning and has the following qualities:

(a) **Learning to learn:** A learning organisation needs to have a leadership that trusts its members, complements their strengths, and tries to compensate for their limitations. Leadership needs to learn to behave in this manner.

(b) **Systems Thinking:** Leadership in learning organisations has the ability to put interrelated parts into a meaningful whole, understand their relationship, and develop a sense of 'big picture' from them.

(c) **Mastery of Leaders:** Leadership in learning organisations have a clear understanding of what really matters, deepened personal vision, focused energy, and high patience; they are realistic and invest their whole selves in the most valuable aspirations of the organisation.

(d) **Shared Vision:** Leaders have a vision that collectively binds all members together; all members move towards this vision in their work. This vision is made and understood collectively. A learning team is one that avoids several factors, which prevent collective thinking and learning.

4.6.8 Micromanagement and its Effects

Micromanagement is the tendency of a leader to control his/her employees, or a situation, by paying extreme attention to small details. It has a detrimental effect on employee engagement and morale. It has the following negative effects:[110,111]

(a) It creates an organisational environment of dependency and inefficiency.

(b) When employees are constantly criticised and made to feel that they cannot do anything right, they may try harder for a while but eventually, stop trying at all. Due to micromanagement, productive employees lose motivation and initiative.

(c) Employees feel afraid to communicate with their leader in situations of difficulty.

(d) It increases stress in employees and affects their work and personal life.

(e) It also increases the feeling of job insecurity among employees.

(f) It leads to increased fatigue from work.

4.6.9 Servant Leadership

The term 'servant leadership' was first coined by Robert K. Greenlief in his essay 'The Servant as Leader' (1970). In his words, "The servant-leader is servant first... It begins with the natural feeling that one wants to serve, to serve first. Then conscious choice brings one to aspire to lead. That person is sharply different from one who is leader first, perhaps because of the need to assuage a usual power drive or to acquire material possessions... ."[112]

A servant-leader focuses primarily on the growth and well-being of people and the communities to which they belong. While traditional leadership generally involves the accumulation and exercise of power by one at the 'top of the pyramid', servant leadership is different. The servant-leader shares power, puts the needs of others first, and helps people develop and perform as highly as possible.

Some of the characteristics of a servant-leader are as described below:[113]

(a) **Listening:** Servant leaders have a commitment to listen intently to subordinates. They identify the will of a group and help to clarify that will. Listening, coupled with periods of reflection, is essential to the growth and well-being of the servant leader.

(b) **Empathy:** The servant leader strives to understand and empathise with others.

(c) **Healing:** One of the great strengths of servant leadership is the potential for healing one's self and one's relationship with others. The healing of relationships is a powerful force for transformation and integration.

(d) **Awareness:** General awareness, and especially self-awareness, is an important quality of a servant leader. Awareness helps one in understanding issues involving ethics, power, and values. It lends itself to being able to view most situations from a more integrated, holistic position.

(e) **Persuasion:** A servant leader relies on persuasion rather than on one's positional authority in making decisions within an organisation. The servant leader seeks to convince others rather than coerce compliance.

(f) **Conceptualisation:** Servant leaders seek to nurture their abilities to dream great dreams. The ability to look at a problem or an organisation from a conceptualising perspective means that one must think beyond day-to-day realities. The traditional leader is consumed by the need to achieve short-term operational goals. The leader who wishes to also be a servant leader must stretch his/her thinking to encompass broader-based conceptual thinking.

(g) **Foresight:** Foresight is a characteristic that enables a servant leader to understand lessons from the past, the realities of the present, and the likely consequence of a decision for the future.

(h) **Stewardship:** This quality describes leaders as playing a significant role in holding their institutions in trust for the greater good of the society. They have a foremost commitment to serve others.

(i) **Commitment to the Growth of People:** The servant leader is deeply committed to the growth of each and every individual within his/her organisation. The servant leader recognises the tremendous responsibility to do everything in his/her power to nurture the personal and professional growth of employees and colleagues. In practice, this can include (but is not limited to) concrete actions such as making funds available for personal and professional development, taking a personal interest in ideas and suggestions from everyone, encouraging worker involvement in decision-making, and actively assisting laid-off employees to find other positions.

(j) **Building Community:** The servant leader tries to build a community among those who work within the institution.

SUMMARY

This chapter described the various aspects of administrative behaviour such as decision-making, communication, motivation, and leadership. It dealt in detail about these factors and their interdependencies. The various models and theories describing these factors were also systematically analysed.

Practice Questions

1. Describe the decision-making process of Simon and Mintzberg.
2. Discuss the behavioural models of decision-making.
3. "A decision-maker chooses that alternative which seems to be favourite to him." (Soelberg) Explain.
4. "Decision-making process is nothing but rational ritualism." Explain in terms of the political model of decision-making.
5. Explain the garbage can model of decision-making with suitable examples.
6. Analytical, judgmental, compromising, and inspiration/authoritarian decision-making are the four types of organisational decision-making. Explain
7. What do you understand by thinking dispositions and other decision-shaping factors?
8. Explain the various models of communication.
9. What is a good feedback? Describe the various models for giving feedback.
10. Explain the term 'persuasive communication'.
11. Is there a direct relationship between motivation and performance? Describe.
12. Motivation is a drive created by unfulfilled needs, deficits, and deprivation. (Hull) Explain.
13. Explain the measures used to improve motivation at the workplace proposed by Frederick Herzberg.
14. "Theory Z advocates establishment of motivational oriented organisational cultures with special emphasis on employee development and participative culture." (William Ouchi) Explain.
15. "Behaviour which is reinforced tends to be repeated and which is not reinforced tends to die out or weaken." (Skinner) Explain.
16. Describe the goal setting theory of motivation.
17. "Satisfaction of an individual is influenced by various factors'. Explain in terms of Porter and Lawler's performance satisfaction model.
18. "Leadership is most conspicuous at points of discontinuities in the organisational structure, where there are breaks between parts of the system." (A.K. Rice) Explain.
19. "Effective leaders are those which match their leadership style with the demands of the situation." Explain the various models of situational leadership.
20. The path goal theory is formed by combining the Ohio studies on leadership and Vroom's expectancy model of motivation. Discuss.
21. "Transformational leadership is a process where one or more persons engage with others in such a way that leaders and followers raise one another to higher levels of motivation and morality." Explain.
22. What is micromanagement? What are its effects?
23. "A servant leader is a servant first." (Greenlief) Explain.

CHAPTER 5 Organisational Dynamics

Learning Objectives: After reading this chapter, you will learn the following:

- Contingency theory of organisation.
- Critical theory of organisation.
- Postmodern and post-structural organisation theory.
- Blacksburg manifesto.
- Basic elements of an organisational structure.
- Organisational structural variables.
- Various organisational structural forms like functional structure form, product division structure form, matrix organisations, networked organisations and process based organisations.
- Organisational culture and its various elements.
- Public Private Partnership (PPP) and its various dimensions.

5.1 Organisational Theories

Organisational theories are those that study organisations to identify the patterns and structures they use to solve problems, maximise efficiency and productivity, and meet the expectations of stakeholders. These patterns are used to formulate normative theories of how organisations function best.

In the literature on public administration, there are various organisational theories. Some of them are enumerated below:

(a) Scientific management theory (discussed in Chapter 3)

(b) Administrative management approach/structural approach (discussed in chapter 3)

(c) Bureaucratic theory (discussed in Chapter 3)

The first three theories (listed above) are classified as *classical organisational theories.*

(d) Human relations theory/neo-classical theory (discussed in Chapter 3)

(e) Decision-making theory (discussed in Chapter 3)

(f) Behavioural approach and participative management approach (discussed in Chapter 3)

(g) Systems approach (discussed in Chapter 3)

(h) Structural functional theory (discussed in Chapter 3)

(i) Contingency theory (will be discussed in this chapter)

The systems theory, structural functional theory, and contingency theory are classified as *modern organisational theories.*

(j) Post-modern theory (will be discussed in this chapter)

5.2 Contingency Theory of Organisation

Contingency theory or situational theory differs from the previous universalistic models of organisational theory. The earlier universalistic models assumed that there is 'one best way' to organise. They considered that organisational performance is optimised by the optimisation of certain organisational variables; for example, specialisation. On the contrary, contingency theory considers that optimum organisational performance is attained by adopting an appropriate, and not optimum, level of the structural variable that fits the contingency. Contingency theory consists of the following three core elements:[1]

(i) There is a relation between contingency factors and the organisational structure.

(ii) The organisational structure is changed as a result of a change in contingency factors. Thus, contingency determines the organisational structure.

(iii) High performance is attained by an appropriate fit between some levels of organisational structure with each level of contingency. A misfit between organisational structure and contingency leads to lower performance.

5.2.1 Contingency Factors Determining Organisational Structure

There are various factors that affect organisational structure. However, the primary contingency factors that determine organisational structure/design are:

(a) Size of organisation

(b) Environment around organisation

(c) Strategy and goals of organisation

(d) Technology of organisation

All these factors will be discussed in subsequent sections.

5.2.2 Effect of Size on Organisational Structure

The size of an organisation is determined by the total number of employees in an organisation. There are two key schools of thought regarding the size of an organisation. The first school considers that bigger organisations are better, as the unit cost of production decreases when the size of an organisation increases. The second school considers that small organisations are more efficient, as oversized organisations suffer from costly behavioural problems. However, recent studies suggest that while designing an organisation, the middle path between these two schools of thought should be considered.

Research by Gooding and Wagner found the following relationship between the size of an organisation and performance:[2]

(a) Organisations having larger assets are more productive in terms of their sales and profits.
(b) There is no positive relationship between organisational size and efficiency.
(c) There is a slightly negative relationship between subunit size and the efficiency of an organisation.
(d) Employee turnover is unrelated to organisational size.

In essence, organisations should be designed according to their sizes.

5.2.3 Effect of Environment on Organisational Structure

Organisations interact continuously with their environment in the form of receiving inputs and supplying back various outputs. This environment can be classified as general or specific. The general environment consists of the cultural, economic, legal-political, and societal factors within which an organisation operates. The specific environment consists of the organisation's owners, suppliers, distributors, government agencies, and competitors with which the organisation interacts to grow and survive.

5.2.3.1 Complexity of Environment

The environmental complexity is determined by the number of problems and opportunities present in it. It is determined by the following three factors:

(a) **Environmental Richness:** A richer environment is one in which there are more opportunities and dynamism (capability for a change).
(b) **Environmental Interdependence:** Environmental interdependence means the dependency of the organisation on outside members and factors.
(c) **Environmental Uncertainty:** Environmental uncertainty means volatility in the environment.

According to research findings, a stable and simple environment permits the development of highly structured bureaucratic-type organisations. On the other hand, uncertain and volatile environments lead to fluidly designed organisations. An organisation tends to be ineffective if it does not adjust its design to the salient features of the environment.

5.2.3.2 Burns and Stalker's Study on the Impact of Environment

Burns and Stalker examined the relationship between environment and organisation. They studied 20 manufacturing units in Scotland and England. They studied the type of organisational structure and management practices that developed in relation to the rates of change in the markets (for the organisation's products) and technological innovation.[3]

As a result of their research, they differentiated between two systems of management—mechanistic and organic. The mechanistic system is characteristic of a stable environment and the organic system is characteristic of a changing environment. Mechanistic systems are rigid bureaucracies with strict rules, narrowly defined tasks, and top-down communication. Organic systems are flexible networks in which individuals perform a variety of tasks. All organisations have certain characteristics of both mechanistic and organic systems. The characteristics of the two systems are described in a tabular form in Mind Map 5.1.

Characteristic	Mechanistic organisations	Organic organisations
Task definition and knowledge required	The task definition is narrow and technical knowledge is required for performing the task	The task definition is broad, and general broad-based knowledge is required for performing the task
Relationship between individual contribution and organisational purpose	The link is vague and indirect	The link is clear and direct
Task flexibility	The task is rigid and routine	The task is flexible and varied
Specialisation of techniques	The specialisation is specific	The specialisation is general in nature
Degree of hierarchical control	There is a high degree of hierarchical control	There is a low degree of hierarchical control and self-control is emphasised
Primary communication pattern	Primary communication pattern is top-down	Primary communication pattern is lateral and between peers.
Primary decision-making style	Primary decision-making style is authoritarian	Primary decision-making style is participative and authoritarian
Emphasis on obedience	There is a high emphasis on obedience and loyalty	There is a low emphasis on obedience and loyalty

Mind Map 5.1: Characteristics of mechanistic and organic systems[4]

Neither system is superior to the other in all circumstances. Organisations need to accommodate the various characteristics of the two systems in accordance with the situation at hand.

5.2.3.3 Lawrence and Lorsch's Study on the impact of Environment

Lawrence and Lorsch's study was based on the plastics, packaged food, and container industries. They came out with the three key concepts of differentiation, integration, and environment.

Differentiation is defined as the level of segmentation of the organisation into subsystems; these subsystems tend to develop particular attributes in relation to the requirements posed by the organisation's external environment.

Integration is defined as the process of achieving unity of efforts among the various subsystems in the accomplishment of the organisation's task.[5] In a stable environment, integration is achieved by the creation of rules and procedures governing the behaviour of members. In a relatively unstable environment, it is better achieved through planning. In a highly unstable environment, it is achieved by mutual adjustment, requiring a great deal of communication through open channels throughout the organisation.

Environment is an independent variable determined from the perspective of the organisational members as they look outwards. There are basically three main sub-environments within the environment—the market, the technical-economic environment, and the scientific environment. These sub-environments correspond to the sales, production, and research and development sub-systems of the organisation.

On the basis of their study, Lawrence and Lorsch proposed the following conclusions:

(a) The degree of differentiation within each sub-system depends on the following attributes of the sub-environment:
   (i) The rate of change of sub-environmental conditions over time
   (ii) The certainty of information about sub-environmental conditions at any particular time
   (iii) The time span of feedback on the results of employees' decisions

(b) The greater the differences between the three sub-environments in terms of rate of change, the certainty of information, and time span of feedback, the greater will be the difference between the three sub-systems in terms of organisational structure and behaviour.

(c) The greater the differentiation among the sub-systems, the more important is the role of integration.

(d) The relative effectiveness of an organisation is directly related to the extent to which it achieves the required differentiation. Given the attainment of an optimal differentiation in a particular sub-environment, the sub-systems must then be integrated to the degree necessitated by the total environment.

(e) There is no one best way to organise. Internal structural adjustments are required to be made in accordance with the state of the environment. Different organisations may adopt different integration mechanisms depending on the environment in which they work.

5.2.4 Effect of Strategy on Organisational Structure

Organisational strategy is defined as the manner in which an organisation positions itself in its setting in relation to its stakeholders, given the organisation's resources, capabilities, and mission. They are of two types—*generic strategies* and *competency-based strategies*.

(a) **Generic Strategies:** Generic strategies are those that are used by all major organisations to build and sustain competitive advantage. There are basically three kinds of generic strategies:
   (i) **Low Cost:** It is a strategy to provide a product or service at a lower cost than the other competitors. For maintaining low cost, a functional organisational design is adopted, where accountability and responsibility are clearly assigned to the various departments.
   (ii) **Differentiation:** It is a strategy to provide unique products or services that are distinctive from the other competitors. To facilitate differentiation, the organisation makes separate departments for the manufacturing, marketing, and research and development (R&D) of separate products or services.
   (iii) **Focused:** It is a strategy to focus or target a specific niche within an industry. For a focused strategy, an organisation utilises any of a variety of organisational designs ranging from functional to product, matrix or network, to satisfy their customers' preferences.

(b) **Competency-based Strategies:** Competency-based strategies are specific administrative and technical competencies used for achieving the organisational purpose. These competencies/skills are developed while learning from the specific opportunities and problems an organisation faces. Senior management recognises these skills and uses them to build upon a generic strategy to develop a competency-based strategy for the organisation.

Strategic Choice: Strategic choice refers to a state in which an organisation takes steps to define and manipulate its environment, rather than allowing the environment to completely determine the organisation's fate. This idea was developed by Alfred Chandler, who proposed that organisational structure follows organisational strategy. He said that organisational structures should be based on the organisational strategy developed by the senior management.

As shown in Fig. 5.1, specific strategic choices reflect how the dominant coalition perceives environmental constraints and the organisation's objectives. These strategic choices are tempered by minor modifications and adjustments to solve specific problems and capitalise on specific opportunities.

In a nutshell, organisational strategy influences organisational structure, and structure influences strategy.

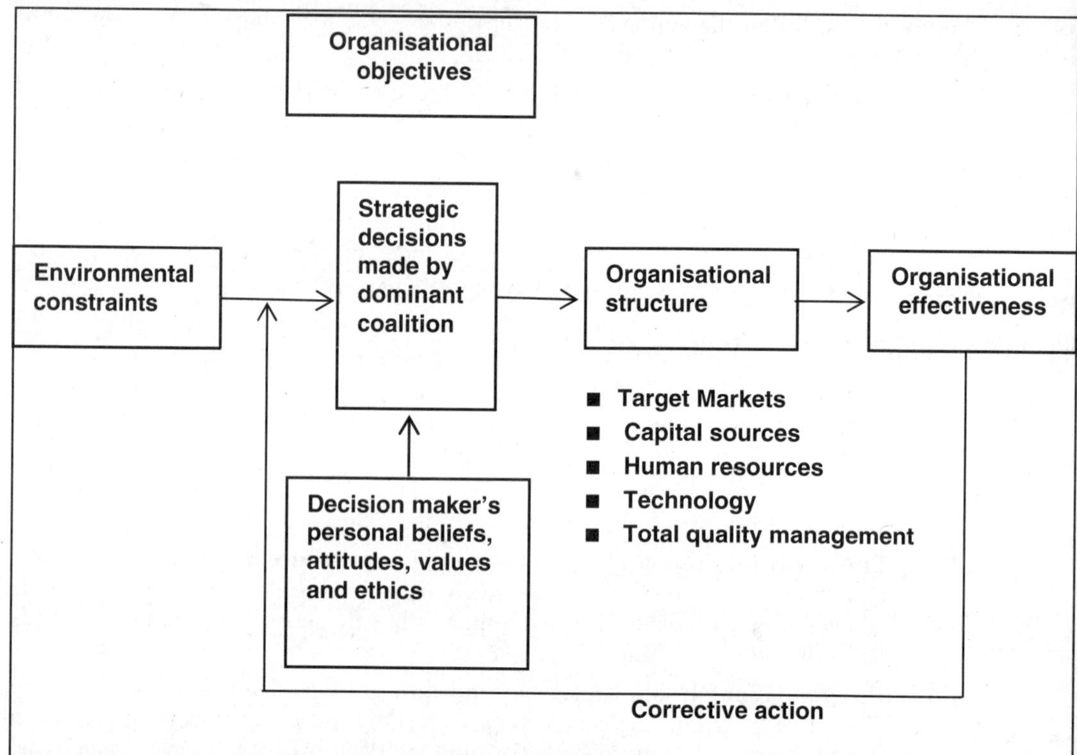

Fig. 5.1: Relationship between strategic choice and organisational structure[6]

5.2.5 Effect of Technology on Organisational Structure

Technology, for an organisation, is defined as the techniques used by it in workflow activities to transform inputs into outputs. It is applicable to all types and kinds of organisations. Technological contingencies also influence the organisational structure. Two important technological contingencies that do so are the *variety* and *analysability* of work activities.

Variety (of technology) refers to the number of exceptions or diversions to standard procedures in the work of the unit.

Analysability (of technology) refers to the extent to which the transformation process (from inputs to outputs) can be reduced into a series of standardised steps.

A work or task may consist of a combination of different levels of variety and analysability of technology. When a task is performed with high variety and low analysability, employees apply their skills to unique situations with little opportunity for repetition. Such situations require an organic organisational structure with low formalisation, decentralised decision-making authority, and a coordination mechanism through informal communication among team members.

On the other hand, tasks having high variety and high analysability have many exceptions to the routine, but their exceptions can be resolved using standard procedures. Such situations also require an organic organisational system, which may involve greater formalisation and centralisation due to the analysis of problems.

5.2.5.1 Woodward's View on Technology and Organisational Structure

John Woodward conducted his research on technology-structure relations by structurally analysing 100 firms in England. These firms were small manufacturing units. Structural indices such as the ratio of managers and supervisors to total personnel, level of authority, a span of control, and so on, were analysed with respect to the relative success of different firms.

All firms were categorised into three primary categories of technology: (1) unit or small batch, (2) mass production or large batch, and (3) continuous process production technology. Woodward came out with the following conclusions in his study:[7]

(a) As the amount of technical complexity increased, the level of authority also increased. Thus, the level of authority was the lowest in unit production and highest in continuous process production, with mass production having an intermediate level of authority.

(b) As the amount of technical complexity increased, the ratio of managers to total personnel also increased.

(c) The span of control of the first line supervisors increased when the technical complexity increased from unit to mass production, but decreased when the technical complexity increased from mass to continuous process production.

(d) Organisations having different technology had different administrative and operational procedures. The organisations having the highest and lowest technical complexity (process and unit firms) tended to have fewer rules, fewer controls, fewer definitions of duties, higher flexibility in interpersonal relations, and higher delegation of authority than those having intermediate technical complexity (mass production firms).

These four principles provided a relationship between technology and structure, and in turn between technology and organisational success. According to the study, successful firms were those that were able to optimally adjust their structural indices with the level of the technical complexity of their work.

5.2.5.2 Thompson's View on Technology and Organisational Structure

Like Woodward, Thompson has also described different types of technologies and their respective organisational structures. He classified three types of technologies—mediating, long-linked, and intensive.[8] These corresponded to three types of interdependence among organisational subunits—pooled, sequential, and reciprocal.

Mediating technology helps in linking categories of customers. For example, a bank links lenders and borrowers. This technology involves *pooled interdependence* among organisational subunits. This means that two organisational subunits (e.g., branches of a bank) have no direct connection but an indirect connection, as they draw resources from the same pool.

In *long-linked technology*, there is sequential interdependence between different tasks, i.e., the output of one task is the input for another task. It requires *sequential interdependence* among subunits, in which the subunits have a direct connection so that the output of one subunit is the input of another subunit.

In *intensive technology*, different techniques are employed based on the feedback received from the environment or that received on intermediate work results. For example, a doctor uses different diagnostic techniques based on the feedback received from a patient's condition. Such technology involves *reciprocal interdependence* among subunits, in which the subunits have a two-way interdependence or connection. The output of each subunit is an input to the other subunit. The subunits have an unpredictable transactional relationship.

According to Thompson, the structure of an organisation has qualities of a mechanistic as well as an organic organisational system, depending upon the nature of interdependence between its various subunits.

5.3 Critical Theory of Organisation

The critical theory of organisation has reiterated the need for the humanization of organisations. It provides an opening for conceptualisation and practice that acknowledges the value-based and normative character of public administration. The origin of critical theory took place from Hegel and Marx to the Frankfurt School.

The critical theory provides an ethical impulse toward substantive equality and democracy in organisations. A major thinker of critical theory, Jurgen Habermas, has criticised the preponderance of technical efficiency in a modern state through the operation of public bureaucracy. As society gets increasingly bureaucratised, social power and discretion tend to be concentrated in the hands of the bureaucratic state apparatus. The expanding role of public bureaucracy is not matched by its popular acceptance. There is increasing criticism of the bureaucracy as a self-aggrandising force alienated from the public, who can rarely repose trust in it. The critical theory urges a replacement of the stifling effect of techno-administrative domination of bureaucracy through de-bureaucratisation and democratisation of administration, based on the free flow of communication and exposure of inherent contradictions in hierarchical relationships.

The aim of critical theory is to improve the quality of organisational life and not let human beings be manipulated for merely attaining organisational goals. It concentrates on the distorted patterns of communication that characterise present-day organisations.

Certain other aspects of the critical theory are as follows:

(a) It regards the organisation-client relationship of modern organisations as filled with distrust and hostility. Modern organisations consider clients as burden, and clients consider organisation as unhelpful. In such a situation, the organisational design and operation run counter to the basic purposes of a democratic public service. The basic thrust of critical theory is to remove the disabilities that have blocked the true needs of the clients from surfacing.

(b) It tries to improve organisational life by advocating self-reflection and self-criticism on the part of the administrators and by pleading for a reordering of priorities so as to give primacy to the growth of individuals as against the productivity of the organisation.

(c) It encourages academicians and practitioners to view social structures and practices not only as vehicles of domination, repression, and manipulation but also as potential starting points for meaningful social change.

(d) It offers a promise for scholars who wish to critique the status quo of professional practice in public organisations, with the intent of imagining better options for the future.

5.4 Postmodern and Poststructural Organisation Theory

The interpretive and the critical theories contributed to paving the way for the postmodern organisation theory. The interpretive theory highlights the subjectivity of the organisational reality and its epistemology (theory of knowledge), while the critical theory provides a critical account of the conditions of power and dependence in organisation theory. The postmodern view continues the criticism of the positivist and functionalist organisation theory but also takes this criticism towards a philosophical criticism of the foundations of modern organisational thought.

There are two branches of the postmodern organisation thought—(1) the theory of postmodern organisations and (2) the postmodern organisational theory. The first one, *theory of postmodern organisations*, refers to certain organisations emerging after modern institutions and structures.[9,10] It is understood as a general analysis of postindustrial society and its organisations. Like critical theory, it takes into consideration the decomposition of modern bureaucracy and the appearance of new and flexible forms of organisations.

The second one, *postmodern organisation theory*, refers to a new kind of theoretical approach to analysing the constitution of societies and organisations. It forms a separate socio-philosophical approach that differs from the ontological and epistemological assumptions held in the modern approach. It understands organisation as a continuous process of articulating and putting into place a stable set of relations and meaningful structures. It considers that the ontological building blocks of organisations, their structure, management, or employees are phenomena constantly being shaped in discursive and material practices.

This act of constantly striving towards order and fracturing the temporary order is not guided by any external force. Unlike the modern approach, postmodernism does not base its view on the societal macrostructures (as in Marxism), the phenomenological powers of the subject (as in the interpretative theory), or the assumed functions of the prevailing order (as in functionalism).[11] The perspective that analyses these ultimate processes and practices of organising is generally referred to as *poststructuralism*.[12]

Poststructuralist thinking about organisations and organising is a subpart of postmodern thinking. However, both can be considered equal for the limited purpose of this book.

5.4.1 Theory of Postmodern Organisations

The theory of postmodern organisations approaches organisations as manifestations of a new era. Industrial organisations had a breaking point after the one-dimensional concept of the market experienced a crisis in the 1960s. The hierarchical Taylorist organisations gave way to more flexible organisations; mechanistic systems gave way to more organic systems. According to Piore and Sabel (1984), this development led to a new kind of organisational rise referred to as flexible specialisation.[13] *Flexible specialisation* describes the transformation of the traditional large corporate structures into a network comprising smaller and flexible business organisations.

This led to flexibility in large organisations, for example, in phenomena such as openness of work tasks and the creative combination of various skills for the development of products and services. Workers no longer remain prisoners of hierarchical structures. Workers can participate in the development of processes and products as equal partners alongside experts and managers. The various forms of postmodern organisations will be discussed later in this chapter in the sections 'Networked Organisations' and 'Matrix Organisations'.

5.4.2 Postmodern Organisational Theory

Postmodern theory can be described as something that eschews modernism. Modernism is described to have extreme faith in rationality. It sees the world as a system that comes increasingly under human control as our knowledge of it increases. However, postmodernism suggests modernism to be a form of intellectual imperialism that ignores the fundamental uncontrollability of meaning. Postmodernism considers that nature is constructed by our discursive conceptions of it and these conceptions are collectively sustained and continually renegotiated in the process of making sense. It advises us to stop systematising, defining, or imposing logic on events. It considers all our attempts to discover 'truth' as forms of discourse. It considers the role of language in constituting 'reality' as central.

The postmodern organisation thought recognises the impossibility of the formal structure.[14] It attempts to uncover the messy edges of the mythical organisational structure; it uncovers the places where the organisation process becomes confused and defies definition by the discourses that are used within it. In the words of Power, "… the postmodernist perspective flows from a denial that there is any single, ultimate or deep language game that is uniquely determinative or organisational stability. The organisation theorist must be sensitive to the diversity and fluidity of the 'life' of organisation and no one model will suffice to orientate research."[15]

This postmodern organisation thought will have the following implications:

(a) It will have no practical use for the organisers since it would be aimed at illustrating the limits of their projects and at providing a critique of the grand codification and systematisation of organisational analysis.

(b) It would seek to undermine all the conventions of administrative/academic discourse.

(c) It would make no claim to be anything more than another language game.

5.5 Blacksburg Manifesto

The Blacksburg Manifesto was a momentous gathering organised by the Centre of Public Administration and Policy (CPAP) of Virginia Polytechnic Institute and the State University of Virginia in January 1982. This Manifesto coincided with the Second Minnowbrook Conference. The

Manifesto was basically a critique of the anti-government attitude that reached its peak during the Reagen administration in America.

A major Blacksburg thinker, Gary Wamsley, considered the process of programme cutbacks, or turnaround in programmes, as depressing. It has led to chaos, confusion, de-legitimisation of government institutions, and damage to the morale, structures, and processes of government. It has damaged the capacity to govern.[16]

The Manifesto discussed various themes and ideas. Some of the very important among them are as described below:

(a) **A Structural/Institutional Stand:** The authors of the Blacksburg Manifesto took a structural/institutional and neo-institutional stand for public administration. According to them, behaviouralism and positivism have led to the cul-de-sac of public administration theory. The Manifesto supports the First Minnowbrook Conference for its support of public administration values and social commitment.

(b) **Institutionally Grounded Minnowbrook Perspective:** The Blacksburg Manifesto is regarded as an 'institutionally grounded Minnowbrook perspective'. It is different from the Minnowbrook perspective in the sense that it does not accept individual responsibility and commitment as the only basis for social change (as is the case with the First Minnowbrook perspective). According to the Blacksburg perspective, social amelioration can be attained both by individuals and institutions. Along with attempts to change individuals, their perceptions, attitudes, and behaviours, institutions also have to be changed. Institutions are the embodiment of collectively held values, perceptions, attitudes, and behaviours.[17]

(c) **Against Public Choice Theory:** The Manifesto has criticised the methodological individualism approach of public choice theory. Methodological individualism discredits the role of collective institutions. Social constructs function best when there is a harmony between self-interest and collective interest.

(d) **Acceptance of Authority as Indispensable:** The Manifesto accepts authority as an inescapable feature of human society. It considers that authority and participation are not antithetical concepts of organisational life. It considers authority to be as important to governance as water is to life on earth.

(e) **Concern with Public Administration History:** The Blacksburg Manifesto has shown great concern with the history of public administration and its constitutional foundation. It makes a bold attempt to rediscover the origins of public administration. It considers that public administration needs to be studied as constitutional governance and, thus, needs to be related to the constitutional framework. Wamsley considers that "adopting Woodrow Wilson, Frank Goodnow and Frederick Taylor as founders of public administration gives us the following pieces of debilitating irrelevant intellectual baggage we must drag about the academic and practical landscape." A public administration outlook based on management (rather than constitutional governance), and borrowed heavily from private sector concepts, is considered debilitating. Such an outlook has hindered the growth of public administration's own theories, concepts, norms, and techniques to suit a constitutional system of polycentric power.[16]

(f) **Post-Behavioural and Post-Positivist:** The authors of the Blacksburg Manifesto had a tendency to overlook the constraints of behaviouralism and positivism. The epistemological bases explored in the Manifesto, such as radical structuralism and radical humanism, are post-behavioural and post-positivist in nature.

(g) **Concern for 'Public Interest':** A distinguishing quality of the Blacksburg perspective is its concern with the idea of public interest. The concept of public interest is as important to bureaucracy as 'due process' is to the judiciary.

(h) **A Bureaucratic as well as Post-Bureaucratic Perspective:** The Blacksburg perspective has been regarded as both bureaucratic and post-bureaucratic. It is bureaucratic as it tries to restore bureaucracy and refurbish its image, expecting it to be more client-serving, value oriented, and constitutionally grounded. It is post-bureaucratic in the sense that it expects administrators to be with higher moral objectives and community consciousness.

Criticism of Blacksburg Perspective: The Blacksburg perspective is criticised to be confusing. It is caught up in a dilemma. The authority and power of public administration are considered important by it; at the same time it emphasises on post-bureaucratic societal concerns. The Manifesto has not thrown light on the manner in which the qualities of social concern and service orientation can be instilled in an authoritarian and power-oriented bureaucracy.

5.6 Organisational Structure—Basic Elements

The structures of organisations have certain basic elements. John Child identified the following five basic elements of the structure of organisations, which are important at the stage of organisation design:[21]

(a) **Specialisation:** The specialisation in an organisation includes functional specialisation and role specialisation. Functional specialisation describes the extent to which the official duties are divided between discrete and identifiable functional areas. Role specialisation describes the extent to which official duties are divided within functional areas between discrete and identifiable positions.

(b) **Standardisation:** It implies the extent to which activities are subject to standard procedures and rules.

(c) **Formalisation:** It implies the extent to which procedures, rules, instructions, and communication are written down.

(d) **Centralisation:** It implies the extent to which the locus of authority to make decisions affecting the organisation is confined to the higher levels of authority.

(e) **Configuration:** It is a composite concept representing the various dimensions of the shape of the organisation. It is generally shown in a detailed organisation chart including every role in the organisation.

5.7 Organisational Structural Variables

Structural variables are one of the important aspects of organisations, others being context variables and design variables. Figure 5.2 describe the relationship between the context variables, design variables, and structural variables in an organisation.

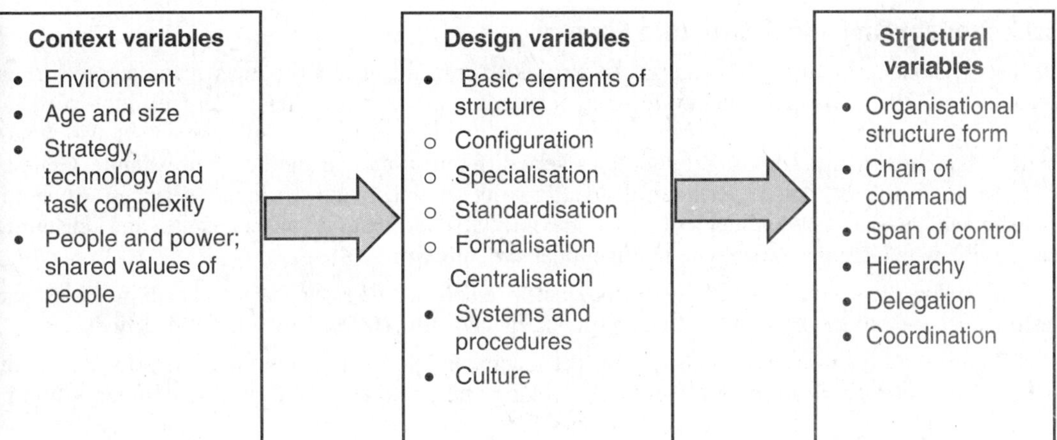

***Fig. 5.2:** Relationship between an organisation's context, design, and structural variables*[22]

The structural variables of an organisation are its chain of command, a span of control, hierarchy, delegation, and so on (they are already discussed in Chapter 3 in the sections 'Principles of Administration' under 'Henri Fayol's Approach to Administration' and 'Explanation of Certain Principles' under 'Gulick and Urwick').

5.8 Departmentalisation in Organisation

An organisation is divided into different departments for ease and efficiency of functioning. The four bases of departmentalisation are discussed in Chapter 3 in the section 'Explanation of Certain Principles' under 'Gulick and Urwick'.

5.9 Organisational Structure Forms

An organisation can be structured in various forms. Many of these forms have been discussed in Chapter 3. However, the important organisational structure forms are functional, divisional, matrix, networked (and virtual organisations), and process-based organisations. All these structures are described in the subsequent sections.

5.9.1 Functional Structure Form

The basic idea in the functional structure form is to club people with functionally similar skills and knowledge together. A functionally structured organisation has departments based on functions, e.g., marketing, finance and accounting, manufacturing, and so on. Over a period of time, the departments develop their own functional specialisation, time horizon, goals, frame of reference, and jargon.[23]

In this arrangement, people become specialised in their tasks and learn the best way of doing their work. However, such an arrangement is not effective in handling growth. The organisation becomes unable to respond to newer demands and opportunities. Communication between different specialised units becomes more and more difficult and complex.

5.9.2 Product Divisional Structure Form

In the divisional structure, an organisation is divided into the major products manufactured in an organisation. The divisional structure form is important in those cases when the organisation needs to pay attention to the expectations of the customers and the changes in the environment. It also works better when the organisation has product lines very different from one another. For example, General Electric has products such as medical imaging, jet engines, and financial services. Such an arrangement possesses qualities such as flexibility, coordination mechanisms, and customer sensitivity, which are unavailable in the functional structure form.

The product divisions are focused on the product-wise core activities such as manufacturing, sales, and distribution. The services of a set of common support functions are shared across the product divisions.

This form of organisation is beneficial, as the planning, goal-setting, and major decisions made by the product divisional heads are more holistic, looking after the interests of the overall organisation in the long term. The divisional heads are responsible for the overall performance of their division, and not just for the cost, size, and investments.

However, this form of organisation has limitations such as integration problems among the various subunits. Strategic integration of the different divisions requires the presence of certain strategic or corporate support staff. However, the divisional members and corporate members of the organisation often develop conflict.

5.9.3 Matrix Organisations

The matrix form of organisation is that form of organisation in which positions are organised as a grid. Horizontally, the arrangement of structure is by functions and, vertically, the arrangement is by projects. Such a structure is required in organisations where the work involves projects with intense and complex, fast and focused activities. Such organisations require the involvement and collaboration of experts in diverse areas in a time-bound manner.

The matrix form of organisation has the following advantages:

(a) It retains the simplicity of functional division of work and yet enhances the agility and flexibility of the organisation.

(b) It enables the organisation to share the expertise of highly skilled employees; on the contrary in the divisional arrangement, expertise is required to be duplicated in all divisions.

(c) It enables employees to do different tasks, take up challenges, and solve more problems.

(d) Contrary to the functional arrangement, the problem is solved with the collaboration of people from different disciplines. This not only enhances the quality of the solution but also makes it more innovative.

However, the matrix form of organisation faces the following difficulties:

(a) There may be confusion due to conflict of a priority between the functional requirement and project requirement.

(b) This form of organisation has minimum control mechanisms vertically and has minimum rules and procedures. This may also create confusion and wastage of resources.

A representation of the matrix form of organisation is shown in Fig. 5.3.

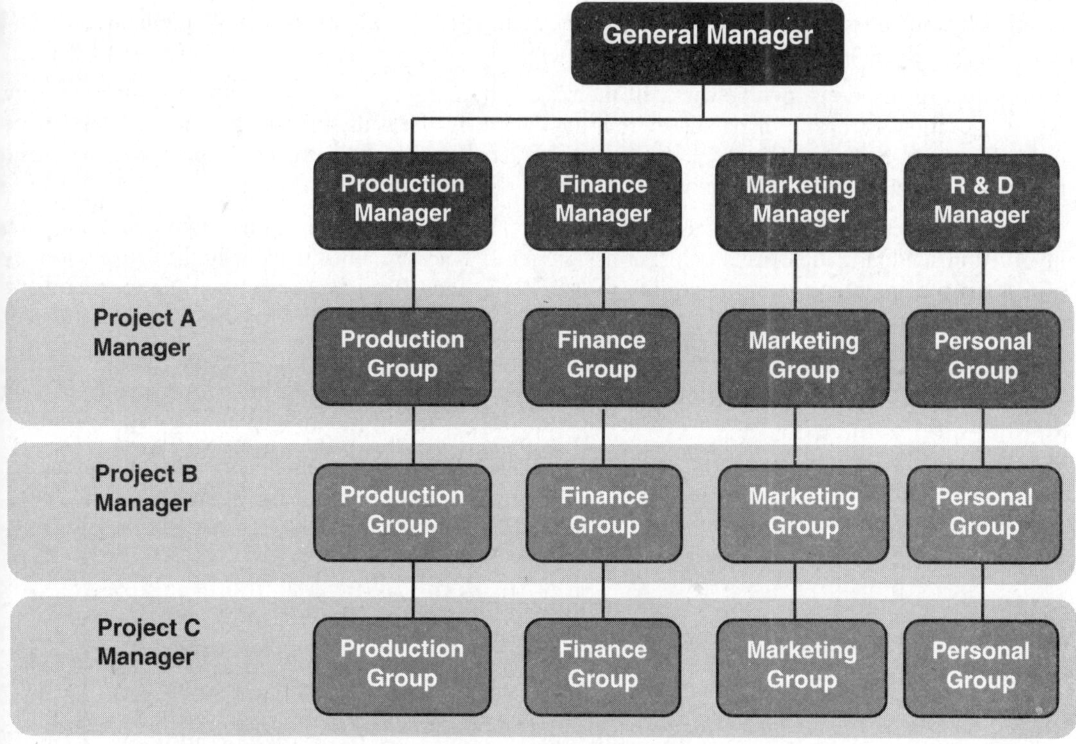

Fig. 5.3: Representation of matrix organisation structure[20]

5.9.4 Networked Organisations/Boundary-less Organisations

A networked organisation involves a highly dynamic environment that has relatively short-lived opportunities. It requires diverse areas of competence to realise these opportunities in a short span of time. Hence, several organisations from different businesses that can be aligned into a new business arrangement come together and create contractual relationships to form a network.

A good example of this is the Amazon or Flipkart online book store. They represent a network of arrangements among the suppliers of books, warehouses, and transportation services, among others. Such arrangement is also seen in organisations that seem like a core or nucleus attracting several other bodies and keeping them together.

In networked organisations, it is difficult to distinguish operationally where one organisation ends and the other starts in terms of teamwork, collaboration, and mutuality. Technology plays a very crucial role in the development and maintenance of such organisations. Second, trust is very important in them; it determines the life and degree of success of such organisations. Opportunistic and self-interested behaviour cannot prosper in such organisations. A representation of the networked structure is shown in Fig. 5.4.

Virtual Organisations

A virtual organisation is a type of networked organisation that is critically dependent on technology and trust for their life and well-being. A virtual organisation is a collection of geographically distributed, functionally, and/or culturally diverse entities that are linked by electronic forms of communication and rely on lateral, dynamic relationships for coordination.[18]

In such organisations, people can start their work by logging into their computers and accessing the organisation's website or database from anywhere. In these organisations, meetings take place through internet-based chat rooms and voice-over-internet facilities. The need for people to meet face to face in a physical setting is minimal.

However, such organisations are very fragile and their form is ever-changing. Employees are often involved in switching their tasks, roles, or assignments. They are advantageous in the sense that they give a sharp edge to speed and flexibility in operations and offer lower response time to customers, over task specialisation.

The effectiveness of a worker in networked and virtual organisations will depend on his/her self-efficacy, experience in working remotely, and information technology capability. A manager of such organisations requires good listening skills, time management, information technology skills, and the ability to maintain ample resources and information available to remote workers.[19]

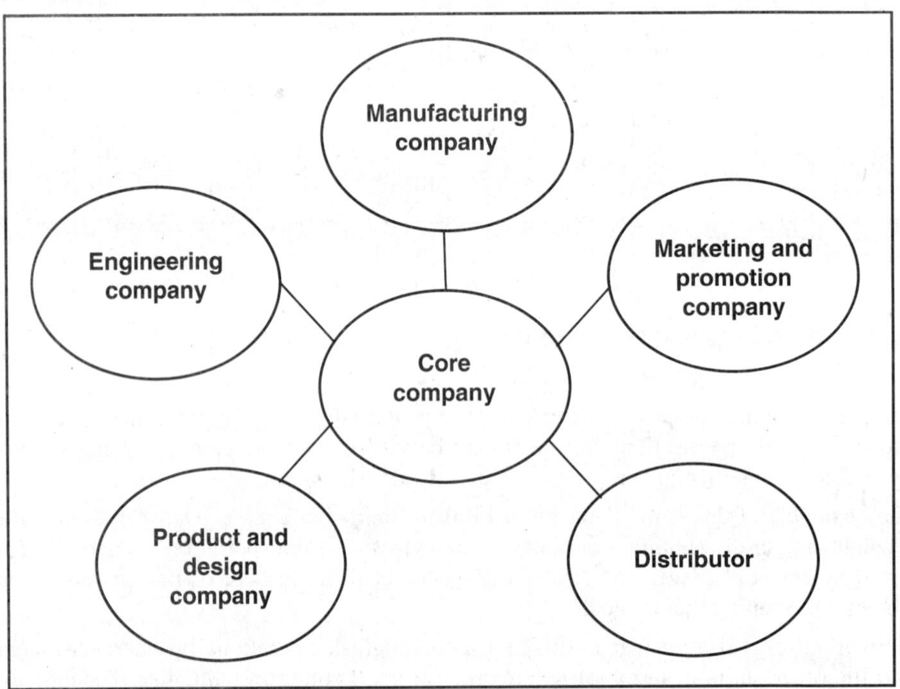

Fig. 5.4: Representation of networked organisation structure

5.9.5 Process-Based Organisations

A process-based organisation has divisions on the basis of the business process. A business process is defined as a structured and measured set of activities designed to produce a specific output for a particular customer or market.[24] Each process is made up of a series of sequential activities or tasks. There are various kinds of processes in an organisation. First, the value-creating processes are those that increase the value of a product/service. Second, developmental processes such as research and development and training are enabling processes. Third, there are management processes that integrate the various value-creating and enabling processes meaningfully to manage the internal and external relationships of the organisation.

A process-based organisation is beneficial in the time of globalisation when the demands of the customers are ever increasing. It is better than traditionally structured organisations, where functional hierarchy and specialisation slow down the decision and action processes. However, a pure process-based organisation faces the problem of activities across different processes, and core-process integration is necessary. Thus, a multidimensional organisation with process ownership as a key dimension is a more beneficial structure (as shown in Fig. 5.5).

A process-based organisation has its customer at the fore and it takes a dynamic view of how it can create and deliver value. In such an organisation, the role of the planning and control process is very important, as it acts as an integrating force and ensures coherence among processes and sub-processes and their contributions to the overall purpose.

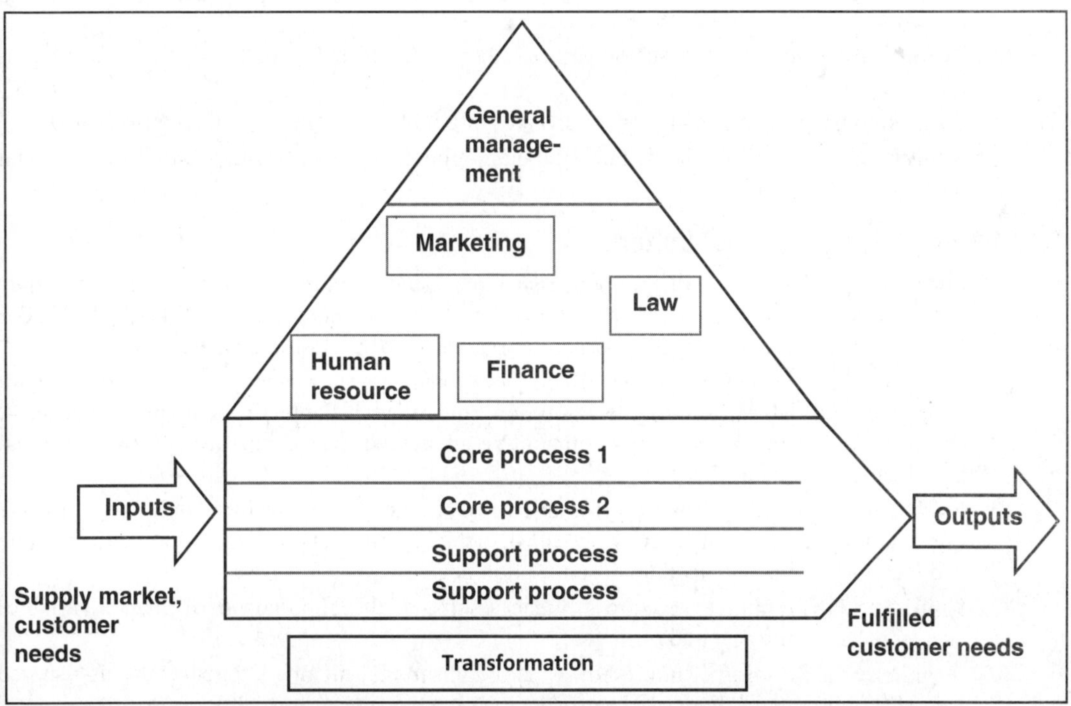

Fig. 5.5: Example of process-based organisation[25]

5.10 Organisational Culture

Organisational culture is a soft and intangible. Organisational characteristic has a real and visible impact on important organisational variables. It is famously defined as "a pattern of basic assumptions—invented, discovered or developed by a given group as it learns to cope with its problems of external adaptation and internal integration—that has worked well enough to be considered valid, and, therefore, to be taught to new members as the correct way to perceive, think and feel in relation to the problems."[26]

The culture of an organisation is similar to the personality of an individual.[27] Just like the profile of the personality of an individual, an organisation also has its cultural profile containing certain basic cultural dimensions.[28] Each dimension represents a set of values that the organisation encourages or discourages. The cultural dimensions are as follows:

(a) **Innovativeness:** It suggests whether an organisation attaches high or low value to being innovative, open to new opportunities, risk taking, willing to experiment, and being less rule oriented.
(b) **Stability:** It suggests whether an organisation attaches high or low value to being rule-oriented and being secure and stable.
(c) **Attention to Detail:** It indicates whether a high or low value is attached to being precise and analytical.
(d) **Respect for People:** It indicates whether the values of fairness, respecting people, and being tolerant are emphasised in the organisation.
(e) **Team Orientation:** It suggests the values of being people-oriented, collaborative, and team-oriented.
(f) **Outcome Orientation:** It suggests the values of being achievement- and result-oriented.
(g) **Aggression:** It suggests the value of being high in competitiveness and low in social responsibility.

5.10.1 Role of Organisational Culture

Organisational culture informs members about issues that need attention, the manner in which they should react emotionally, and the actions they should take.[29] It influences the behaviours and attitudes of individuals. The various roles played by organisational culture are described as follows:

(a) **Financial Performance:** Culture affects the financial performance of a firm. Firms with strong cultures have less volatile cash flow and more reliable financial performance. A strong culture helps in creating a competitive advantage over competitors through internal coordination and control.[30]
(b) **Substitute for Formalisation:** If the employees accept the values and norms of the organisation, a degree of uniformity can be achieved in decisions and actions across time and locations. Thus, the need for formalisation decreases.
(c) **Employee Performance:** Culture influences some of the important performance variables such as job commitment and turnover.[28]
(d) **Organisation Bonding:** Culture binds the organisational members together through shared language, thoughts, feelings, and activities.
(e) **Technology Adoption:** The culture of an organisation determines whether the employees will adopt a technology or not. A culture of innovation, trust, and openness, or a culture where people know they will be cared for by their organisation may secure the required employee support in adopting the new technology.
(f) **Employee Retention:** Organisational culture helps in retaining the employees of an organisation. Employees are retained if the culture contains values of teamwork, respect for individuals, and security.

(g) **Interpretation of the Environment:** Organisational culture helps employees in making sense out of the complex and confusing dynamics around them within and outside the organisation, so that a suitable interpretation can be made and the desired meaning can be drawn.[31]

(h) **Alignment of Employees with Organisational Goals:** Culture helps in fitting the individual needs with the organisational goals.[28]

(i) **Behavioural Control:** Culture controls how employees perceive and feel about a number of issues. Such a control may be beyond the usual control systems.[32]

(j) **Strategy Formulation:** Culture conditions the organisation's internal processes of strategic decision-making and decides the strategy of the organisation.[32]

(k) **Social Efficiency in Organisation:** There are shared meanings, language, and feelings among members due to organisation culture. This makes social processes such as communication very efficient in terms of time and effort.[32]

(l) **Organisational Learning:** Organisational culture gives memory to the organisation. Through it, important knowledge and behavioural patterns, including emotional responses, are stored and shared in the organisation. This helps in organisational learning.[32]

5.10.2 Basic Elements of Organisational Culture

The culture of an organisation consists of three basic elements—its artifacts, values, and basic assumptions.

(a) **Artifacts:** Artifacts are anything that a person can see, hear, or feel while entering into an organisation. They can be seen in physical manifestations, language, stories, technology, and visible traditions. They mark the surface of the culture in every organisation.

(b) **Values:** Values reflect the members' shared opinion on the methodology of doing work in an organisation. They help the members classify situations and actions as undesirable or desirable.

(c) **Basic Assumptions:** Basic assumptions form the core of the culture in an organisation. They are the kind of beliefs that are taken for granted as facts and are never challenged in the organisation.

5.10.3 Strong Culture vs Week Culture

An organisation is said to have a *strong culture* when the manifestation of positive cultural values, beliefs, and behavioural patterns is strong. The stronger the manifestation, the stronger the performance of the organisation.[33] On the contrary, *weak culture* implies that there is no congruence between the values of the top management and the employees of the organisation. There is a contradiction or conflict between the various elements of culture, or the organisational values and interests and the values of the individual employees are contrary to each other. The differences between strong and weak cultures are tabulated in Mind Map 5.2.

Characteristics	Strong culture	Weak culture
Shared traits	Members display the shared traits more frequently and with higher commit-ment[32]	Shared traits are displayed less frequently and with lower commitment

Characteristics	Strong culture	Weak culture
Homogeneity	The values and behavioural patterns are homogenous and uniform across the organisation	The values and behavioural patterns are not homogenous across the organisation
Stability	The values, assumptions, and behavioural patterns are stable across time and situations	The values, assumptions, and behavioural patterns change with time and situations
Bonding	Members are cohesively bonded together	Members are not well-knit as a team
Congruity/ incongruity of expectations	The expectations of the members from one another, the expectations of members and the organisation are in harmony	The expectations of the members and the organisation are not in harmony
Awareness	Beliefs of organisation are fully articulated so that there is common awareness about the values. The values are also differentiated so as to give a distinct identity to the organisation.	There is lesser awareness about the beliefs and values of the organisation. The organisation does not have a distinct identity because of its values.

Mind Map 5.2: Strong culture and weak culture in an organisation[22]

Weak culture is only transactional in nature. In it, members participate only when they receive rewards. They feel alienated and defensive. It limits the potential of individuals and groups.

5.10.4 Measures to Sustain Strong Organisational Culture

Strong organisational culture is preferred to weak organisational culture. The following measures can be adopted to sustain stronger culture in an organisation:

(a) **Better Articulation:** The values and beliefs of the organisation should be articulated completely.

(b) **Better Artifacts:** Artifacts are powerful tools that can bridge the difference between the values that are articulated, communicated, and shared. These artifacts should be displayed and conveyed at various levels of the organisation.

(c) **Better Reward System:** Cultural messages should be reinforced using a reward system. The reward system should create and support organisational values.

(d) **Lead by Example:** The actions of the leaders should be in congruence with the values and assumptions of the organisation.

(e) **Recruitment:** The recruitment process should be designed so that employees with higher degrees of shared values are selected.

(f) **Organisational Socialisation:** Socialisation is defined as an attempt to manage a new employee's identity by clearly defining the organisation in terms of its distinctive characteristics. An employee's identity is aligned with the central characteristics of the organisation. Due to it, an employee identifies himself with the organisational characteristics and shows greater commitment towards organisational values and beliefs.[34]

(g) **Higher Penetration of Culture:** The leaders should ensure that the culture penetrates deeply at the sociological level (cultural values are shared by groups), psychological level (cultural values are deeply internalised in the thoughts of the members), historical level (cultural values are stable over time), and artifactual level (cultural values are deeply communicated by the artifacts).[32]

(h) **Consistency among Cultural Elements:** The values, assumptions, and artifacts of the organisation should be consistent and congruent with each other.[35]

5.11 Public Private Partnership

Public infrastructure and services are very important for a modern society, in terms of roads, education, healthcare, and so on. However, the local public does not show much interest in the funding and daily operation of public infrastructure and services. Thus, there has been an inclination toward the use of private funds for public infrastructure and the growing privatisation of public services. This concept is understood as *public private partnership* (PPP). The PPPs have gained wide interest across the world.

There has been a partnership between the government and the private sector for centuries. PPPs are seen as the main alternative to the earlier practices of contracting out and privatisation and are seen as a qualitative jump ahead in the effort to combine the strong sides of both the public and the private sector. The concept promises a new way of managing and governing organisations that delivers citizen services.

The classic example of the Danish commercial company Falck shows how PPP has evolved from the earlier 'contracting out' model. Falck had a partnership with the Danish public sector for nearly a hundred years. It started its services by providing ambulance services in the city of Copenhagen and then expanded to firefighting and other rescue operations. It has now become the preferred partner for most of Denmark's local governments in providing ambulance and firefighting services. Although the contract to Falck is awarded through a 'contracting out' procedure, the fact that it has remained a market player for many decades makes it more a partner than just 'another business firm'.[36] This kind of transformation of an organisation into an institution through 'infusion with value'[37] describes how PPPs have evolved from the basic contracting out arrangements.

5.11.1 Definition of PPPs

The Department of Economic Affairs, Ministry of Finance, Government of India defines PPPs as "an arrangement between Government or statutory entity or Government owned entity on one side and a private sector entity on the other, for the provision of public assets and/or related services for public benefit, through investments being made by and/or management undertaken by the private sector entity for a specified period of time, where there is a substantial risk sharing with the private sector and the private sector receives performance linked payments that conform (or are benchmarked) to specified, pre-determined and measurable performance standards."

In PPPs, the private partner assumes the traditional role of the public entity, i.e., delivery of public services. However, the ultimate accountability to the public for these services is still that of the public entity. For example, the National Highway Authority of India may contract out the responsibility for the construction and maintenance of a road. However, the ultimate responsibility towards users for providing good quality road services continues to remain with NHAI.

In terms of theory, scholars are divided on how PPPs are perceived. Certain scholars consider PPP as a tool of governance while others think of it as a 'language game'.[38]

5.11.2 PPPs as Organisational and Financial Arrangements

The basic aspect of PPPs is that they are established to benefit both the public and the private sectors. The public and the private sector have certain specific qualities, which, when combined, gives beneficial results for all.[39] One important definition suggests PPPs as "cooperation of some sort of durability between public and private actors in which they jointly develop products and services and share risks, costs and resources which are connected with these products."[40] The following aspects can be deduced from this definition:

(a) The cooperation between public and private actors is of a certain durable time period. Short-term contractual projects cannot be regarded as PPPs.

(b) Risk sharing is a vital component of PPPs. Both the parties bear certain risks involved with the PPP project. These risks can be of many types. Apart from financial risks, there can be democratic risks, political risks, and other substantive risks connected to the subject matter at hand.

(c) Public and private actors jointly produce a product or service. Both of them gain from this mutual effort.

The administrative aspect of PPP has two dimensions—financial and organisational. The *financial dimension* describes how public and private actors are engaged financially. The financial arrangements include a number of financial models such as BOT (build-own-transfer), BOOT (build-own-operate-transfer), and sale-and-lease-back. On the other hand, the *organisational dimension* describes how tightly organised is the relationship between public and private firms. The organisational arrangement emphasises the cooperation of public and private actors in inter-organisational settings. It considers policy networks as a special arrangement of PPP. For example, a policy network in agriculture involves government departments, farmers, farmers' organisations, and other interest groups. Similarly, there are issue networks that are an alliance between various interest groups and individuals who unite in order to promote a common agenda and influence government policy on that.

Figure 5.6 describes the typology of PPPs based on the nature of the financial and organisational relationship between public and private actors.

	Tight organisational relationship	**Loose organisational relationship**
Tight financial relationship	• **Joint venture companies** • **Joint stock companies** • **Joint development projects**	• **BOT** • **BOOT** • **Sale and lease back**
Loose financial relationship	• **Policy communities/policy networks**	• **Issue networks**

Fig. 5.6: Typologies of PPPs based on the nature of financial and organisational arrangement[36]

5.11.3 PPPs as a Language Game

Certain scholars consider PPPs as a language game designed to 'cloud' other strategies and purposes such as privatisation and encouraging private providers to provide public services at the expense of public organisations.[41] The expressions 'contracting out' and 'privatisation' generate opposition from the public. Thus, expressions such as public-private-partnerships are used to get consensus over letting private organisations get a market share of public services.[42] Governments use the term PPP to indicate a new policy direction, apart from privatisation, so as to be not judged inappropriately on the basis of the policy failures of the past.

5.11.4 Key Stakeholders in a PPP

The various key stakeholders associated with a PPP arrangement (especially in an infrastructure project) are as follows:

(i) **Public Entity:** A public entity can include any government department, directorate, government-sponsored board, society, municipal or local body, gram panchayat, government-sponsored education institution, public sector undertaking, government-owned company, statutory authority, or any other entity under government control.

(ii) **Private Entity:** It includes any entity other than a public entity.

(iii) **Concessionaire:** It refers to a private partner who is awarded the tender for the implementation of the PPP project.

(iv) **Special Purpose Vehicle (SPV):** It is an entity created to act as the legal manifestation of a project consortium, with no historical, financial, or operating record that the government can access. An SPV is typically formed by a private partner. The task of the SPV is to sign a contract with the government and with subcontractors to develop a project and maintain it.

(v) **Transaction Advisors:** They are consultants hired through a transparent system of procurement by the sponsoring authorities to assist them in designing the project and/or providing technical, financial, and legal input for the project design.

(vi) **Lead Bank/Lender:** These are financial institutions used for funding the project by providing debt of not less than 25 percent of the total project cost.

(vii) **Lead Financial Institution:** The lead financial institution funds the PPP project.

(viii) **Independent Consultants:** Independent consultants are appointed to ensure that the project work goes on as per the schedule and as per the quality criteria mentioned in the agreement.

(ix) **Users:** These are the project beneficiaries or the end users of the project.

5.11.5 Advantages of PPP

The advantages of PPP projects are enumerated below:

(a) **Higher Efficiency due to the Private Sector:** The private sector is more efficient in carrying out the capital and operating phases of a project. It is well-placed to access quality and skilled manpower and technology and hold its employees, suppliers, and vendors more accountable for performance. In a PPP, the risks and associated performance rewards and penalties are allocated properly between the public and private sectors. Thus, it gains from the efficiency of the private sector.

(b) **Decreased Life Cycle Costs of a PPP Project:** In PPPs, a private partner is responsible for design and construction as well as the operations and maintenance (O&M) management of a project. Thus, the private partner designs the project to take into account the links between construction and operation so that the cost is apportioned over the project's lifetime. In contrast, in traditional 'contracting out' projects, one set of contractors was appointed for design and construction and other unrelated contractors for O&M; thus, they had a narrow perspective and did not focus on the life cycle cost of the project.

(c) **Increased Transparency and Accountability:** In PPPs, there is a clear allocation of risks and responsibilities, where the responsibility of the public entity is to monitor the service provider and that of the private entity is to actually deliver the services. This increases the scope of accountability, as the public entity can always question the private entity over the end delivery of public services. In contrast to this, in traditional procurement projects, the public agency was responsible for both service monitoring and service delivery.

(d) **Access to Private Sector Finance:** PPPs allow public agencies to access private finance for infrastructure and other projects. This allows the government to save its own revenues for social sectors, where the role of government funding is indispensable.

5.11.6 Limitations of PPP

Apart from the advantages, PPPs have the following limitations:

(a) **Complex Procurement Process:** A PPP procurement process is considered complex because the long-term nature of the project requires greater consideration as well as the specification of contingencies in advance. A clear allocation of future risks and service requirements is a complex process. Thus, efficient transaction advisors and consultants are appointed to assist the public entity in handling the challenges involved in this complex process.

(b) **Complex Enforcement and Monitoring Process:** The efficiency of a PPP project depends on the efficient performance monitoring of the private entity against expected performance standards. This again is a complex process requiring the support of independent consultants.

(c) **Legal Hurdles:** The contract and other laws were designed before the concept of PPPs was conceived. Thus, PPPs face various legal hurdles during their project life cycle.

(d) **Financial Contingencies:** There may be contingencies in PPP projects that may require financial support from the government. However, there are generally no provisions in government budgeting for committed and/or contingent liabilities arising out of PPP arrangements.

However, the above limitations can be avoided by the careful design and management of the PPP project by the public entity.

5.11.7 Variants of PPP Models

PPP models are characterised by the identification of risks and their allocation among the various parties to a contract. On the basis of risk allocation, the PPP models (especially in the case of infrastructure projects) are classified into the following three categories:

(a) Management contract
(b) Lease contract
(c) Build-operate-transfer

5.11.7.1 Management Contracts

Management contracts are partnerships in which a private entity is employed only for the management of certain activities for a short duration (3–5 years). They are task-specific and focus only on inputs rather than outputs. The ownership of assets and investments remains with the public sector, although the private sector may be given certain rehabilitation responsibilities. There are several variants of management contracts, as follows:

(a) **Basic Management-for-Fee Contract:** In such projects, a private entity manages designated activities for specified fees. All volume and future value risk is retained by the public entity.
(b) **Management Contract with Performance Incentives:** In such projects, certain risks such as volume risks are retained by the private entity. The private entity is provided with performance incentives against expected cost and quality standards.
(c) **Management and Finance Contract with some Rehabilitation and Expansion:** In such projects, the private entity takes the financial and management risks for a volume incentive.

A Case Study of Management Contract- Karnataka Urban Water Supply Improvement Project

In this project, public entities (Urban Local Bodies, ULBs, of Belgaum, Gulbarga and Hubli, Karnataka Urban Infrastructure Development Finance Company) and a private entity (Veolia Water, France) came into an agreement to improve the distribution and augmentation of bulk water supply. The private partner was entrusted to undertake the rehabilitation/construction of the distribution network across the zones of the three cities. The financing risk, which included all project-related costs, was borne by the public entity, whereas the management risk, which included the operation of the infrastructure created, was transferred to the private partner. The ownership of the created assets remained with the ULBs.

The private partner was responsible for individual house connections, treatment of water, ensuring reduction in distribution losses, and generation and distribution of bills. The payment to the private partner included a 60% fixed component and a 40% variable component based on achieving performance targets.

5.11.7.2 Lease/Affermage Contracts

In lease contracts, the public entity gives an asset on lease to a private entity. Such contracts are valid for a medium term, and the user fees collection risk is transferred to the private partner. The private partner collects the user fees and transfers a percentage of it to the public entity (in case of a lease contract); the private partner may also retain the user fees and transfer an additional surcharge (charged from the consumers) to the public entity (in case of affermage contracts). Such arrangements are generally observed in the case of water supply contracts. The variants of this model are:

(a) **Built-lease-transfer (BLT)**
(b) **Built-own-lease-transfer (BOLT)**
(c) **Built-transfer-lease**

5.11.7.3 Build-Operate-Transfer Agreement

A build-operate-transfer (BOT) agreement is used for the development of greenfield assets in which substantial risks, including volume risk, financial risk, and potential price risks, are allocated to the private entity. A greenfield project is one in which work is done on a new project. For example, in greenfield road projects, the roads are made on unused lands where there is no need to remodel or demolish an existing structure. On the other hand, brownfield projects are those in which work is done to modify or upgrade existing structures. For example, in the case of brownfield road projects, roads are upgraded to improve their quality and efficiency.

The variants of the BOT model are described as follows:

(a) **User Fee Based BOT Model:** In such BOT models, the private entity collects fees from the end users for the delivery of public services. User charges help the private entity to recover the cost incurred on the project. It is prevalent in the case of energy and transport sub-sectors (roads, ports, airports, and so on).

(b) **Annuity-based BOT Model:** In this model, the government transfers an annual fee to the private partner. It is prevalent in those sectors where sizeable cost recovery cannot be made through user charges owing to social, political, or affordability conditions. It is used mostly in rural and urban health and education sectors.

(c) **Modified Design-Build (Turnkey) Contract:** In this model, the payment made by the government to the private sector is linked to the achievement of tangible intermediate construction milestones (instead of lump-sum payment on completion) and short-period maintenance/repair responsibilities.

(d) **Design-Build-Finance-Operate-Transfer:** It is an agreement is which the private partner designs, finances, and constructs a new facility under a long-term lease, and operates the facility during the term of the lease. The facility is transferred back to the public entity at the end of the lease term.

(e) **Buy-Build-Operate:** It is an agreement in which there is the transfer of a public asset to a private or quasi-public entity for upgrading or operating that asset for a specified period of time. Public control is exercised through the contract at the time of transfer.

(f) **Build-Own-Operate:** It is an agreement in which the private sector finances, builds, owns, and operates a facility or service in perpetuity. The public constraints are stated in the original agreement and through on-going regulatory obligations.

Case Study of BOT Model: Tuni Anakapalli Road Project

In the Tuni Anakapalli Road Project, there was an agreement between the National Highways Authority of India (NHAI) and a private partner named GMTAEPL with the objective of improving design, construction, operation, and maintenance of the National Highway road between Tuni and Anakapalli. It was a BOT annuity contract for 15 years. The O&M responsibility was with the private partner. The private player invested in the development of the road stretch and later operated and maintained it. NHAI paid an annual income to the private partner.

5.11.8 Difference between Traditional Contracts and PPPs

Mind Map 5.3 describes the difference between traditional contracts and modern public private partnerships (PPPs).

	Traditional contracts	PPPs
Risk allocation	Public entity bears almost all the risks associated with a project	There is allocation of risks in a manner that a particular kind of risk is allocated to the party most suitable to handle it.
Project management	Public entity is responsible for complete project management	Responsibility for O&M is generally with the private partner
Focus of project	Focus is on building an asset	Focus in on buying of services or output service delivery. The output specifications are clearly mentioned in the partnership agreement
Financing	Financed by public entity through its budgetary resources	The private sector may bring finances in the form of debt or equity to develop a project
Payments	The public entity needs to make frequent and short-term payments to the private entity. Payments may be linked to construction milestones.	The payment made to the private entity is long term and on the basis of the outputs attained. Payments are linked to expected service delivery.

Mind Map 5.3: Differences between traditional contracts and PPPs

5.11.9 PPPs: A Symbiotic Partnership between Public and Private Partner

Public and private entities benefit mutually from PPPs. They both gain respect for different aspects of the partnership. The public entity gets a better economy rate of return and value proposition, whereas the private partner gets financial viability and a better financial rate of return from the project. Thus, a PPP is considered a win-win situation for both the public and private entities. The advantages for a public entity from a PPP are as follows:

(a) PPPs help the public entity in harnessing private sector efficiencies such as on-time and on-budget delivery and access to the latest technology.

(b) It helps the public entity in augmenting public resources.

(c) It ensures better value for the project.

(d) It helps in ensuring continuity in service delivery. This benefits society at large.

(e) It also helps in better compliance with all laws and regulations such as environmental protection.

The advantages for a private entity from a PPP are as follows:

(a) PPP arrangements are usually considered as viable ventures by private entities. They help in creating long-term opportunities and ensuring reasonable profits.

(b) It helps in the fair allocation of risks between public and private entities.

(c) The PPP agreement involves better articulation and implementation of transparent laws and regulations.

5.11.10 Challenges of PPPs in India

The Kelkar Committee on Public Private Partnerships carried out extensive research on the emerging challenges of PPPs in India. It listed challenges as described in the following sections.

5.11.10.1 Challenges from External Factors

PPP projects, especially in the infrastructure sector, are significantly affected by global factors such as economic slowdown and credit crisis.

5.11.10.2 Challenges from Judicial Orders

There are certain judicial or statutory authority orders (e.g., banning of mining activity) that delay the progress of development and implementation of PPP projects and revenue flows.

5.11.10.3 Challenges from Legal and Regulatory Framework

Sectors such as roads, airports, and ports have either no regulator or have multiple regulators (as in the case of airports). The presence of overlap in the functions of several regulatory agencies has led to problems in decision-making. Second, some sectors, such as the urban infrastructure sector, are yet to evolve regulatory frameworks for the sustainable and efficient delivery of PPP projects and services. Third, the dispute resolution mechanism in the case of PPP agreements is slow and not well-developed, often derailing project timelines and freezing funds. Fourth, many PPP projects have been affected by delays in land acquisition and clearances, leading to time and cost overruns.

5.11.10.4 Financing Challenges

Certain issues have been observed in the quality of lending in the case of PPPs. The bank appraisals of PPP projects often suffer from a lack of adequate diligence, sometimes due to inappropriate appraisal skills. Moreover, PPPs also suffer due to a shortfall in equity capital from local sponsors. Apart from this, the underdeveloped debt markets are a cause of concern for Indian PPPs.

5.11.10.5 Overlap in the role of multiple institutions

There is a network of agencies involved in the implementation of PPP projects. However, there is an overlap in the functions of these agencies, leading to inordinate project delays. The inadequate capacity of agencies such as public entity, consultants, financiers, developers, and statutory audit and vigilance agencies has led to coordination issues in PPP projects.

5.11.10.6 Problems in the Private Sector

India has witnessed over-aggressive bidding with inadequate due diligence by private entities. This has sometimes led to unviable PPP offers. Second, the private sector has been unable to develop its skills in the pricing of its risks, despite engaging the best consultants in the field. The quality of consultancy services in PPPs has not kept pace with the growing need for risk assessment and other emerging needs for the PPP sector.

5.11.10.7 Challenges in the Contractual Framework

It is found that PPPs have inadequate provisions for addressing legal and contractual issues such as exit clause provisions, default by parties, and change of scope-related events. This has caused project delays and ineffectiveness in project implementation as anticipated. Most of the PPP agreements are based on model agreements, with little or no project-specific customisations. Furthermore, the traditional long-drawn legal system is unable to adequately deal with matters such as disputes over unanticipated events.

5.11.11 Risk Allocation Framework for PPPs

Proper allocation of risks, in order to reduce the threat of underperformance of PPP projects, is one of the major concerns for PPPs today. The allocation of risk should be taken in a sector and project-specific context. Presently, a 'one-size-fits-all' approach is adopted for risk allocation; failure to adopt project-specific risks has led to project implementation hurdles.

The risk factors associated with a PPP project can be classified in the following manner (Kelkar Committee Report on PPPs):[43]

(a) **Risks to be solely allocated to the Public Sector:**

The *risk of expropriation and nationalisation* is the only risk that can be solely allocated to the public sector. It is defined as a risk in which the government takes over a facility run by a private firm, without giving reasonable compensation, due to unwarranted political, social, or economic pressures.

(b) **Risks to be largely allocated to the Public Sector:**

The following risks can be largely allocated to the public sector:

(i) **Government's Reliability:** It is defined as the reliability and creditworthiness of the government to be able and willing to honour its obligations in the future.

(ii) **Government's Intervention:** It is defined as the unreasonable intervention of the public sector in privatised facilities or services.

(iii) **Poor Political Decision-Making:** Poor political decision-making is observed when PPP decisions are made while considering the political vote bank, personal interests, and short-term goals of political leaders.

(iv) **Land Acquisition:** It is defined as the risk associated with delays in acquiring land for a PPP project.

(v) **Corruption:** Government officials demand bribes for approving a PPP project.

(vi) **Approval and Permit:** This risk is defined as delay or refusal of project approval and permit by the government.

(vii) **Supporting Facilities Risk:** It is a risk in which supporting facilities such as electricity and water may not be available in a timely manner or at fair rates.

(viii) **Uncompetitive Tender:** This is a risk of having non-transparent and uncompetitive tenders.

(ix) **Dishonour of Exclusive Rights:** This is a risk in which the government does not honour its commitment to providing exclusive rights to a private entity and builds another competitive project.

(x) **Change in Law:** It is defined as the risk of project uncertainty due to changes in law and rules.

(xi) **Tax Regulation Changes:** The government's inconsistent application of the tax regulations is a considerable risk for a PPP project.

(xii) **Immature Jurisdiction System:** The absence of a national PPP law may lead to different judicial interpretations of PPPs in different cases.

(c) **Risks to be equally shared by public and private parties:**

The following risks can be said to be equally shared by public and private parties:

(i) **Public/Political Opposition:** Risks may emanate due to opposition from the public to a PPP project because of certain social and cultural values.

(ii) **Change in Tariff:** It is a risk associated with improper tariff design and non-adjustment of the tariff according to the financial requirements of a project.

(iii) **Force Majeure:** It is a risk associated with circumstances such as floods, fires, storms, epidemic diseases, and wars that are out of the control of partners.

(iv) **Payment Risk:** It is a risk in which the consumers or government do not pay for PPP services due to social, political, or other reasons.

(v) **Environmental Protection:** There are certain risks associated with future environmental protection issues.

(vi) **Improper Contracts:** Improper arrangements and improper risk definition and allocation in a contract are risks for both public and private entities.

(vii) **Inflation:** It is a risk associated with unanticipated inflation.

(viii) **Foreign Exchange and Convertibility Risks:** It is the risk associated with fluctuations in the currency exchange rate and difficulty in the convertibility of foreign currency.

(ix) **Change in Market Demand:** It is the risk associated with the changes in market demand for a PPP project.

(x) **Third Party Reliability Risks:** It is the risk associated with the future reliability of the other parties, apart from public and private entities, involved in a PPP project.

(xi) **Change in Interest Rates:** It is the risk associated with an unanticipated changes in interest rates.

(d) **Risks to be largely allocated to the private sector:**

The following risks can be largely allocated to the private sector:

(i) **Construction/Operation Changes Risks:** These are the risks associated with unanticipated changes in the construction or operation of the project.

(ii) **Residual Assets Risk:** It is defined as a risk in which the assets transferred to the government at the end of the partnership period may not be in a good condition or running properly.

(iii) **Organisation and Coordination Risks:** These are the risks associated with disputes arising due to improper organisation and coordination between the different members of a PPP.

(iv) **Consortium Instability Risk:** It is a risk in which the consortium may not be able to perform its obligations as a PPP consortium company.

(v) **Private Investor Change:** It is the risk associated with the an unanticipated entry or exit of a private investor due to certain disputes between private investors or other reasons.

(vi) **Delay in Supply:** It is the risk associated with the inability of subcontractors and suppliers to supply labour and material on time.

(vii) **Construction Completion Risk:** It is the risk associated with a longer construction time than predicted or with the poor quality of a construction.

(viii) **Financial Risk:** It is the risk associated with a poor financial market or unavailability of the financial instrument resulting in difficulty in financing.

(ix) **Operation Cost Overrun:** The operation cost may increase due to improper measurement, ill-planned schedule, or low operational efficiency.

(x) **Technology Risk:** The technology adopted may not be suitable for future project requirements.

Considering the above-mentioned risks, the Kelkar Committee proposed certain suggestions for improving the risk allocation framework of PPPs. First, an entity should bear the risk that is in its normal course of business (for example, land acquisition is a normal course of business for pubic entities). Second, while preparing a contract, the cost-effectiveness of various risks needs to be evaluated.

5.11.12 Obsolescing Bargains in PPPs

Obsolescing bargain is defined as a phenomenon in which the private partner loses its bargaining power related to tariffs and other matters due to abrupt changes in the economic or policy environment. A PPP project spans 20–30 years and it is not possible to accurately estimate project cash flows. The situation leads to government opportunism, giving the government authority an upper hand over the private entity after project completion. This situation is further aggravated because of the absence of an independent regulator in certain PPP sub-sectors.

To guard against this phenomenon, appropriate safeguards for the project developer should be built ab initio into the contract to ensure its say in future negotiations. Moreover, certain conditions should be defined in which bilateral negotiations may be allowed for changing contractual agreements. Such an option will protect the private developer from unexpected changes beyond its control. The establishment of independent sector regulators will also improve the situation of obsolescing bargains.

5.11.13 Government of India's Initiatives for Promoting PPPs

The Government of India has created a PPP programme with several initiatives to promote PPP development and attract private sector participation. Some of the initiatives are classified in the following sections.

5.11.13.1 Institutional and Financial Support Mechanisms

The Government of India has adopted the following institutional and financial support mechanism for promoting PPPs:

(a) **PPP Cell:** A dedicated PPP cell has been created under the Department of Economic Affairs (DEA) to serve as the secretariat for the various committees that appraise and approve central sector projects and for innovative interventions and financial support mechanisms for facilitating PPPs in the country and managing training programmes for capacity building for PPPs.

(b) **PPP Appraisal Committee (PPPAC):** A PPPAC has been established to streamline the appraisal mechanism to ensure speedy appraisal of projects, eliminate delays, adopt international best practices, and ensure uniformity in appraisals.

(c) **Standardised Documents:** The government has notified standardised documents for PPP contracts such as a model request for qualification (RFQ) and model concession agreement (MCA). They lay down the standard terms relating to the allocation of risks, contingent liabilities, guarantees as well as service quality and performance standards.

(d) **India Infrastructure Finance Company Ltd. (IIFCL):** The IIFCL funds' viable infrastructure projects through long-term debt, refinance to banks and financial institutions for loans granted by them, with tenure exceeding 10 years, or any other mode approved by the government.

(e) **Viability Gap Funding:** The government introduced the viability gap funding (VGF) scheme for providing financial support to PPPs for meeting the financial gaps for infrastructure PPP projects. The scheme provides financial support in the form of grants, one time or deferred, to PPP projects to make them commercially viable.

(f) **India Infrastructure Project Development Fund (IIPFD):** The IIPFD has been created by the Government of India to finance the cost incurred towards the development of PPP projects. It supports costs such as those for procuring good quality advisory services.

5.11.13.2 Capacity Building Mechanisms

The Government of India has adopted the following capacity building mechanisms for promoting PPPs:

(a) **www.pppinindia.com:** A dedicated website for PPPs, www.pppinindia.com, giving comprehensive information on the PPP initiatives and various knowledge resources and government guidelines has also been developed along with a web-enabled database, www.infrastructureindia.gov.in, to provide information on infrastructure projects including PPPs.

(b) **Online Toolkits:** The DEA has developed online toolkits to help project authorities design and develop projects and has published several knowledge products for PPP practitioners.

5.11.13.3 Contract Management

Guidance material has been developed for the highways, ports, and education sectors for improving the post-award management of PPPs, with a particular focus on day-to-day monitoring and proactive management of key risks to preserve the interests of the users of infrastructure services and the concessioning authority.

5.11.13.4 PPP Pilot Project Programme

The DEA has a PPP Pilot Projects Programme, where the process of structuring PPP projects in challenging sectors is handheld by the central government to develop demonstrable PPP projects. The objective of the initiative is to develop robust PPP projects and successfully enable bids for them to establish their replication potential in the sectors concerned.

Public private partnerships (PPPs)

PPPs as organisational and financial arrangements
- **Financial dimension**
  - Tight financial relationship
  - Loose financial Relationship
- **Organisational dimension**
  - Tight organisational relationship
  - Loose organisational relationship

PPPs as language game

Advantages
- Higher efficiency
- Lower life cycle cost
- Higher Transparency and accountability
- Private sector finance

Limitations
- Complex procurement process
- Complex enforcement
- Legal hurdles
- Financial contingencies

Key Stakeholders
- Public entity
- Private entity
- Concessionaire
- SPV
- Transaction advisors
- Lead bank/ lender
- Lead financial institution
- Independent consultants
- End users

Variants of PPP
- **Management contracts**
  - Basic management for free contracts
  - Management contract with performance incentives
  - Management contract with rehabilitation and expansion
- **Lease/affermage contracts**
  - Built-lease-transfer (BLT)
  - Built-own-lease-transfer (BOLT)
  - Built-transfer-lease (BTL)
- **Build-operate-transfer (BOT)**
  - User fee based BOT
  - Annuity based BOT
  - Modified design build (Turnkey) contract
  - Design-build-finance-operate-transfer (DBFOT)
  - Buy-build-operate (BBO)
  - Build-own-operate (BOO)

Challenges of PPP in India
- From external factors
- From judicial orders
- From legal and regulatory framework
- Financing challenges
- Overlapping role of institutions
- Problems in private sector
- From contractual framework

Indian initiatives for promoting PPPs
- **Institutional and financial support mechanisms**
  - PPP cell
  - PPP appraisal committee
  - Standardised documents
  - IIFCL
  - VGF
  - IIPFD
- **Capacity building mechanisms**
  - www.pppinindia.com
  - Online toolkits
- **Contract management**
- **PPP pilot project programme**

Mind Map 5.4: Various Aspects of PPPs

5.11.14 Public-Private-People-Partnership (4Ps Model)

The PPP model has not been successfully adopted by social sectors such as education and health because of certain inbuilt deficiencies. For such sectors, the 4Ps model is advocated. PPPs suffer from difficulty in of achieving mutual understanding and coherence between the partners. Moreover, they tend to neglect community engagement and people's participation at the stages of planning, decision-making, and implementation of service provision. Thus, there is a call for engaging the people (in PPPs), i.e., the beneficiaries of the services and the organisations representing them and their interests.[44]

Therefore, considering the difficulties, PPPs are gradually developing into public-private-people-partnership (4Ps) by involving the people in the partnership represented by civil society, NGOs, charitable organisations, and community foundations. The people's dimension is added to PPPs as a solution for the government to advance and promote its services. According to S. Thomas, "the Public Private People Partnership model embraces the bottom-up participative strategies which bring the public engagement clearly visible for infrastructure (and other sectors) planning and policy making."[45]

Thus, the 4Ps model is considered an evolution of the PPP model. In 4Ps, people are engaged from the beginning till achieving the partnership's target; they are treated as the key stakeholder for initiating and implementing developmental programs. With 4Ps, the decision-making power has deviated from the policy makers, who have traditionally held the ultimate decision authority, towards the citizens through proactive engagement.[45]

According to PM Narendra Modi, "Good governance is defined by public-private partnership. If we want to implement good governance, we must look to 4Ps – public private people partnership. People should be kept in the loop by the government."

5.11.15 Public-Public-Partnerships

Public Private Partnerships (PPPs) have been considered as a successful model for infrastructure development and other projects. In case of local infrastructure and other services, they have the advantage of bringing private capital to the table and freeing municipalities from undue risk. However, there are certain problems with PPPs in the case of local infrastructure and public services. First, private entities are unable to borrow money as cheaply as the government can; this may result in higher project costs and discourage borrowing for long-term capital improvements. Second, in the case of PPPs, project implementation is governed by shareholders' returns and not by public good; this raises concerns about adequate and equitable provisions of public service. This has led to rising local dissatisfaction with private water, health, and other infrastructure companies.

Considering these limitations, local governments across the world are exploring public-public partnerships (PPuPs) as a way to provide and maintain infrastructure. PPuPs are defined as partnerships between two or more public or non-governmental entities that pool resources and/or expertise to achieve a common goal. A very common example of PPuPs is an international partnership in which developed nations lend expertise, logistical assistance, and funding to developing nations for infrastructure development.[46]

Some of the examples of PPuPs in which public agencies have partnered with one another and with non-governmental organisations (NGOs) to provide critical public infrastructure are described below:

(a) **Cooperative Purchasing Power:**[46] The local governments in villages provide essential services, such as water supply, to a small population. A population of less than 3000 resides in a village. Supplying essential services to these systems does not have the benefit of economy of scale in supplies and maintenance enjoyed by larger systems. Thus, in the US, local governments have started to partner up and form purchasing cooperatives to help bring down the costs of essential services. For example, a number of villages around Baltimore negotiated a cooperative purchasing agreement with the City of Baltimore resulting in a large amount of savings.

(b) **Fund Pooling and Infrastructure Sharing:**[46] Many of the municipalities are cash strapped. Thus, they may partner with other local agencies to build public infrastructure. For example, the city of Henderson (in Nevada State, US) developed partnerships among city agencies and non-governmental agencies to do many tasks ranging from improving childhood literacy to constructing university campuses. The Henderson officials developed a new aquatics centre with the help of capital funding from the Clark County School District's budget. The School District may have primary use of the facility, but it also serves the community at large.

(c) **Local Renewable Energy Provision:**[46] The idea of PPuPs can also be harnessed for the provision of local renewable energy, such as wind and solar energy, to the same local community. For example, the South Dakota Farmers Unions (of the US) formed an organisation named 'South Dakota Wind Partners'. The organisation was able to partner with several community organisations to leverage public investments in order to provide and maintain a 10.5 MW wind farm. The partnership was beneficial to the local farmers, as it was able to provide cheap and clean energy while shaping policies that protect the farmers' land rights.

There are many such examples of successful PPuPs case studies. They not only help in providing cost-effective and equitable services but also strengthen community capacity and public trust.

Practice Questions

1. What are the factors that determine the complexity of an organisational environment?
2. Differentiate between mechanistic and organic organisational systems (Burns and Stalker).
3. Differentiation, integration, and environment are the three key concepts of organisational dynamics (Lawrence and Lorsch). Discuss.
4. Examine how strategic and technological contingencies influence the organisational structure.
5. Examine the two branches of postmodern organisation theory.
6. Unlike in the modern approach, postmodernism does not base its view on the societal macrostructures (as in Marxism), the phenomenological powers of the subject (as in interpretative theory), or the assumed functions of the prevailing order (as in functionalism). Explain.
7. Postmodern organisation thought recognises the impossibility of the formal structure. Discuss.
8. "Behaviouralism and positivism has led to cul-de-sac of public administration theory." Explain with reference to the Blacksburg Manifesto.
9. "Blacksburg manifesto is regarded as an 'institutionally grounded Minnowbrook perspective'." Explain.
10. What is the relationship between organisational context variables, design variables, and structural variables?
11. What are the different organisational structure forms?
12. The culture of an organisation is similar to the personality of an individual. Explain.
13. What are the differences between PPPs and traditional contracting agreements?
14. "Certain scholars consider PPP as a tool of governance while others think it as a 'language game'." Discuss this statement.
15. Who are the key stakeholders in a PPP project? What are the advantages and limitations of PPPs? Describe the various types of PPP models.
16. What have been the challenges for PPPs in India? What steps has the government taken for providing a suitable environment for the growth of PPPs in India?
17. "The Public Private People Partnership model embraces the bottom-up participative strategies which bring the public engagement clearly visible for infrastructure (and other sectors) planning and policy making." (S. Thomas Ng) Discuss.
18. "Good governance is defined by public-private partnership. If we want to implement good governance, we must look to 4Ps – public private people partnership. People should be kept in the loop by the government." (Narendra Modi) Explain.

CHAPTER 6

Accountability and Control

Learning Objectives: After reading this chapter, you will learn the following:

- Meaning of the term accountability, its various dimensions, forms, purposes, and tools
- Various types of executive controls over administration
- Various types of legislative controls over administration and the difference between control in parliamentary and presidential forms of government
- Judicial control over administration in the US, UK, and India
- Rules of natural justice
- Judicial activism, public interest litigation (PIL), and judicial overreach
- Meaning of citizen-centric administration and various aspects of citizen's charter in India
- Right to Public Service Acts in India
- The concept of social accountability, social audit, its impact on society, and its procedure
- Civil society organisation and social capital in India
- Various types of civil society, their impact on society, challenges faced by them, and their accreditation
- Right to Information in India, its evolution, important provisions of RTI Act, its impact on governance, issues faced in its implementation, and redressal of public grievances
- Media and its role in governmental accountability
- Defects in Indian media and media accountability
- Accountability challenges in the era of new public management (NPM) and post-NPM reforms.

6.1 Meaning of the term 'Accountability'

The term 'accountability' has two connotations—answerability and enforcement. *Answerability* is the obligation of public officials to inform and explain about the work they are doing. *Enforcement*, on the other hand, is the capacity of the government agencies to impose sanctions on officials who violate their public duties.[3]

For enforcing accountability, there are three ways to prevent and redress the abuse of potential power:

(i) Subjecting the official power to the threat of sanctions

(ii) Obliging the official power to be operated in a transparent manner

(iii) Forcing the official to justify his/her acts

The substance of accountability places at least four requirements on the public administrators as described below:

(i) To implement laws as intended with a minimum of waste and delay

(ii) To exercise lawful and sensible administrative discretion

(iii) To recommend new policies and propose changes in existing programmes and policies as needed.

(iv) To enhance citizen confidence in the administrative institutions of the government.

6.2 Accountability to 'Whom'

In a political democracy, the public administrators are accountable to the following stakeholders:

(i) Internal hierarchy of their respective departments

(ii) Political executive

(iii) Legislature

(iv) Judiciary

(v) Media

The mechanism of accountability to all these stakeholders will be discussed in the course of this chapter.

Apart from the above five stakeholders to whom a bureaucrat is accountable, a bureaucrat is also accountable to his/her inner self. This is known as the *moral accountability* of a public administrator and is guided by his/her ethical behaviour. According to Fesler and Kettl, 'accountability to external actors' and 'moral accountability' are generally compatible with each other. However, there are certain instances when they are not compatible.[1] For example, sometimes moral accountability may call for disobedience to internal hierarchy or protesting against the unethical behaviour of the superiors/political executive.

The line of accountability is quite straightforward in a classical democracy. The people elect their representatives based on their stand on certain issues. The administrative agency carries out the policy proposed by the people's representatives. The administrators are responsible to the political executives for the implementation of these policies, who in turn are answerable to the legislature. However, in modern-day democracy, this policymaking and policy implementation dichotomy does not quite hold good. Moreover, the growing nature of the state, and the diffusion of power among bureaucrats and political executives, has led to the complexity of the accountability process. This has led to frequent abuses of power by the bureaucrats. Thus, there have been rising calls for clearer, more transparent public administration and better moral fibre of public officials. Such issues will be discussed extensively in this chapter.

6.3 Dimensions of Accountability

The term accountability has the following dimensions:

(i) **Informational Dimension:** The informational dimension of accountability suggests that accountability involves the right to receive information. It also suggests the obligation of the public officials to release necessary details about their official work.

(ii) **Argumentative Dimension:** The argumentative dimension of accountability suggests that accountability involves the right to receive explanation about the official actions taken by a bureaucrat. It also involves the corresponding duty of the official to justify his/her conduct.

These two dimensions aptly suggest the maxim that *power should be bound not only by legal constraints but also by the logic of public reasoning.* Accountability is antithetical to monologic power. It establishes a dialogic relationship between the accountable and the accounting actors.

6.4 Forms of Accountability

Accountability is a complex process that has various forms and dimensions. The various forms act together as a driving force that generates pressure on the administrators to be responsible for and ensure good public service performance. There are three major forms of accountability, as described below:

(i) **Fiscal Accountability:** It involves the scrutiny of the records of financial transactions made by public administrators. It ensures that the expenditure is made legally by the bureaucrats. It ensures the control of the legislature on public money.

(ii) **Process Accountability:** This form of accountability keeps a check on how the public agencies perform their tasks. It detects, and suggests remedies on, procedural irregularity (such as improper government tenders and contracts) and other governmental activity.

(iii) **Programme Accountability:** This form of accountability focuses on the effectiveness and achievement of goals in a public organisation.[2]

6.5 Purpose of Accountability

According to Wolf et al., there are three important purposes of accountability. They are described below:

(i) **Control on Power:** The most important function of accountability is to control the abuse of bureaucratic power and discretion.

(ii) **Quality Maintenance:** Accountability ensures that the performance of a public official is in accordance with quality standards.

(iii) **Learning Experience:** Another important purpose of accountability is the learning experience it creates for a bureaucrat. An administrator learns effective administration in his/her pursuit of continuous improvement in governance and public management.[4]

6.6 Accountability Tools

Accountability is a multidimensional concept. Thus, multiple tools and means are required to ensure the accountability of public servants. The various tools that serve the different purposes of accountability are mentioned in Mind Map 6.1.

Ends (final goals of accountability)	Means (tools)
Legitimacy of decision-makers	Constitutions, electoral systems for government and decision-making bodies, bureaucratic systems of representation, royal prerogative, legislation, letters of appointment, standing orders, and formal delegation of authority.
Moral conduct	Societal values, concepts of social justice and public interest, professional values, training programmes
Responsiveness	Public participation and consultation, debates, advisory bodies, public meetings, freedom of speech
Openness	Parliamentary questions, right to information, public information services, public hearings, green and white papers, annual reports
Optimal resource utilisation	Budgets, financial procedures, rules of virements (process of transferring funds from one to another account), parliamentary public account committees, auditing, public enquiries and participation, formal planning systems
Improving efficiency and effectiveness	Information systems, value for money audits, setting objectives and standards, programme guidelines, approval feedback from public.

Mind Map 6.1: Tools of accountability (Hayliar, 1991)[5]

6.7 Controls Over Administration

Controls over administration are of two types—internal as well as external. Internal controls are those fitted within the administrative machinery and working automatically as the machinery moves. Both internal and external controls are supplementary and complementary. External controls over administration are of four types—from the executive, from the legislature, from the judiciary, and from the citizens.

6.7.1 Executive Control over Administration

In a parliamentary democracy, bureaucrats are responsible to the elected ministers of their respective departments in the government. The minister in charge of a department is held responsible for the good work and the mistakes committed by the civil servants working in the department. Various executive controls over administrators are exercised in the following manner:[6,7]

(a) **Political Direction:** Civil servants work under the overall direction, control, and supervision of political executives. The policies laid down by the political executives are required to be implemented by the civil servants. Civil servants are responsible to the political executives for the implementation of these policies. Important decisions in a department are made after consultation with and approval of the minister. The ministers possess rewards as well as punitive powers in order to ensure control over bureaucrats. The relationship between political executives and administrators is dealt with in detail in Chapter 1 of the book.

(b) **Budgetary System:** The budgetary system determines the total financial and personnel resources, which no department may exceed. It is an effective means for controlling the work of administrators. The bureaucrats work within the budget allocated to their departments. Every penny is spent after the sanction of the political executive. The money needs to be spent in accordance with the purpose intended in the budget, and it needs to follow the rules of financial and economic propriety. Under an effective budgetary system, the administration is under the constant control of the executive.

(c) **Recruitment System:** In higher positions, ministers have a say in the appointment of officers in key positions. They play an important role in the appointment of key officials such as secretaries of departments, officer-on-special-duty, Director General of Police, and directors of other departments. Thus, only those officers who enjoy the confidence of the political executive are appointed. A senior bureaucrat not performing effectively can also be removed easily after the recommendation of the political executive. Through these powers of appointment and removal, the political executive exercises full control over the administration of a department.

(d) **Executive Legislation:** Political executives have the power to prepare 'delegated legislation' within the purview of the overall legislation prepared by the legislature. The concept of 'delegated legislation' will be dealt with in detail in Chapter 7. In brief, it constitutes the rules and regulations to be followed under a particular legislation. For example, the Minister of Human Resource Department prepares rules and regulations under the Right to Education Act. These rules and regulations control the action of the bureaucrats working for the implementation of a particular legislation.

(e) **Civil Service Code:** The executive has created a civil service code to be observed by all civil servants while doing their official functions. It consists of a set of rules that guide the official behaviour of a civil servant and prevents him/her from misusing his/her official powers. It will be discussed in detail in the chapter on administrative ethics.

(f) **Monitoring by Staff Agencies:** The executive exercises control over administration using the staff agencies. Important staff agencies of India are the Department of Administrative Reforms, NITI Aayog, Cabinet Secretariat, and Prime Minister's Office. Staff agencies serve as the eyes and hands of the executive in executing its control on the administration. They influence the functioning of administrative agencies in an indirect but substantial manner. They also play an important role in coordinating the policies and programmes of different administrative agencies.

(g) **Articulation of Public Opinion:** The political executives are elected by the public and are thus responsible to the public opinion. On the other hand, administrators are appointed by the government and are insulated from public opinion. Thus, administrators become status quo oriented and resist any change in their functioning. Thus, the political executive plays an important role of articulating the public opinion into implementable policies, rules, and regulations. In this manner, the executive ensures the accountability of the bureaucrats towards the public opinion.

These four executive controls give a positive and continuous guidance to the administration. They ensure the alertness, efficiency, and effectiveness of public administrators. Executive control is the closest and most influential form of control over administration.

6.7.2 Legislative Control over Administration

In every form of democracy, the legislature exercises control in different forms over the functioning of different agencies and departments of the government. The parliament and the state legislative bodies are recognised as custodians of public interest. The manner of control in the parliamentary and presidential forms of government is different in certain senses.

6.7.2.1 Legislative Control in Parliamentary form of Government

In the parliamentary form of government, ministers are a part of the legislature and they are directly responsible to the legislature for actions taken by the government. The extent and quality of control depends on the statutory powers in the hands of the minister, the time available for debates in parliament, the quality of performance of a department, and the amount of information available with the parliament. Parliamentary control over the government, in democracies like India, is exercised through two techniques—built-in techniques in parliamentary procedure and committees appointed by the parliament.

6.7.2.1.1 Control Techniques Built into Parliamentary Procedures

There are certain general and specific techniques for parliamentary control built into the procedures of the parliament. They are as described in the following.[7,8]

(a) **Questions:** A question is basically a request made to a legislature to receive an oral explanation for an action/inaction by the government. There are two types of questions—starred and unstarred questions. The starred questions are those that are answered orally and the unstarred ones are those that are answered in written. Each member of the parliament is allowed to ask a maximum of five questions on a particular day. The questions can be on almost any act of the government, whether small or big. The answers to the questions are prepared by the officials of a department. They thus help in keeping an effective control over the officials of a department. They help in focusing attention on the failures, and abuses of authority, by a department. They also force the officials to be cautious and meticulous in their record keeping. There is also a provision to raise supplementary questions together with the main question, with the permission of the speaker. The questions have the potential of uncovering big corruption scams and instances of wide misuse of power. The first hour of every parliamentary sitting is slotted for asking questions and is known as the *Question Hour.*

(b) **Resolutions:** A resolution is moved in a parliament to either recommend a particular course of action to the government or to censure an individual minister or his/her ministry. A resolution is also moved on a matter of public interest. It is used to raise certain definite issues in front of the parliament. The nature of a resolution is only recommendatory in nature and not binding on the government. However, a resolution that is passed in pursuance of any provision in the constitution or in any law of the parliament has a binding effect on the government.

(c) **Motions:** A legislator brings a motion on a matter when he/she feels that a particular matter needs to be discussed in the parliament. After a motion is introduced, the member speaks on the matter, followed by a discussion with other members. This debate over an important matter pressurises the government to take a particular course of action.

(d) **Adjournment Motion:** Adjournment motions are motions that require discussion on urgent and important issues. When an adjournment motion is passed, the ordinary business of the house is adjourned and the urgent matter is discussed. The notice for an adjournment motion should be given to the speaker before 12 pm. The motion is said to be passed if 50 or more members support it. A debate takes place on the motion. After the debate, the speaker puts the motion to vote. If the motion is passed by a majority, it amounts to a censure against the government. The adjournment motion is restricted to certain matters, as listed in the following:

   (i) Specific and important matters requiring urgent attention of the house
   (ii) Matters based on facts not subjected to dispute
   (iii) Matters of recent occurrence
   (iv) Matters of public importance
   (v) Matters not sub judice
   (vi) Matters related to the administrative responsibility of the government and not related to legislative concerns
   (vii) Matters not related to anything already discussed in the house

(e) **Zero Hour:** Zero hour is a device used by legislatures to raise important matters without prior notice. It starts immediately after the question hour and lasts until the regular business of the day is started. It has been in use in India since 1962.

(f) **Calling Attention Motion:** Calling attention motion is introduced by a member of the parliament to call the attention of a minister to a matter of urgent public importance and seek important explanations from him/her on that matter.

(g) **Debates and Discussions:** Debates and discussions take place on various governmental issues in the parliament. They form an effective mechanism of parliamentary control. They are arranged at the government's own initiative or at the request of the opposition. Such discussions compel the government to explain particular issues of its policy and enrich the policy perceptive of the government.

(h) **Annual Financial Statement or Budget:** The annual financial statement or the budget is laid before the parliament for discussion and seeking opinion. Mentioned in Article 112 of the Constitution, it contains the statement of the estimated receipts and expenditure of the government for a year. A discussion over the budget enables effective financial control over governmental expenditure.

(i) **No-confidence Motion:** According to Article 75 of the Indian Constitution, the council of ministers is collectively responsible to the Lok Sabha (or the lower house of the parliament). The ministers can be removed from the office if they lose the confidence of the Lok Sabha.

Such removal of the whole council is done through a *no-confidence motion*. The motion is admitted by the support of at least 50 members of the house.

(j) **Censure Motion:** A censure motion is introduced in the lower house to censure the policies or action/inaction of a single minister, group of ministers, or the whole council. It is admitted only after specific reasons for its admission are stated. Unlike the no-confidence motion, it does not force the removal of the ministers.

6.7.2.1.2 External Control through Audit and Committees

Apart from the in-built mechanisms mentioned in the preceding section, the parliament also exercises its control over the government through audits and committees. Auditing is an important tool of parliamentary control over administration. In India, the Comptroller and Auditor General (CAG) is the chief auditing agency, which audits, on behalf of the parliament, the accounts of the government and submits an annual *audit report* on the financial transactions of the government. This report helps in highlighting the improper, illegal, unwise, uneconomical, and irregular expenditures of the government. In this manner, it helps in maintaining the financial responsibility of the government towards the parliament.

Similarly, there are parliamentary committees such as the Public Accounts Committee (PAC), Estimates Committee, Committee of Public Undertakings, and Committee on Subordinate Legislation, which help the parliament in exercising effective control over the administration. These committees will be discussed in Chapters on Financial Administration & Financial Management and Administrative Law.

6.7.2.2 Legislative Control in Presidential form of Government

In the presidential form of government (prevalent in the USA and some other countries), the control mechanism is very different from the parliamentary form of government. Unlike the parliamentary system, in the presidential system, the executive and the legislature are completely separate. The president and the ministers are not a part of the legislature. They are thus independent of the legislature. The president enjoys a fixed tenure and cannot be removed before the completion of his/her tenure in normal circumstances. S/he also does not require a majority support in the lower house (known as *the Congress* in the USA) for his/her survival in the office. Thus, in-built techniques such as questions, adjournment motions, censure motions, and no-confidence motions are not valid mechanisms of legislative control in the presidential form of government.

In the US, the legislative branch consists of the House and the Senate, known collectively as the Congress. The Congress ensures the accountability of the US administration in the following manner:[7,9,10,11]

(a) **Creation of Government Organisations:** The US Congress creates executive departments, commissions, boards, and other administrative agencies. It determines their structure, organisation, powers, and functions.

(b) **Independent Regulatory Commission:** The Independent Regulatory Commission regulates the various sectors of the US economy such as the Inter State Commerce Commission and the Federal Trade Commission. These commissions report directly to the US Congress and are outside the control of the US President. Thus, they are an important mechanism of Congressional control on the administration.

(c) **Committees:** The US Congress appoints various committees to investigate the functioning and/or malfunctioning of governmental departments and agencies. Such investigation helps the Congress in pointing out the deficiencies in administration.

(d) **Legislative Power:** The laws enacted by the Congress form the basis of the policies and rules framed by the government.

(e) **Budgetary Power and Congressional Budget Office:** The Congress has the power to approve the budget, which is thoroughly examined by its committees and sub-committees. The congressional budget office (CBO) is responsible for producing independent analyses of budgetary and economic issues to support the Congressional budget process. It conducts a non-partisan, objective, and impartial analysis of the governmental budget.

(f) **Auditing and Government Accountability Office (GAO):** The US Government Accountability Office (GAO) is an independent and non-partisan agency that works for the US Congress. It has the responsibility of investigating how the federal government spends the taxpayers' money. Its mission is to support the Congress in meeting its constitutional responsibilities and to help improve its performance and ensure the accountability of the federal government for the benefit of the American people. It supports Congressional supervision by auditing governmental agency operations to determine whether federal funds are being spent efficiently and effectively. It also investigates allegations of illegal and improper activities by government functionaries. Moreover, it performs policy analyses and outlines options for congressional consideration.

(g) **Powers of the Senate:** The Senate has important powers such as confirming the treaties executed by the president and confirming higher appointments made by the president. Such powers help the Senate in controlling the actions of the president.

(h) **Impeachment of President:** Unlike the parliamentary system, the US government cannot be removed by passing a no-confidence motion in the Congress. However, the president can be removed by the process of impeachment on grounds of treason or corruption.

(i) **Doctrine of Co-directorship:** The government agencies of the US are mandated to report their past actions and future plans to the committees of the Congress. This process is described as the *doctrine of co-directorship*, as it ensures direct participation of the Congress in administrative decision-making. Moreover, the departments are also required to submit their annual and special reports to the Congress for its consideration.

6.7.3 Judicial Control over Administration

Judicial control over administration is exercised by various mechanisms, the most important being the judicial review. It is defined as the power of the courts to keep the administrative actions within the limits of law. Its sole purpose is to protect the citizens against unlawful trespass on their constitutional or other rights. Judicial review is the power of the courts to examine the legality and constitutionality of administrative (as well as legislative) acts. It is the power of a court to hold unconstitutional and unenforceable any law or order based upon such law or any other action taken by a public authority, which is inconsistent or in conflict with the basic law of the land.[12] The nature of judicial control is different in different countries.

6.7.3.1 Judicial Control in USA

In the US, it is considered that there is no limit upon the rights of courts to review administrative decisions. The power of judicial review in US can be described under the following heads:[17]

(a) **Finality of Administrative Decisions:** The Supreme Court maintains a watchful eye even on independent regulatory bodies. The courts enjoy the right of final scrutiny on every administrative action.

(b) **Questions of Law and Fact:** The US courts examine questions of law or questions of constitutional or statutory authority in administrative actions. The courts also examine those questions of fact that involve the questions of law.

(c) **Jurisdictional Facts:** The judiciary intervenes in case of jurisdictional fact, when the order given by an authority is beyond its jurisdiction. For example, the US Employees' Compensation Commission has the power to award compensation to injured employees. Here, the employer-employee relation determines the jurisdiction of the commission, and the power of the commission to act is referred to as a jurisdictional fact. In a particular case, the Supreme Court negated an action of the commission when it awarded compensation to an injured person who was not an employee to an employer (the Commission went beyond its jurisdiction). The facts of jurisdiction are not left to be determined by the administrative agencies themselves and are determined by the US courts. The practical result of this doctrine of jurisdictional fact is to permit a complete judicial re-examination of facts, which otherwise would have been conclusively determined by the administrative agency.[13]

(d) **Due Process Clause:** In cases involving police power, or where the individual freedom is restricted in the interest of society as a whole, the due process clause comes into picture. The US courts interpret due process to include matters of substantive law as well as procedure. The 14th amendment of the US Constitution mentions that no state shall "deprive any person of life, liberty or property, without due process of law." This due process clause acts as a bar to all arbitrary governmental actions. However, the US Supreme Court uses this clause to nullify administrative acts and legislations that seem to it contrary to 'good' social, economic, and political policy. Judicial review under this clause has had a widespread effect on the administrative practice and findings of the US.[14]

(e) **Other Mechanisms for Appeal against Administrative Actions:** Apart from the above-mentioned mechanisms, there are several other ways in which an administrative action may be brought before a US court for review. First, an action for damages may be brought on by an aggrieved party. Second, an aggrieved party can approach the courts to enforce the orders of an administrative agency; for example, the Interstate Commerce Commission. Third, extraordinary writs (will be discussed later in this chapter) are also used for bringing administrative actions in front of US courts. Finally, there are also express statutory provisions for appeal; for example, the provision allowing an appeal from the California Railroad Commission directly to the State Supreme Court.

Thus, the US judiciary has the power to review administrative acts to the extent that they seem desirable by the judiciary.

6.7.3.2 Judicial Control in UK

In UK, the theory of judicial control is simpler than that in the US. It is commonly called the *doctrine of ultra vires*. It states that administrative power derives from statute and statute gives power for certain purposes only. Moreover, these powers are subject to some special procedures or limited in certain other ways by the statute. These limits are found not only in the statute but also in the general principles of construction that the courts apply. Any administrative act outside the defined limits (ultra vires) is denoted as an act unjustified by law and has no legal validity in UK. The courts thus declare such acts to be null and void. Apart from this, the courts also intervene in the case of wrongful acts by ordinary law (such as a trespass to person or property).

By acting in the case of wrongful acts, the courts uphold the doctrine of 'rule of law', which requires public authorities of all kinds to show the legal warrant for the actions they take. This doctrine will be discussed in detail in Chapter 7. The various grounds for judicial control in UK are as follows:[17]

(a) **Doing the Wrong Things:** The courts of UK can quash an administrative action if the action taken is wrong according to statute. For example, local bodies in UK have power under the Housing Act, 1936 to acquire land compulsorily for housing, provided that the land is not a part of any park, garden, or pleasure ground. If a body acquires parkland for housing, it will be considered as a wrong act and will be quashed by the Judiciary.[15]

(b) **Acting in a Wrong Manner:** Certain right acts are quashed for taking some false steps or ignoring a mandatory condition. Cases falling under this category are as follows:

   (i) **Breach of Mandatory Conditions:** The statute requires certain conditions/ procedures to be followed by administrative agencies. The power is to be exercised in accordance with that procedure and not otherwise, and any departure from the procedure invalidates the administrative action.

   (ii) **The rule against negligence:** This rule says that administrative power should be exercised with reasonable care. A statutory power to do something does not provide exemption from ordinary law and does not justify any sort of negligence on the part of the administration. Any negligent act of administration is liable to be quashed by the court.

   (iii) **Other Injurious Acts:** Similar to negligence, the administrative power does not justify nuisances, unless it seems that the parliament had intended to authorise such nuisance. For example, the authority to build hospitals in London was provided for the benefit of the poor, but the courts did not allow the operations of a small pox hospital in Hampstead, as it was proved to be a nuisance to the neighbourhood.[16]

(c) **The Rule against Delegation:** The maxim *delegates non protest delegare* says that power must be exercised by a designated authority and cannot be sub-delegated to any other authority or official.[12] For example, under defence regulations, the Minister of Agriculture delegated to the War Agriculture Executive Committee the power of directing what crops should be grown. This delegation was authorised by the statute. However, the Bedfordshire Committee directed the farmers to grow 8 acres of sugar but left it to their executive officer to specify on which field it should be grown. In this manner, the committee sub-delegated its power and its decision was thus quashed by the Judiciary.[16]

(d) **Surrender or Abdication of Discretion:** Abdication of discretion happens when the person entrusted with discretionary power exercises it at the dictation of some other person. Here it is not his/her discretion that governs the act, as intended by the legislation. Any abdication of discretion and adoption of a rigid arbitrary policy is liable to be questioned by the Judiciary.

(e) **Disregard of Natural Justice:** The doctrine of natural justice will be discussed a little later in this chapter. Any administrative act disregarding this doctrine will be questioned in the court.

(f) **Action not in Good Faith:** The abuse of administrative power is not confined only to cases where a wrong thing is done or a right thing is done in the wrong way. Abuse can also said to be done when a right thing is done in the right way, but on the wrong grounds. The motive of the administrator behind every act should be bona fide and not mala fide. The court has the power to quash an administrative action if it is proven that the motive behind it is mala fide.

(g) **Abuse of Discretion:** Administrative power is also said to be abused when the administrator abuses the discretion provided to him/her. If any administrative authority abuses the discretion to exercise its power, its decision/action is considered illegal or unreasonable. For example, in 1920, the Poplar Borough Council, wishing to set an example of a model socialist employer, instituted a minimum weekly wage of £4 for all their employers. The council had the discretion to pay their servants such wages as they thought fit. However, the court considered that the minimum weekly wage of £4 was excessive in relation to the labour market. Thus, the decision of the council was considered as an abuse of its discretion and was quashed by the Judiciary.

(h) **Jurisdictional Question:** The jurisdiction of an administrative authority is determined in a manner similar to what is done in the US. Jurisdictional facts are considered to determine the legality of an administrative action.

6.7.3.3 Judicial Control in India

In India, the mechanisms of judicial control are specifically mentioned in the Constitution in Articles 13, 32, 131–136, 143, 226, and 246. The doctrine of judicial review is firmly rooted in India and has the sanction of the Constitution. Article 13(2) of the Indian Constitution expressly says that "the state shall not make any law which takes away or abridges the rights conferred by the part 3 (fundamental rights) of the Constitution, and any law made in contravention of this clause shall, to the extent of the contravention, be void." This provision of the Constitution has been interpreted widely to review the legislative as well as administrative actions by the Judiciary.

However, the scope of judicial review is not as wide in India as in US. This is because the limitations on fundamental rights are mentioned in the Indian Constitution itself and not left to the courts to be interpreted. The judicial control in India is derived from both the US and the UK model. The grounds for judicial review of administrative decisions in India are as described below:

(a) **Illegality:** The decision of a decision-maker becomes illegal if it is beyond its jurisdiction or if the administrative body has no power to make such a decision. This happens mostly when the legislation does not provide power to a public body to take such a decision. It is similar to UK's ultra vires doctrine and the same term is used in India. Apart from this, the courts declare an administrative action to be illegal when it violates the following conditions:

   (i) If the action/decision does not take into account relevant information (and does not assign appropriate amount of time to this information)

   (ii) If the decision-making is delegated to a body not responsible for taking the decision, similar to UK's rule against delegation

   (iii) If sufficient discretion is not used for taking the decision or the discretion has been fettered by applying a very rigid policy, similar to UK's 'surrender or abdication of discretion' clause

   (iv) If the action of the administrator violates the fundamental rights or human rights of a person. This is somewhat similar to the US 'due process' clause.

(b) **Irrationality:** The Indian judiciary can quash an administrative action if it is considered unreasonable and irrational. To be 'irrational', the administrative decision should be so absurd that no sensible person could ever dream that it is within the powers of the authority.

(c) **Procedural Impropriety:** An administrative decision can be quashed if it is arrived at without following a prescribed procedure. The process to arrive at a certain decision is mentioned in the relevant statute. The 'rule of natural justice' must be applied while arriving at a particular decision. Moreover, procedural impropriety suggests that a public body should act with complete fairness. Furthermore, in the case of judicial and quasi-judicial bodies, procedural impropriety requires a 'fair hearing' before reaching a decision. The public body shall also give reasons for the decision it has taken.

(d) **Proportionality:** Under the principle of proportionality, the Judiciary checks that a legislative or administrative authority maintains a proper balance between the purpose to be attained by an action and the adverse effect such an action may have on the rights, liberties, or interests of the affected persons. If the adverse effect is more severe than the purpose served by an action/decision, such an action/decision can be quashed by the Indian judiciary.

6.7.3.4 Principles of Natural Justice

The principles of natural justice are the foundation on which the whole superstructure of judicial control of administrative action is based. They provide a basis for judicial control of the procedure followed by adjudicatory bodies (administrative, quasi-judicial as well as judicial bodies). They refer to the minimum fair procedure that a public body must follow while taking decisions. There are two basic principles of natural justice, which are described as follows:

(a) ***Nemo in propria causa judex, esse debet:*** No one should be made a judge in their own case, or the rule against bias.

(b) ***Audi alteram partem:*** The other party needs to be heard before giving a decision, also referred to as the rule of fair hearing.

The two principles are described in the following sections.

6.7.3.4.1 Rule against Bias

The principle connotes that the adjudicator in a case should be disinterested and unbiased with respect to the case. No one should be allowed to be a judge in their own case. The judge should be a neutral person having no relations with either party. In this rule, 'bias' connotes an operative prejudice, whether conscious or unconscious, in relation to a party or issue. Such operative prejudice may be the result of a preconceived opinion or a predisposition to decide a case in a particular manner, so much so that the mind is not open while deciding.[18]

A common saying derived from this principle is that 'not only should justice have been done but is should also appear to have done'. This principle is equally applicable to administrative action and the administration.[19] The public should also have confidence that the judge or administrator is not biased. If a reasonable man thinks, on the basis of existing circumstances, that a judge or administrator is likely to be prejudiced, his/her decision is liable to be quashed.[20]

6.7.3.4.2 Rule of Fair Hearing

The rule of fair hearing protects a person from arbitrary administrative actions whenever his/her right to life or property is jeopardised. The main objective of providing a fair hearing is to avoid any illegal action or decision on the part of the administration. Any wrong order can be avoided by giving a reasonable opportunity of explanation before passing an administrative order.[21] The rule suggests that the affected party should have adequate notice of the case against him/her and he/she should be appraised of the evidence on which the case against him/her is based and be given the opportunity to rebut these materials.[22]

6.7.3.5 Extraordinary Remedies or Writs

The extraordinary remedies or writs are the premier source of judicial review of administrative action. The writs are explicitly mentioned in the Indian Constitution. Article 32 of the Constitution authorises the Supreme Court of India to issue writs for the enforcement of the fundamental rights of the citizens and Article 226 authorises the High Courts to issue writs for the enforcement of fundamental rights and otherwise. The writs are of the following six types:

(a) ***Habeas Corpus*:** The meaning of *Habeas Corpus* is 'to have the body of'. It is an order passed by a court to produce the body of a detained person before it. This helps the court in seeing whether the detention of the person was legal or illegal. If found illegal, the detention can be cancelled by the court. It helps in protecting individual liberty against arbitrary detention by any administrative authority.

(b) ***Mandamus*:** The meaning of *mandamus* is 'we command'. It is a command issued by a court to a public official asking him/her to perform the official duties that he/she has failed to perform.

(c) **Prohibition:** The meaning of prohibition is 'to forbid'. It is issued when a higher court forbids a lower court from exceeding its jurisdiction. This writ can be issued only against judicial and quasi-judicial bodies and not against administrative authorities. Thus, it is not an effective tool of judicial control over administrative bodies.

(d) ***Certiorari*:** The meaning of certiorari is 'to be certified'. It is issued by a higher court to a lower court for transferring the records of the proceedings of a case pending with it for the purpose of determining the legality of its proceedings or for giving fuller and a more satisfactory effect to them than could be done in lower courts. Like prohibition, *certiorari* can also be issued only against judicial and quasi-judicial bodies. Thus, it also not an eminent toll of judicial control over administrative bodies.

(e) ***Quo Warranto*:** The meaning of *quo warranto* is 'by what authority or warrant'. It is issued by the courts to enquire into the legality of claim of a person to a public office. It prevents illegal assumption of a public office by a wrong person.

(f) **Injunction:** The writ of injunction is issued by the court directing a person to take an action or refrain from taking an action. Thus, it is both mandatory and preventive in nature. It is different from the *mandamus* writ, as mandamus can only be issued against a public person but an injunction can be issued against any person, either public or private.

6.7.3.6 Judicial Activism

Judicial activism is basically defined as active judicial action in order to realise social justice. It tries to free the judiciary from the constraints of traditional judicial processes in the interests of social justice and permits a more dynamic interpretation of the social values enshrined in the Constitution beyond what the framers of the Constitution had contemplated. A good example of judicial activism is that of the Supreme Court directing the administration to provide free legal aid to the poor accused in a criminal trial. In simple language, judicial activism refers to judges using their power of judicial review, and other powers, to act as social activists for the benefit of society.

An activist judge activates the legislative and administrative mechanisms and makes them play a vital role in the socio-economic process. It helps in articulating concepts such as liberty, equality, or justice. In contrast to the traditional concept of judiciary as a mere umpire, it works as an active catalyst in the constitutional scheme.

Judicial activism can be classified as being of two different types—*reactionary activism* and *progressive activism*. Reactionary activism is associated with instances where the judiciary reacts to a particular political and social situation. The Nehruvian era activism that dealt with issues such as land reforms, right to property, and the pro-emergency activism in the 1970s can be understood as *reactionary activism*.[23] On the other hand, *progressive activism* deals with social action litigation.

Defining judicial activism, Professor Sathe has said that when the political organs of the state fail to discharge their constitutional obligations effectively or if their indifference to certain constitutional objects brings the constitution to a state of no response, if the judiciary steps in to meet the constitutional ends assuming the role of a policymaker, legislator, and even the role of a monitor to oversee the implementation of its directions, then its behaviour or attitude can be rightly summarised as judicial activism.[24]

6.7.3.6.1 Need for Judicial Activism

The following reasons can be said to be responsible for the growth of judicial activism:

(a) **Collapse of Responsible Government:** A responsible government is said to collapse when the legislature and the executive fail to discharge their respective functions. When the legislature fails to make the necessary legislation to suit the changing times and the governmental agencies fail miserably to perform their administrative functions sincerely, it leads to an erosion of confidence of the citizens in the constitutional values and democracy. In such an extraordinary scenario, the judiciary steps into the areas earmarked for the legislature and executive and the result is judicial legislation and government by the judiciary.

(b) **Pressure on Judiciary to Step in for Aid:** When the fundamental rights of the citizens are negatively affected by the government or any other third party, the judiciary becomes responsible for aiding the ameliorating conditions of the citizens. In such circumstances, the citizens look up to the judiciary to step in to aid them and protect their fundamental rights and freedoms. This leads to tremendous pressure on the judiciary to play an active role for the suffering masses.

(c) **Filling the Legislative Vacuum:** Despite the presence of a large number of legislations, there still remain certain areas that may not have been legislated upon. Thus, when a competent legislature fails to act legislatively and make a necessary law to meet the societal needs, the courts often indulge in judicial legislation, thereby encroaching into the domain of the legislature.

(d) **Public Confidence in Judiciary:** The judiciary, especially the Indian judiciary, commands the confidence of the people and inspires faith in their minds in its capacity to provide even-handed justice.[25]

(e) **Enthusiasm of Particular Groups:** Many groups such as women's rights activists, peoples' rights activists, bonded labour groups, citizens for environmental action, and civil rights activists have been responsible for the growth of judicial activism.

6.7.3.7 Public Interest Litigation and Judicial Activism

Public interest litigation (PIL) is an important mechanism for judicial activism. In fact, the PIL is itself the result of judicial activism. PIL refers to a legal action initiated in a court of law by a person or persons other than the affected party for the enforcement of public interest or general interest in which the public or class of the community have some interests and by which their legal rights or liabilities are affected.

In a PIL, the aggrieved person may not be directly affected by the action of the other party before he/she comes to the court to seek relief. The aggrieved person may be any person representing another person(s) affected. This is the community orientation of PIL. PILs are intended to improve access to justice to those who are otherwise poor and unaware of their legal entitlements. For example, social activists and lawyers bring up matters on behalf of the vulnerable and weaker sections of the community.

A PIL petition can also be brought before a court in the form of a letter written by someone on behalf of another affected and vulnerable party, such as a jailed prisoner, a mentally challenged person in a mental institution, or a bonded labourer. This process of initiating proceedings through letters is called *epistolatory jurisdiction*.[26]

Judges play the role of activists in a PIL proceeding and play an active role in meting out justice to the affected party. For the purpose of attaining a solution, courts may also constitute fact-finding commissions on a case-by-case basis for looking into a matter and reporting back to the court. These commissions usually consist of experts in the concerned field or practising lawyers.

The trend of filing PILs in India was started by Justice P.N. Bhagwati and Justice V.R. Krishna Iyer. The earliest example of a PIL was the 1980s' case of *Hussainara Khatoon* v. *State of Bihar*. It was a writ petition filed by an advocate, Mrs Hingorani, on behalf of undertrial prisoners in the Bhagalpur Jail of Bihar. The petition was based on reports that appeared in *Indian Express*, in which it was mentioned that many undertrial prisoners had been languishing in jail for periods longer than the maximum possible sentences for the offences they were charged with. In this PIL, the Supreme Court decided in favour of the undertrial prisoners and observed that they should not be detained without cause, and if it appears that the trial would start after a period of more than 18 years, they should be released.[8]

Similarly, the mechanism of PIL has from time to time brought justice to suffering prisoners, women in protective homes, victims of flesh trade, children of juvenile institutions, exploited bonded and migrant labourers, untouchables, tribals, and so on. Thus, through the mechanism of PIL and judicial activism, the Judiciary has emerged as the guardian of the rights and liberties of the victims of repression, cruelty, and torture. The mechanism has helped bring justice to the doorstep of the weak, underprivileged, and exploited sections of the society.

6.7.3.8 Negative Aspects of Judicial Activism

The mechanism of judicial activism may have the following negative aspects:

(a) **Usurping the Powers of Other Branches of Government:** When overtly exercised, judicial activism may result in usurping the powers of the executive and legislature, the other two important organs of governance. Judicial activism permits the courts to legislate in certain matters and pass administrative directions in others. If not done within proper limits, this amounts to demeaning the other organs of government. For example, the

Supreme Court once gave a judgment in relation to admission to post graduate education in medical science. The Supreme Court went on to lay down the manner in which PG seats in different post graduate medical institutions in India should be filled, the examination for filling those was to be conducted, the seats were to be distributed in every discipline, and the question of the reservation for the backward classes candidates would be dealt with. This judgment was considered as transgressing into the domain of the Department of Education.

(b) **Lack of Domain Competency with the Judiciary:** Professor William Wade noted that the judiciary is the least competent to function as a legislative or administrative agency. Courts lack the facilities to gather detailed data to make probing enquiries. They rely for data on advocates who appear before them, but these data are likely to give them partisan or inadequate information. Moreover, the courts' own knowledge and research is bound to be selective and subjective. Furthermore, the courts have no means for effectively supervising and implementing the aftermath of its orders, schemes, and mandates. Courts also have no method to reverse their orders if these are found unworkable or requiring modification.[27]

(c) **Impact on the Legitimacy of Traditional Judicial Decisions:** Excessive exercise of judicial activism, and serving of impractical orders, may sacrifice the legitimacy attached to the decisions within the traditional judicial sphere. Excessive judicial activism may also make the judiciary vulnerable to assault and reprisals from other branches of the government. This may disable the courts from performing the narrower but nonetheless vital constitutional role that is assigned to them.

(d) **Impact on Political Responsibility:** Excessive reliance upon courts instead of self-government through democratic processes may negatively impact people's sense of moral and political responsibility.[28]

Disregarding the negative aspects, judicial activism is considered the healthiest trend in constitutional interpretation. It makes the Constitution a living and dynamic document and enables the accommodation of the aspirations of the vast masses of our people.

6.7.3.9 Judicial Overreach

When the judiciary, in its enthusiasm of activism, takes over the functions of the legislature and executive, it is referred to as judicial overreach. Judicial overreach starts from the point where legitimate 'activism' ends. Any further exercise of judicial power beyond the point that judicial activism loses its legitimacy is regarded as judicial overreach. In India, there have been several instances where courts have arguably crossed the line. For example, in the case of *Delhi Sealing Drive*, the SC set a monitoring committee to oversee all the executive agencies involved in sealing shops and offices. Similarly, the SC also stayed the government's plan of introducing OBC reservations in central institutions in a staggered manner.[29]

However, it is said that the application of judicial review to determine the constitutionality of legislation and to review executive decisions sometimes creates a tension between the judge and the legislative and executive branches. Such tension is natural and desirable.

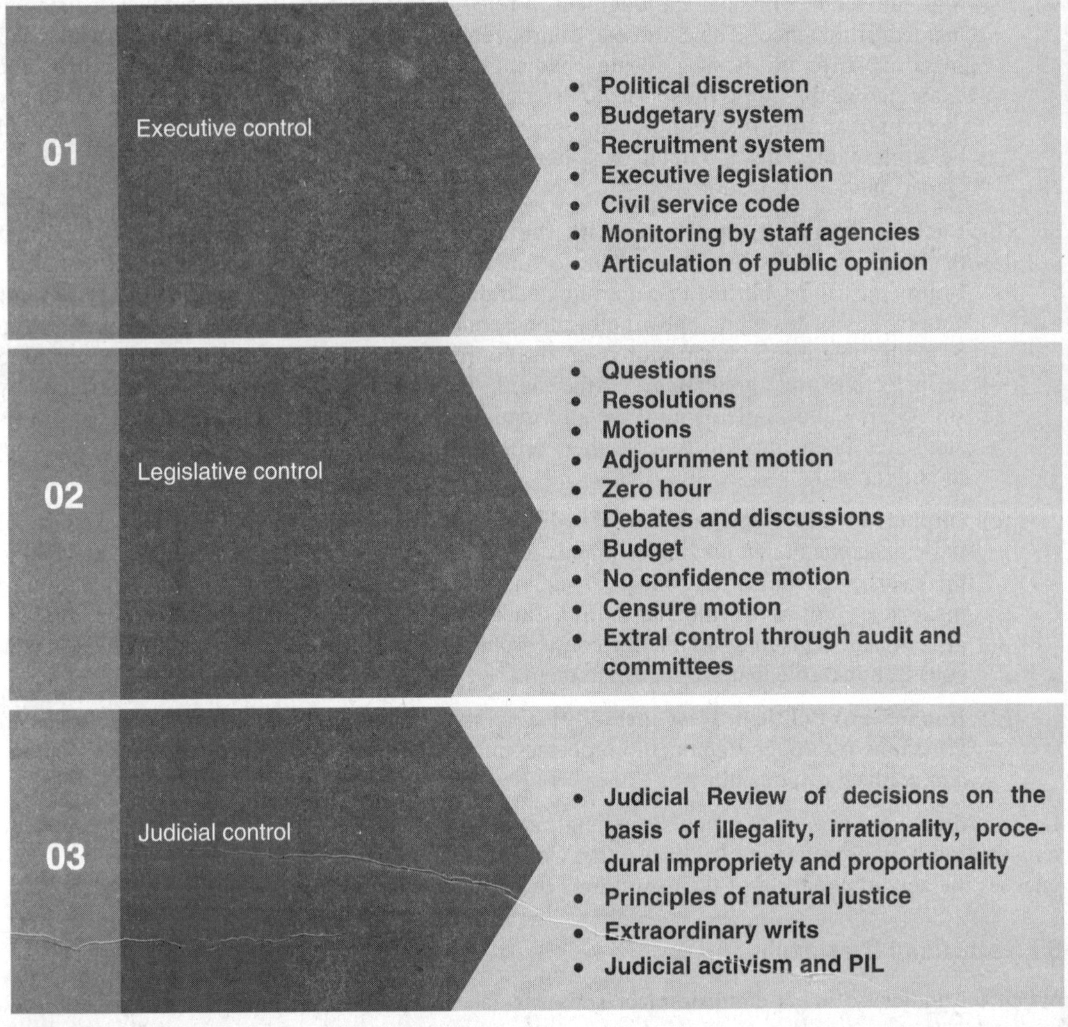

6.8 Citizen-centric Administration and Citizen's Charter

Citizen-centric administration treats citizens as the most important aspect of service delivery. The needs, requirements, and comfort of the citizens are given utmost priority while designing administrative processes and service delivery mechanisms. It is against procedure-centric administration, which focuses on following administrative rules and procedures rather than focusing on the comfort of the citizens. Citizen-centric administration is seen to be associated with good governance.

In India, and across the world, the following tools have been employed for making the administration citizen-centric:

(a) Re-engineering of governmental processes for making the governance citizen-centric (refer to the section 'Business Process Re-engineering' of Chapter 1)

(b) Adoption of modern technology including IT for facilitating service delivery (refer to Chapter 2 on Good Governance, E-Governance, and Emerging Trends)
(c) Implementation of the Right to Information Act
(d) Implementation of the Citizen's Charter
(e) Independent evaluation of services by external agencies
(f) An effective grievance redressal mechanism
(g) Facilitating effective citizen participation in governmental service delivery (refer to Chapter 2)

6.8.1 Citizen's Charter

A citizen's charter is basically defined as a set of commitments made by an organisation regarding the standards of services it delivers. It is an effective tool to improve the trust between service providers and their users. The basic thrust of the citizen's charter is to make public services citizen-centric by ensuring that these services are *demand-driven rather than supply-driven*. Every citizen charter has the following important components:

(a) The vision and mission statement of the organisation is one of the important components of the citizen's charter. This statement gives the outcomes desired from the organisation and its broad strategy to achieve them. It makes the citizens aware of the intent of their service providers, who can then be held accountable.
(b) The organisation states the subjects it deals with and the service area it broadly covers. It contains commitments and promises, which constitute the heart of a citizen's charter. Even though these promises are not enforceable in a court of law, each organisation should ensure that the promises made are kept and, in case of default, a suitable compensatory/remedial mechanism is provided.
(c) The organisation states the details of its client groups and the services provided to each client group.
(d) It states the details of the grievance redressal mechanism to be accessed when there are any lacunae in service delivery by the organisation.
(e) The charter also stipulates the responsibilities of the citizens in the context of the charter.

6.8.2 Principles of Citizen's Charter

The basic objective of the citizen's charter is to empower the citizens in relation to public service delivery. The nine principles of the citizen's charter as envisaged by the 1998 Labour Government of UK are as follows:[30]

(a) **Standards:** Specify the standards of the services to be expected from an organisation. Also specify the remedial measures if the specified standard of service is not provided.
(b) **Choice:** Encourage access and promotion of choice of service wherever possible.
(c) **Quality:** Improve the quality of service delivery according to citizen's expectation. The quality shall be improved by using modern-day technology and innovations.
(d) **Value for Money:** Use the public resources effectively so as to provide value for money to the tax payers.

(e) **Transparency:** The organisation should be open and ready to provide full information. Th citizen should be aware of the rules, procedures, schemes, and grievance redressa mechanism of the organisation.

(f) **Accountability:** Individuals should be held accountable for any lacunae in service delivery The organisation should work towards putting things right if they go wrong and if complaint is brought to its notice. In India, regular monitoring, review, and evaluation of th charter is carried out by internal as well as external agencies.

(g) **Participation:** The public should be consulted and involved during the preparation an implementation of the charter. Involvement of consumer organisations, citizen groups, an other stakeholders is emphasised.

(h) **Equality:** All the citizens/service beneficiaries should be treated equally by the organisation.

(i) **Network:** The organisation should work with other providers to provide efficient and timel services.

6.8.3 Indian History of Citizen's Charter

The Government of India commenced a 'National Debate for Responsive Administration' in 1996. A major recommendation of this debate was to bring out a citizen's charter for all public servic organisations. These ideas received strong support in the Chief Ministers' Conference in 1997 Following this, the Department of Administrative Reforms and Public Grievances (DAR&PG formulated guidelines for structuring a *model charter* as well as a list of dos and don'ts to enable th various governmental departments to bring out focused and effective charters. It also sets out a serie of guidelines to enable the service delivery organisations to formulate precise and meaningfu charters to set the service delivery parameters.

Primarily, an adoption of the UK model of citizens' charter, the Indian model has an additiona component of 'expectations from the client'.

6.8.4 Successful Case Studies of Citizens' Charters in India

The following are certain case studies highlighting examples of successful citizens' charters.

Case 1: Regional Transport Office, Hyderabad

The Regional Transport Office (RTO) of Hyderabad has developed a charter that commits efficien service delivery as per the standards specified in it. A sample of the services provided by it is a mentioned below:

Work to be done	Service charge (INR)	Response time
Learner's license	60	Same day
Fresh driving license	390	Same day
Registration of four–wheelers	400	Same day
Duplicate registration certificate for motorcycles	130	Two hours
Transfer of ownership of motorcycles	130	Same day

Apart from specifying the services, the RTO has taken a number of steps for making itself citizen-friendly, as follows:

(a) It has simplified the procedures of registration and licensing.

(b) It has introduced automation of all services with the aim of providing all the services through a comprehensive and networked solution.

(c) It has created integrated checkposts (ICPs) to provide the checking facility to transport operators at one single point to avoid unnecessary delay and harassment.

(d) It has introduced a token system for simplifying the availability of forms and applications.

(e) It has created public assistance cells/help desks in every office to guide and assist the public in filling forms and furnishing information about the procedures. Finally, it has also installed suggestions and complaints boxes in every office in a prescribed format.

Case 2: Jan Sewa Kendra, Ahmedabad

The district administration of Ahmedabad had standardised all the citizen's charters of the district, which consisted of 75 issues ranging from land matters, issue of licenses and certificates, public distribution system, to widow pension. It contained the issues in a concise and simple application format mentioning the legal provisions, officers responsible for taking decisions, enclosures and annexures expected from the citizens, number of days required for disposal at each stage in the Collectorate and its subordinate offices, and so on. This simplified the range of services to be delivered and established the basic standards of service delivery.

Apart from this, the Jan Sewa Kendras were established as e-governance-enabled civic centres. These centres had the citizen's charter as the main focus of service delivery, which were launched to re-engineer the processes and standardize the application and query formats. These kendras were a part of the 'one day governance programme' of the Gujarat Government.

The facility led to better service delivery, quicker turnaround time, reduced interface of citizens with government officials, and better productivity.

6.8.5 Nodal Officers for Citizen's Charters

The Government of India has mandated that each ministry of a public agency proposing to formulate a citizen's charter may designate an officer, of the rank of joint secretary or equivalent, as the nodal officer for the citizen's charter. His/her role is to be actively involved in the process of formulating and implementing the citizen's charter at each stage.

6.8.6 Evaluation, Monitoring, and Review of Citizen's Charters

Periodical monitoring and evaluation of the citizen's charter is very important for an organisation to maintain excellent service delivery. The evaluation should be IT-enabled so that the data can be analysed in real time and reports on service failure against the charter standards can be generated automatically. The evaluation process shall consist of self-assessment by the staff, feedback from the customers, and surveys from citizen groups and by an external evaluation agency. The surveys can be conducted with the help of questionnaires relating to the quality of the services delivered.

On the basis of the evaluation, the organisation shall have an obligation to correct its wrong procedures in order to implement the charter effectively in the future.

6.8.7 Major Lacunae in Indian Citizen's Charters

After several studies, the following major lacunae had been found in the citizen's charters of Indian publ organisations:

(a) The citizen's charters are not formulated through a consultative process with the low (implementing) staff and the public.

(b) The service providers are not familiar with the philosophy, goals, and main features of th charter.

(c) Adequate publicity is not given to the charters. Extra efforts are not made for the citizen awareness or for orientation of the staff with respect to the various components of the charter.

(d) The charters have by and large not succeeded in appreciably empowering end users demand greater public accountability.

(e) The charters have been implemented without adequate groundwork in terms of assessin and reforming the organisational processes to deliver the promises made in the charter.

(f) The employees of the agencies have shown resistance to change according to th requirements of the charter.

6.8.8 Guidelines for Effective Implementation of Citizen's Charter

The *Handbook on Citizen's Charter* has provided the following guidelines for effectiv implementation of the charter:

(a) **Simple:** The charter must be simple and easy to understand.

(b) **Consultation:** The charter must be framed not only by senior experts but by interaction wi the cutting edge staff, who will finally implement it, and with the users.

(c) **Organisation Climate:** A climate for better service delivery should be created throug regular interaction and training.

(d) **Entitlement of the User:** Against each service, the entitlement of the user, servic standards, and remedies available to the user in case of non-adherence to standards shoul be mentioned.

(e) **Feedback:** A standard structure should be created for obtaining feedback and performanc auditing. Accordingly, the charter should be reviewed periodically.

(f) **Publicity:** The charters should be given wider publicity among the public. A specific budge should be earmarked for awareness generation and orientation of the staff.

6.8.9 Charter Mark: Scheme of Service Excellence

The Charter Mark Scheme was launched in 1992 in UK to improve the efficacy of the citizen' charters, and recognising and encouraging excellence in public service. It contained the nin principles of service delivery (discussed in the previous section 'Principles of Citizen's Charter') a criteria for demonstrating service excellence. An organisation would win a 'charter mark' if it woul be able to meet those criteria.

In India also, DAR&PG has been tasked to develop a charter mark scheme to encourage an reward improvement in public service delivery with reference to the commitments and standard mentioned in the charter. It would give a sense of achievement to better performing organisations an promote competitiveness among the various organisations.

6.8.10 Sevottam Model

Sevottam is a public service delivery excellence model that provides an assessment improvement framework to bring about excellence in service delivery. The need for such a tool arose from the fact that citizen's charters by themselves could not achieve the desired results in improving the quality of public services. It works as an evaluation mechanism to assess the quality of an organisation's internal processes and their impact on the quality of service delivery. The model has three components for evaluation:

(a) **Effective Charter Implementation:** This component requires opening up channels for receiving citizens' inputs on the way organisations determine service delivery requirements.

(b) **Public Grievance Redressal:** This component requires a good grievance redressal system operating in a manner that leaves the citizen more satisfied with how the organisation responds to complaints/grievances, irrespective of the final decision.

(c) **Excellence in Service Delivery:** This component requires that the organisation shall have excellent service delivery by managing the key ingredients for good service delivery well and building its own capacity to continuously improve delivery.

6.9 Right to Public Service Acts

Many States of India have passed the Right to Public Service Act/Public Service Guarantee Act. These are part of a broader rights-based approach to social policy that the Indian Government has been following since 2000. The need for these Acts were felt because the citizen's charters had certain deficiencies as mentioned in the section 'Major Lacunae in Indian Citizen's Charters'. To address these lacunae, the Acts mandate that the covered services are clearly stated and must either be completed or denied (with explanation) within a specified timeframe. They also set a monetary fine to be levied against the responsible officer if they do not complete the service within the timeframe.

Madhya Pradesh was the first state to implement this Act under the title *Public Service Guarantee Act* in 2010. It contains 52 services ranging from applications for ration cards to income certificates. A designated public servant is required to either provide a service or deny it with a written explanation within the designated time period (ranging from 3 to 60 days depending on the service). If they fail to do so, the applicant can appeal to an appeal officer (usually a mid-level official such as a sub-divisional officer and sometimes a higher level official such as the district collector) who must decide the appeal within a stipulated time period and can order the public official to provide the service. The decision of the appeal officer can be further appealed to a second appeal officer (usually a higher level official such as a district collector or, if the first appeal was to the district collector, then to a divisional commissioner). The second appeal officer may fine the designated public official between INR 500 and 5000 if they feel that they failed to provide the service without 'sufficient or reasonable cause'.

The citizen demands generated due to this Act has pushed the government to simplify its application procedures. For example, it has created a single-window application centre in the District Collector's office. The Public Service Management Department oversees the implementation of this Act in Madhya Pradesh. The District Manager, from this department, performs quality control, i.e., he/she checks whether a service has been provided within a designated time period or not. Similar acts have been implemented by states such as Maharashtra and Bihar. The Union Government is also planning to pass a similar act for the Central Government departments as well as for all the state governments.

6.9.1 Brief Assessment of Right to Public Service Acts in India

According to a study by Nick Robinson, published in *Accountability Initiative*, the implementation of the Right to Service Acts in different states has not been encouraging. There had been reports of applications not being accepted by officers and of receipts not being given. Less than 2% of the applicants were aware of the Right to Service Act. Moreover, almost none were aware of the available appeal mechanisms in the Act. Very few officers had been fined for not delivering effective and timely services. The Act has been more about administrative relationships to systemize things at the government level than about being a part of the people.

A disturbing trend has also been found—the lower staff tends to take the maximum allowed time to deliver a service, even if it could be delivered before time. Top officials have also expressed a fear that if these Acts are perceived as a success, their scope may be expanded to services that are not as easy to quantify or track. The Acts cannot be seen as a one-size-fits-all approach to service delivery. Some have also criticised the Acts for not covering difficult services such as health and education.

Disregarding the negative aspects, observers believe that the package of changes brought about by these Acts—such as receipts of applications, computerisation, and clearer requirements and deadlines—has helped improve services by creating simpler and more legible processes for applying for services. Moreover, these Acts have the potential to have a lasting institutional cultural effect of empowering citizens to make demands on their public servants.

6.10 Social Accountability and Social Audit

Apart from accountability to the executive, legislature, and judiciary, social accountability is an important aspect of good governance. This term is a combination of two words—'social' and 'accountability'. It indicates accountability of the administration to the society. According to the World Bank, social accountability is "an approach towards building accountability that relies on 'civil engagement', i.e., in which it is ordinary citizens and/or civil society organisations who participate directly or indirectly in exacting accountability."[49]

Social accountability engages citizens in monitoring government performance, demanding and enhancing transparency, and exposing government failures. The three basic aspects of social accountability are as follows:

(a) **Information to Citizens:** A key aspect of social accountability is generating relevant information and making it available to the public. It calls for transparency of government operations, including the capacity to produce and provide data and accounts for accessing information such as policy statements, budget commitments, and expenditure.

(b) **Voice to Citizens:** Another important aspect of social accountability includes giving voice to the needs, opinions, and concerns of the citizens. This can happen by creating spaces for public debate, citizen–state dialogue, building citizen confidence and rights awareness, and making use of information and communications technology (ICT) for garnering citizen's views.

(c) **Negotiation with Citizens:** Proper negotiations between citizen groups and government officials can help in bringing about crucial improvement in the process of governance. Community-led meetings with government officials, peace committee meetings, or mediated forms of consultation are certain forms of such negotiation.

6.10.1 Benefits of Social Accountability

Social accountability is direct accountability to the citizens. However, these citizens are primarily represented by various civil society organisations, voluntary organisations, NGOs, and so on. Thus, the benefits of social accountability are discussed in the later section 'Roles Played by Civil Society Organisations' of this chapter.

6.10.2 Social Accountability Initiatives

According to Mohit Bhattacharya, the following social accountability initiatives have been found to be practised across the world:[32]

(a) **Participatory Planning and Policy Formulation:** The process of participatory planning and policy formulation engages citizen groups and civil society organisations in the process of planning of governmental schemes and processes. This helps in ensuring optimal and justified allocation of public resources for the welfare of the citizens.

(b) **Participatory Budget Analysis:** Participatory budget analysis involves analysing the impact and implications of budget allocation, demystifying the technical content of the budget, raising awareness about budget-related issues, and undertaking public education campaigns to improve budget literacy. It also involves building awareness about policies in key areas such as poverty reduction, gender equity, environmental protection, employment, and social services.

(c) **Participatory Expenditure Tracking:** This practice allows citizen groups in tracking how the government actually spends funds, with the aim of identifying leakages in the flow of financial resources.

(d) **Citizen's Survey/Citizen Report Cards:** This practice allows citizens to submit report cards and survey reports on a range of governmental issues. These reports can pertain to service delivery assessments, opinion polls, awareness exercises, and so on.

(e) **Citizen's Charter:** This has been discussed in the section 'Citizen's Charter'.

(f) **Community Score Cards:** This practice is used to assess the quality of service delivery in a participatory manner at the community level. The process typically involves ratings of service delivery by users and self-assessment by service providers, who then participate in an interface meeting to identify and sort out issues.

(g) **Social Audit:** The practice of social audit will be discussed in the following section.

6.10.3 Social Audit

Social audit is one of the latest techniques to ensure social accountability of the government. It is basically an auditing process that enables an organisation to assess and demonstrate its social, economic, and environmental benefits and limitations. It is a way of measuring the extent to which an organisation lives up to the shared values and objectives it has committed itself to. As a technique, it includes auditing of organisational processes by various stakeholders including its employees, clients, volunteers, financing agencies, contractors, suppliers, and local residents interested in the organisation.[32]

6.10.3.1 Difference between Social Audit and Regular Audit

As a concept, a social audit is quite different from a regular audit, in which an external auditor checks the financial records of an organisation. The concept of social audit is much more comprehensive and has a much wider scope than the traditional audit. It is a technique for measuring, understanding, and improving the social performance of an activity of an organisation. A financial audit is aimed at verifying the reliability and integrity of the financial information of an organisation. On the contrary, a social audit examines the performance of a department/programme vis-à-vis its stated core values in the light of community values and the distribution of benefits among various social groups reached through good governance principles.

A social audit is a supplement to, and not a replacement for, the conventional audit to help government departments/public agencies to understand and improve their performance as perceived by stakeholders.

6.10.3.2 Importance of Social Audit

The process of social audit has the following benefits for the local community and the organisation:

(a) **Educative Value:** The process of social audit provides an understanding of the administrative system to the local people. It also legitimizes the common practices of the administrative system.

(b) **Independent Evaluation:** Social audit helps in independent evaluation of the attainment of the social goals of an organisation.

(c) **Social Accountability:** It is an important instrument for ensuring the social accountability of an organisation.

(d) **Impact Analysis:** It is an important method for assessing the social, economic, and environmental impact of an organisation. This assessment is carried out through systematic and regular monitoring by the stakeholders.

(e) **Shape Management Strategy:** Social audit helps in shaping the management strategy of an organisation in a socially responsible and accountable way.

(f) **Enhances Reputation:** The information generated from a social audit can provide crucial knowledge about an organisation's ethical performance, i.e., how stakeholders perceive the services offered by it. The social angle of the services delivered enhances the reputation of the organisation. Social auditing helps the legislature and executive in identifying the problem areas and provides an opportunity for them to take a proactive stance and create solutions.

(g) **Helps in Policymaking:** Social audit helps in anticipating the stakeholders' concerns regarding organisational policies. It provides essential information about the interests, perspectives, and expectations of the stakeholders.

6.10.3.3 Process of Social Audit

The process of social audit consists of the following steps:[50]

(I) **Preparatory Activities:** The preparatory activities of social audit include listing the core values of an organisation, listing the social objectives of an organisation, matching the activities with the objectives of the organisation, listing the current practices and delivery systems, and fixing the responsibility for performing social audit in the organisation.

(II) **Defining Audit Boundaries and Identifying Stakeholders:** This step includes identifying the key issues for social audit based on the social objectives of an organisation. It also involves listing key stakeholders for consultation and getting their consensus on the issues for audit.

(III) **Social Accounting and Bookkeeping:** This step involves selecting performance indicators for social accounting. Moreover, it involves identifying the relevant records to be used and the additional data to be collected for auditing. Furthermore, it involves preparing a social accounting plan and timeline.

(IV) **Preparing and using Social Accounts:** This step includes preparation of social accounts using the existing information, data collected, and views of stakeholders. Moreover, it includes identifying the key issues for action and setting targets for the future.

(V) **Social Audit and Dissemination:** This is the most important step, in which social accounts are presented before the social auditors. The social auditors verify the data used, assess the interpretation, and comment on the quality of social accounting and reporting. The social accounts are then revised in accordance with the recommendations of the social auditors. After this, social auditors collect information from the stakeholders regarding programme implementation and the benefits accrued to them. Following this, the social auditor's report is disseminated to a decision-making committee, which includes representatives of all the stakeholders. This report is also disseminated to the civil society.

(VI) **Feedback on the Audit Report:** The feedback received on the report of social auditors is used for fine tuning of policy, administrative functioning, and various other social programmes.

6.11 Civil Society and Social Capital

Civil Society

There are various definitions of civil society. According to Larry Diamond, the civil society is the realm of an organised social life that is voluntary, self-generating, self-supporting, and autonomous from the state, bounded by a legal order or a set of shared rules. It involves citizens acting collectively in a public sphere to express their interests, passions, ideas; exchange information; achieve mutual goals; make demands on the state; and hold the state officials accountable. There are two conceptions of civil society—political and social.

Politically, it is rooted in the liberal democratic theory, which identifies civil institutions and the political activity as an essential component for the emergence of a particular type of political society based on the principles of citizenship, rights, democratic representation, and rule of law.

Its sociological conception is that of an intermediate associational realm situated between the state on the one side and the basic building block of the society on the other (individuals and families), inhabited by sociological organisations with some degree of autonomy and voluntary participation on the part of its members.[32]

Civil society is an important mode of development in society, apart from the state-led mode of development. There has been historically a fairly well-accepted community-centric self-development tradition. The church in the West has long been associated with social development activities along with numerous voluntary organisations such as Rotaries and other organisations. In India, various models of community-based self-development have emerged, such as Gandhiji's *Sevagram* model and Rabindranath Tagore's *Shantiniketan*.

Having numerous advantages, civil society is considered to be an essential prerequisite of a good governance.

Social Capital

Like civil society, social capital is also a term with numerous definitions. According to OECD (Organisation for Economic Co-operation and Development), social capital can be understood as the links, shared values, and understanding in society that enable individuals and groups to trust each other, cooperate, and work together. Such social capital complements the economic capital for the rapid growth of a society.

These collective efforts, known now as social capital, have been a part of human behaviour right from the early civilisation days. Gradually, such collective action led to the formation of small habitations, communities, villages, and thereafter large cities and metropolises. However, in the course of time, the government and society became too big and formalised and somewhat distant from the common man. Thus, today we feel a need for mutual networking and interaction, known collectively as social capital.

6.11.1 History of Civil Society/Social Capital in India

The social regeneration in India is often considered to have begun during the colonial rule but not created by it. Ideas of social reform combined with national sentiments led to the formation of societies and sabhas such as *Brahmo Samaj* and *Arya Samaj*. During the struggle of Independence, the whole emphasis of the Gandhian movement was on self-help and cooperation. Such movements were responsible for the growth of civil society in India.

Towards the end of the nineteenth century, the corporate community in India also began setting up organisations dedicated to the welfare and development of the underprivileged. The JN Tata Endowment Trust was established in 1982, much before Rockefeller and Carnegie set up their philanthropic foundations in the US.

On the socio-political front, Vinoba Bhave's *Bhoodan* and Jai Prakash Narain's *Sarvodaya Movement* were the two major voluntary action initiatives that caught the attention of people across the country in the 1950s and 1960s. Moreover, the inception of cooperative societies took place in the early years of the twentieth century, when the government thought of organising farmers into voluntary groups that could secure cheap farm credit on a collective basis and thus save them from the usurious practices of money lenders.

Such movements and societies led to the birth of the present civil society in India.

6.11.2 Indian Constitutional Position on Social Capital Organisations/Civil Society

The Indian Constitution provides a distinct legal space to social capital/civil society institutions. The following articles of the Constitution are important in this regard:

(a) **Article 19(1)(c):** It provides the right to citizens to form associations or unions.

(b) **Article 43:** It directs the states to make endeavours to promote cooperatives in rural India.

(c) Voluntary organisations have an explicit mention in entries made in the 7th Schedule of the Constitution (schedule dividing the functions between the Union Government and state governments).

(d) **97th Constitutional Amendment Act:** The 91st Constitutional Amendment Act has added the right to form cooperative societies in Article 19(1)(c).

6.11.3 Types of Civil Society Organisations in India

Civil society groups in our country can be divided into the following broad categories:[31]

(a) **Registered Societies:** In India, societies are formed under the Societies Registration Act, 1860 for literary, scientific, or charitable purposes or for any purpose as described in Section 20 of the Societies Registration Act. These societies can be formed by seven or more persons after subscribing to a Memorandum of Association. As societies fall under the state list, many of the state legislations have been enforced to control them.

(b) **Trusts:** A trust is a special form of organisation that emerges owing to the execution of a will. The will-maker exclusively transfers the ownership of a property to be used for a particular purpose. If the purpose is to benefit a particular individual, it becomes a *private trust*, and if it concerns some purpose of the common public or the community at large, it is called a *public trust.* Under Schedule 7 of the Constitution, the subject 'trusts and trustees' find mention in the concurrent list.

(c) **Religious Endowments:** Religious endowments are variants of trusts formed for specific purposes such as for providing support functions relating to the deity, charity, and religion. They arise from the dedication of property for religious purposes. Towards the beginning of the twentieth century, many of the temples and *mathas* across the country had acquired considerable landed property and funds, often comparable to the holding of a *zamindari.* This often led to incidents of social tension and civil disputes in the adjoining areas. The government has enacted the Charitable and Religious Trusts Act, 1920 to deal with this situation. In the Act, the trustees of religious bodies are made accountable for the disclosure of income and the value of their religious trust. Civil courts are also given proactive powers with regard to the management of their property.

(d) **Waqfs:** A *waqf* implies the endowment of property, movable or immovable, tangible or intangible, to God by a Muslim, under the promise that the transfer will benefit the needy. As a legal transaction, the *waqif* (settler) appoints himself or another trustworthy person as *mutwalli* (manager) in an endowment deed (*waqfnamah*) to administer the charitable trust (*waqf*). As it implies a surrender of property to God, a waqf deed is irrevocable and perpetual. A quasi-judicial body, i.e., a *waqf board,* is created to rule over waqf-related disputes. At the national level, there is a *Central Waqf Council* that acts in an advisory capacity.

(e) **Organisations under Section 8 of the Companies Act, 2013:** Section 8 of the Companies Act, 2013 provides for a mechanism through which an association can be registered as a company with a limited liability if such an association is formed for promoting commerce, art, science, religion, or any other useful objective and intends to apply its profits/income in promoting its objectives. The objective of this provision is to provide a corporate personality to such associations but at the same time exempt them from some of the cumbersome legal requirements.

(f) **Trade Unions:** According to the Trade Unions Act, of 1926, a trade union is a combination, whether temporary or permanent, formed primarily to regulate relations between workmen and employers, among workmen, or employers, or for improving the restrictive conditions on the conduct of any trade or business, and includes any federation of two or more trade unions.

(g) **Self-help/Joint Liability Groups:** Self-help groups (SHGs) are created by a group of people to motivate its members to save, persuading them to make a collective plan for generating additional income and act as a conduit for formal banking services to reach them. The first organised initiative in this direction was taken in Gujarat, in 1954, when the Textiles Labour Association of Ahmedabad formed its women's wing to organise women of households belonging to mill workers to train them in primary skills such as sewing, knitting, embroidery, typesetting, and stenography.

Such groups received a more systematised structure in 1972, when the Self-employed Women's Association (SEWA) was formed as a trade union under the leadership of Ela Bhatt. She organised workers—hawkers, vendors, and home-based operators such as weavers, potters, papad/agarbatti makers, manual labourers, and service providers—with the objective of increasing their income and assets and improving their organisational and leadership strengths. The overall intention was to recognise women for full employment.

Such groups are funded by financial institutions such as local banks, microfinance institutions, National Bank for Rural Development (NABARD), Small Industries Development Bank of India (SIDBI), Rashtriya Mahila Kosh (RMK), and Housing and Urban Development Corporation (HUDCO).

(h) **Self-regulatory Authorities:** The self-regulatory authority of a profession means to select body of its members that is responsible for the growth and development of the profession in the background of its responsibility towards the society and the state. Its functions may include issues of professional education, matters connected with licensing and ethical conduct of practitioners, and providing technical advice to the government in conceptualising, formulating, and implementing policies and standards for providing important public services (such as healthcare and education) to the citizens.

(i) **Cooperatives:** A cooperative is an autonomous association of persons united voluntarily to meet their common economic, social, and cultural needs and aspirations through a jointly owned and democratically controlled enterprise. They follow certain broad-based values other than those associated with purely profit-making. These values are self-help, democracy, equality, equity, and solidarity. The need for profitability is balanced by the needs of the members and the wider interest of the community. The cooperatives of India have played a pivotal role in the economy by making a significant contribution to our primary sector production. They have also played an important role in bringing food sufficiency through the green and white revolutions.

6.11.4 Roles Played by Civil Society Organisations

The civil society organisations play the following important roles in governance:.

(a) **Mobilising Communities:** Civil society organisations play a vital role in mobilising particular communities, such as women, labourers, and dalits, to participate fully in politics and public affairs.

(b) **Information Dissemination:** They play an important role in the discovery, publication, and dissemination of information about issues on legislation, legal provisions, public expenditure allocations, implementation of policies, and special enquiries.

(c) **Pressure from Certain Groups:** They represent the interest of certain specific groups in government-citizen interactions. They put pressure on the government to achieve various social goals such as changing forest development policy, transferring erring officials, and providing housing and medical aid to poor and slum dwellers.

(d) **Developmental/Welfare Activities:** These organisations can contribute by working directly with the government in shaping, financing, and delivering public services in a variety of innovative ways. They work closely with state institutions in designing and providing health and educational services by mobilising funds from among client groups and other sources, providing services directly, and monitoring quality and coverage. State institutions acquire greater legitimacy and improve their performance by developing responsive working relationships with the civil society.

(e) **Social Justice:** They play the role of specialist human rights organisations pressing for the implementation of existing laws, for fresh legislative initiatives, and for improving the functioning and accountability of state policing and security organs. They also play a protective role by sheltering individuals threatened by repressive governments and defending their rights.

(f) **Citizen Empowerment:** Citizens get empowered in the process of holding the government accountable through civil society organisations. While holding the government accountable, citizens become familiar with the processes of governmental operations. This has considerable educative value for the citizens.

(g) **Role in Globalised World:** International civil society organisations such as the World Social Forum represent organisations in which the voices of average citizens count in discussions around international social, political, and economic justice. People who feel increasingly alienated from the prevailing global system join together to explore an alternative vision for a more ethical form of globalisation that works for the benefit of average people rather than only for powerful interests. These organisations conduct public campaigns on issues such as landmines, debt relief, and international criminal court.

(h) **Filling the Democracy Deficit:** The era of globalisation is witnessing the emergence of democracy deficit in several countries. Elections are being held, but fewer and fewer people are choosing to vote, and the meaningful interface between the citizens and the elected is becoming minimal in between the elections. Political parties are increasingly being characterised by a lack of internal democracy, failing to address important citizen-related issues. In this era, civil society is helping people find new and more direct ways to get involved in public life and decision-making, marking a shift from representative democracy to participatory democracy.

5.11.5 Challenges Faced by Civil Society Organisations

The civil society faces the following challenges in its functioning:

(a) **Power Imbalance:** The civil society faces the challenge of power and power imbalance within itself. The sector is vibrant and extremely diverse. It compasses both major transnational NGOs with multi-dollar operating budgets and tiny citizen-based organisations with highly constrained resources, limited access to information, and lower capacity.

(b) **Narrow Interests:** Many civil society organisations project their narrow interests without considering other important aspects. For example, human rights organisations do not have a very good dialogue with developmental NGOs.

(c) **Diminished Established Procedure:** It is argued that citizen activism, through civil society organisations, threatens to undermine democratic systems by short-circuiting established procedures for decision-making.

(d) **Issue of Legitimacy and Accountability:** Many organisations face the challenge of legitimacy and related challenges of transparency, representation, and accountability. It is alleged that many organisations do not represent any one else's views but their own. Moreover, it is alleged that they are accountable upwards to their funding organisations rather than downwards to those they purportedly serve. However, many civil society organisations have developed a culture of self-regulation and transparency within them.

(e) **Accountability of Funds:** Civil society organisations derive funding from various sources such as government, individuals, foundations, business organisations, or multi-lateral institutions. Some organisations have dubious funding sources and, accordingly, they work for the dubious interests of their funders. These organisations avoid giving full information about their funding sources.

6.11.6 Revenue Sources of Civil Society Organisations

Civil society organisations raise their funds from the following sources:

(a) **International Aid:** NGOs receive funding from many international agencies such as the Department of International Development (DFID) of the British Government. Some agencies can support directly while others require specific project approval by the government before financing an NGO.

(b) **Corporate Donations:** Many NGOs receive donations from corporates. Among other funds, those falling under corporates'. Corporate social responsibility are the major source of funding for many NGOs.

(c) **Government Funding:** The Government of India funds many civil society organisations, either directly or through certain designated agencies. The Central Social Welfare Board (CSWB) and National Institute of Public Cooperation and Child Development (NIPCCD) are two such prominent bodies dealing with the government–NGO interface in the social welfare sector, while the Council for Advancement of People's Action and Rural Technology (CAPART) is an organisation that finances voluntary organisations to stimulate grass-roots participation and encouragement of rural technology. Moreover, another way in which the state supports NGOs is by tax concessions of various kinds.

(d) **Individual Donations:** NGOs also acquire funds by collecting donations from various individuals, or groups of individuals, of Indian as well as foreign nationality.

6.11.7 Regulation on Foreign Contribution to NGOs

The foreign contributions received by NGOs are regulated by the Foreign Contribution (Regulation) Act (FCRA), 1976. The primary objective of the act is to regulate the acceptance and utilisation of foreign contribution or foreign hospitality by certain persons or associations. This is done with a view to ensure that parliamentary and political associations, academic and other institutions, as well as individuals working in important areas of national life may function in a manner consistent with the values of a sovereign and democratic republic. It allows associations having definite cultural, economic, educational, religious, or social programmes to accept contributions after complying with certain requirements.

The FCRA has a rigorous scheme for compelling the recipients of foreign contributions to adhere to the stated purpose for which such contribution has been obtained. It is mandatory to obtain the funds only through an intimated branch of a bank, to use the funds only through that branch, and to file annual returns. The government has the power to inspect and seize accounts and records, audit associations that has failed to file returns, and confiscate articles and currencies received in contravention of the Act.

6.11.8 Accreditation of NGOs

Accreditation is an important process to ensure the accountability and proper functioning of NGOs and other voluntary sector organisations. It is the formal recognition of the achievements of an organisation, linked to some internal/external norms such as commitment to long-term aims and objectives, organisational ability, adherence to financial norms, and transparency and accountability.

A National Accreditation Council for accrediting the voluntary sector organisations of India has been proposed.

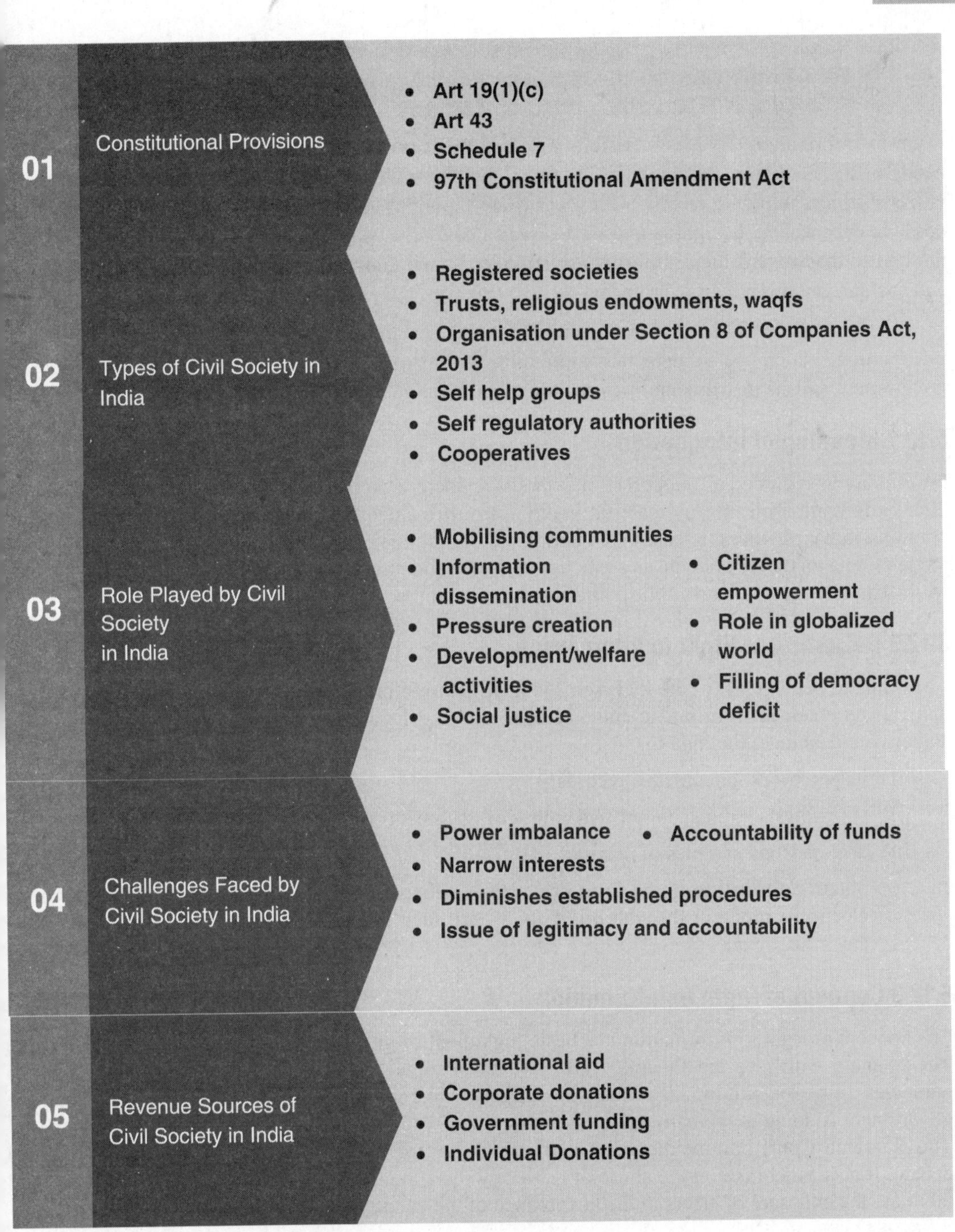

01 Constitutional Provisions
- Art 19(1)(c)
- Art 43
- Schedule 7
- 97th Constitutional Amendment Act

02 Types of Civil Society in India
- Registered societies
- Trusts, religious endowments, waqfs
- Organisation under Section 8 of Companies Act, 2013
- Self help groups
- Self regulatory authorities
- Cooperatives

03 Role Played by Civil Society in India
- Mobilising communities
- Information dissemination
- Pressure creation
- Development/welfare activities
- Social justice
- Citizen empowerment
- Role in globalized world
- Filling of democracy deficit

04 Challenges Faced by Civil Society in India
- Power imbalance
- Accountability of funds
- Narrow interests
- Diminishes established procedures
- Issue of legitimacy and accountability

05 Revenue Sources of Civil Society in India
- International aid
- Corporate donations
- Government funding
- Individual Donations

Mind Map 6.3: Aspects of Civil Society in India

6.12 Right to Information

Right to Information (RTI) is a basic human right that provides an ultimate source of power in the hands of the people of a democratic society. The essential requirement of a modern democracy is citizens' access to public records. Openness is an important quality of a democracy. This openness is possible only when the 'right to know' is exercisable by the people, who can use it to keep a check on the bodies that govern them. Information provides us the knowledge to demand political, economic and social rights from the government.

According to the RTI Act, 2005, democracy requires an informed citizenry and transparency of information, which are vital to its functioning and also help to contain corruption and hold the government and its instrumentalities accountable to the governed.[33]

6.12.1 Meaning of Information

Information is regarded as oxygen for a democratic society. According to Section 2(f) of the RTI Act, 2005, information means any material in any form. It includes records, documents, memos, e-mails, opinions, advices, press releases, circulars, orders, logbooks, contracts, reports, papers, samples, models, data material held in any electronic form, and information relating to any private body, which can be accessed by a public authority under any other law for being in the force.[33]

6.12.2 Definition of Right to Information

According to Section 2(j) of the RTI Act, 2005, 'Right to Information' refers to the right to information that can be obtained from public authorities or which is held by or under the control of any public authority and includes the right to:

(i) inspect work, documents, records

(ii) take notes, extracts, or certified copies of documents or records

(iii) take certified samples of material

(iv) obtain information in the form of diskettes, floppies, tapes, video cassettes, or in any other electronic mode or through printouts, where such information is stored in a computer or in any other device.[33]

6.12.3 Concept of Right to Information

The concept of right to information is a basic ingredient of the Preamble of the Constitution of India. The opening words of the Preamble are "We the People of India"; the final words are "give to ourselves this Constitution."[34] Thus, the citizens have a fundamental right to know what the government is doing in the name of the Constitution. Freedom of speech is the blood of democracy.[34] The Supreme Court has mentioned that the free flow of information and ideas informs political debate. It acts as a brake on the abuse of power by the administration and public officials. It helps to facilitate the exposure of errors in the governance of the country.

The demand for openness in government, the basic motive of the RTI, is based on the following two reasons:

(i) It is well-accepted that democracy does not consist merely in people exercising their franchise once in five years, which leads to passive citizen's participation and lack of interest in governance. It is considered that democracy requires continuous and pervasive participation of citizens.[35] In a democracy, people should not only cast intelligent and rational votes but also exercise sound judgment on the conduct of the government and the merits of the public policies so that democracy becomes a continuous process. Democracy can become a continuous process only when the government is open and there is full access to information with regard to the functioning of the government.[36]

(ii) The working of the government has been shrouded in secrecy from many years. Citizens have struggled for a long time to get even minute information. The demand for openness was strongly directed against this culture of secrecy of the government.

The Supreme Court of India, while interpreting Article 19(1) of the Constitution of India, has laid down in several decisions that the fundamental right to freedom of speech and expression includes the right to acquire information and to disseminate it, which is necessary for self-expression, enabling the people to contribute to debates on social and moral issues.

6.12.4 Evolution of Right to Information

The founders of the US Constitution were inspired by the idea of free flow of information, and they guaranteed this free flow of information in the Constitution.[37] James Madison, a primary author of the American Bill of Rights said, "a popular government, without popular information, or the means of acquiring it, is but a prologue to a farce or a tragedy, or perhaps, both. Knowledge will forever govern ignorance; and a people who mean to be their own governors must arm themselves with the power which knowledge gives." The Federal Freedom of Information Act was passed in 1966 and signed by the then US President in 1973.

Before this, Sweden passed the oldest law for freedom to information in 1766. In the mid-twentieth century, freedom of information received a major push from various international organisations.[38] The United Nations Universal Declaration of Human Rights also declared in its Article 19 that "everyone has the right to freedom of opinion and expression; this right includes freedom to hold opinions without interference and to seek, receive and impart information and ideas through any media and regardless of frontiers."

As of 2005, when India enacted its Right to Information Act, more than 50 countries around the world had passed laws specifying access to information.[39]

6.12.5 RTI Movement in India

The RTI movement in India can be classified into three broad phases as described below:

(a) **Phase 1 (1975 to 1996):** In this phase, there were sporadic demands for information from various sections of the society, culminating in a more focused demand for access to information from environmental movements in the mid-1980s, and from grass-roots movements in rural Rajasthan in the early 1990s. This phase ended with the formation of the National Campaign for People's Right to Information (NCPRI) in 1996. This phase also saw various judicial orders in support of transparency and the judicial pronouncement that the right to information was a fundamental right.

(b) **Phase 2 (1996 to 2005):** In the second phase, a draft bill was prepared by NCPRI and was subsequently processed by the Government and the Parliament. Various states' RTI laws were passed during this period, including Tamil Nadu, Delhi, Maharashtra, Karnataka, Assam, Madhya Pradesh, and Goa. The National Freedom of Information Act was passed in 2002. The phase culminated with the passing of the RTI Act in 2005.

(c) **Phase 3 (2005 to present):** This phase has focused on the consolidation of the Act and on pushing for its proper implementation.

6.12.6 Important Sections of RTI Act

The Right to Information Act of India has the following important provisions:

(a) **Preamble:** The preamble of the RTI Act states it as "an act to provide for setting out the practical regime of right to information for citizens to secure access to information under the control of public authorities, in order to promote transparency and accountability in the working of every public authority, the constitution of a Central Information Commission and State Information Commissions and for matters connected therewith or incidental thereto." It states that democracy requires an informed citizenry and transparency of information.

(b) **Obligation to Proactively Provide Information:** Section 4 of the RTI Act suggests that public authorities should be proactive in disclosing their information via various media such as websites, journals, and reports. If an organisation is proactive in disclosing information, the need for people demanding information will decrease simultaneously. Section 4(1) of the act states that every public authority shall maintain all its records duly catalogued and indexed in a manner and the form that facilitates the right to information under this Act and ensure that all records that are appropriate to be computerised are, within a reasonable time and subject to availability of resources, computerised and connected through a network all over the country on different systems so that access to such records is facilitated.

(c) **Public Authority:** A 'public authority', under the RTI Act, means any authority or body or institution of self-government established or constituted (a) by or under the Constitution, (b) by any other law made by the Parliament, (c) by any other law made by the state legislature, or (d) by notification issued or order made by the appropriate government, and includes any (i) body owned, controlled, or substantially financed or (ii) non-government organisation substantially financed, directly or indirectly, by funds provided by the appropriate government.

(d) **Coverage:** The RTI Act includes the public authorities mentioned above. These public authorities include all three branches of the government, namely, the executive, legislature, and judiciary. It also includes information relating to private bodies that can be accessed under any other law for the time being in force [Section 2(f)].

(e) **Public Information Officer:** Each public authority, or its various subunits, has to appoint a public information officer (PIO) designated to receive information requests and provide information pertaining to them. It is mandatory for the PIO to provide information within 30 days. However, the information needs to be provided within 48 hours if a question of life and liberty is involved. Moreover, information related to a third party can be provided within 40 days and information related to human rights violations from listed security/intelligence agencies are required within 45 days.

(f) **Appellate Authority:** Every public authority, or its various subunits, has to appoint an appellate authority designated to receive appeals against the information provided, or information withheld, by a PIO.

(g) **Central Information Commission and State Information Commissions:** Under the RTI Act, the Central Information Commission is an autonomous body set to inquire into information-related complaints received from citizens. A citizen can complain if he/she has been refused some information, has not received satisfactory information, has not received the information within the stipulated period, or has not received information in the form asked for. State information commissions are also set up in each state for the same purpose.

(h) **Exemption from Disclosure (Section 8):** Section 8 of the RTI Act provides a list of information that is exempted from disclosure under the RTI Act. In brief, it includes information that:

- may prejudicially affect the sovereignty and integrity of India; the security, strategic, scientific, or economic interests of the State; or relations with a foreign state; or lead to incitement of an offence
- has been expressly forbidden to be published by any court of law or tribunal or the disclosure of which may constitute contempt of court
- would cause a breach of privilege of the Parliament or the state legislature
- includes commercial confidence, trade secrets, or intellectual property, the disclosure of which would harm the competitive position of a third party, unless the competent authority is satisfied that larger public interest warrants the disclosure of such information
- includes information that is available to a person in his/her fiduciary relationship, unless the competent authority is satisfied that the larger public interest warrants the disclosure of such information
- includes information that is received in confidence from a foreign government
- includes information that would impede the process of investigation or apprehension or prosecution of offenders
- includes cabinet papers, including records of deliberations of the council of ministers, secretaries, and other officers
- includes information that relates to personal information, the disclosure of which has no relationship to any public activity or interest, or which would cause unwarranted invasion of the privacy of the individual

However, the RTI Act clearly mentions that notwithstanding any of the exemptions, a public authority may allow access to information if public interest in disclosure outweighs the harm to the protected interests.

(i) **Penalty:** The Information Commission can impose a penalty of INR 250 per day, up to INR 25,000, on the PIO for unreasonable delay in providing information beyond the stipulated time period. A fine of INR 25,000 can also be imposed for illegitimate refusal to accept an application, malafide denial, knowingly providing false information, or destruction of information.

6.12.7 Impact of RTI on Governance

Various studies, including those by the Second Administrative Reforms Commission, Society of Participatory Research in Asia, and by various media channels, have studied the impact of RTI on governance and the society of India. The following impacts of RTI have been felt substantially in India:[41]

(a) **Achievement of Transparency and Reduction in Corruption:** RTI has been used as a weapon in areas where citizens have had to struggle to get their rights. A majority of the RTI applications are filed in welfare and developmental issues such as public distribution system, drinking water, human rights, school and education, health, and daily wages. As a result of RTI applications in these areas, a majority of the government departments have taken note of the lacunae in them and have taken rectifying steps. It has been proven that an informed citizenry—even if illiterate and marginalised—can bring in transparency and improvement in the system.[40]

(b) **Assets of Bureaucrats and Ministers:** Various RTI applications have forced ministers and bureaucrats to put their assets and liabilities in the public domain.

(c) **Scams Exposed:** Various corruption scams have been exposed using the RTI Act, including the Adarsh Housing Scam, which resulted in the exit of the then Chief Minister of Maharashtra. RTI has also helped in unearthing scams such as the 2G Scam, Coal Block Allocation Scam, and Commonwealth Games Scam.

(d) **Financial Propriety in Governmental Spending:** RTI has helped in bringing financial propriety in governmental spending by saving money in areas such as foreign trips and recruitment of personal staff. Earlier, ministers and bureaucrats used to travel by air in order to earn mileage points, which were then used by them for private travel. Such malicious practices were checked when it was made mandatory to put the details of foreign trips on respective websites. Similarly, the malicious practice of recruiting relatives as personal staff was checked by RTI applications.

(e) **Accessible File Notings:** File notings were made available under the RTI Act in 2012. This step has pressurised bureaucrats to write properly on their files.

Table 6.1 displays various success stories on the implementation of the RTI Act in India

Attendance of the Village School Teacher	School uniforms distributed at the end of the December Session	Transparency in Public Distribution System for BPL Families
In a Pre-Middle School in Panchampur village, situated 70 kilometers away from the District Headquarters of Banda, a teacher was appointed for the school. However, the teacher was absent for most of the times. The workers and volunteers from the Delhi based organisations like Kabir and Parivartan, along with the local workers from the Chingari Sangathan under the 'Action Research Villages' Campaign, propagated the use of the Right to Information. Finally, the villagers witnessed a ray of hope when they learned that they could question the Government and ask for information related to the attendance records, leave records and medical records of the absconding village school teacher. Fifteen villagers drafted an application regarding the same and filed a number of applications with the Primary Education Officer at the Banda District Head Quarters. They asked for the records of the teacher and also questioned the Primary Education Department about the Department's role and responsibilities in such situations. Immediate action was taken on the issue by the Department. The Primary Education Officer summoned the teacher the next day and	School uniforms distributed at the end of the December Session Despite several claims of the Government, school uniforms of the session – December 2006-07 – were not distributed among the students of the Gulrahai Primary School in Allahabad. Workers from KABIR and ABSSS conducted a meeting with the villagers of Gulrahai and educated them on the RTI Act. Immediately thereafter, nine parents prepared an RTI application and questioned the administration regarding the school uniforms of the children. In the first week of January 2007, the school dresses were distributed to the children. Similarly, in the Bharthaul Village primary school of Chitrakoot district, school dresses were not distributed among the children till December. Under 'Mere Gaon Ke Sawaal' Campaign, KABIR & ABSSS conducted a meeting with the villagers and educated them on the RTI Act. The very next day, parents of these children submitted an RTI application with the District Education Officer and within 15 days, school dresses were distributed and a video shoot of the court was also conducted.	Transparency in Public Distribution System for BPL Families The 'Mere Gaon Ke Sawaal' Campaign volunteers noticed that the residents of Nai Basti (Bahraich, UP) were also facing the same problems as the other economically backward villages of the region. The 'Kotedar' had been apathetic towards their requests. The use of Right to Information by the villagers, the women being in majority, was successful in curbing the corruption that had seeped in the Public Distribution System to some extent. When the campaign volunteers saw the BPL ration cards of the villagers, they found that no entries had been made during February 2006 to December 2006. It was evident that the villagers had not received any ration in the said time period. Immediately, 51 village residents agreed to file group RTI applications on the issue and demanded information regarding the acquisition and the distribution of the ration and also asked for copies of the ration records. The applications were filed by the applicants personally after a lot of difficulty at the District Supply Office. Exactly within a fortnight, the Kotedar reached the village and narrated a long sob story, which moved few of the innocent villagers so much that they even agreed to

Attendance of the Village School Teacher	School uniforms distributed at the end of the December Session	Transparency in Public Distribution System for BPL Families
asked for an explanation. Living up to his accountability and responsibility, the officer appointed a new school teacher for the village school. The school was opened on the next day itself and regular teaching began in the school. An enquiry was ordered against the teacher and he was asked to report to the school immediately. The villagers were overwhelmed with the fact that their use of Right to Information could reap such instant results.		take back their RTI applications. They following day the Kotedar brought a mini bus to the village along with "pooris" made with one quintal flour and asked the villagers to come to the SDM's office and take back their RTI applications. But, the women of the forest village rights forum refused to do so. This initiative by the women of the village encouraged the other villagers and they refused to take back their RTI applications. The Kotedar trying another of his tactics, one day announced in the village that all those who requested for information can collect it from him. When few villagers reached to take the information, they were forced to make thumb imprints on a blank paper. The Dehat Sanstha volunteers immediately reported this scam to the SDM. Finally, the Kotedar was suspended.

6.12.8 Issues in Implementation of RTI Act

The issues and constraints in implementation of the RTI Act come from three sides—demand side, supply side, and from the side of information commissions.

6.12.8.1 Demand Side Issues in RTI Act Implementation

The demand side issues and constraints in the implementation of the RTI Act are as follows:

(a) **Low Public Awareness:** Section 26 of the RTI Act mandates that the appropriate government may develop and organise educational programmes to advance the understanding of the public, especially disadvantaged communities, regarding how to exercise the rights contemplated under the Act. However, a minor proportion of the population is aware of the provisions of the RTI Act. No substantial steps have been taken by the government to promote the awareness of the RTI Act. The efforts made by public authorities have been restricted to publishing rules and FAQs on their websites. The awareness level is comparatively lower among disadvantaged communities such as women, rural population, and SC/ST/OBC community.

(b) **Constraints in Filing Application:** Users face various constraints and difficulties in filing RTI applications. Under Section 26 of the Act, the appropriate governments are mandated to publish and distribute user guides for information seekers. However, these guides have not been published by many public authorities of various states. The lack of user guides results in substantial efforts on the part of the information seeker to gather knowledge about the process for submitting an RTI request. Moreover, inadequate efforts have been made to receive RTI applications through electronic means, i.e., through email/websites, etc. Furthermore, information seekers are rarely provided with any assistance by the PIO to draft and fill their RTI applications; the non-friendly attitude of the PIOs discourages the citizens from filing RTI applications.

(c) **Poor Quality of Information Provided:** A majority of information seekers are found to be dissatisfied with the information provided by the PIO. Incomplete information is provided to a majority of the people.[43]

(d) **Constrains Faced in Inspection of Records:** Under Section 7(9) of the Act, information is to be provided in the form it is requested in, unless it would disproportionately divert the resources of the Public Authority. If information cannot be provided in the form requested, it can be provided through inspection of records.[44] However, there is inadequate awareness of this provision of the RTI Act due to inadequate awareness of the citizens and inadequate training of the PIOs to utilise this provision effectively.

6.12.8.2 Supply Side Issues in RTI Act Implementation

The demand side issues and constraints in the implementation of the RTI Act are as mentioned below:

(a) **Failure to Provide Information Within 30 Days:** Many PIOs face challenges in providing information within the stipulated time period due to inadequate record management procedures with the public authorities.

(b) **Inadequately Trained PIOs and First Appellate Authorities:** PIOs and First Appellate Authorities are not adequately trained with the complete provisions of the RTI Act and the various judgments of the Information Commissions. Moreover, they are also not provided sufficient behavioural training for the implementation of the RTI Act. The training of PIOs is a big challenge, primarily due to the huge number of PIOs and their frequent transfers. Moreover, the public authorities do not feel the urgency to train their PIOs.

(c) **Obsolete Record Management Guidelines:** The current record management guidelines at the Centre and in most states are not geared to meet the requirements specified under the RTI Act. There is lack of any electronic document management system in any of the departments.

(d) **Non-availability of Basic Infrastructure:** Basic infrastructure such as photocopy machines and email service are not available at the level of blocks and panchayats. Moreover, there is inadequate usage of the IT platform for acceptance and delivery of RTI applications.

(e) **Lack of Motivation Among PIOs:** PIOs lack the motivation to implement the RTI Act. They feel that there is no incentive for taking on the responsibility of a PIO; however, penalties are imposed in the case of non-compliance.

(f) **Ineffective Implementation of Section 4:** Section 4 mandates *suo motu* dissemination of information by the public authorities. However, the internal processes within the public authorities are not defined to take care of this requirement of suo motu disclosure of information. Moreover, the information provided on websites is not updated periodically. Furthermore, the quality of *suo motu* disclosure is quite low and does not cater to the information needs of the citizens. Neither the state government nor the information commissions have taken adequate steps to ensure compliance of this basic minimum requirement of the RTI Act.

6.12.8.3 Issues Faced at the side of Information Commissions

The following issues are faced at the side of information commissions:

(a) **Perception of being lenient towards PIOs:** In a survey by PricewaterhouseCoopers, it was found that information commissions have imposed penalties on PIOs in a very few cases. Given that more than half of the RTI applications get processed after 30 days, there is a very strong perception in the citizens and the civil society organisations that the information commission is lenient towards the erring PIOs.

(b) **Lack of Monitoring and Review Mechanism:** One of the most important roles of the information commission is to monitor and review the public authority and initiate actions to make them comply with the spirit of the Act. However, this has been one of the weakest links in the implementation of the Act. It is acknowledged and appreciated that the information commissions have been spending most of their time primarily in 'hearings' and disposing off appeals. However, monitoring the public authority for compliance of the Act is also an important aspect of the role of the information commission, which could result in reducing the number of appeals.

(c) **High Level of Pendency:** The number of RTI appeals with the information commissions has been increasing year by year. This has led to an increase in the 'wait period' of each appeal and has, thus, discouraged citizens from filing appeals. Unless and until the pendency is kept at a manageable level, the objective of the Act would not be met.

(d) **Geographical Spread of Information Commissions:** A majority of the information commissions are situated in the state capitals, which results in appellants undergoing an additional cost in order to attend the hearings. The RTI Act allows information commissions to set up regional offices with the prior approval of state governments. For example, in Maharashtra, SIC offices have been set up in Pune, Aurangabad, Nagpur, Konkan, and Mumbai. The benefits of setting up regional offices far outweigh the initial capital costs involved in setting them up.

6.12.9 Issue of Including Non-Governmental Bodies

The RTI Act mentions that the non-governmental bodies that are substantially financed by the government must be considered as public authorities under the RTI Act. However, the terms 'substantially financed' is not defined under the Act. According to the Second Administrative Reforms Commission, in the wake of outsourcing functions that were traditionally performed by government agencies, it is desirable that institutions enjoy a natural monopoly. The functions that impinge on citizens' lives substantially must come under the provisions of the RTI Act. Moreover, norms should be laid down that any institution or body that has received 50% of its annual operating costs or a sum equal to or greater than INR 1 crore during any of the preceding 3 years should be understood to have obtained 'substantial funding' from the government for the period and purpose of such funding.

6.12.10 Redressal of Public Grievances Associated with Information Sought

It is common knowledge that citizens seek information because of some grievance against a department/agency. This information is the starting point in a citizen's quest for justice and is not an end in itself. It is a means to fight corruption, mis-governance, and to obtain better services. However, it has been observed that departments tend to be defensive rather than proactive in redressing a grievance when it directly pertains to their conduct (or misconduct). This proclivity underlines the need for an independent organisation to hear complaints into acts of omission and commission, harassment, corruption, and so on, which emerges through information collected under the Right to Information Act. Such an independent body should hear the citizen and the public authority, come to an early conclusion about how the complaint can be best redressed, and where the dereliction of duty is established, recommend initiation of disciplinary action and also suggest systemic reforms where required (recommendation of Second Administrative Reforms Commission).

6.13 Media and Governmental Accountability

The role of the Press as an important mechanism of ensuring governmental accountability has been recognised since the seventeenth century. Media has been regarded as a watchdog, a guardian of public interest, and as a conduit between the government and the governed. It is regarded as the fourth branch of the government because of the power it yields and the oversight function it exercises. It can promote democracy by, among other things, educating voters, protecting human rights, promoting tolerance among various social groups, and ensuring that governments are transparent and accountable.[45]

Enlightenment theorists have argued that publicity and openness provide the best protection against tyranny and arbitrary rule. Since the 1700s, the Press has been widely proclaimed as the "Fourth Estate", a co-equal branch of the government that provides the check and balance without which governments cannot be effective. When the legislature, executive, and judiciary are ineffective and corrupt, the media is seen as the only check on the abuse of power.

The important role of media is seen in the following areas:

(a) **Investigative Reporting:** Through the mechanism of investigative reporting, the media act as a watchdog on the government. Sustained investigative reporting on corruption, human rights violations, and other forms of wrongdoings have helped build a culture of accountability in the government. In Latin America, investigative reporting on corruption has led to the downfall of four presidents—Fernando Collor de Mello of Brazil in 1992, Carlos Andres Perez of Venezuela in 1993, Abdala Bucaram of Ecuador in 1997, and Alberto Fujimori in 2000. Similarly, in Southeast Asia, sustained reporting on malfeasance in public life has resulted in the ouster of corrupt officials and raised public awareness on the need for reforms.[45]

(b) **Information Medium and Forum for Discussion:** Various media channels such as newspapers, radio, electronic media, and social media inform, educate, and engage the public. The discussions over media keep the citizens engaged in the business of governance and prompt them to take action. As a tool for information dissemination, the media aid the public in making informed choices, such as whom to vote for, which policies should be endorsed, and which should be opposed. In new democracies, media has helped in public education on elections. Channels organise debates and enable poor candidates to possess air time to articulate their views to a wider audience. The Internet, as the most effective media channel, has been used in many democracies for disseminating information and opinions and mobilising protest actions.

(c) **Consensus Builder:** Media plays the crucial role of building consensus among diverse and separatist groups. It plays an important role in conflict situations via the mechanism of *peace journalism*. Peace journalism endeavours to promote reconciliation through careful reportage, which gives voice to all sides of a conflict and resists explanations for violence in terms of innate enmities or ancient hatreds.

(d) **Watchdog Against Disasters:** Scholars have also regarded media as a watchdog against disasters. Economist Amartya Sen has said that there can never be a famine in a functioning multiparty democracy. He said, "a free press and the practice of democracy contribute greatly to bringing out information that can have an enormous impact on policies for famine prevention… a free press and an active political opposition constitute the best early-warning system a country threatened by famine could have."[46]

(e) **Poverty Reduction:** Positive reporting helps in poverty reduction, as addressing poverty requires not just a transfer of economic resources to the needy but also making information available to the poor, so that they can participate more meaningfully in political and social life.[47] The poor can assert their rights only if they have knowledge about them. Effective media provide essential information to the poor to take part in public life.

6.13.1 Constraints on Effective Media

After the process of liberalisation, privatisation, and globalisation, a wave of private channels has entered, which has brought cut-throat competition with them. With increasing competition, every channel has started providing news that the public wants to hear. Moreover, apart from providing news to people, they have also started framing the opinion of the people. In other words, they have started controlling the minds of the people. It has been observed that the standards of journalism have fallen with rising competition. The present situation is that media are considered as a business without ethics and without any social responsibility. This is because the owners of print and private electronic channels are the owners of either a business establishment, industrial house, or a financial institution.

As a result of this commoditisation of news, the following evils have been associated with present-day media:[48]

(a) **High Levels of Inaccuracies:** As a result of competition, high levels of inaccuracies are found in present-day media reporting. For example, in one case *India Today* regarded common gamblers attacking a church, without verifying their true identity, as people from 'right wing groups'.

(b) **Sensationalism:** The media generally try to highlight sensational stories such as those of crimes, rapes, and what celebrities are doing. Some other issues of public importance are not covered by the media.

(c) **Poor Coverage of Important Issues:** In a mad race to gain popularity, the media tend to show what people want to see, sidelining important news that is of real public importance. Rather than focusing on issues such as poverty, unemployment, and health, the media focus on stories such as the wife of a film actor is pregnant.

(d) **Short Attention Span:** The media cover a story only when a particular incidence occurs but barely provide its necessary and important follow up.

(e) **Focus on Profit and not Public:** The media have been severely affected by the disease of 'paid news'. They publish news favourable to a candidate for monetary or other considerations. The phenomenon has gone beyond the corruption of individual journalists and media companies and has become pervasive, structured, and highly organised.

(f) **Media Trial:** In certain high-profile criminal cases, media create the perception of guilt or innocence of an accused without having any substantial knowledge of the judicial proceedings. Media trials are judicial proceedings that are conducted by media houses even before the actual trial starts. These media trials are one-sided, without any substantial information, and they affect the fundamental rights of the parties involved.

6.13.2 Accountability of Media

The media gather information on the behalf of citizens. Thus, they must observe utmost care while gathering and circulating information. It is the moral duty of journalists to supply correct information and guard the public against misleading and distorted information. Thus, the media need to be accountable to either an internal or an external agency. The Press Council of India, Electronic Media Monitoring Committee, and News Broadcasting Standards Authority are regulatory bodies for media in India.

(a) **Press Council of India:** In India, statutory regulation is maintained over print media by the Press Council of India (PCI). It governs the conduct of the print media. Its chairperson is a retired judge of the Supreme Court of India. This quasi-judicial institution works under the Press Council Act of 1978. It adjudicates the complaints against and by the press for the violation of ethics and for the violation of the freedom of the press, respectively. It is empowered to hold hearings on receipt of complaints and take suitable action where appropriate. It may either warn or censure the errant journalists upon finding them guilty.[51] However, it does not have any legal powers to take any penalising or remedial action against publishers providing wrong news.

(b) **Central Press Accreditation Committee:** The Central Press Accreditation Committee (CPAC) debars a particular media organisation from accreditation for 2–5 years, if it is found to not comply with the The Central News Media Accreditation Guidelines, 1999. These guidelines say that a media organisation shall not provide any false, fraudulent, or forged details or news.[54]

(c) **Electronic Media Monitoring Centre:** The Electronic Media Monitoring Centre (EMMC) is a subordinate office under the Indian Ministry of Information and Broadcasting tasked with monitoring the content of television channels and reporting on the violations of the programme and advertising code. It checks television content in line with the provisions of the Cable Television Network Rules, 1994. The provisions check that the channels do not offend good taste or decency, or attack a particular community. It also ensures that electronic media do not cover anything that is likely to encourage or incite violence, anything that goes against the maintenance of law and order, or anything that results in the contempt of court.[52]

(d) **News Broadcasting Standards Authority:** The News Broadcasting Standards Authority (NBSA) is a self-regulatory authority of broadcasters of India set up by the News Broadcasters Association (NBA). Its task is to consider and adjudicate upon complaints about broadcasts. It is a nine-member committee consisting of an eminent jurist as its chairperson. It receives any complaint on the violation of the code of ethics of media and broadcasting standards laid down by the NBA. These standards include ensuring impartiality and objectivity in reporting, ensuring neutrality, ensuring non-glorification of crime and violence, ensuring utmost discretion while reporting on crime against women and children, abhorring sex and nudity, ensuring privacy of citizens, ensuring that national security is not endangered, refraining from advocating or encouraging superstition and occultism, and ensuring responsible sting operations.[53]

(e) **Other Mechanisms:** Editors of media organisations are tasked with substantiating any news before publishing it in the public domain. Apart from this, an internal mechanism for ensuring authenticity of information is ensured through mechanisms such as the media council of peers and media watch groups, readers editor, internal ombudsman, 'letters to the editor', all of which are intended to highlight and address the wrongs done by media persons, reporters, or the management.[55]

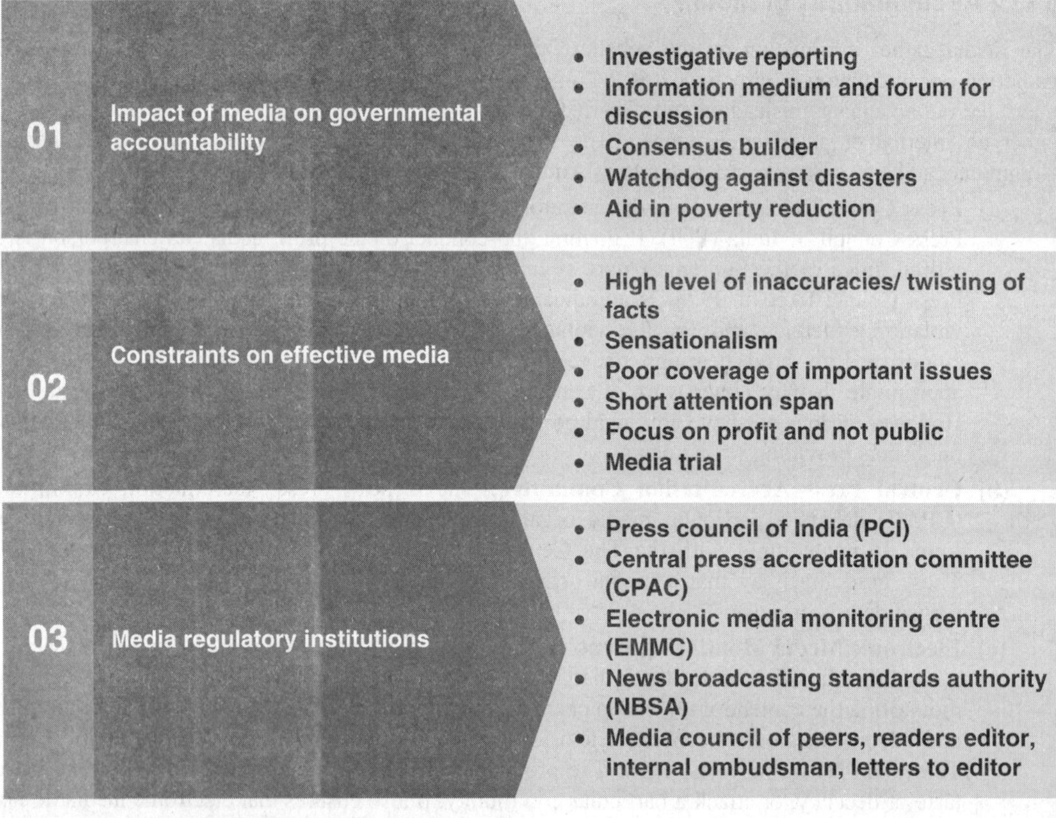

***Mind Map 6.4:** Aspects of Governmental Accountability by Media in India*

6.14 Accountability Challenge in Twenty-First Century Governance

In the era of new public management (NPM) and post-NPM reforms, the concept of accountability has changed drastically. The traditional mechanism of accountability was through ministerial control, parliamentary debates, legislative committees, media scrutiny, ombudsman system, and judicial control. In the post-NPM era, the focus of governance is on economic growth and productivity. Its normative standards are now redirected towards efficiency, competition, profit, and value for money. The values and objectives of NPM and later reforms are already discussed in the Chapters 1 and 2.

In this era of 'entrepreneurial governance', a unique set of challenges have emerged to the concept of accountability. According to Haque, these challenges can be placed into three categories:[56]

(a) **Standards of Accountability (accountability of what):** In present-day governance, more emphasis is laid on procedural and economic criteria such as efficiency and productivity rather than on substantive public concerns such as equality, citizen's rights, representation, justice, and welfare. In other words, the growing primacy of business-like criteria adopted in contemporary public governance has the tendency to displace its accountability in terms of established democratic standards.

(b) **Agents of Accountability (accountability to whom):** In the present scenario, the government is accountable to diverse groups and classes of citizens entitled to social services. The people-centred tradition of accountability has evolved with the emergence of the broader civil society, an organised working class, and an increase in the entitlements or rights of common citizens. However, in the NPM paradigm, citizens have been defined as customers. This has reduced the social rights associated with collective citizenship. Accountability under this paradigm is more to private, affluent customers than to the collective public. Thus, the poor and underprivileged class has lost its role as agents of accountability in the NPM paradigm.[58]

(c) **Means of Accountability (how accountability is ensured):** The means of accountability have also been under challenge in the NPM paradigm. Today, we see over-interference of politicians in the work of civil servants, leading to politicisation of civil services, in violation of the principle of neutrality. Recent NPM-led measures, such as doing away with the permanent nature of civil services and introducing contract-based appointments, has led to undue interference of politicians in civil services. Thus, accountability has become more of ministerial control than control by the general public. Moreover, NPM-led measures such as autonomous public agencies have posed serious challenges to the traditional means of accountability. Furthermore, under the NPM regime, many developed and developing countries have shifted from process-oriented to result-oriented performance of public agencies, with increasing focus on outcome rather than inputs. It is difficult to put such an outcome-based administrative system under legislative scrutiny because the administrative outcomes such as environmental security, poverty alleviation, and community development are difficult to measure. Moreover, the current proliferation of public-private partnership represents a challenge to the various legislative and executive means of accountability.[57]

However, these above challenges can be tackled if good governance initiatives such as right to information, citizen's charter, social audit, citizen's report card, and right to public service are effectively implemented by the government.

SUMMARY

The chapter discussed, we have learnt about various forms of control over administration in India. We gained an understanding about the various modern-day reforms such as citizen's charter, right to information, right to public service, and social audit, which have helped in increasing the accountability of the government to the society. Finally, we learnt how important the role of free flow of information is in securing the accountability of government servants.

Practice Questions

1. " 'Accountability to external actors' and 'moral accountability' are generally compatible with each other. However, there are certain instances when they are not compatible." Comment.
2. "Power should be bound not only by legal constraints but also by the logic of public reasoning." Comment.
3. What are the various tools and ends of accountability?
4. Compare and contrast legislative control over administration in US, UK, and India.
5. Compare and contrast judicial control over administration in US, UK, and India.
6. US judiciary has the power to review administrative acts to the extent that they seem desirable by the judiciary. Comment.
7. Judicial control in India is derived from both the US and the UK models. Comment.
8. The mechanism of PIL has helped in bringing justice to the doorstep of the weak, underprivileged, and exploited sections of the society.
9. What do you understand by the term judicial overreach? Explain with examples.
10. The basic thrust of the citizen's charter is to make public services citizen-centric by ensuring that these services are demand driven rather than supply driven. Explain.
11. Explain the working of the Right to Public Service Acts in the various states of India.
12. What is social accountability and how is it different from other forms of accountability?
13. What is social audit? Explain its benefits and procedures with examples.
14. What are civil society organisations? Describe the different forms of civil society organisations in India.
15. Explain the growth of Right to Information in India while highlighting the major issues faced in its implementation.
16. Media is rightly proclaimed as the "Fourth Estate" of the government. Comment.

CHAPTER 7 Administrative Law

Learning Objectives: After reading this chapter, you will learn the following:

- Various facets of administrative law
- Nature and scope of administrative law
- Reasons for growth of administrative law
- Administrative law in different countries
- Dicey's views on administrative law and the rule of law
- Globalisation of administrative law
- The concept of rule of law and the principle of the legal state (Rechtsstaat)
- Delegated legislation and its rising importance, its scope, types of delegated legislation, and bye-laws
- Procedural, legislative, and judicial control over delegated legislation
- Meaning of administrative tribunals, their evolution in India, Administrative Tribunals Act of 1985, central administrative tribunals, and other tribunals constituted under various statutes in India
- Role of administrative tribunals and judicial review
- Deficiencies in functioning of administrative tribunals and measures for their improvement.

7.1 Introduction to Administrative Law

Administrative law is a very board term and its origin dates back from the time of origin of the administration itself. It refers to the body of laws, procedures, and legal institutions impacting government agencies as they implement legislation and administer public programmes. As a body of law, it is derived partly from constitutional law, partly from statutory law, partly from public policy, and, in some systems, partly from common law.

In all its forms, the main purpose of administrative law is to guide how government authority can and ought to be exercised. At its core, it seeks to influence the behaviour of government employees and organisations in such a way as to promote important social objectives. It is characterised in part by prescriptive measures to design rules that better promote democratic and other values, including fairness, electiveness, and efficiency.[1]

7.2 Nature and Scope of Administrative Law

Administrative law deals with the power, rights, and duties of the administrative authorities and the various remedies available to the persons affected by administrative lacunae and excesses. As the activities of the government have increased with the growth of the welfare state, the administrative and executive powers have enlarged, and delegated legislation has developed in the form of rules, regulations, and so on. Moreover, administrative tribunals have been created to exercise judicial functions to resolve disputes.

This enlarged increase in state power has led to increasing in the abuse of power by administrators. Thus, an increased need has been felt to demarcate administrative power and provide remedies to affected persons for its abuse. This has led to a widening of the scope of administrative law.

In this context, the basic principles of administrative law are a judicial review of administrative actions (discussed in the previous chapter), measures for the prevention of the misuse and abuse of administrative power, and provision of adequate steps for public grievance redressal.

In the words of Bernard Schwartz, the "goal of administrative law is to ensure that the individual and the state are placed on a plane of equality before the Bar of Justice.[2]"

7.3 Reasons for the Growth of Administrative Law

As discussed in the previous topic, the growth of the size and scope of government has led to the growth of administrative law. The various reasons for this growth are explained in the following.

(a) **Emergence of Welfare State:** The nature of the state across the globe has changed from the *laissez faire* state to the welfare state. In the *laissez faire* era, the role of the state was only to prevent crime, maintain law and order, maintain foreign relations, and defence of the country. However, the welfare state has numerous functions such as poverty alleviation, health, education, providing employment, and urban and rural development. Thus, the state has started touching the lives of common citizens in a number of ways.

(b) **Emergence of Delegated Legislation:** With the emergence of the welfare state and the increase in state functions, the rigid legislative processes have made it imperative for the legislatures to delegate their power to administrators in the field of making rules, regulations, and by-laws.

(c) **Emergence of Administrative Tribunals:** The rigid, slow, complex, overburdened, and expensive nature of the judicial system has led to the denial of justice to the common people. This has led to the birth of tribunals and quasi-judicial bodies to provide quick and inexpensive justice in certain areas of administration.

(d) **Theoreticization of Administrative Law:** Earlier administrative law was functional in nature and not much emphasis was laid on its theoreticization. However, with the growth of administrative functions, experts have started focusing on building the theory of administrative law. Thus, present-day administrative law has become more theoretical, technical, legalistic, complex, and, therefore, wider in nature.

(e) **Increase in Preventive Measures:** In today's world, administrative agencies have started taking preventive measures in the cases of law and order, licensing, fixing of minimum wages, and so on. For example, authorities have prevented riots by preventive detention of suspected people rather than taking legal action against them after a riot occurs. However, such preventive action powers are subject to misuse and abuse.

(f) **Proactive Administration Action:** Administrative authorities worldwide have also started taking proactive steps to enforce socio-economic legislations such as suspension and cancellation of licenses and destruction of materials such as narcotic drugs. However, such proactive steps are also subject to misuse.

The growth of administrative law has increased because the possibility of misuse of administrative discretion and power has increased due to the various reasons mentioned above.

7.4 Administrative Law in Different Countries

The nature of administrative law in different countries is defined by the national experience and history of those countries. The two basic aspects of administrative law are procedural law and substantive law. Over the world, the nature of administrative law can be classified into three categories—that is followed in common law countries (such as Britain and its earlier colonies), that is followed in continental law countries (such as France and other European countries), and that is followed in Germany and related countries. The three systems and their sub-systems will be discussed in the following sections.

7.4.1 Administrative Law in England/Common Law System of Administrative Law

Administrative law in England is also determined by its national history. Here, the business of the government was handled by local elites with relatively little central involvement, and the appeals against government officers were heard by courts of general jurisdiction under the same system of common law writs devised for private disputes. A failed attempt was made by the Stuarts to create a separate set of prerogative courts with jurisdiction over complaints against government officers; the attempt failed in 1688.

In 1885, the English scholar Albert Venn Dicey proclaimed that in England, unlike France, there was no such thing called administrative law.[3] Government officers were held accountable for their actions, like private individuals, before ordinary courts. Generalist courts are responsible for hearing disputes between individuals and public administration. This system was considered better for safeguarding individual liberties. It is followed in countries that were a part of the British Empire, such as Australia, New Zealand, India, Ireland, and the United States. It is also followed in other countries, such as Japan and South Korea, due to the influence of American law after World War II.

While considering the administrative law situation in England, it is important to first discuss the views of Albert Dicey on administrative law.

Views of Dicey on Administrative Law

According to Dicey, administrative law is defined as the following:

- The portion of a nation's legal system that determines the legal statutes and liabilities of all state officials.
- A law that defines the right and liabilities of private individuals in their dealings with public officials.
- A law that specifies the procedure by which those rights and liabilities are enforced.4

However, Dicey's view suffers from various deficiencies. For example, his definition does not include the study of the various administrative authorities such as public corporations. It also excludes the study of the various powers and functions of administrative authorities.

Rule of Law

Rule of law is an important aspect of administrative law. The term originated in England. For the sake of comparison with the German *Rechtsstaat*, this concept will be discussed later in this chapter.

Procedural Aspect of English Administrative Law

The common law system of administrative law relies especially on the procedural principles of fair play in judging the correctness of administrative actions. This is one of the main differences between common law and continental administrative law. Here, administrative action is equated with judicial action requiring analogous procedural safeguards. In contrast to this, the administrative law of continental Europe is more focused on the substantive correctness of administrative decisions.[7] This procedural emphasis in English law has originated from the principles of natural justice (discussed in Chapter 6). In American law, these same guarantees have been developed in constitutional case law on procedural due process.

In today's time, the common law countries have institutionalised the judicial procedure within the administrative process. In Britain and Australia, this has taken the shape of administrative tribunals, while in the US it comes under the heading of 'formal adjudication' governed by the Administrative Procedure Act and handled by administrative law judges.[8]

Substantive Aspect of English Administrative Law

The substance of an administrative decision is also considered during the judicial review of the decision. This intervention of courts in bureaucratic activity can be categorised under three headings: rule of law, individual rights, and policy rationality. Basically, the substantive principle of administrative law guides public administration to respect the purposes and limits set down in law.

In the US, the substantive principle helps in overturning administrative action if it is in excess of statutory jurisdiction, authority, or limitations.[9] Similarly, in England, administrative action can be overturned on the grounds of "error of law" or "illegality."[10] For example, in 2000, the US Food and Drugs Authority (FDA) passed a decision restricting the sale and advertisement of tobacco products. This decision was struck down on substantive grounds that the FDA had authority only over medical drugs and not tobacco.

A second type of substantive review of administrative action is the protection of basic liberties against government action. These generally include the protection of fundamental and human rights.

The third form of substantive review of administrative action is a review of policy rationality. The soundness of administrative policymaking is reviewed under this principle. In the US, this principle reviews administrative actions on the ground of being "arbitrary and capricious."[9] This principle has become a demanding test in the US and represents a distinctive feature of the American administrative law system.

In England, the principle of policy irrationality is applied to a decision that is so outrageous in its defiance of logic or accepted moral standards that no sensible person who had applied his/her mind to the question to be decided could have arrived at it.[13]

7.4.2 Administrative Law in France/Continental Administrative Law

The administrative law in France is shaped by its national history. In France, there was a drive to consolidate absolute monarchy in the seventeenth and eighteenth centuries. This was marked by intense conflicts between the royal officers responsible for administering the provinces (*intendants*) and the powerful regional courts in the hold of the local elites (*Parlements*). To insulate the decision of the *intendants* from interference by the *Parlements*, legal supervision was entrusted to a special body directly controlled by the monarchy (*Counceil du Roi).*

This system of a specialised review body/legal supervision body was borrowed during the French Revolution, motivated by a republican theory aimed at destroying the special privileges and vested interests of the *Parlements* and ensuring that government officials would not encounter resistance from the old elites in carrying out the will of the people. This system was embraced by Napoleon by founding the Council of State (*Conseil d'État).*

At this time, a distinctive French separation of powers doctrine was born, according to which "to judge the administration is still to administer" (*juger l'administration c'est encore administrer*). According to it, judicial review by the ordinary courts represented an encroachment upon the executive power, and therefore supervision was entrusted to a specialised body connected to the executive branch.

The basic idea of French administrative law is described in the concept of *droit administratif.* This system is followed in countries influenced by France, such as Belgium, the Netherlands, Luxembourg, Italy, Greece, Turkey, Lebanon, Egypt, Colombia, Morocco, Algeria, and Senegal.[6]

Droit Administratif

French administrative law is known as *droit administratif*; it determines the organisation, powers, and duties of public administration and regulates the relationship of the administration with the citizens of the country. It basically consists of the rules developed by the administrative courts (*Conseil d'État)* of France. Napolean was the founder of *droit administratif.*

The basic characteristics of *droit administratif* are as follows:

(a) **Act *Suo Motu*:** The administration has the power to act *suo motu* and impose directly on the subject the duty to obey its decisions.

(b) **Power within law:** The power of the administration to take decisions and to execute them *suo motu* may be exercised only within the ambit of law protecting individual liberties against administrative arbitrariness.

(c) **Administrative Courts:** As discussed, there are administrative courts to review the decision of administrative authorities. Matters concerning state and administrative litigation fall within the jurisdiction of administrative courts and cannot be decided by the land of the ordinary courts.

(d) **Administrative rules:** Rules, as developed by the administrative courts, are applied to the state and administrative litigations.

(e) **Dual Functions:** The *Conseil d'État* has the dual functions of drafting government laws and rules and hearing cases against government administration.

(f) ***Tribunal des Conflicts:*** If there is any conflict of jurisdiction between ordinary courts and the administrative court, it is decided by the *tribunal des conflicts.*

(g) ***Conseil d'État*:** It is the highest administrative court of the country.

(h) **Difference in Recruitment:** There is a critical difference between the system of recruitment and personnel management of the Council of State and the judicial branch. The members of the Council of State are selected from graduates of the École Nationale d'Administration, the elite, the state-run school designed to train the uppermost echelons of the civil service and from the ranks of experienced individuals already serving in the administration, either in the lower administrative courts or in the upper ranks of the civil service. In contrast, recruitment in the judiciary is made from law school graduates who receive professional training at the state-sponsored school for the judiciary.

(i) **Independence of administrative courts:** The administrative courts enjoy the same freedom from executive meddling as the courts.

(j) **Nature of Litigation:** The nature of litigation in the Council of State is considered different from that in ordinary courts. Traditionally, administrative litigation is understood to be primarily designed to guarantee the legality and propriety of administrative action, and ensure the correct working of the bureaucracy. Until recently, the purpose of promoting justice and safeguarding individual rights was considered secondary.

(k) **Separation of Public and Private Law:** In France, there is a divide between public and private law. In public law, the state administration is granted extraordinary privileges but is also subject to extensive duties designed to safeguard the rights and interests of citizens.

Procedural Aspect of French Administrative Law

The administrative law of France, and other related countries, is more focused on the substantive correctness of administrative decisions than on its procedural correctness. However, the procedural requirements for administrative action have been introduced since 1944, in France, while introducing the rights of defence (*droits de la defense*). However, these rights were limited, as they were applied only to those administrative actions that were made to impose sanctions. Moreover, these rights did not include the right to an oral hearing and the disclosure of documents.

However, the situation has changed since the 1970s. A number of French national laws guarantee individuals, in the context of an administrative decision, the right to receive a notice of the proposed decision, to examine the supporting documents, to respond in writing, and to receive a statement of reasons with the final decision.

Substantive Aspect of French Administrative Law

As far as the substantive aspect is considered, in France, administrative decisions can be overturned on the grounds of 'incompetence' or a 'violation of the law'. It is similar to the US principle of 'excess of jurisdiction' and the English principle of 'illegality'. These concepts have been discussed in detail in Chapter 6.

7.4.3 Administrative Law in Germany

In Germany, an alternative of judicial review has originated, which is different from that of France and England. In this system, a specialised branch of the judiciary is dedicated to hearing administrative law cases.[5] The judicial branch is composed of the Federal Constitutional Court and five discrete judicial hierarchies, one for civil and criminal law, one for labour disputes, one for tax disputes, one for social security disputes, and one for administrative law disputes. The last three judicial branches are responsible for handling administrative law cases. The judges that serve on the tax, social security, and administrative law courts have the same system of recruitment and training as their counterparts in other courts; they also enjoy the same kind of independence as enjoyed by other courts. The only difference is the degree of specialisation and familiarity that the members of these three branches acquire with administrative disputes.

This system of administrative law is closer to the common law model than the French model. In this system, government contracts and tort disputes are heard by civil courts and not by administrative courts. This system is widespread and adopted in countries such as Austria, Portugal, Sweden, Finland, the Czech Republic, Poland, Spain, Switzerland, Hungary, Slovenia, Romania, Estonia, and most of Latin America.

Rechtsstaat/Principle of the Legal State

The German administrative law has a concept similar to that of the English rule of law. It is known as the principle of the legal state/*Rechtsstaat*. This principle is followed in Continental Europe and is also understood as the parallel of the rule of law in Continental Europe. This principle will be discussed in the later part of this chapter.

Procedural Aspect of German Administrative Law

In Germany, administrative procedures for decision-making were made in the post-war period under the heavy influence of constitutional law and were eventually codified with the Federal Administrative Procedure Act of 1977. Thus, in Germany, administrative procedures are codified.

Substantive Aspect of German Administrative Law

As far as the substantive aspect is considered, in Germany, administrative law is thoroughly constitutionalised and fundamental rights are particularly pervasive; this pervasiveness is higher than that in common law countries such as England and US. The most conspicuous sign of this is probably the declaration, made in 1959 by the President of the Federal Administrative Court, that administrative law is "concretised constitutional law" (*konkretisiertes Verfassungsrecht*).[11] As a result, the German courts have developed a number of cross-cutting principles to limit administrative action to the benefit of individual liberties. Important among them are proportionality, equality, and legitimate expectations.

The principle of 'proportionality' suggests that any administrative action that interferes with individual rights must satisfy a proportionality test. For example, the German Federal Constitutional Court has held that the forfeiture of unemployment benefits for two weeks, in response to the recipient's failure to notify regularly the public employment office of his employment status, was disproportionate. The principle of 'equality' requires administrative action to be non-discriminatory on economic and other grounds. The principle of legitimate expectations limits the ability of public administration to reverse benefit-conferring determinations. As a result of this legal doctrine, the beneficiaries of public programmes involving agricultural subsidies, housing benefits, and other types of entitlements have a right to significant notice or compensation before the government may alter the terms of the programme or withdraw a benefit improperly granted.[12]

7.4.4 Administrative Law in India

The existence and application of administrative law in ancient India can be found in the concept of *dharma*. The king and other administrators used to follow dharma. Dharma can be said to be the ancient Indian equivalent of rule of law. Dharma is used to guide the administrators on their righteous, just, and moral duties toward the welfare of the citizens.

The modern system of administrative law in India started during the period of the East India Company with the Stage Carriage Act of 1861, under which the system of granting licenses was initiated. After this, a series of enactments, such as the Bombay Forts Trust Act, of 1879 and the Explosives Act, of 1884 were passed by the British executive to enhance the powers of the executive and increase its interaction with the citizens.

However, the modern concept of a welfare state in India emerged with the passing of the Indian Constitution in 1950 and the establishment of the Supreme Court of India. The philosophy of the welfare state envisaged in the Constitution ushered in new dimensions of growth in the social, economic, and political fields. A number of provisions have been made, since independence, to protect the citizens from the excesses of the administration.

In India, the Constitution is supreme and the rule of law is clearly established in it. Article 39 of the Constitution says that the ownership and control of material resources of the society should be so distributed as to best sub-serve the common good of the community and the economic distribution should not result in the concentration of wealth in the hands of a few individuals. This article protects the common citizens from the economic policies of the administration.

Similarly, Articles 32 and 226 empower the Supreme Court and high court, respectively, to issue extraordinary writs to protect the fundamental rights of the citizens. Moreover, administrative tribunals have been established in India to protect government employees from the wrong actions of the administration against them. Apart from this, the introduction of the concept of public interest litigation (PIL) has added a new dimension to Indian administrative law. All these concepts have been discussed in detail in Chapter 6.

7.4.5 Globalisation of Administrative Law

From the preceding discussions, it is clear that administrative law is profoundly shaped by distinct national experiences with state formation. However, today, the interdependence between nations and the rising power of international organisations has prompted several countries to adopt a common set of good governance reforms involving administrative procedures and the principles of judicial review. These good governance reforms are aimed at the welfare of the citizens and are, thus, a part of administrative law. Therefore, it can be said that the administrative laws of various nations are converging due to globalisation.

One good example of this convergence is the concept of transparency. Legislation on the right of access to government documents was first adopted in Sweden in 1766 and was immediately copied in Finland, which at the time was a Swedish colony. Since the 1990s, the United Nations, the Organisation of American States, and a number of other international organisations have urged their member countries to adopt freedom-of-information laws. As a result, in 2016, 115 nations adopted the freedom of information regime.[14]

Mind Map 7.1 Comparison of Administrative Law in Different Countries		
Common Law Countries (England and Others) • Disputes between citizens and administrators handled by ordinary courts • Countries—Australia, New Zealand, India, Ireland, US, Japan, South Korea, etc. • Important role played by Dicey. • Concept of Rule of Law o Rule against arbitraryness. o Equality before Law o Common Law Rights • Procedural Aspects o Administrative actions require equivalent judicial procedures. o Rules of natural justice in England and Procedural Due Process in US. o Present Status- administrative tribunals in Britain and 'formal adjudication' governed by Administrative Procedure Act. • Substantive Aspect o Three parts-on rule of law/ limits set by law; on individual rights and on policy rationality.	**Continental Law Countries (France and Others)** • Judicial review by ordinary courts considered as encroachment upon administrative powers. • Concept of *droit administratif* • Countries- France, Belgium, Netherlands, Luxembourg, Italy, Greece, Turkey, Lebanon, Egypt, Colombia, Morocco, Algeria and Senegal. • Specialised administrative courts under Conseil d'Etat to review administrative actions. • Members of administrative courts are experienced civil servants. • Procedural Aspect- Procedures introduced since 1944 and 1970s. • Substantive Aspect- Decisions cam be overturned on grounds of 'incompetence' or 'violation of law'.	**In Germany and related countries** • Closer to the common law model than to the French model. • 3 types of judicial courts are dedicated to administrative issues- (1) for tax disputes, (2) for social security disputes and (3) for administrative law disputes. • Judges in these courts have the same system of recruitment, training and independence as those of other courts. • Principle of the Legal State/ Rechtsstaat • Countries- Australia, Portugal, Sweden, Finland, Czech Republic, Poland, Spain, Switzerland, Hungary, Slovenia, Romania, Estonia and most Latin American countries. • Procedural Aspect- administrative procedures are highly codified. • Substantive Aspect—Fundamental rights are pervasive and number of cross-cutting principles developed to limit administrative action to the benefit of individual liberties. o Principles of 'proportionality', 'equality' and 'legitimate expectations'.

7.5 Rule of Law and *Rechtsstaat*

The expression 'rule of law' has been derived from the French phrase 'la principle de legality' i.e., a government based on the principles of law. It heralds the *supremacy of law* and is against the 'rule of man'. The rule makes even rulers subject to the principles of law.

7.5.1 Principles of Rule of Law According to Dicey

As explained by Dicey, the concept of rule of law has the following important factors:

(a) **The rule against arbitrariness:** This rule suggests that every action of an administrator shall have some basis in law or a rule made by a competent authority. The powers of administration shall not be exercised arbitrarily. Only the powers that have been authorised by the legislature shall be exercised. This is called the *operative part of the rule of law.* On the other hand, the *effective part of the rule of law* suggests that the Constitution controls all the powers of the administration. Administrative powers are controlled by the legislature, but the legislature itself is controlled by the people and the Constitution.

(b) **Equality before Law:** This is the second important part of the rule of law. It suggests that among equals, law should be equal and should be administered equally. Dicey has regarded this as 'equality before the law'. It means that no one should be made to suffer in body or goods except for a distinct breach of law. Furthermore, it means that all persons must be amendable to the ordinary jurisdiction of the court. It guides the administrators to exercise their powers without discriminating between persons. This principle of equality is against the French *droit administratif,* which provides special provisions and treatment for government officials while exercising their official power.

(c) **Common Law Rights:** According to Dicey, the Constitution of England is the consequence of the common law rights of the individuals and, hence, common law is the source of all the freedom of the people. Common law refers to the decisions given by the judiciary from time to time. This is the third part of the rule of law. If rights are based on a document such as the Constitution, they can be added, abrogated, or *denied by amending* the Constitution. However, in India, the Supreme Court regards the rule of law as the basic structure of the Constitution, which cannot be amended by amending the Constitution.

7.5.2 Peculiar Aspects of English Rule of Law (in contrast to Continental Rule of Law/*Rechtsstaat*)

The concept of rule of law in England has a very basic difference from that found in other countries of continental Europe. The concept of state is not found in the English concept of rule of law. On the contrary, in the continental European countries, the law is inextricably connected to the state, whether it is *Rechtsstaat* (German for the state of the law; law-governed state), *état de droit* (French), *statto diritto* (Italian), *estado de derecho* (Spanish), *panstwo prawa* (Polish), or *pravovoe gosudarstvo* (Russian).

This is because the concept of state is not a part of the English constitutional jurisprudence.[18] The English tradition has been pluralistic in its conceptions of the sources of law with multiple cumulative and competing authoritative sources, among them customs, court decisions, and statutes.[19] As described by Dicey also, common law (judicial decisions) is the source of all rights in England. Popular custom was seen as a primary source of law and was evidenced in the judgments of the courts in cases brought before them. This was the 'common law' and was preferred over the commands of the king in the seventeenth century.[20] The king, like his subjects, was subject to this 'common law'.

Thus, the notions that the rule of law draws upon sources other than legislative fiat, that the judiciary is a fundamental guardian of it, and that all, even the most powerful, are and should be subject to it, have roots in the common law tradition.[21]

A term similar to 'rule of law' was coined in Germany in the eighteenth century—*Rechtsstaat.* It was coined to capture a new phenomenon, the modern state with its monopoly of force. The term means 'principle of legal state' or 'rule by law'. The state is the subject of this concept and the source of legal power.

As discussed, the English rule of law suggests that general constitutional principles are the result of judicial decisions and not a result of a constitutional assembly.[22] This judge-centeredness is peculiar to English constitutional law because of the common law tradition. The principle of the legal state/ *Rechtsstaat* is, by contrast, more centred on the formal constitution and the formal statute.[23] It contains the requirement of a formal written constitution.[24] It also contains the doctrine of the necessity of the statute (*Vorbehalt des Gesetzes*) and the primacy of the statute (*Vorrang des Gesetzes*).[23] The doctrine of the necessity of the statute (Vorbehalt des Gesetzes) holds that every administrative act with negative consequences for human rights needs to be justified by a formal statute of a parliament. The doctrine of the primacy of the statute (*Vorrang des Gesetzes*) holds that every statute of a parliament is primary to all judgments and administrative acts. These doctrines are the consequences of a statute-centred legal system such as the German system and the French system, but not of a common law system such as the American and British systems.

7.5.2.1 Thin and Thick Aspects of the Rule of Law and *Rechtsstaat*

There are two aspects of the rule of law—'thin' or *formal* and 'thick' or *substantive*. The 'thin' aspect limits itself to formal properties of laws and legal institutions, which are purported to constitute the rule of law. On the other hand, the 'thick' aspect suggests substantive elements from a larger vision of a good society and polity—democratic, free-market, human rights respecting, and so on.

The *Rechtsstaat* has oscillated between this 'thin' and 'thick' definition in its 200 years of evolution. It was first theorised by German liberal constitutional and administrative theorists, prominent among them being Karl Rotteck, Karl Theodor Welcker, and Robert von Mohl, seeking to characterise a legal order in terms of the values it served (those values in their turn to be realised in and not against the state). In the late nineteenth century and early twentieth century, Rechtsstaat did not have any normative concerns and was strictly devoted to elaborating the formal components of a legal order. However, the post-Nazi Rechtsstaat returned to, and richly amplified, a normative characterisation based on the fundamental value of human dignity. This aspect of human dignity is one of the fundamental differences between the English rule of law and the German Rechtsstaat.

7.5.2.2 Anatomical and Teleological Aspects of Rule of Law and Rechtsstaat

The rule of law intends to curb arbitrary power and not to describe the type and structure of government. Whether power is in the hands of a single monarch, a community, or the whole body of people is immaterial. What matters is whether this power is with or without control.[20] Similarly, Rechtsstaat was also not concerned with the form of government in its earlier form. However, in the nineteenth century, it became a formalistic and anatomising concept, stressing the positively characterised features of a state.

On the teleological front, rule of law is concerned not only with certain rules and practices but also with the social contribution of law. It has much to do with what the law does rather than simply with what it has been declared to do.[21] To say that the rule of law exists in a society is to imply an accomplishment: an ideal to which law is taken to contribute has been approached.

7.5.2.3 Rule of Law and Rechtsstaat on Human Dignity

The English principle of the rule of law and the continental Rechtsstaat differ with respect to a very material difference, i.e., on the protection of human dignity. The English rule of law does not explicitly include the protection of human dignity as such, but only some of its main applications, namely, the prohibition of torture, slavery, and so on. Human dignity is neither found originally in common law nor in the American Declaration of Independence, including the Bill of Rights of the American Constitution. On the contrary, according to the continental principle of the legal state, human dignity is inviolable (*Die Würde des Menschen ist unantastbar*).

7.5.2.4 Common Aspects of Rule of Law and Rechtsstaat

The principle of the legal state/Rechtsstaat and the rule of law coincide with respect to their core aspects. According to the rule of law, no man is punishable or can be lawfully made to suffer in body or goods except for a distinct breach of law established in the ordinary legal manner before the ordinary courts of the land.[22] Similarly, the Rechtsstaat focuses on individual human rights, especially protection against arbitrary punishment. This was not the case in the nineteenth century when the Rechtsstaat was in the developing stage. However, this principle of human rights was developed in the Weimar Republic and especially after World War II.

One more common aspect of both principles is that the law is supreme. According to the principle of rule of law, no one is above the law, whatever his/her rank or condition; everyone is subject to the ordinary law of the realm and amenable to the jurisdiction of the ordinary tribunals. Similarly, Rechtsstaat suggests that nobody is above the law and that everybody is subject to ordinary laws.

A third aspect on which the rule of law and the principle of the legal state coincide is the principle of constitutionalism. Both the rule of law and the principle of legal state require that the most important decisions of the political community are made in the form of a legal constitution, which is superior to every other legal, political, and administrative act.[25]

Fourth, both the rule of law and Rechtsstaat require the laws to be accessible, well-published, consistent, clear, and definite. Fifth, both the rule of law and Rechtsstaat have emphasised the principle of separation of powers. In English history, the earlier executive and judiciary were separate arms of the polity with no presence of legislature. However, the legislative appeared later and the separation of the executive, legislature, and judiciary became a core element of the rule of law. On the other hand, the principle of separation of powers has been the initial core element of Rechtsstaat.

Sixth, both the rule of law and Rechtsstaat require an independent, accessible, fair, and effective judiciary. They both require a fair legal procedure, including freedom from political or other external influences on the judges, equal hearing of all parties, and so on.

7.5.3 Criticism of Dicey's Views on the Rule of Law

Dicey's views on the rule of law is subject to the following criticism:

(a) **Discretion is inevitable:** In his concept of rule of law, Dicey has opposed providing discretionary powers to the administration. According to him, discretionary powers create arbitrariness, which, in turn, poses a serious threat to individual freedom. However, providing discretion to administrative authorities is inevitable nowadays. Dicey's concept is considered outdated in this regard.

(b) **Separation of Discretionary and Arbitrary Powers:** Dicey failed to distinguish discretionary powers from arbitrary powers. Arbitrary powers are against the rule of law. Thus, discretionary powers need to be controlled by certain guidelines and principles. This control of discretionary administrative power is one of the main concerns of administrative law.

(c) **Special treatment to officials not recognised**: According to Dicey's concept of rule of law, every person should be subject to the ordinary law of the country and there shall not be special privileges for any person including the administrative authority. This proportion is not valid even in England, where several persons enjoy certain privileges and immunities. For example, judges enjoy immunities from suits in respect of acts done in the discharge of their official function. Moreover, foreign diplomats enjoy immunity before the Court.

(d) **Role of administrative courts not recognised:** Dicey said that there shall be no separate laws and courts for the trial of government servants. He criticised the system of French *droit administratif*, in which disputes between the citizens and administration are decided by administrative courts. However, today various countries, including India, have recognised the importance of the functioning of administrative courts.

(e) **Definition peculiar to England:** Dicey has said that the Constitution is the result of judicial decisions determining the rights of private persons in particular cases brought before the courts. This conception is peculiar to the situation of Great Britain and is not valid in several countries, including India.

Despite the above-mentioned shortcomings, Dicey is appreciated for drawing the attention of various scholars toward controlling the discretionary powers of the administration. The rule of law established by him requires that every action of the administration must be backed by law or must have been done in accordance with the law.

7.5.4 General Principles of Rule of Law

As seen in the preceding section, Dicey's conception of rule of law is peculiar to the historical situation of England. However, the concept is widely accepted in the majority of democracies across the world. Thus, it is important to understand the general principles of rule of law. They are as described below:[4]

(a) Law is supreme, and above everything and everyone. Nobody is above law.

(b) Every action should be in accordance with the law and not based on the whims and fancies of any person.

(c) No person should be made to suffer except for a distinct breach of law.

(d) The rule of law requires the complete absence of the use of arbitrary powers.

(e) The rule of law requires equality before the law and equal protection of the law.

(f) It requires discretionary powers to be exercised within reasonable limits set by law.

(g) There shall be adequate safeguards against the abuse of administrative power.

(h) The judiciary shall be independent and impartial.

(i) The judicial procedure shall be free, fast, and fair.

7.6 Delegated Legislation

Delegated legislation is one of the most significant aspects of administrative law today. It denotes the legislative power of administration. Delegated legislation means the power of the executive to make legislation or supplement the legislation made by the legislature.

7.6.1 Rising Importance of Delegated Legislation

The importance of delegated legislation has increased today because of the following reasons:

(a) **Emergency Situations:** In certain emergency situations, the parliament may not be able to provide speedy and appropriate legislation. This requires administrative agencies to take timely legislative action to supplement the legislature's work.

(b) **Increase in Workload:** The workload of the parliament has increased and much of its time is devoted to political, policy, and foreign affair matters. It gets left with very less time for considering complicated and technical matters. Thus, the executive agencies need to support the parliament in legislating on such technical issues.

(c) **Technical Matters requiring Expert Action:** The technical nature of legislative work has increased due to the increased work of the legislature in the welfare state. Such technical nature of work requires the intervention of experts. In such cases it is inevitable that the power to deal with such matters is given to the appropriate administrative agencies, to be exercised according to the requirements of the subject matter.

(d) **Removal of Difficulty Clause:** When the legislation is prepared, the parliament is unable to foresee the difficulties that will be encountered during its implementation. Therefore, there is a 'removal of difficulty clause', which empowers the administration to remove such difficulties by exercising the powers of making rules and regulations underthe legislation.

(e) **Flexibility in Legislation:** The powers of delegated legislation are given to the executive in order to bring flexibility into the legislation. The rules and regulations made under the legislation can be changed easily by the executive on the basis of the feedback received. Such flexibility cannot be expected from the parliament.

7.6.2 Scope of Delegated Legislation

Delegated legislation means legislation by an executive authority, which has been given delegated power from the legislature to legislate on certain matters. However, delegated legislation takes place only within the proper laid down limitations. The legislature can delegate only its non-essential legislative functions to the executive.

There is a marked difference between the essential and non-essential legislative functions of the executive. The essential legislative functions consist of making law and formulating legislative policy. The task of filling in the details while implementing this legislative policy can be delegated to the executive. The task of designing the legislative policy cannot be delegated to the executive.

In order to avoid the dangers of delegated legislation, the scope of delegation is strictly circumscribed by the legislature by providing for adequate safeguards, controls, and appeals against executive orders and decisions. Such safeguards will be discussed later in the chapter.

The power exercised under delegated legislation in aid of the legislative policy cannot:

(i) Travel beyond the legislative policy

(ii) Run counter to it

(iii) Certainly change the essential features, the identity, structure, or the policy of the act

7.6.3 Types of Delegated Legislation in India

In India, the following types of delegated legislations exist:

(a) **Skeleton Delegation:** In such type of legislative delegation, legislature prepares the broad statute in which broad principles are set out to empower the executive authority to make rules for carrying out the purpose of the act. Mines and Minerals (Regulation and Development) Act, 1948 is an example of such legislation in which the Ministry of Mines prepares various rules and regulations from time to time.

(b) **Machinery Type Delegation:** In this type of delegation, the concerned executive authority is given machinery powers to prescribe:

(i) The kind of forms
(ii) The method of publication
(iii) The manner of making returns
(iv) Such other administrative details

7.6.4 Bye-laws

Bye-laws are the local laws, rules, and regulations that are designed by a local public body, municipality, Panchayati raj institution, the public body concerned with the government, public corporation, or by a society formed for commercial or other purposes. Bye-laws are framed by these bodies to carry out their administration effectively. For example, an urban municipal corporation may place certain restrictions on the construction of buildings, in its jurisdictional area, in order to clear certain areas as open spaces around the buildings. Such restrictions can be considered as bye-laws designed by that municipal corporation. Such bye-laws may help in the disciplined and systematic growth of buildings and towns and prevent haphazard development in the city. Such restrictions can be designed by the local authority only, and the state legislative assembly or the national parliament is not in a position to design such minute rules and regulations.

However, there are certain restrictions on the scope of these bye-laws. They are as follows:

(a) Bye-laws should be made and published in the manner specified by their authorising act.
(b) They should not be repugnant to the law of the land.
(c) They should not be repugnant to the act under which they are framed.
(d) They should not be uncertain.
(e) They should not be unreasonable.

7.6.5 Control over Delegated Legislation

The power of delegated legislation can be abused by the executive. Thus, proper precautions are required to be taken to prevent such abuse. In India, the control over delegated legislation is of the following three types:

(a) Procedural control
(b) Parliamentary control
(c) Judicial control

These three controls over delegated legislation is discussed in the following sections.

7.6.5.1 Procedural Control over Delegated Legislation

Every executive authority needs to follow certain procedures while making any delegated legislation. These procedures are described below:

(a) **Prior Consultation with Citizens:** The executive authority, before making any delegated legislation, needs to consult the affected citizens. This prior consultation is necessary for safeguarding citizens from the potential misuse of the delegated legislation. Certain acts provide for the consultation of interested bodies and advisory committees before the formulation of rules and regulations under them. Prior consultation with interested parties ensures their participation so as to avoid various possible hardships. It also helps the administration in understanding the problems and conditions of the field in which delegated legislation is contemplated.

(b) **Prior Publicity of Rules and Regulations:** The drafted rules and regulations are widely publicised and circulated among the affected parties to enable them to make their representation for any consideration in them.

(c) **Publication of Delegated Legislation:** The delegated legislation needs to be publicised widely so that the law may be ascertained with reasonable certainty by the affected persons. The proposed rules and regulations should not come as a surprise and should not consequently bring hardships.

7.6.5.2 Parliamentary Control over Delegated Legislation

Parliamentary control over delegated legislation takes place in India through the following mechanisms:

(a) **Committee on Subordinate Legislation:** A committee on subordinate legislation is set up under the Rule of Procedure and Conduct of Business of the House of the People (Lok Sabha). Presided over by a member of the Opposition, the committee has the following tasks:

- It scrutinises the statutory rules, regulations, orders, bye-laws, and so on made by any making authority.
- It reports to the House whether the delegated power is being properly exercised within the limits of the delegated authority, within the limits of the Constitution or any act of parliament.
- It examines whether the subordinate legislation is in accord with the general objects of the Constitution or the act pursuant to which it is made.
- It examines whether it contains matter that can be dealt more properly within an act of the parliament.
- It examines whether it contains the imposition of any tax.
- It examines whether it, directly or indirectly, ousts the jurisdiction of the courts of law.
- It examines whether the delegated legislation gives retrospective effect to any of the provisions in respect of which the Constitution or the act does not expressly confer any such power.
- It examines whether the delegated legislation is constitutional and valid.
- It examines whether the subordinate legislation includes expenditure from the Consolidated Fund of India or the Public Revenues.
- It examines whether the form or purpose of the legislation requires any elucidation for any reason.
- It examines whether the legislation appears to make some unusual or unexpected use of the powers conferred by the Constitution or the act pursuant to which it is made.
- It examines whether there appears to have been an unjustifiable delay in the publication of the delegated legislation or in its laying before the parliament.

(b) **Laying rules and regulations on the Table of the Parliament:** The Committee on Subordinate Legislation has recommended that the rules and regulations made by any executive authority shall be laid down in the parliament for a total period of 30 days before the date of their final publication. However, if it is not deemed expedient to lay any rule before the date of publication, such rule shall be laid in the parliament as soon as possible after publication. Such a rule shall be accompanied by an 'explanatory note' explaining why it was not deemed expedient to be laid down before the date of publication. When such delegated legislation is laid down in the parliament, the members have the chance to modify or repeal the enactment under which obnoxious rules and orders, if any, are made. Moreover, they can also revoke the rules and orders made by the executive authority.

(c) **Memoranda of Delegated Legislation:** According to the recommendation of the Committee on Subordinate Legislation, each act shall be accompanied with a Memoranda of Delegated Legislation in which the full purpose and effect of the delegation of power to the subordinate authorities is mentioned. Second, the points that are to be covered by the delegated legislation are mentioned in it. Third, the particulars of the subordinate authorities or the persons who are to exercise the delegated powers are mentioned in it. Fourth, the manner in which such power has to be exercised is mentioned in the memoranda.

(d) **Debates and Discussions:** Any delegated legislation may be debated in the parliament during the normal course or when special motions are introduced on them. Such debates may lead to their acceptance or revocation.

7.6.5.3 Judicial Control over Delegated Legislation

Delegated legislation can be judicially controlled in the following manner:

(a) **Doctrine of Ultra Vires:** The doctrine of ultra vires is the chief instrument in the hands of the judiciary to control delegated legislation. This doctrine is applied with regard to procedural and substantive defects in delegated legislation. They are described in the following.

- **Procedural Defects:** As discussed before, the acts allowing delegated legislation prescribe for certain procedures to be followed while making rules, regulations, and other subordinate legislations. If these formal procedures are mandatory in nature and are disregarded by the said authorities, then the rules etc. so made by these authorities would be turned down by the Judiciary. In short, subordinate legislation in contravention of mandatory procedural requirements would be invalidated by the court as being ultra vires the parent statute.
- **Substantive Defects:** In the case of delegated legislation, a court can inquire whether it is made within the limits laid down by the parent legislation. If a piece of delegated legislation were found to be beyond such limits, the court would declare it to be ultra vires and hence invalid. Moreover, no delegated legislation can be allowed to be inconsistent with the fundamental rights and other important provisions of the Constitution.

(b) **Delegation beyond Permissible Limits:** A legislature cannot delegate the power of legislating on its essential functions or preparing the basic legislative policy. The primary duty of law-making has to be discharged by the legislature itself, but delegation may be resorted to as a subsidiary or ancillary measure. The legislature must declare the legal policy and the legal principles that are to control and guide the actions of the authority on which the power of subordinate legislation is delegated. If the legislature delegates excessively, the delegated legislation thus prepared by the executive authority can be turned down by the judiciary. Excessive delegation can be regarded as the one in which:

- The legislature has not laid down any policy at all.
- The legislature has declared its policy in vague and general terms.
- The legislature has not set down any standard for the guidance of the executive.
- The legislature has conferred arbitrary powers to the executive authority to change or modify the policy laid down by it.

7.7 Administrative Tribunals in India

Administrative tribunals are agencies created under specific enactments for administrative adjudication. The judicial courts are heavily preoccupied with long pending and backlog cases and are, thus, not able to offer a speedy remedy to the people in their disputes with the government. Therefore, the need for administrative tribunals is felt in today's time. These tribunals have the following characteristics:

(a) They are created under a statute passed by the legislature.
(b) They are vested with the judicial power of the State and thereby perform quasi-judicial functions as distinguished from pure administrative functions.
(c) They are required to act judicially and follow the principles of natural justice.
(d) They have some of the trappings of a court and are required to act in an open, fair, and impartial manner.
(e) They are not bound by the strict rules of procedure and evidence prescribed by the civil procedure code.

7.7.1 Tribunal System in India

In India, the function of dispensing justice is entrusted to regularly established courts on the pattern of the common law system (the pattern followed in England and its earlier colonies). The history of tribunals in India dates back to 1941, when the first tribunal was set up in the form of the Income Tax Appellate Tribunal. However, a major push to the tribunal system was brought about by the Constitution (42nd Amendment) Act, 1976, in which Articles 323A and 323B were introduced into the Constitution of India. Under these articles, administrative tribunals are intended to be set up by the parliament and state legislatures.

Article 323A provides for the setting up of administrative tribunals by parliamentary law for determining disputes pertaining to the conditions of service of government servants. It also brings within its ambit employees of any local or other authorities within the territory of India or under the control of the Government of India or a corporation owned or controlled by the government. Further, it authorises the establishment of separate administrative tribunals for each state or a joint administrative tribunal for two or more states.

Similarly, Article 323B provides for setting up of administrative tribunals for adjudication of disputes in matters such as taxation; foreign exchange; industrial and labour disputes; land reforms; the ceiling on urban property; elections to parliament and state legislatures; production, procurement, and distribution of food stuffs; and rent and tenancy issues.

Apart from these Articles, tribunals have been set up under specific statutes to adjudicate upon the various matters as provided in them.

7.7.2 Administrative Tribunals Act, 1985

The various provisions of Article 323A of the Constitution were intended to be implemented by passing the Administrative Tribunals Act in 1985. In its original form, the Act intended to take away the writ jurisdiction of the high court in matters concerned with the administrative tribunals. The Act was challenged in various cases in the Supreme Court. However, the Supreme Court upheld the constitutional validity of Article 323A as well as the Administrative Tribunals Act. It stated that the Constitution permits the parliament to abrogate the jurisdiction of the high courts under Articles 226 and 227, provided the same happens to be exercised effectively and efficiently by a closely comparable institution or body. It suggested that the tribunals need to be a real substitute for high courts, not only in form (*dejure*) but also in content (*defacto*).

Under the Administrative Tribunals Act, a tribunal means a central administrative tribunal, a state administrative tribunal, or a joint administrative tribunal, as defined in Section 3(e) of the Act. The Act vests in the administrative tribunals all the powers of the ordinary civil courts as well as high courts pertaining to service matters. However, the armed forces of the Union are excluded from their jurisdiction.

As the main aim of the administrative tribunals is expeditious disposal of cases, they are not unencumbered with the technicalities of the Civil Procedure Code, 1908 and the Indian Evidence Act, 1872. However, the tribunals have to follow certain procedures, including the principles of natural justice, which cannot be set aside for the sake of expediency. They are not bound by law to observe all the technicalities, complexities, refinements, discriminations, and restrictions that are applicable to the courts of record in conducting trials, but at the same time, they are required to look at all matters from the standpoint of substance as well as form and be certain that the hearing is conducted and the matter is disposed of with fairness, honesty, and impartiality.[15]

7.7.3 Central Administrative Tribunal

The Central Administrative Tribunal (CAT) has been established under Article 323A of the Constitution for adjudication of disputes and complaints with respect to the recruitment and conditions of service of persons appointed to public services and posts in connection with the affairs of the Union or other authorities under the control of the government. The Tribunal presently has 17 benches all across India.

The CAT is headed by a retired chief justice of a high court or the Supreme Court. Half of its strength consists of judicial members and the other half consists of administrative members. Judicial members are required for maintaining the freedom and values of an independent judiciary. Administrative members are required to supply the Tribunal with adequate expertise to dispose of technical and administrative matters. The conditions of service of the chairman and members are the same as those applicable to a high court judge.

7.7.4 Administrative Tribunals in India

At present, the following administrative tribunals have been set up in India under their respective statutes:

(i) Appellate Tribunal for Electricity (ATE)
(ii) Armed Forces Tribunal
(iii) Authority for Advance Rulings
(iv) Central Electricity Regulatory Commission (CERC)
(v) Central Administrative Tribunal
(vi) Company Law Board
(vii) Competition Commission of India (CCI)
(viii) Competition Appellate Tribunal (CAT)
(ix) Copyright Board
(x) Customs Excise and Service Tax Appellate Tribunal
(xi) Cyber Appellate Tribunal
(xii) Employees Provident Fund Appellate Tribunal
(xiii) Income Tax Appellate Tribunal
(xiv) Insurance Regulatory and Development Authority (IRDA)

(xv) Intellectual Property Appellate Board
(xvi) National Green Tribunal
(xvii) Securities and Exchange Board of India (SEBI)
(xviii) Telecom Disputes Settlement & Appellate Tribunal (TDSAT)
(xix) Telecom Regulatory Authority of India (TRAI)

7.7.5 Judicial Review and Administrative Tribunals

The Administrative Tribunals Act and Article 323A of the Constitution were challenged in various cases in the Supreme Court. However, the Supreme Court upheld the constitutional validity of Article 323A as well as the Act in the *SP Sampath Kumar case*. It stated that the Constitution permits the parliament to abrogate the jurisdiction of the high courts under Articles 226 and 227, provided the same happens to be exercised effectively and efficiently by a closely comparable institution or body. It suggested that the tribunals need to be the real substitute for the high courts not only in form (*dejure*) but also in content (*defacto*). It was also ruled that barring Article 226/227 does not totally bar the provision of judicial review, as tribunals can be capable of reviewing the actions of administrative authorities.

However, in *RK Jain* v. *Union of India*, the Supreme Court expressed it anguish over the ineffectiveness of administrative tribunals in exercising the high power of judicial review, and it emphasised on the need to take remedial steps to make the tribunals capable of dispensing effective, inexpensive, and satisfactory justice.[16] Moreover, it held that the tribunals are not effective substitutes of high courts with respect to their powers under Article 226/227 of the Constitution. The Supreme Court also held the power of the high courts and Supreme Court to review the judgments of the administrative tribunals in case they assume wrong jurisdiction, proceed on erroneous assumptions of facts or law, or make a malicious action in law or fact. Thus, the judgment of the Supreme Court in this case was contrary to its own decision in the *SP Sampath Kumar* case.

In the *L Chandra Kumar case*,[17] it was examined whether the tribunals, constituted under Articles 323A and 323B of the Constitution, can act as effective substitutes of the high courts vis-à-vis the power of judicial review. The Supreme Court held that the power of judicial review of the High Courts and the Supreme Court cannot be ousted or excluded "ordinarily." The use of the word 'ordinarily' gives an impression that in exceptional cases or special circumstances ousting or excluding the jurisdiction of these courts may be justified.

It was also held in this case that the tribunals shall perform a "supplemental as opposed to a substitutional role." They cannot act as substitutes for high courts and Supreme Courts in the case of administrative matters. The decisions of the tribunals, created under Articles 323A and 323B of the Constitution of India, shall be subject to scrutiny before a division bench of the high court within whose jurisdiction the concerned tribunal is located.

7.7.6 Deficiencies of Administrative Tribunals in India (with special reference to CAT)

After reviewing the working of administrative tribunals in India, the following deficiencies were found in their functioning:

(a) **Pendency of Cases:** It was found that administrative tribunals, especially CAT and SATs, also suffer from high pendency of cases similar to regular courts. The avowed aim of providing speedy justice is affected by this delay in the disposal of cases. The pendency of cases can be reduced by increasing the strength of the various benches and cutting down unnecessary adjournments on one ground or another.

(b) **Location of Benches:** The location of the various benches of CAT is a matter of concern. It is experienced that the 17 benches are unable to meet the requirements of the government servants in far-flung areas. Moreover, the provision of sitting in circuits has not been very effective. This has resulted in hardships and exorbitant costs incurred by the litigants. The litigant officials could rather easily approach the subordinate courts in far-flung areas instead of approaching the administrative tribunals.

7.7.7 Measures to Improve Efficiency of Administrative Tribunals

According to studies, the following measures have been suggested to improve the functioning of administrative tribunals:

(a) **Speedy Disposal:** The rules framed under the Administrative Tribunals Act should be amended for ensuring speedy disposal of cases by the tribunals, apart from enlarging the strength of the benches to cope with the increase in litigation.

(b) **Circuit Courts:** The circuit courts of CAT should be held at frequent intervals in different locations so as to ensure speedy disposal in far-flung areas.

(c) **Equality with Courts:** Necessary amendments in the Act are also called for to provide equality of status to members of the tribunal in all aspects with that of high court judges. Such amendments will attract better talent to administrative tribunals and will improve their efficiency also.

SUMMARY

This chapter dealt with the meaning, nature, and scope of administrative law. We have learned how administrative law has grown in different regions of the world and how it has been affected by various respective national histories. In a comparative analysis, we have learnt about the administrative law of common law countries, continental countries, and that followed in Germany and related countries. Moreover, we have learnt about the views of scholars such as Dicey on administrative law and the rule of law. We have also learned how the administrative law of different countries is converging in the era of globalisation. Moving forward, we have learned the meaning of delegated legislation and bye-laws. An important point of learning was procedural, legislative, and judicial control over delegated legislation. In the last leg of the chapter, we learnt about administrative tribunals and their evolution in India. We learned about constitutional provisions such as Articles 323A and 323B as well as about the Administrative Tribunals Act of 1985. Moreover, we have learnt about the various administrative tribunals constituted in India, with special emphasis on the Central Administrative Tribunal (CAT). We have also learned about the present status of judicial review with respect to the functioning of administrative tribunals. Finally, we learnt about the deficiencies in the functioning of administrative tribunals in India and measures for improving their functioning.

Practice Questions

1. The goal of administrative law is to ensure that the individual and the state are placed on a plane of equality before the Bar of Justice. Comment.
2. What are the reasons for the growth of administrative law?
3. "The nature of administrative law in different countries is defined by the national experience and history of those countries." Explain with the examples of England, France, and Germany.
4. Compare and contrast the administrative law of common law countries and continental administrative law.
5. Explain the views of Dicey on administrative law and the various criticisms levelled against him.
6. Discuss the various provisions of the rule of law in Indian polity.
7. How is the administrative law of different countries converging in the era of globalisation?
8. Explain the nature of various types of control over delegated legislation in India.
9. Are the decisions of administrative tribunals subjected to review by high courts? Explain the present status of judicial review with respect to matters falling in the domain of administrative tribunals.

CHAPTER 8

Comparative Public Administration

After reading this chapter, you will learn the following:

- Need for and evolution of comparative public administration (CPA)
- Organisational initiatives for CPA
- Theoretical assumptions of CPA
- The nature of studies in CPA
- About the confusion and novelty in CPA and the various models of CPA
- The bureaucratic systems approach in CPA
- The decision-making approach in CPA
- The general systems approach in CPA
- Riggs's ideas on CPA and the ecological approach in CPA, including the structural-functional approach, agrarian-industrial approach, fused-prismatic-diffracted approach, and exogenous and endogenous changes in a prismatic society
- About Riggs's and Weber's contribution to CPA
- The comparison of administration in different countries including a comparison of their political system/Constitution, executives, policymaking, departmental system, administrative structure, relationship between civil servant and political executive, political rights of civil servants, and recruitment and training in different countries
- The current status of CPA

8.1 Introduction to Comparative Public Administration (CPA)

Comparative public administration (CPA) is a subfield of the discipline of public administration. Cross-cultural studies of administration place the discipline of public administration on a firm footing, supply sufficient material for providing satisfactory solutions to administrative issues, and establish the discipline on the strong support of scientific values. As Robert Dahl has mentioned, "the comparative public administration specialist is first and foremost a scholar who is in pursuit of greater knowledge and understanding. In order to establish the science of public administration, it is necessary to be comparative." The discipline of public administration is able to provide satisfactory solutions to the administrative issues of different cultures only with the help of rationality and scientific investigation.[2]

Unlike comparative public administration, traditional public administration is non-comparative. The traditional literature is largely descriptive rather than analytical, explanatory, and problem-oriented. It is non-comparative because it does not consist of cross-temporal and cross-cultural analysis. On the other hand, comparative public administration is more scientific, critical, analytical, and cross-cultural.

Comparative public administration deals with administrative organisations or systems pertaining to different cultures and settings whose similar or dissimilar features or characteristics are studied and compared in order to determine the 'causes' or 'reasons' for the efficient or effective performance or behaviour of administrators, civil servants, or bureaucrats.[3] While comparing different administrations, the ecological perspective is adopted; the various social, economic, political, cultural, and other factors form a part of the ecology of administration.

8.2 Need for Comparison in Public Administration

Comparison is essential in public administration, as it is important for our understanding of public administration.[4] In any discipline, comparison is important for the process of theory building and for the interchange of ideas among human beings. As W.A. Welsh has mentioned, "comparison is the basis of concept formation."

Moreover, in any discipline, comparison helps in classification. If we want to study administration, we need to first understand the characteristics and basis for classifying them. This classification helps in comparing them and in determining the similarities and differences among them. Once the concepts and categories of classification are established, they are put in a particular theoretical framework for use in research.

Furthermore, the comparison is important for induction in public administration. Here, induction means the process of deriving general statements of relationships among specific administrative phenomena within various settings. Comparison is crucial because the validity/applicability of a deduced fact for testing a general proposition depends substantially on the degree of comparability between the concepts of a general statement and those of a specific statement.

8.3 Evolution of Comparative Public Administration

The evolution of comparative public administration can be understood to have taken place in the following stages:

1. **Introduction by Wilson:** Woodrow Wilson is known to have introduced the concept of comparison in the field of public administration. He was the first scholar to compare the administration of America with that of the United Kingdom and demonstrate that the USA lacked unified authority in several fields of administration. He compared the administration of Europe and America on the basis of the presence of democratic values.
2. **Comparative Study before World War II:** Before World War II, the literature on comparative administration emphasised the formal aspects of various countries, such as their

foreign relations, political parties, elections, pressure groups, constitutions, and important institutions. It also focused on certain aspects of foreign governments, such as their central administrative machinery, the extent of decentraliation in them, the structure of civil services, and financial administration. The majority of these studies were concentrated on the institutional aspects of democratic governments only. They were culture bound, limiting themselves to western nations and institutions.

3. **Comparative Study during Scientific Management Era:** The scientific management theories had certain comparative aspects in them. However, the methods of comparison were confined to individual jobs. They measured and compared people holding similar positions. However, such studies were only restricted to large-scale industrial organisations in the USA.
4. **Impetus after World War II:** The comparative administration studies received an impetus after World War II. Various post-war events have changed the state of comparative literature drastically. After the war, there were policy-oriented as well as intellectually oriented catalysts for the progress of comparative public administration.
    - **Policy-oriented Catalysts:** The policy-oriented catalysts include policy concerns such as tackling the governmental problems of third-world countries, interest in the economic recovery of Europe, and an increase in American political and economic commitments abroad.
    - **Intellectually Oriented Catalysts:** Post World War II, various scholars showed interest in supporting international administrative reforms across the globe. Various universities and private foundations showed their active support for these reforms. It was recognised those international reforms required a complete understanding of the cultural context of the administrative institutions and behaviour in foreign countries. Thus, there developed a conscious ecological perspective among the students of public administration working in various developing countries. This emphasis on comparison was also supported by parallel growth in other disciplines such as comparative sociology and anthropology.
5. **Focus on Bureaucracies:** Since the 1980s, comparison in public administration has been centred on public bureaucracies. It is centred on issues such as power of bureaucrats over the government, influence of bureaucrats on political decisions, the quality of public services in different countries, and so on. Such studies were influenced by the work of Max Weber on comparative bureaucracy. Such a comparison of bureaucracies will be discussed while discussing the administrative systems of various countries.
6. **Impact of Behaviouralism on CPA:** Behaviouralism has contributed to growing interest in CPA. Behavioural research has certain features such as being descriptive, analytical, empirical (based on rigorous methods such as field observation, controlled experiments, and laboratory studies), and having a concern for quantification and formal theory construction. It has motivated greater scientific research and systematic theory construction in public administration. Testing these theories in cross-cultural contexts has necessitated the growth of comparative public administration.
7. **Impact of Comparative Politics Movement:** After World War II, there has been interest in the study of comparative politics. The first institutional effort in this direction was the Summer Seminar on Comparative Politics sponsored by the Social Science Research Council.[6] It provided impetus towards the study of comparative public administration

because of the close affinity between comparative politics and CPA. As noted by Robert Holt, the boundary between the political system and the administrative system is the boundary between an analytically defined macrosystem and an analytically defined microsystem.[7] Moreover, comparative politics has led to the treatment of bureaucracy as a subsystem of the political system. This treatment of bureaucracy has led to the study of interactions between a political system and its bureaucracy in cross-cultural settings. On this, Alfred Diamant noted that the students of CPA find in comparative politics "a considerable body of substantive materials directly related to their own concerns, as well as an increasingly sophisticated and self-conscious effort at methodological clarifications."[8]

8. **Organisational Initiatives for CPA:** Various organisational initiatives were taken for CPA, such as the Conference on Comparative Public Administration, Sayre-Kaufmann Outline, and the Comparative Administrative Group. These initiatives will be discussed in the following section.
9. **CPA Movement in Foreign Countries:** USA was the epicentre for the growth of CPA. However, there were other independent international efforts for CPA also. In June 1953, the International Political Science Association sponsored a panel on CPA in Paris. Apart from this, the International Institute on Administrative Sciences conducted studies on administrative experiences in various European countries. Moreover, various Asian and Latin American countries have established institutions of public administration conducting research on CPA.

8.4 Organisational Initiatives for CPA

The following organisational initiatives have been undertaken for the growth of CPA:

(a) **Conference on Comparative Administration:** The first organisational effort for the study of comparative administration was when the Conference on Comparative Administration was organised at Princeton by the Public Administration Clearing House in 1952. The Conference appointed a subcommittee on CPA under the committee on public administration to design the criteria of relevance and methods of field studies in foreign countries.

(b) **Sayre-Kaufman Outline:** In the subcommittee on CPA, Wallace Sayre and Herbert Kaufman prepared the Sayre-Kaufman outline for comparative administration research.[9] The outline gave a three-point strategy for comparison of administrative systems, emphasising:

- the organisation of the administrative system
- the control of the administrative system
- securing control and compliance by the administrative hierarchy

The outline assumed that administrative hierarchical relationships are common in all societies. Thus, it largely focused on western experiences.

(c) **Comparative Administration Group:** The Comparative Administration Group (CAG) was set up in 1963 under the American Society of Public Administration (ASPA). Fred Riggs was its chairman from its inception till the end of 1970. The initial focus of the CAG was on encouraging research, teaching, and public-policy formulation in the area of development administration. It emphasised the administrative problems of developing countries viewed in the context of their social, cultural, political, and economic environments. The group sponsored comparative research in various parts of the globe such as Asia, Latin America, and Europe. It also started a *Journal of Comparative Administration* in 1969. Moreover, the CAG has supported a large number of scholars in conducting research in comparative public administration. It is credited for widening the horizons of public administration, opening its doors to all kinds of social scientists, making its scope more systemic by studying different administrative systems in their ecological settings and stimulating interest in the problems of development administration.

8.5 Theoretical Assumptions of CPA

Robert Jackson[10] has outlined certain theoretical assumptions in the field of comparative public administration. They are described in the following.

(a) CPA tries to achieve a science of public administration. It asserts that there are patterns of administrative behaviour that are susceptible to rigorous systematic analysis and capable of being drawn together into a body of theory.

(b) The science of public administration is possible only by studying administrative patterns in cross-cultural and cross-national contexts.

(c) The empirical findings of such cross-cultural studies are required to be subjected to rigorous systematic comparative analysis.

(d) Such a comparative analysis would help in deriving a general hypothesis of administration applicable to different administrative contexts. A such hypothesis can be integrated into a general theory of public administration.

8.6 Nature of Studies in CPA

Research in comparative public administration is understood as being empirical, nomothetic, and ecological.[12] Here, 'empirical' means studies that are based on real-life experimentation, observations, and their results. 'Nomothetic' is understood as any approach primarily concerned with the formulation of laws and general propositions. It is opposed to the 'ideographic' approach, which is concerned with unique administrative situations, specific historical accounts, a single country, or single culture.[17] Ecological approaches are those that study a subject with respect to its social, political, cultural, economic, and other environmental factors. The empirical, nomothetic, and ecological orientation of CPA provides the following purposes to the subject:

(a) The first purpose of CPA is to learn the distinctive features of a particular system or cluster of systems.

(b) The second purpose is to explain the cross-cultural and cross-national differences in different administrative and bureaucratic systems.

(c) The third purpose is to examine the causes for the success or failure of particular administrative features in their particular ecological settings.

(d) The fourth purpose is to devise strategies for administrative reforms for different administrative systems.

8.7 CPA in a State of Confusion and Novelty

Thomas Kuhn has described comparative public administration (CPA) to be in a *pre-paradigmatic* stage.[12] The field is in a state of confusion and novelty.[13] There is a lot of diversity in the CPA literature. A pre-paradigmatic stage is a stage where there exist a number of competing views languages, and logics, and there is no common research methodology and consensus regarding common field of inquiry.[14] In this state, the study of CPA offers a fertile ground for *poly paradigmatic* research. Various paradigms of CPA are studied and efforts are made to develop systematic coherence among them.

Among these various paradigms, Heady has classified the following four traditions of research in CPA:[15]

(a) **Modified Traditional Approach:** The literature in this approach shows continuity with the earlier public administration literature, which had a parochial character. It basically involves a descriptive comparison of administration in western countries with particular reference to their administrative organisations and civil service systems.

(b) **Developmental Approach:** The developmental approach of CPA is concerned with th problems of public administration in the context of rapid socio-economic and political change in developing countries. It emphasise improving the capabilities of administrativ systems to direct socio-economic progress.

(c) **General System Model Approach:** The general system model approach is related to the study of different administrative systems within the context of their respective social environment. Its focus is on the study of the administrative system with respect to the whol society.

(d) **Middle Range Theory Approach:** The middle range theory approach is not concerned with the whole administrative system. Rather it is concerned only with certain components or characteristics of an administrative system.

Similarly, Henderson has classified the following three traditions of studies in CPA:[16]

(a) **Bureaucratic Systems Approach:** The bureaucratic systems approach is concerned with studying certain specific aspects of different bureaucratic systems. It is similar to Heady's middle range theory approach.

(b) **Input-Output Approach:** The input-output approach is similar to Heady's general system model approach.

(c) **Component Approach:** The component approach described by Henderson consists of th remaining other types of partial approaches dealing with administrative procedures, control responsibility, and informal behaviour in administrative systems.

8.8 Bureaucratic Systems Approach in CPA

The bureaucratic systems approach is best depicted in Max Weber's ideal-type construct of bureaucracy. He has compared authority systems (or administrative systems with different kinds of authority) in three historical and sociological contexts—(a) traditional authority, (b) charismatic authority, and (c) legal-rational authority. It has already been discussed in Chapter 3.

Weber's ideal-type construct is regarded as the single most influential work in the literature on comparative public administration (CPA).[18] While providing the different ideal-type constructs, Max Weber realised that administrative systems in different settings are likely to include a mixture of different types of authority systems.

Apart from Weberian studies, there is an underlying assumption in CPA literature that a public bureaucracy is a subsystem of the political system in which it operates. This implies that the bureaucracy has a greater interaction with the political system than with the economic or socio-cultural systems. This feature is beautifully illustrated in Ferrel Heady's following statement: "The environment of bureaucracy may be visualised as a series of concentric circles, with bureaucracy at the centre. The smallest circle generally has the most decisive influence, and the larger circle represents a descending order of importance as far as bureaucracy is concerned. We may visualise the largest circle as representing all of society or the general social system. The next circle represents the economic system. The inner circle is the political system; it encloses the administrative subsystem and bureaucracy as one of its elements."[15]

This statement suggests an important trend (not always valid) in comparative thinking, which indicates the predominance of political elements in the ecology of public bureaucracies. This interest in studying the interaction between bureaucracy and the political system has been found in comparative literature right from the earlier work of Woodrow Wilson to the modern research of Francis Rourke. This interest is further enhanced while studying the politico-administrative systems of new and developing nations.[19] In developing nations, bureaucracy is closely related to the political system because of its close association with the processes of policymaking, goal-setting, and goal attainment.

Balanced and Unbalanced Polity

The above-mentioned interaction between bureaucracy and the political system varies from country to country. This interaction leads to the formation of different kinds of polities—either balanced or unbalanced. The concept of balance and unbalanced polities is made clear by Riggs' views. According to him, a political system consists of three subsystems—its 'constitutive subsystem', its bureaucracy, and its Head of State, as described in Fig. 8.1.

Political System

Constitutive Sub-System	Bureaucratic Sub-System	Head of the State
• Elected assembly • Electoral system • Political parties	• Career bureaucracy • Non-career bureaucracy • Military	

Fig. 8.1: *Rigg's Description of a Political System*

Referring to Fig. 8.1, a *balanced polity* is said to be attained when a reasonably stable balance of power exists between a bureaucracy and a constitutive system.[20] There are certain consequences of this balance, e.g., cabinet ministers are recruited from the constitutive system, leading to more power being exercised by the constitutive system. Similarly, middle-level positions in the bureaucracy are occupied by career bureaucrats. Such a coexistence of both these structures leads to a balance of power between them.

The constitutive system is more skilled in performing political functions and the bureaucracy is more skilled in performing administrative functions. Many modern state governments such as the Philippines, Malaysia, Singapore, India, Jamaica, and Lebanon can be considered to be balanced because their political leaders exercise power over the bureaucracy without having their protégés appointed in it. A balanced government is understood to be more effective in policy formulation and implementation.

On the other hand, an *unbalanced polity* is one in which either the constitutive subsystem or the bureaucracy is disproportionately powerful over the other. It may be a party-run polity or a bureaucratic polity. In a *party-run polity*, political party workers and favourites hold key positions in the bureaucracy. In a *bureaucratic polity*, the bureaucratic ruling group tries to usurp the powers of the head of the state and the constitutive system. Here, the bureaucracy dominates the policymaking as well as the implementation process. Military regimes such as those in Thailand and Pakistan are examples of this category.

8.9 Decision-making Approach in CPA

Martin Landau is one of the few scholars who have contributed towards the decision-making approach of CPA. While comparing the administrative systems of developing and developed countries, he said that more attention needs to be given to the decision-making process in developing countries. The process of 'muddling through' is not applicable in these countries. A closer scrutiny of the available alternatives and continual observation of consequences is required. Such a requirement is not necessary in the decision-making process of the developed countries.

Apart from this, Landau has used the 'fact' and 'value' premises of Simon (as discussed in Chapter 3) to make his ideal-type constructs. He has discussed two ideal-type constructs—*folk societies* and *urban societies*.[21] In folk societies, decisions are basically value judgments, and in urban societies, the decisions are based on facts.[22] In folk societies, there is a system in which *facts* tend towards zero and decisions are essentially a matter of *values*.[23] Certain primitive societies are an example of this category. On the other hand, in urban societies, there is a system of programmed decision-making. However, Landau admits that, even in urban societies, such programmed decision-making is restricted to certain institutions and not all. What Landau wants to imply is that as society develops, the focus of decision-making moves away from 'value' and is based more on 'fact' judgments.

However, the ideas of Landau do not hold much water in the age of phenomenology in which a fact is understood to be a perception and not an objective reality. Facts are determined by values. Hence, folk societies may rely on the facts as they know them (or the facts determined by their values), similar to urban societies.

8.10 The General Systems Approach in CPA

A general system has already been discussed and defined in Chapter 3. Riggs' ideas (to be discussed in the subsequent sections) are based on this general systems approach. His *agraria-industria* model intends to study the features of an administrative system within its socio-cultural, economic, and political environment. Similarly, Riggs' *prismatic society* model is based on the systems approach.

Another application of the systems approach in CPA is the *Information-Energy Model* of Dorsey.[24] It conceptualises individuals, groups, organisations, and societies as complex information energy converters. In an administrative system, there are various inputs such as demands and intelligence. The conversion process involves screening, selecting, and channelling of alternatives. Finally, the outputs are various forms of administrative and other services for other subsystems of the society. According to Dorsey, the quality and quantity of outputs depends on the availability of information and energy at the input stage.

The degree of development of a society is based on its quality and quantity of outputs, which in turn are based on the size of its information and energy surplus. The administrative systems of developing nations usually possess lesser information input and a lower capacity to process energy. This results in fewer and lower quality outputs in developing countries, which in turn results in an ineffective administrative system and lack of rationality and traditional procedures. The situation is the opposite in developed countries.

Dorsey has emphasised on studying the input, conversion, and output aspects of the various administrative systems in order to effectively compare them with each other. However, the model did not find much attraction among later scholars because of its complex nature.

8.11 Riggs' Ideas on CPA and the Ecological Approach

One of the dominating scholars of CPA, Riggs' focus has been on the interactions between administrative systems and their environment. Thus, his approach is considered ecological in nature. The ecological approach considers public bureaucracies as one of the several basic institutions in a society. Here, the bureaucracy/administrative system is studied in the context of its interrelationship with other societal institutions. The bureaucracy is understood to be a system having an environment with which it interacts.[25] Without understanding this environment and the social setting in which the bureaucracy operates, the nature of public administration of any country cannot be studied. Riggs has applied the *structural-functional* approach to understand the different administrative systems within their ecology.

8.11.1 Application of Riggs' Structural-Functional Approach

The structural-functional approach is briefly discussed in Chapter 3. In this approach, a *structure* is considered any pattern of behaviour that has become a standard feature of a social system.[25] These structures may be concrete such as government agencies and departments; they may also be imaginary such as structures of authority.[26]

Apart from this, *function* in the structural-functional approach is understood to be patterns of interdependencies between two or more structures or the relationship between certain variables of a society. It refers to any consequences of a structure in so far as they affect other structures or the total system of which they are a part. All social structures perform certain functions.[27]

The five basic functions of administrative structures in a society, as highlighted by Riggs, are economic, social, communicational, symbolic, and political functions.[25] In a nutshell, the structural-functional approach emphasises on the interactions between the various parts within a social system. Moreover, it analyses the interaction between the system and its environment. This is known as the *systemic-ecological character* of the structural-functional approach.[28]

The structural-functional approach has brought an understanding that the institutions and practices of the western countries are not necessarily the best in all the cases. The indigenous administrative systems of the developing countries, though dysfunctional from the western perspective, may prove to be 'functional' within their own social setting and environment.[29]

8.11.2 Riggs' Agraria-Industria Model

In the agraria-industria model, Riggs has provided a system of hypothetical categories for the classification and analysis of realities, including the patterns of political and administrative transition.[30] The idea of agrarian and industrial societies was developed from the examples of imperial China and the contemporary United States of America. These ideal types of Riggs resemble Weber's ideal-type constructs of traditional and legal-rational authority systems. Riggs has described the various features of agrarian and industrial society on the basis of four characteristics, namely, social patterns, social mobility, occupational pattern, and social differentiation, as shown in Table 8.1.

Table 8.1: Various features of agrarian and industrial societies

	Agraria Society	Industrial Society
Social patterns	Predominance of ascriptive, particularistic, and diffuse patterns	Predominance of universalistic, specific, and achievement patterns
Social mobility	Stable local groups and limited social mobility	High degree of social mobility
Occupational pattern	Relatively simple and stable occupational differentiation	Well-developed occupational pattern. There is an egalitarian class system based on the generalised pattern of occupational achievement.
Social differentiation	A deferential stratification system of diffuse impact	Associations prevail in the society. Such associations are functionally specific and non-ascriptive structures.

Certain terms used in Table 8.1 require description, as follows:

- **Ascriptive Value:** A society is understood to possess ascriptive values when the status parameters of citizens are determined by factors other than achievement, such as place and family of birth.
- **Particularistic Value:** A society is supposed to have particularistic values when an individual is not judged on a clear measure of achievement or merit. Certain individuals are given priorities because of factors other than merit.
- **Universalistic Value**: A society is supposed to have universalistic values when an individual is judged by a clear measure of achievement (or expectation of behaviour) that is also applied to every other individual in the society.

However, the above model is criticized for lacking sufficient mechanisms to analyse intermediate or mixed-type societies. Generally, societies have mixed agrarian and industrial characteristics. Moreover, Riggs is criticised for applying a unidirectional movement of a society from the agrarian stage to the industrial stage. Such a unidirectional movement is not found in real societies. Furthermore, the ideal-type categories of the model are found to be too abstract and general; administrative systems are not analysed properly within the model.[31]

Despite such weaknesses, the agraria-industria model is considered important, as it has provided a base for further research in ecological studies in CPA.

8.11.3 Fused-Prismatic-Diffracted Model

In the fused-prismatic-diffracted model on the aspect of multi-functionality, Riggs has divided social structures into being *functionally diffuse* and *functionally specific*. The functionally diffuse structures perform a large number of functions. Societies having such structures are called *diffused*. On the other hand, the functionally specific structures perform limited prescribed functions only. Societies having such structures are called *diffracted*. Societies lying in between these two categories are known as *prismatic societies*. The characteristics of fused, prismatic, and diffracted societies are as described in Table 8.2.

Table 8.2: Various characteristics of fused, prismatic, and diffracted societies

	Fused society	Prismatic society	Diffracted society
Social patterns	Predominance of ascriptive and particularistic patterns	Predominance of patterns like selectivism and attainment.	Predominance of universalistic and achievement patterns.
Functionality	Functions are diffused	Social structures are characterised by poly-functionalism.	Social structures perform specific functions.
Social values	Traditional values in society and administration	Society and administration are characterised by *heterogeneity* of values.	Modern values in society and administration.
Administrative subsystem	Courts/chambers	*Sala*	Bureau
Administrative attitude	Administrative attitude characterised by realism	Administrative attitude characterised by *formalism*	Administrative attitude characterised by realism
Administrative functions	All functions performed by one structure (*fused/ undifferentiated administrative structures*)	*Overlapping* of fused and differentiated administrative structures.	Functions performed by different administrative structures (*differentiated administrative structures*)
Administrative recruitment	Administrative recruitment is based on family loyalty and kinship	Administrative recruitment is based on *nepotism*	Administrative recruitment is based on merit and achievement

	Fused society	Prismatic society	Diffracted society
Social mobility	Stable local groups and lack of mass mobilesation	*Poly-communalism* (simultaneous presence of groups living in hostile conditions)	High degree of social mobility. There is national communication.
Economic characteristics	Economy is based on *arena factors*	A state of *price indeterminacy*. A *bazaar-canteen* economy.	Prices determined by market supply and demand
Social norms	Traditional norms	*Poly-normativism/ normlessness*	Modern norms
Authority and control	Both authority and control with a fused structure	Separation of authority and control	Authority and control with different specific structures

As described in Table 8.2, the various characteristics of a prismatic society are as follows:

1. **Social Patterns:** A prismatic society is characterised by selective and attainment. Here, selective is an intermediate category between *particularism* (found in fused societies) and *universalism* (found in diffracted societies). In selective, the facilities and benefits of society are provided only to certain individuals on the basis of certain tests such as the income test or mean test; on the contrary, in universalism, the facilities and benefits of society are provided to everyone equally. On the other hand, attainment is an intermediate category between achievement (found in diffracted societies) and ascription (found in fused societies). A society having the value of *attainment* is supposed to motivate individuals for achieving only certain benchmarks/minimum standards. Apart from that, individuals are judged unequally on the basis of their caste, family, place of birth, sex, and so on. On the other hand, in a society the value of *achievement* is supposed to judge individuals only on the basis of their achievements; the atmosphere is competitive, and merit is the only criterion for evaluating individuals.
2. **Administrative Subsystem:** Riggs has used the term *sala* for the administrative subsystem of a prismatic society. Sala is a Spanish word meaning a room or a government office. It represents a mixture of diffracted 'bureau' and fused 'chamber'. The prominent characteristics of sala are heterogeneity, formalism, and overlapping.
3. **Social Values (Heterogeneity):** A prismatic society is characterised by heterogeneity. This means that there is a simultaneous presence of different systems, practices, and viewpoints.[32] The coexistence of different features is a result of the incomplete and uneven change. In a prismatic society, there are both urban areas (with modern administration) and rural areas (where all the administrative, political, religious, and social functions are performed by the village elders). In the administrative structure of prismatic society (sala), we can find the characteristics of both the bureau and chamber.
4. **Administrative Attitude (Formalism):** The administrative attitude in prismatic societies is characterised by formalism. Formalism refers to the degree of discrepancy between the formally prescribed and the effectively practised procedures.[33] A prismatic administrative system is termed *formal* as there is a major difference between the formal and effective

behaviour of the administrators. Administrative behaviour does not conform to legal statutes, constitutional ideals, and moral principles, although administrators vocally support them. Such formalistic behaviour is caused due to the lack of pressure towards programmes, policies, and laws; the weakness of social power as a guide to bureaucratic performance; and a great permissiveness for arbitrary administration.[33] Such behaviour is supposed to be a major source of corruption in the sala administration. Moreover, due to formalism, the administrative reforms in prismatic societies bring about only a superficial impact.

5. **Overlapping in Administrative Functions:** In a fused society, all the administrative functions are performed by just one structure. On the other hand, in a diffracted society, different administrative functions are performed by different specific administrative structures. However, in prismatic societies, we find overlapping of administrative functions. That is, the formally differentiated structures of a diffracted society coexist with the undifferentiated structures of a fused society.[33] Although modern social structures are created, the fused (or undifferentiated) structures still continue to dominate the social system. Moreover, modern norms and values coexist with the traditional norms and values. Effective administrative behaviour is determined by non-administrative political, social, economic, religious, and other factors.[32] The phenomenon of overlapping leads to certain other features in a diffracted society such as nepotism, poly-communalism, poly-normativism, and separation of authority from control.
6. **Administrative Recruitment Based on Nepotism:** In a fused society, administrative behaviour is based on kinship and family loyalty. On the other hand, in a diffracted society, administrative behaviour is separated from family loyalty. However, in a prismatic society, modern administrative structures are found together with family- and kinship-based administrative values. This often results in administrative recruitment based on nepotism.
7. **Social Mobility:** In a diffracted society, every person is mobilised for mass communication. On the other hand, there is a lack of mass communication in a fused society and each village/tribe exists as a relatively closed system. In a prismatic society, we find the simultaneous presence of various different social groups living in hostile conditions. This condition is known as *poly-communalism*. In this social condition, the membership of various groups is largely community-based. These were termed *clects* by Riggs. They have the characteristics of attainment, selection, and poly-functionalism. They are organised on a modern pattern but carry out the diffuse functions of a traditional society. Moreover, these groups influence the behaviour of the administrators of the sala. The administrators show more loyalty towards the members of their own community than towards the larger community and the government. The sala develops a close relationship with a particular clect and starts adopting the values of that clect. Thus, it functions primarily in the interest of some particular groups, while superficially supporting the modern ideals of achievement and universalism.
8. **Bazaar Canteen Economy:** The economy of a prismatic society is different from that of a fused and a diffracted society. The determination of prices in a diffracted society is based on the market factors of supply and demand. While in a fused society, the economic system is based on *arena factors* such as power balance, prestige, and solidarity. In a prismatic society, the economic system is determined by both the market and arena factors. This produces a state of *price indeterminacy*, where it is generally impossible to determine a common price for a commodity or service. The prices of public services depend on the

nature of the relationship between a public servant and a citizen. It is lower for the members inside the clect and higher for the citizens outside the clect to which a public servant belongs. This condition is similar to that of a subsidised canteen in which prices are lower for the privileged class and higher for the other people. Such a condition of price indeterminacy promotes a bazaar-like atmosphere in which we find considerable bargaining with respect to financial dealings on taxes, fees, rebates, corruption money, and so on. This impacts the process of government revenue collection and budgeting. Thus, the economy of a prismatic society is also known as a *bazaar-canteen economy.*

9. **Poly-normativism/normlessness:** In a prismatic society, we find the condition of poly-normativism, in which modern norms coexist with the traditional form of behaviour. There is a lack of consensus on which norms of behaviour should be followed. Such normlessness also penetrates into the sala, where public officials, while claiming to follow an objective, universalistic, and achievement-oriented practices, actually follow more subjective, ascription-oriented, and particularistic modes of conduct. They laud western rationalistic norms but actually apply traditional practices in their work. Moreover, in a prismatic society, citizens are also in a condition of normlessness, in which they are ready to disregard official rules for their own benefit, while openly supporting the legal-rational character of the government.
10. **Separation of Authority and Control:** In a prismatic society, there is a separation of authority and control. The authority (or officially sanctioned legitimate power) lies with the centralised administrative organisations led by political executives. The control (or real but illegitimate power) lies with the localised and dispersed bureaucracy based on poly-communalism and poly-normativism. This leads to the condition of unbalanced polity (as discussed in the section Bureaucratic Systems Approach in CPA), in which bureaucrats dominate the politics-administrative system. In a prismatic society, the administrators participate more in the decision-making process than their counterparts in a diffracted society. This concentration of power in the hands of the bureaucrats results in a lack of responsiveness to public needs and demands. Moreover, the formal political leadership is often found weak in influencing the behaviour of the sala administrators. They are unable to reward the ideal behaviour and punish the delinquent behaviour of the bureaucrats. Thus, they unintentionally motivate the bureaucrats to disregard public interest and divulge their energies in safeguarding their personal interest. Furthermore, Riggs has suggested that there is an inverse ratio between bureaucratic power and administrative output. The more the power of sala administrators, the less effective is the administration.

8.11.4 Exogenous and Endogenous Change in a Prismatic Society

Every prismatic society undergoes continuous change from a fused state to a diffracted state. This change takes place in two forms—exogenous and endogenous. In an exogenous change, change takes place due to pressure from external sources (e.g., from a foreign government in a foreign assistance programme). In an endogenous change, change takes place due to pressure from internal sources. When both types of pressure for change are relatively equal, then the change is known as *equigenetic change*.

In *exogenetic change*, new formal structures are created before creating a change in the administrative behaviour. On the other hand, in *endogenetic change*, new formal structures are created after bringing about a change in the effective behaviour of the administrators. When the process of change is more exogenetic, it leads to more formalism and heterogeneity in a prismatic society, whereas more endogenetic change leads to less formalism and heterogeneity.

A favourable or better change leads to better development in a society. We have witnessed endogenetic change in western societies because of the relatively longer time span for their development and, thus, their ability to adjust their behaviour gradually to the desired patterns. Therefore, in the process of development, they have experienced less formalism, heterogeneity, and overlapping. On the other hand, there has been rapid socio-economic development, pushed by external forces, in a developing society, leading to greater heterogeneity, formalism, and overlapping.

This process of development is defined by Riggs as "a process of increasing autonomy (discretion) of social systems, made possible by the rising level of diffraction." Here, discretion is the 'ability to choose among alternatives' while diffraction refers to the 'degree of differentiation and integration in a social system'.[38]

The two elements of diffraction—differentiation and integration—are the two key elements in the process of development. Differentiation is the availability of specialised structures for every function. Integration is the ability to tie together and coordinate the functions of different specialised structures.[39]

The nature of a society—either diffracted or prismatic—depends on the nature of differentiation and integration in it. A society is prismatic if there is high differentiation and poor integration. A society is diffracted when high integration accompanies high differentiation. A society with no differentiation is a fused society. Better the differentiation and integration, better is the development in a society. The level of non-alignment between differentiation and integration leads to the different levels of prismatic conditions. The correlation between differentiation and integration is shown in Fig. 8.2.

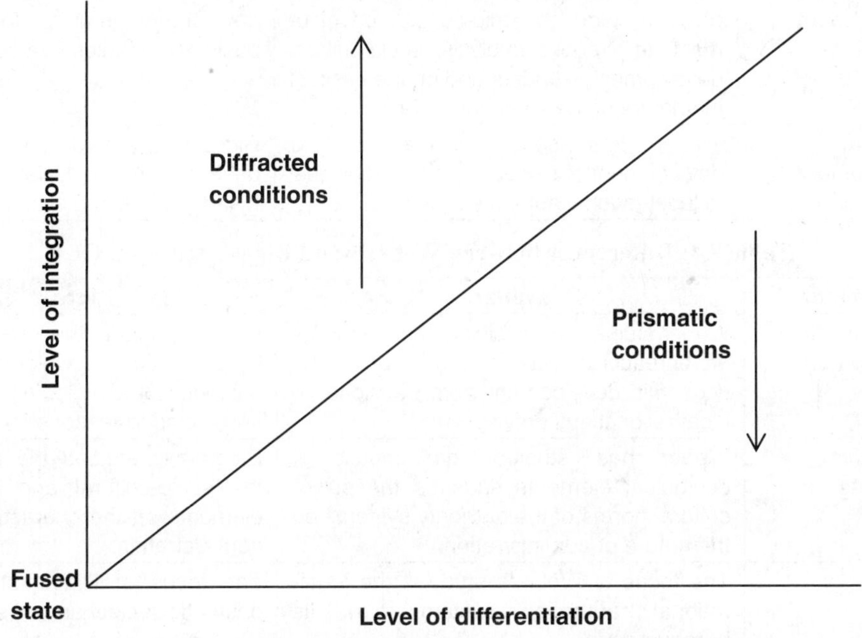

***Fig. 8.2:** Conditions of Integration and Differentiation in Societies*[40]

In Fig. 8.2, differentiation and integration takes place at the two axes. The diagonal represents the ideal state of integration, for the corresponding differentiation, in order to attain perfect coordination between the different functions of the different structures in society. If integration is below this level, then the different functions are not well-coordinated and we find the conditions of a prismatic society. Integration above this level leads to the conditions of a diffracted society. Development is possible only when we attain appropriate integration along with the available differentiation in society.

8.11.5 Comparison of Riggs's and Weber's Contribution to CPA

There are various similarities and contradictions in the studies of Riggs and Weber in CPA. Some of the similarities are enumerated in Table 8.3 and the differences are enumerated in Table 8.4.

Table 8.3: Similarities between Weber's and Riggs's study on CPA

Similarities	Weber	Riggs
Three ideal- type constructs	Weber's three ideal-type constructs are based on the legitimacy of the authority systems. They are traditional, charismatic, and legal-rational authority systems.	The three ideal type constructs of Riggs are based on the criterion of structural differentiation. They are fused, prismatic and diffracted societies.
Similar characteristics	The legal-rational characteristics are found in Riggs' diffracted societies.	The traditional characteristics are found in Riggs's fused societies.
Impact of political system	Weber has studied the impact of political system on administration.	Riggs has studied the impact of political system on administration.
Socio-cultural development	Both have compared nations on the basis of their stage of socio-cultural development. In Weber's analysis, socio-cultural development is understood on the basis of the nature of the authority system.	In Riggs' analysis, socio-cultural development is understood on the basis of diffraction in a society.
Unilinear development	Weber has considered a unilinear development of society from the traditional to legal-rational authority system.	Riggs has considered a unilinear development of society from the fused to diffracted system.

Table 8.4: Differences between Weber's and Riggs's study on CPA

Differences	Weber	Riggs
Bureaucratic development	Weber studied the evolving characteristics of bureaucracy as a result of socio-economic development from traditional to legal-rational authority system.	Riggs studied the absence of bureaucratic development in prismatic or developing societies, and provided reasons for them.
Ecological elements	Weber has studied the impact of ecological elements such as the socio-cultural norms of the authority systems on the nature of administration.	Riggs has studied the impact of the socio-cultural and economic elements on the characteristics of administration.
Focus	The focus of Weber's study is the legal-rational authority system and its bureaucracy.	The focus of Riggs' study is a prismatic society and its sala.

8.11.6 A Critical Analysis of Riggs' Contribution to CPA

Riggs' work in comparative public administration is criticised on the following points:

(a) **Not a Truly Ecological Approach:** Riggs' approach in CPA is not considered completely ecological. A truly ecological approach should study the interaction between an administrative system and its environment, and the way in which both impact each other. However, Riggs has studied only the impact of the environment on the administrative system and not vice versa. In his analysis, the administrative system is considered as a dependent variable unable to bring changes in the environment.

(b) **Relationship between Political System and Administration:** Riggs has not clearly studied the relationship between the political system and administration in a comparative analysis. He has simply described that the bureaucracy is dominant over the political system in all prismatic societies.

(c) **No Comparison between different Prismatic Societies:** Different prismatic societies have different kinds of administrative systems, capable of directing socio-economic change in varying manners. However, Riggs has not studied the varying capabilities of the administrative systems of different prismatic societies.

(d) **Less Study on Administrative System:** Riggs was supposed to study administrative systems in a comparative analysis. However, he ended up studying the structure of the environment and not the administrative system within it. His primary concern has been the input side of the administration and not the internal processes and output of it. Thus, it is said that Riggs has not fully worked out the implications of his theory for public administration.[34]

(e) **Disregarded the Variation between different Social Structures:** While studying the structure of an administrative system, Riggs has understated the possibility that various social structures within an environment can develop independently of each other. In a real situation, however, the environment of a prismatic society may have a prismatic socio-cultural system existing along with a bureaucratic subsystem. For example, in a prismatic society such as India, the administrative system could be considered as diffracted because of considerable role differentiation between the politicians and bureaucrats.

(f) **Mixed-type Societies:** As Weber talked about the need of developing mixed-type authority systems, there is a need to study mixed-type societies within Riggs' analysis of prismatic societies. Such mixed-type societies may take into account the degree of autonomy of the various subsystems within various prismatic societies.

(g) **Invalid Causal Implications:** Riggs has come out with certain causal implications that are not valid in all prismatic societies. For example, it is not always true that formalism may increase the power of bureaucrats, or that the increased power of bureaucracy may lead to inefficiency in administration.

(h) **Restrictive Meaning of Overlapping:** Riggs has provided a restricted meaning of the term 'overlapping', referring only to the simultaneous coexistence of traditional institutions and those patterned on western practices. There can also be a competitive coexistence of institutions providing similar public services (all can be traditional or all can be modern). Such overlapping of functions is also found in diffracted western societies, where the various institutions compete with each other in providing public services.

(i) **Western Bias:** Riggs' analysis has a western bias, in which all the negative qualities of a prismatic society are defined. Riggs' negative outlook is seen first in the terminology used by him to depict social behaviour in a prismatic society. He has used terms with negative connotations such as 'normlessness', 'ritualism', 'mimetic', and 'bazaar-canteen' to describe the characteristics of a prismatic society. On this, Michael Monroe has said that Riggs' theory appears to use developed nations, such as the United States, as the standard for evaluating the activities in prismatic nations. In this way, the development setbacks in prismatic countries are explained as dysfunctional applications of diffracted norms to bewildered and unstable societies.[36]

(j) **Imperfect Comparison:** Riggs' comparison can be considered imperfect, as he has only considered the good features of western societies and the bad features of developing societies. The American society also has a number of prismatic characteristics such as the indifference of public employees, corruption in government, labour union activities, and tax loopholes. Riggs has clearly understated these prismatic traits in diffracted societies. He has, mistakenly, understood the existence of a direct and close relationship between the diffraction of social structures and legal-rationality in the behaviour of their participants. Apart from this, Riggs has also understated the presence of diffracted features in a prismatic society.

(k) **Restrictive Meaning of Formalism:** Similar to overlapping, Riggs has also considered a restrictive and dysfunctional meaning of the term 'formalism'. According to Riggs, formalism leads to corruption and arbitrary administration. However, formalism can also have positive implications in society. According to Valsan,[37] in countries such as India and the Philippines, formalism may help in bringing about a positive and creative effect useful for development by skipping several slow-moving routine steps of the government. Such functional formalism is termed by Valsan as *positive formalism.*

8.12 Comparison of Administration of Different Countries

A comparison of the administrative situation of different countries consists of comparing their political system, policymaking bodies, administrative structures, civil services, and personnel administration. The comparison of these different aspects is made in the subsequent sections.

8.12.1 Comparison of Political System/Constitution

The political system of various countries can be compared on the basis of their nature of legislature, nature of executive, nature of making laws and policies, and the relation between the political executive and administrators.

The most important aspect of comparing the political system is the comparison of the constitutions of different countries. It is the constitution of a country that lays down the basic structure of the political system. It is the constitution that establishes the three organs of the government, i.e., the legislature, executive, and judiciary. It defines their powers, demarcates their responsibilities, and regulates their relationship with each other and the people.[41] A brief comparison of the constitution of different countries is made in Table 8.5.

Table 8.5: Comparison of Constitution of Different Countries

	India	USA	France	UK	China
Written/ unwritten constitution	Written	Written	Written	Unwritten; based on conventions, traditions, and customs	Written
Federal/ unitary	Quasi-federal, i.e., federal with a strong unitary and pro-Centre bias	Federal constitution	Unitary constitution	Unitary constitution	Does not precisely describe the relative power of the Centre and states
Separation of powers	Separation of powers between the three organs of government	Separation of powers between the three organs of government	Less separation of powers	Less separation of powers with the supremacy of the Parliament	No formal separation of power between the three organs of govern-ment, and between the Centre and republic. There is no constitutional limit on the state power and the power of communist party.
Presidential/ parliamentary system	Parliamentary system with the supremacy of the Constitution	Presidential system with the supremacy of the Constitution	Quasi/semi-presidential	Parliamentary system with a monarch as the head	Semi-presidential-type socialist republic system controlled by a single party. The politburo is the most powerful committee, which controls the Commu-nist Party of China as well as the military

	India	USA	France	UK	China
					and security wing of China.
Rigidity of Constitution	Neither flexible nor rigid. Some features are rigid and others are flexible.	Rigid Constitution	More flexible Constitution	More flexible Constitution	Can be modified easily upon the proposal of the communist party.

In Table 8.5, the terms federal and unitary constitution require explanation. A *unitary constitution* is one in which all the powers are vested in the central government and the various units (or states) are subordinate to it. On the other hand, in a *federal constitution*, the powers are divided between the centre and the states. Apart from this, a federal polity has certain features, such as a rigid written constitution and supremacy of the constitution.

8.12.2 Comparison of Executives

The executive is the dominant organ of any political system. Thus, the comparison of executives is an important aspect of comparing the administration of different countries. There is considerable variation in the power of executives of various countries such as the USA, the UK, India, France, and China. A comparison of the executives of different countries is shown in Table 8.6.

Table 8.6: Comparison of executives of different countries

	India	USA	France	UK	China
Nominal/real executive	The president is the nominal head and the prime minister is the real head.	The president is the real and the only head of state.	The president is the real as well as the effective head. The president appoints a prime minister to run the government.	The king/queen is the nominal head and the prime minister is the real head.	The paramount leader is the head of the state. He/she is the general secretary of the Commu-nist Party of China. He/she is also the president of the People's Republic of China. A premier is the head of the state council and that of the govern-ment.

	India	USA	France	UK	China
Responsibility of executive	The prime minister is responsible to the parliament. The council of ministers are collectively responsible to the parliament.	The president is not directly responsible to the legislature. There is no collective res-ponsibility among the US cabinet.	The French president is the most powerful executive. The cabinet, headed by the prime minister, is collectively responsible to the legislature.	The executive is responsible to the legislature and the government decision is taken collectively by the members of the cabinet.	The president is responsible to the politburo as well as to the Polit-buro Standing Commi-ttee. The premier is responsible to the National People's Congress (NPC).
Cabinet members	The elected legislatures are appointed as cabinet ministers by the PM.	Cabinet members are experts from universities, law officers, and politically unknown personalities chosen by the President.	Cabinet members are nominated by the president upon the advice of the PM.	The elected legislat-ures are appointed as cabinet ministers by the PM.	The Chinese cabi-net is known as the state council. It is appointed by the NPC.

8.12.3 Comparison of Policymaking

A comparison of policymaking in different countries consists of comparing their supreme policymaking institution and the nature of their policies. A brief overview of these two aspects is given in Table 8.7.

Table 8.7: Comparison of policymaking in different countries

	India	USA	France	UK	China
Fundamental unit of policymaking	The policies are determined by the prime minister and council of ministers, aided by senior civil servants of important departments such as the Cabinet	Congress has the fundamental role in policymaking, with little intrusion from the bureaucracy.	All major policy decisions are made by the French president. The French parliament prepares the laws and policies; however, the president can return bills	The policies are principally determined by the prime minister and council of ministers. The parliament does not have a significant say in policy	The Communist Party of China (CPC) is the ultimate decision-making body and retains final control over policy formulation. The president and premier are response-

	India	USA	France	UK	China
	Secretariat, Prime Minister's Office, Planning Commission, and Ministry of Finance, Commerce and Industry.		passed by the parlia-ment. Moreover, the president can prepare a legislative policy based on a referendum.	issues.	ble for imple-menting the decisions taken by the CPC.
Nature of policy	The broad aspects of policies are strongly influenced by the political party in power. However, the fundamental aspects of policies are determined by senior bureaucrats.	The policies of US are known for their legitimacy because of their legislative support. There is less influence of political parties over policy issues; it is restricted to few issues.	Due to direct elections of the president, there is a small role of the parlia-ment in policy areas. The influence of political parties is also less. The real power-house of policy-making is that of the president and he/she is not answerable to the parliament.	There is strong influence of political parties over policy issues. The Upper House, i.e., the House of Lords enjoys a suspensory vote over policies.	The party (CPC), the state, and the government are locked in a complicated relationship. The political level of decision-making and the adminis-trative level are thoroughly intert-wined due to the role of the CPC. There is a strong reliance on consensus building during policy formulation. Moreover, policies rely on planning documents such as five-year plans.

8.12.4 Comparison of Departmental System

While comparing the departmental system of different countries, we intend to study their organisations and how various functions are allocated, performed, and coordinated in different countries. Table 8.8 analyses the comparative features of the departmental system of different countries.

Table 8.8: Comparison of departmental system in different countries

	India	USA	France	UK	China
Head of departments	The policies are determined by the prime minister and council of ministers aided by senior civil servants of important departments such as the Cabinet Secretariat, Prime Minister's Office, Planning Commission, and Ministry of Finance, Commerce and Industry.	Some departments are headed by individuals and others by boards.	The departments are usually not headed by a single permanent official. Some departments are also placed under the direct control of a minister.	The policies are principally determined by the prime minister and council of ministers. The parliament does not have a significant say in policy issues.	The Communist Party of China is the ultimate decision-making body and retains final control over policy formulation. The president and premier are responsible for implementing the decisions taken by the CPC.
Number of departments	The total number of departments is not fixed.	The total number of departments is not fixed.	The total number of departments is not fixed.	The total number of departments is not fixed.	The total number of departments is fixed.
Structure of departmental organisation	The departmental structure is hierarchically organised.	The departmental structure is hierarchically organised.	The departmental structure is complex and flexible to accommodate any directions that come from the ministers and the chief executives. The pattern of departmental structure varies from	The departmental structure is hierarchically organised.	The departmental structure is highly rigid and contro-lled by extra-constitu-tional forces such as the Communist Party.

	India	USA	France	UK	China
			department to department. The common major unit of departments is the directorate; while some ministries are divided into directorate generals, others are divided into secretariat generals.		
Type of senior administrators	The Indian departments are occupied by senior members of Indian civil services employed by the mechanism of competitive examinations. However, we find patronage in the transfer and postings of the senior administrators.	The departments are occupied by federal civil servants consisting of two positions—classified (competitive) positions and unclassified (expected) positions. Most of the top administrative posts are filled by political appointments.	There is patronage and political appointment of civil servants. Most of the politicians are erstwhile civil servants, and the present civil servants may become future politicians, leading some departments. Such a system helps in developing an organic link between policymaking and policy execution.	Senior administrators are appointed only on the basis of merit and there is no place of patronage in the case of transfer and postings.	The party bureaucracy operates parallel to and almost penetrates into the state civil services. A Chinese civil servant can either opt for a career in the party apparatus or in the state bureaucracy. Policy formulation and policy execution are not considered as separate functions performed by separate agencies.

8.12.5 Comparison of Administrative Structure

The administrative structure of a country depends on the political situation prevailing in it. Thus, the administrative structures of the five major polities—India, UK, USA, France, and China—vary in form. A comparison of the administrative structure of these policies is shown in Table 8.9.

Table 8.9: Comparison of administrative structures of different countries

	India	USA	France	UK	China
Levels of administ-ration	Three levels of administration —union, state, and local (federal government)	Three levels of administration —union, state, and local (federal government)	Two levels of administration —one central level and other local levels (unitary government)	Two levels of administratio n—one central level and other local levels (unitary government)	China is a com-posite state with a central government, 33 sub-natio-nal units (22 provinces, 2 municipa-lities, 5 auto-nomous regions, and 2 special administra-tive regions).
Unity in administ-ration	There is unity in admini-stration, with all the departments coming under the direct control of the executive.	The federal administrative structure of the USA is not unified. There is lack of unity among various departments, agencies, and bureaus. At the central level, some bodies are created by the president and others are created by the Congress. There is a problem of co-ordination and integration bet-ween these bodies.	There is unity in administ-ration.	The UK admini-stration is highly co-ordinated and centralised.	The Chinese administrative structure has some kind of decentrali-sation, but the decentralised structures are highly unified because of the strong control of the Communist Party.

	India	USA	France	UK	China
Decentralisation of power	There is decentralisation of power in terms of the power to state governments, panchayati raj, and urban municipal bodies.	The USA is an epitome of decentralisation. Power is sufficently delegated to state governments and local bodies.	France has a highly centralised system of administration. Lately some power has been decentralised to districts, can-tons, and comm-unes.	Britain is a unitary government with some amount of decentralisati on to local governments.	We find decentralisation of power in China to sub-national units. However, all these units' function under the direct command of the Communist Party.
Complexity / simplicity of administrative structure	The Indian administration is characterised as complex because various new organisations have been created (apart from the colonial organisations) after independence for attaining rapid socio-economic development.	The USA has the most complex administration. It is a fertile ground for the emergence of new type of organisations, public corporations, and other presidential executive agencies.	The French administrative structure is complex, as departments are based both on area as well as functional principle.	The UK administration is complex with a variety of non-departmental organisations (along with departmental organisations) called *gaungos*.	The Chinese administratio n is not that complex, as various administrative units act as a substitute or agency of the Communist Party.

8.12.6 Relationship between Civil Servant and Political Executive

A very important component of administration is the relationship between the civil servants and other sectors of the political system such as the executive, legislature, political parties, pressure groups, and so on. The relationship between civil servants and political executives varies from system to system. A comparison of this relationship is provided in Table 8.10.

Table 8.10: Comparison of relationship between civil servants and political executives

	India	USA	France	UK	China
Permanency in posting	The postings of civil servants in India are generally politically dependent.	The senior civil servants of the USA are politically appointed, and change with the change of president.	The senior civil servants are given permanent postings.	The senior civil servants are given permanent postings.	Both the ministers and civil servants are not likely to be changed at intervals due to electoral defeat. Thus, they enjoy a good relationship among each other.
Ministerial interaction with civil servants	The ministers spend less time in matters of administration due to the parliamentary form of government in which the executives are a part of the legis-lature.	The interaction of ministers is high in administrative and non-policy matters, as the interaction between the executive and legislature is less evident there, due to a clear sepa-ration of powers.	The ministers interfere in administrative matters.	The ministers spend less time in matters of admi-nistration due to the parliamentary form of government, in which the execu-tives are a part of the legislature.	The ministerial interference depends on the dictates given by the party from time to time.
Nature of relationship	The relationship between civil servants and political executives is limited to the area of policymaking.	The relationship is extended to non-policy matters apart from the regular policy matters.	Apart from regular policy matters, the relationship is extended to non-policy matters.	The relationship between civil ser-vants and political executives is limited to the area of policymaking.	The relationship between civil ser-vants and political executives is in those areas that are prescribed by the party.

8.12.7 Comparison of Political Rights of Civil Servants

The political rights of civil servants are an important aspect of the administration. Civil servants of different countries enjoy a variety of political rights in different ways and degrees. The important political rights of the civil servants, demanding consideration, are the following:

(a) Right to vote in elections
(b) Right to contest in elections
(c) Right to freedom
(d) Right to form associations
(e) Right to strike

A comparison of these political rights is presented in Table 8.11.

Table 8.11: Comparison of political rights of civil servants

	India	USA	France	UK	China
Right to vote in elections	Granted to civil servants	Granted to civil servants	Granted to civil servants	Granted to civil servants	Civil servants are allowed to vote in certain matters but under the strict directions of the Communist Party.
Right to contest in elections	Civil servants are not allowed to become members of political parties and contest in elections.	Civil servants are not allowed to become members of political parties and contest in elections.	Civil servants can become member of political parties and participate in election activities. The only restraint is that they must not disclose the fact that they are civil servants when engaged in political activities.	Civil servants are not allowed to become members of political parties and contest in elections.	There is no question of participating in elections as China is not a democracy.
Right to Freedom of Expression	Civil servants do not enjoy the right to freedom of	The civil servants are allowed to express their	Civil servants are allowed to even criticise government	Civil servants do not enjoy the right to freedom of	Civil servants are strictly prohibited from ex-

	India	USA	France	UK	China
	expression. They are expected to seek the prior permission of the competent authorities for publishing books, articles and speaking to general audiences.	views on political subjects, but not in the capacity of a civil servant and only privately.	policies and the manner of implementtation. But such criticism needs to be outside the official work of a person.	expression. They are expected to seek the prior permission of the competent authorities for publishing books and articles and speaking to general audiences.	pressing their views and criticise the government.
Right to association	Civil servants are allowed to form associations according to Article 19 of the Indian Constitution. However, the government negotiates with only those associations that are recognised by it.	Civil servants are allowed to join any association barring those associations that are indulged in illegal and unlawful activities.	Civil servants enjoy the right to form associations including the right to associate with trade unions. They can uphold their political ideologies by joining any association.	Civil servants are allowed to form associations but with restrictions. They are not allowed to associate with unions believing in communism.	Civil servants are allowed to form professional associations under the strict control of the Communist Party.
Right to strike	The Constitution of India has not granted civil servants the right to strike. However, such a right is not specifically denied to civil servants, except police personnel, foreign service officials, and top bureaucrats.	The US Labor Relations Act does not allow civil servants the right to strike. The law denies employment or retention of any public servant who participates in strikes. However, this act is being diluted due to	Barring certain categories such as top civil servants, foreign service officials and police personnel, all civil servants enjoy the right to strike.	The UK public servants are not specifically denied the right to strike. However, such a right is allowed with various limitations.	Strikes by civil servants are considered as acts against the government.

	India	USA	France	UK	China
		the increasing pressure of various federal unions.			

8.12.8 Comparison of Recruitment and Training in Different Countries

Recruitment and training are the central concerns for an efficient administration. Different countries differ in their recruitment and training policies, principles, and practices. A comparative picture is provided in Table 8.12.

Table 8.12: Comparison of recruitment and training of administrators in different countries

	India	USA	France	UK	China
Recruitment mechanism	Recruitment is based on an open competetive examination for various important civil service positions.	Recruitment is based on a competitive examination, in which candidates are selected on the basis of merit. The senior civil servants or departmental heads are the political executives appointed on the basis of the spoils system.	The recruitment system in France is quite different. The French civil service is organised on the basis of 'Corps'—categories of staff that form the groups from which recruitment occurs.	Recruitment is based on an open competitive examination for various important civil service positions.	Recruitment is based on an open competitive examination.
Minimum educational qualification	Minimum educational qualifycations are required for appearing in government examinations.	In USA, minimum educational qualification is not needed for appearing in civil service entrance examinations.	The civil servants and other government servants are graduates from the National School of Administration (NSA), the Ecole Normale, the	Minimum educational qualifications are required for appearing in government examinations.	Minimum educational qualifycations are required from civil servants, most important being proficiency in Chinese

	India	USA	France	UK	China
			Ecole Poly-technique, and Ecole Centrale des Arts et Manufacturers. Members of the 'grand corps' (which includes the senior level of general administra-tors) are recruited from the graduates of special competitive entry training schools founded by the state.		language.
Generalist versus specialist	Important positions are held by non-specialists recruited by an open competitive examination.	Senior positions are held by specialists of different fields.	France favours technocrats in civil service. Technocrats are bureau-crats possessing technical skills.	Important positions are held by non-specialists recruited by open competitive examination.	Chinese civil servants are specialists allowing little space for generalist party executives.
Training of administrators	Training of administrators is more generalist-oriented.	Training is based on imparting skills to the specialist cadre.	Training is based on imparting skills to the specialist cadre. Unlike other countries, training in France starts before recruit-ment at the various institutions mentioned.	Training of administrators is more generalist-oriented.	Training of civil servants is divi-ded into two parts. In the first part, public admi-nistration educa-tion is provided in the form of formal schooling to undergradua tes. Second, specialised

	India	USA	France	UK	China
					training is provided to the serving civil servants and Communist Party members.

8.13 Current Status of Comparative Public Administration

In recent years, public administration has become increasingly international and comparative. This has happened with respect to four aspects.[42] First, the inclusion of international and comparative perspectives has been of immense value to the development of public administration and our understanding of how and why administration differs across countries. Second, there has been a fundamental change in public administration teaching because of advanced research in comparative public administration (CPA). Third, international comparative public administration fulfils a growing need for administrative tools, strategies, and processes that can better address the policy implementation challenges faced by governments in an increasingly globalised world. Fourth and most important, a CPA perspective on theory, research, and public administration teaching has drastically changed the practice of public administration by directing it towards 'good governance'.

However, there are certain concerns and problems with respect to comparative public administration affecting the international development of public administration. Some of these concerns are enumerated below:

(a) **Lack of Unanimity over Definition**: Over the years, scholars have failed to form a consensus over the definition of comparative public administration.[43]

(b) **Lack of Integration with Public Administration**: Many scholars consider that CPA is not sufficiently integrated with public administration in general and development practice in particular. An effective convergence of CPA with the parent discipline of public administration has not materialised despite the practical need for such convergence.[44]

(c) **Insufficient Base of Theory**: Much of the research on CPA, barring some, is based on theory. Many CPA works are bereft of the theory and thoughtful methodological approaches.[45]

(d) **Lack of Quality Empirical Research**: Because of the inherent nature and complexity of the subject, CPA research suffers from a scarcity of empirical data or quantification.[46]

Notwithstanding the above-mentioned lacunae, the field of CPA has gained new momentum in the age of information and communication technology (ICT) and globalisation.

8.13.1 CPA in the Age of ICT and Globalisation

The current breakthroughs in information and communication technologies (ICTs) have created tremendous opportunities for sharing information on a global scale. In an article by Jreistat, namely, 'Comparative Public Administration is back in, Prudently', the sharing of scientific and technological inventions has accelerated globalism and enabled scholars and practitioners to compare their methodological approaches for the sake of building a grounded body of scientific knowledge in comparative public administration.[47]

This increasingly comparative focus has prompted public administration scholars and practitioners to initiate regular meetings to discuss administrative practices and concerns while producing research that is relevant to a wider set of issues in various parts of the world. Today, public administration research is multi-directional and geared towards exploring pertinent issues related to decentralisation, public-private partnerships, and governance. In particular, the focus of CPA is on enforcing transparency and accountability mechanisms for the ultimate goal of achieving effective development and democratic governance. In this comparative analysis, it is seen that nations lacking a long tradition of functioning under a system of accountability face the challenge of establishing a responsive, equitable, and effective government.[48]

It is seen that with the current trend towards globalisation, most governments are going through structural changes as they adjust to new types of partnerships that are critical to maintain public values alongside socio-economic growth. These partnerships have made the global community less tolerant towards corruption in governance. The ICTs have created an environment in which the demand for an accountable government is intensifying, as recently noticed with the *Arab Spring*.[49]

Apart from accountability and transparency, topics such as public ethics and e-governance are becoming a part of CPA research. These topics are being studied in accordance with each country's contextual conditions. Such contextual conditions include their social values, legal norms, politics, international global accords, literacy level, climate, culture, racial and religious factors, and the state of their economy.[50]

The future research in CPA is monitored and coordinated by the Section on International and Comparative Administration (***SICA***) under the American Society of Public Administration (ASPA). SICA is spearheading an effort to converge CPA in public administration through the annual *Riggs International Symposium*, which provides an opportunity for comparitivists from all over the world to meet and present their research. SICA is also planning to organise regional symposiums that will create opportunities for comparative administration scholars to discuss their research with the ultimate goal of building a regional body of administration knowledge.

The essence of modern comparative public administration is captured in these lines of Jreisat that "countries in all regions of the world are striving for more successful methods of management to deliver public services of better quality and with less cost, and that the processes of accountability, ethics and merit-based appointments to public jobs, for example, have no nationality."[47]

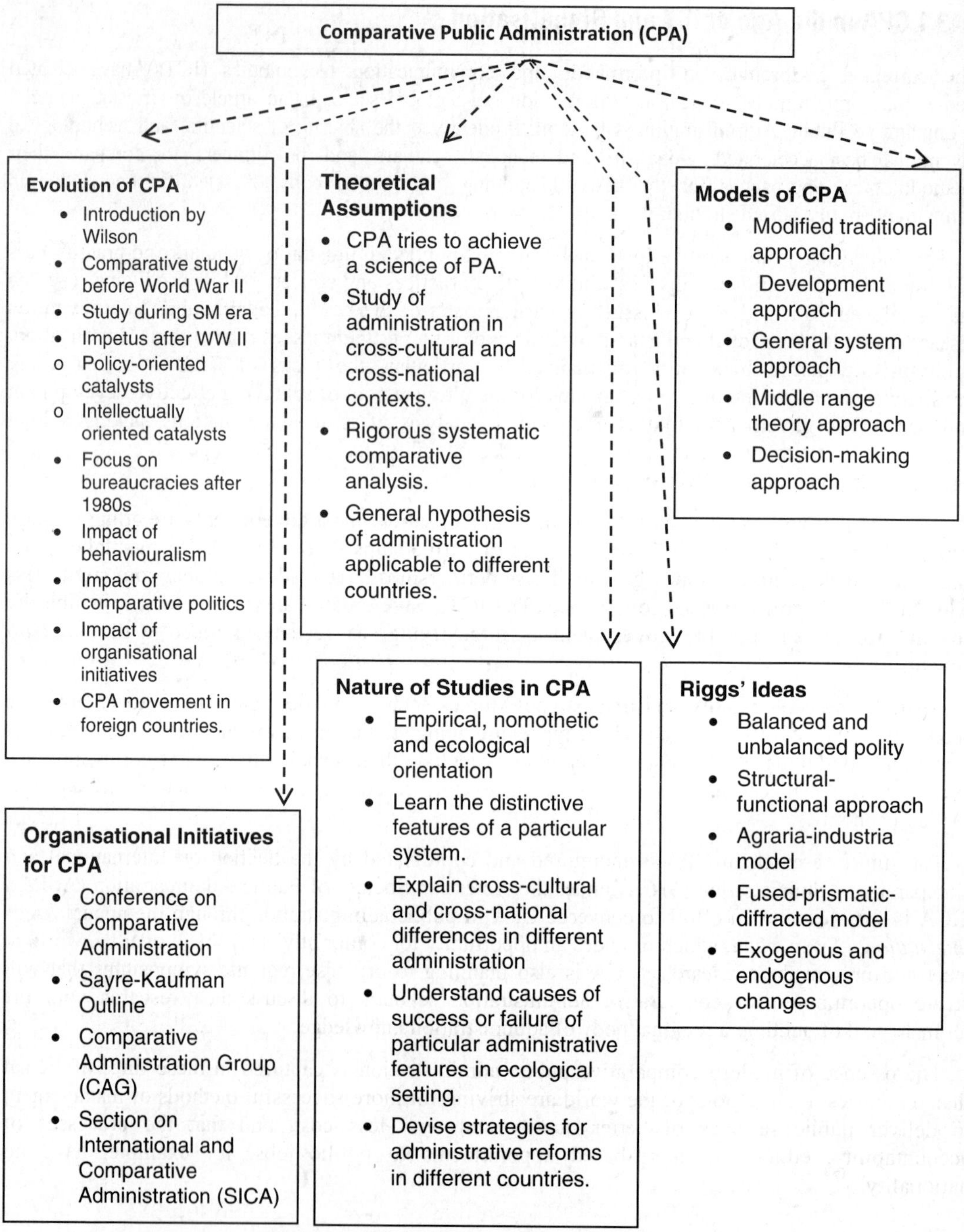

Comparative Public Administration (CPA)

Evolution of CPA

- Introduction by Wilson
- Comparative study before World War II
- Study during SM era
- Impetus after WW II
  - o Policy-oriented catalysts
  - o Intellectually oriented catalysts
- Focus on bureaucracies after 1980s
- Impact of behaviouralism
- Impact of comparative politics
- Impact of organisational initiatives
- CPA movement in foreign countries.

Theoretical Assumptions

- CPA tries to achieve a science of PA.
- Study of administration in cross-cultural and cross-national contexts.
- Rigorous systematic comparative analysis.
- General hypothesis of administration applicable to different countries.

Models of CPA

- Modified traditional approach
- Development approach
- General system approach
- Middle range theory approach
- Decision-making approach

Organisational Initiatives for CPA

- Conference on Comparative Administration
- Sayre-Kaufman Outline
- Comparative Administration Group (CAG)
- Section on International and Comparative Administration (SICA)

Nature of Studies in CPA

- Empirical, nomothetic and ecological orientation
- Learn the distinctive features of a particular system.
- Explain cross-cultural and cross-national differences in different administration
- Understand causes of success or failure of particular administrative features in ecological setting.
- Devise strategies for administrative reforms in different countries.

Riggs' Ideas

- Balanced and unbalanced polity
- Structural-functional approach
- Agraria-industria model
- Fused-prismatic-diffracted model
- Exogenous and endogenous changes

***Mind Map 8.1:** A Brief Overview of CPA*

SUMMARY

This chapter has discussed a special division of the discipline of public administration, known as comparative public administration (CPA). The evolution of the discipline has been discussed along with various models in the field of CPA. The chapter concludes by speaking about the status of CPA in the age of ICT and globalisation.

Practice Questions

1. "In order to establish science of public administration, it is necessary to be comparative." (Robert Dahl) Comment.
2. "Comparison is the basis of concept formation in any discipline." Comment.
3. The students of CPA find in comparative politics "a considerable body of substantive materials directly related to their own concerns, as well as an increasingly sophisticated and self-conscious effort at methodological clarifications." (Diamant) Comment.
4. The nature of research in CPA is empirical, nomothetic, and ecological. Explain.
5. "CPA is in a pre-paradigmatic stage." (Thomas Kuhn) Discuss.
6. Weber's ideal-type construct is regarded as the single most influential work in the literature of comparative public administration. Examine.
7. "The environment of bureaucracy may be visualised as a series of concentric circles, with bureaucracy at the centre." (Heady) Examine.
8. "Weber's ideal-type models are innocent of spatio-temporal cautions and give the impression that bureaucracy has existed in an essentially similar form, regardless of great differences in which it was enmeshed." (Gouldner) Examine.
9. "The sala behaviour is basically wasteful and prodigal." (Riggs) Evaluate.
10. "Development setbacks in the prismatic countries are explained by Riggs as dysfunctional applications of diffracted norms to bewildered and unstable societies." (Michael Monroe) Evaluate.
11. "The heterogeneity also extends its Damocle's sword straight on the administrative system." Discuss.
12. "In recent years, public administration has become increasingly international and comparative. This has happened in four aspects." Comment.
13. "Countries in all regions of the world are striving for more successful methods of management to deliver public services of better quality and with less cost, and that the processes of accountability, ethics and merit-based appointments to public jobs, for example, have no nationality." Explain with focus on the current status of comparative public administration.

CHAPTER 9 Development Dynamics

After reading this chapter, you will learn the following:

- Definition of development administration (DA) including the concepts 'development of administration' and 'administration of development'.
- Comparison and contrast of traditional and development administration.
- Evolution and growth of development administration from the 1950s till date.
- Development administration in 1950–1960, with emphasis on the modernisation theory and the technical assistance programme.
- Development administration in 1960–1970, with emphasis on the contribution of CAG to development administration (DA), contribution of Riggs to DA, empirical approach to DA, and the dependency theory of DA.
- Development administration in 1970–1980, with emphasis on the political economy approach, ecological approach to DA, and basic needs approach to DA.
- Development administration in 1980–1990, with emphasis on the learning process approach, world systems approach, and the ultra-modernist approach to DA.
- Development administration in 1990–2000, with emphasis on the people-centred approach, anti-development thesis, market orientation approach, and sustainable livelihoods approach to DA.
- Development administration since 2000, with emphasis on the capability approach, women and development approach, sustainable development approach, and post-development thought in DA.
- Views of scholars such as Edward Weidner and Ferrel Heady on development administration.
- Human Development Report and indicators such as HDI, GDI, GII, and MPI.
- Concept of women, gender, and development, including an understanding of the subordinate position of women; various theoretical perspectives on women's development including women in development (WID), women and development (WAD), gender and development (GAD), development alternative with women for a new era (DAWN), Martha Nussbaum's capability approach, women's empowerment approach, women's main-streamming approach, and women and sustainable development approach.

- Important international initiatives for women's development and important gender-related indicators.
- The role of women in administration, the advantages they bring, the challenges faced by them, and methodologies to improve their position in administration.
- Concept of sustainable development, sustainable development goals (SDGs), and role of gender in SDGs.

9.1 Definition of Development Administration

Development administration is required for bringing positive change through integrated, organised and properly directed governmental action. Development administration consists of two concepts—administration of development and development of administration. These are described in th following sections.

9.1.1 Administration of Development

Administration of development is a planned transformation of the economy involving the help of th administration, policymaking, and society as a whole. It is an impetus towards bringing improvemen in all spheres of development, including economic, social, political, and cultural development. In thi development, the state administration is supposed to play a leading role. In order to facilitat development, the state administration is required to play a special role and understand the peculia problems of a developing country.

This special role played by state administration should be considered from different operativ levels, i.e., quick and innovative decisions to be taken by the officials, adoption of new an innovative policies, and adoption of path-breaking implementation strategies and activities. Thus, th administration of development is the *action or functioning part of public administration*. In a nutshell, the administration of development consists of the following two elements:

(a) The bureaucratic process that initiates and facilitates socio-economic progress by making th optimum use of talents and expertise available.

(b) Mobilisation of administrative skills to speed up the developmental process.

9.1.2 Development of Administration or Administrative Development

Development of administration is defined as the enlargement of the administrative, structural, an behavioural capabilities of administration in order to bring in development. It aims at bringing abou fundamental changes in administration that lead to political development, economic growth, an social change. It helps in the creation of a new ability in the administration to respond immediately t new stimuli and changes in the environment.

In the words of Caiden, "Administrative development or administrative reform is an essentia ingredient of development in any country, irrespective of the speed and direction of change Administrative capability becomes increasingly important in the implementation of new policies plans, and ideas. Improvement in administrative capacity may involve the removal of environmental obstacles and structural alternatives in traditional and innovatory institutions, bureaucratically organised or otherwise. This would also necessitate changing individual and group attitudes and performance."[1]

Although the two terms have different meanings, administration of development and development of administration are interrelated and well-connected. Administration of development is as important as the development of administration. In the words of Riggs, "Development administration and administrative development have a chicken and egg kind of relationship. The superiority of one concept over the other cannot be established."

9.2 Traditional Administration and Development Administration

Development administration differs from traditional administration in terms of purpose, structure, organisation, attitude, behaviour, capabilities, techniques, and methods. The basic differences between traditional and development administration are mentioned in Table 9.1.

Table 9.1: Differences between traditional and development administration[2]

	Traditional administration	Development administration
Nature of tasks	The nature of tasks is regulatory and routine. It is concerned with fulfilling all the legal requirements of government operations and maintaining social stability. It is confined to maintenance of law and order, collection of revenues, and regulation of national life in accordance with the legal requirements.	The nature of tasks is new and unpredictable in a rapidly changing environment. Its central nature is to bring socio-economic and political change.
Orientation of work	The orientation of work is towards efficiency and economy in individual work.	The orientation of work is towards organisational growth and effectiveness in the achievement of goals, and the emphasis is on group performance and inter-group collaboration. It is basically goal-oriented.
Daily focus	Daily focus is on conformity with rules and procedures. There is concern for security, comfort, and power preservation.	Daily focus is on achieving higher overall performance. Employees are willing to take risks while encouraging innovation and change.
Organisational structure (closed/open)	Organisational structure is rigid, hierarchical, and closed.	Organisational structure is shaped by the requirements of goals and is flexible in nature. It is open and has linkages with experts and people at the grass-roots level. It shapes the environment and is in turn shaped by the environment.

	Traditional administration	Development administration
Nature of decision-making	Decisions are made at a central level and past experience is a major guide for new decisions.	Decisions are made in a participatory manner and emphasis is given to new aids to decision-making.
Organisational change	Traditional administration avoids organisational change and tends to maintain the status quo.	The organisational structure remains dynamic and adaptive to the changing demands of the environment. Changes such as structural reorganisation of administration and innovative programmes to increase production, reduce employment, etc. form an essential part of development administration.
Innovation in administration	Traditional administration is rigid and based on traditional procedures and precedents.	Development is innovative and progressive in thought and action. It emphasises in identifying and applying new structures, methods, procedures, techniques, policies, projects, and programmes so that the objectives and goals of development are achieved using the minimum possible resources and time.
Universal/ targeted approach	Traditional administration is universal in nature and all the people are its beneficiaries.	Development administration is generally targeted to benefit the weaker sections of society such as women, small and marginal farmers, rural artisans, and people below poverty line. It prioritises the needs of its beneficiaries by preparing, reviewing, and, if necessary, changing the programmes, policies, and activities aimed at the satisfaction of the targeted beneficiaries.
Public participation	In traditional administration, generally, people are treated as passive recipients of services.	In development administration, people are considered as active participants in the formulation and execution of development plans, policies, and programmes.
Coordination in work	In traditional administration, generally, the different agencies work in separation.	In development administration, generally, the agencies are required to effectively coordinate their work. This is essential because of the proliferation of agencies working for development (because of the increasing specialisation and professionnalism required in developmental tasks).

There are also some common aspects between traditional administration and developmen administration. Some of these aspects are as follows:[3]

(a) **Dependency on Each Other:** Development administration and traditional administration depend on each other. The robustness of the structure of traditional administration has a decisive role in the strengths and weaknesses of development administration.

(b) **Common Source of Authority:** Both traditional administration and development administration derive their authority and power from a common source. For example, in the Indian Union Government, derive its authority from the central cabinet.

(c) **Under Single Official:** In many areas, developmental and traditional administrative tasks are given under the authority of a single person, e.g., the district collector at the district level.

(d) **Equal in the Eyes of Citizens:** The citizens view traditional and developmental administration as same and equal. They often judge the administration as a whole and are not concerned with the distinction between traditional and developmental administration.

Considering the differences and similarities, the debate on the dichotomy between traditional and development administration is an inconclusive one. Gant has described this debate beautifully in his words. He says, "Development administration is distinguished from, although not independent of, other aspects and concerns of public administration. Certainly, the maintenance of law and order is a prime function of government and is basic to development, although it precedes and is not usually encompassed within that definition of development administration. Similarly, the provision of essential communications and educational facilities and the maintenance of judicial and diplomatic systems would have an impact on, but not be an integral part of, development administration."[4]

9.3 Evolution and Growth of Development Administration

The term 'development administration' has come into focus mainly after the Second World War. It was seen that the problems faced by the Third World countries such as Asia, Africa, and Latin America were completely different from the problems faced by the developed countries. The developed nations started getting involved in preparing special policies and programmes for underdeveloped and developing nations. Thus, the concept of 'development administration' was introduced in public administration to understand and analyse the special problems of developing and underdeveloped nations.

The evolution and growth of development administration are divided into six phases—(a) 1950–1960, (b) 1960–1970, (c) 1970–1980, (d) 1980–1990, (e) 1990–2000, and (f) 2000–present. These phases are discussed in the following sections.

9.3.1 Development Administration in 1950–1960

Two important phenomena took place post the Second World War. First, the countries of Western Europe were reconstructed with the help of the Marshall Plan. Second, many new countries were born due to the process of decolonisation. The theory of development administration originated because of these two major events in world history. The term 'development administration' was coined by an Indian scholar 'Goswami' in 1955.

In the earlier phase, the development administration was preoccupied with the classical economist concept of the gross national product (GNP) or per capita income. It was thought that the Keynesian economic approach (or macroeconomic approach) paved the way for the transformation of *ascriptive*, *particularistic*, and *functionally diffused prismatic* developing societies to modernised, *achievement-oriented*, *universalist*, and *functionally specific* developed societies (the words in italic font are special terms, already discussed in Chapter 8). In this era, disciplines such as economics, political science, and sociology contributed to the growth of the discipline of development administration.

In these starting years, the process of development was sought to be achieved on the basis of a prescriptive or normative approach, in which administrative reforms (or development of administration) were seen as a precondition to development. This approach was also known as the *instrumental theory of administration.* It was said that development could be achieved only if the government deigns monetary and fiscal policies properly. These monetary and fiscal policies were thought to lead to a process of planned development with the aid of Western funds and the technology of administration.

This aid from Western countries was better known as the *Technical Assistance Programme*. The aims of this programme were:

(i) Reformation of administrative structures of developing countries.
(ii) Creation of new developmental agencies in these countries.
(iii) Improving the administrative technology (in terms of methods and procedures) in these countries.
(iv) Transferring the Western administrative thoughts for application in the administrative procedures and practices of developing countries.
(v) Personnel administration reforms in terms of setting up a merit system, implementation of the position classification scheme and central personnel agencies (these terms are discussed in Chapter 10).
(vi) Creation of training institutions for imparting training to the people of developing countries by the scholars and practitioners of Western countries.

The above-mentioned technical assistance programme was a part of the *modernisation thought* that outlined the Western model of development as an indispensable solution to the developmental problems of the Third World countries. This thought was propounded by economists such as W.W. Rostow, Samuel Eisenstadt, Gabriel Almond, Marion Levy, Neil Smelser, and Talcott Parson. In the modernisation theory, the process of modernisation was viewed as a lengthy homogenising process towards irreversible and progressive convergence among societies over long periods of time.5

Another supporter of modernisation thought was the much famous *achievement motivation theory* propounded by D. McClelland (already discussed in Chapter 4). In his view, people living in Western industrialised nations had high levels of achievement motivation, which accounted for their high level of economic growth. They were innovative personalities who displayed self-confidence and satisfaction from problem-solving and achievement. On the other hand, people in Third World countries lacked self-confidence, exhibited a high level of anxiety when faced with new situations, and were content to continue with the status quo. Thus, for effective development, the individual personalities had to undergo a distinctive change towards the Western model of living.[6]

9.3.2 Development Administration in 1960–1970

Since the 1960s, the technical assistance programme was found to fail. It was criticised by many scholars; it was regarded as "a sad waste of scarce human resources" by Dwight Waldo. The various reasons for its failure were as mentioned below:

(a) **One-Size-Fits-All Approach:** The universal approach of the model disregarded the environmental and contextual factors of various countries.

(b) **Different Interpretation of Similar Terms:** The important terms of macroeconomics such as efficiency, economy, and rationality were interpreted in different manners in different countries.

(c) **Planning without Implementation:** Many plans for administrative reforms were not implemented in developing countries because of the lack of political and bureaucratic support.

(d) **Lack of Knowledge:** The experts of the technical assistance programme did not have sufficient knowledge of the administrative problems in the various economic sectors of developing countries such as their agriculture, health, education, industry, population control, and so on.

(e) **Incomplete Transfer of Technology:** It was seen that only basic administrative technologies were transmitted from Western countries to developing countries. Modern administrative techniques such as CMP, PERT, linear programming, network analysis, and cost-benefit analysis were not transmitted.

(f) **Disregard towards Attitudinal Change:** Administrative reforms in this era focused only on structural change and not on attitudinal and behavioural changes.

As the technical assistance programme failed, there were other advancements in the field of development administration between 1960 and 1970. These were importantly based on (1) the contribution of CAG, (2) Riggs' contribution, (3) the empirical approach to development administration, and (4) the dependency theory of development administration. These topics are discussed in the following sections.

9.3.2.1 Contribution of CAG to Development Administration

The Comparative Administrative Group (CAG), as already discussed in Chapter 8, was tasked with carrying out research in comparative administration with a special focus on the problems of development administration. The CAG felt that the classical concepts of administration (as emphasised in the technical assistance programme) were rigid, narrow, and parochial and, thus, unfit to explain the cross-cultural contexts of administration in different countries. It stressed that the sociological and cultural contexts of administration are more important than mere reforms in the organisational structure and personnel administration.

The group provided many new concepts to the field of development administration and public administration, such as systems analysis, patterns variables, information theory, and pluralism.

9.3.2.2 Riggs' Contribution to Development Administration

Riggs has observed that an increase in GNP may not necessarily lead to improvement in the real-life conditions of the people. On the contrary, indicators reflecting the physical, social, and psychological quality of life are more useful for judging the development of a country. He has regarded developing countries as prismatic societies undergoing the social transformation process between fused societies and developed diffracted societies (this topic is discussed in detail in Chapter 8). Further, he has made an attempt to understand the socio-cultural and administrative factors that are important for the effective implementation of the technical assistance programme.

9.3.2.3 Empirical Approach to Development Administration

Between 1960 and 1970, we saw a shift from the normative approach (of the technical assistance programme) to the empirical approach of development administration. The basic units of this empirical approach were the various structures and their functions within different systems (here, 'systems' refer to different societies). It led to numerous reports and studies by experts, visiting consultants, technical assistants, and other public administration scholars. The basic concern of these reports was to search for an ideal administrative pattern and to determine administrative challenges and their solutions in developing societies.

9.3.2.4 The Dependency Theory of Development Administration

The dependency theory has described underdevelopment as the historical result of the functioning of the capitalist system. It stated that colonialism and the continuing colonial structures were responsible for the underdevelopment of the Third World countries. It described the Western countries as the *core countries*, from where the capitalist model has emerged, and the Third World countries as the *periphery countries*, who have been victims of the capitalist paradigm. A schematic of this situation is shown in Fig. 9.1.

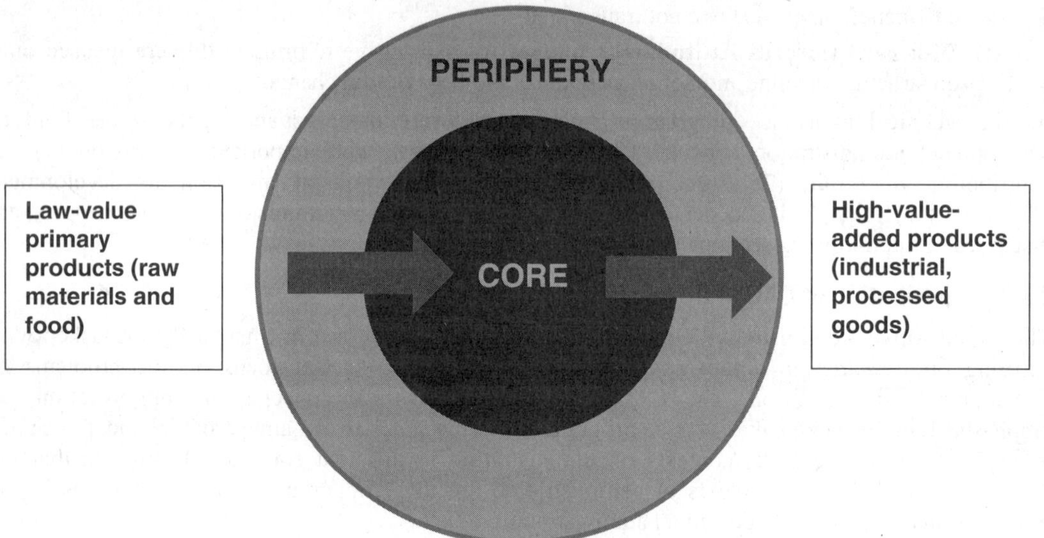

***Fig. 9.1:** Core and Periphery Countries in the Dependency Theory*[7]

In the capitalist model, the low-value primary products (raw materials and food) are supplied from the periphery countries to the core countries. The core countries, in turn, supply back the high-value-added products (industrial and processed goods) to the periphery countries. This capitalist penetration (from the core to the periphery countries) leads to further underdevelopment of the periphery countries. Thus, the dependency theory suggests that indigenous social and economic development in Third World countries must be so organised as to ensure the removal of industrial capitalist penetration and dominance. This simply means that the Third World economies should become self-reliant and be able to control their natural resources effectively.

9.3.3 Development Administration in 1970–1980

By the 1970s, the meaning of development underwent a change; development goals were now framed in terms of meeting basic human needs rather than increasing the per capita income. The development model also underwent a change in terms of strategies and implementation programmes. It started with the report of the Commission on International Development on the Technical Assistance Programme in 1969.

9.3.3.1 UN Report of Commission on International Development on Technical Assistance Programme

The Report of the Commission on International Development on the Technical Assistance Programme, 1969 made it clear that the development strategy of the 1960s, focusing on the technical transportation of administrative methods, procedures, and practices from the Western countries to the developing countries, required a critical review. The important role of the local people in the development and decision-making process was pointed out. It was said that the development problems were related to the political economy of the aid-receiving countries.

9.3.3.2 The Political Economy Approach to Development Administration

The political economy approach sought to combine the political, social, and administrative aspects of society for bringing in development. It sought to relate administration to the political and social environment. Moreover, it examined development administration in terms of power relationships, power conflicts, and their resolution process.

9.3.3.3 The Ecological Approach to Development Administration

The ecological approach (already discussed in Chapter 8) sought to relate public administration to the political, economic, social, and cultural environment. It regarded development as a holistic concept dependent on strong political institutions and practices. Thus, the political, social, and economic framework must be taken into account while analysing developmental activities. It pointed out that the special characteristics of a country are required to be understood before prescribing a developmental role to its government and administration.

9.3.3.4 Basic Needs Approach to Development Administration

The basic needs approach is aimed at restructuring the internal domestic economy in such a manner as to eradicate mass poverty and income inequality and meet the basic needs of people, including their education, health, nutrition, shelter, and clothing. The emphasis was on qualitative change in people's lives rather than just quantitative economic growth in the economy. The development ideology was characterised by need orientation, ecological orientation, self-reliance orientation, and rural development orientation based on the creation of endogenous techniques and institutional structures. The issue of distributive justice was given a major focus along with the goal of increasing in production of goods and services. The approach was based on anti-poverty programmes and policies aimed at the removal of socio-economic disparity.

In these basic needs approach, certain administrative modifications were made as follows:

(a) **Focus on Local Organisations:** Regional and local administrative structures rather than the central institutions were made instrumental for development.

(b) **Rural Development:** Rural development was made the central strategy for development rather than focusing on increasing urbanisation.

(c) **Agriculture Development:** Focus was shifted from increasing industrialisation to developing agriculture in order to address the poverty scenario of the villages.

(d) **Labour-intensive Economy:** Various attempts were made to shift the economy from capital-intensive to labour-intensive.

(e) **Participative Planning:** Planning for development was made more participative and less top-down in nature.

(f) **Self-reliance:** There was a focus on developing the indigenous economy rather tha depending on foreign funds for development.

(g) **Appropriate Technology:** Rather than focusing on advanced technology, the approac focused on adopting appropriate and indigenous technologies for addressing developmenta problems.

(h) **Decentralisation and Delegation:** Decentralisation and delegation of power wer considered necessary for attaining developmental goals.

9.3.4 Development Administration in 1980–1990

Since the 1980s, we have seen a shift towards indigenous concepts, methods, and theories fo development administration. The focus was on the role of non-government, voluntary, an community organisations in the developmental process. Moreover, the focus was further enhanced o the local, decentralised, and participative approaches to development administration. The majo approaches of development administration adopted in this decade were the (a) learning proces approach, (b) world systems approach, and (3) ultra-modernist approach. These approaches ar discussed in the following sections.

9.3.3.1 Learning Process Approach to Development Administration

Before the 1980s, a blueprint approach was followed, in which specific plans of action were prepare in advance for implementing a developmental project. However, this approach was foun inappropriate and too rigid to respond to the changing needs of the environment. Hence, a nev approach, namely, the learning process approach, was recommended; this approach was relativel open-ended to planned social change and involved a cybernetic process through which developmen administration could adapt itself to the changing environment and incorporate mid-cours corrections, based on existing local conditions. The approach emphasised planning with the loca people and planning along with the process of administrating a developmental programme. It lai stress on learning by self-experience and the experience of others.

The approach basically aims at looking for administrative solutions from practical experience rather than expecting help from Western societies in raising them from the impoverished condition in their life.

9.3.3.2 World Systems Approach to Development Administration

The world systems approach is an advancement to the dependency approach to developmen administration. In it, the 'world system' or the historical social system is considered as the unit o analysis. The scholars used historical explanations from the viewpoint of the world system, in whicl the functions and interactions of all the societies were analysed. They examined large-scale change in the world system over long periods of time.

Taking the lead from dependency theorists, they have categorised the world countries into core semi-periphery, and periphery countries, as shown in Fig. 9.2. This is a tri-modal structure of the world described by Wallerstein.[9] When the overall world economic growth increases, the worl system is said to expand. On the other hand, the world system is said to contract when the overal world economic growth decreases.

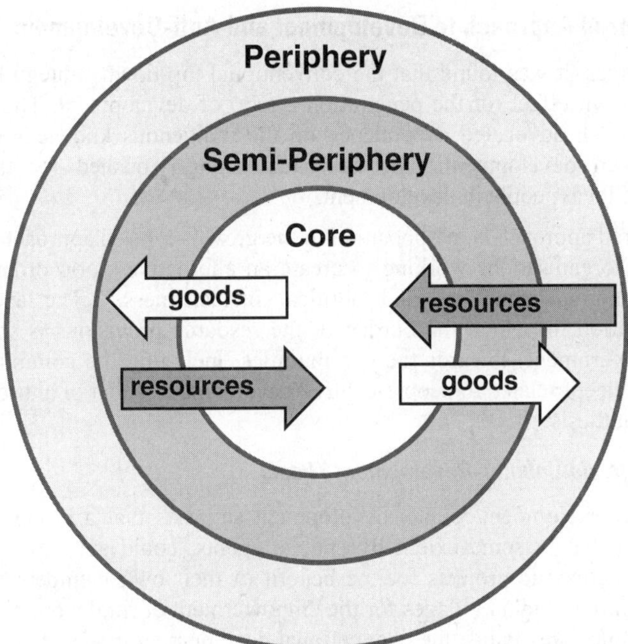

Fig. 9.2: Core, Semi-Periphery and Periphery Countries in World Systems Theory[8]

As the world system expands or contracts in its totality, countries change their positions at different rates and move in different directions. Countries are said to be in upward mobility when they move from a semi-peripheral region to the core region or from a peripheral region to a semi-peripheral region. Similarly, downward-mobility countries move from the core to a semi-peripheral and peripheral regions.

The development of countries is dependent upon the expansion or spread of their market control. The world system theorists ended up recommending a socialist world government as a solution to the problem of unequal development.

However, the theory is criticised for having a single worldview for all countries. Thus, world system theorists have remained largely outside the practical world of policy debates.

9.3.3.3 Ultra-Modernist Approach to Development Administration

Since the 1980s, another approach that emerged in development administration was the ultra-modernist approach. The scholars of this approach advocated for the basic laws of economics and the market mechanisms for the optimal allocation of resources across the world. They said that the role of government and outside agencies makes the working of market forces imperfect and disrupts the process of natural development. Thus, developing countries should be allowed to grow in a free market without any aid from a foreign or national government. The free market allows a condition in which resources are allocated in an optimal manner to all people.

9.3.5 Development Administration in 1990–2000

During the decade between 1990 and 2000, we saw the emergence of (a) people-centred approach to development and the anti-development thesis, (2) a market orientation approach to development, and (3) a sustainable livelihoods approach to development.

9.3.4.1 People-centred Approach to Development and Anti-Development Thesis

In the previous decades, it was found that the conventional top-down strategy had failed to produce the desired trickle-down effect (or the penetration effect) of development. Thus, the scholars of the people-centred approach advocated dependence on the indigenous knowledge system of the local people for their own development. The approach strongly pushed for the participation and empowerment of the local people in development.

This people-centred approach is in opposition to the growth-centred approach to development. It is advanced by citizen organisations working to create an alternative world order based on economic justice, environmental sustainability, and political inclusiveness.[10] The approach is based on community participation, in which the burden of the resource provisions is shifted away from the public sector (or government) towards the communities, including the communities that are in the greatest need.[11] A concept related to people-centred development is that of anti-development thesis or counter-development thesis.

Anti-Development Thesis/Counter-Development Thesis

The concept of anti-development/counter-development suggests that a group of people organise a self-help basis and aided to some extent by change agents, could agree on collective action and operate cooperative economic projects for the benefit of their own members.[12] Women's self-help groups (SHGs) working in Indian villages for the empowerment of rural women are classic examples. Such cooperative groups are against the conventional development models that only took care of the capitalists and the powerful and rejected the genuine interest of the poor.

The counter-development movement got a theoretical basis when the field experiences proved the failure of society-wide structural change programmes. The counter-development approach particularly favoured the development of small groups. It was proved that in relatively small groups, contradictory developmental goals can be reconciled, overall economic growth can be justly distributed among the members of the group, and complete participation of the individuals can be ensured. (Such initiatives, including self-help groups and cooperatives, have already been discussed in Chapter 6).

Moreover, it was also advocated that conventional developmental research (attaching importance to the technical knowledge of external experts over the indigenous knowledge of the people under study) was anti-developmental in nature, as it prevented people from freely thinking and acting for themselves.

Participatory Action Research

An important implementation strategy of the people-centred developmental approach and the counter-development thesis is the methodology of participatory action research. It is a method of promoting the collective intellectual capacity of the disadvantaged people under study. In it, the poor are allowed to investigate their own deprivations and evolve their own science or systematic thinking to improve their standard of living and negotiate with the government and other developmental agencies. In this context, *participatory rural appraisal* (PRA) is a strategy of participatory action research in rural areas, which enables the rural population to undertake their own appraisal, analysis, developmental actions, self-monitoring, and evaluation of their action programmes.

It is basically a way of learning from and with the villagers to investigate, analyse, and evaluate their constraints and opportunities. It helps in making informed and timely decisions regarding the development projects of the rural people.[13] This strategy of PRA will be discussed in detail in the chapter on rural development in the second volume of this book.

Benefits of the People-centred Approach/Anti-development Thesis

There are various benefits of the people-centred approach or the anti-development thesis. They are as follows:

(a) **Congruence between Development Objectives and Community Values:** The people-centred approach ensures congruence between development objectives and community values and preferences, as it maintains a continuous two-way communication between the grass-roots people and the developmental implementers during the planning and implementation process.

(b) **Low Project Cost:** Participatory projects are expected to have a low project cost, as participation helps in the optimum utilisation of manpower and natural resources.

(c) **Acceptance to Community:** The fruit of developmental projects is readily accepted by the community, as they are actively involved in the planning and implementation stages. They are more tolerant of the mistakes made during the project.

(d) **Better Monitoring and Sustainability:** As people are directly involved in their welfare projects, they ensure active monitoring of the projects as well as their sustenance even after withdrawal from the government or the external aid agency.

(e) **Two-way Learning Process:** It becomes a two-way learning process, in which the administrators learn from the local people and the local people learn from the grass-roots implementation done by the administrators.

(f) **Community Cohesion:** People-centred development helps in building community cohesion and instils a sense of dignity among the community members.

Criticism of the People-centred Approach

Notwithstanding the benefits, the people-centred approach is criticised on the following grounds:

(a) **An Egalitarian Concept:** The participation approach is an egalitarian concept, not practical to be implemented completely in all the communities.

(b) **Corruption and Rivalries at the Local Level:** It is naïve to assume that the devolution of authority to the local people would help in removing all the developmental barriers such as corruption and caste and religious rivalries. On the contrary, local people are more sharply divided into the lines of caste, religion, and other political factors. It cannot be said with complete confidence that local people's organisations will work more effectively than central organisations.

(c) **Lack of Clarity:** The people-centred approach suffers from lack of the clarity required to be easily implemented at the grass-roots level. Thus, the approach enjoys popularity only in thought but is difficult to be implemented.

(d) **Important Role of Experts:** The role of external experts is as important as the involvement of the local people. The external experts and social workers are important for organising the local community and mobilising the local people for development. Thus, every people-centred programme requires the initiative of outside activities and experts.

(e) **Requires Widespread Social Change:** Every community-based programme suffers from the caste, class, and communal barriers found at the local level. Thus, for the people-centred approach to be successful, widespread social change is required at the national and international levels. Community mobilisation, cannot, on its own, correct the social imbalances that are deeply rooted in the socio-economic structure of the society.

9.3.4.2 Market Orientation Approach to Development Administration

The market orientation approach advocates the reduced role of the state vis-à-vis the market for development. The approach suggests unilateral opening of the internal economy to foreign trade;

extensive privatisation of state enterprises; deregulation of goods, services, and labour markets; liberalisation of the capital market with extensive privatisation of pension funds; sharp reduction in public expenditure; reduction in state-supported social developmental programmes; an end to industrial policies; and concentration on macroeconomic management.[14]

In this approach, development is understood as the mere success of an economy in the marketplace without paying any attention to the distributive effects of aggregate economic gains either between or within countries. The merits and demerits of this approach will be extensively dealt with in this chapter.

9.3.4.3 Sustainable Livelihoods Approach to Development

The sustainable livelihoods (SL) approach is an important approach to development and poverty reduction. It offers a more coherent and integrated approach to development than the previous approaches. The previous approaches were narrower in the sense that they focused on certain aspects of development such as increasing per capita income, and did not consider other aspects of development such as vulnerability and social exclusion. However, the SL approach pays more attention to the various factors and processes that either constrain or enhance poor people's ability to make a living in an economically, ecologically, and socially sustainable manner.[15]

The idea of the SL approach was first developed by the Bruntland Commission on Environment and Development, in 1987 and the UN Conference on Environment and Development, in 1992. According to scholars, sustainable livelihood is defined as "a livelihood that can cope with and recover from stresses and shocks, maintain or enhance its capabilities and assets, and provide sustainable livelihood opportunities for the next generation, which contributes net benefits to other livelihoods at the local and global levels and in the short and long term, and which can help in integration of population, resources, environment, and development with respect to four aspects: stabilising population, reducing migration, fending off core exploitation, and supporting long-term sustainable resource management."[16]

The SL approach has three important assumptions, as follows:

(a) **No Automatic Relationship between Economic Growth and Development:** Economic growth is essential for development, but there is no automatic relationship between the two. Development depends on the capabilities of the people to take advantage of the expanding economic opportunities.

(b) **Integral Concept of Development:** Development is related not just to an increase in income but also access to improved health, education, other important social services, and so on, and the provision of a feeling of empowerment and dignity to the poor.

(c) **Participation of People:** People know their situation very well and must be involved in the design of policies and projects intended to benefit them.

9.3.6 Development Administration since 2000

There has been considerable growth in the field of development administration since 2000. The major approaches since 2000 have been (1) the capability approach to development, (2) the women and development approach, (3) the sustainable development approach, and (4) post-development thought. The first and fourth approaches will be discussed in this section. The second and third approaches will be discussed as separate topics in the subsequent parts of this chapter.

9.3.5.1 The Capability Approach to Development Administration and Development as Freedom

Amartya Sen's capability approach is based on four terms—capability, functioning, freedom, and agency. These terms are defined below:

(a) **Functioning:** Functioning refers to the various things a person may value and have reason to value doing or being. Examples of functioning are working, resting, being literate, being healthy, being part of a community, being able to travel, and so on.[17] These are aspects of human fulfilment. Some functionings are very basic (such as being nourished, literate, and clothed) and some are complex (such as being able to play music). Functioning can relate to different dimensions of well being, from survival to self-direction and self-actualisation. The different indicators of functioning are per capita income, health indicators, education levels, and so on.

(b) **Capability:** Sen has described capabilities as what people are effectively able to do and be, or the positive freedom that people have to enjoy valuable beings and doings (these valuable beings and doings are the 'functionings'). It describes the real actual possibilities open to a person. Thus, capability has two parts: (1) freedom and (2) valuable beings and doings (functionings).

For example, in the case of food, gaining nutrition from food is its functioning (a person values gaining nutrition) and the ability to get nutrition from food is the capability of a person. A month-old baby is not capable of gaining nutrition from rice but a 10-year-old boy is.

(c) **Freedom:** Freedom is described as the real opportunity we have to accomplish what we value. A good life is one in which a person is free to choose and attain what he/she values rather than being forced into a particular life—however rich it might be in other aspects. Moreover, freedom is authentic *self-direction*—the ability to shape one's own destiny as a person and a part of various communities. For Amartya Sen, freedom has two aspects, as described below:

- **Process Aspect:** The process aspect of freedom is the ability to act on behalf of what matters to a person, such as various movements and democratic practices (an agency of a person).
- **Opportunity Aspect:** The opportunity aspect of freedom refers to the real opportunity to achieve valued functionings, selected from among various good possibilities (capabilities).

(d) **Agency:** Agency is defined as a person's ability to act on what he/she values and has reason to value. The opposite of a person with an agency is someone who is forced, oppressed, or passive. It expands the horizons of a person's concern beyond his/her own well-being to include concerns such as helping others. A person with an agency is viewed to be active, creative, and able to act on behalf of his/her aspirations. Moreover, a person with an agency is able to participate, debate in public, indulge in democratic practices, and be empowered along with being concerned about well-being.

Development as Freedom

Amartya Sen has provided a completely different definition of development. According to him, development should be understood as an expansion of people's freedom. Freedom is not only the primary end of development but also the primary means of attaining development.[18]

Moreover, Sen has claimed that the development or well-being of a person can be evaluated by evaluating the functionings and capabilities s/he possessess. Human development needs to be re-examined from the 'capabilities approach' perspective, as it gives a person the freedom to choose one kind of life over another. The capabilities approach constitutes a broad normative framework for the evaluation of social arrangements and the design of policies on social change issues such as poverty measurement, social cost-benefit analysis, social justice, development ethics, and inequality analysis. While justifying his concept of development as freedom, Sen has quoted Immanuel Kant as "human beings should be seen as ends in themselves rather than as means to other ends."[19]

Sen has delineated freedom into its various realms, namely, social, political, and economic. Further, he has shown how the expansion of freedom is, at the same time, the 'end' we seek and the 'means' to that end. In this expanded and comprehensive perspective, previously unattended domains such as healthcare and education have received importance in the measurement of real development. Moreover, Sen has explained how the expansion of freedom in one domain is instrumental in expanding freedom in another domain. For example, an increase in female literacy can lead to a decrease in the female fertility rate.

In a nutshell, in Sen's neo-developmental vision, the focus is on what people are able to do and be, on the quality of their life, and on removing obstacles in their lives so that they have more freedom to live the kind of life they find valuable. For example, every person should have the opportunity to be part of a community and to practice a religion, but if someone prefers to be a hermit or an atheist, they should have this option also.

Capability Approach vs Utilitarian Approach

Sen's capability approach to development is drastically different from the previous utilitarian approaches to development. The previous approaches suggested that development should maximise income, commodities, and people's happiness. On the other hand, the capability approach claims that the appropriate method of evaluating development is not in terms of primary goods or utilities but rather in terms of a person's capabilities—in terms of the real freedom that they have reason to value. Capabilities are more important than utilities or resource availability.

Sen has made this point clear through the example of a healthy person and a handicapped person needing different kinds of resources to enable them to have the same opportunities in life. The relationship between a certain amount of goods, and what a person can do or can be, may differ from person to person. A person may have more income and more nutritional intake than another person, but less freedom to live a well-nourished existence because of a higher basal metabolic rate, greater vulnerability to diseases, larger body size, or pregnancy.

Thus, the conversion of goods and services into functionings is influenced by personal, social and environmental factors. Resource provision may not always lead to increased capabilities or functionings. Moreover, Sen has introduced a concept of *adaptive preferences* to demonstrate the superiority of capabilities over utility. This concept suggests that our desires and pleasure-taking abilities adjust to circumstances, especially to make life bearable in adverse situations. Thus, the utility calculus can be unfair to those who are persistently deprived.

Capability Approach—A Holistic View on Development

The capability approach is a holistic view of development. It evaluates policies according to their impact on people's capabilities. For example, it asks whether people are being healthy (functioning) and whether the resources necessary for this capability, such as clean water, access to medical facilities, protection from infections and diseases, and basic knowledge of health issues, are present. Similarly, it raises questions on whether people are well-nourished and whether the conditions required for this capability, such as sufficient food supplies and food entitlements, are being met. Financial resources and economic production are, of course, the main input for some of the capabilities. However, the other inputs are political practices such as the protection of freedom of thought, religion or political participation, socio-cultural practices, social norms, traditions, habits, and so on. Thus, the capability approach covers a full terrain of human development and well-being. Development is regarded in a comprehensive and integrated manner and attention is paid to the links between material, mental, spiritual, and social development and well-being, or to the economic, social, political, and cultural dimensions of life.

9.3.5.2 Post-Developmental Thought/Postmodern Critique of Development/Development as Discourse

In the late 1990s and 2000s, we found a complete distrust in the concept and practice of development. This happened as all the developmental efforts failed in ameliorating the real-life conditions of Third World people. This complete distrust in the concept of development is regarded as a post-development thought or a post-development critique.

Post-development thought claims that the concept of development is a Western creation imposed on the people of the Third World countries. The strategies and plans for development created by Western scholars pre-empt any new thinking by the Third World scholars. Western scholars design development strategies such as micro-development, participative development, and sustainable development, which are then posed as alternative development strategies for the Third World. These theories are institutionalised and absorbed into the mainstream development theory and implemented in developing countries. However, they reproduce the same power relationship as found in the era of colonialism and afterward in the era of conventional development theories (e.g., modernisation theory and the technical assistance programme).

This happens because of the very nature of the concept of development. Development is planned, directed, and controlled by specific international and national institutions representing a specific Western ideology. This ideology describes the Third World as being in need of help and provides the legal and moral rationale for development interventions, situating the Third World in the lower rungs of the international system. Thus, development is a product of a perspective that portrays the situation in the Third World as a great problem.

Development as Discourse

The above-mentioned view of postmodern scholars describes the development as a discourse used as an apparatus for surveillance and control over the Third World.[20] It is a historical discourse in which many countries started seeing themselves as 'underdeveloped' in the post World War II period, and 'How to develop?' became the most important question for them. However, as the postmodern critics argue, they ended up 'underdeveloping' themselves. The so-called process of development discourse consists of the following steps:

1. **Portrayal of Problems:** The conditions and situations in the Third World, such as poverty and illiteracy, were perceived as problems by the scholars and politicians of Western countries.
2. **Preparation of Development Strategies:** Understanding these problems led to the emergence of a new domain of thought known as 'development'. This thought resulted in the preparation of new strategies for dealing with the alleged 'problems' of the Third World. These strategies were willingly or forcefully accepted by the Third World in order to 'develop' themselves.
3. **Control over Third World:** As a result, the Third World population was put under a regime of control by these discursive practices. The poor people of the Third World were portrayed as a social problem and subjected to new ways of intervention in the name of development. The management of poverty called for interventions in education, health, hygiene, morality, employment, and instilment of the good habits of association, savings, and so on.
4. **Superior Western Knowledge:** Models of social planning and intervention were formed requiring extensive 'superior' Western knowledge. Such knowledge and planning were

required not only in the field of poverty but also in the field of health, education, employment, and standard of living in urban and rural areas. Such apparatus of knowledge advocated for 'modern' and 'scientific' living conditions for the people of the Third World.

5. **Regarding Third World Countries as Poor:** The result of these strategies and practices was pervasive in the Third World countries. They started defining themselves in relation to the standard of the wealth of the more economically advantaged countries. The economic concept of poverty was measured in terms of per capita income. Thus, two-thirds of the world's population (the poor living in Third World countries) was transformed into poor subjects according to the poverty definition of the World Bank.
6. **Subtle Power Relation:** Such transformation of the Third World countries into poor countries had an inherent power relation behind it.[21] In this power relation, the Third World was distanced from the 'civilised and developed' West. This distance was marked with inferiority and negativity about the Third World. The Third World was branded as backward, underdeveloped, poor, lacking in achievement-motivation, traditional, and so on. When such kinds of negative images were imposed on the people of the Third World, they became permeable to certain interventions on them. Thus, the negative view of the Third World justified the 'developmental' interventions on them. This brought in a kind of 'doctor-patient' or 'father-child' power relationship between the West and the Third World.
7. **New Forms of Power and Control:** The above-mentioned power relation helped in producing an efficient apparatus for knowledge generation and exercising power over the Third World. New forms of power and control, more subtle and refined than the colonial regime, were put into operation over the Third World. The people of the Third World lost the ability to define and take care of their lives.

In the words of Wolfgang Sachs, "Development had become a shapeless amoeba-like word. It had no definitive content. All that it did was allow any intervention to be sanctioned in the name of higher evolutionary goals. Development always implied that there are lead runners who showed the way to latecomers. It suggests that advancement is the result of planned activity by experts and it evokes notions of universality, progress and feasibility. It prevents people to think autonomously and grow in their own milieu and style."[22]

This developmental discourse created a power game in the world, in which the problems of the Third World were analysed, investigated, and worked over by the West. Various policies for the betterment of the Third World were prepared by Western scholars. These policies and practices were accepted by the Third World either due to conditions imposed under various aid programmes or due to the sense of inferiority in the mind of the leaders and people of the Third World with respect to the living conditions prevalent in Western countries.

However, such policies and interventions have failed to uplift the conditions of the Third World because of the inbuilt patriarchy and ethnocentrism in the development discourse. In this discourse, the indigenous people were made to modernise according to Western values. Their own culture was regarded as backward, evil, and inimical to development. In the development discourse, various models and plans were formulated, having no relation to the beneficiary population and the views of the local people on their own problems and solutions. Thus, most development interventions were unsuccessful and led to tensions in the Third World.

Thus, the post-development or postmodern scholars regard 'development' as a strategy by the West to morally subjugate the Third World and establish the same power relationship as was found in the colonial era.

Evolution of Development Administration

1950-1960

Coining of the term in 1955

Technical Assistance Programme
- Modernization thought
- Reformation of administrative structures
- New development agencies
- Administrative technology
- Western administrative thoughts
- Personnel administration reforms

1960-1970

Contribution of CAG to DA

Contribution of Riggs to DA

Empirical Approach to DA
- Reports and studies for searching an ideal administrative pattern

Dependency Theory
- Core and peripheral countries

1970-1980

Political Economy Approach
Combination of political, social and administrative aspects of the society for development.

Ecological Approach to DA

Basic Needs Approach
- Focus on local organisations
- Rural development
- Agriculture development
- Labour Intensive economy
- Participate planning
- Self reliance
- Appropriate technology
- Decentralisation and delegation

1980-1990

Learning Process Approach
- Open ended
- Cybernetic process
- Adjustment of DA to changing environment

World Systems Model
Core, semi- periphery and periphery countries

Ultra Modernist Approach
Development in free market without any aid from government or foreign nation

1990-2000

People Centered Approach
- Community participation in development
- SHGs
- Anti development thesis
- Participatory action research

Market Oriented Approach
Reduced role of state vis-à-vis market

Sustainable Livelihood Approach
- Bruntland commission
- No automatic relationship b/w economic growth and development.
- Integral concept of development
- Participation of people

Since 2000

Capability Approach
- Functioning, capability, freedom and agency
- Development as freedom
- Holistic view of development

Post Development Though
- Distrust with concept and practice of development
- Development as a western concept imposed on people of third world
- **Development Discourse consisting of**
  - Portrayal of third world problems
  - Perpetration of development strategies
  - Control over third world
  - Superior western knowledge
  - Regarding of third world as poor
  - Subtle power relations
  - New forms of power and control.

Mind Map 9.1: *Evolution of Development Administration*

9.4 Edward Weidner on Development Administration

Edward Weidner has described development administration as a goal-oriented and action-oriented public administration. There has been an underemphasis on the study of goals in earlier public administration. On this, Weidner has commented that "traditionally public administration has glorified the means and forgotten the ends. Good administration and good human relations have become ends in themselves, quite apart from the achievement of other values that they may or may not facilitate.[43]

He introduced the concept of development administration to fill such a gap in administrative theory. He has described development administration as "the processes of guiding an organisation toward the achievement of progressive political, economic and social objectives that are authoritatively determined in one manner or another."[43]

To describe the concept further, Weidner has formulated eight development models on the basis of directional growth, system change, and planning. These models are described below:

1. **Ideal Planned Directional Growth with System Change:** In this model, development is understood as a continuous process. Plans are formulated for socio-economic growth and programmes are implemented, with system change, in order to realise this growth. Most developing countries have set up a Planning Commission to attain this development process. However, the model is criticised as the ideal set of conditions of planning, system change, and growth, not often serving as evidence for development. The ability of an administrative system to carry out a planned programme of a major change is often severely restricted.
2. **Planned Directional Growth with No System Change:** In this model, the maximum development is tried to be attained without introducing any major system changes in the administration. Such a model has the maximum payoff in the short run, in terms of nation building and socio-economic progress. Such a model is adopted when the conditions are not suitable for bringing in major system changes, such as weak national leadership, lack of budget and financial assistance, and political instability or demand to show quick results. An example of this model is the promotion of native arts and crafts, such as the cottage industry programmes in India and Pakistan. These programmes were adopted as a part of the plans. They did not disturb the economic or social structures; in turn, they realised economic gains for the country's concern and peasants or other participants. These gains have been small.
3. **Planned System Change with No Directional Growth:** In this model, there is system change, but system change may not necessarily result in directional growth. It may rather have an adverse effect on growth. For example, systemic land reforms have led to lower agricultural growth in many areas.
4. **Planning with No Growth or System Change:** There are certain schemes in which there is planning that lead neither to growth nor to any system change. Such planning concludes in failure. For example, many economists came to a conclusion in 1965 that development planning has neither accelerated economic growth nor made any change in the administrative system of the countries.
5. **Unplanned Directional Growth with System Change:** The model stipulates that nation building and socio-economic progress involving institutional differentiation and

coordination can take place in an unplanned manner also. Such changes emanate from any society as the reaction of leaders or groups to certain environmental factors. For example, most changes in the bureaucratic system are brought about by ad hoc pragmatic adoption of the conditions in which an agency finds itself.

6. **Unplanned Directional Growth with No System Change:** In this model, unplanned growth takes place in the direction of development with no major system changes. It is found in mildly liberalising countries where development is relatively painless. It produces some short-run payoffs and does not require complicated planning mechanisms. It is the most attractive course of action in those countries where there is no integrated attack on poverty and underdevelopment.
7. **Unplanned System Change with No Directional Growth:** In this model, unplanned change comes largely as a result of decentralised initiatives, competition, adaptation, and emulation. However, such changes do not work in the direction of development and socio-economic progress. Such conditions are found in the case of emergencies, during wars, in newly independent states, and in countries suffering from the serious problems of refugees, starvation, uncontrolled epidemics, floods, droughts, and so on. In such conditions, system changes are required to be adjusted to the on-field challenges.
8. **No Plans and No Change:** In certain static societies, there are no plans for bringing about any system change. In such societies, there are certain pockets of change as well as other pockets of resistance to change. There is a possibility of such static conditions in all developmental efforts.

9.5 Ferrel Heady on Development Administration

Ferrel Heady understood public administration to be best studied from a comparative and international perspective. He analysed development administration and international development from a comparativist perspective. As already discussed before, after World War II, development administration aimed at improving economic conditions and governance systems in developing countries by both spurring macroeconomic development through large-scale industrial projects and implementing Western administrative structures and techniques. However, such a model rarely produced any desirable results in developing countries.

Macroeconomic growth and increase in per capita income were considered to be necessary but not sufficient achievements in economic development. As a response to this model, three analytically separate yet interdependent approaches have emerged: comparative administration, development management, and international public management. These approaches are briefly described in the following:

(1) **Comparative Administration:** The traditional development administration was ethnocentric and ignorant to the conditions and culture of developing countries. Comparative administration emerged as a response to these weaknesses of traditional development administration. In contrast to traditional development administration, comparative administration examined alternative development models based on the cultural contexts of different developing countries. It evaluated the relative capacity of different administrative systems based on the unique underlying socio-political and cultural trends and conditions.

(2) **Development Management:** Development management emerged in the 1990s after the collapse of the Soviet Union and the internalisation of insights from comparative administration. It emerged as the underlying structural mechanism for international economic development changed fundamentally from politically motivated state-to-state aid to market-oriented economic development.[44] In this approach, it was realised that macroeconomic growth was not the sole goal of development. There were other important goals such as balanced economic development, growth of civil society, development of NGOs, and increase of public confidence in the government. Strengthening of the capacities of government agencies and NGOs was considered not only a desirable antidote to the dominance of market-based economy but a prerequisite to successful development. In this era, development managers (scholars and consultants) had formed alliances with international donor agencies and, in effect, established a global industry with different clients, sponsors, and objectives.[45]

(3) **International Public Management:** The third offspring of development administration was international public management, also known as new public management (NPM) (discussed extensively in Chapter 1). In this approach, economic and competitive demands pushed governments for development, democratisation, improvement in economic policy decisions, and the use of scarce resources more efficiently. This movement supported development in individual countries, as it tried to make governments more innovative, flexible, problem-solving, and entrepreneurial.

In a nutshell, development administration has changed fundamentally since the 1960s through the above-mentioned three approaches due to the legacy pioneered in part by Ferrel Heady.

9.6 Human Development Report

Since 1990, the United Nations Development Programme (UNDP) started publishing the Human Development Report (HDR). The report introduced a new approach to advancing human well-being. The approach is aimed at expanding the richness of human life rather than expanding the richness of the economy in which human beings live.[23] The approach is focused on people, their opportunities, and their choices. The first HDR introduced the concept of the *human development index (HDI)* as a measure of achievement in the basic dimensions of human development across countries.

HDI consists of three key indicators essential for human life: *long and healthy life, knowledge, and a decent standard of living.* The total HDI is the geometric average of these three indicators. The three indicators are described in the following:

(a) **Long and Healthy Life (Life Expectancy Index):** The life expectancy index is measured using the value of life expectancy at birth. Long life is closely associated with adequate nutrition, good health, and personal safety.

(b) **Knowledge (Education Index):** The education index of a country is measured by taking the average of two key indicators—(a) mean years of schooling and (b) expected years of schooling.

(c) **Decent Standard of Living (GNI Index):** The standard of living of a country is measured in terms of its gross national income per capita (in terms of purchasing power parity, PPP).

A schematic of these three indicators is shown in Fig. 9.3.

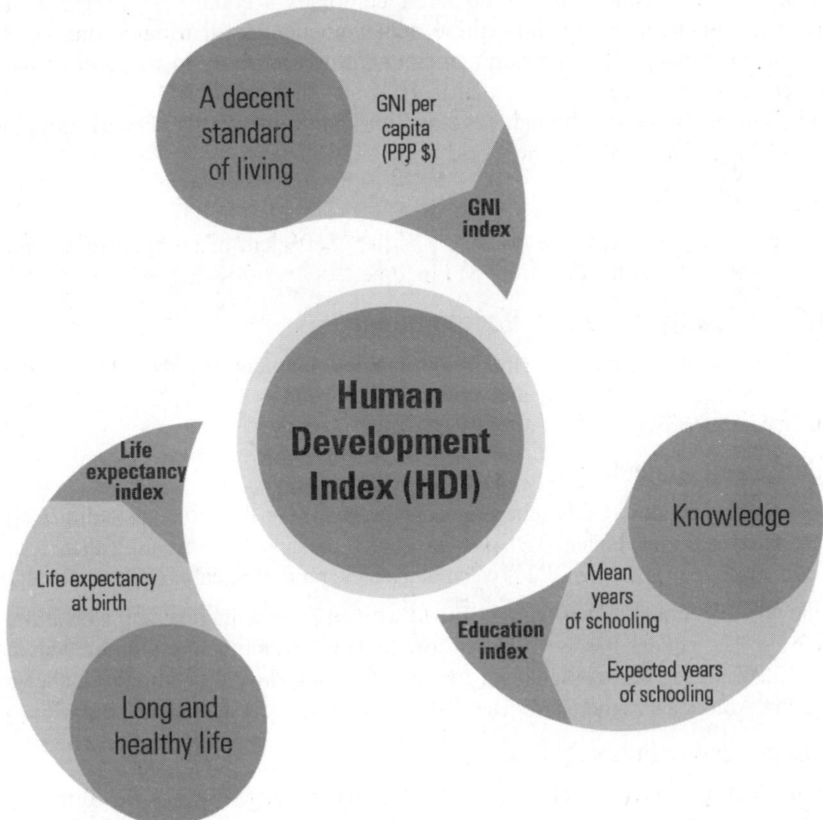

Fig 9.3: Schematic of Human Development Index[24]

Apart from the HDI, the UNDP also publishes three other indicators to measure human development more effectively. They are inequality adjusted human development index, gender inequality index, multidimensional poverty index and gender development index. Ranking countries by their HDI value has transformed the development discourse and discarded per capita income as the sole indicator of development progress.

9.6.1 Inequality in Human Development

In countries across the world, we find deep inequality in human development. These inequalities are not only limited to income but also apply to education, health, voice, access to technology, and exposure to shocks. Human development inequality reflects unequal opportunity in access to education, health, employment, credit, and natural resources due to gender, group identity, income disparities, and location.

Such inequality fuels extremism and undermines support for inclusive and sustainable development. It can lead to adverse consequences for social cohesion and the quality of institutions and policies, which in turn can slow human development progress.

To measure this inequality, UNDP has been measuring the *inequality-adjusted human development index (IHDI)* since 2010. The IHDI combines a country's average achievements in health, education, and income with how these achievements are distributed among the country's population by discounting each dimension's average value according to its level of inequality. In a condition of perfect inequality, IHDI is equal to HDI but falls below HDI in the case of inequality. IHDI is also known as the loss of human development due to inequality. The average loss in human development due to inequality across the world is 20% (2018 data).

Coefficient of Inequality

A specific measure of inequality in development is the coefficient of inequality. It is an unweighted average of inequalities in health, education, and income.

9.6.2 Gender Inequality in Human Development

Gender inequalities are the greatest barriers to human development progress. Two composite indices measure the disparities between men and women—the gender development index (GDI) and the gender inequality index (GII).

9.6.2.1 Gender Development Index

The gender development index (GDI) reports gender inequality in the three basic dimensions of human development.[25] The male and female HDI is calculated separately by estimating their specific share in GNI, health, and education. Then the GDI is calculated as the ratio of female HDI to male HDI.

Much of the gap in gender development is due to women's lower income and educational attainment in many countries. The gender gap is widest in low human development countries, where the average HDI value is 13.8% lower for women than for men. Among developing regions, the gender gap is narrowest in Latin America and the Caribbean and widest in South Asia and the Arab States.[26]

9.6.2.2 Gender Inequality Index

The gender inequality index (GII) reflects gender-based disadvantage in three dimensions—reproductive health, empowerment (education and political representation), and the labour market. It shows the loss in potential human development due to inequality between female and male achievements in these dimensions. It ranges from 0, where women and men fare equally, to 1, where one gender fares as poorly as possible in all the measured dimensions.

While primary and secondary education enrolment indicates that some gender gaps in the early formative years are closing, the gender gaps in adulthood remain high. Women hold only 23.5% of seats in the parliament, and among women, unemployment rates are higher and labour force participation rates are lower.[26] Yet, women provide most unpaid care work in the home—limiting their choices in paid work.

In low human development countries, 39% of women aged 20–24 was married before their 18th birthday. Childhood marriage determines their way of life and—more often than not—undermines their opportunities for education, income, and independence. High adolescent birth rates also undermine young women's opportunities, especially when pregnancies are by chance and not a choice. Worldwide, the adolescent birth rate is 44.0 per 1000 women aged 15–19 and the highest in Sub-Saharan Africa, at 101.3 (2018 data).[26]

9.6.3 Multidimensional Poverty Index

The global multidimensional poverty index (MPI) identifies multiple deprivations at the household level in health, education, and standard of living. It uses micro data from household surveys. It uses

10 indicators in the three dimensions of health, education, and standard of living. Each person is assigned a deprivation score according to his or her household's deprivations in each of the 10 indicators. The maximum deprivation score is 100%, with each dimension equally weighted; thus, the maximum deprivation score in each dimension is 33.3% or, more accurately, 1/3. The 10 indicators of household deprivation are as follows:

- Health:
  1. Nutrition: The nutrition value is calculated using indices such as body mass index (for adults), height-for-age (stunting) (for children), and weight-for-age (underweight) (for children). A household is deprived when any adult under 70 years of age or any child is found undernourished.
  2. Child Mortality: A household is deprived in this field when any child in the household has died in the five years preceding the survey.
- Education:
  1. Years of Schooling: A household is deprived in this field when none of its members above 10 years of age has completed six years of schooling.
  2. School Attendance: Deprivation in this field is calculated when any school aged child (of a household) is not attending school up to the age at which he or she would complete class 8.
- Standard of Living:
  1. Electricity: A household is deprived when it has no electricity.
  2. Sanitation: A household is deprived when it does not have access to improved sanitation such as flush toilets, latrines, ventilated improved pits, or composting toilets that are not shared (according to Sustainable Development Goals guidelines).
  3. Drinking Water: A household is deprived when it does not have access to an improved source of drinking water (according to Sustainable Development Goals guidelines).
  4. Housing: A household is deprived when at least one of its dwelling elements—floor, walls, or roof—is made of inadequate materials.
  5. Cooking Fuel: A household is deprived when it cooks with dung, wood, charcoal, or coal.
  6. Assets: A household is deprived when it does not own a car or truck and does not own more than one of the following assets: radio, television, telephone, computer, animal cart, bicycle, motorbike, or refrigerator.

To identify multidimensionally poor people, the deprivation scores for each indicator are summed to obtain the household deprivation score. A cutoff of 1/3 is used to distinguish between poor and non-poor people. If the deprivation score is 1/3 or higher, that household (and everyone in it) is considered as *multidimensionally poor*. People with a deprivation score of 1/5 or higher, but less than 1/3, are considered to be *vulnerable to multidimensional poverty*. People with a deprivation score of 1/2 or higher are considered to be in *severe multidimensional poverty*.

9.6.4 Quality, not Quantity, of Human Development

Human development should be expressed in terms of quality and not only in terms of quantity. For example, a person may have attended school till the age of 18, but his/her learning should also be meaningful. A person may live till the age of 100 but his/her life should also be meaningful. The additional employment provided must be in safe and secure conditions. From a human development viewpoint, true progress can be achieved only by ensuring quality in health, education, the standard of living, and so on.

- **Quality of Health:** Quality of health can be understood by various input and output factors. The input factors are factors such as access to physicians and hospital beds. The output factors are factors such as healthy life expectancy, which provides information on whether the years lived are expected to be in good health, and lost health expectancy, which is the difference between life expectancy and healthy life expectancy expressed as the percentage of life expectancy at birth.
- **Quality of Education:** The quality of education is understood in terms of skills and capabilities while attending school.

9.7 Women, Gender, and Development

At the outset, when we talk about women, it is very important to differentiate between two terms—sex and gender. While sex is a natural and biological characteristic, gender is a socio-cultural phenomenon, whose definition changes according to the different socio-cultural conditions. In the words of Ann Oakley, "gender is a matter of culture and refers to the social classification of men and women into 'masculine' and 'feminine'. It reflects the existing power relations in any given society. The kinds of power relations reflected by gender are of unequal nature in which women are given secondary position with respect to the men."[27]

9.7.1 Subordinate Position of Women Gender

Historically, it has been seen that women have been given a lower socio-economic and political status in the social hierarchy. The power relation between men and women is defined by the social concept of *patriarchy*, a term that was first defined by Kate Millet in her book *Sexual Politics* in 1974. It describes the way in which a girl child is socialised into accepting the powerful male authority. The various reasons for the subordinate position of women in society are as follows:

(a) **Low Status to Women's Work:** It is seen that the majority of the life-sustaining work such as growing food, cooking, raising children, elderly care, and house maintenance are done by women, and such work is accorded low status and offered no pay in the society. Wherever women work for money, they are invariably limited to low-paying and low-status jobs.

(b) **Unfavourable Laws and Customs:** There are certain laws and customs that prevent women from owning land or other productive assets, from getting loans or credit, or from having the right to inheritance or owning their home. Moreover, they possess no assets to leverage for economic stability and investment in their own future.

(c) **Low Education:** Women form a majority of the population worldwide that cannot read and write. They make up the majority of the children not attending school across the globe.

9.7.2 Women and Development

Women and development is an inclusive term signifying both a concept and a movement. It aims at the well-being of society as a whole, consisting of men, women, and children. It states that the overall development goals will remain unachievable without the full and active participation of women, who constitute more than half of the human resources. Thus, women must possess the legal right and access to the existing means for their own improvement and for the improvement of society as a whole. Therefore, 'women and development' is a holistic concept, wherein the goal of one cannot be attained without the success of the other.

The goal of women's development focuses on three aspects related to women—their rights, resources, and voice.[28] They are as follows:

- **Women's Rights:** Women's development is concerned with ensuring equal social, economic, and legal rights for men and women.
- **Resources:** Women should have command over productive resources, including education, land, information, and financial resources.
- **Voice:** Women should also have influence over resource allocation, investment decisions, and other decisions in their home, community, and at the national level. Their representation should be improved at national, regional, and local representative bodies.

9.7.3 Agencies of Women Development

There are three agencies that can help in women's development: (a) the individual (she herself), (b) the community, and (c) the state. Among the three, the libertarian argument says that it is the individual that counts the most for women's development. Any intervention by the community and the state on her behalf, they say, proves counterproductive and detrimental to her well-being. According to this logic, women need to work for themselves and come up with merit for their own well-being.

The second stand for women's development is the communitarian view. It is favoured for two reasons—(a) the most powerful women's movements over the last three decades have been fought with the help of local communities and (b) the communitarian view is propagated by the Western aid agencies in their programme. The basic argument for this view is that the responsibility for women's development lies with their communities, where women's rights are enshrined. However, upon closer analysis, we find that natural or traditional communities, in most places, are bound by patriarchal normative values, from which women can hardly expect any justice. The religious, village, and artificial communities (such as trade unions) are largely the epitome of inequality between men and women.

Notwithstanding such ideas, it is seen that women communities have successfully contributed to feminist movements. They have helped in providing the much needed free space for the political and social mobilisation of women.

Apart from the individual and the community, in modern times, the state has played a crucial role in enabling women to access better facilities and resources. It plays a significant role for women in developing countries. It is the state that mobilises social resources and provides the largest welfare measures to women. In India, gender and women's development is considered a state responsibility.

However, similar to community, when powers inimical to women capture the state, they are left underdeveloped.

9.7.4 Theoretical Perspectives on Women, Gender, and Development

The three important theoretical perspectives on women, gender, and development are women in development (WID), women and development (WAD), and gender and development (GAD). Apart from these, two important views are *Development Alternatives with Women for a New Era* (DAWN) and *Martha Nussbaum's Capabilities Approach for Women Development*. These approaches are discussed in the following sections.

9.7.4.1 Women in Development

The women in development (WID) approach was first propagated by Ester Boserup's book *Women's Role in Economic Development* published in 1970. The major aspects of this approach were:

(a) **Against Trickle-down Effect:** It challenged the trickle-down effect of development and highlighted how women were affected by economic development. It showed that the trickle-down effect of development does not impact men and women equally.

(b) **Liberal Feminism:** The approach of women in development (WID) was based on the theories of modernisation and liberal feminism. It aimed at integrating women into the overall development process.

(c) **Western Methodologies:** It advocated that women can be developed by adopting Western technologies, institutions, and values.

(d) **Separation of Public and Private Spheres of Women:** It advocated for maintaining a clear line between the public and private spheres. The public sphere is a space that is regulated by the government and the private sphere is a space untouched by the government. Maintaining a clear line between the public and private spheres is necessary for preserving the liberty of women.

(e) **Gender Equality in Institutions:** Apart from this, the WID approach proposed the removal of discriminatory practices in institutions or the creation of alternative institutions that supported women.

(f) **Women's Representation:** It also proposed an increase in the representation of women in elected and appointed positions in the government.

(g) **Women-oriented Policies:** It proposed the preparation of women-oriented policies for increasing women's efficiency and advancing the economic development of women.

(h) **Access to Basic Facilities:** It advocated access to basic facilities for women such as education, training, property, and credit rights. This would help women in improving their employment rate and overall economic development.

Notwithstanding the above aspects, the WID approach is criticised on the following grounds:

(a) **Women as Passive Recipients:** The women were treated as passive recipients of the economic development programme. Moreover, they were integrated with only those activities that were specific to women.

(b) **Unsustainable Approach:** The WID approach was unsustainable, as it disregarded the unequal relationship between men and women. It showed results in the short term but faltered in the long term. The approach was blind to the roles and responsibilities of men regarding women's positions in society. It did not question the existing social structures and the sources of women's oppression. Thus, the approach did not aim at bringing a radical change in the position of women in society.

9.7.4.2 Women and Development

The women and development (WAD) approach is a neo-Marxist approach highlighting the role of the social class and exploitation of Third World countries in the backward status of women. The approach emerged in the 1970s as a response to the criticism of the WID approach. The approach has the following main aspects:

(a) **Against Capitalist Paradigm:** The approach, similar to dependency theory, says that global capitalism has led to the exploitation of women and unequal distribution of wealth between men and women.

(b) **Active Participation of Women:** Women have always been active participants in the development process, and they did not suddenly appear in the 1970s in the development process as a result of the insights of a few scholars and agencies.

(c) **Against Integration of Women:** They were against the idea of integration of women into the development process. They said that 'integrating women into development' was inextricably linked to the maintenance of economic dependency of the Third World countries on the Western countries.

(d) **Relationship between Women and Development Process:** The WAD approach focused on the relationship between women and the development process rather than on the strategies for integrating women into the development process. It says that women have always been integrated into their societies, and the work they do, both inside and outside their households, is central to the maintenance of those societies. However, this integration is responsible for sustaining the international structures of inequality. The WID approach concludes that women's position will improve as and when the development process will become more equitable.

Notwithstanding the above-mentioned aspects, the WAD approach is criticised on the following grounds:

(a) **Influence of Class on Gender:** The WAD approach has failed to analyse the question of gender within classes. It tends to group women together without taking any strong analytical note of class, race, or ethnicity, all of which may exercise a powerful influence on women's actual social status.

(b) **Relationship between Patriarchy and Gender:** It failed to undertake the complete analysis of the relationship between patriarchy, the different modes of production, and women's oppression and subordinate position.

(c) **Men and Women's Problems Considered Together:** It has failed to understand the problems of women independent of those of men since both genders are seen to be disadvantaged within oppressive global capitalist and class structures.

(d) **Disregarded the Reproductive Side of Women:** The approach is completely based on the productive side of women at the expense of the reproductive side of women's work and lives. It has focused on income-generating activities without regarding the time and energy required by the reproductive activities of women.

9.7.4.3 Gender and Development

The gender and development (GAD) approach emerged in the 1980s as an alternative to the WID approach. It has emerged from grass-roots organisations and feminists from developing countries. It is also known as the *empowerment approach* or the *gender aware planning approach.* Having its theoretical roots in socialist feminism, it has taken a complete view of women's lives, including the productive and reproductive aspects of their lives.[29] The various aspects of this theoretical perspective are as follows:

(a) **Against Existing Social Structures:** The GAD approach has identified the social construction of production and reproduction as the basis for women's oppression and has questioned the specific roles ascribed to men and women in different societies.

(b) **Holistic Approach:** The approach is not concerned with women per se but with the social construction of gender and the assignment of specific roles, responsibilities, and expectations to men and women. It looks at the totality of social, economic, and political life in order to understand the particular aspects of gender and society.[30]

(c) **Rejects Public-Private Dichotomy:** The approach completely rejects the public and private dichotomy for women's development. The public-private dichotomy addressed in previous theories has been used as a mechanism to undervalue family and household maintenance work performed by women. The approach analyses women's contribution within the context of work done both inside and outside the household. It places special emphasis on the oppression of women in the family to analyse the assumptions on which conjugal relationships are based.

(d) **Participation of State:** The GAD approach emphasises the participation of the state in promoting women's development. It sees it as the duty of the state to provide some of the social services that women in many countries have been provided on private and individual basis.

(e) **Women as Agents of Change:** The approach sees women as agents of change rather than as passive recipients of development. It stresses the need for women to organise themselves for more effective political vote.

(f) **Inquiry into Class and Caste:** The approach argues that the ideology of patriarchy operates both within and across classes to oppress women. They have tried to explore the connections between gender, class, race, and women's development.

(g) **Legal Rights:** A key work of the GAD approach is on strengthening women's legal rights including the right to inheritance and owning land. It has also analysed the confusion created by the co-existence of customary and statutory legal systems in many countries and the tendency of men to manipulate them to the disadvantage of women.

(h) **Re-examination of Social Structures:** The approach not only proposes affirmative strategies for the integration of women into the development process, but also advocates the fundamental re-examination of social structures and institutions, leading to a change in the status of men and women.

Notwithstanding the above-mentioned aspects, the GAD approach is criticised for its inapplicability to the everyday problems of women, as it proposes a re-examination of the way in which social structures and institutions affect women's oppression.

9.7.4.4 Development Alternative with Women for a New Era

The WID and the WAD approach failed in addressing the fundamental factors that maintain gender inequalities. Thus, a complementary thought, broader in scope and radical in spirit, emerged in the 1980s, known as the Development Alternative with Women for a New Era (DAWN). The idea arose in 1984 in Bengaluru, India, when a group of feminists from Third World countries assembled and mounted a comprehensive critique of the development model. From this meeting, a platform known as *Development, Crisis and Alternative Visions: Third World Women's Perspectives* for future women movements emerged.

DAWN criticizes the role of macroeconomics, neo-liberal international relations, and military relations in perpetuating the marginalisation of women in the developing world. Moreover, DAWN is a network of activist feminist scholars and researchers who work for gender justice and sustainable democratic development. In this research, the feminists of the North and South have collaborated for women's justice.

9.7.4.5 Martha Nussbaum's Women and Human Development: The Capabilities Approach

Women are bearers of human capabilities and basic powers of choice to make a moral claim for opportunities to be realised and flourish. However, their human powers of choice and sociability are frequently thwarted by the societies in which they live. Due to social conditions, women have failed to attain that higher level of capability (refer to the capabilities approach of Amartya Sen discussed previously in this chapter), which may open all the choices of central human functions to them. This is a serious problem of justice for women.

Martha Nussbaum has argued that a political approach based on the ideas of human capability and functioning (refer to Sen's capability approach) supplies a good basis for thinking about the problems of women. It also helps in constructing the basic principles that can serve as the foundation for constitutional guarantees for women.

She says that the world community has been slow to address women's problems because it has lacked a consensus that sex-based inequality is an urgent issue of political justice. The outrages suffered every day by millions of women—hunger, domestic violence, child sexual abuse and child marriage, inequality before the law, poverty, lack of dignity, and self-regard—are the issues requiring urgent attention of the world community.

However, in recent times, the capability failure of women has been highlighted on the national and international agenda.

9.7.4.6 Women Empowerment Approach

The concept of women's empowerment has basically taken birth in the Third World. It is broadly defined as women's control over material assets, intellectual resources, and ideology. It is the process of challenging the existing power relations and women gaining control over the power sources. It is the redistribution of power that challenges patriarchal ideology and male dominance in society. The term became popular as such in the 1980s in the field of women's development. It tends to provide equity and equality to women in a mutually cooperative spirit. It also results with respect to the traditional female values in society. The first ever event for women's empowerment occurred in 1642 when 400 women submitted a representation before the House of Commons about the problems faced by them. It addressed the marginalisation of women in religion, family, and other places.

Empowerment is a power that cannot be given by a third party. The people who want to be empowered must claim it. Thus, development agencies cannot empower women—they can only facilitate women to empower themselves. Empowerment is an ongoing process rather than a final goal. Moreover, empowerment is a relative term. People are empowered or disempowered with regard to each other or with regard to themselves at a previous instance. It represents the ability to act independently or having the ability to make one's own decisions regarding life and society. This idea of making independent decisions was propagated by Amartya Sen and followed up by N. Kabeer.

The empowerment movement was actively supported by many development agencies including the World Bank. As a result, many states have formulated policies and programmes for women's empowerment, in which the active participation of grass-roots NGOs is required. They enable poor women to get out of the poverty trap and rebuild rural society with the new social development philosophy of community care and development. Two important development efforts for women's empowerment are microcredit and self-help groups (SHGs). These concepts have already been discussed in Chapter 6.

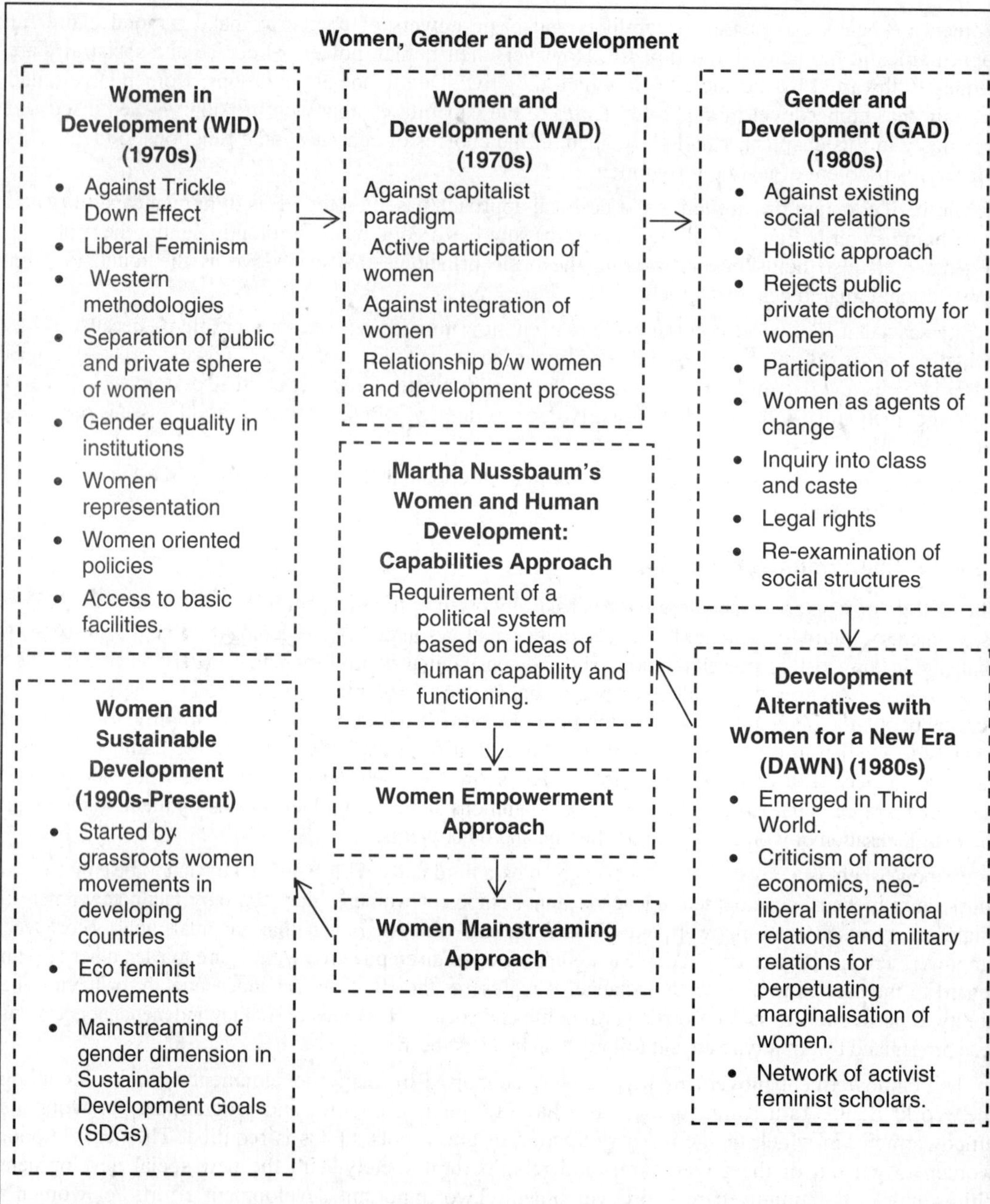

Mind Map 9.2: *Various Theoretical Perspectives on Women, Gender and Development*

9.7.4.7 Gender Mainstreaming Approach

The idea of gender mainstreaming has emerged in development theory and practice in the last few years. The idea has its origin in development studies, which show that initiatives and projects have failed due to the absence of the gender perspective in it. The concept has been defined by the United Nations Economic and Social Council (ECOSOC) as "a process of assessing the implications for women and men of any planned action, including legislation, policies or programmes, in any area and at all levels. It is a strategy for making the concerns and experiences of women as well as of men an integral part of the design, implementation, monitoring, and evaluation of policies and programmes in all political, economic, and social spheres, so that women and men benefit equally, and inequality is not perpetuated. The ultimate goal of gender mainstreaming is to achieve gender equality."

It requires gender to be brought into the centre of discussions about development and not marginalised as a women's issue. It makes gender a central aspect of all development planning and practices. Gender budgeting is an important strategy of the gender mainstreaming approach.

9.7.5 International Initiatives for Women's Development

From time to time, there have been various international forums and conventions for propagating the goal of women's development. A brief of these initiatives is as follows:

1. **Commission on the Status of Women (CSW), 1946:** In 1946, the UN Economic and Social Council (ECOSOC) created CSW as a functional commission dedicated exclusively to gender equality and women's advancement. It is an important global policymaking body on women's development. The basic tasks of CSW are to annually evaluate universal progress on gender equality, identify challenges in it, set global standards, and formulate concrete policies to promote gender equality and the advancement of women worldwide.
2. **Universal Declaration on Human Rights, 1948:** The declaration explicitly states "equal rights for men and women" and includes "equal rights of men and women to marriage, during marriage and at its dissolution."
3. **Declaration on the Protection of Women and Children in Emergency and Armed Conflict, 1974:** The declaration, having its origin in the CSW, called for states that are involved in armed conflicts, military operations in foreign territories, or military operations in territories still under colonial domination to make all efforts to spare women and children from the ravages of war. All the necessary steps must be taken to ensure the prohibition of measures such as persecution, torture, punitive measures, degrading treatment, and violence, particularly against that part of the civilian population that consists of women and children.
4. **The First World Conference on Women, Mexico, 1975:** The First World Conference on Women was convened in Mexico City in 1975. The conference identified three core areas of interest (a) full gender equality and the elimination of gender discrimination, (b) the integration and full participation of women in development, and (c) increased contribution by women towards strengthening world peace.
5. **Formal Establishment of International Women's Day, 1977:** Since 1977, the International Women's Day is celebrated on 8 March when a UN General Assembly (UNGA) Resolution officially designated the date. The day honours women's contributions, celebrates achievements, promotes the status of women worldwide, and draws attention to the current issues that are critical to achieving equality.

6. **Convention on the Elimination of All Forms of Discrimination Against Women (CEDAW), 1979:** The convention was adopted by UNGA in 1979 and entered into force in 1981. In the convention, the states committed themselves to ending discrimination against women in all forms, including legal discrimination.
7. **Third World Conference on Women, Nairobi, 1985:** The second world conference on women was organised in 1980 and the third conference was organised in 1985 in Nairobi, Kenya. It appraised the achievements of the *UN Decade on Women (1976–1985)*. It revealed that not many women have been benefited. Three basic categories were established to measure the progress achieved: (a) constitutional and legal measures, (b) equality in social participation and (3) equality in political participation and decision-making. It realised that gender equality is not an isolated issue and encompasses all aspects of human life.
8. **Convention on the Rights of Child (CRC), 1989:** It is the first legally binding international instrument to incorporate the human rights of children, emphasising on the rights of girl children. It was decided that children require special care and protection that adults do not. It spelled out the basic human rights that children everywhere have—the right to survival, to develop to the fullest, to protection from harmful influences, to safety from abuse and exploitation, and to participate fully in family, cultural, and social life.
9. **UN World Conference on Human Rights, Vienna, 1993:** The Vienna Declaration on Human Rights states "all human rights are universal, indivisible, interdependent and interrelated" and no hierarchy exists within human rights. It also recognised that women's rights are human rights.
10. **The Declaration on the Elimination of Violence Against Women (DEVAW), 1993:** The UNGA adopted the DEVAW in December 1993. Before the declaration, a majority of governments treated violence against women as a private matter between individuals and not as a pervasive human rights problem that required State intervention.
11. **International Conference on Population and Development (ICDP), Cairo, Egypt, 1994:** The conference established a close link between sustainable development, reproductive health, and gender equality. It aimed at empowering women and providing them with more choices through expanded access to education and health services, skill development and employment, and through their full involvement in policymaking and decision-making processes at all levels.
12. **Fourth World Conference on Women: Action for Equality, Development and Peace (Beijing, China): Beijing Platform for Action, 1995:** The fourth world conference on women led to the passing of the Beijing Declaration and Platform for Action (BPfA), the most progressive blueprint for advancing women's rights. The platform advocated for a world where all women could exercise their freedoms and realise their rights such as the right to a life free from violence, education, participation in decision-making, and earning equal pay for equal work. The process unleashed worldwide political will and visibility. Governments, civil society, and the public translated the BPfA promises into concrete changes in individual countries. Recognition of the negative effects on women of major global political and economic changes, including globalisation, liberalisation, use of new technologies, migration, and conflicts had increased. One of the remarkable achievements has been bringing issues of sexual and reproductive health and rights, violence against women, and inequality of power in gender relations to focus on global and national debates.

13. **The Millennium Declaration and eight Millennium Development Goals (MDGs), 2000:** The MDGs were adopted in 2000 as the world's main development challenge. They recognised gender equality as a goal (Goal 3) and included the dimension of gender in all other goals.
14. **UN Action against Sexual Violence in Conflict, 2006:** Established in 2006, UN Action is a coordination body that unites the work of 12 UN entities with the goal of ending sexual violence in conflict. It has three main pillars: country-level action (including peacekeeping operations), advocating for action, and learning by doing (including creating a knowledge hub on sexual violence in conflict).
15. **UNiTE to End Violence Against Women Campaign:** In 2008, the UN launched the *UNiTE to End Violence Against Women Campaign*, a focused effort between 2008 and 2015 aimed at preventing and eliminating violence against women and girls in all parts of the world. The campaign called on governments, civil society, women's organisations, young people, the private sector, media, and the entire UN system to join forces in addressing the global pandemic of violence against women and girls.
16. **UN Women, 2010:** In July 2010, the UN established a new entity for gender equality and women's empowerment, known as UN Women, to accelerate progress in meeting the needs of women and girls worldwide. UN Women merges and will build on the important work of four previously distinct parts of the UN system that focus exclusively on gender equality and women's empowerment—(a) Division for the Advancement of Women (DAW, established in 1946), (b) International Research and Training Institute for the Advancement of Women (INSTRAW, established in 1976), (c) Office of the Special Advisor on Gender Issues and Advancement of Women (OSAGI, established in 1997), and (d) United Nations Development Fund for Women (UNIFEM, established in 1976).

9.7.6 Important Gender Indicators

Gender indicators measure gender-related changes over time. They are sex-disaggregated statistical data and provide separate measures for men and women on various aspects such as literacy and health. They aim at capturing both quantitative and qualitative changes in women's lives. Some of the important gender indicators, used worldwide, are as follows:

1. **Gender Development Index (GDI):** This indicator has already been discussed earlier in this chapter.
2. **Gender Inequality Index (GII):** This indicator has also already been discussed earlier in this chapter.
3. **Gender Empowerment Measure (GEM):** The GEM was introduced by the Human Development Report (HDR), in 1995. It measures the empowerment of women in the following three key areas:
   - *Political power and decision-making power* measured by women's share of seats in the parliament, legislative assemblies and local bodies; the number of female candidates in national parties in parliamentary elections; and the percentage of female voters exercising their right to vote in parliamentary elections.
   - *Economic participation and decision-making power* are measured by the percentage of women in service in the IAS, IPS, and IFS and the percentage share of women enrolled in medical and engineering colleges.

- *Power over economic resources* measured by the percentage of women/girls with operational land holdings, percentage of women/girls with bank accounts in scheduled commercial banks, and the share of women/girls in the national per capita income.

4. **Gender Equity Index (GEI):** GEI was introduced by the international organisation Social Watch in 2007, combining both the indicators GDI and GEM. It has the following three dimensions:
   - *Education* is measured by the literacy gap between men and women and by the male and female enrolment rates in primary, secondary, and tertiary education.
   - *Participation in the economy* is measured by the percentage of women and men in paid jobs, excluding agriculture, and by the income ratio of men to women.
   - *Empowerment* is measured by the percentage of women in professional, technical, managerial, and administrative jobs, and by the number of seats women have in the parliament and in decision-making ministerial posts.
5. **Gender Gap Index (GGI):** The GGI was introduced by the World Economic Forum (WEF) in 2006 as a framework for capturing the magnitude of gender-based disparities and tracking their progress over time. It benchmarks national gender gaps on economic, education, health and political criteria.

9.8 Women in Administration: Opportunities and Challenges

The Constitution of India provides for equal opportunity for men and women in employment. It also guarantees equal pay for men and women. The legal, education, and health support is given to women has led to increased participation of women in administration and higher management over the last few decades. The growing number of women movements has given an impetus to the economic and social participation of women.

9.8.1 Advantages Women Bring to Administration

Women tend to bring substantial diversity, sustainability, increased performance, and creativity to an organisation. The benefits attributed to an organisation because of the increased participation of women are as follows:

(a) **Diversity in Workforce:** In the era of sglobalisation, we require talented and forward-looking administrators who can innovate with new techniques of administering the nation. Women represent a significant but underutilised pool of talent that needs to be tapped by the administration to combat the shortage of skills and lack of innovative practices. Recruitment of women employees brings diversity into the workforce and is extremely important for the success of an organisation.

(b) **Enhancement in Organisational Performance:** A considerable body of evidence suggests that increased female participation at the senior level can enhance the organisational capacity to respond to key shifts in the economy. There is a strong relationship between the number of female executives and the performance of organisations.[40] The presence of women positively impacts an organisation's communication and decision-making processes and encourages a thorough investigation of prevalent procedures.[41]

(c) **Different Management Styles:** In the era of privatisation and outsourcing, management styles that facilitate and support short-term partnerships are preferred. In this environment, stereotypical female skills such as strong communication and collaboration skills are preferred over traditionally male management styles that tend to promote individualism and competition.[42]

9.8.2 Challenges Faced by Women in Administration

It has been seen that there has been a narrow interpretation of the concept of gender equality in administration and higher management. The principle of equal opportunity has remained a marginal concern for senior administrators. The gap between the rhetoric of equal opportunity and organisational reality remains a concern for the academicians and practitioners of public administration. Women face the following hurdles while growing in administration:

(a) **Short-term Organisational Drivers:** The current focus on short-term financial returns creates incentives that do not allow long-tem, sustainable, and inclusive organisational performance in which women are equal partners. Preoccupation with immediate financial performance encourages a left-brain bias that favours hard skills such as rationality, expediency, and numeracy (typically associated with masculinity) over less tangible, soft skills such as relationship-building (typically found in women).

(b) **Masculine Administrative Culture:** The traditional imperatives of the market economy hinder the accommodation of women workers in the workforce. In traditional organisations, the preferred management style is based on masculine stereotypes such as dominance, aggression, rationality, and independence.[34] This style bias mitigates the value of talents widely associated with the feminine such as interpersonal communication and emotional intelligence. In this cultural setting, women are seen as providing support to men but failing to thrive as leaders.[35]

(c) **Hostile Organisational Culture:** Women often face a hostile culture in the organisations they work. Male-dominated organisations have an unstated promotion criterion that favours men over women. There has been a male bias in key economic sectors against the employment of women. Organisations suffer from the stereotypes of both the masculine and the feminine, which inhibits the cultural acceptance of women in leadership positions.

(d) **Long Working Hours:** A 24/7 work ethic at senior administrative levels has low tolerance for the intersection of administrative and domestic life. This round-the-clock working culture particularly impacts women who have the responsibility of parenthood and family care also. As a result, it is often seen that working mothers are excluded from key roles, projects, and opportunities due to a culture that does not accommodate their needs.

(e) **Gender Stereotyping:** In organisations, strong numeric competency is often wrongly confused with higher intelligence. As a result, stereotyping of women as being less numerically competent encourages the view of women as intrinsically lacking organisational skills. Apart from this, women's reluctance to enter into aggressive and strategic personal politics is perceived as a weakness and lack of ambition.

(f) **Difficulty in Managing Strategic Relationships:** A very important aspect of organisational life is managing informal relationships. As men hold positions of power in organisations, women who wish to succeed must establish good relationships with them. However, informal organisational relationships are extended only to employees possessing masculine qualities. Women are seen absent from networking opportunities such as drinks at the pub or a game of golf.

(g) **Sexual Harassment at Workplace:** Women also suffer from the serious problem of sexual harassment at the workplace. Those women who try to manage informal relationships with their men colleagues and seniors are seen in a negative light and are subjected to ridicule and harassment.

9.8.3 Approaches to Understanding Women's Participation

There have been two approaches to understand the participation of women in the workforce: (a) person-centred approach and (b) environment-centred approach. They are as described below:

(1) **Person-centred Approach:** According to this approach, the organisational problems faced by women are related to female attributes, behaviours, and their historical relationship with working life.[36] The onus of change is on women. Interventions are aimed at supporting women in adopting their behaviours to culturally fit in with the male-dominated environment.[37] Leadership training programmes encourage behavioural reform through the acquisition of essential business aligned with masculine traits such as assertive decision-making and self-promotion.

(2) **Environment-centred Approach:** The environment-centred approach understands that the source of gender inequality lies within organisational cultures and work practices rather than in the inherent nature of women.[38] It seeks to fundamentally realign organisational values to accommodate the growing presence of women. It seeks to change organisational culture by adopting interventions that pursue an inclusive organisational culture that is championed by the CEO, driven by senior executives, and holds line managers accountable.[39]

The person-centred approach continues to drive organisational interventions to support women in professional work environments. However, it does not address the source of problems faced by women in management. Thus, we need to move towards an environment-centred approach if women's promotional opportunities are to be increased.

9.8.4 Recommendation for Better Participation of Women

For better participation of women, the narrow demands of day-to-day administration need to be reconciled with the broader consideration of relevance, resilience, and sustainability over the long term. Notions such as sustainability and diversity require awareness beyond daily operational issues. Moreover, the modern organisations are required to respond to the following:

- the need to manage and maintain level playing field dynamics around selection and promotion processes
- the preponderance of caring responsibilities in women's lives
- the need for more flexible arrangements for working mothers

There is a requirement of an honest conversation between men and women to raise awareness of the subtle inhibiters to women's experience at the workplace. Awareness must be created around the principles and values of diversity in organisations. Apart from this, flexible workplace options are required to be discovered in order to allow women to balance work and parent life. Furthermore, the organisational environment should be made more family-friendly.

Women in administration

Advantages brought by women

- Diversity in workforce
- Enhancement in performance
- Different management styles

Approaches for understanding women participation

- Person Centered Approach
- Environment Centered Approach

Challenges faced by women in administration

- Short term organisational directives
- Masculine administrative culture
- Hostile organisational culture
- Long working hours
- Gender stereotyping
- Difficulty in managing strategic relationships
- Sexual harassment at work place

The space is left

Recommendation for better women participation

- Level playing field around selection and promotion processes.
- Consideration of caring responsibilities in women's lives
- Flexible working hours for working mothers.
- Awareness of subtle inhibiters to women.
- Female and family friendly organisational environment.

Mind Map 9.3: *Women in Administration*

9.9 Sustainable Development

The concept of sustainable development was defined by the Bruntland Report, named after the chairperson of the World Commission on Environment and Development (1987), the then Prime Minister of Norway. The report defines sustainable development as "the development that fulfils the needs of the present without compromising the ability of future generations to meet their needs."

The environment emerged as an international issue in development after the 1972 Stockholm Conference. It received further impetus from the 1987 World Commission on Environment and Development and the 1992 Rio Earth Summit.

It has been felt that indiscriminate overconsumption of natural resources by the economic sectors has led to steady resource depletion. The consumerist societal model flaunted by the modern elite has been responsible for eco-destruction and planetary disequilibrium. Sustainable development is a model of development to reverse this trend of over-exploitation of natural resources and allow the fruit of development to be enjoyed by generations to come.

9.9.1 Sustainable Development Goals

The Sustainable Development Goals (SDGs) were born at the United Nations Conference on Sustainable Development in Rio de Janeiro in 2012. Also known as global goals, they are a universal call to action to end poverty, protect the planet, and ensure that all people enjoy peace and prosperity. The goals consist of 17 goals built on the lines of the successful Millennium Development Goals, while including new areas such as climate change, economic inequality, innovation, sustainable consumption, peace, and justice, among other priorities.

The goals came into effect in 2016 and will continue to guide global policy, funding, and action till 2030. The UNDP supports governments to integrate the SDGs into their national development plans and priorities. The 2030 Agenda for Sustainable Development[31] seeks to attain the SDGs by 2030 through the *5Ps*—people, planet, prosperity, peace, and partnership. They are described as follows:

- **People:** The goals are determined to end the poverty and hunger of people, in all their forms and dimensions, and to ensure that all human beings can fulfil their potential in dignity, equality, and in a healthy environment.
- **Planet:** The goals aim at protecting the planet from degradation through sustainable consumption and production, sustainably managing its natural resources, and taking urgent action on climate change, so that it can support the needs of the present and future generations.
- **Prosperity:** The goals are targeted to ensure that all human beings can enjoy prosperous and fulfilling lives and that economic, social, and technological progress occurs in harmony with nature.
- **Peace:** The goals are determined to foster peaceful, just, and inclusive societies that are free from fear and violence. There can be no sustainable development without peace and no peace without sustainable development.
- **Partnership:** The SDGs are to be implemented through a revitalised Global Partnership for Sustainable Development, based on a spirit of strengthened global solidarity, focused in particular on the needs of the poorest and most vulnerable, and with the participation of all countries, all stakeholders, and all people.

The 17 Sustainable Development Goals are as follows:

1. **No Poverty:** End poverty in all its forms everywhere.
2. **Zero Hunger:** End hunger, achieve food security and improved nutrition, and promote sustainable agriculture.
3. **Good Health and Well-being:** Ensure healthy lives and promote well-being for all at all ages.
4. **Quality Education:** Ensure inclusive and equitable quality education and promote lifelong learning opportunities for all.
5. **Gender Equality:** Achieve gender equality and empower all women and girls.
6. **Clean Water and Sanitation:** Ensure availability and sustainable management of water and sanitation for all.

7. **Affordable and Clean Energy:** Ensure access to affordable, reliable, sustainable, and modern energy for all.
8. **Decent Work and Economic Growth:** Promote sustained, inclusive, and sustainable economic growth, full and productive employment, and decent work for all.
9. **Industry, Innovation, and Infrastructure:** Build resilient infrastructure, promote inclusive and sustainable industrialisation, and foster innovation.
10. **Reduce Inequality:** Reduce inequality within and among countries.
11. **Sustainable Cities and Communities:** Make cities and human settlements inclusive, safe, resilient, and sustainable.
12. **Responsible Consumption and Production:** Ensure sustainable consumption and production patterns.
13. **Climate Action:** Take urgent action to combat climate change and its impacts.
14. **Life below Water:** Conserve and sustainably use the oceans, seas, and marine resources for sustainable development.
15. **Life on Land:** Protect, restore, and promote sustainable use of terrestrial ecosystems, sustainably manage forests, combat desertification, halt and reserve land degradation, and halt biodiversity loss.
16. **Peace and Justice Strong Institutions:** Promote peaceful and inclusive societies for sustainable development, provide access to justice for all, and build effective, accountable, and institutions at all levels.
17. **Partnerships to achieve the Goals:** Strengthen the means of implementation and revitalise the Global Partnership for Sustainable Development.

The 169 sub-targets of these 17 SDGs are discussed in Annexure 1.

9.9.2 Women and Sustainable Development

Women have been integrated with sustainable development by the *Women, Environment and Sustainable Development (WED)* approach (started in the 1990s) sparked by grass-roots women's experiences in the developing countries' social movements such as the Chipko Movement, Narmada Bachao Andolan, and Greenbelt Movements.[32] The approach spread into the Western nations through the *eco-feminist movements* that made connections between the dignity of women and respect for the different processes of life. The WED approach included women's relationship with the environment in the context of economic development as well as the harmful effects that the degradation of environment can have on women's lives.

Based on this approach, the agenda for gender equality (Goal 5 of SDGs) is a prominent goal, among the 17 SDGs, building on the commitments and norms contained in the Beijing Declaration and Platform for Action and CEDAW (discussed earlier in this chapter). The 2030 Agenda makes it clear that development will only be sustainable if its benefits accrue equally to both women and men, and women's rights will become a reality only if they are a part of the broader efforts to protect the planet and ensure that all people can live with respect and dignity.

Gender equalities manifest itself in every aspect of sustainable development (as shown in Fig. 9.4). Women are the first to suffer when households do not have sufficient food. While women perform better at school, they are underpaid as compared to men. While women have better inroads into political offices, they are largely under-represented in decision-making positions. Women and girls are also the main water and solid fuel collectors in households without access to an improved water source and clean energy in their homes, with adverse implications for their health and safety. Thus, women's development is an essential ingredient of sustainable development and women's development cannot take place without sustainable development.

GOAL NO. 1	GOAL NO. 2	GOAL NO. 3	GOAL NO. 4
No Poverty  Globally, there are 122 women aged 25-34 living in extreme povery for every 100 men of the same age gropu	**Zero Hunger**  Women are up to 11 percentage points more likely than men to report food insecurity	**Good Health and Well-Being**  Globally, 303,000 women died from pregnancy-related cause in 2015. The rate of death is declining much too slowly to achieve Target 3.1	**Quality Education**  15 million girls of primary-school age will never get the chance to learn to ready or write in primary school compared to 10 million boys

GOAL NO. 5			
Gender Equality  The 2030 Agenda promises to put an end to barriers that prevent women and girls from realising their full potential. But significant challenges the ahead: 5.1 In 18 countries husbands can legally prevent their wives from working; in 39 countries, daughters and sons do	not have equal inheritance rights; and 49 countries lack laws protect-ting women from domestic violence. 5.2 19% of women and girls aged 15 to 49 have experienced physical and/ or sexual violence by an intimate partner in the past 12 months. 5.3 Globally, 750 million women and girls were married before the age of 18 and at least 200 million women and girls in 30 countries have undergone FGM.	5.4 Women do 2.6 times the unpaid care and domestic work that men do. 5.5 Women hold just 23.7% of parliament-tary seats, an increase of 10 percentage points compared to 2000-but still way below parity. 5.6 Only 52% of women married or in a union freely make their own decisions about sexual relations, contraceptive use and health care.	5(a) Globally, women are just 13% of agricultural land holders. 5(b) Women are less likely than men to own a mobile phone, and their internet usage is 5.9 percentage points lower than that of men. 5(c) More than 100 countries have taken action to track budget allocations for gender quality.

GOAL NO. 6	GOAL NO. 7	GOAL NO. 8	GOAL NO. 9
Clean Water and Sanitation	**Affordable and Clean Energy**	**Decent Work and Economic Growth**	**Industry, Innovation and Infrastructure**

Women and girls are responsible for water collection in 80% of households without access to water on premises.	Indoor air pollution from using combustible fuels for household energy caused 4.3 million deaths in 2012, with women and girls accounting for 6 out of every 10 of these.	The global gender pay gap is 23%. Women's labour force participation rate is 63% while that of men is 94%.	Women represent 28.8% of researchers worldwide. Only about 1 in 5 countries have achieved gender parity in this area.

GOAL NO. 10	GOAL NO. 11	GOAL NO. 12	GOAL NO. 13
Reduced Inequalities	**Sustainable Cities and Communities**	**Responsible Consumption and Production**	**Climate Action**

Up to 30% of income inequality is due to inequality within households, including between women and men. Women are also more likely than men to live below 50% of the median income.	Women living in urban slums endure many hardships, with basic needs such as access to clean water and improved sanitation facilities often going unmet.	Investment in public transportion yields large benefits for women, who tend to rely on public transport more than men do.	Climate change has a disproportionate impact on women and children, who are 14 times as likely as men to die during a disaster.

GOAL NO. 14	GOAL NO. 15	GOAL NO. 16	GOAL NO. 17
Life below Water	**Life on Land**	**Peace, Justice and Strong Institutions**	**Partnerships for the Goals**
The contamination of freshwater and marine ecosystems negatively impacts women's and men's livelihoods, their health and the health of their children.	Between 2010 and 2015, the world lost 3.3 million hectares of forest areas. Poor rural women depend on common pool resources and are especially affected by their depletion.	In times of conflict, rates of homicide and other forms of violent crime increase significantly. While men are more likely to be killed on the battlefield, women are subjected during the conflict to sexual violence and abducted, tortured and forced to leave their homes.	In 2012, finances flowing out of developing countries were 2.5 times the amount of aid flowing in, and gender allocations paled in comparison.

Fig 9.4: *Gender Aspects in Sustainable Development Goals (SDGs)*[33]

SUMMARY

Development administration is a new and emerging field of public administration. Differing from traditional administration, development administration is goal-oriented and action-oriented. In this chapter, we have discussed the evolution of development administration from the 1950s to the present, with emphasis on the various important theoretical perspectives. Moreover, we have separately dealt with the issue of women, gender, and development, including the challenges and opportunities faced by women in administration. Finally, chapter concludes with an understanding of the concept of sustainable development and sustainable development goals (SDGs).

Practice Questions

1. Development administration is known as the active part of public administration. Comment
2. The Keynesian economic approach is instrumental in transforming a prismatic developing society into a diffracted developed society. Evaluate.
3. "Development had become a shapeless amoeba-like word. It had no definitive content. All that it did was to allow any intervention to be sanctioned in the name of higher evolutionary goals… It prevents people to think autonomously and grow in their own milieu and style." (Sachs) Evaluate.
4. "The approach is aimed at expanding the richness of human life rather than expanding the richness of the economy in which human beings live." Comment.
5. There can be no sustainable development without peace and no peace without sustainable development. Explain with respect to the implementation of the SDGs.
6. Women's development is an essential ingredient of sustainable development and women's development cannot take place without sustainable development. Discuss.

CHAPTER 10

Personnel Administration and Civil Services

After reading this chapter, you will learn the following:

- Meaning and different dimensions of personnel administration.
- History of personnel administration.
- Various aspects of human resources planning.
- Meaning of recruitment and its various aspects such as types of recruitment, systems of recruitment, steps in recruitment, and examinations for recruitment.
- Meaning of promotion, its essential elements, its principles, and methods of ascertaining merit for determining promotions.
- Civil Services in India, their history, constitutional provisions related to them, types of civil services such as All India Services, Central Civil Services, State Civil Services, and their critical assessment.
- Personnel agencies in India such as the Department of Personnel and Training (DOPT), cadre-controlling authorities, Union Public Service Commission (UPSC), state public service commissions (SPSCs), and Staff Selection Commission (SSC).
- Types of job classification, including position classification and rank classification, their advantages and disadvantages, and their significance in the Indian scenario.
- Performance appraisal, its objectives, performance measurement, tools of performance appraisal, weaknesses of performance appraisal in India and recommendations for improving it, performance management and its comparison with performance appraisal, performance development plan, and performance agreement.
- Good governance initiatives taken in the field of personnel administration.
- Appointment of personnel at senior ranks in India.

- Various aspects of training and development including their advantages to the employees and organisation, methods of training, evaluation of training, training of Civil Services in India, limitations of training in India, and National Training Policy.
- Important aspects of personnel administration such as pay, pay fixation, incentive administration, employer-employee relations, employee welfare, and grievance redressal of public servants in India.
- Importance of generalists and specialists in the Indian government.
- Privatisation of Civil Services and allowing mobility of civil servants to the private sector.

Personnel administration is one of the most important management functions in an organisation, the others being financial management, technology development, business expansion, and so on. It is very important for the successful functioning of an organisation, as it deals with manpower. Without the growth of human capital, the goals and objectives of an organisation can never be achieved. Human resources are the most important constituent of the overall resources of an organisation. Their adequate utilisation leads to the optimum utilisation of financial, physical, technological, and other resources of an organisation. The subject of personnel administration deals with the management of an organisation's human resources.

Personnel administration is defined as the part of an administration that is interested in people at work and their relationships within an organisation.[1] It consists of the entire spectrum of an organisation's interaction with its human resources, from recruitment to retirement. It is an important measure to ensure organisational effectiveness.

Thomas Spates has defined personnel administration as "a code of the ways of organising and treating individuals at work so that they will each get the greatest possible realisation of their intrinsic abilities, thus attaining maximum efficiency for themselves and their group, and thereby giving to the enterprise of which they are a part, its determining competitive advantage and optimum results."

According to Michael Jucius, personnel administration is "the field of management which has to do with planning, organising, and controlling various operative functions of procuring, developing, maintaining and utilising a labour force such that the:

(a) objectives for which the company is established are attained economically and effectively;
(b) objectives of all levels of personnel are served to the highest possible degree; and
(c) objectives of the community are duly considered and served."

In brief, personnel administration consists of the following functions in an organisation:

(a) Planning of manpower within an organisation
(b) Recruitment, selection, and placement in the right job
(c) Training, education, and capacity building of employees
(d) Ensuring mobility of employees by the process of transfers and promotions
(e) Preparation of terms of employment and the methods and standards of remuneration
(f) Maintenance and improvement of working conditions and employee's welfare

(g) Maintenance of communication between the employer and employees and their representative groups—also known as maintaining employee relations
(h) Negotiation with employee groups/unions on wages, working conditions, and disputes resolution
(i) Maintenance of organisational discipline and taking disciplinary action against delinquent employees
(j) Enhancing employee motivation by providing monetary and other incentives to them; enthusing a feeling of organisational commitment and loyalty in employees
(k) Maintenance of communication channels within an organisation
(l) Planning and implementation of organisational reforms for better organisational functioning with respect to its personnel
(m) Optimum utilisation of human resources in order to achieve maximum output with minimum inputs; this happens through effective job designing and placement of right employees in the right jobs
(n) Planning for employees' retirement and providing adequate retirement benefits to them

The functions enumerated above will be discussed in detail in the course of this chapter.

10.1 History of Personnel Administration

The subject of personnel administration can be attributed to having grown in countries such the USA and the UK. As far as administrative thought is considered, the work of F.W. Taylor is considered the first piece of work towards the development of the subject of personnel administration. He laid emphasis on the scientific selection (or recruitment) of employees and their systematic training and development. Taylor was followed by H.L. Gantt who worked towards seeking the willing cooperation of employees within an organisation. Another important scientific management thinker, M.P. Follett, laid stress on the training and development of employees within an organisation.

Following the scientific management movement, an important contribution to the discipline of personnel administration was provided by Elton Mayo and the human relations school. The school helped in understanding the employees' motivation and measures to improve it. This was followed by the contribution of behavioural and other thinkers on administration. These theoretical approaches led to the gradual evolution and development of the subject of personnel administration.

Apart from the theoretical impetus, a great emphasis was given to the subject during the two World Wars when there was an acute labour shortage and various labour problems were faced. At that time, the aim of the administration was the efficient utilisation of human resources with minimum wastage.

The growth of the subject of personnel administration in India has not been voluntary but has taken place due to the special efforts of the government.

10.2 Human Resource Planning

Human resource planning, or manpower planning, is the foremost function of personnel administration. It consists of planning the various jobs within an organisation and the personnel required for them. Before the process of recruitment, an organisation is required to understand the number and nature of jobs, the definition of each job, the number of personnel needed for each job, the skill set required for each job, and so on. These and other activities are together known as human resource planning. It helps in understanding the number and type of personnel an organisation needs to recruit, train, and promote in a given period. It has the following objectives:[2]

(a) To ensure the optimum use of human resources employed.
(b) To assess the skill requirements for the future functioning of an organisation.
(c) To assess the number and nature of personnel required in various jobs within an organisation.
(d) To classify jobs according to their nature and skills required.
(e) To ensure that the necessary human resources are available as and when required by the organisation.
(f) To determine the nature and type of recruitment to be conducted by the organisation to select employees with the right skill set.
(g) To anticipate the weaknesses of organisational procedures and avoid unnecessary removal/resignation of employees.
(h) To determine the nature and type of training required to develop employees according to the skills required for organisational tasks.
(i) To assess the future growth of an organisation concerning its human resources.

Thus, manpower planning is an important task, as it determines the quality and quantity of personnel required for specific jobs within an organisation. Without effective human resource planning, the other functions of personnel administration, namely, recruitment, placement, training, promotion, the welfare of employees, and so on cannot be performed properly. The various techniques of human resource planning will be discussed in the course of this chapter.

10.3 Recruitment into Public Service

Recruitment is the entry point of employees as far as the administration is concerned. It is defined as the process through which suitable candidates are induced to compete for appointments to the public service.[3] The process is linked with the organisational human resource plan for the purposes of economy and ready availability of personnel with the attendant implications for organisational efficiency.

There are two sources of recruitment—from inside and outside of the organisation. Recruitment from inside the organisation means the promotion of employees to higher positions and recruitment from outside the organisation means the recruitment of external talent into the organisation. All organisations take recourse to both methods to meet their organisational requirements.

10.3.1 Direct and Indirect Recruitment

Direct recruitment is a form of recruitment in which vacant posts are filled by suitable and qualified candidates from outside the organisation. On the other hand, in indirect recruitment, vacant posts are filled by suitable and qualified candidates from within the organisation, i.e., through the mechanism of promotion. Posts at lower levels are generally filled by direct recruitment and those at higher levels are generally filled by indirect recruitment. The comparative advantages and disadvantages of direct and indirect recruitment methods are described in Mind Map 10.1.

Variable	Direct recruitment	Indirect recruitment
	Advantages	**Disadvantages**
Democratic/ undemocratic	This principle is democratic, as it gives equal opportunity to all qualified persons outside the organisation.	It is undemocratic, as it gives opportunities only to qualified persons within the organisation.
Source	It has a wider pool of resources for selecting candidates.	It has a narrow pool of resources for selecting candidates.
Competency	Here competency is high, as young and better qualified persons are allowed to compete.	Here competency is less, as young and competent people from outside are not allowed to compete.
Penetration of Ideas	Recruitment from outside allows new ideas to enter the organisation so that the organisation can reflect on the changing technical, administrative, and socio-political conditions of the environment.	Recruitment from inside breeds conservatism and stagnation in the organisation, as new ideas do not enter from outside.
Environment Connection	Due to direct recruitment, Civil Services can keep pace with the changing environmental conditions.	Due to indirect recruitment, the Civil Services are unable to keep pace with the changing environmental conditions.
Qualification	External candidates are better qualified, as they work hard to improve their qualifications due to the stiff competition outside. This also motivates the existing employees to remain up to date so as to compete with external candidates.	The existing employees are less qualified, as they wait for their promotion and do not stiffly compete for it.
Experience	New employees recruited from outside lack confidence in discharging their duties, as they do not have the necessary experience in administration.	The existing employees discharge their duties with responsibility, as they have the necessary experience in administration.
Training	Expensive and prolonged training is required for directly recruited employees.	Indirectly recruited employees do not require prolonged training due to their rich experience.
Progression	The chances of progression for existing employees decrease as employees are inducted from the outside.	It provides ample opportunities for employees to grow and advance in the service.

	Advantages	Disadvantages
Loyalty	The loyalty of existing employees towards the organisation decreases when new employees are inducted from outside at par with them or ranked above them.	As employees get promoted to higher ranks, they work loyally towards the organisation.
Employee attrition	When there is direct recruitment at higher ranks, existing employees tend to look for other job opportunities, as they do not find sufficient opportunities to grow within the same organisation.	When employees are allowed to advance, they tend to remain in the same organisation and benefit from it fully.
Reliability	This method of recruitment is less reliable, as examinations and interviews are not foolproof methods to test the candidates' qualities.	This method of recruitment is more reliable, as the work of long years truly reveals the qualities of employees.
Cost	This method is more time-consuming and costly.	This method is less time-consuming and costly.
Social capital	As direct recruitment may place young people above old and experienced people, it is not conducive to developing positive social capital within the organisation.	In indirect recruitment, old and experienced people are placed above the young and new; this is good for developing a cohesive organisational culture.

Mind Map 10.1: Comparison between direct and indirect recruitment

In India, both these methods of recruitment are used for entry into public services. For example, in the Indian Administrative Service, more than two-thirds of the positions are filled by direct recruitment, whereas around one-third of the posts are filled by the promotion of employees from the Group B services of state revenue departments. This proportion varies from service to service. A detail of recruitment into all the governmental services can be found in the book *An Introduction to Civil Services*.

10.3.2 Systems of Recruitment

In the world, there have been various systems of recruitment into public services. Among them, the most prevalent system at present is the merit system. The various systems of recruitment are enumerated below:

(a) Sale of office

(b) Patronage system

(c) Spoils system

(d) Merit system

All these systems are described below.

(a) **Sale of Office:** It is a system of recruitment in which the vacant posts are sold by public auction to the higher bidder. This system was followed in pre-revolutionary France. It brings revenue to the state, enables the rich people to acquire government posts, and frees the government from patronage, favouritism, and political interference.[4]

(b) **Patronage System:** It is a system of recruitment in which the vacant posts are filled by those candidates who are favoured on certain personal or political grounds. The system was followed earlier in Britain and other countries. It involves the selection of candidates on the basis of family, kinship, relation, personal loyalty, political links, and so on.

(c) **Spoils System:** It is a system of recruitment in which the governmental posts are filled by the supporters of the winning party. The system was followed in the USA, where appointments in the government were considered as spoils for the winning party. The party coming into power used to dismiss all the government servants appointed by the earlier government and fill up all the vacancies by recruiting its supporters. This system continued till 1883 when the Pendleton Act was passed and the merit system was introduced in the USA.

(d) **Merit System:** It is a system of recruitment in which vacant posts are filled by selecting the most suitable and qualified candidates on the basis of the principle of merit tested through open competitive examinations. Competitive examinations allow meritorious and more qualified candidates to enter into government service. The system of merit was introduced in 1854 in India, in 1855 in Britain, and in 1883 in the USA. This system has now been adopted by all democratic countries.

10.3.3 Steps in Recruitment

The process of recruitment consists of the following steps:[5]

(a) **Job Requisition:** It is the first step of the recruitment process, which describes the nature of a job. The nature of a job is described in terms of the following criteria:

- General educational and technical qualifications required for the job.
- Special skills are required for the job, which helps in designing the selection test for recruiting the candidates.
- Previous work experience, if any, required for doing the job.
- Personal and physical attributes desired from the candidates.
- Age and domicile requirements, if any, required from the candidates.

These criteria are used for submitting the requisition for the staff required.

(b) **Application Forms:** Application forms are designed to procure the desired information from the applicants as per the job description and specifications.

(c) **Job Advertisement:** The vacancies are notified to the candidates through well-articulated advertisements. Advertisement is a method to secure the best talent for the post and fulfil the constitutional requirement of giving equal opportunity to all eligible candidates.

(d) **Scrutiny of Applications:** The applications are scrutinised to eliminate the less qualified candidates. Scrutiny ensures that the information provided by the candidates is complete and that they fulfil all the requisite criteria of eligibility.

(e) **Selection:** Suitable candidates are selected via the mechanism of an open competitive written examination or interview.

(f) **Communication:** The selected and non-selected candidates are then informed about the status of their results. Appointment letters are provided to the selected candidates, wherein the terms and conditions governing the appointment are clearly mentioned.

(g) **Placement:** After selection, the employees are made to undergo a fixed period of probation. Once the probation is complete, the candidates deemed fit are placed in the job.

10.3.4 Types of Examination for Recruitment

In India, and elsewhere, the following types of examination are conducted for recruiting candidates on the basis of the merit system.

(a) **Essay-type Examination:** In this examination, the candidates are required to write long essay-type answers to questions. Its purpose is to judge the command of the candidates over factual knowledge and their ability to logically reason and argue. However, this examination consists of certain subjectivity, as a judgment of a subject matter differs from examination to examination.

(b) **Short-answer-type Examination:** In this examination, short or one-word answers are required to be given to a large number of questions. It is objective in nature, as there is only one correct answer to a given question. It is a cheap form of examination, allowing the use of electronic means for result compilation. However, this examination does not offer any scope for testing the creativity and imaginativeness of the candidates.

(c) **Intelligence Test:** The inherent intellectual capability of a candidate is measured by the mechanism of intelligence tests. These are used to assess the mental maturity of a candidate. They consist of multiple-choice questions on language skills, quantitative skills, analytical reasoning, common sense, and so on. The intelligence quotient (IQ), an indicator of the mental age of a person, is calculated through this examination. It helps to ensure that the persons with the right intelligence are recruited for the job. It ensures that neither a person with higher intelligence nor a person with lower intelligence is recruited.

(d) **Personality Test:** Different types of personality tests are used to measure the temperament and emotional stability of the candidates.

(e) **Aptitude Test:** Aptitude tests help in discovering the natural talent of a candidate in a specific area associated with the job. Different jobs require different aptitudes. This examination helps in selecting the right candidate with the required job-related aptitude.

(f) **Performance Test:** In this examination, the candidates are asked to perform a particular task and their performance is measured in terms of the output. It is useful in the recruitment of personnel for skilled trades or jobs; for example, the job of a stenographer, typist, machine operator, and so on.

(g) **Interview:** An interview is a form of an oral test, in which the knowledge, skills, and views of a candidate are sought to be assessed by the examiner. It is also designed to assess intangible qualities such as smartness, integrity, alacrity, emotional stability, and confidence. The nature of interview is that of a natural purposeful conversation intended to reveal the qualities of a candidate.

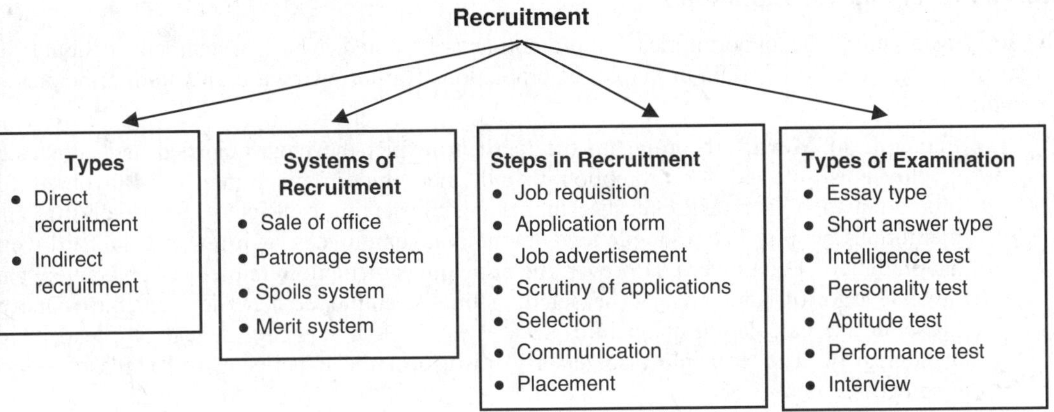

Mind Map 10.2 : Various aspects of recruitment

10.4 Promotion

Promotion is defined as an appointment from a given position to a position of higher grade, involving a change of duties to a more difficult type of work with greater responsibility, accompanied by a change of title and usually an increase in pay.[7] It is important to meet the basic urge of human beings for recognition and advancement in work. It also develops the feeling of belongingness in employees.

An inappropriate promotion policy tends to breed discontent and decrease the morale of the employees. This eventually hurts the overall efficiency of the organisation. Thus, promotion is a very important tool in organisational dynamics.

10.4.1 Essentials of a Sound Promotion System

The essentials of a sound promotion system have been laid down by W.F. Willoughby in the form of the following guidelines:[8]

1. **Standard Specifications:** Promotion should be based on standard specifications valid for everyone.
2. **Classification of Positions:** For a sound promotion, the positions within an organisation should be classified into distinct services, classes, and grades.
3. **Inclusion of all Positions:** All the positions should be included in the above-mentioned classification except those having a political character.
4. **Indirect Recruitment:** As far as possible, the principle of recruitment from lower positions to higher positions should be adopted.
5. **Merit System:** Promotions should be done after determining the relative merits of the eligible employees.

10.4.2 Principles of Promotion

In any organisation, the opportunities for promotion are limited. Thus, to maintain equality, an organisation has to follow certain principles of promotion. The following are important principles of promotion:

(a) **Principle of Merit:** According to the merit principle, the most qualified and competent employee is selected for promotion to a higher grade. This principle is favoured for promotion to higher ranks because higher positions require efficient, hard working, and meritorious people. The principle tends to motivate employees, as it rewards the hard work and initiative of employees. However, the principle is difficult to implement objectively and involves a lot of subjectivity. The determination of employee merit is a complex concept involving the calculation of qualities such as intellectual capacity, personality, leadership, and integrity. The principle also tends to disrespect the experience and skills of senior employees.

(b) **Principle of Seniority:** Seniority refers to the length of service in a particular post, scale, or grade. According to this principle, seniority is the sole basis of promotion. To implement this principle, a seniority list is prepared and an order of preference is decided on the basis of age and experience. It is a simple and objective principle to apply for promotion. It leaves no room for favouritism and promotion. It respects age and experience. Moreover, it is a democratic principle, as it gives a chance of promotion to everyone irrespective of merit. However, this principle does not motivate employees to work hard and efficiently. With this system in place, inefficient and conservative persons may get promoted to higher positions, adversely affecting the overall performance of the organisation. This principle is generally applied for a promotion at lower ranks.

(c) **Principle of Seniority cum Merit:** As both the above-mentioned principles have certain merits and demerits, a combination of both principles is applied for promotion in certain cases. For example, after fixing a certain necessary seniority, the most meritorious candidate is chosen for promotion. On the other hand, the organisation may also fix the minimum qualifications required and choose the most senior candidate for promotion. Promotions to middle ranks are based on this principle.

10.4.3 Ascertaining Merit

As discussed, ascertaining the merit of employees is a complex phenomenon. It is decided by the overall performance of an employee in the organisation. We will further discuss performance management in the latter part of this chapter. Here, we will discuss the various methods utilised to ascertain the merit of employees. They are as described below:

1. **Written Examination: A** written examination is conducted for promotion when few candidates are to be selected from many applicants. In this system, the chances of corruption, favouritism, and arbitrariness are minimised. However, it makes no distinction between older candidates with rich experience and younger candidates with less work experience.

2. **Personal Judgment of the Head of Agency:** In this system, the head of the agency applies his/her personal judgment for selecting fit candidates for promotion. This system is advantageous, as the head of the department is expected to have full knowledge about the

capabilities of his/her subordinates. However, this system is criticised for being subjective. It can be made more effective by taking steps such as appointing a board to review the performance of employees and allowing appeals against the decisions taken by the board.

3. **Service Record and Efficiency Rating:** In civil services as well as in other big organisations, the service record of each employee is maintained. The service record, also known as the confidential record, personal record, or personal file, is a file containing the record of all the good and bad aspects of an employee's work. It is used for assessing the relative merit of the employees for the purpose of promotion. It also provides sufficient data for evaluating the efficiency of the employees.

   Such evaluation helps in determining the efficiency rating of the personnel. An efficient rating is a scientific tool to assess the suitability of personnel for promotion. It is a fair and reliable system to reward the most efficient person. However, it is criticised for not being completely objective. It depends on the subjective judgment of the superior officers. Moreover, it is difficult to prepare a proper rating form consisting of all the qualities, traits, or criteria necessary for an efficiency rating.

   In efficiency rating, qualities such as knowledge of work, personality, judgment, initiative, accuracy, willingness to take responsibility, and neatness are rated on the basis of the service record of the employees. In India, the following efficiency ratings are given to the employees:

   (a) Outstanding
   (b) Very Good
   (c) Satisfactory
   (d) Indifferent
   (e) Poor

4. **Viva Voce:** The viva voce is the oral examination of the employees taken to assess their suitability for promotion. It has the advantage of being a holistic appreciation of a person and his/her work by a group of seniors. However, it is subjective in nature.

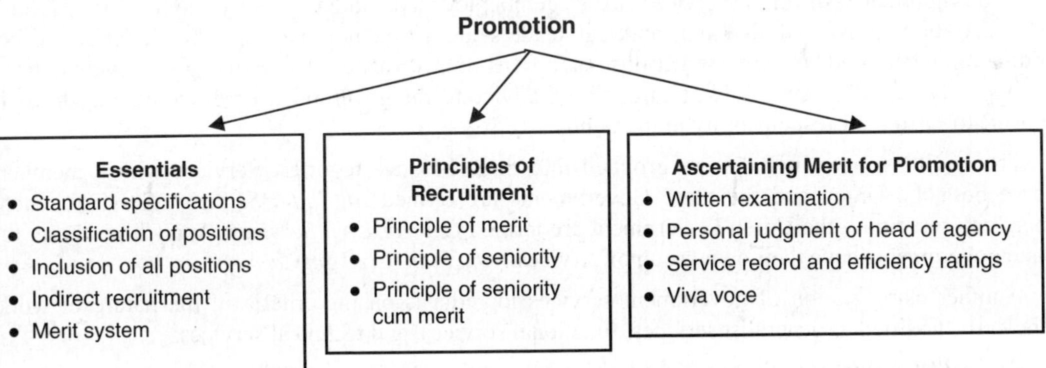

Mind Map 10.3 : Various aspects of promotion

10.5 Civil Services in India

The roots of civil services go back a long way in human history. The key to the survival of the ancient Egyptian civilisation, which flourished as early as 3000 BC, was the civil service—the historical model of all the later bureaucracies. The waterways for the whole country needed central management, which required a body of scribes and officials. Once in place, the scribes and officials found their second rung of business in extensive construction activities, which were organised along military lines. It was only a matter of time before they took over the administration of the entire state.

In India, the legends of the Aryans speak of the evolution of the administrative apparatus. The Gods, at war with the demons, were on the verge of defeat. In desperation, they got together and elected a king to lead them. The origins of the early Aryan administrative system may perhaps be traced to these legends.

After this, the bureaucratic system of India evolved in the period of the Delhi Sultanate, the Mauryan Empire, the Mughal Rule, and the British Colonial Empire.

The present civil service structure of India traces its origin to the Macaulay Committee under Lord Macaulay. The committee that gave India its first modern civil service in 1854 recommended that the patronage-based system of the East India Company should be replaced by a permanent civil service based on a merit-based system through a competitive entrance examination. While designing the civil services after Independence, the Indian political leaders chose to retain certain elements of the British structure of a unified administrative system such as an open-entry system based on academic achievements, elaborate training arrangements, permanency of tenure, important posts at Union, state, and district levels reserved for the Civil Service, a regular graduated scale of pay with pension and other benefits, and a system of promotions and transfers based predominantly on seniority.

Civil services are far superior to any job in the private sector. They run the entire administration of the country. The elected ministers of India lay down the policies required to properly run the administrative machinery, which is then carried out by the civil servants in various Central Government and state government agencies.

The importance of civil services in a democracy like India is very high. For effective administration, it is vital that our political leaders are given non-partisan advice. Effective co-ordination is required between the various institutions of governance. The Indian government expects civil servants to offer free, frank, and unbiased advice to the government (irrespective of who is in power) to fulfil their responsibility to the public.

The Civil Services in India are grouped into three broad categories. Services whose members serve both the Union and the State Governments are termed *All India Services*. Services whose members serve only the Union Government are termed *Central Civil Services*. Apart from these, the state governments have their own group of services—*the State Civil Services*.

Another classification of government services in India is on the criteria of the nature of work. They are classified as generalist services, functional services, and technical services.

Generalist Services are those in which the nature of the task to be performed is general. It includes services such as the Indian Administrative Service (IAS), Indian Police Service (IPS), and Central Secretariat Service. There is no specific qualification required for recruitment into these services.

Functional Services are those in which the task to be performed is a specialist in nature. It includes services such as the Indian Revenue Service, Indian Civil Accounts Service, and Indian Defence Accounts Service. There is no specific qualification required for recruitment into these services.

Technical Services are those in which the task to be performed is technical in nature. It includes services such as the Indian Engineering Service and the Indian Ordnance Factories Service (Technical). Specific qualifications, such as an engineering or medical degree, are required for recruitment into these services.

10.5.1 All India Services

All India Services are those services that are appointed by the Central Government and serve both the Central Government and state governments. They generally work under the state government but go on deputation under the Central Government. They are controlled jointly by the Central Government and the state governments. The ultimate control lies with the Central Government, while the immediate control lies with the state governments. At present, there are three All India Services in India:

(a) Indian Administrative Service (IAS)
(b) Indian Police Service (IPS)
(c) Indian Forest Service (IFS)

These All India Services have been created under Article 312 of the Indian Constitution. The article empowers the Parliament of India to create new All India Services on the basis of a resolution passed by the Rajya Sabha to that effect. New All India Services cannot be created without the recommendation of the Rajya Sabha, as the role of the Rajya Sabha is to protect the interest of the states in the Indian federal system.

Sardar Vallabhbhai Patel is known as the 'Father of All India Services', as he was the chief protagonist of the All India Services in the Constituent Assembly of India.

The rules for the recruitment and service conditions of All India Services are framed by the Union Government under the All India Services Act, 1951.

10.5.1.1 Importance of All India Services

The All India Services has been very important for the functioning of India democracy, as mentioned below:

(a) **Impartiality:** Most of the members of the All India Services are posted in states other than their home states. Thus, they work at locations far away from their home states. Thus, their functioning is considered to be objective and impartial.
(b) **Rich Field Experience:** AIS officers serve at the district, state, as well as at Central Government level. Thus, they gain rich experience of three tiers of governance at the grass-roots level (Panchayati raj and municipal bodies), state level, and Union level. This rich experience helps them in formulating balanced and holistic policies in different fields.
(c) **National Perspective:** As the officers of AIS serve at different levels and in different positions, they develop a national perspective as opposed to the parochial perspective of some state service officers. This, along with exposure to certain international institutions, helps them in making quality decisions in the national interest.

(d) **National Integration:** The All India Services have been instrumental in integrating the diverse parts of India into an integral whole. As the members of the AIS are recruited by the Central Government and serve in the state government, their most important task is to integrate the various parts of India within the national developmental plan. After Independence, they played a very important task in integrating around 550 princely states into the mainstream Indian government. Moreover, whenever Presidential Rule is imposed in any state, the AIS officers act as representatives of the Union Government and help in quickly restoring normalcy in that state.

(e) **Uniform Administration:** As the members of the AIS are recruited by the Central government and serve in the state government, this helps in developing a uniform pattern of administration across India. All the developmental schemes are uniformly and effectively implemented because of the role of AIS officers.

(f) **Cooperative Federalism:** The members of the AIS act as a bridge between the Central Government and the state governments. They help in increasing cooperation between the Union and the state governments for the development of the nation.

(g) **Policy Advice:** The members of the AIS play an important role of providing crucial policy advice to the political executives heading different ministries/departments of the Union Government and state governments.

10.5.2 Central Civil Services

The Central Services are those that work under the jurisdiction of the Central Government. Their personnel occupy specialised positions (functional and technical) under the various departments of the Central Government. They are classified into four categories, based on their seniority, Group A, Group B, Group C, and Group D Central Civil Services. Presently, there are 59 Central Civil Services, as mentioned below:

1. Indian Foreign Service (IFS)
2. Indian Post and Telecommunication Accounts and Finance Service (IP&T AFS)
3. Indian Audit and Account Service (IAAS)
4. Indian Revenue Service—Customs and Central Excise
5. Indian Defence Accounts Service (IDAS)
6. Indian Revenue Service—Income Tax (IRS-IT)
7. Indian Ordnance Factories Service (IOFS)
8. Indian Corporate Law Service (ICLS)
9. Indian Civil Accounts Service (ICAS)
10. Indian Railway Traffic Service (IRTS)
11. Indian Railway Accounts Service (IRAS)
12. Indian Railway Personnel Service (IRPS)
13. Indian Railway Protection Force (RPF)
14. Indian Defence Estates Service (IDES)
15. Indian Information Service (IIS)

16. Indian Trade Service (ITS)
17. Indian Postal Service (IPoS)
18. Armed Forces Headquarter Civil Service (AFHQCS)
19. Central Secretariat Service
20. Indian Railway Service of Mechanical Engineers
21. Indian Railway Service of Electrical Engineers
22. Indian Railway Service of Engineers
23. Indian Railway Service of Signal Engineers
24. Indian Railway Stores Service
25. Indian Telecommunication Service
26. Military Engineering Service (MES)
27. Indian Ordnance Factories Service (Technical)
28. Indian Naval Armament Service
29. Central Power Engineering Service
30. Indian Supply Service (ISS)
31. Indian Inspection Service (IIS)
32. Indian Salt Service
33. Indian Electrical and Mechanical Engineering Service
34. Indian Water Engineering Service (Civil)
35. Indian Engineering Service
36. Indian Engineering Service (Roads)
37. Border Roads Engineering Service
38. Indian Broadcasting (Engs.) Service
39. Overseas Communication Service
40. Central Health Service
41. Railway Medical Service
42. Indian Ordnance Factories Health Service
43. Indian Economic Service
44. Indian Statistical Service
45. Indian Cost Accounts Service
46. Defence Quality Assurance Service
47. Defence Research and Development Service
48. Defence Aeronautical Quality Assurance Service
49. Central Legal Service
50. Survey of India Service

51. Military Engineers Service of Architects
52. Military Engineers Service of Surveyors
53. Indian Water Engineering Service (Mechanical)
54. Indian Defence Service of Engineers
55. P&T Building Works Service
56. Central Labour Service
57. Indian Broadcasting (Programme) Service
58. Railway Board Secretariat Service
59. Defence Lands and Cantonment Service

10.5.3 Constitutional Provisions Related to Recruitment in India

Article 309 of the Indian Constitution deals with recruitment to public services in India.

Article 309 (Recruitment and Conditions of Service of Persons Serving the Union or a State): This article empowers the Parliament or the state legislature to make laws to regulate the recruitment and conditions of service of persons appointed to public services and posts in connection with the affairs of the Union or the state, as the case may be. It also authorises the president or the governor to make rules for these purposes until a provision to this effect is made by or under an Act of Parliament or the state legislature. Rules such as the All India Services (Conduct) Rules, 1968 are framed under this article only.

10.5.4 History of Civil Service Recruitment in India

Due to extensive emphasis on recruitment, the Civil Services in India have progressed from an elitist service to a service representative of the Indian society. It consists of many officers from the rural and disadvantaged sections of the society. As they come from the disadvantaged sections, they are in a better position to serve the disadvantaged sections of the society.

Before 1922, the Indian Civil Service Examination was conducted in England by the British Public Service Commission. After 1922, the examination began to be held in India. In 1926, the first Public Service Commission was established in India to conduct the Indian Civil Service (ICS) Examination on behalf of the British Public Service Commission. Subsequently, the Federal Public Service Commission (FPSC) of India was established in 1937 under the Government of India Act, of 1935. The FPSC was established to conduct the Indian Civil Service Examination independently of the British Commission.

In 1950, the FPSC was renamed as the Union Public Service Commission (UPSC) to conduct the examination for prestigious civil services including the Indian Administrative Service (IAS), Indian Foreign Service (IFS), and Indian Police Service (IPS). The syllabus for the examination, the number of attempts allowed, and the age requirements of the candidates have changed from time to time based on the recommendations of the various committees constituted for the same.

Certain important committees formed for recommending the scheme of the Civil Services Examination are as follows:

(a) **Macaulay Committee:** In 1854, the report of the Macaulay Committee on the Indian Civil Service laid down the basic policy for recruitment to the Civil Service in India. The most important recommendation was on recruitment through the merit system consisting of open competition and searching for well-qualified candidates. It established the principle of 'transferability of academic talent to administration'.[6]

(b) **Kothari Committee (Committee on Recruitment Policy and Selection Methods):** The Kothari Committee recommended a new scheme for the Civil Services Examination in 1976. This consisted of three sequential stages. First, the preliminary examination (objective type) for selecting the candidates for the main examination. Second, the main examination (written examination followed by an interview) for selecting candidates for entry into the Civil Services. Third, the post-training test at the end of the Foundation Course at the academy, including an interview by a board constituted by the UPSC. It was proposed that the result of the stage-three test, combined with the result of the stage-two examination would determine the ranking and, therefore, allocation of services. The government did not accept the recommendation regarding the allocation of services after the foundation course, but accepted other recommendations. The sequential system of examination recommended by the Committee was based on the dictum that 'the average quality would get richer as the stream proceeds from one stage to the next'.[6] The scheme recommended by the Kothari Committee was implemented in 1979.

(c) **Satish Chandra Committee:** This committee, in 1989, recommended the continuance of the earlier structure while recommending the introduction of the Essay paper in the main examination.

(d) **Alagh Committee, 2001 and Administrative Reforms Commission, 2008:** In 2001, the Y.K. Alagh Committee recommended that a civil services aptitude test should be introduced at the preliminary stage of the Civil Services Examination. The same recommendation was also made by the Administrative Reforms Commission report in 2008. Following the recommendations of these two committees, the Civil Services Aptitude Test (CSAT) was introduced in 2011 to replace the 'optional subject' paper at the preliminary stage of the examination.

(e) **Nigvekar Committee:** The Nigvekar committee gave certain radical recommendations in 2013 on the structure of the Civil Services Examination. Based on some of its recommendations, the Civil Services Main Examination was modified to some extent. An optional subject paper was removed and two new general studies papers were introduced. After the implementation of the changes, there are four papers on general studies now, including one on ethics and integrity, two papers on one optional subject, one paper on essay writing, and compulsory papers on English and one Indian language.

10.6 Personnel Agencies in India

A personnel agency is an organisation that deals with all aspects of personnel administration including recruitment, selection, placement, training and development, compensation, promotion, motivation, and disciplinary action. The Central Personnel Agency in India is the Department of Personal and Training. Apart from it, various issues of personnel administration are handled by the cadre-controlling authorities of the various civil services. Then there is the UPSC, which is an advisory body with the task of recruiting and selecting personnel into the Civil Services. Similarly, the lower level grades in administration are recruited through the Staff Selection Commission (SSC).

10.6.1 Department of Personnel and Training

The Department of Personnel and Training (DOPT) is the central personnel agency of India. Its role can be described as follows:

(a) **Personnel Policy Formulation:** The department is responsible for policy formulation for all the ministries/departments on various aspects of personnel administration such as recruitment, training, placement, promotion, motivation, and disciplinary action.

(b) **Watchdog for Government:** The department ensures that certain standards and norms, made by it, of personnel administration, are followed and maintained by all the ministries and departments of the Government of India.

(c) **Issuance of Guidelines:** The department issues guidelines from time to time regarding various aspects of personnel administration for the benefit of the different ministries and departments of the Central Government. It also ensures the implementation of these guidelines.

(d) **Advisory Role:** The DOPT advises all departments and ministries on the issue of personnel administration.

(e) **Cadre-controlling Authority:** The department is the cadre-controlling authority of the IAS and three secretariat services in the Central Secretariat.

(f) **Placement and Posting:** The department operate the Central Staffing Scheme, under which suitable officers from the All India Services and Group 'A' Central Services are selected and then placed in posts at the level of deputy secretary/director and joint secretary on the basis of tenure deputation. It also deals with appointments to the posts of chairman, managing director, full-time functional director/member of the board of management of various public sector undertakings/enterprises, corporations, banks, and financial institutions.

(g) **Training Policies:** The DOPT is also responsible for the formulation and coordination of the training policies for the All India and Central Services and for providing support for the capacity building of state government officials. It also sponsors a number of training programmes on a variety of subjects for different categories of Central Government and state government employees.

(h) **Administrative Vigilance:** The department determines the government policy for the maintenance of the integrity of the public services and eradication of corruption, and coordinates the activities of the various ministries/departments in that area.

10.6.2 Cadre-controlling Authorities

Different All India Services and other Civil Services are managed by their respective cadre-controlling authorities. For example, the cadre-controlling authority for the IAS is the DOPT, for the IPS is the Ministry of Home Affairs, and for the IFS is the Ministry of External Affairs. These cadre-controlling authorities are responsible for the various aspects of personnel administration of the respective services, including recruitment, selection, placement, service confirmation, promotion, disciplinary action, awards, and punishment.

10.6.3 Union Public Service Commission and State Public Service Commissions

The UPSC is the central recruitment agency for recruitment into the Group A public services of the Union Government. The first ever Public Service Commission was set up in India in 1926. After the passing of the Government of India Act, of 1935, the Public Service Commission was renamed the Federal Public Service Commission (FPSC) on 1 April 1937. After the promulgation of the Indian Constitution on 26 January 1950, the Federal Public Service Commission came to be known as the Union Public Service Commission (UPSC).

10.6.3.1 Constitutional Provisions

Article 315 (Public Service Commission for Union and states): Article 315 of the Indian Constitution[22] provides for a public service commission for the Union and a public service commission for each state. Moreover, the Parliament may by law provide for the appointment of a joint public service commission if two or more states agree that there can be one public service commission for that group of states and if a resolution to that effect is passed by the house, or where there are two houses, by each house of the legislature of each of those states.

Article 316 (Appointment and Term of Office of Members): It provides that the chairman and other members of the UPSC are appointed by the president, and those of the state public service commissions (SPSC) are appointed by their respective governors. It also provides that (as nearly as may be) one-half of the members of every public service commission shall be persons who at the dates of their respective appointments have held office for at least 10 years either under the Government of India or under a state government. Further, it provides that a member of a public service commission shall hold office for a term of six years from the date on which s/he enters her/his office or until s/he attains, in the case of the Union Commission, the age of 65 years, and, in the case of a state commission or a joint commission, the age of 62 years, whichever is earlier. A person who holds office as a member of a public service commission shall, on the expiration of his/her term of office, be ineligible for reappointment to that office.

Article 317 (Removal and Suspension of a member): The chairman or any other member of the public service commission can be removed from their office by the order of the president on the grounds of proven misbehaviour after the Supreme Court's inquiry and confirmation of guilt in accordance with the procedure prescribed under Article 145 of the Constitution. The president, in the case of the UPSC or joint commission, or the governor, in the case of the state commission, may suspend the Chairman or any other member of the Commission from office in respect of whom a reference has been made to the Supreme Court until the president has passed appropriate orders on the Supreme Court's report. The president has the authority to remove by order the chairman or any other member of a public service commission if:

(i) S/he is adjudged an insolvent

(ii) S/he engages herself/himself in any paid employment outside the duties of her/his office

(iii) S/he is unfit to continue in office by reason of infirmity of mind or body

Article 319 (Prohibition as to the holding of offices by members of Commission on ceasing to be such members): This article provides that the chairman of the UPSC shall be ineligible for further employment either under the Government of India or under the government of a state. The chairman of a state public service commission shall be eligible for appointment as the chairman or any other member of the UPSC or as the chairman of any other state public service commission, but not for any other employment either under the Government of India or under the government of a state. However, a member other than the chairman of the UPSC would be eligible for appointment as the chairman or any other member of the UPSC, or as the chairman of any other state public service commission, but not for any other employment under the Government of India or under the government of a state. Similarly, a member of an SPSC would be eligible for appointment as the chairman or member of the UPSC or as a chairman of that or any other SPSC, but not for any other employment under the Government of India or under the government of a state.

Article 320 (Functions of Public Service Commissions): This article provides for the functions of the UPSC and SPSCs. They can be described as mentioned below:

1. **Conducting Examination:** It is the duty of the UPSC and the SPSCs to conduct examinations for appointments to the services of the Union and the states, respectively.
2. **Assistance to States:** It is the duty of the UPSC to assist two or more states, if requested by them, in framing and operating the schemes of recruitment for any services for which candidates possessing specific qualifications are required.
3. **Advisory Role:** It is the duty of the UPSC and SPSCs to provide advice to the Central Government and state governments, respectively, if asked for, in the following matters:
   (a) Matters relating to the methods of recruitment to Civil Services and for civil posts
   (b) On the principles to be followed in making appointments to the Civil Services and posts and in making promotions and transfers from one service to another, and on the suitability of candidates for such appointments, promotions, or transfers
   (c) On all disciplinary matters affecting a person serving under the Government of India or the government of a state in a civil capacity, including memorials or petitions relating to such matters
   (d) On any claim by or in respect of a person who is serving or has served under the Government of India or the government of a state or under the Crown in India or under the government of an Indian state, in a civil capacity, that any costs incurred by him/her in defending legal proceedings instituted against him/her in respect of acts done or purporting to be done in the execution of his/her duty should be paid out of the Consolidated Fund of India, or, as the case may be, out of the consolidated fund of the state
   (e) On any claim for the award of a pension in respect of injuries sustained by a person while serving under the Government of India or the government of a state or under the Crown in India or under the government of an Indian state, in a civil capacity, and any question as to the amount of any such award
   (f) On any other matter referred by the president of the governor of any state.

Article 323 (Reports of the Public Service Commissions): The PSCs will be required to present a report on the work done by the commission annually to the president (or governor, as the case may be) and such a report shall be caused to be laid before each House of Parliament (or the legislature of the state), together with a memorandum explaining the cases of non-acceptance by the government of the advice of the commission and the reasons therefore.

10.6.3.2 Advisory Role of Public Service Commissions

The UPSC and SPSCs are entrusted only with advisory roles under the Constitution of India. They render advice to the government on the recruitment and regulation of service conditions. However, the government is under no legal obligation to act according to their advice. They have been provided with merely advisory roles, as the Constitution-makers did not want the cabinet or the executive to be bound by the advice of the PSCs.

However, necessary safeguards have been provided in the Constitution against possible disregard of the advice of the commissions by the government. As stated in Article 323 of the Constitution, the president (or the governor) is required to lay down the annual report of the UPSC (or SPSC) in each house of the Parliament (or state legislature). Along with this report, the president (or governor) is required to present a memorandum explaining those cases where the advice of the PSC was not accepted, along with reasons for such non-acceptance. Further, any advice tendered by the Commission cannot be rejected without the approval of the Appointments Committee of the Cabinet.

Such checks have ensured that the cases of non-acceptance of the advice of the PSCs have remained low since Independence.

10.6.3.3 Important Role Played by UPSC

Since Independence, the UPSC has played a very important role in ensuring transparency, objectivity, and integrity in recruitment to public services in India. The important role played by it can be described under the following heads:

(a) **Objectivity and Impartiality:** The UPSC has developed a clear and documented procedure of recruitment into the Civil Services. The candidates can easily understand the recruitment process and predict their selection on the basis of their performance in the examinations conducted by the UPSC. The role of the UPSC has ensured that evils such as nepotism and favouritism have been completely eliminated from the process of recruitment into the Central Government services. The UPSC enjoys the reputation of being a completely objective and impartial organisation unaffected by any sort of political or other pressures on the recruitment system.

(b) **Equality in Recruitment:** In British times, the Indian Civil Service (ICS) was considered an elite service, in which only candidates from urban areas and well-to-do families were recruited. However, the recruitment process has now been redesigned by the UPSC in such a manner that it provides equal chances for candidates from rural backgrounds to compete with urban candidates. Moreover, it allows the candidate to write their examination in any one of the languages mentioned in Schedule 8 of the Indian Constitution. As a result, the proportion of rural background candidates in the government has increased substantially since Independence.

(c) **Representation of all Communities:** The UPSC has effectively implemented the reservation policy of the government. As a result, the backward communities of SCs, STs, and OBCs are adequately represented at all levels of the government. The advice provided by the UPSC in the case of the promotion of civil servants is also in tune with the affirmative action policy of the government. In addition, the UPSC has also played an instrumental role in improving the representation of women and minorities in the government.

(d) **Improving Recruitment in State Services:** The UPSC provides crucial advice to state public service commissions (SPSCs) to improve their recruitment process. The advice provided by the UPSC has helped in attaining a uniform system of recruitment across all the states. It has also helped in freeing state recruitment from the evils of nepotism, favouritism, and political interference.

10.6.3.4 Assessment of State Public Service Commissions

In the earlier years of independent India, the SPSCs functioned well throughout the country. They maintained objectivity, transparency, and fair play in the states' recruitment procedures. Competent and experienced people were appointed as their chairpersons and members. They were either senior government servants or academicians of high standing in the field. However, in recent times, the SPSCs have suffered extensive loss of reputation and their functioning has been negatively impacted by a number of factors. Some of the reasons for their negative image are as follows:

(a) **Corruption in Recruitment:** It is perceived that the members of the SPSCs have been involved in corrupt activities while selecting state civil service officers and specialist officers. Charges of nepotism and favouritism have also been levelled against them in various instances.

(b) **Slow Procedure:** The procedure of recruitment in the SPSCs is far slower than that of the UPSC. The archaic procedure followed by them results in an inordinate delay in the recruitment process. The civil services examination conducted by them takes a minimum time period of one and a half years to a maximum of 4 years in some states. This demotivates bright and ambitious candidates from applying for state government jobs.

(c) **Issues in Appointing Chairperson and Members:** The chairperson and the members of the SPSCs are appointed by the governor of the state in accordance with the provisions of Article 316 of the Indian Constitution. Accordingly, members are recruited in two categories. In the first category, half of the total members are to be government servants (serving or retired) who have served for at least 10 years in the government. In the second category, the Constitution does not stipulate any minimum qualification for another half of the members.

Some states have misused this Constitutional provision. It is seen that junior employees, who are weak in merit and professional ability to do justice to their roles, are appointed as members of SPSCs. In the second category, it is seen that members do not have the appropriate background, training, or experience to hold their posts. This has led to considerable erosion in the reputation and credibility of the SPSCs of some states.

(d) **Strength of SPSCs:** The Constitution has not prescribed a fixed strength for the SPSCs. As a result, the staff strength of some SPSCs is very low and of others is very high. It is seen that SPSCs with low staff strength suffer from delays in the recruitment process and those with higher strength suffer from inefficiency.

(e) **Late Submission of Annual Reports:** Many SPSCs do not prepare their annual reports on time. These reports are also not given priority by the respective state legislatures.

Notwithstanding this criticism, the various SPSCs have shown incredible efficiency and integrity in their functioning. Moreover, many others have improved their functioning. However, the task of the SPSCs is such that any minor mistake committed by them can affect their whole reputation.

The Second Administrative Reforms Commission has given certain recommendations to improve the functioning of the SPSCs. According to it, steps should be taken to ensure that persons of high standing, intellectual ability, and reputation are selected as chairman/members of the state public service commissions. A limit should also be imposed on the strength of its membership. Moreover, there is a need to evolve a national consensus among the states on the issues of (a) appointment of chairman/members and (b) limit on the membership of the commission, through discussions/ deliberations at the Inter-State Council.[35]

10.6.4 Staff Selection Commission

The Staff Selection Commission (SSC) has been set up to make appointments to lower level non-technical positions of the Government of India. It was formed after the recommendations of the 47th report of the Estimates Committee of the Parliament, which advised for the creation of a commission for recruitment to the lower categories of posts.

The Commission is an attached office of the Department of Personnel and Training and comprises of a chairman, two members, and a secretary-cum-controller of examinations, who are appointed on such terms and conditions as may be prescribed by the Central Government from time to time.[23]

10.7 Job Classification

Classification of jobs is understood as the grouping of various job positions on the basis of their roles and responsibilities. This classification helps in increasing the efficiency of the recruitment process, rationalising the promotion system, and in the equitable treatment of persons working in different departments.[24] The following functions are said to be served due to job classification:

1. **Similarity of Treatment:** All the employees grouped under one class are kept under similar conditions of pay, benefits, and other service conditions. This helps in minimising the influence of individuals to change or modify their service conditions. It ensures the enforcement of the principle of equal pay for equal work.
2. **Ease in Budget Management:** It helps in simplifying the task of budgetary sanctions and ensures meaningful control by the legislature on personnel issues.
3. **Division of Work:** The classification system helps in properly dividing work among various classes and among different hierarchical levels.
4. **Task Clarification:** It helps the employees in understanding their duties and responsibilities clearly. This also helps in promoting better management-employee relations and better supervision by the superior authority.
5. **Avoids Duplication:** Proper classification of work helps in avoiding duplication and inconsistencies in the work process.
6. **Better Performance Appraisal:** As the jobs are classified on objective parameters, it helps in the objective appraisal of the performance of the employees.
7. **Better Personnel Administration:** Classification of jobs facilitates the process of recruitment, training, promotion, and transfer.

There are two well-known systems of job classification—position classification and rank classification. The system of position classification was developed in the USA and that of rank classification was developed in the UK.

10.7.1 Position Classification

In position classification, position connotes a group of current duties and responsibilities assigned to a person by the competent authority. Here, an employee's service conditions (salary, rank, etc.) are dependent on the position he/she holds. The duties and responsibilities that are attached to the job are more important than the person discharging those duties. The positions that are comparable are grouped together in a common class.

This class of positions is made up of positions that are sufficiently similar in terms of:[25]

(a) Subject matter of work
(b) Importance, scope, and complexity of the work
(c) Level of difficulty and responsibility
(d) Qualifications required for the performance of the duties of the post
(e) Extent and nature of authority to take decisions

Grade: One important term related to position classification is the grade. A grade denotes all classes of positions that are different with respect to the subject matter of work but similar with respect to the level of difficulty of work and the level of qualification required for the work. Thus, a grade is used to group those positions, which require employees with similar work potential and similar qualifications.

Class Series: Different classes of the same occupational group are brought together in a class series. These classes in a series define the hierarchy of responsibility for that occupational group.

10.7.2 Rank Classification

In rank classification, the service conditions (salary, rank, status, etc.) of an employee are determined by the service he/she is assigned after recruitment. For example, an IAS officer would draw the same salary and hold the same status while s/he serves in a district or in a secretariat. The service conditions do not depend on the position held or the work done by the employee. Rank classification has the following merits:

(a) It is easier to understand and administer.
(b) It encourages career opportunities and promotes mobility.
(c) It encourages the employee to be loyal to the service rather than to a narrow position.
(d) It attracts competent and well-qualified persons to apply for government services.

However, rank classification has the following demerits:

(a) It violates the principle of equal pay for equal work.
(b) It does not describe the duties, roles, and responsibilities of any job in detail. It does not clearly describe the expectations from an employee serving at a particular position. Thus, it becomes difficult to appraise the performance of the employees.
(c) The lines of division run horizontally across the service, resulting in the grouping of services and posts on a non-departmental and non-occupational basis.[26]
(d) The system of rank classification promotes class consciousness and a sort of 'caste system' within the government service.[26]

(e) The system is not conducive to formulating scientific standards for different aspects of personnel administration such as recruitment, training, transfer, and promotion. It is not designed for the orderly grouping of services.

As can be seen from the preceding analysis, position classification is a better method of job classification. As a result, many countries across the world have adopted position classification in government services. The system of classification of Indian government services is fundamentally based on the rank system. The classification of services in India is described in detail in Section 10.5. However, we are moving towards the system of position classification by classifying the various jobs in a department/ministry and allocating them to the officers who possess the kind of expertise or 'domain competence' required.

10.8 Performance Appraisal and Performance Management

Performance appraisal is understood as the assessment of an employee's performance with respect to his/her job. It involves measuring an employee's past and present performance quantitatively and qualitatively with reference to his/her specified role and the potential he/she imparts to an organisation.

According to Hegel, "Performance appraisal is the process of evaluating the performance and qualifications of the employees in terms of the requirements of the job for which they are employed; for purposes of administration; including placement, selection for promotion, providing financial rewards and other actions which require differential treatment among the members of a group as distinguished from actions affecting all members equally."[9]

An important part of the performance appraisal is to apprise the employees of the standard and level of performance, both quantitative and qualitative, expected from them. This helps in matching their personal contribution with the output expected from them.

10.8.1 Objectives of Performance Appraisal

There are three basic objectives of performance appraisal—monitoring, evaluating, and controlling the performance of employees in an organisation. It is more than mere work assessment. It is a management development activity that facilitates the development of an organisational climate of mutuality, openness, and collaboration toward the achievement of the individual as well as organisational goals. The objectives of performance appraisal can be classified as being work-related, career-development-related, communication-related, and administration-related. These are described as follows:[10]

(a) **Work-related Objectives:** The following are the work-related objectives of performance appraisal:

- o **Control over Work:** Measurement of the employees' personal work with respect to the expected organisational standards help in controlling the work of the employees.
- o **Work Efficiency:** This measurement increases the output of the employees with respect to the inputs required for doing any work.
- o **Scientific Assignment of Work:** Appraisal of the employees' performance helps to scientifically assign organisational work to employees as per their proclivities and specialisations.

- **Job Evaluation:** Appraisal of the employees' performance helps in overall evaluation of the work as per the prescribed outcomes expected from the organisation in a given period.

(b) **Career-development-related Objectives:** The following are the career-development-related objectives of performance appraisals:

- **Employee Improvement:** Performance appraisals help in identifying the strong and weak points of the personnel and, thus, in supplying them with the requisite training to improve on their weaknesses.
- **Employee Motivation and Job Satisfaction:** Scientific performance appraisal (PA) motivates the employees to take the right course of action and modify their behaviour to attain organisational goals successfully. Employees also feel satisfied when they find that they are working in higher performing agencies or workgroups.
- **Employee Potential Determination:** PA helps in determining the career potential of an employee as per his/her specialisation and aptitude.
- **Performance Development:** PA also helps in planning for performance development activities for improving the overall performance of the organisation.

(c) **Communication-related Objectives:** The following are the communication-related objectives of performance appraisal:

- **Timely Feedback:** Performance appraisals help in providing timely feedback to the employees on their performance and developing an informal communication channel between the head and his/her junior workers.
- **Mutual Setting of Goals:** It helps the employer and employees to clearly and mutually set the organisational goals. This, in turn, helps in a better understanding of the expected outcomes and thereby enriching the jobs of the employees.
- **Job Counselling:** It allows the senior employees to counsel their junior employees on improving their work through open and free discussions between them.
- **Self-Assessment of Employees:** It also helps employees in self-assessing their work in terms of their actual performance and what is expected from them.

(d) **Administration-related Objectives:** The following are the administration-related objectives of performance appraisals:

- **Basis for Assessment:** Performance appraisals act as the basic assessment tool for providing promotions, rewards, and penalties to employees.
- **Incentive Administration:** Performance appraisals serve as the basic tool for incentive administration. Various incentive schemes such as rewards, welfare measures, and employee benefit schemes are designed on the basis of performance appraisals.
- **Basis for Transfer and Placement:** PAs act as an important tool for deciding the transfers and placements of suitable employees in jobs matching their proclivity, specialisation, and aptitude.

- **Maintaining Continuity:** Proper performance measurement helps in maintaining organisational continuity when its leadership changes. This happens because the new leader is able to understand the organisational situation from the appraisal reports of the employees and the previous achievements of the organisation as a whole.[12]
- **Basis for Termination:** PAs also act as an important tool for deciding the termination of non-performing employees.

10.8.2 Performance Measurement

Performance measurement is an important aspect of performance appraisal. An employee's/organisation's performance can be evaluated and assessed only after measuring it in terms of certain specified standards. Performance measurement aims at measuring performance by using certain objective indices. These objective indices are used to measure the 'ends' or results of the employees' actions and behaviour in an organisation. The emphasis of this concept is on the tangible contribution of the employees to the organisation, which can be expressed in numbers. It is a necessary tool to ensure the accountability of employees towards pre-established organisational goals.

According to Osborne and Gaebler, "what gets measured gets done and measured results help in telling success from failure."[11]

Limitations of Performance Measurement

Some of the major weaknesses and issues involved in performance measurement are described in the following:

(a) **Difficulty in Measurement:** Measuring performance in governmental organisations is a complex phenomenon. Some agencies may find measuring performance far easier than others. For example, performance measurement is easier for the National Highway Authority than for child care agencies.[13]

(b) **Unreliable Results:** Performance measurement may lead to unreliable results. This happens when public agencies resort to unreliable data for measuring performance. For example, too much reliance on crime statistics may lead to the under-reporting of crime by junior officers. This under-reported crime may project a false and unreliable picture of the prevailing crime situation. Such unreliability or cheating in data generation happens when any organisation resorts to management-by-fear or management-by-greed.[14]

(c) **Barriers in Measurement:** While measuring performance, variables other than the goals of the organisation come into the picture. Among these variables, the organisational and social cultures impact the measurement process the most. They act as a barrier to performance measurement. Moreover, it is difficult to measure human desires and interactions.[15]

(d) **Obsolete Indicators:** As organisations change rapidly, the indicators used by them, and the results obtained, become obsolete from time to time.

(e) **Employees' Resistance:** Employees resist performance measurement on the grounds that the job is too creative and professional to be measured.

(f) **Measuring the Wrong Parameters:** If there is imprecision in defining what the organisation wants to measure, it may result in measuring something entirely different from what is required to be measured.

(g) **Goal Displacement:** Excessive reliance on performance measurement may also lead to goal displacement. Goal displacement is a phenomenon in which organisational goals are superseded by new goals during the course of time. For example, if a furniture factory measures its performance in terms of the weight of furniture sold, it may start manufacturing heavier furniture rather than focusing on increasing its sales.

(h) **Unethical Practices:** Excessive reliance on performance measurement may also lead to unethical practices. For example, when income tax officers are forced to increase their tax collection amount, they may resort to dubious practices for tax collection, resulting in discomfort to the tax payers.

(i) **Projecting the Incorrect Picture:** Performance measurement may not project the right picture when lower/higher performance is beyond the capabilities of the employees. The underperformance may be due to insufficient resources, unrealistic organisational strategy, poor management, and other constraints. Thus, it is very important to understand the reasons behind an increase or decrease in performance.

10.8.3 Tools of Performance Appraisal

The tools of performance appraisal are described below:

1. **Graphic Scale:** In the graphic scale method, the degree of merit of an employee is noted on certain articulated traits such as quality of work, the quantity of work, dependability, attitude, and integrity. A form is designed in which the appraising authority appraises the various traits of the employees as 'excellent', 'good', 'poor', and so on. Many scales have been designed to suit different work situations.
    - **Advantage:** The advantage of this technique is that it is less subjective, as it considers different traits of an employee rather than rating an employee by one measure. The subjectivity is further decreased when the traits are defined precisely and the uncertainty in their definition is minimised. Moreover, as it mentions the degree to which each trait is present in an employee, it is a precise technique of appraisal.
    - **Disadvantage:** The technique has the disadvantage that it is difficult to measure the relative weights of the different traits. Moreover, the opinion of the appraising authority on the presence of the different traits in an employee is subjective and cannot be validated easily. Furthermore, it is hard to maintain uniformity in trait articulation and consistency in rating from one appraising authority to another.
2. **Ranking of Employees:** In this technique, the employees in a group, or an organisation, are ranked according to their performance in the order of their merit. Various techniques are used for this ranking, the most common being paired comparison. In paired comparison, the appraising officer compares each employee with every other in the group. The final ranking is based on the number of times an employee is ranked better than others.
    - **Advantage:** The method is advantageous, as each employee is compared with every other. Moreover, as all employees are rated among themselves, it decreases subjectivity.
    - **Disadvantage:** The method becomes difficult when there are more than 20 employees in a group. Moreover, the comparison of employees involves the judgment of the appraising officer, which may be based on subjective criteria.

3. **Forced Distribution Method:** In this method, a job performance scale is formed, in which the employees of a group are rated as best performers, middle performers, worst performers, and so on. For example, on a five-point scale, employees are categorised as poorest (10% of the employees), poorer (20%), average (40%), better (20%), and best (10%) performers. Here, 10% of the employees are placed in the poorest category, 40% in the average category, 10% in the best category, and so on.
   - **Advantage:** The method classifies employees into groups and helps in easily assigning the right kind of work to employees based on their capability to perform.
   - **Disadvantage:** The method is subjective, as it involves the judgment of the appraising authority.
4. **Critical Incident Method:** In this method, the good and bad instances of an employee's job performance, in a particular review period, are noted down. Such good and bad incidents are examined to understand the strengths and skills of an employee. Accordingly, an employee can be helped to overcome his/her weaknesses and rise up in his/her career. It is a technique based on the description of particular events and does not rely on the assignment of ratings or rankings. It demands more effort from the appraising officer, as it is much more than just ticking off items on a form.
   - **Advantage:** The technique is very useful in improving the performance of the employees, since the information provided by it is detailed and specific.
   - **Disadvantage:** The technique requires additional effort and is time-consuming. If the incidents are recorded after a delay, the detail and accuracy may be lost.
5. **Forced Choice Rating Method:** In this method, the appraising officer is asked to select two statements (out of 4–6 statements) with respect to an employee—one that is most characteristic of the employee and another that is the least characteristic of him/her. Likewise, employees are rated on a number of characteristic questions about them. The list contains only positive or only negative sets of behaviours to choose from.

   As an example, an employee is rated on the following statements:
   - Is friendly with colleagues (most characteristic)
   - Is cool-headed
   - Is indifferent (least characteristic)
   - Is overbearing

   Here, the term checked as a most characteristic gives positive credit to the employee.
   - **Advantage:** This method is considered a less biased way of appraising. The supervisor does not have much control over deciding whether an employee's performance is good or bad, as it is decided after answering multiple questions. Thus, it provides a more realistic scenario of the performance of an employee.
   - **Disadvantage:** The method is difficult to apply and sometimes the appraiser is forced to make a decision that closely, but not entirely, relates to the behaviour of an employee.

6. **Group Appraisal Method:** In this method, the appraisal is done collectively by a group of four to five officers, including the immediate supervisor. The group members can be managers at higher levels, colleagues, or subordinates.
   - **Advantage:** This method is free from bias, as the decision is made by a group of people.
   - **Disadvantage:** This method is more time-consuming than appraisals done by a single person.
7. **Nomination Method:** In this method, the appraisers are asked to identify exceptionally good and exceptionally bad performers in the organisation. The good performers are studied to understand their causes of motivation and efficiency. The exceptionally bad performers are separated out to undergo corrective training and improvement courses.
8. **Work Sample Tests:** In this method, the employees are assessed based on their performance in certain sample tests relating to their work. These sample tests mirror the tasks the employees perform in their actual work. The results provide important practical inputs for training and employee development programmes.
   - **Advantage:** As the tests mirror the actual work tasks, a good performance in these tests reflects good performance in actual work. Moreover, these tests are considered as unbiased and fair by all the employees. They are best suited for positions for which the measured competencies are highly critical for successful performance on the job.[16]
   - **Disadvantage:** The method is time-consuming and expensive.
9. **Annual Confidential Report:** Annual confidential reports (ACRs) are confidential reports written annually by supervisory officers in order to appraise the performance of their subordinate employees. The format of these reports differs from organisation to organisation, depending on their work requirement. These reports describe the performance, ability, and character of a person. The defects mentioned in the report are communicated to the concerned employee in order to make improvements. The report, as prepared by the immediate supervisory authority, is reviewed and countersigned by a higher authority. The higher authority may also take a different view than the immediate supervisory authority.
   - **Advantage:** It is a comprehensive method of performance appraisal. Moreover, any bias in the appraisal is removed because of a review of the appraisal by the reviewing authority.
10. **Result-oriented Performance Appraisal System/Management by Objectives:** In this method, the merit of an employee is ascertained by his/her contribution towards the overall goals of the organisation. The superior and the subordinate managers jointly determine their common goals, define each individual's major areas of responsibility in terms of the results expected of him/her, and use these measures as guides for operating the unit and assessing the contribution of each of its members.[17] The value added by an employee to the overall organisational goals is considered as an indicator for appraisal. The method of MBO (management by objectives) is discussed in detail in Chapter 3.
    - **Advantage:** The method is useful, as improving the performance of an employee results in an overall improvement in the performance of the organisation.
    - **Disadvantage:** It is difficult to find objective indices to calculate the value added by a person to the overall organisational goals.

11. **360-Degree Appraisal:** The 360-degree appraisal or *multi-source feedback* is a management practice in which feedback is received from multiple sources including:
    - o Self
    - o Superiors
    - o Peers
    - o Subordinates
    - o Internal customers
    - o External customers/citizens
    - o Others

    This method of appraisal by multiple sources helps in behavioural change and better assessment of the employees. It is more of a development tool than an evaluation tool.
    - **Advantage:** The technique helps in career improvement and behavioural change in the employees. The review provided by citizens/customers and subordinates is important for the overall personality growth of the employees. Moreover, it is seen that, in the case of the Civil Services, citizens are in a better position to judge the integrity of serving bureaucrats than their superior officers.
    - **Disadvantage:** The tool is difficult to use for evaluating performance, as the feedback provided by citizens and subordinates may be subjective and confined to their own narrow interests.

10.8.4 Performance Appraisal in Indian Public Administration

Performance appraisal of civil servants in India is done by the controlling authority, which is generally the head of the department. Different departments follow different kinds of annual confidential reports (ACRs) in order to rate the strengths and weaknesses of their employees. The employees are rated on various parameters such as competence, punctuality, efficiency, capability, ability to work with a team, leadership qualities, technical skills, and physical strength. Efficiency ratings are also provided, as discussed in the preceding sections. One important part of the assessment is the rating of the integrity of the employees. Integrity is rated as 'totally beyond reproach', 'of unquestionable integrity', or 'doubtful integrity'. Any negative comment in terms of integrity affects the further promotion of an employee.

10.8.4.1 Weaknesses of Performance Appraisal System in India

The performance appraisal system in India has several weaknesses. Some of them are as follows:

1. **Limited Idea of Efficiency:** The performance appraisal of employees in the Indian Civil Services is generally based on the limiting idea of efficiency. Other important factors do not impact the appraisal report and, in turn, promotions in a substantial manner. The 'integrity' factor affects promotion and career growth only when it is marked as negative. The integrity rating needs to be given due weight in the appraisal report and, in turn, in promotions to improve the ethical situation of public personnel in India.
2. **High Subjectivity:** In India, it is found that there is a high degree of subjectivity in the performance appraisal of employees. Thus, it is used more as an instrument of subservience than as that of measuring employee effectiveness.
3. **Delay in Assessment:** It is also observed that there is often a delay in completing the assessment of employees, especially when promotions are due. The concerned employee has to continuously follow up with his/her reporting, reviewing, and accepting authority to

ensure that his/her appraisal report is written within time. Moreover, due to delays in assessment, the reporting and reviewing authority forgets the good and bad qualities of the employee under assessment.

4. **Frequent Transfers:** Indian government services are affected by the problem of frequent transfers. When an employee is transferred frequently, within an assessment period, his/her assessment becomes very difficult.
5. **Not Target Based:** It has been found that only general assessments are made in the annual appraisal reports. Specific targets are not fixed by the superior officers, on which employee assessment can be based.
6. **Delay in Feedback:** In departments where ACRs are not filled online, there is a delay in communicating negative and positive feedback to the employees. This delay hinders any substantial improvement in the performance of the employees on the basis of their appraisal reports.
7. **Politicisation of Appraisal:** As the appraisal process is important for determining the promotion of employees, a large measure of politicisation and unethical practices have been observed during employee appraisal report writing in India.
8. **Undue Care and Supervision:** It has also been found in many cases that the superior authority shows a lack of care and supervision while writing the appraisal report of subordinate employees. This generally happens due to their large span of supervision, which requires them to write ACRs for many employees, some of whom they do not even recognise personally.
9. **System of Appeal:** The reporting officer avoids giving adverse remarks in ACRs because of the system of representation against adverse remarks. Any adverse remark requires evidence and justification by the reporting authority.
10. **Uniform Format:** While All India Service officers and other officers are posted in different departments, it has been found that their appraisal reports are written in the same format and they are assessed on the same parameters. It does not recognise the difference in performance parameters applicable for civil servants working in completely different departments or agencies.
11. **Lack of Focus on Employee Development:** The focus of the appraisal report is on rating and evaluating performance rather than on performance planning, analysis, and helping the employees improving their performance.

10.8.4.2 Recommendations for Improving Performance Appraisal System in India

Various committees and commissions have made various recommendations to improve the performance appraisal system of government services in India. These recommendations are compiled and mentioned below.

1. **Computerisation:** The process of writing and reviewing appraisal reports should be computerised for all positions and ranks. At present, computerisation has been implemented for Group A employees. Computerisation helps in the immediate communication of feedback to the employees and, thus, in taking corrective steps speedily.[18]
2. **Different Formats:** Employees posted in different departments, and at different levels of the government, should be subjected to different formats of ACR. It is seen that officers of the same service are subjected to the same format of ACR even when they are posted in different ministries/departments. Thus, the ACR form should have a component reflecting their parent service and a component reflecting the goals and targets of the department in which they are working.[20]

3. **10-point Scale:** Grading should be made on a 10-point or 7-point scale rather than on broad categories of very good, good, etc. The rating should be done on the basis of detailed written guidelines.[20] This helps in further differentiating between good performing, average performing, and bad performing employees, thus motivating the real performers in the department.
4. **Training:** All levels of officers should be trained to write ACRs objectively, with due care, and without bias.
5. **Action on Delay:** Action should be taken against officers who delay in writing ACRs, whether he/she is reporting, reviewing, or accepting authority.
6. **Career Development and Counselling:** The comments in the ACR should be used for imparting training to and planning the career development of the employees.[18] Counselling should be provided to the employees on the basis of the feedback provided in the appraisal reports.
7. **Continuous Process:** Rather than being an annual activity, the performance appraisal should be a continuous process. The officers responsible for reporting on their subordinates should maintain a weekly or monthly record of their impressions about the performance and contribution of their subordinates, including important achievements and shortcomings. This would help them in writing effective ACRs at the end of the year.[19]
8. **Consultative and Transparent:** It is advised that the reporting officer shall set tangible targets at the beginning of the year in consultation with all the employees. The appraisal should be based in a transparent manner on the achievement of these targets. This two-way consultation process leads to the fixing of more realistic targets having greater acceptability.[20]

10.8.5 Performance Management

The new public management (NPM) reforms have had a significant impact on public administration theory and practice. The emphasis of governance in the NPM era is on customer orientation, end orientation, goal orientation, innovation, and citizen satisfaction. In this era, certain modifications are warranted in the traditional performance appraisal procedure. It is important to replace the practice of performance appraisal with the modern practice of performance management, which is a result-oriented performance assessment exercise. Employee performance is related to the long-term and strategic goals of the organisation as a whole. The employees' goals and objectives are derived from their departments, which in turn are derived from the overall mission and goals of the organisation.

For creating targets for employees, all organisational and departmental goals are linked together. These employee targets are monitored continuously to provide timely feedback to the employees. The main aim of performance management is not to measure performance but improvement in the performance of the employees. It provides an opportunity for the employee and performance manager to discuss development goals and jointly create a plan for achieving those goals. The developmental plan prepared contributes to the organisation as well as personal goals of the employees.

The process of performance management helps in performance improvement due to the stress it lays on informal work relations, the use of positive social capital in performance management, and periodic adjustment in the performance measurement processes. The emphasis is more on improving the overall organisational performance than on impacting the behaviour and activities of the employees.

The process of performance management is performed step by step in a logical manner, as follows:

1. **Articulation of Results:** The targeted results of the overall organisation is articulated in terms of quality, quantity, timeliness, and cost incurred.
2. **Alignment of Goals:** The above-mentioned organisational goals are translated in terms of results to be attained by the discrete departments and the employees within them. These results are described objectively in terms of quantity, quality, timeliness, and cost incurred. The results of all the parts and departments of the organisation is aligned with the overall preferred results of the organisation.
3. **Prioritisation of Results:** The desired results are prioritised through their different subunits—the desired results are broken down into sub-results and doable activities to the extent possible. The sub-results and doable activities are weighted in terms of ranking, percentage, or time to be spent on each of them.
4. **Cathe USAl Relationship:** A Cathe USAl (cause and effect) relationship is established between the desired activities performed by the employees and the achievement of the overall desired goals and values of the organisation.
5. **Regular Monitoring:** The employees' performance is regularly monitored on the basis of the targeted results. The divergent employees are provided with timely feedback in order to improve their performance.
6. **Rewarding Good Performance:** The well-performing employees are rewarded in different manners according to the situation of the organisation.

10.8.5.1 Performance Appraisal vs Performance Management

Performance appraisal is a component of the performance management cycle, which consists of assessing the employee's performance in his/her current position. Table 10.1 compares the two concepts.

Table 10.1 Comparison of performance appraisal and performance management[20, 21]

Characteristics	Performance management	Performance appraisal
Objectives	The objectives of individuals, groups (departments), and the organisation are integrated.	Only individual objectives are emphasised.
Frequency	Performance review is done continuously throughout the year.	Performance review is done once a year.
Rating system	Employees are rated in a joint and participative manner. Less emphasis is given to rating employees.	High emphasis is placed on rating employees in a top-down manner.
Reward linkage	The process is not directly linked to rewards, as the main aim is an employee development and achievement of organisational goals.	There is a direct link between the appraisal report and promotion, pay, etc.
Ownership	The process is owned and implemented by the line management.	The process is owned by the personnel department.
Corporate alignment	The system is completely integrated, and aimed at organisational and employee development.	The system is isolated and not linked with organisational goals.

Characteristics	Performance management	Performance appraisal
Focus of performance review	The focus is on improving the future performance of the employees.	The focus is on assessing the past performance of the employees.
Emphasis	The emphasis is on career development and organisational improvement.	The emphasis is on rating and evaluating individuals.

According to the Second Administrative Reforms Commission Report, the performance management system can be introduced into the Indian government by designing a performance management system (PMS) for each department/organisation within its overall strategic framework. The PMS of each department/organisation should be customised to its own working conditions; a general PMS cannot be adopted for the entire government.

10.8.6 Performance Development Plan

A performance development plan is aimed at filling the gaps in the performance of the employees and the organisation as a whole. The plan aims at detecting the areas in which performance is below expectations, identify the underlying causes of below-par performance in those areas, search for corrective action in order to improve performance, and review the performance in order to improve continuously. The plan is typically a subpart of the performance management system.

10.8.7 Performance Agreements

A performance agreement is signed between the head of a department/agency and the respective minister about the expected performance (and desired results) from the department/executive agency within an assessment period. The key ingredients of such an agreement are the objectives to be achieved, provision of resources for achieving those objectives, accountability and control mechanism in case of diversion from the desired results, and autonomy or flexibility is given to civil servants to attain those objectives. It is the most common accountability mechanism in countries that have reformed their public administration systems, such as New Zealand and France.

In the agreement, the head of a department/agency is held responsible for the attainment of targets. The head devises suitable mechanisms to ensure the accountability of the personnel working under him. After an assessment period is over, the results are assessed by an independent agency such as the public service commission or a public service authority.

The second administrative reforms commission suggests that the annual performance agreement shall be signed between the departmental minister and the secretary of the ministry/head of department, providing the physical and verifiable details of the work to be done well before the start of a financial year. The details of the annual performance agreements and the result of the assessment by the third party should be provided to the legislature to decide the budget of the respective ministry/department for the next financial year.

10.8.8 Good Governance Initiatives in Performance Appraisals

Various good governance initiatives have been taken to improve the performance appraisal system used in public services in India. Some of them are as follows:

1. **e-Service Book:** The government has taken steps to computerise, and make available online, the service books of government employees. The purpose of the service book has already been discussed in the preceding sections. The data entered in the e-service book is available to the employees to enable them to cross-check and report any discrepancies. The Controller General of Accounts (CGA) also considers e-service books as legal tender for all purposes.
2. **SPARROW Portal:** Smart Performance Appraisal Report Recording Online Window (SPARROW) is an online portal for online appraisal reporting. It started with the performance appraisal reports of IAS and IPS officers but is intended to be extended to all the employees of the Central Government and state governments. It will help in reducing the paperwork in performance appraisals. It would also help in the immediate communication of feedback, and in taking corrective steps, on the basis of appraisal reports. Moreover, it will be helpful in speeding up the process of performance appraisals.
3. **Employees Online App:** The Department of Personnel and Training (DOPT) has launched the *Employees Online App* to update on governmental appointments and postings on real-time basis. The aim of the application is to bring in transparency in appointments and postings. It enables its users to stay updated on real-time basis with appointments, postings, and vacancies at senior levels in the Central Government. It also intends to eliminate the information symmetry in appointments and postings and to reduce speculations in transfers and postings in the Union Government. It will make the system completely transparent, as all the relevant orders and notifications will be instantly available in the public domain. Furthermore, it will provide online documents such as the Annual Performance Appraisal Report, Immovable Property Return, and Executive Record Sheet of all the government officers.
4. **Online Probity Management System:** The DOPT has launched the Online Probity Management System (also known as the Probity Portal) in association with other ministries to assess the integrity and performance level of officers. The integrity and performance level of officers in the age group of 50–55 years (or those who have completed 30 years of service) will be assessed to take a decision on their continuity in service. The non-performing officers will be made to retire compulsorily. The online portal will expedite the assessment process, as the relevant ministries would be able to upload positive/negative reports about an officer online on the portal. The government would be able to get a bird's eye view of the performance of the officers by referring to this portal. The portal also monitors the rotation of officers in sensitive and non-sensitive posts to identify officers occupying sensitive positions for more than three months.
5. **SUPREMO Portal:** The Single User Platform Related to Employees Online (SUPREMO) is a portal that can be used to access certain details about senior government officers, including their executive record sheets. The system, presently applicable to IAS officers, is intended to be applied for all senior government servants. The portal helps the general public to know the credentials of each government servant, including their source of recruitment, place of domicile, educational background, work experience, and awards and punishments received. This helps the general public, and the governmental authorities, to be aware of the performance and integrity of senior government servants.
6. **SOLVE Portal:** The Central Government has launched the System for Online Vigilance Clearance Enquiries (SOLVE) portal for swiftly providing vigilance clearance certificates,

which are required for the appointment of officers at senior government levels. The service was started initially for board appointments for Central Public Sector Enterprises (CPSEs). It is intended to be expanded to all senior appointments in the Government and in banks. The online vigilance clearance is concerned with the integrity of the officers considered for appointment to senior positions.

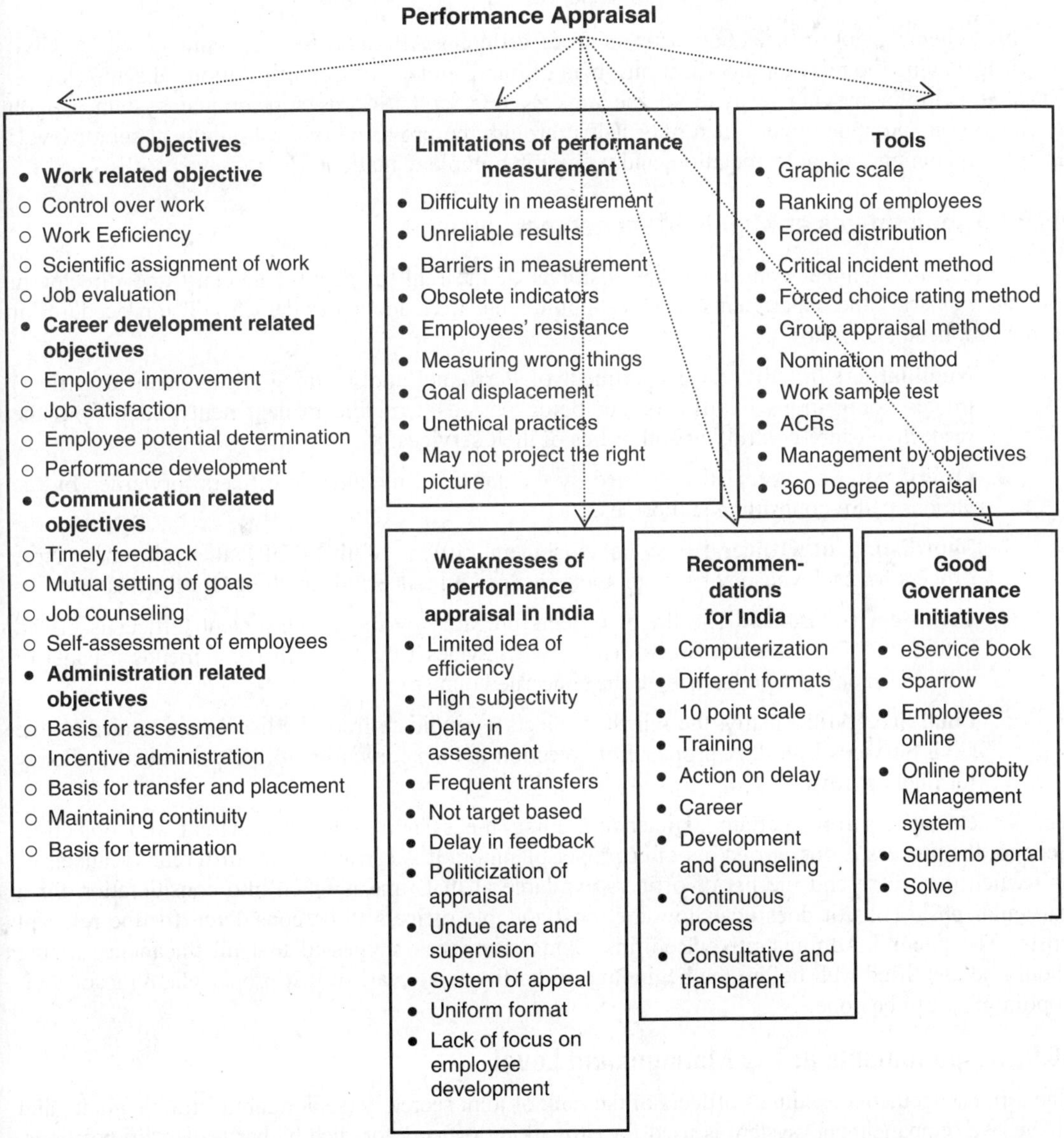

Performance Appraisal

Objectives

- **Work related objective**
  - Control over work
  - Work Eeficiency
  - Scientific assignment of work
  - Job evaluation
- **Career development related objectives**
  - Employee improvement
  - Job satisfaction
  - Employee potential determination
  - Performance development
- **Communication related objectives**
  - Timely feedback
  - Mutual setting of goals
  - Job counseling
  - Self-assessment of employees
- **Administration related objectives**
  - Basis for assessment
  - Incentive administration
  - Basis for transfer and placement
  - Maintaining continuity
  - Basis for termination

Limitations of performance measurement

- Difficulty in measurement
- Unreliable results
- Barriers in measurement
- Obsolete indicators
- Employees' resistance
- Measuring wrong things
- Goal displacement
- Unethical practices
- May not project the right picture

Tools

- Graphic scale
- Ranking of employees
- Forced distribution
- Critical incident method
- Forced choice rating method
- Group appraisal method
- Nomination method
- Work sample test
- ACRs
- Management by objectives
- 360 Degree appraisal

Weaknesses of performance appraisal in India

- Limited idea of efficiency
- High subjectivity
- Delay in assessment
- Frequent transfers
- Not target based
- Delay in feedback
- Politicization of appraisal
- Undue care and supervision
- System of appeal
- Uniform format
- Lack of focus on employee development

Recommen-dations for India

- Computerization
- Different formats
- 10 point scale
- Training
- Action on delay
- Career
- Development and counseling
- Continuous process
- Consultative and transparent

Good Governance Initiatives

- eService book
- Sparrow
- Employees online
- Online probity Management system
- Supremo portal
- Solve

Mind Map 10.4 : Various aspects of performance appraisal

10.9 Appointment of Personnel at Senior Ranks in India

Appointments at senior levels in the Government of India are decided by the *Appointments Committee of the Cabinet* (ACC). These appointments are made under the *Centre Staffing Scheme* (CSS), which provides a mechanism for the selection and placement of officers to senior administrative posts in the Government of India.

This scheme helps in selecting officers from different All India Services and Group A Civil Services, having the relevant qualifications, bent of mind, and expertise, for positions at senior levels. Thus, it helps in moving away from the rank system, and towards a positional system, of job classification and appointment. It further helps through the provision of fresh inputs at senior levels in policy planning, policy formulation, and programme implementation.

10.9.1 Appointments at Middle Management Level

The middle management constitutes the positions of the rank of deputy secretary and director in various ministries and departments. These appointments are made under the CSS. The procedure for an appointment is as follows:

1. **Nomination:** Initially, the Department of Personnel and Training (Establishment Officer) invites nominations of officers, for being posted at middle management ranks, from the respective cadre-controlling authorities of their services.
2. **Offer List:** An 'offer list' is formed by the names of the eligible officers forwarded by the various cadre-controlling authorities.
3. **Shortlisting of Officers:** The Establishment Officer of the DOPT then shortlists three officers for each vacancy based on their past performance and suitability for the post.
4. **Civil Services Board:** The list of officers prepared by the Establishment Officer is placed before the Civil Services Board. The Civil Services Board in turn recommends a panel of officers (in order of preference) to the concerned ministry.
5. **Final Selection:** Finally, the ministry selects a candidate from the list recommended by the Civil Services Board. A proposal of selection is then forwarded to the competent authority for final approval.

The system suffers from certain deficiencies. First, the system is not transparent and objective. Second, the process is not carried out after proper planning. It is carried out for different vacancies as and when they arise and the list of officers available at that time is taken into consideration for a particular post. Thus, it does not allow the most suitable officers to be considered for the relevant posts. The Second Administrative Reforms Commission has suggested that all vacancies arising should be identified well before the beginning of the financial year, so that proper planning for their appointment can be done.

10.9.2 Appointments at Top Management Level

The top management constitutes officers of the rank of joint secretary (senior administrative grade) and above. An 'empanelment' system is used for earmarking officers for such higher leadership positions. The procedure followed is described below:

1. **Empanelment:** A panel of suitable officers, having superior career records, is prepared by a group of secretaries after closely evaluating the service records of the eligible officers. Here, a panel is a list of suitable officers from All India Services and Group A Central Services participating in the CSS. This exercise is conducted on an annual basis and officers with the same year of allotment are grouped together. For the empanelment of officers for the ranks of higher administrative grades (additional secretary and above), a Special Committee of Secretaries (SCOC) is constituted to assess (on a scale of 10) the service records as well as experience profiles of officers and evaluate such qualities as general reputation, merit, competence, leadership, and aptitude for participating in the policymaking process. For being empanelled at this rank, the fulfilment of conditions such as a minimum service period (2 years), work experience of at least 3 years at JAG (Junior Administrative Grade) in the Union Government, mandatory vigilance clearance, etc. is necessary. Moreover, it is also necessary that the panel of officers must represent officers from the weaker sections such as women, SCs, STs, and OBCs.
2. **Finalisation by CSB:** The Civil Services Board (CSB) finalises the panel prepared by the group of secretaries and forwards it to the Appointments Committee of the Cabinet (ACC).
3. **Approval by ACC:** The ACC approves the panel of officers, after making necessary modifications, upon the recommendations of the CSB. This panel is utilised for appointing officers for the various top management posts under the Government of India.
4. **Final Selection:** Officers are selected by the various ministries from the panel of officers approved by the ACC.

10.10 Training and Development

Training is an important component of the functioning of every organisation. Every well-functioning organisation needs to have well-trained and experienced employees to perform their job-related activities and attain their goals.

More precisely, training is the process through which employees are made capable of doing the jobs prescribed to them. It helps in improving the productivity of newly recruited workers in minimum time. It helps in refreshing the competency of old employees and making them conversant with the required work methodologies and technologies.

10.10.1 Training, Development, and Education

Training, development, and education are related terms and are often used interchangeably. However, there are certain fundamental differences among these terms that are important to understand. Table 10.2 schematically compares the three terms in terms of parameters such as their objectives, time duration, nature of personnel, nature of knowledge imparted, and institutional arrangement.[27]

Table 10.2: Comparison of the terms training, development, and education

	Training	Development	Education
Objective	The intention of training is to improve the performance of an employee in the current or intended job.	The intention is not only to improve performance in the current job but to bring in personality growth, and help individuals in progress toward maturity and the actualisation of their potential capacities.	The intention is to develop a logical and rational mind that can determine the relationship among pertinent variables and understand various phenomena.
Time duration	It is a short-term process.	It is a long-term process.	It is a very long term process.
Nature of personnel	It is generally imparted to non-managerial personnel for gaining technical skills for a definite purpose.	It is generally imparted to managerial personnel.	It is imparted to personnel at higher positions as well as to newly recruited personnel.
Nature of knowledge Imparted	Knowledge of technical and mechanical operations is imparted through it. This knowledge is strictly job-related.	Knowledge of theoretical concepts and ideas is imparted through it. This knowledge is general in nature.	More than imparting knowledge, it aims at imparting the qualities of mind and character, understanding basic principles, and learning objectivity.
Institutional arrangement	It is imparted on the job and at technical training institutions.	It is imparted on the job and at administrative/ general training institutions.	It is imparted in educational institutions.

10.10.2 Advantages of Training

Training is a vital function, with important advantages for the organisation as well as the employees. It plays a large role in determining the effectiveness and efficiency of an organisation.[28] The various advantages of training are described below.

10.10.2.1 Advantages of Training to the Organisation

The major advantages incurred to an organisation by training is as mentioned below:

1. **Improvement in Job Selection:** An effective training programme helps in selecting personnel with requisite skills for the corresponding job. It acts as a follow up of the selection procedure. It helps not only in imparting the necessary skills but also in identifying promising individuals during the training programme.
2. **Improvement in Organisational Performance:** Training improves the skills of the employees, which in turn help in improving the output of the organisation.

3. **Reduction in Cost of Production/Service:** Training helps employees to understand better and economical use of the material and equipment of the organisation, which helps to decrease the cost of goods and services provided by the organisation.
4. **Improvement in Supervision:** If the employees are well-trained, they are not required to be supervised on the minor aspects of the job, i.e., close supervision is not required for trained employees. Thus, the management is able to focus on the broader and futuristic aspects of supervision.
5. **Employee Morale:** Training programmes help in aligning individual goals with organisational goals. This increases the employees' loyalty, support, and commitment towards organisational goals.
6. **Organisational Stability:** As training creates a pool of learned employees, the organisation feels safe in times of employee movement, cut-down, and transfers. This provides stability to the organisation.

10.10.2.2 Advantages of Training to the Employees

The major advantages incurred to employees by training are as follows:

1. **Increase in Importance:** Training helps a person in gaining new knowledge and skills. This increases his/her importance both inside and outside the organisation.
2. **Job Security:** Training helps an employee to adjust to the changing working conditions and to adapt to the new technologies in the job. This helps improve job security.
3. **Promotional Aspects:** Adequate and timely training helps the employees to gain the required skills for being promoted to a position of greater responsibility.

10.10.3 Methods of Training

A number of ways have been devised to train employees. These methods can be classified as being 'on the job' and 'off the job'.

10.10.3.1 On-the-job Training

In this methodology of training, the trainees learn the skills of the job while performing the job under the guidance of his/her immediate boss. The trainees get the advantage of gaining firsthand knowledge and experience in the actual working conditions. The various methodologies of on-the-job training are as follows:

1. **Training on Specific Job:** In this method, training about a specific job is provided while working in the conditions of that specific job. It is conducted through the following methods:
   (a) **Job Experience:** In this method, the trainee learns by performing the actual job, solving actual problems, and interacting with colleagues in the organisation. It is the oldest method. It is considered wasteful if not combined with other methods of training.
   (b) **Coaching:** In this method, the trainee is coached by his/her immediate boss who provides him/her with requisite feedback on the performance on the job. The boss

addresses the various questions, doubts, and apprehensions in the mind of the trainee about the actual job. It is an interactive method, in which the boss uses his/her experience in order to train the trainee.

(c) **Understudy:** In this method, a trainee is placed as an assistant of an experienced employee. The trainee learns by experience, observation, and imitation of the style of the experienced employee. Being an assistant, the trainee learns about all the practical aspects of the job he/she would be working on in the future.

2. **Job Rotation:** In this method, the trainee is made to visit and learn from the various jobs being performed in the different sections of an organisation. He/she interacts with the employees of the different sections and learns the working skills of the different departments. The method helps in broadening the outlook of the trainee and understanding the functioning of the overall organisational unit.

3. **Special Assignment:** In this method, the weaknesses of an employee are highlighted based on his/her performance. To eradicate these weaknesses, the employee is asked to perform a special assignment in a particular time frame. The motive of this special assignment is to help the employee overcome his/her weaknesses while performing the assignment.

4. **Selective Reading:** In this method, the organisation establishes dedicated libraries for its employees and stocks them with advanced journals and books related to the organisation's work. Moreover, it allows its employees time to visit the library and read books. After reading the journals and books, the employees are able to learn about the various aspects of the job and the advanced methods to perform it. It also helps in broadening the knowledge of the employees.

5. **Apprenticeship:** Apprenticeship training basically provides job-related skills to a craftsman or a worker. In this method, the trainee learns trade-related skills by doing actual work under the guidance of a master craftsman. A large number of skilled workers in industrial organisations are trained by this technique.

6. **Vestibule Training:** In this method, training is provided in a simulated work environment. Organisations create vestibule schools, in which the actual working conditions are simulated under the close watch of a mentor. Trainees learn skills by working in these vestibule schools. It is generally used for the training of clerical staff and factory workers.

10.10.3.2 Off-the-job Training

In off-the-job training, the trainee learns about the various skills in an environment that is separated from the actual job. The entire concentration is on gaining knowledge and skills rather than spending a certain amount of time in completing a job. Off-the-job training is of the following types:

1. **Lectures Methodology:** It is the most traditional form of training, in which trainees are made to attend various lectures organised by the training department. These lectures are intended to transmit work-related knowledge and skills to the trainees.

2. **Conferences:** In conferences, there is a discussion on various problems faced by the participants while working in the field. The participants intensively discuss methods to improve their functioning and come out with relevant and practical solutions.

3. **Case Studies:** In this technique, a real case is discussed among a group of participants. A case is an account of a real incident written and analysed by the training officer. The various aspects of and problems encountered in a case are discussed by the participants under the guidance of the trainer. This discussion helps the trainees face a similar situation in a better manner in the future.
4. **Brainstorming:** It is a method of training where new ideas are sought from the trainees in an open environment. The trainees are given a problem and asked to think of innovative solutions. Full participation of the trainees is encouraged without criticising their ideas in any manner. A chain reaction develops from ideas to ideas. All the ideas are then collated and critically examined to determine new and practical solutions. The main aim of brainstorming is to generate new ideas rather than bringing about a change in the behaviour of the participants.
5. **Simulated Training:** In simulated training, the conditions/situations of the field are simulated in the training session. Real situations are simulated and the participants are asked to play relevant roles to deal with those situations effectively. There are two methods of simulated training—role playing and business game.
   (a) **Role Playing:** It is a technique in which participants are asked to play certain roles in real-life simulated situations. Trainees get involved in active dialogue with each other, which helps in improving their human relations skills such as effective communication and group bonding. Other trainees in the group serve as observers and examine the role played by the participants. A trainee plays the role of positions other than his/her official position in the organisation. This helps in broadening his/her experience of the work situations.
   (b) **Business Game:** A business game is a training method in which the problem of running a company or a department is simulated in the classroom, and the various participants are given various positions in this simulated company situation. The participants are divided into several teams, and each team is given the task to run a company in competition with other companies. Each team makes decisions on several issues such as fixing price levels, levels of production, and inventory levels. All these decisions are fed into a computer, which acts like a real market. According to the results of the computer, the team with the maximum profit is declared as the winning team. The strengths and weaknesses of the decisions of the various teams are then analysed in light of the profits earned by each team. The basic aim of this technique is to impart certain administrative skills such as learning investment strategies, collective bargaining techniques, and dealing with the morale of clerical staff. It is different from the 'role playing' technique, as the former aims at solving administrative problems and the latter aims at improving the human interactions within an organisation.
6. **Syndicate Training:** In syndicate training, a syndicate or a workgroup is formed by the trainees. Various groups are formed by the trainees among themselves. A problem is assigned to each syndicate for study and solution. Each syndicate has a chairperson and a secretary from among themselves. Each group looks for a solution to the problem by deeply studying the problem, reading selective material, referring to best practices, collecting data, and writing down various alternative solutions to the problem. For

determining the solution, they also consult with specialists. The final solution is then submitted in the form of a report by each group. The report of each syndicate is presented to an assembly of the training faculty and all the syndicates in the training programme for comments and discussion.

7. **Sensitivity Training:** This method of training is already discussed in Section '*Sensitivity Training (or T Group Training)*' under the topic of '*Chris Argyris*'.

10.10.4 Training Evaluation

Training evaluation is defined as a study to find out whether the various objectives of a training programme are attained or not and in what measure. The evaluation of a training programme is of the following two types:[29]

1. **Formative Evaluation:** The formative evaluation of a training is conducted at the early stage of a programme. It addresses the questions of effective training implementation and planning. It helps in determining problems in the early stages of implementation so that they can be rectified well in time.
2. **Summative Evaluation:** Summative evaluation assesses the outcomes or impacts of a training programme in the short as well as long term. It establishes the relationship between different training factors and the overall outcome once the training programme is finished. It provides evidence for establishing a cause-and-effect relationship.

10.10.4.1 Levels of Training Evaluation

Hamblin has described five levels of training evaluation. They are as described as follows:[30]

1. **Reaction Level:** In this level, the reactions of the trainees towards the training programme are assessed. These reactions are complex and a result of many factors such as training content and methods, training context, location, and the trainees' perceived success at attaining certain goals using the training programme. The reactions are generally recorded using a rating questionnaire followed by an informal discussion and interview. The method is subjective in nature, as the views of the trainees may depend on a number of factors unrelated to the objectives of the training programme.
2. **Learning Level:** In this level, the various skills and knowledge acquired by the trainees are assessed by observing the improvement in their performance. This assessment of their learning can be done either immediately after the training programme or after a certain time gap. Immediate assessment of learning is done by conducting a post-training test. A more detailed assessment can be done later using various techniques, including the performance appraisal of the employees. However, it needs to be ensured that the employees' performance is a true reflection of the training and not owing to some unrelated factors.
3. **Job Behaviour:** In this level, the extent of translation of training programmes into improvement in the actual job performance is assessed. This evaluation is done in collaboration between the trainer and the organisation's management.
4. **Organisation:** In this level, the immediate effect of the training programme on organisational factors are studied. The immediate effect is studied in the case of the organisational factors such as the following:

- o Quality and quantity of production
- o Safety in the production
- o Absenteeism
- o Labour turnover
- o Attitude towards work
- o Job satisfaction
- o Improvement in work methods

5. **Ultimate Level:** In this level, the ultimate effect of the training on the financial improvement of the organisation is studied. The overall improvement in the financial condition of the organisation due to the skills transmitted during the training is studied.

10.10.5 Training of Public Services in India

The Indian Civil Services (ICS) have a well-established method of training. The history of public service training dates back to 1805 when the British government established Haileybury College for the training of young civil servants. After 1855, when recruitment through competitive examinations started, successful ICS officers were made to go through a course of 1–2 years in British University in the subjects of Indian history, law, language, and so on. During the Second World War, a camp school was set up at Dehradun to impart training to the new entrants into the ICS. After Independence, the Indian Civil Service was converted into the Indian Administrative Service, and institutional training was imparted to the new recruits at the IAS Training School, Metcalfe House, Delhi. The Indian Administrative Service Staff College was set up at Shimla to train senior officials and recruits other than direct recruits. Both these training institutions were subsequently merged and the National Academy of Administration was set up in September 1959 at Mussoorie. The academy is now named as Lal Bahadur Shastri National Academy of Administration (LBSNAA), which is the most important central institution of training for higher civil services, including the All India services.

In the pre-Independence era, officers were expected to learn from their field experience, and training was not recognised as a major capacity-building tool. However, after Independence, the role of the government, number of the government departments, and the number of public services increased. Thus, an imminent need was felt to structure training programmes for different civil services.

Since Independence, the Indian system of training has largely been based on the British model, in which the civil servants recruited at higher ranks undergo well-planned institutional/university training. Such systemic training arrangements do not exist for the public servants of Group B and lower ranks. They are expected to learn from their job experience.

10.10.6 Training of Higher Civil Services in India

The training of higher civil services is divided into two elements—institutional (or off-the-job) training and departmental (or on-the-job) training.

10.10.6.1 Institutional/Off-the-job Training

Institutional training for the Civil Services, especially for the All India Services, is divided into the following elements.

Foundation Course

The Foundation Course marks the beginning of the training of civil servants recruited by various examinations conducted by the UPSC, especially the Civil Services Examination. It is conducted jointly by LBSNAA and its allied institutions. The raison d'être for it is to instil a shared understanding of the government and build camaraderie among the various civil services for smoother conduct of the affairs of government. Its objectives are to instil values of self-discipline, integrity, sensitivity to the weaker sections, constitutional values, public service, and so on. It is further aimed at the overall development of the personality of young officers.

Professional Training

The professional training course of various civil services is conducted in their parent institutions. The parent institution for the IAS is LBSNAA, for the IPS is Sardar Vallabhbhai Patel National Police Academy (SVPNPA), for the Indian Foreign Service (IFS) is the Foreign Service Institute (FSI), Delhi. Professional training involves imparting skills and knowledge in the subjects relevant for performing the actual job in the field in the whole career of the civil servants. For example, the IPS officer trainees are imparted training in subjects such as investigation, human rights, forensic science, forensic medicine, cybercrime investigation, and police leadership.

For the All India Services, the professional training programme is divided into two phases—phase 1 and phase 2. In between the two phases, the district/departmental/on-the-job training is sandwiched. The training programme also involves attachment with various other institutions, agencies, and training organisations to gather real-life experience of functioning in them. These organisations are generally those where a civil servant may work in his/her future postings.

10.10.6.2 District/Departmental/On-the-job Training

During the probation period itself, the civil servants are exposed to their real work situations. IAS and IPS officers are attached under a District Magistrate and Superintendent of the Police, respectively. Similarly, IRS officers are given junior-level work in the Income Tax Department, ISS officers are attached in the statistics wings of various ministries, IES officers are attached in the economic division of various ministries, and so on.

The principal style of training in district/departmental training is 'learning by watching'. For example, an IPS officer observes the work of various district-level organisations such as the superintendent of police office, police headquarters, subdivisional police office, urban police station, rural police station, district magistrate officer, zila parishad, district court, local crime branch, district special branch, and traffic branch. He/she is also given an opportunity to hold independent charge of a rural police station. Similar methods of on-the-job learning are adopted by all the civil services.

10.10.6.3 Mid Career Training

As a civil servant goes up in the hierarchy, the nature of his/her job changes. Mid-career training is conducted to fulfil the skill requirements for this change in the nature of the job. Mid-career training programmes are conducted for all civil services, but they are more structured in the case of IAS and IPS.

In the case of IAS, for the first 8–10 years, an officer is primarily concerned with the implementation and coordination of programmes at the district level. In the next 8–10 years, s/he is concerned with project/programme formulation and in the management of programmes on a large state-wide basis. In the further 8–10 years, s/he is directly responsible for policy formulation functions. Thus, the nature of the job changes every 8–10 years, for which adequate mid-career training is required after every 8–10 years of service.

The duration of the mid-career training programme ranges from 4 to 6 weeks and may/may not involve a foreign component. In the case of IAS and IPS, the total training programme is divided into five phases. Phase 1 and phase 2 are conducted at the time of induction of the officer into the service. Phases 3–5 are mid-career training programmes held during the 7–9th years, 14–16th years, and 26–28th years of service, respectively.

10.10.6.4 In-service Training

Apart from the structured training programmes, various intermittent in-service training programmes are conducted by the training academies in which interested officers can apply. Such programmes include officers of different ranks all across India.

10.10.6.5 Institutional Arrangement for Training in India

There are six broad categories of training institutions involved in training civil servants in India. They are as follows:

1. **Service-specific Parent Institutions:** Every civil service has a service-specific parent institution whose sole responsibility is to impart training to the officers of that service. The service-specific institutions of some of the civil services recruited by the UPSC are listed in Table 10.3.

Table 10.3: Parent training institutions of some civil services recruited by the UPSC

Service	Parent institution
Indian Administrative Service (IAS)	Lal Bahadur Shastri National Academy of Administration (LBSNAA), Mussoorie
Indian Foreign Service (IFS)	Foreign Service Institute (FSI), New Delhi
Indian Police Service (IPS)	Sardar Vallabhbhai Patel National Police Academy (SVPNPA), Hyderabad
Indian Forest Service (IFoS)	Indira Gandhi National Forest Academy (IGNFA), Dehradun
Indian Post and Telecommunication Accounts and Finance Service (IP&T AFS)	Institute of Financial Management (NIFM), Faridabad
Indian Audit and Account Service (IAAS)	National Academy of Audit and Accounts, Shimla

Service	Parent institution
Indian Revenue Service - Customs and Central Excise	National Academy of Customs, Excise and Narcotics (NACEN), Faridabad
Indian Defence Accounts Service (IDAS)	National Academy of Defence Financial Management (NADFM), Pune
Indian Revenue Service - Income Tax (IRS-IT)	National Academy of Direct Taxes (NADT), Nagpur
Indian Ordnance Factories Service (IOFS)	National Academy of Defence Production (NADP), Nagpur
Indian Corporate Law Service (ICLS)	ICLS Academy in Indian Institute of Corporate Affairs, Manesar
Indian Civil Accounts Service (ICAS)	Institute of Government Accounts and Finance (INGAF), Delhi
Indian Railway Traffic Service (IRTS)	Indian Railway Institute of Transportation Management (IRITM), Lucknow
Indian Railway Account Service (IRAS)	Railway Staff College, Vadodara
Indian Railway Personnel Service (IRPS)	National Academy of Indian Railways (NAIR), Vadodara
Indian Railway Protection Force (RPF)	Jagjivan Ram RPF Academy, Lucknow
Indian Defence Estates Service (IDES)	National Institute of Defence Estates Management (NIDEM), New Delhi
Indian Information Service (IIS)	Indian Institute of Mass Communication (IIMC), New Delhi
Indian Trade Service (ITS)	Indian Institute of Foreign Trade (IIFT), New Delhi
Indian Postal Service (IPoS)	Rafi Ahmed Kidwai National Postal Academy, Ghaziabad
Armed Forces Headquarters Civil Service (AFHQCS)	Defence Headquarters Training Institute (DHTI), New Delhi
Indian Economic Service (IES)	Institute of Economic Growth (IEG), New Delhi
Indian Statistical Service (ISS)	National Statistical Systems Training Academy (NSSTA), Greater Noida

2. **General-purpose Training Institutions:** General-purpose training institutions are those that are involved in providing training of broad aspects of governance and administration to all the public services in India. They include government-aided institutions such as the Indian Institute of Public Administration (IIPA) and privately owned institutions such as the Administrative Staff College of India (ASCI), Hyderabad.
3. **Educational Institutions:** These institutions serve as training institutions as part of their management development activities. They include institutions such as the Indian Institutes of Management (IIMs) and the Indian Institute of Foreign Trade (IIFT).
4. **Sector-specific Institutes:** These are lead institutions for providing training in certain specific sectors such as the National Institute of Rural Development and the Central Institute of Road Transport.
5. **State-level Institutions:** These are training institutions that are either general-purpose or specific in nature. They include the Yashwantrao Chavan Academy of Development Administration (YASHDA), Pune, Dr Marri Channa Reddy Institute of Human Resource Development (MCRHRD), Hyderabad, and the Centre for Good Governance, Hyderabad.

However, there is a feeling that a lot of resources are wasted due to the non-coordinated functioning of these training institutions.

10.10.7 Limitations of Civil Services Training in India

The present-day Civil Services training sessions often result in failing to attain their desired objectives. This happens basically due to the following reasons:

1. **Minimum Value Attached:** The line management of an organisation does not have faith in the training methodologies to improve the performance of their employees. The minimum value is attached to training by the senior officers.
2. **Lack of Clarity:** It is seen that the training objectives are not clear, specific, and easy-to-understand for the participants. The training policy is not comprehensive and not linked with the other human resources objectives such as recruitment, promotion, transfer, and performance appraisal.
3. **Lack of Coordination:** The training personnel does not maintain adequate coordination with the regular personnel and line department of the organisation.
4. **Lack of Seriousness:** A less amount of seriousness is shown in the various aspects of training such as identification of training needs, selection of trainees, and using trainees on the job. These aspects are considered mere formalities rather than intensive activities. Moreover, there is lack of expertise among the trainers in using the various methods and resources of training. Furthermore, the trainees also often show less seriousness in learning from the training sessions.
5. **Not Linked to Performance:** Once the trainees join their parent departments, there are often inadequate efforts to use their training in order to enhance the overall work performance. Moreover, neither is an increase in performance (due to training) rewarded nor is the change in performance due to training monitored. Furthermore, promotions are based on the performance of an employee on the task given to him/her and not on his/her performance in developing skills through training programmes or other academic pursuits.

6. **Lack of Proper Evaluation:** The world across, not many steps have been taken to properly evaluate the various outcomes of a training programme. In India also, there is no formal evaluation of the performance of the trainees. The mid-career training is general in nature and no evaluation is done to suggest improvement in the performance of the officers after passing through mid-career training.
7. **Resource Problem:** An organisation encounters various problems during training such as a lack of budgetary allocation, less dedicated staff, and other organisational arrangements.
8. **Lack of focus on Domain Competency:** The induction training programmes of the Civil Services focus on the immediate duties to be performed by the civil servants. Neither do they adequately take into account the need for development of domain expertise nor are they responsive to an officer's individual interests and academic qualifications.
9. **Focus on Senior Civil Services:** The training programmes focus on senior civil services and much less efforts are made to train the middle and lower levels of government.
10. **Less focus on Attitudinal Change:** Conventional training programmes focus largely on enhancing the professional skills and knowledge of civil servants. However, they overlook helping civil servants understand and analyse their environment and bring about the desired attitudinal and behavioural change.

10.10.8 National Training Policy, 2012

The National Training Policy[31] was passed in 2012 to guide the training of civil servants by the various departments and training institutions. The need for such a policy was felt because of changes such as rapid economic growth, devolution of funds, functions and functionaries to the panchayats and municipalities, enhanced transparency through the right to information, globalisation, climate change, and extremism. These changes had created an environment in which expectations from the civil services to work efficiently and effectively had increased since earlier times.

The Policy has tried to address the major weaknesses in the training programmes mentioned in the preceding section. It has advised a move towards a strategic human resource management system, which should look at the individual as a vital resource to be valued, motivated, developed, and enabled to achieve organisational objectives. The Policy has provided the following guidelines:

1. **Competency Framework:** The Policy has guided all departments to move towards a competency-based approach of training. Here, competencies encompass knowledge, skills, and behaviour required in an individual for effectively performing the functions of a post. The competencies can be core skills (leadership, people management, etc.) and specialised skills (civil aviation, medical care, etc.). There has been no comprehensive review or classification of all the posts in accordance with the functions that are to be performed and the competencies required for them. Thus, the issue of whether an individual has the necessary competencies to be able to perform the functions of a post has not been addressed. For moving to a competency framework, it is required to classify the distinct type of posts and indicates the competency required for each of them. Then the departments need to address the gap between the existing and the required competencies and provide opportunities for the employees to develop their competencies.
2. **Training Schedule:** The training should be imparted at the induction as well as at regular intervals in order to address the gap between the existing and the required competencies.

3. **Role of Ministries/Departments:** The Policy has guided each ministry/department to adopt a systematic approach to training, in which all posts are classified with clear job descriptions and competencies required. Moreover, it has asked them to develop *Cadre Training Plans* (CTPs) based on the training needs and the competencies required and to ensure that all cadres/offices under them have a clearly defined scheme of competency development through training. Further, it has guided the departments to link the career progression of the employees with the competencies gained during training.
4. **Role of Training Institutions:** The Policy has guided training institutions to become models of excellence in imparting training and learning through the process of self-assessment and benchmarking. Moreover, they should provide technical assistance to departments in preparation of their annual training plans and help them in moving towards a competency-based framework for training. Furthermore, they are required to facilitate the development of domain-specific trainers and provide opportunities for faculty development.
5. **Trainer Development:** It is required to identify the current best practices in training skills and techniques and develop a cadre of trainers in such skills and techniques. The Policy has guided the development of a cadre of trainers in different sectoral and functional specialisations.
6. **Foreign Training:** The Policy has urged the maintenance and strengthening of the Domestic Funding of Foreign Training (DFFT, a scheme for funding foreign training) scheme as well as other similar schemes of various cadre-controlling authorities so that the employees gain access to both long-term and short-term programmes to develop in-depth competencies through foreign exposure.
7. **Training for Urban and Rural Development:** The Policy has noted the urgent need to train urban and rural local body functionaries to help them in playing their roles effectively. Moreover, IAS and state civil services officers are required to be well-versed in the functioning of the grass-roots institutions of rural and urban governance. Thus, trainees should be given 'hands-on experience' of grass-roots level administration in Panchayati raj bodies and urban local bodies.
8. **Implementation and Coordination:** The policy has noted the requirement for the establishment of a National Training Council for providing the overall direction for the implementation of this policy.
9. **Distance and E-Learning:** The policy has emphasised the importance of distance and e-learning for meeting the training needs of a large number of civil servants dispersed across the country in different cities, towns, and villages. The government has taken a decision in this direction by tying up with IGNOU to facilitate distance learning in a wide range of subjects and courses.
10. **Monitoring and Evaluation:** The policy has mentioned the need to embed comprehensive impact evaluation in the training ecosystem, where the evaluation not only judges the quality of training programmes or the learning derived to the participants but also evaluates the changes in the job behaviour that result from the programmes and their impact on organisational effectiveness and improvement in the satisfaction level of the clients/citizens.

Training and development

Methods of training

- **On-the-Job Training**
  - Training on specific job – job experience; coaching; understudy
  - Job rotation
  - Special assignment
  - Selective reading
  - Apprenticeship
  - Vestibule training
- **Off-the-job training**
  - Lectures
  - Conference
  - Case studies
  - Brainstorming
  - Simulated training-role playing; Business game;
  - Sensitivity training

Advantages

- **To Organisation**
  - Improvement in job selection
  - Improvement in organisational performance
  - Reduction in cost of production / service
  - Improvement in supervision
  - Employee morale
  - Organisational stability
- **To employee**
  - Increase in importance
  - Job security
  - Promotional aspects

Training evaluation

- **Types**
  - Formative evaluation
  - Summative evaluation
- **Levels of evaluation**
  - Reaction level
  - Learning level
  - Job behavior
  - Organisation level
  - Ultimate level

Training of civil servants

- Foundation course
- Professional training
- Departmental / District/On-the-job training
- Mid career training
- In service training

Institutional arrangement

- Service specific parent institutions
- General purpose institutions
- Educational institutions
- Sector specific institutes
- State level institutes

Limitations of training in India

- Minimum value attached
- Lack of clarity
- Lack of coordination
- Lack of seriousness
- Not linked to performance
- Lack of proper evaluation
- Resource problem
- Lack of focus on domain competency
- Focus on senior civil services
- Less focus on attitudinal change

National Training Policy, 2012

- Competency framework
- Training schedule
- Role of ministries / departments
- Role of training institutions
- Trainer development
- Foreign training
- Training for urban and rural development
- Implementation and coordination
- Distance and e-learning
- Monitoring and evaluation

Mind Map 10.5 : Various aspects of training

10.11 Salary

Salary of employees is an important part of personnel administration and is based on the classification of jobs in an organisation. It impacts organisational recruitment, the prestige associated with public services, and the attraction of youngsters towards public service. A person chooses a career based on the salary s/he expects to receive from a job. Salary is, in one form or another, certainly one of the mainsprings of motivation in our society.

10.11.1 Principles of Salary Fixation

There are various methods for deciding the salary of public sector employees. It is generally decided on the basis of the following factors:[32]

(a) **Economic Position of the Country:** The salary of public service officials is decided on the basis of the per capita income and the economic position of the country.

(b) **Cost of Living:** Salaries in public services bear a direct relationship with the cost of living in the country. The salaries are revised on the basis of changes in price levels in the country. The regional variations in price levels are kept in mind while deciding the pay scales.

(c) **State as the Modal Employer:** Government salaries are fixed in such a manner that the people should consider the state as the model employer. For this, the government considers the salaries of private sector enterprises while deciding its pay scales. The salaries are finalised by analysing the minimum and maximum salaries for the same kind of job in the private sector.

(d) **Equal Pay for Equal Work:** Salaries are decided on the basis of the positions and not the individuals occupying those positions. The principle of 'equal pay for equal work' ensures that no favouritism is shown while fixing salaries.

(e) **Governmental Policy:** Salaries are also determined by the governmental policy on salary fixation. The governmental policy is in turn determined by the political orientation of the government, the ideology professed by it, and the level of opposition faced in practising that ideology.

10.12 Incentives in Public Service

Incentives are used to describe the material and non-material benefits given to employees in addition to their normal salaries to induce them to put in extra effort towards promoting the productivity and efficiency of the organisation. Their main purpose is to increase the morale and motivation of the employees to contribute to the goals of the organisation.[33] Apart from motivating, incentives reinforce positive behaviour on the part of the employees by rewarding good performance to promote a healthier organisational climate.

10.12.1 Types of Incentives

Different types of incentives are offered by the government depending upon the profile of the employees and the situation of the organisation. Incentives are classified as material and non-material incentives. They are as follows:

1. **Material Incentives:** Material incentives are those in which employees are supplied with material advantages for performing better on the job. Material incentives are of the following types:
   (a) **Individual Incentives:** An individual, or a group of individuals, is encouraged by providing them extra income for performing extra on the job. Monetary and other rewards are provided on the basis of the personal efforts and efficiency of an individual.
   (b) **Group Incentives:** In a group incentive scheme, incentives are paid to a group of individuals engaged in a particular organisational activity.
   (c) **Profit Sharing:** In a profit sharing programme, the additional profit generated by the organisation is distributed among the employees as incentives in the form of bonus. The programme works more effectively in established firms with relatively stable earnings. It has various advantages such as fostering teamwork and focusing on the sustainability and profitability of the organisation. However, the programme is not valid for small companies with erratic earnings. Apart from providing bonuses, profit sharing can take place in the following forms:
      - ***Salary-at-risk Plans:*** In this plan, the employees receive their full base pay only if their performance meets the minimum goals. Moreover, larger payments are provided for meeting additional goals.
      - ***Gain Sharing:*** In the gain sharing plan, a portion of the money generated due to an increase in efficiency is shared with the employees. The gains are measured and distributed using predetermined formulae. It is used mostly in manufacturing firms.
      - ***Stock Options:*** Some companies provide stock options as incentives to their employees. Stock options mean the right to purchase company stocks at a given price at some time in the future. An option is created, specifying that the owner of the option may exercise the right to purchase a company's stock at a certain price (the *grant price*) by a certain (*expiration*) date in the future.
2. **Non-Material Incentives:** Non-material incentives include incentives such as appreciation letters, awards, medals, and certificates. These incentives are more suited for civil services, where the service aspect is more emphasised than the business or commercial aspect. It helps in sustaining the moral of self-motivated and hard-working employees.

10.12.2 Grievance Redressal of Public Servants

The public servants in India are deprived of certain rights, as will be discussed in Chapter 11. Most importantly they are not allowed to protest and strike for their grievances. As they are a member of the government, they are not allowed to criticise or protest against the state. However, often individual civil servants are affected by the decisions/actions of their department. Thus, certain in-built mechanisms for dealing with the grievances of the aggrieved civil servants are required. The various mechanisms available to affected civil servants are as follows:

1. **Call on to the Head of the Department:** Any individual civil servant affected by the wrong decisions/actions of his/her senior officers can 'call on' to the Head of the Department

he/she is serving in. Here 'call on' means arranging a one-on-one meeting with the head of the department and expressing their grievances in it. The grievances are addressed in such a meeting if the solution is not against the general public interest.

2. **Administrative Tribunals:** An aggrieved civil servant can approach the state administrative tribunal or Central Administrative Tribunal, as the case may be, in order to complain against the decision/action of the department. Administrative tribunals are discussed in detail in Chapter 7.
3. **High Court/Supreme Court:** An aggrieved civil servant can also approach a high court or the Supreme Court against governmental action/decision if such action or decision tends to impact the fundamental rights of the civil servant.
4. **Employee Union/Association:** Civil servants organise themselves into various unions/associations. The role of these associations is to negotiate with the government, on behalf of the employees, in order to protect the rights of the employees including ventilation of their grievances. They also indulge in settling the employees' disputes through joint consultation/collective bargaining.
5. **Joint Consultative Machinery (JCM):** Joint consultation is an important scheme for addressing the grievances of the employees. It is designed with the objective of promoting harmonious relations and securing cooperation between the government and its employees in matters of common concern. In the scheme, joint councils are created to have a full and frank discussion on important matters. The staff associations and government representatives are members of this joint council.

   The Joint Consultative Machinery (JCM) scheme provides for a three-tier structure of joint councils at the national (for matters affecting central government employees), departmental (for employees of one department), and regional/office (for employees of a region or a local office) level. The joint councils deal with employees' grievances related to conditions of work, standards of work, and staff welfare. The decisions taken by the council become operative after receiving the nod of the government.

   Moreover, if the matters are arbitrable and both the parties agree to it, they can also be resolved by arbitration. The government can appoint a *Board of Arbitration* under the JCM scheme. The board consists of members from the government, staff, and the independent side. The recommendations of this board are binding on both the parties, but the Parliament may modify or reject them on grounds of the national economy or social justice.

However, the jurisdiction of arbitration matters is limited to grievances related to pay and allowance, hours of work, and leaves of employees.

10.13 Generalist versus Specialist Debate in Public Service

The two broad functional categories of the government are generalists and specialists. There has been a long-standing controversy between these two groups of functionaries. In India, following the tradition of the Indian Civil Service (ICS) from the British days, there has been a strong debate on the question of supremacy between generalists and specialists. There are various facets of this debate, which will be analysed in subsequent topics.

10.13.1 Generalists

Generalists are the personnel dealing with general administration. According to Leonard White, general administration is understood to mean the duties that are concerned with the formulation of policy, coordination and improvement of government machinery, and general management and control of the departments.[34] Generalists are personnel whose postings in certain departments have nothing to do with their educational background or work experience. They are professional administrators possessing the skills of professional administration and management. Moreover, they are capable of taking flexible assignments and furnishing essential administrative advice and policy support to the government. As generalists are required to perform the tasks of policymaking and overall coordination, they are supposed to possess rich administrative experience gained after serving in various different departments.

10.13.1.1 Functions of Generalists

Generalists are required to perform the following tasks:

(a) **Leadership:** Generalists are usually made to lead various governmental departments. This principle of generalists dominating administrative departments can be traced to the nineteenth century British philosophy, where generalism was considered an absolute principle of administration. The Northcote Treveleyan Report on the Organisation of Permanent Civil Service (1854) and the Macaulay Report on the Indian Civil Service (1854) established the supremacy of generalists for leadership positions in the administration.

(b) **Policy Formulation:** Generalists are assumed to have a vibrant mind and a wide understanding of the entire administration. Thus, they are given the important task of assisting political executives in policy formulation.

(c) **Coordination:** Generalists serve as secretaries or heads of departments. In this position, they coordinate the work of the various specialists posted in the department and take the necessary measures to achieve the expected results with the help of the members of the department.

(d) **Balancing Role:** Generalists play a balancing role, in which they reconcile the conflicting viewpoints of the various members of a department/organisation. This is possible because they have the ability to view things in an overall perspective, generated on account of their non-specialist background and exposure to administrative reality.

(e) **Problem Solving:** A department often encounters certain problems that require quick and practical solutions. As the work of most departments is interdisciplinary in nature, the task of problem solving can be best done by a generalist. A generalist helps in identifying a rational, cost-effective, and beneficial solution to any problem.

(f) **Decision Making:** Due to their varied field experience, generalists possess certain qualities such as prompt decision-making, objectivity in decision-making, and looking for the most practical and implementable decisions. The decisions made by them are considered to be in accordance with the various environmental factors affecting a situation. Thus, they are preferred for the decision-making positions in a department.

10.13.2 Specialists

A specialist is a person who has special and in-depth knowledge of a particular field and who works in that field for his/her entire career. In the government, specialists are those who are recruited to posts requiring professional, scientific, technical, or other specialist qualifications. The posts include those of engineers, doctors, lawyers, statisticians, and economists.

In a department, specialists are required to work for their discipline without bothering about the functioning of the other disciplines. For example, a lawyer posted in the Ministry of Commerce is required to work only on the various aspects of corporate law. S/he is not expected to worry about the other aspects of the ministry such as annual budget or number of startup firms established in a year.

10.13.2.1 Functions of Specialists

Specialists are required to perform the following tasks:

(a) **Professional Functioning:** Each organisation/department requires certain employees who can function effectively in a particular field so that the policies are implemented in the right manner. For example, the role of scientists is very important in the Department of Atomic Energy to establish quality nuclear power projects in India. A generalist can coordinate the work of the various scientists but the role of scientists is indispensable in the professional working of the department.

(b) **Technical Tasks:** The present-day administration, where the role of the government has grown by leaps and bounds, consists of a vast majority of technical tasks. For example, the Department of Atomic Energy, Science and Technology, Agriculture, Health, and so on are those departments in which the majority of work is technical in nature. In such cases, specialists are required to have a holistic approach while performing their technical tasks.

(c) **Programme Planning in Technical Fields:** The advice of specialists is very important for policymaking in scientific and technical fields.

(d) **Programme Execution:** The specialists play a major role in the implementation of various programmes of the government. They, in a sense, lead the implementation wings of the department. For example, the policy of sending space missions to Mars is implemented by a team of scientists led by a head scientist (a specialist).

(e) **Expert Advice:** An important function of specialists is to provide expert advice to the generalists in carrying out their administrative functions. For example, at the district level, a district magistrate (a generalist) requires the advice of district-level specialists such as district health officers and district agriculture officers to discharge his/her functions effectively.

10.13.3 Debate Between the Role of Generalists and Specialists

Generalists and specialists have to work together to increase the efficiency and effectiveness of the government. However, as their functions tend to overlap, certain controversies get generated based on their work on the grounds of ego and ambition to occupy top positions. In India, generalists, in the form of the Indian Administrative Service (IAS), occupy the top positions in all the major governmental departments, and specialists are left to occupy the subordinate positions. The various arguments that have cropped up are as follows:

(a) **Suitability for Policymaking:** The specialists question the suitability of the generalists for all policymaking positions. According to them, the functions of policymaking in the government in today's time call for a certain level of professionalism, which is not possessed substantially by generalists.

(b) **Deprivation of Expert Advice:** According to critics, the government is deprived of expert advice and specialised knowledge, as all senior managerial positions are reserved for generalist IAS officers. However, generalists argue that the field experience gained by them at the district and state level is instrumental in effective decision-making and policy formulation.

(c) **Parity in Field Experience:** Specialists contest that they also possess the same amount of field experience as the generalists to provide policy advice in their field of specialisation. For example, a doctor working in a primary health centre is exposed to all sorts of field problems as experienced by a district collector. Thus, he/she acquires certain administrative skills, in addition to technical competence, in order to advice the government in case of health-related policies.

(d) **Separate Hierarchies:** A major point of contention between generalists and specialists is their organisation into separate hierarchies. This leads to situations where the expert advice rendered by the specialist is submitted to the generalist for his/her approval. This approval is required as the generalists are considered to have a broader view than the specialists. However, such a mechanism tends to demotivate the specialists.

(e) **Privileged Position of the Generalists:** In India, generalist IAS officers occupy a privileged position in the government. They are supposed to have higher salaries, better career prospects, and a monopoly over the top administrative positions. In fact, it is seen that the post of the heads of various executive departments is also reserved for IAS officers. This makes specialists feel that their position and status in the administrative hierarchy is not commensurate with the contribution they make to the advancement of the country.

However, the above-mentioned points are being addressed gradually by the government. Measures are being taken to encourage the cooperation of generalists as well as specialists for the advancement of the country.

10.13.4 Measures to Improve Cooperation between Generalists and Specialists

Various suitable measures have been practised across the world to improve the cooperation between generalists and specialists in government. Some of these measures are as follows:

(a) **Integrated Hierarchies:** Presently the hierarchies of generalists and specialists are separated and parallel to each other. On the contrary, an integrated hierarchy can be formed by encouraging the liberal entry of specialists as administrative and policy functionaries at key governmental levels. Specialists should be integrated into the main hierarchy to share equal responsibilities, with generalists, in policy formulation and management.

(b) **Senior Executive Service:** The Second Administrative Reforms Commission (ARC) has recommended the formation of a Senior Executive Service (SES). The SES would consist of public servants, both generalists and specialists, for high-level government positions.

(c) **Specialist Department:** Certain departments have been earmarked where specialists occupy senior positions. The Department of Atomic Energy, Department of Science and Technology, and Department of Space have technical personnel as their secretaries.

(d) **Ex-Officio Status:** In certain executive departments, specialists are given an ex-officio status of joint/additional secretary to the Government of India. This helps in giving the specialists the position due to them in policymaking and administration. For example, members of the Railway Board, who are heads of the operating departments, are ex-officio secretaries in the Ministry of Railways.

(e) **Domain Competency:** The Second ARC has also advised that generalist civil servants should develop their domain competency. The increasingly complex challenges of modern administration demand higher levels of knowledge and deeper insights from public servants. This would mean that civil servants, especially in policymaking positions, should possess in-depth knowledge of the sector, acquired through academic qualification, field experience, managerial exposure, training, and self-study. This type of in-depth knowledge and skills is often termed domain competence. The generalist officers with the required domain competence should be placed only in the policymaking positions in the respective departments. For example, an IAS officer having domain competence in rural development should be posted as the secretary of the Ministry of Rural Development.

(f) **Intermingling of Skills:** In today's time, it is desirable that generalists should possess functional specialism and specialists should possess general administrative skills. This can be done by providing adequate training to them on domain specialisation and generalised administration, respectively.

(g) **Minister-Specialist Interaction:** While making important policy decisions, the ministers should seek the advice of generalists as well as specialists. The specialists should not have a feeling of being ignored by the political class. They should also participate in the meetings in which important policies are decided by political executives.

(h) **Pay Parity:** At a higher level, the income of the generalist IAS officer is higher than that of other specialist service officers. However, this disparity should be removed, and specialists should be provided with the same salary, allowance, and status as generalists. Seven pay commissions have tried to address this issue of disparity in salary, but some amount of disparity still exists.

10.14 Privatisation of Civil Services

There have been suggestions from various quarters, including from the NITI Aayog, for allowing private entry into senior civil service positions. The measure has been suggested in order to reduce dependency on the government's administrative machinery.

The present structure of the Civil Services in India is cadre-based, in which civil servants are recruited at a young age, and they occupy key governmental positions as they mature in their careers. The senior administrative positions are occupied by them. As discussed already, we have a system of rank classification, in which positions are allotted according to rank and not based on the qualifications of civil servants.

However, the present-day government requires the service of specialists and professionals. Thus, it has been recommended that specialists be inducted into the governance system through lateral entry from the private sector. The move is expected to have the following advantages:

(a) **Bring in Competition:** This step is expected to bring in the much-needed competition among career-based civil servants. In the career-based civil service, the assurance of a secure career path discourages initiative by reducing competition in the higher administrative positions.

(b) **Remove Complacency:** The present quasi-monopolistic hold of the career-based civil services on senior management positions breeds complacency, inhibiting innovative thinking and preventing the inflow of new ideas. Lateral entry from the private sector can help in removing this complacency.

(c) **Modernisation:** All the modernisation reforms of the government, including the NPM reforms, have been inspired by reforms in the private sector. The entry of professionals from the private sector may help in accelerating the technological and management reforms process of the government.

(d) **Innovative Methodology:** The private sector personnel would bring along with them innovative and new ideas to attain the government's goals.

However, the idea of privatisation of senior civil service positions is also criticised on various counts. Some of these are as follows:

(a) **Bridging Role of AIS:** It is argued that the All India Services (and the IAS, in particular) provide a unique link between cutting-edge employees at the field level and the top policymaking positions. This bridge between policymaking and implementation, while crucial to all systems, has been of strategic significance in the Indian context, given the regional diversity of the country.

(b) **Rich Experience of Career-based Civil Servants:** The career-based civil servants (particularly the IAS officers) have an exposure and sensitivity to the country's complex socio-political milieu and the problems of the common people. This is due to their rich field experience. However, the people from the private sector may not have the same amount of exposure and experience.

(c) **Little Impact on Implementation:** Lateral entry at the top management level may have little impact on field-level implementation, given the multiple links in the chain of command from the Union Government to a rural village or urban locality.

(d) **Impact on Affirmative Action:** The entry of professionals from the private sector may have a possible impact on the constitutional mandate for affirmative action. This may happen as the backward communities are not as adequately represented in the private sector as they are in the government civil services.

(e) **Demotivation to Career-based Civil Servants:** Entry from the private sector would lead to the wastage of internal talent in the civil services and to atrophy of the existing career-based services. This would demotivate the civil servants from performing to their full potential at the field level.

10.15 Mobility of Civil Servants to Outside Government

In the debate on the privatisation of civil services, career-based civil servants have argued that they should be allowed to work in the private sector and non-governmental organisations for a fixed period of deputation. According to them, if private sector personnel are allowed to enter the government service, then career-based civil servants should also be allowed to serve in the private sector for a fixed deputation period. Such a policy would be fair to both the civil servants and the private sector personnel. Allowing entry of private sector personnel, for a fixed period, without allowing the exit of career-based civil servants, for a fixed period, would be unfair to career-based civil servants.

In many countries, there is a well-established practice of civil servants being permitted to work in the private sector as well as in academic and non-governmental institutions while retaining a position in the government service. It helps the civil servants to acquire a wider perspective. It also leads to the mixing of the values and culture of the public and private sectors, helping in the growth of both the sectors.

However, such a measure is opposed on the ground that such avenues of moving to the private sector would be available only to those civil servants serving in sectors such as finance, information and broadcasting, and commerce. A vast majority of civil servants, especially those serving in the social sectors and sectors such as rural development, would be unaffected by such a policy. This would increase the reluctance of career-based civil servants to develop their competence in these crucial developmental areas.

At present, the deputation of civil servants is allowed to registered societies, trusts, foundations, non-profit organisations, NGOs, cooperatives, international intergovernmental organisations, and apex bodies of industries and commerce. However, deputation is not allowed for profit-oriented companies registered under the Companies Act. According to the author, such a policy should be maintained, as the core task of the civil servant is to serve in the social sector and work for the equitable development of India. An opportunity to serve in profit-making private firms would shift their core values from being people-oriented to becoming self-oriented.

SUMMARY

This chapter discussed the various aspects of personnel administration such as recruitment, training, promotion, performance appraisal, job classification, appointments, employer-employee relations, grievance redressal of employees, pay, and incentive administration. We have analysed these aspects of personnel administration with respect to the Indian Civil Services and their role in national development. It was also discussed the role of important institutions such as DOPT and UPSC in personnel administration. Moreover, we have learnt about the various good governance initiatives, taken and proposed, in the field of personnel administration and Civil Services in India.

Practice Questions

1. "Personnel administration is interested in people at work and their relationship with an organisation." Discuss.
2. "The thoughts of Taylor were the founding stones of the subject of personnel administration." Examine.
3. "Indirect recruitment increases the morale of the workforce and is good for the health of the organisation." Examine.
4. "In India, promotions are not based on merit but on other irrelevant factors." Examine.
5. "The roots of civil services can be traced back to 3000 BC." Discuss the growth of civil services in India and across the world.
6. "Various committees and commissions have modified the pattern of the Civil Service Examination." Discuss.
7. "Although UPSC is an advisory body, its advice cannot be easily rejected." Discuss.
8. "UPSC has been instrumental in realising the Constitutional ideal of social justice in recruitment." Examine.
9. "Rank classification is an archaic form of job classification and should be immediately done away with in India." Examine.
10. "What gets measured gets done and measured results help in telling success from failure." Discuss.
11. "Management by objectives is the most effective technique of performance appraisal." Examine.
12. "Performance appraisal in Indian Government requires a complete overhaul." Examine.
13. "Performance management is future oriented and performance appraisal is past oriented." Why should performance appraisal be replaced by performance management in Indian Civil Services?
14. Discuss the good governance initiatives taken in the field of personnel administration.
15. "The appointments at senior levels in Indian Government favour generalists over specialists." Examine.
16. "Training evaluation is an important aspect of training delivery." Discuss.
17. "The whole of Indian administration should not revolve around the Indian Administrative Service (IAS)." Discuss.
18. "Privatisation of civil services is a much needed reform." Discuss.

CHAPTER

11 Ethics in Public Administration

After reading this chapter, you will learn the following:

- Definition of ethics, values, and morality
- Approaches to ethics and frameworks of ethics
- Values required in the administration
- Competence required in public administration
- Importance of ethics in public administration
- Ethics philosophies to guide administrative action
- Morality and methods to determine morality of human actions
- Use of conscience in taking ethical decisions
- Indian thoughts on ethics and values
- Gandhian ethics
- Civil service values and civil service activism
- Code of conduct for civil servants
- Code of ethics for civil servants
- Definition, types, and causes of corruption
- Criminalisation of politics and its impact on corruption in the administration
- Legal and institutional measures to tackle corruption
- Corruption in the private sector
- Role of citizens and systemic reforms in tackling and preventing corruption
- Grievance redressal mechanism(s) in India
- Relation between the political executive and civil servants and measures to improve them
- Discipline and disciplinary action in India

11.1 Ethics, Values, and Morality

Ethics, values, and morality are considered as the most important concepts for good administration or good governance. An unethical person cannot be considered a good administrator notwithstanding the person's qualifications and intelligence. An ethical administrator is what the public seeks. A morally upright person tends to enjoy the general confidence of the public he/she serves.

In this context, there are three related terms—ethics, values, and morality—that need to be made clear.

11.1.1 Ethics

There are various definitions of ethics because it is a complex concept. One definition describes ethics as a science that offers general principles that govern human behaviour applicable to all human beings. These principles are developed through human reasons. These are limited because human reasoning is limited to the extent that it cannot discover hidden laws or principles.[1] A major area of ethics is to develop standards for conduct, or a code of behaviour, to guide human behaviour in the right manner.

11.1.1.1 Approaches to Ethics

There are two approaches to understanding ethics: objectivist/deontological and interpretivist/teleological.

- **Objectivist/Deontological Approach:** The deontological approach of ethics advocates searching for objective, ultimate, and/or absolute standards or criteria for assessing the morality (goodness/badness) of human actions. Such objective and normative standards are derived from the philosophical and religious traditions of the society.[2]
- **Interpretivist/Teleological Approach:** The interpretivist/teleological approach of ethics does not offer any absolute standard for assessing the rightness or wrongness of human actions. It introduces a radical kind of doubt into everyday actions and tries to justify the goodness and badness of human actions by looking into the results of past actions. The past is considered for predicting the consequences of the future. It tries to find meaning in human actions and, through reflection, finds out how right or wrong are a person's actions. Thus, this approach concludes with the rightness/wrongness of human actions on the basis of reflection and not on the basis of objective rules, laws, and/or standards.[4]

11.1.1.2 Framework of Ethics

There are two major frameworks of ethical standards applicable to public administration. These are bureaucratic ethos and democratic ethos.[5]

- **Bureaucratic Ethos:** Bureaucratic ethos can be traced back to the Weberian model of bureaucracy. It emphasises values or standards such as efficiency, efficacy, expertise, loyalty, and accountability.

- **Democratic Ethos:** Democratic ethos emphasises values such as those of the Constitution, citizenship, public interest, and social inquiry. Such values are discussed within the framework of political theory.[6]

Both these standards/values are important in determining the ethical standard of a public administrator.

11.1.2 Values

The word 'value' means a belief, standard, criteria, or preference that is held by an individual. For each one of us, there are values rooted in the finest part of the self from where we radiate outwards. These values are an inbuilt mechanism that helps us in distinguishing right from wrong even when no one is watching us. These values are also imbibed from the environment, society, and family. However, the source of values is within, which guides us in exercising choice as we acquire learning from the environment, society, and family.

There are certain uniform/universal values inbuilt into each one of us, for example, nonviolence, peace, love, truth, honesty, integrity, gratitude, and innocence. Apart from these, there are individual/personal values that vary to the extent we are conscious of our inner self and to the extent, we tend to compromise with them in a cultural environment and under compulsion. For example, honesty is a universal value found in all human beings; its source lies deep within us. However, there are some individuals who disregard this inner source and compromise because of greed and dishonesty present in the environment and, thus, possess the undesirable value of greed and dishonesty.

Values in Administration

Many thinkers have talked about values in administration. Paul Appleby advocated for honesty and loyalty in public administration.[7] Similarly, Stephen Bailey has argued for values such as optimism, courage, and fairness in the public sector.[8] A wider study on public service values brings out a mix of institutional values (e.g., accountability), instrumental values (e.g., effectiveness), and fundamental values (e.g., honesty and fairness).

11.1.3 Morality

As already discussed, an important function of ethics is to determine whether particular human actions are moral or otherwise. It examines the purpose of human action, especially its ultimate end. On the other hand, morality is the conformity or lack of conformity of human action with the actor's purpose. It is the relationship of the person's action with his/her purpose. It involves the examination of human action to decide if it is good, bad, or indifferent.

For example, we can say that one of the purposes of human beings is to spread peace. Peace leads to the welfare of the whole society. Now, if the action of a person is to help poor people, then it is in conformity with the human purpose. On the other hand, if the action of a person is to kill human beings, it is not in conformity with the human purpose. Thus, the first person would be acting morally, whereas the other person would be acting immorally.

Thus, we can say that an action is moral if it is in harmony with or fits his/her purpose. If the action of a person is not in harmony with his/her purpose, it leads to the situation of the *knower-doer split*. The situation of a knower-doer split arises when a person ignores the general ethical principles valid for all human beings. For example, if an administrator ignores the principle of remaining honest, he/she creates a knower-doer split in himself/herself. When he/she takes illegal money he/she becomes a doer. He/she is aware that what he/she is doing is contradictory to what he/she is supposed to do. There, he/she, the 'knower', is in one position and he/she, the 'doer', is in another position. Thus, he/she is not integrated. He/she has divided himself/herself into an 'ideal knower' who values one course of action and the 'actual doer' who does something else. The 'knower' begins condemning the 'doer'. The person tells himself/herself that he/she is useless, that he/she cannot do what he/she wants to do, and that he/she is not the person he/she wants to be.

When a person is split, the person cannot fully enjoy anything. To appreciate the beauty of life and really be available to enjoy its comforts, a person needs to be 'together'; the person needs to act in a moral manner.

Morality of Human Action

A human action can be termed either morally good or morally bad. There are different schools of thought that suggest how to determine the moral goodness and badness of human actions. Three of these schools are *divine positivists*, *human positivists*, and *scholastics.*

- **Divine Positivists:** According to divine positivists, God had already commanded some actions to be good and some to be bad. The morality of human actions is decided by the positive laws of God. For example, God has declared lying to be morally bad and speaking truth to be morally good.
- **Human Positivists:** According to human positivists, the difference between right and wrong arises from tribal customs, education, and/or social influences. Jean-Jacques Rosseau states that actions are good when the state commands them and evil when the state forbids them. Thomas Hobbes, in his classical book, *Leviathan*, stated that humans established the state because of the troubles encountered in the free state of nature. To establish peace, harmony, and longer life, the state described some actions to be good and some to be bad. Thus, the criteria of morality are based on the laws enacted by the state. Moreover, Emile Durkheim has conceived that the Gods were nothing more than the tribal society conceived symbolically. Religious rites, worship, and dogma were nothing but various ways and means to make people accept and submit themselves to the laws and customs of their closed tribal group. Moral laws, then, are nothing but positive laws enacted by a given society to ensure its stability and preservation.
- **Scholastics:** Scholastic philosophers believe that there is an intrinsic difference between morally good and morally bad acts. Some actions are intrinsically good (e.g., caring for human beings and speaking the truth) and some are intrinsically bad (e.g., murder, robbery, and treachery). Actions that lead a human being towards his/her goals are good and actions that lead a human away from his/her goals are evil.

11.2 Competence for Public Administration

The competence of public administrators is determined by their skills and values. A good public administrator is one who is high on skills and possesses deep-rooted values. Here, skills are the ability to do a task; for example, to manage a database, disburse salaries on time, and so on. On the other hand, values are the standards that guide our actions using our skills. For example, Mahatma Gandhi was a skilled advocate. His values (of truth and ahimsa) guided him to use his law-related skills in fighting for the rights of Indians in South Africa. Osama Bin Laden was a skilled orator. His values (hatred and terror) guided him to use his oratory skills to spread the message of terrorism and to recruit youth for terrorism.

Figure 11.1 describes the competence framework based on skills and values. We can see that a person can be high or low in skills and values. Accordingly, there are four kinds of people in society:

(a) **High-skills and High-values People:** Persons with high skills and high values are an asset to society and the administration. Such people use their skills to do good work for the country and its people. For example, T.N. Seshan was an able administrator and a person possessing democratic values. Thus, he used his administrative skills to fulfil his values and, thus, brought about many election-related reforms in India. People in this category are said to possess *holistic competence.*

(b) **High-values and Low-skills People:** These are persons having strong inbuilt values of honesty, loyalty, love, and so on, but they do not possess adequate technical and administrative skills. Such people need adequate training and education to make them competent for administrative roles. The new recruits to an organisation generally fall into this category, and it is the duty of the organisation to hone their skills for the development and well-being of the organisation and society.

(c) **Low-values and Low-skills People:** Persons in this category have neither any skills nor values. Such persons are not a threat to the society as they do not possess the necessary skills to do anything wrong. However, we need to protect such persons from coming under the influence of terrorist/criminal organisations.

(d) **High-skills and Low-values People:** The people in this category are intelligent and highly skilled but do not possess the universal values of love, peace, truth, integrity, fairness, honesty, and so on. Such persons are the biggest threat to society. Take the example of a police officer who has a huge intelligence network with the local transport companies, village people, other government departments, criminal organisations, and airport security authorities. He is skilled in making secret contacts and seeking information from them. However, this person is low in values and does not care about the peace and tranquillity of the country. Such as person can use his/her strong network to increase drugs trade in the country and, thus, earn illegal money from it. Thus, persons in this category are a big threat not only to the police department but also to the entire nation. Such persons need to be identified and immediately removed from the administration. Persons in this category are *professionally competent* but not *holistically competent.* Effective public administration requires people with not only professional competence but also holistic competence.

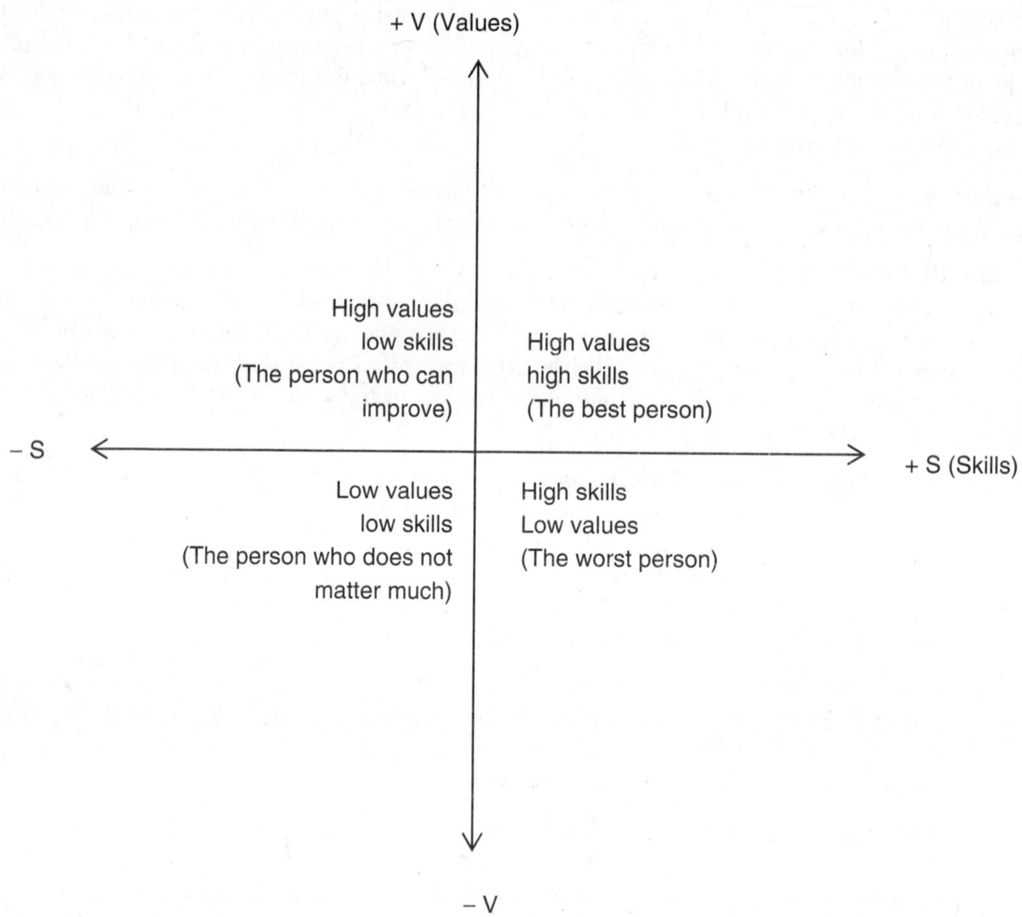

Fig. 11.1: Competence Framework on the basis of Skills and Values

In the 21st century, it is very important to understand this competence framework. Phenomena such as globalisation and the spread of technology have immensely impacted the administration. Today a good decision can benefit millions of people; likewise, an unethical decision can ruin the future of many people. In the past, poor ethical judgments have produced such devastations as the meltdown of the Chernobyl Reactor, the Bhopal Gas Tragedy, and so on. Such devastating events are expected to increase in the 21st century with the decreasing moral values of people and the spread of technological skills. Thus, it is very important to identify the people falling in the fourth category.

11.3 Importance of Ethics in Public Administration

Ethics are the most important aspect of public administration. An ethical public administration is an effective public administration. If a government allows unethical activities to prosper under it, it leads to greater damage to citizens and/or businesses and a high number of complaints are received from the public. On the other hand, the public is satisfied with a government that implements high ethical standards. Moreover, employees are more motivated, tend to take fewer leaves, feel proud that they serve the citizens in a better manner, and tend to work for their organisation for a longer tenure.[9]

Organisations that have ethical administrators have a strong bonding with the citizens and are more likely to implement productivity reforms with the support of the public than those organisations that are administered by people who are less ethical. Unethical administrators try innovative activities but do not succeed because of the lack of accountability and responsiveness in their work.

Similarly, the most important quality for a successful administrator is his/her strong ethical base. An ethical administrator tends to better lead organisations and is able to convince the employees in an effective manner. In short, higher ethics are associated with better governance and more successful public careers.[10]

11.4 Public Interest and Administrative Action

The most important duty of a public administrator is to work in the 'public interest'. However, whether a public administrator is working in the public interest or cannot be determined easily. Among the three branches of the government (i.e., legislature, executive, and judiciary), determining the public interest is the most difficult task in executive functioning.

One mechanism to ensure that administrative actions are in the public interest is the mechanism of bureaucratic accountability. The concept of accountability is discussed in detail in Chapter 6. Accountability ensures that the administrative actions are in tune with laws, rules, democratic values, and the principle of fairness. Conformity with such laws, rules, values, and fairness ensures that administrative actions are in the public interest.

However, critics contend that these mechanisms of external accountability are not sufficient to ensure that an administrator acts in the public interest. Internal accountability is required, whereby an administrator is guided by his/her inner values. A combination of both external accountability and internal accountability is important to ensure that the actions of a public administrator are in the public interest.[11]

11.5 Ethics Philosophies to Guide Administrative Action

Administrative decision-making can be based on a number of ethical philosophies. Such philosophies can help the administrator in understanding the various ethical issues involved in an administrative decision-making situation. Some of the ethical philosophies that can guide bureaucratic decision-making are described in the following sections.

11.5.1 Intuitionism

Aristotle advocated the philosophy of intuitionism to guide human actions. According to it, human beings have a special sense faculty that enables them to directly perceive and distinguish the right from the wrong. Just as human beings have a sense of taste to distinguish bitter from sweet, they have a moral faculty to enable them to distinguish what is right and what is wrong. This moral faculty is based on the universal values inbuilt into all human beings. What brings pleasure to this moral faculty is good and what brings displeasure is evil. Thus, Aristotle claims that morality can be determined by using common sense.

On the basis of common sense and reflection of the mind, people form their principles instinctively, though they cannot explain them. These principles help them intuitively discern what is good or what is evil.

The disadvantage of this philosophy is that a number of ethical principles may develop in a person's mind, which may be in conflict with each other when applied to specific situations. Moreover, intuitionism tells us how to know what is good and what is bad. It does not tell us why it is good or bad. The philosophy is not rational and systemic in guiding human action.

11.5.2 Rationalism

Rationalism is a deontological theory propounded by Immanuel Kant. According to him, no action is moral if it is done for pleasure or any motive other than duty or respect for the law. In human beings, there are *a priori* (universal and necessary) principles of speculative knowledge and similar principles of practical knowledge. Kant has termed these *a priori gates* or principles as a *categorical imperative.*

The categorical imperative can be discussed by contrasting it with another term—*hypothetical imperative.* A hypothetical imperative uses instrumental reasoning to take a decision. It uses an if-then statement; if we want X, then we do Y. It is something that is based on one or many conditions. On the other hand, a *categorical imperative* is unconditional, and it is the command for everyone everywhere with no exceptions. In other words, if the action is good in itself and justifiable with reason, then it is a categorical imperative. Kant has talked about two categorical imperatives:

- **Concept of Universal Law:** Kant has said that a person should act on the basis of those personal codes of conduct that can be universalised. In simpler terms, one should act according to those personal codes of conduct that he/she would want to become the code of conduct for all people to follow.
- **Treat People as Ends:** According to Kant, morality is about respecting people as ends in themselves, and treating a person like a person and not just an object for gain.

These categorical imperative orders a person to do good and avoid bad. Acts are categorised as good or bad with respect to the categorical imperative. An act is good according to the motive of the actor, and the only motive that makes an act good is respect for duty or laws. The essential element in determining the morality of motive is human reason.

Let us see a practical example of the implementation of the Kantian theory in a specific situation of unpaid internship in Case Study 11.1.

Case Study 11.1: Unpaid Internship

Many of the private sector companies have started the concept of unpaid internship in which interns are selected from various colleges to learn and work in the organisation for a specific period of time. Students look out for such opportunities as they get to learn from the experience gained while working in a company. The students do internship during their summer and winter vacations and, thus, do not lose out on their university education. The students look out for specific learning experiences from these organisations.

Companies have used this concept as a business strategy. They use these interns on important projects and give them full-time tasks. The interns are energetic and eager to learn. Thus, they work very hard to complete the tasks given to them. Sometimes, the work done by them is much better than the work done by regular employees. Thus, the companies save a lot of their money by recruiting these interns as they are not required to be paid.

Moreover, the interns are not allowed to act autonomously. They are guided by their immediate managers. They do not enjoy the privileges given to a regular employee.

The question here is whether the companies are acting ethically while recruiting unpaid interns.

Kantian Perspective: According to the Kantian perspective, the act of recruiting unpaid interns is unethical because of the following reasons:

- The companies are using young students as a means to increase their profits. They are not respecting them as ends in themselves. The motive of the company is to earn profit by recruiting unpaid interns. However, the motive of the interns is to learn and gain experience. Thus, the motive of the company is not aligned with the motive of the interns and thus the companies are not respecting the interns as ends in themselves.
- The motive of the company is not a duty towards the society or the law. By earning profits using unpaid interns, the companies are not doing any duty to the society. Moreover, they are not respecting the law of minimum wages by recruiting unpaid interns. If the work of interns is helping the companies in gaining profits, the interns should be given a part of the profit. However, companies try to show that the interns are there just for gaining experience and they do not contribute anything meaningful to the company. By doing this, the companies are disrespecting the law of the land.

11.5.3 Scholasticism

According to scholastic philosophers, the morality of human actions lies in the human nature considered in its totality—that is, in all its parts and all its relationships, including those with other human beings, the universe, and the supreme being. The theory considers several criteria, including the body and the soul, the intellect and the senses, human relationships with various entities, and the circumstances in which humans find themselves. All these elements are considered in deciding what is right and what is wrong. In a sense, this philosophy joins together the deontological and teleological approaches to ethics.

11.5.4 Utilitarianism

Utilitarianism is a teleological theory of ethics, which claims that the test of goodness or badness of human action is the usefulness of the action. The philosophy of utilitarianism was propounded by

John Stuart Mills. It says that the decision of a person should be such that it makes most people better off, even when some people are left worse off. An action is morally good if it is useful for the community, i.e., it brings the greatest good to the greatest number of people.

However, the theory is criticised, as it promotes selfishness and does not respect the rights of minorities.

Let us see a practical example of the implementation of the utilitarian theory in a specific case of torture practices in Case Study 11.2.

Case Study 11.2: Is Torture Justified[12]

Mr XYZ is the Assistant Commissioner of Police (ACP) of Mumbai city. His commissioner gave him an intelligence input that bombs have been planted at various places in the city. Late in the night at 2:00 am, after receiving the information, Mr XYZ goes out with his team to search for those who planted these bombs. After putting in strenuous hard work he raids a house in the Mahim area of Mumbai, where he finds two people with 2 kg of explosives and IED devices. He immediately arrests them and brings them to the police station.

He suspects that these people might be aware of where the bombs have been planted. When he asks them about the whereabouts of the bombs and their plans, they say they have no information. In this situation, he has an option of using torture techniques on them. The torture committed on them might help in getting crucial information about the planted bombs. This torture may also lead to the death of these people. Moreover, he is not sure about the role to these people in planting the bombs.

Ethical Question Involved: Is the use of torture justified in this situation?

From the Utilitarian Perspective: The use of torture in this situation would be justified on the basis of the utilitarian theory. Furthermore, swift action is required to be taken by the ACP to locate and defuse the bombs to prevent mass destruction of lives and property. If these people can give crucial information about the whereabouts of the planted bombs, many lives can be saved. Thus, the torture of few can be useful to save many lives. Even if those people do not have information, then also torture can be justified on the assumption that these people may have crucial information.

From other perspectives: The torture can be justified according to the utilitarian theory but cannot be justified because of the disadvantages of the utilitarian theory with respect to this particular example.

- Torture violates the intrinsic dignity of the human being.
- Torture mistreats the vulnerable and thus violates the demands of public justice.
- Torture erodes the character of the nation that tortures.
- Allowing torture will act as a slippery slope and may lead to extra judicial executions.
- Legalising torture will provide a license to use torture against every person suspected, without confirmation.

11.5.5 Theory of Justice/Fairness

As discussed, one of the major lacunae of the utilitarian theory is that it disregards the rights of minorities and the people living at the bottom of society.

To counter this problem, John Rawls propounded a theory of justice. He gave two principles of justice:

(a) Each person is to have an equal right to the most extensive basic liberty compatible with a similar liberty for others.

(b) Social and economic inequalities are to be arranged so that they are reasonably expected to be to everyone's advantage and attached to positions and offices open to all.[13] Only those social and economic inequalities are permitted that work to the benefit of the least advantaged members of society. This principle is known as the *difference principle of justice.*

Thus, the principles support a progressive tax system, which taxes the rich to provide for the health, education, and welfare of the poor. Rawls has spoken against the aristocracies and caste systems, as they distribute income, wealth, opportunity, and power according to the accident of birth.

Let us see an example of the implementation of the Justice theory in a specific case of reservation in government jobs, in Case Study 11.3.

Case Study 11.3: Reservation in Government Jobs

Our Constitution provides for reservation for scheduled caste (SC) and scheduled tribe (ST) communities in government educational institutions and government jobs. The members of the SC and ST communities are considered disadvantaged as they have historically suffered from the age-old caste system that prevailed in the Indian society. They are generally from a poor background and are not represented adequately in the education system and in government jobs.

By providing reservations to them, the government provides them opportunities to compete with students from the forward castes.

Ethical question involved: Is it ethical to provide reservation to the SC and ST people?

From the Utilitarian Perspective: The utilitarian philosophy would regard the reservation policy as unethical as it makes the majority people worse off for the benefit of the minority (SC and ST) people. Moreover, due to reservation, candidates below merit are selected for government jobs and government educational institutions. This may affect the efficiency and effectiveness of the government.

From the Perspective of Justice Theory: Rawl's theory of justice supports the reservation policy, as it suggests that if the disadvantaged sections are not recruited through reservation, they would become further deprived in the society. Recruiting and promoting them would facilitate the full realisation of their basic dignity without demeaning the dignity of the others. Moreover, recruiting them assures that all government offices are open to all communities. Furthermore, it also ensures that privileges innate to government offices work for the advantage of all in a reasonable equal way, because they are extended to the disadvantaged sections of the society.[10]

11.6 How to Determine Morality of Human Actions

In public administration, it is very important to determine whether a particular action is moral or not. An analysis of the morality of actions in the past helps in taking moral and ethical decisions in the future. There are three parts of every human action to determine its morality: the object of the action, the circumstances in which the action was performed, and the end or purpose of the action. These three parts are described below:

(a) **Object of Action:** The essence of every human action is known as its object.[14] The object distinguishes an act from other acts. The object of action can be good, bad, or indifferent. An action whose object is bad by its very nature is bad and cannot be improved under any circumstances. For example, the object of speaking a lie is bad and remains bad despite the circumstances and the intention/purpose behind the action.

An action whose object is good may become good or bad because of the purpose or circumstances involved. For example, telling the truth is good. However, telling the truth, when silence would have sufficed, to destroy another person's character makes the act of telling the truth a bad act because of the person's intention. Further, an indifferent action could become good or bad according to the circumstance and the purpose involved.

(b) **Circumstances that surround the action:** The circumstance of an action are qualities such as the manner in which the act is done, the time of the act, the place where the act is done, the person by whom the act is done, and so on. These circumstances affect the goodness and badness of an action.

Circumstances may aggravate the badness of an act. For example, stealing is a bad act. However, stealing from a poor person is a very bad act. Similarly, the circumstances may extenuate an act. For example, stealing from a rich person to serve the poor is a lesser bad act. In a similar manner, circumstances may make an indifferent act good or bad.

According to some scholars, particularly from the teleological school, circumstances are the sole criteria for judging the morality of human actions.[15] Such scholars are regarded as scholars of *situation ethics*.

(c) **Intention/Purpose behind Action:** The intention/purpose in the mind of the person while doing an act is very important in determining its morality. An action with an indifferent object can become good or bad depending on the intention behind it. For example, running is an indifferent act, but running to catch a dreaded criminal is a good act.

A good act may become good or bad because of the intention behind it. For example, giving money to a young poor woman is a good act. However, giving money to a young poor woman with the intention of luring her into an illicit sexual relation is a bad act.

A bad act may become less bad or worse because of the purpose of the act. However, an intrinsically bad act cannot become a good act because of the intention behind the act. For example, telling a lie is a bad act. However, when a police officer speaks a lie to an accused in order to confuse him/her and gather information from him/her, the act becomes less bad.

Let us see the working of this object-circumstances-intention framework to determine the morality of human action in a case study of fake encounters (Case Study 11.4).

Actions of Double Effect

There are certain actions that have two effects/consequences—good and bad. Thus, it is complicated to determine the morality of such actions. To determine their morality, the following criteria are followed:

(a) The object of the action must be good or indifferent. An action with a bad object is always bad.

(b) The good effect produced must be immediate and should not be obtained through the evil effect.

(c) The intention behind the action must be good.

(d) The purpose of performing the act must be strong and good.

An example of an act of double effect is a situation in which a doctor can save the life of either a pregnant mother about to give birth or the child inside her womb. In this case, a bad effect (death of mother/child) has to take place with the good effect (life of child/ mother).

In this case, the doctor will be acting morally if she intends to perform a good act (i.e., to save the life of both mother and child) although she foresees that the evil effect is possible and probable. Moreover, she should not intend an evil effect.

Furthermore, it is moral if saving the life of the mother (the good effect) is the immediate effect and it is not obtained by not saving the child (i.e., through the evil effect).

Such situations of double effects are encountered by police officers, doctors, military officers, public administrators, and politicians very frequently.

Case Study 11.4: Fake Encounter

There was a gruesome murder of a landlord during the night of 12 December 1980 within the limits of Police Station X in district Gadchiroli of Maharashtra. Very soon, news spread and there was scare in the village and neighbouring villages. The deceased landlord happened to be a close relative of a senior police officer occupying a key position in the Police Head Quarters. The reputation of the deceased in the village was not good. In fact, he was hated by most of the villagers, particularly belonging to the working class, as he was known to be exploiting the labourers and manipulating cases to be registered in the Police Station against those who were not amenable to him. Pressure was brought on the SP of the district by the senior police officer for immediate arrest of the accused. Within about 2 months of his taking charge, clues to the identity of the accused could be gathered through sustained collection of intelligence and the interrogation of suspects. Very soon one of the main accused was arrested.

On sharing this information with the senior officer, the senior officer asked the SP to bump off the accused. He said that the accused is a hardcore Naxalite and has committed a gruesome murder and should be taught a lesson. The arrest of the accused was known to the public in the village and bumping him off was not possible according to the SP.

The Home Minister also called the SP in this regard. He said, "I heard that the Naxalite is arrested. You know that the people of the village were very much scared of the Naxalites and you have to restore confidence among the people by teaching the Naxalites a lesson. Our party people will give you full support. Take deterrent action."

Ethical Question: Is it ethically justified to kill the accused Naxalite after he is arrested? The Naxalite has committed various murders and other crimes. He also has a strong support of urban Maoist supporters, who would help him in taking advantage of the loopholes in the legal system and get bail in a few days. Killing the Naxalite would make the SP a public hero and would advance his career opportunities.

Ethical Analysis of the Situation: Let us analyse this situation using the object-circumstances-intention framework discussed above.

- **Object:** If the SP decides to kill the accused Naxalite after arresting him, the object of the act itself is morally bad. Killing a person who is in our custody cannot be morally justified, no matter what the circumstances and the intention.
- **Circumstances:** The circumstances in this situation may make the act less evil because the Naxalite is a dreaded criminal and deserves to be treated in the manner he treats common people. Moreover, there is a situation where he may take advantage of the loopholes in the legal system and start his criminal activities again. Furthermore, there is pressure from the politicians, senior officers, and public to kill the Naxalite. So, in short, the circumstances are such that the SP should kill the Naxalite.
- **Intention:** The intention of the SP should be to maintain public peace and order. If the SP kills the Naxalite with this intention in mind, his act can become less morally bad. However, if the intention of the SP behind the killing of the Naxalite is to earn higher career opportunities for himself, then his act becomes morally worse.

It can be said that the circumstances and the intention behind the act can make the act less morally bad. However, the act of killing someone in our custody is intrinsically bad and cannot be justified due to the circumstances involved. Thus, the SP should not kill the accused. He should take him on police remand, interrogate him, and recover the weapons used in the offence. He should investigate the crime committed by the accused properly and ensure that appropriate punishment is awarded by the court as soon as possible. He should put all his efforts, while avoiding any unethical act on his part. The police should not indulge in fake encounters as they provide an opportunity to Naxalites to indulge in propaganda around police excesses.

11.7 Conscience

There are many factors such as laws, rules, regulations, codes of conduct, codes of ethics, precedents, and ethical philosophies that help in guiding our ethical behaviour. However, a major factor that always guides our ethical behaviour is our conscience. Conscience is nothing but our inner voice that speaks up when we are going to do something morally bad. It stops us and guides us. The person who hears this inner voice does not commit an ethically wrong act. However, the person who neglects his/her inner voice commits unethical acts.

The conscience is something within us and determines the morality of our actions. It is a special act of the mind that comes into being when the intellect passes judgment on the goodness or badness of a particular act. It is a practical judgment on specific and concrete human actions.

For every specific action, the conscience lays down a practical rule. It applies all laws, rules, codes, ethical philosophies, and previous ethical learnings to a specific situation. It also involves reflection on a set of values developed by a human being since his/her birth.

Types of Conscience

Our conscience is our own judgment in a particular situation. Thus, the conscience can be true or erroneous.

- **True Conscience:** A conscience is said to be true if it is a correct judgment according to the prevalent laws and rules.
- **Erroneous Conscience:** A conscience is said to be erroneous if it is a false judgment on the course of action in a specific situation; when a conscience incorrectly applies laws and rules to an action. The judgment can be vincibly false (i.e., the actor can understand the error in judgment through ordinary care and common sense) or invincibly false (i.e., the actor cannot understand the error in judgment through ordinary care and common sense).

Apart from this, conscience can be classified as being certain, doubtful, or probable.

- **Certain Conscience:** A conscience is said to be certain when the judgment on the morality of the human action is without prudent fear or error.
- **Doubtful Conscience:** A conscience is said to be doubtful when there are prudent fears/doubts about the judgment of the morality of an action.
- **Probable Conscience:** A conscience is said to be probable when the judgment almost excludes all prudent fears or errors. A person is almost certain that the judgment is correct.

Principles of Conscience

The following ethical principles govern conscience:

- If a human conscience says something, the person is bound to follow it even if it is false. For example, if the conscience guides that telling a lie for saving someone's life is correct, then the actor is bound to follow this decision.
- A person, while making a decision, should take reasonable care to ensure that his/her conscience is correct.
- A person should not act on a doubtful conscience. He/she should make all possible efforts to clear his/her doubts.

11.8 Indian Thoughts on Ethics and Values

Vedic Indian thoughts describe the *guna dynamics*. The *guna dynamics* help us to understand the interplay of the different types of values of a personality and give us an insight into how to undertake to improve our ethical personality.

The *Bhagwat Gita* has explained human nature as a combination of three types of *gunas*. These are the *sattwa guna, rajas guna,* and *tamas guna.*

- ***Sattwa*** represents values such as purity, fineness, goodness, compassion, and gratitude.
- ***Rajas*** represent values such as restlessness, activity, passion, lust, greed, and pride.
- ***Tamas*** represents values such as darkness, obstruction, laziness, procrastination, confusion, and so on.

The human mind is the synthesis of these three *gunas*. The personality of a human being is along these three trends. The *tamas guna* is associated with emotional people who are sensitive, day-dreaming, sentimental, and soft-hearted. Most of the artists belong to this group. However, when pushed to the extreme, these temperaments bring imbalance in the personality, and people can sink into lethargy and depression.

On the other hand, the people with *rajas guna* is regarded as active and are the builders of civilisations and committed to the common cause. As long as these people act with fairness, firmness, constancy, and moderation, without overloading themselves with stress, they remain in balance. However, when they start going to extremes by neglecting others and becoming ego-centric, they become impatient and greedy.

Finally, the people with *sattwa guna* are people with moderate tendencies. They possess the ability to watch with detachment the consequences of their actions. They try to take the middle path, in which extreme positions are avoided. In an organisation, some of the essential qualities for a successful leader are integrity, accountability, openness, honesty, objectivity, selflessness, innovativeness, intelligence, decision-making ability, skills of planning and organisation, emotional stability, and self-control. These qualities are rooted in and sustained in an awakened *sattwa.* It is the activated *sattwa* in an administrator that enhances conciliation between discipline and obedience on one hand and self-respect on the other. Such people possess the capacity to reflect on their actions and take decisions cautiously. It is a very important quality to be inculcated in administrators.

11.8.1 Working on Self to Improve Personal Ethics

In order to increase the *satvic* qualities in an individual (or to improve the personal ethics in an individual), the following things can be done:

(a) **Look at the Good in Others:** We imbibe in ourselves those qualities that we pay our attention to. Thus, if we start observing the good qualities (or *satvic* qualities) in others, we are likely to gain from them. We need conscious cultivation of counter-thoughts to weed out perverse thoughts.

(b) **Introspection:** When negative emotions overpower us, our consciousness lapses. To regain control of our negative emotions and to make positive emotions a priority, we need to move our consciousness inwards. This inward movement of consciousness, or introspection, is very important for maintaining balance and ethics in life. It helps in maintaining our connection with our inner selves. If this connection is lost, we get swayed in the direction of the wrong things in the outer world. While introspecting, first we need to shift our attention to our inner self (*anter mukhita)*. Then, we need to develop an insight into our inner selves (*anterdrishti)*. Finally, we require steps to purify our inner self (*anter chitt shuddhi)*.

(c) **Reading and Watching Good Things:** We can improve our ethical conduct by regulating what we hear, see, read, and so on. We should read inspiring books and autobiographies of ethical leaders and hang portraits of great personalities and divine people.

(d) **Bring Purity in Our Action:** According to Indian philosophy, our mind takes us away from the real world into myth. It gives a particular perception of our vision of the outer world. Thus, our vision gets distorted. Our mind reacts to whatever we receive in our brain through our five senses from the external world (a) based on our past experiences and habits, which we may call as our conditioning and/or (b) out of our ego, our own desires, feelings of jealousy, envy, pride, and so on. If the mind becomes still, it will not react to all these situations and we will be able to witness things in *thoughtlessness*. When there is no thought, we may call it a state of pure mind. Such a state is a *satvic state.*

Action in this state is not a reaction of the mind but an automatic response in the given situation and, thus, a pure action. It is an unconscious action, such as all activities of nature. An outright approach in ethical governance is towards developing service orientation in public service. The government servants are expected to serve with the 'at your service attitude'. Such a temperament (basic human nature while reacting to situations) can be an outcome of a pure mind only, which is neither influenced by preconditions and preconceived ideas nor by ego or selfish interests.

11.8.2 Learning the Art of Administration from Nature

The art of administration and public service can be learned in a substantial manner from nature. Natural objects such as trees, flowers, earth, etc. keep on performing their own duty the way they are supposed to. Through their actions, they unfold or observe their own *dharma*—the 'law of being'. They do not calculate or work out the outcomes. However, we human beings have the capability to decide and to make a choice.

With the excessive exercise of our power of intellect, we have failed to maintain consonance with cosmic consciousness—the natural harmony. The whole infrastructure of nature is so beautifully made that each object of nature is fully taken care of by the ecosystems. In these systems, each individual is fulfilling its own dharma for the benevolence of all and is, in turn, automatically getting everything that is required for its sustenance from the system.

However, we humans have become calculative because of our self-interests. We have deviated from *swadharma* (our duty) to *swarthadharma* (self-interest). Consequently, all the public affairs in administration, which are required to bring about social welfare, are resulting in *swarthadharma.* Such pursuance of self-interest also sidelines *lok-hit*, i.e., benevolence for all. This self-interest is the main cause of corruption, red-tapism, misuse of power, and so on. However, if we maintain natural harmony in all our deeds and start working for *lok-hit*, all the bigger and higher interests will automatically be taken care of. And if there is benevolence prevailing all over, the self-interest can never remain unfulfilled.

11.8.2.1 Nishkam Karma

In the Indian philosophy, a desireless action is known as *nishkam karma.* It is the principle of detached involvement in work; this means involvement in work and detachment from personal rewards or gains. If we learn to profess *nishkam karma,* our organisations would benefit from our work. On the other hand, *sakam karma* is the principle of work in which we work with an expectation of a quick return.

In *nishkam karma*, the emphasis is on *karma* (work) and not on the desired result. The reduction of concern for results psychologically leads to the conservation of energy. Once a person has taken a decision to act after due deliberation about the ends and the means, all our energies should be focused on execution and not on the end results. Then if the result is not according to our expectations, it will not dishearten us or make us hopeless. Moreover, the attainment of the result would also not puff us with euphoria and pride.

The strengths of *nishkam karma* are the *sattwic gunas* that give us mental equilibrium, i.e., *samatwa*—the state in which one accepts the positive results gracefully and does not get derailed in case of failure. *Sakam karma* is driven by the *rajasic* forces of ego, greed, and anger, which lead to inequilibrium and can prompt the doer to trust the means to ensure the desired results.

In *sakam karma*, the goals are ego-centric, whereas in *nishkam karma* they go beyond to the socio-centric and cosmo-centric causes. Here the work is performed in a natural way like the flowers that give fragrance and the sun that gives sunlight without asking for rewards. The management of our ego helps us in becoming wholesome workers.

The modern concept of success treats man as a rational being. Work is performed in a competitive spirit quoting the law of jungle and survival of the fittest. Everyone tries to excel through competitive rivalries. As against this, in *nishkam karma,* excellence is achieved through the principle of 'work is worship'.

11.8.2.2 Concept of Work is Worship

An able administrator is one who can practice the principle of 'work is worship'. The concept is derived from the practice of *nishkam karma.* It means that work is a man's homage to the supreme. The person following this principle is internally autonomous and self-motivating.

The spiritual meaning of the principle can be understood by understanding the following three sequential steps:

(a) **Work and Worship:** When a person treats work and prayer differently, he/she is understood to be doing work and worship daily. For him/her, work and worship are two different things and are done at different times of the day. He/she does not derive spiritual pleasure from work.

(b) **Work as Worship:** This happens when a person is able, in a conscious way, to offer his/her work as a prayer to the supreme power. This brings a touch of purity in the means employed and some extra dedication and humility while doing work.

(c) **Work is Worship:** This happens when a person's entire life and conduct become unending worship. No work remains higher or lower for the person. The nature of work becomes less important, but the manner in which it is performed becomes more important. The importance of work is decided by the dedication with which it is done.

We need to teach the principle of work is worship to public administrators. This method of working can be attained through the purification of the mind, which helps us to keep aside ego-driven self-interests.

11.8.2.3 Giving Model of Inspiration

The nature derives pleasure in giving and not taking. It is important for an administrator to learn this art of giving from nature. Giving benefits our health. Ultimate fulfilment comes from giving and not receiving.

Giving is a natural law of the universe. We get in lieu of what we give, though we may not recognise it because the return may come sooner or later than we expect it to. For example, we get oxygen only when we give out carbon dioxide. We will not get oxygen without giving out carbon dioxide. Without getting carbon dioxide, the trees cannot make food, which we human beings consume. Thus, our living starts when we give something (carbon dioxide in this case).

The giving model is based on the theory that there is a large network of interconnected forces, which contribute to the existence and nurturance of us all. As good human beings, we must think of all these forces and our duty towards them.

The *Brihadarnyaka Upanishad* mentions the obligations/debts we owe to the nature. These are as follows:

(a) ***Deva Hrin***: It is our obligation towards all universal forces or divine forces that are beyond human control, such as air, water, sun, earth, and space. Our surrender and service to these natural forces helps in valuing them. It also helps us in leading our life in harmony with the natural laws. An administrator should learn that, like divine giving, we should give as much as possible without any prejudice for who the receiver is.

(b) ***Rishi Hrin***: It is our duty to study the contribution of the seers and great personalities, and practice their teachings and also to enrich them for the coming generations. From this, administrators must learn to read the best practices of experienced leaders and practitioners, and then practice them in the organisations they work in.

(c) ***Pitri Hrin***: It is our moral duty to serve our parents, learn from their experience in life, and look after them in their old age. For an administrator, it is important to give special care to senior citizens when they approach them for any help.

(d) ***Nri Hrin***: It is our moral duty to humankind. We should carefully ensure that whatever we do is for the well-being of humankind. We should not indulge in means that are detrimental to humanity as a whole. Means such as corruption, environmental degradation, and sexual harassment are detrimental to humanity as a whole.

(e) ***Bhuta Hrin***: It is our moral duty to all subhuman species, i.e.. the whole flora and fauna of the world. Our duty towards them is to take care of them with gratitude. Thus, it is important for an administrator to take care of the environment while implementing developmental projects.

The giving model inspires us to work for the accomplishment of our duties and not for any external incentive. Our selfishness is the chief source of evil, diminished morals, and unethical behaviour. Selfishness springs from the non-cultivation and non-realisation of the feeling of oneness with all.

If we can attain equality at the level of feelings, we can achieve natural harmony amongst unequal individuals. This can help us in not using unethical means to attain our ends.

According to the Western scholars, the motivating factors in an organisation are autonomy for work, the scope for career development, the scope to shoulder responsibility, self-actualisation, interpersonal relations, the scope for challenges, and so on. On the other hand, according to the giving model, the motivating factors for an employee are meeting his/her standards of self-respect for quality and rate of work done; performing any given task as a token of discharge of his/her debt to society; enjoying the happiness from keeping promises made, without giving excuses for failure; to be convinced that good work is bound to reap rewards; and so on. When an administrator has such motivating factors, he/she is bound to remain away from unethical activities.

11.8.3 Doctrine of Karma

The doctrine of karma refers to the moral law of cause and effect. Similar to the law of conservation of energy in the physical world, there is a law of conservation of moral energy in the moral world. Every act—good or bad—has its energy level, which is never lost. It may remain stored for a long or short period, but at some point in time, it emerges and gets activated. Thus, no act of ours, morally right or wrong, gets lost.

The doctrine of karma has the following principles:

(a) A cause at present may produce an effect in the future.

(b) An effect at present must have had a cause in the past.

(c) The effect returns to the source of the cause.

(d) Similar to the cause, similar is the effect.

(e) Each cause produces its own effect; there is no mutual cancellation.

These principles are found operative for a group of people. A collective cause brings a collective effect. We do see the effect of right or wrong doings at the level of family, society, organisation, or country.

11.8.3.1 Doctrine of Karma and Nishkam Karma

There are infinite factors that have an impact on a given situation. Thus, we cannot be sure about the effect of a cause. The outcome or the effect is decided by the net result of all the permutations and combinations of the various factors in the universe. Therefore, we cannot be sure of a good effect from a good cause.

Thus, it is always better to act in a manner that is most appropriate to a pure mind (which is not prejudiced by ego, desire, or greed) and leave the result or effect to the all-pervading cosmic power.

11.8.3.2 Organisational Illustration of Doctrine of Karma

If corrupt functionaries are educated in the doctrine of karma, and if its inevitability becomes alive in their consciousness, they might desist from ethically reckless ventures. There are classes of low/wrong deeds that are imposed on the employees during their daily functioning. For example, an employee may be offered a bribe for quickly clearing files upon the order of his/her superior. If the employee takes his/her cut in the bribe, he/she becomes an accomplice. However, if his/her sensitivity and mental purity are sufficiently aroused, he/she would reject accepting the bribe and take the step that is most appropriate according to a pure mind.

The reward one gets for following the doctrine of karma is nothing but the protection of the inner conscience and the resultant inner peace and harmony.

11.8.4 Gandhian Ethics

Mahatma Gandhi is considered an eminent philosopher for ethical leanings across the world. His teachings are very important for implementing ethical conduct in administration. Gandhiji's ethics are based on the three cardinal values of love, truth, and non-violence. His principles are as follows:

(a) **Truth:** Gandhiji has put the greatest emphasis on the value of truth. For him, being truthful is the greatest service to God. It is the biggest virtue of humankind. His idea of truth is that of ideal human conduct. It is a principle of how humans should order their social, political, and economic world. All social, political, and economic affairs should be aligned on the principle of truth. The principle applies not only to individuals but also to entities such as political and social causes and movements. Thus, Gandhiji regarded the Indian struggle for independence as standing for truth because it represented a just struggle for national and individual autonomy.

In the case of administration, truth should become a part of the value system of the organisation. All the dealings of the administrators should be based on the principle of truth. The public should be served with complete truthfulness and without any scope for greed and self-interest.

(b) **Service to Society:** Another important ethical principle given by Gandhiji is that of service to society. According to him, the only way to see God is through his creation and by identifying oneself with it. This is possible only through service to humanity.

(c) **Purity of Heart:** Gandhiji advocated self-purification from the inside. A person with a pure heart does every task without thinking of his/her narrow self-interest. The concept of purity of heart is further discussed in Section 11.8.1.

(d) **Ends and Means:** Gandhiji constantly emphasised the purity of means. This follows from his view that God is the embodiment of all virtues. The means for attaining any end need to be good no matter howsoever good is the end purpose. If the means are not good, the act is unethical. According to Gandhiji, following unethical means in any matter amounts to acting in opposition to divine injunctions.

(e) **Human Nature:** According to Gandhiji, humans have a divine spark in them. Violence and self-assertion are alien to them. If a person goes on the path of selfishness and violence, s/he goes against her/his inner self.

(f) **Non-violence (*Ahimsa*):** *Ahimsa* is an important value propagated by Gandhiji. In the negative sense, ahimsa guides us to refrain from killing or injuring other beings. One should not harm anyone by thoughts, words or deeds. Violence has to be shunned in all its aspects. In the positive sense, ahimsa guides us to show overflowing love to humankind and all living beings. The concept is closely linked with the concept of truth and man's search for God. A prerequisite to attaining ahimsa is developing the value of truthfulness and fearlessness in us. Human beings should fear only God and no one else. This follows Gandhiji's principle of *Satyagraha*, i.e., the fearless pursuit of truth.

Ahimsa requires complete purification of the mind and heart. The concept of ahimsa subsumes values such as truthfulness; selflessness; absence of anger, pride, and hate; benevolence; altruism; courage; magnanimity; humility; and total submission to God. Thus, it is very important for present-day administrators to cultivate the value of ahimsa.

(g) **Qualities of a Satyagrahi:** The qualities of a satyagrahi are required to be cultivated in our administrators in order to stop them from moving on unethical paths. The qualities of a satyagrahi are humility, self-sacrifice, universal benevolence, silence, thought control, non-use of drinks and drugs, renunciation, non-violence, and so on.

(h) **Seven Social and Political Sins:** Mahatma Gandhi mentioned seven deadly sins that have the potential of destroying any person. These sins are very relevant in our social and political affairs. Thus, every administrator is required to prevent himself/herself from indulging in these deadly sins, which are as follows:

- **Wealth without Work:** People earn wealth without working by indulging in activities such as corruption, non-payment of taxes, claiming undue government subsidies and reservations, designing fraudulent ponzi schemes, and so on. Earning wealth without working is motivated by the value of greed and is bound to destroy the life of the individual indulging in it.
- **Pleasure without Conscience:** Some people seek pleasure or happiness in everything without a conscience or sense of responsibility for it. They become so greedy and selfish that they start enjoying pleasures without understanding their disadvantages. Pleasure without conscience leads to the loss of reputation and disregard for public service.
- **Knowledge without Character:** As discussed before, a person with knowledge and skills but without strong values is the most dangerous person in the society.
- **Commerce without Morality:** If economic systems and businesses ignore their moral foundations, then we can expect nothing but an immoral society. Fairness and benevolence in business are the underpinnings of the free market system.
- **Science without Humanity:** If science and technology losses its value of humanity, soon it starts functioning to the disadvantage of humanity. Scientific inventions such as dynamite and the computer viruses are invented without having any regard for the human race. Such technological advancements are dangerous for the whole of society.
- **Religion without Sacrifice:** A religious practice becomes successful only when we can sacrifice our wrong habits and unethical means while practising it.
- **Politics without Principle:** Politics should be based on the laid-down principles and codes of the political party. Any party that frequently violates its principles is bound to suffer in the long run and earn the anger of the public.

11.9 Civil Service Values

Civil service values are the guiding principles for the conduct of civil servants. Civil servants do not have the time to test their decisions on the basis of ethical philosophies. Thus, civil service values provide them with a standard against which they can evaluate their own values and actions.

Such values are very important in the new public management (NPM) and post-NPM era, where the citizen–public servant equation is fast changing. The discretionary powers of civil servants are fast increasing and need to be checked by certain principles. The civil service values help in forming these principles.

The Nolan Committee of England, 1996, recommended the following civil service values:

(a) Leadership
(b) Honesty
(c) Selflessness
(d) Openness
(e) Accountability
(f) Integrity
(g) Objectivity

Values such as leadership and accountability have already been discussed in previous chapters of this book.

Similarly, the Second Administrative Reforms Commission has provided for certain civil service values such as integrity, objectivity, dedication to public service, empathy, tolerance, compassion towards weaker sections, and impartiality/non-partisanship.

Some of these civil service values will be discussed in the following sections.

11.9.1 Integrity

Integrity is the quality of taking action according to one's conscience. A person with integrity is one who does not allow a *knower-doer split* (as discussed in Section 11.1.3) to take place in himself/herself. The person does not follow his/her duties blindly but takes only those actions that his/her conscience allows. For such a person, his/her behaviour would match his/her value system. For example, if a person believes that taking bribes is wrong, he/she would not take bribes. Moreover, his value system would be internally consistent.

11.9.2 Objectivity

Objectivity is the quality that requires a civil servant to make his/her decisions on the basis of certain policies, rules, or criteria. This quality avoids subjectivity in decision-making. It is very important in procedures such as recruitment, transfers, promotions, postings, selection of contracting agencies, selection of persons for granting awards, and also in daily administrative work.

Objectivity can be promoted by promoting critical thinking among civil servants. Moreover, administrators should be alert to the complaints received from the public while making a decision. Furthermore, it is important to manage the total information within an organisation in order to advance objectivity in decision-making.

11.9.3 Dedication to Public Service

Public service is the value to provide services to the public in the right manner, according to the duties of the organisation. For example, the duty of a judge is to deliver justice. Thus, he/she would be doing public service if he/she delivers justice at the right time. Similarly, the duty of a legislator is to prepare legislation. He/she would be doing public service if he/she dedicates most of his/her working time to legislative discussions over laws and public policies. Public service is not as easily determined for an administrator as for a judge or legislator. Here, the public is served when a public servant follows all the civil service values.

11.9.4 Empathy

Empathy is the quality to think from the mind of the other person or to think after putting oneself in another person's position. Empathy makes a person feel the emotions and conditions/plight of others. It is one of the many bases for pro-social and pro-people behaviour adopted by administrators.

It is very important for intelligent Indian civil servants to cultivate empathy. Intelligence without empathy has led to high levels of corruption in India, where administrators use their intelligence to generate illegal money, not for the welfare of the poor. Lack of empathy leads to a situation of bullying, intolerance, and lack of compassion towards animals, environment, the poor, minorities, women, children, and so on.

The quality of empathy can be imbibed with the help of art, literature, and cinema. Moreover, if administrators interact freely with poor people, their empathy levels could increase. Furthermore, training activities such as perspective talking and role playing can help in increasing the quality of empathy among civil servants.

11.9.5 Compassion Towards Weaker Sections

Compassion is a quality far stronger than empathy. Empathy can be for any person, higher or lower in the social order. However, compassion is sympathy and empathy only towards the weaker sections. It is this quality that made Mother Teresa leave her motherland and serve the poor people of Kolkata selflessly.

Compassion is required in administrators towards the weaker sections of the society such as victims of crime, women, children, the poor and the socially disadvantaged, disabled people, and transgenders. Compassion can be inculcated by teaching the philosophies of great leaders to administrators.

11.9.6 Neutrality and Impartiality

Civil service neutrality is the value to serve different regimes/political parties with the same enthusiasm. It also necessitates that public administrators must stay away from political affiliations. Civil servants must not be associated with any political party or ideology. However, civil servant is expected to cooperate with any political party in power and follow the policy advocated by them. They must not allow their own political values/ideology to interfere with their day-to-day work.

A civil servant must faithfully implement public policies. The quality of neutrality is very important to maintain the confidence of the public. It is also important to win and retain the confidence of political executives after a change in regime.

Neutrality is of two types:

(a) **Passive Neutrality:** In passive neutrality, the officers blindly follow the orders of the political executives in power. However, this may lead them to violate certain legal or constitutional provisions.

(b) **Active Neutrality:** In active neutrality, the officers take action on the basis of the Constitution, laws, rules, and office manuals. They do not blindly follow the orders of political executives.

To know more about civil service neutrality, read the sub-topic *'Neutrality and Commitment of Bureaucrats'* under the topic *'Politics and Bureaucracy by Weber'* in Chapter 3 of this book.

However, the value of neutrality is extremely endangered in the Indian Civil Service, as is evidenced by the mass transfers of public servants after a change in regime. The reasons for such mass transfers are as follows:

(a) **Election-related Corruption:** During elections, political candidates require a lot of money to fund their election campaigns. This money is generated, as well as distributed, through illegal means. An upright and neutral officer may become a big threat to such generation and distribution of money during elections. Thus, political executives prefer to post those candidates who would listen to their oral (and not written) dictates and not interfere in their nefarious means of money generation. Therefore, pliable officers are selected for important postings and others are sidelined. Such politicisation in transfers and postings is a serious threat to civil service neutrality.

(b) **Competition among civil servants:** There is constant rivalry and competition among civil servants to get the most desirable postings. The departmental postings are based purely on merit. Thus, non-meritorious candidates turn towards politicians to seek their favour in getting good postings. This, in turn, demoralises the whole civil service community and pushes even meritorious candidates to seek political recommendations. Such a phenomenon makes civil servants align politically with various political parties.

11.9.7 Civil Service Anonymity

A concept connected to neutrality is that of civil service anonymity. It is a value of working silently behind the scenes and avoiding the media limelight and public gaze. A civil servant has to implement public policies with full commitment but is expected to receive neither credit for its success nor blame for its failure. It is the responsibility of political executives to receive public applause and/or criticism.

The value of anonymity also suggests that a civil servant shall not hold any press conference (or use social media) to air his/her grievance against a government policy or action.

However, the principle of anonymity is often criticised. Ministers are often seen to be openly criticising bureaucrats, but the bureaucrats are unable to defend themselves because of this principle. Once an officer earns a bad name, he/she is unable to work efficiently with the public. Moreover, he/she is also unable to defend himself/herself because of the requirement of anonymity.

Another criticism is that media is one of the most efficient channels for an honest and efficient bureaucrat to seek justice. Seeking justice through official grievance redressal mechanisms can be difficult, time-consuming, and demoralising. However, the anonymity criterion bars the civil servants from approaching the media to air their grievances.

11.9.8 Civil Service Commitment

A civil servant is required to be committed towards implementing the policies and programmes of the government. This quality is discussed at length in the sub-topic *'Neutrality and Commitment of Bureaucrats'* under the topic *'Politics and Bureaucracy by Weber'* in Chapter 3 of this book.

11.10 Civil Service Activism

Civil service activism refers to the active, self-initiated, and committed acts of civil servants in order to serve society effectively and work for its development. It is, however, a deviation from the principle of civil service neutrality and anonymity.

It includes all, or any, of those proactive steps that are taken by civil servants to make the governmental system more citizen-centric, transparent, and effective. A gamut of activities come under its purview such as holding regular public meetings, taking people's feedback, making the public aware of their rights, ensuring the quality of goods and services provided by the government, vigilant working (checking corruption), and checking strict action against the illegal and unconstitutional actions of the political leaders.

11.10.1 Instances of Civil Service Activism

The instances of civil service activism are increasing across India. Some of the famous civil servants who have resorted to civil service activism are as mentioned below:

(a) **T.N. Seshan:** T.N. Seshan is a former Chief Election Commissioner of India. He played an activist role in bringing down electoral malpractices and making the Election Commission a powerful, efficient, and transparent body.

(b) **Kiran Bedi:** Kiran Bedi brought activism into police service by collaborating actively with the local public to curb crimes and create a sense of safety among the public. She also actively brought reforms into the prison system through various innovative methods such as vocational courses in prison, yoga, and meditation.

11.10.2 Reasons for Increasing Civil Service Activism

The phenomenon of civil service activism has increased tremendously because of the following reasons:

(a) **Declining Standards of Political Executive:** The ethical standards of the political executive have declined due to the increasing corruption and criminalisation of politics. The diminishing standards of politics have led to dwindling standards of administration. Hence, some civil servants have taken an active role to protect the faith of the public in administration.

(b) **Role of Media:** The role of media in protecting democracy has increased by leaps and bounds. Media has helped civil servants in exposing various corruption scams and scandals. It has played the role of a medium to blow the whistle against corrupt practices. Thus, civil servants have been actively seeking the help of the media in playing an active role against maladministration and corruption in India.

(c) **Civil Servants from different Socio-Cultural Backgrounds:** The proactive role of the Union Public Service Commission has led to civil servants increasingly being recruited from rural and disadvantaged backgrounds. Such civil servants tend to play an active role in serving the communities they come from.

(d) **Exposure to Ground Reality:** Civil servants (especially, All India Services officers) are posted in rural areas in their initial assignments. Here they understand the ground realities and difficulties faced by people in taking benefits of government programmes. Such understanding helps them in playing an activist role at senior levels.

11.10.3 Benefits of Civil Service Activism

There are numerous benefits of civil service activism. Some of them are as follows:

(a) **Welfare of Weaker Sections:** Civil service activism is directed towards providing administrative justice to the poor and disadvantaged people. For example, an activist civil servant implemented the fingerprint-based payment model for proper and timely payment to MGNREGA workers.

(b) **Good Governance:** Civil service activism helps in brining innovative solutions for service delivery. Some of the innovative measures taken by activist civil servants are the formation of 'Mohalla Committees' in Maharashtra, the use of local tribal language to teach tribal students in Chhattisgarh, the use of dance-drama techniques to spread awareness about forest protection among the tribal communities, and so on.

(c) **Attracting Talent Towards Civil Services:** The wonderful role played by activist civil servants helps in attracting intelligent, socially inclined and responsible, committed, and ethical youth to join the civil services.

11.10.4 Limitations of Civil Services

Although civil service activism has various advantages, it has certain limitations in the Indian scenario. Some of its limitations are as follows:

(a) **Tends to Interfere with Conduct Rules:** Steps taken by activist civil servants are in the long-term interest of democracy and the rule of law. However, their direct interactions with media and whistleblower activities interfere with the conduct rules of neutrality and anonymity. Thus, activist civil servants are said to be doing the right things in a wrong way. However, such civil servants are better than those civil servants who act as mute spectators of corruption and other irregularities. They are a ray of hope to improve the value system of the administration.

(b) **Complications in Politician-Civil Servant Relations:** Political executives are expected to serve the public while playing an active role. However, when civil servants play such an active role, it tends to strain their relation with the political executives.

(c) **Politicisation of Civil Services:** The activist and populist roles played by civil servants tend to align them towards one political party or another.

(d) **Voluntary Retirement and Suicide Attempts:** Activist civil servants tend to strain their relations with their senior officers and politicians. They are also targeted for taking on a pro-people role. They are often transferred frequently and given non-important positions. Such a stance leads to an increasing number of voluntary retirements and suicide attempts among the civil servants.

11.11 Code of Conduct

The conduct of civil servants in India is restricted and directed according to certain conduct rules. These rules are meant to guide the manner of conduct of behaviour of civil servants. In India, there are three types of conduct rules: (1) All India Services (Conduct) Rules, 1954 for the officers of All India Services, (2) Central Civil Services (Conduct) Rules, 1955 for the officers of Central Civil Services, and (3) Railway Services (Conduct) Rules, 1956 for the government servants posted in Indian Railways. Similarly, there are conduct rules for government servants and public servants of all categories in all states. The content of all the conduct rules is more or less similar.

11.11.1 Brief Description of Conduct Rules

All the conduct rules are pretty exhaustive, and describing them in totality is beyond the scope of this book. Thus, we will discuss them in brief in this section. The major areas covered by the various conduct rules are as follows:[16]

(a) **Maintaining Integrity:** Every civil servant is required to maintain the highest standards of ethics, integrity, honesty, neutrality, fairness, impartiality, accountability, transparency, responsiveness to the public, compassion to the weaker sections, and so on. Moreover, every civil servant is required to take all possible steps to ensure the integrity of all government servants working under his/her control.

(b) **Restriction on Political Activities:** The conduct rules restrict a civil servant from behaving like an ordinary citizen who can resort to any sort of political activity. Public interest demands political impartiality and neutrality from civil servants. Civil servants have the right to vote and form associations, but they are prohibited from participating in political activities. They cannot become members of any political party. They can also neither accumulate funds for, nor receive funds from, any political party. However, civil servants are allowed to form associations with the aim to promote their work and the welfare of their members.

(c) **Behaviour with respect to Media:** The conduct of civil servants with respect to media is restricted. Some of the criteria that guide their relationship with media are as follows:

- Under the Official Secrets Act, 1923, civil servants are prohibited to communicate any official document or information to anyone whom they are not authorised to communicate such information with.
- Civil servants are not allowed to make any public criticism of any policy or decision taken by the Government.
- The rules do not bar press conferences to be held by civil servants but state that these conferences should be held only to propagate government programmes and not to make any political statement or propaganda.

(d) **Duty with respect to Subversive Activities:** In the interest of the security of the State, it is the duty of the government servants to endeavour to prevent any member of their family from participating or assisting in any activity that tends directly or indirectly to be subversive of the government.

(e) **Restriction on Public Demonstrations:** The conduct rules prohibit civil servants from participating in any demonstration or form of strike in connection with any matter related to the conditions of service. However, the Indian government allows strikes to be conducted by certain government employees. Further, strikes are banned in case of essential services such as posts, transportation, police, and so on.

(f) **Restriction on Receiving Presents:** The conduct rules say that no civil servant shall, except with the previous sanction of the government, accept or permit his/her family members to accept from any person any gift of more than a trifling value (this value changes from time to time and is INR 25,000 right now).

(g) **Restriction on Matters of Property and Investment:** In the case of property and investment, the conduct rules restrict the civil servants in the following manner:

- Civil servants are not allowed to take part in speculative investments.
- Information about every movable and immovable property acquired by a civil servant needs to be communicated to the government.

(h) **Restriction on Private Trade or Employment:** Civil servants are not allowed, except with the previous sanction of the government, to engage in any private trade or business. They are also not allowed to negotiate for, or undertake, any other employment. However, they are allowed to do the following things without the sanction of the Government:[17]

- undertake honorary work of a social or charitable nature
- undertake occasional work of a literary, artistic, or scientific character
- participate in sports activities as an amateur
- take part in the registration, promotion, or management (not involving the holding of an elective office) of a literary, scientific, or charitable society, club, or similar organisation, the aims or objectives of which relate to promotion of sports, cultural, or recreation activities, registered under the Societies Registration Act, 1860 or any other law for the time being in force
- take part in the registration, promotion, or management (not involving the holding of an elective office) of a co-operative society substantially for the benefit of the members of the Service or government servants registered under the Co-operative Societies Act, 1912 or any other law for the time being in force in any State

Apart from these, the conduct rules direct the civil servants to report to the government if any member of their family is engaged in a trade or business, or owns or manages an insurance agency or commission agency.

(i) **Restriction on Employment of Close Relatives:** Civil servants are restricted from using their position or influence, directly or indirectly, to secure employment for any member of their family or other close relatives with any private undertaking or non-governmental organisation.

(j) **Evidence before Committees:** The conduct rules guide that no member of the service shall, except with the previous sanction of the government, give evidence in connection with any inquiry conducted by any person, committee, or other authority. When a sanction is received, they are not allowed to criticise any policy or action of the government while giving evidence. However, this rule does not apply while giving evidence in any inquiry before an authority appointed by the government, Parliament, or state legislature, while giving evidence in any judicial inquiry, and while giving evidence at any departmental inquiry ordered by any authority subordinate to the government.

(k) **Subscriptions or Raising of Funds:** Conduct rules guide that no civil servant shall, except with the previous sanction of the government, ask for, or accept, contributions to or otherwise associate himself/herself with the raising of any fund or other collections in cash or in kind in pursuance of any object whatsoever.

(l) **Restrictions Regarding Marriage:** Regarding marriage, civil servants are not allowed to enter into or contract a marriage with a person having a spouse living. Moreover, they are also not allowed to enter into a marriage with any person if they already have a spouse living. Furthermore, they are not allowed to take, give, demand, and/or abet the taking, giving, and demanding of dowry.

11.11.2 Code of Ethics

In India, the Code of Conduct rules guide the behaviour of civil servants in specific situations. However, in our country, there is no Code of Ethics to guide the general ethical conduct of the civil servants. The conduct rules while containing some general norms, such as 'maintaining integrity and devotion to duty', are mostly directed towards cataloguing specific activities deemed undesirable for government servants. They do not constitute a code of ethics.

Such codes of ethics exist for civil servants of other countries such as New Zealand, Australia, and UK. According to the Second Administrative Reforms Commission, a Code of Ethics (or a comprehensive Civil Services Code) can be conceptualised at three levels. At the apex level, there should be a clear and concise statement of the values and ethical standards that a civil servant should imbibe. These should contain the civil services values described in the earlier sections of this chapter.

At the second level, there should be broad principles guiding the behaviour of civil servants. This would consist of the principles of ethics and morality. At the third level, there should be specific rules of conduct describing the acceptable and unacceptable behaviour of civil servants in specific situations. The Second Administrative Reforms Commission (ARC) also recommended providing a legal backing to the Code of Ethics. However, such a move has not been initiated by the government yet.

Apart from just designing the code of ethics, efforts are required to be made by the persons at leadership positions to inculcate the civil services values in all employees in their organisation. Moreover, according to the Second ARC, an independent agency should be appointed to audit organisations and evaluate the measures taken to uphold the civil services values in organisations.

11.12 Corruption

Corruption is the most serious issue in public administration today. It is the very reason for administrators forgetting the 'public' in public administration and working for their self-interests. It has spread like a plague in all government institutions and has tended to impact their efficiency and effectiveness. Transparency International, an international watchdog monitoring corruption across nations, has defined corruption as the abuse of entrusted power for private gain.[18]

The Prevention of Corruption Act, 1988 has also extensively defined the term corruption. The Second ARC has also described certain acts as acts of corruption. Accordingly, corruption consists of the following offences:

- Accepting of illegal gratification as a motive or reward for doing or forbearing to do any official act or for favouring or disfavouring any person
- Public officials obtaining a valuable thing without consideration or inadequate consideration
- Public officials involving in criminal misconduct including receiving gratification, misappropriation, obtaining any pecuniary advantage from any person without public interest, or being in possession of pecuniary resources or property disproportionate to their known sources of income
- Public officials indulging in acts leading to gross perversion of the Constitution and democratic institutions, amounting to wilful violation of the oath of office
- Officials indulging in the abuse of authority unduly favouring or harming someone without receiving any gratification
- Officials indulging in acts leading to the obstruction of justice to citizens
- Officials indulging in any act leading to squandering of public money

11.12.1 Types of Corruption

Corruption is of two types: collusive and coercive corruption. In *coercive corruption*, corruption is said to be done when the bribe-taker forcefully takes a bribe from a bribe-giver for doing/not doing some official work. Here, the bribe-giver is the victim and the bribe-taker is the accused. For example, the illegal money paid to obtain government permits, such as driving licences and shop licences, comes under the purview of coercive corruption. This form of corruption is easy to be detected and contained, as the victim can approach the authorities to complain against the corrupt public official.

In *collusive corruption*, corruption is said to be done when both the bribe-giver and the bribe-taker are guilty of a wrong act/offence. The bribe-giver wilfully pays a bribe to a public official in order to commit an illegal activity together with the bribe-taker. For example, sand mafias give bribes to local politicians, revenue departments, and police officials in order to let them continue their acts of illegal sand mining. Similarly, in PPPs, the private party pays bribes to government officials to facilitate and approve certification of substandard work as part of projects. In collusive corruption, the general public is the victim. It is a more dangerous form of corruption, as it leads to long-term impacts on the society, economy, community, and environment.

The coercive form of corruption is more easily punishable, as there is an aggrieved party in it. Collusive corruption, on the other hand, is not easily punishable, as there is no direct aggrieved party in it.

11.12.2 Major Causes of Corruption

There are various socio-economic and personal causes for the existence of corruption. The broad causes of corruption are as follows:

(a) **Authority without Responsibility:** In our country, there is a colonial legacy of unchallenged authority and the propensity to exercise power arbitrarily. We live in a society where power is worshiped above everything else. As Lord Acton has stated, "power corrupts and absolute power corrupts absolutely." We have a tradition of providing our public officials (and political executives) with absolute power. In such a culture, officials find it easier to deviate from ethical conduct.

(b) **Power Asymmetry in Society:** There is an enormous asymmetry of power in our society Nearly 90% of the people are employed in the unorganised sector. Such asymmetry o power reduces the societal pressures to conform to ethical behaviour and makes it easy t indulge in corruption.

(c) **Master–Servant Relation:** The historical system of governance in India has been that of master and a servant. We have adopted those policies whose unintended consequences have bee to put the citizen at the mercy of the government. Governmental services have been a sort c favour to the people rather than being their rights. In such a governance system, the publi officials consider themselves as the master and indulge in any sort of wrong acts they desire.

(d) **Centralisation of Power:** Since a long, power has been centralised in a few institutions i India. The power (or authority) of getting work done (or delivering any service) has been fa away from the people. The governments have been very large, with the decision-makin power lying at the top of the hierarchy. Such centralisation of power correlates with highe corruption.[19]

(e) **Constitutional Protection to Civil Service:** Article 311 protects civil servants from bein removed by any other authority except the President of India. Moreover, the procedur followed for removal is cumbersome and time-taking. No other constitution of the worl provides the type of protection provided to Indian civil servants. This has created a climat of excessive security, without the fear of penalty for wrongdoing, among civil servants.

(f) **Personal Greed:** The personal greed of public officials is also an important reason for risin corruption. The desire for money is followed by the desire for friendship, status, and makin an impression. People indulge in corruption for all these personal reasons.[20]

(g) **Criminalisation of Politics and Election-related Corruption:** The quality of politic determines the level of corruption in our society. The criminalisation and corruption in ou politics are increasing day by day. These are major reasons for corruption in the whol government. We will discuss this in detail in the following section.

11.12.3 Criminalisation of Politics

The most disturbing factor in Indian politics today is the criminalisation of politics, that is, people wit criminal backgrounds are becoming politicians and ministers. This happens due to the nature of election in our country. The elections in our country are mostly based on money, religion, caste, and violence. Th money and influence required to win the elections is generated by the criminal elements of the society. Th hardcore criminals provide the necessary muscle power and illegal money required during the time o elections to political parties. Some of the criminals are, in turn, provided tickets to contest as MLAs an MPs by political parties. The criminals who win the seats are also appointed to lead crucial governmer departments because of their influence and threat to the people.

The most important determinant of the integrity of a society or the prevalence of corruption is th quality of politics in it. If politics attracts and rewards men and women of integrity, then the society i safe, and social and national integrity is maintained. However, if honesty is incompatible wit survival in politics and if public life attracts corrupt/criminal elements seeking private gains, the abuse of authority and corruption become the norm. The latter is the situation in public life in Indi where corrupt politicians are rewarded with important positions in the government.

This phenomenon of criminalisation of politics is said to be the fountainhead of all corruption in ou country. The aims of criminal politicians are to earn back the money they have spent during th elections, to misuse the government system for the advantage of the criminal world, and to further cement their clout amongst the people by all means. When criminal politicians lead crucial government departments, ethical conduct cannot be expected from the civil servants working under them.

The Vohra Committee was constituted to identify the political-criminal nexus and recommend ways in which the menace can be effectively dealt with. The report highlighted the political and government patronage received by crime syndicates. Over the years, criminals have been elected to local bodies, state assemblies, and the Parliament.

Types of Criminalisation of Politics

The scope of the term 'criminalisation' extends to criminalisation in electoral politics, policymaking politics, judiciary, executive, and administration. The types of criminalisation are as follows:

(i) **Electoral Fraud:** Electoral fraud refers to acts that disrupt the process of fair elections. One such act is criminal elements entering politics. According to the Association for Democratic Reforms (ADR), 34% of members of parliament (MPs) in the 14th Lok Sabha faced criminal charges against them. Most of these MPs were previously members of organised syndicates. Electoral frauds also include the use of muscle power to garner votes. Political parties take the help of muscle men from crime syndicates to create a fear psychosis among the public to garner votes. Once these political parties win, they return the favour by either providing political patronage to crime syndicates or giving them crucial positions in the government.

(ii) **Political Scams:** India has witnessed a high number of political scams such as petrol pump allocations, the Bofors scandal, 2G and 3G spectrum allocations, and coal allocations at the central level and scams in municipal corporations at the state level. Such scams occur because the parties in power have to return the favour to crime syndicates in cash or kind.

(iii) **Political Patronage to Criminal Gangs:** As already discussed, many of the members of criminal gangs have entered into politics. Thus, they truly and effectively enjoy the patronage of political leaders. This is how their syndicates survive.

Measures to break this criminal-politician nexus

The following measures have been taken or are proposed to be taken to break the criminal-political nexus:

(i) **Negative Voting System:** In the 2014 elections, the system of NOTA (None of the Above) was introduced wherein a voter can choose to vote for none of the candidates (if he/she feels that all the candidates are unworthy of his/her vote). However, his/her vote will be counted as an invalid vote and not as a negative vote. In negative voting, if the number of negative votes exceeds the majority of votes polled, then the election process of that constituency has to be repeated. This system would act as an eye opener to the criminalisation situation in that constituency.

(ii) **Right to Recall:** This system can provide an opportunity to the voters to recall their elected representatives if he/she indulges in corruption or any criminal act. This can also be done if he/she fails to fulfil his/her electoral promises.

(iii) **Need to have Value-based Politics:** Presently, political parties want to capture power by any means whatsoever without regard to the basic democratic, moral, and ethical values. This has led to the criminalisation of politics. We need to bring in a code of conduct (or code of ethics) for political parties and prefer value-based politics over muscle and money-based politics.

(iv) **Deliberation on the report of Poll Observers:** The report of the poll observer contains information on whether the contesting candidates have followed the code of conduct and other norms laid down by the Election Commission. The common public should deliberate on this report at the local level.

(v) **Minimising Election Expenditure:** The candidates spend more money than that allowed by the Election Commission norms. This money, being illegal and routed through various channels, is difficult to monitor by the Commission. However, the Commission should take stringent and innovative steps to curb the excessive flow of money during elections. If this flow of money is curbed, then criminalisation of politics will reduce significantly.

(vi) **Auditing of Accounts of Political Parties:** The whole process of collecting funds by the political parties and the way the money is spent during the elections goes without auditing. Funds being raised by the political parties to meet election expenditure from industrialists, business houses, and criminal syndicates is leading to political corruption. The funds of the political parties should be audited by the Comptroller and Auditor General of India (CAG) and its audit report made public.

(vii) **Special Courts for Election Matters**: Election offences such as booth capturing and rigging are tried by normal courts and thus the judgments are delayed. This creates a negative image in the public about the Indian democratic system. Thus, election-related offences should be tried in special courts using special procedures so that justice is delivered swiftly and the democratic process remains healthy.

(viii) **Creating Public Awareness:** The public needs to be educated about the proper utilisation of their right to vote. The public should better know and understand the person they are voting for. Election Commission publishes the background of all the candidates. The public should be made aware to make an informed choice after seeing this database.

(ix) **State Funding of Elections:** The world over, there are three patterns of funding of elections. First, there is the *minimalist pattern*, in which elections are partially subsidised through specific grants or state-rendered services. Candidates are made accountable to the public authority for observance, reporting, and disclosure of expenditure for the limited election period. Such a pattern is followed in countries such as the UK, Ireland, Australia, New Zealand, and Canada. Second, there is the *maximalist pattern*, in which public funding is provided not only for elections but also for other party-related activities. Such a system is followed in countries such as Sweden and Germany. In this system, less detailed regulation on monetary contributions and expenditures is required, because political parties are largely dependent on state support. Third, there is the *mixed pattern*, in which there is a partial reimbursement of the money spent during elections on a matching grant basis. This system is followed in countries such as France, the Netherlands, and South Korea.

In India also, state support is provided to political parties in certain manners during elections, such as providing full tax exemption on contributions made to political parties, free supply of electoral rolls, and free air time to political candidates on government channels. However, the funding of political parties is largely based on private donations. We need to think of innovative measures for state funding of elections in India so that the dependency of the parties on private donations is reduced.

(x) **Disqualification of Criminal Candidates:** The elected Members of Parliament and MLAs are disqualified from their seats if they are convicted in any criminal offence. In 2013, the Supreme Court ruled that this disqualification should be immediate without being given three months' time for appeal in a higher court. However, given the delay in our criminal justice system, disqualification after conviction is an insufficient safeguard against criminalisation of politics. The Election Commission has suggested that candidates against whom charges have been framed in a court should be disqualified. As a safeguard, it has been suggested that only those cases filed six months prior to an election should lead to such disqualification.

However, the Supreme Court has not accepted this suggestion and has directed that a candidate cannot be disqualified unless he/she is proven guilty. Thus, the Parliament needs to amend the Representation of the People Act and introduce some mechanism to preliminarily determine the criminality of a candidate and disqualify him/her on that basis.

(xi) **Expediting Disposal of Election Petitions:** Under the Representation of the People Act, election petitions are required to be disposed of within a period of six months. However, in actual practice such petitions remain pending for years, and in the mean time even the term of the house expires, thus rendering the election petition infructuous. It is recommended that special benches shall be constituted in high courts earmarked exclusively for the disposal of election petitions. Special tribunals can also be formed for election petitions under Article 323B of the Constitution.

11.12.4 Legal Measures to Tackle Corruption

In India, there are three laws to tackle corruption in the private sector: the Prevention of Corruption Act, 1988, the Benami Transactions (Amendment) Act, 1988, and the Whistle Blowers Protection Act, 2014. These measures will be discussed in the following sections.

11.12.4.1 Prevention of Corruption Act, 1988

The Prevention of Corruption Act was enacted in September, 1988. It was enacted because the provisions of the Indian Penal Code were considered insufficient to fight against the growing menace of corruption. The various provisions of this act are as follows:

1. **Special Courts:** Special courts of the rank of a sessions judge/additional sessions judge/assistant sessions judge are appointed to try cases under the Act.
2. **Cognizable Offence:** The offence of corruption is a cognizable offence in which the police can arrest without an arrest warrant from a court.
3. **Punishment:** The punishment for indulging in an act of corruption is a minimum of six months and a maximum of six years.
4. **Sanction to Prosecution:** Section 19 of the Act provides that previous sanction of a competent authority is necessary before a competent court takes cognizance of an offence under the Act. The objective of this provision is to protect honest public servants from malicious and vexatious complaints. However, such a clause also leads to delays in the process of justice.

11.12.4.2 Benami Transactions (Prohibition) Act, 1988

The Benami Transactions (Prohibition) Act, 1988 precludes the person who acquired the property in the name of another person from claiming it as his/her own. The wealth assessed by corrupt public servants is often kept in 'benami' accounts or invested in properties in others' names. Strict enforcement of the Act could unearth such property and work as a deterrent against corrupt practices.

11.12.4.3 Whistle Blowers Protection Act, 2014

There are many honest public servants who want to disclose the corrupt activities of other public servants. However, they require protection upon disclosing such corrupt activities. A strong protection provided to such whistle blowers can go a long way in eliminating corruption in India. In this light, the Whistle Blowers Protection Act was passed in 2014. The various provisions of the act are as follows:

(a) **Disclosure of Information:** Under the Act, disclosure is defined as a complaint relating to an attempt to commit an offence under the Prevention of Corruption Act, 1988; a complaint relating to wilful misuse of power or of virtue by which demonstrable loss is caused to the government or demonstrable wrongful gain accrues to the public servant or any third party; or a complaint relating to an attempt to commission of a criminal offence by a public servant.

(b) **Official Secrets Act:** The provisions of the Official Secrets Act will not be applied to any disclosure made under this Act. Any public servant, private person, or non-governmental organisation can make a disclosure.

(c) **Competent Authority:** The Act provides for competent authorities at various levels to receive public interest disclosures. These authorities are to be notified by the Central Vigilance Commission or state vigilance commissions. The competent authority shall not reveal the name of the complainant, and upon receiving the complaint it may conduct a discreet inquiry to examine its veracity and forward it to the concerned head of department without revealing the name of the complainant.

(d) **Designated Authority:** The Central Vigilance Commission has been made the designated authority under the Act to receive written complaints for disclosure on any allegations of corruption.

(e) **Role of Head of Department:** The head of the department is required to conduct an inquiry and submit an inquiry report within the stipulated time to the competent authority. On this inquiry report, the competent authority may recommend action against the accused, which might include prosecution, and the government shall take a decision on it within a period of three months.

(f) **Punishment for Negligence:** If any public servant shows negligence under the Act or intentionally reveals the name of the complainant, he/she will be liable for punishment by way of imprisonment up to three years and a fine.

(g) **Mala Fide Disclosure:** The Act also provides a punishment of up to two years for mala fide disclosures.

(h) **Protection to Complainant:** The Central Government shall ensure that no person or a public servant making a disclosure is victimised by the initiation of any proceedings or otherwise merely on the ground that such person has made a disclosure. If required, the competent authority can order for police protection to be given to a complainant or a witness.

11.12.5 Institutions to Check Corruption

There are various institutions to tackle corruption at the central, state, and local levels in India. These institutions are discussed in the following sections.

11.12.5.1 Administrative Vigilance Division of DoPT

This division is the nodal agency to deal with vigilance and anti-corruption measures in the Central Government.

11.12.5.2 Central Vigilance Commission

The Central Vigilance Commission (CVC) was set up in February 1964 on the recommendations of the Committee on Prevention of Corruption headed by K. Santhanam. It is conceived to be the apex vigilance institution, free of control from any executive authority, monitoring all vigilance activity under the Central Government and advising various authorities in Central Government organisations in planning, executing, reviewing, and reforming their vigilance work.

It exercises superintendence over the Central Bureau of Investigation (CBI) in the investigation of offences relating to the Prevention of Corruption Act. It also inquires or causes an inquiry or investigation into any complaint received against any public servant.

11.12.5.3 Vigilance Units

Vigilance units are set up in all ministries, departments, public sector undertakings, and other public organisations. These vigilance units are headed by a chief vigilance officer (CVO) appointed on the advice of the Central Vigilance Commission. These units deal with the vigilance functions of their respective organisations.

11.12.5.4 Central Bureau of Investigation

The Central Bureau of Investigation traces its origin to the Special Police Establishment (SPE), which was set up in 1941 by the Government of India. The functions of the SPE then were to investigate cases of bribery and corruption in transactions with the War & Supply Department of India during World War II. After Independence, the Delhi Special Police Establishment Act, 1946 was passed to give SPE a legal backing. Its functions were then enlarged to cover all departments. The SPE was renamed CBI in 1963, and its functions were also enlarged. It now functions under the Department of Personnel, Ministry of Personnel, Pensions & Public Grievances.

The CBI has an Anticorruption Division that deals with the investigation of cases of bribery and corruption involving the employees of Central Government, public sector undertakings, and central financial institutions.

11.12.5.5 Comptroller and Auditor General

The Comptroller and Auditor General (CAG) audits the receipts and expenditures of the government. Through this audit, it unearths the various corruption scams in the government.

11.12.5.6 Anticorruption Bureau

Every state has an anticorruption bureau (ACB) for preventing corruption and creating deterrence through education and awareness campaigns. These bureaus combat corruption by conducting enquiries on complaints received against corrupt officials. They also lay traps to catch the bribe-takers red-handed. Furthermore, they investigate crimes of trap cases, criminal misconduct, and disproportionate assets cases and prosecute corrupt public servants.

State ACBs have their units in every district. All the complaints against district-level officers are received by the ACB only.

11.12.5.7 Lokpal and Lokayuktas

Globally, the ombudsman is an important institution for tackling corruption. In India, the ombudsman is known as the *Lokpal*. The concept was first introduced by L.M. Singhvi in Parliament. The First ARC recommended setting up a Lokpal at the Central level and Lokayuktas at the state level. Subsequently, eight bills had been introduced in the Lok Sabha for the formation of the Lokpal. However, success was achieved in 2014, when the President gave his assent for the Lokpal and Lokayuktas Act, 2013. The key provisions of the Act are as follows:

(a) **Composition of Lokpal:** The Lokpal is required to have a chairperson and up to eight members. Four of these members are judicial members and the rest are non-judicial members. The chairperson can be (a) a serving or retired Chief Justice of India, (b) a serving or retired Supreme Court judge, or (c) an eminent person. A judicial member can be (a) a serving or retired judge of the Supreme Court or (b) a serving or retired chief justice of a high court. A non-judicial member must be a person of impeccable integrity and outstanding ability having special knowledge and expertise of not less than 25 years in matters relating to anti-corruption policy, public administration, vigilance, finance including insurance and banking, law, and management. The Act further provides that not less than 50% of the members shall be from amongst the persons belonging to scheduled castes, scheduled tribes, other backward classes, minorities, and women.

(b) **Selection Committee:** The chairperson and members of the Lokpal are to be appointed by the president on the recommendations of the Selection Committee. The members of the Selection Committee are:

(i) Prime Minister as Chairperson

(ii) Speaker of the Lok Sabha

(iii) Leader of Opposition in the Lok Sabha

(iv) Chief Justice of India or a judge of the Supreme Court nominated by him/her

(v) One eminent jurist as recommended by a committee of first three members

(c) **Search Committee:** Under the Act, a search committee is required to be formed, whose role is to prepare a panel of names from which the selection committee will appoint the chairperson and members of the Lokpal. This search committee shall have at least seven persons including experts in anti-corruption policy, public administration, vigilance, and finance including insurance and banking, law, and management. However, the selection committee may also consider any person other than the persons recommended by the search committee.

(d) **Duration of Office:** The chairperson and the members of Lokpal can hold office for five years or until they attain the age of 70 years. They are barred from holding any other office in the Central or state governments. They cannot fight state and general elections for a period of five years after completing their tenure in the Lokpal.

(e) **Jurisdiction:** The Lokpal can receive complaints against public functionaries and public servants at all levels of the government. Here, public functionaries refer to persons other than civil servants holding public offices such as ministers and other political persons. Thus, apart from government servants, the Act includes the prime minister, ministers, Members of Parliament, members of boards, bodies financed by the government and societies/associations/trusts receiving more than INR 10 lakhs from foreign donors.

(f) **Safeguard for Prime Minister:** The Act has provided certain safeguards for the PM. Accordingly, the Lokpal cannot inquire into any allegation of corruption against the PM if it relates to international relations, external and internal security, public order, and atomic energy and space. Any inquiry into such matters can be made if the full bench of the Lokpal initiates such an inquiry and at least two-thirds of the members approve such inquiry.

(g) **Inquiry Wing:** The Lokpal will have an inquiry wing for conducting a preliminary inquiry into any allegations of corruption. If it finds some material in a complaint, it can forward it for a preliminary inquiry to the inquiry wing. This inquiry can also be conducted by the CVC.

(h) **Prosecution Wing:** The prosecution wing will be responsible for prosecuting public servants after an investigation before a special court.

(i) **Procedure for Handling Complaints:** After the preliminary inquiry, a report will be submitted to Lokpal. A bench of not less than three members will consider this report. After this, the bench will summon the public servant and give him/her an opportunity to justify his/her actions. Then the bench will decide the merits of the case and, accordingly, either send it to the CBI for investigation, initiate departmental proceedings against the person, or close the case. After the investigation by the CBI, the bench will consider the investigation report and, accordingly, either file a charge sheet or closure report before the Special Court or initiate departmental proceedings against the public servant.

(j) **Prior Sanction not Required:** Whenever the Lokpal sends a case for prosecution, no prior sanction of the competent authority for prosecution is required under section 197 of the Criminal Procedure Code.

(k) **Attachment of Property:** The Lokpal has the power to attach the proceeds of corruption in the possession of a public servant.

(l) **Lokayuktas:** The Act has provided for the formation of Lokayuktas in all states within 365 days of the passing of the Act. The functioning and composition of the Lokayuktas will be similar to that of the Lokpal.

Functioning of Lokayuktas

The Lokpal and Lokayuktas Act, 2013 has made it mandatory for all the states to create a Lokayukta to prevent corruption. However, several states already had a functioning Lokayukta since many years before. The Lokayuktas in the states functions with the support of the Income Tax Department and the ACBs. By 2018, 10 states and union territories had still not created a Lokayukta. Maharashtra was the first state to introduce the institution in 1971. Karnataka's Lokayukta is considered one of the strongest. N. Santosh Hegde, former Lokayukta of Karnataka, uncovered one of the biggest mining scams in the country in 2011.

The powers of the Lokayuktas have varied from state to state. In some states, the Lokayukta inquires into the allegations against public functionaries including the chief minister, ministers, and MLAs. While in some others, the Lokayuktas investigate complaints against the civil servants, judiciary, and police.

However, there are certain problems that the Lokayuktas of many States face. They lack prosecution powers, adequate staff, funds, and independence in functioning. In some states, the office has remained vacant for many years. For example, in Gujarat, there was no Lokayukta for eight years until the then Governor Kamla Beniwal appointed the Lokayukta. Thus, it is necessary that Lokayuktas should be upgraded in all the states in accordance with the provisions of the Lokpal and Lokayuktas Act, 2013.

11.12.6 Corruption in the Private Sector

We always talk about corruption in the government. However, corruption has spread to the private sector also, particularly in the era of privatisation and public private partnerships (PPPs). The private sector comes under the Prevention of Corruption Act (PCA) only when it involves in abetting bribery with a public servant.

Today a large number of public services are being entrusted to private companies and non-governmental organisations (NGOs). The Companies Act, 2013 provides the statutory framework that governs the internal processes and corruption within a private organisation. It also contains penal provisions against offences by companies and their directors and officers. Though the offence of corruption or bribery is not mentioned under the Companies Act, instances of wrongdoing by companies and their officers are addressed through the mechanisms of accounts, audits, inspection, technical scrutiny of balance sheets, and so on. Besides, companies are also required to have audit committees of the board of management to look into various aspects related to financial propriety.

Thus, corruption in the private sector can be tackled by the effective implementation of the Companies Act.

Serious Economic Offences

An important aspect of corruption in the private sector and in the PPPs is the phenomenon of the serious economic offence. Serious economic offences include offences of tax evasion, counterfeiting, distorting share markets, falsification of books of accounts of companies, frauds in the banking system, smuggling, money laundering, insider trading, and bribery.

To tackle such offences, the *Serious Frauds Investigation Office* (SFIO) was set up in 2003 as a multidisciplinary organisation to deal with cases of serious corporate frauds. It was formed on the recommendation of the Naresh Chandra Committee on Corporate Audit and Finance. The need for such an institution was felt because of an increase in stock market scams. A fragmented approach was found to be inadequate in tackling such offences. Though there were a number of agencies to investigate these frauds, none of them were able to adopt a holistic approach to such crimes.

Financial frauds in the corporate world are very complex and can be properly and adequately investigated only by a multidisciplinary team of experts. Thus, the SFIO consists of experts from the financial sector, capital market, banks, accountancy, audit, taxation, law, information technology, company law, customs, and investigation. The SFIO is mandated to carry out an investigation under the Companies Act. It also sends its reports to other agencies to act under their own laws.

After investigating cases of serious fraud, the SFIO initiates prosecution against the culprits after receiving approval from the Central Government. The investigation report filed by the SFIO with the criminal court is deemed to be a report filed by the police under the Criminal Procedure Code.

The SFIO also has powers to arrest persons under the Companies Act. When a case is taken up by the SFIO for investigation, no other investigating agency is allowed to investigate that case.

However, a concern with SFIO is that it initiates investigation only under the direction of the Central Government. Thus, there can be hindrances in cases where influential politicians and ministers are involved.

11.12.7 Role of Citizens in Tackling Corruption

Public servants and politicians are the members of our society. They come from the same society they serve. Thus, the level of corruption in government is a reflection of the standard of ethics of our citizens. Citizens have a very important role to play in containing corruption in the government, as the government works for them and they are the victims of corruption.

The Whistle Blowers Protection Act provides an opportunity for citizens to secretly lodge complaints against public servants. Apart from this, the citizens have been given ample ways to complain against the corrupt activities of public servants. At the local and state levels, they can approach the anticorruption bureau and Lokayukta. At the national level, they can approach the Central Vigilance Commission and Lokpal. Moreover, they can also approach the head of a department to complain against the public servants working under him/her. Such a complaint can also be made to the political head of a ministry or department.

In India, there are statutory provisions casting obligations on the citizens to report any instance of corruption that comes to their knowledge. Such provisions apply to both citizens and public servants and are backed with penal provisions in the event of failure to comply with such obligations. The Code of Civil Procedure makes it mandatory for any person to report to a magistrate or officer of the law any alleged corrupt offence by a public servant, failing which he/she shall be liable for prosecution.

However, this provision has remained a dead letter because the informant protection mechanisms are very weak in India.

11.12.8 Systemic Reforms for Tackling Corruption

There are many laws, codes of conduct, and agencies in India to tackle corruption. However, it is seen that corruption is on the rise. New legal or institutional initiatives to tackle corruption have had little impact and are often seen as politically expedient ways of reacting to societal pressures to contain corruption.

Systemic reforms go a long way to eradicate corruption in government. For example, systemic reforms such as online railway ticket booking, online common entrance tests, and direct cash based subsidies are aimed at upgrading the system of service delivery. Such upgradations in the systems of service delivery are aimed at removing all opportunities for corruption from the system. When there are no opportunities, there would not be any corruption. Some of the systemic reforms that can be implemented in all the government departments are as follows:

(a) **E-Governance:** E-governance helps in decreasing the public servant–citizen contact during service delivery. When personal contact decreases, opportunities for corruption also decrease. In Chapter 2, we have discussed e-governance in detail.

(b) **Integrity Pacts:** The term 'integrity pact' refers to an agreement between the public agency involved in procuring goods and services and the bidder for a public contract to the effect that the bidders have not paid and shall not pay any illegal gratification to secure the contract in question. The public agency calling for bids commits to ensuring a level playing field and fair play in the procurement process. An important feature of such pacts is that they often involve oversight and scrutiny by independent, third-party observers.

(c) **Risk Management for Preventive Vigilance:** An important aspect of organisational vigilance is to prevent corruption in organisations rather than reacting after an incidence of corruption. For this, various positions in the government can be classified as being at 'high risk of corruption', 'medium risk of corruption', and 'low risk of corruption'. Similarly, individual government servants vary in their level of integrity, ranging from those who indulge in outright extortion to those who are absolutely upright. A risk management system to prevent corruption should seek to ensure that 'low risk personnel' are posted at 'high risk positions' and vice versa. Such preventive vigilance helps in identifying suspected corrupt public servants and not allowing them to occupy sensitive positions.

(d) **Intelligence Gathering in respect of Corrupt Officials:** Intelligence gathering is an important mechanism to gain information about the unethical activities of public servants. It includes keeping surveillance over suspected public servants, studying their lifestyles, studying the decisions they have made, analysing the complaints against them, and feedback of their work from citizens and peer groups. Such intelligence gathering can be done by the head of the department or by the state and central intelligence agencies. Such intelligence can help in grading public servants on a scale from being 'completely ethical' to 'highly prone to corrupt activities'. On the basis of this scale, public servants can be given sensitive and less sensitive positions as discussed in the previous section.

(e) **Good Governance Initiatives:** Some of the good governance initiatives taken to promote an ethical government system are the SPARROW system, Employees Online, Online Probity Management System, SUPREMO portal, and SOLVE portal. These initiatives have been discussed in Section 10.8.8 under the topic '*Good Governance Initiatives in Performance Appraisal*' of in Chapter 10.

11.13 Grievance Redressal Mechanism in India

A grievance is defined as an indignation or resentment arising out of a feeling of being wronged. It is also defined as an expression of dissatisfaction with an organisation and its products, services, and/or processes, where a response or resolution is explicitly or implicitly expected.[21] The grievances can be classified into three broad categories as described in the following:

(a) Grievances arising out of the abuse of office and corruption. An example of it is a police officer demanding money for registering an FIR.

(b) Grievances arise out of systemic deficiencies within an organisation. An example is frequent power cuts in an area in the monsoon season due to poor power distribution infrastructure.

(c) Grievances arising from non-fulfilment of needs or demands. An example is when labourers demand an increase in their daily wages but the management does not agree to their demands.

While the first category of grievances can be dealt with through statutory interventions such as the RTI Act and Prevention of Corruption Act, the second and third categories require internal reforms and organisational capacity building.

Apart from institutions such as the Central Vigilance Commission and Lokpal, every organisation has set up its own grievance redressal mechanism. Institutions such as the Reserve Bank of India have set up ombudsman to deal with public grievances. Moreover, there are institutions such as the National Human Rights Commission (NHRC), National Women Commission (NWC), National Commission for Scheduled Castes (NCSC), National Commission for Scheduled Tribes (NCST), and National Commission for Minorities (NCM) that deal with public grievances in their respective domains.

The basic principle of the grievance redressal system is that if the promised level of service delivery is not achieved or if a citizen's right is not honoured, the citizen should be able to take recourse to a mechanism to get his/her grievance redressed.

11.13.1 Grievance Redressal Mechanism in Central Government

The mechanisms for handling grievances in the Central Government are as follows:

(a) **Department of Administrative Reforms and Public Grievances (DAR&PG):** The DAR&PG receives complaints from the public. After receiving complaints, it forwards them to the concerned ministry/department/state government/union territory, which in turn deals with the substantive functions linked with the grievance for redress. The department follows up on the redressal of grievances till their final disposal.

(b) **Central Public Grievance Redress and Monitoring System (CPGRAMS)**: The CPGRAMS was launched in 2007 for receiving, redressing, and monitoring grievances from the public. It provides the facility to lodge a grievance online. It also enables a citizen to track online his/her grievance being followed up with the departments concerned. Moreover, it also enables the DAR&PG to monitor grievances.

(c) **Directorate of Public Grievances (DPG)**: The DPG was set up under the Cabinet Secretariat in 1988 to look into individual complaints pertaining to four Central Government departments prone to public complaints. It was envisaged as an appellate body for investigating grievances selectively and, particularly, those grievances where the complainant has failed to get redress from the internal redressal machinery and the hierarchical authorities.

(d) **Grievance Redressal Machinery of Individual Organisations**: Every important Central Government ministry, department, their attached and subordinate office, public sector undertaking, and autonomous body have their own grievance redressal machineries.

11.13.2 Grievance Redressal Mechanisms at State Level

The mechanisms of grievance redressal vary from state to state. Generally, the chief minister's office has a *public grievance cell*, which receives complaints from citizens. It forwards these to concerned departments and follows their progress. Apart from this, some chief ministers hold regular public hearings as well as use electronic media to hear and respond to public grievances. In some states, ministers and senior officers visit districts and villages to hear and resolve the grievances of citizens.

At the district level, the district magistrate is generally designated as the district public grievance officer. In some states, the *zila parishad* (or *zila panchayats*) have constituted their own public grievance redressal mechanisms.

11.13.3 Grievance-prone Areas

In order to eliminate the underlying causes that lead to public grievances, government organisations need to be proactively engaged in a rigorous and periodic exercise towards analysing the nature of grievances received by them. For this, the grievances need to be identified, correlated, and linked with different processes involved in the functioning of an organisation. This would provide a clear mapping of public grievances based on both functions and functionaries. Such mapping of grievances can be improved by taking the help of public opinion and expert advice. Once the mapping is done, it would be easy to identify grievance-prone areas, processes, functions, and functionaries within an organisation.

This would help in devising corrective measures in order to eliminate the very *raison d'être* of grievances.

11.14 Relation between Political Executives and Civil Servants

The tasks of political executives and civil servants are different. Their roles overlap at some points in their duties. The roles of political executive and administration are described under the topic *'Politics and Administration'* of Chapter 1.

However, there has not been a clear outline of the relationship between civil servants and political executives. The absence of such a relationship has led to the servile nature of civil servants in India. Sardar Patel had predicted danger to the unity of India due to the servile nature of civil service in India. However, the Indian Constitution did not devise a new scheme for the selection, appointment, transfer, promotion, and other service matters in order to avoid ministerial interference in the work of civil servants.

In this regard, Paul Appleby was called as a consultant to study the state of Indian administration in 1950. In his report, he said, "civil servants should be in no danger of reprisals for opinions freely and vigorously expressed to ministers and they shall have firm support in the exercise of discretion ministers delegate and should delegate to them."[22] Following this, a number of committees and commissions have recommended to clearly define and delimit the role of ministers and civil servants. However, no concrete action has been taken in this direction.

Inaction in defining the relationship between civil servants and political executives has many ramifications. Some of these are as follows:[23]

(a) Impact on the concept of neutrality
(b) Impact on the advisory role of civil servants in policymaking
(c) Impact on the statutory role of civil servants
(d) Impact on the appointments/recruitment to civil services
(e) Impact on the transfers and postings of civil servants
(f) Cowardly nature of civil servants

11.14.1 Impact on the Concept of Neutrality

As already discussed, civil servants have to behave in a politically neutral manner. However, the situation in India has not been encouraging. The top level of civil servants, with a few exceptions, have generally tended to follow their political bosses and carry out their commands rather than risk their displeasure and jeopardise their own careers by offering them unpalatable advice. Civil servants have tended to become mere puppets in the hands of the political leadership.

P.S. Appu, an IAS Officer of the 1951 batch, has described the time periods that have negatively impacted the neutrality of civil servants.[24] According to him, 1947–1962 was a period of good governance and cordial ministerial–civil servant relations. The degeneration started in 1967 due to extreme political corruption. In 1967, the Congress party was defeated in Bihar and a few other states and a number of amorphous parties with conflicting goals and ideologies came to power. Political decline was also generated due to coalition politics, where the chief ministers had to oblige to all sorts of unfair, unreasonable demands of their coalition partners who included a good number of criminals. These illegal demands were communicated by the chief ministers to administrators, thereby decreasing the standard of administration.

Apart from this, the actions of Mrs Indira Gandhi led to the subversion of inner party democracy. She advocated for a committed bureaucracy and a committed judiciary. This also had a deleterious impact on the neutrality of the civil servants. From 1971–74, the administration started declining at the Centre. It was found that administrators of integrity, ability, and vision were sidelined from Mrs Gandhi's inner council. This coincided with the usurpation of political power by a small coterie headed by her son, Sanjay Gandhi. These developments adversely affected public administration and the neutrality of civil servants.

Things have deteriorated to such an extent that it can be said that neutrality in civil services is only an exception. There have been civil servants who immediately after their retirement became head of the same corporate entity with which they have had some interaction when they were in the government. Moreover, there have also been civil servants who secured party tickets for elections immediately after their retirement.

11.14.2 Impact on Advisory Role of Civil Servants in Policymaking

Considering the advisory role, there have been instances where the policy formulated is against the public interest. In such a case, it is the duty of the civil servant to convince the political executive about the adverse implications of such policies. However, as discussed, most civil servants have not shown the courage to give unpalatable advice to the ministers. As per good practices, if the political executive does not agree with the advice of the civil servant, he/she has to put his/her views clearly on record.

11.14.3 Impact on Statutory Role of Civil Servants

There is an increasing political interference in the statutory functions of civil servants. Such interference had led to the demeaning of democratic institutions during the Emergency Period. The perverse personnel policies followed by the political executives had forced the civil servants to allow the interference of political executives in their daily work. As a result, the morale of the civil servants has gone down, and the law-and-order administration has suffered a major jolt in various parts of the country. The executive magistrate and the police have increasingly become spectators to communal, class, and caste-based conflicts.

Such has been the partisanship of police officers that they have also played the role of adding fuel to communal riots. The serious communal riots of Meerut, Bhagalpur, and the anti-Sikh riots of 1984 have shown serious failures on the part of the administration. Due to politicisation, administrations have failed to take deterrent actions against criminal elements to protect innocent and unsuspecting citizens.[24]

The situation has worsened in recent times when the IAS and IPS officers have shown a marked tendency to carry out the wishes of their political masters without regard to law and propriety.

Under the Criminal Procedure Code and the Police Act, the sole responsibility for the maintenance of public order rests with the executive magistrate and the police. It assigns no role to the political executive in the maintenance of the public order. If illegal orders are received from the political executives, it was the duty of the Chief Secretary and DGP to ignore such orders.

The partisan role of the bureaucracy was also found in the ineffective implementation of the land laws in some states. It was found that the bureaucracy joined hands with zamindars and sabotaged the abolition of zamindari sytem in some states.[25]

11.14.4 Impact on Appointments/Recruitment to Civil Services

Although the UPSC enjoys an untarnished image, the state public service commissions (SPSCs) suffer from political interference. Many of the appointments from state civil services and state police services to IAS and IPS, respectively, are based on political considerations. The state of affairs of the SPSCs is discussed in the topic *'Union Public Service Commission (UPSC) and State Public Service Commissions (SPSC)'* of the Chapter 10.

Political interference has also been found in government recruitments to lower positions such as those of police constables, teachers, bus drivers, village accountants, and so on.

11.14.5 Impact on Transfers and Postings of Civil Servants

In India, the transfer is considered as the politician's basic weapon of control over the bureaucracy and thus a lever for surplus extraction from the clients of the bureaucracy. With this weapon, not only can the politicians raise money by direct sale of office, they can also remove someone who is not being responsive enough to their monetary/political demands or to their requests for favours to those from whom they get money and electoral support. This unhealthy symbiosis between politicians and civil servants has deepened. It can be said that the politicians in power and civil servants have come to share a mutually beneficial relationship in pursuit of self-interested behaviour.[26]

Apart from this, the politicians use a number of methods to coerce the civil servants to align with them. They post honest and upright civil servants to insignificant positions which had been occupied by officers far junior in rank to them. After doing this they declare the said post to be equal in rank and responsibilities to that of a higher rank by issuing a revised circular under the Civil Services Pay Rules.

11.14.6 Cowardly Nature of Civil Servants

Another disturbing trend that has been observed due to political interference in civil service is the decreasing courage of civil servants. Officers are losing the courage to stand for the truth. They have an unknown fear that something terrible may happen to them if they do not align with the dictates of their political masters. This fear makes them apathetic towards the real governance issues. The tragedy is that such pliable civil servants are rewarded with important positions.

Many social scientists believe that the absence of a code guiding the relationship between civil servants and politicians has led to the chaos in the administration and governance of the country.

11.14.7 Civil Service Board and Security of Tenure

As discussed, political transfers and postings are the biggest reasons for the partisan nature of civil servants. To end this, the Supreme Court in *TSR Subramaniam and Others* vs *the Union of India* directed the Centre and the states to set up Civil Services Boards (CSBs) for the management of transfers, postings, inquiries, the process of promotion, reward, punishment, and disciplinary matters.

The Supreme Court also directed that the civil servants should not act on the verbal orders of the politicians and their tenure should be fixed. It was directed that the CSBs should be headed by the Cabinet Secretary at the Central level and the chief secretaries at the state level. The political executive will have to record reasons while overruling the suggestions of the CSBs on transfers, postings, promotions, and other service matters. Such a step will ensure good governance, transparency, and accountability in governmental functions.[27]

It was said that a fixed minimum tenure would not only enable the civil servants to achieve their professional targets but also help them to function as effective instruments of public policy. The Bench directed the Centre, states, and union territories to issue appropriate directions to secure the provision of minimum tenure of service to various civil servants.

11.14.8 Output–Outcome Framework in Minister–Civil Servant Relationship

The Second ARC Report has suggested an output–outcome framework to improve the minister–civil servant relationship. Outputs or key results are specific services that the civil servants produce and deliver, and, therefore, they should be held to account for the delivery of key results, which becomes the basis for the evaluation of their performance.

On the other hand, the outcome is the success in achieving social goals, and the political executive decides what outputs should be included so that the desired outcomes or social goals can be achieved. In such a scheme, the political executive becomes accountable to the legislature and the electorate for the outcomes. The political executive is judged on the basis of whether it has chosen the right outputs to achieve the social goals. For example, if the political executive wants to a attain the objective of reduction in the maternal mortality rate in the country, the actions decided by them could be to increase the number of health centres, doctors, and ASHA workers; improvement in the training of ASHA workers; and so on. Attaining these outputs would be the responsibility of the civil servants. However, the outcomes attained (decrease in the maternal mortality rate) by proper implementation of these outputs would be the responsibility of the political executive.

If this framework is implemented properly, the relationship between the political executive and permanent civil service can be objectively defined.

11.15 Discipline and Disciplinary Action

Employee discipline is very important for the smooth functioning of an organisation. It helps in establishing a harmonious relationship between the employer and its employees. It refers to the quality of self-control and self-direction at work. It helps in the development of teamwork and proper appreciation of the hierarchical superior–subordinate relationship.

There are two aspects of the discipline: positive and negative. The positive aspect of discipline is related to self-discipline. It is related to the idea of self-actualisation at work under which employees are committed to work and take personal initiatives in the progress of the organisation. Such positive discipline is found in organisations where the management applies the principles of positive motivation. This kind of discipline is also known as *co-operative discipline* and *determinative discipline.*

On the other hand, in *negative discipline*, the employees are forced to obey orders. Compliance from employees is obtained by the use of coercive means such as penalties, threats, and fear of authority. This kind of discipline is also known as *punitive discipline*, *corrective discipline,* or *autocratic discipline.* This kind of discipline inhibits positive behaviour and ensures only a minimum standard of performance on the part of the employees.

11.15.1 Disciplinary Action

Disciplinary action is the official process to deal with an employee's indiscipline in an organisation. It is based on the *hot stove rule*. According to this rule, disciplinary action behaves like a 'hot stove' as described hereafter:

- **Burns Immediately:** If we put our hand on a hot stove, it will get burnt immediately. Similarly, disciplinary action is taken immediately when any employee commits a wrong.
- **Provides Warning:** If we bring our hand close to the hot stove, we feel the heat and get a warning to move away. Similarly, disciplinary action provides a warning to the errant employees to improve their behaviour to avoid future punitive action.
- **Equity in Punishment:** The hot stove burns every person equally. Similarly, the punishment provided by the disciplinary action is equal to the equal delinquent action of the employees.
- **Burns Impersonally:** As the hot stove behaves impersonally, the disciplinary action also acts in an impersonal manner.

This formal system of disciplinary action is adopted so that the motivation and morale of employees are not affected by disciplinary punishments.

11.15.2 Discipline in Civil Services

In civil services, disciplinary action is initiated against employees indulging in corrupt activities, delinquent action, violation of conduct rules, and so on. The disciplinary inquiry is conducted in accordance with Article 311 of the Indian Constitution. The provisions of this article are as follows:[28]

Article 311: Dismissal, removal, or reduction in rank of persons employed in civil capacities under the Union or a state:

1. No person who is a member of a civil service of the Union or an all India service or a civil service of a state or who holds a civil post under the Union or a state shall be dismissed or removed by an authority subordinate to that by which s/he was appointed.
2. No such person as aforesaid shall be dismissed or removed or reduced in rank except after an inquiry in which he/she has been informed of the charges against him/her and given a reasonable opportunity of being heard in respect of those charges. Provided that where it is proposed after such inquiry to impose upon him/her any such penalty, such penalty may be imposed on the basis of the evidence adduced during such inquiry and it shall not be necessary to give such person any opportunity of making representation on the penalty proposed. Provided further that this clause shall not apply:
   (a) where a person is dismissed or removed or reduced in rank on the ground of conduct that has led to his/her conviction on a criminal charge; or
   (b) where the authority empowered to dismiss or remove a person or to reduce him/her in rank is satisfied that for some reason, to be recorded by that authority in writing, it is not reasonably practicable to hold such inquiry; or
   (c) where the President or the Governor, as the case may be, is satisfied that in the interest of the security of the State, it is not expedient to hold such inquiry.
3. If, in respect of any such person as aforesaid, a question arises whether it is reasonably practicable to hold such inquiry as is referred to in clause (2), the decision thereon of the authority empowered to dismiss or remove such person or to reduce him/her in rank shall be final.

Accordingly, punishment cannot be awarded to a civil servant by any authority subordinate to the authority that has appointed him/her. Moreover, the power under Article 311 cannot be delegated to a lower authority. However, the power to inquire on the charges made against the employee can be delegated to a subordinate authority, an independent individual, or a tribunal. The inquiry made by the subordinate authority is then submitted to the appointing authority for final consideration and action. Moreover, the advice of the UPSC is taken in every case of disciplinary action where it is important to consult the commission before passing a penal order.

11.15.3 Suspension

Suspension is an action that can be taken by an authority subordinate to the appointing authority. Suspension is defined as sending an employee on compulsory and underpaid leave in order to conduct inquiries against him/her in a free and fair manner.

According to Central Civil Services (Classification, Control, and Appeal) Rules, 1965, "The appointing authority or any authority to which it is subordinate or the disciplinary authority empowered in that behalf by the President, by general or special order, may place a Government servant under suspension:

1. where a disciplinary proceeding against him/her is contemplated or pending;
2. where, in the opinion of the authority aforesaid, he/she has engaged himself in activities prejudicial to the interest of the security of the state; or
3. where a case against him/her in respect of any criminal offence is under investigation, inquiry, or trial.

Provided that, except in case of an order of suspension made by the Comptroller and Auditor-General in regard to a member of the Indian Audit and Accounts Service and in regard to an Assistant Accountant General or equivalent (other than a regular member of the Indian Audit and Accounts Service), where the order of suspension is made by an authority lower than the appointing authority, such authority shall forthwith report to the appointing authority the circumstances in which the order was made."

11.15.4 Types of Penalties

Rule 11 of Central Civil Services (Classification, Control, and Appeal) Rules, 1965 has described the type of punishment to be awarded to civil servants after an inquiry. Accordingly, the penalties are classified as follows:

I. **Minor Penalties:** The minor penalties are as described below:
   (i) Censure
   (ii) Withholding of promotion
   (iii) Recovery from pay of the whole or part of any pecuniary loss caused to the government by negligence or breach of orders by the delinquent officer
   (iv) Withholding of increments of pay

II. **Major Penalties:** The major penalties are as described below:
   (i) Reduction to a lower stage in the time scale of pay for a specified period.
   (ii) Reduction to the lower timescale of pay, grade, post, or service which shall ordinarily be a bar to the promotion of the government servant to the timescale of pay, grade, post, or service from which s/he was reduced.
   (iii) Compulsory retirement.
   (iv) Removal from service, which shall not be a disqualification for future employment under the government.
   (v) Dismissal from service, which shall ordinarily be a disqualification for future employment under the government.

Here it is important to understand the distinction between 'dismissal' and 'removal'. In 'dismissal', the person is ineligible for reemployment in government service, while in 'removal' he/she is eligible for further employment.

11.15.5 Lacunae in Disciplinary Action in India

The disciplinary proceedings in India suffer from inordinate delay and inequity in awarding punishment. Moreover, the protection provided in Article 311 tends to protect delinquent civil servants. No other Constitution of the world contains such guarantees as Article 311 of the Indian Constitution. With the provision of judicial review on administrative decisions, the protection available to delinquent civil servants is even more formidable.

This has created a climate of excessive job security without fear of penalty for incompetence or wrongdoing. A rough estimate suggests that the average time taken to complete disciplinary enquiries ranges from 10 months to 16 months. Moreover, with the formation of the Central Administrative Tribunal in the 1980s, most of the judicial proceedings arising out of departmental inquiries are landed in these administrative tribunals for which they, not infrequently, entertain pleas to stay disciplinary proceedings on technical grounds and even entertain pleas against interlocutory orders. Apart from this, public servants are also allowed to challenge the order of the tribunals in high courts. There is, in addition, recourse to the Supreme Court under Article 136 of the Constitution. Thus, a delinquent civil servant has ample options to delay and avoid the punishment awarded to him/her through disciplinary action.

Apart from this, consultation with the UPSC further delays the process of disciplinary proceedings.

To improve the status of disciplinary proceedings in India, the Hota Committee has given the following recommendations:

(a) The UPSC need not be consulted in case of a civil servant facing charges of corrupt practice and whose case has already been referred to the CVC.

(b) An inquiry officer should be relieved from his/her normal duties for a sufficient period to enable him/her to complete the departmental enquiry expeditiously and submit the report in time.

(c) In case of serious corruption, if the president/governor is satisfied, the civil servant should be removed and be given an opportunity in a post-decisional hearing to defend himself/herself.

SUMMARY

This chapter dealt withthe various dimensions of ethics, morality, and values as applicable to civil servants and administrators. Based on Western as well as Indian philosophies, we have learned the art of leading an ethical lifestyle. Moreover, we have discussed the malaise of corruption in public life and the measures to deal with it. Finally, we have discussed the an important concept of relations between political executives and civil servants.

Practice Questions

1. Discuss the values important in public life.
2. We can say that a thing is moral if it is in harmony with or fits a nature. Explain with real life examples.
3. Holistic competence is what is required from public administrators. Explain with administrative examples.
4. Can ethics philosophies help in taking moral decisions? Explain with the help of real-life administrative examples.
5. What is the role of conscience in taking decisions?
6. According to Indian philosophy, what steps can be taken to improve ethics in administration?
7. What is the importance of civil services values in public administration?
8. Civil service activism is the opposite of civil service neutrality. Evaluate with examples.
9. Criminalisation of politics is the *gangotri* of corruption in India. Evaluate with examples.
10. What is the role of citizens in tackling corruption in public life?
11. Non-determination of political executive-civil servant relations has led to major problems for public administration in India. Evaluate.

CHAPTER

12 Public Policy

After reading this chapter, you will learn the following:

- Definition of public policy and its comparison with political science and public administration.
- Comparison of the term 'policy' with related terms such as mega policy, decisions, and goals.
- Descriptive models of public policy such as functional process model, elite/mass model, group model, systems model, institutional model, neo-institutional model, organised anarchy model, public goods and services model, technology assessment model, political policy process model, and mixed approach of public policy by Hogwood and Gunn.
- Prescriptive models of public policy such as rational comprehensive model, incremental model, mixed scanning model, strategic planning model, Hogwood and Gunn model, and normative-optimum model of public policy.
- Policy cycle, policy implementation process, and various top-down and bottom-up models of implementation.
- Top-down models of implementation such as policy implementation relationship model, system building model, implementation game model, and policy implementation framework model.
- Bottom-up models of implementation such as street-level bureaucracy model and policy implementation structure model.
- Synthesis of top-down and bottom-up approach to implementation and its variant models such as Elmore's forward and backward mapping model, Matland's ambiguity and conflict model, Goggin's communication model, Thomas and Grindle's interactive model, and Sabatier and Mazmanian's advocacy coalition framework.
- First-, second-, and third-generation research into policy implementation.

- The process of policy monitoring; its various techniques such as business technique, systems technique, formative technique, performance management technique, and social systems accounting technique; limitations in policy monitoring; and steps to improve monitoring.
- Meaning of policy evaluation and its procedure.
- Effectiveness models of policy evaluation including goal attainment model and side-effects model.
- Professional models of policy evaluation including client-oriented evaluation, stakeholder-oriented evaluation, and peer review evaluation.
- Economic models of evaluation including productivity model and efficiency model.
- Policy evaluation framework in India including policy evaluation by the Planning Commission, performance management and evaluation system (PMES), independent evaluation office (IEO), and development monitoring and evaluation office (DMEO).
- Various emerging tools and methods of policy analysis.

Similar to public administration, public policy is a governmental function as well as an academic discipline. As a governmental function, it is defined as a course of action adopted and pursued by the government. As an academic discipline, it is a subject to study the policy cycle right from policy conceptualisation, planning, and implementation to monitoring, evaluation, and review. The subject gained momentum in the 1950s. As a discipline, it gains subject matter from other disciplines such as political science, public administration, economics, management, and science and technology. Thus, public policy is an interdisciplinary subject.

As a governmental function, public policy is a frequently used term in our daily lives, when we refer to the national health policy, education policy, wage policy, farmers policy, water policy, and so on. A public policy can take the following forms:

- A declaration of goals
- A declaration of course of action
- A declaration of general purpose
- An authoritative decision

Apart from the general understanding of public policy discussed, different scholars have provided different definitions for public policy. Some of them are as follows:

Y. Dror: "Public policies are general directives on the main lines of action to be followed."[1]

Peter Self: "Public policies are changing directives as to how tasks should be interpreted and performed."

Geoffrey Vickers: "Public policies are decisions giving direction, coherence, and continuity to the course of action for which the decision-making body is responsible."[2]

Carl Friedrich: "A public policy is a proposed course of action of a person, a group, or government within a given environment providing obstacles and opportunities which the policy was proposed to utilise and overcome in an effort to reach a goal or realise an objective or purpose."[3]

James Anderson: "A public policy is a purposive course of action followed by an actor in dealing with a problem or a matter of concern."[4]

David Easton: "Public policies are the authoritative allocation of values for the whole society. Public policies are formulated by elders, paramount chiefs, executives, legislators, judges, administrators, councillors, monarchs, and the like. These are the people who engage in the daily affairs of a political system and are recognised by most members of the system as having responsibility for those matters and take actions that are accepted as binding most of the time by most of the members so long as they act within the limits of their roles."[5]

Thomas Dye: "Public policy is whatever governments choose to do or not to do."[6]

Robert Lineberry: "Public policy is what governments do and fail to do for their citizens."[7]

Political Science, Public Administration, and Public Policy

There are two approaches to public policy— political science and of public administration. The political science approach to public policy is substantive, descriptive, and objective. It is also known as the *incrementalist approach* (which will be discussed later) and relates to the study of how government policies are formulated and implemented. It is dominated by researchers and students of political science. The focus is less on policies and more on the institutions in which the policies are formulated. The linkages between important institutional structures and the public policy context are largely unexplored in this field.[6]

On the other hand, the public administration approach to public policy is theoretical, effectual, prescriptive, and normative. It is also known as the *rationalist approach* to public policy and it relates to the application of available knowledge to governmental policies for the purpose of improving their formulation and implementation.

However, at the present time, independent research has started in the field of public policy. There is no need to be dependent on scholars of political science and public administration for the effective study of public policy. The modern schools of public policy mix both these approaches of public policy.

Mega Policy

A mega policy consists of the general guidelines to be followed while formulating and framing policies in specific areas such as agriculture and science and technology. According to Y. Dror, "mega policies form a kind of master policy, as distinct from concrete discrete policies, and involve the establishment of overall goals to serve as guidelines for the larger sets of concrete and specific policies."[1]

Distinction between Policy and Decision

Policymaking is related to decision-making but is not the same as decision-making. Decision-making involves the identification of a problem, the identification of suitable rational alternatives to solve the problem, and then adopting an optimum alternative to solve the problem. The process of policymaking may consist of taking a number of such decisions on certain issues. Thus, policymaking consists of decision-making but all decisions are not policies or not part of a public policy.

Administrators take decisions in their day-to-day work on a number of matters. Among them, the decisions that are taken while formulating a public policy are regarded as policy decisions. Other decisions are regarded as routine decisions. According to Anderson, "Policy decisions are decisions made by public officials that authorise or give direction and content to public policy actions."[4]

Distinction between Policy and Goals

Polices can be distinguished from goals, as policies are the means to achieve the goals (the end purpose of the government). The goals are the objectives towards which governmental actions are directed. On the other hand, the public policy indicates the direction and manner in which the actions are to be performed to attain the goals.

Inputs, Outputs, and Outcomes of Public Policy

Three basic and important terms related to public policy are policy input, policy output, and policy outcome. *Policy inputs* are defined as the demands made on the political system by individuals or groups of individuals for action or inaction on certain problematic issues. For example, India Against Corruption movement (under Anna Hazare) in 2011 made aggressive demands (policy input) on the government to take measures against rising corruption in the country. Accordingly, the government passed the Lokpal and Lokayukta Act and took a number of policy decisions on curbing black money in India.

Policy outputs are the actual decisions taken by the government under a public policy. They are what the government actually does as distinguished from what it says it is going to do. For example, the number of schools built, the number of teachers recruited, and the number of food items increased in school meals are the actual outputs of an education policy.

Policy outcomes are the actual effect of public policy on the target groups or beneficiaries. For example, in the above case of education policy, the policy outcomes will be an increase in literacy rate, a decrease in the dropout rate, an improvement in learning outcomes of children, and so on.

12.1 Models of Public Policy

A model of public policy is a representation of a complex reality that has been oversimplified to describe and explain the relationships among different variables; it prescribes how policies should be made.[8] The models of public policy are of two types—descriptive and prescriptive. The descriptive models analyse the public policymaking process and the prescriptive model describes public policy options.[9] These two categories of public policy models are described in the subsequent topics.

12.1.1 Descriptive Models of Public Policy

The descriptive models of public policy analyse the public policy process in terms of who is involved and how and why are policies made.[8] The various descriptive models of public policy are the following:

(1) Functional process model
(2) Elite/mass model
(3) Group model
(4) Systems model
(5) Institutional model

(6) Neo-institutional model
(7) Organised anarchy model
(8) Public goods and services model
(9) Technology assessment model
(10) Political policy process model
(11) Mixed approach of public policy by Hogwood and Gunn

These models are described in the following sections.

12.1.1.1 Functional Process Model

The functional process model deals with the 'how' aspect of public policy. It suggests how public policy alternatives (or choices) are effectively generated through active grass-roots participation during the public policy process. An analysis of the functional activities required in policymaking involves a consideration of the following variables:[11]

- Alternative solutions
- Participants in policymaking and execution
- Adjudication measures to ensure adherence to the law
- Judgment pertaining to the success or failure of a specific policy
- Adaption of legislative measures for policy implementation

The model is a comparative and all-inclusive approach aimed at forging collaboration with the public policy process.

Advantages: This model has various advantages. It helps in enhancing public policy by consulting actors involved at the grass-roots level in the public policy process. Second, the model is suitable for a comparative study of policymaking. Third, the consideration of the functional activities can help in increasing rationality in the process of policymaking.

Disadvantages: The model tends to show that the process of public policymaking is nothing more than an intellectual activity. This is not true in real life.

Case Study 12.1 describes an example of the functional process model.

Case Study 12.1: Functional Process Model in American Heath Policy

The formulation of the American Healthcare Policy can be considered as an example of the functional process model. American Health Decisions is a developing social movement that aims to work at the grass-roots level to educate people about the issues and problems in healthcare and to promote public involvement in decision-making about health policy. The movement offers nurses the opportunities to expand their traditional commitment to involving people in decisions about their health. By promoting the development of the movement, nurses can contribute to the creation of a structured process of direct public participation in policy decisions related to healthcare.

12.1.1.2 Elite/Mass Model (Kings and Kingmakers Model)

The elite/mass model of public policy focuses on the 'who' aspect of public policy. It suggests that there is a policymaking elite group, whose members share common values and have more power than the masses. The elite govern the passive masses in an environment characterised by apathy and lack of information. The public policies are designed by the elite and implemented in a top-down manner (Fig. 12.1). The policies are aimed at preserving the status quo in the system.

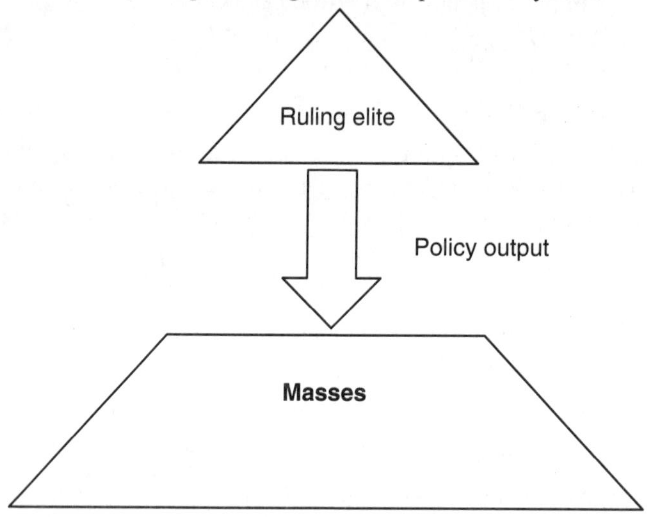

Fig. 12.1: Elite/mass model of public policy[8]

This model is valid in sectors where the policymaking process is influenced by the ruling intellectuals. Case Study 12.2 illustrates an example.

Case Study 12.2: Elite/Mass Model in Space Policy

As an example of the elite/mass model, the Space Policy of India is determined by the senior scientists of ISRO (Indian Space Research Organisation) and the political executives posted at the higher levels of the Ministry of Science and Technology. The masses have little say in determining the Space Policy of India. This is appropriate, as the subject of space is guided by the views of intellectuals and the masses have little understanding about the uses of space research.

Advantages: The advantage of this model is that it helps in identifying the contribution of specific groups involved in policy formulation and policy execution. It makes it possible to determine who is responsible for making policies and for whom. Moreover, such a model is beneficial in sectors where the common people have less knowledge about the subject matter of the policy.[12]

Disadvantage: The disadvantage of this model is that it advocates that society is divided into those who have power (elites) and those who are powerless and uninformed (masses). The model suggests a top-down model of policy implementation, which is considered less effective in social sectors such as urban and rural development.

12.1.1.3 Group Model of Public Policy

According to Nicholas Henry, the group model of public policy is based on the *hydraulic theory of politics*, in which the policy is conceived of being a system of forces and pressures pushing against one another in the formulation of public policy. The public policy is derived from interest groups who continuously interact with policymakers to influence the policymaking process.[9] Thus, public policy is a product of group struggle.

The group model suggests that the interaction and struggle among groups are the central facts of political life. An individual is significant only as a member of a political group. S/he seeks to secure her/his political preferences only through membership in a group.

A central concept of this model is access to policymaking institutions. Access may result from the groups being organised, their status, good leadership, or resources such as money. It suggests that some groups may have more access than others. Thus, public policy at any given time reflects the interests of those who are dominant (see Fig. 12.2). Case Study 12.3 illustrates an example of this model.

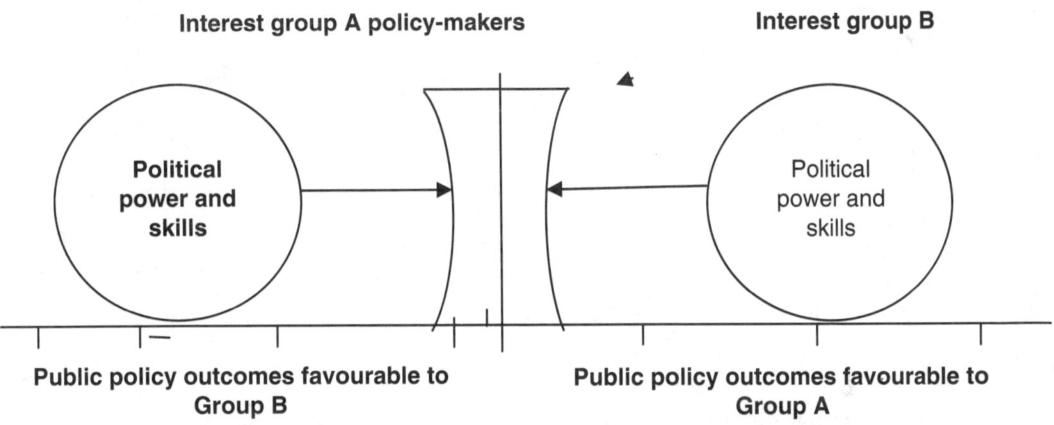

Fig. 12.2: Group model of public policy[13]

Case Study 12.3: Group Model in Struggle for Policy Favouring LGBT Community

There is a struggle between groups favouring the rights of the LGBT (lesbian, gay, bisexual, and transgender) community (such as Queer India Campaign and Gaysi and Gaylaxy) and those campaigning against providing equal rights to the LGBT community (right-wing groups). For a long time, the opposition groups were more active, which led to the suppression of equal rights to the LGBT community. However, since 2010, the groups favouring LGBT rights have gained dominance and pushed the government to secure their legal rights. As a result, in 2017, the Supreme Court of India declared that sexual orientation is an essential attribute of the privacy of an individual. Discrimination against an individual on the basis of sexual orientation is deeply offensive to the dignity and self-worth of the individual. Equality demands that the sexual orientation of each individual in the society must be protected on an even platform. The judgment essentially helped in ensuring that freedom of orientation is a fundamental right of each individual.

The group model of public policy has the following advantages and disadvantages:

Advantage: The advantage of the group model of the public policy lies in the identification of pressure groups and the acceptance that they do have the power to influence policy. As a result, they cannot be disregarded when a specific policy is being analysed.

Disadvantage: The model suggests that public policy is tilted towards the more influential groups of society. Following such a model can be against the interests of society, as, in actuality, many people (e.g., the poor and disadvantaged) and interests (such as natural beauty and social justice) are either not represented or are poorly represented in group struggle.

12.1.1.4 Systems Model of Public Policy

The systems model of public policy suggests how the political system responds to problems, needs, goals, wants, and demands of the society comprising both individuals and interest groups.[9] David Easton is regarded as the originator of this model. In the model, the policymaking process is regarded as the 'black box', which converts the demands of the society into policies. The systems approach is shown in Fig. 12.3.

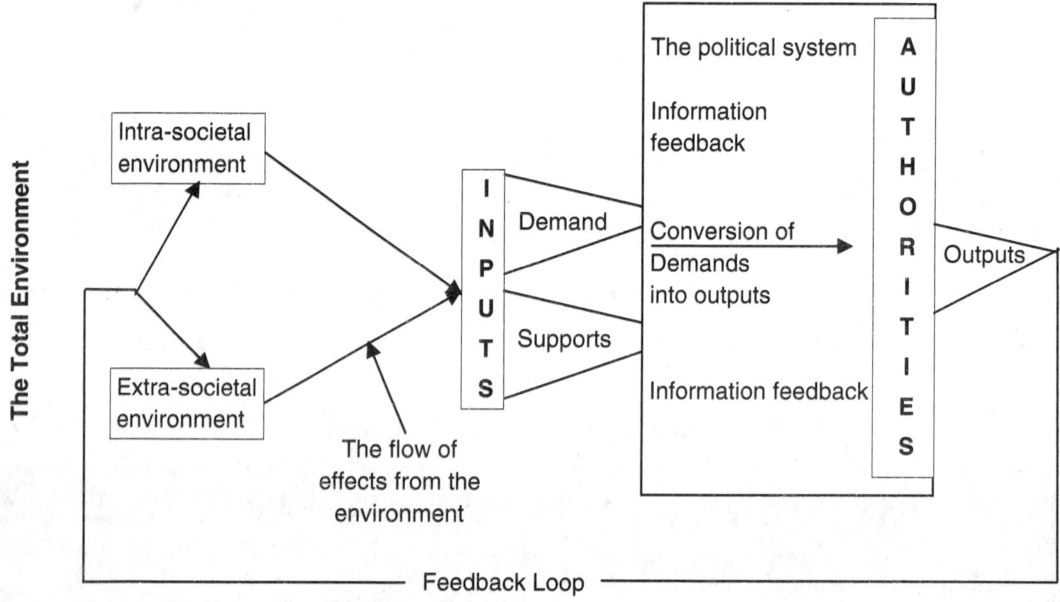

Figure 12.3: David Easton's systems model[14]

According to Easton's model,[14] a policy system has the following components:

(a) **Inputs:** Inputs are the physical, social, economic, and political conditions of the environment of an organisation or society. These inputs are received into the political system in the form of demands on and supports for the political system. Here, *demands* are the claims made on the political system by individuals and groups to alter some aspects of the environment. These demands occur when individuals and groups pressurize the political system to make public policy as a response to certain environmental conditions.

On the other hand, the *support* to a political system consist of the rules, laws, and customs that provide a basis for the existence of a political community and political authorities. This support is seen when individuals and groups accept the decisions of the authorities and the law of the land. Such support is seen in the form of gestures such as citizens obeying laws and paying taxes.

(b) **Environment:** The environment surrounding a political system is defined as any condition or event external to the boundaries of the political system. Environmental conditions are the major source of inputs to a political system. According to Easton, there are two types of environments—intra-societal and extra-societal. The *intra-societal environment* consists of the social system, ecological system, personality system, and biological system. On the other hand, the *extra-societal system* consists of the international political system, international ecological systems, international social systems, and so on.

(c) **Political System:** The political system consists of the institutions and important personnel responsible for policymaking for the whole society. These institutions include the chief executive, legislatures, civil servants, and judges. This political system is responsible for translating inputs into outputs.

(d) **Outputs:** The outputs of a political system are the public policies prepared by it. Easton described this public policy as authoritative value allocation by the political system.

(e) **Feedback:** Feedback is the modifying impact created by the public policy (output) on the environment and the resultant change in the inputs to the political system. Thus, the feedback helps in changing the inputs and the functioning of the political system on the basis of the experience from the previous output (or public policy). Policy outputs may generate new demands and new support for the political system. Feedback also helps in generating a suitable environment for future public policy formulation.

An example of the functioning of the systems model is discussed in Case Study 12.4.

Case Study 12.4: Use of Systems Model for Analysing the Levee Effect on Brahmaputra River Floods[15]

Levees (embankments) are created on rivers to control floods and protect people and assets from river overflow. Now there arose a situation in which flood losses increased due to the Brahmaputra river, and people suffered social and economic losses. People also suffered from various diseases due to frequent floods. (This is the 'environment' surrounding the political system.)

Thus, there were 'demands' on the political system to take adequate policy decisions to avoid flood-related losses in the catchment area of the Brahmaputra river. The 'political system' (in this case, the state governments of the north-eastern states and the Central Government) decided to consider building levees on various points of the river. The 'support' to the political system is the community readiness to participate in flood-related disaster preparedness.

For a long time, levees have been built on flood-prone rivers and there are successful stories attached with them. Thus, there was successful 'feedback' from the implementation of previous policies of building levees. However, there was also some negative 'feedback' from this implementation. Levees, and other flood protection structures, may increase flood losses because they spur new developments in the floodplains, which causes catastrophic losses when flood protection fails. This is known as the levee effect. Empirical results from Upper Assam suggested that vulnerability to large floods increases when levees are constructed.

Another feedback to the political system was the increase/decrease in flood-related deaths after the construction of levees on rivers. The political system decided the future policy to protect floods based on the 'environment', 'inputs', and 'feedback' (essential ingredients of the systems model). As a result of the analysis in this case, it was decided that structural measures have little impact on preventing floods, and non-structural measures are also required to offset the negative consequences of levees. The non-structural measures included public awareness of not developing structures in the floodplains, training people to deal with floods, and so on.

The advantages and disadvantages of the systems model are as follows:

Advantages: The systems model allows effective debates, discussions, written proposals, counter proposals, and other methods to attain consensus on public policy. The final policy is effective, as it is made after reviewing previous implementation experience and feedback from it. The continuous feedback obtained while implementing the policy helps in the continuous improvement of the policy. This also helps in determining whether a specific policy has had the effect intended by the policymaker.

Disadvantages: The systems model has the following limitations:

- **Simplistic:** The input-output model is too simplistic an aid for understanding public policy.
- **Value-laden:** The policy outcome of the model is often loaded with and influenced by the values held by the policymakers and is not completely rational.
- **Not Holistic:** The systems model does not consider the role of important variables such as power, personnel, and institutions in policymaking.
- **Dominant Role played by Bureaucracy:** In a developing country like India, where the State's objectives are not fully articulated and clear, the bureaucracy can easily capitalise on the process of policy selection.

12.1.1.5 Institutional Model of Public Policy

The institutional model of the public policy highlights the integral role of the public sector and other institutions in the public policy process. The model is premised on the basis that public policy is the product of public institutions, whose structures are responsible for public policy implementation.[9]

In our society, the activities of individuals and groups are generally directed toward government institutions such as the legislature, executive, judiciary, and bureaucracy. The executive includes institutions such as the Prime Minister's Office, Cabinet Secretariat, Election Commission, Reserve Bank of India, and so on. Public policy is formulated, implemented, and enforced by these governmental institutions, either in coordination or individually. Each institution influences the public policy process. The government institutions accord three different characteristics to public policies, as follows:

- o Legal authority
- o Universal character (which is extended to all the citizens)
- o Coercive character

The institutional model suggests a close relationship between public policy and government institutions. Thus, research is based on the study of institutional structures in order to analyse public policies. An example of the influence of various institutions on public policy is described in Case Study 12.5.

Case Study 12.5: Institutional Approach in Case of Decision in River Water Disputes16

India is a federal democracy, where rivers cross state boundaries. Thus, developing an efficient and equitable mechanism for allocating river water flow is an important policy issue for India. Numerous interstate river disputes have erupted since independence, including the Cauvery water dispute and Krishna–Godavari water dispute.

There is a plethora of institutions involved in taking decisions over interstate river water disputes. The various interested actors include state governments (which in turn include professional politicians, political parties, and interest groups), the Indian Parliament, Central Government ministries, the courts, and ad hoc water tribunals. These institutions negotiate to reach an agreeable decision. However, sometimes the involvement of so many institutions create obstacles in reaching a final decision.

Apart from this, Article 262 of the Constitution explicitly grants the Parliament the right to legislate over matters of river water disputes. However, no river water managing body has yet been created by the Parliament with powers of management over river water disputes. Instead, river bodies with only advisory powers have been created by the Parliament.

In the present situation, decisions over interstate river water disputes are taken after long negotiations among the various institutions mentioned. Ad hoc river water tribunals pass final decisions, which are also sometimes not followed by the involved state governments. Sometimes the orders of the Supreme Court are also not followed by the state governments. A high-level coordination meeting under the Central Government is the required to be conducted to reach a final policy decision in the case of river water disputes.

Thus, river water disputes are a classic example in which various institutions are involved in reaching a final policy decision. If we want to reduce the delay due to the influence of the various institutions, a strong body should be created under Article 262 of the Constitution.

The advantages and disadvantages of the institutional approach to public policy are as follows:

Advantages:

(a) The institutional approach helps in structuring government institutions in a manner that will facilitate certain policy outcomes.

(b) The approach helps in examining policy issues in a systematic fashion, focusing on institutional arrangements.

(c) It helps in analysing the relationship between institutional arrangements and the content of public policy as well as in investigating these relationships in a comparative fashion.

(d) The model also helps in formulating uniform policies, across sectors and jurisdictions, which are made legitimate by the legislature.

Disadvantages: The criticism against the institutional approach is that it largely focuses on the description of governmental structures and institutions. The approach does not devote adequate attention to developing linkages between governmental structures and the content of the public policy.

12.1.1.6 Neo-Institutional Model of Public Policy

The neo-institutional model is an improvement over the institutional model. It tends to categorise public policies according to policymaking subsystems and predicts institutional behaviour accordingly. Theodore J. Lowi classified public policies into four policy issues/'arenas of power'. These policy issues/policy arenas help in predicting the behaviour of political institutions.[17] These policy arenas are as follows:

(a) **Redistributive Policy Arena:** Redistributive policy issues are concerned with changing the distribution of existing resources and bringing about basic socio-economic changes. The policies are highly ideological and involve a fight between the 'haves' and 'have-nots'. Such issues are secretive and have low partisan visibility.[18] An example of a redistributive policy is the income tax.

(b) **Distributive Policy Arena:** Distributive policy issues are those concerned with the distribution of new resources. They are meant for the benefit of a specific section of society. They can be concerned with the grant of subsidies, loans, provision of education, welfare, health, and so on.

(c) **Regulative Policy Arena:** Regulative policy issues are those concerned with the regulation and control of activities. They deal with issues such as regulation of trade, business, safety measures, and public utilities. They provide benefits to the people but also impose visible costs on them. For example, airport safety regulations may provide security benefits but also impose fine on the violators of the rules.

(d) **Constituent Policy Arena:** Constituent policy issues are those concerned with the setting up or reorganisation of institutions.

12.1.1.7 Organised Anarchy Model of Public Policy

The 'organised anarchy' model of public policy is based on the 'garbage can' theory of decision-making (discussed in Chapter 4). The model suggests that a policy is formulated in a 'window of opportunity', where three streams—problem stream, policy stream, and political stream—come together at the same time. These three streams are described as follows:

(a) **Problem Stream:** Problems are policy issues requiring attention. Problems get attention based on how they are 'framed' or defined by participants who compete for attention. In some cases, issues receive attention because of a crisis or change in the scale of a problem.

Once a problem is identified, it requires either the application of a new policy for resolution or letting the problem fade from sight. This stream consists of the following phases:

- **Getting Attention**: Attention to problems is sought in the form of setting up study groups, budgetary allocations, and so on.
- **Definition of Problem:** The problem is defined according to the values, issues involved, and comparison with other issues.
- **Fading of Problem**

(b) **Policy Stream:** A policy is a solution to a problem receiving attention as well as a future anticipated problem. Viable policy solutions are attained through a process that takes time to develop. Initially, the solution ideas are proposed by one actor; then reconsidered and modified by a large number of participants. As a result, widely accepted solutions are developed in the anticipation of future problems. This stream consists of the following phases:

- **Formulation of Decision Agenda**: In this stage, ideas are sought from the participants to reach solutions to the anticipated problems.
- **Softening Phase:** In the softening phase, various ideas are tried (*trial balloons* are released) and a variety of suggestions are made about how to resolve a particular issue.
- **Survival of Ideas:** Some ideas survive and some ideas are rejected as being infeasible.
- **Consensus Building:** Consensus is built on a few ideas.
- **Tilt Effect:** The tilt effect refers to a final solution being reached among the participants.

(c) **Political Stream:** In this stream, policymakers (or political executives) have the motive and opportunity to take policy decisions. They pay attention to the problem and are receptive to the proposed solutions. This stream consists of the following phases:

- **Formulation of Governmental Agenda:** A governmental agenda, i.e., a list of issues to be resolved, is formed based on the national mood, the role of pressure groups, and the role of important institutions.
- **Window of Opportunity:** A window is an opportunity to create a policy. This window is typically opened by a shift in the national mood. Opening the window requires the convergence of all three streams.
- **Consensus Building:** Consensus is built, by bargaining, among the governmental actors on a few policy alternatives.
- **Tilt Effect**: The final policy decision is taken by the government.

The organised anarchy model is different from the rational model of policy formulation, as it does not analyse all the possible alternatives. In the rational model, the policymakers identify problems, the bureaucrats perform a comprehensive analysis to produce solutions, and the policymakers select the best solution.

On the other hand, in the organised anarchy model, problems are ambiguous, and bureaucrats struggle to research issues and produce viable solutions. In this model, sometimes readymade solutions are available, but there is no problem to apply them to. Sometimes there are problems but no solutions. Still sometimes, there are problems and solutions, but policymakers do not have a consensus over a policy solution. A policy is successfully formed only when the problem, solution, and policy consensus are reached at the same time. A description of the organised anarchy model is shown in Fig. 12.4.

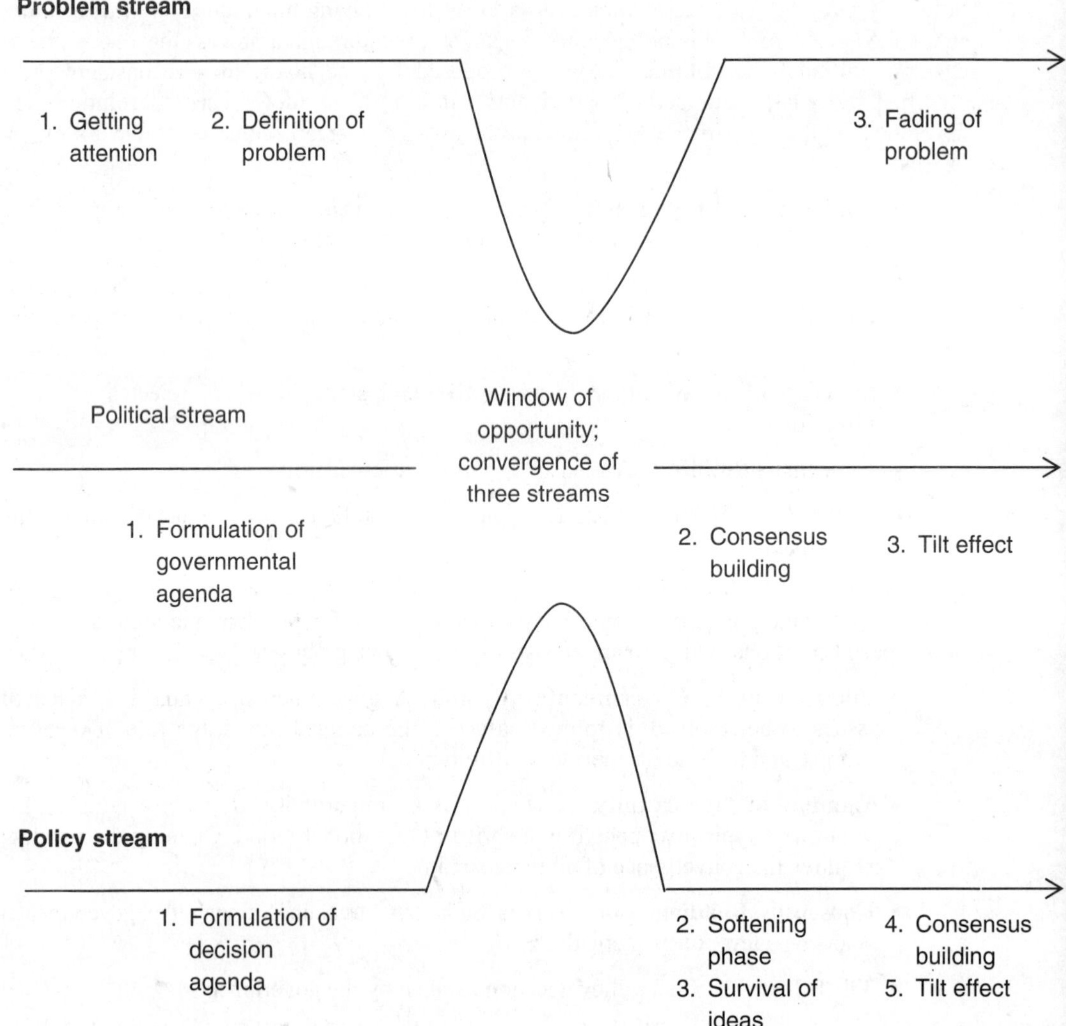

Figure 12.4: The organised anarchy model of public policy[19]

A practical understanding of the organised anarchy model can be attained by reading Case Study 12.6.

Case Study 12.6: Organised Anarchy Approach in Case of US Public Policymaking[19]

Kingdom19 showed the presence of organised anarchy in American policies during 1976–1980 under the presidency of Jimmy Carter. According to him, policy proposals are not necessarily written in response to a particular event. Rather, at any given time, there exists a multitude of proposals ready to go and waiting for the best opportunity for their introduction. An idea's time comes via the process of organised anarchy.

In the US, the policy participants are the Congress, the President, civil servants, interest groups, academics and researchers, media, and voters/citizens. While explaining the policies made during 1976–1980, Kingdom said that action was taken before identifying problem preferences. There was disagreement between participants on national problems and priorities.

Second, there was no clear strategy to solve national problems. For example, in the case of education, there was no clearly defined way to eliminate the learning gap and adult illiteracy. Third, there was 'fluid participation' and a good deal of turnover in personnel. Moreover, the importance of participants did not match their job description. Participants outside the government entered and exited the decision-making process all the time, and the access given to them varied. Thus, the situation in the US Federal Government was one of organised anarchy.

Kingdom had conceptualised the problem, policy, and political streams in the case of the US government. Problems flowed in and out of focus in the news and during legislative debates. Policies were generated and kept in abeyance for years. The opportunities for decisions arose at different times, when the three streams converged.

The three streams were independent. Policy solutions were developed whether or not they responded to an actual problem. The political stream was not necessarily dependent on the identified problems. The three streams converged only when a policy opened. That is, only when the conditions were right would an issue find itself on a policy agenda.

12.1.1.8 Public Goods and Services Model

The public goods and services model deals with those goods and services for which public policy is necessary to be formulated. Public goods and services are those that are most efficiently delivered by the government. They have two characteristics: non-rival competition and non-exclusion. The description of public goods and services can be found in Chapter 1.

12.1.1.9 Technology Assessment Model

The technology assessment model is useful in studying the current and future impacts of new technical and scientific innovations on society. According to Joe Coates,[20] technology assessment is a class of policy studies that systematically examines the effects on society that may occur when a technology is introduced, extended, or modified. It emphasises those consequences that are unintended, indirect, or delayed.

The model is used for assessing the impact of technology on society. A study of the impact of technology helps in understanding the complex and technical issues affecting society. For example, television was a technological innovation that had the intended effects of entertainment and education. However, it also had unintended effects on society such as an increase in sedentary lifestyle, reduced involvement in community programmes, less interaction with neighbours, and isolation.

The aim of technology assessment is to identify the probable major concerns (and benefits) to alert technology developers to potential issues and help them in taking mitigation measures. It also helps the government in taking important policy steps to avoid the unintended consequences of technology.

12.1.1.10 Political Policy Process Model

Lawrence Lynn and Peter de Leon are the founders of the political policy process approach.[38] It describes public policymaking as a political process and not a technical process. The difference between the two processes is that technical policy analysis chooses the best or satisfactory alternative from a set of alternatives. On the other hand, political public policy sees information in an advocacy role, that is, information is supplied from many perspectives into the political process.

According to Lynn, public policy can be characterised as the output of the diffuse made up of individuals who interact with each other in a small group in a framework dominated by formal organisations. Those organisations function in a system of political institutions, rules, and practices, all subject to societal and cultural influences. To understand public policy, it is necessary to understand the behaviour of interactions among these structures: individuals holding particular positions, groups, organisations, the political system, and the wider society of which they are all a part.

The managers of public policy (policymaking executives) pursue their policy goals within the following three kinds of limits:

(a) Limits imposed by the external environment

(b) Limits imposed by the organisation

(c) Limits imposed by their own personalities and cognitive styles[39]

These managers of public policy do the following tasks while formulating public policies:

(a) Establish *understandable premises* for their organisation's objectives.

(b) Attain an intellectual grasp of *strategically important issues*, and identify and focus attention on those activities that give meaning to the organisation's employees.

(c) Remain alert to and *exploit all opportunities*, whether deliberately created or fortuitous, to further their purposes.

(d) Consciously employ the strong features of their personalities as instruments of *leadership and influence.*

(e) Manage, within the framework of the economy, personal resources to govern how much they attempt to accomplish and how they go about it.

12.1.1.11 Mixed Approach of Public Policy by Hogwood and Gunn

The mixed approach of public policy, advocated by Hogwood and Gunn, considers two aspects of public policy together—the application of technical analysis and the political process associated with public policy.[40] The approach is both a descriptive as well as a prescriptive approach of policy analysis. Hogwood and Gunn set out a nine-step approach to the policy process, which they say is mixed. The nine steps are as follows:

1. ***Deciding to Decide***: This step consists of searching for issues and setting the agenda.
2. ***Deciding how to Decide:*** This step ponders upon how the plan of action is to be determined. For example, should the issue be left to political mechanisms and normal administrative processes for resolution or is there a need for fundamental analysis to understand the issue?
3. ***Issue Definition***: Issue definition is the process by which an issue (which could be a problem, opportunity, or trend) on the public policy agenda is perceived, explored, articulated, and defined in terms of causes, components, and consequences by interested parties.[40]
4. ***Forecasting and Projecting Outcomes:*** Forecasting attempts to quantify some of the more important variables that will affect an issue and its suggested resolution by making implicit and explicit assumptions that will guide better decision-making.
5. ***Setting objectives and priorities:*** Objectives and priorities are set after the forecasting stage.
6. ***Policy option analysis and selection***: Several possible routes are analysed for achieving the set of objectives.
7. ***Policy implementation, monitoring and control***: These topics will be discussed later in chapter.
8. ***Policy evaluation and review***: These topics will be discussed later in chapter.
9. ***Policy maintenance and succession***: These topics will be discussed later in chapter.

This model has its roots in the rational model, but it also deals with the political aspects of the policy process.

12.1.2 Prescriptive Models of Public Policy

The prescriptive models of public policy help in taking important decisions in public policy after determining the impact of public policy and eliminating the negative consequences before, during, and after policy implementation. These models help guide policymakers while designing public policies. These models focus on the analysis of policy approaches for determining the most appropriate policy options.[8] The following prescriptive models will be described in the subsequent sections:

(a) Rational comprehensive model of public policy

(b) Incremental model of public policy

(c) Mixed scanning model of public policy

(d) Strategic planning model of public policy
(e) Hogwood and Gunn model of public policy
(f) Normative-optimum model of public policy

12.1.2.1 Rational Comprehensive Model of Public Policy

The rational comprehensive model helps in deciding public policies from a full range of options. The choice from among the various options is made on rational grounds. According to Robert Haveman, the rational policy maximises the net value achievement in a policy.[21]

The biggest question is how to make a rational choice among the various alternatives. According to Thomas Dye, the various alternatives are compared on the basis of the ratio between the value achieved and the value sacrificed. The alternative with the highest positive value of this ratio is considered the best alternative. The value in this ratio is the social, political, and economic value achieved/sacrificed by a public policy.

The process of rational policymaking consists of the following steps:

(a) Identification and determination of goals
(b) Ranking of goals in the order of importance
(c) Identification of possible policy alternatives for achieving these goals
(d) Comparing the ratio of values achieved/values sacrificed of all the alternatives or performing the cost-benefit analysis for all the alternatives.

According to Nicholas Henry, while comparing the various alternatives, the policymaker has to consider the following aspects of the various alternatives:

(a) **Optimality:** The optimality of each alternative is measured by the 'pareto optimality' or 'pareto improvement' (these terms are discussed in Chapter 1) of each alternative. It suggests the change brought out by an alternative in which one or more members of the society are made better off without making any one worse off.

(b) **Trade-off:** Trade-off is defined as the exchange/loss of one value for the attainment of another value.

(c) **Externalities:** Externalities are the unintended consequences caused on a third party by a policy alternative. The concept of externality has been discussed in Chapter 1.

After selecting a policy alternative, it is very important to monitor its implementation to find out the accuracy of expectations and estimates. If the implementation is not as expected, the policy choices can be modified. Such modification is made by using the feedback.

The advantages and disadvantages of the rational model of public policy are as follows:

Advantages: The rational model provides the most rational and best policy solution. Although rationality is difficult to attain, the whole exercise leads to an efficient public policy. According to Lineberry,[22] "as democracy is the measuring rod of virtue in a political system, so too is rationality the yardstick of wisdom in policymaking."

Disadvantages: In the rational model, it is very difficult to identify all the alternatives on the basis of rationality. Moreover, there is no consensus on community values. It is almost impossible to formulate an extensive range of alternatives to satisfy the needs or to calculate the results of each alternative. Further, the technical myopia attached with rational policymaking leads to distorted and wrong policies.

An example of the rational comprehensive model of public policy is described Case Study 12.7.

Case Study 12.7: Rational Comprehensive Policymaking in Stanford University Budget Process[23]

The rational approach for policymaking is applicable only in areas where decision alternatives are completely measurable, e.g., in the case of budgets. This case study is on the budget process of the University of Stanford from 1970 to 1979 and is concerned with the allocation of funds to 38 academic departments within the University.

The five steps used by the University in the budget process were as follows:

(a) **Values and Objectives:** There were two major objectives in the allocation of budget resources. The first was to achieve budget equilibrium in which the growth rates of the income and expense were in balance. The second was to allocate funds on the basis of well-defined academic criteria such as academic importance, student interest, possibility for excellence in the programme, and funding potential.

Alternatives: The University was required to simultaneously consider a wide array of spending alternatives every year. The alternatives were based on the 'equilibrium' objective and the 'academic criteria' objective. According to the 'equilibrium' objective, alternative were listed on the basis of future increase in project income and expenses. This was done on the basis of a computerised model known as the *long-range functional forecast model* (LRFF). The model extrapolated the budgets of the next five years. The assessment of the alternatives on the basis of the 'academic criteria' objective was constrained by the result of the LRFF model. Accordingly, the dean of each academic department communicated his/her alternatives (or requests) to the Vice Chancellor (VC) of the University. The VC made a list of all the alternatives received. These alternatives were then analysed on the basis of the LRFF model.

(b) **Consequences:** The next step was to consider the consequences of the array of available alternatives. One criterion for assessing the alternatives was that of financial equilibrium. Computer models were used to estimate how budget alternatives would alter the University's financial picture for 3, 5, 10, and 25 years. Apart from this, discussions and meetings were conducted to assess the financial aspects of each alternative. Another criterion for assessing the alternatives was the academic criterion. The alternatives for academic expenditure were presented to the VC by the Deans in letters setting forth compelling arguments in favour of funding each request (or alternative). Annual letters from the Deans from the preceding 7 years were considered.

(c) **Choice:** Finally, the choice of alternatives was made on the basis of two criteria—financial equilibrium and academic importance.

12.1.2.2 Incremental Model/Branch Model of Public Policy

Charles Lindblom introduced the incremental model of public policy, in his article the 'Science of Muddling Through', as an alternative to the difficult-to-implement rational model of public policy. According to Lindblom, various constraints come in the way of making a completely rational policy decision. As an alternative, the incremental approach of policymaking involves a process of continually building out from the current situation, step-by-step and in small increments.[24]

The following are the basic features of incremental decision-making:

(a) The incremental decision is taken through a succession of incremental changes. Policymakers accept the legitimacy of the existing policies because of the uncertainty about the consequences of completely new policies.

(b) The process of decision-making involves mutual adjustment and negotiation. The achievement of agreement among the parties is the hallmark of a good decision.

(c) The approach involves the trial and error method for testing alternatives. Policymakers do not try to maximise all their values; rather, they try to satisfy certain important demands. It is similar to Herbert Simon's 'satisficing' model of decision-making.

(d) The search for a 'satisficing' alternative begins with options that are closer to the original policy, slowly diverting to newer alternatives.

Methods to Improve Incrementalism

One of the arguments supporting the incremental approach is that it allows mutual adjustment and negotiation. However, Etzioni criticises this pluralist decision-making as biased because of the pre-existing inequities in the power of the participating interests and individuals. Not all participants in the incrementalist approach are equal; the power of some is considerably more than others. Businessess and large corporations occupy a predominant position in the policymaking process.

Lindblom recognised the power equity in pluralist decision-making under the incrementalist approach. Thus, he advocated for *analytical incrementalism*[25] as a method for securing the balance of power in the process of pluralist policymaking under the incrementalist approach. He suggested three major forms of incrementalism:

(a) **Simple Incremental Analysis:** In simple incremental analysis, only those alternatives that are marginally different from the existing policy are considered.

(b) **Strategic Incremental Analysis:** In strategic incremental analysis, the policymakers use certain methods, such as trial and error learning, systems analysis, operations research, management by objectives, and programme evaluation and review techniques, to analyse the various policy alternatives that emerge by making certain modifications to the existing public policy.

(c) **Disjointed Incremental Analysis:** Lindblom suggested disjointed and incremental experimentation on the margins of the existing policy. Here, 'disjointed' means non-connected. Thus, 'disjointed incrementalism' means incremental steps that are not connected to each other. Moreover, it refers to various incrementalist decisions that are less subject to some kind of control or coordination.[26]

In disjointed incrementalism, public policy is shaped by a fragmented decision-making process, where numerous smaller decisions add up to the final policy. Each decision is taken in response to specific demands and pressures. These small decisions are either incrementalist, rationalist, or based on trial or error. Then each decision is joined by the process of partisan mutual adjustment.

Partisan Mutual Adjustment

Lindblom said that decision-making involves adjustment and compromise between disjointed decisions. Such adjustment leads to agreement and coordination. Such partisan mutual adjustment is the democratic and practical alternative to centralised hierarchical control.[27] Such mutual adjustment takes place between various participants such as bureaucrats, political executives, and interest groups.[28]

Advantages and Disadvantages

The advantages and disadvantages of the incremental approach are as follows:

Advantages:

1. The incremental model of public policy has greatly helped in exploring the constraints that shape the decision-making process in modern policies.
2. The incremental approach has a low conflict potential, a relatively expeditious adaptation to changing circumstances, and flexibility. In the model, it is quite possible to make adaptations and then return to the initial policy at a later stage.

Disadvantages:

1. The incremental model accepts that the existing policy is satisfactory without analysing the policy and all its ramifications in totality. Y. Dror recognises the incremental model as conservative; suitable in situations where policy is deemed to be working or is satisfactory, where problems are quite stable over time, and where there are ample resources available.
2. In the incremental approach, it is difficult to specify what an increment actually is. The model seems to be too crude in the complex environment of public policy.

An example of the rational comprehensive model of public policy is described in Case Study 12.8.

Case Study 12.8: A Case of Disjointed Incremental Policymaking in the Protracted/ Controversial War of US-NATO Forces in Afghanistan[29]

After the 9/11 attacks on the World Trade Centre in 2001, the US military planned for a quick engagement in Afghanistan. The mission planned at that time was a small one with only 10,000 troops, in which minor support of NATO was sought. The NATO, which was earlier not interested in an out-of-area conflict, gave its consent because of the short nature of the mission.

However, in 2014 the mission expanded to a protracted and controversial war in Afghanistan, which was never expected by the NATO and US. The growth of the mission to such a deep level was a result of the piecemeal decision-making process (disjointed decision-making), self-perpetuating dynamics (incremental decision-making), and steady goal expansion.

The initial short engagement policy was based on the following two objectives:

1. *War on Terror*: The short engagement was decided upon to eliminate terrorists from Afghanistan.

2. *Liberal Internationalism*: Liberal internationalism was a support for peace building and post-conflict economic recovery in Afghanistan.

Now let us see how a number of 'disjointed' decisions incrementally expanded the earlier policy of short engagement based on the above-mentioned two objectives. The following disjointed decisions were taken to expand the engagement:

(i) The invasion of Iraq in 2003 enhanced the demands for increase in NATO troops in Afghanistan. Thus, the International Security Assistance Force (ISAF) was enlarged in 2003 to accommodate more NATO troops.

(ii) There was an array of aid agencies, NGOs, and human rights activists, along with the UN Mission, that created the pressure to decide to increase ISAF presence in Afghanistan. Thus, it was decided to expand ISAF presence beyond Kabul in order to improve security and facilitate relief and reconstruction.

(iii) In 2003, it was also decided that NATO would take over the command of ISAF because of its strong command structure.

(iv) Then, another decision (again disjointed but incremental) was taken by the then NATO General to geographically expand NATO's presence to the entire Afghanistan, with a regional command structure and timetable. By the end of 2006, NATO's command structure extended to the entire country. As a result, by 2010, 47 countries had sent troops to Afghanistan, serving under the ISAF flag.

(v) After this, another resolution added quality to the mission, in which the ISAF was tasked with providing security assistance for the performance of tasks in support of the Bonn Agreement. A few items under the Bonn Agreement were—to disarm all Afghan armed factions, programmes to reconstitute the national armed forces and the police, and other security sector reforms. The mandate was broad enough to include any activity to be done by the ISAF.

(vi) Another factor responsible for further expanding the mission was the slow progress in achieving desired results. It was felt that increase in troops and funding can help in attaining the desired results.

(vii) Another decision was taken to learn about unconventional operations from the Afghanistan war. Growing involvement in combat operations in Afghanistan gave the NATO operational experience in dealing with unconventional threats.

(viii) Moreover, another decision was taken to protect the military bases post removal of troops from Afghanistan in 2014. By 2011, the USA had developed a huge, modern base infrastructure in Afghanistan. Understanding the value of access to such bases in the new strategic picture in Southwest Asia, the US military negotiated with the Afghan government for a base presence after the scheduled end date of 2014.

Thus, we saw a displacement of goals due to the 'disjointed incremental' policy of the US and NATO in Afghanistan. A search for foreign bases was certainly not the reason for the US invasion in 2001. The deepening military commitment appeared to be less the product of a deliberate strategy than the result of 'disjointed incrementalism', where the sub-rationalities of organised interests, vested interests, and rhetoric traps were prominent.

12.1.2.3 Mixed Scanning Model of Public Policy

The mixed scanning model integrates the good characteristics of the rational comprehensive model with those of the incremental model. The approach is devised to address the inherent inadequacies of both the rational and incremental policymaking models.

It provides for rational decision-making and policymaking processes to establish the basic policy goals and directions. Administrators are then required to apply incremental processes to choose and effectively carry out decisions. The mixed scanning approach allows for the rational or incremental approach, depending upon the situation. A very well explained example of the mixed scanning approach, in the case of a weather observatory, is provided in Chapter 4.

Public administrators can use the mixed scanning policymaking approach to superficially scan the whole organisation. Due to this superficial scanning, problem areas are identified and fresh rational policies are formulated in those problematic areas. In the rest of the areas, incremental policies are formulated.

More can be understood about incremental policymaking from Case Study 12.9.

Case Study 12.9: Mixed Scanning Approach in the Game of Chess[30, 31]

In a game of chess, a chess player is unable to review all the options (i.e., rational approach is not possible). Moreover, it is not good to merely think one or two steps ahead (i.e., taking an incremental approach will not lead to an efficient decision). Thus, a chess player first decides on his/her fundamental approach (e.g., ready to attack, need to develop further forces, or attack on the queen or attack on the king) and then examines only the options within the chosen approach in detail. In effect, this form of scanning takes place at two levels, i.e., choosing a major strategy or sub-strategy and then examining in detail some options within that major strategy/sub-strategy.

The advantages and disadvantages of the mixed scanning model are as follows:

Advantages: In the mixed scanning model, an overall picture is obtained before concentrating on any deviation with a view to adaptation. Thus, the model is beneficial in formulating a comprehensive policy with limited resources of time and manpower.

Disadvantages: The model makes a superficial scanning of the total policy before concentrating on problematic areas. Such superficial analysis may lead to missing out on important problematic (but less glaring) areas requiring a fresh policy perspective.

12.1.2.4 Strategic Planning Model of Public Policy

In the government sector, it is important to make coherent public policies. Thus, it is important to coordinate the decision-making process of various governmental departments. Such coordination is attained via the mechanism of strategic planning.

Such coordination is required within executive public institutions on one hand, and between public institutions and interest groups on the other. From a historical perspective, the strategic approach originated in the military domain. It is an attempt to systemise the chaotic process of decision-making in administration.[32]

According to Dean Acheason, strategic planning is to "look forward, not to a too distant future, but beyond the decision-makers vision caught in the current crisis battles; far enough to see those things in progress and to highlight what should be done to materialise or predict."[33] It helps policymakers in discerning what to do, how to do, and why to do it.

It is also considered as a management tool consisting of planning the following activities: institutional mandate, institutional values, analysis of the internal and external environment, medium-term priorities, and the key activities to achieve them. From an institutional perspective, strategic planning is understood as a process that describes the general direction of an institution in the future. The Five-Year Plan prepared by the Planning Commission is an example of strategic planning. The policies of individual ministries are formulated under these Plans. These strategic plans include the priorities for a period of time (generally 1–5 years) and the foundations of human resource and financial allocations for that period.

The strategic plan aims at the following things in an organisation:

(a) Improvement in performance
(b) Creation of a more relevant institutional structure
(c) Enhancement of institutional, departmental, and individual responsibility
(d) Improvement of transparency and communication between management, employees, and stakeholders
(e) Establishing priorities for allocating resources efficiently and effectively[34]

The strategic planning model has the following advantages and disadvantages:

Advantages:

1. The model helps in improving public sector performance, sharpens the focus on the organisations' goals, and improves the chances of effective implementation. Quantified strategic priorities lead to better organisational outcomes.[35]
2. It also helps in clarifying organisational priorities and the direction in which management is required.[36]

Disadvantages:

Strategic planning is less effective in public sector organisations as public agencies' missions are characterised by vagueness and the agencies are wide open to environmental constraints, time constraints, and unexpected aberrations such as elections that can rush or delay strategic decisions.[37]

12.1.2.5 Normative-optimum Model of Public Policy

Yehezkel Dror founded the normative-optimum model of public policy. He advocated this model based on the weaknesses he found in both the incremental and rational models of public policy. The model has the following characteristics:

(a) It accepts the need for rationality.

(b) It applies management techniques for enhancing the rationality of decision-making at low levels.
(c) It applies the *policy science* approach for dealing with complex problems requiring decisions at higher levels.
(d) It accepts the need to take into account of values and irrational elements in decision-making.

Policy Science

Policy science is a systematic and scientific study of public policy. Laswell has extensively described policy science. His vision of policy science is multidisciplinary, contextual, problem-oriented, and explicitly normative.

Laswell identified two separate approaches to policy science. One emphasises knowledge of policy and the other emphasises knowledge for use in the policy process. According to Dror, policy science encourages alternative features in policies such as values, judgment, and 'organised creativity'.

The model integrates and supplements the strengths of the various models of public policy, at the same time avoiding their weaknesses. The model is termed *normative-optimum* as it combines the core elements of the rational model (such as the measurement of costs and benefits) with 'extra-rational' features that are not a part of the pure rational model. The rational part of the model deals with gathering information on the feasibility and opportunity costs of the model. The extra-rational part of the model deals with value judgement and bargaining among policymakers. The model is destined to fit reality and at the same time directed to improve reality.

Rationality and Extra-rationality[43]

Dror described pure rationality in a manner similar to what Simon had done (discussed in Chapters 3 and 4). He further described four variants of pure rationality as follows:

(a) **Economically Rational Model:** The economically rational model is similar to the pure rational model but deviates from it in the sense that it accepts the restraints that limited resources put on the attempt to achieve pure rationality.

(b) **Sequential-Decision Rationality Model:** Sequential decisions are those in which the result of one decision affects the alternatives for the subsequent decision.

(c) **Incremental-change Model:** The incremental-change model deviates from pure rationality on the grounds that innovative policies are necessarily risky and unpredictable, and that the unexpected results of such policies will likely be very costly.

(d) **Satisfying Model:** The satisfying model deviates from pure rationality on the grounds that, for social-psychological reasons, policymakers do not look for new alternatives after they have found the one they consider satisfactory.

Extra-rationality: Dror described extra-rationality as subconscious intuition and judgment. The importance of extra-rationality in policymaking/decision-making is described in Case Study 12.10.

Case Study 12.10: Prisoner's Dilemma

The well-known example of 'prisoner's dilemma' shows the importance of extra-rationality in decision-making. Prisoners A and B have committed two crimes, bank robbery and car theft. They are picked up on suspicion but the police have no definite evidence of the bank holdup. The prisoners are interrogated separately—the crucial implication being that neither knows if the other has confessed. What each prisoner does know is the probable consequences of their joint responses: (1) if neither confesses, they get light sentences on a reduced charge (the car theft is the lighter sentence), (2) if both confess, they get medium sentences on the original charge (bank robbery), (3) if one confesses (i.e., turns state evidence), he gets off but the other gets convicted for both crimes. The following is an illustration of the dilemma:

(a) If both A and B keep quiet, then both will get one year punishment for car theft.

(b) If A keeps quiet and B confesses for bank robbery, then A gets three years' punishment and B gets no punishment.

(c) If B keeps quiet and A confesses for bank robbery, then B gets three years' punishment and A gets no punishment.

(d) If both A and B confess, then both will get two years' punishment for robbery.

The dilemma is that the assumed nature of competition inherent in rational choice (i.e., goal is to maximise personal gain) would make each prisoner, in isolation of the other, confess to robbing the bank. The assumed object of the game is to get more and avoid getting less than the other prisoner. By confessing, neither prisoner can do worse and may do better than the other. However, if both prisoners play an 'extra-rational hunch' and keep quiet, then they have cooperated (even if in isolation) and this maximisation of joint gains exceeds the individual reward/punishment calculation. This shows that better choice outcomes could be the result of subjective calculation, as opposed to the assumption of rational competitiveness.

The model is accustomed to deal with the complexities in real-life situations and it accounts for extra-rational factors. As it is required to deal with real situations, the model is very comprehensive, consisting of several stages.

The model has three broad stages, which are further divided into 18 stages. The three broad stages are meta-policymaking, policymaking, and post-policymaking. The three broad stages are as described in the following:[41]

I. **Meta-policymaking**: This stage requires the policymaker to consider the best approach in a given context. For example, it may be more appropriate to take an incremental approach or a rational approach on different occasions. Here the extra-rational dimension is important, as it allows for some intuitive processes, though they should be as informed and rational as possible.[42] This stage consists of the following substages:

(i) Processing values
(ii) Processing reality
(iii) Processing problems
(iv) Surveying, processing, and developing resources
(v) Designing, evaluating, and redesigning the policymaking system
(vi) Allocating problems, values, and resources
(vii) Determining the policymaking strategy

II. **Policymaking:** This stage consists of the following substages:
(i) Sub-allocating resources
(ii) Establishing operational goals, with some order of priority
(iii) Establishing a set of major alternative policies, including some 'good ones'
(iv) Preparing a set of major alternative policies, including some 'good ones'
(v) Preparing reliable predictions of the significant benefits and cost of the various alternatives
(vi) Comparing the predicted benefits and costs of the various alternatives and identifying the 'best' ones.
(vii) Evaluating the benefits and costs of the 'best' alternatives and deciding whether they are 'good' or not.

III. **Post-policymaking:** This stage consists of policy evaluation and feedback on the policy. It has the following substages:
(i) Motivating the execution of policy
(ii) Executing the policy
(iii) Evaluating policymaking after executing the policy
(iv) Communication and feedback channels interconnecting all phases.

The model has five major characteristics, as follows:

(a) It is qualitative, not quantitative.
(b) It has both rational and extra-rational components.
(c) It is basic rational to economically rational.
(d) It deals with meta-policymaking.
(e) It has a built-in feedback mechanism.

12.2 Policy Cycle

Policy cycle describes the various stages that a policy undergoes (Fig. 12.5). It is a continuous process. A policy does not come to an end once it is set out or approved. The figure shows that policy is an ever-continuing process. In the words of Anderson, "policy is made as it is administered and administered as it is made."

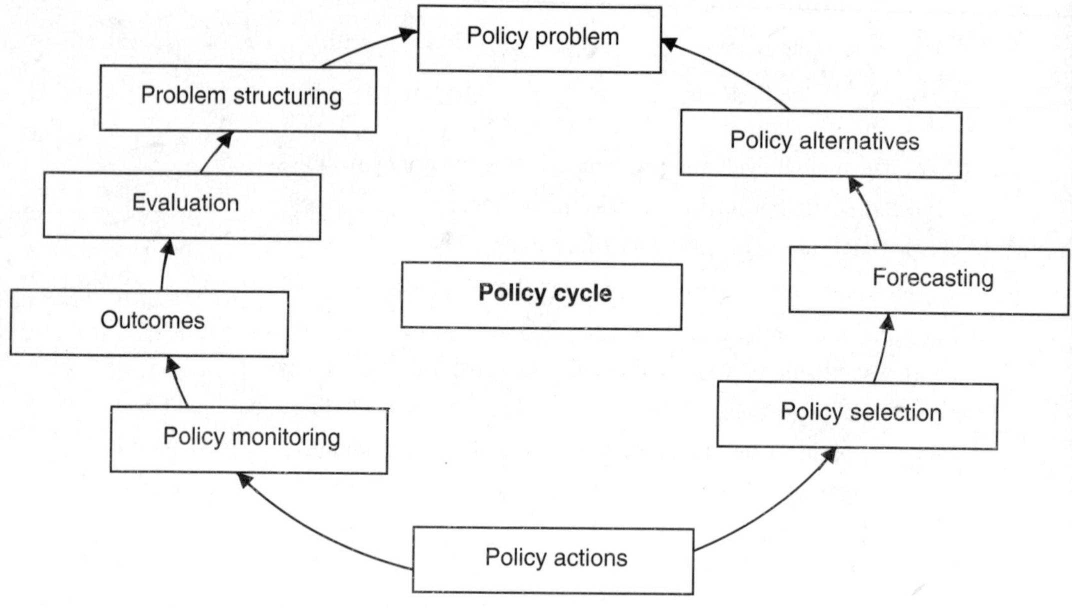

Figure 12.5: A schematic of policy cycle

12.3 Public Policy Implementation

Policy implementation is of vital importance to policymakers and the government. Implementation is defined as the realisation of the outputs of a public policy. It is also defined as "a process of interaction between the setting of goals and actions geared towards achieving them."[44] It is also considered as a conversion of physical, financial, and other resources into concrete service delivery outputs aimed at achieving public policy outcomes.[45]

For effective implementation, visionary management is required to accompany the process of public policy implementation.

12.3.1 Methods of Public Policy Implementation

There are many methods of implementing a public policy. Some of them are as follows:

(a) **Big Bang Method:** In the big bang (or sudden) method, there is a complete and sudden change from the old policy to a new policy. The method carries the risk of causing chaos within the system.

(b) **Parallel Method:** In the parallel method, the new policy is implemented while the old policy is still running. It allows the organisation to check whether or not the new policy is working satisfactorily.

(c) **Phased Implementation Method:** In this method, the policy is implemented in various stages to minimise the risks associated with the policy.

(d) **Pilot Method:** In this method, the policy is implemented on a small scale over a period of time. Implementation on a small scale allows one to determine the challenges associated with implementation and the consequent improvements required. Finally, the improved policy is implemented on the full scale.

12.3.2 Generations of Research on Public Policy Implementation

Research on public policy implementation has occurred over three generations, as described in the following:[46]

(a) **First Generation:** The first generation assumed that public policy implementation may happen automatically once a policy is formulated.

(b) **Second Generation:** Second-generation scholars said that policy implementation is a complex process that does not happen automatically. Thus, these scholars understood the implementation failures and devised various theories and models to improve the policy implementation process. These models will be discussed in the subsequent sections of this chapter.

(c) **Third Generation:** The third-generation scholars were less concerned with the implementation failures but focused on how implementation works and how its prospects can be improved.

12.3.3 Variables for Studying Public Policy Implementation

There are five critical variables for studying the process of public policy implementation. They are also known as the 5C's of public policy implementation. They are as follows:[46]

(a) **Content:** The content of public policy is an important variable to determine whether the policy will be implemented properly or not.

(b) **Context:** Every public policy is implemented under a certain social, political, economic, and legal context. While implementing a policy, it is important to focus on its context.

(c) **Commitment:** Commitment of the policy executors is of vital importance to policy implementation. This commitment is important not only at the street level but also at all levels through which the policy passes.

(d) **Capacity:** Capacity refers to the structural, functional, and cultural ability of an organisation to implement public policy objectives. Local knowledge and expertise are required to predict the difficulties to be encountered while implementing. This prediction helps in interpreting theoretical public policy into workable and predictable programmes.

(e) **Clients and Collaboration:** Collaborating with various interest groups, leaders, and other important parties during policy implementation helps in attaining efficiency, cost-effectiveness, and transparency in implementation. Collaboration provides a viable platform for sharing ideas and predicting feasible alternatives through which optimum results could be achieved.

12.3.4 Models of Public Policy Implementation

The various models for studying the process of public policy implementation can be divided into two types—top-down models and bottom-up models. The *top-down approach* is also known as *forward mapping* or *programmed approach*. This approach emphasises on the careful and explicit preprogramming of the implementation procedures by the policy designers.[49] It accepts the concept of politics-administration dichotomy by assuming that policy formation and implementation are discrete steps in the policy process; political executives determine policy and the administrators implement it. According to it, the ability of the policy to structure the implementation is the key to the success of the implementation. The model envisions a centrally controlled, hierarchical system of government, where the federal government maintains a high degree of control over the state and local government actions, whether it is through law or through the use of money to coerce state and local government action.[52]

On the other hand, the *bottom-up approach* says that implementation is effective when the policy is adapted based on the unfolding interaction of the policy with its institutional setting. It is also known as the *backward mapping* or *adaptive approach*. The approach views implementation as the result of a bargaining process rather than that of the control of the central policymakers.[50] They reject the concept of politics-administration dichotomy and argue that implementation is associated with politics. Policy is what is formulated during the implementation stage. Successful implementation happens when the implementers reach an agreement on the scope and substance of a policy or programme.[51] In the model, central control is decentralised to the state or local governments as a result of bargaining, conflict, and compromise.

12.3.5 Top-Down Models of Policy Implementation

The various models with top-down approach are described in the following sections.

12.3.5.1 Policy Implementation Relationship by Pressman and Wildavsky

Jeffrey Pressman and Aaron Wildavsky are considered the founding fathers of policy implementation studies. According to them, successful implementation depends upon the linkages between the different organisations and departments at the local level. For effective implementation, a top-down system of control and communication is required. The working of this model will become clearer from Case Study 12.11 on the implementation of the economic development programme in Oakland, California. The recommendations provided in this case study are the major strategies for successful implementation of the public policy provided by Pressman and Wildavsky.

Case Study 12.11: Learning from the Failures of EDA Project in California[47]

The main objective of the Economic Development Agency (EDA) project was to help stimulate the economy of devastated Oakland by creating public work projects that would create jobs for the unemployed African-American people. Initially, the EDA had four projects. However, other projects were added later during the planning and implementation process. Everything looked positive during the early years of the project. The formulation was proper, participants agreed on the overall goals and the employment plan was set in place. Financial allocations were also done in a proper manner.

However, the project started to fail when the EDA began to experience delays during the implementation process. Deals that had been made with outside companies were being compromised by new cost estimates. As the delays began to pile up, management changes were also happening. The head of the project resigned in 1966. As the management changed, the enthusiasm of the employees to continue the project deteriorated. The funding was diverted to partner agencies. Only few jobs were offered to the African-American community. Eventually, the project was declared a complete failure in the 1970s.

Case Study 12.2: Elite/Mass Model in Space Policy

In the analysis, it was found that there was a deficit of linkage between different organisations and departments at the local level. The reasons for the failure were described as follows:

(a) **Multiple Goals with Lack of Linkage:** While there was one goal—to reduce unemployment—the solution actually involved the implementation of two separate decision paths: (a) financing the construction of the public works project and (b) developing a hiring plan to ensure that the firms would actually involve the targeted workers.

(b) **Correlating the Number of Decisions to Programme Success:** Adding more decisions, without linkages, led to failure. As the number of decisions seeking approval for a programme to be implemented increases, the chance for overall programme success decreases drastically.

(c) **Decreasing Commitment of Participants:** As there were disagreements to come to a decision, the sense of commitment of the participants decreased. This led to delay in implementing the policy.

(d) **Bargaining:** There was growing bargaining among the partner agencies. Each agency wanted to implement a programme that was most favourable to it. This bargaining consumed time and resources, causing delays in implementation.

(e) **Separate Organisation:** A separate task force was created for the implementation of the EDA programme. This led to the creation of new guidelines, hiring of new people, establishment of new conduct rules, and so on.

Thus, the project failed, and the following improvements were suggested for the successful implementation of a public policy:

(a) Implementation should not be divorced from policymaking and should not be considered as a process that is independent from the process of policy design.

(b) The policymakers must consider direct means for implementing a policy. In the EDA project, implementation was intended to be done by intermediaries, and the multiplicity of decision points and clearances resulted in a complexity of 'joint actions' that paralysed the implementation process.

(c) The theory underlying a decision must be clear to the policymakers. In the EDA, there were many deficiencies at the concept stage itself.

(d) It is important to maintain continuity of leadership for successful implementation.

(e) A policy must be designed as simple as possible.

12.3.5.2 System Building Approach for Policy Implementation by Donald Van Meter and Carl Van Horn

The contribution of American scholars Donald Van Meter and Carl Van Horn consists in moving forward from the more general approach of Pressman and Wildavsky to offer a model for the analysis of the policy implementation process.

Their approach starts with the consideration of the need to classify policies in terms of difficulties faced during the implementation stage. They said that implementation is most successful only when the goal consensus is high and there is a marginal change in policy. In their model, they have suggested six independent variables that are dynamically linked to the performance of a public policy. They are as described below:

(a) **Policy Objectives:** Policy objectives are the overall goals of a public policy that help in assessing the performance of a policy.

(b) **Resources Available:** The human and physical resources available, along with timely incentives, decide the performance of a policy.

(c) **Inter-organisational Relationship:** The quality of relationships among the different organisations responsible for policy implementation determines the overall quality of implementation of a public policy.

(d) **Quality of Implementation Agencies:** The quality of implementation agencies, including control of employees and linkage with the policymaking body, determines the quality of policy implementation.

(e) **Environment:** The economic, social, and political environment of the implementation agencies determines the extent of policy implementation.

(f) **Disposition of Implementers:** The disposition of implementers, including their cognition of the policy, and the direction and intensity of their response determine the quality of implementation of a policy.

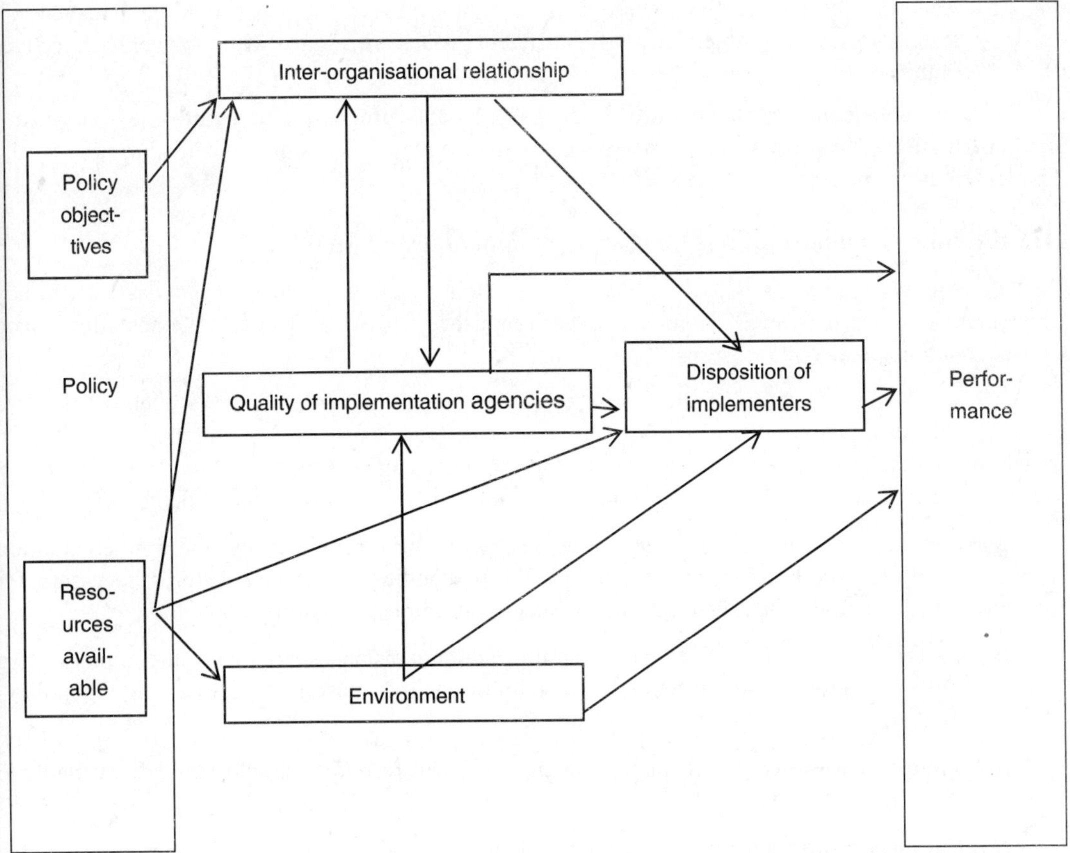

Figure 12.6: Schematic representing the implementation process in the system building model[48]

The process of policy implementation is made clear in Fig. 12.6. The process is presented as going through a series of stages with the arrows pointing forward or sideways and not back to the policy. Accordingly, Van Meter and Van Horn said that the study of implementation should be conducted longitudinally. Thus, the model is a top-down approach to policy implementation.

12.3.5.3 Implementation of Game Model by Eugene Bardach

Eugene Bardach, in his book *The Implementation Game*, suggested that the implementation process consists of 'political games'. According to him, implementation is a game of bargaining, persuasion, and manoeuvring under conditions of uncertainty. The various groups and individuals involved in implementation seek to maximise their power and influence during the implementation process. Thus, policy implementation is a game in which implementers seek to win as much control as possible and achieve their sub-objectives.

Bardach gave two recommendations for better implementation:

(a) Taking care of the *scenario-writing* process so as to structure the implementation games.

(b) Attention needs to be given while *fixing* the games, i.e., the games should be managed in a manner that the sub-objectives of the different groups are aligned with the overall objectives of the policy.

Bardach considers implementation as a political process and that the successful implementation from a top-down perspective must involve a complete full-through of the implementation process.

12.3.5.4 Policy Implementation Framework by Hogwood and Gunn

In their book *Policy Analysis for the Real World*, Hogwood and Gunn have advocated a policy implementation framework. They have distinguished between 'non-implementation' and 'unsuccessful implementation'.

Non-Implementation refers to the fact that policies are not put into effect as intended because those involved in the implementation are inefficient or because it has not been possible to overcome obstacles despite their best efforts. On the other hand, *unsuccessful implementation* is a situation where the policy is fully implemented but fails to produce the intended outcomes.[53]

Apart from this, a notion of *perfect implementation* is provided by the implementation framework of Hogwood and Gunn. It provides the preconditions and key features necessary for perfect implementation. The preconditions for successful implementation are as follows:[53]

(a) **External Constraints:** External constraints are circumstances external to the implementing agency. These constraints should be minimised and must be addressed at the policy-designing stage itself.

(b) **Time and Resources:** Adequate time and sufficient resources should be made available to the programme.

(c) **Resource Combination**: The required combination of resources should be made available for policy implementation.

(d) **Theory-based Policy:** The policy to be implemented should be based on the valid theory of cause and effect.

(e) **Cause/Effect Relation:** The relationship between cause and effect should be direct and there should be few, if any, intervening links.

(f) **Dependency Relationships**: The dependency relationships should be minimal.

(g) **Agreements of Objectives:** There should be an agreement of, and understanding on, the objectives.

(h) **Events Sequencing**: The tasks should be fully specified in the correct sequence.

(i) **Communication/Coordination:** There should be perfect communication and coordination.

(j) **Total Compliance:** Those in authority should demand and obtain perfect compliance.

This framework is made clear in Case Study 12.12.

Case Study 12.12: Application of Hogwood and Gunn Implementation Framework in OSD Scheme

In 2007, the South African Government introduced Occupation Specific Dispensation (OSD), a financial incentive strategy to attract, motivate, and retain health professionals in the public sector. The implementation commenced with all categories of nurses, as they are the majority healthcare providers. However, there were numerous problems with the implementation of the OSD policy, ranging from inadequate planning, budget overruns, and some unintended negative consequences such as unmet nurses' expectations, inequities in the amount received, perceived unfairness, and dissatisfaction among the various categories of nurses.55 These failures in implementation were analysed using Hogwood and Gunn's framework.54 Accordingly, the following factors were held responsible:

(a) **External Constraints**: Widespread public sector strike led to hurried implementation without sufficient planning beforehand. There was some contestation over prioritisation of nurses as the first health-provider category to benefit from OSD.

(b) **Time and Resources**: The OSD policy implementation was rushed, and adequate time was not given for gradual implementation. Financial resources were insufficient and human resources were limited. Moreover, the implementers were not trained adequately.

(c) **Resource Combination:** The human resource information system was inadequate.

(d) **Theory-based Policy:** The OSD policy was philosophy-based and not evidence-based.

(e) **Cause/Effect Relationship:** The OSD policy provided clear career paths and salary progression for nurses. Increase in salary was supposed to increase motivation and retention.

(f) **Minimal Dependency Relationships:** There was a complex series of events dependent on nurses submitting proof of Nursing Council qualifications.

(g) **Agreement of objectives**: The objective of OSD was to retain nurses within clinical areas. However, there was vagueness in the definition of what constitutes specialisation.

(h) **Events Sequencing:** The roles of the implementation stakeholders were not specified explicitly even though prior announcements were made to ensure sufficient combination of resources.

(i) **Communication and Coordination:** There was weak communication to frontline nurses. Moreover, there was poor coordination amongst the key actors.

(j) **Total Compliance:** There was varied interpretation of the policy at the institution and provincial level. There was also the problem of overpayments and underpayments to the nurses.

12.3.5.5 Weaknesses of Top-down Models

The top-down approach of policy implementation suffers from the following weaknesses:

(a) Top-down models are normative in nature and fail to recognise the significance of actions taken earlier in the policymaking process.

(b) Top-down models regard implementation as a purely administrative process and ignore the political aspects associated with it.[63]

(c) The top-down approach excessively emphasises the role of the legislatures/political executives as key actors in the implementation process. It denies the importance of the local service delivery institutions/people, who are experts and are aware of the actual circumstances/problems.

(d) The approach neglects the reality of policy modification or distortion at the hands of the implementers.

(e) The models very simplistically assume that policy priorities are known beforehand and can be ranked before implementation.

(f) The approach has no behavioural basis. Thus, it can lead to resistance, disregard, and pro forma compliance.[64]

12.3.6 Bottom-Up Models of Policy Implementation

As discussed previously, the bottom-up approach suggests that the implementation process should involve policymaking by the implementers. The various models of the bottom-up approach are described in the following sections.

12.3.6.1 Street-level Bureaucracy by Michael Lipsky

Michael Lipsky is considered the founding father of the bottom-up approach of public policy implementation. Lipsky defined street-level bureaucrats as public service workers who interact directly with citizens in the course of their jobs and who have substantial discretion in the execution of their work.[56] They share the following characteristics:

(a) Need to process workload expeditiously

(b) Substantial autonomy in their individual interactions with clients and an interest in furthering that autonomy

(c) Conditions of work include inadequate resources

(d) A demand that exceeds supply

(e) Ambiguous and multiple objectives

(f) Difficulties in defining or measuring good performance

(g) Requirement for rapid decision-making

(h) Non-voluntary clients

Lipsky said that policies cannot be implemented effectively through control over street-level bureaucrats. He pointed out that policies are not designed by senior policymakers. The decisions of street-level bureaucrats, the routines they establish, and the devices they invent to cope with uncertainties and work pressures effectively become the public policies they carry out. In order to cope with the work pressure, street-level bureaucrats develop methods of processing the work of citizens in relatively routine and stereotyped ways. They develop such conceptions of their work and clients that help in narrowing down the gap between their work/personal limitations and the service ideal.

Street-level bureaucrats tend to avoid being controlled by the managerial staff. Attempts to control them hierarchically increase their tendency to stereotype and disregard the needs of their clients. Thus, diverse methods are required to ensure their accountability.

The model of street-level bureaucracy considers the implementation process as involving negotiation and consensus-building with the implementers. Street-level service providers such as doctors, teachers, engineers, and social workers shape policies and have an important role to play in ensuring their implementation.

In Dunleavy's words, "policymaking process may be skewed by policy implementation, which is largely dominated by the professionals."[57] For example, doctors may develop ways of implementing health policies that actually result in outcomes that are quite different from the intentions of the policymakers. Case Study 12.13 illustrates the working of this model.

Case Study 12.13: Nurses as Street-level Bureaucrats

Nurses can be considered as street-level bureaucrats for implementing a health policy. They fulfil all the conditions of street-level bureaucracy mentioned by Lipsky. Nurses working within the health scheme interact with citizens on a daily basis and can influence citizens' treatment and experience through their own discretion, thus influencing and producing policy.58

To understand this concept, a study was conducted in Scotland for the three-month period of June–August 2010. Semi-structured interviews of 31 front-line nursing staff were taken. The participants belonged to different health departments. The findings were as follows:

- **Use of Discretion in Interpretation of Policy:** It was found that there was often ambiguity and confusion as to what was actually meant by the term 'policy'. The different understandings of the term meant that the nurses would use differing levels of discretion when interpreting and following what they perceived as policy.
- **Conflicting Goals of Managers and Nurses:** Managers wanted to restrict the nurses' discretion to ensure that the desired results were achieved. However, the nurses wanted to exercise their clinical autonomy to make critical discretionary decisions; the restrictions imposed by the managers were often seen as illegitimate by the nurses. Thus, there was tension between the managers and nurses. In order to cope up with such tensions, the nurses used the rules, regulations, and administrative provisions to evade or change the policies that would limit their discretion.

12.3.6.2 Policy Implementation Structures by Benny Hjern

The approach given by Benny Hjern suggested that a policy is implemented via 'implementation structures' formed along with various organisations, pooled through the process of consensual self-selection.[59] These structures consist of the actors/organisations that are involved in a problem, mapping the relations among these actors. These actors/organisations form a network within which field-level decision-making actors carry out their activities without predetermining the assumptions about the structures within which they occur.

In these networks, both public and private players are essential. Hjern[60] focused on the role of local networks in affecting the implementation process of a given problem and propounded the ways of identifying these networks (the methods of identifying these networks are beyond the scope of this book). These structures help in evaluating the significance of government programmes vis-à-vis other influences such as the market. They also enable one to discern strategic coalitions, the unintended effects of policy, and the dynamic nature of policy implementation.[61]

According to Hjern, the success of a policy depends on the skills of the individuals involved in the local implementation structure, which can help in adapting a national policy to local conditions.

12.3.6.3 Weaknesses of Bottom-up Models

Bottom-up models of policy implementation suffer from the following weaknesses:

(a) They do not provide satisfactory solutions to the problems of public policy, as they reject the authority of policymakers on policy implementation. In a democratically elected government, the accountability of policy success lies on the democratically elected political executives. However, the bottom-up approach assigns the power of efficient policy implementation to the implementers, who are not directly accountable to the voters in a democracy.

(b) The bottom-up approach does not suggest ways to control the discretion of the policy implementers in order to improve the implementation process. It also does not suggest ways to use discretion as a device for improving the effectiveness of policies at the street level.[62]

12.3.7 Synthesis of Top-down and Bottom-up Approaches to Policy Implementation

As discussed in the preceding sections, the top-down and bottom-up models differ in their basic approach to policy implementation. Each tends to ignore the implementation reality explained by the other. The basic differences between these two approaches are enumerated in Table 12.1.

Table 12.1: Basic differences between the top-down and bottom-up approach of policy implementation

Variables	Top-down approach	Bottom-up approach
Policy decision-makers	Policymakers	Street-level bureaucrats
Starting point	Normative language	Social problems
Structure	Formal	Both formal and informal

Variables	Top-down approach	Bottom-up approach
Process	Purely administrative	Networking including administrative
Authority	Centralisation	Decentralisation
Output/outcomes	Prescriptive	Descriptive
Discretion	Top-level bureaucrats	Bottom-level bureaucrats

Some scholars have attempted to synthesise the top-down and bottom-up approaches of policy implementation. Their work is described in the following sections.

12.3.7.1 Elmore's Forward and Backward Mapping

While combining the top-down and bottom-up approaches, Elmore said that the policy designers should choose policy instruments on the basis of the incentive structure of the target groups. The model is a combination of forward mapping and backward mapping for policy implementation. Forward mapping consists of stating precise policy objectives and specifying explicit outcomes criteria to judge policy[65] (basis of the top-down approach).

On the other hand, a backward mapping consists of stating precisely the behaviour to be changed at the lowest level, describing a set of operations that can bring about this change, and repeating the procedure upwards in steps until the central level is reached. The use of backward mapping may help policy designers to find more appropriate tools for policy implementation.

The combination of forward and backward mapping helps in considering micro implementers' interpretation of policy problems and the possible solutions.

12.3.7.2 Matland's Ambiguity and Conflict Model

Richard E. Matland's ambiguity and conflict model suggest that the value of the policy can be described through the degree of ambiguity in the means and goals of a policy and the degree of conflict in them. Accordingly, he suggested the following four policy implementation paradigms:[61]

(a) **Low Conflict, Low Ambiguity (Administrative Implementation):** Low ambiguity and low conflict are prerequisite conditions for a rational decision-making process. Simon referred to such decisions as *programmed decisions*. Such implementation is known as administrative implementation, where the quality of implementation is directly proportional to the resources supplied for implementation. Here, the implementation process closely parallels that of traditional top-down approaches.

(b) **High Conflict, Low Ambiguity (Political Implementation):** A political policymaking situation has clearly defined goals, but dissension occurs as these clearly defined goals are incompatible. Conflict occurs at the design of the policy implementation stage itself. The implementation outcomes are decided by power. The group having more power is able to shape the implementation goals. Such a situation consists of active bargaining by the participants. Such a system is more open to influences from the environment than from internal administration.

Successful implementation depends on either having sufficient power to force one's will on the other participants or having sufficient resources to bargain an agreement based on means.

(c) **Low Conflict, High Ambiguity (Experimental Implementation):** In an experimental implementation, the policy outcomes depend on which actors are active and most involved. The contextual conditions dominate the process of implementation. This kind of implementation closely parallels a 'garbage can' process with streams of actors, problems, solutions, and choice opportunities combining to produce outcomes that are hard to predict.

(d) **High Conflict, High Ambiguity (Symbolic Implementation):** Symbolic policies are those that receive exposure at the adoption stage but ultimately have little substantive effect.[66, 67] Symbolic policies have an important role in confirming new goals, in re-affirming a commitment to old goals, or in emphasising important values and principles.[68] In such policies, the local-level coalition strength determines the policy outcomes. The course of the policy is decided by the coalition of actors who control the available resources at the local level.

These four policy implementation paradigms are schematically described in Fig. 12.7.

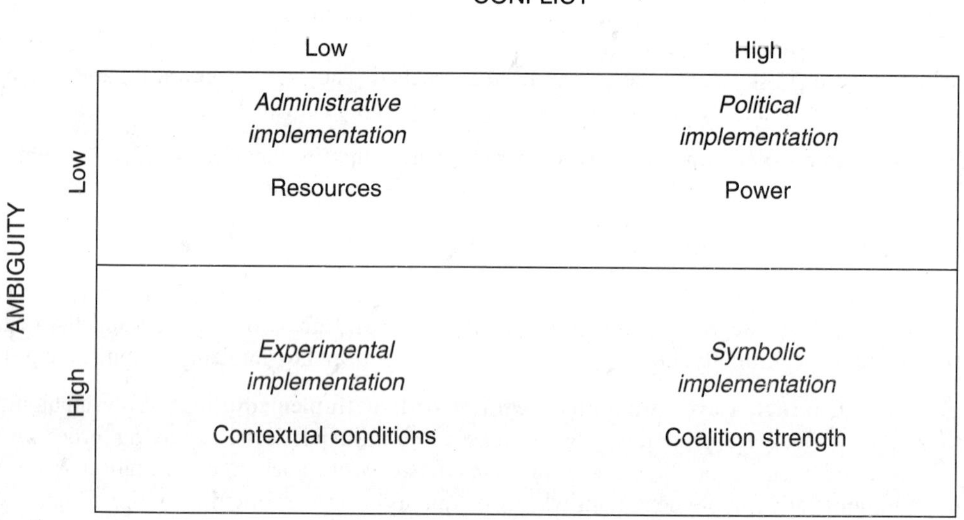

Figure 12.7: Matland's conflict-ambiguity matrix[61]

12.3.7.3 Malcolm Goggin's Communication Model of Policy Implementation

The communication model by Malcolm Goggin suggests that policy implementation is a nexus of a series of communication channels. In the model, the messages, their senders, and their recipients are the critical ingredients, and decoding these messages and absorbing them into a routine is what implementation is all about. Accordingly, the differences in the state-level implementation of national policies are explained by variations in the clarity and consistency of the communication of the intent of the policy. Goggin described three clusters of variables that affect state-level policy implementation:[69]

(a) Inducements and constraints from the top level (Central Government/Federal Government)
(b) Inducements and constraints from the bottom level (state and local level)
(c) State-specific factors defined as decisional outcomes and state capacity

2.3.7.4 Thomas and Grindle's Interactive Model of Policy Implementation

his model is designed for the implementation of reforms-based policies. It suggests that the process f implementing reforms is interactive rather than linear.[70] In the interactive model, policy quilibrium results from the acceptance of an existing policy or institutional arrangement by those at are affected either positively or negatively by the policy. A policy reform initiative may be tered or reversed at any stage in its life cycle by pressures and reactions from those who oppose it. nlike the linear model, the interactive model views policy reform as a process, one in which iterested parties can exert pressure for change at various points. Understanding the location, rength, and stakes involved in these attempts to promote, alter, or reverse policy reform initiatives is entral to understanding the policy outcomes. The interactive model helps the policymakers to think itically about crucial supporting or threatening issues.

The analysis in this model starts with analysing the characteristics of any public policy in terms of e reactions it will generate. Next, the available resources and how these resources can be mobilised or successful implementation are analysed. Decision-makers evaluate political resources while ublic managers evaluate bureaucratic resources.

Such analysis leads to a realistic approach to the policy, where the question of implementation ssumes major importance. Failure can be anticipated, modifications can be judged, and resources an be more efficiently and effectively allocated.[71]

2.3.7.5 Sabatier and Mazmanian's Advocacy Coalition Framework

abatier and Mazmanian proposed a strictly top-down model in 1981. However, they changed their pproach later on to formulate a synthesis of the top-down and bottom-up approaches.

In their top-down perspective, Mazmanian and Sabatier argued that three general sets of factors ractability of the problem, ability of statute to structure implementation, and non-statutory variables ffecting implementation) determine the success of policy implementation.[72]

Later on, in their combined model, they argued that policy needs to be analysed in a cycle of 10 ears to allow policy learning for proper policy implementation. According to them, policies operate ithin the parameters identified by a top-down approach, such as socio-economic conditions, legal istruments, and the basic government structure.

However, there are sets of core ideas about the causation and values in public policy that shape its nplementation. These core ideas are held by certain groups of people known as *advocacy coalitions*. hese advocacy coalitions are actors from a variety of public and private organisations who are ctively concerned with a policy problem or issue. These people from a variety of positions (elected presentatives, public servants, interest groups, leaders, researchers, and so on) shape the particular elief system—a set of basic values, causal assumptions, and problem perceptions—and exemplify a gnificant degree of coordination activity over time.[73]

These networks of actors can be mapped to a policy sector. The policy change comes from the bility of the core ideas (held by the advocacy coalitions) to adapt to the broad top-down guidelines, nging around a whole series of operational questions and what works at any one time or place.[74]

12.3.8 Third Generation Research into Policy Implementation

The models of public policy implementation discussed are a result of second-generation research on polic implementation. However, the second-generation models suffer from the following weaknesses:

(a) **No Common Definition:** Second-generation researchers do not agree on a commo definition of the term 'implementation'. In different models, there are vast differences in th role of the implementers.

(b) **Does not Explain the Nature of Implementation:** The second-generation models hav failed to explain why implementation occurs as it does or to predict how implementers ar likely to behave in the future.[69]

(c) **Lack of Validation:** There are too many case studies to prove that second-generatio models lack enough validation and replication.[75] Thus, they have failed to provide comprehensive approach to implementation analysis.[76]

Third-generation research in policy implementation has attempted to overcome the above-mentione lacunae. Third-generation studies have attempted to test implementation theories on the basis of mo comparative case studies and statistical research designs.[77] In this research, the macro-world (policymakers has been integrated with the micro-world of individual implementers.[78] The macro-lev research operates at the systems level and focuses on the regularities of processes and organisation structures as stable outlines of the policy process and frames individual actions in terms of position in relational network. It provides only broad guidance to the policymakers on understanding polic outcomes, evaluating alternatives, and so on.

On the other hand, micro-level research is focused on individual action and understands th actions in policy implementation as the efforts of autonomous actors. It does not address the systen wide qualities and lacunae and, thus, does not say anything about expected organisation consequences or the system-wide effects of a policy. It, thus, provides limited guidance policymakers faced with system-wide decisions.

A combination of both macro-level and micro-level implementation analysis is realised in thir generation research.

12.4 Public Policy Monitoring

Policy monitoring is the process of observing the progress of policy implementation and reportir any deviations from the intended implementation path.[80] It is defined as an analytical procedure th produces information on the cause and consequences of public policies.[79] It goes along with th implementation stage and is integral for effective implementation. It ensures that anticipate implementation is attained within the anticipated time and budget.

The key requirements for effective implementation are that the policy progress should b measurable in terms of some indicators. Second, different personnel should be made accountable f deviations from the expected intermediate outcomes. Third, proper tools and techniques are require to identify deviations from the anticipated policy performance. Fourth, and most important, a effective information system is necessary, which gives policy implementers the required informatic for understanding deviations and taking timely corrective actions.

12.4.1 Techniques of Policy Monitoring

The various techniques for policy monitoring can be classified as business techniques, systems techniques, formative techniques, performance management techniques, and social systems accounting techniques of policy monitoring. These techniques are discussed in the following sections.

12.4.1.1 Business Techniques for Policy Monitoring

The various business techniques for public policy monitoring are applicable to public sector policy monitoring as well. Important among them are the critical path method (CPM), programme evaluation and review technique (PERT), activity bar chart and planning programming budgeting system (PPBS). The first three techniques are discussed in Chapter 13 and the fourth technique is discussed in Chapter 14.

12.4.1.2 Systems Technique for Policy Monitoring

The systems approach of policy monitoring addresses the deviations in the policy implementation structure as a whole. Implementation gaps are analysed in the policy implementation system. The policy implementation system consists of the network of organisations responsible for implementation, their interrelationships, the sequence of planned implementation activities, desired inputs, and expected outputs. These systemic factors are studied, during the course of implementation, in order to address the failures in policy implementation. Thus, the systems technique is a wide-ranging method for addressing implementation problems that consider multiple and interacting relationships.

12.4.1.3 Formative Technique for Policy Monitoring

The formative approach is a method in which a schedule for policy implementation is designed and then the management information system (MIS) is utilised to ensure that implementation adheres to the desired schedule. We will study the details of MIS in Chapter 13, which is used to study the conditions that promote successful policy implementation. The technique helps the managerial decision-making process by analysing the acquired information at every stage of policy implementation.

12.4.1.4 Performance Management Technique of Policy Monitoring

In the performance measurement approach, a policy is monitored by measuring certain policy indicators. The measurement of policy indicators helps in understanding the deviations from the anticipated values of these indicators. The performance indicators of all the parameters of a public policy are observed to detect the earliest available signs of any deviations from the desired results. Whenever any deviations are found, the policy implementers work on the deviated parameters to return to the anticipated course of implementation.

This technique is very helpful in the case of social sector policies, wherever simple indicators such as profit are inadequate for the effective implementation of a policy. It has the following advantages:

- The measurement of performance indicators enhances the accountability of the implementers.
- The indicators provide a basis for adequate policy planning and control.

- The performance indicators provide important information for monitoring organisationa activities.
- Performance measurement also provides a strong base for an effective performanc appraisal system (discussed in Chapter 10).

However, the method of performance measurement has many limitations, as discussed in Chapter 10.

12.4.1.5 Social Systems Accounting Technique for Policy Monitoring

Social systems accounting is a technique for measuring changes in social conditions, over time, as result of the policy implementation process. Here *social indicators* are studies in order to monitor policy; social indicators are statistics that measure social conditions, and changes in it, over time fo the various segments of a population. These social indicators can be both objective as well a subjective. Table 12.2 lists some examples of social indicators.

Table 12.2: Examples of social indicators[79]

Area	Indicator
Health and illness	Persons in hospital at a given point of time
Public safety	Number of persons afraid to walk alone at night
Women's employment	Labour force participation by women
Income	Percentage of population below poverty line
Housing	Households living in substandard units
Social values and attitudes	Overall life satisfaction and alienation
Physical environment	Air pollution index

Social indicators are imperative for supplying information on the impact of policies on the targe groups and, thus, help in modifying the course of implementation if needed.

12.4.2 Limitations in Policy Monitoring

Policy monitoring suffers from various internal and external factors. These factors are described i the following:

(a) **Improper Design:** When the implementation process is not suitably designed, then there i an inadequate flow of information for a good monitoring scheme.

(b) **Lack of Time:** In the case of important mission mode policies, very little time is allocated t the process of monitoring and control.

(c) **Lack of Corrective Actions:** Even when deviations are found, the implementers often d not know the corrective actions to be taken in order to return to the anticipated course o policy implementation.

(d) **Lack of Skills:** The implementers often lack the skills of effective monitoring. There i general ignorance on the part of the officials about the role and techniques of polic monitoring.

12.4.3 Measures for Effective Monitoring

Various measures can be taken to avoid the above-mentioned limitations in policy monitoring. These measures are described in the following:[82]

(a) **Effective Designing of the Monitoring System:** For effective monitoring, it is important to design the specific parameters (or characteristics) based on which performance is to be monitored. Policy parameters can be monitored in terms of three variables—anticipated activities (technical performance), within anticipated schedule (time performance), and within anticipated budget (cost performance).

(b) **Policy Communication:** The various deviations in a policy are required to be widely communicated within the implementation structure. Apart from the deviations, corrective actions are also required to be communicated timely. The objective of communication is to keep the implementers informed so that they are on the right track and to provide feedback to those who deviate from the right track.

(c) **Systematic Review:** The monitoring process should be conducted in a systematic manner at regular intervals and not in a haphazard manner. Any significant deviations from the planned performance should be analysed and reported timely.

(d) **Capacity Building of Personnel:** Policy monitoring requires the skills of planning, accounting, statistics, auditing, and general management. The key monitoring functionaries are required to be trained in these skills.

(e) **Taking Corrective Actions:** It is important to work on the corrective actions to be taken once a deviation is observed from the planned course of policy implementation.

12.5 Policy Evaluation

Policy evaluation is a complex term with various kinds of definitions. In a holistic definition, it is defined as a tool to determine the worth and value of public policies/programmes with the purpose of providing information to decision-makers and improving institutional performance in the spirit of looking backwards to improve forward directions.[82]

In the modern era, policy evaluation was first used by the United States in three important social sectors. In the 1960s, many countries, such as the USA, Germany, Canada, and the UK, started feeling the need to evaluate the government's programmes. Scientific methods were applied to policy evaluations, leading to the birth of traditional evaluation. Following this, the 1970s were characterised by a predominantly social science approach to programme evaluation. The focus on evaluation increased in the 1990s when there was an increased emphasis on accountability, performance, and result orientation of the government.[86]

12.5.1 Procedure for Policy Evaluation

The procedure for policy evaluation works through various phases, as shown in Fig. 12.8.

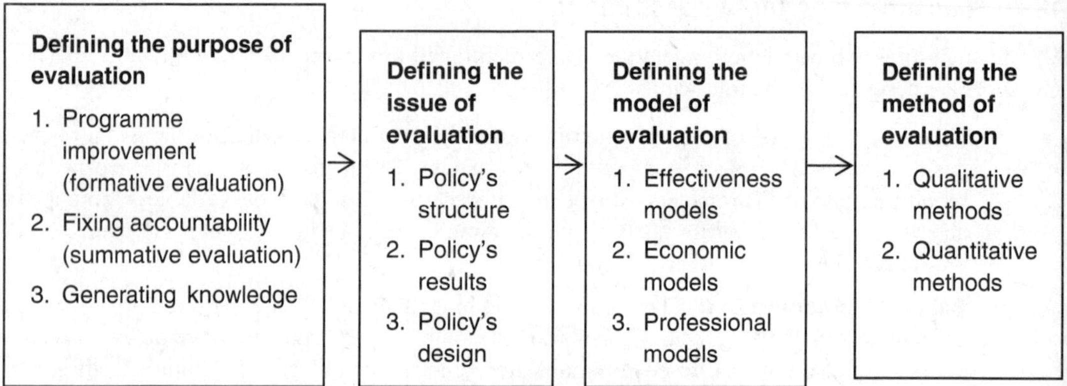

Figure 12.8: The procedure of evaluation[87]

Various permutations of the different steps in the evaluation procedure leads to a vast number of evaluation techniques. The first step in the evaluation procedure is defining the purpose of evaluation. There can be three purposes of the evaluation, as follows:

(a) **Evaluation for Improvement:** Evaluation done in order to bring improvement in policy performance is known as *formative evaluation* or evaluation for improvement.

(b) **Evaluation for Fixing Accountability:** Evaluation aimed at providing information for holding policymakers and implementers accountable is known as *summative evaluation* or evaluation for fixing accountability.

(c) **Evaluation for Knowledge Generation:** Evaluation done to understand the policy procedures is known as evaluation for knowledge generation.

12.5.2 Models for Policy Evaluation

There are a large number of alternative approaches in the policy evaluation literature. These approaches can be classified into three broad categories, as mentioned below:

(a) Effectiveness models/results models of evaluation

(b) Professional models of evaluation

(c) Economic models of evaluation

These three models are discussed in the following sections.

12.5.2.1 Effectiveness Models of Evaluation

The effectiveness models of evaluation focus on the results attained by a given policy. They also emphasise on the possible effects of a policy—both foreseen and unforeseen. The two important models under this category are the goal-attainment model and the side-effects model. These are described in the following.

Goal-attainment Model of Evaluation

The goal-attainment model of evaluation consists of the measurement of the extent of goal achievement and an assessment of the impact of the policy. Here, the goal-achievement measurement considers whether the results are in accordance with the policy goals. On the other hand, impact assessment considers whether the results achieved are produced by the policy under evaluation or by something else. The method consists of three steps as follows:

(a) **Identifying Goals:** The first step consists of identifying the policy goals, understanding their meaning and prioritising them, turning them into measurable objectives, and determining the extent to which they can be realised in practice.

(b) **Ascertaining the Effect:** This step involves ascertaining the degree to which the policy has promoted or dampened goal realisation.

(c) **Success of Policy:** The success of the policy is then measured as the discrepancy between the stated goals and actual outcomes.[88]

The model is an effective model because it deals with the substantive content, output, and outcomes of a policy and not with policy procedures such as equity of treatment and due process. A simple anatomy of the model is described in Fig. 12.9. The model can be better understood after reading Case Study 12.14.

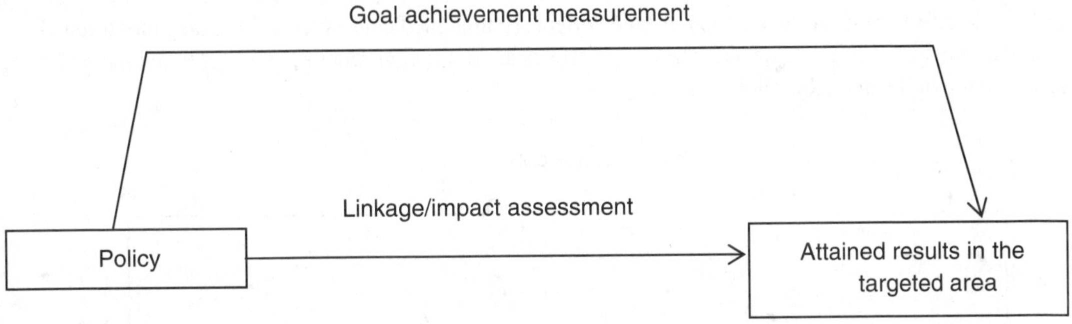

Figure 12.9: Schematic representing the goal-attainment model of policy implementation[89]

Case Study 12.14: Goal Attainment in Building Energy Saving Plan[82]

In a building energy saving plan, the goal was that annual net energy consumption should decrease by 30% in 10 years. To achieve this goal, various policy steps were taken, such as home insulation, retrofitting of industrial and commercial buildings, and energy auditing and counselling. A goal-attainment evaluation of this policy would consist of evaluating whether energy consumption had actually decreased by 30% in 10 years and whether this outcome was attributed to the adopted reforms.

The goal-attainment model is also known as *goal-achievement evaluation, rational evaluation model, objectives-oriented approach,* and *behavioural objectives approach.* The various advantages and disadvantages of this model are as follows.

Advantages:

(a) **Democratically Grounded:** The model recognises the goals prepared by a democratically elected government as the first steps to measure policy effectiveness.

(b) **Objective Nature:** The model is assumed to use impartial and unbiased social research for policy evaluation.

Disadvantages:

(a) **Obscurity of Policy Goals:** In most of the government policies, the goals are obscure and are, thus, not sufficient criteria of merit.

(b) **Unintended Consequences:** The model does not study any unintended effects of a policy.

(c) **Role of Hidden Agendas:** The model disregards the role of hidden agendas in public policymaking. There are various hidden agendas besides the goals enumerated in a policy. For example, the hidden agenda behind a privatisation policy may not be to increase efficiency in the best interests of the consumers but to strengthen the power network supporting conservative political parties.

Side Effects Model of Evaluation

In the side effects model of evaluation, the side effects (unintended consequences) are also measured along with the anticipated goals achieved. These side effects are defined in relation to the intended main effects. A schematic of this model is shown in Fig. 12.10.

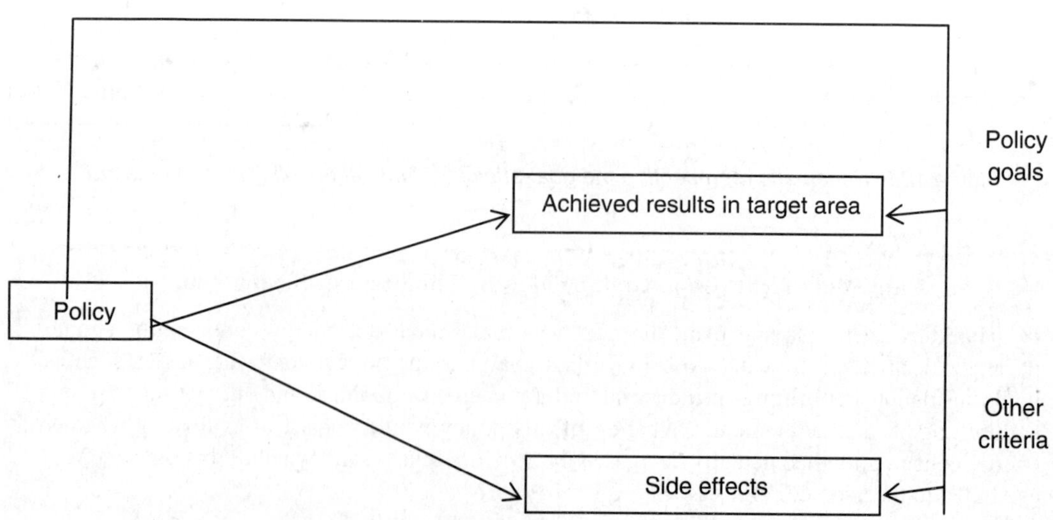

Figure 12.10: Schematic representation of the side effects model of policy evaluation

Apart from the side effects, there can be *perverse effects*, which are exactly counter to the very intentions of the policy investigators. Since these counter effects occur in the target area of the public programme, they are not considered as side effects, neither are they the main effects. Moreover, there are *null effects*.[90] This means that the programme wholly failed to show any intended effects. No impacts were produced in the target area.

The perverse and null effects are calculated by the goal-attainment model, as they fall in the targeted area. However, the model does not handle the side effects, as they do not fall in the targeted areas. The side effects can be detrimental as well as beneficial. An example of the side effects can be seen in Case Study 12.15.

Case Study 12.15: Side Effects in Energy Conservation Policy[82]

As discussed in Case Study 12.14, as a part of the Energy Savings Plan for Existing Buildings, state subsidies were offered to people wanting to retrofit their buildings. The intended outcome was to achieve more energy efficiency in the existing buildings. However, one side effect was anticipated. The programme was expected to have an unfavourable impact on the distribution of wealth in the country, since the home owners and other prospective recipients of the programme were generally wealthier than people at large.

Apart from this, certain spillovers were expected from the scheme. It was expected to boost economic activity and create new employment. The evaluation of wealth distribution and economic activity generated were considered as the side effects evaluation of the main policy.

The advantages and disadvantages of this model are as follows.

Advantages: Side effects are crucial factors in every inclusive judgment on the worth of a policy. The approach is beneficial, as the majority of governmental activities have unpredictable effects. It is important to assess the worth of these side effects.

Disadvantages: It is difficult to judge the merit of a side effect. A good judgment requires value criteria for the main effects, the side effects, and for a trade-off between the two.

12.5.2.2 Professional Models of Evaluation

The professional models of evaluation are actor-oriented. They consider the view of a person or a group of persons for evaluating the value of a policy. The professional models discussed here are the client-oriented evaluation model, stakeholder-oriented evaluation model, and peer review evaluation model.

Client-oriented Evaluation

In the client-oriented evaluation model, the criteria for evaluation of a policy are the desires, values, objectives, concerns, expectations, and assumptions of the service users about the policy. The model is based on two arguments. First, the market place needs are superior to the public sector provisions. While buying a service, the customer pays no attention to the producer's goals and objectives. In the same way, clients are concerned with their service satisfaction and not with the goals of the government. Second, the model allows the democratic participation of clients in policy implementation and assessment. The participatory and deliberative features suggest that the clients may voice their complaints and desires to the service providers, discuss with each other and with the service providers, and to some extent influence and take responsibility for the service content. This feature is not present in the goal-attainment model of policy evaluation.

Client-oriented evaluation is done in the following steps:

(a) **Location of Clients:** First, the clients of a policy are located. Here, the clients are the intended target population as well as the non-intended affected population. A sample from the target population is picked up for analysis.

(b) **Clients' Views:** The clients' views on the impact of the policy are sought. Clients are asked to give their judgments on some aspects of the policy, such as policy outcome, policy output, service availability, and service quality.

(c) **Policy Impacts:** The policy impacts are assessed based on the views of the clients. What would have happened had there been no policy is compared to what has actually happened with the policy in place.

Apart from this, a distinguishing feature of this evaluation is its *value pluralism*, in which consumers may have conflicting opinions on the different aspects of the policy. Such a model of evaluation is employed in the case of public service provisions such as urban transport, public utilities, education, parks and recreation, health services, child care, public housing, and nursing homes for the elderly, where clientele participation is crucial to the operation of the programme.

This model of evaluation has the following advantages and disadvantages:

Advantages: This model of evaluation is superior to the previous model, as it considers the views of the end users. It provides an additional dimension to the evaluation process. It makes the government responsive to the needs of the citizens.

Disadvantages: This model has certain limitations and it cannot replace the previous models of evaluation. The clients have a tendency to exaggerate their complaints in order to get more service. Moreover, greater client involvement in the evaluation may surrender power to groups with vested and narrow interests.

Stakeholder-oriented Evaluation Model

In the stakeholders' model, the concerns of the stakeholders are the criteria for assessing the merits of a policy. Here, the stakeholders are all those people who have an interest in or are affected by the policy intervention. The scope of this model is much larger than the client-oriented model, as the evaluator population in the case of the latter is just a part of the total stakeholder (client) population. Table 12.3 provides an example of the total population of stakeholders in a policy.

Table 12.3: Different kinds of stakeholders in a policy[82]

Stakeholders	Description
Citizenry	Citizens are important as they elect the policymakers.
Decision-makers	Policymakers are responsible for deciding whether an evaluated policy is to be instituted, continued, discontinued, expanded, or curtailed.
Political opposition	Political opponents are important for pointing out the perverse and unintended consequences of a policy.
Central bureaucrats	Central bureaucrats are responsible for providing important policy advice to the policymakers.

Stakeholders	Description
Policy directors	Policy directors are the technical heads of the various implementation organisations.
Private/non-governmental organisations	Private/non-governmental organisations are given important roles in policy implementation.
Local government	The local governments are responsible for the implementation of a majority of the policies.
Street-level bureaucrats	These are the front-line staff responsible for policy implementation. They decide the course of the actual policy.
Clients	These are the individuals, households, business organisations, and so on, who are the beneficiaries/target groups of a policy.
Neighbouring agencies	These agencies are those that are related to the agencies responsible for implementation.

Considering the views of all the stakeholders in an evaluation makes the evaluation process holistic. The process of evaluation in this model passes through the following steps:

(a) **Mapping of Stakeholders:** All the major groups that have an interest in the execution and results of a policy are identified. Apart from the policymakers and implementers, the target groups, affected groups, and other stakeholders are also identified.

(b) **Concerns and Issues:** The concerns (any matter of interest or importance including claims, doubts, fears, difficulties, and so on) and issues (any statement or proposition that allows for the presentation of different points of view) of different stakeholders are analysed.[83]

(c) **Qualitative Methodology:** A qualitative methodology is used to seek the views of the stakeholders. This methodology includes talking to the stakeholders to elicit their narrative histories and observational data. This helps in getting involved with the views of the stakeholders. The evaluators are required to search extensively for the crucial problems faced by the stakeholders. To do this, the approach is not limited to certain pre-defined questions. It is rather open to seek the views of the evaluators. This sort of evaluation is known as *responsive evaluation.*

(d) **Reporting Results:** After collecting data from all the stakeholders, the results are summarised using pictures, anecdotes, thick descriptions, and quotes. A holistic view is portrayed in the result. The approach is pluralist in nature.

The model has the following advantages and disadvantages:

Advantages:

(a) The model is democratic in nature as it allows for the stakeholders' participation, deliberation, dialogue, and debate.

(b) The evaluation process leads to the generation of a lot of knowledge about the policy under evaluation.

(c) The results of this model are of practical importance to the policymakers and implementers.

(d) The model helps in situations where there are no written pre-defined goals or where the stated goals are lofty and difficult to trade-off against each other. It provides a practical solution to the problem of eliciting concerns and issues using quality criteria.

(e) The model is supposed to promote compromises, agreement, and support and forestall bitter political struggles.

Disadvantages:

(a) The model is accused of being impractical and resource-demanding, as every stakeholder is required to be contacted and nurtured.

(b) The strategy of the model is accused of being unclear. The stakeholders can be varied on a case-to-case basis and their identification depends on the capacity and orientation of the evaluators.

(c) The model gives equal weightage to all the stakeholders. However, some stakeholders are more important than the others. For example, the views of the elected policymakers are more important than the carrier bureaucrats.

Peer Review Evaluation Model

In the peer review model, the other members of a profession evaluate the performance of a policy on the basis of certain professional criteria and quality standards. For peer review, a group of evaluators is formed by the members of a profession having equal status. For example, lawyers evaluate the implementation of a legal policy, doctors evaluate the implementation of a health policy, and so on. This model is often used in the evaluation of research and higher education plans.

In this model, the process of evaluation is based less on scientific measures and more on the process of deliberation, discussion, and dialogue. The process of evaluation starts with self-evaluation, in which professionals carry out an appraisal of their own performance and the achievements of the policy implemented by them. Then, external evaluators are tasked to assess their performance on the basis of self-evaluation, additional material, documentary evidence, site visits, and so on. After this step, the observations of the evaluators are discussed with the evaluatees in order to hear their views. Following this, a final evaluation report is prepared by the evaluators. As the process includes hearing the opinions of the evaluatees, the approach is regarded as interactive and participative.

For example, peer review is the most accepted method of judging the merit of a research article. Articles submitted to a journal are subject to peer review to decide whether they ought to be accepted for publication or not.

The model has the following advantages and disadvantages:

Advantages: The model is the best approach for evaluating policies relating to technical fields, as it solicits the opinion of technical experts.

Disadvantages: The model can produce unreliable results, as a similar group of evaluators can use different criteria of evaluation in the case of different policies.

12.5.2.3 Economic Models of Evaluation

Economic models of evaluation consider only the measurable economic aspects of a policy for evaluation. The economic models discussed in this chapter are the productivity model and efficiency models of evaluation.

Productivity Model of Evaluation

The substance models discussed previously focus only on the results produced by a policy and ignore the costs involved in the implementation of a policy. However, the economic models of evaluation also consider the costs involved in the implementation of a policy.

Among the economic models, the productivity model of policy evaluation is derived from private business practices. Just as in the private sector, profit is the main criterion of assessment, in the productivity model, productivity is the main criterion to assess the performance of a policy. Productivity is defined as the ratio between the output of products and services to the input of resources.

Productivity = Output of Products and Services/Input of Resources

For example, in the case of a library programme of municipal corporations, the cost productivity can be defined as:

Cost Productivity = Number of Books Borrowed/Cost of Books

After the productivity ratio is computed, it is compared with a reference case. Evaluators select performance standards based on the productivity criterion to suggest what is high productivity and what is low productivity. For this, several performance standards are used, such as comparing with past performance, similar institutions in the same country, similar institutions in other countries, goals of political bodies, client goals, or stakeholder goals.

The various advantages and disadvantages of the productivity model of evaluation are described below.

Advantages: The productivity criterion is technically easier to calculate and compare. It is applicable in cases where the costs are easy to calculate.

Disadvantages: In certain programmes, it is difficult to calculate the relevant costs incurred. Similarly, it may be difficult to calculate and compare the outputs in the case of social sector policies. Conflicting opinions may come in the way of selecting a relevant criterion for the output. Moreover, productivity is not considered an ideal measuring tool for assessing the worth and merit of public sector policies. In the public sector, even when decided outputs are attained, the desired outcome may not have been achieved.

Efficiency Models of Evaluation

The efficiency models of evaluation are those that are used for evaluating the outcomes of a public policy. There are two types of efficiency models—the *cost-benefit model* and the *cost-effectiveness model.*

In the cost-benefit evaluation, efficiency is measured as the ratio of the monetised value of the outcomes produced by the programme to the monetised costs incurred. On the other hand, in cost-effectiveness evaluation, the criterion of evaluation is the ratio of the policy effects in physical terms to the costs incurred in monetised terms. The physical effects are basically the consequences produced by the policy.

The efficiency models have the following advantages and disadvantages:

Advantages: The evaluation in efficiency models is objective in nature and it is easier to compare the results of different policies using these models.

Disadvantages: The efficiency models consider only limited aspects of evaluation. They disregard those criteria of evaluation that are important in public sector policies, such as legal equity, procedural fairness, representativeness, participatory values, and publicity rules.

12.5.3 Policy Evaluation Organisations in India

In India, several initiatives have been taken to improve the evaluation of public policies. We have taken several institutional steps to tie the evaluation system with our regular planning, budget-making, and accountability activities. Among the major steps are outcome budgeting by the Ministry of Finance, the Independent Evaluation Office under the Planning Commission, and the Performance

Management and Evaluation System under the Cabinet Secretariat.[91] The second and third initiatives will be discussed in this chapter. Outcome budgeting will be discussed in Chapter 14.

The various systems of evaluation in India are discussed in the following sections.

12.5.3.1 Policy Evaluation by Planning Commission

Evaluation policies in India came into being with the onset of 'planning'. The *Programme Evaluation Organisation* (PEO) was created under the Planning Commission in 1952 as an independent agency to evaluate programmes funded by the plans. The PEO was conceived of as an elaborately structured, nationwide organisation with field units, regional offices usually located in state capitals, and the headquarters in the Planning Commission. The organisation was autonomous, with its own state-level offices. The PEO's reports each year were an important agenda item at the annual conference of the state development commissioners, enabling them to undertake follow-up action on policies and plans.

However, the role of the PEO decreased in the 1970s, when the First Administrative Reforms Commission (ARC) recommended reducing the role of the Planning Commission in the Central Government's decision-making process. The role of the Planning Commission was substantially reduced in the implementation of schemes. After the 1970s, the role of the Planning Commission remained limited to the areas of funds allocation and policy designing. The role of the PEO also decreased because of the diminishing role of the Planning Commission in policy implementation.

The first ARC recommended that the PEO's substantive evaluation work should mainly concern the operational, financial, and administrative aspects of schemes and programmes rather than issues related to the overall design of programmes and their impact on the community.

The role of the PEO was revived in 1995, with the appointment of a professional economist as the head of the PEO and a marked improvement in the evaluation studies conducted by it. However, the importance of the PEO has diminished with time. It hardly responds to the significant challenges of assessing the effectiveness of public expenditure.

Seeing the mediocre role played by the PEO, the Planning Commission created a new Independent Evaluation Office (IEO), at an arm's length from itself, in 2013.

12.5.3.2 Performance Management and Evaluation System

A Performance Management and Evaluation System (PMES) was set up in 2009 under the Cabinet Secretariat. The system requires each department of the Government of India to prepare a Results Framework Document (RFD). The RFD is a summary of the important results expected to be achieved by a department in a financial year. It has two objectives: move the emphasis of the department from the process to results and provide an objective and fair basis to evaluate the department's overall performance at the end of the year. The process involved in PMES is as follows:

(a) **Set Targets:** All the departments are required to set their targets in accordance with the decisions laid down by the Planning Commission (or NITI Aayog) and Finance Ministry.

(b) **Plan Preparation:** The departments are then required to set their outcome-oriented plans to be assessed at the end of the financial year.

(c) **Placing on Website:** The RFDs are placed on the website of each department.

(d) **Assessment of Results:** The targets achieved at the end of the year are assessed in accordance with the RFDs laid down.

The RFDs differ from the earlier performance assessment in four ways. First, the targets are prioritised. Second, the interpretation of deviations from targets is agreed upon ex-ante. For this, there is a five-point scale. Third, there is an independent vetting of the RFD at the beginning of the ear by an independent non-government body of experts. This independent body also reviews the esults at the end of the year. Fourth, RFDs allow the departments to calculate their composite score, etween 0% and 100%, on the basis of the results attained. This allows them to employ a erformance-related incentive scheme for the employees.

Notwithstanding the advantages, the PMES and RFD suffer from certain limitations. These are as ollows:

(a) **Centre–state Relations:** In a federal country like India, the policies of the union government are implemented by the state governments. Thus, the success of implementation depends on the structural arrangement between the Centre and the state governments.

(b) **Inter-ministerial Coordination:** It is often found that there is a lack of inter-ministerial support and coordination for achieving the targets stated in the RFD. Such a challenge is addressed by ex-ante clarification of the importance of inter-ministerial coordination for the achievement of RFD targets.

(c) **Political Will:** It is also found that there is a lack of political will to use the full potential of performance management in India.

(d) **Alignment with overall goals:** It is also a challenge to align the targets mentioned in the RFD with the overall plans and goals of the Central Government.

(e) **Alignment with PAR (Performance Appraisal Report):** Further, it is a challenge to align the goals of the RFD with the annual performance appraisal of the employees.

(f) **Alignment with Incentive System:** Furthermore, it is also a challenge to align the RFD with the incentive system of the employees.

12.5.3.3 Independent Evaluation Office

The Independent Evaluation Office (IEO) started functioning in 2013. Its structure and functioning is superior to the PEO functioning under the Planning Commission for several reasons. They are as mentioned below:

(a) **Arm's-length Relationship:** The IEO functions at an arm's length from the Planning Commission, unlike the PEO. This arm's-length relationship helps in making it independent from the government.

(b) **Influence over Line Ministries:** The IEO is intended to exercise its influence over the line ministries. There are two features built into the IEO's structure that give it more influence over the line ministries than the PEO. First, the head of the IEO is an ex-officio member of the Planning Commission. As the Planning Commission is the funding body of the line ministries' programmes, the head of the IEO is able to exercise influence over the line ministries through the Planning Commission. Second, the head of the IEO holds the rank of minister of state and is, thus, one level above the line ministries' civil service head.

(c) **Expert Professionals:** The IEO is staffed with professionals in the fields of health, education, statistics, and so on, whereas the PEO was staffed with generalist officers from the Indian Economic Service and Indian Administrative Service.

(d) **Independent Budget:** The budget of IEO is entirely independent of the Planning Commission (or NITI Aayog).

(e) **Expert Reporting:** The head of the IEO reports to the deputy chairperson of the Planning Commission (or NITI Aayog) who is a technocrat and not a political executive.

Mandate of IEO

The mandate of the IEO is to conduct evaluations of planned programmes, especially the larg flagship programmes, to assess their effectiveness, relevance, and impact. The evaluation reports ar submitted to the Parliament and the Prime Minister's Office. The findings can also be made publi without any interference from the government.

Functions of IEO

The functions of the IEO include the following:

- To help improve the effectiveness of government policies and programmes by assessin their impact and outcomes.
- To set the guidelines and methodology for all evaluations done by various departments an agencies and encourage a culture of openness and learning in government systems.
- To connect India to the best internationally evaluated evidence in development practice an knowledge; to learn from others' successes and mistakes.

12.5.3.4 Development Monitoring and Evaluation Office

The Development Monitoring and Evaluation Office (DMEO) was created under the NITI Aayog or 18 September 2015 to subsume the work of the PEO and IEO.

12.6 Emerging Tools and Methods of Policy Analysis

The emerging field of big data and data analysis has had a tremendous impact on various socia science fields including policy sciences. Thus, it has found a place in the field of policymaking anc policy analysis. Some of the modern analytical tools used in policy analysis are discussed in the following.[94]

(a) **Randomised Control Trials:** Randomised control trials (RCTs) are the most familiar tools for medical and psychology research. In these trials, there is a control group and a group that receives the treatment. These studies enable causal interference by randomly assigning a policy intervention to some people or areas and comparing the results to the control group's parameters. This helps in examining the effects of policy implementation.[95]

For example, in the case of education, RCTs are used for examining the impact of policies such as distribution of free textbooks and out-of-school tutoring. RCT research helps in reaching certain inferences, which cannot be deduced from the traditional methods of evaluation. For example, it was found in research that distributing free textbooks to African students did not lead to an improvement in their test scores.[96]

(a) **Policy Informatics:** In policy informatics, cutting-edge data science techniques are applied to a wide range of policy analysis and implementation issues. It applies a combination of computational thinking, complex systems modelling, data analysis, and participatory science to help governments deal with complex governance problems.[97]

Policy informatics is an analytical approach that comprises concepts, methods, and processes for understanding complex public policy and management problems. Policy informatics uses modern computational methods to process vast quantities of data, mine data from single and multiple sources, seek patterns in multidimensional data, and develop models of various phenomena. It helps in stakeholder engagement and model building and interpretation at various stages of the policy process.[98]

(c) **Process Mining:** Almost all policy implementations involve creating at least one process. In fact, much of policy analysis involves examining a policy's processes to determine how to implement the policy more effectively. Process mining is an emerging management field that examines workflow data to discover how processes work and to determine ways to improve them. Process miners use data for events that occur as a part of the process, as work is passed from one participant node to another. This data, which is collected into an event log, is analysed with specialised software to map workflows. Policy analysts can create policy event logs to map how work and information flow in a policy process or even in policy networks.

(d) **Design Thinking:** Design thinking is a solution-based method of problem solving or policy implementation. It differs from the traditional problem-oriented approach to policy analysis because design thinking focuses on iterating toward a solution that fulfils a desired outcome. Design thinkers use various methods to develop empathy with the people who will use future solution or policy outputs. Stakeholders are interviewed to find out what they perceive as problems. Design thinker practitioners then create prototypes to gain feedback from the stakeholders. The advantage of design thinking is that the almost constant feedback from the eventual users of the solution guarantees acceptance of that solution.

(e) **Agile Project Management:** There are various similarities between project management and policy implementation. Both of them share the goal of solving a problem or introducing something new. Moreover, both involve creating a temporary organisation that implements a solution within a specific time period. Agile project management is different from traditional project management in the sense that agile project practitioners iterate toward the eventual project product based on stakeholder feedback. Iterating toward an eventual policy solution, based on stakeholder feedback, could also be more effective than the traditional method of policymaking.

SUMMARY

The modern tools of policy analysis and implementation discussed in this chapter and otherwise are important in the times of complex policy and governance issues. These tools introduce new data analysis methods to better test policy assumptions and determine the causal factors for policy analysis and implementation. Moreover, they use well-tested management methods to improve policy implementation.

Practice Questions

1. "Mega policies form a kind of master policy, as distinct from concrete discrete policies." Comment.
2. Explain the systems model of public policy.
3. "Public policy is the product of public institutions, whose structures are responsible for public policy implementation." Explain in the light of the institutional model of public policy.
4. "There are four arenas of power for public policies." (Lowi) Explain.
5. "Policy is formulated in a window of opportunity." Discuss.
6. "Public policy can be characterised as the output of the diffuse made up of individuals who interact with each other in a small group in a framework dominated by formal organisations." Explain in the light of the political policy process model of public policy.
7. "The mixed approach of public policy, advocated by Hogwood and Gunn, considers two aspects of public policy together—application of technical analysis and the political process associated with public policy." Discuss.
8. "Rational policy is one that maximises the net value achievement in a policy." (Robert Haveman) Discuss.
9. "Strategic planning is an attempt to systemise the chaotic process of decision-making in administration." Explain.
10. What are the various methods of public policy implementation?
11. Explain the various top-down and bottom-up models of policy implementation.
12. "Policymaking process may be skewed by policy implementation, which is largely dominated by the professionals." (Dunleavy) Discuss.
13. "Success of a policy depends on the skills of individuals in the local implementation structure, which can help in adapting a national policy to local conditions." (Hjern) Discuss with reference to policy implementation structures.
14. "The value of policy can be described in the degree of ambiguity in means and goals of a policy and the degree of conflict in it." (Matland) Examine.
15. "Implementation is a nexus of a series of communication channels." (Goggin) Discuss.
16. "The process of implementing policy reforms is interactive rather than linear." Examine.
17. Explain the different models of policy evaluation.
18. Discuss the institutions involved in policy implementation in India.

CHAPTER 13

Techniques for Administrative Improvement

After reading this chapter, you will learn the following:

- Organisation and methods (O&M)
- Work study and work management
- Network analysis such as programme evaluation and review technique (PERT) and critical path method (CPM)
- Management information system (MIS)

Apart from these, there are some important techniques of administrative improvement such as e-governance, impact assessment, programme monitoring and evaluation system (PMES), and results framework document (RFD), which have already been discussed in the previous chapters of this book.

As administration is becoming complex and widespread, there is an ongoing quest for developing scientific techniques for administrative improvement. Every organisation, private or public, is interested in these techniques, as these techniques bring economy and efficiency to organisational functioning. At a broader level, these techniques are targeted towards the following:

(a) Fixing a standard of work in the organisation

(b) Assigning the responsibility and accountability of different personnel and units in an organisation

(c) Suggesting measures towards bringing economy and efficiency in work processes and eliminating wasteful expenditure and unnecessary activities in the organisation

(d) Providing tools to employees for efficient discharge of their duties, ensuring harmony in employer-employee relations

(e) Suggesting proper channels of communication in an organisation to understand the views of both the employer and the employees

(f) Suggesting methods for improving the budget and financial control processes in the organisation.

13.1 Organisation and Methods

There are two meanings of organisation and methods (O&M). The first meaning is narrower in its approach and deals with the internal structuring of an organisational unit. This meaning is generally adopted in countries such as India and England. The second meaning is broader in its meaning and connotes it as a technique of administrative importance. This meaning is generally adopted in countries such as the US. Both approaches are discussed in the following sections.

Narrow Definition of O&M

Organisation and method is a technique for improving the work procedures and structure of organisations to bring efficiency and improvement in both. It helps in eliminating duplication, waste, and delay by restructuring the organisation and simplifying its processes. A formal definition of O&M describes it as "the examination of the structure of the organisation under review and the studying of administrative and clerical methods, office mechanisation and equipment, office layout and working conditions in order to improve the efficiency of the organisation."[1]

In a nutshell, it is an important tool to streamline the functioning of an organisation. However, it is concerned only with a single unit of an organisation and does not deal with the rearrangement of different units within an organisation.

In O&M, 'O' stands for organisation or internal structure and 'M' stands for the methods or work processes of a unit. As far as the 'organisation' part is concerned, O&M deals with the restructuring of the internal structure of a unit for bringing in efficiency. The 'methods' part deals with reviewing the procedures and systems of transacting work to improve the functioning of a unit.

Broad Definition of O&M

In the broader sense, O&M is aimed at improving the entire process of management, including planning, organising, coordinating, motivating, directing, and controlling. In the words of L.D. White, "O&M is regarded as the improvement of all aspects of transacting business with special emphasis upon procedures and relationships."[4] While recommending O&M for India, Paul Appleby emphasised the broader definition of O&M. He said, "I recommend that the Government of India give consideration to the establishment of a Central Office (Office of O&M) charged with the responsibility for giving both extensive and intensive leadership in respect to structure, management and procedures. At one level of the highly technical and scientific sort, it would give attention to work measurement, work flow, office management, filing systems, space arrangements and the like; at another level, it would be charged with general governmental structural studies and proposals."[5]

13.1.1 Origin of O&M

The need for O&M was first felt in industries in the eighteenth century to increase production and profits. It was introduced in public administration at the end of the nineteenth century. In modern times, F.W. Taylor laid down the foundation of O&M in his treatise *The Principles of Scientific*

Management. The basic principles formulated by Taylor, such as the standard of work and differential wage scheme, are the origins of O&M.

O&M was introduced in the United Kingdom during the First World War. In the US, the Federal Government set up a Bureau of Efficiency in 1913 for doing O&M work. In India, the Central Government set up the O&M division in 1954 consequent to the recommendations of A.D. Gorwala and Paul H. Appleby.

13.1.2 Functions of O&M

The O&M department is a staff department whose sole purpose is to recommend changes in the internal functioning of an organisational unit. The responsibility of taking actions on these recommendations is that of the chief executive of a unit and not that of the O&M department. The functions of O&M are as follows:

(a) **Research:** One of the main functions of O&M is to conduct research for developing new ideas for administrative improvement. Such research deals with honing techniques such as work management, work simplification, quality control, improvement in office management, sound record management, measurement of work, and cost control.

(b) **Investigation:** The O&M office conducts investigations into analysing the procedures and methods of administrative units.

(c) **Training:** The O&M office provides training to the O&M staff for better research and investigation for O&M.

(d) **Information:** The O&M office is the clearing house of all information regarding O&M work transacted at all levels in the government. It collects relevant information, builds a library, and makes available information to those who require it.

(e) **Publication:** The O&M office publishes guides, manuals, research material, and other literature related to the theory and practice of O&M.

(f) **Coordination:** The O&M department plays a major role in the coordination of O&M activities so that overlapping, duplication, and contradictions are avoided. It assists the efforts of the line departments in planning and implementing their O&M activities.

In the words of E.D. Melrose, the role of O&M can be described as "to get the best organisation and best method to obtain a desired and necessary end with the minimum of outlay and effort."[5]

13.1.3 Techniques of O&M

The O&M specialists have developed a number of techniques for simplifying procedures, measuring work performance, and assisting efficient management. Some of these techniques are described as follows:

(a) **Survey:** One of the most important techniques of O&M is the management survey into the functioning of different departments. A management survey is a systematic examination of one or more related organisations, functions, and procedures. It is initiated for the purpose of identifying problems, determining their causes, and developing solutions.[6] It is instrumental in determining the suitability of personnel policies, appropriateness of organisational arrangements, the effectiveness of supervision, and the requisites for better performance.

(b) **Inspections:** Inspections are used to find faults in the functioning of a unit and to suggest measures for improvement in the future. Through periodical inspections, in collaboration with the chief executive of a unit, the O&M analysts can assist in work improvement.

(c) **Forms Control:** O&M analysts periodically upgrade the nature of forms used in a department to improve internal communication and simplify procedures. The forms play an important role in the effective management of an agency as they furnish information for formulating policies, controlling subordinate staff, and evaluating their performance. Forms constitute the basis for clerical and executive actions.

(d) **File Operations:** A filing system denotes a method of arranging records in a systematic sequence. Such a system is important for the easy location of any particular record in a file and is instrumental for the proper functioning of a department. Unorganised file operations lead to delayed decision-making and inefficient operations. O&M specialists deal with problems in file operations such as file classification, training of unit staff, issuing and controlling of files, and retention and disposal of files.

(e) **Work Simplification:** Work simplification means the use of different methodologies to break down the complex work of an organisation into simple procedures. The various techniques of work simplification include work distribution charts and process charts. The work distribution chart is used to distribute the total activities of a unit among the employees working in it. Every employee is held responsible for the activity assigned to him/her and necessary time is allocated for performing that activity. A process chart furnishes a detailed record of the successive steps involved in a particular activity. Various process charts such as PERT and CPM will be discussed later in this chapter.

(f) **Work Measurement:** Work measurement is a technique used to set up a standard between work produced by an operating unit and the human resources used in the process. It is the application of techniques designed to accomplish the work content of a specific task by determining the time required to carry it out while conforming to a defined standard of performance by a qualified worker. It is an important technique to measure the volume of work and establish an equitable relationship between the work output and human resources. Various methodologies of work measurement will be discussed later in this chapter.

(g) **Automation:** Automation is the use of mechanical processes for doing office work. It is used for accounting, filing, tabulating, punching, sorting, stamping, and various types of computational work. Mechanisation of routine and repetitive work is economical both from the point of view of money and human resources. E-governance is one of the largest mechanisms of automation of government services.

13.1.4 O&M in India

O&M was introduced in India in 1954 and the O&M Division is a part of the Department of Administrative Reforms and Public Grievances (DAR&PG) at present. It is headed by a director of the rank of joint secretary. Apart from this, there is an O&M cell/unit in each ministry that is headed by an officer of the rank of deputy secretary.

The work of the O&M Division was very important in the early years of the independence of India. At that time, it gave crucial suggestions on the ways and means of simplification of office procedures and removal of delays and bottlenecks. It also suggested means for expeditious movement of files and papers from one end to the other. It also suggested ways and means to decide the extent of delegation of work to lower authorities. Moreover, it helped in suggesting the preservation of old records.

At present, the O&M Division performs all the functions mentioned in Section 13.1.2.

13.1.5 Advantages of O&M

The advantages of O&M are as follows:

(a) **Improvement in Administration:** O&M serves as an important device for improvement in the administration of a unit. It critically reviews the various branches of an organisation and the methods of work adopted by them.

(b) **Updating of Structure and Procedure:** The machinery of O&M helps in keeping the structure of the government office and procedures adopted by it up-to-date. It helps in recommending ways for a government organisation to adapt itself to the changing times.

(c) **Reservoir of Experience:** The O&M Division functions as the reservoir of best practices and successful administrative experiences. This wealth proves conducive to offices and institutions with regard to problems pertaining to organisation and methods.

13.1.6 Disadvantages of O&M

The disadvantages of O&M are as follows:

(a) **Fault-finding Exercise:** It is contended that O&M often degenerates into a fault-finding exercise. It is seen that the O&M analysts start behaving as inspectors rather than playing the role of supporting the administration. When they start finding faults in an organisation, the organisation concerned develops resistance to working with them.

(b) **Usurping of Line Functions:** Rather than being advisors, O&M analysts often try to encroach upon the powers of administrators and managers.

(c) **Technical in Nature:** Sometimes the work of the O&M division becomes too technical in nature. The more technical their work, the less can they win the confidence of the head of a department.

13.2 Work Study and Work Management

Work study is the study of the measurement of work and its improvement. It is based on Taylor's basic ideas about work, method, and time management (discussed in the Chapter 3 on *'Administrative Thought*). It is a generic term for all methodologies used for the examination of human work in all its contexts. It is useful in the investigation of all the factors that affect the efficiency and economy of a work situation. Work study has two important components:

(a) Method study

(b) Time and motion study

13.2.1 Method Study

Method study is the study of the method or process of work to achieve improvements in layout design, and working environment. It enables an administrator to subject each operation to systematic analysis. Its main purpose is to eliminate unnecessary operations and achieve the best method of performing a task. In the standard definition, method study is "the systematic recording and critical examination of existing and proposed ways of doing work as a means of developing and applying easier and more effective methods and reducing cost."[7]

13.2.1.1 Objectives of Method Study

Method study plays an important role in adding value and increasing efficiency in the work by eliminating unnecessary operations, avoiding delays, and avoiding other forms of wastage. It has the following objectives:

- Improvement of work processes and procedures
- Improvement of the design of the organisational unit and equipment used to do work
- Improvement in the layout of organisational unit
- Improvement in the use of the human resource, material resource, machines, and other resources
- Economy in human efforts and reduction of unnecessary fatigue
- Improvement in safety standards
- Development of better working environment

13.2.1.2 Steps Involved in Method Study

A basic approach to method study consists of the following eight steps (see Figure 13.1):

1. **Select:** The work to be studied is selected and its boundaries are defined.
2. **Record:** The relevant facts about the work are recorded by direct observation and from other sources.
3. **Examine:** The way the job is being performed is examined and its challenges, procedure, and method of performance are analysed.
4. **Develop:** Some practical, economic, and effective alternative methods are developed based on the contributions of the concerned employees.
5. **Evaluate:** The different alternatives for developing a new improved method are evaluated by comparing the cost effectiveness of the selected new method with that of the existing method.
6. **Define:** A new method is defined based on the evaluation of different alternatives. This new method is presented to the management, supervisors, and workers.

7. **Install:** The involved employees are trained and the new method is installed as a standard practice.
8. **Maintain:** The new method is maintained and various control procedures are adopted to prevent drifting back to the previous method of work.

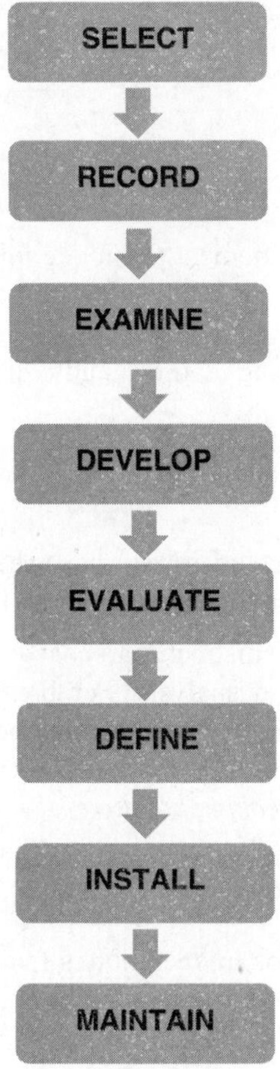

Fig. 13.1: *Flow Chart Representing the Procedure of Method Study*

13.2.1.3 Tools of Method Study

The tools of method study can be classified as *exploratory tools* and *recording and analysis tools.* The exploratory tools are:

- o Pareto analysis
- o Fish bone diagram
- o Gantt, PERT, and CPM charts

The recording and analysis tools are:

- o Outline process chart
- o Flow process chart
- o Flow diagram
- o Worker and machine process charts
- o Gang process charts
- o Synchronous servicing

13.2.2 Time and Motion Study

Time and motion study is a work measurement technique for recording the time taken for performin a certain job or its elements carried out under specific conditions. It is a direct and continuou observation of a task using a timekeeping device (e.g., a stopwatch) to record the time taken t accomplish the task. Before conducting a time study, it should be ensured that the work ha undergone method study.

In the time study, there are certain terms that need to be understood first. These terms are a follows:

(a) **Rating:** Rating is a technique to assess the speed and effectiveness of a worker. It i subjective and relies on the skill of the observer carrying out the rating exercise.

(b) **Element:** An element is a distinct part of a specified job selected for convenien observation, measurement, and analysis. For breaking down a job into its elements, th elements should be easily identified with definite beginnings and endings. Once established these elements should be repeatedly recognised. The point at which one element ends an another begins is called the *breaking point.*

(c) **Standard Time:** Standard time is the time that is allowed to perform the job satisfactorily:

Standard Time = Basic Time + Allowances

(d) **Basic Time:** The basic time for an operation is found by relating the observed time with th observed rate of working:

Basic Time = Observed Time × Observed Rating

(e) **Allowances:** In the operation, there are certain kinds of allowances, such as relaxatio allowances, contingency allowances (time to meet expected items of work or delays), polic allowances, and special allowances.

13.2.2.1 Steps required for Time and Motion Study

For conducting a time study, the following steps are followed:

(a) **Recording Information:** All information about the job is obtained and recorded. Moreover information about the operative and surrounding environment is also recorded.

(b) **Recording Method:** A description of the work method is recorded by breaking down th whole operation into elements.

(c) **Examination of Breakdown:** The breakdown is examined to ensure that the most effective method and motions are used.

(d) **Time Measurement:** The time taken to perform each element of the operation is measured using a timing device.

(e) **Speed Measurement:** The effective speed of working of the worker relative to the observer's concept of the standard rate is measured.

(f) **Basic Time:** Basic time is calculated using the observed time and the observed rate.

(g) **Determining Allowances:** The allowances are determined over and above the basic time for the operation.

(h) **Determining Standard Time:** The standard time for the operation is then determined.

(i) **Determining Ineffective Time:** The ineffective time is determined by the time lost due to inefficiency caused by material, method, and human resources.

(j) **Improvement Measures:** Measures are adopted to reduce the ineffective time and complete the task in the standard time.

A simple example of time study and motion study is given in Case Study 13.1.

Case Study 13.1: Time and Motion Study for Making Steel Bar[8]

A steel bar making operation can be divided into various elements, as shown in Table 13.1. The average time for completing the various elements and the whole job is calculated in the table. The total time calculated in Table 13.1 (2345.4 sec) is the observed time. This is not the standard time for performing the work.

Table 13.1: Average time taken for making steel bars (in seconds)

Labour	Transfer steel bar	Straight steel bar	Cutting bar	Cutting ring	Bending bar (1 ring)	Bending bar (20 ring)	Apply ring to beam	Fit ring on beam
1	40	220	50	45	35	750	75	990
2	49	225	52	49	48	960	78	975
3	43	286	48	43	39	800	80	956
4	39	246	46	41	45	956	72	980
5	42	276	51	39	42	863	70	983
Average	42.6	250.6	49.4	43.4	41.8	865.8	75	976.8

The standard time for the basic work is only 2052.2 sec. The rest of the time is ineffective time that id lost in unnecessary activities, as shown in Table 13.2.

Table 13.2: Time for basic work and ineffective time in steel making (in seconds)

Time for basic work	2052.2
Time added by poor material utilisation/management	42.6
Time added by inefficient method of operation	200.2
Time added by inefficient contribution of human resources	50.4
Total time	2345.4

Then the reasons for this ineffective time are explored. This is illustrated in Table 13.3.

Table 13.3: Causes for ineffective time

Work content added by poor material utilisation/management	A1: poor design and frequent design changes
	A2: waste of materials
	A3: incorrect quality standards
Work content added by inefficient method of operation	B1: poor layout and utilisation of space
	B2: frequent stoppages
	B3: improper handling of materials z
	B4: ineffective method of work
	B5: poor planning of inventory
	B6: frequent breakdown of machines and equipment
Work content added by inefficient contribution of human resources	C1: absenteeism and lateness
	C2: poor workmanship
	C3: accidents and occupational hazards

The work method can be improved by taking measures to reduce the time wasted. Some of the following measures can be taken to reduce this ineffective time:

(a) The work content due to poor design can be reduced by proper product development.

(b) Waste can be reduced by proper material utilisation.

(c) Unnecessary movements can be reduced by better planning, work area layout, and processes.

(d) Proper materials handling can be adapted to reduce time and effort.

(e) Method study can help in reducing work content due to poor methods of work.

(f) Inventory control can help in defining the appropriate and most economical inventory level.

(g) Training can help in reducing the time wasted owing to unskilled human resources.

13.3 Network Analysis

In public administration, complex projects are adopted, which require the interdependence of the efforts of a variety of people and organisations. Thus, understanding this network is very important for effective administration. Such a network has already been discussed in the topic 'Networked Organisations/ Boundary Less Organisations' of Chapter 5 on '*Organisational Dynamics*'.

In network analysis, networks model the interrelated workflows that must be accomplished to complete a project. They visually portray the events and activities that are planned for the project and show their sequential relationships and interdependencies. The analysis of such a network for improving project implementation is known as *network analysis*, in which a systems approach is adopted for completing a programme/project.

There are four basic steps in network analysis:

(a) **Network Generation:** A network is generated for a project implementation cycle. The first step in this regard is the specification of the project's goals and objectives. In the second step, the specific events and activities to be carried out for achieving these goals and objectives are specified. A network consisting of these events and activities is made with the corresponding time and cost estimates.

(b) **Network Evaluation:** The network generated is evaluated by a manager/specialist to determine its soundness.

(c) **Network Monitoring:** The network is then monitored to determine the extent to which the project is proceeding as planned and whether managerial interventions are required to correct the course of the project. Where such interventions are necessary, the network provides useful data for weighing the possible alternative managerial actions.

(d) **Network Modification:** The network plan may be modified to attain the project objectives and improve managerial control over the project.

13.3.1 Basic Concepts in Network Analysis

The basic concepts used in network analysis are the following:

(a) **Network:** A network consists of a series of events (represented by circles) and activities (represented by arrows), with time and/or cost data associated with each of these activities.

(b) **Event:** An event is represented by a circle. In networks, an event is an identifiable point in time at which an activity is begun or completed. These points are described by placing a few keywords within the circles, as shown in Figure 13.2. An event does not consume any time or effort. It is just a point in time.

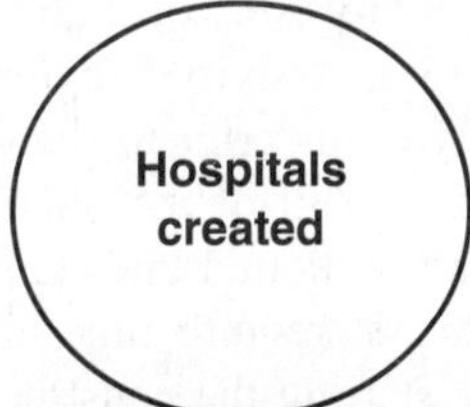

Fig. 13.2: *Example of an 'Event'*

(c) **Activities:** Activities are represented by arrows (see Figure 13.3). They are the time- and resource-consuming efforts required to complete an event.

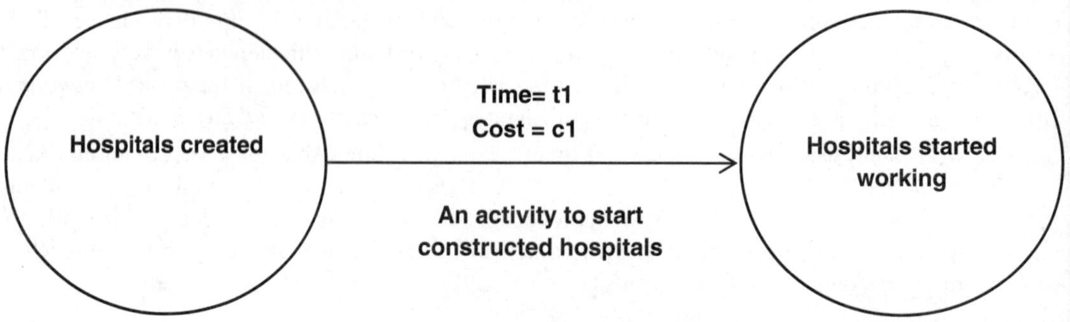

***Fig. 13.3:** Example of an 'Activity'*

(d) **Generation of Network:** A network is made up of activities and events that are interconnected in accordance with the logic underlying the actual work. Each predecessor event must be completed before subsequent activities can be initiated in a network. Figure 13.4 represents a simple network. When an activity is directly dependent on an event, the arrow of that activity emanates from that event. In Figure 13.4, the logic of the network indicates that Activity B is directly dependent on Event 2 and indirectly dependent on Event 1. However, Activities C and F are directly dependent on Event 3. The work going on sequentially can be depicted by a serial or linear network. The work going on simultaneously can be depicted by a parallel network.

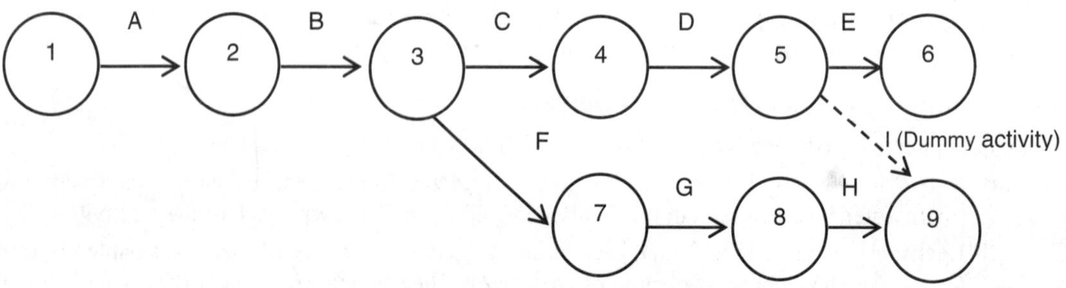

***Fig. 13.4:** Example of a Simple Network*

(e) **Dummy Activity:** A dummy activity is a constraint that hinders the accomplishment of an event. For example, in Figure 13.4, Activity I represent a dummy activity. It indicates that the completion of Event 5 must occur prior to the completion of Event 9 even though no resource or time is required as a result of the relationship between the two events. These dummy activities are represented by dotted lines to show dependency relationships that are important even though they do not require time and resources. For example, a building permit must be required before starting the construction of a hospital but no resources are consumed as a result of this relationship.

(f) **Time Estimates:** A time estimate is a forecast of the time required for an activity. There are three types of time estimates that are used to account for the uncertainty involved in any plan. They are as follows:

- **Optimistic Time:** It is an estimate of the shortest time an activity will take. It is represented by a.
- **Pessimistic Time:** It is an estimate of the longest time an activity is likely to take. It is represented by b.
- **Most Likely Time:** It is an estimate of the amount of time an activity would normally take. It is represented by m.
- **Expected Time:** Expected time is the time an activity is expected to take for completion. It is represented by the symbol t_e and is calculated using optimistic time, pessimistic time, and most likely time:

  $t_e = (a + 4m + b)/6$

(g) **Other Time Concepts:** Other relevant concepts related to time are as follows:

- **Standard Deviation:** Standard deviation is calculated as the amount of uncertainty involved in the activity estimate:

  Standard deviation (σ) = $(b - a)/6$

  Variance = σ^2
- **Earliest Expected Time:** It is the time by which an event can be completed. It is obtained by adding the calculated time estimates (t_e) of each activity on the longest path prior to the event.
- **Latest Allowable Time:** It is the time by which an event must be completed to prevent delaying the completion of the total project. It is obtained for an event by tracking back from the final event along the longest path to the event in question. The expected times of all the activities on this path are added, and the sum is subtracted from the total time on the critical path. The resulting number is the maximum time that can elapse from the beginning of the project to the completion of this event without compelling a delay in the completion of the project.

(h) **Critical Path:** The critical path is the longest path (in terms of time) through the network. Any time delay in this path will result in a delay in the accomplishment of the whole project.

(i) **Slack:** Slack refers to the difference between the latest allowable time T_L and the earliest expected time T_E for the completion of a given event. The amount of slack available tells about the path on which an event is located. An event on the critical path has 0 slack. All other events have ascertainable amounts of slack, the knowledge of which provides managers with an understanding of their available flexibility:

Slack for an event = $T_L - T_E$

(j) **Standard Deviation of Critical Path:** The standard deviation of the critical path provides a measure of the extent of uncertainty involved in the plan's scheduled completion time (IT$_S$I) for the total project. It is obtained by summing the variances for each activity on the critical path and then taking the square root of the sum to obtain the desired standard deviation.

(k) **Probability to Complete Project on Time:** It is possible to calculate the probability to complete the project on time. This probability is calculated by first subtracting the sum of the expected times ($t_e s$) for the activities in the critical path from the completion time $IT_S I$ and then dividing this figure by the standard deviation of the initial path. This calculation provides the slack in the critical path, expressed in terms of the standard deviation of the initial path. The larger this quotient, the less likely it is that the scheduled completion date will be missed.

13.3.2 Critical Path Method

The various techniques of network analysis include the critical path method (CPM) and programme evaluation and review technique (PERT). These techniques are derived from the Gantt chart (as discussed in the topic 'Henry Gantt' in Chapter 3 of this book).

The CPM was originally founded by the engineers of the Du Pont company in the 1950s. In the CPM, a network of the programme is made, as explained already, by breaking down the whole programme into events and activities. The programme is divided into its elementary parts in chronological order. It helps in finding out the more strategic elements of a plan for the purpose of better designing, planning, coordinating, and controlling of the entire programme.

In the CPM, the critical path is computed as explained already. The calculation of this critical path helps in shortening the time span of the whole programme by various methods and in its timely completion. Furthermore, breaking the programme down helps in the optimum utilisation of the resources. Moreover, it helps the administrators in making advance planning for all the activities, identifying strategic events, detecting potential bottlenecks, and so on. In a nutshell, the CPM helps in improving the quality of planning, organisation, and control because of concentrated thinking and attention on each activity of a project.

However, the CPM has certain limitations. It is not useful for routine projects. Its time estimates do not account for future contingencies and impending difficulties.

13.3.3 Programme Evaluation and Review Technique

PERT is an advancement of the CPM technique. It attempts to address the limitations of the CPM technique. It was first used in the US defence projects in connection with the execution of the Polaris Missile Programme in 1958. As an advancement of the CPM, it uses statistical methods for estimating the time required for each activity. Instead of using one single time as in the CPM, PERT calculates the expected time for each activity on the basis of the optimum time, pessimistic time, and most likely time.

Thus, the PERT system can be applied to new projects with no past data. Apart from this, the technique of PERT is similar to the CPM. Thus, like CPM, it allows for systematic planning of the project. It allows concentrating attention on critical elements that need correction or modification. It also helps in effectively coordinating all the activities and events in a complex project.

However, the PERT system also has certain limitations. The expected time for each activity of a new programme cannot be calculated with certainty. Further, like CPM, PERT has limited application in planning routine activities. Among various resources, PERT considers only the time element. Thus, it is suitable for only those projects where only time is of essential consideration.

Case Study 13.2: Application of Network Analysis to Manufacture of Fuel Engine[10]

A car manufacturing company decided to redesign its fuel engine. The project involved various activities as shown in Table 13.4.

Table 13.4: Activities and their sequence for manufacturing fuel engine

Activity	Description of activity	Predecessor activity	Time estimates (weeks)
A	Evolve the design of the fuel engine	--	5
B	Develop marketing strategy	A	4
C	Design manufacturing process	A	7
D	Select advertising media	B	8
E	Initial product run	C	9
F	Release fuel pump to market	D, E	4

A network diagram for this project is as shown in Figure 13.5.

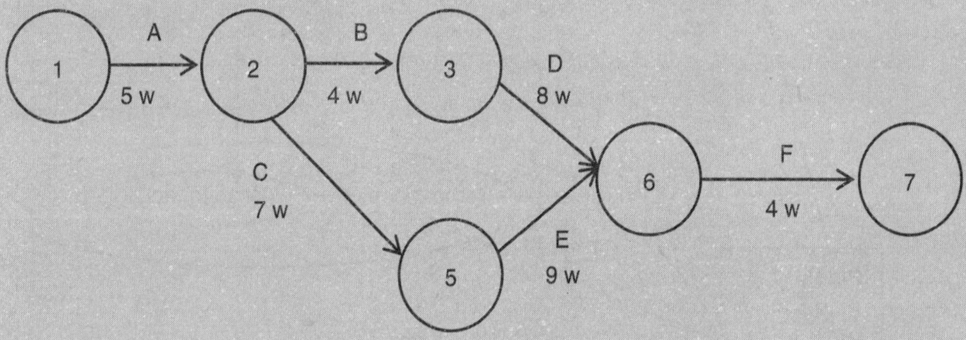

Points 1, 2, 3, 4, 5, 6 and 7 represent different events in time like 5th weak (point 2), 9th weak (point 3rd), and so on. Here w stands for weak.

Fig. 13.5: Network for making fuel pump according to table 13.4

In this simple network, A → C → E → F is the critical path as it requires 25 weeks to complete, whereas path A → B → D → F requires only 21 weeks to complete. It is called critical because a delay in the activities on this path would delay the whole project.

This is a simple example with a simple network. However, complex networks can be constructed in a similar manner.

13.4 Management Information System

A management information system (MIS) is a system to support the decision-making functions in an organisation. It is also known as an information system, information and decision system, and computer-based information system. It is a computerised business processing system that generates information to meet the information needs of the people in the organisation. It assists in decision-making and improving service delivery for all concerned.

It is also defined as an information system that provides reports to assist the managerial monitoring and control of organisational functions, resources, and other responsibilities. Dealing with a broader picture, among other management functions, the MIS aids the process of monitoring and control, as shown in Figure 13.6. In this figure, monitoring and control represent a feedback loop, in which information about a later stage is fed back into the control unit of an earlier stage. As shown in the figure, MIS can be of the following types:

(a) **Monitoring MIS:** The monitoring MIS gathers information about output performance and presents it to the managers, who then use it for comparison themselves.

(b) **Monitoring and Control MIS:** In this MIS, the preset standards for output performance are fed into the computer system. The MIS is thus able to perform the comparisons itself.

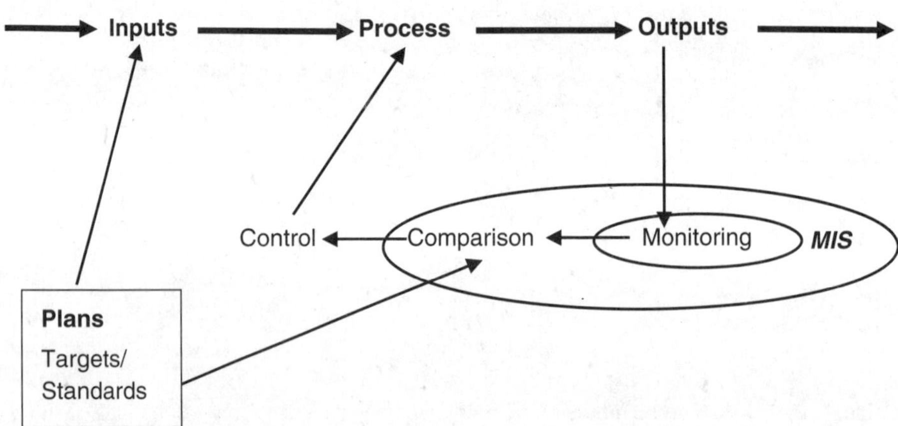

Fig. 13.6: *Role of Management in the whole process of Monitoring and Control*[11]

Apart from this, the main features of the MIS are its linkage to the data gathering system and generation of reports. The MIS often relies on monitoring data produced by an organisational database. Reports are central to the monitoring and controlling roles of MIS. They provide much of the organisational value to the MIS.

13.4.1 Role of MIS in an Organisation

The role of the MIS in an organisation is the same as that of the heart in the body. The information is the blood and the MIS is the heart. Much like the heart supplies blood to all parts, the MIS supplies information to all parts of an organisation. It ensures that appropriate data are collected from various sources, processed, and sent further to all destinations. The information needs are satisfied by a variety of systems such as query systems, analysis systems, modelling systems, and decision support systems. By providing timely information, the MIS helps in strategic planning, management control, operational control, and transaction processing.

The MIS helps different levels of personnel in different ways:

(a) **Clerical Personnel:** The MIS helps the clerical personnel in transaction processing and answering their queries on the data pertaining to transactions, the status of a particular record, and references to a variety of documents.

(b) **Junior Management:** It helps the junior management by providing operational data for planning, scheduling, and controlling, and helps them in decision-making at the operations level to correct an out-of-control situation.

(c) **Middle Management:** It helps the middle management in short-term planning, target setting, and controlling their divisional functions.

(d) **Top Management:** It helps the top management in goal setting, strategic planning, evolving organisational plans, and ensuring their implementation. Further, it plays the role of information generation, communication, and problem identification and helps in the decision-making process.

13.4.2 Automation of Decision-Making using MIS

In the MIS, the output from the comparison stage forms an input to human decision-making. This process of decision-making is automated in some systems. For example, inventory information systems gather data on the level of stocks and suggest the decision that particular items should be re-ordered if stocks fall below a certain level. Such an automated decision-making system is depicted in Figure 13.7.

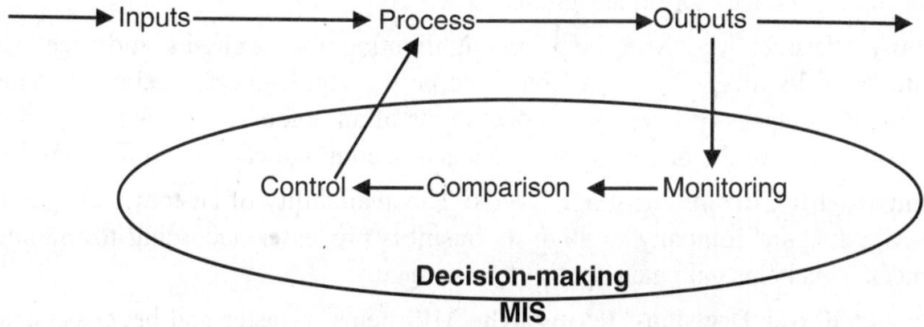

Fig. 13.7: Automated Decision Making using MIS[11]

13.4.3 Factors Responsible for Success of MIS

In an organisation, the following factors are responsible for the success of the MIS:

(a) **Integration of MIS with Managerial Functions:** The MIS of an organisation must be integrated with its managerial functions. The MIS should focus on the major issues of the organisation.

(b) **Appropriate Technology:** For a successful MIS, appropriate information technology is required to meet the data and analysis needs of the users.

(c) **Operational Viability:** The MIS should be operationally viable and should be oriented defined, and designed in terms of the users' requirements.

(d) **Continuous Surveillance:** The MIS should be kept under continuous surveillance so that its open system design can be constantly modified according to the changing information needs.

(e) **Focus on Results:** The focus of the MIS should be on the results, goals, and factors for thei achievement.

(f) **Consider Human Factors:** An efficient MIS recognises that a manager is a human being, and the system must consider all the human behavioural factors in the process of management.

(g) **Information related to Objectives:** A successful MIS recognises that the various organisational objectives have their specific information needs. If information is generated in isolation from the specific needs based on the objectives, it leads to the generation of useless information.

(h) **User-friendly:** A good MIS is easy to operate, and its design features are user-friendly.

(i) **Ability to Upgrade:** In an organisation, new information needs emerge constantly and old needs become obsolete. Thus, the MIS design must have the potential to upgrade itself and quickly meet the changing information needs.

(j) **Focus on Critical Success Factors:** The emphasis of an effective MIS is on the critical success factors of an organisation.

13.4.4 Advantages of MIS

The MIS has several advantages for organisations:

(a) **Company Picture:** The MIS helps in highlighting the strengths and weaknesses of company from its revenue reports, employee performance reports, and so on. This helps in improving the business processes and operations of an organisation. Moreover, it provides macroscopic view of the organisation and acts as a communication and planning tool.

(b) **Alignment with Citizen/Customer Needs:** The availability of customer data and feedback in the MIS helps a company to align its business processes according to the needs of th customers. This helps gain a competitive advantage.

(c) **Faster and Better Decision-Making:** The MIS helps in faster and better decision-making by providing relevant information on time.

13.4.5 Factors Responsible for Failure of MIS

The following factors are responsible for the failure of MIS in an organisation:

(a) **MIS as an impersonal system:** Many times, the MIS is conceived as a data-processing tool and not an information-processing tool. When the MIS processes data only and does no provide relevant information to managers it becomes an impersonal system providing general information. It does not provide the information needed by the managers, but tends to provide the general information that the function calls for. Such an impersonal system is of no use to an organisation.

(b) **MIS not linked to the organisational system:** The MIS fails when it underestimates the complexity in the organisational system and does not incorporate that complexity in its design.

(c) **Inadequate attention to quality control:** The MIS also fails when adequate attention is not given to the quality control aspects of the inputs, process, and outputs, thereby leading to insufficient checks and controls in the MIS.

(d) **Inadequate Training:** The MIS is unsuccessful when it is deployed without providing adequate training to all the stakeholders. The generators of data and the users of information are different sets of people, and both are required to be brought on the same footing by the medium of regular training.

(e) **Non-user-friendly:** The MIS fails when it does not meet certain critical and key factors for its users, such as response to a database query, inability to get the processing done in a particular manner, lack of a user-friendly system, and dependence on the system personnel.

(f) **Lack of Discipline:** A lack of administrative discipline in following the standard systems and procedures may result in incomplete and incorrect information and the subsequent failure of the MIS.

13.4.6 Examples of Management Information Systems

The MIS can help in supporting a variety of public sector functions. Among others, it is useful for internal transaction functions, regulation functions, and service delivery functions.

13.4.6.1 Internal Transaction Based MIS

As far as organisational internal transactions are concerned, the MIS helps in accounting, human resource management, and other functions. Some of the examples of these are as follows:

(a) **MIS for Accounting:** The MIS is very useful for activities related to monetary control, control on money spent, comparison with the budget, and control of expenditure to bring it close to that sanctioned in the budget. To this end, the MIS generates reports such as statements of accounts, warning on budgets, and statements of cash requirements.

(b) **MIS for Human Resource Management:** The MIS is used in the entire human resource lifecycle, from recruitment to termination or retirement. Reports for this include vacancies, recruitment and selection, performance appraisal, payroll management, training, promotion, turnover, and pensions.

(c) **MIS Inventory Management:** The MIS is used for monitoring stock levels and controlling stocks to ensure that all items are neither overstocked nor understocked.

13.4.6.2 MIS for Regulating Activities

The MIS helps in supporting and regulating a whole range of activities in public administration. For example, in the US, the National Drivers Register has MIS facilities to report on driver license details, such as information about those driver licenses that have been revoked or suspended.[13] Similarly, the US Environment Protection Agency uses the MIS to monitor and control environmental risks.[12]

Similarly, the MIS is also used in regulating taxation activities. Based on data recorded about individual taxpaying entities, the MIS helps in monitoring tax payments and producing reports on matters such as details of individual taxpayers, a summary of sales tax receipts, and patterns of non-payment to target enforcement efforts.

13.4.6.3 Public Service Delivery MIS

The MIS is also used by governments to monitor and control public services. It is used in important public services such as education and health. In the case of education, based on the data gathered from schools and other educational institutions, the MIS helps in monitoring the provision of education and producing reports on matters such as details of individual schools, a summary of the average staff, student ratio for each state, and name and location of schools without sports facilities. It also helps in pointing towards the improvement/degradation in the performance of schools over a period of time and a comparison with the standards set by the government.

SUMMARY

The essence of this chapter has been to discuss the various techniques for reforming the administrative system such as Organisation and Methods (O&M), Work Study, Method Study, Performance Evaluation and Review Technique (PERT), Critical Path Method (CPM) and Management Information System (MIS). These modern techniques have evolved from the work of scholars like Frederick Taylor. As tools of administrative reforms, they help in simplification of work, preservation of time, increase in efficiency and effectiveness of work, improvement in managerial monitoring of work, and in faster and better decision making in an organisation.

CHAPTER

14 Financial Administration

After reading this chapter, you will learn the following:

- Importance, scope, and objectives of financial administration
- Various aspects of fiscal policy and monetary policy such as their objectives and instruments
- Phenomenon of public expenditure, its different types, its determinants and theories, its effects, and its status in India
- Concept of public revenue, types of public revenue including tax and non-tax revenue, and overview of tax system in India
- Concept of goods and service tax (GST), its salient features, its benefits, Indian indirect tax structure in the pre-GST and post-GST era, and GST council
- Direct taxes code as a reform in the Indian direct tax structure
- Deficit financing, its advantages, its limitations, and the measures to control it
- Concealed deficit financing or 'March Rush'
- Concept of public debt and public borrowing, methods of public debt payment, negative impacts of public debt, positive impacts of public debt, and the role of the Reserve Bank of India (RBI) in public debt management
- Status of public debt and public deficit in India
- Definition and importance of budget
- Various types and forms of budgets such as line-item budget, programme/performance budget system, planning–programming budget system, budgeting by objectives, zero-based budget, target-based budget, performance-based budget, and outcome-based budget
- Complete budgetary cycle and the various processes involved in it such as budget formulation, approval by Parliament, execution of budget, and legislative review of budget implementation

- Various mechanisms for parliamentary oversight over the executive including committees such as Public Accounts Committee (PAC), Estimates Committee (EC), Committee on Public Undertakings (COPU), and Departmentally Related Standing Committees (DRSCs)
- Various weaknesses in the Indian budgetary system and measures for improving it
- Concept of government accounting, its weaknesses, and measures for moving from a cash-based to an accrual-based system of accounting
- Concept of auditing, differences between external and internal audit, weaknesses in the internal audit system, and measures to improve the system.
- Types of audits such as financial audit, regularity audit, receipts audit, propriety audit, and performance audit/value for money audit.
- Concept of Supreme Audit Institutions (SAIs) and its various types across the world.
- About the office of Comptroller and Auditor General (CAG); its powers, duties, and responsibilities; its discretionary power to expand the scope of audit; its constitutionally guaranteed independence; its power to audit private sector records; its relationship with social audit; its strengths and weaknesses; various reforms brought about in its functioning; and other reforms that are required to be implemented for its enhanced functioning.

Financial administration is an important aspect of public administration. Every administrative act may have some financial implications. Its significance is witnessed in Lloyd George's statement that "government is finance."[1] Financial administration consists of *activities that* are *concerned with making money available to the various branches of an organisation to support it in carrying out its objectives*. A more comprehensive definition describes financial administration as including *all the activities that generate, regulate, and distribute the monetary resources needed for the sustenance and growth of the members of a political community*.

14.1 Significance and Scope of Financial Administration

The significance of financial administration increased drastically after the Industrial Revolution when social life became more complex and the importance of government increased. This significance has further increased after the introduction of welfare functions in the government. Financial administration has become responsible for exploring the ways and means for generating resources to meet the ever-increasing expenditure of the government.

In this context, the scope of financial administration has increased by leaps and bounds. The following aspects fall in the core scope of financial administration:

(a) Financial planning
(b) Budgeting

(c) Resource mobilisation
(d) Investment decisions
(e) Expenditure control
(f) Accounting and auditing

We will discuss these aspects in detail in the subsequent sections of this chapter.

14.2 Objectives of Financial Administration

The objectives of financial administration depend on the nature and sise of the polity within which it functions. However, there are certain objectives that are applicable to all societies and all polities. They are as follows:

(a) **Management of Public Household Finances:** Financial administration is concerned with managing public funds in such a way as to satisfy human wants and needs.
(b) **Implementation of Public Policies and Programmes:** A major focus of financial administration is to take investment decisions for implementing various public policies and programmes within the stipulated time schedule and expenditure ceiling.
(c) **Provision of Public Goods and Services:** Financial administration is instrumental in providing the necessary funds for public goods and services.
(d) **Growth, employment, and price stability:** An increasing emphasis of financial administration is on ensuring optimum growth, employment, and price stability in the national economy.
(e) **Capital Formation:** Financial administration supports capital formation in the country through increased savings, taxation, and other fiscal and monetary policy instruments.
(f) **Productive Deployment of Funds:** Financial administration ensures that scarce national resources and funds are deployed in those projects and programmes that are economically viable and in the national interest.
(g) **Facilitates Legislative Control over Public Funds:** Financial administration helps in ensuring a strong control of the Parliament (and state legislature) over the use of public funds, through the procedures of budgetary control and public audit.
(h) **Achievement of social equality and equity:** Financial administration, through its policies such as progressive taxation, grants, subsidies, and so on, helps in attaining greater equality of wealth and opportunities.

14.3 Fiscal Policy and Monetary Policy

14.3.1 Fiscal Policy

Fiscal policy is a government policy concerned with raising and spending financial resources and public debt operations to influence the economic activities of the community in desired ways. It is also concerned with the allocation of resources between the public and private sectors and their use in accordance with national objectives and priorities. It refers to the government's choices regarding the overall level of government expenditure, taxes, and debt.

In the long run, it influences savings, investment, and growth in a country. In the short run, it primarily affects the aggregate demand in an economy. It is often referred to as the revenue and expenditure policy of the government, which is generally used in maintaining economic stability in the country.

14.3.1.1 Objectives of Fiscal Policy

The basic objectives of a fiscal policy are as follows:

(a) **Increase in Capital Formation:** Capital formation is instrumental in sustaining economic development in a country. A core objective of fiscal policy is to allocate national resources for public investment and decrease consumption to attain the desired level of economic growth and standard of living.

(b) **Attaining Economic Equality:** A major emphasis of fiscal policy is to minimise economic inequalities by improving the distributional impact of government policies. It is an important objective of fiscal policy to finance the anti-poverty programmes of the government.

(c) **Attaining Balanced Economic Growth:** Fiscal policy aims at the balanced growth of the three crucial sectors of the economy—agriculture, industry, and services. This balance in development is also emphasised geographically, across income groups, and between the public and private sectors.

(d) **Economic and Social Funding:** Fiscal policy has to ensure adequate availability of national resources for funding social expenditure benefiting the poor. For benefiting the downtrodden, it focuses investment in agriculture, infrastructure, transportation, communication, water management, health, education, and so on. Such investments are heavy and generally beyond the capacity of the private sector.

(e) **Inflation Control:** High inflation results either from increased demand for limited goods/services or from an increase in the input cost of goods/services. An appropriate fiscal policy aims at decreasing demand as well as input cost to control the overall inflation rate.

(f) **Attaining a Progressive Tax Structure:** Fiscal policy aims at converting the tax structure of a country into a progressive one. In a progressive tax structure, the economically stronger people are taxed for the benefit of the economically weak.

14.3.1.2 Instruments of Fiscal Policy

The instruments of fiscal policy are as follows:

1. Reducing government expenditure
2. Increasing government taxation
3. Imposing new taxes
4. Controlling wages
5. Rationing public goods and services
6. Controlling public debt
7. Increasing savings
8. Maintaining surplus budget
9. Increasing/decreasing imports and exports
10. Increasing the productivity of goods and services
11. Providing subsidies

12. Introducing and using the latest technologies
13. Rationalising industrial policy, and so on

Some of these instruments will be discussed in the subsequent sections of this chapter.

14.3.2 Monetary Policy

Monetary policy is broadly understood to be the policies, objectives, and instruments directed toward regulating money supplies and the cost of the availability of credit in the economy. The Reserve Bank of India (RBI) is responsible for formulating the monetary policy of the country. According to *classical economic theory*, controlling the money supply is very important for managing the output, employment, and price stability in an economy. Thus, monetary policy is considered a very effective instrument in the hands of the RBI. This classical view is encapsulated in the well-known *equation of exchange*:

$$MV = PY$$

where M denotes the supply of money, V denotes the income velocity of money, P denotes the general price level, and Y denotes the aggregate output in an economy.

In this equation, the total value of payments, i.e., money stock times the velocity (MV) must equal the total value of sales, i.e., output, times price (PY). All values in the equation except price level are determined elsewhere—output in the real sector by non-monetary factors, money stock by policymakers, and velocity of money by institutional factors. Since the velocity of money is constant and the output is determined by the full employment level in the short run, the entire effect of enlarged money supply is reflected in an upward movement of the price level, leaving the real economic activity unaffected. *This is the classical view of monetary policy*. However, the modern view says that monetary policy also impacts the employment and output levels apart from impacting the general price level.

14.3.2.1 Monetary Policy in India

The monetary policy in India has evolved over the years, from the regulation and direction of credit to liquidity management in a market environment. Earlier, the monetary policy was conducted through direct instruments of monetary control such as prescribing deposit and lending rates of commercial banks, selective credit control over sensitive commodities, sector-specific standing facilities, statutory liquidity ratio (SLR) and cash reserve ratio (CRR), though the bank rate was used as a general instrument of interest rate policy.

However, after the 1990s, open market operations were introduced. Apart from this, the *liquidity adjustment facility* (LAF) was introduced in 2000 as the principal operating instrument for modulating short-term liquidity. Lately, repo and reverse repo rates have emerged as the key instruments for signalling the monetary policy stance. These instruments will be discussed in detail in the following sections.

14.3.2.2 Instruments of Monetary Policy

The various instruments of monetary policy are as follows:

1. **Cash Reserve Ratio (CRR):** The cash reserve ratio is the number of funds that the banks are bound to keep with the RBI as a portion of their net demand and time liabilities (NDTL). The objective of CRR is to ensure the liquidity and solvency of banks. When the CRR is reduced, more money is available with the banks for deploying in the economy. This leads to a reduction in the interest rates on loans provided by the banks, which leads to price rise.

On the other hand, when the CRR is increased, fewer funds are available with banks, leading to an increase in the interest rates and a decrease in inflation.

2. **Statutory Liquidity Ratio (SLR):** The SLR is defined as the fraction of the total net time and demand liabilities of the banks that they have to keep in the form of liquid assets such as gold, cash, approved securities, and so on. Apart from CRR, banks are required to maintain SLR with them. The major objectives of SLR are to
   - control the expansion of bank credit
   - ensure the solvency of commercial banks
   - compel banks to invest in government securities and bonds
   - control inflation and suck liquidity in the market to tighten the measures to safeguard customers' money
3. **Bank Rate:** Bank rate is the standard rate at which the Reserve Bank is prepared to buy or rediscount bills of exchange or other commercial papers eligible for purchase under the provisions of various acts. In other words, it is the official interest rate at which RBI provides loans to the banking system. It is used as a signal by the RBI to commercial banks on what the interest rates should be according to RBI.
4. **Open Market Operations:** The money market plays a pivotal role in the deployment of short-term funds and in signalling trends in liquidity and interest rates. RBI, being the main constituent in the money market, aims at ensuring that liquidity and short-term interest rates are commensurate with the monetary policy objectives. Open market operations refer to the purchase and sale of certain instruments, such as government securities (G-Secs), T-bills, and so on, by the RBI from and to the market. The operations help the RBI in either sucking or supplying liquidity in the economy.
5. **Liquidity Adjustment Facility (LAF):** LAF is an instrument of the RBI for modulating liquidity and transmitting interest rate signals to the market. It refers to the difference between the two key rates, namely, repo rate and reverse repo rate. Repo rate and reverse repo rate are the two components of the LAF. The *repo rate* is the rate at which banks borrow money from RBI to meet short-term needs by putting government securities (G-Secs) as collateral. On the other hand, the *reverse repo rate* is the rate at which RBI borrows money from banks by lending securities. While the repo injects liquidity into the system, the reverse repo absorbs liquidity from the system. RBI decides the repo rate based on the prevalent market conditions and other relevant factors.
6. **Marginal Standing Facility (MSF):** MSF is a new liquidity adjustment facility (LAF) window created by RBI in its credit policy of 2011. It is the rate at which banks can borrow overnight funds from RBI against approved government securities. Accordingly, banks can borrow overnight up to 1% of their NDTL outstanding at the end of the second preceding fortnight. At present, MSF is 100 basis points (1%) above the repo rate. MSF helps the RBI in curbing volatility in the overnight lending rates in the banking system.

14.4 Public Finance

Public finance is the branch of economics that deals with the income and expenditure of a government. In the words of Adams Smith, "public finance is the investigation into the nature and principles of state expenditure and state revenue." The objectives of public finance are to ensure macroeconomic stability, achieve the desired state of distribution, and provide public services to accelerate growth and development.[2] The discipline of public finance consists of three important subjects—public expenditure, public debt, and public revenue.

14.4.1 Public Expenditure

Public expenditure is an important government process through which the welfare of the people is ensured. It helps in overcoming the inefficiencies of the market system in allocating economic resources. There are three types of public expenditure—purchase of goods and services, transfer payments, and providing loans. By purchasing goods and services, the government directly buys economic resources such as military aircraft. In transfer payments, the government provides direct money and subsidies to the people to improve their purchasing capacity. Through loans, the government provides money on credit to provide certain important facilities to the public such as employment, housing, education, health, and transportation.

14.4.2 Different Types of Public Expenditure

Public expenditure is classified based on various criteria. Some of these classifications are (a) revenue and capital expenditure, (b) developmental and non-developmental expenditure, and (c) plan and non-plan expenditure. These classifications are described in the following sections.

14.4.2.1 Revenue and Capital Expenditure

Capital expenditure leads to the creation of new assets, such as expenditure on the acquisition of assets—such as land, buildings, machinery, equipment, and investment in shares and loans—and advances granted by the Central Government to state and union territory governments. On the other hand, *revenue expenditure* is an expenditure that is incurred for the normal running of government departments and various services, interest charges on debt incurred by the government, and so on. Such expenditure does not lead to the creation of new assets.

14.4.2.2 Developmental and Non-Developmental Expenditure

Developmental expenditure is incurred on developmental activities such as public health, education, family planning, employment generation, and education. *Non-developmental expenditure*, on the other hand, is incurred on non-developmental activities such as defence, collection of revenue, administrative services, and interest on the debt. Developmental expenditure constitutes the main target of a plan. It helps in focusing on the economic aspirations of people.

14.4.2.3 Plan and Non-Plan Expenditure

Plan expenditure is the expenditure incurred by the government on planned programmes and projects recommended by the Planning Commission. On the other hand, *non-plan expenditure* refers to all expenditures that are not a part of the plan of the Planning Commission. It consists of many obligatory expenditures such as interest payments, pension charges, statutory transfer to states, defence, internal security, and subsidies. The distinction between plan and non-plan expenditure is a pure administrative classification. A plan expenditure becomes non-plan once the plan is over.

14.4.3 Determinants of Public Expenditure

The various aspects of public expenditure are described on the basis of various theories and approaches to public expenditure. Some of these approaches are discussed in the following sections.

14.4.3.1 Marginal Utility Approach

Developed in the 1920s, the marginal utility approach proposes an economic method to determine the composition of government expenditure. According to it, the government spends its limited income on alternative services in such a way that the marginal benefit is the same on all the items. It is similar to individual spending, in which different types of expenditures are incurred to ensure some marginal satisfaction from all of them. It is described in the words of the famous scholar Pigou: "expenditure should be so distributed among wars and poverty programmes so that the last shilling devoted to each of them yields the same real return."[3]

However, the approach has certain problems:

(1) It is difficult to quantitatively measure the benefits flowing from diverse items of public expenditure.

(2) Evaluation of government activities is difficult due to the vast array of services and goals of the government.

(3) Community satisfaction cannot be the only principle of public expenditure; the future interests of the community are also important.

14.4.3.2 Public Goods Approach

Public and non-public goods have already been discussed in the topic *'Public Goods and Services'* of Chapter 1 of this book on '*Introduction to Public Administration*'. The demand for public goods is an important element in the determination of public expenditure.

14.4.3.2 Public Choice Approach

It has been discussed in the topic '*Public Choice Approach to Public Administration*' (of Chapter 1 of this book) which discusses how public choice theory determines the preference and nature of public expenditure. It says that public expenditure is so determined to maximise the government's chances of winning elections. The budget expenditure is determined not with reference to overall spending and taxation but through a series of separate policy decisions based on the estimates of vote gain and vote loss. To fulfil voters' demands, promises made at election time, and their aspirations for projects or services, public expenditure gives way to larger governments, larger bureaucracies, and bigger budgets.[4]

14.4.3.3 Wagner's Law

Wagner's law, also known as the *law of increasing expansion of fiscal requirements*, propounded by Adolph Wagner in 1876, states that the share of the public expenditure in the economy rises as the economic growth proceeds, owing to the intensification of existing activities and extension of new government activities. Wagner predicted an increase in the ratio of government expenditure to national income as the per capita income rises. Such an increase in public expenditure is the result of the growing administrative and protective actions of the government in response to more complex legal and economic relations, increased urbanisation, and rising cultural and welfare expenditures.

14.4.3.4 Peacock and Wiseman's Displacement Effect of Public Expenditure

In their theory, Peacock and Wiseman[5] provided an explanation of fluctuations in public expenditure over time. The theory, also known as the *displacement effect hypothesis*, states that public expenditure grows due to growth in revenue. In normal times, there is an acceptable level of taxation that is tolerated by people. When economic growth increases, this stable level of taxation produces more revenue for the government. An increase in revenue leads to an increase in expenditure.

Apart from this, public expenditure increases due to wars, threats of wars, social upheavals, natural calamities, and other unexpected events leading to substantial fluctuations in public expenditure. These events create new demands on the government in the form of new welfare schemes, war pensions, and so on.

14.4.3.5 Approach of Equal Economic Distribution

This approach is an important public expenditure policy for securing better distribution of wealth among the citizens. Public expenditure is aimed at reducing the inequalities in income through a progressive tax structure, public distribution system, poverty alleviation programmes, and large-scale transfer payments such as pensions and subsidies.

14.4.4 Effects of Public Expenditure

Public expenditure has many widespread effects on the economy and society. Its aim is to divert economic resources into various channels determined by the government in accordance with national objectives and public policy. It has the following impacts:

(i) **Impact on Public Consumption:** Public expenditure helps in improving public consumption and, thus, enhances the quality of life of individuals.

(ii) **Proper Allocation of Resources:** Public expenditure helps in the allocation of resources according to national priorities. Changes in national priorities, from time to time, get reflected in the pattern of public expenditure.

(iii) **Increase in Economic Production:** Public expenditure helps in the generation of crucial infrastructure, health, and education programmes. Such expenditure helps the private sector in improving the production of their goods and services.

(iv) **Economic Distribution:** Public expenditure serves the purpose of reducing income inequalities. In Dalton's words, "other things being equal, the system of public expenditure is best when it has the strongest tendency to reduce income inequalities."[6] Through the mechanism of grants and subsidies, public expenditure tries to bring the income of individuals above a basic minimal level, say, the below poverty line.

(v) **Economic Stabilisation:** The business activities in an economy are usually characterised by fluctuations of a cyclic nature. During an economic boom, inflation increases beyond the reach of the common person. On the other hand, due to depression, employment and production levels fall down, creating colossal damage. In such situations, public spending leads to economic stabilisation. For example, during the depression, public expenditure in public works programmes improves employment and per capita income. During a boom, public expenditure is curtailed to decrease the flow of money in the economy, leading to reduced inflation levels.

14.4.5 Public Revenue

Public revenue or *government revenue* is an important tool for planned economic development. It covers the various sources of the government's income including taxation, income from public services, public enterprises, and public utilities.

The various types of public revenue are broadly classified as tax revenue and non-tax revenue.

14.4.6 Tax Revenue

Taxes are the most important source of government income. They are compulsory charges imposed by a public authority on the citizens. Taxes are basically classified into direct and indirect types. *Direct taxes* are those that are imposed and collected directly from the individual/organisation on whom they are legally imposed. Some of the direct taxes are income tax, corporation tax, capital gains tax, expenditure tax, wealth tax, gift tax, estate duty, and so on.

On the other hand, *indirect taxes* are those that are collected by an entity in the supply chain (usually a producer or retailer) and paid to the government, but they are passed on to the consumer as part of the purchase price of goods or services. The consumers pay the taxes ultimately, which are indirectly collected from them. Goods and service tax (GST) is an example of an indirect tax.

14.4.7 Non-tax Revenue

Non-tax revenue includes those government incomes that are collected from sources other than taxes, including:

(a) Administrative receipts and user charges for government services.
(b) Net contribution of public sector undertakings
(c) Other revenue, including that from forests, opium, irrigation, electricity, and dividends due from commercial and other undertakings.

14.4.8 Overview of Public Expenditure in India

In India, the share of public expenditure in the GDP has remained remarkably stable, varying from 25% to 28% since 1991. However, a certain increase has taken place in public expenditure recently in terms of pre-election decisions to revise the pay scale of government employees, farm loan waivers, expansion of the National Rural Employment Guarantee Act, and increase in subsidies.

The analysis of public spending in India shows that allocation to essential social services and physical infrastructure is low by international standards. The Indian government's expenditure on health and family welfare is only 1.4% of GDP (according to 2015–16 data) as compared to the international standard of 3% of GDP. Similarly, the government's expenditure on education is only 3.5% of GDP (according to 2011–12 data) as compared to the international standard of 6% of GDP. The public expenditure on physical infrastructure in India has also decreased from 4% of GDP (in 2003–04) to 1.8% of GDP (in 2015–16).

The low levels of expenditure on education and healthcare explain the government's failure to provide adequate health and education infrastructure. Moreover, public expenditure on subsidies and transfers has shown a substantial increase over time. Over the years, there has been a significant increase in transfers such as for employment guarantee, food security, housing, loan waivers, and recapitalisation of banks.

Public spending on social and physical infrastructures, besides low allocation, is marked with poor productivity. They are beset with time and cost overruns. Public private partnership projects, for which the government provides viability gap funding, often take an inordinately long time owing to delayed land acquisition and disputes.

Thus, much needs to be done to achieve development objectives through public expenditure in India. The inability to increase tax revenues and the proliferation of expenditure on subsidies and transfers have crowded out capital expenditures relative to the GDP, leading to its steady erosion.

14.4.9 Overview of Tax System in India

A good tax system is one that is supposed to raise the required revenues by minimising the collection cost, compliance cost, and cost in terms of the distortions it creates. A good tax system should have the following qualities:

(a) Broad base (higher number of taxpaying people)

(b) Low rate

(c) Minimum rate of differentiation

(d) Simple and transparent tax system

(e) Progressive distribution of tax system

However, the revenue system in India is the one generating low revenues for the nation. The tax-GDP ratio was 15.8% in 1991–92, which decreased to 10.2% in 2001–02. Due to certain tax reforms in 2004–05, the tax-GDP ratio increased to 17.5% in 2007–08. In 2016–17, it was around 17%. Compared to India, the average tax-GDP ratio for middle-income countries is 22%. Thus, the current tax-GDP ratio in India is much lower than the international standard.

The main reason for low revenue in the Indian tax system is its *narrow tax base*. The various causes for such a narrow tax base are as follows:

(a) Fragmented constitutional distribution of taxes between the Centre and the states

(b) Wide-ranging tax preferences

(c) Multiplicity of objectives assigned to the tax policy, resulting in complicated tax laws, wide avenues for evasion and avoidance, and large and increasing amounts held in disputes.

(d) Tax abuse by multinational companies, resulting in base erosion and profit sharing

(e) Poor capacity of the tax administration, including the information system, to effectively administer and enforce taxes

(f) A plethora of exemptions, concessions, and deductions given in direct and indirect taxes

A closer look at the number of objectives pursued by the tax system is enough to understand the reasons for the complications and ineffectiveness in achieving its multiple objectives. Besides raising tax revenue, the tax system is required to achieve certain revenues such as incentivising savings, promoting exports, achieving balanced regional development, promoting infrastructure investment, expanding employment, promoting scientific research and development, and encouraging cooperatives and charitable activities. The incorporation of such objectives creates enormous avenues for the evasion and avoidance of tax.

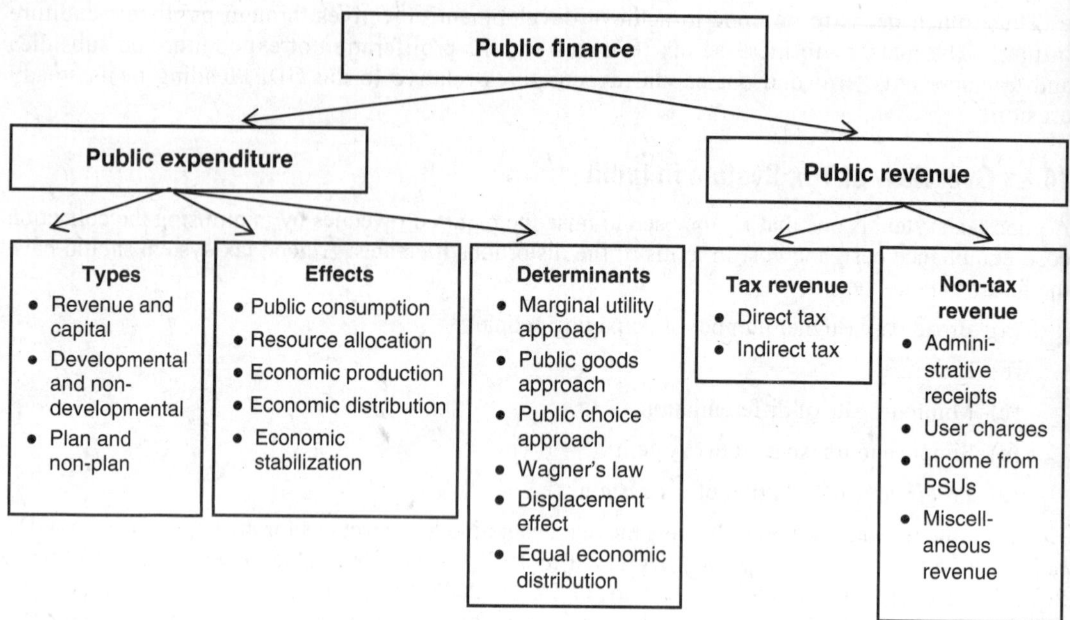

Mind Map 14.1: Public Finance in India

14.4.10 Goods and Services Tax

Good and services tax (GST) refers to any tax on the supply of goods, services, or both, except taxes on the supply of alcoholic liquor for human consumption. It is included in Article 366 (12A) of the Constitution of India in the 101st Constitutional Amendment Act. The tax has constituents of previous Central and state laws. The 101st Constitutional Amendment Act was notified on 8 September 2016.

14.4.10.1 Pre-GST and GST Indirect Tax Structure

Before GST, certain indirect taxes were collected by the Centre and others by the state governments. These are mentioned in Table 14.1. After the introduction of the GST, all the taxes mentioned in Table 14.1 have been subsumed under it.

Table 14.1: Pre-GST indirect tax structure[7]

Central taxes	State taxes
Central excise duty	State VAT/sales tax
Additional duties of excise	Central sales tax
Excise duty levied under Medicinal and Toilet Preparation Act	Purchase tax
Customs duty	Entertainment tax (other than that levied by local bodies)

Additional duties of customs	Luxury tax
Service tax	Entry tax
Surcharges and cesses	Taxes on lottery, betting, and gambling

With respect to the GST, the Constitution was amended to provide concurrent powers to both the Centre and the states to levy and collect GST, which is provided for by Article 246A of the Constitution.

Moreover, Article 269A of the Constitution allows the Centre to levy and collect Integrated GST (IGST) on supplies in the course of interstate trade or commerce including exports. The loss caused to the states due to this is to be compensated by the Centre upon the recommendation of the GST Council (GSTC).

In the initial version of the GST, this tax is not levied on items such as petroleum crude, high-speed diesel, motor spirit (commonly known as petrol), natural gas, and aviation turbine fuel. However, these items may be included at a later date upon the recommendations of the GSTC. Apart from this, tobacco and entertainment tax are outside the purview of the GST presently. As of now, the power to levy additional excise duty on tobacco lies with the Central Government and the power to levy entertainment tax lies with local bodies. Figure 14.1 compares the pre-GST and GST tax structure in India.

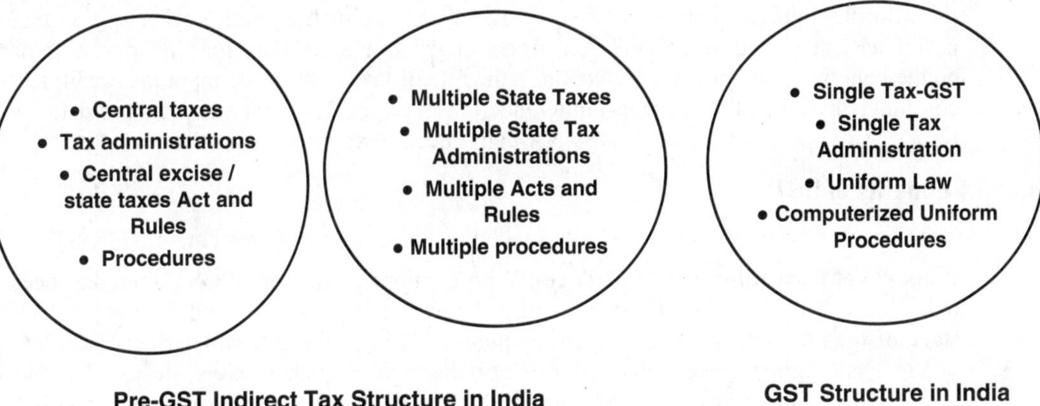

Fig. 14.1 : Pre-GST and GST Tax Structure in India[7]

14.4.10.2 GST Council

The GST Council (GSTC) has been created under Article 279A of the Constitution. The Union finance minister is its chairperson and the vice chairperson is chosen from among the ministers of state governments. Its members are the minister of state (finance) and all ministers of finance/taxation of each state.

In the council, the states enjoy a weightage of two-thirds of the votes and the Centre is accorded a weightage of one-third of the votes. It is tasked with making recommendations on everything related to GST including laws, rules, and rates.

According to the decision of the GSTC, tax rates of 5%, 12%, 18%, and 28% are levied in GST. Above these rates, specific cesses are levied on specific luxury and sin goods.

14.4.10.3 Salient Features of GST

The GST has the following salient features:

1. **Concurrent Jurisdiction:** The Centre and states have concurrent jurisdiction to levy GST.
2. **Compensation to States:** The Centre will compensate the states for their loss in revenue due to the introduction of GST for the first five years.
3. **Tax in Territorial Waters:** The power to collect GST in territorial waters is delegated to the states.
4. **Registration Limit:** At present, the providers of goods and services are to be registered for GST only when their turnover is more than INR 20 lakhs per annum (INR 10 lakhs for special category states except for J&K).
5. **Voluntary Registration:** There is an option of voluntary registration for providers whose turnover is less than INR 20 lakhs per annum.
6. **Anti-Profiteering:** The concept of anti-profiteering is introduced under the GST. It has a multi-tier tax structure, and it has been found internationally that there is inflation and price rise after the implementation of GST. To avoid such a situation, anti-profiteering measures have been introduced in the GST Act. Accordingly, it is mandatory for GST payers to pass on the benefit gained due to a reduction in the rate of tax, or from the input tax credit, to the consumers by way of a commensurate reduction in prices. To implement this provision, the *National Anti-profiteering Authority* (NAA) has been established under the GST Act.

14.4.10.4 Benefits of GST

The following benefits have resulted, or are expected to result, from the implementation of GST:

1. **Removal of Cascading Effect of Taxes:** With the implementation of GST, there has been a reduction in the cascading of taxes. A cascade tax is a tax that is levied on a good at each stage of the production process up to the point of being sold to the final consumer. In the previous tax regime, there were a number of indirect taxes such as excise duty, value-added tax (VAT), Central Sales Tax (CST), and entertainment tax. This wide variety of taxes led to many regulatory compliance procedures and to the cascading effect of taxes. In this regime, the manufacturers had to pay tax at every stage of the supply chain, without any deduction for the tax paid at earlier stages. However, GST has introduced a concept of the input tax credit, in which the tax paid by the manufacturer or seller on their purchase of raw materials, etc. is reduced from their output tax. Thus, the cascading effect is removed in GST.
2. **Decrease in Inflation:** Full implementation will lead to an overall reduction in prices and inflation.
3. **Common National Market:** One GST across the nation will support the creation of a common national market.
4. **Ease of Doing Business:** Implementation of GST will benefit small taxpayers and improve the ease of doing business in India.
5. **Decrease in Black Transactions:** GST is a self-regulating and non-intrusive electronic tax system leading to a decrease in 'black' transactions in the tax system.

6. **Simplified Tax Regime:** A single tax administration in the GST regime has led to a simplification of the tax regime in India.
7. **Decrease in the Number of Taxes:** Implementation of GST has led to a reduction in the multiplicity of taxes in India.
8. **Consumption-based Tax:** GST is a consumption-based tax that is applied after the consumption of goods or services. On the other hand, the previous taxes were supply-based and were applied whether or not the goods and services were consumed.
9. **Benefit to Poorer States:** GST provides benefits to the poorer states, as it has abolished the provisions of the Central Sales Tax (CST).
10. **Benefit to Exporters:** GST has decreased the tax on exports to zero and has employed other measures to promote the domestic production of goods and services in India.

14.4.11 Direct Taxes Code

Just as GST is a tax reform of indirect taxes, the direct taxes code (DTC) is a tax reform of direct taxes. Presently, there are many complications in the Income Tax Act, as mentioned below:[8]

1. **Overlapping and Contradictory Provisions:** The Act is replete with overlapping and contradictory provisions.
2. **Allows Administrative Discretion:** There are many provisions allowing administrative discretion, leading to inconsistent application of law and various opportunities for corruption.
3. **Inconsistent with Basic Tax Principles:** Various provisions of the Income Tax Act are inconsistent with the basic tax principles.
4. **Not at par with International Practices:** It has not adopted international best practices and fails to deal with many common commercial transactions.
5. **Opportunities for Tax Avoidance:** The present Act provides ample opportunities for tax planning and tax avoidance resulting in serious revenue repercussions.
6. **Higher Cost of Compliance:** The complexity of the present tax legislation increases the overall cost of compliance and administration.

To avoid the above-mentioned issues, the Government of India is planning to introduce the DTC, which will be a comprehensive exercise for reforming the direct tax system. It will be a single code for all direct taxes including wealth tax. Apart from other things, it will try to achieve the following benefits:[9]

1. **Broadening of Tax Base:** It will attempt to broaden the base of direct tax and bring more assessees into the tax net.
2. **Equitable Tax System:** It will make the tax system more equitable for different classes of taxpayers.
3. **Ease of Doing Business:** It will make businesses more competitive by lowering the rate of corporate tax.
4. **Removal of Tax Exemptions:** It will remove the various exemptions from the net of direct tax. The removal of exemptions will lead to a higher tax-GDP ratio and enhance the GDP growth rate.
5. **Reduce Legal Cost:** It is expected to reduce legal costs due to the simple and lucid manner of the code.

14.5 Public Deficit and Deficit Financing

14.5.1 Deficit Financing

As discussed in the previous section, the sources of public finance can be divided into domestic and foreign sources. The domestic sources of finance are taxation, public borrowing, government savings, and public expenditure surpluses. The foreign sources consist of loans, grants, and private investments. These sources are very important for financing the planned socio-economic development of India.

However, the above-mentioned sources have generally remained inadequate for financing the development of India. There is an excess of expenditure over revenue. Thus, a new method of deficit financing has emerged to meet the resource gap in development financing.

In general, *deficit financing* is referred to as the financing of expenditure over income through the printing of currency notes or through public borrowings. This is the globally accepted definition of deficit financing, in which the excess expenditure is filled up by borrowing from the central bank of the country, withdrawing accumulated cash balances, and issuing new currency notes. However, borrowing from public and commercial banks does not form a part of deficit financing in India.

This sort of deficit financing is resorted to in three situations—during the war, during depressions, and for financing economic development.

14.5.2 Advantages of Deficit Financing

Deficit financing is said to have the following benefits on the economy:

1. **Increase in Production:** Deficit financing supports national production by increasing the money supply for transactions. For example, if the land is to be reclaimed, deficit financing helps in injecting more money to finance that activity. Moreover, when deficit financing is used for productive purposes, its inflationary side effects are very low.
2. **Recovery from Depression:** In times of depression, when there is a decrease in the demand for goods and services, deficit financing increases the money supply to increase demand and refurbish the economy.
3. **Economic Development:** Deficit financing for development provides stimulus to economic growth by financing investment, employment, and output in the economy. In deficit financing for development, the government invests money in basic heavy industries and in economic and social overheads.
4. **Financing of War:** At the time of war, every government has to spend more than its revenue. Such spending is met by the mechanism of deficit financing.
5. **Increase in savings:** A properly managed programme of deficit financing can lead to an increase in public savings due to an increase in monetary income.
6. **Restructuring of Economy:** Certain underdeveloped economies having low incomes, negative savings, inadequate investments, and resistance to change need to be restructured. Such restructuring can be done by money supply and a stimulus of inflation caused by deficit financing.
7. **Increased Investment and Capital Formation:** Deficit financing increases inflation. Such inflation may stimulate economic activity, and price rise induces more investment in

different sectors. Such an increase in investment leads to rapid capital formation. The increase in inflation due to deficit financing reduces real consumption and provides resources for investment.

However, any deficit financing needs to be undertaken in the context of an efficient and well-executed plan for economic development to avoid its limitations.

14.5.3 Limitations of Deficit Financing

As mentioned, there are certain limitations and side effects of deficit financing. The most important drawback of deficit financing is that it is inflationary in nature. When inflation crosses a tolerable limit, it directly impacts the poor and downtrodden people.

Such inflationary effects of deficit financing are more prominent in developing countries than in developed countries. In developed countries, there is underutilisation of natural resources; these resources are employed by raising government investment through deficit financing, leading to an increase in output, income, and employment without any danger of inflation. An increase in money supply brings about a corresponding increase in the supply of commodities and hence no increase in the price level.

However, in developing countries, the standard of living is low and there is a marginal propensity for consumption. Thus, the money generated due to deficit financing immediately leads to an increase in the demand for goods and services. This increase in demand leads to price rise because of the following four reasons:

(a) **Delay in Goods Production:** Monetary incomes increase immediately (increasing the demand for goods and services) while the production of consumption goods takes time.

(b) **Investment on Capital Goods:** Generally, public investment is on capital goods and the increased public demand for consumption goods is not satisfied by such an investment. It takes a long time to convert investment in capital goods, such as heavy industries, into consumption goods in developing economies. This happens due to a lack of technical and entrepreneurial skills in developing countries, leading to the under-deployment of the capital assets created by deficit financing. Such conditions lead to high inflation as a result of deficit financing in developing countries.

(c) **Multiplier Effect:** In developing economies, there exists the multiplier effect, in which the velocity of circulation of money increases as a result of deficit financing for economic development. This leads to a condition in which the increase in demand is more than the initial increase in the money supply.

(d) **Expansion of Bank Credit:** With deficit financing, the credit condition of commercial banks improves and they start providing loans to the public and businesses. This happens because the liquidity of the bank increases owing to the creation of new money. Due to the expansion of bank credit in a developing economy, the total money supply in the economy tends to increase much more than the amount of deficit financing.

Thus, deficit financing can be tolerated in a developing economy only to the extent that it promotes the capital formation and economic development. This extent of tolerance is called the *safe limit of deficit financing*. Such a safe limit is attained only when the supply of money (due to deficit financing) equals the demand for money in the economy.

14.5.4 Concealed Deficit Financing and 'March Rush'

Apart from the phenomenon of deficit financing, there is a phenomenon of *concealed deficit financing*, which takes place in the economy of developing countries. In a budget, all government departments are allocated certain amounts to be spent in the upcoming year. However, government departments avoid spending money throughout the year and recklessly spend it in the last few weeks of the financial year so that the amount sanctioned may not lapse.

This reckless expenditure is largely a waste and does not lead to the expected results. As it is not productive, it leads to a price rise and operates in a manner similar to deficit financing. Thus, it is known as concealed deficit financing. As this reckless spending happens in the month of March, which is also known as the *March Rush.*

If, by efficient and honest administration, this wasteful expenditure is avoided, then the officially acknowledged deficit financing will not be so inflationary.

Ministry of Finance Memorandum on March Rush

To avoid this March Rush, in 2018, the Ministry of Finance came out with a circular in which it regarded the rush of expenditure in the closing months of a financing year as a breach of financial propriety. In the memorandum, the ministry directed that the last-quarter expenditure must be limited to the actual procurement of goods and services and reimbursement of expenditures that already occurred. It has restricted the last-quarter expenditure to a 33% ceiling and the last-month (March) expenditure to a 15% ceiling.

14.5.5 Measures to Control Deficit Financing

Deficit financing is very important for economic development, but its inflationary effects need to be curtailed. These inflationary effects can be controlled through the following steps:

(a) **Higher Savings and Taxation:** The government should take measures to increase public savings and increase taxation so that the large proportion of funds created due to deficit financing is easily drained off.

(b) **Last Resort:** Deficit financing should be adopted as a step of last resort, after exhausting all other possible sources of development finance.

(c) **Low Capital Output Ratio Sectors:** The capital output ratio is the amount of capital needed to produce one unit of output. Investment should be channelled into areas where the capital output ratio is low so that the returns are quick and price rise is not provoked.

(d) **Policies for Price Control:** The government should simultaneously adopt various policies for price control along with deficit financing.

(e) **Efficient Import Policy:** The import policy should be so formulated that it encourages the import of only necessary capital equipment for economic development and consumer goods required by the masses. It should discourage the import of luxury and semi-luxury goods.

(f) **Integration of Deficit Financing and Credit Policy:** The credit creation policy and deficit financing should be integrated in such a way that neither of the two sectors (public and private) feel handicapped due to shortage of financial resources and, at the same time, inflation is kept under check.

(g) **Public Cooperation in Public Policies:** To reduce the ill effects of deficit financing, the government should try to seek full public cooperation in the implementation of public policies.

Thus, deficit financing must be undertaken efficiently and should be executed well to achieve economic development.

14.6 Public Debt and Public Borrowing

So far, we have discussed taxation and deficit financing as mechanisms for financing the government's development programmes. However, there are certain limitations to both these mechanisms. Thus, a third mechanism of public borrowing is resorted to. The increase in public borrowing leads to an increase in the public debt of the nation.

Formally, *public debt is the debt incurred by the government in mobilising the savings of the people in the form of loans, which are to be repaid at a future date with interest to them*. Public debt mainly resorts to investing money in infrastructural projects, development projects, meeting budget deficits, during times of war, economic crises, unexpected disasters, and so on.

14.6.1 Public Debt Management

Management of public debt is an important task, as it significantly impacts the economy of India. According to the International Monetary Fund (IMF), public debt management is described as the process of establishing and executing a strategy for managing the government's debt to raise the required amount of funding, achieve its risk and cost objectives, and meet any other public debt management goals the government may have set, such as developing and maintaining an efficient market for government securities.

As a sound macroeconomic policy, the government should seek to ensure that both the level and rate of growth in public debt are fundamentally sustainable. The main objective of public debt management is to ensure that the government's financing needs and its payment obligations are met at the lowest possible cost over the medium to long run, consistent with a prudent degree of risk.

14.6.2 Methods of Public Debt Payment

The following methods are used for paying public debt:

(a) **Refunding:** In the mechanism of refunding, new bonds and securities are issued by the government to repay the matured loans. In this process, short-term securities are replaced by long-term securities. The money burden of debt is not finished but postponed to a future date. This leads to the accumulation of public debt.

(b) **Conversion:** In conversion, the existing loans are converted into new loans before their maturity, at an advantage. For example, the higher rate of interest of public debt is converted to a lower rate of interest. The advantage of this procedure is that it reduces the burden on taxpayers. However, the success of conversion depends upon factors such as (a) the credit-worthiness of the government, (b) the maintenance of adequate stock of securities, and (c) efficient management of public debt.

(c) **Surplus Budget:** A surplus budget is that budget in which the public expenditure is less than the public revenue. It is utilised for clearing public debts. However, this method is not considered suitable in today's time.

(d) **Sinking Fund:** A sinking fund is a fund created by the government from the public revenue. Money is deposited in this fund periodically to be used for paying off the debt at the time of its maturity. This is the most systematic method for the redemption of public debt. The burden of repaying public debt is least felt, as the burden of taxing the people to repay the debts is spread evenly over a period of time. An adequate amount of sinking fund also improves the credit-worthiness of the government.

(e) **Terminable Annuities:** In this method, debt is repaid every year by issuing terminable annuities to the bond-holders, which mature annually. In this method, the burden of debt diminishes annually and is fully paid by the time of maturity.

(f) **New Taxation:** Newer taxes are imposed on the public to repay the public debt. This method causes a redistribution of the income by transferring resources from the taxpayers to the hands of the bond-holders. It imposes a burden on the future generations, who repay the long-term debts of the previous generations.

(g) **Capital Levy:** Capital levy refers to heavy taxation on property and wealth as a method of repaying public debt. Such a method imposes the least burden on the society for debt repayment. It is generally imposed after a war to repay unproductive war debts.

(h) **Surplus Balance of Payments:** A surplus balance of payments is created when a country's exports are higher than its imports. This creates an excess of foreign exchange reserve, which is used in the payment of the country's external debt.

14.6.3 Positive Impacts of Public Debt

The positive aspect of public debt is that it helps in raising household and other savings in the economy. People save their money by investing in government bonds. In an economy, if aggregate demand is to be maintained at a high level of employment, the volume of savings needs to be increased and these savings need to be transferred to the government and private businesses for spending on the economy. Debt creation is the process by which savings are transferred to spenders. As the availability of bonds (created to raise money by public borrowing) encourages savings, more resources are freed for investment and economic growth tends to be enhanced. However, such a situation results only when the savings are invested in capital generating, developmental, employment generating, and other economically beneficial activities.

For public borrowing, the international norm is that the current expenditures of paying salaries, interest, maintenance of capital assets, subsidies, and other transfers should be financed from the current revenues from tax and non-tax sources, and capital expenditure could be financed from borrowings. This rule ensures that borrowed funds are used for financing those expenditures that would accelerate the growth rate of the economy at least equivalent to the interest rate on the borrowing. This rule further suggests that borrowings can be resorted to so long as they lead to a net increase in employment and incomes.

14.6.4 Negative Impacts of Public Debt

A non-managed public debt has the following negative consequences:

1. **Transfer of Resources to Other Nations:** Every external debt has to be paid at a future date. To meet its interest and repayment charges owed to the outside world, the government is required to reduce future spending or raise taxes and thereby reduce private spending. Thus, it cuts total internal resource use.

2. **Loss of Real Output:** To finance the interest payments of public debt, extra taxes are imposed on the public. These taxes lead to a loss of real output because of their distorting and disincentive effects.
3. **Decrease in Private Investment:** Under conditions of full employment and unchanged monetary policy, government borrowing competes with private borrowing. The government increases the interest rates, leading to a reduction in private investment. This is also known as the *crowding out effect* of public debt. Apart from this, private investment also reduces because of the presence of an existing public debt. The existence of a large public debt has a psychological influence on business behaviour. As debt increases, people lose their confidence and curtail their investments.
4. **Decrease in Public Savings:** People decrease their investments and savings when taxes increase to finance the interest payments of public debt.
5. **Increase in Inflation:** Public debt represents the amount of past expenditure which was not matched by taxes. It represents the past government's claim to resources that it could not pay for. In the case of full employment, such a debt is a burden on the future governments for the funds raised by the previous governments. This shift in burden is often inflationary in nature and leads to price rise in the future. The debt is inflationary in nature because it is raised by selling government bonds. Government bonds, by their very nature, can be converted into money easily, as they have little or no risk of loss. Thus, they constitute a potential backlog of purchasing power, which can add materially to inflationary pressures.

14.6.5 Role of RBI in Public Debt Management

The role of RBI in public debt management is paramount, as it works in the following manner:

1. It helps the Central and state governments to float new loans and manage public debt.
2. RBI provides money to the Central Government and, thus, is the major owner of public debt. It is the single largest holder of Central Government securities. When RBI buys government securities, it prevents the government from borrowing from other sources at a higher rate of interest.
3. RBI imposes credit control measures from time to time on banks via mechanisms such as CRR and SLR, as explained before. This maintained reserve helps the government in borrowing from banks.

A large public debt imposes certain constraints on the effective monetary policy of the RBI. The basic dilemma is between the government's desire for low-interest costs on the one hand and the goals of economic stability on the other.

14.6.6 State of Public Deficit and Public Debt in India

India has persistently suffered from huge debt because of the building up of large fiscal deficits. At an average of over 75% of GDP, India's debt is significantly higher than that of other middle-income countries. A higher deficit and debt are serious concerns in India. The 1991 economic crisis was attributed to the lax fiscal policy of India. Before 1991, the rapid growth of debt, together with the political instability that delayed response to the rising debt, made it impossible to finance the balance of the payment deficit.

The same problem came up in 2001-02 when the fiscal deficit reached the level of 10.3% of GDP. With the outstanding liabilities of the government at 72.5% of GDP and interest payment at nearly 35% of the total revenue receipts, there were serious questions on the sustainability of the debt.

This led the central government to pass the *Fiscal Responsibility and Budget Management Act* (FRBMA) in 2003. The state governments also passed their fiscal responsibility legislation based on the recommendations of the 12th Finance Commission. The fiscal deficit targets were set at 3% of GDP each at the Central and state levels, and the revenue deficit was targeted to come down to zero.

As a result, substantial fiscal consolidation was witnessed from 2004–05 to 2007–08. However, the revenue deficit was not completely phased out. By 2007–08, the fiscal deficit was 4.5% of GDP and the revenue deficit was 0.5% of GDP.

However, the central government's fiscal position changed drastically after 2008-09, mainly owing to the sharp increases in subsidies and transfers. The central government's expenditure increased substantially because of the expansion of the Mahatma Gandhi National Rural Employment Guarantee Act, 2005 (MGNREGA), the introduction of farm loan waiver, implementation of the sixth pay commission, and the increase in international crude oil price leading to an increase in fuel subsidies. The problem was exacerbated by the decline in the Centre's tax-GDP ratio by more than two percentage points of GDP—from 11.8% in 2007–08 to 9.6% in 2010–11. Consequently, the consolidated revenue and fiscal deficits in 2008–09 increased to 4.4% and 10.6%, respectively. Thus, there was a significant slippage in achieving fiscal consolidation at the Central level.

Subsequently, targets were breached in continuously in the subsequent years until 2016–17, when the setting up of the FRBM review committee was announced in the Union Budget. The mandate of the committee was to (a) review the FRBM targets, (b) examine the range rather than a point estimate of fiscal targets, and (c) explore the possibility of linking fiscal expansion or contraction to credit expansion or contraction.

Considering the nature of savings in India, only household sector savings are available for investment in corporate and government sectors. A target of 6% of the fiscal deficit of GDP for unions and states combined would leave enough borrowing space for the private sector and avoid financial crowding out. However, over the years, it has been observed that the household sector's financial savings have declined and fallen to around 7.8% of GDP. Thus, in the present scenario, with the combined fiscal deficit of 6% (3.5% at the union level and 2.5% at the state level), and with public enterprises requiring 1.5% of GDP, there is hardly any borrowing space left for private sector investment. Added to this is the problem of the huge volume of non-performing loans from commercial banks. This has led to both lack of demand for viable investment projects by the corporates and a reluctance to lend by commercial banks.

Worldwide experience has shown a preference towards finance-expanding expenditures by borrowing owing to the myopic view of the policymakers and, in particular, electoral budget cycles. This is aided further by the lack of transparency and fiscal illusion. Thus, the world over, there has been a movement towards a rule-based fiscal policy. There has also been a trend of the creation of an independent fiscal institution to review and monitor the conduct of fiscal policy. Thus, the 14th Finance Commission (2014) recommended that an independent fiscal council should be established through an amendment to the FRBM Act to undertake the ex-ante assessment of budget proposals and to ensure their consistency with the fiscal policy and rules.

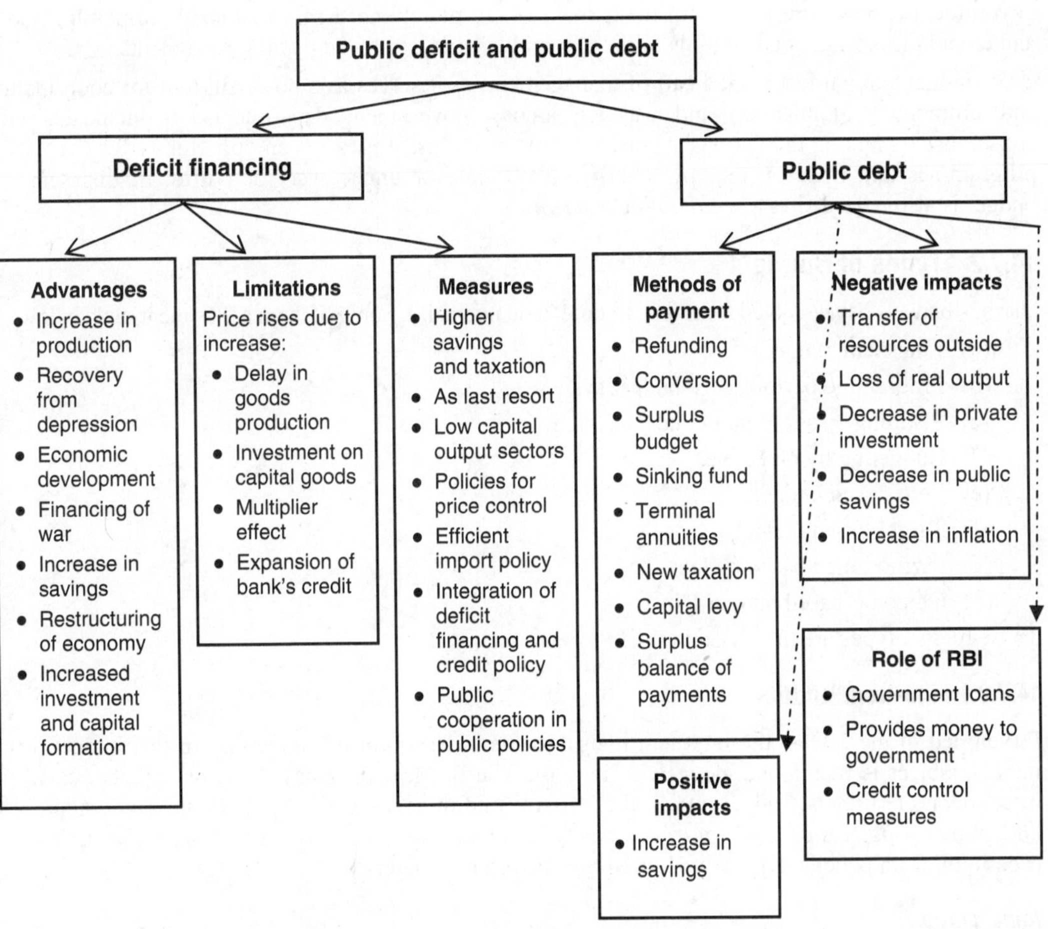

Mind Map 14.2 : Public Deficit and Public Debt

14.7 Budget: Types and Forms

A budget is an estimation of the government's revenue and expenditure over a specified future period of time (generally a year). It consists of a series of goals with price tags attached. These budgetary goals are beyond money; they are budgetary choices, budgetary policies, and budgetary philosophies. Thus, the policies and the intent of the government are laid down via the mechanism of the annual budget.

14.7.1 Importance of a Budget

A transparent and efficient budget is instrumental for a sound democracy. In a democracy, there is an unmistakable urge to evolve sound financial management, as the democracy stands discredited if there is extravagance and other ill practices in the government. The unprecedented increase in government expenditure in modern times makes it absolutely necessary that sound principles, tools, and techniques of financial administration are evolved and employed by all governments.

A budget is regarded as the heart of management, as it serves as a powerful tool for coordination and eliminating duplication and wastage among government departments. It inculcates cost consciousness among the various subordinate organisations. It presents an opportunity for evaluating programmes and policies, thereby identifying obsolete or unnecessary activities. In this sense, a budget is also regarded as a *pre-audit instrument.*

14.7.2 Types of Budgets

Various budgets have evolved from time to time in democracies. Some of them are as mentioned below:

(a) Line-item budget
(b) Programme/performance budget system
(c) Planning–programming budget system
(d) Budgeting by objectives
(e) Zero-based budget
(f) Target-based budget
(g) Performance-based budget
(h) Outcome-based budget

These budget types are discussed in the following sections.

14.7.2.1 Line-Item Budget

Developed in the 1920s, the line-item budget is the oldest form of budgeting. In this budget, each item or object is mentioned along with its cost. The budget paper has items or objects (scientific instruments, fertilizers, and so on) on the left side and their respective costs on the right side. Also known as the *objects-of-expenditure budget,* it is the allocation of resources according to the cost of each item, from pencils to personnel, used by a government agency.

Importance:

The importance of the line item budget is that it shows in detail what public administrators are spending their money on. Thus, it is still used in many countries in conjunction with other types of budget formats. It brings honesty and efficiency into the budgetary system.

Disadvantage

1. **Inflexible:** The line-item budget is inflexible, as the individual departments are not allowed to spend according to the contingent circumstances.
2. **Absence of Policy:** This form of budgeting deals only with the input items of a budget; it does not deal with any policy to be laid down in the budget. While dealing with inputs, it only deals with what it takes to make a project continue; it does not give direction to the government. The only policy-related question dealing with this form of the budget is the number of items (and their cost) required to run a programme or project. For example, the number of parks required in a locality and what will it cost to build and maintain them.
3. **Programme Problem:** It does not show for what programmes public money is being spent. Thus, it does not facilitate the public management of funds.

4. **Performance Problem:** It also does not show whether the money being budgeted for public policies was actually spent for doing the right job or not. Thus, it does not help in assessing the performance of the departments.

14.7.2.2 Programme/Performance Budget System

The programme/performance budget system (P/PBS) emerged from the recommendations of the Hoover Commission in 1949; the report encouraged performance measures and standards. It was initially started for the US Defence Department in 1950.

P/PBS is a system of resource allocation that organises the budget document by operations and links the productivity of those operations with specific budget amounts. Thus, it deals with the 'performance problem' of the line-item budget. It considers the outputs as well as the inputs for the various departments. In it, the various government programmes for which government money is to be spent are laid down. It asks questions such as for what programmes we need to build public parks and hospitals. On the performance side, it asks questions such as how many people will be served by the parks and how many patients will be treated in the hospitals.

Thus, in a nutshell, P/PBS deals with the inputs for various programmes in the budget and the outputs (or performance) to be expected from these programmes.

Importance

P/PBS is the first of its kind budget that introduced the organisation of the budget by the programmes to be carried out in the upcoming year. It also introduced the concept of measuring and linking the results of programmes with individual agency budgets.

Disadvantage

1. **Performance Problem:** Although the P/PBS focused on the performance of the programmes while providing funds, the performance part of the budget did not work systematically. This was mentioned in the report of the Second Hoover Commission.
2. **Policy Problem:** Although P/PBS tried to reward efficiency in implementing public policies, it did not throw light on whether those policies are worth having in the first place.

14.7.2.3 Planning–Programming Budgeting System

The planning–programming budgeting system (PPBS) emerged in the General Motors industry. It was first implemented in government functioning during World War II by Robert McNamara. It became an active part of government budgeting since 1965. In India, it has been adopted for various developmental programmes after the recommendations of the reports of the 20th Estimates Committee and the First Administrative Reforms Commission.

Formally, *PPBS is a system of resource allocation designed to improve government efficiency and effectiveness by establishing long-range planning goals, analysing the costs and benefits of alternating programmes that would meet these goals, and articulating programmes as budgetary and legislative proposals and long-term projections.*

The system is concerned not only with the inputs and outputs of a department but also with the outcomes of the various programmes adopted by a department and their alternatives. The budget-making agency is seen as a centralised systemic, planning and policymaking body. Considering the previous example, PPBS does not emphasise on questions such as the number of parks built for public recreation. However, it asks questions such as whether there can be alternatives to parks, such as fitness centres and yoga centres, for better public recreation. Finding alternatives to building parks requires the budget agency to reconsider the whole recreation policy annually.

Importance

PPBS is described as the first most comprehensive rational budgeting system, as it augments not only the resource allocation on the basis of the performance of various programmes but also the significance of listed programmes and the need to change them to attain the national goals. It provides a system of better information, better systems analysis, better amount and quality of programme evaluation.

Disadvantage

PPBS is difficult to adopt by all departments because of its complexity, rigidity, and obsession with details and uniformity.

14.7.2.4 Budgeting by Objectives

This form of budgeting, started in 1972, has its roots in the management by objectives technique of programme management (discussed in the topic 'Management by Objectives (MBO)' in Chapter 3 of this book). It is a process in which organisational goals are set through the participation of organisational members in terms of the results expected, and resources are allocated according to the extent to which those goals are achieved. Thus, it is concerned with the inputs, outputs, and outcomes of an organisation. However, it is not concerned with alternative policies or paths in attaining the expected outcomes.

Importance

It is the first system of budgeting that deals with the achievement of broader goals. The earlier systems emphasised only on the performance of the various programmes designed for the achievement of the broader goals. However, BBO directly emphasises on the achievement of the broader goals, and the setting up of these goals with the full participation of departmental/organisational members.

Disadvantage

The biggest disadvantage of this budgeting system is that it is not concerned with the various policy alternatives in attaining the broader goals of the government. It deals primarily with the effectiveness of governmental programmes, but when it comes to pushing the policymakers to ask what else the government can do to accomplish a particular social mission, it is somewhat at loss.

14.7.2.5 Zero-based Budgeting

Introduced in 1977, zero-based budgeting (ZBO) is a system of allocation of resources to organisations on the basis of those organisations that periodically reevaluate, through intense consultation, the need for all the programmes for which they are responsible and justify the continuance or termination of each programme in the organisation's budget programme. In other words, an organisation reassesses what it is doing from top to bottom from a hypothetical *zero base*. This form of budgeting does not pay much attention to the inputs, outputs, and outcomes of a department. Rather, it completely emphasises on fixing the various alternative programmes to be adopted by a department.

Considering the previous example of the recreation policy, in a zero-based budget, the head of different districts would decide on the number of parks, fitness centres, yoga centres, and so on, to be built. However, the central budget-making agency would decide whether parks, fitness centres, yoga centres, or any other mechanism of recreation will be better suited. Accordingly, it will order for starting new mechanisms of recreation and closing down older inefficient mechanisms. It will rank-order the various mechanisms of recreation in terms of their relative usefulness to the government's overall mission of making the population physically fit and mentally strong.

It was first adopted in India in the year 1983 by the Department of Science and Technology (DST).

Importance

In a department in which ZBB is implemented, the programme managers are given a better choice of participation in the budgetary process, as there is a complete overhaul of all the programmes. Moreover, it creates better communication among all levels of the bureaucracy while formulating the budget. The most lasting benefit of the ZBB is that it prioritises the various programmes on the basis of their expected effectiveness and efficiency.

Disadvantage

1. Although the ZBB intends to plan the budget from the zero base, programmes are virtually never cut to zero. Organisations submit their zero-based budgets at levels ranging from 75% to 90% of the previous year's budget. Thus, initially intended to get away from incrementalism, it finally ended up being the most incremental form of budgeting.
2. It does not focus on reducing the spending of an organisation, as it is not concerned with outputs. Rather, a pure zero-based budget requires a lot of paperwork, which increases the cost of the budget-making process itself.

14.7.2.6 Target-based Budgeting

Introduced in 1981, target-based budgeting (TBB), also known as *target budgeting*, *fixed ceiling budgeting*, and *top-down budgeting*), is a method of allocating resources to departments in which the departments' spending limits, and sometimes their goals too, or targets are set by the central budget-making agency. It is the reversal of the traditional bottom-up budgeting process, in which the goals and targets are set by the individual departments and the central budget-making agency allocates resources according to those individual targets. In TBB, the individual departments have to adjust their spending targets according to the ceiling fixed by the central budget-making agency. Instead of departments sending their budget requests up the hierarchy, the central agency sends down the budget that they may request and then leaves the achievements of departmental goals to the heads of the departments.

The TBB focuses on the Central Government's, or the head of the nation's, sole mission (e.g., achieving a clean India), and the mission is achieved by redirecting resources (i.e., inputs) to that mission to assure the desired outputs and outcomes. In this budgeting system, there is no consideration for policy alternatives at the departmental level. For example, in the Central scheme of *Swachh Bharat*, the mission of the Prime Minister is to make India open-defecation-free. To achieve this mission, money is transferred to state governments and local governments with the particular target to build toilets in each home. Thus, the goal and the target is prefixed by the Prime Minister.

Cutback Management in TBB

The most important aspect of TBB is cutback management. TBB is based on revenue availability at the Central level. Whenever revenue declines, the costs of departments are cut down. There are two types of cutbacks: short-term cutbacks and long-term cutbacks. The *short-term cutbacks* include temporarily reducing employees, deferring maintenance, and postponing equipment purchases.

On the other hand, *long-term cutbacks* signify reorganising governmental departments so that they can manage policy areas more effectively. This is difficult to attain in all the departments. The methods of long-term cutbacks include improving productivity to manage cutbacks, using alternative delivery systems such as service delivery through non-employees, rearranging intergovernmental relations, e.g., by shifting a programme to another government (e.g., a problem on health, when shifted from the Central to the state government, cuts back the spending of the Central Government), and prioritising programmes and then cutting the lowest ranked programmes.

Importance

Target-based budgeting has the following advantages:

1. **Cutback Management:** The concept of cutback management was introduced with TBB. In today's time, managing public funds is the most important issue in budgeting. Cutback management helps in managing crucial and limited government resources.
2. **Budgetary Realism:** It is an unusually realistic budgeting system because it is driven by revenue.
3. **Big Picture:** It helps in visualising the big picture through the common language of the budget. It has helped in smoothening communication between public administrators and legislators by providing them with a common budget vocabulary. This, in turn, has enhanced the ability of top executives to understand through a budgetary lens the 'big picture' of how the whole government spends its funds.
4. **Executive Control:** TBB helps in enhancing the control of the Central executive on all the departments via the mechanism of budget.

Disadvantage

Target-based budgeting suppresses the initiatives of the individual departments and subordinate governments. The goals and targets set by the Central executive may not suit the conditions and circumstances of all the departments and subordinate governments.

14.7.2.7 Performance-based Budgeting

Introduced in 1993, performance-based budgeting, also known as *budgeting for results*, *results budgeting*, *mission budgeting*, *entrepreneurial budgeting*, and *performance-informed budgeting*, is a system of resource allocation that links the performance levels of programmes with specific budget amounts.

Like P/PBS, PBB is essentially limited to inputs and outputs and perhaps emphasises on the quality of output more than P/PBS. In the case of alternatives, PBB addresses only the alternative policy implementation mechanisms and not the alternative policies per se.

The Indian version of PBB is known as *outcome budgeting*. It was introduced in India in the budget of 2005–06.

Importance

Performance-based budgeting tends to reward good performing departments with larger budgets and sanction poor performing departments with lower budgets. This leads to the emergence of a more efficient and effective government.

Disadvantage

As discussed in the previous chapters, it is very difficult to objectively measure the performance of government programmes. Thus, PBB is not helpful in effectively measuring the performance and accordingly reward or sanction different departments. Moreover, as PBB is based on measuring the department's performance, it is fraught with difficult and sometimes insurmountable problems.

14.8 Process of Budget in India and Improvements Required

14.8.1 Budget and Various Government Funds

The procedure for the budget is laid down by Articles 112 to 117 of the Indian Constitution. Article 112 states that the President of India causes to be laid before both Houses of Parliament an *annual financial statement* containing the statement of the estimated receipts and expenditures from the Consolidated Fund of India for that year.

The government accounts are kept under three funds. They are:

(i) Consolidated fund
(ii) Contingency fund
(iii) Public accounts

Consolidated Fund

The Consolidated Fund of India consists of all revenues received by the government, loans raised by it, and also its receipts from recoveries of the loans granted by it from the Consolidated Fund. All expenditures of the government are incurred from the Consolidated Fund, and no amount can be withdrawn from the fund without authorisation from the Parliament. Apart from the regular expenditures, there are certain expenditures from the Consolidated Fund that do not require the sanction of the Parliament. These expenditures are known to be charged to the Consolidated Fund. Article 112(3) mentions such expenditures, which include the following:

(a) the emoluments and allowances of the president and other expenditure relating to his/her office

(b) the salaries and allowances of the chairman and the deputy chairman of the Council of States and the speaker and the deputy speaker of the house of the people

(c) debt charges for which the Government of India is liable, including interest, sinking fund charges, and redemption charges, and other expenditure relating to the raising of loans and the service and redemption of debt

(d) the salaries, allowances, and pensions payable to or in respect of judges of the Supreme Court
(e) the pensions payable to or in respect of judges of the Federal Court of India
(f) the pensions payable to or in respect of judges of any high court that exercises jurisdiction in relation to any area included in the territory of India or which, at any time before the commencement of the Constitution, exercises jurisdiction in relation to any area included in a governor's province of the Dominion of India
(g) the salary, allowances, and pension payable to or in respect of the Comptroller and Auditor General of India
(h) any sums required to satisfy any judgment, decree, or award of any court or arbitral tribunal
(i) any other expenditure declared by the Constitution or by Parliament by law to be so charged

Contingency Fund

Under Article 267(1) of the Constitution, the Contingency Fund is created for meeting urgent unforeseen expenditure pending authorisation from the Parliament. The president is authorised to spend from this fund. Parliamentary approval for such expenditure and for withdrawal of an equivalent amount from the Consolidated Fund can be obtained subsequently.

Public Account

The Public Account is created under Article 266(2) of the Constitution. It is that fund of the government which receives receipts apart from those received by the Consolidated Fund. These receipts are in the form of provident funds, small savings collection, other banking-related citizen's deposits, and so on. The money is kept in the Public Account, and the connected disbursements are also made therefrom. Parliamentary authorisation is not required for payments from the Public Account, as it consists of the deposits of the citizens.

14.8.2 Budgetary Process in India

The whole budgetary process in India goes through a cycle, making it robust and accountable to the executive and the legislature. This cycle consists of the following four phases:

(a) Budget formulation
(b) Approval of Parliament
(c) Execution of budget
(d) Legislative review of budget implementation (audit of government's financial operations)

These phases are discussed in detail below.

14.8.2.1 Budget Formulation

The budget formulation process in the Government of India consists of the following steps:

Step 1: Commencement of Process in August-September

The budget formulation process commences in the month of August-September. To get the process started, the budget division in the Department of Economic Affairs (Ministry of

Finance) issues the annual budget circular to all Union Government ministries/departments in August-September. The circular contains detailed instructions in the form and content of the statement of budget estimates to be prepared by these ministries/departments.

Step 2: Three Kinds of Figures Sought

In their forms, the ministries/departments are required to provide three kinds of figures, i.e., their budget estimates, revised estimates, and actuals. For example, for the budget of 2019–20, the process started in August 2018. While preparing this budget, the *budget estimate* is that estimate of the budget for the upcoming year of 2019–2020 for which approval is sought by the Parliament. Second, the *revised estimate* is the revised estimate of the first six months of the ongoing year, i.e., 2018–19 on the basis of the initial experience of implementation of the budget of 2018-19. The *actuals* are the actual expenditure in the previous year of 2017–18.

Step 3: Role of Planning Commission/ Other Central Planning Agency

The budget estimates are prepared after discussion with the Planning Commission or any other planning agency for the time being in force. The Planning Commission depends on the Ministry of Finance to first arrive at the size of the gross budgetary support (GBS), which would be provided in the next year. In principle, the size of each annual plan should be derived from the approved size of the Five-Year Plan prepared by the Planning Commission (or any other medium-term plan prepared by the Government).

Step 4: Measures to Reduce Deficit

Certain measures are then taken by the government to reduce the fiscal deficit in the upcoming budget.

Step 5: Finalisation of Estimated Receipts

In the month of January, more attention is paid to the finalisation of the estimated receipts. At this stage of budget preparation, the finance minister examines the budget proposals prepared by the Ministry and makes the required changes. S/he consults the prime minister and the Cabinet for the same.

Step 6: Consultation with Crucial Stakeholders

Pre-budget consultations are held with the finance ministers of the states/Union Territories as well as trade and industry representatives. On the basis of the consultations, decisions are taken on suitable fiscal policy changes to be announced in the budget.

Step 7: Consolidation of Budget Data

Finally, the whole data is compiled with the help of the National Informatics Centre (NIC). The compiled budget is then presented in the Parliament after receiving the permission of the President of India.

14.8.2.2 Approval of Parliament

The budget so formulated is presented to the Parliament generally on the last working day of February (being presented on the first day of February from 2017). It consists of the following stages:

Stage 1: General Discussion

In this stage, there is a general discussion on the broad economic and fiscal policies of the government as reflected in the budget. It lasts for 20–25 hours.

Stage 2: Demand for Grant

In this stage, there is a detailed discussion on the demand for grants in respect of the different ministries and departments. The demands for grants are the estimates of expenditure from the Consolidated Fund included in the budget and required to be voted on by the Lok Sabha. One demand for grants is presented in respect of each ministry or department. While voting on the demands for grants, the Members of Parliament may pass various motions showing their approval or disapproval. These motions will be discussed in the subsequent sections of this chapter. These demands for grants are submitted only to the lower house of the Parliament.

Stage 3: Appropriation Bill

After the demands for grants are voted on by the Lok Sabha, the Parliament's approval is sought on the withdrawal of the amount so voted from the Consolidated Fund through the Appropriation Bill. After receiving the consent of the President, the Appropriation Bill becomes the Appropriation Act.

Intermediate Stage: Vote on Account

A vote on the account is an intermediate step to ensure the functioning of the government until the Appropriation Bill is passed by the Parliament. As the financial year lasts from 1 April to 31 March, no expenditure can be incurred by the government after 31 March if the Appropriation Act has not been passed till then. However, the discussion on the budget generally goes on up to the end of April or the first week of May. To allow effective government functioning in this delayed period, a vote on account is obtained by the Parliament through an Appropriation (Vote on Account) Bill.

Vote on account was frequently used until 2016 when the budget was presented on the last working day of February. However, in 2017, the budget presentation date was advanced to 1 February. Thus, since 2017, voting on the account is not usually used unless in special cases such as an election year.

Intermediate Budget

The interim budget is nothing but a 'vote on account' presented by a government in an election year. As general elections take place between April and May, the previous government is required to present a budget only for a short duration of 3–4 months, before the next government takes charge.

The previous government presents an interim budget and gets the funds required for spending via the vote on account route. However, it is not mandatory to pass an interim budget during an election year. The government can even prepare a full budget and get the appropriation bill passed to get the finance.

However, the route of interim budget is mostly followed, as it is considered inappropriate to impose policies that may or may not be acceptable to the incoming government taking over in the same year.

14.8.2.3 Execution of Budget

As soon as the Appropriation Act is passed, the Ministry of Finance advises individual ministries/departments about their respective allocation of funds. The heads of different ministries/departments then allocate the funds to various subordinate disbursing officers. The expenditure is monitored to ensure that the amounts spent do not exceed their limit without obtaining additional funds within time.

The system for execution of the budget consists of the following levels:

(a) The head of the ministry/department acts as the controlling officer for budget execution
(b) Certain competent authorities are designated in the ministry, who issue the financial sanction for spending any money from the budget
(c) Certain officers are designated as drawing and disbursing officers who allow disbursement of money for the activities of the ministries, departments, and subordinate offices
(d) There is a system of payments, receipts, and accounts to ensure the accountability of each and every penny spent by every department or subordinate office.

14.8.2.4 Legislative Review of Budget Implementation (Audit of Government)

To ensure executive accountability to the legislature over the correct spending of public funds, public expenditure is audited by an independent agency, i.e., the Comptroller and Auditor General (CAG). Its duties will be discussed in the subsequent sections.

14.8.3 Parliamentary Control over Budget

Parliamentary sanction is required for every function of public finance. It is required for levying new taxes, increasing the rates of existing taxes, withdrawing money from the Consolidated Fund, and raising of loans by the government. The control exercised by the Parliament is in two forms:

(a) Through built-in techniques in parliamentary procedures
(b) Through committees appointed by the Parliament

The built-in techniques are already discussed in Chapter 6. In the present chapter, we will discuss the various committees appointed by the Parliament.

14.8.3.1 Public Accounts Committee

The Public Accounts Committee (PAC) is a panel of the Parliament tasked with examining the reports of the Comptroller and Auditor General (CAG) of India. Its main purpose is to examine the accounts showing the appropriation of sums granted by the Lok Sabha for the expenditure of the Government of India and the Annual Financial Accounts of the Central Government. While examining these accounts, PAC satisfies itself that:

- The money shown in the accounts was made available legally through voting by the Lok Sabha. Moreover, the available money was applied to the service or purpose for which it has been intended by the Lok Sabha.
- The expenditure conforms to the authority that governs it.
- The money spent for a particular purpose has been spent fruitfully and not wasted.
- The principle of the economy has been followed and a high standard of public morality has been maintained while spending the money.
- The money spent has been useful and serviceable to the nation.

Apart from examining the accounts of the government, the PAC also examines the accounts showing the income and expenditure of state corporations, trading and manufacturing schemes, and autonomous and semi-autonomous bodies, the audit of which may be conducted by the CAG.

Composition of PAC

The PAC consists of 22 members—15 from Lok Sabha and 7 from Rajya Sabha. These members are elected every year by the MPs themselves, according to the principle of proportional representation, by means of a single transferable vote, with a view that all major political parties are adequately represented in it. According to Lok Sabha rules, a minister is prohibited from becoming a member of the PAC. The members are selected to represent a cross section of the Parliament, ensuring that all shades of opinions are brought to bear on the working of the committee.

The chairperson is appointed by the speaker of the Lok Sabha. If the deputy speaker is a member, he/she is designated as the chairperson of the committee. Generally, an MP of an opposition party is nominated as the chairperson of the committee.

Functioning of PAC and the Role of CAG

PAC examines the reports of CAG by calling officers from different departments as witnesses. After examining the statements of the witnesses and the reports of CAG, PAC comes out with its own reports. The PAC's reports are then presented in the House and published widely in the media. These reports are generally accepted by the government and implemented completely. The findings of the committee and its periodical reports are then compiled by CAG into *epitomes*. These epitomes, which contain case laws in respect of all financial matters, are a guide to all the departments for the future.

In its functioning, the PAC is actively assisted by the CAG. The CAG assists it in its deliberations by preparing a list of the most urgent and important matters that deserve the attention of the PAC. The CAG helps in making the action of the PAC clear to the government witnesses and in making the action of the government clear to the PAC. Thus, the position of the CAG is sometimes understood to be one of a translator and an interpreter, explaining the officials' views to the politicians and vice versa.

Apart from this, the CAG also checks whether the corrective actions suggested by the PAC are taken up by the government or not. In case the suggestions are not implemented, the CAG reports the same to the PAC, which takes up the matter in the Parliament.

Achievement of PAC

Since its starting, the PAC has benefitted the nation in the following ways:

1. **Systemic Reforms:** The PAC has suggested various reforms in the government procedure from time to time. It focuses its attention on the weaknesses in the government system and serves as an agitator for systemic reforms.
2. **Separation of Accounting and Auditing:** In one of the reforms suggested, it emphasised on the separation of accounts from audit and the introduction of a proper scheme of accounting and financial control. This suggested reform was implemented by the government in 1976.
3. **Capacity Building:** The functioning and environment of the committee leads to the training of the politician and bureaucrat. It brings the politician and the bureaucrat together—the former in the task of constructive criticism and the latter in responsiveness to public opinion.[10]
4. **Introduction of Administrative Audit:** The suggestion of PAC has led to the introduction of administrative audit and performance review in large departments such as the Central Public Works Department.

5. **Changes in Taxation Laws:** The PAC's suggestions have also led to various constructive changes in the functioning of the taxation laws and procedures.
6. **Financial Discipline:** It has been instrumental in pointing out financial irregularities, curbing wasteful expenditure, toning up the fiscal administration, and strengthening the financial discipline of the government.[11]

Disadvantages of PAC

The PAC faces the following disadvantages in its functioning:

1. **Advisory in Nature:** The reforms suggested by the PAC are only advisory in nature. It cannot interfere with the internal administration of departments. There is no obligation on the part of the executive to adopt its reports. It can point to various financial irregularities but does not have the authority to disallow any item of wasteful expenditure.
2. **Cannot Question Policy Decisions:** The committee can point out various financial irregularities in administrative action, but is not allowed to question the very policy on the basis of which such an administrative action is taken. Thus, wasteful policy decisions are outside the ambit of the PAC. However, there is a very thin line between policy and non-policy decisions, and any enquiry into an administrative decision often touches upon the underlying policy decision. Thus, the PAC has to face various difficulties and criticism while pointing out the irregularities.
3. **Dependent on CAG:** The functioning of the PAC is dependent on the work of the CAG. Any inquiry carried out by the PAC is done based on the demand of the CAG. Generally, no inquiry is done by the PAC at its own initiative. Thus, its powers are derived from the audit conducted by the CAG.
4. **Delay in Presentation of Reports:** The reports of the PAC are presented after analysing and conducting an enquiry on the reports of the CAG. This leads to a delay in the presentation of the PAC reports in the Parliament. The utility of the reports is generally reduced due to this time delay.
5. ***Post Facto* Functioning:** The functioning of the committee is like a postmortem into financial irregularities. It unearths the irregularities of financial transactions some years after they have occurred, thus making it very difficult to effect measures against those responsible.
6. **Inadequate Discussion in Parliament:** The Parliament does not adequately discuss the reports of the PAC. Most of the points of the reports are addressed at an informal level between the individual departments and the PAC. Such informal addressing of the issues does not bring the crucial findings of the Committee into the active public domain.

Notwithstanding this criticism, it is found that most of the suggestions of the PAC are accepted by the government. To address the weakness of its postmortem investigations, some experts have suggested that on cases deserving urgent attention, PAC reports should be prepared concurrently during the year, so that the Parliament and the PAC can look into a specific matter then and there and not *post facto*.[12]

14.8.3.2 Estimates Committee

The Estimates Committee (EC) is a committee of the Parliament responsible for scrutinising the estimates included in the budget and to make suggestions to introduce economy in government expenditure. The functions of the EC are as follows:

(a) **Improvements for Better Policy Implementation:** The EC reports what economies, improvements in organisation, efficiency or administrative reform, consistent with the policy underlying the estimates may be affected.

(b) **Alternative Policies for Better Administration:** It suggests alternative policies to bring about efficiency and economy in administration.

(c) **Improvement in Financial Allocation within a Policy:** It examines whether the money is well laid out within the limits of the policy implied in the estimates.

(d) **Improvement in Form of Estimate:** It suggests the form in which the estimates shall be presented to the Parliament.

However, it needs to be pointed out that the committee is concerned with estimates only after they have been presented to the House. Thus, voting on grants in the Lok Sabha does not depend on the EC's report. Therefore, the examination of the EC is of a *post facto* character. Its suggestions serve as guidelines for future budget estimates.

Composition of EC

The EC has 30 members, all of whom are elected from the Lok Sabha alone. They are elected according to the principle of proportional representation by means of a single transferable vote so as to represent the interests of all the political parties represented in the Parliament. No minister is allowed to become a member of the committee. The tenure of each member is one year.

The chairperson is appointed by the speaker from amongst the members. If the deputy speaker is one of the members, he/she automatically becomes the chairperson of the EC. Generally, a senior member of the ruling party is nominated as the chairperson.

Functioning of EC

The reports of the EC are prepared by analysing the functioning and expenditure incurred by a ministry in the last 3 years. This information is sought from individual ministries by the EC. It also examines different officers as witnesses while making its reports. Each EC report generally contains the following three types of information:

(a) Information for improving the organisation of different ministries/departments

(b) Information on securing budget formulation and execution of different ministries/departments

(c) Guidelines for preparing better budget estimates by different ministries/departments

The reports prepared are then presented in the House. In general practice, these reports are not discussed in the Parliament, but individual members are free to refer to them in their discussions. The receiving ministries are mandated to reply, from time to time, regarding the action they have taken on the EC's reports.

Achievement of EC

The EC has benefitted the nation in the following ways:

1. **Check on Public Expenditure:** The EC has maintained a moral check on the activities of all the ministries and departments. It has ensured that the taxpayers' money is spent efficiently and adequate return is given back on the tax paid by them (in the form of government services).

2. **Training of Members:** Like the PAC, the EC also serves as a valuable training ground for the members of the Lok Sabha. During the working of the Committee, the members become conversant with the problems the government has to face daily.
3. **Educative Value for Public:** The reports of the Committee tend to educate the public on the functioning and performance of the government. It creates an intelligent and informed public opinion, which goes a long way in strengthening our democracy.

Disadvantages of EC

The EC faces the following disadvantages in its functioning:

1. **Lack of Expertise:** The members of the EC get a tenure of only one year. Thus, they do not get an expert's hold over the government functioning. By the time they get a grip of the situation, their tenure is about to end. Moreover, subject experts are not made members of the Committee.
2. **No Assistance from CAG:** Unlike the PAC, the EC lacks the expert assistance of the CAG.
3. **Regular Criticism:** The Committee is often criticised for arrogating powers that do not belong to it constitutionally. It is said that while commenting on the economic aspects of a ministry, it starts finding faults within the administrative structure, procedures, and distribution of functions of a department. Such criticism creates difficulty in the smooth functioning of the EC.
4. **Advisory in Nature:** The suggestions of the Committee are advisory and not binding on the government.

14.8.3.3 Committee on Public Undertakings

The Committee on Public Undertakings (COPU) is a parliamentary committee to scrutinise the financial and administrative functioning of different public sector undertakings (PSUs). It has the following functions:[14]

(a) **Examination of Accounts:** It examines the reports and accounts of public undertakings.

(b) **Examination of CAG Reports:** It examines the reports, if any, of the Comptroller and Auditor General of India on public undertakings.

(c) **Economy in affairs of PSUs:** It examines, in the context of the autonomy and efficiency of public undertakings, whether their affairs are being managed in accordance with sound business principles and prudent commercial practices.

(d) **Miscellaneous Functions:** It exercises such other functions vested in the Public Accounts Committee and the Estimates Committee in relation to the public undertakings as are not covered by the above-mentioned functions.

During its functioning, the COPU comes out with two kinds of reports—micro-level reports and horizontal reports. They are as described below:

(a) **Horizontal Report:** The horizontal report of the COPU is a report on the various public undertakings, which focuses on their issues such as personnel policies, financial management, foreign collaboration, and board structure. They are deductive in nature and prove to be quite useful to the entire domain of public undertakings.

(b) **Micro Level Report:** The micro-level report of the COPU focuses on individual enterprises and makes references to all significant aspects of an undertaking such as administration, finance, contracting practices, and inventory control.

(c) **Action Taken Report:** An action taken report lists the action taken by the government on the recommendations contained in the Committee's reports.

Composition of COPU

The COPU consists of 22 members, 15 of whom are elected by the Lok Sabha every year from amongst its members according to the principle of proportional representation by means of a single transferable vote; 7 members are nominated from the Rajya Sabha for being associated with the Committee. The chairperson is appointed by the speaker from amongst the members of the Committee. A minister is not eligible to become a member. The term of the Committee does not exceed one year.

Achievements of COPU

The COPU has had the following achievements since its inception:

(a) **Public Accountability:** The COPU has ensured the accountability of public undertakings to the general public.

(b) **Financial Advisor:** The COPU has suggested the creation of the post of a *financial advisor* in public undertakings and specified its roles and responsibilities.

(c) **Streamlining of Financial Procedures:** It has helped in streamlining the procedures relating to budgeting, costing, inventory control, and internal audit of public undertakings.

(d) **Streamlining of Personnel Policies:** It has made useful recommendations relating to the personnel policies, manpower requirements, recruitment, training, promotion, labour unions, grievance redressal machinery, worker's participation, incentives, labour welfare schemes, and so on, in public undertakings.

(e) **Combination of PAC and EC:** It combines the role of the PAC and EC for public undertakings. While the PAC is backward-looking and the EC is forward-looking, the COPU represents a synthesis of both for public undertakings.

(f) **Promotes Understanding between Politician and Management:** It promotes greater understanding between the Members of Parliament and the management of public undertakings.

Disadvantages of COPU

COPU faces the following constraints in its effective functioning:

(a) It is unable to examine the functioning of all the undertakings falling under its purview. Moreover, it is unable to examine all the aspects of the individual undertakings under its review.

(b) As the committee is advisory in nature, remedial action taken on its reports is not ensured completely.

(c) There is no discussion on the reports of the COPU in Parliament. Hence, the issue of non-acceptance or non-implementation of the COPU's reports does not figure in parliamentary proceedings.

14.8.3.4 Departmentally Related Standing Committees

Initiated on 31 March 1993, departmentally related standing committees (DRSCs) are responsible for overseeing the functioning of one to three union ministries. The system was introduced to ensure specialised and specific scrutiny of the individual ministries/departments by the Parliament. At present, there are 24 DRSCs on subjects such as agriculture, finance, IT, and home affairs.

Functions of DRSCs

The DRSCs have been entrusted with the following functions:

(a) **Scrutiny of Demands for Grants:** They scrutinise the demands for grants of the concerned ministries/departments and report to the Parliament. When the demands are scrutinised beforehand by the DRSCs, the Parliament has to spend less time on discussing the grants of each ministry.

(b) **Examination of Bills:** They examine bills pertaining to the concerned ministries/departments as are referred to them by the speaker of the Lok Sabha or the chairman of the Rajya Sabha, as the case may be, and make reports thereon.

(c) **Examination of Annual Reports:** They consider the Annual Reports of the concerned ministries/departments and make reports thereon. They verify the claims made by the ministries and departments in their annual reports.

(d) **Examination of Policy Documents:** They consider national basic long-term policy documents presented to the houses, if referred to them by the speaker of the Lok Sabha or the chairman of the Rajya Sabha, as the case may be, and make reports thereon.

Composition of DRSCs

The DRSCs consist of 31 members—21 members from the Lok Sabha, nominated by the speaker of the Lok Sabha and 10 members from the Rajya Sabha nominated by the chairman of the Rajya Sabha. The chairpersons of the DRSCs are appointed by the Speaker from amongst the members of the Committee from the Lok Sabha. It is roughly agreed that the chairpersons of half the DRSCs will be from the opposition political parties. The term of office of the members of the DRSCs does not exceed one year.

Advantages of DRSCS:

(a) **Strengthening of Parliament wrt Executive:** The DRSCs have helped in radically altering the way the Parliament functions and strengthened the position of the legislature vis-à-vis the executive.

(b) **Training of MPs:** It has led to active training of MPs on government functioning, leading to better informed parliamentarians.

14.8.4 Weaknesses in the Indian Budgetary Process

Various studies have been conducted, including the report of the Second Administrative Reforms Commission (ARC), to highlight the weaknesses in the Indian budgetary process. Some of these weaknesses are as follows:

1. **Excessive Focus on Inputs:** The budgetary processes are focused almost exclusively on inputs, with less focus on outputs and outcomes. The performance of the departments is judged on spending as much as that appropriated in the budget. There is very low correlation between expenditure and actual policy implementation. The expenditure figures do not reflect the actual expenditure made towards the receipt of goods and services.
2. **Short-term Perspective**: The focus on inputs leads to a short-term perspective to budget decision-making. It fails to take into account the long-term costs and biases in the choice of policy instruments. Though the Five-Year Plans (or any medium-term plan of the government) provide the basis for a long-term perspective, often *ad hoc* deviations from them distort the long-term plan perspective.
3. **Bottom-up Approach:** There is more than required emphasis on the bottom-up approach of budget-making. In this approach, the transaction costs are very high due to game playing between the line and central agencies. Due to this higher transaction cost, the overall budgetary goals are not attained perfectly.
4. **Micro-decision-making:** It is seen that the Central Government/central budget-making agency is involved in micro-decision-making on all aspects of funding of the ongoing policy. Micro-decision-making curbs the initiatives of the individual departments.
5. **Last-minute Cuts:** It is seen that sometimes, due to focus on reducing the fiscal deficit, last-minute budgetary cuts are resorted to. The last-minute cuts cause unpredictability of funding for the existing government policy.
6. **Incentive for Mindless Spending:** Government often resorts to incrementalism in budget-making. In incremental budget-making, additional funds are provided to a department in the next year based on the spending in the ongoing year. Thus, there is a strong incentive to spend everything in the budget, mindlessly, early in the year and as quickly as possible, since the current year's spending is the starting point of the annual budget bargaining between various departments.
7. **Incrementalism:** The policies laid down in the budget are subjected to very little scrutiny from one year to the next. Even when the policy outcomes are not encouraging, incremental funds are provided to a policy.
8. **Poor Linkage between Policy and Resources:** Due to excessive dependence on incremental budgeting, there are poor linkages between policy and the resources at the centre, between the centre and line agencies, and within the line agencies.
9. **Unrealistic Budget Estimates**: The budget estimates are often unrealistic. Weaknesses in preparing proper estimates lead to frequent revisions and supplementaries.
10. **Policies with Low Funds**: Many policies and schemes are announced in the budget. However, the resources are thinly spread among them, with only token provisions in some cases. This leads to an inordinate delay in the execution of these policies.

11. **Mis-stating of Financial Position**: Sometimes it is seen that government funds are transferred from the government accountable to the account of private goods and service providers without providing that good or service in reality. This parking of funds by implementing agencies outside the government accounts portrays an incorrect picture of the financial position of the government.

14.8.5 Measures for Overcoming Weaknesses in Budgetary Process

The Second Administrative Reforms Commission has recommended various changes for overcoming the weaknesses in the Indian budgetary process. Many of these recommendations have been implemented by the Government of India. As a result, the following reforms have been made in the budgetary process:

1. **Realistic Budget Estimates:** Efforts are being made to formulate realistic budget estimates. The DRSCs have been playing an important role in this regard. At the end of each year, the reasons for the gap between the estimates and the actuals is ascertained and efforts are made to minimise the gap.
2. **Top-down Budgeting:** A top-down method of budgeting is adopted, in which the overall budgetary targets are decided beforehand (as explained in Section 14.7.2.6) by the Central Government. These expenditure targets are indicated to each agency, based on which these agencies prepare and adjust their budgets. This leads to the formulation of realistic targets in the central budget.
3. **Outcome Budgeting:** Since 2005, the system of outcome-based budgeting has been implemented in various government departments for budgeting in case of certain flagship schemes and activities of national importance. In this form of budgeting, the emphasis is on the outcomes attained from the various policies on which funds were spent.

Apart from the above-mentioned implemented reforms, the following reforms need to be implemented in the Indian budgetary process:

1. **Scrutiny of Projects:** Projects and schemes should be included in the budget only after detailed consideration. The norms for formulating the budget should be strictly adhered to, to avoid making token provisions and spreading resources thin over a large number of projects/schemes.
2. **Alignment between Five-Year Plans (or any Medium-Term Plan) and Annual Budget:** to bring long-term perspective into budget-making, there should be alignment between the Five-Year Plans (or any medium-term plan) and the annual budget. There should be medium-term expenditure limits for ministries/departments through the Five-Year Plans, linking them to the annual budgets. These medium-term expenditure limits should be monitored by a high powered committee.
3. **Stoppage to *Ad Hoc* Announcement of Projects:** The practice of announcing projects and schemes on an *ad hoc* basis in budgets and on important National Days, and during visits of dignitaries to the states needs to be stopped. Projects/schemes that are considered absolutely essential may be considered in the annual plans or at the time of the mid-term appraisal.

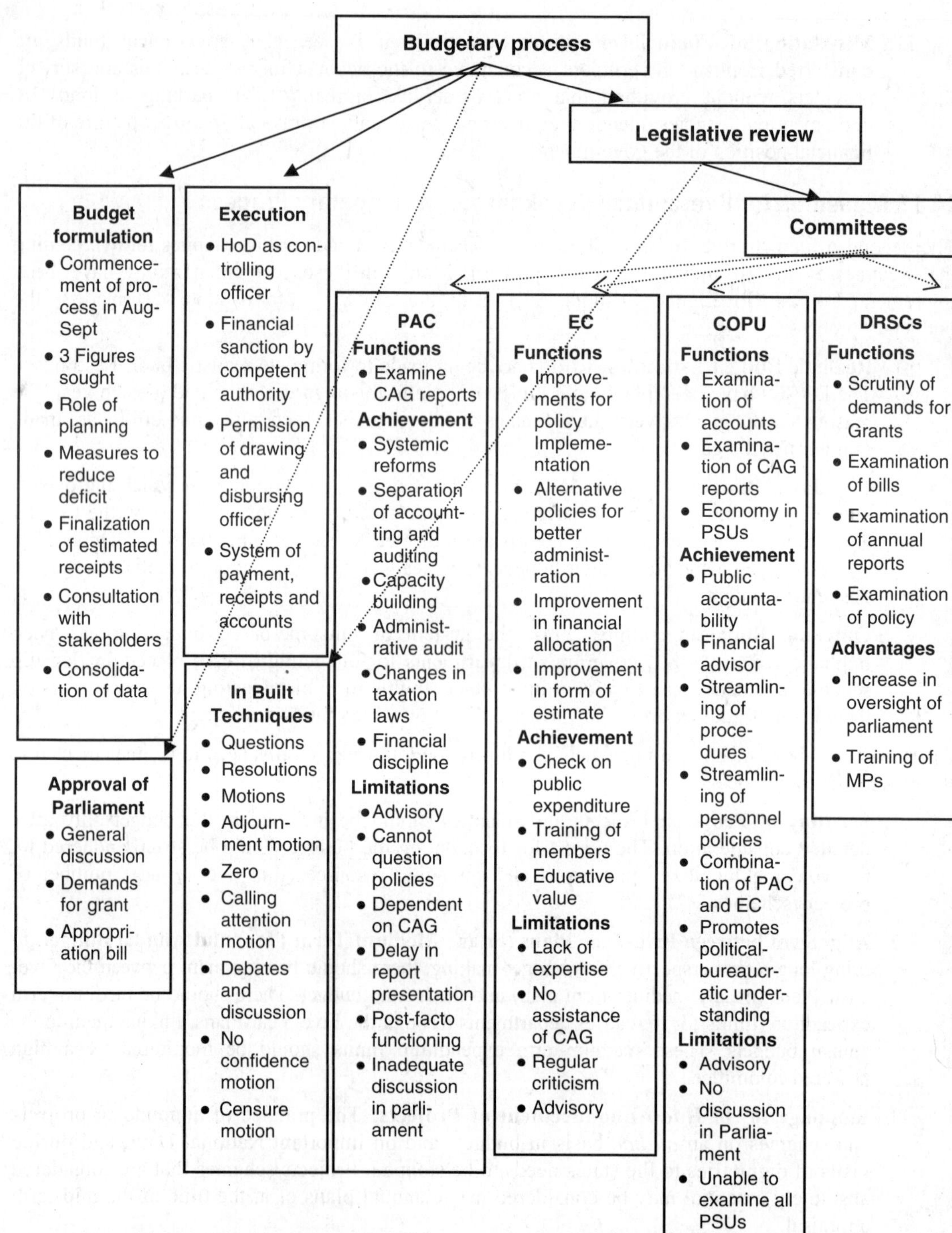

Mind Map 14.3: Budgetary Process in India

14.9 Budget as a Political Document

Nicholas Henry[15] has described a budget as meaning different things for different persons. For an economist, it is a device for influencing the country's economy. For a politician, it is a device for defending or criticising the government's programmes. For an administrator, it is a framework for communication and coordination as well as for exercising administrative discipline.

However, above all, a budget is a political document. W.F. Willoughbhy has regarded the budget as "an instrument of political reform."[16] It is regarded as a political document because of the following reasons:

(a) **Determines the Political Power of Elected Executives:** Public budgeting is a political process and influences the extent and exercise of political power by elected officials. It is regarded as a political instrument, as the power of political leaders depends on the various policies and schemes implemented by them. The funds for implementing these popular schemes are, in turn, provided by the annual budgets. Thus, it serves as a way in which the elected executives demonstrate their political clout to the rest of the political system.

(b) **Device for Undertaking Popular Measures:** The budgetary process acts as an arena in which various popular measures are taken by the political executives. These popular measures help them in enhancing their political power. They do this in two ways:[17]

- They show their concern for taxpayers by limiting the amount of money allocated to the public sector, especially to the less popular government programmes. This, in turn, helps in reducing the tax burden on the taxpayers.
- They lend their political and budgetary support to agencies that are supported by major interest groups. As a result, they attain political backing from these interest groups.

(c) **Creates Loyalty of Public Agencies towards Political Programmes:** To receive more funds, public agencies also become politically sensitive and cater to the prevailing political agenda. In fact, many public representatives demand that public agencies should seek the necessary budgetary appropriations to ensure agency survival and service provision for the representative's constituency. For example, if a minister of agriculture is from a particular constituency, say, X, then s/he will pressurise more funds for the ministry's programmes in X constituency.

(d) **Device for Governmental Reforms:** The budgetary process helps in the removal of defects in the governmental machinery and, therefore, profoundly affects our whole political system.

(e) **Strengthens Democracy:** The budget helps in the formulation of an intelligent popular will, as it provides a means to the public to know how government affairs have been conducted in the past, what the present conditions are, and what policies for work in the future are under consideration. Moreover, it locates responsibility for future government actions and furnishes the means of control for them. Thus, the budgetary process helps in the attainment of a real democracy.

(f) **Strengthens Legislative Control:** The budgetary system constitutes an effective means of giving legislative bodies effective control over the executive. The Parliament gains its true position and function in a political system due to the budgetary process.

14.10 Government Accounting

Accounting is a systematic process of identifying, recording, measuring, classifying, verifying, summarising, interpreting, and communicating financial information. It provides a convenient form to the various levels of management in an organisation for decision-making purposes.

In the government, accounting helps in providing information for preparation of the annual budget. It helps in determining the taxes to be levied for meeting the committed expenditures.

14.10.1 Government Accounting and Commercial Accounting

Accounting can be classified as government accounting and commercial accounting. Government accounting is done for government departments and commercial accounting is done for private/public sector companies. The key differences between these two types of accounting are enumerated in Table 14.2.

Table 14.2: Difference between government accounting and commercial accounting:

	Government accounting	Commercial accounting
Purpose	The purpose is to help govern the country and administer various functions in the best possible way in the interest of the larger society.	The purpose is to help produce goods/services and sell them to earn profit.
Revelation	It reveals the status of the government in relation to the citizens.	It reveals the status of the firm in relation to its debtors and creditors.
Relevant information	It indicates the funds required to carry out the government's activities.	It indicates whether a firm is gaining or losing and what the sources of its gain or loss are.
Nature of transaction	The transactions in the government accounts are determined by administrative classification of the activities. The accounts are, therefore, quite elaborate and kept on a single-entry basis.	Commercial accounts are maintained in the double-entry system, in which two parties are involved in every transaction—one giving and the other receiving. Every transaction requires two entries in the books—one against the party or account giving and the other against the party or account receiving.

14.10.2 Methods of Accounting

There are two methods of keeping accounts—accrual based and cash based.

14.10.2.1 Accrual-based Accounting

Accrual-based accounting is defined as a system of accounting in which transactions are entered into the books of accounts when they become due. The transactions are recognised as soon as a right to receive revenue and/or an obligation to pay liability is created. The expenses are recognised when the resources are consumed, and incomes are booked when they are earned. Therefore, the focus is on recording the flow of resources, i.e., labour, goods, services, and capital. The related cash flow may take place after some time (of the event); it may or may not take place in the same accounting period.[18]

14.10.2.2 Cash-based Accounting

Cash-based accounting is defined as a system of accounting in which transactions are recorded when there is an actual flow of cash. Revenue is recognised only when it is actually received. Expenditure is recognised only upon the outflow of cash. No consideration is given to the 'due' fact of the transaction. This system of accounting is simple to understand and as such needs fewer skills on the part of the accountant. Its whole focus is on cash management. Budgetary and legislative compliance is easier.[18]

14.10.2.3 Comparison of Accrual-based and Cash-based Accounting

The differences between cash-based and accrual-based accounting are mentioned in Table 14.3. It also shows how accrual-based accounting is better than cash-based accounting.

Table 14.3: Difference between cash-based and accrual-based accounting

Cash-based Accounting	Accrual-based Accounting
A statement of receipts and payments is prepared based on actual cash receipts and cash payments recorded in the cash book of a year.	The statements of receipts and payments are based on the amount 'due' in a particular year. It does not include those items of receipts and payments of the past and future years but those for which cash has been deposited/paid in the present year.
There is no distinction between capital and revenue receipts or payments.	There is a distinction between capital and revenue receipts and payments.
The receipt and payment statement commences with the opening balance showing both cash in hand and cash at bank.	The revenue and expenditure statement does not commence with any balance.
The statement is not necessarily accompanied by a statement of assets and liabilities.	The statement is necessarily accompanied by a statement of assets and liabilities.
The difference between the two sides, debit and credit, indicates the cash balance at the end of the period.	The difference between the two sides, debit or credit, indicates the excess income over expenditure or vice versa.
Accounting for assets creation/acquisition, depreciation, and written-down value are not taken cognizance of.	Accounting for assets creation/acquisition, depreciation, and written-down value are well-recorded and used for the right decisions.
It does not provide basic information such as the total assets of an organisation.	It provides different kinds of accounting information on significant dimensions of an organisation.
The system is not as transparent and efficient as expected.	Having a double-entry system, this method of accounting is highly transparent and efficient.

14.10.3 Accounting System in Government of India

The cash-based accounting system is used for accounting in all government agencies, i.e., the transactions in government accounts represent the actual cash receipts and disbursements during a financial year, as distinguished from the amounts due to or by the government during the same period.

Apart from this, government accounting is based on a single-entry system, which does not capture the dual impact of a transaction and is, thus, not arithmetically accurate.

The following problems are observed in the present government accounting system:

1. **Inaccurate Financial Position:** The accurate financial position of the government is not reflected in the cash-based accounting system because of a lack of scientific and structured information.
2. **No Balance Sheet:** The present system of accounting does not provide any balance sheet pertaining to the government showing the assets/liabilities and receivables/payables of the government.
3. **Lack of Skills and Training:** There are personnels who are trained in accounting and understand the financial aspects of all administrative issues.
4. **Lack of Guidelines:** The absence of any accounting manual or regulations to guide the accounting process has led to improper approaches to accounting and budgeting.
5. **Lack of MIS:** The government accounting system is not based on a strong management information system (MIS), leading to a lack of data support for facilitating decision-making.

14.10.4 Benefits of Accrual-Based Accounting

The accrual-based accounting system has the following benefits over the system that is adopted by the Government of India (cash-based accounting):

1. The accrual-based system recognises the financial flows at the time economic value is created, transformed, exchanged, transferred, or extinguished, whether or not cash is exchanged at that time. It records the flow of resources; in addition to cash flows, unpaid consumptions (payables) and unrealised incomes (receivables) are also recorded.
2. The system allows better cost–price calculations, records capital use properly, distinguishes between current and capital expenditures, presents a complete picture of debt and other liabilities, and focuses policy attention on the financial position, as shown in the whole balance sheet, not just cash flows or debts. It gives a complete measure of the cost of various services, takes care of disinvestment receipts, and provides adequate information on both fiscal balance and net worth and their changes over time.[19]

14.10.5 Reforms in Accounting System of India

The Second ARC has recommended introducing accrual-based accounting in the Government of India in a step-by-step procedure.

14.10.6 Separation of Accounting and Auditing

In 1971, the Comptroller and Auditor-General's (Duties, Powers and Conditions of Service) Act was passed to separate accounting and auditing in the Government of India. It relieved the CAG from compiling the accounts of any department of the Union Government.

The audit and accounts functions were separated in the Union Government because of the following reasons:

1. **Constitutionally Valid:** The combination of accounting and auditing under CAG used to violate the fundamental provisions of the Constitution and the CAG Act, 1971, which expected that the duties of the CAG shall be only auditorial. The separation made the role of the CAG constitutionally valid.
2. **Independence of CAG:** The combination of auditing and accounting functions used to bring the CAG under the indirect control of the finance ministry. However, the CAG is expected to be an independent institution under the Parliament. The separation ensured this independence.
3. **Improvement in Accounting Duties:** The combined accounts and auditing functions in a single office led to the slow performance of accounting duties such as timely payment of dues such as salary, pension, and provident fund.
4. **Federally Correct:** When the CAG was responsible for the auditing and accounting of the states, the accounting functions of the states used to lie with the president through the CAG. This used to disturb the federal character of Indian polity. The separation allowed the role of the CAG to be federally correct.
5. **Accountability of Individual Departments:** Separation of accounting functions from CAG and giving them as a responsibility to respective individual departments establishes an accountability on the decision-making departments for the expenditure incurred by them.
6. **Improved Performance of CAG:** Separation of the auditing and accounting functions enables the CAG to confine its attention to audit matters and focus on higher auditing activities such as efficiency audit and performance audit.

14.11 Auditing

The term 'audit' is derived from the Latin word '*audire*' (meaning to hear). In historical times, the auditors used to hear the accounts from the accounting parties. Thus, the word 'audit' was formed. Formally, *an audit is an examination of accounting records undertaken with a view to establishing whether or not they correctly and completely reflect the transactions to which they purport to relate.* It ensures that expenditure has been incurred with the sanction of the competent authority and applied for the purpose for which it was sanctioned.

14.11.1 Statutory Audit (External Audit) and Internal Audit

Statutory audit (external audit) is the audit conducted by the CAG through the Indian Audit and Accounts Department. On the other hand, an internal audit is an audit conducted by an agency created by the internal management of an organisation. The differences between the two are tabulated in Table 14.4.

Table 14.4: Difference between statutory audit and internal audit

	Statutory audit	Internal audit
Agency	It is an audit of different departments/organisations done by the CAG.	It is an audit of a department done by an agency created by the management of the same department.
Purpose	The purpose is to ensure the financial accountability of the executive to the Parliament.	The purpose is to serve the executive for smooth and efficient functioning and for reviewing and improving its performance.
Common objectives	(a) To see that all payments are supported by receipt vouchers (accountability audit) and detect fraud, technical errors, and other errors. (b) To check that the items have been charged on the proper heads of accounts and further that the appropriation of these heads have not exceeded their limit. (appropriation audit). (c) To check whether the expenditure has been incurred according to the rules and regulations and sanctioned by a competent authority (administrative audit).	(a) To check the adequacy, soundness, and applicability of the systems of internal controls such as accounting controls, financial controls, and other operative controls. (b) To prevent and detect frauds in a department. (c) To check the adequacy and reliability of the accounting and reporting systems. (d) To improve the performance and efficiency of an organisation.
Independence	It is independent in nature.	It is not independent in nature.
Nature	It does not audit all the transactions. It test-checks certain transactions randomly.	It checks all the transactions of an organisation.

14.11.2 Weaknesses of Internal Audit

In the Government of India, there are certain deficiencies in the internal audit system of different departments. These weaknesses are as follows:

1. **Untrained Internal Audit Staff:** The internal audit staff lacks the requisite skills for internal audit. Moreover, specific training programmes for upgrading their skills are not conducted regularly.
2. **Audit of Schemes and PSUs:** The audit of developmental schemes and PSUs is kept outside the purview of the internal audit of ministries.

3. **Lack of Audit Plan:** Internal audit is generally done in an *ad hoc* manner without any monthly or annual plan.
4. **Lack of Response by Auditee Units:** A tendency has been seen in the ministries to not comply with the recommendations of the internal audit report.
5. **Outdated Guidelines:** It is found that the internal audit guidelines are outdated in many ministries. There are no prescribed internal audit standards.
6. **Fault-finding Reports:** It is often seen that internal audit reports have a fault-finding nature with few positive recommendations.

14.11.3 Integrated Financial Adviser

Prior to 1975, there were two types of financial advisers in all ministries. The first one, the *internal financial adviser*, was in charge of the budgets and accounts and was required to be consulted in all cases of exercise of those financial powers that are delegated to a ministry. The second one, the *associate financial adviser*, was based in the Department of Expenditure (Ministry of Finance) and was required to be consulted by a ministry/department in matters falling outside its delegated field.

In 1975, it was felt that combining the functions of the two advisers would enable him/her to play a more effective and constructive role in the developmental activities of the ministries and provide better financial expertise in assisting the secretary of administrative ministries. Thus, the post of an *integrated financial adviser* (IFA) was created to combine the roles of the two types of financial advisers mentioned. He/she is responsible both to the Ministry of Finance and to the relevant administrative ministry.

The duties of the IFA were reformulated in 2006. They are as follows:

1. Support in the budget formulation of a ministry/ department
2. Support in outcome budgeting and performance budgeting in a ministry/ department
3. Expenditure and cash management work
4. Project/programme formulation, appraisal, monitoring, and evaluation
5. Screening of proposals
6. Leveraging of non-budgetary resources for sectoral development
7. Non-tax receipts for a ministry/department
8. Evaluating the tax expenditure
9. Monitoring of assets and liabilities of a ministry/department
10. Support in accounting and auditing of a ministry/department
11. Procurement of materials/services and awarding of work contracts
12. Monitoring the financial management system of a ministry/department
13. Support in improving the use of technology in various financial matters

The purpose of IFAs is to assist the secretary in the achievement of the goals/objectives of the respective administrative ministry/department with due financial prudence and ensure that the funds allocated are spent on time to achieve the intended outcomes. Their role is akin to that of a chief financial adviser (CFA) in a corporate firm.

14.11.4 Types of Audits

Audits are of the following types:

1. **Financial Audit:** A financial audit is conducted to check whether the executive action is in conformity with the prescribed law, financial rules, and procedures and does not lead to extravagance. For example, in a canal construction project, the financial audit would concern itself with whether the canal's alignments have been drawn up on insufficient data necessitating a subsequent change leading to additional expenditure. Similarly, it would check whether the anticipated financial results were obtained and what circumstances led to the fall, if any, in the financial results. However, a financial audit will not deal with administrative matters such as proper construction of the canal and whether it passes through the expected areas or not. However, it may interfere with administrative matters when administrative actions have serious financial implications and are not in conformity with the prescribed financial principles.
2. **Regularity Audit:** A regularity audit checks whether or not payments are duly authorised and supported by proper vouchers in the prescribed formats. It ensures conformity of executive action with the relevant administrative, financial, budgetary, and accounting rules and regulations provided in the Constitution and parliamentary laws.

   It checks whether the funds spent were authorised by a competent authority, whether they were sanctioned and incurred by a competent officer, whether the rules regulating the method of payment have been duly observed by the disbursing officer, and so on.
3. **Receipts Audit:** Receipts audit is the audit of income tax, customs, and excise receipts at the Union level. It ensures that adequate procedures and regulations have been framed and are being observed by the revenue department, to secure an effective check on the assessment, collection, and proper allocation of resources.
4. **Propriety Audit:** Propriety audit is an audit that checks the decisions of the executive with an emphasis on public interest and financial discipline to verify that such decisions are not only within the framework of legislative sanctions, laws, rules, and procedures but also within the broad framework of financial propriety. It checks whether the commonly recognised standards of financial propriety and the quality, quantity, morality, and ethics of expenditure are observed by the sanctioning, spending, and dispensing authorities.[21] It ensures not only that the spending is based on a sanction from the Parliament but also the wisdom, faithfulness, and economy of such spending.[21] Beyond ensuring that any expenditure is duly sanctioned by an appropriate authority, it investigates the justification and necessity of it.

6. **Performance Audit/Value for Money Audit:** In today's time, when the government is indulged in several developmental works, programmes, and schemes, the financial and regulatory audits are not found sufficient for auditing.

   Financial and regularity audits only audit individual transactions. However, a performance audit evaluates the performance of an organisation in terms of its goals and objectives. It seeks to check whether all the input resources have been utilised efficiently by deploying them in an optimum manner. It highlights the extent of productive use of national resources in achieving programme goals and objectives.

However, there are certain problems in conducting performance audits, as follows:

- It is not easy to do performance evaluations of developmental activities, as their objectives are not easily quantifiable.
- Apart from measuring the visible outputs, it is necessary to consider the non-measurable social benefits of a programme. Such social cost-benefit analysis is difficult to be carried out by an audit agency.
- There may be certain objectives of developmental schemes that may be socially desirable but financially undesirable. Performance audit is unable to take account of such objectives. For example, by selling air tickets at a lower price, Air India serves the social objective of connecting Tier II and Tier III cities via air. However, such an objective does not fit the criteria of financial propriety.

Therefore, for a successful performance audit, two things are necessary. First, there should be a developed information system in an organisation, giving weightage to all kinds of objectives. It should supply accurate information about the achievements and costs incurred. Moreover, it requires the framing of precise yardsticks against which resources can be evaluated.

14.12 Comptroller and Auditor General and other Supreme Audit Institutions

14.12.1 Types of Supreme Audit Institutions

A Supreme Audit Institution (SAI) is the central audit institution of any country. In India, the CAG is the SAI. Depending on the historical and legal legacy of different countries, three models of SAIs are in use worldwide. They are as follows:

(a) The judicial or Napoleonic model

(b) The parliamentarian or Westminster model

(c) The board or collegiate model

These models are discussed in the following sections.

14.12.1.1 Napoleonic/Judicial Model

The Napoleonic/judicial model of the Supreme Audit Institution (SAI) has the following features:

(a) This type of SAI is also known as the *cour de comptes* (court of accounts). It has judicial as well as administrative authority.

(b) It is independent of the legislative and executive branches of the government.

(c) It is an integral part of the judiciary. It passes judgments on the government's compliance with laws and regulations, ensuring that public funds are well spent.

(d) This type of model is used in the Latin countries of Europe (France, Italy, Spain, Portugal, and so on), Turkey, and most Latin American and Francophone countries (French-speaking African countries such as Algeria, Benin, Burkina Faso, and Burundi).

14.12.1.2 Westminster/Parliamentarian Model

The Westminster/parliamentarian model of SAI has the following features:

(a) The SAI is an independent body reporting to the Parliament.

(b) It consists of professional auditors and technical experts who submit periodic reports on the financial statements and operations of government entities.

(c) Their emphasis on legal compliance is less than that in the Napoleonic system. The Westminster model emphasises more on financial compliance more than on legal compliance.

(d) The SAI serves no judicial function but, when warranted, its reports may be used by the legal authorities for any legal/judicial function.

(e) It is prevalent in the Commonwealth countries such as Australia, Canada, India, the UK, and many Caribbean, Pacific, and Sub-Saharan African countries.

14.12.1.3 Board/Collegiate Model

The board/collegiate model of Supreme Audit Institution (SAI) has the following features:

(a) Like the Westminster model, in the board model, the SAI is independent of the executive and helps the Parliament in its oversight over the executive.

(b) SAI consists of an audit commission (the decision-making body) and a general executive bureau (the executive organ). The president of the board is the *de facto* Auditor General.

(c) The board's mandate is to analyse the government's spending and revenue and report its findings to the Parliament.

(d) It is found in Asian countries such as Indonesia, Japan, and South Korea.

14.12.2 SAI of India—Comptroller and Auditor General

The Comptroller and Auditor General (CAG) is the Supreme Audit Institution (SAI) of India. The office came into the picture in 1857 following a major reorganisation of the government by Lord Cannings, in which the office of the *accountant general* was created by merging the accounting offices of Bombay, Bengal, and Madras. The Indian Councils Act, of 1919 made the auditor general independent of the Government of India. It was given a status of a Federal Court in the Government of India Act, 1935.

In the Constitution of India, 1950, the designation of auditor general was changed to Comptroller and Auditor General (CAG). The word 'comptroller' means the one who restrains, governs, and checks the exchequer and all expenses of the government.

Article 148 of the Constitution provides the provisions regarding the appointment and conditions of service of the CAG. Articles 148–151 ensure that the CAG is able to conduct its work in an impartial and upright manner.

14.12.3 Duties, Powers, and Responsibilities of CAG

The constitutional purpose of CAG is to promote accountability, transparency, and good governance in administration through its auditing and accounting functions. It is also mandated to provide independent assurance to the legislature, executive, and the public, in general, that the public funds are used efficiently and effectively. The duties, powers, and responsibilities of the CAG are as follows:

I. Audit Functions of Government Bodies

CAG conducts the following audits at the Central and state levels:

- Receipts and expenditures of the Union and the state governments accounted for in the respective Consolidated Funds.
- Transactions relating to the Contingency Funds (created for use in emergency circumstances) and the Public Accounts (used mainly for loans, deposits, and remittances).

- Trading, manufacturing, profit and loss accounts, balance sheets, and other subsidiary accounts kept in any government department.
- Accounts of stores and stocks kept in government organisations, government companies, and government corporations, whose statutes provide for audit by the CAG.
- Authorities and bodies substantially financed from the Consolidated Funds of the Union and the states.
- Any authority or body even though not substantially financed from the Consolidated Fund at the request of the President of India or the governor of a state.
- Accounts of bodies and authorities receiving loans and grants from the government for specific purposes.

II. Audit Functions of Government Companies

In government companies (companies in which the share of government companies is more than 51%), the CAG advises for the appointment of chartered accountants (CAs) for the audit. The Indian Audit and Accounts Department (IAAD) (CAG is the head of IAAD) officers give directions to these chartered accountants on the manner in which the audit should be conducted. They also intervene and conduct the audit of such companies, and their audit report is tabled in the Parliament and state legislative bodies. These officers also form Audit Boards for periodically appraising the working of such government companies or public sector undertakings (PSUs).

The Office of the AG (Audit) is in charge of auditing the activities of the state government, while the Office of Principal Director (Audit) takes care of auditing the activities of the Central Government. Each state has an Office of the AG (Audit), while the Office of PD (Audit) is located regionwise, which may contain more than one state. All these offices fall under the jurisdiction of the CAG.

III. Account Functions

The CAG lays down the general principles of government accounting and the broad principles applicable to the audit of receipts and expenditure. It ascertains and certifies the net proceeds of taxes levied and collected by the Union Government but assigned to states or distributed between the Union and the states.

IV. CAG Reports

The CAG brings out a number of reports relating to a number of Central and state departments. In these reports, they communicate their major findings and observations. The following types of audit reports are prepared by the CAG:

- **Inspection Report:** The CAG prepares inspection reports of individual agencies/departments/organisations while doing their regular inspection. These reports are sent to the head of these organisations, who are asked to take corrective actions based on these reports. These corrective actions are monitored by the CAG.
- **Audit Reports:** According to Article 151 of the Constitution, the CAG prepares audit reports and submits them to the president or governors for presentation in the Parliament or state legislative assembly, respectively. These reports consist of two parts. The first part is the report on appropriation accounts, in which it is checked whether the money spent by the government is spent for the purpose for which it was granted. The second part is the report on financial accounts, in which the accounts of annual receipts and expenditures during the last year are audited.

These audit reports highlight cases involving financial irregularities, losses, frauds, and wasteful expenditure by the government. They also suggest corrective measures to be taken by the government to avoid such waste in the future. The CAG provides *audit paras* in which it criticizes public expenditure by the delinquent organisations. These 'paras' are brought to the notice of the concerned parliamentary committees, which conduct an inquiry and dispose off each 'para' one by one.

- **Annual Activity Report:** The CAG assesses the overall functioning of each department and brings out their annual activity report. It highlights the detailed functioning of a department and any irregularities observed by it, which helps provide the real picture of the functioning of a department. Moreover, it also helps in future planning and improving the work of the departments.

V. Audit of Grants and Loans

When any grant or loan is given for any specific purpose from the Consolidated Fund of India or of any state or Union Territory having a legislative assembly to any authority or body, the CAG scrutinises the procedures by which the sanctioning authority satisfies itself about the fulfilment of the conditions subject to which such grants or loans were given.

VI. Powers to Call Documents

While auditing the accounting records of any organisation, the CAG has the power to demand the production of any account, book, paper, or other document relevant to her/his audit, to put such questions or make such observations, and to call for information required for any account or report that s/he has to prepare.[20]

VII. Audit of International Organisations

International agencies such as the UN envisage that their audit should be conducted by the SAI of its member countries. In this regard, the CAG is also involved in the audit of international agencies. However, there is no provision in the CAG Act that empowers it to conduct the audit of international bodies.

14.12.4 Audits Conducted by CAG

Section 23 of the CAG's (Duties, Powers and Conditions of Service) Act gives full independence and discretion to the CAG to regulate and decide the scope of his/her audit. In its functioning, due to this discretionary power, it has invented various new forms of auditing such as efficiency-cum-performance auditing. The various types of audits conducted by the CAG have already been discussed in Section 14.11.4.

14.12.5 Independence of CAG

The Constitution has various provisions for safeguarding the independence of the CAG, which is important for ensuring the highest standard of integrity in the administration. These provisions are as follows:

(a) **Appointment and Fixed Tenure:** Article 148 of the Constitution lays down that the CAG of India would be appointed by the President of India. S/he will hold office for a period of six years or until the age of 65 is attained, whichever is earlier. Further, s/he can be removed from office only in the same manner and on the same grounds as a Supreme Court judge, i.e., by impeachment in the Parliament.

(b) **Conditions of Service:** Article 148(3) provides that the salary and other conditions of service of the CAG are such as determined by the law and cannot be varied to his/her disadvantage after his/her appointment.

(c) **Debarment from Further Office:** Under Article 148(4), the CAG is debarred from holding any office either under the Government of India or the state governments after retirement.

(d) **Salaries Charged to the Consolidated Fund:** According to Article 148(6), all salaries, allowances, and pensions payable to or in respect of persons serving in the office of the CAG shall be charged upon the Consolidated Fund of India.

14.12.6 Private Sector Records Audit by CAG

There has been a constant debate on the power of the CAG to access private sector records while performing audit duties. The issue was settled by the Supreme Court in the case of access of records of private telecom companies by the CAG while auditing the 2G spectrum allocation case. In its judgment, the honourable court recognised that the records of private players entrusted with the responsibility of delivering public goods and services by utilising state-owned resources should be accessible to the CAG for audit. The judgment has the following wider implications for a CAG audit:

1. **Principle of *Res Communes*:** The doctrine of *res communes* claims that some things are common to all mankind—air, water, and so on. Thus, the titles of these resources are vested with the state as the sovereign, in trust for the people. Even if a private party provides the resources, the CAG can check its records. When the nation's wealth/resources, such as spectrum, are being dealt with by the government or by private players, they are accountable to the people and to the Parliament.
2. **Accountability of the Licensees:** Licensees are the accountants of the government and are expected to maintain complete, accurate, and honest books of accounts as to any transaction(s) involving revenue as a fiduciary duty.
3. **Audit in case of Revenue Sharing:** Any revenue shared by the licensees with the government flowing into the Consolidated Fund of India is the income of the nation and is subject to CAG audit. The CAG's examination of the accounts of private service providers in a revenue-sharing contract is important to ascertain whether there is an unlawful gain to the private provider or an unlawful loss to the government.

   The judgment, in essence, emphasises that the duties of the CAG are required to be interpreted to meet the changing needs and requirements of accountability. The CAG audit of private sector records would:

   - Provide an independent assurance that the terms and conditions of an agreement (between the government and a private player) have been complied with in letter and spirit
   - Assist in protecting the larger public interest
   - Strengthen parliamentary oversight over those projects in which the government and private sector collaborate to provide public goods and services

14.12.7 Social Audit and Performance Audit

The concept of social audit is already discussed in the topic *'social audit'* of chapter 6 of this book. For conducting the performance audit (as discussed in the topic 'Performance Audit/Value for Money Audit of this chapter) of government schemes by the CAG, it is very important that the social audit be carried out effectively at the gram panchayat and gram sabha level. Moreover, it is mandatory that a summary of the findings of the social audit conducted during a financial year be submitted by state governments to the CAG.

An effective social audit forms the basis of the performance audit by the CAG. For example, in the case of MGNREGA, it was mandated by the Ministry of Rural Development (MoRD) in April 2013 that one percent of the total annual expenditure under the MGNREGS in the states/UTs must be used for meeting the cost of establishing social audit units (SAUs) and the conduct of social audit work. Similarly, a social audit has been made mandatory in all Central Government schemes.

The CAG conducts the performance audit with the help of the social audit by checking the following things:

1. **Diversion of Adequate Funds:** The role of the CAG is to check whether or not the required funds under the central schemes have been diverted for the social audit. For example, in the case of MGNREGS, the CAG reported underutilisation of social audit funds in 2013–14 and 2014–15 due to the non-availability of field-level staff and the shortfall in achieving social audit coverage.
2. **Setting up of Effective SAUs:** As per social audit guidelines, especially in the case of MGNREGS, it is mandated that social audit units (SAUs) shall identify the appropriate number of resource persons at state/district/block/village levels to facilitate the conduct of social audits. The CAG checks whether or not adequate resource persons are recruited for effective social audit. It also checks whether or not full-time directors of SAUs are recruited at district levels. Moreover, the social audit reports are checked to determine whether the prescribed formats for conducting social audits and preparing social audit reports are being followed, which helps the CAG in finding out whether or not the social audit staff is well-trained on the various aspects of the audit.
3. **Planning of Social Audit:** The CAG checks whether, at the beginning of the year, an annual calendar to conduct a regular social audit in each gram panchayat is laid down or not. Apart from this, the CAG also checks whether, while conducting the social audit, the social audit teams visited the project sites and physically verified the completed projects vis-à-vis the information contained in the records of the implementing agencies. Moreover, it verifies whether the social audit teams have checked all the mandatory details of a centrally sponsored scheme. For example, in the case of MGNREGS, it is mandatory that the gram panchayats have to paint the money paid to all job card holders on its wall. The CAG checks whether all social audit teams have verified this mandatory condition in their reports.
4. **Conduct of Social Audit Gram Sabhas:** A gram sabha has to be convened to discuss the findings of the social audit. The CAG checks whether the social audit reports were laid out in front of the gram sabha or not. Moreover, in the social audit reports, the CAG also checks the proceedings of the social audit gram sabhas. Their proceedings should mention the details of the issues discussed.
5. **Action Taken on Social Audit Reports:** It is mandatory that the state governments take action on the findings of the social audit and incorporate the action taken reports in the annual reports of the respective departments, to be laid down before the respective state legislatures. The CAG checks that this mandatory requirement is fulfilled.

Thus, the CAG plays the pivotal role of ensuring the quality of social audits conducted in each gram panchayat. As social audits check the performance of developmental schemes at the village level, the CAG indirectly conducts a performance audit by auditing the social audit conducted by the SAUs.

14.12.8 Strengths of CAG Audit

The statutory audit conducted by the CAG has the following advantages:

1. **Independence of CAG:** As discussed, the Constitution has guaranteed independence to the CAG for its functioning. It is often regarded as the fourth pillar of the democratic setup and an essential instrument of financial control and accountability.
2. **Discretion to Audit:** The CAG's (DPC) Act, 1971 provides discretion to the CAG to expand the scope of an audit conducted by it. Thus, the audit conducted by it can respond to changes, reforms, new initiatives, changing patterns of government activities, international developments in the profession, and rising expectations of the stakeholders regarding public accountability.
3. **No Interference in Audit Reports:** The CAG has the right to determine what should be included in the audit reports without any intervention from any side.
4. **Wide Publicity:** The CAG's audit reports are tabled in the Parliament and widely publicised.
5. **Manuals and Guidelines:** The auditors of IAAD have documented the audit manuals and guidelines to be followed.
6. **International Standard:** The auditing standards in India are framed on the lines of the International Organisation of SAIs (INTOSAI).
7. **Parliamentary Committees:** As discussed, the CAG's audit reports are discussed in the various Parliamentary committees such as PAC and COPU. These committees interview government officers, as witnesses, based on the reports. The functioning of these committees puts the CAG's reports in the political arena.

14.12.9 Weakness of CAG Audit

The statutory audit conducted by the CAG has the following weaknesses:

1. **Dependent on Parliamentary Committees:** The entire 'audit paras' included in the CAG's audit reports are not submitted to the Parliament by the PAC. Only 1.5% to 2% of the paras are submitted by the PAC. Moreover, it is seen that the ministries/departments do not take the cognisance of the CAG paras directly. They take the CAG paras seriously only when they are taken up for discussion in the PAC. Thus, the impact of the CAG is dependent on the efficient functioning of the PAC. In the words of Shri R.R. Murarka, "the ineffectiveness of the PAC or COPU in the moulding of financial management and correcting them in the light of irregularities brought out in Audit Reports is one of the greatest setbacks to the improvement in the financial management of the country. One can suppose that these things occur because of very loose accountability on the part of the executive and the lack of willingness to put the house in order."
2. **Formal Action Taken Reports:** All the ministries/departments are required to submit *action taken reports* on the audit paras of the CAG. Apart from the paras discussed by the PAC, the action taken reports on other paras are largely formal and not substantial.
3. **Insufficient Action on Inspection Reports:** Many of the inspection reports prepared by the CAG are kept unattended in the departments of the Union and state governments. There is low accountability for taking timely corrective actions on the audit observations made in the inspection reports.
4. **Delay in CAG Reports:** It is often seen that there is a substantial time gap between the occurrence of a financial irregularity and the tabling of a CAG report on it. Thus, the recommendations made by the CAG are available too late to take any corrective action.

5. **Based on Documentary Evidence:** The CAG's audit reports are based on documentary evidence and not on the ground-level conditions and situations. Sometimes, the situation on the ground is quite different from what is reflected in the documents. Thus, the CAG's findings are criticised as being idealistic and not real.
6. **Fault-finding in Nature:** It is often criticised that, rather than being constructive, the CAG's reports are negative and fault-finding in nature. They do not recognise the practical constraints in the functioning of government organisations. They do not recognise the unforeseen contingencies that the government departments have to face. Thus, the CAG is criticised for dampening the initiatives and risk-taking abilities of government employees. It is also criticised for policing government organisations rather than being a management aid to them. Paul Appleby also criticised the CAG on these lines. He said that auditors are not expected to know about good administration and that auditing is a necessary but highly pedestrian function with a narrow perspective and limited utility.
7. **Indifference by the Government Departments:** The CAG reports can be of immense value to policymakers, administrators, and others. However, it is seen that the senior officers of the Government have some apathy to the audit reports and the corrective actions taken based on them. They consider audit as an extraneous and alien activity. This apathy is because of very little interaction between the senior officers of the auditee organisation and the IAAD.
8. **Internal and External Audit:** There is inadequate coordination between the internal audit done by the respective organisations and the external audit done by the CAG.
9. **Overreach by CAG:** The CAG is often accused of overreach when it uses its discretion to widen its scope and conduct higher level audits such as performance audits. Such unwarranted criticism decreases the motivation of the IAAD officers.

14.12.10 Measures Taken for Improving CAG's Functioning

The following measures have been taken to improve the functioning of the CAG:

1. **Rapport between Administration and CAG:** To improve the understanding between the officers of IAAD and the senior officers of the government, a system was devised in 1965 to provide personal contacts between them. Under this system, the secretary of each ministry/department has the authority to take up those points directly with the CAG that he/she considers unjustified and objectionable.
2. **Constructive Reports:** The CAG's reports have moved from being of a fault-finding nature to being constructive in nature. The various policy suggestions made by the CAG (such as those made in the report on the 2G spectrum and coal block allocation) are constructive and very helpful for administrators. Moreover, the CAG has started auditing issues of public importance on a priority basis. Thus, the delay in submitting reports in the case of urgent issues has decreased by a considerable amount.
3. **Lucid Reports:** The language of the reports has been made lucid and easily understandable for the public. This has increased the knowledge value of the reports and helped in shaping informed public opinions.
4. **Focus on Systemic Irregularities:** There is an effort by the CAG to move away from pointing out individual irregularities to pointing out systemic irregularities in its reports. This systemic audit done by CAG is helpful in playing a constructive role in the overall functioning of a department.

14.12.11 Recommendations for Improving CAG's Functioning

Various commissions and committees, including the Second Administrative Reforms Commission and the CAG itself, have provided various recommendations for improving the impact of the CAG. Some of these recommendations are as follows:

1. **Time Limit for Audit Paras Examination:** The examination of the audit paras of the CAG must be completed in a maximum period of one year. For this, the PAC and COPU may decide, at the beginning of the year itself, which paras would be examined by them, which by their sub-committees, and which they may consider assigning to the respective departmentally related standing committees (DPSCs).
2. **Time Limit for CAG Audit:** The second ARC has said that the CAG audit needs to be timely in inspecting and reporting so that the reports can be used for timely corrective action. All audits for the year under review should be completed by the 30th of September of the following year.
3. **Time Limit for taking Remedial Actions:** The government agencies should be sensitised on responding promptly to the observations made in the inspection and audit reports. They should ensure timely remedial and corrective action not only on settling the irregularities reported but also on addressing the systemic deficiencies mentioned in the reports.
4. **Database on Unattended Paras:** The Second ARC has recommended the creation of a database to list the paras pending for taking corrective action. In the case of persistent default in submitting replies to the audit paras, a procedure should be laid down for action against the concerned officer(s).
5. **Deterrent Action in case of Non-Cooperation:** At present, there is no deterrent action available if the individual departments do not cooperate with the CAG in conducting the audit. Thus, there is a need to strengthen the CAG's (DPC) Act to the effect that no document can be refused on the grounds of confidentiality, and penal action can be taken by the CAG in the case of non-compliance to such requests. Such powers are provided to the SAIs of Japan and Turkey.
6. **Power to Summon:** Like a civil/criminal court, the CAG shall have the power to summon persons and documents while conducting its enquiry. The SAIs of Thailand and Japan have such power.
7. **Power of Search and Seizure:** The CAG shall have the power of search and seizure in the following cases:[20]
    - In relation to government contracts to enter any land/building and inspect the property. The SAI of New Zealand has such a power.
    - Power to enter any premises to search and seize any document. The SAIs of Thailand and Malaysia have such power.
    - Power to seal books of accounts and assets in case the auditee is obstructing or sabotaging the audit work. The SAI of China has such power.
    - Power to confiscate illegal gains/embezzled assets in the case of violation of economic regulations. The SAI of China has such power.
8. **Power of Penal Actions:** Like the SAIs of China, Japan, Korea, and Israel, the CAG shall have the power to recommend disciplinary action against the delinquent officers involved in financial irregularities and those who have obstructed the smooth functioning of the CAG. Like the SAI of New Zealand, it must also have the power of imposing a surcharge on any officer due to whom a loss has been caused to the state exchequer.

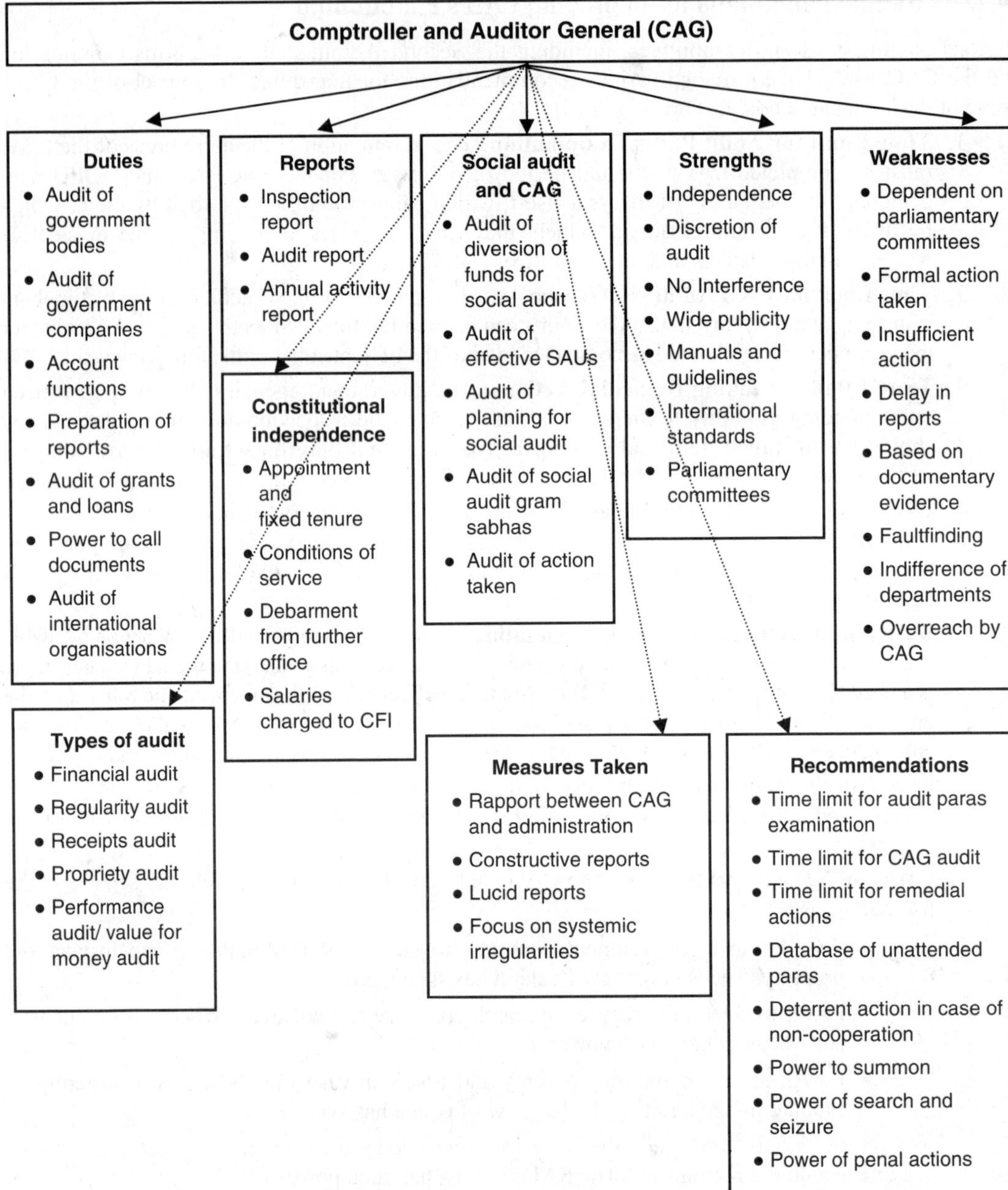

Mind Map 14.4: Various Aspects of CAG

SUMMARY

This chapter dealt with the various aspects of financial administration in India as well as internationally. Starting with the objectives of financial administration, the chapter has ended up discussing the importance of auditing and the role of Supreme Audit Institutions (SAIs) across the world. In between, the chapter has dealt with concepts such as fiscal policy and monetary policy; public expenditure, public revenue, and various reforms in the public revenue system; public debt, deficit financing, and the status of Indian public debt; various types of budgets and the budgetary cycle in India; importance of accounting and auditing with special emphasis on the role of the Comptroller and Auditor General (CAG); and various parliamentary committees to improve the legislative oversight over the executive.

Practice Questions

1. What are the objectives and instruments of fiscal policy and monetary policy in India?
2. "Public finance is the investigation into the nature and principles of state expenditure and state revenue." Comment.
3. Explain the different theories for determination of public expenditure.
4. "The system of public expenditure is best when it has the strongest tendency to reduce income inequalities." (Dalton) Explain.
5. There are numerous issues in the Indian public expenditure and revenue collection system. Enumerate some of the current problems.
6. Explain the anti-profiteering clause of GST.
7. "Deficit financing should be resorted to only in times of emergency." Examine.
8. What do you understand by concealed deficit financing? What are the guidelines of the Ministry of Finance on it?
9. What is the status of public debt and public deficit in India?
10. How is a budget described as a pre-audit instrument?
11. "Cutback management is the most important outcome of the target-based budget." Comment.
12. "The functioning of PAC and CAG is interdependent. The efficiency of one depends on the efficiency of the other, and vice versa." Explain.
13. "Departmentally related standing committee is the most effective advancement in the Indian Parliamentary system." Explain.
14. "Budget is an instrument of political reform." (Willloughbhy) Explain.
15. "The value for money audit/performance audit is the recent advancement in the functioning of CAG. CAG requires the support of social audit units in order to carry out performance audit effectively." Examine.
16. "Many changes are required to be made in order to provide the Indian CAG with the same teeth as the Supreme Audit Institutions (SAIs) of other countries." Examine.

Previous Years' Questions

Chapter 1. Introduction to Public Administration

1. The essence of new public administration is "some sort of movement in the direction of normative theory, philosophy, social concern and activism" (Waldo). Comment. (1989)
2. Management of the flow of work upward and downward within human hierarchies and between human hierarchies is the art of administration (Appelby). Comment. (1989)
3. Public administration today stands at the crossroads of public choice theory, pluralism, corporatism, and elitism. Discuss. (1989)
4. Popular belief is that ownership change from public to private brings about improved performance. Comment. (1989)
5. "… the development, if not survival of civilization depends on the science and practice of administration." Comment. (1990)
6. The identity and scope of public administration both as an academic discipline and government in operation have always been matters of continuing debate and controversy. Discuss. (1991)
7. Waldo speaks of the fears of F.M. Marx that public administration has grown so broad and is so much involved at its periphery that it stands "in danger of disappearing completely as a recognizable focus of study." Comment. (1993)
8. Explicate the theoretical premises of new public administration and show how far their concerns were accommodated in public administration. (1994)
9. A theory of public administration means in our time a theory of politics also. Comment. (1995)
10. New public administrationists are likely to be forthright advocates for social equity and would doubtless seek a supporting clientele. Comment. (1995)
11. The scope of public administration is ever expanding. Comment. (1996)
12. How far is it true to state that the bureaucratic state began to displace the administrative state when the predominant function of the government changed from regulation to operation of business? (1996)
13. In the science of administration, whether public or private, the basic 'good' is efficiency. Comment. (1997)
14. The scope of administration is determined by the scope of government functions which is decided politically. Comment. (1998)
15. The themes developed at 1998 Minnowbrook Conference (20 years after the first conference) largely focus on the current and future visions in the field of public administration. Elucidate. (1998)

16. Examine the growth of the discipline of public administration as a response to the developing capitalist system in USA. (1999)
17. Critically comment on the function of administrative capabilities with reference to developing countries. (1999)
18. What do you understand by the term 'under administration'? What are the issues involved in it? (1999)
19. "...The paradigms of public administration may be understood in terms of locus and focus" (Golembiewski). In the light of the above statement, describe the "five paradigms" of Nicholas Henry about the evolution of the discipline of public administration. (2000)
20. Minnowbrook Conference in USA identified four features crucial to 'new public administration'. Explain. (2001)
21. "Publicness" of public administration in an ideal democratic government remains the ultimate value in theory and practice. Elucidate. (2001)
22. Though there are certain points of similarity between public and private administration yet no private organization can ever be exactly the same as a public one. Examine. (2002)
23. Describe the evolution of the discipline of public administration with special emphasis on post-1970 developments. (2002)
24. The new public management (NPM) is an incarnation of a new model of public sector management in response to the challenges of liberalization, international competitiveness and technological changes. Explain. (2003)
25. Give an account of major landmarks in the growth of the discipline of public administration in the 20th century. What are the possible trends in its growth in the first decade of 21st century? (2003)
26. Administrative questions are not political questions. Discuss. (2005)
27. If public administration is to play a major legitimizing role in governing our complex society, it needs to be more fully conceptualized. Discuss. (2006)
28. Public and private administrations are two species of the same genus, but they also have special values and techniques of their own. Comment. (2007)
29. The widening gap in the emoluments of government employees versus public sector corporations and private sector employees has a strong bearing on the motivation and ability to work. Comment. (2007)
30. Calling Woodrow Wilson the father of public administration is doing injustice to equally or even more eminent contributions made prior to him. Comment. (2008)
31. In the last two decades, almost all countries have experienced transformations in their administrative systems. Explain this phenomenon with examples from the developed and the developing nations in the context of new public management movement. (2008)
32. New Public Administration is ... a revolution or radicalism in words, and (at best) status-quo in skills or technologies. Comment. (2009)
33. It is said that "the perspective of public administration, developed over a century, with a tradition of management of public institutions and services

has received a jolt from the novelty of new public management." Bring out the core values, approaches, and assumptions of traditional public administration and show how the new public management has attempted to change or retain them, and to what extent. (2009)

34. The study of administration should start from the base of management rather than the foundation of law. Explain. (2010)
35. 'A crisis of credibility' in the administrative system can be overcome only by 'reinventing government'. Comment. (2011)
36. In an evolution of the discipline of public administration, Minnowbrook Conferences I, II, and III reflect the discipline's reconceptualization and its changing values. Elucidate. (2011)
37. How would you trace the development of public administration in terms of different paradigms from the politics-administration dichotomy of 1900-1926 to the rise of public administration as public administration after the formation of the National Association of Schools of Public Affairs and Administration (NASPAA) in the USA in 1970? (2012)
38. New Public Administration may have neither been the savior its enthusiasts promised, nor the devil its critics worried it would be. Discuss (2013)
39. New public management and post new public management reforms initiatives ever affected the balance between managerial, political, administrative, legal, professional and social accountability, Analyze (2014)
40. Discuss how the public choice theory promotes the concept of 'Steering' and undermines the concept of 'Rowing' in visualizing efficient and effective administration. (2015)
41. Globalization has transformed the nature and character of state from traditional administrative welfare state to a corporate state. Analyse the changes in the nature of public administration in this context. (2015)
42. "Public Administration is the translation of politics into reality that citizens see everyday" (Donald F. Kettl and James W. Fesler). Explain. (2016)
43. "The New Public Administration has seriously jolted the traditional concepts and outlook of the discipline and enriched the subject by imparting wider perspective by linking it closely to the society" (Felix A. Nigro and Lloyd G. Nigro). Elucidate. (2016)
44. Bureau-shaping model has been developed as a response to the budget-maximizing model. (2016)
45. The problem is to achieve the right balance between a competitive market economy and an effective state: Markets where possible, the state where necessary. Justify your answer. (2016)
46. "Even after 130 years of its publication, Woodrow Wilson's essay 'The Study of Administration' continues to have great relevance even today." Comment. (2017)
47. New Public Management has been branded by certain scholars as `Neo-Taylorism'. Is it a justified comparison? What factors have led to the decline of NPM so soon after its birth? (2017)

48. "The scope of the discipline of Public Administration is determined by what an administrative system does." Does it mean that the scope of this discipline is boundary less? Explain. (2018)
49. "New Public Service approach is an improvement over its predecessor, New Public Management." Discuss. (2018)
50. Dwight Waldo in his book, The Administrative State emphatically mentions that the roots of administrative theory lie in political theory. Critically examine Waldo's contention. (2018)
51. "The Phenomenological Approach advocated by the New Public Administration has obstructed the path of theory building in Public Administration." Comment. (2018)
52. "Political and administrative systems have reciprocal relationship." Discuss. (2018)
53. "Public Administration is constantly being reinvented because it is contextual." Elaborate. (2019)
54. "Bureau pathology denigrates competence in organizations." Explain. (2019)
55. "If there js ever to be a science of Public Administration it must derive from an understanding of man's behaviour." Explain. (2019)
56. Has New Public Management failed in promoting a democratic polity? Analyse in the contexts of individual as a citizen and individual as a customer. (2019)
57. "Globalization has constructed the administrative state to save and serve corporate power structure." Discuss how transnational corporations impact government and public administration in the contemporary era. (2019)
58. "The strength of Public Administration is in its exploration of the complexities and nuances of public policy making and implementation." Discuss. (2020)
59. New Public Service emphasizes democracy and citizenship as the basis for public administration theory and practice. Elucidate. (2020)
60. "Accountability under New Public Management has undergone a radical change, although the focus has continued to remain on management." Comment. (2020)
61. "Administrative ideas must be seen in the context of environment in which they develop." In the light of the above statement, examine the influence of New Public Management and Information and Communication Technologies on comparative study of Public Administration. (2020)
62. "Globalization is impacting the context of national policy making. The national policy agenda is becoming international." Explain. (2020)
63. Public administration has been viewed as a socially embedded process of collective relationship, dialogue and action. Examine the statement in light of the consensus achieved in the Third Minnowbrook Conference. (2021)
64. The new public service model approaches governance on the premises of an active and involved citizenship, wherein the role of public officials is to facilitate opportunities for citizens' engagement in governance. Explain. (2021)

65. Nothing in public administration is more important, interesting, or mysterious than leadership. Analyze the statement in the context of strategic leadership. (2021)
66. Public Management takes 'what' and 'why' from Public Administration and 'how' from Business Management. Elaborate. (2022)
67. New public service celebrates what is distinctive, important and meaningful about public service. Discuss. (2022)

Chapter 2. Good Governance, E-Governance, and Emerging Trends

1. Do you think that sudden eruption of 'information society' has adapted and accelerated administrative development? (1989)
2. Elaborate the World Bank's concept of 'Good Governance'. (1999)
3. "Civil society exists to ensure that government does provide good governance." Discuss. (2002)
4. Democracy and good governance are contradictions in terms. Discuss with examples. (2004)
5. In what ways and how can information technology play a crucial role in effective government-citizen interaction in the context of good governance? (2005)
6. "Not merely governance but good governance is the key factor in achieving the United Nations Millennium Goals (2000)." Explain. (2010)
7. "Organizations today seem to invest in information and information systems, but their investments often do not seem to make sense." Comment. (2003)
8. What is information technology? Describe its impact on public administration. (2004)
9. "The rise of information technology is an opportunity to overcome historical disabilities." Explain. (2006)
10. "E-governance has the potentiality to emerge as the most effective instrument of efficiency, transparency and accountability." Comment. (2008)
11. Do you think there is a sort of paradox between e-governance and good governance? Explain fully. (2010)
12. 'New Public Management is Dead- Long Live Digital Era Governance'. Explain this in terms of reforms and impact brought by the first and second wave of Digital Era Governance. (2010)

    'The apparent demise of –Government and e-Business as the main organizing principles of society has created the conditions for the rise of e-Governance from the ashes'. In the context of the above statement show the distinctions between e-Government and e-Governance. (2012)
13. 'Good governance is closely aligned with effective democratic governance.' Elaborate (2012)
14. Gandhian model of decentralization is similar to the process of reinventing governance. Analyze in the context of good governance. (2013)
15. "Governance theory and the notion of governmentality have many points of convergence, but they run on parallel lines." Comment (2014)

16. The bottom line for governance is outcome rather than the outputs of government. Analyze in the context of e-government and e-governance. (2014)
17. The technical and multi-disciplinary nature of e-governance has created an interdependent relationship within government between policymakers, program administrators and technical specialists. Analyze in context of generalist-specialist relationship. (2014)
18. "E-governance creates a direct relationship between the citizen and the state." In this context, explain the changing role of the elected representatives. (2015)
19. "Good governance is ensuring respect for human rights and strengthening democracy, promoting transparency and capacity in public administration."—Kofi Annan

    In the light of this statement, critically examine the criteria of good governance as provided by the United Nations and Nayef Al-Rodhan. (2016)
20. "Information Technology brings efficiency and transparency to Public Administration." Examine the statement with suitable examples. (2016)
21. "Digitalisation provides great impetus to E-governance." Discuss. (2017)
22. To what extent has e-governance made the administrative system more citizen-oriented? Can it (e-governance) be made more participative? (2018
23. "Governance is neither a paradigm nor a panacea for all the ills of government. It may be a more useful approach when other methods fail in providing public service." Critically evaluate. (2019)
24. With the entry of the concept of 'good governance' the discipline of Public Administration has shed its statist character. Explain. (2019)
25. Has e-governance led to debureaucratization and decentralization? Assess its impact on bureaucratic inertia. (2019)
26. "Media, the fourth estate, is in chains." Examine the statement in the context of governmental accountability. (2019)
27. "Arbitrariness in the application of rule of law is a primary cause of poor governance." Discuss. (2020)
28. "Disruptive nature of developments in Information Technology has changed the contours of e-governance in the last one decade." Analyse. (2020)
29. "Governance is about managing self-organizing networks." Elaborate. (2021)
30. Regulatory governance frameworks have become essential building blocks of world society. Discuss their potential and impact in fulfilling the hopes and demands. (2022)
31. Social auditing is not just saving the money; it creates positive impact on governance. Comment. (2022)

Chapter 3. Administrative Thought

1. "From Taylorism to Mayoism, the organizational theory has travelled a long road in quest of organizational effectiveness." Comment (1989)
2. Argue for and against the Simonian perspective that the 'decisional science envelopes decisional structure, decisions and their feedback not in an integrated manner but anything other than that.' (1989)

3. Elucidate whether increasing organizational size gives rise to dialectical forces having opposite organizational effects. (1989)
4. Compare the relative merits of the classical theory of organization and the systems approach. (1990)
5. 'Mayo was a behavioral scientist long before the term became popular.' Comment (1990)
6. 'Taylor's scientific management had a major influence on the growing reform and economy movements in Public Administration'. Comment (1992)
7. Evaluate the contributions of George Elton Mayo to Administrative organization. Do you consider his contributions as great innovations of modern times? (1992)
8. 'Simon explains that decision making basically involves choice between alternative plans of action and choice in turn, involves facts and values.' Comment (1992)
9. 'The transition to a study of the negative aspects of bureaucracy is afforded by the application of Veblen's concept of trained incapacity.' Examine (1993)
10. 'Though somewhat unwittingly, Herbert Simon and James March have provided the muscle and the flesh to the Weberian (bureaucratic) skeleton.' Comment (1993)
11. 'Taylor's Scientific Management already offered a 'humanistic' theory of motivation, with its democratic and participatory emphases that was hardly improved on by Elton Mayo and others.' Comment (1994)
12. In a hierarchy every employee tends to rise to his level of incompetence. Comment (1996)
13. Examine the view that systems theory, despite its promises to the contrary, followed similar patterns that characterized the structural classical thinkers. (1996)
14. Show how Barnard while analyzing the multiplicity of satisfactions, clearly identifies four specific inducements. (1996)
15. 'In the science of administration, whether public or private, the basic 'good' is efficiency.' Comment (1997)
16. 'Once fully established, bureaucracy is among those social structures which are the hardest to destroy.' Comment (1997)
17. Examine the basic postulates of the Human Relations Theory and show how far it differs from the classical theory of organization. (1997)
18. 'That is, to be a successful administrator one must have a catholic curiosity.' Comment (1997)
19. Why is it that the behavioral approach to the study of organizations is a continuous phenomenon? Discuss Chester Barnard's contributions to this approach. (1998)
20. 'The process of change may create crisis in a system'. (1999)
21. 'A science of administration would be a body of formal statements describing invariant relationships between measurable objects, units or

elements. Unquestionably, administrative research has produced definite precepts and hypotheses that are applicable to concrete situation.'(Fritz Morstein Marx) (2000)

22. ..."a more thorough consideration leads to the understanding that communication, authority, specialization and purpose are all aspects comprehended in coordination.' (Chester Barnard). Comment (2000)
23. Administrative efficiency is enhanced by keeping at a minimum the number of organizational levels through which a matter must pass before it is acted upon.' (Herbert A. Simon) Comment (2000)
24. Critically examine the models of Max Weber and Chester I Barnard with reference to bureaucratic authority. (2001)
25. Why do all administrative organizations consider 'hierarchy' as the many splendoured technique? Discuss (2001)
26. The 'decision-making scheme' and 'satisficing model' of Herbert A. Simon is the major component of administrative theory. Comment (2001)
27. Explain the contributions of George Elton Mayo to the development of the Human Relations School. How did behavioral scientists modify his basic findings? (2002)
28. 'Weberian model of bureaucracy lacks empirical validity when applied to modern democratic administration.' Examine (2003)
29. Weber's ideas of impersonal detachment and espirit de corps are incompatible. Explain (2004)
30. 'Bureaucracy can exist only where the whole service of the state is removed from the common political life of the people, its chiefs as well as rank and file. Its motives, its objectives, its policy, its standards must bureaucratic'. Discuss (2004)
31. 'Administrative questions are not political questions.' Discuss (2005)
32. 'The failure of classical science of administration lies in its incapacity to confront theory with evidence.' Discuss (2005)
33. In Follett's views, 'authority belongs to the job and stays with the job.' Explain (2005)
34. 'Organization is a system of consciously coordinated activities or forces of two or more persons.' Comment (2005)
35. 'The main problem with Mary Parker Follett's work is that her idealism is showing'. Explain (2006)
36. 'Simon's work has had major implications for the study of public administration and the practice of public administration professionalism.' Comment (2006)
37. 'Taylor's scientific management ignored social and psychological factors'. Comment (2007)
38. Analyze McGregor's Theory X and Theory Y. Do you agree with the view that with every passing year, McGregor's message has become more relevant and more important? Substantiate your answer. (2007)

39. 'Calling Woodrow Wilson, the father of Public Administration is doing injustice to equally or even more eminent contributions made prior to him.' Comment (2008)
40. 'Mary Parker Follett was far ahead of her time.' Discuss (2008)
41. Examine the respective roles of facts and values in the decision making process. Is it possible to make value-free decisions in government system? How can government decisions be made more rational? (2008)
42. 'The field of Public Administration is a field of business.' (Woodrow Wilson) Comment (2009)
43. From Woodrow Wilson to Herbert Simon most writers on administration have taken the achievement of efficiency as the central objective. Justify the statement with references to the work of major writers. (2009)
44. Consider the following statements below
    (i) 'Technically, the bureaucracy represents the purest type of legal-rational authority.'
    (ii) 'Bureaucracy does not represent the only type of legal authority.'

    Identify the theoretical context and analyze the above statements. (2009)
45. 'The Barnard-Simon Theory of Organization is essentially a theory of motivation.' Comment (2009)
46. 'Taylor's contribution was not a set of general principles for organizing work efficiency, but a set of operating procedures that could be employed in each concrete situation to secure their application.' Comment (2009)
47. 'Simon's identifying decision making as the core field of public administration appears logical, acceptable. But his positivist underpinning is problematic.' Critically examine the statement. (2010)
48. 'In McGregor's view, the managerial cosmology meaningfully addresses the understanding of manager and his role perceptions.' Explain (2010)
49. 'The successful management leaders are found in Likert's 'System-4' approach to organizational leadership.' Examine. (2010)
50. E-Governance is the final arrival of the Max Weber's iron cage of rationality. Discuss (2011)
51. The Systems Approach is relevant even today for organizational analysis. Discuss how Chester Barnard and David Easton adopted this approach in their respective areas of study. (2011)
52. In what respects is Taylor's 'Scientific Management' of classical motivational theory different from the classical organizational theory expounded by Gullick, Urwick etc? (2012)
53. What light does Antonio Gramsci's critique of Taylorism throw on its socio-psychological underpinnings? (2012)
54. 'In the canonization of this abstract idea of 'Staatstraison' are inseparably woven the sure instincts of the bureaucracy for the conditions which preserve its own power in the state' (Weber) Explain (2012)

55. 'Man's motives….. in different subparts of the same organizations may be different'. (Edgar Schein). Discuss (2012)
56. 'Three features characterize Simon's original view of bounded rationality: search of alternatives, satisficing and aspiration adaptation.' Elucidate (2012)
57. "The design of physical structures, the anatomy of the organization came first, and was indeed the principle consideration." "An organization is a system of interrelated social behaviors of participants" Analyses these statements and evaluate the contribution of the respective approach to Administrative theory. (2013)
58. Decisions are not made by organizations, but by human beings behaving as the members of organizations. How do Bernard and Herbert A. Simon conceptualize the relation between decision of the individual employee and the organizational authority? (2013)
59. The theory of organizational incompetence has two separate and distinct faces. Examine Chris Argyris' views on this. (2013)
60. According to Macgregor, "true professional help is not in playing God with the client, but in placing professional knowledge and skills at the client's disposal." In the light of above statement, justify how theory-Y is indicative and not prescriptive. (2014)
61. Is Peter Drucker justified in saying, "Management principles should not tell us what to do, but only tell us what not to do"? (2014)
62. 'Weberian model of bureaucracy lacks emotional validity when applied to modern democratic administration.' Comment (2015)
63. 'Democracy within bureaucracy is likely to reduce its effectiveness.' Do you agree with this view? Argue your case. (2015)
64. "Follett's work was not directed towards the resolution of the conflict of ideas, but towards the resolution of structural conflicts between workers and capitalists." In the light of the statement critically evaluate Follett's idea of dynamic administration. (2015)
65. "Contemporary Organisational theory seems further afield of Chester Barnard's Functions of the Executive than of organisational ecology." Examine the statement in the light of ecological elements in Barnard's thought. (2015)
66. "Taylorism is considered very controversial despite its popularity." (Stephen P. Waring) Comment (2016)
67. "Douglas McGregor's Theory X and Theory Y describe two contrasting models of workforce motivation applied by managers in an organization." *Examine.* (2016)
68. *The Participative Management School of Argyris and Likert advocates democracy within the administrative system. Will this approach be equally useful to developing countries with evolving democracies?* (2017)
69. "What is distinctive about the Classical and Human Relations schools of administration is their complementarily to each other." Analyse. (2017)

70. "Conflict is the appearance of differences — differences of opinions and of interests" — (Mary Parker Follett). Comment. (2017)
71. "The concepts of rationality and efficiency are intertwined in the bureaucratic analysis of Max Weber." Comment. (2018)
72. "Herbert Simon's book Administrative Behavior presents a synthesis of the classical and behavioural approaches to the study of Public Administration." Explain. (2018)
73. "Chester Barnard's model of 'Contribution-Satisfaction Equilibrium' is still considered a logical model of organisational motivation." Do you agree? Give arguments. (2018)
74. "Chester Barnard in 'The Functions of the Executive' injected 'the social' in the study of organization. Explain in this context how the executive is expected to play a much greater role than a manager." (2019)
75. Contingency theory of organization is founded on the interplay of 'external fit' and 'internal fit'. Discuss. (2019)
76. Mary Parker Follett traced the foundational value of business and enterprise on her way to understand the organism of governmental machinery. Comment. (2019)
77. "Principles of analysis and principles of action were not differentiated in Taylor's scientific management." Comment. (2020)
78. "The movement towards governance as an organizing concept for public administration and management is because the focus of administration has been shifting from the bureaucratic state to the 'hollow state' and 'third-party government'." Critically examine. (2020)
79. "Productivity is not the result of working conditions but the result of emotional response of workers to work performed." Are Elton Mayo's findings relevant in contemporary organizations? (2020)
80. "The content and process theories of motivation have the same focus but are different in approaches." Do you agree? Give reasons. (2020)
81. "Two-dimensional taxonomy was used by Herbert Simon to describe the degree to which decisions are programmed or non-programmed." Explain. (2021)
82. Fayol and Taylor had different management perspectives, while having similar goal of organizational efficiency. Comment. (2021)
83. Integration of different streams of administrative thought to propound a universal administrative theory is hindered by the impact of culture. Critically examine. (2021)
84. Neo-Weberian State involves changing the model of operation of administrative structures into a model focussed on meeting citizens' needs. Discuss. (2021)
85. In modern context, Riggsian terms have not altogether disappeared, but have emerged in different forms with newer meanings. Discuss. (2021)
86. Every human organisation shall start from System-I and ultimately end up with System-IV. Comment on Likert's statement. (2022)

87. Weber's construct of bureaucracy has served a great heuristic purpose in furthering research in the field of Comparative Public Administration. Do you agree with the statement? Give reasons. (2022)
88. 'The more exogenetic the process of diffraction, the more formalistic and heterogenous its prismatic phase; the more endogenetic, the less formalistic and heterogenous.' Examine this hypothesis of Riggs. (2022)
89. 'Lindblom regarded rational decision-making as an unattainable goal.' In the light of the statement, suggest measures to avoid policy failures. (2022)
90. Classical Organisation Theory formed the bedrock for the modern organisation theories. Analyse. (2022)
91. Barnard posits the zone of indifference as the human condition that animates authority relationships and cooperation modern organisations. Examine. (2022)

Chapter 4. Administrative Behaviour

1. Outline the intrinsic and extrinsic rewards that motivate the public employees to achieve personal and organizational goals. (1989)
2. 'A leader must always adapt his behavior to take account of the persons whom he leads.' Comment (1990)
3. 'A management which takes its environment as given… is pursuing a dangerous course.' Comment on the environment of decision making. (1990)
4. "Without communication, there can be no organization". Discuss the importance of communication in Public Administration. (1990)
5. Compare the relative merits of Maslow's Theory of Human Needs and Herzberg's conception of Motivation and Hygiene Theory. (1991)
6. 'The Chief Executive is a trouble shooter, a supervisor, and a promoter of the future programme.' Comment (1991)
7. 'While the entrepreneur makes strategic decisions, the manager makes tactical ones.' Elucidate (1993)
8. 'A managerial leader should effectively communicate to motivate his team,' Comment. How do Maslow and Herzberg see this inter linkage between motivation and communication? (1993)
9. 'Thus the endurance of organization depends upon the quality of leadership.' Comment (1994)
10. "As March and Simon put out, there seems to exist a 'Gresham's Law' of decision making." Explain (1994)
11. Bring out the importance of communication in administrative organizations. What are the drawbacks in upward communication? (1994)
12. "The study of decision-making is proceeding in so many directions that we can lose sight of the basic administrative processes that Barnard and Simon were trying to describe and that so many men have been trying to improve." Elucidate (1995)

13. 'Frederick Herzberg's Two-Factor Theory is more or less an extension of Abraham Maslow's theory of motivation'. Explain (1997)
14. "Communication holds the organization together." Comment (1998)
15. "Information constitutes the life-blood of the functioning of an organisation." Explain the utility and significance of communication in decision-making. (2000)
16. The nature and role of communication in administration indicates that 'communication is authority'. Comment (2001)
17. Compare Abraham Maslow's theory of motivation and Herzberg's motivation hygiene theory. Do you think that they are universally applicable? If so, why? If not, why not? (2002)
18. 'Motivation theory is not synonymous with behavior theory. The motivations are only one class of determinants of behavior while behavior is almost always motivated, it is also almost always biologically, culturally and situationally determined as well.' Comment (2004)
19. What is meant by morale? There is a belief that 'morale and productivity go hand in hand and higher the morale, higher the productivity.' Do you agree? Substantiate. (2007)
20. 'Leaders do the right things, managers do them rightly.' (Bennis) Comment (2008)
21. Leadership is the 'influential increment over and above mechanical compliance with the routine directive of the organization' [Katz and Kahn] (2012)
22. Decisions are not made by organizations, but by human beings behaving as the members of organizations. How do Bernard and Herbert A. Simon conceptualize the relation between decision of the individual employee and the organizational authority? (2013)
23. Read following instances carefully and suggest what specific perspectives on organizational psychology of motivation would help the concerned organization to reconcile the needs of the following four persons with the needs of organization:
    (a) Mr.A comes to his office with clocklike punctuality; does his work with impeccable honesty and integrity; takes orders from above gladly; responds well to overtures by peers; but neither mixes with anyone himself nor seeks anyone's company. What is more, he seem quite happy in his isolation.
    (b) Mr.B is an efficient charge hand at the welding shop. He is very outgoing and makes friends fast, but falls out with them very fast too. He is, however, easily pacified when anyone asks him to calm down in the name of the organization.
    (c) Mr.C is completely happy and absorbed when he is teaching in the classes, and doesn't at all mind when is workload gets heavier and covers new areas. But he gets angry when the finance section raises objection about his medical bills; and is furious that the higher administration is yet to give him full tenure.

(d) Mr.D is a metallurgist in the forge shop of the steel plan, and has received honors for his innovativeness in modifying conventional alloys. He also paints well and values his painting skills far more than his metallurgy and is extremely unhappy that company house journal did not finally carry his water sketch on its front cover. (2013)

24. Do you agree with the view that the charismatic approach of the mid-1970s is a "new version" of the Classical Trait Theory of Leadership? Give reasons. (2015)
25. "Information constitutes the life-blood of the functioning of an organisation." Explain the utility and significance of communication in decision-making. (2015)
26. Morale can drive an organization forward or can lead to employees' discontent, poor job performance and absenteeism.' Examine (2016)
27. "Blake and Mouton defined leadership styles based on two dimensions-concern for people and concern for production." In the light of statement, discuss the Managerial Grid Model. Explain with reason which one of the styles is the best. (2016)
28. 'Abraham Maslow's 'Hierarchy of Needs' and Frederick Herzberg' 'Two Factor Theory' have commonalities in the analysis of human motivation.' Comment (2017)
29. 'Leaders do the right things; managers do them rightly' (Warren Bennis). Is this distinction by him valid? Explain. (2017)
30. "A leader is a people's developer" (Napoleon). Which aspects of subordinates' development can be positively influenced by a leader? Discuss. (2018)
31. Communication represents the "Nerves of Government" (Karl Deutsch). How can the communication system in the government be made more effective, responsive and motivational? (2018)
32. Behavioural approach has been questioned on the basis of its utility in the analysis of administrative problems. Discuss the weaknesses of the approach and the shifts made therein. (2021)

Chapter 5. Organizational Dynamics

1. Account for the growing tendency of centralization in the modern state. (1991)
2. "Decentralisation has a more important justification than mere administrative efficiency". Comment. (1992)
3. "It is difficult to state any demarcating principle to differentiate between Line and Staff functions of agencies." Discuss. (1992)
4. "Decentralisation is never just a technical exercise, with intentions and effects neatly confined to questions of economy and efficiency." Comment. (1993)
5. "The distinction between line authority and professional expertness is also less clear cut in reality than the abstract concepts of line and staff make it appear." Discuss. (1994)

6. Hierarchical control, whereby instructions are passed down the line is not the only dimension of control. Comment. (1995)
7. Although the theory of V.A. Graičiūnas is admittedly crude, it is useful as a reference against which variations between organizations as well as within organizations can be examined. Comment. (1996)
8. "Centralisation inclines towards power and domination. Decentralisation, on the other hand, inclines towards competition and self-determination." Discuss. (1997)
9. Differentiate between managerial and functional aspects of coordination. How is coordination achieved? (1998)
10. "Voluntarism is not anti-thesis of state centricism." Comment. (1999)
11. "The distinction between line and staff is relative rather than absolute." Discuss. (2007)
12. "There is no doubt that departmentalization is fraught with complexities. They are in part technical, in part political." Discuss. (2009)
13. "Man's motives… in different subparts of the same organizations may be different." (Edgar Schein) Discuss. (2012)
14. "The essence of the contingency theory paradigm is that organizational effectiveness results from fitting characteristics of the organization, such as its structure, to contingencies that reflect the situations of the organization." Give your reactions to this statement. (2012)
15. In the context of Q. 14, also show where and how this 'fitting' differs essentially from 'coping with stress' from the environment emphasized by the systems theory of organization. (2012)
16. "To talk about the regulatory framework is to talk about short governance." Analyse the statement in the context of public private partnership and identify the elements of regulation. (2013)
17. Structure theory is by and large grounded in classical principles of efficiency, effectiveness, and productivity. Explain. (2013)
18. What is the nature of psychological contract pursued by organizational management through authority and employees through exertion of upward influence? (2013)
19. A variety of different organizational arrangements can be used to provide different public goods and services. Examine the theory underlying this proposition and its potential contribution. (2013)
20. "The design of physical structures, the anatomy of the organization came first, and was indeed the principle consideration." "An organization is a system of interrelated social behaviours of participants." Analyse these statements and evaluate the contribution of the respective approach to administrative theory. (2013)
21. What are the implications of the post-structuralist perspective on the discrete aspects of Public Administration, coming from its epistemological positions? (2014)

22. "Adaptive, problem-solving, temporary systems of diverse specialists, linked together by coordinating executives in an organic flux—this is original form that will gradually replace bureaucracy." Discuss, in the light of this statement, the 'end of bureaucracy' thesis and its strengths and limitations. (2014)
23. How does the Strategic Contingencies Theory of organizational design deal with problems arising from sub-unit centrality and non-substitutability? (2014)
24. "Contemporary Organisational theory seems further afield of Chester Barnard's Functions of the Executive than of organisational ecology." Examine the statement in the light of ecological elements in Barnard's thought. (2015)
25. "PPPs serve too many parties and too many interests… to be focussed." Identify in the context of the statement, the parties involved in Public Private Partnerships and their conflicting aims. (2015)
26. "Systems Theory in essence is not a theory, but an approach to the study of administrative phenomena." Comment. (2017)
27. Discuss the essential characteristics of public sector-centred and market-centred perspectives in Public Private Partnerships and also compare the two. (2018)
28. "Form of an organisation influences the success of a public enterprise, but the choice of a form has always remained problematic." Discuss the statement in the context of the comparative merits and limitations of departments, corporations, companies and boards. Give illustrations. (2018)
29. "Organizations of the future will be organic-adaptive structures but temporary systems." Discuss how Warren Bennis characterises the new form of organization. (2020)
30. "'Performance information use' is a form of organizational behaviour that is influenced by individual, job, organizational and environmental factors." Critically analyse. (2020)
31. Public-private partnership phenomenon has been transformed into a type of governance scheme or mechanism. Discuss its capacity to overcome future challenges. (2021)
32. ICT has immense potential to transform governance and empower citizens. Examine. (2021)
33. Transformational leadership requires high degree of coordination, communication, and cooperation. Explain. (2022)
34. Human relationists postulate that 'what is important to a worker and what influences his/her productivity level may not be the organizational chart but his or her associations with other workers'. Is it more relevant today? (2022)
35. 'Leadership is seen as dealing with change, whereas administration is viewed as coping with complexity.' In this context, discuss the contextuality of leadership and administration for the success of organisations. (2022)

Chapter 6. Accountability and Control

1. Comment on the following in not more than 200 words: "It would be fatal for administration if public functionaries indulge in procrastination, betray inaction, or more in circles simply because the demand for accountability has overawed and benumbed them." (1992)
2. Comment: Bureaucracy is "a system of government the control of which is so completely in the hands of officials that their power jeopardizes the liberties of ordinary citizens." (1996)
3. Comment: At one extreme, the vigour of judicial control may paralyze effective administration, at the other the result may be offensive bureaucratic tyranny, exactly where the balance may be best struck is a major problem of judicial administration relationship. (1996)
4. Comment: "The controls exercised over administration by legislature are, in sum, of greater theoretical than practical efficiency." (1997)
5. Comment: "Executive control over administration is much more real." (1998)
6. "It is not weak but strong bureaucracy that creates concern in democracy." Comment (1999)
7. Comment: "Public Interest Litigation is an effective innovation in realizing social justice." (1999)
8. Comment on judicial control over administration in India and the concept of judicial activism. (2000)
9. "The weakest aspect of Indian administrative system is utter disregard of accountability." Examine the current mechanism for enforcing accountability. What steps are necessary to make it more effective? (2000)
10. "Citizen's Charter is the most important innovation in the context of promotion of customer-orientation of administration." Discuss. (2003)
11. Discuss the legal and political implication of Right to Information. Is it feasible in developing countries? (2004)
12. What is judicial activism? How far has it been successful in exercising a check over administration? (2005)
13. Define the term 'civil society'. How does civil society influence the public policy? (2006)
14. "Right to Information promotes transparency and accountability in the working of every public authority." Explain. (2007)
15. "Instruments of public accountability can be truly effective only if people and their associations, backed by responsible media, are assertively proactive." Comment. (2008)
16. Examine the basic principles underlying citizen's charter with special reference to
    - (a) Its administrative philosophy
    - (b) Promoting public accountability
    - (c) Ensuring standards of public service (2010)

17. Should media exposure be included in rules for administrative accountability in India? State your views. (2012)
18. Comment on the role of Civil Society in facilitating administrative accountability with special reference to the 'Janlokpal' issue in India. (2012)
19. Public Administration in the neo-liberal era is governed less by instruments of internal accountability and more by those of external accountability. Elaborate. (2013)
20. "Strong state and strong civil society are the need to develop both participatory democracy and responsive government as mutually reinforcing and supportive." Bring out the myths and realities associated with public participation. (2013)
21. "The Right to Information is not all about citizen's empowerment; it is essentially redefining the concept of accountability." Discuss. (2014)
22. "New Public Management and post-NPM reforms initiatives have affected the balance between managerial, political, administrative, legal, professional and social accountability." Analyse. (2014)
23. "Voluntary organizations have become tools of sensitization of governmental agencies." Comment. (2014)
24. "Right from the days of the 'Peoples' Charter' to the new concept of 'Precariat Charter', the concept of Citizen's Charter and its scope is constantly evolving." Comment. (2015)
25. How far do you agree with the view that the growing influence of media comes in the way of agenda-setting by the Government? (2015)
26. "In spite of certain advantages, Social Audit arrangements have mostly been ineffective because there is no legal provision for punitive action." (2016)
27. "The legislative control over administration is not as effective as it ought to be." (2016)
28. "Civil Society performs a key role in defending people against the state and market and in asserting the democratic will to influence the State." Analyse the statement with suitable examples. (2016)
29. "Self-Help Groups are considered as one of the most significant tools to adopt participatory approach for economic empowerment of women." Comment. (2016)
30. Civil society supplements and complements the state. However, its capacity and role depends upon the will of the state. Comment. (2017)
31. When the media is controlled by vested interests, how can it control the vested interests in the government? How can the media become more responsible and impartial? (2017)
32. Can we say that statutory audit and social audit are two sides of the same coin? Or, are they two separate coins with varying values? Discuss. (2017)
33. "The advent of the regulatory regimes indicates the demise of the arbitrator state." Comment. (2019)
34. "Departments, Boards and Commissions as forms of organization are dissimilar in the context of accountability and responsibility." Analyse. (2020)
35. Thrust on the citizen centricity and Right based approaches, aim to. empower the citizens. In the light of the above, has the administrative accountability improved? Justify your argument. (2020)

36. "Collaboration and its cognates for public service delivery need to be viewed from the governance lenses." Comment. (2020)
37. Regulation is an old but increasingly necessary mode of social coordination and political intervention into societal processes. Examine it in the context of globalization. (2021)
38. Strategic communication ought to be an agile management process. Discuss the conceptualization of strategic communication for the government actions. (2022)

Chapter 7. Administrative Law

1. "Administrative Law has the obligation to observe the principles of natural justice and fairness." Elaborate. (1989)
2. "... administrative law, with its creature administrative tribunals, is like martial law, the negation of law." Comment. (1990)
3. Comment: "The essence of delegation is to confer discretion upon others, to use their judgment in meeting specific problems within the framework of their duties." (1991)
4. Administrative tribunals are authorities outside the ordinary court system that interpret and apply the laws when acts of public administration are attacked in formal suits or by other established methods. Discuss. (1991)
5. Comment: "Rule of law is the base of India's constitutional life, and administrative law seeks to ensure that this basic premise remains upheld and protected." (1992)
6. "Increased legislative delegation should be considered as a phenomenon of the modern positive state." Discuss. (1992)
7. Comment: "The most effective safeguard against the abuse of delegated legislation is not to delegate it in such a manner that it may invite abuse." (1993)
8. How has the interest of judiciary in administrative decisions grown over the years? Has it extended the frontiers of administrative law? (1993)
9. "Administrative law is not a rigid, rule-bound barrier to good management." Discuss. (1994)
10. Comment: "The field of administrative law, after a century of litigation and adjudication, remains alive with simmering issues." (1995)
11. Bring out the reasons for the growth of delegated legislation and mention its dangers. (1995)
12. Comment: "The central concern of administrative law has been the legal limitation of administrative discretion." (1997)
13. How far is it true to state that delegated legislation has become a present day necessity and has come to stay; it is both inevitable and indispensable? (1997)
14. Comment: "Administrative law in modern government system is inevitable." (1998)

15. "Increased delegated legislation is a phenomenon of a modern positive state." Elucidate. (1999)
16. Write a short note on the effectiveness and utility of the Central and State Administrative Tribunals. (2000)
17. "Dicey was wrong not only in his concept of the rule of law, but he also overlooked the significance of the administrative law." Comment. (2002)
18. Delegated legislation is not absolute. Explain. (2004)
19. "Today the content of administrative law is driven primarily by the scope of public administration activity." Explain. (2005)
20. "Delegated legislation is a necessary evil." Examine. (2007)
21. Make a critical assessment of Dicey's understanding of the rule of law and droit administratif. (2011)
22. Make out a case for delegated legislation. (2011)
23. Do you think that there is an unresolved and often overlooked tension in Dicey's concept of rule of law, considering that the other principle of parliamentary sovereignty in the English constitutional system runs counter to it? (2012)
24. Would you agree that the strong Rechtsstaat version of the rule of law found on the continent never existed in England because of its particular history? (2012)
25. Why is le droit administratif regarded alongside the Napoleonic code as the most notable achievement of French legal science? (2012)
26. Discuss the view that 'tribunals' should have the same degree of independence from the executive as that enjoyed by the Supreme Court and the high courts, especially for those tribunals that look over the functions of high courts. (2013)
27. "The conceptual division between administrative and constitutional law is quite porous, and that along many dimensions, administrative law can be considered more constitutional in character than the constitutions." How would you justify the statement? (2014)
28. "Legislative action is not subject to the rules of natural justice." Explain the exceptions to the rule of natural justice. (2015)
29. "The central concern of Administrative Law has been the legal limitation of administrative discretion." Give reasons. (2016)
30. "Administrative law is recognized by its substance rather than its form." Discuss. (2017)
31. The principle of delegated legislation, is I think right, but I must emphasize that it is well for Parliament to keep a watchful and even zealous eye on it at all stages. (Herbert Morrison). Analyse. (2017)
32. "The Journey of Administrative Law has moved much beyond A. V. Dicey." Comment. (2018)

33. "Red light and Green light theories provide contrasting approaches to the role of administrative law." Which of the two theories will be effective in achieving the objectives of administrative law? Justify your choice. (2019)
34. "Developments in the field of Administrative Law reflect an increasingly blurred boundary between the state and society, and between justice and administration." Has administrative law become more constitutional than the Constitution itself? Argue. (2020)
35. Judicial review, prevention of misuse or abuse of administrative power and provision of suitable remedies are the basic principles of administrative law. Justify as how various organs of the State are able to uphold these principles. (2021)
36. All tribunals are courts, but all courts are not tribunals. Explain. (2022)
37. 'The administrative state is the creation of a power to bind us, with rules ... that are not made by legislature.' Discuss the constitutionality of the administrative state and its future. (2022)

Chapter 8. Comparative Public Administration

1. The prismatic sala model "enables us to cope with many problems of transitional societies…" (Riggs). What are these problems and how can this model enable us to cope with them? (1989)
2. Discuss the major conceptual approaches to the study of comparative public administration and explain how Max Weber is considered to be the foremost mentor in the field. (1990)
3. Explain how the concepts of 'clects' and 'bazaar-canteen' model explain the working of the administrative system in a developing society. In this context, compare the working of the administrative system in a developed and a developing society. (1990)
4. Comment: "The growth of comparative public administration is a continuing process and is of relevance for both operational and academic study of public administration." (1991)
5. "Riggs' approach and models may be considered as more sophisticated tools for describing and diagnosing administrative situations." Discuss. (1992)
6. Comment: "The emphasis in most of the writings on comparative bureaucracy appears to be on the interaction between the administrative subsystem and the political system in which it exists." (1994)
7. Comment: "Riggs' key concepts have altered the research that Weberian bureaucracy might not be entirely predictive of behaviour in most Third World countries." (1995)
8. Comment: "A major problem with comparative public administration is that it has been behavioural." (1995)
9. What, according to Riggs, are the three important characteristic features of the prismatic society? (1996)
10. "As long as the study of public administration is not comparative, claim for a 'science of public administration' sounds rather hollow." Explain. (1998)

11. Comment: "Instead of looking inward in their own values and requirements, the Asian countries looked outward." (1999
12. Comment: "Political environment conditions administrative system." (F.W. Riggs) (2000
13. Critically examine the approach and methodology adopted by Fred W. Riggs in his study of prismatic and sala societies. What is the valid content of Raj Krishna's criticism of refraction? (2000
14. Critically comment on the Riggsian prismatic sala model of administration of developing societies. To what extent does the Indian Administrative system exhibit prismatic characteristics? (2001
15. How did Fred W. Riggs conceptualize the interactions between administrative systems and their environment? (2002
16. Explain the meaning, significance, and models of comparative public administration. (2004
17. "No science of public administration is possible unless… there is a body of comparative studies from which it may be possible to discover principles and generalities that transcend national boundaries and peculiar historical experiences." Discuss. (2005
18. "Not to be comparative is to be naively parochial." (Riggs) Comment. (2007
19. "Truly comparative administrative studies are empirical, nomothetic and ecological." (Riggs) In this perspective, examine the current status of comparative public administration. (2008
20. Which of the models in development administration are characterized by selectivism, attainment and polyfunctionalism? Describe the corresponding theoretical roots and attributes. (2009
21. "…non-western states often, if not always, have unbalanced politics, but these may not necessarily be bureaucratic politics." Discuss. (2009
22. "The Prismatic model of Riggs is equally applicable to developing as well as developed society." Comment. (2010
23. "Riggs' classification of societies into fused, prismatic and diffracted is built around the concept of differentiation." Analyse. (2012
24. Comment on the reason why universal theory remains elusive in comparative public administration. (2012
25. "Comparative Public Administration both resembles and differs from modern organization theory." Elaborate. (2013
26. Critically examine the Riggsian concept of differentiation in the context of post-globalization era. (2014
27. Comparative performance measurement (CPM) bridges everyday work experience with the broader horizons of comparativism. Comment (2015
28. "Riggs observed that three 'trends' could be discerned in the comparative study of public administration." Discuss. (2016
29. "Fred Riggs continuously changed his theory in order to create the perfect model." Comment. (2016

30. "The Riggsian models of fused-prismatic-diffracted societies and their administrative systems have been inspired by Max Weber's typology of traditional, charismatic and legal-rational authorities." Analyse. (2017)
31. "Administrative systems across the world can be understood only in their respective historical and social contexts." Explain the statement giving examples. (2018)
32. The failure to discard its elitist character and west-centric orientation has led to the decline of Comparative Public Administration. Explain. (2019)
33. "Comparative Public Administration started with no paradigm of its own and developed none." Comment (2020)

Chapter 9. Development Dynamics

1. Development administration is "an action-oriented, goal-oriented administrative system." (Edward Weidner) Comment. (1989, 1997)
2. Comment: "Development administration calls for some revolutionary changes in the attitudes, behaviour, orientation and outlook of public services at all levels of administration." (1991)
3. Outline the features of development administration and explain the reasons for its marginal performance. (1995)
4. 'What are the basic objectives of Development Administration? Also examine the demands placed by DA on the structures and practices of administration. (1998)
5. "Development administration is concerned with maximizing innovation for development." Discuss. (2002)
6. "Development Administration has two aspects, namely, 'the administration of development' and 'the development of administration'." Explain. (2003)
7. Describe the changing profile of DA and identify its efforts towards people's empowerment (2004)
8. "Development administration is starved for theories that will guide the pooling of empirical knowledge, orient new research, and recommend administrative policy." Explain. (2005)
9. Do you agree with the view that DA has in recent years lost its impetus without making any significant intellectual breakthrough? Discuss. (2006)
10. "People's participation is crucial to development administration." Comment. (2007)
11. "In certain discourses, there is a reflected basic distrust against bureaucracy as an instrument of development." Do you think bureaucracy is more appropriate for regulatory administration than for development administration? In the changing profile of development administration in a liberalizing environment, what role of bureaucracy can be envisaged? (2008)
12. "The concept of development is multidimensional and ever-expanding." Explain. (2010)
13. "The market has become the new icon of developmentalism." Comment. (2010)

14. Neither Edward Weidner not Fred Riggs was able to describe the process of development administration adequately. Explain the drawbacks and weaknesses in their theoretical analysis. (2011)
15. "The anti-development thesis… reduces development to an idea without history, impervious to change, but fails to take account of the fact that for all its faults, development can be empowering." Discuss. (2012)
16. Given the importance of the issue of sex equality in development do you think the self-help group movement adequately addresses absence of women in the former mainstream development agenda? (2012)
17. "… In most cases… Newly independent states, of the nations of Africa, Asia and Latin America, despite their differences … are in transition." (Ferrel Heady) What common features are indicative of characteristics of their administrative patterns (cultures)? (2013)
18. "The term development administration can be used only in a broad sense to mark the variety of approaches and points of view." Discuss. (2014)
19. 'Self-help groups have not only empowered women, but have also brought about attitudinal change among all stakeholders towards women development." Discuss (2014)
20. Show in what way the gender and development approach differs from the woman and development approach. (2015)
21. How does Ferrel Heady rationalize the three stages of development in comparative administration? (2015)
22. "Self-help groups are considered as one of the most significant tools to adopt participatory approach for economic empowerment of women." Comment. (2016)
23. "The idea of development stands like a ruin in the intellectual landscape." and "It is time to dismantle this mental structure." (Wolfgang Sachs) In the light of these statements, critically examine the anti-development thesis. (2016)
24. Development administration and administrative development have a chicken and egg kind of relationship. (Riggs) Comment. (2017)
25. "Liberalization, Privatization and Globalization have transformed the nature of development administration." Discuss. (2017)
26. "Bureaucracy has inbuilt limitations to act as the prime catalyst to multi-faceted development in a democratic country." Analyse this statement with appropriate examples. (2017)
27. "The issue of development of women is closely related to the issue of women in development." How can women become equal partners in the process of socio-economic development? (2018)
28. "The process of administrative development is generally slower than the process of socio-economic development." How can the speed of administrative development be made faster? (2018)

29. In order to be development-oriented, bureaucracies need to be innovative, flexible, citizen-centric, and result-oriented, but they are slow in imbibing these virtues in a democratic system. Do we need to go beyond the traditional models of bureaucracy and create alternative structures? Elaborate. (2018)
30. "Development dynamics is marked by a dilemma: the concept of development has a built-in participatory orientation, but the practice of development has been inherently exclusionary." Discuss. (2019)
31. In a society marked by social inequity and gender inequality women self-help groups are bound to play a marginal role. Do you agree? Give reasons for your answer. (2019)
32. Affirmative action in socio-economic development has not altogether eliminated discrimination. Discuss it in the context of women empowerment. (2020)
33. The approach to the study of administration in its environmental context is especially more useful for developing countries. Comment. (2021)
34. Gender equality and women's rights have laid down a strong foundation of development. Elaborate. (2021)
35. The successful attainment of SDGs objectives largely depends upon the wisdom, experience and farsightedness of the actors involved and their willingness to cooperate in the implementation process. Analyze. (2021)
36. Interaction between the State and Civil society has hitherto been largely neglected, especially in developing countries. Examine. (2022)
37. The environment and situational conditions under which the government operates have an important bearing on its human resource development practices. Examine. (2022)
38. Development Administration 'embraces the array of new functions assumed by the developing countries. Explain. (2022)

Chapter 10. Personnel Administration and Civil Services

1. "The Union Public Service Commission should have an integrative and coordinating role vis-à-vis state public service commissions in more or less the same way as is the case of Supreme Court of India vis-à-vis the high courts in the states. A sound case exists for an institutional linkage between UPSC and SPSCs for evolving a national policy, a uniform approach and common work procedures.' Discuss. (1989)
2. "Training is viewed as a paid holiday by a large number of public officials in India. It essentially betrays a crisis of motivation: in the process of administration, and on the part of both the trainers and trainees." Comment. (1990, 2016)
3. "Government has been slow in using modern methods for discovering executive talent." Examine the validity of the statement with reference to recruitment to higher civil services in India, USA, and France. (1990)
4. Comment: "Systematic training of higher civil servants has been conducive to promoting stability, skills and integrity of the civil services, but the objectives of training have not been realized to the desired extent." (1991)

5. Differentiate between the open and closed career systems. Do you favour the coexistence of both the systems for a balanced career development? (1992)
6. "Reservation Policy in public services as a mandate from the Constitution has been conducive to the promotion of social justice." Discuss and illustrate. (1992)
7. "The recruitment of recruiters in the public service commissions of India needs streamlining." Examine the statement. (1992)
8. Comment: "Professionalism of the Civil Services demands that their training programmes should be tagged with the personnel policies of promotion, placement and career planning at each level." (1993)
9. "The incumbents to civil service posts and political offices, who derive their legitimacy and strength from intellectual merit and popular support, respectively, cannot have identical perspectives on development. Naturally, therefore, the former has a higher and heavier responsibility to avoid conflict and preserve integrity in development administration." Comment. (1993)
10. Comment: "The administrator is a layman rather than a specialist or at least he has about him something of the qualities of a layman." (1994)
11. "Be it an occupation or a profession, public personnel have certainly developed a series of subspecialists and techniques that, over the years, have combined to produce an organizational subsystem that must be staffed with experts if it is to meet the standards set by public personnel administration." Explain. (1995)
12. "Much of what the recruits learn in an organization is communicated in the fashion of Bentham's 'dog law'." Discuss. (1995)
13. "It is said that the generalist rationale was part of a revealed truth. All of us should have known better, for in a world of increasing scientific and technical complexity, it has compelling inadequacies." Discuss. (1996)
14. Comment: "Public agencies have used a number of sources and procedures for measuring performance." (1996)
15. Comment: "The public services in India have been conferred a constitutional status." (1996)
16. "Independence of the public service commissions has been ensured under specific provisions of the Constitution." Examine. (1996)
17. "Public personnel administration is concerned with a number of functions." Elaborate. Why are the procurement and development functions important? (1998)
18. Comment: "Central services are more 'All India' in character than are the All India Services." (1998)
19. It is argued that the recruitment and training of All India Services and Central Services have not kept pace with the changing needs and times. Give suggestions for improving these processes in order to make administrators more effective, committed, and honest. (1998)
20. "The generalist will always have an edge over the specialist." Substantiate this view. (1999)
21. Comment: "Article 320 states that the Government shall consult the UPSC on certain specific matters." (1999)

22. Comment: "The All India Services have, naturally, to be remunerated on a higher level than services recruited purely on a local basis." (1999)
23. What opportunities are available to All India Services and state services in career development? Do you agree that the days of generalists in the modern administrative state are numbered? (2000)
24. "All India Services play a crucial unifying role in the whole administrative system of the country." Explain. (2000)
25. What techniques has the Government of India employed to evaluate (appraise) the performance of senior level, i.e., Class I and Class II, employees? Are you satisfied with these techniques? (2001)
26. Comment: "The need and significance of All India Services has been well-recognized in political as well as administrative circles." (2001)
27. Comment: "All India Services as an institution is the result of history." (2002)
28. "Training is practical education in any profession, not only to improve skills but also to develop attitudes and the scheme of values necessary for effective performance." Elaborate. (2003)
29. "In-service training of officers belonging to higher civil services has been perhaps the most conspicuous development in Indian administration." Discuss with reference to training designed for the Indian Administrative Service officers. (2003)
30. Recruitment is the backbone of public administration. Explain. (2004)
31. "If positions are the raw material of classification, the class is the operating unit." Discuss. (2005)
32. Why do public organizations evaluate employees' performance? How can performance evaluation system affect employees' behaviour? How can administration effectively evaluate employees? (2005)
33. Comment: "One of the most distinctive characteristics of Indian Administrative Service is its multipurpose character." (2005)
34. To what extent has the human relations movement contributed to the knowledge and practice within the field of personnel administration? (2006)
35. "The generalist character of IAS is its chief characteristic as well as its chief criticism." Comment. (2006)
36. "Training is essential not only for efficiency and effectiveness but also for broadening the vision of employees." Substantiate. (2007)
37. "A well-designed module-based training for civil servants is the best way to achieve the goals of good governance.' Analyse. (2007)
38. "To talk of administrative modernization and still continue with the conventional practice of public personnel administration is a gross incongruity." Offer suggestions to initiate radical reforms in human resource management of public administrative systems. (2008)
39. "Training has proved its incapacity to change the attitudes, behaviour and values of civil servants." Do you agree with this statement? (2008)

40. "Training of civil servants for capacity building should be in consonance with the needs of the socio-economic and technological development of the country." Explain. (2008)
41. It is said that 'position classification', as originally conceived, is sound in terms of its operational characteristics, but complicated and unresponsive in practice. Why is it still considered better than the other models of civil service classification? (2009)
42. Do state services suffer in comparison with the All India Services and Central Services? Suggest measures for enhancing the role, competence and impact of state services. (2009)
43. Discuss the case for and against promotion based on seniority. (2010)
44. Distinguish fully among the syndicate method, role playing method and T-Group training method in personnel management. (2010)
45. "Position Classification can be problematic. A serious complaint in its practice is that it dehumanizes the employee." Discuss. (2010)
46. The "selection model of recruitment rests on the assumption that the primary needs to be met are those of the organization." Examine. (2012)
47. Civil service neutrality is founded on the application of the principles of rule of law. Comment (2013)
48. "The position-classification attempts to establish a triangular relationship among duties and responsibilities, working conditions and qualification requirements." Elucidate. (2015)
49. "A central reason for utilization of performance appraisal is performance improvement of the employees." In the light of the statement, analyse the needs of performance appraisal in an organization. (2016)
50. "Autonomy granted to higher civil servants tends to increase their creativity and productivity." Argue the case to make the civil service more accountable as well as innovative. (2016)
51. "360 degree appraisal is a rational idea, but it involves complex and inauthentic procedures." How can it be made foolproof? (2017)
52. "Lateral entry of competent experts into the government will promote freshness and innovation, but is can create problems of accountability." Discuss. (2017)
53. "The idea of lateral entry into the Civil Services would energize Indian administration." What are its possible advantages and limitations? (2017)
54. Indianization of public services is a slow but steady process. Explain. (2017)
55. "There is a need for greater inclusion of technocrats into bureaucracy to ensure effective governance in India." Do you agree? Elucidate. (2017)
56. "Civil servants should avoid airing grievances in media." In this context, discuss the grievance redressal mechanism available to the Civil Servants in India. (2017)
57. Currently, administrative training focusses more on improving efficiency than on transforming the attitudes and behaviour of civil servants. What type of training will you suggest to fill this gap ? Elaborate (2018)
58. "Lateral entry is an antidote to the complacency in civil service." Discuss. (2018)

59. "Competency mapping is important for effective allocation of responsibilities to administrators." Do you think that a generalist administrator can handle all issues as effectively as a specialist Discuss. (2018)
60. "Performance management requires identification of indicators and measures to ensure that goals are achieved efficiently." Discuss. (2018)
61. "Delegated legislation has become a strategic tool in the hands of the executive despite its utility." Comment. (2019)

Chapter 11. Ethics in Public Administration

1. "Public interest demands the maintenance of political impartiality in the civil services." Comment (1990)
2. "Professional standards, ethics, philosophy, attitudes, and ideology of public service are the means to promote accountability of public administration." Explain how career and non-career public services are accountable to judiciary. (1990)
3. "A civil servant must not forget that s/he is the servant, not the master of the community and that the official competence need not, and should not, involve the loss of human touch." Examine. (1991)
4. How far is it true to state that for a developing democracy the concept of civil service neutrality is outdated; instead there is a need for a civil service with professional competence and commitment? (1997)
5. Comment: "The principle of bureaucratic neutrality is more superfluous and redundant in the context of developing countries." (1999)
6. "The doctrine of political neutrality and anonymity is no more relevant to modern civil service." Comment. (2002)
7. Account for the increasing corruption in administration. Suggest remedies to curb administrative corruption. (2003)
8. What are the various institutional devices available for the redressal of citizens' grievances against the excesses and malfunctioning of administration? How successful have these been? (2003)
9. Civil service neutrality is a thing of the past. Discuss. (2004)
10. Briefly discuss the principles of ensuring ethics in public service as recommended in the Nolan Committee Report. (2010)
11. "Civil services neutrality is founded on the application of the principles of Rule of Law." Comment. (2013)
12. "The basic ethical problem for an administrator is to determine how s/he can use discretionary power in a way that is consistent with democratic values." Comment with respect to corruption in administration. (2013)
13. "British philosophy of administration is based on unification of science of administration with ethics." Analyse. (2014)
14. Discuss the need for civil services neutrality in development administration. Suggest some measures for achieving and strengthening it in practice. (2014)

15. The Supreme Court ruling on 31st October, 2013 in respect of bureaucracy's functioning would help achieve good governance. Analyse this ruling and add your comments on it. (2014)
16. "Administrative ethics is a process of independently critiquing decision standards, based on core social values that can be discovered, within reasonable organizational boundaries that can be defined, subject to the personal and professional accountability." (Denhardt). Explain. (2015)
17. Distinguish between 'Codes of Conduct' and 'Codes of Ethics'. Justify your answer. (2015)
18. "Disciplinary action may be informal and formal." Explain and point out the provisions made in the Constitution or Statute to check the misuse of power to take disciplinary action. (2016)
19. "Administrative ethics includes the code of conduct of civil servants, but goes beyond it as well." Discuss. (2017)
20. "The 'policy of non-action' regarding the institutional mechanisms and legal provisions to eradicate corruption is a feature of Indian administration." Examine critically. (2017)
21. The imperatives of administrative ethics are necessarily an antidote to "I was only obeying the orders" argument by public officials. Explain. (2019)
22. "Prevention of misconduct requires institutionalization of ethical values at the political and administrative levels." Justify. (2020)
23. Examine the approach of public service motivation as an inducement to bring the desired level of efficiency in public service delivery. (2021)
24. Most civil service regimes still equate 'Public Sector Ethics' with anti-corruption efforts. Discuss the insufficiency of Ethics-code in this background. (2022)

Chapter 12. Public Policy

1. 'Policy process must take account of the political complexion of an authority, demography and the historical pattern of service.' Comment (1989)
2. 'The emerging discipline of policy science aims to work out solutions to problems in policy making.' Comment (1990)
3. Comment: 'Public administration consists of all these operations having for their purpose the fulfillment or enforcement of public policy.' (1991)
4. Comment: 'Every public policy is a government decision aimed at solving a problem of society and calls for collective approach to its planning and implementation.' (1991)
5. 'There has been an increasing emphasis on the need for policy formulation and policy analysis in order to ensure improved performance and to avoid ad hoc or fragmented approach to administration, particularly in the context of active role of the state in economic, social, defence and scientific areas.' Discuss (1991)
6. 'Policy making is a series of continuing dynamic processes which are plural and composite.' Explain (1992)
7. Comment: 'The activities of public administrators at various stages of the policy process illustrate the difficulty of divorcing politics from administration.' (1993)

8. "One way of analyzing implementation problems is to begin by thinking about what 'perfect administration' would be like, comparable to the way in which economists employ the model of perfect competition." Discuss (1993)
9. Comment: "The postwar formulations of White and Pfiffner reflect the new 'public policy' orientation- the conception of administration as a political process." (1994)
10. 'The basic issue of administrative accountability relates to that part of public administration which has something concrete to contribute towards not only policy execution but also policy formulation and policy adjudication.' Comment (1994)
11. Elucidate the concept of policy implementation. How does implementation assessment focus on the operation of a public policy? (1994)
12. 'The interest or power group base provides a member of an organization with negotiable goods that can be cashed in for recognition, status and rewards.' Examine (1995)
13. Explain how factors such as communications, resources, self interests and bureaucratic structures affect implementation of public policies. (1995)
14. Comment: "An attack has been made on the 'top down' character of the kind of implementation studies and an alternative 'bottom up' approach has been developed." (1996)
15. Sketch and overview the state of public policy analysis as it is most likely to interest those who have a public administration perspective. (1996)
16. 'Policy making does not end once a decision is made. The implementation of the decision can have just as great an impact on public policy as the decision itself.' Discuss (1997)
17. Comment: 'Policy implementation in less developed countries needs to be effective.' (1998)
18. 'All policy making is decision making, but all decision making is not policy making.' Elaborate. How does a policy emanate and what course does policy-making in government follow? (1998)
19. Elucidate the political process of policy formulation. Bring out its distinguishing features in developing countries. (1999)
20. 'Public policy is what politics is about.' Substantiate (2002)
21. Comment on the role of public administration in policy making and its implementation. What are the other factors influencing the policy process? (2003)
22. Public policy is not an independent variable and human history shows little evidence of systematic learning from policy experience. Discuss (2004)
23. Policy is a decision driven model of research use. Explain (2004)
24. Give an assessment of the processes of policy formulation and discuss the problems of policy implementation. (2005)
25. 'Nothing comes across more strongly than the great naiveté about policy implementation.' Discuss (2006)

26. 'Implementing a public policy is a process of discovering what works and what does not.' Examine (2007)
27. 'Laxity in monitoring and evaluation can render even the best policies infructuous.' Discuss (2008)
28. 'Yehezkel Dror's normative models of policy making tend to be academic in perspective with poor operational utility.' Comment (2009)
29. '... even if policies are well-organized, efficiently operated, widely utilized, adequately financed and supported, we may still ask, so what? Do they work? ... What about their costs, outputs and impacts?' Discuss (2009)
30. 'Cost-benefit analysis is a very unsatisfactory view of evaluating public policy.' Comment (2010)
31. 'Public administration can be portrayed as a wheel or relationships focused on the formulation and implementation of public policy.' Explain (2010)
32. Explain the 'Peter Principle' in respect of promotion policy in a hierarchical organization. (2010)
33. 'Policy is being made as it is being administered and administered as it is being made.' Comment (2011)
34. The incrementalist paradigm posits a conservative tendency in public policy making. (2011)
35. Dror's optimum model is a fusion of the economically rational model with the extra-rational model. (2011)
36. 'Policy judgments comprise reality judgments, value judgments and instrumental judgments.' (Geoffrey Vickers). Elucidate
37. Would you agree with Bachrach and Baratz that along with decisions, non-decisions are also part of policy? Give reasons for your answer. (2012)
38. "Our normal expectation should be that new programs will fail to get off the ground and that, at best, they will take considerable time to get started. The cards in this world are stacked against things happening." (Pressman and Wildavsky) Comment. (2012)
39. "The policy process was not structured in the way required by bureaucratic planning." "Arguably, instrumentalism now stands most in contrast to neo liberal nationality that impose market against both gradual change and democratic liberalism." Analyse these two statements. (2013)
40. "Policies determine politics as governments constrain." Attempt a critique of this statement. (2014)
41. The output studies approach to public policy analyses overstresses the rational techniques and allocative dimension of public policy. Analyse the statement. (2014)
42. According to Y. Dror, "The science of mudelling through is essentially a reinforcement of pro inertia and anti-innovation ideas in policymaking." Comment. (2014)
43. "In the appreciative systems of policymakers, goals are subsidiary to norms and values." (Vickers) Comment. (2015)

44. Policy analysis is incomplete without taking into account policy delivery. (2015)
45. "The concept of political feasibility in policy alternative is a probabilistic concept and is related to each policy alternative." In the context of this statement, analyse Dror's contribution. (2015)
46. "In public policy marking, 'rationalism' is the opposite of 'incrementalism'." (2016)
47. "Of all the processes involved in public policy, implementation is of greatest importance." Examine the impediments in policy implementation. (2017)
48. "A public policy without the active involvement of people in its formulation, implementation and evaluation is only a facade." How can this anomaly be corrected? (2018)
49. Contractualism has become a favourite policy of the neoliberal forces, but not without its share of controversy. Argue. (2019)
50. "Maximum social gain" in public policy making is an attractive goal which is rarely found in practice. Discuss. (2019)
51. Has policy analysis become a major source of legitimation of status quo in political and social order? Discuss. (2020)
52. Have political realities thwarted the move towards evidence-based policy making? Critically examine. (2020)
53. Groups work to elevate issues on the policy agenda or seek to deny other groups the opportunity to place issues. In this background, discuss the role of interest groups in agenda setting in the developing countries. (2021)
54. Failure of public policies has often been attributed to problems of implementation, while implementors question the policy design. Discuss the contestation. (2022)
55. Policy evaluation contributes fundamentally to sound public governance. Discuss. (2022)

Chapter 13. Techniques for Administrative Improvement

1. Do you think that sudden eruption of 'information society' has adapted and accelerated administrative development? (1989)
2. Work study comprises all 'systematic activities concerned with the investigation, recording, measurement and improvement of work.' Comment (1990)
3. 'There are widely different views not only about the context of O and M, but also concerning its relationship with other techniques concerned with improving effectiveness and efficiency.' Discuss (1991)
4. Comment: 'Administrative reform, by its very definition, seeks to apply new ideas to administration and thus entails new values.' (1992)
5. 'Administrative reforms represent efforts, intended to enhance and/ or expand the administrative and managerial capacity of public administration to achieve national objectives or goals.' Elucidate (1993)

6. Comment: 'The entire process of development and nation building hinges on the effectiveness of administrative reforms.' (1994)
7. 'Whatever is the purpose it is true that reforms always takes place against 'resistance' and that failure to recognize the various sources of opposition, and to plan and to neutralize them, is a major reason for the widespread failure of reform efforts.' Examine (1996)
8. Comment: 'Administrative reforms are induced changes in the machinery of government undertaken in order to bridge the gap between reality and desirability.' (1997)
9. Bring out the importance of Organization and Methods (O&M). Do you think that there should be a separate O&M organization? (1997)
10. 'Work study succeeds because it is systematic in investigating a problem an also in developing a solution for it.' Explain. Also discuss the components of work study and their usefulness. (1998)
11. Write short note in about 200 words on work study and work-measurement in Indian administration. (2000)
12. Examine the needs and facts of administrative reforms in the fast changing scenario of the 21st century. What are the obstacles to administrative reforms? Give suggestions to overcome them. (2003)
13. 'Organizations today seem to invest in information and information systems, but their investments often do not seem to make sense.' Comment (2003)
14. Discuss the main approaches to increase the efficiency of government and public administration. (2007)
15. Bring out the various techniques of O&M adopted in India to improve efficiency in administration. (2007)
16. 'Techniques like PERT and CPM help in effective office management.' Elaborate (2009)
17. A system of information ties planning and control by managers to the operational system of implementation. Elaborate. (2011)
18. "Relations are the building blocks of network analysis." In the light of this statement, summarize the form and content of relations in 'network analysis'. (2012)
19. Trace the background and development of PERT and enumerate the steps involved in its application. (2012)
20. Draw a simple PERT chart for a seminar planning project. (2012)
21. The field of MIS is not necessarily an extension of computer science but of management and organization theory. Elucidate. (2014)
22. "MIS, PERT, and CPM have accelerated the process of reinventing O&M." In the context of this statement, explain the recent developments in managerial techniques. (2015)
23. "The term 'work study' may be used in narrower and wider senses." Elucidate. (2016)

24. "An effective Management Information System (MIS) is the key to successful headquarter-field relationships."Comment. (2018)
25. In the absence of a merit-based, fair and objective civil service a more partisan and corrupt government will emerge. Is the statement justified? Give reasons. (2019)
26. A narrow view of information comes in the way of successful implementation of MIS in organizations. Analyse. (2019)
27. A more effective system of performance appraisal should acknowledge the subjective elements in it and be less obsessed with the objective criteria. Elucidate. (2019)
28. In the era of increasing stress on productivity work study provides the road ahead for the administrators. Identify the positive attributes of work study in the light of the statement. (2019)
29. Administrative man bridges the psychological man and the rational man. Explain. (2020)
30. "Markets, hierarchies and networks represent modem governing structures in government." Explain. (2020)
31. Administrative reform is "an artificial inducement of administrative transformation against resistance." (Gerald Caiden). Identify the nature of resistance and inducements required to overcome it. (2020)
32. In theory, the 'civil society organizations' promote cooperation between people and public service organizations, but in practice, their activities restrict the promotion of government programmes. Analyze. (2021)
33. MIS has evolved and gone far beyond its traditional advantages due to technological advancements. Comment. (2021)
34. Performance appraisal needs to be seen beyond the mere suitability of the official for vertical promotion. Explain. (2021)
35. It is widely agreed that the government ought to provide the goods that market fails to provide or does not provide efficiently. Argue. (2021)
36. Civil servants generally tend to exhibit the values and ethical framework of the political executives under whom they function. Explain. (2021)
37. Standards are the foundation which do not replace regulations but complement them. Comment. (2022)

Chapter 14. Financial Administration

1. "Public bureaucracies have not grown yet to adopt their accounting and auditing mechanisms to the ever growing automation within them." Comment. (1989)
2. Give reasons for the failures on the part of bureaucracy and the legislature to supervise the enactment of the budgetary provisions. (1989)
3. "… Budget office needs accountants, statisticians and procedure analysis; it must provide a working climate in which these specialist skills are applied in a general context." Comment. (1990)

4. "What the auditors know is auditing which is not administration." Comment on the nature, importance and role of audit in administration. (1990)
5. "Whereas the control over expenditure, as well as on actual expenditure, incurred after the accounts are closed and audited, is essential, it appears to be neither necessary nor desirable to scrutinize the estimate before their inclusion in the budget in a parliament system of government." Comment. (1990)
6. Comment: "It (audit) is the process of ascertaining whether the administrator has spent or is spending its fund in accordance with the terms of legislature which appropriated money." (1991)
7. Examine the nature of parliamentary control over the National Finances in India. (1991)
8. Comment: "The office of the Comptroller and Auditor General of India is a Constitutional device to ensure parliamentary accountability, federal supervision and expert administrative control over expenditure in the financial administration of the nation." (1991)
9. Analyse the role and functions of the Ministry of Finance of the Government of India. What steps would you visualize to improve its performance of the functions of financial management? Suggest measures to streamline its relationship with ministries. (1991)
10. Comment: "Financial administration is a vital institution for economic and social change in a poor country." (1992)
11. What is performance budgeting? Do you agree with the statement that it is a tool of business management? (1992)
12. Comment: "Public Accounts Committee of Parliament is the real watchdog of the finances of Union Government." (1992)
13. Comment: "Government has numerous ideal objectives, and three of these are closely linked to accounting and finance: efficiency, effectiveness and equality." (1993)
14. Explain the principles involved in the preparation of budget. Assess the scope of budgetary techniques in financial management. (1993)
15. Examine the view that during the last two decades programming, planning and budgeting system and zero base budgeting have been driven out by political dissentions. (1994)
16. Comment: "As an auditor, the CAG's functions and authority are wider and more comprehensive than those exercised by professional auditors." (1994)
17. Comment: Programme budgeting is often considered interchangeable with performance budgeting, but there is a significant difference, at least in theory. (1995)
18. Describe the methods by which the Public Accounts Committee and the Estimates Committee control administration. (1995)
19. Comment: "The Estimates Committee merely gives a big list of advices." (1995)
20. "Budgeting and fiscal administration require the public administration to resolve a variety of operational, managerial and strategic issues." Examine. (1996)
21. Comment: "The CAG is the friend, philosopher and guide of the PAC." (1996)

22. "Time-honoured and yet often not sufficiently appreciated are the fiscal techniques for securing responsible conduct of administrative business." Discuss. (1997)
23. Comment: "The main function of the PAC is to ascertain that the money granted by Parliament has been spent by the government within the scope of the demand." (1997)
24. Critically examine the role of the Finance Ministry as the custodian of all public revenues. (1997)
25. Comment: "Budget is a tool which serves many purposes." (1998)
26. Comment: "CAG should be watchdog and not a bloodhound." (1998)
27. Comment: "The PAC is probably the best medium through the eyes of which the taxpayers see what has been done with their money." (1999)
28. Do you think that the CAG's role is to maintain the dignity, independence, detachment of outlook and fearlessness necessary for a fair, impartial and dispassionate assessment of the actions of the executive in the financial field? Give arguments. (1999)
29. Comment: Budget as an instrument of socio-economic transformation. (2000)
30. Give reasons for the failure of Government of India to introduce the performance programme budgetary technique in Union ministries. What type of budgetary system is being practiced in India and why? (2000)
31. Burkeliead says: "Budget in government is a vehicle of fiscal policy and a tool of management." Examine this statement. (2001)
32. Critically examine the monetary and fiscal policies of Government of India in the decade 1991–2001. Do you think world financial institutions had a role to play in opening Indian economy to global forces? Give reasons to substantiate your argument. (2001)
33. "Statutory External Auditing is one of the protectors of democracy in the parliamentary form of government." Comment. (2001)
34. Comment: "It is the audit of propriety that distinguishes the audit by the CAG from the audit made by any professional auditor." (2001)
35. "Control over public expenditure is an essential feature of accountable and responsible financial administration." In the light of this statement, discuss various methods of control over public expenditure which are exercised by the Indian Parliament. (2001)
36. "The policy of the government is reflected by various items of the budget." Explain by distinguishing between a commercial budget and a government budget. (2001)
37. "Auditing in government is an exercise in post-mortem." Examine. (2002)
38. Examine the government budget as an instrument of public policy and a tool of legislative control. (2002)
39. Comment: "The role of CAG is a limited one." (2002)
40. "Legislative controls over finances are inadequate and incomplete." Comment. (2003)
41. Comment: "Questions represent a powerful technique of parliamentary control over expenditure." (2003, 2012)

42. Comment: "The Estimates Committee is a continuous economic committee." (2004)
43. "The budget is an instrument of coordination." Explain. (2005)
44. Why does the issue of budgeting as politics versus budgeting as analysis remain important in the budgeting process? Do you agree that some synthesis of the two positions seems possible? Illustrate. (2005)
45. Comment: "Public Accounts Committee conducts a post-mortem examination of public accounts." (2005)
46. "Audit provides a healthy safeguard against public money going down the drain." Comment. (2005)
47. "Audit continues to be considered as something alien and something extraneous and something of the nature of an impediment." Explain. (2006)
48. "Successfully implementing budgeting approach requires favourable incentive structures." Discuss. (2006)
49. "Audit, like the judiciary, the executive and the legislature is one of the important ingredients of democracy." Comment. (2006)
50. What is performance budgeting? Bring out its merits, limitations and difficulties. (2007)
51. "Parliamentary Departmental Committees have played their role effectively in analysing the demands for grants." Evaluate. (2007)
52. "Good economics and bad politics cannot coexist in a sound budgetary process." Discuss this statement in the context of the developmental challenges in countries experiencing competitive politics. (2008)
53. "The Budget is more than the economic horoscope of the nation." Comment. (2008)
54. Examine the role of the Finance Ministry of the Government in designing and implementing monetary and fiscal policies. (2009)
55. Distinguish between PPBS and performance budgeting. (2010)
56. The optimism expressed by the proponents of the Fiscal Responsibility and Budget Management Act, 2003, in ensuring fiscal discipline appears to be unwarranted. (2010)
57. Whereas 'value for money audit' aims at economy and 'performance audit' seeks efficiency, 'social audit' goes beyond both, to examine the effectiveness of a programme or activity. Examine this statement with suitable illustrations. (2011)
58. "Budget is a series of goals with price tags attached." Explain. (2011)
59. An administrator used the budget as a framework for communication and coordination, as well as for exercising administrative discipline throughout the administrative structure. Explain. (2011)
60. "Those who budget, deal with their overwhelming burdens by adopting heuristic aids to calculation." (Wildavsky) Explain. (2012)
61. What is an output based performance budgeting system? Analyse this system in the context of India. (2012)
62. What new models of budgetary capacity and incapacity have emerged after the decline of planning, programming budgeting and zero-based budgeting? (2013)

63. Budget allocation involves a series of tensors between actors with different background, orientations and interests and between short-term goals and long-term institutional requirements. Discuss. (2013)
64. Instead of reforms to budgetary process, Wildavsky proposes to redefine the role of political institutions and rules by which politics leads to agreement on budget. Explain. (2014)
65. "The fact that we call something performance auditing means that we imply salient features which can distinguish it from other forms of inquiry." Discuss with reference to the main measures of indicators of performance measurement. (2014)
66. Identify the elements of programme budgeting, output budgeting and 'new' performance budgeting. What do they have in common with PPBS? (2014)
67. Discuss the changes in the powers of the CAG following a recent Supreme Court judgment in a case concerning a private sector provider. (2014)
68. Parliamentary committees bring about accountability in public expenditure. Discuss. (2014)
69. "Social audit of flagship programmes of Central Government facilitates the performance of CAG." Elaborate the statement with appropriate examples. (2014)
70. "No significant change can be made in the budgetary process without affecting the political process." (Wildavsky) Analyse. (2015)
71. "Public borrowing produces different effects on the economy." Examine. (2016)
72. "Fiscal policy and monetary policy are the two tools used by the state to achieve its macroeconomic objectives." Examine the statement and point out the differences between the tools. (2016)
73. "The key to understanding performance-based budgeting lies beneath the word 'result'." In the light of the statement, examine the elements of performance-based budgeting. (2016)
74. "Budget is a political process." (Wildavsky) Examine. (2017)
75. There can be no performance auditing without performance budgeting. Elucidate. (2017)
76. Can we say that statutory audit and social audit are two ideas of the same coin? Or, are they two separate coins with varying values? Discuss. (2017)
77. The office of Controller General of Accounts (CGA) is expected to strengthen the financial management in India. Discuss its mandate. (2017)
78. Implementation of Goods and Services Act (GST) has led to a paradigm shift in Centre–state relations, both financially and politically. Analyse with examples. (2017)
79. "Monetary policy of a country can help or hinder its development process." Discuss. (2018)
80. "Sound performance auditing is impossible without systematic performance or outcome budgeting." Explain the relationship between the two. (2018)
81. Is William Niskanen's "Budget Maximising Model" relevant today? Argue. (2019)
82. Performance measurement remains an emerging issue, but it is relegated to exclusively monitor and assess the use of funds. In light of the statement

discuss various nonfinancial parameters of performance measurement to evaluate public sector organizations. (2019)

83. Discuss the major areas of change in the Tax-Reforms of the post liberisation era. How do you justify the importance of the direct tax reform in this context? (2019)
84. "Fiscal policy should address the issues of inequity, intricacy and obscurantism." Explain. (2020)
85. "Performance Management Framework enables a clear line of sight between planning, measuring and monitoring performance." Critically analyse. (2020)
86. "Objectives of performance budgeting include improving expenditure prioritization, effectiveness and efficiency." Has performance budgeting worked effectively in governmental system? Argue. (2020)
87. Emphasis on cost control and reducing public expenditure has diverted the focus of government budgets from the basic objectives of reallocation of resources, bringing economic stability and promoting social equity. Examine. (2021)
88. A striking feature of economic development is an apparent symbiotic evolution of strong States and strong market economies. Analyze. (2021)
89. Policy problems are increasingly tending towards being wicked. Discuss the capacity and preparedness of the State to tackle such problems. (2021)
90. Zero-based budgeting was intended to get away from incrementalism but ended up being the most incremental of any budgetary approach. Discuss. (2021)
91. Performance problems are rarely caused simply by lack of training and rarely can performance be improved by training alone. Critically analyse the statement. (2022)
92. The audit function has always been viewed as an integral part of government financial management. Discuss the significance of internal audit in improving the performance of the government sector. (2022)
93. A sound budgeting system is one which engenders trust among citizens that the government is listening to their concerns. Elaborate this in the context of budgetary governance. (2022)
94. The results of Washington Consensus were far from optimal for transitional economies. In this background, discuss the change of direction towards post-Washington Consensus. (2022)
95. 'Outcome budgeting addresses the weaknesses of performance budgeting.' Elaborate. (2022)

Important People and Scholars

Important Books, Papers, Articles and Reports

Important Organisations, Commissions and Conferences

Important Terms

B

C

D

E

F

G

H

I

Q

R

S

T

U

V

W

Z

References

Chapter 1. Introduction to Public Administration

1. IGNOU- Public Administration- Meaning, Nature, Scope and Importance.
2. Baker, R.J.S., 1972, Administrative Theory and Public Administration, Hutchinson University Library, London.
3. Suyash Verma, Nature of Public Administration, Desi Kanoon- Law, Economics and Politics, December, 2012.
4. Suyash Verma, Public Administration vs Private Administration, Desi Kanoon- Law, Economics and Politics, December, 2012.
5. University of North Florida, Department of Political Science, PAD 4003 Public Administration Fall 2016, Paradigms of Public Administration.
6. Nicholas Henry, Paradigms of Public Administration, Public Administration Review, Vol. 35, No.4, (Jul. to Aug. 1975), pp. 378-386.
7. Nicholas Henry, Public Administration and Public Affairs.
8. Mohit Bhattacharya, Politics and Administration, New Horizons of Public Administration, 2013, Jawahar Publishers and Distributors.
9. Woodrow Wilson, The Study of Administration, Political Science Quarterly, June 1887, Vol.2, pp.197-222.
10. R.B Jain, Politicization of Bureaucracy: A Framework for Comparative Movement, The Indian Journal of Public Administration, Vol XX, No.4, Oct-Dec, 1974.
11. Shanti Kothari, Ramashray Roy, Relations between Politicians and Administration at the District Level, Indian Institute of Public Administration, 1969.
12. Thomas L. Bertone, Public Administration and the Prevailing Political Regime, PA Times, March 15, 2012.
13. Richard Clay Wilson Jr., Politics and Administration: Where Does Leaks Fit In?, PA Times, March 28, 2017.
14. IGNOU, MPA 012, Administrative Theory, Unit 18, New Public Administration.
15. Frederickson George H, Minnowbrook II: Changing Epochs of Public Administration, Public Administration Review, March-April, 1989.
16. Guy, Mary Ellen, Minnowbrook II: Conclusions, Public Administration Review, March-April, 1989.
17. Y. Pardhasaradhi, Revisiting Minnowbrook: Praxis and Change, Indian Journal of Public Administration, Vol. LIX, No.2, April-June, 2013.
18. IGNOU, MPA 012, Administrative Theory, Unit 19, Perspective of Public Choice.
19. Eamonn Butler, Public Choice- A Primer, The Institute of Economic Affairs, 2012.
20. Mohit Bhattacharya, Restructuring Public Administration: A New Look, 2012, Jawahar Publishers and Distributors.

21. Christopher Hood and Michael Jackson, 1991, *Administrative Argument*, Dartmouth, Aldershot.
22. IGNOU, MPA 012, Administrative Theory, Unit 21, New Public Management Perspective.
23. Osborne, David and Ted Gaebler, 1992, Reinventing Government: How the Entrepreneurial Spirit is Transforming the Public Sector, Addison-Wesley, Reading (MA).
24. Dr M. Veerappa Moily and others, Reorganizing Government- International Experiences, Chapter 2, Organizational Structure of Government of India, Second Administrative Reforms Commission, Thirteenth Report, April 2009.
25. Public Management Reforms in Developing Countries, Shodh Ganga.
26. New Public Management Concept and Review of Literature, Shodh Ganga.
27. Denhardt, Robert B. and Janet Vinzant Denhardt, 2000, The New Public Service: Serving Rather Than Steering, Public Administration Review, November/December, Vol. 60, No. 6.
28. IGNOU, MPA 011, Unit 14, Impact of Globalization on Public Administration.
29. Sheila Rai, Fragmented Response Towards Global Governance: The Indian Context, Indian Journal of Public Administration, 63(1) 63-84, 2017.
30. Lohit Matani (IPS), Internal Security: Concepts, Dynamics, Challenges, Knowracle Publications, January 2017.

Chapter 2. Good Governance, E-Governance, and Emerging Trends

1. Bhattacharya, M. (2012). *Restructuring public administration: A new look*. Jawahar Publishers and Distributors.
2. The World Bank. (1992). *Governance and Development* (Report No. 10650). Retrieved from http://documents.worldbank.org/curated/en/604951468739447676/Governance-and-development.
3. United Nations Development Programme. (1997). *Reconceptualizing Governance* (Discussion Paper No. 2). Retrieved from ftp://pogar.org/LocalUser/pogarp/other/undp/governance/reconceptualizing.pdf.
4. Chakrabarty, B., & Bhattacharya, M. (2008). *The governance discourse*. New Delhi: Oxford University Press.
5. Rhodes, R.A.W. (1996). The new governance: Governing without government. *Political Studies, 44*, 652–667.
6. United Nations Development Programme. (1997). *Governance for Sustainable Human Development*. New York: UNDP.
7. Arora, D. (2014, July). *Good Governance: A Study of the Concept in Indian Context*. Paper presented at the 23rd IPSA World Congress, Montreal, Canada.
8. IGNOU Master of Public Administration (MPA), Concept of Good Governance.
9. Leftwich, A. (1993). Governance, democracy and development in the third world. *The Third World Quarterly, 14*(3).
10. Jayal, N. (1997, February 22). The governance agenda: Making democracy dispensable. *Economic and Political Weekly*.
11. Dunleavy, P., Margetts, H., Bastow, S., & Tinkler, J. (2006). New public management is dead—Long live digital-era governance. *Journal of Public Administration Research and Theory, 16*(3).

12. Margetts, H., & Dunleavy, P. (2013). The second wave of digital-era governance: A quasi-paradigm for government on the web. *Philosophical Transactions of the Royal Society, A 371*: 20120382.
13. Bhattacharya, M. (2008). *New Horizons of Public Administration* (7th ed.). Jawahar Publishers and Distributors.
14. Second Administrative Reforms Commission. (2008). *Promoting e-Governance: The Smart Way Forward* (Report No. 11, Chapter 5). http://ijlt.in/wp-content/uploads/2015/09/E-Governance_Open-Standards. compressed.pdf.
15. Khan, I., Khan, N., & Nazia. (2015). E-governance reforms in India: Issues, challenges and strategies—An overview. *International Journal of Computer Science Issues, 12*(1), no. 2.
16. Ministry of Electronics & Information Technology. (2018). *Digital India Programme*. Retrieved from digitalindia.gov.in/
17. Matani, L. (2017). *Internal security: Concepts, dynamics, challenges*. New Delhi: Knowracle Publications.
18. Srivastava, M. (2013). Social media and its use by the government. *Journal of Public Administration and Governance, 3*(2).
19. Schaefer, M. (2018). *Five mega trends: How social media is transforming governance*. Retrieved from www.businessesgrow.com/2011/04/04/five-mega-trends-how-social-media-is-transforming-government/.
20. Department of Electronics and Information Technology. (n.d.). *Framework and guidelines for use of social media for government organizations*. Retrieved from http://meity.gov.in/writereaddata/files/ Approved%20Social%20Media%20 Framework%20and%20Guidelines%20_2_.pdf.
21. O'Flynn, J. (2007). From new public management to public value: Paradigmatic change and managerial implications. *The Australian Journal of Public Administration, 66*(3), 353–366.
22. Moore, M. (1995). *Creating public value: Strategic management in government*. Cambridge, MA: Harvard University Press.
23. Philip Marcel Karre, Cor van Montfort, 'Public Value Management and Public Entrepreneurship', Nov. 2010.
24. Stoker, G. (2006). Public value management. A new narrative for networked governance. *The American Review of Public Administration 36*(1), 41-57.

Chapter 3. Administrative Thought

1. Bailey Stephen, "Objective of the Theory of Public Administration," in Charlesworth James C., Theory and Practice of Public Administration: Scope, Objectives and Methods, American Academy of Political and Social Sciences, 1968. Pp. 128-139.
2. Woodrow Wilson, "The Study of Administration", Political Science Quarterly, Vol. 2, (June 1887), pp. 197-222.
3. Shafritz, Jay M., and Hyde Albert C., Classics of Public Administration, Fort Worth, Harcourt Brace Publishers, 1997, p.5.
4. Bragden Henry A., "Woodrow Wilson as Administrator", Public Administration Review, Vol. XVI, No. 4, 1956, p.249.

5. Prasad Ravindra D., Prasad V.S., Satyanarayana P., Pardhasaradhi Y., Administrative Thinkers, Sterling Publications Pvt. Ltd., 2010.
6. Nicholas Henry, Public Administration and Public Affairs, Englewood Cliffs, Prentice Hall, 1975.
7. Dwight Waldo, Ideas and Issues in Public Administration, McGraw Hill Book Company Inc, 1953, p. 406.
8. Woodrow Wilson, The New Meaning of Government, Public Administration Review, May-June, 1984.
9. Van Viper Paul P. 'The Politics Administration Dichotomy: Concept or Reality?', Politics and Administration: Woodrow Wilson and American Public Administration, Marcel Dekker Inc, 1984, pp. 203-218.
10. Claude S. George Jr., The History of Management Thought, New Delhi, Prentice Hall of India Pvt. Ltd, 1972, p.92.
11. Taylor Frederick W., Principles of Scientific Management, Harper Brothers, 1947.
12. 'Hearing before Special Committee of the House of Representatives to Investigate the Taylor and other Systems of Shop Management under Authority of House Resolution 90', Washington DC, US Government Printing Office, 1912.
13. Gross Bertram M., The Managing of Organizations: The Administrative Struggle, The Free Press, 1964.
14. Hopkins G.B, The New York Bureau of Municipal Research, The Annals of the American Academy of Political and Social Science, 1912: 41, pp. 235-244.
15. Darell Myrick, Frederick Taylor as a Contributor to Public Administration, Mediterranean Journal of Social Sciences, Vol. 3(12) November, 2012, ISSN 2039-9340.
16. Marx FM, Fesler JW, James WG and Key VO Jr, Elements of Public Administration, Prentice Hall, 1946.
17. Schachter HL, Frederick Taylor and the Public Administration Community, Albany, State University of New York Press, 1989.
18. Appleby PH, Policy and Administration, Tuscaloosa, University of Alabama Press, 1949.
19. *Society of Industrial Psychology, 2012, What is I-O,* http://www.siop.org/.
20. Pitts DW, Diversity, representativeness and performance: Evidence about race and ethnicity in public organizations. Paper presented at the 7th national public management research conference, Washington DC, 2003.
21. Henry Laurence Gantt, The Gantt Chart, Thinker 022, Chartered Management Institute, March 2002.
22. Frank Bunker Gilbreth, Robert Thurston Kent, Motion Study: A Method for Increasing The Efficiency of the Workman, D.Van Nostrand Company, New York, 1911.
23. Frank Bunker Gilbreth, Lillian M. Gilbreth, Fatigue Study, the Elimination of Humanity's Greatest Unnecessary Waste, Macmillan Publication, 1916.
24. Harrington Emmerson, The Twelve Principles of Efficiency, Wentworth Press, 2016.
25. Braverman Harry, Labour and Monopoly Capital, The Degradation of Work in the Twentieth Century, Social Scientist Press, Trivandrum, 1981.
26. Scientific Management Approach, Unit 4, Administrative Thought, Indira Gandhi National Open University.

27. Prasad D. Ravindra, Prasad V.S, Satyanarayan P., Pardhasaradhi Y., Administrative Thinkers, Sterling Publishers Private Limited, New Delhi, 2010.
28. Taylorism and Mechanization of the Worker, Antonio Gramsci Reader: IX Americanism and Fordism, SPN, 308-10, 1934, http://marxism.halkcephesi.net/Antonio%20Gramsci/prison_notebooks/reader/index.htm.
29. Henri Fayol, The Administrative Theory in the State, in Luther Gulick and Urwick, Papers in Science of Administration, New York, Columbia University Press, 1937.
30. Indira Gandhi National Open University, Unit 5, Administrative Management Approach, Administrative Thought, Master of Public Administration Module.
31. Sheldrake John, Management Theory, London, Thomson Learning, 2003.
32. Gross Bertram M, The Managing of Organizations, The Administrative Struggle, The Free Press of Glencoe, Collier-Macmillan, London, 1964.
33. Study of Fayol and Taylor, Management Study Guide, http://www.managementstudyguide.com/taylor_fayol.htm.
34. Tompkins JR, Organization Theory and Public Management, Belmont CA: Wadsworth, Cengage Learning.
35. Michelle N Thomas, Administrative Management Theory, Ball State University.
36. Urwick L, The Functions of Administration with special reference to the work of Henri Fayol', in Gulick and Urwick, The Papers on the Science of Administration, New York Institute of Public Administration, 1937.
37. Urwick L, The Elements of Administration, London, Sir Issac Pitman and Sons Ltd., 1947.
38. Drucker Peter F, Management: Tasks, Responsibilities, Practices, London, Heineman, 1974.
39. Denhardt Robert B., quoted in Paul P. Van Riper.
40. Diamond Alfred, The Temporal Dimensions in Models of Administration and Organization, in Waldo Dwight, Temporal Dimensions of Development Administration, Durham, North Carolina, Duke University Press, 1970.
41. Subramaniam V, The Classical Organizational Theory and its Critics, Public Administration Review, Vol 44, 1966, pp. 435-42.
42. Luther Gulick, The Dynamics of Public Administration as Guidelines for the Future, Public Administration Review, No. 3, May-June, 1983.
43. Gulick Luther, Time and Public Administration, Public Administration Review, No.1, Jan-Feb, 1987, pp. 115-116.
44. Clegg, Steward & David Dunkerley, 1980, Organisation, Class and Control, Routledge & Kegan Paul, London.
45. Gerth HH and Mills Wright C, "Introduction," in Essays, p/59; Bendix Reinhard, "Max Weber," International Encyclopedia of Social Sciences, XVI, p.499.
46. Alfred Diamant, The Bureaucratic Model: Max Weber Rejected, Rediscovered, Reformed, in Ferrel Heady and Sybil Stokes, Papers in Comparative Administration, Ann Arbor, Institute of Public Administration, University of Michigan, 1962.
47. Parsons Talcott, Structure and Process of Modern Societies, Glencoe, Free Press.
48. Gouldner Alvin, Patterns of Industrial Bureaucracy, Glencoe, Free Press, 1954.
49. Blau Peter M, Bureaucracy in Modern Society, Random House, New York, 1962.

50. Arora Ramesh K, Comparative Public Administration, Associated Publishing House, New Delhi, 2011.
51. Kaufman Herbert, Emerging Conflicts in the Doctrine of Public Administration, American Political Science Review, 1956, pp. 1060.
52. Max Weber, Essays in Sociology, translated and edited by HH Gerth and C. Wright Mills.
53. Bendix Reinhard, Max Weber: An Intellectual Portrait, Garden City, New York, 1962.
54. Neutrality Versus Committed Bureaucracy, IGNOU Bachelors of Public Administration.
55. Robert K Merton, Social Theory and Social Structure, Glencoe, IL, Free Press, 1957.
56. Philip Selznick, Leadership in Administration: A Sociological Perspective, 1957.
57. Philip Selznick, Foundations of the Theory of Organization, 1948.
58. Jackall Robert, Moral Mazes: The World of Corporate Managers, Oxford University Press, 1989.
59. Bureaucracy and Modernization: The Russian and Soviet Case, in La Palombara.
60. Hegel GWF, Philosophy of Right, London, Oxford University Press, 1967.
61. McLellan D, Karl Marx: Selected Writings, New York, Oxford University Press, 1977.
62. Urwick L and Brech EFL, The Making of Scientific Management, Vol 1, Thirteen Pioneers, London, Management Publications Trust, 1949 (Sir Isaac Pitman & Sons, Ltd., London, 1951.)
63. Urwick, Lyndall F, The Pattern of Management, Minneapolis: University of Minnesota Press, 1956.
64. Metcalf and Urwick, Dynamic Administration: The Collected Papers of Mary Parker Follett, New York, Harper and Brothers, 1942.
65. Mary Parker Follett, Creative Experience, New York, Longmans Green and Company, 1924.
66. Fox E, Marry Parker Follett: The Enduring Contribution, Public Administration Review, 28(6), pp 520-529.
67. Follett Mary Parker, The Process of Control, in Gulick, Luther and Lyndall, Urwick, Papers on Science of Administration, Columbia University, 1937.
68. Sapre SA, Mary Parker Follett: Her Dynamic Philosophy of Management, Mumbai, Government Central Press, 1975.
69. deLeon L and deLeon P, The Democratic Ethos and Public Management, Administration and Society, 34(2), 2002, pp. 229-250.
70. Hendricks C, Institutions of Deliberative Democratic Processes and Interest Groups: Roles Tensions and Incentives, Australian Journal of Public Administration, 61(1), pp. 64-75.
71. Mary Ann Feldheim, Mary Parker Follett Lost and Found- Again and Again and Again International Journal of Organization Theory and Behaviour, 6(4), 2004, pp. 341-362.
72. Ventriss C, Radical Democratic Thought and Contemporary American Public Administration: A Substantive Perspective, American Review of Public Administration 28(3), pp. 227-245.
73. Stivers C, The Listening Bureaucrat: Responsiveness in Public Administration, Public Administration Review, 54(4), pp/ 364-369.
74. Morton and Lindquist, Revealing the Feminist in Mary Parker Follett, Administration and Society, 29(3), pp. 348-371.
75. Domenec Mele, Ethics in Management: Exploring the Contribution of Mary Parker Follett Working Paper no 618, March, 2006, IESE Business School, University of Navarra.

76. Elton Mayo, The Social Problems of an Industrial Civilization, Cambridge, 1949.
77. Bell Daniel, Adjusting Men to Machines, Commentary, III, January, 1947.
78. Larke Alfred G., 'Human Relations Research: Academic Wool-Gathering, or Guide to Increased Productivity?' Dun's Review and Modern Industry, LXVIII, July, 1956.
79. Roethlisberger Fritz J and Dickson William J, Management and the Worker, Cambridge, 1943.
80. Homans George C, My Meta Sociology, in the Study of Behaviour: Psychology as Science/ Science as Psychology, 1978.
81. Homans George C, Sentiments and Activities: Essays in Social Science, Glencoe, IL, The Free Press of Glencoe.
82. Homans George C, Steps to a Theory of Social Behaviour: An Autobiographical Account, Theory and Society.
83. Homans George C, A Conceptual Scheme for the Study of Social Organization, American Sociological Review, 1947.
84. Infed.org, George C. Homans, The Human Group and Elementary Social Behavior, http://infed.org/mobi/george-c-homans-the-human-group-and-elementary-social-behaviour/.
85. Homans George C, Social Behaviour: Its Elementary Forms, 1974, New York, Harcourt Brace Jovanovich Inc.
86. Ickis John C, William F. Whyte: Contributions to Management, Journal of Business Research, 67(2014), pp. 1493-1500.
87. Whyte WF, Participant Observer: An Autobiography, 1994, Ithaca, New York, ILR Press.
88. Trahair Richard CS, Bruce Kyle, Human Relations and Management Consulting: Elton Mayo and Eric Trist.
89. Trahair R, The Humanist Temper: The Life and Work of Elton Mayo, New Brunswick, New Jersey, Transaction Publishers, 1984.
90. Clark Kerr and Lloyd Fisher, Plant Sociology: The Elite and the Aborigines, Common Frontiers of the Social Sciences, Glencoe, Illinois, 1957.
91. Whyte William H Jr, The Organization Man, New York, 1956.
92. Whitehead Thomas N, Leadership in a Free Society, Cambridge, 1936.
93. Abraham Siegal, The Economic Environment in Human Relations Research, Arensberg.
94. Easton David, A Framework of Political Analysis, 1965, Prentice Hall, New Jersey.
95. IGNOU Maters of Public Administration, Administrative Theory, Systems Approach: Views of David Easton and Chester Barnard.
96. Gvishiani D, Organization and Management: A Sociological Analysis of Western Theories, Moscow, Progress Publishers, 1972.
97. Barnard I Chester, The Functions of Executive, Harvard University Press, Cambridge.
98. Fry Brain R, Mastering Public Administration: From Max Weber to Dwight Waldo, Chatham House Publishers, 1989.
99. Principles of Administrative Theory, Rai Technology University.
100. Chikere Cornell C and Nwoka Jude, The Systems Theory of Management in Modern Day Organizations- A Study of Aldgate Congress Resort Limited Port Harcourt, International Journal of Scientific and Research Publications, Vol 5, Issue 9, September 2015.

101. Espejo Raul and Gill Antonia, The Viable System Model as a Framework for Understanding Organizations.
102. Beer Stafford, Diagnosing the System for Organizations, Wiley, Chichester, 1985.
103. Espejo R and Harnden R, The Viable Systems Model-Interpretations and Applications of Staffor Beer's VSM, Wiley, Chichester, 1989.
104. Tanuja A, System Approach Theory of Management: Features and Evaluation, Business Management Ideas, http://www.businessmanagementideas.com/management/system-approach-theory-of-management-features-and-evaluation/4703.
105. Ishiyama John T, Breuning Marijke, 21st Century Political Science: A Reference Handbook, Vol. 1, University of North Texas.
106. Parsons T and Shils A, Toward a General Theory of Action, Harvard University Press, Cambridge, 1976.
107. Parsons T, Theories of Society: Foundations of Modern Sociological Theory, Free Press, New York, 1961.
108. Cuff E and Payne G, Perspectives in Sociology, Allen and Unwin, London, 1984.
109. Gingrich P, Functionalism and Parsons, in Sociology 250 subject notes, University of Regina, 1999.
110. Ritzer G, Sociological Theory, Knofp Inc, New York, 1983.
111. Holmwood J, Functionalism and its Critics, in Harrington A, Modern Social Theory: An Introduction, Oxford University Press, Oxford, 2005.
112. Almond GA and Coleman JS, The Politics of the Developing Areas, Princeton, NJ, Prince University Press, 1960.
113. Almond GB and Powell GB, Comparative Politics: A Developmental Approach, Boston, Little Brown, 1966.
114. IGNOU Maters of Public Administration, Administrative Theory, 'Views of Herbert A. Simon on Decision Making in an Organization'.
115. Hoselitz Bert F, A Reader's Guide to the Social Sciences, New York, The Free Press, 1970.
116. Brain R. Fry, Mastering Public Administration: From Max Weber to Dwight Waldo, Chatham, NJ, Chatham House Publishers, 1989.
117. Simon Herbert A, The New Science of Management Decision, New York, Harper and Row Publishers, 1960.
118. Simon Herbert A, Administrative Behavior: A Study of Decision Making Processes in Administrative Organization, New York, The Free Press, 1957.
119. Gustavo Barros, Herbert A. Simon and the concept of rationality: Boundaries and Procedures, Brazilian Journal of Political Economy, Vol 30(3), 2010, pp 455-472.
120. Subramaniam V, "Fact and Value in Decision Making" Public Administration Review, Vol. XXIII, No.4, December 1963.
121. Selten Reinhard, What is Bounded Rationality?, Paper prepared for the Dahlem Conference 1999, May 1999.
122. Hong Zhang, On 'A behavioral theory of the firm' by Richard Cyert and James March.
123. McGregor Douglas, The Human Side of the Enterprise, New York, McGraw-Hill Book Company, 1960.

124. Leavitt Harold J, Managerial Psychology, New York, McGraw Hill, 1948.
125. Harold Koontz, Cyril O Donnel and Heinz Weihrich, Management, McGraw Hill International, eighth edition, 1984.
126. Argyris Chris, Personality and Organization, New York, Harper, 1957.
127. Hampton DR, Summer CE and Webber RA, Organizational Behavior and the Practice of Management, Glenview (III) Scott, Foreman and Co., 1968.
128. Argyris Chris, Intervention Theory and Method: A Behavioral Science View, Addison Wesley, 1970.
129. Argyris Chris and Schon Donald A, Organizational Learning: A Theory of Action Perspective, Massachusetts, Addison-Wesley Publishing Company, 1978.
130. Likert Rensis, Likert Jane Gibson, New Ways of Managing Conflicts, New York, McGraw-Hill Book Co., 1976.
131. Pollard Harold R, Developments in Management Thought, London, Heinemann, 1974.
132. Jenkins WO, A Review of Leadership Studies with Particular Reference to Military Problems, Psychology Bulletin, 44(1).
133. Latham Gary P, Saari Lise M, Importance of Supportive Relationships in Goal Setting, Journal of App. Psychology, 1979, Vol 64(2), pp. 151-156.
134. Likert Rensis, New Patterns of Management, New York, McGraw-Hill Book Co., 1961.
135. Likert Rensis, The Relationship between Management Behavior and Social Structure, CLOSXV Session, Symposium C-3.
136. Likert Rensis, An Improvement Cycle for Human Resource Development, Training and Development Journal, July 1978, Vol.32, No.7.
137. Luthas Fred, Organizational Behavior, New York, McGraw-Hill Company, 1973.
138. Drucker Peter F, Management Challenges for the 21st Century, New York, Harper Business, 2001.
139. https://www.linkedin.com/pulse/6-major-contributions-peter-drucker-management-murali-mohan-rao/.
140. Drucker Peter F, The deadly Sins in Public Administration, Public Administration Review, 40(2), March-April, 1980, pp. 103-106.
141. Drucker Peter F, Really Reinventing Government, The Atlantic Online, 2009.
142. Drucker Peter F, The Practice of Management, London, Heinemann, 1955.
143. Drucker Peter F, Managing for the Future, Oxford, Butterworth- Heinemann, Classic Edition, 2000.
144. Behling O, Schriesheim C, Organizational Behavior: Theory, research, and application, Boston: Allyn and Bacon, 1976.

Chapter 4. Administrative Behaviour

1. Handbook of Organizational behaviour, Prentice Hall.
2. Butler R, Designing Organizations: A Decision-making Perspective, Taylor and Francis, 1991.
3. Garvin DA and Roberto MA, What you don't about managing decisions, Harvard Business Review, Sept, 2001, Electronic Version.

4. Mintzberg Henry, Raisinghani Duru, Theoret Andre, The structure of unstructured decision process, Adm. Sc. Quarterly, 21(2), Jun, 1976, pp. 246-275.
5. IGNOU, Decision-making Models, Techniques and Processes.
6. Behling O, Schriesheim C, Organizational behaviour: Theory, research, and application, Boston: Allyn and Bacon, 1976.
7. Thompson James D, Arthur Tuden, Strategies, structures and processes of organizational decision, in James D Thompson, Peter B Hammond, Robert W Hawkes, Buford H Junker and Arthur Tuden, Comparative Studies in Administration, pp. 195-216, 1959, University of Pittsburgh Press.
8. Allison GT, Essence of Decision: Explaining the Cuban Missile Crisis, Boston, Little, Brown and Company, 1971.
9. Etzioni A, Humble Decision-making, in Harvard Business Review no. 89406, July-Aug, 1989, Harvard Business School Publishing, pp. 122-126.
10. Cohen MD, March JG, Olsen JP, A garbage can model of organizational choice, Administrative Science Quarterly, 1972, Vol.17, pp. 1-25.
11. Cheshire JD and Feroz EH, Allison's models and the FASB statements no's 2,5,13 and 19, Journal of Business Finance and Accounting, 16(1), pp. 119-130.
12. Henry Nicholas, Public Administration and Public Affairs, 12th Edition, Georgia Southern University, PHI Learning Private Limited, New Delhi, 2012.
13. Twerky A, Kahneman D, Judgment under Uncertainty: Heuristics and Biases, Science, 185, 4157 (1974), pp. 1124-1131.
14. Hammond JS, Kerry RL, Raiffa H, Thinking About… The Hidden Traps in Decision-making, Harvard Business Review, Sept-Oct, 1998.
15. Parikh Margie, Gupta Rajen, Organizational behaviour, McGraw Hill Education, New Delhi.
16. Staw BM, Knee-deep in the big muddy: A study of escalating commitment to a chosen course of action, Organizational behaviour and Human Performance, 16(1), 1976, pp. 27-44.
17. Robert H Ennis, Critical Thinking, Upper Saddle River, NJ: Prentice Hall, 1996.
18. Paul C. Nutt, Comparing Public and Private Sector Decision-making Process, Journal of Public Administration Research and Theory, April 2006, pp. 289-318.
19. Antonsen and Jorgensen, The Publicness of Public Organizations.
20. Myung Jae Moon, The Pursuit of Managerial Innovation: Does Organization Matter?, Public Administration Review, 59, Jan-Feb, 1999, pp. 31-43.
21. Bryson John M, Anderson Sharon R, Applying Large-Group Interaction Methods in the Planning and Implementation of Major Change Efforts, Public Administration Review, 60, March-April, 2000, pp. 143-162.
22. Amabile TM, Conti R, Coon H, Lazenby J, Herron M, Assessing the Work Environment for Creativity, Academy for Management Journal, 39(5), pp. 1154-1184.
23. Hender JM, Dean DL, Rodgers TL, Nunamaker JF Jr, An Examination of the Impact of Stimuli Type and GSS Structure on Creativity: Brainstorming Vs Non-Brainstorming Techniques in a GSS Environment, Journal of Management Information Systems, Springer, 18:4, 2002, pp. 55-59.

24. Nemeth CJ, Managing Innovation: Where Less is More, California Management Review, Vol. 40(1), 1997, pp. 59-64.
25. Argyris C, Interpersonal Barriers in Decision-making, Harvard Business Review, no 66201, March-April, 1966, pp. 84-96.
26. James K, Chen J, Goldberg C, Organizational Conflict and Individual Creativity, Journal of Applied and Social Psychology, 22(7), 1992, pp. 545-566.
27. Euske NA, Roberts KH, Evolving perspectives in organizational Theory: Communication Implications in Jablin FM, Putnam LL, Roberts KH, Porter LW, Handbook of Organizational Communication, 1987, pp. 41-69, Newbury Park, CA: Sage.
28. Sigband N, Communication for Management, Glenview, IL, Scott, Foresman & Co., 1980.
29. Baumeister RF, Leary MR, The need to belong: Desire for interpersonal attachments as a fundamental human motivation, Psychological Bulletin, 1995, 117, pp. 497-529.
30. Bhattacharya Mohit, New Horizons of Public Administration, Jawahar Pub and Dist, New Print, 2015.
31. Joseph Devito, The Interpersonal Communication Book, Harper and Row, 1976.
32. Gerbner G, A Generalized Graphical Model of Communication, In Communication Studies: An Introductory Reader, by Corner J and Hawthorn J, Arnold, 1993, pp. 15-16.
33. Communication, Indira Gandhi National Open University.
34. Models and Processes of Communication, Indira Gandhi National Open University.
35. Heyes J, Interpersonal Skills at Workplace, Routledge, 2002.
36. Taiguri R, On Good Communication, Taiguri, Harvard Business School, 1993, Note 9-493-080.
37. Stauffer D, Yo, Listen Up: A Brief Hearing on the most neglected communication skill, Harvard Management Update, Article Reprint No. 9807D, HBS Publishing, 1998.
38. Arisgueta Maria P, Denhardht R, Denhardt J, Managing Human behaviour in Public and Non-Profit Organizations, SAGE Publications, Aug, 2015.
39. Leach AH, The Keys to Effective Communication in Public Organizations, PA Times, April 19, 2016.
40. Luft J and Ingham H, The Johari Window: A Graphical Model of Interpersonal Awareness, Proceedings of the Western Training Laboratory in Group Development, Los Angeles, UCLA, 1955.
41. Pinder CC, Work Motivation in Organizational behaviour, Upper Saddle River, NJ, Prentice Hall, 1998.
42. Frey BS, Osterloh M, Successful Management by Motivation: Balancing Intrinsic and Extrinsic Incentives, Springer, 2001.
43. Hebb DO, The Organization of behaviour: A Neuropsychological Theory, Wiley, New York, 1949.
44. Locke EA, Motivation by Goal Setting in the Handbook of Organizational behaviour, Robert T Golemievski, CRC Press, 2000, pp. 43-56.
45. Rainey HG, Work Motivation in the Handbook of Organizational behaviour, Robert T Golemievski, CRC Press, 2000, pp. 19-42.
46. Work Motivation, Personality and Attitudes in Organizational behaviour, IGNOU.
47. Ritcher CP, Animal behaviour and Internal Drives, Quarterly Review of Biology, 1927, 2, pp. 307-343.
48. McClelland D, The Achieving Society, New Jersey, Van Nostrand, 1961.

49. Prasad DR, Prasad VS, Satyanarayana P, Pardhasaradhi Y, Administrative Thinkers, Sterling, New Delhi, 2012.
50. Maslow AH, Motivation and Personality, New York, Harper & Row, 1954.
51. Maslow AH, Religions, Values and Peak Experiences, Penguin Books, 1994.
52. Motivation, Indira Gandhi National Open University.
53. Harvey P, Martinko MJ, Attribution Theory and Motivation, Jones and Barlett.
54. Weiner B, An attribution theory of achievement motivation and emotion, 1985, Psychological Review, 97, pp. 548-573.
55. Gundlach MJ, Douglas SC, Martinko MJ, The decision to blow the whistle: a social information processing framework, Academy of Management Review, 2003, 28, pp. 107-123.
56. Kovenklioglu G, Greenhaus JH, Causal Attributes- Expectations and Task Performance, Journal of Applied Psychology, 1978, 63, pp. 698-705.
57. Abramson LY, Seligman MEP, Teasdale JD, Learned Helplessness in Humans: Critique and Reformulation, Journal of Abnormal Psychology, 1978, 87, pp. 49-74.
58. Douglas SC, Martinko MJ, Exploring the role of individual differences in the prediction of workplace aggression, Journal of Applied Psychology, 2001, 86, pp. 547-559.
59. Martinko MJ, Gardner WL, The leader-member attribution process, Academy of Management Review, 1987, 12, pp. 23-249.
60. Conger JA, Kanungo RN, Charismatic leadership in organizations: perceived behavioural attributes and their measurement, Journal of Organizational behaviour, 1994, 15, pp. 439-452.
61. Coutu DL, How resilience works, Harvard Business Review, 2002, 80, pp. 46-55.
62. Huey SJ, Weisz JR, Ego control, ego resiliency and the five factor model as predictors of behavioural and emotional problems in clinic-referred children and adolescents, Journal of Abnormal Psychology, 1997, 106, pp. 404-415.
63. Campbell CR, Martinko MJ, An integrative attributional perspective of empowerment and learned helplessness: A multi method field study, Journal of Management, 1998, 24, pp. 173-200.
64. Kanungo RM, Mendonca M, Evaluating employee compensation, California Management Review, 1988, Fall, pp. 23-39.
65. Vroom VH, Work and Motivation, New York, Wiley, 1964.
66. Pinder CC, Work motivation in organizational behaviour, Prentice Hall, Upper Saddle River, NJ, 1998.
67. Tubbs ME, Commitment as a moderator of goal performance relation: A case for clearer construct definition, Journal of Applied Psychology, 1993, 78, pp. 86-97.
68. Earley PC, Northcraft, GB, Lee C, Lituchy TR, Impact of process and outcome feedback on the relation of goal setting to task performance, Academy of Management Journal, 1990, 33, pp. 87-105.
69. Locke EA, Motivation through conscious goal setting, Applied and Preventive Psychology, 1996, 5, pp. 117-124.
70. Gililand SW, Landis RS, Quality and quantity goals in a complex decision task: Strategies and outcomes, Journal of Applied Psychology, 1992, 77, pp. 672-681.
71. Guion RM, Some Definitions of Morale, Personnel Psychology, 11, 1958, pp. 59-61.
72. Lawler, Edward E, Lyman Porter, The effect of performance on job satisfaction, Industrial Relations, Oct, 1967.

73. McElroy JC, A Typology of Attribution Leadership Research, Academy of Management Review, July, 1982, pp. 413-417.
74. Katz D, Kahn Robert L, The Social Psychology of Organizations, John Wiley and Sons, New York, 1978.
75. Philip Selznick, Leadership in Administration, Quid Pro Quo Books, 2011.
76. Rice AK, Learning for Leadership: Interpersonal and Intergroup Relations, Karnac Books, 1999.
77. Calder BJ, An attribution theory of leadership, In B Staw and G. Salancik, New Directions in Organizational behaviour, Chicago, St. Clair Press, pp. 179-204.
78. Yulk GA, Leadership in Organizations, Pearson Education Inc, 2003.
79. Stogdill RM, Handbook of Leadership: A Survey of the Literature, New York, Free Press, 1974.
80. Kuhnert KW, Lewis P, Transactional and Transformational Leadership: A Constructive/ Developmental Analysis, The Academy of Management Review, 1987, 12(4), pp. 648-657.
81. Hemphill JK and Coons AE, Development of the Leader behaviour Questionnaire, in Leader behaviour: Its description and measurement, edited by Stogdill RM, Coons AE, 1957, pp. 6-38, Columbus, Ohio State University, Bureau of Business Research.
82. Kahn RL, The Prediction of Productivity, Journal of Social Issues, 1956, 12, pp. 41-49.
83. Fiedler FE, Chemers MM, Mahar L, Improving leadership effectiveness: The leader match concept, New York, Wiley, 1976.
84. Gannon MJ, Management: An Integrated Framework, Boston, Little Brown, 1982.
85. Gray JL, Starke FA, Organizational behaviour, Merrill Publishers, 1984.
86. Hersey P, Blanchard KH, Management and Organizational behaviour, Englewood Cliffs, NJ, Prentice-Hall, 1988.
87. Caskey F, Leadership style and team process: A comparison of the managerial grid and situational leadership, Training and Development Research Centre Project, 1988.
88. Aldag RJ, Brief AP, Managing Organizational behaviour, West, 1981.
89. Blake RR, Mouton JS, The Managerial Grid, Advance Management Office Executive, 1962
90. Sahni P, Vayunandan E, Administrative Theory, New Delhi, PHI Learning Pvt. Ltd, 2010.
91. Kerr S, Jermier JM, Substitutes for Leadership: Their meaning and measurement, Organizational behaviour and Human Performance, 22(3), Dec, 1970.
92. J.P. *Howell*, P.W. Dorfman, S. KerrModerator variables in *leadership* research. Academy of Management Review, 11 (*1986*), pp. 88-102.
93. Theories of Leadership, Indira Gandhi National Open University.
94. House RJ, Woyke J, Fedor E, Charismatic and non-charismatic leaders: Differences in behaviour and effectiveness, In Conger J, Kanungo R, Charismatic Leadership, San Francisco, CA, Jossey-Bass.
95. Verma A, Ekkirala SS, Linda KS, A comparative study of the impact of leader-member exchange in US and Indian samples, Cross Cultural Management, 2005, 12(1), pp. 84-95.
96. Dansereau F, Garen G, Haga WJ, A vertical dyad linkage approach to leadership within formal organizations: A longitudinal investigation of the role making process, Organizational behaviour and human performance, 1975, vol 13, pp. 46-78.
97. Dienesch RM, Liden RC, Leader member exchange model of leadership: A critique and further development, Academy of Management Review, 1986, 11(3), pp. 618-634.

98. Burns JM, Leadership, New York, Harper and Row, 1978.
99. Yulk G, Managerial leadership: A review of theory and research, Journal of management, 1989, 15(2), pp. 251-289.
100. Bass BM, Avolio BJ, Jung DI, Berson Y, Predicting unit performance by assessing transformational and transactional leadership, Journal of applied psychology, 2003, 88(2), pp. 207-218.
101. Parikh M, Gupta R, Leading for change and organizational effectiveness, in Organizational behaviour, New Delhi, McGraw Hill Education, pp. 515-566.
102. House RJ, A theory of charismatic leadership, In Leadership: The Cutting Edge, Hunt, Larson, Carbondale, Southern Illinois University Press, 1977.
103. Willner AR, The spellbinders: Charismatic political leadership, New Haven, CT, Yale University Press, 1984.
104. Peters T, Austin N, A Passion for Excellence: The Leadership Difference, New York, Random House, 1985.
105. Ayas K, Zeniuk N, Project based learning: building communities of reflective practitioners, Management Learning, 2001, 32(1), pp. 61-76.
106. Dewey J, How we think, Henrey Regnery, Chicago, IL, 1933.
107. Klenke K, Women in Leadership: Contextual Dynamic and Boundaries, Bingely, UK, Emerald Group Publishing Ltd, 2011.
108. Yulk (2002) and Zalenick (1992).
109. Jerry Newfarmer, Are You a Leader or a Manager?, PA Times, July 21, 2015.
110. Linda Barnes, Damaging Effects of Micromanagement, PA Times, March 31, 2015.
111. Kathleen Rao, My Boss is Jerk: How to Survive and Thrive in a Difficult Work Environment Under the Control of a Bad Boss.
112. Greenleaf RK, Servant Leadership: A journey into the nature of legitimate power and greatness, Mahwah, NJ: Paulist Press, 1977.
113. Larry CS, Character and Servant Leadership: Ten Characteristics of Effective, Caring Leaders, The Journal of Virtues and Leadership, 1(1), 2010, pp. 25-30.

Chapter 5. Organizational Dynamics

1. Factors affecting organizational design, Indira Gandhi National Open University.
2. Gooding RZ, Wagner JA III, A Meta Analytical Review of the Relationship between Size and Performance: The productivity and efficiency of organizations and their subunits, Administrative Science Quarterly, 30(4), Dec, 1985, pp. 462-481.
3. Mohit Bhattacharya, Behavioural and Systems Approach, New Horizons of Public Administration, 2013, Jawahar Publishers and Distributors, pp 64-78.
4. Burns T, Stalker GM, The Management of Innovation, London, Tavistock, 1962.
5. Lawrence PR, Lorsch JW, Organization and Environment, Harvard Business School, 1967.
6. Kreitner R, Kinichi A, Organizational Behaviour, Irwin McGraw-Hill, USA, 1998.
7. Woodward J, Industrial Organization: Theory and Practice, London, 1965.
8. Thompson JD, Organizations in Action: Social Science Bases of Administrative Theory, McGraw Hill, USA, 1967.
9. Bauman Z, Sociology and Postmodernity, The Sociological Review, Nov 1988.

10. Parker I, Discourse Dynamics: Critical Analysis for Social and Individual Psychology, Routledge, 1992.
11. Peltonen T, Organization Theory: Critical and Philosophical Engagements, Emerald Group Publishing, 2016.
12. Cooper R, Organization/ Disorganization, Social Science Information, 1986, 25(2), pp. 299-335.
13. Piore MJ, Charles FS, The Second Industrial Divide, New York, Basic Books, 1984.
14. Parker M, Postmodern Organizations or Postmodern Organization Theory?, Organization Studies, 1992, 13(1).
15. Power M, Modernism, Postmodernism and Organization, in The Theory and Philosophy of Organizations, Hassard J, Pym D, Routledge, 1990, pp. 109-124.
16. Wamsley GL, Refounding Public Administration, European Institute of Public Administration Series, Sage, 1990.
17. Bhattacharya M, Restructuring Public Administration: A New Look, Jawahar Publishers and Distributors, New Delhi, 2012.
18. Desanctis G, Monge P, Introduction to the Special Issue: Communication Process for Virtual Organizations, Organization Science, 1999, 10(6), pp. 693-703.
19. Staples DS, Hulland JS, Higgins CA, A Self-Efficacy Theory Explanation for the Management of Remote Workers in Virtual Organizations, Journal of Computer Mediated Communication, 1998, 3(4).
20. https://analysisproject.blogspot.in/2015/07/matrix-organization-structure.html.
21. Child J, Organizational Structure, Environment and Performance: The Role of Strategic Choice, Sage Journals, 6(1), 1972.
22. Parikh M, Gupta R, Creating Structures to Support Effective Behaviour, Organizational Behaviour, McGraw Hills, New Delhi, 2010.
23. Shrivastava P, Mitroff II, Enhancing Organization Research Utilization: The Role of Decision Maker's Assumptions, Academy of Management Review, 1984, 9, pp. 18-26.
24. Davenport TH, Process Innovation: Reengineering Work Through Information Technology, Harvard Business Press, 1993.
25. Henrikki T, The Process Movement: A Critical Review, LTA, 1998, pp 204-226.
26. Schein EH, Organizational Culture and Leadership, John Wiley and Sons, 2010.
27. Benedict R, Patterns of Culture, 1934, Boston, Houghton-Mifflin.
28. O'Reilly CA III, Chatman J, Caldwell DF, People and Organizational Culture: A Profile Comparison Approach to Assessing Person-Organization Fit, Academy of Management Journal, 34(3), pp. 487-516.
29. Ashkanasy NN, Wilderom C, Peterson MF, The Handbook of Organizational Culture and Climate, 2010, Sage, Newbury Park, CA.
30. Sorensen JB, The Strength of Corporate Culture and the Reliability of Firm Performance, Administrative Science Quarterly, 47(1), 2002, pp. 70-91.
31. Martin J, Feldman MS, Hatch MJ, Sitkin SB, The Uniqueness Paradox in Organizational Stories, Administrative Science Quarterly, 1983, 23(3), Organizational Culture, pp. 438-453.
32. Saffold GS III, Culture Traits, Strength and Organizational Performance: Moving Beyond 'Strong' Culture Source, The Academy of Management Review, 1988, 13(4), pp. 546-558.

33. Denison DR, Bringing Corporate Culture to the Bottomline, 1984, http://www.denisonconsulting.com/.
34. Ashforth BE, Mael F, Social Identity and the Organization, Academy of Management Review, 1989, 14(1), pp. 20-39.
35. Whorton JW, Worthley JA, A perspective on the challenge of public management: Environmental paradox and organizational culture, Academy of Management Review, 1981, 6, pp. 357-363.
36. Hodge GA, Greve C, The Challenge of Public-Private Partnerships: Learning from International Experience, Edward Elgar Publishing, 2005.
37. Selznick P, Leadership in Administration: A Sociological Interpretation, University of California Press, 1984.
38. Teisman, G.R. and E.H. Klijn. 2000. "Public-Private Partnerships in the European Union." In S. Osborne (ed.). Public-Private Partnerships: Theory and Practice in International Perspective. London: Routledge, pages.
39. Rosenau PV, Introduction: The Strengths and Weaknesses of Public-Private Policy Partnerships. American Behavioural Scientist - AMER BEHAV SCI. 1999, 43. 10-34. 10.1177/0002764299043001002.
40. Van Ham Hans, Koppenjan Joop, Building Public-Private Partnerships: Assessing and Managing Risks in Port Development, Routledge.
41. Linder S 'Coming to Terms with the Public–Private Partnership: A Grammar of Multiple Meanings', American Behavioural Scientist, 1999, 43, 1, 35–51.
42. Savas E. S., Privatization and Public–Private Partnerships, New York: Chatham House Publishers and Seven Bridges Press, 2000.
43. Kelkar V et al, Report of the Committee on Revisiting and Revitalising Public Private Partnership Model of Government of India, Department of Economic Affairs, Min. of Finance, Nov 2015.
44. Farahat SMM, Potential Uses of Public-Private-People-Partnership for Improving the Health Services in Egypt: A Case Study of Egypt free from Virus C Program, MPA Thesis, Master of Public Policy and Administration Department.
45. Ng ST, Wong JM, Wong KK, A public private people partnerships (P4) process framework for infrastructure development in Hong Kong, Cities, 2013, 31, pp. 370-381.
46. Voshell K, Public-Public Partnerships: Innovative Partnerships Advancing Community Goals, PA Times, Sept 27, 2016, http://patimes.org/public-public-partnerships-innovative-partnerships-advancing-community-goals/.

Chapter 6. Accountability and Control

1. Fesler JW, Kettl DF, The Politics of the Administrative Process, Chatham House Publishers, 1991.
2. Jabbra JG, Dwivedi OP, Government Response to Environmental Challenges in Global Perspective, IOS Free Press, 1998.

3. Romzek BS, Dubnick MJ, Accountability in the Public Sector: Lessons from the Challenger Tragedy, JSTOR, 1987, 47(3), pp. 227-238.
4. Wolf A, Symposium on *Accountability* in Public administration: Reconciling Democracy, Efficiency and Ethics, Sage Journals, 2000.
5. Hayllar MR, Accountability: Ends, Means and Resources, Asian Review of Public Administration, 1991, Vol 3(2), pp 10-22.
6. Nayar P, Control Over Public Administration, Essay, Public Administration, http://www.politicalsciencenotes.com/essay/ public-administration/control-over-public-administration-essay-public-administration/13698.
7. Laxmikanth M, Public Administration, Tata McGraw Hill, New Delhi, 2011.
8. Arora R, Goyal R, New Age International Publishers, New Delhi, 2013.
9. https://www.house.gov/the-house-explained/branches-of-government
10. https://www.cbo.gov/.
11. https://www.gao.gov/.
12. Takwani CK, Lectures on Administrative Law, Lucknow, Eastern Book Company, 2001.
13. Lutrin C E, Settle A, *American Public Administration Concepts & Cases*, 2nd Ed. California: Mayfield Publishing Company, 1980, pp. 297-304.
14. Massey I.P, *Administrative Law*, Eastern Book Company, Lucknow, 2001.
15. Pfiffner JM, Presthus, *Public Administration*, New York : Ronald Press Co, 1953, 3rd Edition, Vol.10, pp. 504-520.
16. Wade H.W.R., *Administrative Law*, Oxford: Clarendon Press, 1971, pp. 46-105.
17. Mollah Hossain MA, Judicial Control over Administration and Protection of Citizen's Rights: An Analytical Overview, University of Rajshahi, Bangladesh, April, 2006.
18. Nayak GN, Goa University, 2002, 2, SCC, pp 290.
19. Centre for Public Interest Litigation v UOI, (2005), 8, SCC, pp 202.
20. S Parthsarathi v. State of AP, AIR 1973 SC 2701: (1974)3 SCC 459.
21. BALCO Employees Union v UOI, (2002)2 SCC 33.
22. D.C Mills vs Commercial Income Tax, AIR 1955 SC 65.
23. Sathe SP, Judicial Activism in India 1 (2002).
24. Baxi, Judicial Discourse: Dialectics of the Face and the Mask, 35, JILI, 9 (1993).
25. Baxi U, The Avatars of Indian Judicial Activism: Explorations in the Geographies of (in) justice, in SK Verma and Kusum, Fifty Years of Supreme Court of India- Its Grasp and Reach, 2000, 173.
26. Balakrishnan KG, Judicial Activism Under the Indian Constitution, Trinity College, Ireland, 14th Oct, 2009.
27. Prof. William Wade on "Judicial Activism and Constitutional Democracy in India".
28. ShodhGanga, Public Interest Litigation and Judicial Activism.
29. MC Mehta vs Union of India AIR 2006 SC 1325: (2006) 3 SCC 399.
30. Handbook of Citizens' Charter, http://www.goicharters.nic.in/cchandbook.htm.
31. Second Administrative Reforms Commission Report on 'Social Capital- A Shared Destiny', Ninth Report, Aug, 2008.

32. Bhattacharya M, New Horizons of Public Administration, Jawahar Publishers and Distributors, New Delhi.
33. Right to Information Act, 2005.
34. The Constitution of India, 1950.
35. Coopel P, Information Rights 62 (2004).
36. Ponting Clive, The Right to Know, 47 (2001).
37. Escalante RP, Coordination of the Mechanism for the Protection of Human Rights in the American Convention with those Established by the United Nations, American University Law Review, Vol 3, 1980, pp. 167-201.
38. Bhatia S, Freedom of Press: Politico-Legal Aspects of Press Legislation in India, 45 (1997).
39. Barowalia JN, Commentary on the Right to Information, 42 (2007).
40. Price Water House Coopers, Progress in Implementation of RTI.
41. http://indianexpress.com/article/explained/10-ways-in-which-rti-has-changed-the-functioning-of-govt-officials/.
42. Poorest Area Civil Society (PACS) Report on RTI.
43. Price Water House Coopers, Issues and Constraints in Implementation of RTI.
44. As per section 2(j)(1), "inspection of work, documents and records" is a means to provide information under Right to Information Act.
45. Coronel SS, The Role of Media in Deepening Democracy Coronel, 2002, from http://unpan1.un.org/intradoc/groups/ public/documents/ UN/UNP AN010194.pdf.
46. Amartya Sen, Development and Freedom, New York: Anchor Books, 1999.
47. "Corruption and Good Governance: Discussion Paper 3," published by the Management Development and Governance Division, Bureau for Policy and Programme Support, United Nations Development Programme, 1997.
48. Shringarpure S, Role of Media in Indian Democracy, E-ISSN No : 2454-9916, Vol 2 (6), June 2016, from https://archive.org/stream/03SalilShringarpure/03-Salil%20Shringarpure_djvu.txt.
49. Malena C, Forster R, Singh J, Social Accountability: An Introduction to the Concept and Emerging Practice, World Bank Report No 31042, Vol 1, Dec 2004.
50. IGNOU, Social Audit and Gender Audit, from http://egyankosh.ac.in/bitstream/123456789/42358/1/Unit%207.pdf.
51. https://en.wikipedia.org/wiki/Press_Council_of_India.
52. https://en.wikipedia.org/wiki/Electronic_Media_Monitoring_Centre.
53. http://www.ibfindia.com/news-broadcasting-standards-authority-nbsa.
54. The Central News media Accreditation Guidelines, 1999.
55. Mathew M, Media Self-Regulation in India: A Critical Analysis, ILI Law Review, Winter Issue, 2016.
56. Haque SM "Significance of accountability under the new approach to public governance" International Review of Administrative Services, Vol 66, 2000.
57. Hayllar M "Accountability: Ends, Means and Resources", Asian Review of Public Administration, Vol. 3(2), 1991.
58. IGNOU, Accountability.

Chapter 7. Administrative Law

1. Administrative Law notes of Harvard University from https://sites.hks.harvard.edu/m-rcbg/research/c. coglianese_international.encyclopedia_administrative.law.pdf.
2. Schwartz Bernard, Administrative Law, Little Brown, 1991.
3. Introduction to the Study of the Law of the Constitution (London: Macmillan, 1885).
4. Zalpuri Sunita, Training Package on Administrative Law, DOPT-UNDP.
5. Fromont, Droit administratif des États européens.
6. Gaudemet Y, 'L'exportation du droit administratif français: Breves remarques en forme de paradoxe', in Mélanges Philippe Ardant: Droit et politique a la croisée des cultures (Paris: LGDJ, 1999).
7. Custos D, 'Droits administratifs:américain et français: sources et procédure', (2007) Revue international de droit compare.
8. Peter Cane, 'Judicial Review in the Age of Tribunals', (2009) Public Law 479.
9. Administrative Procedure Act of US.
10. P. Craig, Administrative Law, (London: Sweet & Maxwell, 2008.
11. G. Nolte, 'General Principles of German and European Administrative Law—A Comparison in Historical Perspective', (1994).
12. E.J. Eberle, 'The West German Administrative Procedure Act: A Study in Administrative Decision Making', Dickinson Journal of International Law, 1984,3, pp. 67.
13. Council of Civil Service Unions v Minister for the Civil Service [1985] AC 374, Lord Diplock.
14. www.freedomofinfo.org.
15. Mc. Mohan, Omar T., "A Fair Trial before quasi-judicial Tribunals as required by due process" 29 MLR 105 (1946).
16. AIR 1993 SC 1769.
17. https://indiankanoon.org/doc/1152518/.
18. MacCormick, D. Neil, Der Rechtsstaat und die rule of law. Juristenzeitung, 1984, 50 (50), 65–70.
19. Rosenfeld M, The rule of law and the legitimacy of constitutional democracy. Southern California Law Review, 2001, 74, 1307–1352.
20. Reid, John Philip, The Rule of Law. Northern Illinois University Press, De Kalb, 2004.
21. Martin EJ Krygier, Rule of Law (and Rechtsstaat), International Encyclopedia of the Social & Behavioral Sciences, 2nd edition, Volume 20.
22. A.V. Dicey, Introduction to the Study of the Law of the Constitution Macmillan, London, 1959.
23. Dietmar von der Pfordten, On the Foundations of the Rule of Law and the Principle of the Legal State/ Rechtsataat, in Silkenat, James R., Hickey Jr., James E., Barenboim, Peter D The Legal Doctrines of the Rule of Law and the Legal State (Rechtsstaat), Springer, 2014.
24. Grzeszick, in: Maunz-Dürig, Grundgesetzkommentar, Art. 20, VII, at nr. 30.
25. Tom Bingham, The Rule of Law (2011), Allen Lane, London.

Chapter 8. Comparative Public Administration

1. Arora RK, Comparative Public Administration, Associated Publishing House, New Delhi, 1979.
2. Riggs FW, Ecology of Public Administration, Asia, New Delhi, 1961.
3. Joseph La Palombare, Bureaucracy and Political Development.
4. Benge E, Job Evaluation and Merit Rating, National Foreman's Institute, New York, 1941, pp. 240-45.
5. Martin DW, The Guide to the Foundation of Public Administration, Marcel Deckker, Inc, New York, 1989, p. 219.
6. Report of the Inter-University Summer Seminar on Comparative Politics, Social Science Research Council, American Political Science Review, 54, 1953.
7. Holt RT, Comparative Politics and Comparative Administration, in Riggs F, Frontiers of Development Administration, Durham, Duke University Press, 1970, pp. 309-10.
8. Diamant A, The Relevance of Comparative Politics to the Study of Comparative Administration, Administrative Science Quarterly, 5, 1960, pp. 87.
9. Sayre-Kaufman Outline: A Research Design for a Pilot Study in Comparative Administration, CAG Occasional Papers, January, 1966.
10. Jackson RH, An Analysis of the Comparative Administrative Movement, Canadian Public Administration, 9, 1966, pp. 114-115.
11. Riggs FW, Administration in Developing Countries, Boston, Houghton Mifflin Co, 1964.
12. Kuhn TS, The Structure of Scientific Revolutions, Chicago, University of Chicago Press, 1970.
13. Siffin W, Toward the Comparative Study of Public Administration, Bloomington, Indiana University, 1957.
14. Landau M, Sociology and the Study of Formal Organization, in Waldo D, Landau M, The Study of Organizational Behaviour: Status, Problems and Trends, Washington, Comparative Administration Group, ASPA, 1966, pp. 37-50.
15. Public Administration: A Comparative Perspective, Englewood Cliffs, Prentice Hall, 1966, pp. 9-13.
16. Emerging Synthesis in American Public Administration, Bombay Asia Publishing House, 1966.
17. Trends in the Comparative Study of Public Administration, International Review of Administrative Sciences, 1962, Vol 28, pp. 9-15.
18. Readings in Comparative Public Administration, Boston, Allyn and Bacon, 1967, pp. 7-8.
19. Rourke FE, Bureaucracy, Politics and Public Policy, Boston, Little Brown and Co, 1969.
20. Journal of Comparative Administration, 1969, Vol 1.
21. Redfield R, The Folk Society, American Journal of Sociology, 1947, Vol 52, pp. 293-308.
22. Miner H, The Folk Urban Continuum, in Lazarfald PF, Rosenberg M, The Language of Social Research, Glencoe, Free Press, 1955.
23. Development Administration and Decision Theory.
24. Dorsey JT, An Information-Energy Model, in Heady and Stokes, Papers in Comparative Public Administration, pp. 37-57.

25. Riggs FW, Administration in Developing Countries: The Theory of Prismatic Society, Boston, Houghton Mifflin Company, 1964.
26. Inkeles A, What is Sociology, Englewood Cliffs, NJ, Prentice Hall, 1964.
27. Merton R, Manifest and Latest Functions, in Demearth NJ III, Peterson RA, System, Change and Conflict, New York, Free Press, 1967, pp. 10-75.
28. Young O, Systems of Political Science, Englewood Cliffs, NJ, Prentice Hall, 1968, pp. 27-37.
29. Caldwell L, Conjectures on Comparative Public Administration, in Stiffin WJ, Toward a Comparative Study of Public Administration, Bloomington, Indiana University Press, 1957, pp. 23-119.
30. Siffin WJ, Toward the Comparative Study of Public Administration, Bloomington, Indiana University Press, 1957.
31. Tickner FJ, Comparative Administrative Systems, Public Administration Review, 1959, Vol 9th, pp. 19-25.
32. Heady, Stokes, The Ecological Approach: The Sala Model, Papers in Comparative Public Administration, pp. 19-36.
33. Riggs FW, The Sala Model, Phillipine Journal of Public Administration.
34. Chapman RA, Prismatic Theory in Public Administration: A Review of the Theories of Fred W Riggs, Public Administration, London, 1966, Vol 44, pp. 423.
35. Shor EL, Comparative Administration: Static Study versus Dynamic Reform, Public Administration Reform, 1962, Vol 22, pp. 160.
36. Prismatic Behaviour in the United States, Journal of Comparative Administration, 1970, Vol 2, pp. 230.
37. Valsan EH, Positive Formalism: A Desideration for Development, Philippine Journal of Public Administration, 1968, Vol 12, pp. 3-6.
38. Riggs FW, The Idea of Development Administration, in Weiner EW, Development Administration in Asia, Durham, NC, Duke University Press, 1970, pp. 25-72.
39. Riggs FW, Further Considerations on Development, Administrative Change, July-December, 1976, Vol 4(1).
40. Riggs FW, Administrative Change, Jan-June 1975, Vol 2(2).
41. Sakwa R, Soviet Politics-An Introduction, Routledge, London, 1990.
42. Argyriades D, Pagaza IP, Winning the needed change: Saving our planet earth- A global public service, New York, IOS Press, 2009.
43. Jreisat JE, Comparative public administration and policy boulder, CO, Westview Press, 2002.
44. Heady F, Public Administration: A Comparative Perspective, Englewood Cliffs, NJ: Prentice Hall, 2001.
45. Van Wart M, Cayer NJ, Comparative Public Administration: Defunct, Dispersed or Redefined? Public Administration Review, 1990, 50(2), pp. 238-248.
46. Eglene O, Dawes SS, Challenges and Strategies for Conducting International Public Management Research, Administration and Society, 2006, 38(5), pp. 596-622.
47. Jreisat JE, Comparative Public Administration is Back in, Prudently, Public Administration Review, 2005, 65(2), pp. 231-242.

48. Huque AS, Accountability and Governance: Strengthening Governance: Strengthening Extra Bureaucratic Mechanisms in Bangladesh, International Journal of Productivity and Performance Management, 2011, 60(1), pp. 59-74.
49. Madacumura GM, Ferreira M, Toward a Comparative Public Administration: The Brazilian Experience, PA Times, June 9, 2015.
50. Olukoju SA, Global Perspectives of Public Administration: How Adaptable Are They to Contextual Conditions?, PA Times.

Chapter 9. Development Dynamics

1. Caiden GE, Public Administration, Palisades Publisher, 1982.
2. Sharma SK, Verma SP, Comparative Public Administration, Indian Institute of Public Administration, 1985.
3. Panandikar VA Pai, A Survey of Research in Public Administration 1980-1990, Konark Publications, 1997.
4. Gant GF, Development Administration: Concepts, Goals, Methods, University of Wisconsin, Madison, 1979.
5. Rostow WW, The Stages of Economic Growth, The Economic History Review, Vol 12(1), 1959, pp. 1-16.
6. Hagen EE, How Economic Growth Begins: A Theory of Social Change, Journal of Social Issues, Vol 19(1), 1963, pp. 20-34.
7. https://www.slideshare.net/jodiecmills/superpowergeographies.
8. https://faridanazg.wordpress.com/2016/03/15/dependency-theory/.
9. Wallerstein I, The Capitalist World Economy, Cambridge University Press, 1979.
10. Korten DC, Steps towards People-Centered Development: Vision and Strategies, in Heyzen N, Riker JV, Quizon AB, Government-NGO Relations in Asia: Prospects and Challenges for People-Centered Development, Asian and Pacific Development Centre, Kuala Lampur, 1995.
11. UN Human Development Report, 1993.
12. Galjart B, Counter-development: Possibilities and Constraints, in Craig G, Mayo M, Community Empowerment: A Reader in Participation and Development, Zed Books, London and New Jersey, 1995.
13. Mukherjee N, Participatory Rural Appraisal: Methodology and Application, Concept Publishers Co, New Delhi, 1994.
14. Portes A, Neoliberalism and the Sociology of Development: Emerging Trends and Unanticipated Fact, Population and Development Review, 1997, Vol 23(3), pp. 229-259.
15. Krantz L, The Sustainable Livelihood Approach to Poverty Reduction: An Introduction, SIDA, 2001.
16. Chambers R, Conway G, Sustainable Rural Livelihoods: Practical Concept for the 21st Century, IDS Discussion Paper 296, IDS, Brighton, UK, Feb 1992.
17. Sen AK, The Standard of Living, in Hawthorn G, The Standard of Living, Cambridge University Press, 1987.
18. Sen AK, Development as Freedom, Oxford University Press, New York, 1999.
19. Sen AK, Inequality Re-examined, Claredon Press, Oxford, 1992.

20. Escobar A, Encountering Development: The Making and Unmaking of the Third World, Princeton University Press, 1995.
21. Islam MS, Paradigms of Development and Their Power Dynamics: A Review, Journal of Sustainable Development, Vol 2(2), July, 2009.
22. Sachs W, The Archaeology of Development Idea, Earthcare Books, 2008.
23. http://www.hdr.undp.org/en/humandev.
24. http://www.hdr.undp.org/en/humandev.
25. Technical Notes on Human Development Indices and Indicators: 2018 Statistical Report at http://hdr.undp.org/ sites/default/files/hdr2018_technical_notes.pdf.
26. Human Development Indices and Indicators: 2018 Statistical Report, UNDP, New York, USA, 2018.
27. Oakley A, The Ann Oakley Reader: Gender, Women and Social Science, Policy Press, Bristol University Press, 2005.
28. The World Bank Report on Engendering Development Through Gender Equality in Rights Resources and Voice, Washington DC, 2001.
29. Jaquette JS, Women and Modernization Theory: A Decade of Feminist Criticism, In World Politics 1982, 34(2).
30. Young K, Gender and Development, Notes for a Training Course on Gender and Development sponsored by the Aga Khan Foundation, Toronto, 1987
31. UN Transforming our World, The 2030 Agenda for Sustainable Development, A/Res/70/1.
32. Shiva V, Staying Alive: Women, Ecology and Development, Kali for Women, New Delhi, India, Zed Books, London, 1988.
33. UN Women, Turning Promises into Action: Gender Equality in the 2030 Agenda for Sustainable Development, US, 2018.
34. Palermo J, Breaking the Cultural Mode: The Key to Women's Career Success, Hudson 20:20 Series Whitepaper: Hudson Global Resources and Human Capital Solutions, 2004.
35. Chesterman C, Ross-Smith A, Peters, M, Senior Women Executives and the Cultures of Management: A brief cross-comparison of public, private and higher education organisations, June, 2004.
36. Meyerson DE, Fletcher JK, A Modest Manifesto for Shattering the Glass Ceiling, Harvard Business Review, January – February, 2000.
37. Simpson R, Gender Mix and Organisational Fit: How gender imbalance at different levels of the organization impacts on women managers, Women in Management Review, 200 15 (1): 5 – 18.
38. Tharenou P, Correlates of Women's Chief Executive Status: comparisons with men chief executives and women top managers', Journal of Career Development, 1995, 21 (3): 201-212.
39. EOWA Website (2007): www.eowa.gov.au.
40. The Economist, The conundrum of the glass ceiling – Women in Business: London, 2005, Jul 23,.Vol. 376, Iss. 8436; p. 67.
41. Konrad AM, Kramer VW, How Many Women Do Boards Need?, Harvard Business Review., 2006, 84 (12): 22.
42. Sands S, Why Aren't Women at the Top Yet?,New Statesman, 1996, 135: 40 –1.

43. Weidner E, Development Administration: A New Focus for Research, in Heady F, Stokes, Papers on Comparative Public Administration, Ann Arbor Institute of Public Administration, University of Michigan, 1962.
44. Fredland R, Technology Transfer to the Public Sector in Developing States: Three Phases, Journal of Technology Transfer, 2000, Vol 25, pp. 265-175.
45. Brinkerhoff D, Coston J, International Development Management in a Globalized World, Public Administration Review, 1999, Vol 59(4), pp. 346-361.

Chapter 10. Personnel Administration and Civil Services

1. IGNOU, Concept, Nature and Scope of Personnel Administration, Personnel Administration, Bachelor of Arts (Public Administration).
2. IGNOU, Functions and Significance of Personnel Administration, Personnel Administration, Bachelor of Arts (Public Administration).
3. Kingsley JD, Recruiting applications for the public service, a report submitted to the Civil Service Assembly by the Committee on Recruiting Applications for the Public Service, Civil Service Assembly of the United States and Canada, 1942, Chicago.
4. IGNOU, Recruitment (Reservation in Services), Personnel Administration, Bachelor of Arts (Public Administration).
5. IGNOU, Recruitment, Selection, Appointment and Promotion, Masters of Arts (Public Administration).
6. http://www.thehindu.com/features/education/Civil-services-test-in-for-a-revamp/article16627687.ece.
7. LD White, Introduction to the Study of Public Administration, New York, Macmillan Co, 1926.
8. Willoughby W.F., Principles of Public Administration, Allahabad, Central Book Depot.
9. Hegel C, The Encyclopedia of Management, Reinhold Publishing Corporation, New York, 1973.
10. IGNOU, Performance Appraisal, Masters of Arts (Public Administration).
11. Osborne, Gaebler, Reinventing Government, Addison Wesley Publishing Company, 1992.
12. US General Accounting Office, Managing for Results: Emerging Benefits from Selected Agencies' Use of Performance Agreements, Washington DC, US Government Printing Office, 2000.
13. Lynch J, Skewed Results, Governing, December 2004, pp. 42-45.
14. Miller K, Ditching the Carrot and Stick, Governing, June 201, pp. 50-53.
15. McNamara C, Performance Management: Benefits and Concerns.
16. Work Sample and Simulations, Assessment and Selection, opm.gov on https://www.opm.gov/policy-data-oversight/assessment-and-selection/other-assessment-methods/work-samples-and-simulations/.
17. Odiorne G, Management by Objectives, Pitman, New York, 1965.
18. Karnataka Administrative Reforms Commission Report, 2001.
19. Report of the Fifth Central Pay Commission, Vol 1, Part 2, Section III, pp. 182-187.
20. Chapter on Performance Management, Second Administrative Commission Report on Refurbishing of Personnel Administration- Scaling New Heights.

21. Michael A, B, Performance Management of the Civil Servants, Jaico Publishing House, 2002.
22. http://www.upsc.gov.in/about-us/constitutional-provisions.
23. http://ssc.nic.in/.
24. Finer H, The Theory and Practice of Modern Government, Methuen & Co., Ltd. London.
25. United Nations, International Civil Service Advisory Board Ninth Session, June, 1966, P.l (ICSAB/IX/5-Coord/CC/S0/ 156).
26. Report of the Second Pay Commission.
27. IGNOU, Training and Development, Masters of Arts (Public Administration).
28. Dale Y, Personnel Management and Industrial Relations, Prentice Hal, 1969.
29. Shodhganga, Evaluation and Effectiveness of Training, http://shodhganga.inflibnet.ac.in/bitstream/10603/ 4405/11/11_chapter%204.pdf.
30. Hamblin, A. C., Evaluation and control of training. Maidenhead, McGraw-Hill, 1974.
31. National Training Policy 2012, Office Memorandum, Jan 19th, 2012, Department of Personnel and Training (Training Division).
32. IGNOU, Salary Administration (Including Incentives and Other Benefits), Personnel Administration, Bachelor of Arts (Public Administration).
33. French Wendell, Human Resource Management, Third Edition, Houghton Mifflin Company, USA, 1997.
34. White LD, Introduction to the study of public administration, McMillan, New York, 1948
35. Second Administrative Commission Report on District and State Administration, Fifteenth Report, Department of Administrative Reforms and Public Grievances, April 2009.

Chapter 11. Ethics in Public Administration

1. Means CL, The Ethical Imperative, New York, Anchor Books, 1970.
2. Sheeran PJ, Ethics in Public Administration- A Philosophical Approach, Rawat Publications, Jaipur, 2006, chapter 4 on ‘the focus of ethics in human actions’.
3. Gibson W, Elements for a Social Ethic: The Role of Social Sciences in Public Policy, New York, McMillan, 1966.
4. Cynthia J, McSwain and White OF Jr, The case of lying, cheating and stealing- personal development as ethical guidance for managers, Administration and society 18, 4, Feb 1987.
5. Bhattacharya M, New Horizons of Public Administration, Administrative Ethics, pp. 293, Jawahar Publishers and Distributors, New Delhi, 2015.
6. Pugh DL, The origins of Ethical Framework in Public Administration, in Bowman JS, Ethical Frontiers in Public Management, Jossey-Bass, San Francisco, Oxford, 1991.
7. Appleby P, Morality and Administration in a Democratic Government, Louisiana State University Press, 1959.
8. Bailey S, Ethics and the Public Service, Public Administration Review, December 1965.
9. Waring CG, Daughterty CA, Auditing Ethics-Make Them an Offer They Can’t Refuse, Journal of Government Financial Management, 53, Spring, 2004, pp. 34-40.
10. Henry N, Public Administration and Public Affairs, Toward a Bureaucratic Ethic, Indian Edition, PHI Learning Private Ltd, New Delhi, 2012.

11. Cooper TL, The Responsible Administrator, San Francisco, CA, Jossey-Bass, 1990.
12. Matani Lohit, Vishal, An Introduction to Civil Services, OakBridge Publications, New Delhi, 2018.
13. Rawls John, A Theory of Justice, Belknap Press of Harvard University Press, Cambridge, 1971.
14. Pegis, Basic Writings of Saint Thoman Acquinas.
15. Fletcher J, Situation Ethics: The New Morality, New York, Westminster, 1966.
16. Conduct and Discipline, IGNOU, MA, Personnel Administration.
17. All India Services (Conduct) Rules, 1968.
18. https://www.transparency.org/what-is-corruption.
19. Goel RK, Nelson MA, Causes of Corruption: History, Geography and Government, Helsinki, Bank of Finland Institute for Economics in Transition, Finland, 2008.
20. Graff D, Huberts, Portraying the Nature of Corruption Using an Exploratory Case Study Design, pp. 647.
21. Quality Management Systems – Requirements for Service Quality by Public Service Organizations, IS 15700:2005, Bureau of Indian Standards, December 2005, New Delhi.
22. Appleby P, in the article of Raghavan RK, Unfulfilled Hopes, June 14th, 2001.
23. Relationship between the Political Executive and the Civil Servants, Tenth Report on Refurbishing of Personnel Administration, Second Administrative Reforms Commission Report, Nov, 2008.
24. Appu PS, The All India Services-Decline, Debasement and Destruction, Economic and Political Weekly, Feb 26th, 2005.
25. Barik BK, Decline of All India Services, Economic and Political Weekly, April 23rd, 2005.
26. Wade R, Canal Irrigation in South India, Mohan Jag, Soul and Structure of Governance in India, pp. 75.
27. Venkatesan J, Officials told not to act on oral orders from political executive, The Hindu, October 31, 2016, http://www.thehindu.com/news/national/in-major-reform-sc-orders-fixed-tenure-for-bureaucrats/article5299939.ece.
28. https://indiankanoon.org/doc/47623/.

Chapter 12. Public Policy

1. Dror Y, Public Policymaking Reexamined, Transaction Publishers, 1983.
2. Vickers G, The Art of Judgment: A Study of Policymaking, SAGE Publications, 1995.
3. Friedrich CJ, Mason ES, Public Policy, Harvard University Press, Cambridge, 1940.
4. Anderson JE, Public Policymaking, Cengage Learning, 2014.
5. Easton D, The Political System, An Inquiry into the state of Political Science, Calcutta: Scientific Book Agency, 1971.
6. Dye TR, Understanding Public Policy, Pearson Education, 2016.
7. Lineberry RL, Sharkansky I, Urban Politics and Public Policy, Harper & Row, 1978.
8. Cloete F, Conning CD, Improving Public Policy: Theory, Practice and Results, Van Schaik, Pretoria, 2011.
9. Fox T, Ward H, Howard B, Public Sector Roles in Strengthening Corporate Social Responsibility: A Baseline Study. Washington D.C, 2002.

10. Williams DM, Policy at the Grassroots: Community-Based Participation in Heath Care Policy, J Prof Nurs. 1991 Sep-Oct;7(5):271-6.
11. Anderson JE, Public Policymaking, New York: Halt, Rine and Winston, 1979.
12. Marume SBM, Mutongi C, Jubekanda RR, Chikasha AS, Public Policy Analysis Models, The International Journal of Humanities and Social Studies, 2016 March, Vol 4, Issue 3, pp. 306.
13. Bentley AF, The Process of Government, Bloomington, IN, Principia Press, 1949.
14. Easton D, A Framework for Policy Analysis, University of Chicago Press, 1979.
15. Wasson R, Leong C, Buurman J, A System Dynamic Anaysis of the Levee Effect on the Brahmaputra River and Policy Implications, Institute of Water Policy, Lee Kuan Yew School of Public Policy, Singapore, in eHealth-enabled Health, Vol. 216.
16. Richards A, Singh N, Interstate Water Disputes in India: Institutions and Policies, Department of Environmental Studies and Department of Economics, University of California, October, 2001.
17. Henry N, Public Administration and Public Affairs, PHI Learning Pvt. Ltd., New Delhi, 2012.
18. Lowi TJ, American Business, Public Policy, Case Studies and Political Theory, World Politics, 16, July 1964, pp. 677-693.
19. Kingdon JW, Agendas, Alternatives and Public Policies, New York, Longman, 2003.
20. Coates JF, Technology Assessment- A Tool Kit, Chemtek, June, 1976, pp. 372-383.
21. Haveman RH, Evaluating the impact of public policies on regional welfare, Journal of Regional Studies, 10(4), 1876.
22. Lineberry RL, Urban politics and public policy, Harper and Row, 1978.
23. Ellen EC, Rational Decision-making in Higher Education, US Department of Education, 1983.
24. Lindblom CE, The science of 'muddling through'. *Public Administration Review*, 1959, **19**, pp. 79–88.
25. Lindblom C E, *Still muddling, not yet through,* "Public Administration Review", **39**, 1979, pp. 517–526.
26. Lindblom C E, Braybrooke D, *A strategy of decision: policy evaluation as a social process*, 1963, Free Press.
27. Lindblom CE,*The intelligence of democracy*, Free Press, 1965.
28. Lindblom CE, Woodhouse EJ, *The policymaking process,*1993, *3rd. ed.* Englewood Cliffs, New Jersey: Prentice Hall.
29. Suhrke A, Disjointed Incrementalism: NATO in Afghanistan, PRIO Policy Brief, 3/2011.
30. Haynes PA, Towards a Concept of Monitoring, Town Planning Review, Vol 45, Jan 1974, pp. 6-29.
31. Etzioni A, Mixed Scanning Revisited, Public Administration Review, Jan-Feb, 1986.
32. Hintia C, Cristiana M, Management Strategic in Administratia Publica, Transylvanian Review of Administrative Sciences, 2003, 9, p. 25.
33. Acheason D, Present at the Creation, Ed. WW Norton, New York, 1969, p. 214.
34. General Secretariat of the Government of Romania, 2009, Strategic Planning Guide.

35. Boyne GA, Chen AA, Performance Targets and Public Service Improvement, Journal of Public Administration Research and Theory, 17, July 2007, pp. 455-478.
36. Berry FS, Weschler B, State Agencies' Experience with Strategic Planning: Findings from a National Survey, Public Administration Review, 55, March/ April, 1995, pp. 159-168.
37. Miller, Unique Public Sector Strategies, pp. 137-138.
38. Leon P, Democracy and the Policy Sciences, Albany: Sunny Press, 1977.
39. Lawrence L, Managing Public Policy, Boston: Little Brown, 1987.
40. Hogwood B, Gunn LA, Policy Analysis for the Real World, Oxford University Press, Oxford, 1984.
41. Dror Y, Public policymaking re-examined, New York: Chandler, 1989.
42. Fromholtz M, Public Policy Course Manual, Commonwealth of Learning, 2012, Vancouver, Canada.
43. Wiles DK, The viability of extrarationality as a framework for educational policy analysis, American Educational Research Association Annual Convention, California, April 1976.
44. Pressman J, Wildavsky A, Implementation, University of California, Berkeley, 1984.
45. Brynard P, Coning De C, Policy implementation: Improving public policy from theory to practice. Pretoria: Van Schaik, 2006.
46. Mokhaba MB, Outcomes Based Education in South Africa Since 1994: Policy Objectives and Implementation Complexities, PhD Thesis in the Faculty of Economics and Management Studies, University if Pretoria, September 2004.
47. http://paissues.blogspot.com/2011/11/pressman-and-wildavsky-policy.html.
48. Hill M, Hupe M, Implementing Public Policy, Sage Publications.
49. Sabatier PA, Daniel AM, Can Regulation Work? The Implementation of the 1972 California Coastal Initiative, New York, NY: Plenum, 1983.
50. Elmore RF, Instruments and Strategy in Public Policy, Policy Studies Review, 1987, 7 (no. 1): 174-186.
51. Imperial MT, Intergovernmental Policy Implementation: Examining Inter-organizational Networks and Measuring Network Performance, School of Public and Environmental Affairs, Indian University, Bloomington, July, 1998.
52. Chubb J, The Political Economy of Federalism, American Political Science Review, 1985, 79 (December), pp. 994 – 1015.
53. Hogwood B, Gunn L, Policy Analysis for the Real World, New York, Oxford University Press, 1984.
54. Ditlopo P, Blaauw D, Rispel LC, Thomas D, Bidwell P, Policy Implementation and Financial Incentives for Nurses in South Africa: A Case Study on the Occupation-Specific Dispensation, Global Health Action, Jan 2013.
55. Ditlopo P, Blaauw D, The Impact of Human Resource Intervention on the Motivation and Retention of Health Professionals in South Africa, Johannesburg, The Centre for Health Policy, University of Witwatersrand, 2010.
56. Lipsky M, Street Level Bureaucracy: Dilemmas of the Individual in Public Services, 2010, New York, Russels Stage.

57. Dunleavy P, Professions and Policy Change: Some Notes Towards a Model of Ideological Corporatism, Public Administration Bulletin, 1981, Vol. 36.

58. Meyers MK, Vorsanger S, Street-Level Bureaucrats and the Implementation of Public Policy, in Peters BG, Pierre J, Handbook of public administration, London: Sage, 1981, 153-64.

59. Hjern B, Porter DO, Implementation Structures: A New Unit of Administrative Analysis, Organization Studies, Sage Publications, 2(3), pp. 211-217, July 1, 1981.

60. Hjern B, Hull C, Implementation Research as Empirical Constitutionalism, European Journal of Political Research, Vol 10(2), June 1982, pp. 105-115.

61. Matland RE, Synthesizing the Implementation Literature: The Ambiguity Conflict Model of Policy Implementation, Journal of Public Administration Research and Theory: J-PART, Vol.5, No.2 (Apr. 1995) pp. 145-174.

62. Elmore RE, Organizational Models of Social Program Implementation, Public Policy, 1978, Vol.26, No. 2, pp. 185-228.

63. Saetren H, Facts and Myths about Research on Public Policy Implementation: Out of Fashion, Allegedly Dead, But Still Very Much Alive and Relevant, Policy Studies Journal, 2005, Vol. 33, No. 4, pp. 559-582.

64. Berman P, The Study of Macro-and Micro- Implementation, Public Policy, 1978, 26(2), pp. 157-184.

65. Elmore R F, Backward Mapping: Implementation Research and Policy Decisions, Political Science Quarterly, 1979, Volume 94, No. 4, pp. 601-616.

66. Edelman MS, The Symbolic Use of Politics. Champaign: University of Illinois Press, 1964.

67. Edelman MS, Political Language: Words That Succeed and Policies That Fail. New York: Academic Press, 1977.

68. Olsen JP, Local Budgeting-Decision- Making or Ritual Act?, Scandinavian Political Studies, 1970, 5: 85-118.

69. Goggin ML, Bowman AOM, James PL, Toole LJ Jr., Implementation Theory and Practice: Towards a Third Generation, USA: Harper Collins Publishers, 1990.

70. Thomas JW, Grindle MS, After the Decision: Implementing Policy Reforms in Developing Countries, World Development, 1990, Vol. 18, No. 8, pp. 1163-1181.

71. Turner M, Hulme D, Governance, Administration and Development: Making the State Work, 1997, London: Macmillan Press Ltd.

72. Mazmanian DA, Sabatier PA, Implementation and Public Policy. Glenview, III.: Scott, Foresman, 1983.

73. Sabatier PA, Pelkey N, Incorporating Multiple Actors and Guidance Instruments into Models of Regulatory Policy- making: An Advocacy Coalition Framework, 1987, Administration and Society 19(2), pp. 236-63.

74. John P, Is there a Life after Policy Streams, Advocacy Coalitions and Punctuations: Using Evolutionary Theory to Explain Policy Change?, Policy Studies Journal, 2003, 31(4), pp. 481-498.

75. Goggin ML, The 'Too Few Cases/Too Many Variables' Problem in Implementation Research, Western Political Quarterly, 1990, pp. 328-347.

76. Schofield J, Time for a revival? Public Policy Implementation: A Review of the Literature and An Agenda for Future Research, International Journal of Management Review, 2001, Vol 3, Issue 3, pp. 245-263.
77. Winter SC, Implementation, (Section 5) In Handbook of Public Administration, (ed.) BG Peter and J Pierre. London, Thousand Oaks, CA and New Delhi: Sage, 2003, pp. 206-211.
78. McLaughlin MW, Learning From Experience: Lessons From Policy Implementation, Educational Evaluation and Policy Analysis, 1987, Vol.9, No. 2, pp. 171-178.
79. Dunn WA, Public Policy Analysis: An Introduction, Pearson Prentice Hall, 2004.
80. Sapru RK, Public Policy: Formulation, Implementation and Evaluation, Sterling Publishers, 2012.
81. Indira Gandhi National Open University, Masters of Arts in Public Administration, Unit on Monitoring of Public Policy-I.
82. Vedung E, Public Policy and Program Evaluation, Transaction Publications, USA.
83. Guba EG, Lincoln YS, Effective Evaluation, Jossey Bass Publishers, Michigan, 1981.
84. Wolcott, The art of Fieldwork. Walnut Creek, CA, Altamira Press, 1995.
85. Wolcott, Ethnography: A Way of Seeing. Walnut Creek, CA, Altamira Press, 1999.
86. Fine T, Coghlan A T, Program Evaluation Practice in the Non-Profit Sector. Non-Profit Management and Leadership, 2000, 10(3), pp. 331-339.
87. Federica CL, Evaluation: Definition, Methods and Models, An ITPS Framework, Working Paper, R 2006:002.
88. Ernest RH, Evaluating with Validity, Sage Publications, 1980, Michigan.
89. Lane JE, Implementation, Accountability and Trust, European Journal of Political Research, 1987, 15(5), pp. 527-546.
90. Seiber SD, Fatal Remedies: The Ironies of Social Intervention, Plenum Press, New York, 1981.
91. Mehrotra S, The Government Monitoring and Evaluation System in India: A Work in Progress, Oct 2013, ECD Working Paper Series No. 28, Independent Evaluation Group, The World Bank Group, Washington.
92. http://ieo.gov.in/pds.
93. Sabine GH, Thorson TL, A History of Political Theory, Oxford and IBH Publishing, New Delhi, 4th Edition.
94. Brantley B, Five Emerging Tools and Methods for Policymaking, PA Times, April 7, 2015.
95. Bichay N, Randomized Controlled Trials of Public Policy, Michigan Policy Work, Michigan State University, August 8th, 2016, on https://www.ippsr.msu.edu/public-policy/michigan-wonk-blog/randomized-controlled-trials-public-policy.
96. https://www.wired.com/2013/11/jpal-randomized-trials/.
97. Johnston EW, Governance in the Information Era: Theory and Practice of Policy Informatics, Routledge, New York, 2015.
98. Dawes SS, Janssen M, Policy informatics: addressing complex problems with rich data, computational tools, and stakeholder engagement, Proceedings of the 14th Annual International Conference on Digital Government Research, pp. 251-253.

Chapter 13. Techniques for Administrative Improvement

1. Milward HB, Provan KG, Governing the Hollow State, Journal of Public Administration Research and Theory, Vol 10(2), 2000, pp. 359-379.
2. Jayapalan N, Atlantic Publishers and Distributors, New Delhi, 2000.
3. White LD, Introduction to the Study of Public Administration, New York, Macmillan Co, 1926.
4. Appleby PH, Public Administration in India: Report of a Survey, New Delhi, Cabinet Secretariat, GoI, Manager of Publications, 1953.
5. Melrose ED, Organization and Methods, Public Administration, Vol 38(2), June 1960, pp. 119-130.
6. Hudson CS, Organization and Management Theory and Practice, American University Press, 1955.
7. Glossary of Terms Used in Management Services, BS 3138:92.
8. Naik M, Agola J, Rathod H, Time and Motion Study: A Case Study on a Commercial Building at Kadodara, IJARESM, ISSN: 2394-1766.
9. Godderis L et al, Prevention Pathways: Application of the Critical Path Methodology in Occupational Health Services, JOEM, Vol 46(1), Jan 2004.
10. PERT/ CPM, Indira Gandhi National Open University.
11. Heeks R, Information Systems for Public Sector Management, Sept 1998, Institute of Development Policy and Management, University of Manchester, UK.
12. Sparrow MK, Informing Enforcement, Information and the Public Sector, 1992, 2(3), pp. 197-212.
13. Danziger JN, Management Information Systems and Inter-organizational relations with the American Government System, Information and the Public Sector, 1991, 1(3), pp. 169-187.

Chapter 14. Financial Administration

1. Groves HM, Financing Government, Henry Colt and Co, New York, 1958.
2. Musgrave RM, The Theory of Public Finance, Mc-Graw Hill Book Company, 1959.
3. Pigou AC, A Study in Public Finance, Macmillan, London, 1928.
4. Singh MP, Economics of Government Expenditure and Growth, Reliance Publishing House: New Delhi, 1988.
5. Peacock AT, Wiseman J, The Growth of Public Expenditure in the United Kingdom, George Allen and Unwin Ltd, London, 1967.
6. Dalton H, Principles of Public Finance, Allied Publishers, 1922.
7. Government of India document on GST-An Update, Dec, 2018.
8. https://www.livemint.com/Politics/FNfN2HppUNVZ9IGvGFOA6N/The-new-direct-tax-code-Heres-all-you-need-to-know.html.
9. Modi A, Direct Taxes Code, National Institute of Public Finance and Policy, One Pager No 012, May 2014.
10. Jones M, Parliament in India.
11. Mukherjee HN, The Public Account Committee, in Shakdar SL, The Constitution and Parliament in India, Delhi, National, 1967.

12. Arora RK, Goyal R, Indian Public Administration, New Age International Publishers, Delhi, 2013.
13. Parliament of India Website, http://164.100.47.194/Loksabha/Committee/Committee Information.aspx?comm_code= 10&tab=0.
14. Parliament of India Website, http://164.100.47.194/Loksabha/Committee/Committee Information.aspx?comm_code=27 &tab=0.
15. Henry N, Public Administration and Public Affairs, PHI Learning, New Delhi, 2012.
16. Willoughbhy WF, The Budget as an Instrument of Political Reform, Proceedings of the Academy of Political Science in the City of New York, Vol 8(1), National Conference on War Economy, Jul 1918, pp. 56-63.
17. https://www.angelo.edu/faculty/ljones/gov3301/block6/objective4.htm.
18. Primer on Accrual Accounting, GASAB Secretariat, Office of the CAG, New Delhi.
19. 14th Report of Second Administrative Reforms Commission on Financial Management.
20. CAG Report on Public Audit in India, https://cag.gov.in/content/public-audit-india-and-ought.
21. Chanda A, Indian Administration, Allen and Unwin, Dec 1967.